THE
OXFORD COMPAN[...]
CHESS

THE OXFORD COMPANION TO
CHESS

SECOND EDITION

■

DAVID HOOPER
AND
KENNETH WHYLD

Oxford New York
OXFORD UNIVERSITY PRESS
1996

Oxford University Press, Walton Street, Oxford OX2 6DP
Oxford New York
Athens Auckland Bangkok Bogota Bombay
Buenos Aires Calcutta Cape Town Dar es Salaam
Delhi Florence Hong Kong Istanbul Karachi
Kuala Lumpur Madras Madrid Melbourne
Mexico City Nairobi Paris Singapore
Taipei Tokyo Toronto
and associated companies in
Berlin Ibadan

Oxford is a trade mark of Oxford University Press

First published 1992 by Oxford University Press
First issued as an Oxford University Press paperback 1996

British Library Cataloguing in Publication Data
Data available

Library of Congress Cataloging in Publication Data
Data available
ISBN 0-19-280049-3

1 3 5 7 9 10 8 6 4 2

Printed in Great Britain by
The Bath Press Ltd.
Bath

For
Joan Roma Hooper
and
Abigail Whyld

PREFACE

FOR this second edition we have maintained the tradition of the *Oxford Companion* series: to provide an overview of the subject that is suitable for experts and non-experts alike. Instruction is not our purpose, although a newcomer could learn to play and to follow the game by referring to laws, notation, and conventional symbols.

Compared to the first edition about 70 entries of a biographical kind have been omitted, and more than 160, most of them contemporary players, have been added. For a player's most noteworthy performances the score is given in wins, draws, and losses (+ = −). Nearly all of the game scores and compositions are different from those in the first edition, and there are more of them. A larger number of technical terms used by both players and composers is included. We have also added some hundreds more names of openings.

Tournaments are indicated by their labels, e.g. 'London 1851'; a game not from formal competition would be described as 'played at London in 1851', or simply 'London, 1851'. A 'minor tournament' may be understood as an event of category 7 or weaker. The standard reference work is the multi-volume *Chess Tournament Crosstables* by Jeremy Gaige. When titles of books are quoted they are suggestions for further reading, and are not intended as bibliographies.

Many entries have been revised to take account of new research, and because of comments by a large number of correspondents, who have willingly helped. Of these we are particularly indebted to: John Beasley, Chris Becker, Peter Blommers, Ivan Bottlik, Dale Brandreth, Norman Brenner, Bernard Cafferty, Calle Erlandsson, Arpad Foldéäk, Jeremy Gaige, George Jelliss, Jan Kalendovský, Cedric Lytton, Michael McDowell, Michael Mark, Egbert Meissenburg, Kevin O'Connell, René Olthof, Isaak Romanov, John Roycroft, Lothar Schmid, Frank Skoff, Paul Valois, Rob Verhoeven, Gareth Williams, and Edward Winter.

Such a compilation inevitably leaves room for error, and amendments by readers will be welcome.

Taunton　　　　　　　　　　　　　　　　　　　DAVID HOOPER
Caistor　　　　　　　　　　　　　　　　　　　KENNETH WHYLD

ACKNOWLEDGEMENTS

THE authors and publishers thank the following who have kindly lent the subjects illustrated on the pages listed:

Mr Gareth Williams, 41, 200, 203, 294, 328, 343, 351, 392; Just Games, 369.

They are also indebted to the following for permission to reproduce the illustrations on the pages given below:

B. T. Batsford, 230; Bodleian Library, 257, 417; British Chess Magazine, 409; British Museum, 225; Thomas E. Cook, 82; Richard Cross, 78, 427; John Gaughan, 432; Mark Huba, 193; Lloyds Bank, 381; Michael Mark, 312; Novosti Press Agency, 191, 300; Kevin O'Connell, 105; Patrimonio Nacional, Madrid, 11; Philadelphia Museum of Art: The Louise and Walter Arensberg Collection (Copyright ADAGP), 116; Royal Asiatic Society, 367; Royal Dutch Library, 19; Russell Collection, 451; Lothar Schmid, 138, 362; Society for Cultural Relations with USSR, 54; Staatliche Museen Preussischer Kulturbesitz, Berlin, 96; Comptroller of Her Majesty's Stationery Office (Crown Copyright), 291.

NOTE TO THE READER

ENTRIES are in simple letter-by-letter alphabetical order, with spaces and hyphens ignored; all names beginning with Mc are arranged as though they were prefaced Mac, and St is ordered as though it were spelt Saint. In a few difficult cases a guide to approximate pronunciation is given, without indication of stress. Cross-references are indicated by the use of small capital letters: if a name or term is printed in this form on its first appearance in an article, it will be found to have its own entry. The numbers that accompany names of openings or variations refer to Appendix I, where the moves of the line are listed. Appendix II provides a glossary of chess terms in French, German, Italian, Magyar, Russian, and Spanish.

A

Abbazia Defence, 1117, standard line, known to POLERIO, first published by SILBERSCHMIDT, 1829, and played in a tournament at Abbazia (now Opatija) 1912; all games in this event had to begin with the KING'S GAMBIT Accepted. The defence is also known as the Scandinavian Variation, or Modern Defence.

Abdurahmanović, Fadil (1939–), Yugoslav problemist, International Judge of Chess Compositions (1972), International Master for Chess Compositions (1980). His best work is in the field of HELPMATES; he also composes FAIRY PROBLEMS.

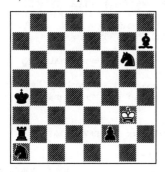

rp2

A reflex stalemate minimal by Abdurahmanović, first prize, *Feenschach* 1981. Either player must give stalemate if this is possible. The key is 1 Kg2, and variations show ALLUMWANDLUNG:

   1 ... f1 = Q +   2 Kg3 Qf5
   1 ... f1 = R +   2 Kh3 Rg1
   1 ... f1 = B +   2 Kh1 Rg2
   1 ... f1 = N +   2 Kg1 Ng3.
Other variations begin 1 ... Ra3 2 Kh2; 1 ... ~ 2 Kf1.

Abonyi Variation, 296, a BUDAPEST DEFENCE line advocated and analysed by the Hungarian master István Abonyi (1886–1942) in *Deutsches Wochenschach* (1922).

Abrahams Variation, 136 in the QUEEN'S GAMBIT Declined. The English player Gerald Abrahams (1907–80) introduced the move when playing against Holmes in the Lancashire County Championship in 1925. Abrahams played the variation against his countryman William Winter (1898–1955) in 1929 and in the same year Winter played it against Noteboom, after whom it is sometimes named.

The precursor, known from a 16th-century manuscript, was published by SALVIO in 1604: 1 d4 d5 2 c4 dxc4 3 e4 b5 4 a4 c6 5 axb5 cxb5 6 b3 b4 7 bxc4 a5 8 Bf4 Nd7 9 Nf3. Writing in 1617, CARRERA made his only criticism of Salvio's analysis in this variation. He suggested 8 ... Bd7 instead of 8 ... Nd7, or 9 Qa4 instead of 9 Nf3. Salvio nursed his injured pride for 17 years and then devoted a chapter of his book to a bitter attack on Carrera. The argument was pointless: all these variations give White a won game.

Abū 'l-fath Aḥmad as-Sinjārī (*fl. c.*1100), player and author. The surviving copies of his 11th- or 12th-century manuscript, made in the Tadzhik language, indicate that he came from Sīstān, a land on the eastern border of Iran; a 16th-century Persian manuscript suggests that he was an Indian. Three copies of his manuscript were discovered in 1951, the earliest dating from 1665; two are in Bukhara, one in Samarkand, and they may not be exactly as the original, written more than 500 years earlier. The contents include the usual legends of the game's origin, poems, puzzles, ten TA'BI'ĀT (opening systems), and 287 MANṢŪBĀT. Soviet sources indicate that 127 of the manṣūbāt are not among those in MURRAY's *History of Chess*; but their style, judging from those known outside the USSR, is similar, which is not surprising, for the compilation was made from the same sources, the libraries of Isfahan, Ray (near Tehran), and other Islamic cities.

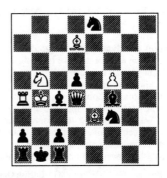

=

A study given by Abū 'l-fath (manṣūba no. 214). The pieces shown as queen and bishops are FIRZĀN (F) and FĪLS (A) respectively. White draws by forcing a situation where Black has to repeat checks with the firzān. 1 Kb3 (threatening 2 Na3 mate, and so acting as a DECOY to the N on f3, which might

otherwise defend from e1 at a later stage)
1...Nd2+ 2 Ka3 (threatening 2 Rb4+ Nb3 3
Rxb3 mate) 2...Ad6 3 Rb4+ (SQUARE VACA-
TION) Axb4 (SELF-BLOCK preventing Fb4+ later) 4
Nc3+ (to free the square b5 for the fīl) 4...Fxc3
5 Ab5 (threatening 6 Ad3 mate) 5...Fb2+ 6 Ka4
Fc3 7 Ka3 Fb2+ etc.

In 1024 Abū 'l-Qăsim Mahmūd rebuilt Ghazna
(Afghanistan) as the capital of his newly-won empire, and the great libraries, brought there within
ten years, were destroyed when the city was sacked,
c.1150. Abū 'l-fath made his collection in Ghazna,
and states that he travelled to India, Iraq, and
Khorāsān, meeting none who could match him in
play. He probably composed few manṣūbāt himself; specifically he laid claim to four, three of which
are based on the work of aṣ-ṣūlī.

académies des jeux, a name common in the 17th
and 18th centuries for compendia of indoor games
and amusements. *Hoyle's Games* was the most
popular example in English. The compilers often
borrowed extensively, even giving the complete
content of works by GRECO, STAMMA, or PHILIDOR.
Such general books may have historical value,
sometimes as the last surviving evidence of obsolete
rules.

Accelerated Dragon, 493 in the SICILIAN DEFENCE,
also known as the Accelerated Fianchetto Variation.

Accelerated Fianchetto Variation, alternative
name for two lines in the SICILIAN DEFENCE, 493, the
ACCELERATED DRAGON, and 563, the HUNGARIAN
VARIATION.

Accelerated Meran, 139, the ALEKHINE VARIATION
of the QUEEN'S GAMBIT Declined.

Accelerated Tarrasch, 223, the KRAUSE VARIATION
of the QUEEN'S PAWN OPENING.

accumulation of advantages, the gradual gain of
advantages which are not decisive individually, but
collectively may be so. Put forward by STEINITZ and
sometimes called his accumulation theory, this procedure remains sound. Confusing means with ends,
NIMZOWITSCH stated that the accumulation of
advantages was subordinate to PROPHYLAXIS, the
prevention of freeing moves by the opponent. Steinitz, like PHILIDOR before him, understood the use of
prophylaxis as one means of obtaining advantage.

Andersson-Browne Wijk aan Zee 1983 English Opening

1 Nf3 c5 2 c4 Nf6 3 Nc3 e6 4 g3 b6 5 Bg2 Bb7 6 0-0
Be7 7 b3 0-0 8 Bb2 a6 9 e3 d6 10 d4 Nbd7 11 d5 exd5
12 Nh4 g6 13 Nxd5 Nxd5 14 Bxd5 Bxd5 15 Qxd5
(White has two advantages: a STRONG SQUARE at d5, and a
potentially more active pawn MAJORITY.) 15...b5 16 Ng2
Nb6 17 Qd3 bxc4 18 bxc4 Rb8 19 Rab1 Qd7 20 e4 f5
21 Ne3 fxe4 22 Qxe4 Rbe8 23 Qd3 Rf3 24 Bc3 Bd8 25

Ba5 Qc6 26 Bxb6 Bxb6 (Black is saddled with a BAD
BISHOP, another advantage to White, whose overall advantage is now probably sufficient for victory.) 27 Rfd1 Bc7
28 Rb3 Ba5 29 Qc2 Bd8 30 Nd5 Rff8 31 Qb2 Qa4 32
Rc1 Re6 33 Rb8 Qe8 34 Kf1 Qf7 35 Rb7 Bf6.

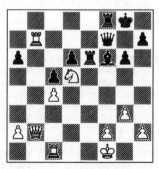

The following SIMPLIFICATION brings about a won endgame. 36 Rxf7 Bxb2 37 Rxf8+ Kxf8 38 Rc1 Rxc1 + 39
Kxe1 Kf7 40 Ke2 Bd4 41 f4 h5 42 Kf3 Ke6 43 h3 Bb2
44 Ke4 Bc1 45 g4 hxg4 46 hxg4 Bb2 47 a4 Ba1 48 Nb6
Bb2 49 f5+ gxf5+ 50 gxf5+ Kf6 51 Nc8 d5+ 52
Kxd5 Kxf5 53 Nd6+ Kf6 54 Ne4+ Ke7 55 Nxc5 a5
56 Kc6 Bc3 57 Nb7 Black resigns.

action chess, the US term for ALLEGRO.

active chess, FIDE's original term for RAPID CHESS.
The unpopular first choice, made in 1987, was
altered in 1989.

actual play, see POST-KEY PLAY.

Adams, Michael (1971–), British player who in
1989, at the age of 17, won the British championship and became a Grandmaster. He ended his full-
time education at the age of 16 and immediately
became a chess professional with the French club
Clichy.

Kindermann–Adams Novi Sad 1990 Olympiad Spanish
Opening Close Defence

1 e4 e5 2 Nf3 Nc6 3 Bb5 a6 4 Ba4 Nf6 5 0-0 Be7 6 Re1
b5 7 Bb3 0-0 8 d3 d6 9 c3 Bb7 10 Nbd2 Na5 11 Bc2 c5
12 Nf1 Re8 13 a3 h6 14 Ng3 Bf8 15 h3 g6 16 Nh2 d5
17 Ng4 Nxg4 18 Qxg4 c4 19 dxc4 bxc4 20 exd5 Qxd5
21 Be4 Qe6 22 Qh4 Bxe4 23 Nxe4 g5 24 Qh5 f5 25 Ng3
Nb3 26 Rb1

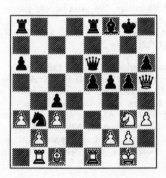

26 ... f4 27 Ne4 Kg7 28 h4 Qg6 29 Qe2 Rac8 30 hxg5 hxg5 31 Rd1 Rcd8 32 Bd2 Rd3 33 Be1 Red8 34 f3 g4 35 Kf1 g3 White resigns.

In August 1988 he shared first place in two successive tournaments played in London, Lloyds Bank (110 players in a Swiss) and NatWest Young Masters. In 1989 he won a strong tournament at Preston (+4=5), and in 1990, on his first appearance in the English Olympiad team, he scored +2=4−2 at Novi Sad. At Groningen 1990 he was first (+3=5−1) equal with KHALIFMAN and Piket, and at Wijk aan Zee 1991 he was second equal with CHERNIN, Khalifman, and HANSEN, after NUNN.

Adams Attack, 515, line for White in the SICILIAN DEFENCE pioneered by the American player Weaver Adams (1901–63). It was played by FISCHER against BOLBOCHÁN at the Stockholm Interzonal 1962, against NAJDORF in the Varna Olympiad 1962, and against RESHEVSKY in the USA championship, 1962–3: hence the alternative name, Fischer Attack.

Adams Gambit, 626, a speculative line in the VIENNA GAME, introduced by Weaver Adams in the early 1960s.

Adam Variation, 724, ingenious line in the HOWELL ATTACK of the SPANISH OPENING, introduced by the German player Edmund Adam (1894–1958) in a correspondence game against MALMGREN, 1939.

Adianto, Utut (1965–), the first Indonesian to become an International Grandmaster (1986). In 1987 he shared first place in a strong tournament at San Francisco.

adjournment, the closure of a playing session; the period after a game has been broken off and before its resumption. For the adjournment procedure under FIDE rules see SEALED MOVE.

In some early tournaments players were forbidden to analyse their games during adjournments. The rule, difficult to enforce, was soon abandoned, but for a long time help from others was considered unethical. In the 1930s analytical assistance became accepted practice, and today teams armed with literature and computers are employed at major events. However, committees are as fallible as individuals and consultation is less effective than supposed.

adjudication, an independent decision as to whether an unfinished game should be scored as a draw or as a win for one of the players; used in situations where conditions prevent the completion of a game.

adjust, see J'ADOUBE.

al-'Adlī ar-Rūmī (*fl.* 840). Patronized by several caliphs, including a son of HĀRŪN AR-RASHĪD, al-'Adlī was regarded as the strongest player of his time until defeated, not later than 848, by ar-RĀZĪ. al-'Adlī wrote a book on chess, severely criticized by aṣ-ṢŪLĪ, and also a book on nard, an old board

game in the backgammon family, often confused with chess by historians. His books have long since been lost, but some of his problems, endgames, and opening systems have survived. His name indicates that he came from some part of the eastern Roman Empire, possibly Turkey.

ad libitum. Represented by the symbol ~, the term means any one of the available legal moves except those, if any, mentioned in the context, and, on occasion, limited to the moves of one piece, e.g. K~.

Adorján (pron. a-door-yan), András (1950–), Hungarian player, International Grandmaster (1973). As a youth he played under the name Jocha. He was second, after KARPOV, in the world junior championship, Stockholm 1969, and won or shared first prizes at Varna 1972, Luhačovice 1973, Osijek 1978, Budapest 1982 (+6=5), Gjovik 1983 (+4=4−1), Gladsaxe 1983 (+4=4−1), Esbjerg 1985 (+5=6), and the New York Open 1987. In 1984 he won the Hungarian 'Super-championship'. After scoring +7=8−2 to share third place in the interzonal tournament, Riga 1979, Adorján became a CANDIDATE, but he lost the quarter-final match to HÜBNER.

Ribli–Adorján Hungarian Team Championship 1983
English Opening

1 Nf3 c5 2 c4 Nf6 3 Nc3 b6 4 e3 e6 5 d4 cxd4 6 exd4 Bb7 7 a3 d5 8 cxd5 Nxd5 9 Ne5 a6 10 Qa4+ Nd7 11 Nxd5 b5 12 Qb3 Nxe5 13 dxe5 Bxd5 14 Qg3 h5 15 h4 Rc8 16 b4 g6 17 Bg5 Be7 18 Bxe7 Qxe7 19 Be2 Bc4 20 Rc1 0-0 21 Bxh5 a5 22 bxa5 Qa7 23 Bd1 Qxa5+ 24 Qc3 Qa8 25 Qe3 Rfd8 26 Bf3 Qa5+ 27 Qc3

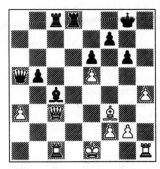

27 ... Bf1 White resigns.

advanced pawn, a pawn on its fifth rank or beyond. It may be weak because it is hard to defend, or strong because it restricts the opponent's mobility. Sometimes an advanced pawn provides an essential link in a COMBINATION.

advance point, a square on a player's fifth rank, other than a HOLE, that can be attacked by an enemy pawn from only one of the adjoining files. A piece, usually defended by a pawn, is often well placed on such a square.

After 1 e4 e6 2 d4 d5 3 exd5 exd5, for example, White has advance points at e5 and c5, Black at e4 and c4. The following example shows how such squares might be occupied. 4 Bd3 Bd6 5 Nf3 Nf6 6 0-0 0-0 7 Nc3 c6 8 Ne2 Re8 9 Ng3 Nbd7 (9 . . . Ne4 equalizes) 10 Nf5 Nf8 11 Nxd6 Qxd6 12 Ne5! and White has the better position. The game Larsen–Petrosyan, Havana Olympiad 1966, continued from this position 12 . . . Nfd7 13 Bd2 f6 (13 . . . Nxe5 14 Bf4) 14 Qh5, but Larsen misplayed later.

For examples showing the importance (and use of) such squares, see BIRD; FIXED CENTRE; MIESES.

Advance Variation, 589, also known as the Classical Variation, a line in the CARO–KANN DEFENCE characterized by the advance of White's e-pawn to e5. Tried by ZUKERTORT in 1864, it was played eight times by TAL, without much success, in his world championship match against BOTVINNIK, 1961.

The name is occasionally used for a similar advance in the FRENCH DEFENCE, the NIMZOWITSCH VARIATION, 1238, or for a line in the ALEKHINE DEFENCE, the LASKER VARIATION, 1256, in which the c-pawn is moved forward to c5.

advantage. To have *an* advantage is to have the better situation regarding one of the factors that are considered when making an EVALUATION OF POSITION. The value of White's advantages may be weighed against that of Black's; if the comparison shows that one player has the better prospect of winning, then that player is said to have *the* advantage.

During the course of a game one kind of advantage is often exchanged for another. A gain of time, by nature transitory, will be lost if not converted; a positional advantage may be ceded for material gain, or the reverse might happen; any number of advantages might be conceded in order to make a decisive attack on the king.

Afek, Yochanan (*né* Yohanan Kopelovich) (1952–), Israeli player and composer, International Judge of Chess Compositions (1988), International Master for Chess Compositions (1989). Much of his work consists of problems but he also composes studies.

+

A study by Afek, first prize, Israel Ring tourney 1975. 1 b7 Bc5 2 Bxc5 Rh8+ 3 Ka7 Kc6 4 Bd4 Rh7 5 Bg7! Rxg7 6 Nd4+ .

affidatus, see FIDATED.

Agdestein, Simen (1967–), winner of the 1982 Norwegian championship, after a play-off, and again in 1986, Nordic champion and International Grandmaster in 1985. Among the stronger international tournaments won by Agdestein are Jerusalem 1986, Lyons 1988 (both being shared victories), and Espoo 1989. In parallel with his chess career Agdestein is an international footballer.

Agdestein–Benjamin   Match Nordic–USA   Reykjavik 1986   Benko Gambit

1 d4 Nf6 2 c4 c5 3 d5 b5 4 Nf3 Bb7 5 Nfd2 d6 6 e4 b4 7 a3 Na6 8 axb4 Nxb4 9 Be2 g6 10 0-0 Bg7 11 Nc3 0-0 12 Nb3 Qb6 13 Be3 Rab8 14 Ra3 Bc8 15 f3 Ne8 16 Qd2 f5 17 Rc1 fxe4 18 Nxe4 Bf5

19 Nexc5 dxc5 20 Bxc5 Qf6 21 Bd4 Qh4 22 Bf2 Qf6 23 Bd4 Qh4 24 Bf2 Qf6 25 Nd4 Nd6 26 Rxa7 Bc8 27 Rf1 Nf5 28 Nb5 Na6 29 b4 Bh6 30 Qd3 Nxb4 31 Qb3 Qe5 32 Bd1 Na6 33 Re1 Nc8 34 c5 Bd2 35 Re2 Bf4 36 d6+ e6 37 Qc4 Rxb5 38 Qxb5 Nd4 39 Qc4 Nxe2+ 40 Bxe2 Nb8 41 g3 Be5 42 f4 Nc6 43 Rc7 Nd4 44 Bg4 Kh8 45 Rxc8 Rxc8 46 fxe5 Nf3+ 47 Kg2 Black resigns.

agreed draw, a game of which the outcome, and perhaps even the moves, have been agreed beforehand. Usually the intention is to save effort, but sometimes it is the result of a financial transaction. A game in which, after a normal contest, the players agree to draw is not an 'agreed draw' in this sense (see THEORETICAL NOVELTY).

Agzamov, Georgy Tadzhiyevich (1954–86), Uzbek player, International Grandmaster (1984) who died in a fall from a cliff. The strongest tournament he won was Sochi 1984 (+7=7−0). (See FAMILY CHECK.)

Ahlhausen Opening, 1322, the GROB OPENING. Carl Ahlhausen (1835–92), one of the first to adopt this unusual opening, was librarian of the Berlin Chess Association.

Ahues, Herbert Siegfried Oskar (1922–), German problemist, son of the well-known player Carl

Oscar Ahues (1883–1968), International Judge of Chess Compositions (1962), International Grandmaster for Chess Compositions (1989), teacher. One of the leading TWO-MOVER composers of his time, he published *Meine besten Schachproblemen* (1988) containing 603 compositions. (See CORRECTION.)

Ahues Variation, 556, the KOCH VARIATION, of the SICILIAN DEFENCE, advocated by the German player Carl Oscar Ahues (1883–1968).

Aitken Variation, 916, a line in the ITALIAN OPENING recommended in the *British Chess Magazine*, 1937, by the Scottish player James Macrae Aitken (1908–83).

Ajeeb, the second AUTOMATON to become famous, was made in 1868 by a Bristol cabinet-maker, Charles Alfred Hooper (1825–c.1900). Ajeeb, a life-size dark-skinned Indian figure with mobile head, trunk, and right arm, sat on a cushion mounted on a large box. Before a display the box was opened to show an elaborate clockwork mechanism, wound conspicuously by a huge key. Many of the wheels were of rubber, pushed aside when the operator descended from inside the cushion. After a long and successful run in London Hooper took Ajeeb to Germany, Belgium, France, and, in 1885, to New York where it was a great attraction: so great that Hooper made another Ajeeb which performed concurrently in other cities, and the existence of this copy and some unauthorized copies makes the story hard to trace. Among the masters who operated an 'official' Ajeeb in the USA were Charles Moehle (1859–98), Albert Beauregard Hodges (1861–1944), Constant Ferdinand Burille (1866–1914) and PILLSBURY. Hooper retired to England in 1895 but Ajeeb continued successfully, although an angry Westerner emptied his six-gun into its torso on one occasion, wounding the operator. After 1915 Ajeeb concentrated on draughts and one operator, Jesse B. Hanson, together with Frank Frain, purchased it in 1932. They toured the USA in 1936 to sponsor a radio set, one to be given free to each winner. Of the thousands of games he played Hanson conceded eight draws but never lost. Frain came to believe the automaton had supernatural qualities and had it blessed at a shrine in Quebec. During the Second World War Ajeeb disappeared.

K. Whyld, 'The Oriental Wonder', *British Chess Magazine*, Jan. 1978.

Akopyan, Vladimir Eduardovich (1971–), Armenian player, World Under-16 Champion 1986, International Grandmaster 1991, World Junior Champion 1991. His first major success was a shared third place (+4=6−1), at Yerevan, in 1989.

Alaikov, Venelin (1933–), Bulgarian problemist, International Judge of Chess Compositions (1977), International Master for Chess Compositions (1988). He composes problems of all kinds; for an example, see STAR-FLIGHTS.

Alapin, Semyon Zinovievich (1856–1923), player and openings analyst. He was born in Vilnius but spent the later years of his life in Heidelberg. While a student at St Petersburg he tied with CHIGORIN for first place, ahead of SCHIFFERS, in a national tournament, St Petersburg 1878–9; his only loss was to Chigorin, who also won both games of the play-off. Beginning with Frankfurt 1887, Alapin entered nearly a score of international tournaments during the following 25 years; his best results were fifth place at Monte Carlo 1901, the strongest tournament of the year, and first (+3=3) ahead of ROTLEWI, SPIELMANN, and FAHRNI at Munich 1911. In a national tournament, St Petersburg 1906, he took first prize, two and a half points ahead of his nearest rival. He is better known as a writer, publishing, until the end of his days, openings analyses and often illustrating them with fictitious games between 'Attakinsky' (White) and 'Defendarov'.

Alapin Defence, 766, rarely played line in the SPANISH OPENING analysed by ALAPIN in *La Stratégie*, 1896.

Alapin Defence Deferred, 675, the ALAPIN DEFENCE played after 3 . . . a6.

Alapin Gambit, 764, a line in the EXCHANGE VARIATION of the SPANISH OPENING, condemned in the 7th edition of the HANDBUCH 1891, played in the games Albin–von Scheve, Dresden 1892, and Pollock–Mieses, Hastings 1895, and praised by FINE in the 7th edition of MCO as refuting 5 0-0.

Alapin Opening, 671, played with the intention of continuing 3 f4. Analysed by Carl Mayerhofer (1828–1913) in *Schachzeitung*, 1849, this uncommon opening was played by Ljubojević at Groningen 1970 and (with transposition, i.e. 2 f4 exf4 3 Ne2) by Alapin at Manchester 1890. At one time it was jokingly called the HIPPOPOTAMUS GAME.

Alapin–Steinitz Variation, 888 in the EVANS GAMBIT, recommended by ALAPIN in *Deutsche Schachzeitung* in 1892 and played by STEINITZ in his match against CHIGORIN later in the same year.

Alapin–Sveshnikov Variation, 448, the ALAPIN VARIATION of the SICILIAN DEFENCE.

Alapin Variation, 112, standard play in the QUEEN'S GAMBIT Declined as in the game Alapin–Marshall, Monte Carlo 1901 (see RAZUVAYEV); 448 (sometimes called the Alapin–Sveshnikov Variation) in the SICILIAN DEFENCE, CARRERA'S interesting invention; 688, a sound line in the SPANISH OPENING.

Other lines named after this diligent analyst are 85 and 117 (sometimes called the Tartakower

Variation) in the Queen's Gambit Declined; 257 in the DUTCH DEFENCE; 623 in the VIENNA GAMBIT; two lines in the Spanish Opening, 763, and 806 (analysed by Alapin but first played Chigorin–Janowski, London 1899); 843 and 847 in the SPANISH FOUR KNIGHTS GAME; 881 (sometimes called the Lasker Variation) in the EVANS GAMBIT analysed by Alapin in *Schachfreund* in 1898; 1088 in the FALKBEER COUNTER-GAMBIT; 1125 in the KING'S KNIGHT GAMBIT; 1215, 1232 (GUIMARD VARIATION), and 1237 (also known as the Janowski Variation) in the FRENCH DEFENCE.

Alatortsev, Vladimir Alexeyevich (1909–87), honorary International Grandmaster (1983), International Arbiter (1953), born in St Petersburg, but living in Moscow for the greater part of his life. He was second, after BOTVINNIK, in the USSR championship, 1933, and shared three city championships: Leningrad 1933–4, with LISITSIN; Moscow 1936, with KAN; and Moscow 1937, with BELAVENETS. He also shared the last pre-war championship of the Trades Unions in 1938. Although Alatortsev played in several USSR championships and other tournaments he is better known as a writer and organiser. In 1958, when full-time chess research began in Moscow at the Central Research Institute for Physical Culture, Alatortsev was put in charge. His book *Problemui sovremennoi teory shakhmat* (1960) deals with the development of chess ideas from PHILIDOR to modern times, with emphasis on CO-OPERATION.

Alatortsev Variation, 64 in the QUEEN'S GAMBIT Accepted; 544 in the SICILIAN DEFENCE; 848 in the SPANISH FOUR KNIGHTS; 1190 in the FRENCH DEFENCE; also 157, the PETROSYAN VARIATION of the QUEEN'S GAMBIT Declined.

Albin, Adolf (1848–1920), Romanian-born player who spent most of his life in Vienna, where he died. Not a great player, perhaps because he learned the game at 22 and did not enter the international arena until he was 43, after his business career faltered, Albin had his best results during a temporary residence in America. He came second, some way behind LASKER, at New York 1893, and in the same year drew a match with A. B. Hodges (1861–1944), each player winning 4 games. (See CHATARD–ALEKHINE ATTACK; FLAG.)

Albin Attack, 1221, the CHATARD–ALEKHINE ATTACK, introduced in the game Albin–Csánk, Vienna 1890.

Albin Counter-gambit, 110, provocative reply to the QUEEN'S GAMBIT introduced by Cavallotti (after whom it is sometimes named) in a game against Salvioli at the Milan tournament of 1881, and reintroduced in the game Lasker–Albin, New York 1893. See LASKER TRAP, in this opening, for a plausible line which gives Black a winning UNDER-PROMOTION, a feature not found as early as the seventh move in any other opening.

albino, a problem TASK. A white pawn on the second rank, other than a rook's pawn, is moved, in different variations, in each of four possible ways, two forward moves and two captures, each preceded or followed by a different black move. The task was first achieved by LOYD in 1858. (See STARFLIGHTS, and compare PICKANINNY.)

Albin Variation, an alternative to the DILWORTH VARIATION (714) in the SPANISH OPENING introduced in the early 1890s in a match game Csánk–Albin. Instead of 11...Nxf2 Albin played 11...Nxd2 12 Qxd2 Be7. Also, 1043 in the PHILIDOR DEFENCE, first played by Albin in a simultaneous display in 1885, when the spectators unsuccessfully wagered that Albin's gambit would fail, and less happily in master play a month later, against Popiel, Vienna 1886.

Albrecht, Hermann (1915–82), German problemist, International Judge of Chess Compositions (1957), journalist. By 1980 he had collected about 80,000 orthodox TWO-MOVERS, a task he began in 1933; he invented his own classification system without reference to that used by A. C. WHITE. Since Albrecht's death it has been maintained and augmented by the German composer Hans-Dieter Leiss (1941–94). Tourney judges seeking advice regarding ANTICIPATION frequently refer to this collection.

Album, see FIDE ALBUMS.

Alburt, Lev Osipovich (1945–), International Grandmaster (1977), a teacher in Odessa until he emigrated to the USA in 1979. In 1974 he won the championship of the Ukraine and came equal fifth in the third of his five attempts in the USSR championship. He won the USA championship (+9=7−1) in 1984 and (+7=5−1) again in 1985. He also won a strong Swiss tournament at Portland in 1987 ahead of 534 other players.

In 1978 Alburt was 5th of 16 players at a tournament in Kiev. A Russian book of the tournament, in preparation at the time of Alburt's defection, became a literary curiosity. The book was published with all of Alburt's games omitted, no crosstable, and no index. Only a detailed examination of the scores after each round reveal to the innocent reader that the player who appeared to have a bye that round might have won, drawn, or lost a game during the round.

Alburt–Weinstein New York 1984 Catalan Opening

1 d4 Nf6 2 c4 e6 3 g3 d5 4 Bg2 Be7 5 Nf3 0-0 6 0-0 dxc4 7 Qc2 a6 8 Qxc4 b5 9 Qc2 Bb7 10 Bd2 Be4 11 Qc1 Nc6 12 Be3 Rc8 13 Nbd2 Bd5 14 Rd1 Na5 15 Ne5 c6 16 Ndf3 Qb6 17 Bg5 Rfd8 18 Qf4 Bxf3 19 Bxf3 h6 20 Bh4 Nc4 21 b3 Nxe5 22 dxe5 g5? (Alburt recommends 22...Nd5)

23 exf6 gxf4 24 fxe7 Re8 25 Rd7 Kg7 26 Rad1 Rc7 27 gxf4 Qb7 28 Kh1 Rxd7 29 Rg1+ Kh7 30 Bf6 Rd5 31 Rg7+ (The SEE-SAW begins.) 31...Kh8 32 Rxf7+ Kg8 33 Rg7+ Kh8 34 e4 Rd7 35 Bh5 Rd1+ 36 Rg1+ (The interrupted see-saw ends with the gaining of a piece.) 36...Kh7 37 Bg6+ Kg8 38 Rxd1 Black resigns.

Alekhine (pron. al-yekh-een), Alexander Alexandrovich (1892–1946), the only man to die while holding the world championship. Not everyone liked his personal character but all admired his chess genius. His father was a landowner, a Marshal of Nobility, and a member of the Duma, his mother, heiress of an industrial fortune. Both he and his brother Alexei (1888–1939) were taught chess by their mother. Alexander became addicted to the game when about 11, playing in his head during lessons, and by the light of a candle when in bed. While nominally studying law he developed his chess talent. He gained a master title at St Petersburg 1909, then played at Hamburg 1910, Carlsbad 1911, Vilnius 1912, and several lesser tournaments before his first big test came in 1914: it was the historic St Petersburg tournament, won by LASKER half a point ahead of CAPABLANCA, while Alekhine lost two games to each of these masters and came a poor third (+6=8−4).

Around this time he gave serious thought to the world championship, which he expected to win, and the problem of how to beat Capablanca dominated his thoughts for the next 13 years. His first task, to win strong tournaments, was checked by the outbreak of war; while he was playing in the Mannheim tournament of 1914, and leading, war began, and he and a number of other foreigners were interned. Accounts of his next few years mix fact and fancy. He is said to have made a dramatic escape from internment, feigning madness, using a false passport, and so on. Certified by a German medical commission as unfit for military service, he was officially released on 14 September. Returning to Russia in October 1914, via Switzerland, Italy, England, Sweden, and Finland, he completed his legal training and then served for a time in the Union of Cities (a voluntary service) on the Austrian front.

After the revolution he used his legal training to work as a magistrate. He played in a few tournaments and in 1920 won what was later called the first Soviet championship, but he knew that he needed to play abroad. A notorious trimmer if anything stood in the way of his two loves, Alekhine and chess, he joined the Communist Party in 1921 and became an official interpreter (he spoke several languages); undeterred by his marriage of the previous year to a Russian baroness (which legitimized their seven-year-old daughter), he married a Swiss Comintern delegate, Anneliese Rüegg, and obtained permission to leave Russia. They soon parted (she died in 1934) and Alekhine settled in Paris to become, in time, a naturalized French citizen. In 1928 he publicly attacked the Soviet regime; realizing, however, the growing strength of Russian chess (and, perhaps, the generosity of Soviet patronage), he later tried to ingratiate himself with the Soviet authorities, renouncing the label 'White'; but the breach was not repaired. He never returned to his homeland, and he was rehabilitated only in the 1950s.

Alekhine's first objective in his quest for a match with Capablanca was to destroy RUBINSTEIN'S claims. When that was achieved, by 1925, a new threat appeared in the shape of NIMZOWITSCH, and

Alekhine a year or two after winning the world championship. His signature shows a German form of his name—Aljechin

he, too, was closely studied. From 1921 to 1927 Alekhine won or shared first place in 8 of the 15 strongest tournaments in which he competed. His best victory was at Baden-Baden 1925 (+12=8), ahead of Rubinstein and BOGOLJUBOW. The two strongest events of this period were at New York: in 1924 Alekhine took third prize (+6=12−2), after Lasker and Capablanca; in 1927 he was second (+5=13−2), after Capablanca. He found time to take a third wife, Nadezda Vasilieva, the widow of a high-ranking Russian officer, and to commence law studies at the Sorbonne. His thesis was on the penal system in China, but he completed only the first two of four stages required. Although, like ZUKERTORT, he did not become a doctor, he was able to pass himself unchallenged as such.

Tarrasch–Alekhine   Piešt'any 1922   Blumenfeld Counter-gambit

1 d4 Nf6 2 Nf3 e6 3 c4 c5 4 d5 b5 5 dxe6 fxe6 6 cxb5 d5 7 e3 Bd6 8 Nc3 0-0 9 Be2 Bb7 10 b3 Nbd7 11 Bb2 Qe7 12 0-0 Rad8 13 Qc2 e5 (Black mobilizes his central pawn MAJORITY.) 14 Rfe1 e4 15 Nd2 Ne5 16 Nd1 Nfg4 17 Bxg4 Nxg4 18 Nf1 Qg5 19 h3 Nh6 20 Kh1 Nf5 21 Nh2 d4 22 Bc1 d3 23 Qc4+ Kh8 24 Bb2 Ng3+ 25 Kg1 Bd5 26 Qa4 Ne2+ 27 Kh1 Rf7 28 Qa6 h5 29 b6 Ng3+ 30 Kg1 axb6 31 Qxb6 d2 32 Rf1 Nxf1 33 Nxf1 Be6.

The game ended 34 Kh1 Bxh3 35 gxh3 Rf3 36 Ng3 h4 37 Bf6 Qxf6 38 Nxe4 Rxh3+ White resigns. If instead 34 Qc6 Rf3 35 Qxe4 Bd5 36 Qa4 Qxg2+ 37 Kxg2 Rg3+ (a STAIRCASE MOVEMENT begins) 38 Kh2 Rg2+ 39 Kh1 Rh2+ 40 Kg1 Rh1 mate.

Besides playing and studying chess ('eight hours a day on principle') he prepared for his challenge in other ways. He wrote *My Best Games of Chess 1908–1923* (1927), probably his best book, and *The Book of the New York International Chess Tournament 1924* (1925); the detailed annotations he made were an excellent form of training. He also toured the chess world making himself popular with its devotees, especially in South America, in the hope of obtaining financial backing, the lack of which had barred the way for many challengers. He studied the games of Capablanca, with whom he was careful to maintain cordial relations. When Nimzowitsch's challenge expired in January 1927, Capablanca agreed to play Alekhine for the world championship, and the match began at Buenos Aires in September.

The contestants differed in many respects. Capablanca was a man of his word, abstemious, a non-smoker; possessed of exceptional talent, he rarely studied and he played confidently and, apparently, with ease; away from the board he pursued the life of a playboy. Alekhine was devious, nervous, restless, a heavy smoker, and fond of drink; he had great combinative talent and had studied ceaselessly for many years to make himself the complete player. A patron who took both players to a show during the London Congress of 1922, noted: 'Capablanca never took his eyes off the chorus, Alekhine never looked up from his pocket chess set.' Above all, Alekhine learnt to rein his fertile imagination, for he knew that against Capablanca he would be unable to disturb the equilibrium favourably by violent means, however ingenious. Capablanca's failure to study was of little consequence, for his talent sufficed; but his failure to prepare psychologically was fatal; Alekhine won the match (+6=25−3), playing much of it in his opponent's solid positional style. Both in time and in number of games it was one of the longest of all championship matches.

Having spent 13 years before the match praising Capablanca and courting his friendship, Alekhine spent the next 13 years derogating his rival in annotations, articles, and books. His purpose in doing so may have been to avoid a return match. 'Somehow the match will never take place', he remarked soon after he won the title; and so it happened. He used Capablanca's own weapon, the LONDON RULES, demanding $10,000 in gold, but after the Wall Street crash such backing was unobtainable.

Alekhine also refused to play in any tournament with Capablanca, and the two did not meet again until 1936, at Nottingham, when Capablanca won. There had been a positive side to this campaign. To prove the supremacy he claimed, Alekhine won five strong tournaments: San Remo 1930 (+13=2); Bled 1931 (+15=11); London 1932 (+7=4); Pasadena 1932 (+7=3−1); and Zurich 1934 (+12=2−1). He defeated Bogoljubow in two matches, 1929 (+11=9−5) and 1934 (+8=15−3). On 15 June 1934, before the second of these matches was finished, he accepted a challenge from EUWE. Perhaps made complacent by his chess successes he gave way to a long-standing weakness for drink, and when he came to play Euwe in 1935 he was in poor condition and he lost the match.

If Alekhine loved alcohol, he loved chess and the championship more. With determination he regained much of his fitness and former playing strength, and convincingly defeated Euwe (+10=11−4) in the return match of 1937. In 1936 Alekhine came first in two very strong tournaments, Bad Nauheim (+4=5), a tie with KERES, and Dresden (+5=3−1). His results in the two major events of this time were less impressive; Nottingham 1936, sixth (+6=6−2), after BOTVINNIK, Capablanca, Euwe, FINE, and RESHEVSKY; and

AVRO 1938 (+3=8−3), fourth equal with Euwe. In 1939 Alekhine published *My Best Games of Chess 1924–1937*, a fitting companion to his earlier book of games.

Around June 1939 Alekhine accepted a challenge from Botvinnik, but shortly afterwards the Second World War began. Alekhine was then in Buenos Aires, playing for France in the Olympiad; as captain, he refused to allow his team to play Germany. Returning to France, he joined the army as an interpreter, and, when France fell in 1940, fled to Marseille. In the autumn of 1940 he sought permission to enter Cuba, promising, if it were granted, to play a match with Capablanca. This gambit having failed, he went to Lisbon in April 1941, seeking a visa to the USA. Meanwhile six articles directed against Jewish chessplayers appeared under Alekhine's name in the Nazi press. This anti-Semitism brought a hostile reaction, particularly in America and Britain, possibly a reason no visa was granted. In an interview quoted in a Madrid paper, *El Alcázar*, 3 Sept. 1941, Alekhine spoke proudly of these articles. When the tide turned he said, in December 1945, 'there is nothing that was written by me'.

In September 1941 Alekhine went to Munich and, somewhat out of practice, could do no better in a tournament than share second place with Lundin, a point and a half after STOLTZ. From 1941 to 1943 he played in another seven tournaments in Germany or German-occupied countries, winning or sharing first place in all of them. After the war the anti-Semitic articles and his participation in these events were construed as collaboration with the enemy. Perhaps he played because he needed the money; he claimed to have been acting under duress, 'the price of my wife's liberty'. This was his fourth wife, the American-born Grace Wishard; the widow of an Englishman, she retained her British nationality. In 1956 the manuscripts of the six articles, in Alekhine's own handwriting, were found among her effects.

From 1943 he lived in Spain and Portugal, earning no more than a pittance by chess; moreover he suffered from cirrhosis of the liver, duodenitis, and hardening of the arteries, and in 1945 his health worsened. He was asked to play in a tournament in London in 1946 but, largely on account of pressure from the USA, the invitation was withdrawn because of his wartime record. Nor could he return to France. He had resumed negotiations for a match with Botvinnik, and agreed conditions. The match was to take place in England, under the auspices of the British Chess Federation, which confirmed the arrangements on 23 March 1946, so informing Alekhine by telegram. He died of a heart attack the next day. For three weeks his body lay unburied at Estoril, Portugal. A few years after his death the Soviet authorities proclaimed him the greatest star of Russian chess, and requested his reburial in Russia. His widow objected, and in 1956 his body was re-interred in Montparnasse cemetery, Paris. The ceremony was attended by Alekhine's son by Anneliese Rüegg, who came from Switzerland, and by the Soviet Ambassador. France, Russia, and FIDE provided a tombstone.

Alekhine had been anxious not to lose his title to one of his own generation, but realized that he would lose to Botvinnik, Keres, or Fine. He had called MORPHY 'the man born too soon', and PILLSBURY 'the man born too late'. Alekhine died at the right time.

After gaining his master title in 1909 Alekhine had played in 44 strong tournaments and won or shared 25 first and 8 second prizes; and he had come first in all but 5 of 39 minor tournaments. His games remain universally admired. As well as the games collections, he wrote many other books, notably on his matches with Euwe, and on the tournaments at New York 1924, New York 1927, and Nottingham 1936. A. A. Kotov, *Alexander Alekhine* (1975) contains a biography and 75 games. P. Morán *A. Alekhine, Agony of a Chess Genius* (1989) is an account, translated and edited by F. X. Mur, of Alekhine's visits to Spain, and his last years, and includes 148 games, mostly unfamiliar. (See FIXED CENTRE; GRIGORIEV VARIATION.)

Alekhine–Junge   Prague 1942   Catalan Opening

1 d4 d5 2 c4 e6 3 Nf3 Nf6 4 g3 dxc4 5 Qa4+ Nbd7 6 Bg2 a6 7 Qxc4 b5 8 Qc6 Rb8 9 0-0 Bb7 10 Qc2 c5 11 a4 (This POSITIONAL SACRIFICE gives White command of an open file and a lead in development.) 11 ... Bxf3 12 Bxf3 cxd4 13 axb5 axb5 14 Rd1 Qb6 15 Nd2 e5 16 Nb3 Nc5? (After the better move 16 ... Be7 White plays 17 e3 dxe3 18 Bxe3, with sufficient compensation for his pawn.) 17 Nxc5 Bxc5

18 Ra6 Qxa6 19 Qxc5 Qe6 20 Bc6+ Nd7 21 Bxd7+ Kxd7 22 Qa7+ Kc6 23 Bd2 Rhc8 24 e4 Qb3 25 Ra1 b4 26 Ra6+ Kb5 27 Ra5+ Kc6 28 Qc5+ Kd7 29 Ra7+ Black resigns.

Alekhine Attack, 1221, the CHATARD–ALEKHINE ATTACK in the FRENCH DEFENCE.

Alekhine Defence, 1248. Play usually continues 2 e5 Nd5 3 d4 d6, when Black hopes to gain counterplay by attacking White's pawn centre. Analysed and found wanting by ALLGAIER in 1819, the defence did not become popular until promoted by Alekhine in 1921, although it had occasional airings. It was tried in a correspondence game

Berwick–Edinburgh 1860–1. Charles Pearson, receiving knight odds, played it twice against ANDERSSEN in the London 1862 handicap tournament, and level against PAULSEN during a blindfold display at the same event. The English player John Edmund Hall (1853–1941) was perhaps the first to play the line regularly. Some early players had retreated the knight, 2 e5 Ng8, content to have forced what they saw as a weakness in White's pawn skeleton.

Alekhine may have derived his idea from the variation 1 e4 c5 2 Nf3 Nf6, (561), in which Black also tempts White to advance the e-pawn, but he is said to have been shown the defence by the Moscow player Mikhail Gertsovich Klyatskin (1897–1926). (See ÓLAFSSON, F.; SCHMID.)

Alekhine Gambit, 579, a line in the CARO–KANN DEFENCE, played Alekhine–Winter, Hastings 1936–7; 1259, in ALEKHINE DEFENCE, as Alekhine–Reshevsky, Kemeri 1937.

Alekhine System, 32, the NIMZOWITSCH VARIATION of the ENGLISH OPENING. The name arises because of the line's resemblance to the ALEKHINE DEFENCE, but it is not an opening system.

Alekhine Variation, 63 in the QUEEN'S GAMBIT Accepted, from the third game of the Bogoljubow–Alekhine championship match of 1929; 79 in the SLAV DEFENCE; 96, also in the Slav Defence, introduced by ALEKHINE around 1922; 139 (sometimes called the Accelerated Meran) in the SEMI-SLAV DEFENCE, from the game Bogoljubow–Alekhine, Bern 1932; 183 and 211 in the QUEEN'S GAMBIT Declined; 199 in the Queen's Gambit Declined, played nine times by Alekhine in his championship match with CAPABLANCA in 1927; 228 in the QUEEN'S PAWN OPENING; 255 in the DUTCH DEFENCE, introduced by Alekhine in 1936; 250 also in the Dutch Defence; 265 in the STAUNTON GAMBIT; 358 in the QUEEN'S INDIAN DEFENCE; 479 and 529 in the SICILIAN DEFENCE; 627 in the VIENNA GAMBIT; 719 and 762 in the SPANISH OPENING; 1189 in the FRENCH DEFENCE, played in the 7th match game Alekhine–Euwe, 1935.

Others among the many variations that sometimes bear Alekhine's name are 294 CENTRE PLAY VARIATION; 304 SPIELMANN VARIATION; 309 CLASSICAL VARIATION; 907 CLOSE VARIATION.

Aleppo Gambit, 59, obsolete name for the QUEEN'S GAMBIT, bestowed because of its association with STAMMA.

Alexander, Conel Hugh O'Donel (1909–74), International Master (1950), International Correspondence Chess Master (1970). Born in Cork, he moved to England as a boy, after the death of his father. In spite or because of his intense application at the board his tournament performances were erratic. From about 1937 to the mid-1950s he was regarded as the strongest player in Great Britain, although of the 13 British championships in which he competed he won only two (1938, 1956); he played in six Olympiads from 1933 to 1958. His best tournament result was at Hastings 1937–8, when he was second (+4=5) equal with KERES, after RESHEVSKY, ahead of FINE and FLOHR, but later generations remember him better for his tie with BRONSTEIN for first place at Hastings 1953–4. He won his game against Bronstein in 120 moves, after several adjournments. The outcome became a kind of serial in the daily press, arousing great national interest even among those who did not play chess.

During the war Alexander became a leading cryptanalyst, one of the three men who cracked the German Enigma code. When war ended he had a brief encounter with the business world but was soon back in intelligence work, based in Cheltenham. Because of the nature of his work he was not allowed to play chess in countries under Soviet influence, and in his relatively few tournaments abroad he achieved only moderate results.

Golombek and Hartston, *The Best Games of C. H. O'D. Alexander* (1976) contains 70 annotated games and a touching personal memoir from Milner-Barry.

Alexandre, Aaron (1766–1850), writer and teacher. A Bavarian, the eldest of three brothers, he became a rabbi. In 1793 he went to Paris and, impressed by the new regime's tolerance of Jews, became a naturalized Frenchman, teaching German at several colleges and privately. For years chess was a pastime, but he was strong enough to operate the TURK although he disliked the cramped working space. His other hobbies included the making of mechanical devices, children's toys, and furniture with secret drawers. His nephew Lämlein, who walked from Würzburg to Paris to be placed under his care, some years later depicted Staunton playing Saint-Amant. The engraving hung for a century in the CAFÉ DE LA RÉGENCE.

Alexandre's importance to chess lies in his two books, which might never have been written had he been able to manage his affairs. He owned the hotel L'Echiquier where his pupils lodged. After his wife's death he forgot to collect from his debtors (an old chess teacher, Castinel, lived free of charge for ten years under his roof) and he went bankrupt.

He turned to chess for support and, at 70, worked day and night to finish his *Encylopédie des échecs* (1837), as well as travelling through Germany, England, Scotland, and Ireland to enlist subscribers. The book was intended to be a collection of all the openings variations then known; he drew from about 37 books, dating from LÓPEZ in the 16th century to WALKER and LEWIS in the 1830s. Although some sources were not available to him, his book is a remarkable compilation which gives a fair representation of the development of the openings. Anticipating *Chess Informant*, Alexandre gave an introduction in English, French, German, and Italian, and used STANDARD NOTATION.

Settling in London for the rest of his days, Alexandre gave German lessons, opened another unsuccessful chess club, and wrote *The Beauties of Chess* (1846). It contains 1,884 problems and 136 endgames, the first large compilation of its kind, but has many errors. (A facsimile edition published in 1979 includes thirty pages of corrections.) The accelerating pace of change (see PROBLEM HISTORY) soon made the collection look out of date. Its historical value would be greater had sources been quoted, a practice which did not become standard until well into the 20th century.

alfil, a European name for the piece known to players of SHAṬRANJ as a FĪL, a 2,2, ($\sqrt{8}$) LEAPER; also known in medieval times as an AUFIN or alfin.

Alfonso manuscript. An important historical source of information about chess and other indoor diversions, this beautifully illustrated manuscript of 98 leaves was completed in 1283 by order of Alfonso the Wise (1221–84), King of Castile and León 1251–84. The first of the seven parts (ff. 1–64b) is devoted wholly to chess, and contains 103 problems both Arabic (MANṢŪBAT) and European. The fourth part (ff. 81a–85b) contains 14 FAIRY PROBLEMS, and descriptions of several unorthodox games, including forms of GREAT CHESS and MUST-CAPTURE CHESS. Two significant departures from the laws of SHAṬRANJ are noted: the FERS'S leap (previously mentioned by EZRA) and the pawn's double move.

algebraic notation, see STANDARD NOTATION.

Alice chess, an unorthodox game invented in 1954 by the English puzzle expert Vernon Rylands Parton (1897–1974) and named after the principal character in Lewis Carroll's *Through the Looking Glass*. Two boards and one set of men are required. The game begins from the ARRAY with all the men on one board. Every time a man is moved it is transferred ('through the looking glass') to its corresponding arrival square on the other board. A move need be legal only on the board from which the moved man departs, but the square on the other board to which the man is transferred must be vacant. A man can capture only on the board from which it departs and check only on the board to which it is moved. Some examples follow.

One of the fine illustrations from the Alfonso MS. A conditional problem, Black to move and mate in three with the pawn on d4. Black has K on d3, R on f8, N on c4, firzān on d2, pawns on d4 and g3. White has K on d1, R on h1, fīl on c1. Solution: 1 Kc3, fīl or rook moves, 2 Nb2+ Ke2 3 d3 mate. 1 Nb2+ would be mate, but not by the pawn on d4.

1 Nf3 d5 2 f4. White's second move is legal, for his king's knight has been transferred to the other board.

1 Nc3 d5 2 g3 e6 3 Bh3 Qxd2 (this is not check) 4 Be3. Black's queen can be saved only if it is moved to g2.

1 e4 d5 2 Be2 dxe4 3 Bb5 mate.

1 d4 e5 2 dxe5 Be7 3 Qxd7 Qd4 4 f3 Bh4 mate. A check from a line-piece can never be met by the interposition of a man on the same board, while 5 Kd1, Kd2 would leave White's king in check after transferral. This is an 'Alice mate' of the kind required by problemists: FLIGHTS are guarded on the other board.

allegories, stories ostensibly about chess but aimed at other targets. Medieval chess MORALITIES frequently took this form. A famous political allegory is the play *A Game at Chess* by Thomas Middleton. Acted at the Globe theatre in August 1624, it was performed on nine successive days, Sundays excluded, and took £1,500, a great sum for the time. It was the first long run in the history of English theatre, and would have continued had it not been suppressed by order of James I. The Spanish Ambassador, who said 'there were more than three thousand persons there on the day that the audience was smallest', protested at the veiled attack on the Roman Catholic Church and the Spanish crown. Tradition has it that Middleton was imprisoned, but obtained his freedom by petitioning the king:

> A Harmless game, coin'd only for delight,
> Was play'd 'twixt the Black house and the White.
> The White house won; yet still the Black doth brag,
> They had the power to put me in the bag.
> Use but your Royal hand, 'twill set me free,
> 'Tis but the removing of a man—that's me.

(See also CESSOLE; ÉCHECS AMOUREUX; GESTA ROMANORUM; INNOCENT MORALITY.)

allegro, a game in which each player has a total of thirty minutes for the game. The term, particularly favoured in Scotland, is used also for a finish in which the clocks of the players are set back by half an hour after they have successfully reached the time control. Then the game must be completed before the TIME-LIMIT. In England the term Quickplay is often used instead of allegro.

Allen, George (1808–76), American professor of Greek who wrote *The Life of Philidor, musician and chess-player* (1858). A reprint of the second American edition (1863) was published in 1971. Allen had an excellent chess library, which was acquired by the Library Company of Philadelphia, and he contributed scholarly items to various chess periodicals. He was grand-nephew of Ethan Allen, hero of the American revolution.

Allgaier, Johann Baptist (1763–1823), player and author. He was born in southern Germany and intended to become a Catholic priest, but while travelling in Poland discovered chess. He went to live in Vienna, operated the TURK for a time, won an important match, and became chess tutor to the Emperor's sons and brothers. A big strong man, he gained respect for his direct and honest manner. He served as quartermaster-accountant in the Austrian army from 1798 to 1816, and after his retirement became the strongest chess master in Vienna, where he made a living from chess lessons and stakegames. Like DESCHAPELLES and BOURDONNAIS, he died of dropsy.

Allgaier's most outstanding work was *Neue theoretisch-praktische Anweisung zum Schachspiele* (1795). He published revised editions in 1802, 1811, and 1819, and several other editions were published after his death. The first systematic treatise in the German language, it contains much useful playing advice and many openings variations with detailed annotations. Allgaier stresses his preference for a king's-side majority of pawns, a view shared by his contemporaries. (The idea that, other things being equal, a queen's-side majority might be preferable was not mooted until the 1840s.) In 1811 the openings were printed in tabular form, an innovation that has since become customary; in 1819 he analysed the gambit named after him and the ALEKHINE DEFENCE. Although this book was not widely read in England and France it was rightly regarded in several parts of Europe as the best textbook of its time. (See PROMOTION.)

Allgaier Gambit, 1166 in the KING'S GAMBIT Accepted, played around 1780 by the Englishman Cotter, after whom it is sometimes named. White sacrifices a knight in the hope of obtaining a strong attack. Allgaier was the first to publish a detailed analysis, which appeared in the fourth edition of his book, 1819; five years later his main line was refuted by the HORNY DEFENCE, 1173. Afterwards the WALKER ATTACK, 1169, and THOROLD VARIATION, 1171, gave new life to the gambit which, however, has never been as popular as White's alternative choice, the KIESERITZKY GAMBIT, 1151.

allies, two or more players in consultation taking either the white or black pieces; chessmen of the same colour.

all-play-all, or American tournament, a contest in which each player meets every other player at least once. If they meet twice it is a double-round tournament, if more often it may be called a MATCH TOURNAMENT. At first it was thought that such a system would not work because players out of the running would not play at full strength or even at all. This appeared to be confirmed by the first international tournament of this kind, which began in London on 28 July 1851. Players agreed between themselves when they would play and ANDERSSEN, anxious to return to Breslau, quickly won seven games and took the only prize, a cup valued at £100. The other competitors played a mere handful of games between themselves. Nevertheless, the KNOCK-OUT TOURNAMENT, then fashionable, was soon superseded by all-play-all events, which often took less time and were fairer: a player, who might have travelled a considerable distance, could not be eliminated after losing just one game. In the second all-play-all international tournament, London 1862, six prizes were offered and there were fewer defaults.

Allumwandlung, or AUW, a German term (lit. omni-promotion) that describes a composition TASK consisting of the promotion of a pawn or pawns to Q, R, B, and N. In a FAIRY PROBLEM the term could also include promotion to every kind of fairy piece that is in the set position. Promotions may be concurrent (i.e. in the variations), preferably with the same pawn, or consecutive. Fairy problemists sometimes vary the definition, but always to include at least four different promotions. The first problem to show the task was composed in 1882, the first study in 1933.

For examples, see ABDURAHMANOVIĆ; BABSON TASK; CHINESE FAMILY; LOMMER; MADRASI; PETROVIĆ; SERIES-MOVER.

alquerque, a generic name (from the Arabic *qirq*) for a group of board games played on the intersections of lines rather than on squares. Three forms are given in the ALFONSO MS. *Alquerque de tres* is a version of three men's morris. *Alquerque de nueve* is akin to nine men's morris. The other, *alquerque de doze*, has a board of 5 × 5 points, joined orthogonally and diagonally. Each player has twelve men, filling the five points on the first two ranks and the right-hand pair in the centre rank. Thus only the central point is vacant in the initial array. The object is to eliminate the opponent's men. The move of a man is to any vacant adjacent point, while a capture is made by leaping over an adjacent enemy man to a vacant point. This move was adopted for the game of DRAUGHTS.

Altschul, Frank (1887–1981), American, originally from San Francisco, who became interested in printing as an art. When working as a New York banker he set up his private Overbrook Press at his country home at Stamford, Connecticut. Between 1941 and 1945 he printed eight problem books for A. C. WHITE. They were beautifully produced, with special typefaces, paper, and even binding paste; the pages of one book were individually damped after printing to remove the gloss. All are in limited editions of 150 to 400 copies.

Amar Gambit, 1326, a line played in the 1930s by the Parisian amateur Charles Amar. Sometimes the name is given to 1325, the PARIS GAMBIT.

Amar Opening, 1324, usually known as the PARIS OPENING.

amateur, one who does not live by chess. There are no restrictions on amateurs in chess: they win cash prizes, can accept appearance money, and may reach any standard. There have been amateurs at CANDIDATE level, and even one world champion, EUWE. Sometimes the term is used for one below a master. In the 19th century games were often printed showing a win by a master against 'Amateur' because it was thought improper in some quarters to publish a player's name without permission, and the professional player did not want to lose a customer.

amaurosis scachistica, an ailment diagnosed by the physician TARRASCH in his book *Die moderne Schachpartie*. There is no sure preventive treatment and there is some evidence that it may be infectious. Dr Tarrasch described its various forms, such as *amaurosis scachistica chronica communis, amaurosis scachistica acutissima,* and *amaurosis scachistica totalis duplex benigna ridicula.* The main symptom is the making of obvious but uncharacteristic blunders, a complaint more often known as chess blindness.

amazon, an unorthodox piece that combines the powers of rook, bishop, and knight. First described in a 16th-century manuscript now in Perugia, this piece was sometimes used in the next two centuries as a substitute for the queen in otherwise orthodox chess. In VIDA'S famous poem the queen was sometimes called an amazon, probably the first use of this word to describe a chess piece.

ambush, a composition term for a situation in which a line-piece would control a line if another man, of either colour, were moved out of the way. Problemists use the word BATTERY to describe an ambush in which both pieces are of the same colour, as in the INDIAN THEME.

American Attack, 558, in the SICILIAN DEFENCE, advocated by Philip Richardson of New York in the 1880s but soon superseded by ENGLISCH'S move (7 a3). The name is sometimes used for 632, the PAULSEN ATTACK in the VIENNA GAMBIT.

American Defence, 182, a title occasionally used for the MANHATTAN DEFENCE.

American tournament, see ALL-PLAY-ALL.

Amsterdam Variation, 527, sound way of attacking the DRAGON VARIATION of the SICILIAN DEFENCE, known since the 1880s but named much later. Also 107 in the SLAV DEFENCE.

analysis, a detailed examination of the variations that could arise from a given position.

analyst, one who analyses the game, especially the opening or the endgame.

Anand, Viswanathan (1969–), Indian player, International Grandmaster (1988) who won the World Junior Championship in 1987. His next major success was equal first (+4=7−2) in the very strong top tournament at Wijk aan Zee, 1989. In the interzonal tournament at Manila 1990 he was third, equal with SHORT out of 64 players, and became a CANDIDATE. At Madras in 1991 he defeated DREYEV (+4=1−1) in the first round of Candidates' matches, but then lost narrowly to KARPOV. In the meantime he shared first prize (+5=6) with KAMSKY at New Delhi 1990.

Anand–Badea Manchester 1990 Sicilian Defence Najdorf Variation

1 e4 c5 2 Nf3 d6 3 d4 cxd4 4 Nxd4 Nf6 5 Nc3 a6 6 Bc4 e6 7 0-0 b5 8 Bb3 Be7 9 Qf3 Qb6 10 Be3 Qb7 11 Qg3 Nc6 12 f4 Nxd4 13 Bxd4 b4 14 e5 Nh5 15 Qg4 bxc3 16 Qxh5 cxb2 17 Bxb2 g6 18 Qh6 Bf8 19 Qh3 d5 20 Bd4 Qc6 21 Kh1 Bd7 22 c3 Bg7

23 f5 gxf5 24 g4 Qc7 25 Rae1 Bb5 26 gxf5 Bxf1 27 Rxf1 Qd7 28 fxe6 Qxe6 29 Qg2 Black resigns.

Anastasia's mate. The name is taken from a novel by Wilhelm Heinse (1746–1803), *Anastasia und das Schachspiel* (Frankfurt, 1803). The book takes the form of letters from Italy in which the writer uses positions from LOLLI.

1 ... Ka7 2 b5 Ka8 3 Kc7 Ka7 4 Bc8 Ka8 5 Bb7+ Ka7 6 b6 mate. The author calls this, originally by DAMIANO, Anastasia's mate, but the name is now used for another kind of mate, an example of which is given in his book and described by him as comparable in beauty to a classical Greek epigram.

#2

Lolli ascribes this position to a Turin officer, 'Count NN'. The moves are 1 Qc5+ dxc5 2 Rd8 mate. When Anastasia's mate occurs in play the mated king is usually on the edge of the board, as in this example.

Leonhardt–Englund Stockholm 1908 Two Knights Defence Fritz Variation

1 e4 e5 2 Nf3 Nc6 3 Bc4 Nf6 4 Ng5 d5 5 exd5 Nd4 6 c3 b5 7 Bf1 Nxd5 8 cxd4 Qxg5 9 Bxb5+ Kd8 10 Qf3? Bb7 11 0-0 Rb8 12 d3 Qg6 13 Qg3 exd4 14 Na3 Bxa3 15 bxa3 Nc3 16 Qxg6 hxg6 17 Bc4 Ne2+ 18 Kh1

18 ... Ke7 White resigns because there is no satisfactory way of avoiding Anastasia's mate, 19 ... Rxh2+ 20 Kxh2 Rh8 mate.

anchor ring, a combination of vertical and horizontal CYLINDER BOARDS, used for FAIRY PROBLEMS. It could be depicted on the external surface of a solid body the shape of a lifebelt, or the figure known to mathematicians as a torus. There are no edges: each rank, file, and diagonal is continuous.

Anderson, Gerald Frank (1898–1983), English composer born in South Africa, International Judge of Chess Compositions (1960), International Master for Chess Compositions (1975), best known for his THREE-MOVERS and FAIRY PROBLEMS. He published 120 of his problems in *Adventures of My Chessmen (1914–1923)* (1924). In 1938 he began composing KRIEGSPIEL problems, and in 1959 published *Are There Any?*, the first book on the subject, containing 44 examples. He made his career in the British Foreign Office, and while in Lisbon played the following FRIENDLY GAME at the British Embassy on 9 March 1946, the last recorded game by ALEKHINE. (See PROBLEM HISTORY.)

Anderson–Alekhine   Lisbon, 1946   Queen's Gambit Declined

1 d4 Nf6 2 c4 e6 3 Nc3 d5 4 Bg5 c6 5 e3 h6 6 Bxf6 Qxf6 7 Bd3 Nd7 8 Nf3 Bb4 9 0-0 0-0 10 a3 Ba5 11 e4 dxc4 12 e5 Qe7 13 Bxc4 Rd8 14 Qc2 Nb6 15 Ba2 Nd5 16 Ne2 Bd7 17 Rad1 Rac8 18 b4 Bc7 19 Bb1 f5 20 g4 Rf8 21 gxf5 exf5 22 Kh1 g5 23 Rg1 Kh8 24 Qd2 f4 25 Nh4 gxh4 26 Rg6 Qh7 27 e6 Be8 28 Rg4 Qe7 29 Qd3 h5 30 Rg5 Nf6 31 d5 cxd5 32 Nd4 Ne4 White resigns.

Chandler, Flood, and Matthews, *A Tribute to G. F. Anderson* (1974) contains 112 problems.

Anderson, Magnus Victor (1884–1966), Australian accountant and bibliophile. He built up a collection of 6,000 chess books which he presented to the library of his home city, Melbourne. During his lifetime he would make the journey from his office to the Public Library, usually twice daily, in order to refile any book misplaced after use. No officer of the library was permitted to do the work.

Anderssen, Karl Ernst Adolf (1818–79), winner of three great international tournaments: London 1851, London 1862, and Baden-Baden 1870. After the first he was regarded as the world's leading player. First known as a composer, he published *Aufgaben für Schachspieler* (1842); his problems (see PROBLEM HISTORY) were popular because of their short and lively solutions. They compare well with those of his contemporaries, and he invented one kind of FOCAL PLAY. He continued to compose, but soon became more interested in play, his inspiration being the games of the Bourdonnais-McDonnell matches of 1834. In 1846 he joined the editorial staff of Germany's newly founded magazine *Schachzeitung* (later *Deutsche Schachzeitung*). The following year he returned to his native city, Breslau (now Wrocław), where he lived for the rest of his life, a teacher of mathematics at the Friedrichs Gymnasium.

When the first international tournament was held, London 1851, Anderssen's only notable playing achievement, a drawn match with HARRWITZ in 1848 (+5−5), seemed modest enough, and no one expected him to defeat the acknowledged experts then assembled to play a series of knock-out matches; yet he won decisively, defeating KIESERITZKY, SZÉN, STAUNTON, and WYVILL in that order. At Christmas 1858, after seven years with very little practice, Anderssen went to Paris to meet MORPHY. A match of 11 games lasting nine days ended with Anderssen's defeat. 'It is impossible', he remarked, 'to keep one's skill [*Meisterschaft*] in a showcase, like a jewel.' Anderssen might well have given a better account of himself, under less adverse conditions, had Morphy kept his promise to play a return match in Breslau.

He now began to take chess more seriously. Primarily an attacking player, he superimposed some positional skills and improved his play

throughout the 1860s. In 1861 he defeated KOLISCH in match play (+4=2−3) and in the international tournament, London 1862, he came first ahead of the principal rival, PAULSEN. Afterwards these two played a match which was abandoned as drawn (+3=2−3) when Anderssen was obliged to return to Breslau. He took his work conscientiously and around 1862 was entitled professor of mathematics and of the German language; in January 1865 he was given an honorary degree, Doctor of Philosophy and Master of Liberal Arts. (This doctorate was not awarded for his chess achievements, as commonly supposed.)

In 1866 Anderssen narrowly lost a match to STEINITZ (+6−8) after a series of stirring games. (Neither Steinitz nor anyone else suggested that any kind of championship was involved.) Baden-Baden 1870 was the strongest tournament held up to that time. Anderssen's victory, ahead of Steinitz, BLACKBURNE, and NEUMANN, was the best of his career. He remained among the top half-dozen players until his death, his last notable achievement being at Leipzig 1877 when he came second equal with ZUKERTORT, hard on the heels of his old rival Paulsen.

Anderssen–Zukertort   Barmen 1869   Evans Gambit

1 e4 e5 2 Nf3 Nc6 3 Bc4 Bc5 4 b4 Bxb4 5 c3 Ba5 6 d4 exd4 7 0-0 Bb6 8 cxd4 d6 9 d5 Na5 10 Bb2 Ne7 11 Bd3 0-0 12 Nc3 Ng6 13 Ne2 c5 14 Qd2 f6 15 Kh1 Bc7 16 Rac1 Rb8 17 Ng3 b5 18 Nf5 b4 19 Rg1 Bb6 20 g4 Ne5 21 Bxe5 dxe5? 22 Rg3 Rf7 23 g5 Bxf5 24 exf5 Qxd5.

25 gxf6 Rd8 (25...Rxf6 26 Bc4) 26 Rcg1 Kh8 (26...Qxd3 27 Rxg7+) 27 fxg7+ Kg8 28 Qh6 Qd6 (28...Qxd3 29 Qxh7+) and White announced mate in 5 by 29 Qxh7+ Kxh7 30 f6+ Kg8 31 Bh7+ etc.

A tall man with a stoop, clean-shaven, prematurely bald, Anderssen lived quietly with his mother and sister; he never married. In the holidays he would often travel to Berlin or other cities; in term-time players often came to Breslau, many hoping to learn from him. In 1925 RIEMANN wrote a book about the achievements of Anderssen's pupils, among whom were Neumann and Zukertort. Apart from his work, Anderssen seemed to have no interests other than chess or having a drink with friends. At London in 1851, asked why he had not seen the

Great Exhibition, he replied: 'I came to London to play chess.'

He contested numerous friendly games against beginners and experts alike, never fearing for his reputation; he may have preferred this kind of chess, in which his flair for brilliant tactical play could have full rein. (See EVERGREEN GAME; IMMORTAL GAME.) Although he was rather shy with strangers, the characteristic which emerges most frequently is Anderssen's pleasant nature. Steinitz wrote: 'Anderssen was honest and honourable to the core. Without fear or favour he straightforwardly gave his opinion, and his sincere disinterestedness became so patent ... that his word alone was usually sufficient to quell disputes ... for he had often given his decision in favour of a rival ...'. When Anderssen died, the *Deutsche Schachzeitung* gave an obituary that ran to 19 black-lined pages; and POTTER wrote that 'no one ever speaks ill of Anderssen. In death as in life all chess-players are his friends.'

H. von Gottschall, *Adolf Anderssen* (1912, repr. 1980) contains 80 problems, 787 games, and a biography, with text in German; G. Pollak, *Weltgeschichte des Schachs: Anderssen I* (1968) contains 604 games played from 1844 to 1875, with biographical material.

Anderssen Attack, 1229, an alternative name for the RICHTER VARIATION of the FRENCH DEFENCE.

Anderssen Counterattack, 979, standard line (sometimes called the Paulsen Variation, or Suhle Variation) in the SCOTCH GAMBIT, introduced in a game Cochrane–Staunton, 1841. Also 1134 in the KING'S GAMBIT Accepted, played by ANDERSSEN four times in his match with STEINITZ, 1866. Anderssen lost three of these games. His choice of a defence, long known to be inferior, was probably anticipated by his opponent, who might not otherwise have opened with the SALVIO GAMBIT. Instead of 7 ... d6 (attributed by POLERIO to Sadoleto, *c*.1590) Anderssen could have obtained the better game by SALVIO's move 7 ... f3.

Sometimes the name is given to 1095, the BLEDOW VARIATION of the King's Gambit.

Anderssen Focal, see FOCAL PLAY.

Anderssen Opening, 1, played by ANDERSSEN three times in his match with MORPHY, 1858. Anderssen expected the reply 1 ... e5 after which he believed 2 c4 would favour White; he also wanted to avoid well-known openings which his opponent had studied extensively.

Anderssen Variation, 464 in the SICILIAN DEFENCE, from the game Winawer–Anderssen, Leipzig 1877; 597 in the CENTRE COUNTER GAME, from the 7th match game Morphy–Anderssen, 1858; 694, sometimes known as the Steinitz Attack, in the SPANISH OPENING, given in the second (1852) edition of the HANDBUCH and played by ANDERSSEN throughout his career; 792 in the same opening, at one time often played by him, e.g. Anderssen–Paulsen, London 1862; 920 in the ITALIAN OPENING, as Staunton–Anderssen, London 1851; 1228, sometimes styled Attack, in the FRENCH DEFENCE, favoured by Anderssen in the 1870s, and played with the intention of preparing an attack on Black's king.

Also, 690, the COZIO DEFENCE DEFERRED, first played in a casual game Neumann–Anderssen, 1864; 895, MAYET DEFENCE as played informally Anderssen–Mayet, 1867, but not recommended by Anderssen.

Andersson, Ulf (1951–), Swedish player, International Grandmaster (1972). He won or shared first prizes at Göteborg 1971 (+6=5), Dortmund 1973, Camagüey 1974 (+9−5−1), and Cienfuegos 1975 (+10=7). After this last tournament he married a Cuban and stayed in her country for a year as national trainer. His tournament successes since than have included seven victories in strong tournaments: Buenos Aires 1978 (+5=8); London 1980 (+6=5−2), equal with KORCHNOI and MILES; Johannesburg 1981 (+3=8−1), ahead of HÜBNER and Korchnoi; London 1982 (+5=7−1), equal with KARPOV; Turin 1982 (+1=10 and one win by default), equal with Karpov; Wijk aan Zee 1983 (+5=8); and Reggio Emilia 1985–6 (+3=8) equal with LJUBOJEVIĆ and ROMANISHIN. These successes placed him among the world's best dozen players.

Andersson plays with great concentration and determination; the ACCUMULATION OF ADVANTAGES is the basis of his style (see the game under that heading). This sound and noncommittal approach sometimes encourages his opponents to overreach themselves, but it leads to a high proportion of drawn games. As a consequence, in the 16 important tournaments in which he played between 1985 and 1990 he was first only once, but second, or equal second, on 8 occasions and made a total score of +45=145−9.

Byrne–Andersson   Amsterdam 1979   Sicilian Defence Paulsen Variation

1 e4 c5 2 Nf3 e6 3 d4 cxd4 4 Nxd4 a6 5 Bd3 g6 6 b3 d6 7 0-0 Bg7 8 Bb2 Nf6 9 c4 0-0 10 Nc3 Nbd7 11 Re1 Re8 12 Bf1 b6 13 Qd2 Bb7 14 Rad1 Qc7 15 f3 Rad8 16 Qf2 Ne5 17 Rc1

17...d5 18 exd5 Nfg4 19 Qg3 Nxf3+ 20 gxf3 Bxd4+ 21 Kh1 Qxg3 22 hxg3 Ne3 23 Bd3 exd5 24 cxd5 Nxd5 25 Rxe8+ Rxe8 26 Be4 Bxc3 27 Bxc3 Nxc3 28 Bxb7 Nxa2 29 Rc6 a5 30 Rxb6 Rb8 31 Kg2 Kf8 32 Rb5 Nb4 33 Kf2 Ke7 34 Ke3 Kd6 35 Kd4 Kc7 36 Rxb4 axb4 37 Bd5 Kd6 38 Bxf7 Rf8 39 Bd5 Rf5 40 Be4 Rg5 41 g4 h5 White resigns.

Andreaschek Gambit, 458, a cousin of the MORRA GAMBIT in the SICILIAN DEFENCE pioneered by the Czech player Karl Andreaschek (1880–1910) in a match game Andreaschek–Göbel, 1900.

Anglo-Dutch Defence, 34, the DUTCH DEFENCE move, 1 . . . f5, in response to the ENGLISH OPENING.

Anglo-Indian Defence, 35, the move 1 . . . Nf6, typical of the INDIAN DEFENCE to 1 d4, played in response to the ENGLISH OPENING.

annihilation, a problem manœuvre: the sacrifice of a piece on a line so that another man of the same colour can be moved along the line when the capturing piece is moved out of the way.

#3

A problem by LOYD, *Wilkes's Spirit of the Times*, 1868. 1 Bc5 Nxc5 (1 . . . Nd6 2 Qd7) 2 Qa7 N~ (opening the diagonal a7-g1) 3 Qg1 mate. For other examples, see BAKCSI; DIJK.

annotation, a comment on one or more moves of a game. The best annotations explain what is happening and reveal each decisive error or that part of the game in which such an error occurs. Until the last third of the 19th century annotators frequently failed to explain how the advantage passed from a player to the opponent. As LASKER pointed out, they believed that talented players were able to conjure winning positions from thin air. However, a precondition for victory is an error by the opponent, an insight that is central to the THEORY proposed by STEINITZ; and his annotations marked a distinct advance on those of his predecessors. From then the standard of annotations by grandmasters continued to improve. The fashion for peppering annotations with exhaustive variations, set by MARCO and such imaginative writers as ALEKHINE

and TARTAKOWER, is giving way to one placing greater emphasis on positional assessment.

annotation symbols, see CONVENTIONAL SYMBOLS.

announced mate, a player's claim to be able to force mate in a stated number of moves. In over-the-board play such claims are neither fashionable nor sanctioned by the laws; if incorrect they carry no penalty other than humiliation, but frequent use of such false calls could be treated as an attempt to 'distract or annoy the opponent'. In correspondence play the benefits of an announced mate include the saving of time and money, but there is a penalty for a false claim. The opponent may follow the proposed variation as far as convenient and then play a move not envisaged by the first player.

In this position, from a correspondence game between the Liverpool and Edinburgh chess clubs in 1901, White announced mate in 45 should Black exchange bishops (the best move), whereupon Black (Edinburgh) resigned. White's PROTECTED PASSED PAWN is a decisive advantage because it severely restricts the freedom of Black's king. After 53 . . . Bxf4 54 Kxf4 Kd6 55 Ke4 Ke6 56 Kd4 c5+ (56 . . . Kd6 57 c5+) 57 Kc3 Kd7 58 Kb3 Kd6 59 Ka4 Kd7 60 Kb5 Kd6 61 f7 Ke7 62 Kc6 Kxf7 63 Kb7 b5 64 cxb5 c4 65 b6 White promotes first and wins the QUEEN ENDING. An extensive analysis was published in the *Liverpool Weekly Mercury*, 17 Aug. 1901. (See GILBERT.)

Antal Defence, 237, the PIRC DEFENCE. In 1934 Aladár Antal (1893–1975) of Hungary wrote a book on openings entitled *Dé hat* (which means d6).

anti-, a prefix added to the name of a move or manœuvre to indicate either its opposite or its prevention, e.g. ANTI-MERAN GAMBIT. The prefix is much used by problemists; for an example, see CRITICAL PLAY.

anticipation. A composition is said to have been anticipated if a similar one (the anticipation) has been published previously. Composers rarely intend this to happen, although PLAGIARISM is not unknown. The judge of a composing tourney might disqualify an entry on grounds of anticipation, or might find the later composition acceptable if it were to show new features or a more economical setting. (See COINCIDENCE.)

Anti-Grünfeld Variation, 412, a way of ensuring that a KING'S INDIAN DEFENCE does not develop into a GRÜNFELD DEFENCE.

Anti-Marshall Variation, 753, a line in the SPANISH OPENING intended to thwart the MARSHALL COUNTERATTACK. Black has to meet the threat of 9 axb5. (See EHLVEST; KHOLMOV.)

Anti-Meran Gambit, 153, popular way of avoiding the MERAN VARIATION. The gambit's acceptance, 5 dxc4, was examined by BOTVINNIK, and is sometimes named after him.

Anti-Meran Variation, 151, the RUBINSTEIN VARIATION of the QUEEN'S GAMBIT, forestalling the MERAN VARIATION.

Anti-neo-orthodox Variation, 185 in the QUEEN'S GAMBIT Declined. This is a representative example of jargon used to coin new names. When first given, the label ORTHODOX DEFENCE was intended to be sarcastic.

anti-positional move, a move that is part of a strategically incorrect plan, as distinct from an error made in faulty execution of a correctly conceived plan.

In the game given under MYSTERIOUS ROOK MOVE, for example, White attempts a king's-side attack. Black sets up an unbreakable stronghold for his king, and the continuation of the attack is anti-positional, although White did not realize this at the time.

Even great masters sometimes make the wrong strategic decisions. See EM. LASKER for a game in which Alekhine himself says of his 15th move 'White loses quickly because at any cost he strives for [a king's-side] attack . . .' i.e. wrongly thinking he had the prerequisite advantage.

Most anti-positional moves are pawn advances, by nature irreversible, and the error may not be obvious until later in the game. Of course, every move must be examined in context, but students attempting to discover why one player lost might well begin by suspecting pawn moves.

Antoshin, Vladimir Sergeyevich (1929–94), International Grandmaster (1963), technical designer. He played in the USSR championships of 1955, 1956, 1957, 1967, and 1970, his best result being in 1967, when he was equal sixth. He won ($+8=6-1$) an international event, Zinnowitz 1966.

Tolush–Antoshin   23rd USSR Championship 1956
Nimzo-Indian Defence Three Knights Variation

1 d4 Nf6 2 c4 e6 3 Nc3 Bb4 4 Nf3 d5 5 e3 0-0 6 Bd3 b6
7 0-0 Bb7 8 cxd5 exd5 9 Ne5 Nbd7 10 f4 c5 11 Rf3 Ne4
12 Rh3 Nxe5 13 Qh5 h6 14 dxe5 Bxc3 15 bxc3 f6

16 c4 d4 17 Bb2 fxe5 18 Qxe5 Re8 19 Qh5 Qf6 20 Rf1
Re7 21 Rh4 Qc6 22 exd4 cxd4 23 Qg4 Nf6 24 Qg6 Re3
25 Rd1 Rae8 26 Bxd4 Rxd3 27 Rxd3 Re1+ 28 Kf2
Ne4+ 29 Kxe1 Qxg6 30 h3 Nf6 31 Rd2 Qg3+ 32 Bf2
Qxg2 33 f5 Qh1+ 34 Ke2 Qf3+ 35 Ke1 Ne4 36 Rg4
Nxd2 White resigns.

any? A question addressed to a KRIEGSPIEL umpire by a player who wishes to know whether he or she may make a pawn capture.

apparent play, see SET PLAY.

Apšenieks, Fricis (German spelling Franz Apscheneek) (1894–1941), Latvian champion 1926–7, and again, after play-off with PETROV, in 1934. (See LATVIAN COUNTER-GAMBIT.)

Arabian chess, see SHATRANJ.

Arabian mate, a mate given by a rook and knight unaided by other men, possible only when the king is on a corner square, e.g. Wh: Rb8 (or a7) Nc6; Bl: Ka8. This modern name may have arisen because the powers of the rook and knight have not been changed since the days of SHATRANJ.

arbiter, a supervisor who enforces the laws and rules in a match or tournament and has the power to penalize infringements and settle disputes. Competitors seeking international titles expect events to be recognized by FIDE if the results are to count. An arbiter is not required to have the title INTERNATIONAL ARBITER but must abide by FIDE's rules if the event is to be accepted.

Archangelsk Variation, 698 in the SPANISH OPENING, played in MORPHY's time and recently much analysed by the Soviet players Abram Isaakovich Rabinovich (1878–1943), Anatoly Alexandrovich Matsukevich (1938–), and Rashid Nezhmetdinov (1912–74).

Argentine Defence, 188, the HENNEBERGER VARIATION of the QUEEN'S GAMBIT Declined used in the world championship match played in Buenos Aires, 1927.

Argentine Variation, 178 in the QUEEN'S GAMBIT Declined, as in the 7th match game Capablanca–Alekhine, Buenos Aires 1927. In the SICILIAN DEFENCE, 513, sometimes called the Göteborg Variation, a PREPARED VARIATION which the Argentine players NAJDORF, PANNO, and PILNIK introduced simultaneously in the 14th round of the Interzonal tournament at Göteborg, 1955. Their Soviet opponents, KERES, GELLER, and SPASSKY respectively, were able to follow one another's games by observing the demonstration board from their seats. All three games continued 10 fxg5 Nfd7 11 Nxe6 (played first by Geller) 11 ... fxe6 12 Qh5+ Kf8 13 Bb5 (played first by Keres). Then play varied: Panno continued 13 ... Ne5 expecting 14 0-0+ which the Argentinians, when preparing the line believed would favour Black: but Geller replied 14 Bg3. Najdorf and Pilnik tried 13 ... Kg7. White won all three games.

The name is sometimes used for 202, the RUBINSTEIN VARIATION of the Queen's Gambit Declined; 503, the NAJDORF VARIATION of the Sicilian Defence; 581, EXCHANGE VARIATION of the Caro–Kann Defence; 1220, the POLLOCK VARIATION of the French Defence.

Arlauskas, Romanas (1917–), International Grandmaster of Correspondence Chess (1965). He earned the title by his performance in the 4th World Correspondence Championship 1962–5, in which he came third after ZAGOROVSKY and BORISENKO. A native of Lithuania, where he was second in the national championship in 1938, third in 1941, and equal first in 1943, Arlauskas settled in Australia early in 1948.

Árnason, Jón Loftur (1960–), Icelandic Champion 1977, World Under-16 Champion 1977. In 1986 he won two strong tournaments, Plovdiv (+4=7) and Helsinki, shared (+7=2−2), and became an International Grandmaster.

Aronin, Lev Solomonovich (1920–82), Soviet player from Kuibyshev, International Master (1950), engineer-meteorologist. Beginning in 1947 he played in eight Soviet championships; in 1950, at his fourth attempt, he tied for second place (+9=4−4), half a point behind the winner, KERES, but with the most victories. He shared first place with KROGIUS in the RSFSR (Russian Federation) championship in 1952 and won the Moscow championship in 1965.

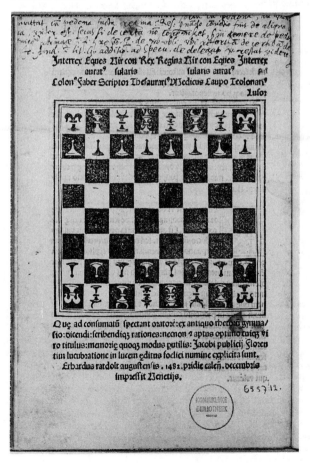

The earliest printed illustration of the array. It is from *Oratoriae artis Epitomata* by Jacobus Publicius, published in Venice in 1482

Aronin–Flohr 18th USSR Championship 1950 Caro–Kann Defence Two Knights Variation

1 e4 c6 2 Nc3 d5 3 Nf3 Bg4 4 h3 Bxf3 5 Qxf3 e6 6 d3 Nf6 7 Qg3 Na6 8 Be2 d4 9 Nb1 Nb4 10 Na3 c5 11 0-0 a6 12 Bf4 b5 13 c4 dxc3 14 bxc3 Nc6 15 Nc2 h5 16 d4 h4 17 Qd3 cxd4 18 cxd4 Be7 19 Rad1 e5 20 Be3 0-0

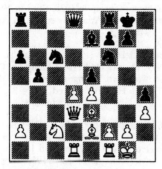

21 f4 exd4 22 Nxd4 Nxd4 23 Bxd4 Qa5 24 e5 Nd7 25 f5 Bc5 26 Bxc5 Nxc5 27 Qe3 Qb6 28 Kh1 Rae8 29 f6 gxf6 30 Qh6 Ne4 31 Rf4 Rxe5 32 Rxh4 Black resigns.

Aronin–Taimanov Variation, 402, standard line in the KING'S INDIAN DEFENCE that first became popular in the 1950s. (See TAIMANOV.)

array, the arrangement of pieces and pawns at the beginning of a game. Each player has a king, a queen, two bishops, two knights, two rooks, and eight pawns arranged as shown in the diagram. If during a game the array is found to have been set up incorrectly then the game shall be annulled.

art and chess. Since medieval times chess has been a popular subject of the visual arts. At first used allegorically, it later became a vehicle for portraying human emotions and perhaps a means of keeping models relatively still for lengthy periods. The state of the game was commonly indicated by facial expressions from mutual happiness to physical violence. Sometimes the players are a man and a woman using chess to disguise a more popular game. There are courtly scenes, family scenes, and group portraits. Abstract artists have also used chess, notably Willi Baumeister, Juan Gris, and Paul Klee. The contemporary Italian artist Johnny

Baldini creates paintings by first tracing the moves of a specific game on a board-like graph and then developing colour and line as the given material seems to demand.

Among the more famous artists to use chess are Sophonisba Anguisciola, Paris Bordone, Georges Braque, Richard Dadd, Honoré Daumier, Eugène Delacroix, DUCHAMP, Thomas Eakins, Francesco di Giorgio, Lucas van Leyden, van Loo, René Magritte, Henri Matisse, Karel van Mander, Jean-Louis-Ernest Meissonier, John Singer Sargent, and Victor Vasarely. There have been sculptures, notably by Max Ernst. Cartoons, posters, mosaics, tapestries, book-plates, glass, and illuminated manuscripts also show chess themes.

Roesler, *Chess in Art* (1973) lists 316 paintings and water-colours.

ashṭāpada, an ancient Indian race game played with dice on an 8 × 8 board; the board on which this game was played. The Sanskrit name, meaning 'having eight legs', is used for a spider and also a legendary being with eight legs, as well as for the board. The rules of the game, disused for many centuries, are no longer known. The board has crosses on the 1st, 4th, 5th, and 8th squares of the a, d, e, and h files. When proto-chess originated the ashṭāpada board was taken into use and some Indian chessboards still have the characteristic marks. (See HISTORY OF CHESS.)

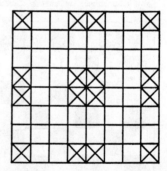

Asperling, B., author of the only important textbook on chess to be written in the second half of the 17th century. The *Traité du Ieu Royal des Echets ...par B.A.D.R.G.S.* was published in Lausanne around 1690 and generally known as the 'Traité de Lausanne'. For many years the authorship was a mystery, but the copy in the White collection at Cleveland, Ohio, is inscribed in contemporary handwriting 'B. Asperling de Raroyne [a misreading of Rarogne in Canton Valais], Garde Suisse'. Much of the contents is derived from GRECO and other early writers but Asperling's own contribution shows him to have been a strong player. The book is of importance for three reasons: the medieval king's leap makes its last appearance; openings are classified in an orderly way for the first time;

and it is extremely rare. Van der LINDE reprinted the whole text in *Deutsche Schachzeitung*, 1872.

assize, a medieval term for regulation in general and, in the chess context, a particular set of rules. At that time the rules varied from country to country, or even within a country, and players had to agree which assize they were observing. Even the array was not standardized. There was the long assize, with men arranged as they are today, and various kinds of short assize, with pawns on the third rank and an unorthodox arrangement of the pieces. A short assize was so named because it curtailed the opening phase, particularly lengthy in the days when the pawn did not have the option of moving two squares initially.

asymmetry, the disturbance of a position's symmetry that occurs when moving a piece to one side of the axis produces a different result from moving the same piece in a similar way to the other side. For examples, see LOSING CHESS; RIFLE CHESS. Dawson and Pauly, *Asymmetry* (1927) deals fully with the subject, which is chiefly of interest to problemists.

Asztalos, Lajos (1889–1956), Hungarian player, International Master (1950), International Arbiter (1951). In 1913 he won the championship of Hungary, ahead of BREYER (the holder) and RÉTI. Between the First and Second World Wars he lived in Yugoslavia, taking a post as professor of philosophy, and playing for that country in two Olympiads (1927, 1931). In 1942 he returned to Hungary and became a journalist. Dr Asztalos was secretary of FIDE's Qualification Committee, and for the last five years of his life, during which he suffered a long illness, was president of the Hungarian Chess Federation. A series of annual memorial tournaments in his honour began in 1958.

Atkins, Henry Ernest (1872–1955), English player, International Master (1950), schoolmaster. Between 1895 and 1901 he played in seven minor tournaments, winning four and taking second place in the others. Of the 70 games he lost only 3. In one of these events, Amsterdam 1899, he made a clean score against 15 opponents. In his first major international tournament, Hanover 1902, he came third (+8 = 7−2), after JANOWSKI and PILLSBURY, ahead of MIESES, CHIGORIN, and MARSHALL. Because of his dedication to his profession he preferred not to give more of his life to chess. Had he done so, LASKER believed that he would have joined the leading grandmasters, but he played in only one more big tournament (London 1922). By the time FIDE awarded its first titles, in 1950, Atkins was largely forgotten outside Britain. The Soviet delegate, confusing him with the Scottish player Aitken, objected to the award of the IM title until it was pointed out that the player under discussion was the one who finished ahead of Chigorin in 1902.

Atkins won the British championship nine times (1905–11, 1924, 1925), on the last occasion scoring +8 = 3. He represented the British Chess Federation in the Olympiads of 1927 and 1935 and played in 12 of the Anglo–American cable matches.

R. N. Coles, *H. E. Atkins: Doyen of British Chess Champions* (1952).

Atkins–Rubinstein London 1922 Queen's Gambit Declined Orthodox Variation

1 d4 Nf6 2 Nf3 e6 3 c4 d5 4 Bg5 Nbd7 5 e3 Be7 6 Nc3 0-0 7 Bd3 dxc4 8 Bxc4 a6 9 a4 c5 10 0-0 Qa5 11 Qe2 cxd4 12 exd4 Nb6 13 Bd3 Rd8 14 Rfd1 Bd7 15 Ne5 Be8 16 Qe3 Nfd5 17 Qg3 Bxg5 18 Qxg5 Nxc3 (saddling White with HANGING PAWNS instead of an ISOLATED PAWN) 19 bxc3 Nd5 20 Qh4 Nf6 21 c4 h6 22 Qg3 Rac8 23 Bc2 Bc6 24 Qe3 b6 25 Ra3 Ba8 26 Qf4 b5 27 Rh3 bxc4

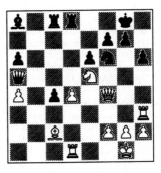

28 Rxh6 Rc5 (Black cleverly forestalls 29 Rxf6; thus preoccupied, he overlooks, on his next move, 29 ... Be4, maintaining his advantage.) 29 Rh3 Rcd5? 30 Kf1 Qb6 31 Rg3 Rxd4 32 Rxd4 Qxd4 33 Qxf6 Qa1+ 34 Ke2 Bf3+ (a SPITE CHECK) 35 gxf3 Black resigns.

Atkins Variation, 184, the LASKER VARIATION in the QUEEN'S GAMBIT Declined, played in the game Marshall–Atkins, Cable Match 1902.

attack, (1) an active THREAT. Its proportion may range from a single move to a sustained attack on the enemy king or some other target lasting for most of the game. Attacks of short duration are usually called threats and they occur frequently in all games. Attacks of longer duration, often localized on a flank or in the centre, are not necessarily tactical throughout. A player may pause, perhaps to prevent counterattack; and there are some attacks, e.g. the MINORITY ATTACK, which may be carried out by means of seemingly quiet manœuvres.

attack, (2) a term for an opening variation initiated by White. Compare DEFENCE (2).

Atwood, George (1745–1807), distinguished English mathematician whose pupil, William Pitt the Younger, rewarded him in 1784 with the post of Patent Searcher for the Customs, a sinecure, and employed him as private secretary for financial affairs. Atwood contested many games with PHILI-DOR, including the last that the Frenchman played, and with VERDONI, and recorded the moves of games at a time when this was not customary. When Atwood died these scores and other chess manuscripts passed to his friend Joseph Wilson 'on whose library shelves, for many years, they quietly slumbered'. On Wilson's death in 1832, 15 manuscript volumes by Atwood were bought by WALKER, who published many of the games.

aufin, a Middle English term for the ALFIL or FĪL, a 2,2, (√8) LEAPER. Because contemporary players were often caught out by the leap of this weak piece the term passed into common usage to denote a coward or contemptible person.

Austrian Attack, 240, or, by another sequence, 1278, one of the most popular lines for White in the PIRC-ROBATSCH SYSTEM. Known since the game Tarrasch–Charousek, Nuremberg 1896, the line was developed by the Viennese players Hans Müller (1896–1971) and Andreas Dückstein (1927–   ).

Austrian Defence, 77 in the QUEEN'S GAMBIT Declined, sometimes called the Symmetrical Defence. Stemming from SALVIO, it was studied by the Austrians Hans Haberditz (c.1901–57), Hans Müller (1896–1971, and GRÜNFELD.

automaton, a machine that plays or appears to play chess. The original and most famous, the TURK, unveiled in 1769, is also important in the history of magic as the first great cabinet illusion. Its maker was proud of the mechanism for the arm and hand and they had a part in the development of prosthetics. The exhibitor of the Turk, as with its successors, such as AJEEB or MEPHISTO, opened the apparatus and convinced onlookers that no one was concealed inside. After being closed up the machine moved the chessmen when it played members of the public.

The only genuine chess playing machine before the modern computer was Ajedrecista, first shown in 1914. Altered several times, it is still in working order in the Polytechnic Museum, Madrid. Much of the work of its inventor, Leonardo Torres Quevedo (1852–1936), was subsidized by the Spanish government, and the purpose of Ajedrecista was to demonstrate the possibility of making a machine carry out what we now call a program. Its play was restricted to the endgame king and rook versus king because exact rules for the winning procedure were known. Ajedrecista always takes White and is switched on when Black's king is moved. The machine does not check the validity of Black's move, but its permanent program calculates the best move from the new position and physically moves a piece by electro-magnetism before switching off. When the inventor's son exhibited the machine in Paris in 1951 TARTAKOWER was persuaded to put it through its paces and thus has a rather strained claim to be the first grandmaster to be defeated by a computer.

Bradley Ewart, *Chess: Man vs Machine* (San Diego, 1980).

AUW, see ALLUMWANDLUNG.

auxiliary scoring methods, ways of refining, or even supplanting, the placings that result from normal scoring (win 1, draw ½, loss 0); often called TIE-BREAKING methods, after their more common application today. The early examples were intended to displace completely the traditional way of determining places. There is an unprovable assumption implicit in many of these methods. If two players in a tournament draw with each other and have identical results against the rest, except that Player A beats the winner and loses to the lowest placed opponent while player B does the opposite, then A's result is more meritorious than B's. The GELBFUHS SCORE and NEUSTADTL SCORE work on this basis, as does the abortive SONNEBORN–BERGER method.

The first documented proposal was made by Dr Zbrožek of Prague, writing in *Schachzeitung*, 1869. Each player's normal score was divided by the number of games played to produce a weighted score. This weighted score was multiplied by the sum of the weighted scores of defeated opponents to give a 'Zbrožek score'. Thus sensible tournament placings could be obtained for events in which all players did not complete their programmes, not an unusual occurence at the time.

Not only did the rival innovators fight each other, they also had to contend with strident defenders of normal scoring such as METGER. When Ludwig Weinbrenner published *Neuer Modus zur Bestimmung der Reihenfolge der Priesträger bei Schachturnieren* (1887), Metger pointed out that the method was so complicated that in some cases a player would score better by losing than winning.

The underlying issue, the allocation of tournament funds, came under the spotlight around 1900 and the unrivalled TIETZ SYSTEM was used at several major events. An excellent summary of the whole subject was made by Dr Ahrens in *Wiener Schachzeitung*, 1901, and the substance of the article was reprinted in the *British Chess Magazine* in 1902.

The introduction of the SWISS SYSTEM led to a new requirement because players were facing unlike sets of opponents. An evaluation of the strength of the different sets was needed, and so BUCHHOLZ, COONS, HARKNESS, MEDIAN, and SOLKOFF scores were developed. (See also SUM OF PROGRESSIVE SCORES.)

The Mannheim 1914 tournament was abandoned on the outbreak of the First World War, an eventuality foreseen by no auxiliary scoring method. The first prize went to ALEKHINE; evidently, however, VIDMAR had met stronger opposition. The crosstable provides a means of comparing the more important methods.

Mannheim 1914

		1	2	3	4	5	6	7	8	9	10	11	12	13	14	15	16	17	18
1	Alekhine	x	–	–	1	–	–	0	1	1	1	–	–	1	1	1	½	1	1
2	Vidmar	–	x	½	½	½	1	1	–	–	½	1	½	–	1	1	1	–	–
3	Spielmann	–	½	x	–	1	½	0	–	1	½	1	½	1	–	–	–	1	1
4	Breyer	0	½	–	x	–	½	½	0	1	–	–	–	1	½	1	–	1	1
5	Marshall	–	½	0	–	x	1	1	½	½	–	1	½	1	–	–	–	½	½
6	Réti	–	0	½	½	0	x	½	–	–	1	1	1	1	½	–	1	–	–
7	Janowski	1	0	1	½	0	½	x	1	–	–	0	1	–	–	½	–	1	–
8	Bogoljubow	0	–	–	1	½	–	0	x	½	0	–	–	–	1	1	½	0	1
9	Tarrasch	0	–	0	0	½	–	–	½	x	1	0	–	–	1	1	1	½	–
10	Duras	0	½	½	–	–	0	–	1	0	x	1	0	0	–	–	–	1	1
11	John	–	0	0	–	0	0	1	–	1	0	x	1	1	–	–	1	–	0
12	Tartakower	–	½	½	–	½	0	0	–	–	1	0	x	½	0	–	½	–	1
13	Fahrni	0	–	0	0	0	0	–	–	–	1	0	½	x	1	1	½	–	–
14	Post	0	0	–	½	–	½	–	0	0	–	–	1	0	x	0	–	1	1
15	Carls	0	0	–	0	–	–	½	0	0	–	–	–	0	1	x	½	½	1
16	Krüger	½	0	–	–	–	0	–	½	0	–	0	½	½	–	½	x	½	½
17	Flamberg	0	–	0	0	½	–	0	1	½	0	–	–	–	0	½	½	x	–
18	Mieses	0	–	0	0	½	–	–	0	–	0	1	0	–	0	0	½	–	x

A dash (–) indicates that the game was not played.

In this table the six columns are: 1. score by addition of points; 2. Neustadtl score; 3. real Sonneborn–Berger score; 4. Coons score; 5. Solkoff score; 6. Buchholz score.

	1	2	3	4	5	6
Alekhine	9½	41¼	131½	42.55	49½	470¼
Vidmar	8½	45¼	117½	45.25	61	518½
Spielmann	8	39	103	40.30	58	464
Breyer	7	31	80	34.00	59	413
Marshall	7	37	86	38.60	59½	416½
Réti	7	34¾	83¾	37.85	63	441
Janowski	6½	39¼	81½	43.35	68½	445¼
Bogoljubow	5½	24½	54¾	29.30	56½	310¾
Tarrasch	5½	23¾	54	29.65	61	335½
Duras	5	23¾	48¾	29.85	62½	312½
John	5	24	49	31.50	61½	307½
Tartakower	4½	22½	42¾	27.00	60½	272¼
Fahrni	4	16½	32½	25.20	64	256
Post	4	16½	32½	23.80	60	240
Carls	3½	12½	24¾	20.50	59	206½
Krüger	3½	16	28¼	21.20	58	203
Flamberg	3	15¼	24¼	23.25	65	195
Mieses	2	10¼	14¼	19.65	62½	125

Averbakh, Yuri Lvovich (1922–), Russian player and author, International Grandmaster (1952), International Judge of Chess Compositions (1956), International Arbiter (1969). At Neuhausen–Zurich 1953, probably the strongest ever CANDIDATES tournament, he scored +5=17−6 to share 10th place. His best victories in international tournaments were Vienna 1961 (+7=4) and Moscow 1962 (+5=10) where he shared the place with VASYUKOV. In his own country he entered the USSR championship 15 times from 1949 to 1969. In 1954 he became champion (+10=9), in 1956 he was first (+7=9−1) equal with SPASSKY and TAIMANOV, but came second after the play-off, and in 1958 he was fourth (+6=10−2). He won or shared the Moscow championship three times (1949, 1950, 1962).

Averbakh's literary contribution is significant. In addition to editorial work on *Shakhmaty v SSSR* and *Shakmatny biuletin*, he has written the standard work on the endgame. In 1956–62 this appeared in three volumes, all bearing the title *Shakhmatnye okonchaniya*, and was revised, translated, and published in many other countries. A substantially revised edition appeared, still with the same title, in 5 volumes, 1980–4, one each year. In sequence the volumes cover endgames involving bishop versus knight, bishop or knight, queen, pawn, rook. (See AŞ-ŞŪLĪ.)

Averbakh–Furman 28th USSR Championship 1961
Spanish Opening Breyer Variation

1 e4 e5 2 Nf3 Nc6 3 Bb5 a6 4 Ba4 Nf6 5 0-0 Be7 6 Re1

b5 7 Bb3 d6 8 c3 0-0 9 h3 Nb8 10 d4 Nbd7 11 c4 c6 12 c5 dxc5 (After this White gains the more effective pawn MAJORITY.) 13 dxe5 Ne8 14 e6 fxe6 15 Bxe6+ Kh8 16 Nc3 Nc7 17 Bf5 c4 18 Bf4 Ne6 19 Bg3 Nec5 20 Nd4 Qb6 21 e5 Rd8 (Black's intention to defend by 22 . . . Nf8 is anticipated by a GREEK GIFT.)

22 Bxh7 Kxh7 23 Qh5+ Kg8 24 Nf5 Bf8 25 Qg6 Kh8 26 Ne4 Ne6 27 Nf6 Nxf6 28 exf6 Ra7 29 Re4 Nf4 30 Rxf4 Bxf5 31 Rxf5 Rd5 32 Rxd5 Black resigns.

Averbakh Variation, 342 in the QUEEN'S INDIAN DEFENCE; 395, in the KING'S INDIAN DEFENCE, introduced to master play by AVERBAKH in 1952; 755, a line in the SPANISH OPENING reaching an indifferent position in the STEINITZ DEFENCE.

Avner, Uri (1941–), Israeli problem composer, International Judge of Chess Compositions (1979). A representative of his country in the annual world solving championships, he was awarded the title of International Solving Master in 1982. (See CYCLIC PLAY; DUPLEX.)

AVRO, a Dutch broadcasting company, Algemene Vereniging Radio Omroep, which has sponsored tournaments in the Netherlands. The first of these, 1938, in which the world's best eight players competed, was the strongest tournament held up to that time. The joint winners were the youngest, KERES and FINE; BOTVINNIK was third, ALEKHINE, EUWE, and RESHEVSKY shared fourth place; CAPABLANCA and FLOHR followed. Keres, having the higher NEUSTADTL SCORE, challenged Alekhine for the world title, but no match took place, for Alekhine was already negotiating secretly with Botvinnik. (See CROSSTABLE.)

Azmaiparashvili, Zurab Alexeyevich (1960–), Georgian player, International Grandmaster (1988), whose best results include sharing first place with TAL at Tbilisi 1986, and winning the strong Havana 1988 tournament (+5=6) and the fractionally weaker Berlin 1989 (+3=6).

Azmaiparashvili–Wahls Dortmund 1990 King's Fianchetto Opening

1 g3 g6 2 Bg2 Bg7 3 Nf3 Nf6 4 c4 0-0 5 0-0 c6 6 b3 Ne4 7 d4 d5 8 Bb2 Nd7 9 Qc2 Ndf6 10 Ne5 Bf5 11 Qc1 Nd7 12 f3 Nd6 13 Nd2 Be6 14 e4 a5 15 Nd3 Re8 16 Nc5 Nxc5 17 dxc5 Bxb2 18 Qxb2 Nc8 19 cxd5 cxd5 20 f4 Qc7 21 Rac1 dxe4 22 Nxe4 Na7 23 Ng5 Bf5 24 g4 Bxg4 25 Bd5 Rf8

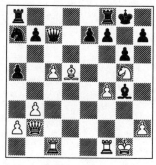

26 f5 gxf5 27 Rc4 h5 28 Rxg4 hxg4 29 Rxf5 e6 30 Ne4 Rfd8 31 Rh5 e5 32 Rxe5 Nc6 33 Rg5+ Kf8 34 Qh8+ Ke7 35 Qf6+ Kd7 36 Qf5+ Ke7 37 Qxf7+ mate.

B

Babson Task, a problem theme: in each of four variations different promotions by one side (usually Black) are answered by similar promotions by the other side, a kind of reciprocal ALLUMWANDLUNG. Using orthodox pieces (Q, R, B, N), Allumwandlung for White was shown in 1882, for Black in 1907. In 1912 A. C. WHITE published *The Theory of Pawn Promotion*, his second book on the subject, and this inspired the American composer Joseph Ney Babson (1852–1929), long interested in problems showing promotions, to formulate his task. The two of them organized a tourney in 1913, but none of the entrants, among them such giants as DAWSON and PAULY, succeeded.

In 1914 Babson himself composed a problem with all the promotions, but using for the purpose three white pawns. He improved in 1924 with two white pawns, and again with one white pawn but using OBTRUSIVE PIECES. The task was first achieved by the American composer Henry Wald Bettmann (1868–1935), whose entry for the Babson tourney of 1925–6 was submitted in June 1925. Two further tourneys were held, 1926–7 and 1929. The successful entries, like all their predecessors, were SELF-MATES. Meanwhile Dawson had achieved the task in fairy problems. Then interest faded for about 20 years, and from the 1950s the Babson Task appeared only occasionally in helpmates or in fairy problems.

In 1983 the Soviet composer and football coach Leonid Yarosh (1957–   ) gained instant fame by composing a direct mate orthodox Babson Task, a feat that had been thought impossible for the preceding 70 years. Subsequently many composers showed this task in orthodox or fairy form, sometimes extending it to five or more echoed promotions. For examples, see CHINESE FAMILY; MADRASI.

The pioneer problem by Yarosh, *Shakhmaty v SSSR*, March 1983. 1 Rxh4

1 . . . cxb1 = Q	2 axb8 = Q	Qxb2	3 Qb3
1 . . . cxb1 = R	2 axb8 = R	Rxb2	3 Rb3
1 . . . cxb1 = B	2 axb8 = B	Be4	3 Bxf4
1 . . . cxb1 = N	2 axb8 = N	Nxd2	3 Nc6 + .

Yarosh composed two more Babson Tasks in the same year, one of which won a first prize in the same magazine.

'The Babson Task', *The Problemist*, Sept. 1988.

Bachmann, Ludwig Ernst August (1856–1937), a German author who was one of the early chroniclers of chess. At a time when it was unusual to create a record of contemporary events, Bachmann launched a series of yearbooks: from 1891 to 1896 they covered sequentially the events of modern chess; from 1897 to 1930 each year's events were covered in one or more volumes, making a total of 44. He also compiled a four-volume work intended to include all of the games of STEINITZ, and less ambitious works on ANDERSSEN, PILLSBURY, and CHAROUSEK. He wrote historical studies of which *Aus vergangenen Zeiten* (1920–2) and *Das Schachspiel und seine historische Entwicklung* (1924) are the best known. Bachmann was a senior official on the Bavarian railway and chess was a spare-time activity. His records contain many errors, but he attempted much and was breaking new ground; he earned his nickname, the 'Chess Herodotus'.

back game, a game that is consciously commenced from a position arrived at in a game previously played, usually between the same players; an old name for a variation, especially one that continues for many moves. For example, PHILIDOR, in the first edition of his book, gives 9 games and, returning to certain positions, 32 back games, one of which has its own subvariation, misleadingly called a sequel. Most of the back games revert to the opening phase, but one picks up from the 26th move, and another from the 37th.

back-rank mate, a king mated on its back (first) rank by a rook or queen on the same rank. Sometimes the king cannot be moved forward because it is obstructed by its own pawns. Such mates rarely occur in master play but are commonly threatened. See how such a threat is used in games given under OUTPOST (control of the open file), KNAAK (a decisive regrouping), MACKENZIE, and RÉTI (part of a winning combination).

#4

A game Bubnov–Yaroslavtsev, play-off for the championship of Voronezh, 1949, continued 28...Nd7 (expecting 29 Ne7+ Kf8 30 Ng6+ Kg8—not 30...Ke8 31 Rxd7) 29 Nb8 Nf6 (29...Qh3 30 Rb2; 29...Rxb8 30 Rxb8+

Nxb8 31 Rd8+; 29...Nf8 30 Rd8) 30 Rd8+ Ne8 31 Rb6 and wins, although 31 Nd7 is stronger.

backward pawn, a pawn that can neither be guarded by, nor be advanced with the support of another pawn; is not blocked by an enemy pawn; and is restrained from advancing by an enemy pawn on an adjoining file. Such a pawn often lacks mobility, and may become a source of weakness. However, its latent power discounted by an adversary, it may sometimes be advanced unexpectedly. A capture which transfers a pawn to an adjacent file may mobilize the backward pawn. (See MINORITY ATTACK; WEAKNESS, all three games.)

Lasker–Rubinstein St Petersburg 1914 Spanish Opening Open Defence

1 e4 e5 2 Nf3 Nc6 3 Bb5 a6 4 Ba4 Nf6 5 0-0 Nxe4 6 d4 b5 7 Bb3 d5 8 dxe5 Be6 9 c3 Bc5 10 Nbd2 0-0 11 Bc2 Nxd2 12 Qxd2 f6 13 exf6 Rxf6 14 Nd4 Nxd4 15 cxd4 Bb6 16 a4 Rb8 17 axb5 axb5 18 Qc3 Qd6 19 Be3

Black, hindered by the need to defend the backward pawn on the c-file, is eventually forced to permit weaknesses elsewhere. 19...Bf5 20 Rfc1 Bxc2 21 Rxc2 Re8 22 Rac1 Rfe6 23 h3 Re4 24 Qd2 R8e6 25 Rc6 Qd7 26 Rxe6 Qxe6 27 Qd3 Qe8 28 Qc3 Kf7 29 Qd3 Kg8 30 Qc3 Qe6 31 Ra1 Qe8 32 Kf1 h6 33 Qd3 Kf7 34 Rc1 Kg8 35 Qb3 Qf7 36 Rd1 c6 37 f3 Qf6 38 Qd3 Re7 39

Bf2 Qd6 40 Qc2 Kf7 41 Rc1 Re6 42 Qf5+ Rf6 43 Qe5 Re6 44 Qxd6 Rxd6 45 Ke2 Ke7 46 Kd3 Rg6 47 g3 Rf6 48 f4 Kd7 49 Re1 Rf8 50 Ra1 h5 51 Be3 g6 52 Rf1 Kd6 53 g4 hxg4 54 hxg4 c5 (Black gets rid of his backward pawn at last, but the rook ending that follows is lost. Dogged defence by 54...Ke6 is better.) 55 dxc5+ Bxc5 56 Bxc5+ Kxc5 57 f5 gxf5 58 gxf5 Rf6 59 Rf4 b4 60 b3 Rf7 61 f6 Kd6 62 Kd4 Ke6 63 Rf2 Kd6 64 Ra2 Rc7 65 Ra6+ Kd7 66 Rb6 Black resigns.

bad bishop, one obstructed by pawns belonging to its own forces. If these cannot be moved out of the way there will be squares of one colour that neither they nor the bishop can control; the disadvantage of such a COLOUR-WEAKNESS combined with the bad bishop's restricted mobility may be fatal, as in the games under ACCUMULATION OF ADVANTAGES, HARRWITZ, and SHORT.

On rare occasions a 'bad' bishop may not be bad at all.

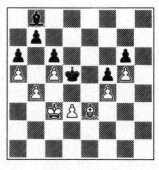

A position from the game P. Blatný–Flear, Oakham 1988.
50 Kd2 Bc7 51 Ke2 Bb8 52 Bc1 Bc7 53 Ke3 Bb8 54 Bb2 Bc7 55 Bf6 Ke6 56 d4 Kd5 57 Be5 Bd8 58 Kd3 Be7 59 Bh8 (TO LOSE THE MOVE) 59...Bd8 60 Bg7 Bc7 61 Be5 Bxe5 (61...Bd8 62 Bd6) 62 fxe5, and White has a won pawn ending. Black loses only because he runs out of moves for his bishop. Were all the men on the board moved one rank south, the position would be drawn, White's extra pawn counting for nothing because of the bad bishop.

Even when a blocked centre pawn alone obstructs a bishop the term 'bad bishop' may be appropriate. For examples, see FIXED CENTRE, ISOLATED QUEEN'S PAWN (Capablanca's game), and WEAKNESS (Taimanov's game).

Bagirov, Vladimir Konstantinovich (1936–), Latvian player, International Grandmaster (1978). From 1960 to 1978 he competed in nine USSR championships, achieving his best result (+7=10−2 and fourth place) in 1960. His playing activity reduced, he trained KASPAROV from 1975 for a while. However he continued to play occasionally, and in 1986 won the tournament at Cascais.

Bagirov–Malanyuk   Baku 1983   Hromádka Defence
Modern Benoni

1 d4 Nf6 2 c4 c5 3 d5 e6 4 Nc3 exd5 5 cxd5 d6 6 e4 g6
7 f4 Bg7 8 Bb5+ Nfd7 9 a4 Qh4+ 10 g3 Qe7 11 Nf3
0-0 12 0-0 Na6 13 e5 Nb4 14 Ne4 Nb6 15 Nxd6 N6xd5
16 Bd2 Bg4 17 Qb3 Rad8 18 Bc4 Nb6 19 Bxb4 cxb4

20 Bxf7+ Rxf7 21 Ng5 Rxd6 22 exd6 Bd4+ 23 Kh1
Qe8 24 h3 Bd7 25 Rae1 Qf8 26 Re7 Bc6+ 27 Kh2 Bd5
28 Qxb4 Bf6 29 Nxf7 Bxf7 30 Rxb7 Qe8 31 Re1 Qc6
32 Rc7 Qf3 33 Qd2 h5 34 Qe2 Qd5 35 Rd1 Qf5 36 d7
Nd5 37 Rc8+ Kh7 38 d8=Q h4 39 Rxd5 hxg3+ 40
Kxg3 Bxd5 41 Rc7+ Black resigns.

Baguio Variation, 11 ... Bf5, an alternative to the
DILWORTH VARIATION (714) in the SPANISH OPENING,
used three times in the 1978 Karpov–Korchnoi
match held in Baguio City. Played Bronstein–
Flohr, USSR championship 1944, the line had
fallen out of use. The variation had a revival when
LARSEN defeated FISCHER at Santa Monica 1966,
using it. At that time 'Keres shows sympathy, Euwe
has little faith, Pachman considers this move weak'
said Larsen.

Baird, Edith Elina Helen (*née* Winter Wood) (1859–
1924), British problem composer. Her parents, two
brothers, and daughter were all good players or
clever problemists. She composed more than 2,000
problems which were not profound but were noted
for their soundness; only a dozen or so were
faulted. Her *Seven Hundred Chess Problems* was
published in 1902. She became deeply absorbed in
help-RETRACTORS, and her other book, *The Twentieth Century Retractor* appeared in 1907. They are
two of the most elegant chess books ever to appear,
printed and bound by the King's printer, Henry
Sotheran, and sold at less than cost.

Bakcsi (pron. bak-shi), György (*né* Bartók)
(1933–), Hungarian composer, International
Grandmaster for Chess Compositions (1980), International Judge of Chess Compositions (1979),
editor for a publishing house. He has composed
more than 1,200 problems, won about 125 first
prizes, is a specialist in TWO- and THREE-MOVERS and
HELPMATES, and is noted for his humorous style of
composition. He published 116 of his problems in

Gondolat és stratégia (1970) and *Stratégia és gondolat* (1981). Among his other books is *En passant
felügyelő visszatér* (1985), more than 400 pages of
RETROGRADE ANALYSIS and other entertaining problems. He was chief editor of *Uj magyar sakkfelad-
vány antológia* (1979), a collection of 473 problems
and 199 studies by Hungarian composers.

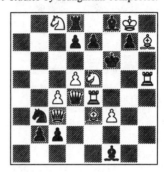

s#4

This problem by Bakcsi, first prize, *Magyar Sakkélet*, 1980, shows cyclic ANNIHILATION on the e-file.
The key is 1 Qe1, threatening 2 Qh4+ g5 3 Rh6+.

1 ... Qxe5 2 Bg5+ Qxg5   3 Rf4+ Qxf4
                          4 Qxe7+ Bxe7#
1 ... Qxe3 2 Rf4+ Qxf4   3 Ng4+
1 ... Qxe4 2 Ng4+ Qxg4   3 Bg5+ .

balance of position, see EQUILIBRIUM.

Balashov, Yuri Sergeyevich (1949–), Russian
player, International Grandmaster (1973). From
1969 to 1990 he played in fifteen USSR championships and had a number of good results, notably in
1976 when he was second (+6=10−1) behind
KARPOV, then world champion, and ahead of three
ex-champions, PETROSYAN, SMYSLOV, and TAL.
Balashov was Moscow champion in 1970 and
achieved good results in a number of other strong
tournaments: Wijk aan Zee 1973, second
(+6=8−1), after Tal; Cienfuegos 1975, second
(+9=7−1 equal with VASYUKOV, after ANDERSSON;
Vilnius 1975, a zonal event, first (+6=6−3) equal
with GULKO, SAVON, and TSESHKOVSKY; Halle 1976,
first; Lvov 1978, zonal tournament, first
(+5=8−1); Munich 1979, first equal with Andersson, HÜBNER, and SPASSKY; Karlovac 1979, first
(+7=6); Wijk aan Zee 1982, first (+4=9) equal
with NUNN; Minsk 1986, first; Dortmund 1987, first
(+5=6), in front of Andersson and TUKMAKOV;
Reykjavik 1989, first; Berlin 1990, first equal with
ROMANISHIN.

Andersson–Balashov   Tallinn 1973   Réti Opening
Wing Blumenfeld

1 Nf3 d5 2 c4 d4 3 d3 Nc6 4 g3 e5 5 Bg2 Nf6 6 0-0
Nd7 7 Nbd2 Be7 8 Rb1 a5 9 Ne1 0-0 10 b3 Nc5 11 Nc2
Bg4 12 Ne4 Nxe4 13 Bxe4 f5 14 Bd5+ Kh8 15 a3 Qe8
16 b4 Qh5 17 Bf3 f4 18 Bxg4 Qxg4 19 Kg2 axb4 20
axb4 h5 21 b5 Nd8 22 Ne1 Ne6 23 Nf3 Bd6 24 Bd2
fxg3 25 hxg3 Nf4+ 26 Bxf4 exf4 27 c5

27...fxg3 28 cxd6 gxf2+ 29 Kh2 h4 30 Rxf2 Qg3+
31 Kh1 Qxf2 32 dxc7 b6 33 Qf1 Qxf1+ 34 Rxf1 Rac8
35 Rc1 Rf7 36 Rc4 Rd7 37 Nxd4 Rcxc7 38 Nc6 g5 39
Kg2 Rd5 40 Rb4 Rf7 41 Kh3 Kg7 42 Nd4 Kg6 43 Rc4
Kh5 White resigns.

Balla Variation, 739, analysed by the Hungarian player Zoltán Balla (1883–1945) and played by him against ASZTALOS at Budapest in 1912.

ballet and chess, see THEATRE AND CHESS.

Balogh Attack, 1267, a line in the ALEKHINE DEFENCE analysed by the Hungarian player János Balogh (1892–1980) in 1925, and introduced into master play in the game Showalter–Torre, Chicago 1926. Also known as the Canal Variation.

Balogh Defence, 236 or 259, an old opening line given by COZIO (1 e4 d6 2 d4 f5), played in the 5th match game Kieseritzky–Horwitz, 1846, much analysed by Balogh in *Wiener Schachzeitung*, 1930.

Balogh Gambit, 295, a BUDAPEST DEFENCE variation of dubious merit introduced by Balogh in the 1920s.

Balogh Variation, 113, a sound line in the ALBIN COUNTER-GAMBIT which had some popularity around 1950.

Baltic Opening, 8, another name for the HEINRICH-SEN OPENING arising from its Lithuanian origin.

Barcza (pron. bartsa), Gedeon (1911–86), International Grandmaster (1954), International Correspondence Chess Master (1966), professor of mathematics. He won the Hungarian championship eight times and represented his country in seven Olympiads in one of which, Amsterdam 1954, he won the prize for the best score (+10=5−1) at third board. In strong tournaments the first prize eluded his grasp, but he often came high, notably (shared) fifth place at Havana 1963 (+12=7−2) and third place at Leningrad 1967 (+6=9−1).

In his later years Barcza worked diligently on a highly regarded history of Hungarian chess, *Magyar sakktörténet*. Two volumes appeared in his lifetime, 1975 and 1977, but the third was delayed until 1989 by his declining health.

Sämisch–Barcza Gablonz 1938 Nimzo–Indian Defence
Three Knights Variation

1 d4 Nf6 2 c4 e6 3 Nc3 Bb4 4 Nf3 b6 5 Bg5 h6 6 Bh4
Bxc3+ 7 bxc3 Bb7 8 e3 d6 9 a4 a5 10 Bd3 Nbd7 11
0-0 Qe7 12 Nd2 g5 13 Bg3 h5 14 h3 0-0-0 15 Bh2 Rdg8
16 Re1 Ne8 17 e4 g4 18 h4 Qxh4 19 c5 dxc5 20 Nc4
Qg5 21 Rb1

21...g3 22 fxg3 h4 23 g4 Qxg4 24 Re2 h3 25 g3 f5 26
Ne3 Qf3 27 Qc2 Nef6 28 Rf1 Rxg3+ White resigns.

Barcza Opening, 1300 or 1310, which may be a prelude to a system completed by White's playing 3 Bg2 and 4 0-0, as in 1321, delaying action in the centre until Black's intentions are known. Transpositions into other openings are not uncommon. The HYPERMODERN movement created a vogue for the opening in the 1920s, but it had been played in the 19th century. Describing the opening moves of the game Capablanca–Janowski, New York 1924, as a 'white' Indian Opening, ALEKHINE noted that after 1 Nf3 d5 2 g3 c5 3 Bg2 Nc6 a Grünfeld variation could be forced here by 4 d4.

Bardeleben, Curt von (1861–1924), German master and writer. After winning the minor tournament held concurrently with the master tournament at London 1883 he gave up serious chess to study law, which he never practised. 'He studies chess and plays at law' said a contemporary. Returning to the game a few years later he became a regular tournament competitor for the rest of his life, notably sharing three first prizes: Leipzig 1888 (+4=3) equal with RIEMANN; Kiel 1893 (+5=2−1) equal with WALBRODT; and Coburg 1904, a tie with SCHLECHTER and Swiderski. His temperament, however, was unsuited to long hard contests, and he often made indifferent results. He was a careful man in chess and in dress, but for such a meticulous person he had a surprising number of withdrawals from tournaments and matches. At the great Hastings tournament of 1895 STEINITZ won a brilliancy prize for his game against Bardeleben who, at the culmination of his opponent's combination, left the room and lost on time rather than resign. Up to that point he had scored six wins and three draws, but this reversal so upset him that only with difficulty was he persuaded not to abandon the competition. Scoring only 4½ points in the next eleven rounds, he shared seventh place with TEICHMANN. Bardeleben wrote many books, usually about openings, although his last work was a pamphlet on the history of the game. Suffering hardship during the difficult years in Germany that followed the First World War, he committed suicide.

Steinitz–Bardeleben   Hastings 1895   Italian Opening

1 e4 e5 2 Nf3 Nc6 3 Bc4 Bc5 4 c3 Nf6 5 d4 exd4 6 cxd4 Bb4+ 7 Nc3 d5 8 exd5 Nxd5 9 0-0 Be6 10 Bg5 Be7 11 Bxd5 Bxd5 12 Nxd5 Qxd5 13 Bxe7 Nxe7 14 Re1 f6 15 Qe2 Qd7 16 Rac1 c6 17 d5 cxd5 18 Nd4 Kf7 19 Ne6 Rhc8 20 Qg4 g6 21 Ng5+ Ke8

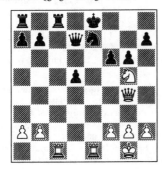

White now begins a long combination during which all or most of his pieces remain *en prise.* 22 Rxe7+ Kf8 23 Rf7+ Kg8 24 Rg7+ Kh8 25 Rxh7+, and Black lost on time. The game might have continued 25 ... Kg8 26 Rg7+ Kh8 27 Qh4+ Kxg7 28 Qh7+ Kf8 29 Qh8+ Ke7 30 Qg7+ Ke8 31 Qg8+ Ke7 32 Qf7+ Kd8 33 Qf8+ Qe8 34 Nf7+ Kd7 35 Qd6+ mate.

Bardeleben Variation, 633, continuation in the VIENNA GAME recommended by BARDELEBEN in *Deutsche Schachzeitung,* 1889; 852 in the SPANISH FOUR KNIGHTS GAME, given by Bardeleben in his book *Kritik der Spanischen Partie* (1885); 973, a GÖRING GAMBIT line given by STEINITZ in *Modern Chess Instructor* (1889); 1060 in the PETROFF DEFENCE, given by Bardeleben in 1889.

Barden, Leonard William (1929–), British joint champion 1954, and equal first in 1958, but unsuccessful in the play-off. (See NEWSPAPER COLUMNS; SLATER.)

bare king, a king without any other men of the same colour on the board. In SHAṬRANJ and in chess of early medieval times one way to win was by leaving the opponent with a bare king (baring chess). The difficulty of mating with the old pieces may have made this win desirable. In some countries, e.g. Iceland, the bare king was considered an inferior form of win and the winner did not receive the full stake money. See MEDINESE VICTORY for an account of situations in which a bare king would not bring a victory.

The FIDE rules for RAPID CHESS state that a player having a bare king cannot win on time-limit.

Bareyev, Yevgeny Ilgizovich (1966–), Russian player, International Grandmaster (1989), World Under-16 Champion 1982, winner of a strong tournament at Trnava 1989 (+3=7). Shortly afterwards, in the same year, he was third (+5=7−1) in an equally strong tournament held at Ljubljana and Rogaška Slatina. In 1990 he won (+4=3) the Moscow semi-final of the USSR championship, was equal first (+5=3−1) with CHERNIN in a strong tournament at Marseille, and won the 1990–1 Hastings tournament (+9=3−2).

baring chess, see BARE KING.

Barlov, Dragan (1957–), Yugoslav champion (1986), International Grandmaster (1986), equal first (+5=4) in the zonal tournament at Pucarevo 1987.

Barnes, Thomas Wilson (1825–74), one of the strongest players in England during the 1850s. He made little impression in his one and only tournament, London 1862, but is remembered for having scored more wins than anyone else in friendly play against MORPHY in 1858. He went on a diet, lost 130 pounds in ten months, and died as a result.

Barnes Defence, 812, sometimes called the Fianchetto Defence or Pillsbury Defence to the SPANISH OPENING. Examined by Albert P. Barnes in the *Canadian Spectator* on 3 July 1880 and later in *Brentano's Chess Monthly,* this rarely played line first occurred in tournament play in Loyd–From, Paris 1867, but attracted little attention until successfully used by STEINITZ in 1883. (See DEFENSIVE CENTRE.) Also 1247, sometimes called the Winawer Defence, played successfully by T. W. BARNES against MORPHY in 1858 and with a less happy outcome against ANDERSSEN in 1862.

Barnes Defence Deferred, 759 in the SPANISH OPENING, the BARNES DEFENCE (812) played after 3 ... a6. Sometimes it is called the Fianchetto Defence Deferred.

Barnes Opening, 1282, an opening move of little merit, so named because of its parallel with the BARNES DEFENCE (1247).

Bartmański Variation, 919, the CRACOW VARIATION of the ITALIAN OPENING. Henryk Bartmański (1875–1911), a member of the Cracow club, played it in the 5th correspondence tournament of the *Wiener Schachzeitung,* and in 1910 that periodical gave two games in which he used this line.

Bartolović, Vojko (1932–), leading Yugoslav composer specializing in orthodox TWO-MOVERS, International Judge of Chess Compositions (1956), International Grandmaster for Chess Compositions (1980), engineer.

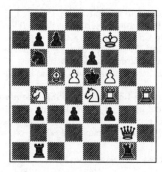

#2

A problem by Bartolović, first prize, British Chess Federation 1979. The key is 1 Nd6, threatening Re4 #.

1 ... cxd6	2 Bd4 #
1 ... exd5	2 Nxd3 #
1 ... exf5	2 Rxf5 #
1 ... Rbe1	2 Qb2 #
1 ... Rge1	2 Qg7 #.

The key, together with the following six tries, form the better part of a White KNIGHT WHEEL: 1 Nf6? Rgd1; 1 Ng5? Rgf1; 1 Ng3? Rge1; 1 Nf2(c3)? Rbd1; 1 Nd2? Rbf1.

baseline chess, a form of RANDOMIZED CHESS.

basic centre, the four squares in the centre of the board.

basic endgame, a phase of the game in which there are few or no pawns on the board, and differing from earlier phases mainly because the normal way of assessing the value of the pieces is often inapplicable. For example, a minor piece may be worth more than a pawn, or a pawn might be stronger than a rook (as in the SAAVEDRA study). From the beginning of modern chess (c.1475) the OPPOSITION and a few simple endgames were understood. Little progress was made until PHILIDOR contributed useful analysis to the endings Q v. R+P, R+B v. R, and R+P v. R. Subsequently LOLLI investigated the endings R+B v. R and Q v. B+B. Then nothing much happened until the 1840s when KLING and others initiated a period of steady progress which accelerated after the middle of the 20th century and has been computer-aided since the 1970s. Some grey areas, mostly of endgames unlikely to arise in play, remain to be investigated, but for practical purposes knowledge of the basic endgame is largely complete. The following summary indicates the normal result to be expected, but there are, of course, exceptions. In all cases White is assumed to be the player with the greater force.

(1) *Black has a bare king*
Mate is impossible if White has one minor piece, unenforceable if White has N+N. (See BASIC MATES.)

(2) *Other pawnless endings*
Two minor pieces v. one. Generally drawn except for KB+QB v. N, for which the American computer expert Ken Thompson demonstrated the win in 1983. Some variations take more than 50 moves. B+N v. N may sometimes be won if the black king is confined on or near a corner square, or if the black knight can be trapped. (See FIFTY-MOVE LAW.)

Three minor pieces v. one. A win with KB+QB+N v. B (or N), or with B+N+N v. B (or N). Otherwise B+B of the same colour +N v. N can be won if Black's king is confined to the edge, as shown by the English composers Charles Michael Bent (1919–) and Walter Veitch (1923–) in 1971, but the result when Black's king has the freedom of the board is not clear. It was TROITZKY's belief that three knights win against one.

R v. N. This ending has attracted attention since the days of RABRAB. In 1970 Thomas Ströhlein of Munich gained his doctorate for a thesis entitled *Untersuchungen über kombinatorische Spiele*, which included a computer analysis of this ending. Although generally drawn there may be winning chances when the knight has strayed far from its king. See DIDACTIC POSITION for a draw that occasionally arises in play.

R v. B. A definitive analysis by computer was made by Ströhlein and L. Zagler, 1967–9, and published in *Ergebnisse einer vollständigen Analyse von Schachendspielen König und Turm gegen König, König und Turm gegen König und Läufer* (Munich, 1978). White may win if Black's king is confined in or near a corner square that the bishop could control. If driven to the edge Black's king should therefore be moved to one of the other corners.

Two minor pieces v. R. Drawn.

Three minor pieces v. R. QB+KB+N wins. B+N+N draws.

R+N+N v. R. White wins.

R+N v. R. Drawn, with exceptions if Black's king can be confined in or near a corner square, when there are winning chances, as shown by Charles Forth of Carlow (d. 1845) in the 1840s and by Luigi Centurini (1820–1900).

R+B v. R. This difficult ending occurs in play more frequently than any other pawnless endgame. More often than not Black should draw. Analysed by Philidor, who at one time believed that White should always win, this ending was also examined by Lolli, COCHRANE, and SZÉN. A definitive analysis, the first of its kind, was published by Kling in *Chess Player's Chronicle*, 1842. The win cannot always be achieved in fewer than 50 moves — see CROSSKILL.

Q v. minor piece. White wins.

Q v. two minor pieces. According to computer analysis by Thompson in 1985 White wins more often than not. Having B+B, Black draws if the

FORTRESS given by Lolli can be set up. With B + N there is one fortress and one BLOCKADE that draw, but White can usually prevent Black's reaching either of them. With N + N several blockades leading to a draw are known, but other drawing resources await discovery. White cannot always win against B + B or N + N in fewer than 50 moves.

Q v. three minor pieces. Drawn.

QB + KB + N + N v. Q. White wins.

Q v. R. White wins. A definitive analysis was published by Crosskill in 1895. A computer analysis by Ströhlein and Zagler shows that the winning process should take at most 31 moves.

Q v. R and minor piece. Normally drawn. Black's simplest plan is to form a barrier or fortress keeping the white king out. White may win against scattered men.

R and two minor pieces v. Q. Usually regarded as drawn, but if Black's king can be confined to the edge of the board White often wins.

R + R v. Q. Drawn.

R + R and minor piece v. Q. White wins.

Q and minor piece v. Q. More than half of all possible positions are drawn. White to play wins 53% of them when the minor piece is a bishop, 48% when it is a knight; these figures are given by the computer analyst Thompson.

(3) *Pawn endings*
The results with only one or two pawns on the board have long been known, and are detailed in many textbooks.

P + P v. P. Many books, from those of Lolli (1763) and STEIN (1789) to those of RABINOVICH (1938) and FINE (1941), contain errors. The endgame was mastered by GRIGORIEV in the 1920s and 1930s.

(4) *Pieces against pawns*
Minor piece v. pawn. Drawn.

N + N v. P. This, the most difficult of all basic endgames, was brilliantly researched by Troitzky, who published his analysis in book form in 1934. The winning procedure consists of blocking the pawn with one knight, using the other knight and the king to corner Black's king, and bringing up the blocking knight to deliver mate. The pawn's newly found freedom to move prevents a stalemate defence. White wins if the black pawn, securely blocked by a knight, is no further foward than a4, b6, c5, d4, e4, f5, g6, or h4—known as the Troitzky line. If Black's king is in certain defined areas White may win when the pawn is further advanced. Many such endings cannot be won in fewer than 50 moves.

R v. P. The result mainly depends upon the position of White's king: if near the pawn White wins, if far away a draw is likely. See DIDACTIC POSITION for an example; for a rare exception, see SAAVEDRA.

R v. two pawns. If the pawns are isolated the results are not very different from those with R v. P. If the pawns are united the position of the white king may be decisive: if near the pawns, White wins, if far away White may lose.

R v. three united pawns. When the white king is unable to confront the pawns and the black king supports them, then Black has winning chances and at worst a draw. Having the king in front of the pawns, White has winning chances. The Soviet analyst Nikolai Antonovich Kopayev (1914–78), adding important discoveries to work by others, made a thorough examination, publishing his results in AVERBAKH'S treatises.

=

Black to play and draw. Analysis by the British lightning chess champion of 1990, Colin Stamford Crouch (1956–   ), given in *EG* in 1987, shows that even when the white king confronts the pawns a win is not always possible.

1 ... g5 2 Rh5 f6 3 Kg2 Kg7· 4 Kf3 Kg6 5 Rh1 f5 6 Ke3 h5 7 Kd4 g4! 8 Ke3 Kg5 9 Ra1 f4+ 10 Kf2 Kg6 11 Ra8 Kg7 12 Ra4 f3 13 Ra5 Kg6 14 Kg3 Kh6 15 Kh4 Kg6 16 Rg5+ Kf6 17 Rg8 Kf7 18 Rh8 Kg6 (White is now in ZUGZWANG.) 19 Kg3 Kg5 20 Rg8+ Kf6 21 Kf2 Kf5 22 Ke3 Kf6 23 Ke4 Ke7 24 Rg5 f2 25 Re5+ Kd6 26 Rd5+ Ke6 27 Rd1 g3 28 Kf3 h4 29 Rh1 Kf5 30 Ra1 = . When Black loses such endings it is usually because the pawns are mishandled.

Q v. P. Normally White wins easily. Black draws with BP or RP on the seventh rank when the white king is far away.

Q v. two or three pawns. White usually wins against isolated pawns. If the pawns are united, well advanced, and supported by their king, Black at least draws unless the white king is nearby.

(5) *Pieces and pawns*
Minor piece and pawn v. minor piece. Normally drawn if Black's king confronts the pawn, or if there are bishops of opposite colour; however, the black king may be endangered if White has a knight. Having an advanced pawn, especially one on the flank, which the black king cannot confront, White may win (except when there are bishops of opposite colour). With a less advanced pawn, White may win if Black has a king or knight far

from the scene of action; for an example see EXCEL-SIOR. The principal analysts include Kling, Centurini, RÉTI, and Averbakh.

R+P v. B. Normally a win when the white king is in touch with the pawn which, however, should not be advanced prematurely. When the king cannot defend the pawn, Black has good drawing chances, as shown in analysis by KOPNIN. Other analysts of this ending include GURETZKY-CORNITZ and the Czech composer Josef Vančura (1898–1921).

R+P v. B+P. There are many drawing positions, but when this ending occurs in play the pawns are frequently blocked on the same file with Black's pawn guarded by the bishop, and White can win most of these positions, with some exceptions for the rook's pawn. In the 1950s CHÉRON discovered one winning position of this type in which the pawns remain unmoved for more than 50 moves.

R+P v. R. When the black king is in front of the pawn the game is normally drawn. White has winning chances when the black king is cut off from the pawn by the white rook's control of a file or rank; for an example, see LUCENA POSITION. Examining this ending periodically from 1922 to 1971, Chéron published a comprehensive analysis in his endgame treatise. (The contribution made by many others, notably Grigoriev, is greater than one would suppose from reading this book.) In 1979 V. L. Arlazarov and A. L. Futer of the Moscow Institute of Control Sciences made a definitive analysis by computer.

Q v. R+P. When the pawn guards the rook, White normally wins if the pawn stands on a7, c6, d6, a5, c5, d5, a4, or d4 (or on the similar king's side squares). In other situations in which the pawn guards the rook, and in which the black king is favourably placed, the game is drawn; for an example, see FORTRESS. Black also draws (except with a rook's pawn) if the pawn is well advanced and guarded by the rook from the rear, and if the black king is well placed. White wins most positions in which the pawn is guarded by the rook from the side. Philidor, Guretzky-Cornitz, and Chéron made the most important contributions to this ending.

Q+P v. Q. Because Black has so many chances of perpetual check, most positions were thought to be drawn until the middle of the 20th century. Then the researches of Averbakh, BOTVINNIK, the Swiss analyst Robert Fontana (1928–), and KERES revealed hitherto unsuspected winning chances. These advances were confirmed in 1986 when Thompson made a definitive analysis by computer. White to play wins about 85% of the possible positions when the pawn is on the seventh rank, decreasing to 74%, 65%, and 60% for a pawn on the sixth, fifth, and fourth rank respectively, and 55% for a pawn on the second or third rank. The BP is the most favourable pawn, the RP the least.

The black king is best placed either near the pawn or near the corner of the board furthest from the queening square. Presumably, Black to play has better drawing chances. The white king often has to make long tours of the board to evade perpetual check, and there are many winning situations in which the pawn cannot be favourably advanced until more than 50 moves have been played.

Limited information about basic endgames is given in many textbooks, but few writers have specialized on the subject. The treatises by Averbakh and Chéron give the most extensive coverage. A summary of such endgames in one small volume is D. Hooper's *A Guide to Chess Endgames* (rev. edn., 1973). Computer analyses are inaccessible to the practical player, and, as yet, give little help to the side attempting to draw.

basic mates, four kinds of decisive pawnless endgames in which the defender has only a king: K+Q v. K, K+R v. K, K+QB+KB v. K, and K+B+N v. K. Except in stalemate positions, or ones in which a piece can be captured, checkmate can be given in, at most, 10, 16, 19, or 33 moves respectively.

The endgame K+N+N v. K should be drawn. Mate cannot be forced but the defending king can be stalemated. It is one of the curiosities of chess that with an extra pawn the defender sometimes loses because the pawn's freedom to move prevents stalemate.

Basman Variation, 272 in the DUTCH DEFENCE, as played Rellstab–Basman, Hastings 1973–4. The English IM, Michael John Basman (1946–), is a fertile researcher of openings.

Basque Gambit, 736, an old line in the SPANISH OPENING, as Lelie & Pinedo–Anderssen, Amsterdam 1861, and Bird–Boden, Westminster Chess Club, 1869. It was briefly revived in the 1930s and given its name in a book, *Eröffnungen* (1936), by the German player Ludwig Rellstab (1904–83), but others called it the North Spanish Variation.

Bastrikov Variation, 552, also known as the Taimanov Variation, a SICILIAN DEFENCE line that became popular in the 1960s and was named after the Soviet player Georgy Vladimirovich Bastrikov (1914–79).

battery, a problem term for one of the two kinds of AMBUSH; a line piece would command a line if another man of the same colour were moved off that line. Discovered checks arise from this kind of ambush, as shown in the INDIAN THEME. For some examples, see DOBRESCU; GULIAYEV; LINDGREN; MATTHEWS; SHINKMAN.

Bauer, Johann Hermann (1861–91). Born in Prague, he settled in Vienna as a youth, and gained his

master title by winning the Frankfurt HAUPTTUR-
NIER, 1887. His most notable achievement was a
second place (+3=3), after MAKOVETZ, ahead of
LASKER and MARCO, at Graz 1890. In a triangular
contest at Vienna 1891 Bauer defeated ALBIN (+4)
and Marco (+2=2). He then played in a double-
round tournament at Vienna, but when sharing the
lead with Albin after half the games had been
played, his health broke down and he withdrew,
dying of tuberculosis shortly afterwards. Like KIE-
SERITZKY and BARDELEBEN, Bauer is chiefly remembered for a game that he lost.

Lasker–Bauer   Amsterdam 1889   Bird Opening

1 f4 d5 2 e3 Nf6 3 b3 e6 4 Bb2 Be7 5 Bd3 b6 6 Nf3
Bb7 7 Nc3 Nbd7 8 0-0 0-0 9 Ne2 c5 10 Ng3 Qc7 11
Ne5 Nxe5 12 Bxe5 Qc6 13 Qe2 a6 14 Nh5 Nxh5

White now makes a DOUBLE BISHOP SACRIFICE. 15 Bxh7+
Kxh7 16 Qxh5+ Kg8 17 Bxg7 Kxg7 18 Qg4+ Kh7 19
Rf3 e5 20 Rh3+ Qh6 21 Rxh6+ Kxh6 22 Qd7 Bf6 23
Qxb7 Kg7 24 Rf1 Rab8 25 Qd7 Rfd8 26 Qg4+ Kf8 27
fxe5 Bg7 28 e6 Rb7 29 Qg6 f6 30 Rxf6+ Bxf6 31
Qxf6+ Ke8 32 Qh8+ Ke7 33 Qg7+ Kxe6 34 Qxb7
Rd6 35 Qxa6 d4 36 cxd4 cxd4 37 h4 d3 38 Qxd3 Black
resigns.

Bauer Variation, 616 in the VIENNA GAMBIT, proposed by the German writer Wilhelm Bauer, who
co-edited the chess column in the *Frankfurter Journal* in the 1880s.

Baumbach, Friedrich (1935–), German correspondence player, winner (on tie-break) of the 11th
World Correspondence Chess Championship,
which ended in 1989. By profession Baumbach is a
chemist, researching molecular biology.

Bayer, Conrad (1828–97), problemist from Olo-
mouc, Czechoslovakia, then part of the Austro-
Hungarian Empire, pharmacist. With the advent of
composing tourneys in the 1850s he became the
most successful prize-winner of the time. The example below, first published anonymously in the
Leipziger Illustrierte Zeitung, 1855, shows play
reminiscent of the manşuba-type positions of
STAMMA. Considered to be the 'last word' in this
genre, the problem was immediately dubbed 'the
Immortal Problem'; and almost as immediately
forgotten, for the problem art was fast changing to
its modern form.

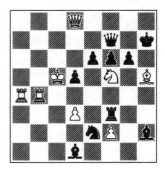

#9

1 Rb7 Qxb7 2 Bxg6+ Kxg6 3 Qg8+ Kxf5 4
Qg4+ Ke5 5 Qh5+ Rf5 6 f4+ Bxf4 7 Qxe2+
Bxe2 8 Re4+ dxe4 9 d4#. White sacrifices five
pieces and a pawn to mate with the lone pawn.

The Dutch composer Hendrik Hermanus Kam-
stra (1899–1971) published a problem in this long
outmoded style (*Tijdschrift v.d. K.N.S.B.*, 1950)
showing mate by a lone pawn after the sacrifice of
seven pieces.

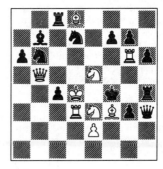

#8

1 Bg4 Rxg4 2 Bg5+ hxg5 3 Rf6+ gxf6 4 Ng6+
fxg6 5 Qf5+ gxf5 6 Nd5+ Bxd5 7 Rf3+ Bxf3
8 e3#.

These two problems illustrate the great strides
made in composing techniques during the intervening years. (See TOURNEY.)

Bayonet Attack, 590 in the CARO–KANN DEFENCE
and 914 in the ITALIAN OPENING, both characterized
by the thrusting move Pg4. An alternative to the
latter is the THERKATZ–HERZOG VARIATION.

Bazlov, Yuri Vasilyevich (1947–), Russian study
composer from the Far East, almost on the border
between Korea and Russia, winner of the 15th
USSR study-composing championship, 1979–80,
journalist. His compositions are often characterized
by dynamic play of all or almost all the men, so that
the final position may look wholly different from
the set-position. (See IDEAL MATE.)

BCF, the British Chess Federation, governing body of English chess with occasional responsibility for other parts of the United Kingdom on certain aspects of the game. Much controversy and considerable opposition from the powerful City of London Chess Club, which regarded itself as the controlling authority of British chess, preceded the foundation of the BCF in 1904. (See ORGANIZATION.)

Beasley, John Derek (1940–   ), English problemist, computer consultant. He has written excellent books on D'ORVILLE and KLETT, and also writes on mathematical recreations. See CONSTRUCTION TASK; IMITATOR; aṣ-ṢŪLĪ.

beauty prize, see BRILLIANCY PRIZE.

Becker, Albert (1896–1984), Austrian-born player, International Master (1953). At Carlsbad 1929, the strongest tournament of the year, he shared fifth place with EUWE and VIDMAR, beating both these grandmasters as well as BOGOLJUBOW and MARSHALL among others. He won two Trebitsch Memorial tournaments at Vienna, coming ahead of GRÜNFELD in 1931, and ahead of Grünfeld and ELISKASES in 1932; but his best achievement was at Tatatóváros (now Tata) 1935, when he came equal second (+10=5−2) after SZABÓ. Becker played in two Olympiads: for Austria in 1931, when he made best fourth-board score (+10=1−3), and for Germany in 1939.

Editor of *Wiener Schachzeitung* from 1926 to 1935, he is also remembered for many monographs on openings which he continued to write when he retired from international chess after settling in Argentina on the outbreak of the Second World War. (He was not a refugee, but a supporter of Germany who was unable to return.) M. A. Lachaga of Buenos Aires published a small book, *Albert Becker Praxis eines Theoretikers* (1975), containing 66 of Becker's games and details of his chess career.

Becker Defence, 1174, variation in the KING'S GAMBIT Accepted named after BECKER. Black may transpose to lines 1145–1147 while avoiding the ALLGAIER and KIESERITZKY GAMBITS, 1166, 1151. (Compare FISCHER DEFENCE.)

Been and Koomen Variation, 171, sharp defence to the QUEEN'S GAMBIT, named after the Amsterdam players Jan Been (1913–   ) and Wim Koomen (1910–88); sometimes called the Dutch Variation.

behaviour. Article 15 of the FIDE rules states that while a game is in progress a player is forbidden to refer to written or printed material, to discuss the game with or take advice from a third party, to analyse on another board, or to distract the opponent. The ARBITER has authority to decide what constitutes distraction, and in the event of misbehaviour of any kind may impose a penalty reaching as far as loss of the game.

Behting Variation, 1046, a GRECO COUNTER-GAMBIT line analysed in the *St Petersburger Zeitung* (1909) by the Latvian writer Karl Behting, or Kārlis Bētiņš (1867–1943).

Belavenets, Sergey Vsevolodovich (1910–42), Soviet master, joint champion of Moscow in 1932, 1937, and 1938, RSFSR (Russian Federation) champion in 1934, third in the USSR championship in 1939. He was killed in action. In *Shakhmaty v SSSR* and *64* Belavenets published endgame analyses and many other articles. They have been catalogued by his daughter Ludmilla (1940–   ), an International Master of Correspondence Chess.

Belgrade Gambit, 861 in the SCOTCH FOUR KNIGHTS GAME, played by the Yugoslav master Nikola Karaklajić (1926–   ) in 1945 and probably introduced by him. Sometimes called the Four Knights Gambit.

Bellón Gambit, 28, in the ENGLISH OPENING, played in the early 1970s by the Spanish Grandmaster Juan Manuel Bellón (1950–   ).

Belyavsky, Alexander Henrikhovich (1953–   ), Ukrainian player, International Grandmaster (1975). He won the World Junior Championship in 1973, and at his second attempt in the USSR championship, Leningrad 1974, came first (+7=6−2) equal with TAL, with whom he shared the title. After a four-year period of adjustment, during which his play was uneven, Belyavsky achieved consistently good tournament results: Kiev 1978, first (+9=4−2), two points clear of the field; Bucharest 1980, first (+10=5), three points ahead of his nearest rival; Baku 1980, second (+7=8), half a point below KASPAROV; Tashkent 1980, first (+7=9−1); Baden-bei-Wien 1980, first (+7=7−1) equal with SPASSKY; USSR championship 1980–1, first (+6=9−2) equal with PSAKHIS; Tilburg 1981, first (+5=5−1), ahead of TIMMAN and Kasparov; Sarajevo 1982, first (+10=5). After taking second place (+7=3−3) in the interzonal tournament, Moscow 1982, Belyavsky became a CANDIDATE but lost the quarter-final match in 1983 to Kasparov.

Later successes in very strong tournaments include Wijk aan Zee 1984, first (+7=6) equal with KORCHNOI; Tilburg 1986, first (+5=7−2), ahead of LJUBOJEVIĆ and KARPOV; USSR championship 1987, first (+7=8−2) equal with SALOV, whom he defeated in the play-off; Reykjavik 1988, second (+6=9−2), behind Karpov; Amsterdam (OHRA) 1989, first (+4=6); Amsterdam (OHRA) 1990, first (+4=5−1); USSR championship 1990,

first ($+5=7-1$) equal with BAREYEV, VYZHMAN-
AVIN, and YUDASIN; Reggio Emilia 1991, fourth
($+3=6-3$) equal with ROMANISHIN and YEPISHIN,
after Ljubojević, VAGANYAN, and GULKO; Linares
1991, third after IVANCHUK and Kasparov; Munich
1991, second ($+5=6-2$) equal with HÜBNER,
GELFAND, and Hertneck, after CHRISTIANSEN. In
the Candidates tournament at Montpellier 1985
he finished equal sixth, half a point too low to
go through to the quarter-finals. (See OPPOSITION;
STALEMATE.)

Belyavsky–Pintér   Luzern 1982 Olympiad   Sicilian
Defence Najdorf Variation

1 e4 c5 2 Nf3 d6 3 d4 cxd4 4 Nxd4 Nf6 5 Nc3 a6 6
Bg5 e6 7 f4 Qb6 8 Qd2 Qxb2 9 Nb3 Nc6 10 Bd3 Be7
11 0-0 Qa3 12 Rae1 h6 13 Bh4 Qb4 14 Bf2 Na5 15 a3
Nxb3 16 cxb3 Qa5 17 b4 Qd8 18 e5 dxe5 19 fxe5 Nd5
20 Ne4 0-0 21 Bb1 Bd7 22 Qc2 Rc8 23 Bc5 g6 24 Qd2
Kg7 25 Bxe7 Qxe7 26 Rf3 Bb5 27 Nf6

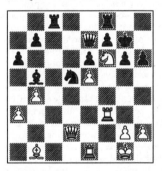

27 ... Rh8 28 Nxd5 exd5 29 e6 f6 30 Rg3 g5 31 Qxd5
Be8 32 Qf5 Rc4 33 Rf3 h5 34 Rd1 Rh6 35 Rfd3 Rc7
36 Rd7 Bxd7 37 exd7 Qd8 38 Qe6 Rh8 39 Qe4 Rh6 40
Qe8 Rh8 41 Qg6+ Kf8 42 Ba2 Black resigns.

Benedict, Clare (1871–1961), American chess
patron who sponsored a series of tournaments for
teams of four, from West European countries.
Most of them, taking place between 1953 and 1979,
were held in Switzerland where she lived during the
latter part of her life. She also sponsored an individual tournament at Zurich 1954. A grand-
daughter of Fenimore Cooper, she was a writer
herself.

Benelux Variation, 771 in the SPANISH OPENING,
analysed by O'KELLY of Belgium, Tjeerd Daniel van
Scheltinga (1914–94) of the Netherlands, and the
Austrian Hans Haberditz (c.1901–57). The line
usually arises by transposition from the BEVERWIJK
VARIATION, 797. The name was coined around 1950,
when the economic union of Belgium, Netherlands,
and Luxemburg (Benelux) was leading the way to
the formation of the EEC.

Benima Defence, 981, a SCOTCH GAMBIT line having
an affinity with the HUNGARIAN DEFENCE, 937.
Played by LÖWENTHAL in 1856, this variation was
later named after Levi Benima (1837–1922), Dutch
champion in 1881.

Benjamin, Joel Lawrence (1964–), International
Grandmaster (1986) from New York, equal first
($+3=10$) in the American championship 1987. He
was second ($+6=4-1$) in a strong tournament at
Toronto 1990.

Browne–Benjamin   USA Championship 1985   Queen's
Indian Defence Petrosyan Variation

1 d4 Nf6 2 c4 e6 3 Nf3 b6 4 a3 c5 5 d5 Ba6 6 Qc2 exd5
7 cxd5 g6 8 Nc3 Bg7 9 g3 0-0 10 Bg2 d6 11 0-0 Re8 12
Re1 Nbd7 13 Bf4 Qe7 14 h3 Ne4 15 Nxe4 Qxe4 16
Qd2 Nf6 17 Rad1 Rad8 18 Nh2 Qc4 19 Bg5 Rc8 20
Bxf6 Bxf6 21 Ng4 Bg7 22 e4 Qa4 23 Qf4

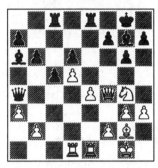

23 ... Be2 24 Rd2 Bxg4 25 hxg4 Be5 26 Qe3 c4 27 Rc1
Rc5 28 Rdc2 Qb3 29 Rxc4 Qxe3 30 fxe3 Bxb2 31 Rxc5
bxc5 32 Rb1 Bxa3 33 Ra1 Bb2 34 Rxa7 Be5 35 Kf2 c4
36 Bf1 c3 37 Bd3 Rb8 38 Ra2 Rb2+ 39 Rxb2 cxb2 40
g5 White lost on time. Black's plan is to play 40 ... f6,
forcing a passed pawn on the king's side, and then to
march the king to c1.

Benko, Pal Charles (1928–), International Grandmaster (1958). A French-born Hungarian player
and composer, he won the Hungarian championship at the age of twenty (1948) and played for his
country in the Moscow Olympiad, 1956. Shortly
afterwards he settled in the USA where he became
naturalized. He became a CANDIDATE for the first
time after sharing third place in the Portorož interzonal, 1958, and for the second time after scoring
$+8=11-3$ to share sixth place in the Stockholm
interzonal, 1962, but he made only moderate scores
in the Candidates tournaments of 1959 and 1962.
Perhaps realizing he had reached his limit, he ceded
his place in the interzonal, 1970, to FISCHER, who
then proceeded on his path to the world championship.

Benko took second place ($+7=8$) after LEIN at
Novi Sad 1972, and shared first prize with QUIN-
TEROS at Torremolinos 1973. In the USA he won or
shared first place in eight Swiss system Open Championships from 1961 to 1975, and from 1962 to
1972 he played for his adopted country in six
Olympiads. Later he re-established a base in Hungary and divided his time between the two countries.

Benko–Gligorić   New York 1963 Piatigorsky Cup   King's
Indian Defence Four Pawns Attack

1 d4 Nf6 2 c4 g6 3 Nc3 Bg7 4 e4 d6 5 Be2 0-0 6 f4 c5
7 Nf3 cxd4 8 Nxd4 Nc6 9 Be3 e5 10 Nxc6 bxc6 11 fxe5
dxe5 12 0-0 Qc7 13 Qe1 a5 14 Qh4 Ne8 15 Bc5 Nd6

16 Rad1 Nb7 17 Bxf8 Bxf8 18 Na4 Be6 19 b3 Nc5 20 Nxc5 Bxc5+ 21 Kh1 Rf8 22 Bg4 f5 23 exf5 gxf5

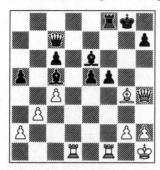

24 Bxf5 Rxf5 25 Qg4+ Qg7 26 Rd8+ Bf8 27 Qxf5 Bxf5 28 Rxf5 Qe7 29 Rdxf8+ Kg7 30 R5f7+ Qxf7 31 Rxf7+ Kxf7 32 Kg1 Kf6 33 Kf2 Kf5 34 Ke3 h5 35 c5 e4 36 a3 Ke5 37 g3 Kd5 38 b4 axb4 39 axb4 Ke5 40 h3 Kd5 41 g4 hxg4 42 hxg4 Ke5 43 g5 Kf5 44 b5 Black resigns.

Benko Attack, 405 in the KING'S INDIAN DEFENCE, introduced by BENKO at Portorož 1958.

Benko Gambit, 279. Arising, by transposition, in the game Rubinstein–Spielmann, Vienna 1922, played in the 1930s by OPOČENSKÝ and sometimes named after him, analysed in 1946 in the USSR where it was called the Volga Gambit, this enterprising variation of the HROMÁDKA DEFENCE was used occasionally from 1947 by BRONSTEIN, KERES, and other players. The gambit's acceptance as a standard line owes much to BENKO who published analysis in the 1960s and wrote a book, *The Benko Gambit* (1973). (See AGDESTEIN; STÅHLBERG.)

Benko Opening, a name occasionally given to 1318, the KING'S FIANCHETTO OPENING.

Benoni Defence, 50, sometimes miscalled the Staunton Defence, one of a group of Queen's Pawn openings (50–52, 278–287, 352–355) in which Black plays a pawn to c5 inviting White to reply Pd4–d5. Making this advance gains space in the centre for White, after which Black usually seeks compensating pressure on the queen's-side, often fianchettoing his king's bishop to this end. In 1617 CARRERA noted that (1 d4 c5) 2 d5 confined the adversary's game, and as late as 1939 FINE wrote that defences of the Benoni type left Black with a 'hopelessly cramped game'; but since the 1950s such defences have been widely accepted. The most popular of these lines is the MODERN BENONI, 282.

The name comes from *Ben-Oni oder die Vertheidigungen die Gambitzüge im Schach* by Aaron Reinganum, published in 1825. Ben-Oni is Hebrew for 'child of my sorrow'. When he was depressed Reinganum turned to his chessboard, and the book was the result of his analysis. He looked at defences against gambits, mainly the KING'S GAMBIT, in some cases as far as move 29. He was the first to examine 1 d4 c5, and gave the following lines, none of which

he called Ben-Oni: 2 c4 cxd4 3 Qxd4 Nc6 4 Qd1 f5; 2 dxc5 e5 3 b4 d5 4 Bb2 f6; and 2 d5 f5. (See SHORT GAME.)

Benoni Deferred, 278, the HROMÁDKA DEFENCE.

Berger, Johann Nepomuk (1845–1933), accomplished all-rounder. In 1870 he won the first tournament (other than club events) in the Austro-Hungarian Empire; this was held at Graz, his home town, during a congress to form an Austrian chess federation. From 1883 to 1908 he entered international tournaments intermittently, swearing after each one that he would not enter another. His best achievement was at Frankfurt 1887, a fifth place shared with TARRASCH, three points behind the winner G. H. MACKENZIE. A keen correspondence player, Berger won the *Monde Illustré* tournament, 1889–92, with a remarkable score, +45=3. From his youth, when he submitted two problems for the London 1862 composing tourney, he maintained a lifelong interest in the problem art. A leading composer of the Old German school, he disliked KOHTZ and KOCKELKORN'S proposed changes. (See PROBLEM HISTORY.) These he opposed in the pages of the *Deutsche Schachzeitung* of which he was co-editor from 1898 to 1907 (with LIPKE in 1898 and then with SCHLECHTER) and sole editor from 1908 to 1911. Berger proposed an AUXILIARY SCORING METHOD almost identical to that mooted by Sonneborn, apparently unaware of the precedent.

Besides all these activities Berger was a keen student of the endgame, and it was in this department of the game that he made his most important contribution. For many years his *Theorie und Praxis der Endspiele* (1890), revised in 1922, was the best textbook on this subject. (See SQUEEZE.) He lived all his life in Graz where he was director of the commercial school. Shortly before his death he was made a Privy Councillor.

Berger tables, see PAIRING TABLES.

Berger Variation, 668 in the CENTRE GAME, recommended by BERGER in *Deutsche Schachzeitung*, 1884; 693, 710, 730, 774, and 785, five lines in the SPANISH OPENING, much analysed by Berger; 947, an old line in the TWO KNIGHTS DEFENCE, given by STAUNTON in his *Chess Praxis* (1860); 998 and 1004 in the SCOTCH GAME, the first proposed by Berger in *International Chess Magazine*, 1887; 1027, 1033, and 1035 in the PHILIDOR DEFENCE, the first given by Berger in *Deutsche Schachzeitung*, 1910, the second, similarly, in 1880.

Berg Variation, 427 in the QUEEN'S INDIAN DEFENCE. The Latvian player Theodor Berg, or Teodors Bergs (1902–66) played it against ALEKHINE in the Kemeri tournament 1937.

Berlin Defence, 625, the FALKBEER VARIATION in the VIENNA GAME; 653 in BISHOP'S OPENING; 788 in SPANISH OPENING; 1160 (also known as Philidor Defence) in the KING'S GAMBIT. All have in common the move ... Ng8-f6 whereby Black attacks the white e-pawn: this sound stratagem was recommended around 1840 by LASA and other Germans.

In the 19th century 788 became one of the principal defences to the Spanish Opening. After 4 0-0 Black plays 4 ... Nxe4, the main line of the Berlin Defence; although the knight may be awkwardly placed if driven from e4 to b7 Black gains compensation: without the king's pawn White cannot set up a CLASSICAL CENTRE. This variation, practised by LASKER, went out of fashion around 1914, probably because Black gets few opportunities for counter-play. (See KUZMIN; MARCO.)

Berliner, Hans (1929–), International Correspondence Chess Grandmaster (1968), computer scientist. Born in Berlin, he was taken to the USA at the age of eight and was naturalized in 1943. A competent over-the-board player, he won at various times the championships of Washington, DC, and New York State, and he played at the Helsinki Olympiad 1952. He was more successful at postal play, winning the 5th World Correspondence Championship, 1965–8, scoring +12=4, three points ahead of his nearest rival.

Berliner–Nyman   5th World Correspondence Championship   Hromádka Defence Petrosyan System

1 d4 Nf6 2 c4 c5 3 d5 e5 4 Nc3 d6 5 e4 g6 6 Bd3 Bg7 7 Nge2 0-0 8 f3 Na6 9 h4 Nc7 10 Bg5 h6 11 Be3 Bd7 12 Qd2 Kh7 13 h5 g5 14 a3 b6 15 g4 Ng8 16 b4 Kh8 17 Kf2 Qf6 18 Kg2 Rfb8 19 Rhb1 Qd8 20 Ra2 Qc8 21 Bc2 Bf8 22 Rab2 Ne8 23 Qd3 Ngf6 24 Ng3 Ng8 25 Bf2 f6 26 Nf5 Ne7 27 Ng3 Qc7 28 Qd1 Kh7 29 Ba4 Nc8 30 Nf5 Ng7

31 bxc5 Bxa4 32 cxb6 Qxc4 33 Nxa4 axb6 34 Rb4 Qc7 35 Nxg7 Bxg7 36 Qb3 b5 37 Nc3 Na7 38 Nxb5 Nxb5 39 Rxb5 Rxb5 40 Qxb5 Qc2 41 Rb4 Qa2 42 Qd7 Qxa3 43 Rb7 Rg8 44 Qe7 Qa8 45 Rd7 Qf8 46 Qe6 Black resigns.

Berlin Variation, 717 in the SPANISH OPENING, analysed and played in the 1950s by Heinz Gerhard Lehmann (1921–95) and Rudolf Teschner (1922–), both living in Berlin at the time.

Bernard, Henry D'Oyly (1878–1954), English problemist. (See BERNARD DEFENCE; MODEL MATE; SISTER SQUARES.)

Bernard Defence, 477, named after H. D'O. BERNARD, who analysed it in the *British Chess Magazine*, Oct. 1940. The position can arise from another sequence, 530. The idea is to meet 14 e5 by 14 ... Nxb3 15 exf6 Bxf6 or 14 Na5 Qxa5 15 e5 by 15 ... d4.

Bernstein, Ossip Samoilovich (1882–1962), Ukrainian born player, International Grandmaster (1950), International Arbiter (1952). He came from a rich family and was able to give much of his time to chess while studying law (he obtained a doctorate at Heidelberg in 1906) and while establishing a practice in Moscow. In 1903 he came second after CHIGORIN, whom he beat, in the All-Russia championship at Kiev. From 1905 to 1914, his best years, Bernstein entered nine international tournaments, six of them major events, notably sharing first prize with RUBINSTEIN at Ostend 1907, and taking second place after Rubinstein at Vilnius 1912. He won the Moscow championship in 1911. After losing his fortune in the revolution of 1917 he settled in Paris, becoming an outstanding financial lawyer and wealthy again, only to be impoverished by the financial crash in 1929–30.

In 1932, after an absence of 18 years, he took up chess again and drew a training match (+1=2–1) with ALEKHINE in 1933. He built up his practice and fortune again, but lost both when Paris fell in 1940. He fled to Spain, returned to Paris when the Second World War ended, competed in tournaments from time to time, and played first board for France in the Amsterdam Olympiad, 1954. There were occasional flashes of his earlier skill, as at Montevideo 1954 when, at the age of 72, he won a brilliancy prize for his game against NAJDORF (see below). In 1956 he took part in a small tournament at Ostend, 50 years after he had first played there. There is an anecdote that at the Zurich tournament, 1934, he missed a winning line against the Swiss player Fritz Gygli (1896–1980), exclaiming 'Am I not a chess idiot?' Hearing this, LASKER agreed, and Bernstein drew up a quasi-legal document to that effect, which Lasker endorsed.

Bernstein–Najdorf   Montevideo 1954 Brilliancy Prize   Old Indian Defence

1 d4 Nf6 2 c4 d6 3 Nc3 Nbd7 4 e4 e5 5 Nf3 g6 6 dxe5 dxe5 7 Be2 c6 8 0-0 Qc7 9 h3 Nc5 10 Qc2 Nh5 11 Re1 Ne6 12 Be3 Be7 13 Rad1 0-0 14 Bf1 Nhg7 15 a3 f5 16 b4 f4 17 Bc1 Bf6 18 c5 g5 19 Bc4 Kh8 20 Bb2 h5?

21 Nd5 cxd5 22 exd5 Nd4 23 Nxd4 exd4 24 d6 Qd7 25 Rxd4 f3 26 Rde4 Qf5 27 g4 hxg4 28 hxg4 Qg6 29 Re8 Bf5 30 Rxa8 Rxa8 31 gxf5 Qh5 32 Re4 Qh3 33 Bf1 Qxf5 34 Rh4+ gxh4 35 Qxf5 Nxf5 36 Bxf6+ Kg8 37 d7 Black resigns.

Bernstein Variation, 210 in the QUEEN'S GAMBIT, proposed in the early 1930s by BERNSTEIN and made popular by ELISKASES (an alternative is the COTLAR VARIATION); 781 in the SPANISH OPENING, from the game Bernstein–Lasker, St Petersburg 1909; 917 in the ITALIAN OPENING, an improvement on GRECO'S 10 ... Bxa1, given by Bernstein in *Tidskrift för Schack*, 1922, but to be found in POLERIO; 1212 in the FRENCH DEFENCE, from the game Bernstein–Swiderski, Coburg 1904, but played earlier in Janowski–Lee, London 1899.

Berolina pawn, an unorthodox kind of pawn used in FAIRY PROBLEMS as well as games; its move is forward diagonally one square at a time (or two for its first move), but it captures on, or attacks, the square directly ahead on the file. Invented by Edmund Nebermann who named it after the city of Berlin, where he worked as a radio officer, it was first published in *Funkschach*, 15 Aug. 1926. A tournament was held in 1957 using Berolina pawns and the following example illustrates their power when connected and passed.

C. F. Snook–K. M. Oliff

1 c2-e4 f7-d5 2 Nf3 Nc6 3 Nc3 d5-c4 4 Nb5 d7-f5 5 d2-f4 a7-b6 (threatening White's knight) 6 Qxd8+ Kxd8 7 Nbd4 Nxd4 8 Nxd4 f5xf4 9 Bxf4 b7-d5 10 Nf3 e7-c5 11 h2-g3 (White should play e2-d3, blocking the enemy pawns.) 11 ... Bf5 12 f2-e3 c5-d4 13 Ng5 Bb4+ 14 Kd1 d4-c3 15 e3-d4 (After 15 Nf7+ Ke7 16 Nxh8 c3-d2+ Black will promote a pawn.) 15 ... d5xd4 16 e2-g4 c4-d3 17 Ke1 c3-d2 18 Rc1 d3-c2 and White resigns; if 19 Rxc2 d2-c1 = Q+ or if 19 Bd3, d4xd3.

Bertin, Joseph, author of the first worthwhile chess textbook in the English language. A Huguenot born at Castelmoron-sur-Lôt in the 1690s, he came to England as a youth, became naturalized in 1713, and married about 1719. In 1726 he joined a line regiment (38th Foot) then serving in the West Indies, was promoted to the rank of Captain, and subsequently invalided out of the army. Then he wrote *The Noble Game of Chess* (1735). In the same year and through the influence of Lord Harrington (later STAMMA's patron) he was recommissioned in a Regiment of Invalids. In all probability he died soon afterwards.

His book, now rare, was sold only at Slaughter's coffee house. (Most of the contents were published by LANGE in *Schachzeitung*, 1860.) Besides openings analysis and useful advice about the middlegame Bertin laid down 19 rules:

1. The King's Pawn, the Bishop's Pawn, and the Queen's Pawn must move before the Knights; otherwise if the pawns move last, the game will be much crouded by useless moves.

2. Never play your Queen, till your game is tolerably well opened, that you may not lose any moves; and a game well opened gives a good situation.

3. You must not give useless checks, for the same reason.

4. When you are well posted, either for attack or defence, you must not be tempted to take any of your adversary's men, which may divert you from the main design.

5. Do not Castle, but when very necessary, because the move is often lost by it. [For 'move' read 'initiative'; STEINITZ later emphasised this point.]

6. Never attack, or defend the King, without a sufficient force; and take care of ambushes and traps.

7. Never croud your game by too many men in one place.

8. Consider well before you play, what harm your adversary is able to do to you, that you may oppose his designs.

9. To free your game, take off some of your adversary's men, if possible for nothing; tho' to succeed in your design, you must often give away some of your own, as occasion serves.

10. He that plays first, is understood to have the attack. When your game is well opened you must endeavour to attack in your turn, as soon as you can do it with safety. But the defence, if well played, is still best against the gambets, in which you will exchange all your pieces except the gambet that gives three Pawns, which will be necessary to keep a Rook, to conduct your Pawns to the Queen.

11. A good player ought to foresee the concealed move, from three to five and seven moves. [The numbers refer to SINGLE-MOVES, the usual way of counting at that time.] The concealed move is a piece that does not play for a long time, but lies snug, in hopes of getting an advantage.

12. At the beginning of a game, you may play any Pawn two moves, without danger.

13. The gambet is, when he that first gives the Pawn of the King's Bishop, in the second move for nothing, the other keeps it, or taking another for it, if he is obliged to lose.

14. The close game is, when he that plays first gives no men, unless to make a good advantage; but in giving a Pawn first he loses his advantage.

15. He that Castles first, the other must advance his three Pawns, on the side of his adversary's King, and back them with some pieces, in order to force him that way, provided his own King, or pieces, are not in danger in other places.

16. When your game is well opened, to gain the attack, you must present your pieces to change; and if your adversary that has the attack, refuses to change, he loses a good situation; and neither in exchanging, or retiring, the defence gets the move.

17. For example: In the beginning of a game, to shew the necessity of playing the Pawns before the pieces, if there were but two Pawns on each side of the board, that is to say the Pawns of the Rooks, the first that should play would soon win the game,

by taking the other's pieces by check; and that situation may come in less number of pieces.

18. To play well the latter end of a game, you must calculate who has the move, on which the game always depends. [A reference to ZUGZWANG.]

19. To learn well and fast, you must be resolute to guard the gambet Pawn, or any other advantage against the attack; and when you have the least advantage, you must change all, man for man. A draw-game shows both sides played it well to the last move.

Except for 1 and 15, and perhaps the incomprehensible 17, these rules are still sound. The seventh rule envisages the possibility that bunched pieces would be endangered by an advancing phalanx of pawns. After noting that his rules would be of great use Bertin adds 'I wish I could give Rules to avoid over-sights.'

Bertin Gambit, 1122, a variation of the KING'S GAMBIT Accepted first published by BERTIN in 1735. It is sometimes called the Three Pawns Gambit, but that name is appropriate only when the line reaches 1123.

best game prize, a prize for a game that is well played throughout, chosen from the games of a particular match or tournament. The first such prize was awarded to GUNSBERG for his game against MASON, New York 1889. Prizes have since been awarded for the best strategic game, best attack on the king, best endgame, best game using a specific opening, and so on. A prize for the best draw is shared between the players. Compare BRILLIANCY PRIZE.

Betbeder Variation, 56, the RICHTER ATTACK. Also 58, the VERESOV VARIATION, frequently played, for example at the London Olympiad, 1927, by Louis Betbeder (1901–) of France.

Beverwijk Variation, 797 in the SPANISH OPENING, a kind of CORDEL DEFENCE Deferred, played by JAENISCH in 1850, and in the game Vlagsma–O'Kelly, Beverwijk 1946. Transposition to the BENELUX VARIATION, 771, is common.

bibliographies. There is not, and perhaps never can be, a complete bibliography of chess titles. The largest single list was published in 1964 when the Cleveland Public Library reproduced the 12,000 catalogue cards of the J. G. WHITE chess collection in two large volumes. The chess collection of the Royal Dutch Library was listed in *Bibliotheca Van der Linde–Niemeijeriana* (1955) showing 6,493 numbered entries. A more comprehensive replacement ceased after the first part appeared in 1974; there were 1,300 entries on bibliography, history, and chessmen, compared to 373 entries given in 1955. There are specialized bibliographies, often confined to one country or language. Among the most important are *Chess, an Annotated Bibliography of Works Published in the English Language 1850–1968* (1974) by D. A. Betts; *Chess: an Annotated Bibliography, 1969–1988* (1991) by Andy Lusis; *Shakhmatnaya literatura SSSR* (1968) by N. I. Sakharov, covering the period 1775–1966; and *Lineamenti di una Bibliografia Italiana degli Scacci* (1987) by A. Chicco and A. Sanvito. The first has 2,568 titles, the second 3,231, the third 1,108, and the fourth 1,032.

Bidev, Pavle (1912–88), Yugoslav professor of philosophy who made a reappraisal of chess history by travelling in a direction opposite to that taken by traditional historians. Instead of taking evidence and then forming a theory, he formed a theory and then made a rigorous examination of the evidence that appeared to confound that theory.

A good player, Bidev beat PIRC and KOSTIĆ in the Yugoslav championship in 1946 and repeated the achievement the following year, but he had what he believed was a divine mission to enquire into CHATURANGA. After twenty years of study, and publication of some of his ideas, he brought together his thesis in *Šah simbol kosmosa* (1972), in Croatian with a 25-page summary in German. A Macedonian version, without the summary, was published simultaneously. (See MAGIC SQUARE.)

Bidev demonstrated convincingly that chaturanga, in the form in which it reached Persia, was created in the period AD 606–620, but, impatient at the slow acceptance of his beliefs, he became increasingly personal in his attacks on those who might have supported him in due course.

Bielicki, Carlos (1940–), Junior World Champion in 1959, the Argentinian player reduced his commitment to the game and never became a great player.

Bilek, István (1932–), Hungarian player, International Grandmaster (1962), champion of his country in 1963, 1965, and 1970, competitor in nine Olympiads from 1958 to 1974, scoring +52=56–11. He played in the interzonals of 1962, 1964 and 1967 with modest results, and in many international tournaments, notably taking third prize (+6=9) at Beverwijk 1966 after POLUGAYEVSKY and SZABÓ and sharing first prize with SAVON at Debrecen 1970. He has a reputation for being economical with his effort. At Slupsk 1979 he drew all ten of his games in a grand total of 125 moves, taking 109 minutes in all. At one time he was married to the Hungarian women's champion of 1958 and 1963, Edith Láng (1938–), IWM (1965).

Örökös sakkban (1987) is an autobiography with games, results, and various essays, in Hungarian.

Bilguer, Paul Rudolf von (1815–40), see HANDBUCH; PRUSSIAN DEFENCE.

Bilguer Defence, 940, the TWO KNIGHTS DEFENCE, in 1839 the subject of a monograph by BILGUER, *Das Zweispringerspiel im Nachzuge.*

bind, a grip, usually held by pawns, from which the opponent cannot easily escape. See MARÓCZY BIND for an example.

Bird, Henry Edward (1830–1908), English player, accountant. He played in 13 strong tournaments, with erratic results. His best achievements were: Vienna 1873, a tie with PAULSEN for fifth place; Paris 1878, fourth place shared with MACKENZIE; Manchester 1890, third prize shared with Mackenzie, after TARRASCH and BLACKBURNE. He also played in numerous minor tournaments, notably tying with GUNSBERG for first place at London 1889. His most important match was against STEINITZ in 1866, for the first to win eleven games. He was adjudged the loser when he was called to the USA on business, the score standing +5 = 5 − 7 in favour of his opponent. Although Steinitz was not as strong a player as he later became this was a creditable result for Bird in the circumstances, for he played each game after a day's work. In 1886 he drew a match with BURN (+9 − 9). One of the most ingenious tacticians of his time, Bird played in the attacking style prevalent in his youth. He usually chose openings that were regarded as bizarre, although many of them, e.g. the DRAGON VARIATION, have since gained acceptance.

Bird was probably the best known and longest serving habitué of the London COFFEE HOUSE known as Simpson's Divan. 'A rosy-cheeked, blue-eyed, fair-headed boy', he first attended around 1846, and was a constant visitor for more than 50 years, after which he was described as 'majestic in stature, in girth, in the baldness of his great head, less majestic in the litter of tobacco-ash upon his waistcoat... with a pleasant smiling countenance'. For the last years of his life he was largely confined to home because of gout.

Besides writing booklets on railway finance, he wrote six books on chess. They are not without interest although the content is somewhat inaccurate and often disorganized. His *Modern Chess and Chess Masterpieces* (1887) contains more than 200 games, about half of them his own. *Chess History and Reminiscences* (1893) contains useful accounts of contemporary players and chess affairs, but its only original contribution to history is ill-conceived. Bird argued that the theologian Alcuin must have introduced chess to Britain after visiting Charlemagne's court in the 8th century, assuming, falsely, that the game was known there. The book also contains such useful advice as 'It is bad form for spectators to remove the pieces from the board without the consent of the players ...'.

Bird–Mason   New York 1876   French Defence Exchange Variation

1 e4 e6   2 d4 d5   3 Nc3 Nf6   4 exd5 exd5   5 Nf3 Bd6   6 Bd3 0-0   7 0-0 h6   8 Re1 Nc6   9 Nb5 Bb4   10 c3 Ba5   11 Na3 Bg4   12 Nc2 Qd7   13 b4 Bb6   14 h3 Bh5   15 Ne3 Rfe8   16 b5 Ne7   17 g4 Bg6   18 Ne5 (ADVANCE POINT) 18...Qc8   19 a4 c6   20 bxc6 bxc6   21 Ba3 Ne4   22 Qc2 Ng5   23 Bxe7 Rxe7   24 Bxg6 fxg6   25 Qxg6 Nxh3+   26 Kh2 Nf4   27 Qf5 Ne6   28 Ng2 Qc7

29 a5 Bxa5   30 Rxa5 Rf8   31 Ra6 Rxf5   32 gxf5 Nd8   33 Nf4 Qc8   34 Nfg6 Re8   35 Nxc6 Qc7+   36 Nce5 Qxc3   37 Re3 Qd2   38 Kg2 Qxd4   39 f6 gxf6   40 Rxf6 Ne6   41 Rg3 Ng5   42 Ng4 Kg7   43 Nf4 Qe4+   44 Kh2 Nh7   45 Nh5+ Kh8   46 Rxh6 Qc2   47 Nhf6 Re7   48 Kg2 d4   49 Ne5 Qc8   50 Ng6+ Black resigns. For this game Bird was awarded the BRILLIANCY PRIZE.

Bird Attack, 911 in the ITALIAN OPENING, strongly advocated by STAMMA and no less strongly by BIRD. In May 1843 SAINT-AMANT played it against STAUNTON in their first match and five years later Bird adopted the variation, playing it in many tournaments, notably with fair success at Vienna 1882, London 1883, and Nuremberg 1883.

Bird Defence, 773, reply to the SPANISH OPENING given in the first edition of the HANDBUCH, 1843. Pioneered by BIRD, e.g. against ANDERSSEN in 1854, and used on occasion by grandmasters such as TARRASCH, SPASSKY, and MALANYUK, this defence has not gained wide acceptance.

Bird Opening, 1312, sometimes called the Stein Opening or, by analogy with the DUTCH DEFENCE, the Dutch Attack. In 1873, after an absence of six years from chess, BIRD played a match with WISKER. 'Having forgotten familiar openings, I commenced adopting KBP for first move, and finding it led to highly interesting games out of the usual groove, I became partial to it.' Bird had also forgotten unfamiliar openings, for 1 f4 (given by LUCENA) had been played by BOURDONNAIS, WILLIAMS, and others of that period. However, because of Bird's consistent adoption of the move, it became a standard opening, although never popular, and it was named after him in 1885 by the *Hereford Times*. (See BAUER; STAUNTON; WILLIAMS.)

Bird Variation, 491 in the PELIKÁN VARIATION of the SICILIAN DEFENCE, from the game Selman–Bird, London 1883. On that occasion each side played an extra move, Selman playing his bishop to f4 and then g5, and Bird playing his pawn to e5 in two steps.

bishop, a minor piece represented by the symbol B or the figurine ♝. It is a line piece that is moved on diagonals of one colour and can neither occupy nor attack the 32 squares of the opposite colour. On an otherwise empty board it controls an odd number of squares in the range 7 to 13 depending on its position. In the ARRAY White's bishops stand on c1 and f1, Black's on c8 and f8. Those on c1 and f8 are dark bishops (the dark squares are their domain) and the other two are light bishops. The bishops on c1 and c8 are called queen's bishops and those on f1 and f8 king's bishops. In descriptive notation they have the symbols QB or KB.

The TWO BISHOPS, which can attack squares of either colour, are generally more than double the worth of one. For a comparison of the bishop with the knight, see MINOR EXCHANGE.

The origin of the name is obscure. The bishop, introduced in the 15th century, took the move of the COURIER and the place in the array of the ALFIL. The appearance of the Muslim fīl was somewhat formless but with two protuberances said to symbolize the elephant from which the piece derives its name. Perhaps these suggested the bishop's mitre, hence bishop, the name used in English-speaking countries since the new game gained acceptance. On the other hand it might simply be a recognition of the political status of the medieval church.

bishop ending, an endgame with kings and bishop(s) and one or more pawns.

bishop of the wrong colour, a phrase used only in the situation where a bishop cannot assist the promotion of a rook's pawn because it cannot attack the queening square.

White to play wins by 1 Kb8 Kb5 2 Kb7. Black to play draws by 1 ... Ka7 2 Bb6+ Ka8 and Black's king can be stalemated but cannot be driven from the queening square to make way for the pawn.

Bishop's Gambit, 1093, the KING'S GAMBIT Accepted with Bf1-c4 as White's third move, introduced by Ruy LÓPEZ. The first extensive analysis of this opening was by JAENISCH, who discovered so many complicated possibilities that he was moved to write: 'We even think we do not exaggerate in looking upon the Bishop's Gambit, with certain other chess openings, as an imperishable monument to human wisdom.' Neither then nor since has it been much played. (See IMMORTAL GAME; SPIELMANN.)

bishops of opposite colour, a light bishop opposed by a dark bishop, there being no other bishops on the board. Both players suffer COLOUR-WEAKNESS on the squares their bishops cannot control. Middlegame positions in which such bishops may combine with other pieces favour the attacker, but endgames are frequently drawn. (See BENJAMIN.)

This position is drawn. Despite having two extra pawns White cannot gain control of the dark squares f4 and c7.

Bogoljubow–Alekhine   Salzburg 1942   Caro–Kann Defence Knight Variation

1 e4 c6 2 d4 d5 3 Nc3 dxe4 4 Nxe4 Nf6 5 Nxf6+ exf6
6 Bc4 Bd6 7 Qe2+ Be7 8 Nf3 Bg4 9 c3 Nd7 10 h3 Bh5
11 g4 Bg6 12 Nh4 Nb6 13 Bb3 Nd5 14 Bd2 Qd6 15
Nf5 Bxf5 16 gxf5 g6 17 0-0-0 0-0-0 18 Qf3 g5 19 Rhe1
Rhe8 20 Re4 Bf8 21 Rxe8 Rxe8 22 Qh5 Qd7 23 Qxh7
Re4 24 Qh8 Qd8 25 Qh5 Qd7 26 Qh8 Qd8 27 Re1
Rxe1 (27 ... Rh4 28 Qg8 also favours White) 28 Bxe1 Kc7
29 Bd2 Qe7 30 Qh5 Qd7 31 Qf3 Bh6

32 h4 Nf4 33 Bxf4 gxf4 34 Qh5 Bf8 35 Bxf7 c5 36 Be6
Qd6 37 Qf7+ Be7 38 dxc5 Qxc5 39 h5 f3 40 h6 Kb6
41 Bc4 (not 41 h7? Qxf2, threatening perpetual check)
41 ... Bd6 42 Bd5 Qc8 43 Qe6 Qf8 44 h7 Ka5 45 Bxf3
Qh6+ 46 Kc2 Black resigns.

Bishop's Opening, 638, given by LUCENA. Until the
middle of the 19th century most authorities held
that after 1 e4 e5 the only good square for White's
light bishop was c4; here, on the ITALIAN DIAGONAL,
the bishop would be poised for attack, eyeing f7.
Believing that White retains more options, including that of advancing the f-pawn, PHILIDOR preferred to play 2 Bc4 rather than delay by 2 Nf3 Nc6
3 Bc4, and his influence made the Bishop's Opening
popular for a long time. Following improvements
for Black in the PHILIDOR VARIATION, 643 (2 ... Bc5
3 c3), and the introduction of the BERLIN DEFENCE,
653 (2 ... Nf6), around 1840, the opening fell out of
favour. In the 1960s LARSEN played it a few times,
usually answering the Berlin Defence with 3 d3, a
long-neglected move recommended by Philidor,
and now the cornerstone of the MODERN BISHOP'S
OPENING. Among later practitioners of the opening
are DOLMATOV and NUNN. (See DOUBLE ROOK SACRI-
FICE.)

Bishop Variation, 572, the CLASSICAL VARIATION of
the CARO–KANN DEFENCE.

bivalve, a problemist's description of a move, made
by Black, that opens a file for one black line-piece
and closes a line commanded by another black line-
piece. The term was coined in 1930 by A. C. WHITE.

\#2

A problem by the Austrian composer Helmut
Maria Zajic (1934–   ), fourth prize, *Die Schwalbe*,
1981. White needs to move B from f6 to threaten
Qe5 mate. There are four tries: 1 Bh4? Nh3, 1 Bg5?
Ng2, 1 Be7? Nd5, 1 Bxd4? Nd3, The key is 1 Bd8:

1 ... Nh3	2 Nh4 #
1 ... Ng2	2 Rg5 #
1 ... Nd5	2 Bxe6 #
1 ... Nd3	2 Nxd4 #.

The first variation shows a VALVE, the others
show bivalves.

Black, the player who moves the darker coloured
pieces. If the difference in COLOUR does not readily
lend itself to a light/dark dichotomy the players
agree who is White or Black.

Blackburne, Joseph Henry (1841–1924), for more
than 20 years one of the first six players in the
world, and for even longer the leading English-born
player. Draughts was the most popular indoor
game in his home town, Manchester, and he
learned the game as a child, becoming expert in his
youth. He was about 18 when, inspired by MOR-
PHY's exploits, he learned the moves of chess. In
July 1861 he lost all five games of a match against
Manchester chess club's Russian-born champion,
Edward Pindar, but he improved so rapidly that
three months later he defeated Pindar (+5=2−1),
and in 1862 he became champion of the club, ahead
of Pindar and HORWITZ. Instructed by Horwitz,
Blackburne became one of the leading ENDGAME
players of his time. Wishing to emulate the feats of
PAULSEN, who visited the club in November 1861,
he developed exceptional skill at BLINDFOLD CHESS.
He spent most of the 1860s developing his chess and
toying with various occupations. After winning the
British championship, 1868–9, ahead of DE VERE, he
became a full-time professional player.

Blackburne achieved excellent results in many
tournaments: Baden-Baden 1870, third equal with
NEUMANN, after ANDERSSEN and STEINITZ; London
1872, second (+5−2) after Steinitz, ahead of
ZUKERTORT; Vienna 1873, second to Steinitz after
a play-off; Paris 1878, third after WINAWER
and Zukertort; Wiesbaden 1880, first equal with
ENGLISCH and SCHWARZ; Berlin 1881, first
(+13=2−1), three points ahead of Zukertort,
the second-prize winner (Blackburne's greatest
achievement); London 1883, third after Zukertort
and Steinitz; Hamburg 1885, second equal with
Englisch, MASON, TARRASCH, and WEISS, half a point
after GUNSBERG; Frankfurt 1887, second equal with
Weiss, after MACKENZIE; Manchester 1890, second
after Tarrasch; Belfast 1892, first equal with
Mason; London 1892, second (+6−2) after
LASKER; London 1893, first (+2=3). He was in
the British team in 11 of the Anglo-American
cable matches, meeting PILLSBURY on first board six
times (+2=3−1), and he continued to play internationally until he was 72, long enough to
meet the pioneer of the hypermodern movement,

NIMZOWITSCH, whom he defeated at St Petersburg 1914 (see below). In the same year he tied with YATES for first place in the British championship, but did not feel well enough to play-off for the title.

Blackburne had remarkable combinative powers, and is remembered for his swingeing king's-side attacks, often well prepared, but occasionally consisting of an ingenious SWINDLE that would deceive even the greatest of his contemporaries. The tournament book of Vienna 1873 called him 'der schwarze Tod' (Black Death), a nickname that became popular. His unflappable temperament also earned him the soubriquet 'the man with the iron nerves'. Even so, neither his temperament nor his style were suited to set matches, in which he was rarely successful against world-class players.

He had other chess talents: a problem composer, he was also a fast solver, allegedly capable of outpacing the great Sam LOYD. Blackburne earned his livelihood by means of simultaneous displays. For more than 50 years he toured Britain twice yearly, with two breaks, for this purpose. Before his time such displays were solemn affairs; LÖWENTHAL, who would turn up in formal dress and play for several hours in silence, was shocked when Blackburne turned up in ordinary clothes, chatting and making jokes as he played, and refreshing himself with whisky. Once, walking round the boards, he drained his opponent's glass saying, when rebuked, 'he left it en prise and I took it en passant'. He played his blindfold displays quickly, and with little sign of the stress that besets most blindfold players. Usually he played eight boards, never seeking for record numbers. Probably the leading blindfold expert of his time, he challenged Zukertort, a close rival in this field, to a match of ten games, played simultaneously, both players blindfold, but Zukertort declined. He was sustained in his last years by funds subscribed by his admirers. P. W. SERGEANT wrote 'Blackburne will always be remembered with affection in his own country and probably was always so regarded in many other lands he visited. He was a "good mixer". He was a very entertaining companion who had picked up much in life besides chess.' (See PURE MATE; STEMGAME.)

P. A. Graham, *Mr Blackburne's Games at Chess* (1899) contains 407 games with notes by Blackburne, and 28 three- and four-movers composed by him. A reprint, styled *Blackburne's Games at Chess* (1979), has a new introduction and two more games.

Blackburne–Nimzowitsch   St Petersburg 1914   van 't Kruijs Opening

1 e3 d6 2 f4 e5 3 fxe5 dxe5 4 Nc3 Bd6 5 e4 Be6 6 Nf3 f6 7 d3 Ne7 8 Be3 c5 9 Qd2 Nbc6 10 Be2 Nd4 11 0-0 0-0 12 Nd1 Nec6 13 c3 Nxe2+ 14 Qxe2 Re8 (Nimzowitsch calls this a MYSTERIOUS ROOK MOVE) 15 Nh4 Bf8 16 Nf5 Kh8 17 g4 Qd7 18 Nf2 a5 19 a3 b5 20 Rad1 Rab8 21 Rd2 b4 22 axb4 axb4 23 c4 Ra8 24 Qf3 Ra2? 25 g5 g6

26 Ng4 gxf5 27 Nxf6 Nd4 28 Qf2 Qc6 29 Nxe8 Qxe8 30 Bxd4 exd4 31 exf5 Bd7 32 Re1 Qf7 33 Qh4 Ra8 34 Rf2 Bc6 35 Qg4 Re8 36 Rxe8 Qxe8 37 Re2 Qd7 38 Re6 Ba8 39 g6 hxg6 40 Rxg6 Qh7 41 Qg3 Qh5 42 Rg4 Black resigns.

Blackburne Attack, 990, a line in the SCOTCH GAME perhaps invented by PAULSEN who played it, for example, at the Wiesbaden tournament 1880, and whose name it sometimes bears. It was taken up by BLACKBURNE in 1882 and became associated with his name. The TARTAKOWER VARIATION (999) of the same opening is sometimes called the Blackburne Attack.

Blackburne Gambit, 1168, a line in the ALLGAIER GAMBIT played by BLACKBURNE in many simultaneous displays but not in master play.

Blackburne–Marco Gambit, 692, the TARRASCH VARIATION of the SPANISH OPENING.

Blackburne–Mieses Attack, 1000, the MIESES VARIATION of the SCOTCH GAME.

Blackburne Shilling Gambit, 935, a fruitful source of income for BLACKBURNE when playing café visitors, the usual stake being one shilling. Black's third move may not be good enough for master chess but it is not an outright error and cannot be refuted by violence. A quiet continuation such as 4 0-0 maintains White's lead in development. The line continues to catch victims, including two in successive rounds at Blackpool 1987.

Blackburne Variation, 269, a sound line in the DUTCH DEFENCE, from the game Blackburne–Gelbfuhs, Vienna 1873; 636 in the SICILIAN DEFENCE, from the 5th match game, Steinitz–Blackburne 1876; 957 in the TWO KNIGHTS DEFENCE, played by BLACKBURNE but described by him as 'an old move revived by Mr. Bird'. Also 601, the MARSHALL GAMBIT in the Sicilian Defence; 987, the PAULSEN ATTACK in the SCOTCH GAME.

black correction, see CORRECTION.

Blackmar–Diemer Gambit, 55 or 221, a variation of the BLACKMAR GAMBIT. Ignacy Popiel (1863–1941) noted in *Deutsches Wochenschach*, 1893, that the Blackmar Gambit (1 d4 d5 2 e4 dxe4 3 f3) could be answered effectively by 3 . . . e5; instead of 3 f3 he recommended 3 Nc3, which he called the Polish Gambit in honour of his native land. In 1932 the German player Emil Josef Diemer (1908–90), following Popiel's analysis, 3 Nc3 Nf6, advocated the continuation 4 f3. The gambit thus modified (which may occur by transposition when the game begins 1 d4 Nf6) has been played occasionally by grandmasters such as SPASSKY, but its soundness is doubtful.

Blackmar Gambit, 222 in the QUEEN'S PAWN OPEN-ING, an opening of doubtful merit. Armand Edward Blackmar (1826–88), an American music publisher (whose company first printed 'The Bonny Blue Flag' and 'Maryland My Maryland'), originated his gambit in 1881. It was analysed in *Brentano's Chess Monthly* for July 1882 and in the *American Supplement*, 1884, of Cook's *Synopsis of Chess Openings*.

Blake, Percy Francis (1873–1936), English problemist who was a player strong enough to win the Lancashire championship in 1911. He composed about 500 orthodox direct-mate problems of which about 100 won first prizes, and is best remembered for three-movers in the early years of the 20th century and four-movers subsequently. Inspired by one of HEATHCOTE's early problems, he began composing at the age of 17, the two of them becoming the leading exponents of the English School (see PROBLEM HISTORY; see also CUTTING-POINT THEMES).

#3

A problem by Blake, first prize, German chess association 1910. The key is 1 Qc4 threatening 2 Qf1+, with variations showing several model mates.

1 . . . dxc4	2 Rxd4
1 . . . Qa6	2 Rxe3
1 . . . Kxe4	2 Bg6+
1 . . . dxe4	2 Qf7+
1 . . . e2	2 Nh6+ .

G. W. Chandler, *P. F. Blake, A Tribute Overdue* (1971) contains 76 problems.

Blake Variation, 846 in the SPANISH FOUR KNIGHTS GAME, played by Joseph Henry Blake (1859–1951) against Atkins in the British championship, 1911.

Bláthy, Ottó Titusz (1860–1939), Hungarian composer with an international reputation as an electrical engineer. One of his specialities was problems with a large number of moves in their solutions, frequently more than 100, and in one case, a mate in 290 moves. In 1889 he published *Vielzügige Schachaufgaben*, a collection of such works. Bláthy also pioneered minimal problems, although the name, given by Josef Halumbirek (1891–1968), came some years later. (See LONG-RANGE PROBLEM.)

Bledow, Ludwig Erdmann (1795–1846), German professor of mathematics who was probably the strongest Berlin player around 1840. He was founder of the PLEIADES, and the driving force behind the Berliner Schachgesellschaft, the chess society of which he became president in 1836. At a time when Paris and London were the chess centres of Europe, and when there were no outstanding players in Germany, the Schachgesellschaft set itself the task of raising the standard of chess in Germany and, as a means to this end, of producing a comprehensive textbook and founding a chess magazine, aims which were successfully achieved. While Bilguer was to edit the HANDBUCH, Bledow was to produce the magazine; he lived just long enough to see the first number of the monthly *Schachzeitung*. Bledow played a few matches, notably defeating JAENISCH in 1842. His large collection of chess books became part of the Royal Library in Berlin. (See PERIODICALS.)

Bledow Variation, 1095, sometimes called countergambit, a standard defence to the BISHOP'S GAMBIT, known from a game Bilguer–Bledow, Berlin, 1840. The line is sometimes called the Anderssen Counterattack, and sometimes named after MORPHY, who probably gleaned his information from the first edition of the HANDBUCH, 1843.

Bled Variation, 1291, a line in the RÉTI GAMBIT introduced by SPIELMANN at Bled 1931.

blind, chess for the, is played with special equipment. In the *British Chess Magazine*, 1889, a correspondent suggested that chessmen and boards should be made to meet the needs of the blind. A reply from William Wood stated that he had made such apparatus since 1848: his design forms the basis of the sets now used. 'The Black squares are raised about an eighth of an inch above the White. The pieces have large pegs at the bottom fitting into holes, so that they may be felt without being overturned. The pieces are the ordinary shape, which is well suited to the touch . . . The Black pieces have a little point at the top, so that the difference in colour can easily be felt.' The 'ordinary shape' was that of the ST GEORGE CHESSMEN, but later sets used a type of STAUNTON CHESSMEN and in some cases the white men had the identifying point on top. As the set is used only by the unsighted, the actual colour is immaterial.

Players call out their moves and record them in braille or on a sound recorder. For play between blind and sighted players there is a FIDE supplement to the laws of chess, with special reference to the TOUCH AND MOVE LAW. A blind player may finger the chessmen of either colour and is deemed to have touched a man only when it has been removed from its socket. A move is completed when the man is secured in its new socket and a move has been called out; only then is the opponent's clock started. Exceptionally, some blind players play 'blindfold', neither using special equipment nor touching the normal board or men.

There have been many strong blind players. One of them, Reginald Walter Bonham (1906–84), formed the International Braille Chess Association in 1951 and won its first international championship in 1956. He also won the first Correspondence World Championship for blind players, 1955–7, and the next five. IBCA was affiliated to FIDE in 1964 and organizes world championships every four years and also Olympiads midway between them. Both types of events, now styled as being 'for the visually handicapped', have been won by either Soviet or Yugoslav entrants so far.

The most famous blind problemist was A. F. MACKENZIE. In 1902 he said: 'I have lately come to think that problem composition is peculiarly a mental work, and that employment of board and men is in many ways a nuisance. It cramps the imaginative faculties. Certainly, the three-movers I have composed since I lost my sight are infinitely superior, as a whole, to those composed before.'

blindfold chess, chess played without sight of the board. This is not difficult for a strong player but others find it astonishing, perhaps uncanny. Some masters have specialized in playing many such games simultaneously. When asked to explain how this is done they have given varied and conflicting answers. Few claimed to have seen the board as a kind of photograph in the mind, but all will have possessed good powers of VISUALIZATION. Although blindfold exhibitions have been a source of income for professional players, especially in the period 1860–1940, their value is open to question. 'The service of chess does not profit by it. He who plays well without seeing the board will play even better if he does look at it. Therefore these displays are merely shows to dazzle the public' (PETROFF). Blindfold play is stressful and some exponents find that the images of board and men persist in their minds after a display. The Soviet authorities, not alone in believing that mental health could be endangered by blindfold displays, banned them from 1930.

Nearly as old as the game itself, blindfold play originally called for the player's eyes to be covered but allowed the pieces to be touched. The great black African player JUBAIR was one of the first to turn his back on the board, now the usual practice. All the great masters of SHAṬRANJ were able to play at least one game blindfold. The earliest known example in Europe was by a Saracen named Buzecca (variously Buchecha or Borzaga) who visited Florence in 1266 and played three games simultaneously, one over-the-board and two unseen. The last accounts of the old game played this way are given by Sukaikir in the middle of the 16th century. He saw a Greek professional, Yusuf Chelebi who had toured India and the Near East, playing blindfold by touch, and he had heard of a player who could manage ten boards, winning all of them and correcting his adversaries' false moves. The famous 16th-century players of modern chess, LÓPEZ, BOI, CERON, and SALVIO, were skilled in this form of chess. An Italian priest, Giovanni Girolamo Saccheri (1667–1733), was well known for playing three games without sight of the board and calling back all the moves afterwards.

In spite of this continuous record of blindfold play, PHILIDOR'S display against two opponents at Paris in 1744 was thought to be unprecedented. At Berlin in 1750 he played three games at once and later in his life gave many such displays. Since then many masters have been willing to play blindfold, notably PAULSEN, MORPHY, BLACKBURNE, ZUKERTORT, PILLSBURY, BREYER, RÉTI, ALEKHINE, and KOLTANOWSKI. One of the most astonishing performances was by Pillsbury on a free day during the Hanover tournament of 1902. Playing simultaneously against 21 opponents, all of whom were competing in the HAUPTTURNIER, he allowed them to consult one another and to try out moves at the board. His score after twelve hours, $+3=11-7$, was remarkable in view of the opposition's strength. Curiously, he achieved better results in the master tournament after the display $(+6=2)$ than he did before $(+2=1-2)$. In 1937 Koltanowski played 34 opponents at Edinburgh, scoring $+24=10$ in $13\frac{1}{2}$ hours. Subsequent claims to records are based on performances lacking the kind of controls expected in such events, and the idea of attaching merit to mere numbers is out of fashion.

blitz, (1) LIGHTNING CHESS (from German *Blitz*, 'lightning'), or, on occasion, a quick FRIENDLY GAME. (See BROWNE.)

blitz, (2) to play a sequence of moves rapidly. This may be done to demoralize the opponent, or as a consequence of TIME-TROUBLE.

blitzkrieg, see PROGRESSIVE CHESS.

block, a problem position in which Black is under no threat (in the problemist's sense of the word) but must become exposed to a threat if obliged to move. This is the problemist's equivalent of the player's (and study composer's) ZUGZWANG or SQUEEZE, but the terms are not interchangeable.

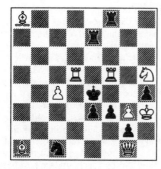

#2

An incomplete block problem by A. F. MACKENZIE, *American Chess Bulletin*, 1905. The block is completed by the key 1 Rf6. White threatens nothing; but mate follows because (and only because) Black is under the necessity of having to make a move:

1 ... Rf on rank	2 Rf4#
1 ... Rff7	2 Rd7#
1 ... Rxf6	2 Nxf6#
1 ... Re on rank	2 Re6#
1 ... Ree8	2 Rd8#
1 ... Re5	2 Rd4#

Also 1 ... Nd3 2 Re5#, 1 ... N~ 2 Qb1#, 1 ... e2 2 Qd4#, 1 ... f2 2 Qxg2#, and 1 ... hxg3 2 Nxg3#.

Complete block problems (in which the set position is a block) are of three kinds:

(1) a waiter; the key is a waiting move, maintaining the status quo—White simply transfers the move to Black.
(2) a mutate; having no waiting move White makes a key that sets up a different block—see FOCAL PLAY.
(3) a block-threat problem; having no waiting move and unable to set up a new block, White makes a key move that creates a threat.

blockade, the mechanical obstruction of an enemy pawn by a piece, a definition given by NIMZOWITSCH in his booklet *Die Blockade* (1925). An English translation, *Blockade*, was published in 1980, and included in it are complete translations of two articles and a note cited by Nimzowitsch in the text. These are from *Wiener Schachzeitung*, 1913, (*Das neue System*), *Kagan's neueste Schachnachrichten*, 1924, and again from *Kagan's*, 1925. The term might also describe any position that is hard to break, e.g. a BLOCKED CENTRE.

Euwe–Pilnik Amsterdam 1950 Grünfeld Defence

1 d4 Nf6 2 c4 g6 3 g3 d5 4 cxd5 Nxd5 5 Bg2 Bg7 6 e4 Nb6 7 Ne2 c5 8 d5 0-0 9 0-0 e6 10 Nbc3 Na6 11 Nf4 e5 12 Nfe2 Nc4 13 b3 Nd6 14 Be3 b6 15 Qd2 Re8 16 f4 Nc7 17 Rf2 exf4 (White has a HANGING CENTRE.) 18 Bxf4 Ba6 19 Re1 Qe7 20 g4 Be5 21 Bxe5 Qxe5

The knight is an excellent piece to use as a blockader, but the queen is not ideal for this purpose, so Black will try to use a different piece. Meanwhile White will try to remove the blockaders. 22 Ng3 Re7 23 Bf1 Bc8 24 Be2 Bd7 25 Ref1 Rf8 26 Qc1 Nce8 27 Kh1 f6 28 Rg1 Ng7 29 Bf3 Qg5 30 Qxg5 fxg5 31 Rgf1 Nge8 32 Be2 Rxf2 33 Rxf2 Kg7 34 h3 Nf6 35 Bf3 Be8 36 Re2 Nd7 37 Rd2 Ne5 38 Be2 b5 39 Rc2 Rc7 40 Nd1 c4 41 bxc4 bxc4 42 Nc3 Kf6 43 Nb1 Rb7 44 Nd2 Ba4 45 Rc1 Rb2 46 Nxc4 Nexc4 47 Bxc4 Bc2 48 Bb3 Rb1 49 Rxb1 Bxb1 50 Ne2 Bxe4+ 51 Kh2 Ke5 52 Nc3 Bd3 53 Kg3 Ne4+ 54 Nxe4 Bxe4 55 d6 Kxd6 56 Bg8 h6 57 Bf7 Bd5 58 Bxg6 Bxa2 59 h4 a5 60 hxg5 hxg5 61 Kf3 a4 62 Ke3 Be6 63 Kd4 Bxg4 64 Kc3 Bd1 65 Bf5 Ke5 66 Bd7 Kf4 67 Kb4 Bc2 68 Kc3 Bb3 69 Kb4 Bf7 70 Kxa4 Bg6 71 Kb4 Bf5 72 Bc6 g4 73 Kc5 Be4 74 Bd7 g3 75 Bh3 Ke3 76 Kd6 Bf5 77 Bg2 Kf2 White resigns.

For analysts of the BASIC ENDGAME the word 'blockade' has a somewhat different meaning: a position in which the defender's pieces confine the attacker's king to a small area. For example, White Ka8, Qf5; Black Kc7, Na5, Nc6, is drawn because the white king cannot get out of the corner. If the black king were at g3 White could win: 1 Qf1 Kg4 2 Qf6 (a ZUGZWANG discovered in 1832 by the German composer Julius Mendheim, (*c*.1788–1836) 2 ... Kg3 3 Qf5 Kg2 4 Qf4 Kg1 5 Qf3 Kh2 6 Qg4 Kh1 7 Qg3, and Black must relieve the blockade. The distinction between an endgame blockade and a FORTRESS is fuzzy: in one a king is held in; in the other, held out. Another blockade, after PONZIANI (1782): White Kh1, Qg7; Black Kf2, Bh3, Nf3.

Blockade Variation, 52, sometimes called the Semi-Benoni, in the BENONI DEFENCE.

blocked centre, an arrangement of pawns in which some of those pawns in the CENTRAL ZONE are blocked so that they have little or no mobility. To break through such a centre may be difficult or impossible, and attacks are likely to be directed towards one or both flanks. (See CLOSE GAME.)

Petrosyan–Pilnik Amsterdam 1956 Candidates tournament Hromádka Defence Petrosyan System

1 d4 Nf6 2 c4 c5 3 d5 e5 4 Nc3 d6 5 e4 g6 6 Nf3 Bg7 7 Bg5 Na6 8 Be2 Nc7 9 Nd2 Bd7 10 a4 b6 11 Nb5 Bxb5 12 cxb5 0-0

13 b4 h6 14 Bxf6 Qxf6 15 0-0 Rfd8 16 Nc4 Bf8 17 g3
cxb4 18 Qb3 Kg7 19 Rfc1 h5 20 Ne3 Ne8 21 Qxb4
Rdc8 22 Rc6 (outpost) 22...Qd8 23 Rac1 Nf6 24 Bf1
Rcb8 25 Bh3 a6 26 Re1 axb5 27 axb5 Nh7 28 Nc4 Ra2
29 Bg2 Qf6 30 Rf1 Ng5 31 Qb3 Rba8 32 h4 Nh7 33
Rxb6 Ra1 34 Rc6 R8a2 35 Qe3 Qd8 36 Rxa1 Rxa1+
37 Kh2 Nf6 38 f3 Qb8 39 Qb3 Nd7 40 b6 Nc5 41 Qb2
Ra4 42 Qb5 Ra2 43 Rc7 g5 44 Ne3 gxh4 45 Nf5+
Kg8 46 gxh4 Ra6 47 b7 Ra7 48 Rc8 Qxb7 49 Qe8 Nd7
50 Nxd6 Black resigns.

blocked pawn, a pawn that cannot advance
because it is obstructed by an enemy piece or pawn.
In NIMZOWITSCH'S words, a blocked pawn has a
'lust to expand'. He observed that a player often
advances such a pawn advantageously when the
obstructing man is removed: the opponent's men
are often arranged on the assumption that the
blocked pawn is rooted to its post, and they become
misplaced when it is moved.

block-threat, see BLOCK.

Blumenfeld Counter-gambit, 353 or 431, an invention of the Russian master Beniamin Markovich
Blumenfeld (1884–1947) that was launched trium-
phantly in master chess by ALEKHINE against TAR-
RASCH (White) at Piešt'any 1922 and was played a
few days later in the game Kostić–Maróczy, Wes-
ton-super-Mare 1922. (See ALEKHINE for the STEM-
GAME.)

Blumenfeld Variation, 145, standard play in the
MERAN VARIATION from the game Blumenfeld–A.
Rabinovich, Moscow Championship 1924–5. Con-
tinuations include the BOTVINNIK VARIATION, the
GLIGORIĆ VARIATION, or the SOZIN VARIATION which
can, in turn, lead to the RELLSTAB VARIATION or the
STÅHLBERG VARIATION.

Also 352, sometimes known as the Spielmann
Variation, a line that might lead to the MODERN
BENONI or the BLUMENFELD COUNTER-GAMBIT (see
SZABÓ); 986, a discredited line in the SCOTCH GAME
introduced by Blumenfeld in 1904.

Blümich Variation, 1296, the NEO-CATALAN OPEN-
ING. In 1925 the German player Reinhold Max
Blümich (1886–1942) played, as a SYSTEM, these
moves for White: g3, Bg2, 0-0, d3 and e4. Examples

are Blümich–Nimzowitsch, Breslau 1925, Blümich–
Sämisch, Breslau 1925, and Blümich–Nimzowitsch,
Dresden 1926.

blunder, a bad move, usually a decisive error; but
whether a decisive error is called a blunder depends
on how difficult it is to detect, and this may depend
upon the strength of the players. Some blunders are
obvious to all; others so labelled by grandmasters
might pass unnoticed by lesser mortals.

A position from the game Keres–Botvinnik, World
Championship match tournament 1948. Play continued 53 Rd3? Rc4 54 Ra3 a5 and Black eventually won by bringing his king to the queen's-side.
Some time afterwards it was shown that 53 Rd5
draws, e.g. 53...Rc3+ 54 Kg2 Kh4 55 Rd6 a5
56 Rd5 Rc2+ 57 Kf1 g4 58 Rxa5 Kg3 59 Ra8
Rc1+ 60 Ke2 Kh2 61 a5 g3 62 Rh8+ Kg1 63
a6 Ra1 64 Rh6 g2 65 Rg6. There are many other
blunders discovered after the event, perhaps years
later.

All players make blunders on occasion; indeed,
there has never been a world championship match
without such lapses. Many causes, including TIME-
TROUBLE and the KOTOV SYNDROME have been
blamed. Some merely refer to chess-blindness
(AMAUROSIS SCACHISTICA). In *Chess Fundamentals*
Capablanca refers to 'the dangers of a safe [advan-
tageous?] position', adding '...even with a good
position a player, no matter how strong, cannot
afford to relax his attention even for one move.' For
two such lapses, see USELESS CHECK.

board, or chess-board, a square board of 64 alternately coloured smaller squares in eight rows of
eight. At the outset of the game the men are
arranged on the squares of the board in the manner
shown under ARRAY. The two players sit on opposite sides of a board placed so that each has a
light-coloured square on the right-hand side, a
convention dating from medieval times and
endorsed by DAMIANO. White's queen stands on a
light square, Black's on a dark square. (Beginners
are told 'white on the right' and 'queen on her
colour'.) If the board is placed otherwise and this is
discovered during a game then the position should
be reset on a correctly placed board and the game
continued.

The ASHṬĀPADA board, 8 × 8 squares, was used in the earliest forms of chess. In CHINESE CHESS, and Korean, the pieces are placed on intersections, in effect a 10 × 9 board, and SHOGI utilizes a 9 × 9 board; but in almost every other country the 8 × 8 board has remained standard throughout the ages. The chequered board with its distinctive light and dark squares was a European invention dating from at least the 11th century, before which time the squares were not differentiated by colour. Chequering may have been useful for the counting boards of the Norman exchequers, and is certainly helpful to players of the modern game with its long-range diagonal moves by the new pieces (Q, B).

board games, the general group to which chess belongs. Such games have been played for at least 4,000 years, but it is possible only to guess from illustrations and literary references how the earlier games were played. In his book *A History of Board-games other than Chess* (1952) MURRAY identified five categories: alignment and configuration (e.g. merels), hunt (e.g. fox and geese), race (e.g. backgammon), mancala, and war games. He subdivided the last category: battle games (e.g. chess), territory games (e.g. go), clearance games (e.g. solitaire), and blockade games. Research into the history of chess and other early games is hampered by the tendency of uninformed observers to describe as 'chess' any board game that looks difficult.

Bobotsov, Milko Georgiev (1931–), a university sports lecturer, the first Bulgarian to become an International Grandmaster (1961). Bulgarian champion in 1958, his best international results are: Pécs 1964, first (+6=9) equal with GIPSLIS; Beverwijk 1965, third (+5=10), after GELLER and POR-

TISCH; and Moscow 1967, second (+3=14) equal with Gipslis, SMYSLOV, and TAL, after STEIN and ahead of PETROSYAN and SPASSKY. In 1972, not long after playing in his eighth Olympiad, Bobotsov suffered a stroke and has played little since then.

Boden, Samuel Standidge (1826–82), English player active in the 1850s. In 1851 he wrote *A Popular Introduction to the Study and Practice of Chess,* an excellent guide, introducing the BODEN–KIESERITZKY GAMBIT, which at once became popular. In the same year he won the 'provincial tournament' run concurrently with the London international tournament. At Manchester 1857, a knock-out event, he came second to LÖWENTHAL—he drew one game of the final match and then retired. In 1858 Boden defeated OWEN in a match (+7=2−3) and he played many friendly games with MORPHY, who declared him to be the strongest English player. This judgement was probably right, STAUNTON and BUCKLE having retired. Also in 1858 he restarted the chess column in *The Field,* handing over to DE VERE in 1872. The column has continued uninterruptedly ever since and is now the oldest column in Britain. Besides chess and his work as a railway employee, Boden found time to become a competent amateur painter and an art critic.

Boden–Kieseritzky Gambit, 657 or 1055, an interesting line suggested by KIESERITZKY in 1848 and sometimes called the Kieseritzky Variation. It was first published in BODEN'S *Popular Introduction . . .* (1851). After the usual 4 . . . Nxc3 5 dxc3 White has a lasting but perhaps inadequate attack for his pawn. A similar gambit occurs in 942.

Boden–Max Lange Variation, 896, the EVANS GAMBIT Declined, an obvious way of declining the

Wall-painting from an Egyptian tomb, c.2000 BC

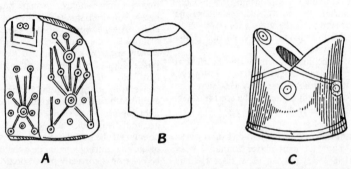

B

A   C

Hnefatafl pieces: A, B, jet pieces found at Warrington, Lancashire; C, bone piece from Woodperry, Oxfordshire.

gambit, but recommended, at a time when acceptance was usual, by the two players whose names it bears.

Boden's mate, a mate given to a king on the edge of the board by the crossfire of two bishops, sometimes preceded by a queen sacrifice. The name stems from the following FRIENDLY GAME.

Schulder–Boden London, 1853 Philidor Defence

1 e4 e5 2 Nf3 d6 3 c3 f5 4 Bc4 Nf6 5 d4 fxe4 6 dxe5 exf3 7 exf6 Qxf6 8 gxf3 Nc6 9 f4 Bd7 10 Be3 0-0-0 11 Nd2 Re8 12 Qf3 Bf5 13 0-0-0 d5 14 Bxd5 Qxc3+ 15 bxc3 Ba3 mate.

However, this type of mate was known earlier.

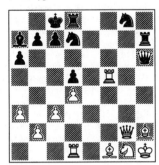

In this position, from a game Horwitz–Popert, Hamburg, 1844, Black set a trap, playing 1 ... Bb8, and White duly 'fell into it' 2 Rxd5 c6. White cannot save his rook because of the threatened mate in two, but 3 Rh5 Qxh5 is followed by 4 Qxc6+ bxc6 5 Bxa6 mate, and the trapper is trapped.

Boden Variation, 769 in the SPANISH OPENING, given by Ruy LÓPEZ, played by STANLEY against ROUSSEAU, 4th match game, in 1845; 1021 in the PHILIDOR DEFENCE, played by BODEN against MORPHY in 1858. Both variations are largely forgotten.

Boey, Jozef Martin (1934–), Belgian player, International Master (1973), International Correspondence Chess Grandmaster (1975). In 1959 he shared the Belgian championship with O'KELLY after tying in the tournament and the play-off match. He won the title in 1964 and again in 1971, and played in seven Olympiads from 1954 to 1974, on the last three occasions on first board. Pressure of work, as a research chemist, limited his over-the-board activities and he turned to postal play, coming second, after ESTRIN in the 7th World Correspondence Championship, 1972–5.

Bogoljubow, Efim Dmitriyevich (1889–1952), International Grandmaster (1951), one of the world's best six players in the 1920s. A Ukrainian by birth, he became a German citizen in 1929 and used German spelling for his name, pronounced Bogolyubov and meaning 'beloved of God'. He studied theology, then agriculture, before finding his true calling as a chess professional. His career began

with minor successes at Kiev, near his birthplace, in 1911, and at the Łódź tournament, 1912–13. In two Russian championships contested at St Petersburg in 1911 and 1914 his results were modest, but he earned the Russian Master title by defeating SALWE +5=2−3 at Łódź, 1913.

While he was playing in the Mannheim tournament in 1914, the First World War began and he was interned. For him this was a stroke of fortune. In a pleasant area of the Black Forest he found a permanent home, a wife, and, eventually, a last resting place. One of the few who substantially improved his playing strength during the war, Bogoljubow won five of the eight tournaments arranged by and for the internees. In 1920 he won a match against NIMZOWITSCH (+3−1) and lost narrowly to RUBINSTEIN (+4=3−5).

Bogoljubow's greatest successes came in the years 1922–8, although his results were erratic. He played in 17 strong tournaments, winning eight first prizes but on occasions scoring less than fifty per cent. His first important wins were at Piešt'any 1922 (+13=4−1), ahead of ALEKHINE, and at Carlsbad 1923, when he tied with Alekhine (both scored +9=5−3) and MARÓCZY. Still a Soviet citizen, Bogoljubow won the USSR championship in 1924 by a margin of two and a half points. At Breslau in the following year he won the German Open Championship (+9=1−1) ahead of Rubinstein and Nimzowitsch, thus becoming the only player to hold the Soviet and German championships at the same time. He again won the USSR championship in 1925, and at the end of the year the great Moscow tournament produced his finest achievement: first prize (+13=5−2) ahead of LASKER, CAPABLANCA, and Rubinstein.

His vigorous and ingenious style was in conformity with Soviet ideals, and he was not hostile to the USSR, but as its citizen he was unable to get visas to a number of countries and was thus restricted in the choice of tournaments for which he could enter. After winning (+6=2−1) the Berlin 1926 tournament, he failed to return to the USSR and was accounted a traitor. (Twenty-five years after his death he was 'rehabilitated'.) He then won several strong tournaments: Bad Homburg 1927 (+5=4−1); Berlin Sept. 1928 (+7=3−1); and Bad Kissingen 1928 (+6=4−1), ahead of Capablanca, Rubinstein, and EUWE. These victories encouraged him to challenge Alekhine for the world title (1929) and, although he was in his prime, he was outclassed (+5=9−11). His ENDGAME play was noticeably below world championship standard.

After this defeat Bogoljubow's successes were fewer. He came a poor second (+12=6−8) to Alekhine in the Bled tournament of 1931. In the German championship, then stronger than any other national championship, he won in 1931 after a play-off, and again in 1933 (+9=5−1). When he played for Germany in the Prague Olympiad 1931, Bogoljubow's score at first board (+9=7−1) was bettered only by Alekhine's (+10=7−1). In 1934 Bogoljubow came fourth (+9=5−1) in the Zurich tournament, and lost another title match against Alekhine (+3=15−8). The optimism which had spurred his imagination began to diminish. Subsequently he played in more than 50 tournaments, finishing first in almost half of them. His best wins were at Bad Nauheim 1935 (+4=4−1), Berlin 1935 (shared with RICHTER), Bad Elster 1938, Stuttgart 1939, and Bad Pyrmont 1949 where he won the German championship for the fourth and last time.

Euwe, writing in *The Development of Chess Style* (1968), describes Bogoljubow's chess: 'His play was sound and his style primarily positional. In addition he had a tactical talent which came into its own especially when the opponent had been outplayed strategically. His weak point lay in his optimism and lack of objectivity.' This weak point, above all else, lay at the root of his inconsistency in play, and perhaps the modest quality of his few literary contributions. A popular, jovial figure, who greatly influenced German players, Bogoljubow died in harness. Returning from a simultaneous display he suffered a fatal heart attack. (See BISHOPS OF OPPOSITE COLOUR; WYVILL FORMATION.)

A. Brinckmann, *Grossmeister Bogoljubow* (1953) contains 64 games; J. Spence, *The Chess Career of Bogoljubow*, 2 vols. (1971–5), contains 100 games in each volume.

Bogoljubow–Spielmann Dortmund 1928 Queen's Gambit Declined Manhattan Defence

1 d4 e6 2 Nf3 d5 3 c4 Nd7 4 Nc3 Ngf6 5 Bg5 Bb4 6 e3 c5 7 cxd5 exd5 8 Bd3 Qa5 9 Qc2 c4 10 Bf5 0-0 11 0-0 Re8 12 a3 Bxc3 13 Qxc3 Qxc3 14 bxc3 Nb6 15 Bxc8 Nxc8 16 Bxf6 gxf6 17 Nd2 Nd6 18 Rfe1 f5 19 f3 Re6 20 Kf2 Rae8 21 Nf1 Kf8 22 a4 b5 23 a5 a6 24 Ng3 f4 25 exf4 Rxe1 26 Rxe1 Rxe1 27 Kxe1 Ke7

28 Nf1 Nb7 29 Ne3 Kd6 30 Nc2 Nxa5 31 Nb4 Nc6 32 Nxa6 Ne7 33 Kd2 Nf5 34 g3 Ng7 35 Nb4 Nh5 36 Nc2 f5 37 Ne3 Ke6 38 Kc2 Nf6 39 Kb2 h5 40 Ka3 h4 41 Kb4 Black resigns.

Bogoljubow Defence, 334 or 430, a sound alternative to the QUEEN'S INDIAN DEFENCE and sometimes called the Bogoljubow Indian, although it does not necessarily lead to an 'Indian' game. It was played by BOGOLJUBOW in his match against RUBINSTEIN, 1920. (See OPPOSITION.)

Bogoljubow Variation, 67 in the QUEEN'S GAMBIT ACCEPTED, an inferior line used by BOGOLJUBOW in his 1934 match against ALEKHINE; 129 in the QUEEN'S GAMBIT Declined, TARRASCH VARIATION, recommended by Bogoljubow in the 1920s; 149 in the SLAV DEFENCE, played in the 21st match game Alekhine–Bogoljubow, 1929, although known earlier; 177, another line in the QGD played before Bogoljubow's time (e.g. by SALWE at Nuremberg 1906); 594 in the NIMZOWITSCH DEFENCE, recommended by Bogoljubow but played earlier in a Nenarokov–Alekhine match game 1909; 744 in the SPANISH OPENING, from the game Capablanca–Bogoljubow, London 1922 (but, again, known earlier); 856 in the SPANISH FOUR KNIGHTS GAME introduced in the third match game Bogoljubow–Rubinstein, Stockholm 1920; 1193 in the FRENCH DEFENCE, as Bogoljubow–Buerger, Scarborough 1927, and Bogoljubow–Thomas, London 1927; 1199 and 1206, in the same opening, as Mieses–Bogoljubow, Berlin 1920, and Capablanca–Bogoljubow, New York 1924 respectively; 1292 and 1295, in the RÉTI OPENING, played Réti–Bogoljubow, Moscow 1925, and Levenfish–Bogoljubow, Moscow 1924.

Also 93, the WIESBADEN VARIATION in the Queen's Gambit Declined; 146, the LUNDIN VARIATION of the QGD; 329, the THREE KNIGHTS VARIATION of the NIMZO-INDIAN DEFENCE, a favourite of Bogoljubow, although played earlier (Kostić–Maróczy, Teplitz-Schönau 1922); 958, the COLMAN VARIATION of the TWO KNIGHTS DEFENCE; 1104, JAENISCH VARIATION, another line that Bogoljubow believed he had invented.

Bohatirchuk, Fedor Parfenovich (1892–1984), International Master (1954). A native of Kiev, he worked there as a radiologist and became director of a research institute. His chess career began when he played in tournaments at Kiev and in the Russian championship. From 1923 to 1934 he entered the Soviet championship six times, tying for first place in 1927, when he and ROMANOVSKY became co-champions, and sharing third place on four other occasions. In 1938 he took second place in one of the qualifying tournaments for the USSR championship. He entered reluctantly and angered officials by not taking his place in the finals. His best playing days were over, and he wanted to give more time to his profession.

When Kiev fell (Sept. 1941) in the Second World War, Bohatirchuk willingly joined a German medical research institute which was moved to various cities, including Kraków, Berlin, and Potsdam. After further travels he arrived in American-occupied Bayreuth in May 1945 to join his family. For a time he lived in Munich, playing in German chess events under the name Bogenko 'to throw Soviet investigators off the scent'. He emigrated to Canada in 1949, became naturalized, and played in a few tournaments, including the Olympiad of 1954. In his seventies he took up correspondence chess, winning the title of International Correspondence Master in 1967. An autobiography, in Russian,

Moi zhiznenny put k Vlasovu i Prazhskomu mani-festu (San Francisco, 1978) focuses largely on the years during and immediately after the Second World War.

Bohemian, a style of problem composition. All Bohemian problems have several variations of about equal merit that lead to MODEL MATES, often with pin-model mates and sometimes with ECHOES; but a problem with model mates is not necessarily Bohemian. Composers in this style seek elegance rather than difficulty; White usually has few pieces and they are combined in different ways so that each has plenty of work to do; spectacular play is avoided so that one variation shall not steal the thunder from another; the black king must not be in an obvious MATING NET, nor too limited in its choice of moves. There should be few, if any, white pawns, thus differing from problems of the old German school (see PROBLEM HISTORY) in which white pawns were often used to guard flight squares. By their nature some of these requirements cannot be defined precisely.

This style was fathered by Antonín König (1836–1911) in the 1860s, although its ancestry may be traced back to the work of D'ORVILLE and BROWN. König, who came from Bohemia, was followed by many of his countrymen including Jan Dobruský (1853–1907), Jiří Chocolouš (1856–1930), Josef Pospíšil (1861–1916), Zdenék Mach (1877–1954), and HAVEL.

#4

A problem by the Soviet composer Vatslav Yevgenievich Gebelt (1913–), first hononary mention, USSR Team Championship 1982. The key is 1 Nc8 followed by three model mate variations:
1 ... Bg3   2 Nb6+ Qxb6 3 Nf2+ Kc5 4 Ne4 #
1 ... Bc5   2 Qf7+ Qxf7 3 Ne5+ Kb5 4 Bc6 #
1 ... ~   2 Nd6+ Qxd6 3 Nb2+ Kc5 4 Na4 #.

Boi, Paolo (1528–98), Italian player nicknamed 'Il Siracusano' after his birthplace. He travelled abroad for 20 years, defeating Ruy LÓPEZ when in Spain. An accomplished blindfold player, he could handle three games simultaneously, chatting with the bystanders meanwhile. He was a favourite of the Duke of Urbino, and Pope Pius V offered him a priesthood which he declined. He played before Philip II of Spain, who gave him a letter of introduction to Don John of Austria. King Sebastian of Portugal also honoured him. The accounts of his life have become tinged with romance, and it is not clear how much is true; whether he was captured by pirates, earned freedom by his chess skill, and died of poison, are matters of speculation. (Much the same was said of his colleague and rival LEONARDO.) 'I knew him in my youth', writes CARRERA, 'when I was at Palermo in the year 1597. His hair was quite white, his form robust, and his mind firm. He dressed very fashionably, like a young man, and was very capricious; nevertheless, he had many excellent qualities, he was extremely chaste and modest—he would never marry . . . he attended mass every day. . . . In stature he was rather tall, well proportioned, handsome, and lively; eloquent in conversation, and gay and affable with everyone.' Carrera, who regarded Boi as the greatest player of his time, ends a long testimonial: 'I have thought it proper to give a full account of such a man, that his name may be known to posterity.'

Bolbochán, Julio (1920–), International Grandmaster (1977), champion of Argentina in 1946 and 1948. His few appearances in European events brought him little success, but he came first in several South American tournaments, notably Mar del Plata–Buenos Aires 1951 (a tie with ELISKASES), Mar del Plata 1952 (a tie with Rossetto ahead of TRIFUNOVIĆ), and Mar del Plata 1956 (a tie with NAJDORF ahead of Eliskases). Bolbochán qualified for an interzonal tournament on three occasions, but competed only once, at Stockholm in 1962, when he came thirteenth. He played in seven Olympiads from 1950 to 1970, and when Argentina took the silver medal in 1950 he scored +9=5, the best second-board result.

Bolbochán–Evans   Helsinki Olympiad 1952   Queen's Gambit Accepted

1 d4 d5 2 Nf3 Nf6 3 c4 dxc4 4 e3 a6 5 Bxc4 e6 6 0-0 c5 7 Qe2 Nc6 8 Nc3 b5 9 Bb3 cxd4 10 exd4 Nxd4 11 Nxd4 Qxd4

12 Nd5 Nxd5 13 Rd1 Nc3 14 bxc3 Qb6 15 Qe5 Bb7 16 Be3 Qc6 17 Bd5 Qc8 18 Bxb7 Qxb7 19 a4 Rc8 20 axb5 Qxb5 21 Qd4 e5 22 Qg4 Rd8 23 Rxd8+ Kxd8 24 Rd1+ Ke7 25 Qf5 Black resigns.

His brother Jácobo (1906–84) won the Argentinian championship in 1932 and 1933, played in three Olympiads (1935, 1937, 1939), and became an International Master in 1965.

Boleslavsky, Isaak Yefremovich (1919–77), Soviet player and theorist, International Grandmaster (1950), journalist. He had several excellent tournament results during the 1940s: Moscow 1942, second (+9=4−2), after SMYSLOV; USSR championship 1945, second (+9=6−2), after BOTVINNIK; USSR championship 1947, second (+7=12), after KERES; Saltsjöbaden interzonal 1948, third (+6=12−1), after BRONSTEIN and SZABÓ; and USSR championship 1949, fifth (+6=11−2) equal with FURMAN and KOTOV. Boleslavsky scored +6=12 and shared first place with Bronstein in the very strong CANDIDATES tournament, 1950, but lost the play off. (His daughter, Tatiana, then four years old, married Bronstein much later.)

He put on weight ('his only physical activity now is walking in the woods looking for mushrooms', wrote GELLER), and his play became more sedate. He scored +8=7−4 to share fourth place in the USSR championship 1952, and +4=19−5 to share tenth place in the Candidates tournament 1953. From then, writes Kotov, 'an overestimation of technique and a desire to avoid complications . . . led to a considerable drop in his performances.' Boleslavsky played in one Olympiad (1952) but attended many as a 'backroom boy' to provide ideas that would assist the Soviet team. The success of PETROSYAN's challenge for the world title in 1963 owed much to Boleslavsky's pre-match training; he was also Petrosyan's second in the world championships of 1966 and 1969.

A simple, unpushful man, he was one of the most creative chess thinkers. Like NIMZOWITSCH, he conceived new strategic ideas, demonstrated their soundness in play, and wrote books and articles about them. In particular his discovery of new resources for Black in the KING'S INDIAN DEFENCE made this opening one of the most popular; and the strategy underlying the Boleslavsky Variation of the Sicilian Defence (see below) remains of interest, especially in the analogous lines of play such as the PELIKÁN VARIATION. In 1957 he published *Izbrannye party*, containing 100 games or part games, and a modest autobiography of 2 pages. An English edition, by Jimmy Adams, with a further 80 games and 15 pages of biography and results, appeared in 1988 as *Isaak Boleslavsky: Selected Games*.

Boleslavsky–Karaklajić USSR–Yugoslavia match 1957
Spanish Opening Open Defence

1 e4 e5 2 Nf3 Nc6 3 Bb5 a6 4 Ba4 Nf6 5 0-0 Nxe4 6 d4 b5 7 Bb3 d5 8 dxe5 Be6 9 Qe2 Be7 10 Rd1 Nc5 11 Bxd5 Bxd5 12 Nc3 Bc4 13 Qxd8+ Rxd8 14 Qe3 b4 15 b3 Be6 16 Ne4 Rd1+ 17 Ne1 Nd4 18 Bb2 Nxc2 19 Qe2 Rxa1 20 Bxa1 Nxa1 21 Nxc5 Bxc5 22 Nd3 Bb6 23 Nxb4 0-0 24 Nc6 f6 25 h4 Kh8 26 Kh2 Bd7

27 exf6 Bxc6 28 Qe7 Rg8 29 fxg7+ Rxg7 30 Qf8+ Rg8 31 Qf6+ Rg7 32 h5 Kg8 33 Qxc6 Rf7 34 Qc3 Nxb3 35 Qxb3 Bxf2 36 Qe6 Bc5 37 Qxa6 Bd6+ 38 Kh3 Re7 39 Qd3 Re5 40 g4 Kg7 41 a4 Kf6 42 Qd2 Ke6 43 a5 Kd7 44 a6 Kc8 45 Qb2 Re3+ 46 Kg2 Rg3+ 47 Kf1 Bc5 48 Qb7+ Kd7 49 Qd5+ Black resigns.

Boleslavsky Variation, 473, in the SICILIAN DEFENCE. Black makes a HOLE at d5 and a BACKWARD PAWN at d6, but he establishes a wedge in the centre and free play for his pieces; if he is able to move his d-pawn safely from d6 to d5 he will probably obtain an advantage in the centre. The move had been played by PAULSEN in the 1880s (against GUNSBERG at Frankfurt 1887, and TARRASCH at Breslau 1889), and a similar line had been played by LASKER, always sceptical of dogma, in 1910. By the 1930s most masters would have regarded 6 . . . e5 as anti-positional but in the early 1940s, when BOLESLAVSKY resuscitated the move, the variation soon became popular, and masters subsequently revived the BOURDONNAIS and PELIKÁN VARIATIONS of the Sicilian Defence (468, 488) in both of which Black advances Pe7-e5. (See WEAKNESS.)

Also 705 in the SPANISH OPENING, introduced Boleslavsky–Smyslov USSR championship 1941, when BOTVINNIK said, 'if a successful reply to the move 10 Nc3 is not found the entire variation will disappear from tournament practice'; 1203 in the FRENCH DEFENCE, as Boleslavsky–Lyublinsky, USSR championship 1950, and Boleslavsky–Guimard, USSR–Argentina match 1954; and 384, the SZABÓ VARIATION of the GRÜNFELD DEFENCE.

Bondarevsky, Igor Zakharovich (1913–79), Soviet player, International Grandmaster (1950), International Arbiter (1954), International Correspondence Chess Grandmaster (1961), economist. He competed in nine Soviet championships from 1937 to 1963, and at his third attempt, Moscow 1940, he came first (+10=7−2) equal with LILIENTHAL. They shared the title. Bondarevsky's best outright victory was in a tournament at Moscow 1942 (+7=6−1). In 1948 he scored +5=11−3, shared sixth place in the Saltsjöbaden interzonal, and thus became a CANDIDATE. Two years later he withdrew from the Candidates tournament before it began. For many years he was SPASSKY's trainer, and his second in the world championship matches of 1966 and 1969. *Combination in the Middle Game* (1967) is from a Russian original of 1960, revised 1965.

Bondarevsky–Gligorić   Saltsjöbaden 1948   Queen's Gambit Declined Slav Defence
1 d4 d5 2 c4 c6 3 Nf3 Nf6 4 e3 Bf5 5 Nc3 e6 6 Bd3 Bxd3 7 Qxd3 Nbd7 8 0-0 Bb4 9 Bd2 Bxc3 10 Bxc3 0-0 11 Nd2 c5 12 dxc5 Nxc5 13 Qd4 Rc8 14 Rad1 dxc4 15 Nxc4 Qxd4 16 Bxd4 Nce4 17 Ne5 a6 18 f3 Nd6 19 Rc1 Rxc1 20 Rxc1 Rc8 21 Rxc8+ Nxc8 22 e4 Kf8 23 Kf2 Ke7 24 Bc5+ Ke8 25 Ke3 Ng8 26 Nc4 Nge7 27 a4 Nc6 28 a5 e5 29 b4 Kd7 30 Kd3 f6 31 Ne3 Nd8 32 Kc4 Kc6 33 Nd5 Ne6 34 h4 Nxc5 35 bxc5 Kd7 36 h5 h6 37 Ne3 Ne7 38 Nf5 Nxf5 39 exf5 Kc6

40 g3 Kc7 41 Kd5 Black resigns. White wins after 41...Kd7 42 g4 (another TEMPO-MOVE) 42...Kc7 (42...Ke7 43 c6) 43 Ke6.

Bondarevsky Variation, 487 in the SICILIAN DEFENCE, played Gromek–Bondarevsky, Poland–USSR match 1955, but it failed to find popular backing.

Bönsch, Uwe (1958–), German player, International Grandmaster (1986) with a good record in Eastern Europe, including first prizes in 1987 at Polanica Zdrój (+5=6), and (shared) Portorož (+7=5−1). He tied for first in the DDR championship of 1976, but lost the play-off.

Chekhov–Bönsch   Leipzig 1986   Queen's Gambit Declined
1 d4 d5 2 c4 e6 3 Nf3 Nf6 4 Nc3 Be7 5 Bg5 0-0 6 Qc2 h6 7 Bxf6 Bxf6 8 0-0-0 c5 9 dxc5 d4 10 Ne4 e5 11 e3 Nc6 12 exd4 exd4 13 a3 Bg4 14 Be2 b6 15 cxb6 axb6 16 h3 Bxf3 17 Bxf3 Rc8 18 Kb1 Be5 19 Be2 Na5 20 Nd2 b5 21 c5 Qe7 22 Bxb5 (22 b4 is better) 22...Rxc5 23 Qd3

23...Rc3 24 Qe4 Qc5 25 a4 f5 26 Qe2 d3 27 Bxd3 Rxd3 28 Qxd3 Rb8 29 b3 Bf6 30 Qc2 Qe5 31 Ka2 Nc6 32 Qc4+ Kh8 33 Rb1 Qd6 34 Rbd1 Nb4+ 35 Kb1 Qe5 White resigns.

Bonus Socius, a 13th-century manuscript written in Lombardy and comprising 119 leaves. The first 99 of these contain 194 chess positions or problems of the old game, some Arabic, some European. The text, including names of pieces, is in Latin. The rest of the work is devoted to backgammon and merels. The name of the manuscript suggests that the author, perhaps Nicholas de St Nicholai, was a university teacher. Many copies of the manuscript were made in Italy and France. Van der LINDE, using a source from which one leaf was missing, published 192 Bonus Socius positions in his *Quellenstudien* (1881). (See COMBINED PIECE; MEDIEVAL PROBLEMS.)

book, known information about the openings or the endgame derived from published sources. Book win (draw): an endgame position for which the technique required to bring about a win (draw) is known, or presumed to be known, to both players. Book player: one who plays according to the book, implying a formal and unimaginative style.

Böök (pron. bek), Eero Einar (1910–90), International Master (1950), honorary Grandmaster (1984), engineer. A leading Finnish player for many years, he won the national championship six times, played for his country in six Olympiads from 1935 to 1960, and shared the Nordic championship in 1947 with STOLTZ. His results in strong tournaments were modest, the best, perhaps, his sharing of eleventh place in the interzonal, Saltsjöbaden 1948.

Borén–Svenonius Variation, 1097, a KING'S GAMBIT Accepted line given in *Nordisk skaktidende* (Denmark), 1873, by the Swedish analysts Per Gustaf Borén (1838–1923) and Ludvig Oskar Svenonius (1853–1926).

Borg Opening, 1275, the GROB OPENING (1322) played in reverse, hence the name, given by Basman (see BASMAN VARIATION) who has had considerable success with this wild line.

Borisenko, Georgy Konstantinovich (1922–), Ukrainian player, International Correspondence Chess Grandmaster (1965). He played in eight Soviet championships with indifferent results, but fared better when he took to postal chess. In the 4th World Correspondence Championship, 1962–5, he was runner-up to ZAGOROVSKY.

Borisenko–Furman Variation, 65, a sharp line in the QUEEN'S GAMBIT ACCEPTED conceived by FURMAN and introduced in the game Borisenko–Flohr, USSR championship 1950.

Borisenko Variation, 11 ... Nc6, an alternative to the CHIGORIN VARIATION, 746, in the SPANISH OPENING, as in the game Bronstein–Borisenko, USSR championship 1958.

Botvinnik, Mikhail Moiseyevich (1911–95), International Grandmaster (1950), World Champion 1948–57, 1958–60, and 1961–3, electrical engineer. Born in Kuokkala (now Repino), near St Petersburg, the younger son of a dental technician, Botvinnik learned chess at the age of 12. He describes himself as having been a round-shouldered, flat-chested, bespectacled boy, a bookworm not fond of sport; but his chess talent developed fast. He had several successes in Leningrad, notably first place in a strong tournament in 1930 ($+6=1-1$), probably the best performance up to that time by an 18-year-old, and first place in the USSR championships of 1931 ($+12=3-2$) and 1933 ($+11=6-2$). Also in 1933 he drew a match with FLOHR ($+2=8-2$). Already he identified his own chess prospects with those of the USSR, and perhaps because he felt this responsibility he failed badly in his first international tournament, Hastings 1934–5 (equal fifth among ten competitors). Nikolai KRYLENKO, who had in vain sent him an encouraging telegram, then organized two international tournaments at Moscow: 1935, when Botvinnik scored $+9=8-2$, to share first prize with Flohr, ahead of LASKER and CAPABLANCA; and 1936, when he took second place ($+7=10-1$), after Capablanca, ahead of Flohr. Then, at Nottingham 1936, he came first ($+6=8$) equal with Capablanca, ahead of EUWE, FINE, RESHEVSKY, ALEKHINE, and Flohr. His achievements in these three major events established his position as a world class player, an aspirant to the champion's title, then held by Euwe.

Botvinnik playing in the World Championship Match, Moscow 1951

Botvinnik remained an amateur, continuing post-graduate studies in Leningrad, and he had other responsibilities, having married a ballet dancer, but he systematically pursued his chess ambitions. He devised a training programme of unprecedented thoroughness: practice with strong players (RAGOZIN was a sparring partner for a long time), the study of master games, the publication of analyses to be criticized by others, learning to handle the clock to avoid time-trouble, and to concentrate in spite of disturbance (a non-smoker, part of his practice was with heavy smokers), the art of ADJOURNMENT analysis, and regular physical activity to maintain fitness. Noting that most innovations in the opening depended on the element of surprise, soon losing their usefulness, he devised opening systems that could be used repeatedly. Two of them are the Rubinstein Variation of the Nimzo-Indian Defence, and the Winawer Variation of the French Defence. The lines he chose often brought about a fixed or blocked centre with promise of a good struggle characterized by flank manœuvring.

In the strongest tournament held up to that time, AVRO 1938, Botvinnik came third ($+3=9-2$). Immediately afterwards he challenged Alekhine, who had regained the world title. After the official challenge was sent, and before the location could be agreed, the Second World War began. He also suffered set-backs within the USSR. In 1937 he could only draw a match ($+5=3-5$) with LEVENFISH, currently the national champion, and, although he won the 1939 championship ($+8=9$), he was only fifth in 1940. Fearing that the Soviet authorities might no longer regard him as their chosen representative, Botvinnik persuaded V. Snegirov, head of the Soviet chess department, to promote a special tournament, a so-called 'absolute championship' of the USSR. It was held at Leningrad and Moscow in 1941. The competitors were those who took the first six places in the championship tournament of 1940, and Botvinnik won handsomely ($+9=9-2$). 'It is clear', he wrote, 'who should play Alekhine.'

Shortly afterwards the USSR was invaded. Exempted from military service on account of poor eyesight, Botvinnik was permitted to leave Leningrad, and on 17 August 1941, two days before the Germans cut the rail link, he and his wife travelled to the Urals. His wife's ballet company, the Kirov, was evacuated to Perm, and there he obtained a post with the Urals Energy Organization, soon becoming head of a high-tension department. He wrote a book on the absolute championship, with excellent annotations to all the games, which was published in 1947; an English version, *Championship Chess*, appeared three years later.

In January 1943, believing that his chess future, and therefore the future of Soviet chess, was threatened because he could not find enough time for study, he wrote to Molotov, the Commissar for Foreign Affairs (after whom Perm was named in those days). As a consequence his employer was instructed to allow him three days a week for chess study. The following year he was transferred to Moscow. From 1943 to 1947 he won five tournaments: Sverdlovsk 1943 (+7=7) and the USSR championship 1944 (+11=3−2), both times ahead of SMYSLOV and BOLESLAVSKY; USSR championship 1945 (+13=4), ahead of Boleslavsky, BRONSTEIN, and Smyslov; Groningen 1946 (+13=3−3), ahead of Euwe, Smyslov, NAJDORF, and Boleslavsky; and Moscow 1947 (+8=6−1), ahead of Smyslov and KERES. In 1945 Botvinnik had renewed negotiations with Alekhine but these ended with the latter's death in March 1946. To fill the vacant title of world champion FIDE organized a match tournament, The Hague–Moscow 1948, won decisively (+10=8−2) by Botvinnik, ahead of Smyslov, Keres, Reshevsky, and Euwe. His seven successive wins in major tournaments from 1941 to 1948 indicate that he was the world's best player in the 1940s, and it was his misfortune that the title of world champion fell to him only towards the end of the decade.

Botvinnik then took a break from chess to gain his doctorate of science. In 1951 he drew a match with his first challenger, Bronstein (+5=14−5), and in 1954 he drew with Smyslov (+7=10−7), both times retaining the title in accordance with FIDE rules. Meanwhile he came first (+9=9−1) equal with TAIMANOV in the USSR championship of 1952 and won the play-off (+2=3−1). At Moscow 1956 he came first (+8=6−1) equal with Smyslov. This was Botvinnik's only first place during his championship years. He lost his title to Smyslov in 1957, regained it in the return match of 1958 (+7=11−5), lost it to TAL in 1960, regained it in 1961 (+10=6−5), and was finally defeated by PETROSYAN two years later. Resentful that FIDE had abolished the privilege of a return match, Botvinnik made no attempt to enter the lists again. Referring to the times when he was champion, Botvinnik described himself as first among equals; more precisely, he was one of the best four players. Before his retirement in 1970 he competed in several tournaments, achieving his best result (+6=9), a share of first prize at Wijk aan Zee 1969.

Botvinnik's style was characterized by good JUDGEMENT OF POSITION, painstaking adjournment analysis, excellent ENDGAME technique, and, above all, thorough preparation. Asked in 1947 why he spent so much time studying endgames that rarely occurred, he replied that to succeed in becoming champion he had to be master of every kind of endgame. Apart from the opening systems he used, and the variations named after him, he made a special study of the GRÜNFELD DEFENCE and the ANTI-MERAN GAMBIT. From the 1960s he spent much of his time training young players and devising chess-playing programs for computers. His approach to the latter (see COMPUTERS AND CHESS) differs fundamentally from that of American programmers.

He published *Izbrannye party 1926–1946* (1949), translated as *One Hundred Selected Games 1926–1946* (1951); two autobiographical works, *Polveka v*

shahkmatakh (1978) and *K dotizheniyu tseli* (1978), the latter translated as *Achieving the Aim* (1981); and a four-volume set, *Analiticheskie i kriticheskie raboti* (1984–7). His later writings, penned with surprising candour, underscore his relentless pursuit of the world chess championship. (See BLUNDER; SPIELMANN COUNTERATTACK.)

B. Cafferty, *Botvinnik's Best Games 1947–1970* (1972) contains biography and 111 games; V. D. Baturinsky, *Shakhmatnoye tvorchestvo Botvinnika* (1965–8) contains 700 annotated games in three volumes.

Makogonov–Botvinnik Sverdlovsk 1943 Queen's Gambit Declined Semi-Slav Defence

1 d4 d5 2 c4 e6 3 Nc3 c6 4 e3 Nf6 5 Nf3 Nbd7 6 Ne5 Nxe5 7 dxe5 Nd7 8 f4 Bb4 9 cxd5 exd5 10 Bd3 Nc5 11 Bc2 Qh4+ 12 g3 Qh3 13 Kf2 Bxc3 14 bxc3 Bf5 15 Bxf5 Qxf5 16 g4 Qe6 17 Ba3 Ne4+ 18 Kf3 h5 19 h3 f6 20 c4 hxg4+ 21 hxg4 Rxh1 22 Qxh1 0-0-0 23 Rd1 fxe5 24 cxd5 cxd5 25 Rc1+ Kb8 26 Qh4 Re8 27 f5 Qf7 28 Rc2 g6 29 Bb2 a6 30 Ke2

30...Ka7 31 Qh2 Qf6 32 fxg6 Qxg6 33 Qg2 Rf8 34 Bxe5 Rf2+ 35 Qxf2 Nxf2 36 Bd4+ b6 37 Rc7+ Kb8 38 Be5 Nxg4 39 Bf4 Ne5 40 Re7 Qc2+ 41 Ke1 Kc8 42 Bxe5 Qxa2 43 Rc7+ Kd8 44 Rc1 a5 45 Bd4 b5 46 Ra1 Qb3 47 Kf2 a4 48 Kf3 Qc2 49 Kf4 Kd7 50 Ke5 Qe4+ 51 Kf6 Qe7+ 52 Kg6 a3 53 Rf1 b4 54 Rf7 Qxf7+ 55 Kxf7 b3 White resigns.

Botvinnik Variation, 13 in the ENGLISH OPENING, and although the square d4 appears weak, BOTVINNIK, who believed that White can control it, frequently adopted this formation here or in other variations; 11...axb5 12 exf6 Qb6 13 fxg7 Bxg7 14 0-0, a possible continuation from the BLUMENFELD VARIATION (145) in the MERAN VARIATION, played Botvinnik–Euwe, world championship 1948, but the line had already been played in 1943 by BOGOLJUBOW and twice by the Austrian Hans Müller (1896–1971).

Also 203, sometimes called the Janowski Variation, in the QUEEN'S GAMBIT Declined, as Botvinnik–Vidmar, Nottingham 1936 (but also Steinitz–Pillsbury, Nuremberg 1896, and Rauzer–Verlinsky, USSR championship 1931); 252 in the DUTCH DEFENCE, as Botvinnik–Bronstein, match, 1951; 303 in the NIMZO–INDIAN DEFENCE, as Lilienthal–

Botvinnik, Moscow 1935; 314 also in the Nimzo–Indian, as Bogoljubow–Botvinnik, Bled 1931; 341 in the QUEEN'S INDIAN DEFENCE, introduced in Uhlmann–Botvinnik, Leipzig Olympiad 1960; 361 in the CATALAN OPENING, as Botvinnik–Tylor, Nottingham 1936; 391 in the GRÜNFELD DEFENCE, played Botvinnik–Gligorić, Tel Aviv Olympiad 1964; 452 in the SICILIAN DEFENCE, as Smyslov–Botvinnik, match, 1954; 584 (also known as the Panov Variation or Rabinovich Variation) in the CARO–KANN DEFENCE, as Botvinnik–Flohr, match 1933, and as recommended by KRAUSE, after whom it is sometimes named, in 1911; 1119 in the KING'S GAMBIT Accepted, as Bronstein–Botvinnik, USSR championship 1952; 1234 in the FRENCH DEFENCE, as Abramyan–Botvinnik, Leningrad 1938. Also 153, the ANTI-MERAN GAMBIT; 364, the RUSSIAN VARIATION of the KING'S INDIAN DEFENCE.

Bourdonnais, Louis Charles de la (1795–1840), for nearly twenty years the most famous player in the world. Born in the Ile Bourbon (Réunion), where his grandfather had been Governor, he was sent to the Lycée Henri IV in Paris where, in 1814, he learnt chess. He began to take the game seriously in 1818, playing regularly at the CAFÉ DE LA RÉGENCE and becoming a player of the first rank within two years. Around 1820 DESCHAPELLES took Bourdonnais as a pupil. A visit to Paris by COCHRANE in 1821 was the occasion for a triangular contest, Deschapelles conceding pawn and two moves to Cochrane and Bourdonnais who themselves met on even terms. There were seven rounds each of three games, each player contributing one napoleon (a 20 fr. gold piece) to a pool for the round. 'When I saw three napoleons on the chess board,' recounts Bourdonnais, 'I went to work in earnest.' He won six of the seven pools, scoring +6−1 against Deschapelles and +7 against Cochrane. A year or so later Deschapelles retired from chess, and Bourdonnais became the undisputed champion of France, then the home of the world's best players.

In the spring of 1825 Bourdonnais made the first of three visits to England. There he played many games against LEWIS, winning the majority, and, conceding odds, defeating all others he met. There too he married an English girl, Eliza Waller Gordon, in July. For a time they lived in a château at St Malo with 'five servants and two carriages'. In the early 1830s, however, Bourdonnais lost his fortune, by neglect or speculation. He was obliged, with increasing insecurity, to try to earn a living at chess.

The first serious challenge to his supremacy came from McDONNELL, England's best player, and in 1834 the two met at the Westminster Chess Club. In a struggle extending from June to October six matches were played. Bourdonnais won the first +16=4−5, lost the second +4=0−5, won the next three, +6=1−5, +8=7−3, +7=1−4, and was trailing +4−5 in the last when it was broken off or ended. The last match was probably to be decided in favour of the first to win eight games. Some reports suggest that it was unfinished but

more plausible, not least on account of the need to settle bets, is the explanation given by Bourdonnais that he conceded his opponent three games start. This account, totalling +45=13−27, is the most widely accepted version of the match results. The games are commonly referred to by their place in the series. For example, the famous fiftieth game (see McDONNELL) was the fourth game of the fourth match.

Both players knew their openings well. Lewis had trained McDonnell while Bourdonnais had read Lewis's books and written one of his own; yet McDonnell's failure was in a fair measure caused by his poor judgement of position in the opening phase. Bourdonnais was described by WALKER, a spectator, as 'the first player, though perhaps not the most modest man; but a jolly fellow [who] talked and laughed a good deal at intervals when winning, and swore tolerably round oaths . . . when fate ran counter to his schemes'. The oaths may not have affected his opponent (according to Walker's dubious testimony, neither spoke the other's language) but they might well have been justified by McDonnell's slowness of play. Bourdonnais played fast, as was his habit and so that he might have more free time to meet all-comers at half a crown a game; thus he would play into the early hours in spite of next day's match.

This series of matches was a landmark in the history of the game, the first important contest of modern times. The games were recorded and made available in book form to a wide public, and analysed by leading masters to an extent not previously known. The result was a process that has continued ever since, the fashioning of openings from actual play. In the EVANS GAMBIT Bourdonnais introduced the LASKER DEFENCE (26th game) and the MORPHY ATTACK (84th game); to the McDONNELL DOUBLE GAMBIT he introduced the reply 4 . . . d5, a move that still holds its own; and he made other improvements.

This was the last time Bourdonnais played even. In 1836 he met SZÉN, conceded odds of pawn and two moves and lost more games than he won, but he held his own at odds of pawn and move against SAINT-AMANT and other leading players. In the same year Bourdonnais became editor of the world's first chess magazine, Le Palamède. In 1838 he became ill, first with a stroke, for which he was frequently bled, and later with dropsy, for which he was tapped every three or four weeks. The following year the Paris Chess Club was disbanded and his secretary's salary (1,200 fr.) ceased abruptly. Unable to play regularly on account of his illness, he could no longer earn a living and bit by bit he sold his books, his furniture, and even his clothes.

An offer of employment at Simpson's Divan brought him to London in November 1840. Watched by large crowds he played in public for two days, conceding pawn and two moves at half a crown a game. Then his illness became too severe. Walker, finding Bourdonnais and his wife living in a garret, facing both eviction and starvation, raised a fund, moved them to more comfortable premises, and provided medical aid, but within three weeks Bourdonnais was dead. Belatedly (8 Dec. 1840) the Réunion Island authorities granted him a pension of 3,000 fr. No money was paid, nor was the pension passed to his widow, for whom Walker set out to raise a fund of £200. (She re-married in 1842.) Bourdonnais, like his rival McDonnell, was buried at Kensal Green.

Bourdonnais–McDonnell   4th match game 1834   Italian Opening

1 e4 e5 2 Nf3 Nc6 3 Bc4 Bc5 4 c3 d6 5 d4 exd4 6 cxd4 Bb6 7 d5 Ne5 8 Nxe5 dxe5 9 Nc3 Nf6 10 Bg5 0-0 11 Qf3 Qd6 12 Bxf6 Qxf6 13 Qxf6 gxf6 (In the following play Black tries to free his BACKWARD PAWN at f6. He achieves this at too high a price, for his king is left defenceless.) 14 g4 Kg7 15 Ne2 Rh8 16 Rg1 Kf8 17 Rg2 Ke7 18 0-0-0 h5 19 g5 f5 20 Nc3 Bc5 21 g6 Bd6 22 gxf7 Kxf7 23 f4 exf4 24 Rdg1 Kf8 25 Rg6 f3 26 exf5 Be5

27 d6 cxd6 28 Rg8+ Rxg8 29 Rxg8+ Ke7 30 Nd5+ Kd7 31 Bb5+ mate.

Bourdonnais Attack, 1246 in the FRENCH DEFENCE, recommended by BOURDONNAIS on page 118 of his book (1833) as better than 2 d4, although he later changed his mind. Occasionally called the Romantic Attack. (See DE VERE.)

Bourdonnais Variation, 468, a line for Black, occasionally called the Modern Variation, in the SICILIAN DEFENCE that was played three times by BOURDONNAIS in his fourth match against McDONNELL, 1834, and was later recommended by LÖWENTHAL whose name it sometimes bears. (Compare BOLESLAVSKY VARIATION, 473); 906 in the ITALIAN OPENING, played three times in the Bourdonnais–McDonnell series. See game under BOURDONNAIS.

Bradford Attack, 1201, a variation of the FRENCH DEFENCE played by BLACKBURNE against Lee at Bradford 1888. Black usually avoids this attack by playing 6 . . . Nc6 instead of 6 . . . Bxc5.

Bradley Beach Variation, 25, a line for Black in the ENGLISH OPENING played by ALEKHINE against Bigelow in a tournament at Bradley Beach, New Jersey, 1929. The line was analysed in *Shakhmaty*, 1929, by the Soviet player N. A. Sudnitsin.

Brandreth, Dale Alden (1931–), American author, bibliophile, and publisher. See SPURIOUS GAMES.

Brazilian System, 805, the RIO DE JANEIRO VARIATION.

breakthrough, the penetration of an apparently well defended position, often by means of sacrifice.

A position from MSS Magliabechiani xix, 51, Biblioteche Nazionale Centrale, Florence, dated *c.*1500. White queens a pawn after 1 g6 hxg6 2 f6 or 1 . . . fxg6 2 h6, an example of a breakthrough given in many textbooks subsequently. For examples of middlegame breakthroughs, see PHILIDOR SACRIFICE.

In a broader sense, many games are decided by a break into enemy territory, with or without sacrifice.

Brede, Ferdinand Julius (1800–49), German problemist whose book, *Almanach für Freunde vom Schachspiel* (1844), includes 113 of his problems (which he calls endgames), 24 knight's tours, 12 correspondence games, poems, and various other matters. He is remembered for the BREDE THEME and a handful of problems showing variation play, rare in his time; but most of his work consists of directmates of an older style, conditional problems, and helpmates. (See GBR CODE; PROBLEM HISTORY.)

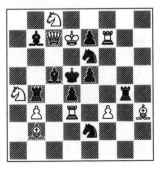

#2

A problem by Brede, no. 3 in his book. The key is 1 Rxd4+, and six different replies lead to six different mates.

Brede theme, a problem manœuvre first shown by BREDE, no. 16 in *Almanach für Freunde vom Schachspiel* (1844). A check from a black piece is answered by the SELF-PIN of an interposed piece which, subsequently unpinned, is freed to make the mating move.

#3

A problem by the Soviet composers Leonid Ivanovich Zagoruiko (1923–) and Viacheslav Georgievich Kopayev (1938–), third special mention, Visserman Memorial Tourney 1981. The key is 1 Kxb2 and the three main variations show CROSS-PINS.

1 ... Re6+ 2 Qe5 Rf6 3 Qh2#
1 ... Rd6+ 2 Qd4 Rf6 3 Qh4#
1 ... Rxc6+ 2 Qc3 Rf6 3 Qh3#

Bremen Variation, 29 in the ENGLISH OPENING, also known as the Carls, Close, Keres, or Szabó Variations.

Brentano Defence, 811, a dubious reply to the SPANISH OPENING dating from 1900, when Brentano published his analysis in the *Wiener Schachzeitung*; 1139, in the KING'S GAMBIT Accepted from the second edition of the HANDBUCH. Franz Clemens Honoratus Hermann Josef Brentano (1838–1917), a well-known German philosopher who lived in Vienna, frequently published analyses of the openings.

Brentano Gambit, 1153, the CAMPBELL VARIATION of the KING'S GAMBIT Accepted, analysed in great detail by Brentano in *Deutsche Schachzeitung*, 1882, 1883, and 1887.

Brentano Variation, 758, the modern way of playing the BRENTANO DEFENCE to the SPANISH OPENING.

Breslau Variation, 722 in the SPANISH OPENING. Black sacrifices a piece (12 f3 Bd6 13 fxe4) but gets sufficient compensation from an attack. Carl Bergmann of Breslau (now Wrocław) analysed the line

with local players and published the result in *Deutsches Wochenschach*, 1913. He added that he wanted it to be known as the Breslau Variation, causing TARRASCH to protest that he had thought of the idea first, and had published it in a lecture given in Stockholm a few days before the magazine appeared. He did not pursue his accusation when it was revealed that Bergmann's paper had been delivered some time earlier. If, instead, 11 ... Qd7, White springs the TARRASCH TRAP, 12 Nxe6.

Breuer, Johann Josef (1903–81) German composer, International Judge of Chess Compositions (1957), International Master for Chess Compositions (1973), teacher. His *magnum opus*, published posthumously in 1982, is *Beispiele zur Ideengeschichte* containing 1,800 diagrams representing the most significant problems published up to 1968.

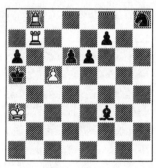

#7

A problem by Breuer, first prize, *Schach-Express*, 1950–51. 1 Rc7 (threatening 2 cxd6) 1 ... d5 2 Rb6 d4 3 Ra7 Be2 4 Rab7 ~ 5 Rb4 Bd1 6 R4b5+ axb5 7 Ra7#.

brevity, interesting game of a few moves. For example, 1 d4 d6 2 c4 e5 3 Nf3 e4 4 Ng5 f5 5 Nc3 c6 6 Nh3 Na6 7 e3 Nf6 8 d5 g6 9 b3 Bg7 10 Bb2 0-0 11 Qd2 Ng4 12 Be2 Nc5 13 Rd1 Qh4 14 Na4 f4 15 Bxg7 fxe3 16 Qc3 Rxf2 17 Bh8 Rxg2+ 18 Kf1 Ne5 and White resigned (Knaak–Speelman, Thessaloniki Olympiad, 1988). (See DANGEROUS DIAGONAL.)

Breyer, Gyula (1893–1921), Hungarian player, national champion in 1912. His play improved rapidly after the First World War, and in a tournament at Berlin, Dec. 1920, he was first (+6=1−2) ahead of BOGOLJUBOW, TARTAKOWER, RÉTI, MARÓCZY, and TARRASCH. In 1921 he made a new blindfold chess record, playing 25 games simultaneously. A career that seemed set for high honours ended abruptly when he died from heart disease.

Breyer has achieved more fame as a pioneer of the so-called HYPERMODERN movement, and for his aphorism 'after 1 e4 White's game is in its last throes'. He is suggesting that the unguarded pawn at e4 could become a target for Black, that White should begin 1 d4, or attempt to control the centre in other ways. (He did not himself abandon the move 1 e4.) Although Breyer's name is not associated with any new opening or variation of a 'hypermodern' type, his enquiring mind, stimulated by new chess ideas of any kind, was a source of inspiration to some of his contemporaries, not least to his close friend Réti. He edited *Szellemi Sport*, a magazine devoted to all kinds of puzzles, including chess, from April to July 1920, and composed at least one brilliant retro-analytical study.

Breyer Gambit, 1175, a dubious line in the KING'S GAMBIT Accepted, analysed by CARRERA whose name it sometimes bears, and played Charousek–Showalter, Nuremberg 1896. When BREYER reintroduced it his idea was to answer 3 ... Qh4+ by Qf2.

Breyer Variation, 101 in the QUEEN'S GAMBIT Declined, as Breyer–Havasi, Budapest 1918; 105 in the same opening, a way, also playable on White's 4th or 5th move, of avoiding the MERAN VARIATION; 497 in the SICILIAN DEFENCE, as Kostić–Breyer, Göteborg 1920; 570 in the CARO–KANN DEFENCE, as Breyer–Bogoljubow, Berlin 1920; 630 in the VIENNA GAME, introduced in Blackburne–Judd, New York 1889; 1223 in the FRENCH DEFENCE, recommended by BREYER.

Also 748 in the SPANISH OPENING, allegedly suggested by Breyer around 1920 and neglected until the 1960s when it became one of the accepted lines in the CLOSE DEFENCE, 732. Black usually redevelops his queen's knight at d7 which, said EUWE, gives the position more flexibility. Presumably Breyer wished to avoid the move Pc7–c5 which was fashionable in his time (see CHIGORIN VARIATION, 746). (See AVERBAKH.)

brilliancy prize, or beauty prize, a prize for a game that contains a brilliant combination, chosen from those played in a tournament or match. Such a game is not necessarily distinguished on account of the sound strategy or excellence of play throughout, the characteristics required for a BEST GAME PRIZE. The first brilliancy prize was given by the proprietor of the Café International, New York, where a tournament was held in September and October 1876. 'This spirited offer should have a marked influence in protecting us from the wearying round of French, Sicilian, and irregular openings ... ' (See BIRD for the prize-winning game, a FRENCH DEFENCE.) The first award for a match game was given to STEINITZ for the eighth game of his world championship match against CHIGORIN in 1889.

F. LeLionnais, *Les Prix de beauté aux échecs* (2nd edn. 1951).

Bristol Clearance, a problem manœuvre: a piece is moved along a line, clearing the way so that in its wake another line-piece may follow.

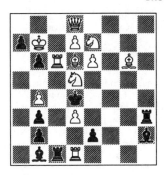

#3

A problem by VUKCEVICH, first prize, Stošić Memorial tourney 1982. The key is 1 Qc7, threatening 2 Rc4+; two variations show Bristol Clearance.

1 ... Rxd3	2 Rc2 Bxc2	3 Qc3 #
	(2 ... Rxc2	3 Rxd3 #)
1 ... Bxd3	2 Bg3 Rxg3	3 Qf4 #
	(2 ... Bxg3	3 Rxd3 #).

The play also shows Nowotny Interference (see CRITICAL PLAY) on d3, c2, and g3. The manœuvre was first shown by the English composer Frank Healey (1828–1906) in one of a set of problems that was awarded first prize in the Bristol tourney, 1861.

Brodsky–Jones Variation, 1202, a line in the FRENCH DEFENCE discovered independently in 1897 by Adolf Brodsky (1851–1929) and Edward Owen Jones (1861–1911). Subsequently masters came to prefer 9 ... Nd4 to 9 ... f6. Brodsky, leader of the Hallé Orchestra and later Principal of Manchester College of Music, gave the first performance of Tchaikovsky's violin concerto when its dedicatee refused, saying it was too difficult to play.

Bron, Vladimir Akimovich (1909–85), Soviet composer, International Judge of Chess Compositions (1956), International Grandmaster for Chess Compositions (1975), a doctor of technical science who specialized in fire research. He became interested in studies at an early age, and gained an award in the first tourney of the All-Union chess section in 1925.

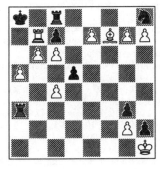

+

A study by Bron, first prize, *Magyar Sakkélet*, 1948. 1 Ra7+ Kb8 2 Ra8+ Kxa8 3 b7+ Ka7 4 bxc8=N+ Ka6 5 gxh8=B d4 6 Bxd4 Rd3 7 Bh5 Rb3 8 Bg6 Rc3 9 Be3 Ra3 10 h8=B Rxe3 11 e8=R.

Although he also composed problems he was better known as the first outstanding study composer from the Ukraine. His book *Izbrannye etyudy i zadachi* (1969) contains a selection of 150 of his studies and 90 of his problems. O. N. Averkin and Bron, *V poiskakh shakhmatnoi istiny* (1979) contains 45 games by Ukrainian masters, and 170 studies by Bron.

Bronstein, David Ionovich (1924–   ), International Grandmaster (1950), one of the best four players in the world for about ten years from 1948. 'Bronstein was a key figure in chess [in the 1950s]. Without him neither TAL, nor even FISCHER, could have played such important roles in the history of chess', said BARCZA in 1986. He learned the game in Kiev and, in 1940 after some local successes, became one of the youngest Soviet players to be awarded the national master title. In 1946 he won a strong Moscow championship tournament (+10=3−2). Between 1947 and 1982 he finished first or equal first a further six times in this event. Bronstein's swift progress from 1946 has few precedents. He won the first (and strongest) interzonal in 1948 (+8=11); came first in two USSR championships, sharing the title with KOTOV in 1948 and (+8=10−1) with SMYSLOV in 1949; came first (+8=8−2) equal with BOLESLAVSKY in the very strong CANDIDATES tournament, Budapest 1950; and won the play-off to become the first challenger for the world championship under the control of FIDE.

The match against BOTVINNIK took place in 1951. Bronstein often outwitted his opponent in the MIDDLEGAME (usually the decisive phase) but lacked adequate ENDGAME technique, and the match was drawn (+5=14−5). Botvinnik retained the title under FIDE rules. In 1953 Bronstein played in the great Candidates tournament at Neuhausen and Zurich, and came second (+6=20−2) equal with KERES and RESHEVSKY after Smyslov. After first prizes at Belgrade 1954 (+8=11) and the interzonal tournament at Göteborg 1955 (+10=10), Bronstein scored +4=11−3 to share third place in the Candidates tournament at Amsterdam 1956.

Bronstein played in 18 USSR championships in addition to the two he won, his best results being second in 1957 (+9=9−3), equal with Keres, and in 1964–5 (+10=6−3), and third in 1958 (+7=9−2) and 1961 (+6=13−1). He played in four Olympiads (1952, 1954, 1956, and 1958), making a total score of +30=18−1, and winning the prize for the best third- or fourth-board score three times. He was first or equal first at Gotha 1957; Moscow 1959 (+3=8), a tie with Smyslov and

SPASSKY; Szombathely 1966 (+9=5−1); Moscow 1968 (+7=7−1), a tie with PETROSYAN who won the play-off; Berlin 1968 (+7=7−1); Sarajevo 1971; Hastings 1975–6 (+6=8−1); Sandomierz 1976; Budapest 1977 (+6=10); Jurmala 1978. He was equal second (+2=9−1) with STEIN, after Spassky, at Moscow 1964, a very strong zonal tournament.

Bronstein has made several contributions to openings knowledge; in particular, he and Boleslavsky introduced new strategic ideas in the KING'S INDIAN DEFENCE, as a consequence of which this opening, regarded as inadequate since the 1930s, became fashionable in the 1950s.

A small neat man, sociable and friendly, Bronstein has a ready smile. He is popular among chess players, who also admire his creative middlegame play and the recondite manœuvres he sometimes finds. His first and best book, published in 1954, contains the games of the Neuhausen–Zurich Candidates tournament, 1953. 'I started', he writes, 'from the premise that every full-bodied game of chess is an artistic endeavour arising out of . . . the battle of chess ideas,' and adds that he wishes to display the richness and limitless extent of these ideas. The book is unencumbered by laborious variations showing what might have occurred. He writes that 'the moves played in each game serve to annotate the author's ideas', a reversal of the normal practice, and that 'the format is that of a literary work.' Bronstein has a great interest in literature, and especially Shakespeare (his English is fluent), and has the approach of an artist. 'The author', wrote Spassky, 'is present in its pages.' Improved by a revision of 1960 the book has become a classic, perhaps the best of all tournament books. The need for an English translation was obvious, and two different ones appeared within a few weeks of each other: *Zurich International Chess Tournament 1953* (1979) and *The Chess Struggle in Practice* (1980). A third Russian edition appeared in 1984.

In 1981 Bronstein published *Samouchitel shakhmatnoi igry* in an edition of 100,000. This attractive 'teach yourself' guide for youngsters has a unique type of chess diagram. They are oblong, pieces move across the page, and lines of attack and defence are shown in various colours, weak squares and king's defensive zones are marked, and so on. Whether this novelty was too difficult to understand, or too costly to print, when a new edition appeared in 1987, familiar diagrams were used, but the number of pages was increased from 248 to 352 and the print run to 150,000 copies.

Tal–Bronstein   33rd USSR Championship   Tallinn 1965
French Defence Winawer Variation

1 e4 e6 2 d4 d5 3 Nc3 Bb4 4 e5 Ne7 5 a3 Bxc3+ 6 bxc3 c5 7 Qg4 cxd4 8 Bd3 Qa5 9 Ne2 Ng6 10 h4 Nc6 11 h5 Ncxe5 12 Qxd4 Nxd3+ 13 cxd3 e5 14 Qe3 d4 15 Qg3 Ne7 16 Qxg7 Rg8 17 Qf6 dxc3 18 0-0 Qc7 19 d4 Bg4 20 f3 Nd5 21 Qh4 Be6 22 dxe5 Qxe5 23 Re1

23 ... Rc8 24 Rb1 b6 25 Rb5 a6 26 Rb3 Qg7 27 Qf2 Rc4 28 h6 Qf6 29 Nxc3 Nxc3 30 Rxb6 Qd8 31 Rxa6 Rg6 32 Qb2 Ke7 33 Ra7+ Kf6 34 Re4 Qd1+ 35 Kh2 Rxe4 36 Qxc3+ Re5 37 Bf4 Qe2 38 Bxe5+ Qxe5+ 39 Qxe5+ Kxe5 40 Ra5+ Kd4 41 Rh5 Bd5 42 Kh3 f5 White resigns.

Bronstein Gambit, 501 in the SICILIAN DEFENCE.

Bronstein–Larsen Variation, 578 in the CARO-KANN DEFENCE, played also by Nimzowitsch, and sometimes named after him.

Bronstein Variation, 317, 323, and 324, all in the NIMZO-INDIAN DEFENCE. The first was introduced by BRONSTEIN in his world championship match with BOTVINNIK in 1951 (see FISCHER), and the last in games played in the USSR championship 1957; 397 and 418 in the KING'S INDIAN DEFENCE, the first from Spassky–Bronstein, Amsterdam 1954; 548 and 553 in the SICILIAN DEFENCE, the first introduced in the game Bronstein–Boleslavsky, USSR championship 1958, and the second in Bronstein–Ivkov, USSR v. Yugoslavia 1962; 602 in the SCANDINAVIAN OPEN-ING, as Bronstein–Lutikov, USSR championship 1959; 683 in the SPANISH OPENING, played by ALEK-HINE and revived by Bronstein in the 1950s.

Brown, John (1827–63), usually known as J. B. of Bridport to avoid confusion with John Brown of the Temple, another problemist active at the same time. His father lived in Bridport, Dorset, and was apparently the proprietor of a private school, where the son may have taught. J. B. married and settled in the town, where he died of tuberculosis.

#3

A problem by J. B., no. 25 in his collection. The key is 1 Nd4, and each of the three white pieces may give mate:

   1 ... Kxh3   2 Nxf5~   3 Rg3#
   1 ... Kh5   2 Nxf5~   3 Bg4#
   1 ... f4 (a self-block)   2 Bg4 Kg3   3 Nf5#.

Few white men, all of which take part, even fewer white pawns, and elegant mates are factors which are alleged to have influenced the founding of the BOHEMIAN style.

Chess Strategy—a collection of the most beautiful problems composed by J. B. of Bridport, containing 174 positions, was published in 1865, 'solely for the benefit of the widow and orphans of its estimable author'.

Browne, Walter Shawn (1949–), International Grandmaster (1970), professional chessplayer from the age of 18. Born in Sydney, Australia, and taken to USA before he joined the Manhattan Chess Club at the age of 13. There he polished his chess, and in 1968 he went back to his homeland for about five years and represented it in the Olympiads of 1970 and 1972. He then settled in the USA where he won the championship in 1974 (+6=7), 1975, and 1977, and shared the title in 1980 (+5=5−2) with CHRISTIANSEN and EVANS, in 1981 (+6=6−2) with SEIRAWAN, and in 1983 (+5=8) with Christiansen and DZINDZICHASHVILI. His major victories in international chess are Venice 1971 (+7=3−1); Wijk aan Zee 1974 (+8=6−1); Reykjavik 1978 (+7=4−2); Wijk aan Zee 1980 (+7=6), equal with Sierawan ahead of KORCHNOI and TIMMAN; Santiago 1981 (+6=4); Surakarta–Denpasar 1982 (+11=13−1), shared with Henley; Gjovik 1983 (+4=4−1), shared with NUNN and ADORJÁN; and Næstved 1985 (+3=7−1), shared with VAGANYAN and LARSEN.

Browne is the driving force behind the World Blitz Chess Association, a body which has its own rating system and issues its own magazine, *Blitz Chess.*

Browne–Byrne   Mentor 1977 USA Championship
Dutch Defence

1 d4 f5 2 Nc3 Nf6 3 Bg5 d5 4 Bxf6 exf6 5 e3 Be6 6 Bd3 g6 7 Qf3 c6 8 Nge2 Nd7 9 h3 Qb6 10 g4 Qxb2 11 Rb1 Qa3 12 gxf5 Bf7 13 Rxb7 Bb4 14 0-0 0-0-0

15 Rxb4 Qxb4 16 Ba6+ Kc7 17 Rb1 Qd6 18 Rb7+
Kc8 19 Rb3+ Kc7 20 Rb7+ Kc8 21 e4 Nb8 22 Nb5
cxb5 23 Qc3+ Nc6 24 e5 Qc7 25 e6 Black resigns.

Brown Opening, 1322, the GROB OPENING. Brown
has not identified himself in order to justify his
claim to the opening.

Brühl, Hans Moritz (1736–1809), Saxon diplomat
who made London his home. He made significant
contributions to the study of astronomy, was
deeply interested in music (devising an improvement in the construction of the pianoforte), and,
judging from the approximately 30 games of his
that have survived, one of the strongest players of
his day. Possibly his love of music first drew him to
PHILIDOR: they became regular opponents at the
chess-board. Twenty of their games are known.

Brunner chess, a form of RANDOMIZED CHESS.

Brunner–Turton, see DOUBLING THEMES.

Bryan Counter-gambit, 1094 or 1105, a variation
of the KING'S GAMBIT Accepted analysed by the
American amateur Thomas Jefferson Bryan
(c.1800–70), who was active in the chess circles of
Paris and London in the middle of the 19th century.
This dubious counter-gambit was also analysed by
KIESERITZKY and sometimes bears his name, or the
name King's Bishop Counter-gambit. (See IMMOR-
TAL GAME.)

Buchholz score, an AUXILIARY SCORING METHOD for
use in Swiss system tournaments, devised to supplant that of Constantin Svenson (1872–1932)
which followed the same lines as NEUSTADTL'S. A
Buchholz score is a player's score multiplied by the
sum of the opponents' scores. The method was
used, probably for the first time, in a tournament at
Bitterfeld 1932, in which the originator, Bruno
Buchholz (d. c.1958) of Magdeburg competed. An
account is given in *Ranneforths Schachkalender
1933*.

Buckle, Henry Thomas (1821–62), English player,
historian. He is usually classed as second only to
STAUNTON among English players during the 1840s,
and STEINITZ regarded Buckle as the better player.
In 1843 Buckle won a match (+6=1) against
Staunton, who conceded pawn and move, and in
1848 he defeated KIESERITZKY (+3=3−2). He won
a knock-out tournament, London 1849, defeating
WILLIAMS (+2) in the second round. In 1851 Buckle
defeated LÖWENTHAL (+4=3−1) and held his own
against ANDERSSEN, who declared him to be the
strongest player he had met so far.

In his youth Buckle suffered ill-health which
interfered with his schooling, and on account of

which he was sent to fairer climates. Nevertheless
he read widely, successfully educating himself and
learning to speak seven languages. His father, a
merchant, died in 1840 leaving him an ample fortune. In the 1850s Buckle largely gave up serious
chess in favour of literary pursuits, and he began his
great work for which he is still remembered, *A
History of Civilization in England*. The first two
volumes were published in 1857 and 1861. At
Damascus, on one of his many trips abroad, he
contracted a fatal illness, allegedly crying as he
died: 'My book! I haven't finished my book.'

Budapest Defence, 290, an aggressive counter-
gambit, played in the game Adler–Maróczy, Buda-
pest 1896, but first taken up seriously in 1916 when
Zsigmond Barász (c.1878–1935) proposed its use,
Abonyi sponsored it, and BREYER played it against
Esser in a small tournament at Budapest in
November 1916.

Buerger Variation, 347, a line in the QUEEN'S
INDIAN DEFENCE played in the game Buerger–Colle,
Tunbridge Wells 1927. The originator later altered
the spelling of his name to Victor Berger (1904–   ).

building a bridge, making a path for a king by
providing cover from attack by enemy line-pieces.
For the best-known example, see LUCENA POSITION.
Problemists frequently use this device in the solution of a SERIES-MOVER.

Bundesliga, the German chess league, a team competition initiated in 1975. Originally there were four
regional groups within West Germany, North,
South, West, and South-West. In 1980 a first division was introduced, covering the whole country,
the second division remaining regional. Each year
there is promotion or demotion between the divi-
sions. There is great public interest in the matches,
some of the teams being chess sections of famous
football clubs. Consequently there are, in chess
terms, high fees available to the best players, and
the top teams engage foreign grandmasters, up to a
maximum of two per team. The fees paid can be as
much as 20,000 DM for the 14 games in a season.

Burn, Amos (1848–1925), one of the world's top ten
players at the end of the 19th century. Born in Hull,
he learned chess when he was 16, went to London at
the age of 21, and rapidly established himself as a
leading English player. A pupil of STEINITZ, he
developed a similar style: both he and his master
were among the world's best defensive players,
according to NIMZOWITSCH. Not wishing to become
yet another impecunious professional, Burn decided to put his work (he was first a cotton broker,
then a sugar broker) before his chess, and he
remained an amateur. He made several long visits
to America, and was often out of practice when he
played serious chess. Until his thirty-eighth year he

played infrequently and only in national events, always taking first or second place.

From 1886 to 1889 Burn played more often. In 1886 he drew matches with BIRD ($+9-9$) and MACKENZIE ($+4=2-4$); at London 1887 he achieved his best tournament result up to this time, first ($+8-1$) equal with GUNSBERG (a play-off was drawn ($+1=3-1$)); and at Breslau 1889 he took second place after TARRASCH, ahead of Gunsberg. After an isolated appearance at Hastings 1895 he entered another spell of chess activity, 1897–1901. The best achievement of his career was at Cologne 1898, first prize ($+9=5-1$) ahead of CHAROUSEK, CHIGORIN, Steinitz, SCHLECHTER, and JANOWSKI. At Munich 1900 he was fourth ($+9=3-1$).

Burn's last seven international tournaments began with Ostend 1905 and ended with Breslau 1912. A comparative success, in view of his age, was his fourth prize shared with BERNSTEIN and TEICHMANN, after Schlechter, MARÓCZY, and RUBINSTEIN at Ostend 1906; 36 players competed in a five-stage event, requiring thirty games in all from those who completed the course. Retired from both business and play, he made his home in London and edited the chess column of *The Field* from 1913 until his death. A shy and withdrawn man, a loyal companion to those who came to know him, he freely gave advice to young and aspiring players.

R. N. Coles, *Amos Burn, the Quiet Chessmaster* (1983), a posthumous publication, contains a biography and 62 annotated games.

Marco–Burn   Hastings 1895   French Defence Burn Variation

1 e4 e6 2 d4 d5 3 Nc3 Nf6 4 Bg5 dxe4 5 Nxe4 Be7 6 Bxf6 gxf6 7 c3 f5 8 Ng3 c5 9 Nf3 Nc6 10 Bb5 Qb6 11 Bxc6+ bxc6 12 0-0 h5 13 Qd2 h4 14 Ne2 Ba6 15 Rfe1 0-0-0 16 a3 Rh7 17 b4 c4 18 a4 Rg7 19 Reb1 Rdg8 20 Ne1 Bb7 21 f3 Qd8 22 b5?

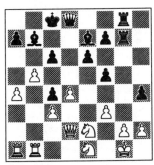

22 ... c5 23 Qe3 Qc7 24 a5 Bg5 25 f4 Be7 26 g3 Qd7 27 dxc5 hxg3 28 hxg3 Qd5 29 c6 Bc5 30 cxb7+ Kxb7 31 Nd4 Rxg3+ White resigns.

Burn Variation, 1213, a line in the FRENCH DEFENCE dating from the 1870s, played regularly by BURN at the tournaments of Hastings 1895, Cologne 1898, and Vienna 1898, and much later by PETROSYAN. See game under BURN.

bust, originally 'burst', the demonstration that an opening variation is unsatisfactory, that a combination is faulty, or that a study has no solution; to make such a demonstration; to demolish.

Bwee, Touw Hian (1943–   ), International Judge of Chess Compositions (1977), International Grandmaster for Chess Compositions (1984). Born in Pekalongan (Java), Bwee was taken to Jakarta when he was five years old. There, in 1958, he discovered chess problems and within three years he began to win tourney awards. In 1965 he went to Germany to study architecture and civil engineering, and while there he became one of the foremost TWO-MOVER composers of his generation, with more than 80 first prizes to his credit. He returned to Jakarta in 1979 and took a planning post with the timber industry.

#2

A problem by Bwee, first prize, Visserman Memorial tourney 1980. The key is 1 Rg6 threatening 2 Kd6#

1 ... Qa6   2 Nd6#
1 ... Bxf7   2 Nf6#
1 ... Rxh5   2 Rg4#.

The TRY 1 cxb6?, threatening 2 Kc5#, is answered by 1 ... Qb4, but there is CHANGED PLAY after other replies: 1 ... Qa6? 2 Nc3#; 1 ... Bxf7? 2 Nc5#; 1 ... Rxh5 2 Rd4#.

bye, a term applied to the situation of a player who has no opponent in a particular round. In a KNOCKOUT TOURNAMENT byes are used to bring the entrants to a number capable of successive halvings. Thus, if 36 players entered, 28 could be awarded byes in the first round, leaving 32 players to go forward to the second round. In an ALL-PLAY-ALL, byes usually arise from there being an odd number of entrants, the player with the bye having no score for that round. When the bye arises from a withdrawal, the player without an opponent may receive a full point should the controller decide that the defaulting player had completed sufficient games to be classed as a participant.

In a SWISS SYSTEM event a bye arising as in an all-play-all scores a full point. There is also the half-point bye, common in a weekend event when a player asks to be excused one round, often the first, and is awarded half a point. In neither case is the player with the bye classed as having had a colour for the round.

Bykova, Yelizavyeta Ivanovna (1913–89), Women's World Champion 1953–6, 1958–62; USSR Women's Champion 1947, 1948, 1950; IM 1953.

by-play, variations of a problem solution that are not central to the composer's idea. Compare FRINGE VARIATION.

Byrne, Robert Eugene (1928–), International Grandmaster (1964). Winner of the US Open Championship in 1960, and co-winner with BENKO in 1967, Byrne finished in a three-way tie, with RESHEVSKY and KAVALEK, for the more important closed US championship in 1972. Because it was a zonal tournament there had to be a play-off, which Byrne won (+2=2). However, his second place (+5=5−1), shared with Reshevsky, behind FISCHER, in 1965 was perhaps a more meritorious result. Byrne played in many Olympiads from 1952, making the best third-board score (+9=6) at Leipzig in 1960.

Towards the end of the 1960s Byrne gave up his position as a college lecturer to become a chess professional and later an excellent columnist in the *New York Times*. His best win in international events was Torremolinos 1976 (+6=7), but more importantly he was third (+9=7−1), after KORCHNOI and KARPOV, ahead of LARSEN, TAL, and TAIMANOV, in the stronger Leningrad interzonal 1973. However, in the ensuing CANDIDATES quarter-final match he lost to Spassky. In the next interzonal, Biel 1976, Byrne again did well, finishing 5th

(+6=11−2) equal with SMYSLOV and HÜBNER, but half a point out of contention for a Candidate place.

Byrne's brother, Donald (1930–76), won the US Open Championship in 1953, and played for the USA in three Olympiads (1962, 1964, 1968).

Larsen–Byrne Leningrad Interzonal 1973 King's Indian Defence Sämisch Variation

1 c4 g6 2 d4 Nf6 3 Nc3 Bg7 4 e4 d6 5 f3 a6 6 Be3 c6 7 c5 0-0 8 Nge2 Nbd7 9 Nc1 b5 10 Be2 dxc5 11 dxc5 Ne5 12 Qc2 Be6 13 0-0 Bc4 14 Rd1 Qc7 15 b3 Bxe2 16 N1xe2 Rfd8 17 h3 Rxd1+ 18 Rxd1 Rd8 19 f4 Rxd1+ 20 Qxd1 Ned7 21 e5 Ne8 22 b4 Nb8 23 a4 Qd7 24 Nd4 Nc7 25 Qb3

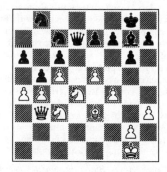

25 ... g5 26 fxg5 Bxe5 27 Nf3 Bxc3 28 Qxc3 Qd1+ 29 Kh2 Nd5 30 Qe5 Nd7 31 Qe4 Qe2 White resigns.

Byrne Variation, 506, a sound line against the NAJDORF VARIATION of the SICILIAN DEFENCE named after Robert BYRNE; 534 in the SICILIAN DEFENCE, played by Donald Byrne (1930–76) in the US championship, 1962.

C

cable match, a match at TELEGRAPH CHESS using electric cable and for which players are present throughout the playing session. The most famous matches of this kind were between Great Britain and the USA. The first, between the British Chess Club and the Manhattan Chess Club in 1895, was marred by inexperience of the medium. Only about 22 moves were played in each of the ten games, of which one was agreed drawn and the others adjudicated as drawn by the referee LASKER. The series is regarded as having begun properly with the 1896 match, and as time went by the teams came to be looked upon as national sides. The competitors included MARSHALL, PILLSBURY, and SHOWALTER for the USA, ATKINS, BLACKBURNE, BURN, and MASON for Great Britain. The series of thirteen matches ended when Britain won in three consecutive years (1909–11) and retained the cup presented by Sir George Newnes (1851–1910). In total the score in games was 64:64, in matches one drawn and six wins each.

A series of Anglo-American university matches was played 1899–1903, 1906–1910, and 1924; each side won four and three were drawn. From 1926 to 1931 a series of matches was played between London and a city of the United States. A match between the House of Commons and the House of Representatives in 1897 was drawn.

Café de la Régence, Paris, perhaps the most famous of meeting places for chess players. Opened around 1688, and named in 1718, the café was one of the first in Europe. Around 1740 chess players moved there from the Café Procope and in the following hundred years it was frequented by LEGALL, PHILIDOR, DESCHAPELLES, BOURDONNAIS, and SAINT-AMANT as well as amateurs such as Voltaire, Rousseau, Robespierre, FRANKLIN, and Napoleon. Its last great days were in the 1850s when MORPHY played there. The Café was relocated in 1855 but after 1916, when the chess room was closed, ceased to have any chess importance.

Cafferty, Bernard (1934–), British Correspondence Chess Champion 1960, editor of the *British Chess Magazine* from 1981.

Caillaud, Michel (1957–), French problemist, International Solving Master (1987), International Master for Chess Compositions (1989). He specializes in fairy problems, and is one of the world's leaders in this field. (See CHINESE FAMILY; STOCCHI THEME.)

Caïssa, the muse or goddess of chess, originally a nymph in a poem of that name composed by JONES in 1763. After a description of the game the nymph is introduced:

> A lovely Dryad rang'd the Thracian wild,
>   Her air enchanting, and her aspect mild:
> To chase the bounding hart was all her joy,
>   Adverse from Hymen and the Cyprian boy:
> O'er hills and valleys was her beauty fam'd,
>   And fair Caïssa was the damsel nam'd.

It is modelled on VIDA'S *Scacchia ludus* in which the nymph is called Scacchis. Mars, whose love for the nymph is not returned, persuades the god of sport to invent a game (chess) that might soften her heart.

Calabrian Counter-gambit, 651. Given by POLERIO, named after GRECO's homeland, it was analysed in detail by ALLGAIER. This dubious defence has had no place in master chess for more than a century.

Calabrian Gambit, 1146, the GRECO GAMBIT.

Caldas Vianna Variation, 805, the RIO DE JANEIRO VARIATION, whose inventor is remembered in this less common name.

Calvi, Ignazio (1797–1872), Italian player and composer. During a stay of about 4 years in France as a political refugee he became a leading player and teacher at the CAFÉ DE LA RÉGENCE and was able to save 40,000 francs, an astonishing sum for the time. In 1845 he drew a match (+ 7 = 1 − 7) with KIESERITZKY. His many contributions to *Le Palamède* include openings analyses and original compositions. Returning to Italy he joined the army in 1848, rose to the rank of major, retired in 1862, and, putting to use his early training in chemistry, became a pharmacist.

+

A version of a study by Calvi (*Le Palamède*, 1836) showing, perhaps for the first time, two different UNDERPROMOTIONS. 1 g8 = N Bxe3 2 h8 = B Nd4 3 Ne7 Bd2 4 Nd5, and not 2 h8 = Q? Nd4 3 Ne7 Nc2 + 4 Bxc2 Bd4 + 5 Qxd4 stalemate.

Calvi Variation, 654, the PONZIANI GAMBIT; 1176, the STAMMA GAMBIT.

Cambridge Springs Defence, 176, sometimes called the Pillsbury Variation, in the QUEEN'S GAMBIT Declined. Black counterattacks on the queen's-side, which cannot be defended by White's DARK BISHOP for this is outside the PAWN CHAIN on the other side. Introduced in a game against Albert Beauregard Hodges (1861–1944) in 1892, this defence was used several times during the tournament held in 1904 at Cambridge Springs (a spa in Pennsylvania). In the world championship match of 1927 ALEKHINE used the defence five times, but since then it has occurred less often, partly because White usually plays the EXCHANGE VARIATION.

Camel, an unorthodox LEAPER used in some forms of GREAT CHESS. The co-ordinates of its leaps are 3,1, and the length of its move √10. A camel attacks from two to eight squares on the normal board depending on its position. If placed on d4 it would attack a3, a5, c7, e7, g5, g3, e1, and c1. (In Tibet and Mongolia camel is the name used for the bishop.)

Campbell Variation, 1153, a reply, also known as the Brentano Defence or Morphy Variation, to the KIESERITZKY GAMBIT, recommended by Campbell in *Chess World*, 1865. He did not give an exact sequence, but proposed d7-d5 as Black's fifth move.

Joseph Graham Campbell (1830–91), one of London's strongest players, was a problemist of note and achieved some notoriety through a problem tourney run in connection with the London 1862 tournament. A prize of £20 was offered for the best set of six problems, £10 for the second best set, etc. Campbell was given the first prize but then one of his compositions was found to be COOKED, and he was declared second-prize winner. The decision was published only for the public to point out that another problem was faulty, and Campbell was struck from the prize list. He refused to pay back the prize money and the angry committee had to provide from their own pockets for the new first prize winner (BAYER).

Campomanes, Florencio (1927–), a Filipino who represented his country at first board in the Leipzig OLYMPIAD, 1960. In 1982 he succeeded ÓLAFSSON as president of FIDE and, during a period of tension between both individuals and groups, displayed exceptional political flair.

Cámpora, Daniel Hugo (1957–), Argentinian champion 1986 and 1989, International Grandmas-

ter (1986), winner of tournaments at Tuzla 1983 (+7=2−2), Niš 1985, Pančevo (+7=6), also 1985, Biel 1989, and third (+5=6−3) at the much stronger Biel 1987.

Canal, Esteban (1896–1981), Peruvian-born player who spent much of his life in Europe. As a thirteen-year-old student he travelled to Europe, first to Spain and then, two years later, to France. After a spell in Belgium he moved to Germany in 1914 where he learned chess and first became known as a player when he won the championship of Leipzig in 1916. In 1917, while in Switzerland, he played a number of serious games with TEICHMANN and H. Johner, with mixed results.

After the war Canal made Italy his home, and he made his international debut at Trieste 1923, taking second place after Hans Johner, and ahead of YATES and TARRASCH. He moved to Budapest around 1930, and achieved his best results in 1933 when he came third, after E. STEINER and ELISKASES, at Kecskemét, and took first prize ahead of LILIENTHAL, L. STEINER, Eliskases, and E. Steiner at Budapest. In the mid-1930s he went back to Peru, but returned to play for his country at the Dubrovnik Olympiad, 1950, and compete in a number of minor events. In 1977 he was made honorary International Grandmaster.

L. Steiner–Canal   Ostrava 1933   Queen's Gambit Declined
Slav Defence

1 d4 d5 2 c4 c6 3 Nf3 Nf6 4 Nc3 dxc4 5 a4 Bf5 6 Ne5 Na6 7 f3 Nd7 8 Nxc4 e5 9 e4 exd4 10 exf5 dxc3 11 bxc3 Qf6 12 Qc2 Nb4 13 Qe4+ Be7 14 Bd2 0-0-0 15 Qb1

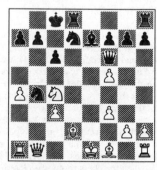

15 ... Ne5 16 cxb4 Nxc4 17 Bxc4 Qh4+ 18 g3 Qxc4 19 Qe4 Qxe4+ 20 fxe4 Rd4 21 b5 Rxe4+ 22 Kf2 Re5 23 g4 Rd8 24 Bf4 Bc5+ 25 Kg2 Re2+ 26 Kh3 Bd6 27 Bg3 Bxg3 28 hxg3 g5 29 bxc6 Rd6 30 cxb7+ Kb8 White resigns.

Canal Variation, 926 in the ITALIAN OPENING, reintroduced by CANAL in 1929 with a new idea in mind (6 ... h6 7 Bxf6 Qxf6 8 Nd5 Qd8 9 c3); 951 in the TWO KNIGHTS DEFENCE, as Canal–Johner, Trieste 1923; 172, the VENICE VARIATION of the QUEEN'S GAMBIT Declined; 1267, the BALOGH ATTACK in the ALEKHINE DEFENCE.

candidate, (1) one of a group of players who competes in the final eliminating contest for the right to challenge the world champion. To become a candidate a player must qualify in a manner prescribed by FIDE, originally through an INTERZONAL TOURNAMENT. To decide who should be challenger five Candidates tournaments were held (winners in brackets): Budapest 1950 (BRONSTEIN after a play-off), Neuhausen–Zurich 1953 (SMYSLOV), Amsterdam 1956 (Smyslov), Bled–Zagreb–Belgrade 1959 (TAL), and Curaçao 1962 (PETROSYAN). Since then Candidates have played matches on a knock-out basis. The winners of the final matches who thus became challengers are SPASSKY (1965, 1968), FISCHER (1971), KARPOV (1974), KORCHNOI (1977, 1980), KASPAROV (1984), and Karpov (1987, 1990).

candidate, (2) NIMZOWITSCH'S name for a HALF-PASSED PAWN.

candidate, (3) a move selected for consideration. In *Think Like a Grandmaster*, KOTOV explains the process of analysing only candidate moves. The ability to select the right candidates is a measure of playing strength.

Candidate Master, a national title in some countries, ranking immediately below that of National Master.

Capablanca, José Raúl (1888–1942), World Champion 1921–7. Born in Cuba, the second surviving son of an army officer, he learnt chess at the age of four, but was not allowed to play frequently until the autumn of 1901, when he defeated Juan Corzo (1873–1941) in an informal match (+4−6−3). Four months later, when Corzo won the national championship, Capablanca took fourth place.

A Cuban industrialist, seeking management talent, offered to pay for Capablanca's education in the USA, and there he went to school in 1904 and to Columbia University in 1906. During term and holiday alike Capablanca spent much spare time at the Manhattan Chess Club, where he played hundreds of friendly games against the leading players of New York. There too he played many games against LASKER, then world champion, from whom he learned to approach the game pragmatically, rather than with the preconceived ideas that characterized the teachings of TARRASCH. Even in his student days Capablanca showed outstanding endgame skill and an extraordinary quick SIGHT OF THE BOARD. (Writing *c*.1946, ALEKHINE stated that he had never seen in any other player such a 'flabbergasting quickness of chess comprehension'.) Capablanca was studying engineering, which he found onerous, especially disliking draughtsmanship, because the drawings which had to be prepared so carefully would have no use after the machines had been made from them; whatever ends he sought he found the means tedious, and often skimped them: in short, he was lazy. A chess-playing classmate, Louis Jacob Wolff (1886–1985), remarked that Capablanca never 'learnt to learn'; even at chess he wanted only to play, and he never studied books on the game.

Early in 1908 his patron, believing (correctly) that Capablanca was giving too much time to chess, withdrew his support. Capablanca attempted to live by means of chess and, feeling a duty towards his parents, to continue his studies; but chess got the upper hand, and he was dropped (sent down) in November 1908. His earnings were meagre and he suffered hardship, but he would not return home until he had made some kind of success at chess. An unexpected opportunity came in 1909. Needing money after an unprofitable trip to Europe, MARSHALL agreed to a match, expecting easy victory. Capablanca won decisively (+8=14−1), an achievement without precedent for one with so little experience of serious play, and he went home, an established master, to a rapturous reception. Capablanca was invited, at Marshall's insistence, to play at San Sebastián 1911, one of the strongest five tournaments held up to that time. He was first (+6=7−1) ahead of RUBINSTEIN, VIDMAR, and SCHLECHTER. Winning a major tournament at his first attempt is a distinction he shares only with PILLSBURY.

Capablanca challenged the world champion in 1911. Lasker replied with 17 conditions, some of which (summarized) were as follows: 1. The match to be for six games up, draws not counting, and to consist of not more than thirty games in all. 2. If

A portrait of Capablanca made in 1938

after thirty games either player should lead by 3:2, 2:1, or 1:0 (in terms of won games) the match should be declared drawn and Lasker would retain the title. 6. Lasker would give four weeks' notice of the date for the commencement of play and two weeks' notice if he decided to change the venue. 9. The time limit to be twelve moves an hour. 10. The playing sessions to be no longer than two and a half hours. Capablanca objected to these conditions and one or two others, and referred to the 'obvious unfairness' of a match limited to thirty games. Lasker, claiming that 'obvious' meant 'deliberate', broke off and refused to renew negotiations.

In September 1913 Capablanca obtained a post in the Cuban Foreign Office, thus relieving him from the necessity of earning a living at chess. He had no specific duties, but was expected to act as a kind of ambassador-at-large, a well-known figure who would put Cuba on the map wherever he travelled. His passport describes him as 5ft. 8in., of dark complexion, blue-eyed, clean-shaven, with black hair. Well fitted for the part, he dressed immaculately, bore himself well, had a natural reserve, a sense of honour and duty ('his word was his bond', said Lasker), and was both courteous and charming. In October he commenced his famous tour of Europe, visiting many cities and playing short matches or exhibition games against leading masters, scoring $+19=4-1$. Staying in his country's embassies he met the 'best people' (Lasker), and was the 'darling of the ladies' (Alekhine); he enjoyed such company, in which he conducted himself well.

In 1914 Capablanca played in the strong St Petersburg tournament, and met Lasker in serious play for the first time. Capablanca forged ahead in the preliminaries to lead by one and a half points $(+6=4)$, but he lost a historic game to Lasker in the finals. Lasker made a questionable pawn advance, and noted that he saw his opponent relax, confident of his advantage; Capablanca's judgement was sound, but his lack of application fatal. Upset by this reverse, he blundered and lost to Tarrasch in the next round. Thus Lasker won $(+10=7-1)$, narrowly ahead of Capablanca $(+10=6-2)$. A crestfallen Capablanca was consoled by the renewed prospect of a championship match which, however, was thwarted by the outbreak of war. Lasker's magnificent finish $(+6=2$ in the finals) impressed Capablanca who came to admire Lasker above all other players, a sentiment that was reciprocated. Capablanca realized that talent alone was not enough; that any deficiencies of Lasker in this respect were balanced or even outweighed by his skill in manœuvre, his tactical awareness, and not least by his great strength of character.

With new resolve, Capablanca strengthened his play to such effect that he lost only one game in the next ten years. He earned the soubriquet 'the chess machine', a compliment and not, as it might seem today, a reference to lack of imagination. He won three strong wartime tournaments at New York:

1915 $(+12=2)$, 1916, and 1918 $(+9=3)$; and in 1919 he crushed KOSTIĆ in a match $(+5)$. Lasker, challenged again, 'resigned' the title to Capablanca in 1920, but the public wanted a match. It took place at Havana in 1921 for a then record stake of $25,000, just over half of which was paid to Lasker. Playing impeccably, Capablanca won $(+4=10)$, the most decisive victory ever obtained by a challenger for the world championship.

He remained in Cuba, where he married Gloria Simoni Beautucourt in December 1921. A son, José Raúl, was born in 1923, a daughter, Gloria, in 1925. In 1922 he played in the London tournament and was first $(+11=4)$, one and a half points ahead of Alekhine, who was followed by Vidmar, Rubinstein, and BOGOLJUBOW. Capablanca found the going hard, but this experience did not prevent him from presuming upon his talents in subsequent tournaments. Sometimes he attended when out of practice, and met with less success. At the strong tournament in New York 1924 he came second $(+10=9-1)$ to Lasker and ahead of Alekhine; at Moscow 1925 he came only third $(+9=9-2)$, after Bogoljubow and Lasker; but he was first $(+8=12)$, two and a half points ahead of Alekhine, in the quadruple-round tournament at New York 1927, from which only Lasker of the world's best players was absent. Winning this tournament with ease, Capablanca conceded several draws in positions that favoured him.

Capablanca was regarded as practically invincible. Of the 158 match and tournament games he had played since his defeat by Tarrasch in 1914 he had lost only four. His name was recognized by millions who had little or no knowledge of chess, a distinction shared only by PHILIDOR, MORPHY, and FISCHER. Although universally admired, Capablanca had no close friends among the other players, from whom he seemed to distance himself. The leading simultaneous player of his time, he visited many clubs to play his games, collect his fee, and depart without stopping to talk to the players, as Lasker or Alekhine might have done. Nor did he discuss his games with other masters. When not playing he preferred tennis, bridge, reading, or the life of a playboy.

He accepted challenges from Rubinstein and NIMZOWITSCH, but neither was able to raise the stake money, $10,000 (see LONDON RULES). In 1927, however, Capablanca and Alekhine agreed to a match, having raised the stakes by their joint influence in Argentina; the match took place towards the end of 1927. To almost universal surprise, Capablanca lost, $+3=25-6$. Years later Alekhine wrote: 'I did not believe I was superior to him. Perhaps the chief reason for his defeat was the overestimation of his own powers arising out of his overwhelming victory in New York, 1927, and his underestimation of mine.

The years 1928 to 1931 were not happy for Capablanca. His marriage was foundering, his title lost. Based in Paris for most of this time, he strove in vain for a return match. He played in nine tournaments, winning six of them (including Berlin, Oct. 1928, +5=7), but failing in two other major tournaments: Bad Kissingen 1928, second (+4=6−1), after Bogoljubow; and Carlsbad 1929, second (+10=9−2) equal with SPIELMANN, after Nimzowitsch. Capablanca came second (+5=3−1) to EUWE in a small tournament at Hastings 1930–1, and shortly afterwards these two met in match play, Capablanca winning +2=8. He then practically retired from the game for more than three years.

Resuming play, he failed in two tournaments, taking fourth place at Hastings 1934–5, and fourth (+7=10−2), after BOTVINNIK, FLOHR, and Lasker, at Moscow 1935. In 1936, however, he made a real effort, winning (+8=10) the strong Moscow tournament one point ahead of Botvinnik, and, at the even stronger tournament at Nottingham, scoring +7=6−1 to tie with Botvinnik, ahead of Euwe (then world champion), FINE, RESHEVSKY, Alekhine (whom he defeated), and Flohr. But chess was no longer easy for him. There were more world-class players, the study of the openings (an idea which would have appalled him) was becoming of greater consequence, and, worse, he was suffering from high blood pressure.

A year or so later he obtained a divorce from his first wife, whose family succeeded in having Capablanca demoted to the post of commercial attaché; he was obliged, for the first time, to do a little work at the office, which, said his second wife, Olga Chagodayev (née Choubarov), he carried out conscientiously. Halfway through the great AVRO tournament of 1938 he suffered a slight stroke, and scored only three draws in the last six games, taking seventh place out of eight. His last serious games were at the Buenos Aires Olympiad 1939, when he played first board for the Cuban team. He died of a stroke in New York.

Alekhine wrote that the world would never see the like of such a genius again; Botvinnik said that of all the players he met, Capablanca made the greatest impression, and another world champion, Euwe, wrote in 1975, 'I honestly feel very humble when I study Capablanca's games.' He played in 29 strong tournaments, winning or sharing 15 first and 9 second prizes. In match, team match, and tournament play from 1909 to 1939 he scored +318=249−34, and he is known to have played 42 exhibition games (+38=4) and 31 consultation games (+22=9). No other master sustained so few losses.

Capablanca's style was direct and classical. He liked to have everything under control and would steer his way through complications to bring about a clear position, retaining only those elements that could be used to maintain or lead to advantage. And he possessed the necessary concomitants: faultless JUDGEMENT OF POSITION and unrivalled endgame skill. He never dissembled; and against his strongest opponents he never speculated, embarking upon a COMBINATION only when he could foresee every possibility. Of his rapid judgement many

tales are told. Botvinnik recalled that he and RAGO-ZIN, after 'thorough analysis' of a position, consulted Capablanca who listened, smiled, shook his head, and immediately pinpointed their errors: 'We went into a long analysis and it turned out that Capablanca was right.' (See MYSTERIOUS ROOK MOVE; POSITIONAL SACRIFICE; SIMPLIFICATION.)

The best known books by Capablanca are *My Chess Career* (1920) and *Chess Fundamentals* (1921). The former is an autobiography in which his candour and honesty were taken for conceit, and the latter is an instructional book which included six of the ten losses he had sustained up to that time. He also wrote a textbook in Spanish (1913), a book of the Havana tournament of 1913, and *A Primer of Chess* (1935). He gave a series of chess lectures on the radio which were published posthumously.

H. Golombek, *Capablanca's Hundred Best Games of Chess* (1947); M. Euwe and L. Prins, *Het schaakphenomeen José Raoul Capablanca* (1949); J. Gilchrist and D. Hooper, *Weltgeschichte des Schachs: Capablanca* (1963) contains 571 match and tournament games; D. Brandreth and D. Hooper, *The Unknown Capablanca* (1975) contains 209 games complementing those in the Gilchrist and Hooper book; A. I. Sizonenko, *Capablanca vstrechi c Rossiey* (1988) and V. & I. Linder, *Capablanca v Rossy* (1988) both deal with Capablanca's visits to the USSR; E. Winter, *Capablanca* (1989), is a meticulously researched and definitive compilation of archival materials including Capablanca's writings and many game annotations by him.

Capablanca–Janowski San Sebastián 1911 Queen's Gambit Declined Tarrasch Defence

1 d4 d5 2 e3 Nf6 3 Nf3 c5 4 c4 e6 5 Nc3 Be7 6 dxc5 0-0 7 a3 Bxc5 8 b4 Be7 9 Bb2 a5 10 b5 b6 11 cxd5 exd5 12 Nd4 Bd6 13 Be2 Be6 14 Bf3 Ra7 15 0-0 Rc7 16 Qb3 Nbd7 17 Rfd1 Ne5 18 Be2 Qe7 19 Racl Rfc8 20 Na4 Rxc1 21 Rxc1 Rxc1+ 22 Bxc1 Ne4 23 Bb2 Nc4 24 Bxc4 Bxh2+ 25 Kxh2 Qh4+ 26 Kg1 Qxf2+ 27 Kh2 Qg3+ 28 Kg1 dxc4 29 Qc2 Qxe3+ 30 Kh2 Qg3+ 31 Kg1 Qe1+ 32 Kh2 Qg3+ 33 Kg1 Qe1+ 34 Kh2 Nf6 35 Nxe6 Qh4+ 36 Kg1 Qe1+ 37 Kh2 Qh4+ 38 Kg1 Ng4 39 Qd2 Qh2+ 40 Kf1 Qh1+ 41 Ke2 Qxg2+ 42 Kd1 Nf2+ 43 Kc2 Qg6+ 44 Kc1 Qg1+ 45 Kc2 Qg6+ 46 Kc1 Nd3+ 47 Kb1 fxe6 48 Qc2? h5 49 Bd4 h4 50 Bxb6 h3 51 Bc7 e5 52 b6 Qe4 53 Bxe5 Qe1+? (53 ... Qh1+ wins) 54 Ka2 Nxe5? (54 ... Nc1+ draws)

55 b7 Nd7   56 Nc5 Nb8   57 Qxc4+ Kh8   58 Ne4 Kh7   59 Qd3 g6   60 Qxh3+ Kg7   61 Qf3 Qc1   62 Qf6+ Kh7   63 Qf7+ Kh6   64 Qf8+ Kh5   65 Qh8+ Kg4   66 Qc8+ Black resigns.

Capablanca Anti-Cambridge, 174, a move, preventing the CAMBRIDGE SPRINGS DEFENCE, played by CAPABLANCA and later by ALEKHINE in their world championship match, 1927.

Capablanca Freeing Manœuvre, 198 in the QUEEN'S GAMBIT Declined (play might continue 10 Bxe7 Qxe7   11 0-0 Nxc3   12 Rxc3 e5). Around 1917 CAPABLANCA was seeking a way by which Black could complete his development without the need to advance and perhaps weaken his queen's-side pawns. He came up with an idea (beginning 7 . . . c6) that had been tried by SHOWALTER in the 1890s, and this became the main line of the ORTHODOX DEFENCE, supplanting the older fianchetto 7 . . . b6. The manœuvre is sometimes known as the Showalter–Capablanca System.

Capablanca Variation, 23 in the ENGLISH OPENING, as Capablanca–Reshevsky, Semmering–Baden 1937, an idea that came into popularity in the 1970s. In his other games with this opening CAPABLANCA fianchettoed on the king's-side before playing Pd2-d3; 181 in the CAMBRIDGE SPRINGS DEFENCE, played in Capablanca–Ed. Lasker, New York 1924; 190, an attacking line in the QUEEN'S GAMBIT Declined introduced by Capablanca against TEICHMANN at Berlin in 1913; 214, in the same opening, introduced by Capablanca, also in 1913, this time in an exhibition game with ALEKHINE; 300 in the NIMZO-INDIAN DEFENCE, as Johner–Capablanca, Carlsbad 1929; 390 in the GRÜNFELD DEFENCE, as Capablanca–Reshevsky, AVRO 1938; 842 in the SPANISH FOUR KNIGHTS GAME, as J. Bernstein–Capablanca, New York 1916.

Also the RUBINSTEIN VARIATION, reached through the CLASSICAL VARIATION (200) of the QGD; 309, the CLASSICAL VARIATION, and 313, the NOA VARIATION, of the Nimzo-Indian Defence; 572, another Classicial Variation, this time in the CARO-KANN DEFENCE; 1266, the KMOCH VARIATION in the ALEKHINE DEFENCE; 1290, the TORRE VARIATION in the RÉTI OPENING.

capped pawn, see PION COIFFÉ.

capture, a move that consists of playing a man to a square occupied by an enemy man, other than a king, and removing the enemy man from the board (for the only exception in orthodox chess, see EN PASSANT; for others see CHINESE CHESS, CIRCE CHESS, GRASSHOPPER, and RIFLE CHESS); to make such a move. Capturing is not compulsory unless there is no other legal move (except in some unorthodox games such as LOSING CHESS).

Carlsbad Variation, 92, a line in the SLAV DEFENCE that came into prominence during the tournament at Carlsbad (now Karlovy Vary) 1929; 194, in the QUEEN'S GAMBIT Declined, played many times at the Carlsbad tournament 1923, but known earlier; 273, a line, similar to the BLACKBURNE VARIATION of the DUTCH DEFENCE, played at the same event; 307 in the NIMZO-INDIAN DEFENCE, played by SPIELMANN at Carlsbad 1929; 446, a line in the SICILIAN DEFENCE first given by JAENISCH and played in the Carlsbad 1923 tournament. Also 467, the NIMZOWITSCH VARIATION of the SICILIAN DEFENCE, played at Carlsbad 1923 on its originator's only adoption.

Carls Variation, 29, the BREMEN VARIATION of the ENGLISH OPENING. Carl Carls (1880–1958) of Bremen analysed this line extensively at the beginning of the 20th century; 40, the FLOHR–MIKENAS VARIATION of the same opening—an old line.

Caro–Kann Defence, 567. Black's intention is to play 2 . . . d7-d5 challenging White's e-pawn (compare FRENCH DEFENCE). After 2 d4 d5   3 Nc3 or 3 Nd2, however, Black probably has nothing better than 3 . . . dxe4, giving up the centre. For this reason the prospects seem, at first sight, to be less satisfactory than those offered by the French Defence, but there is a compensating advantage: Black can develop the LIGHT BISHOP on the king's side (Bf5) after 4 Nxe4, the CLASSICAL VARIATION, or after 2 d4 d5   3 e5, the ADVANCE VARIATION. Other lines include the KNIGHT VARIATION favoured by NIMZOWITSCH, and the EXCHANGE VARIATION which is sometimes followed by the PANOV–BOTVINNIK ATTACK.

This defence, mentioned by POLERIO c.1590, was reintroduced in the 1880s, notably by WEISS who played it several times at Nuremberg 1883. The name refers to the British player Horatio Caro (1862–1920) and the Viennese player Marcus Kann (1820–86) whose recommendations appeared in the magazine *Brüderschaft* in 1886. However, the Caro–Kann was not accepted as a standard defence until its adoption by Nimzowitsch and CAPABLANCA, and was not played in a world championship match until used by BOTVINNIK in 1958. (See ARONIN; BISHOPS OF OPPOSITE COLOUR; DANGEROUS DIAGONAL; EUWE; ILLEGAL POSITION (1).)

Caro–Masi Defence, 592, a treatment of the CARO–KANN based on the ideas of the ALEKHINE DEFENCE, but here the pawn on c6 is not well placed. It was played three times at Bled 1931 by TARTAKOWER, who said that the line was very popular at the time in Buenos Aires. The champion of that city, Dr Masi Elizalde, was acknowledged in the name of the variation.

Caro Variation, 676, a line in the SPANISH OPENING played twice by Caro at Vienna 1898, but adopted many times previously by PAULSEN, and even earlier by STANLEY, after whom it is sometimes named; 815 in the PONZIANI OPENING, known since the 1850s and recommended by Caro in *Deutsches Wochen-*

schach, 1893; 1155 in the KIESERITZKY GAMBIT, recommended by Caro.

Carrera, Pietro (1573–1647), player and author from Militello, Sicily; priest. He is one of a group of writers who recorded the numerous new openings and variations developed by the great Italian masters of the late 16th century. (See GIANUTIO; GRECO; POLERIO; SALVIO.) Carrera's book *Il gioco degli scacchi* (1617) also has chapters dealing with the supposed origin of chess, the giving of odds, the practical endgame, problems, BLINDFOLD play, an unorthodox game on a board of 96 squares, and biographical information about many chessplayers of his own and earlier generations.

He also advises how a player should prepare for a hard match: 'He must abstain some days from meat to clear his brain as also to let blood, he should take both purgatives and emetics to drive the humours from his body, and he must above all be sure to confess his sins and receive spiritual absolution before sitting down to play in order to counteract the demoniacal influence of magic spells.' Although reputedly a less able analyst than Salvio, his outlook was more broadly based, his temper less arrogant, his book better arranged and hardly less informative. The greater part of this book was translated into English by LEWIS and published in 1822.

In 1634 Salvio bitterly attacked Carrera (see ABRAHAMS VARIATION). Carrera replied under a pseudonym in a pamphlet, *Riposta in difesa di D. Pietro Carrera contra l'Apologia di Alessandro Salvio* (1635), of which only ten copies, all incomplete, are known to exist.

Carrera Gambit, 1115, one of four queen moves (after 1 e4 e5 2 f4 exf4) examined by CARRERA; all have fallen out of use except 1175, the BREYER GAMBIT, which sometimes bears Carrera's name.

castle, (1) a colloquial name for the ROOK.

castle, (2) to make the move known as CASTLING.

castling, a combined move of the king and one of the rooks: the king is moved two squares along the first rank towards the rook which is then placed on the square crossed by the king. Castling is not permitted if (a) the king has been moved previously, (b) the rook has been moved previously, (c) the king is in check, (d) the square the king crosses or reaches is attacked, or (e) there is a piece of either colour between the king and the rook. Castling is allowed if the king has been in check, if the rook is under attack, or if the rook crosses a square controlled by an enemy man.

For castling on the king's side White plays Ke1-g1 and Rh1-f1; Black plays Ke8-g8 and Rh8-f8. Known as short castling, this is shown by the symbol 0-0 or 00. For queen's side or long castling White plays Ke1-c1 and Ra1-d1; Black plays Ke8-c8 and Ra8-d8, shown by the symbol 0-0-0 or 000.

Although both king and rook are moved castling is technically a move of the king, which should be touched first; or both king and rook may be touched simultaneously. Playing the rook first may lead to claims that only a rook's move is intended.

In SHAṬRANJ the king could be moved only one square in any direction. The first extension of its powers came in medieval times, perhaps in the 13th century. According to CESSOLE, a previously unmoved king at e1 could be played in one move to c1, c2, c3, d3, e3, f3, g3, g2, or g1, or could even make a longer leap to b1 or b2. There were however various restrictions and no widespread uniformity. (See POLERIO GAMBIT.) Castling was a natural development from this leap; LUCENA shows modern castling in two moves: 1 e4 e5 2 Nf3 Nc6 3 Bc4 Bc5 4 d3 Nf6 5 h3 d6 6 Bb5 a6 7 Ba4 Rf8 8 Nc3 Kg8 (the leap) 9 Be3 Bxe3 10 fxe3 h6 11 Qd2 Qe7 12 Rd1 Be6 13 Kc1 (the leap).

By the end of the 16th century castling was firmly established as a single move but there were 16 versions: Kf1 & Re1, Kg1 & Re1, Kg1 & Rf1, Kh1 & Re1, Kh1 & Rf1, Kh1 & Rg1 on the king's side and the 10 similar queen's side permutations. There were also regional versions. In some castling was forbidden if the moved rook would attack an enemy man, of if the king had been in check previously. In others a king could pass over an attacked square, or a player could castle a king that had been moved but not checked. Sometimes the g- or h-pawn could be moved at the same time. Ruy LÓPEZ, in his book of 1561, quoted castling as it is now played and this became generally established by the 17th century except in Italy, where many versions of castling remained in use until the 20th century. This 'free castling' aroused the sharp tongue of van der LINDE; 'free—as in free love', he said. By mistake or otherwise a player sometimes castles after the king has been moved away from and back to its square. A more frequent occurrence at master level is for an annotator to condemn a player for 'overlooking' castling when it would be illegal.

Hanspeter Suwe, 'Die historische Entwicklung der Rochade', in *Schachwissenschaftliche Forschungen*, Dec. 1975.

casual game, see FRIENDLY GAME; SKITTLES.

Catalan Opening, 357. White continues Bf1-g2 and Ng1-f3, moves that complete what is sometimes called the Catalan System, a standard opening since the 1930s. (The moves are not necessarily played in the sequence given.) At the Barcelona tournament in 1929 TARTAKOWER, as White, played the moves Pd4, Nf3, Pg3, and Bg2, and named the opening, which was not original, after the region. The move Pc2-c4 later became an essential part of the system, a means by which the range of White's LIGHT BISHOP might be extended. (See ALBURT; ALEKHINE; CHERNIN; STALEMATE.)

Catalan Queen's Gambit, 212. White's fourth move transposes from the QUEEN'S GAMBIT Declined to a line in the CATALAN OPENING.

categories, see CLASSIFICATION OF PLAYERS; TOURNAMENT CATEGORY.

Cavallotti Counter-gambit, 110, the ALBIN COUNTER-GAMBIT which first appeared in the Milan tournament 1881. Its originator, Mattia Cavallotti (c.1855–c.1915), edited a book of the event; he subsequently ran a chess column in the Milan papers *Lo Sport Illustrato* and *L'Illustrazione Italiana.*

Cebalo, Mišo (1945–), International Grandmaster (1985), tied for first place in the Yugoslav championship, 1985, but lost the play-off. Winner at Kavala 1985, Bern 1988, and Zagreb 1990 (Swiss system, 220 players), he won the supporting tournament at Reggio Emilia 1991.

centralization, the act of bringing pieces to the centre or moving them so that they control central squares. Queens, bishops, and knights are likely to gain mobility when placed on central squares, but rooks are less often moved there because they perform well from the edges of the board. In the endgame the king is often moved to the centre because it can then be brought more readily to any part of the board.

central zone, the 16 squares in the centre of the board.

centre, the area in the centre of the board varying from 4 squares (the basic centre) to 16 squares (the central zone); the PAWN CENTRE. The central squares are of major strategical importance throughout the game: in the opening, players struggle to control them; in the middlegame the central situation determines the course of play; in the endgame, pieces may be centralized ready for action on any part of the board. The manner in which the central squares are controlled normally depends upon the kind of pawn centre that the players contrive to bring about, but the central squares remain important even when all the centre pawns have been exchanged, a situation known as a VANISHED CENTRE.

Centre Attack, 735, a descriptive name for a line in the CLOSE DEFENCE to the SPANISH OPENING.

Centre Counter Game, 595, the SCANDINAVIAN OPENING.

Centre Game, 664, an opening dating back at least to 1590.

centre pawn, the d- or e-pawn.

Centre Pawn Opening, 607, an unusual opening, but played by Nicholas Menelaus MacLeod (1870–1965) 17 times in the New York 1889 tournament.

Centre Play Variation, 294 in the BUDAPEST DEFENCE, a graphic name for a line also known as the Alekhine Variation.

Ceriani, Luigi (1894–1969), Italian composer, doctor of engineering, manufacturer. Ceriani began composing around 1924 and became one of the world's leading exponents of the art of RETROGRADE ANALYSIS. His *32 Personaggi e 1 autore* (1955) is a book of 657 pages containing more than 400 problems of various kinds, most of them composed by him; and his *La genesi delle posizioni* (1969) contains 155 retro-analytical problems. The so-called Ceriani Theme refers to a problem in which there are two or more UNCAPTURES of pieces created by promotion, usually knights. For an example, see ONE-MOVER.

Ceron, Alfonso (16th cent.), also known as Zerone, Xeron, or Girone, Spanish player from Granada, reputedly the equal of Ruy LÓPEZ, and author of an unpublished chess book. In matches played in the court of Philip II of Spain around 1575 Ceron drew with LEONARDO of Calabria and lost to BOI of Sicily.

Cessole, Jacopo da (13th–14th cent.), Dominican monk who was the author of the most famous of chess MORALITIES. More than a hundred manuscript copies are extant. Caxton's famous *Game and Playe of the Chesse*, one of the first printed books in English and widely admired for the woodcuts of the second edition, was one of the numerous translations.

The appearance of Cessole's name in about 30 forms has led to assertions that he was French, Spanish, or Greek, but most likely he came from Cessole near Asti, Italy, and lived in Lombardy. In

An illustration from *The Game and playe of the chesse*, Caxton's translation of Cessole's *Liber de ludo scacchorum*

1317–18 he was in charge of the inquisition in Genoa.

In the last quarter of the 13th century Cessole gave a series of sermons using chess as a framework. Because they were so popular Cessole made a book of them, using *De Regimine Principum* by Egidius Romanus (Guido Colonna) as his basis. The result was *Liber de moribus Hominum et officiis Nobilum ac Popularium super ludo scacchorum*. The first of many printed versions appeared in Utrecht in 1473. Caxton's first edition was printed in Bruges around 1475, and the second edition in London around 1481.

Because Cessole wanted to extend his ALLEGORIES he gave each pawn a distinct character, which led some later readers to suppose, incorrectly, that real pawns were unmatched.

Chameleon Variation, 159 in the QUEEN'S GAMBIT Declined, a line where the consequence of castling on opposite wings can lead to a rapidly changing game.

Chandler, Murray Graham (1960–), International Grandmaster (1983). He won the New Zealand championship 1975–6 and then settled in England, subsequently playing for his adopted country in five OLYMPIADS, 1982–90, with good results, particularly at Novi Sad 1990 where his score of + 7 = 4 as first reserve was the second best rating performance in the whole Olympiad.

Chandler–Timman   Linares 1988   French Defence
Winawer Variation

1 e4 e6 2 d4 d5 3 Nc3 Bb4 4 e5 c5 5 a3 Bxc3 + 6 bxc3
Ne7 7 Qg4 Qc7 8 Qxg7 Rg8 9 Qxh7 cxd4 10 Ne2 Nbc6
11 f4 dxc3 12 Qd3 Bd7 13 Nxc3 a6 14 Ne2 Rc8 15 Rb1
Nf5 16 h3 Nce7 17 g4 Nh4 18 Nd4 Nc6 19 Nxc6 Qxc6
20 Rh2 Rh8

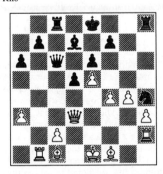

21 Kd1 Qc7 22 Qb3 Qc5 23 Qb6 Qxb6 24 Rxb6 Bc6 25
Rf2 d4 26 Bb2 Bd5 27 Bxd4 Nf3 28 c4 Be4 29 Rd6
Ng1 30 Kd2 Kf8 31 Ke3 Bc6 32 f5 exf5 33 Rxf5 Rh7
34 e6 Re8 35 Kf2 Nxh3 + 36 Bxh3 Rxh3 37 exf7 Rh2 +
38 Kg3 Black resigns. White delays his DEVELOPMENT while
STRONG SQUARES are being established.

In international tournaments his best results are: New York 1980, equal first (+4=6); Dortmund 1983 (+5=5−1), second equal with HORT, after ŞUBA; Amsterdam 1983 (Swiss) (+5=6), equal first; London 1984 (+6=4−3),

second equal with POLUGAYEVSKY, after KARPOV; London 1986 (+5=6−2), second equal with SHORT; Hastings 1986–7, first equal with LARSEN, LPUTYAN, and SPEELMAN; Linares 1988, fourth (+4=4−3) equal with LJUBOJEVIĆ, after TIMMAN, BELYAVSKY, and YUSUPOV; Wellington 1988, first (+5=5) equal with SPASSKY; Hastings 1990–1, second (+5=6−3) behind BAREYEV. Chandler has also been involved with *Tournament Chess*, and the London Chess Centre, and became editor-in-chief of the *British Chess Magazine* in 1991. (See ILLEGAL MOVE; KING HUNT.)

changed mate, see CHANGED PLAY.

changed play, the play in one PHASE of a problem that relates to play in another phase, usually in one of the following two ways: (1) changed mate: a black move may occur in two or more phases, and the mating replies (or continuations) differ in each case. For some examples, see BWEE; FOCAL PLAY; GOLDSCHMEDING; MYLLYNIEMI. (2) mate transference: a mating move occurs in two or more phases, and the preceding black moves differ in each case.

The minimum requirements for the Zagoruiko theme are changed mates for two moves in three phases. For an example, see PACHL. First shown by the English composer George Frederick Harold Packer (1886–1956) in 1919, the theme was named after the Soviet composer Leonid Ivanovich Zagoruiko (1923–), who won the USSR composition championship for three-movers for 1969–70.

The minimum requirements for the Rukhlis theme are two phases showing two changed mates and two mate transferences. For an example, see KELLER. The theme, named after the Soviet composer Yefim Naumovich Rukhlis (1925–), was first shown by the Australian composer Arthur James Mosely (1867–1930) in 1914. (See also CYCLIC PLAY; RECIPROCAL PLAY.)

First investigated extensively in the period 1910–20, largely by British composers, changed play has become a common feature of problems, often combined with other themes.

Charlick Gambit, 241, sometimes called the Englund Counterattack. Henry Charlick (1845–1916) introduced this dubious line in the early 1890s with the object of preventing White from playing a close game. He hoped to gain a lead in development after 2 dxe5 d6? e.g. 3 exd6? Bxd6; instead of 2 . . . d6 Black should play 2 . . . Nc6 as in the ENGLUND GAMBIT.

Charlick won the first tournament to decide the Australian championship, Adelaide 1887, but was the second player to hold the title. In 1885 F. K. Esling was recognized as champion after having won the only match game concluded before his opponent, GOSSIP, defaulted.

Charousek (pron. kharoosek), Rezsö (Rudolf) (1873–1900), law student, born in Bohemia and brought to Hungary when an infant, whose chess career was short but brilliant. He left a legacy of fine games, many of them stemming from gambits, which suited his attacking style. His first strong tournament was Nuremberg 1896, when he was brought in as a substitute for BURN. Subsequently he played in three other major events: Budapest 1896, first (+ 7 = 3 − 2) equal with CHIGORIN (who won the play-off), ahead of PILLSBURY, JANOWSKI, SCHLECHTER, and TARRASCH; Berlin 1897 (Sept.–Oct.), first (+ 12 = 5 − 2), ahead of Janowski, Schlechter, and Chigorin; Cologne 1898, second equal with Chigorin and W. Cohn, after Burn, ahead of STEINITZ, Schlechter, and Janowski. Throughout these years he suffered from tuberculosis, which caused his early death. He was attended by a Dr Sydlauer, whose son, Károly, played master chess under the name Takács.

P. W. Sergeant, *Charousek's Games of Chess* (1919) contains 146 games; L. Bachmann, *Rudolf Charousek* (2nd edn, 1930) is a collection of 101 games with German text; G. Barcza and A. Földeák, *Magyar sakktörténet* vol. 3 (1989), the major work on Hungarian chess history, includes a substantial section, pp. 33–91, on Charousek, with 127 games or part games.

Charousek–Janowski   Cologne 1898   Two Knights Defence

1 e4 e5 2 Nf3 Nc6 3 Bc4 Nf6 4 d3 Bc5 5 Nc3 d6 6 Bg5 h6 7 Be3 Bb6 8 Qd2 Bg4 9 0-0-0 Ba5 10 Qe2 Qd7 11 Nd5 Nxd5 12 Bxd5 Ne7 13 Bb3 c5 14 c3 Be6 15 Nd2 b5 16 f4 Bb6 17 Bxe6 Qxe6 18 Kb1 exf4 19 Bxf4 0-0 20 g4 a5 21 g5 h5 22 Rhe1 a4 23 c4 a3 24 cxb5 axb2 25 Nc4 Ba5

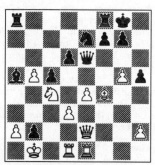

26 Bxd6 Bxe1 27 Qxe1 Rfd8 28 Bxc5 Ng6 29 Qc3 Nf4 30 Kxb2 Qd7 31 Qb3 Qh3 32 Bd6 Ne6 33 Qb4 Nd4 34 b6 Nc6 35 Qc5 Qd7 36 g6 fxg6 37 Bc7 Rf8 38 Qd5+ Qxd5 39 exd5 Nd8 40 Kb3 Nb7 41 a4 Rf5 42 Be5 Kf8 43 Kb4 Ke7 44 Ra1 Rff8 45 Rg1 Kf7 46 Rf1+ Ke7 47 Rxf8 Rxf8 48 a5 Rc8 49 Bc7 Black resigns.

Charousek Gambit, 1086 in the FALKBEER COUNTER-GAMBIT.

Charousek Variation, 666 in the CENTRE GAME, as Winawer–Charousek, Berlin 1897; 768, a rarely played line in the SPANISH OPENING tried by CHAROUSEK against MARÓCZY, Nagytétény 1897, and on a few other occasions; 1087 in the FALKBEER COUNTER-GAMBIT, as Charousek–Pillsbury, Nuremberg

1896, the natural continuation of the CHAROUSEK GAMBIT.

Chatard–Alekhine Attack, or Albin Attack, 1221, a popular line in the FRENCH DEFENCE originated by ALBIN in the 1890s and analysed a few years later by the French player Eugène Chatard (1850–1924). His analysis may have influenced ALEKHINE to play it against FAHRNI at Mannheim 1914, and so it is sometimes called the Alekhine Attack.

chatrang, the old Persian word for chess, derived from the Sanskrit CHATURANGA. Following the Islamic conquest of Persia in the 7th century the Arabic word SHAṬRANJ gradually gained ground.

chaturanga, the earliest precursor of modern chess that can be clearly defined. The Sanskrit name means 'quadripartite' and was also used to describe the Indian army of Vedic times in which a platoon had one elephant, one chariot, three soldiers on horseback, and five foot-soldiers. The 'army game' with its analogous elephants, horses, chariots, and pawns had the same name. The date of the game's origin is uncertain, but documentary evidence exists from *c.* AD 620. Claims for earlier accounts have proved mistaken. The men were rajah (king), mantri (counsellor, ancestor of the FERS), gaja (elephant, later called FĪL), asva (horse), ratha (chariot, later called rook), and pedati (infantry or pawns). For a description of the game see SHAṬRANJ, the Islamic version for which there is a greater abundance of evidence. On account of the false trail laid by FORBES, the ancestor of chaturanga was once thought to be a four-handed chess, no evidence of which exists before the 11th century.

check, the situation of a king under attack; to make such an attack. If a king is attacked it or its player are said to be in check and this must be relieved immediately. There are up to three possible ways. For example, after 1 e4 e5 2 f4 exf4 3 Nf3 Be7 4 Be2 Bh4+ , White may capture the checking piece (5 Nxh4), interpose a man (5 g3), or move the king (5 Kf1). A pinned piece may give check. A player may not castle to get out of check, nor move and remain in check. The two kings can never occupy adjoining squares. If a player cannot get out of check it is CHECKMATE and the game is over.

Until the early years of the 20th century a player was expected to announce a check; this was mandatory in some codes of law but is not required by the FIDE LAWS. Another long-standing practice, saying 'check to the queen' when it was attacked, was largely abandoned in the 19th century. For an older custom, see CHECK-ROOK. The word check is derived from the Persian shah, meaning king.

checkless chess, or prohibition chess, an UNORTHODOX CHESS game, dating from the middle of the 19th century, in which neither player may check except to give checkmate. The consequence of this special rule is that a player may use the king as an attacking piece, perhaps advancing it far into the enemy position. A king may be played so that it would be in check if a man were captured, and can thus protect a piece at a distance. For problems a FAIRY MATE is usually required.

checkmate, or mate, a position in which the king cannot be moved out of check; to make a move that brings about such a position. The object of the game is to checkmate one's opponent. When this happens the game ends and no subsequent event, e.g. a player's failure to stop the clock, can alter the result. According to article 11 of the LAWS there is no other way to win, although players usually resign when they believe that mate cannot be avoided sooner or later. However, in a competition the ARBITER may award victory to a player whose opponent exceeds the time limit or otherwise infringes the laws and rules.

Checkmate is a characteristic not found in other board games where SACRIFICE is justified only if material can be regained. In chess any number of men may be sacrificed, all kinds of advantages ceded, if checkmate can be given. The word is derived from the Persian shah, meaning king, and mat, meaning helpless or defeated.

check-rook, a term used, according to MURRAY, in the old game (that is, before the queen was introduced) for a move that both gave check and attacked the rook. The rook was then the most powerful piece and its capture by a lesser man was often decisive, as is often the case with a FAMILY CHECK in the modern game. The Mongol emperor TIMUR is said to have given a check-rook in a game when news arrived of the birth of a son and the completion of a new town by the river Jaxartes (Syr Darya in USSR). He gave both the son and the town the name, in Persian, of the move, Shah-rukh. This tale is from Herbelot's *Bibliothèque orientale* (1697), in which the author says that shah-rukh means a check given by a rook.

Chekhov, Valery Alexandrovich (1955–), Russian player, World Junior Champion 1975, International Grandmaster (1984). Chekhov won tournaments at Lvov 1983 (+6=7), Barcelona 1984, Leipzig 1988, Moscow 1988, and was second (+3=6) at the strong Berlin 1988 event.

Chekhover, Vitaly Alexandrovich (1908–65), Soviet player, composer, and analyst, International Master (1950), International Judge of Chess Compositions (1956), International Master for Chess Compositions (1961), musician and pianist. An active player in the 1930s, he achieved his best two tournament victories in 1936, both shared: with LISITSIN in the championship of the Trade Unions, and with RAUZER at Leningrad. He played five times in the USSR championship and several times in the Leningrad championship, which he won in 1949. In 1936, the year he turned to the composition of studies, he lost a match to KASPARYAN. In 1959 he published 70 of his studies together with 14 endgames from his play in *Shakhmatnye etyudy i okonchaniya*, and with KOROLKOV he wrote *Izbrannye etyudy A. A. Troitskogo* (1959). (See SYSTEMATIC MOVEMENT.)

Chekhover–Rabinovich Variation, 349, the FINE VARIATION in the QUEEN'S INDIAN DEFENCE, analysed by the Leningrad players CHEKHOVER and RABINOVICH in the 1930s, but first played in master chess by FINE.

Chekhover Variation, 542 in the SICILIAN DEFENCE, played Chekhover–Lisitsin, Leningrad 1938, but sometimes called the Szily or Hungarian Variation.

chekker, perhaps a kind of musical chessboard in the 15th century. Musicologists have not satisfactorily identified the nature of the instrument. A number of illustrations appear in a manuscript by Jean Charlier de Gerson (1363–1429). Each of the squares occupied by pieces and pawns on one side has a virtue attributed to it while those of the opposite side have negative qualities. How the board was made to emit music is unclear, but it was a keyboard of some kind, perhaps a kind of harpsichord. The term chekker may have been used for any kind of keyboard at that period, and it is possible that texts which have been thought to refer to chess may relate to a musical instrument.

A. Chicco, 'Uno "scacchiero" musicale', in *Scacchi e scienze applicate*, No. 5 (1987), pp. 6–7.

Chelyabinsk Variation, 489 in the SICILIAN DEFENCE. Although not new, the move owes much to two grandmasters from Chelyabinsk, SVESHNIKOV and Gennady Anatolievich Timoshchenko (1949–).

Chepizhny, Viktor Ivanovich (1934–), Ukrainian composer, International Judge of Chess Compositions (1965), International Grandmaster for Chess Compositions (1989). Trained as an engineer, he subsequently took a post as head of the chess department in a publishing house. He specializes in orthodox TWO- and THREE-MOVERS and has won the two-mover section of the seventh (1962–4), eighth (1965–6), ninth (1967–8), sixteenth (1981–2), and seventeenth (1983–4) USSR composing championships. (See PICKANINNY.)

Chernin, Alexander Mikhailovich (1960–), Soviet player, International Grandmaster (1985), European Junior Champion 1979–80. Chernin was equal first in the 1985 USSR championship, but lost the play-off. He was first at Copenhagen 1984, and at Polanica Zdrój 1988 (+8=5–1), but a better result was equal second (+1=10) at the very strong tournament at Reggio Emilia 1986–7. He won tournaments at Prague 1989 (+5=10), Dortmund 1990 (+7=4), and Altensteig 1990, and was second (+3=10) equal with ADAMS, KHALIFMAN, and HANSEN, after NUNN, at Wijk aan Zee 1991.

Chernin–Yudasin Sverdlovsk 1984 Catalan Opening

1 d4 Nf6 2 c4 e6 3 g3 d5 4 Bg2 dxc4 5 Nf3 b5 6 a4 c6
7 axb5 cxb5 8 Ne5 Nd5 9 Nc3 Bb4 10 0-0 Bxc3 11 e4
Bxb2

12 exd5 Bxa1 13 Ba3 a5 14 Qg4 b4 15 Qxg7 Rf8 16
Rxa1 bxa3 17 dxe6 Bxe6 18 Bxa8 Qxd4 19 Rb1 Nd7
20 Bc6 Qd6? (*Informator* recommends 20 ... a2) 21 Bxd7+
Bxd7 22 Nxc4 Qc5 23 Rb8+ Bc8 24 Rxc8+ Black
resigns.

Chéron, André (1895-1980), French player, analyst,
and composer, International Judge of Chess Compositions (1957), International Master for Chess
Compositions, *honoris causa* (1959). In his youth he
moved to the Swiss Alps on account of frail health
and from then on gave most of his time to the study
of chess. Champion of France in 1926, 1927, and
1929, he played for his country in the London
Olympiad 1927. He composed both studies and
problems, but above all he investigated the BASIC
ENDGAME. A four-volume treatise, *Lehr- und Handbuch der Endspiele* (1952–71), was the culmination
of many years' work. His aim was to present all
known information about the basic endgame,
together with a selection of the best studies that
relate to this phase. He drew from many sources
and added, without excessive modesty, a considerable contribution of his own. The work is essential
reading for students of the game.

+

A study by Chéron, *Journal de Genève*, 1964. 1 Nf4
d4 2 Bf6 e2 3 Nd3 Kc2 4 Ne1+ Kd2 5 Bh4 d3
6 Kg6 Kc3 7 Bd8 Kd2 8 Ba5+ Ke3 9 Kf5 d2
10 Bb6, an IDEAL MATE.

Chéron spent his last years assembling records in
the field of orthodox problems (he would not
countenance fairy chess), and published posthumously *Le Joueur d'échecs au pays de merveilles*
(1982), showing 564 diagrams of TASK compositions. 'You can't criticize a record', he said; 'you
either admire it or beat it.' (See KRAUSE VARIATION.)

chess blindness, see AMAUROSIS SCACHISTICA.

chess-board, see BOARD.

chess clock, see CLOCK.

Chess Collectors International, an organization set
up to further the aims of collectors with varied
interests, but primarily concerned with chess sets.
Meeting in Florida in 1984 a group of enthusiasts
decided there was a need for such a body, and
founded the CCI. Biennial gatherings since then
have been London in 1986, Munich in 1988,
New York 1990, and Paris 1992.

chessmen, or men, the pieces and pawns. Many
decorative sets have been made showing great
beauty, power, or wit. Made for ceremonial or
artistic purposes, they are outside the mainstream
of chess development, although they provide a life
interest for specialists such as members of CHESS
COLLECTORS INTERNATIONAL. Illustrations depicting
chess being played have, throughout the centuries,
shown only plain sets. Other than in CHINESE CHESS,
where all the men are the same flat shape (distinguished by ideograms) and SHOGI, sets have
always differentiated the men by shape. It is often
said that the shape of chessmen became simple
because of Muslim religious objection to the making of images of living creatures, but, with the
exception of the relatively recent horse's head for
the knight, this has always been the case with
playing sets. The main criteria have been simplicity
of design and ease of production. In more recent
centuries this has included the use of the lathe. The
SAINT GEORGE CHESSMEN and others of similar patterns were popular from the 18th century, but in the
second half of the 19th century STAUNTON CHESSMEN
became the standard design. (See also LEWIS CHESS-
MEN.)

Hans and Siegfried Wichmann, *Chess, the Story of
Chesspieces from Antiquity to Modern Times* (1964);
Victor Keats, *Chessmen for Collectors* (1985);
Michael Mark, *Chessmen Practical and Ornamental*
(1986).

Chiburdanidze, Maia Grigorievna (1961–),
USSR Women's Champion 1977, Women's World
Champion 1978–91, International Grandmaster
(1984). In addition to winning tournaments at New
Delhi 1984 and Banja Luka 1985, Chiburdanidze
was equal third (+2=7) at the strong Bilbao 1987.

Chicago Gambit, 1012, an unsound line, sometimes
called the Irish Gambit, played against PILLSBURY

in a simultaneous display, Chicago 1898. (See also SCHULTZE–MÜLLER GAMBIT.)

Chicco (pron. key-co), Adriano (1907–90), Italian chess historian and problem composer, International Judge of Chess Compositions (1956), International Master for Chess Compositions (1967), state advocate. He was the problem editor of *L'Italia Scacchistica* for 16 years and wrote *Il problema degli scacchi* (1943). The author of about 200 careful papers, mostly on chess history, he discovered a number of chess manuscripts, of which the most important is a CIVIS BONONIAE of 1454 from Modena. With the Italian IM Giorgio Porreca (1927–88) he wrote *Il Libro completo degli scacchi* (1959) and *Dizionario enciclopedico degli scacchi* (1971). With the Italian chess historian Alessandro Sanvito (1938–) he wrote *Lineamenti di una Bibliografia Italiana degli scacchi* (1987) and, with the Italian player Antonio Rosino (1942–), *Storia degli scacchi in Italia* (1990), a work which, with photographs, extends to more than 700 pages.

Chigorin, Mikhail Ivanovich (1850–1908), from about 1883 to 1898 one of the best four or five players in the world. Born near St Petersburg, he settled there after completing his education. His schoolteacher, one of KIESERITZKY'S boyhood friends, taught him the moves at the age of 16. Not at first attracted to the game, he finished his studies and took a government post. In 1873, however, he began to play in the Café Dominik, developed a passion for chess and not long afterwards gave up his job for the impecunious life of a chess professional.

After playing matches against SCHIFFERS in 1878 ($+7-3$ and $+6=1-7$), in 1879 ($+7=2-4$), and in 1880 ($+7=3-1$), and against ALAPIN in 1880 ($+7-3$), Chigorin was regarded as the best player in the city, if not in Russia. In his first international tournament (Berlin 1881) he shared third place with WINAWER, after BLACKBURNE and ZUKERTORT, and at the great London tournament of 1883 took fourth place after Zukertort, STEINITZ, and Blackburne, ahead of MASON, MACKENZIE, and Winawer. He played a prominent part in St Petersburg's victory in both games of a telegraph match against London 1886–7.

In 1889 Chigorin unsuccessfully challenged Steinitz for the world championship ($+6=1-10$). At New York, a month or so later, he shared first prize with WEISS in America's first international tournament, and in 1890 he drew a match with the third-prize winner GUNSBERG ($+9=5-9$). In two famous transatlantic telegraph games, 1890–1, Chigorin defeated Steinitz ($+2$). Of the many opening variations that Steinitz had advocated in his writings, Chigorin was permitted to choose two for these games, a circumstance that greatly favoured him. In 1892 Chigorin again challenged Steinitz and again lost ($+8=5-10$). In 1893 he drew with TARRASCH ($+9=4-9$) a fine series of games noted both for

their fighting quality and the clash of ideas. In 1895 he defeated Schiffers ($+7=3-3$).

Chigorin had now reached the highest point of his career, marked by his best two tournament achievements: Hastings 1895, second ($+14=4-3$), after PILLSBURY, ahead of LASKER, Tarrasch, and Steinitz; and Budapest 1896, first ($+7=3-2$) equal with CHAROUSEK, whom he defeated in a play-off ($+3-1$). In 1897 he played his sixth match against Schiffers ($+7=6-1$).

The best of his subsequent achievements were: Cologne 1898, second equal with Charousek and Wilhelm Cohn (1859–1913), after BURN; Monte Carlo 1901, third equal with SCHEVE, after JANOWSKI and SCHLECHTER; and Łódź 1906 (four players), second ($+5=1-3$), after RUBINSTEIN. Chigorin confirmed his position as Russia's leading player by winning the first three All-Russia tournaments (1899, 1900–1, 1903). After SALWE won the fourth in 1906, Chigorin defeated him in a match ($+7=3-5$). In 1907 he failed badly in tournament play, and while taking the cure at Carlsbad in the autumn was told that he had only a few months to live. At the very end of his life he returned to his estranged wife and his daughter, then living in Lublin; he died of diabetes in the following January.

Chigorin's style was marked by fine tactical skill and an imaginative approach to the problems of the opening phase. At Vienna 1903, when everyone had to play the unfashionable KING'S GAMBIT Accepted, he came first, well ahead of MARSHALL, Pillsbury, and MARÓCZY. Chigorin rejected the doctrinal approach of Steinitz and Tarrasch, but he accepted some of Steinitz's ideas, notably a belief in the soundness of the defensive centre, in which respect his investigations of the CLOSE DEFENCE to the SPANISH OPENING have proved of lasting value. He also pioneered some variations of the SLAV DEFENCE. His original talent produced many lively games, and Russians, both then and since, have regarded him as the founder of their so-called school of chess.

A burly man with a beard, Chigorin was 'decidedly handsome' although 'in difficult positions [he] gets very excited and at times seems quite fierce'. He was a 'bundle of nerves', writes Marshall, 'constantly swinging his crossed leg back and forth'. He was fond of drink, and in his world title matches was supplied with free brandy, the bottle standing by the chessboard. (Meanwhile Steinitz drank champagne for his nerves 'on doctor's orders'.)

Chigorin contributed significantly to the cause of chess in Russia, founding a chess club in St Petersburg, lecturing in many cities, and writing for several magazines and chess columns. Russia's second chess magazine, *Shakhmatny Listok* (1876–81), with a circulation of under 200, was subsidized by him, and he was the main support of two other magazines: *Shakhmatny Vestnik* (1885–7) and *Shakhmaty* (1894.) The founding of a national chess association, a cause he espoused, took place six years after his death. (See SCHOOLS OF CHESS.)

N. I. Grekov, *M. I. Chigorin* (1949) contains 350 games and biography, with text in Russian; I. Romanov, *Tvorcheskoe nasledie Chigorin* (1960) contains 177 games (complementing those in Grekov's book) and 90 pages of well researched biography; Jimmy Adams, *Mikhail Chigorin, the Creative Chess Genius* (1987) contains 100 games and biographical material taken from the above and other Russian sources; M. Yudovich, *Mikhail Chigorin* (1985) is a detailed examination, in Russian, of Chigorin's life and style of play.

Chigorin–Steinitz World Championship 1892 1st game
Evans Gambit

1 e4 e5   2 Nf3 Nc6   3 Bc4 Bc5   4 b4 Bxb4   5 c3 Ba5   6 0-0 d6   7 d4 Bg4   8 Bb5 exd4   9 cxd4 Bd7   10 Bb2 Nce7   11 Bxd7+ Qxd7   12 Na3 Nh6   13 Nc4 Bb6   14 a4 c6   15 e5 d5   16 Nd6+ Kf8   17 Ba3 Kg8   18 Rb1 Nhf5

19 Nxf7 Kxf7   20 e6+ Kxe6   21 Ne5 Qc8   22 Re1 Kf6   23 Qh5 g6   24 Bxe7+ Kxe7   25 Nxg6+ Kf6   26 Nxh8 Bxd4   27 Rb3 Qd7   28 Rf3 Rxh8   29 g4 Rg8   30 Qh6+ Rg6   31 Rxf5+ Black resigns.

Chigorin Defence, 109, an unusual way of declining the QUEEN'S GAMBIT, introduced by CHIGORIN towards the end of the 19th century. Also 224, apparently so named because of its resemblance to 109 rather than evidence that Chigorin played it; he played 2 ... Bg4 in several games, and perhaps that move has greater claims to being named after the Russian grandmaster.

Chigorin Indian Defence, 289, the OLD INDIAN DEFENCE.

Chigorin Variation, 54 in the QUEEN'S PAWN OPENING, sometimes called the Richter Variation, or sometimes named after PONZIANI who first analysed it. Also 148 in the SEMI-SLAV DEFENCE of the QUEEN'S GAMBIT Declined, favoured by Chigorin in the 1890s. Black's first six moves constitute the COLLE SYSTEM, a preparation for the advance of the king's pawn (... e6-e5).

In the STAUNTON GAMBIT, 262 as Gunsberg–Chigorin 10th match game 1890; 618, a VIENNA GAMBIT line played Chigorin–Winawer, Berlin 1897; 798 in the SPANISH OPENING, employed successfully in the 3rd match game Tarrasch–Chigorin 1893, and often used by the victor (also known from the game Minckwitz–Noa, Graz 1880); 1244, Chigorin's ingenious attack against the FRENCH DEFENCE, played by him in master chess more than 30 times.

Also 738 in the Spanish Opening. Chigorin polished ENGLISCH'S defensive system which involved the Black moves Nc6-a5 and Pc7-c5, shown in another form, 746, e.g. Duras–Chigorin, Nuremberg 1906, which may lead to 12 Nbd2 Nc6 (RUBINSTEIN VARIATION) 13 Nf1 (LASKER VARIATION), or, here, 13 dxc5 dxc5 (or 13 dxe5 dxe5) 14 a4 (RAUZER VARIATION); or 12 Nbd2 Bb7 (PANOV VARIATION). Instead of 746 Black can play 11 ... Nc6 (BORISENKO VARIATION), or 11 ... Nd7 (KERES VARIATION). (See SPASSKY; TAL.)

Chinese chess (*Xiangqi*), after international chess the most important variety of the game. The

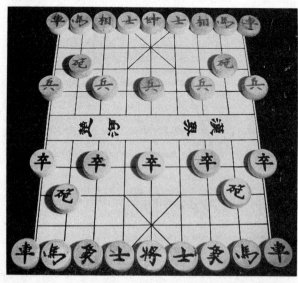

A Chinese set showing the array

modern Chinese form is here described. The men are moved on the line-intersections (points) of a board that has nine files and ten ranks. The space between the fifth and sixth ranks is called the river. Each side has a nine-point fortress, defined by diagonal lines. The men are shaped like draughtsmen, identified by characters on the face, and coloured red for the player who usually moves first, and green (or blue) for the opponent, often called black. (The beautifully carved Chinese sets to be found in antique shops were made for export.) The photograph shows the array; a description of the men and the way they move follows.

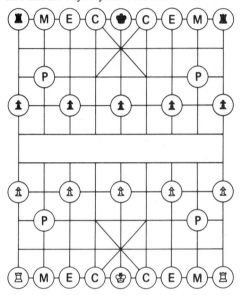

Chinese Chess array

The general, depicted as a king (K), has the move of a WAZIR but may not leave the fortress.
The counsellor (C), or mandarin, has the move of a FERS but is also confined to the fortress.
The elephant (E) is moved like the FĪL but can neither leap nor cross the river.
The horse has the same move as the MAO (M).
The chariot is the same as the ROOK (R).
The cannon is the same as the PAO (P).
The soldier, depicted in the diagram as a pawn, moves or captures one point directly forward, or, after crossing the river, one point sideways. On the tenth rank it can be moved sideways only. The pawn is not promoted.
The cannon was a 13th-century invention; the moves of the other men have much in common with those used in CHATURANGA.
A player can win either by mating the opposing general or by administering stalemate. Perpetual check is not permitted. Generals may not face each other with no man intervening. For example, a green king on e1 and a pawn on c9 would stalemate a red king at d10; add a green pawn at c10 and Red

is checkmated. The shortest game ending in mate: 1 Ph5 Phe8 2 Pg5 Pe9 3 Pxg10. These examples use extended STANDARD NOTATION, but the Chinese identify the files by numbers, 1 to 9, each player counting from the right-hand side.

Terence Donnelly, *Hsiang ch'i The Chinese Game of Chess* (1974); H. T. Lau, *Chinese Chess* (1985); for the more adventurous, *Chinese Chess Dictionary* (1985) (in Chinese).

Chinese family, four fairy chess pieces: the MAO and PAO, derived from CHINESE CHESS and introduced into fairy chess in 1935, the LEO and VAO, invented in 1947 and 1939 respectively.

·hp3 4sols

A HELP-STALEMATE (corrected) by CAILLAUD, first prize *Feenschach*, 1981. There is also a leo on c1, a pao on e3, a vao on g1, and maos on f8 and g3. Set-play: 1 fxg e1=Mao 2 gxf8=Pao Mao-g2 3 Pao-f2=. The four solutions together show the BABSON TASK.
1 e1 = Leo fxg7 2 Leoxb4 gxf8 = Leo 3 Leo-c4
　　　　　　　　　　　　　　　 Leo-b4 = (Black's leo is pinned)
1 e1 = Pao fxg7 2 Pao-c2 gxf8 = Pao 3 Pao g2
　　　　　　　　　　　　　　　　　　　 Pao-f2 =
1 e1 = Vao fxg7 2 Vaoxb4 gxf8 = Vao 3 Vao-a5
　　　　　　　　　　　　　　　　　　　 Vao-b4 =
1 e1 = Mao fxg7 2 Mao-f3 gxf8 = Mao 3 Mao-g5
　　　　　　　　　　　　　　　　 Mao-g6 = (Black's mao is pinned).

Chinese Variation, 238, a line in the PIRC DEFENCE played in the game Liu Wen Che–Donner, Buenos Aires Olympiad, 1978. It was the first defeat of a FIDE grandmaster by a Chinese player.

Christiansen, Larry Mark (1956–), International Grandmaster (1977), US Junior Champion 1973, 1974 (shared), and 1975, US Champion 1980 (shared with BROWNE and EVANS). He also shared the US Open Championship in 1983 with KORCHNOI. His best international results are: Linares 1979, first (+6=4−1), ahead of Korchnoi; Linares 1981, first (+6=4−1) equal with KARPOV; Reggio Emilia 1987–8, equal second (+3=5−1) with BELYAVSKY, half a point behind TUKMAKOV. In 1983 he became editor of *Players Chess News* but gave it up two years later in order to concentrate on becoming a CANDIDATE. However, although consistently among the best, Christiansen was not able to join the small group of players capable of making a serious challenge for the world championship.

Christiansen–Spassky Linares 1981 Queen's Gambit Declined Exchange Variation

1 d4 d5 2 c4 e6 3 Nc3 Nf6 4 cxd5 exd5 5 Bg5 Be7 6 e3 Nbd7 7 Bd3 0-0 8 Nge2 c6 9 Qc2 Re8 10 h3 Nf8 11 g4 Bd7 12 0-0-0 Rc8 13 Kb1 b5 14 Nf4 a5 15 Bf5 a4 16 Nd3 Bxf5 17 gxf5 N8d7 18 Rhg1 Bf8 19 Rg2 c5 20 dxc5 Nxc5 21 Nxc5 Rxc5 22 Qd3 Kh8

23 Ne4 Rxe4 24 Qxe4 Qc8 25 Qd3 Ne4 26 f3 Nxg5 27 Rxg5 Be7 28 f6 Bxf6 29 Rxd5 h6 30 Rxc5 Qxc5 31 Rc1 Black resigns.

Christmas Series, see WHITE, A. C.

cinema and chess. Some films have had chess as a central theme. The first significant one, *Chess Fever*, made in Moscow in 1925 during the international tournament, had CAPABLANCA in a leading role. Another silent film, *Le Joueur d'échecs*, France 1926, was about the TURK, and was so successful that it was made again in 1938, with sound. *White Snows of Russia* (1979) is a biography of ALEKHINE written by KOTOV and filmed in the USSR. Another biography, *Chess Games* (1964), is of DUCHAMP. *Die Schachnovelle*, Germany 1960, is from the story by Stefan Zweig (see LITERATURE AND CHESS). *Black and White as Day is Knight* studies paranoia in world chess champions using facts from the 1972 and 1978 title matches. *Return from the Ashes* (1965) revolves around a professional chessplayer. A Canadian documentary, *The Great Chess Movie*, was made in 1983, and *La Diagonale du Fou* in 1985. A film in Hindi and English, *The Chess Players* (1972), uses chess metaphorically to represent the break-up of a society. A collector's item among films using chess incidentally is *The Black Cat* (1934) in which Bela Lugosi and Boris Karloff play a game for which the stake is the life of an innocent girl. The erotic overtones of a game in *The Thomas Crown Affair* (1968) are also memorable; so, in a different way, is the image of the Knight playing against Death in medieval Sweden in *The Seventh Seal* (1957).

cinéma des échecs, a technique for printing a game by giving a diagram after each move, making it possible to follow a game without knowledge of NOTATION and first used in 1819 when an edition of

PHILIDOR's book was published in London by J. G. Pohlman. The name was made popular by the French writer A. Geoffroy-Daussay (1865–1934) who used the pen-name Alphonse Goetz. His magazine, *Cinéma du jeu des échecs*, had eight monthly issues in 1922.

Circe chess, an unorthodox game invented by the French composer Pierre Monréal (1916–) in 1967. Captured men are replaced on their supposed squares of origin: rook, bishop, and knight on a square of the same colour as that on which they are captured, pawns on the same file as that on which they were taken, pieces obtained by promotion as for other pieces. Kings cannot be captured. If the replacement square is occupied the captured man is removed from the board in the usual way. A man cannot be taken if its replacement would place the capturer in check. Circe chess is less used by players than by composers, who have established a rule for the capture of unorthodox pieces: these are to be replaced on the queening square of the file on which they are captured. For an example, see GANDEV. Composers have invented numerous variations of the rules, four of which follow. Circe Alsacien: a capture is not permitted if replacement creates an illegal position. Kamikaze Circe: the man making the capture is also 'reborn'. Cuckoo Circe: a captured man is reborn as if it were of the opposite colour; a pawn captured by a piece is reborn as if it were that piece, and thus promoted to a piece chosen by the other side, but such a capture is not permitted if any of the possible promotions would leave the capturer in check. Anti-Circe: the capturing man is removed from the board; captures cannot be made if the captured man cannot be replaced; a pawn capturing on its eighth rank is reborn as if it were of the opposite colour.

circular chess, see ROUND CHESS.

Ćirić, Dragoljub Miladin (1935–), International Grandmaster (1965), professional player and writer. A leading Yugoslav player in the 1960s, he came third (+5=10) after SPASSKY and UNZICKER at Sochi 1965, and shared first place at Sarajevo 1966 (+9=4−2) with TAL, and at Sarajevo 1968 with LEIN. Ćirić played in the Olympiads of 1966 (winning eight consecutive games) and 1968, but not long after the last of these events his health deteriorated and he largely withdrew from international chess.

Civis Bononiae (i.e. citizen of Bologna), the pen name of the author of a manuscript collection of 288 problems written before 1450. The author, who includes 191 problems from the earlier BONUS SOCIUS, states that he gave all the problems known to him. He concealed his identity, as yet undiscovered, in a Latin poem of 24 lines. Many positions were designed for wagering purposes. Civis Bononiae gives two pages of tips for tricking the victim, such as pretending to be unsure of the position so that if, on being offered the choice of sides, the antagonist chooses the winning one, some apparently harmless changes can be made to restore the advantage. Proving the absence or presence of a solution may be equally difficult and some problems, following a practice acceptable at the time, were intentionally composed without a solution.

The 288 problems were published in MURRAY'S *History of Chess* (1913). Perhaps the best copy of the manuscript is one made in 1454, now in the Estense Library of Modena. It has an additional 245 problems; for these 192 solutions are in Latin, 53 in Italian. (See ZERO-POSITION.)

Clarke, Richard William Barnes (1910–75), creator of the British system of GRADING. He gave up active chess after leaving Cambridge University, where he played second board between C. H. O'D. ALEXANDER and Jacob Bronowski (1908–74). At first a financial journalist (one of the two who created the *Financial Times Index*), he became, at the outbreak of the Second World War, a 'temporary' civil servant, remaining to become one of the most distinguished of them, and to receive a knighthood. (See RATING.)

Classical Attack, Defence, or Variation, a name given to a line which is or seems to be traditional, or was once much played and thought at the time to represent best play on both sides.

Of some antiquity are three lines given by Ruy LÓPEZ: 639 in the BISHOP'S OPENING; 1071 (see RUBINSTEIN; TARTAKOWER), a sound way of declining the KING'S GAMBIT; and 1107, also called the López Defence, in the King's Gambit Accepted. A line given by LUCENA but sometimes called the Cordel Defence, 767 in the SPANISH OPENING; 1127 in the King's Gambit Declined, given by POLERIO; and 643, the PHILIDOR VARIATION of the Bishop's Opening, also dating from the beginnings of modern chess.

From the second half of the 19th century there are: 68 in the QUEEN'S GAMBIT ACCEPTED; 192 in the QUEEN'S GAMBIT Declined; 572, sometimes known as the Capablanca Variation, in the CARO–KANN DEFENCE; 679 in the Spanish Opening, a deferred version of 767; 718, also in the Spanish Opening; 850 in the FOUR KNIGHTS OPENING (see PAULSEN); 1214, one of the main variations of the FRENCH DEFENCE (see DOUBLE CHECK).

From the 20th century are 200 in the Queen's Gambit Declined (which may lead to the MARÓCZY VARIATION, the RUBINSTEIN VARIATION, or the VIDMAR VARIATION); 309, also known as the Alekhine, Capablanca, or Teichmann Variation, in the NIMZO-INDIAN DEFENCE (see KERES); 589, the ADVANCE VARIATION of the Caro–Kann Defence.

classical centre, two centre pawns of the same colour, abreast on the fourth rank. They attack four squares on the fifth rank and may thus restrict the opponent's mobility. Early attempts to make such a centre are often foiled, e.g. 1 e4 e5 2 Nf3 Nc6 3 Bc4 Bc5 4 c3 Nf6 5 d4 exd4 6 cxd4 Bb4+ 7 Bd2 Bxd2+ 8 Nbxd2, and Black can strike back by 8 . . . d5. A subtler strategy is first to play to prevent such counter-play and then to establish the pawns on the fourth rank. This happens, for example, in many variations of the CLOSE DEFENCE to the SPANISH OPENING in which White plays Pd2-d4 on his 10th or 11th move. In some openings a player encourages the opponent to set up a classical centre early in the game so that the pawns become a target for a counterattack, as happens, for example, in the EXCHANGE VARIATION of the GRÜNFELD DEFENCE.

classification of players. Since the middle of the 20th century classification has been based on GRADING or RATING and the latter has been one of the bases on which FIDE TITLES are awarded.

Classification, however, was used at the dawn of the game. In the Islamic world of the 9th century leading players were called 'Alīyāt, of whom only two or three would be active at any time. Writing in 1617, CARRERA compares many Italians and a few Spanish players by means of the HANDICAP they might receive from a first-class player: 'I have heard he received the odds of two moves.' Similar comparisons were made in the middle of the 19th century. Thus someone might be described as a rook player or a player of the knight class. In the first half of the 20th century players were acknowledged as grandmasters or masters, usually without any qualifications. Classification at lower levels such as county or club play sometimes includes 'top board', meaning accepted (by some) as best player for the team.

clean mate, see PURE MATE.

clean score, the score in a tournament or match in which the victor has won every game. Not easily done when the opposition is comparatively weak, it is an outstanding achievement when grandmasters meet. There have been five notable match victories of this kind: STAUNTON v. HARRWITZ, 1846 (+7), STEINITZ v. BLACKBURNE, 1876 (+7), CAPABLANCA v. KOSTIĆ, 1919 (+5), FISCHER v. TAIMANOV, 1971 (+6), and Fischer v. LARSEN, 1971 (+6). These last two were consecutive world championship events, quarter- and semi-finals respectively. In tournaments at New York LASKER made a clean score in 1893 (+13), Capablanca in 1913 (+13 including one default); but Fischer made the most remarkable achievement of this kind (+11) in the strong US championship of 1963. Although her opposition was weaker, MENCHIK had clean scores in four consecutive world championship tournaments between 1931 and 1937, a total of 45 games.

clearance, see ANNIHILATION; BRISTOL CLEARANCE.

Clemenz Opening, 1323, named after the Estonian player Hermann Clemenz (1846–1908).

clock, or chess clock, a device for recording separately the time taken for each player's moves. (For an earlier timing device, see SANDGLASS.) When clocks first began to be used the rules were sometimes based on a maximum time for each move (as is the case in draughts today), and a single clock sufficed. Often when two clocks were used one was a standard time-piece, the other a stopwatch, the stopwatch reading being subtracted from that of the ordinary watch to give the time for the latter. For the 1866 match between ANDERSSEN and STEINITZ the time for each move was recorded and the total time calculated by addition. Gradually it became the custom to use two pendulum clocks, one for each player. One clock ticked while the other, on its side, was silent.

Prompted by a discussion with BLACKBURNE, Thomas Bright Wilson (1843–1915), secretary of the Manchester Chess Club, devised a stand with a movable beam, like a seesaw, to hold two pendulum clocks. This was used for the London 1883 international tournament. The tipping of the beam caused one clock to stop while the other, in an upright position, was going, 'which saves time and cannot well go wrong. So much cannot be said of the minor tournament clocks which, unless care was taken, had a trick of going on even when

turned on their backs.' A counter totted up the number of times the beam had been tipped and a bell rang when the required number of moves had been made. In 1887 Fattorini of Bradford brought out a similar stand but without the counter and bell. This cheap device sold well, but users sometimes complained that it was difficult to stop both clocks at the same time, and that the upright clock might not start unless the beam was moved at the right speed.

The first chess patent taken out in the United Kingdom, in 1884, was for a clock designed by Amandus Schierwater, a watch and clock maker from Liverpool. He made 'improvements in time-pieces, applicable for indicating the time spent by each player . . . chiefly for recording the movements of a game of chess'. The large dial showed the total time while small dials on either side showed each player's individual time. A large finger on the central dial showed the total number of moves played, and a small finger pointed to the side whose clock was ticking. This, the first true chess clock, was well liked but had a short life.

Of a clock used at Leipzig 1894, HOFFER wrote: 'A novel kind of clock was provided by a German firm, and pronounced a great improvement. The clocks are fixed upon a stand, not movable like

A chess clock of the 1890s; the acorn-shaped pendulums were stopped and started by rocking the pair of clocks from one side to the other

ours. A lever is provided, which upon being pressed down stops one clock and sets the other in motion, and vice versa. The clocks are of a superior make to ours, and the price is lower.' These clocks, made by Gustav Herzog of Leipzig, were the first balance-wheel chess clocks of a type that became general. The following year Theodore Grossé, an engineer from Sale, patented a chess timing device using two pendulum clocks with magnets to restrain the inactive pendulum, but this kind of mechanism gave way to the balance wheel over the next 20 years.

In 1899 H. D. B. Meijer, secretary of the Netherlands chess association, circulated a leaflet proposing that a flag be suspended above the third minute before XII, to be lifted by the minute hand and to fall on the hour. This would obviate unseemly squabbles such as the use of a penknife blade to see if the hand had reached its zenith. Many players felt that rigid insistence on time controls verged on sharp practice and about 20 years passed before the use of flags became general. With the electronic revolution clocks providing a wide range of functions and great precision were developed, and chess-boards were made which automatically timed each player's moves. Special clocks, capable of buzzing every five or ten seconds, have been made for LIGHTNING CHESS. (See PATENTS; TIMING OF MOVES.)

Close Defence, 732 in the SPANISH OPENING. A common continuation is 6 Re1 b5 7 Bb3 d6 8 c3 0-0 9 h3. White prepares to play Pd2-d4, setting up a CLASSICAL CENTRE, while Black holds the pawn at e5, maintaining a DEFENSIVE CENTRE. This variation first became popular at the beginning of the 20th century and has since become favoured above all others. (See ADAMS; AVERBAKH; CLOSE GAME; EHLVEST; KARPOV; KHOLMOV; ROMANOVSKY; SAX; SPASSKY; TAL.) The name is descriptive, indicating a war of attrition and manœuvre as contrasted with the direct play that usually occurs in the less fashionable OPEN DEFENCE, 707. However, one variation of the Close Defence, the MARSHALL COUNTER-ATTACK, 754, leads to an open game.

close game, or closed game, a game characterized by manœuvres behind the lines. The game frequently becomes open later, a transition brought about by pawn exchanges. White does not necessarily cede the initiative by setting up a close game at the beginning but its impact is delayed; meanwhile Black has the task of preparing to meet a variety of white options by means of which the game might be opened. On the other hand Black might seek a close game with the idea of minimizing the advantage in time that having the first move gives to White. In either case a player seeking a close game will place the men where their powers will be enhanced when the game becomes open.

Karpov–Gligorić Milan 1975 Spanish Opening Close Defence

1 e4 e5 2 Nf3 Nc6 3 Bb5 a6 4 Ba4 Nf6 5 0-0 Be7 6 Re1 b5 7 Bb3 0-0 8 c3 d6 9 h3 Nb8 10 d4 Nbd7 11 Nbd2

Bb7 12 Bc2 Re8 13 Nf1 Bf8 14 Ng3 g6 15 a4 c5 16 d5 Nb6 17 Qe2 Nxa4 18 Bxa4 bxa4 19 Rxa4 Bg7 20 c4 Bc8 21 Bd2 Rb8 22 Rb1 Re7

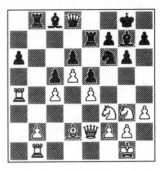

23 Ne1 Reb7 24 Nd3 Rb3 25 Rba1 Ne8 26 Bc3 Qh4 27 R4a3 f5 28 Be1 Qe7 29 Rxb3 Rxb3 30 Nc1 Rb8 31 Nd3 Rb3 32 f3 Qg5 33 Kh2 Nf6 34 Qc2 Rb8 35 b4 fxe4 36 Nxe4 Nxe4 37 fxe4 Qe3 38 bxc5 Qxe4 39 cxd6 Bf5 40 Ra3 Rc8 41 Rc3 Bf8 42 Bf2 Bxd6 43 Qa2 a5 44 c5 Bd7 45 Ra3 Bb5 46 cxd6 Bxd3 47 d7 Rd8 48 Rxd3 Qxd3 49 d6+ Kh8 50 Qxa5 Black resigns.

close opening, one that begins 1 d4 d5, a term of no strategic significance.

Close Variation, 449, sometimes called the Nimzowitsch Variation, a line in the SICILIAN DEFENCE (see WEAKNESS). White usually continues 3 g3, 4 Bg2, 5 d3, and these moves, not always played in this sequence, constitute the Close System as practised by PAULSEN (see ENGLISCH; MECKING). Also 907, sometimes called the Alekhine Variation, in the ITALIAN OPENING. The BREMEN VARIATION, 29, and the NIMZOWITSCH VARIATION, 1238, of the FRENCH DEFENCE are sometimes called Close Variations.

Cochrane, John (1798–1878), Scottish player, barrister, called to the bar in 1822. If the so-called romantic style existed, then Cochrane has a claim to be regarded as its founder. A dashing player, he attacked at all costs often sacrificing pieces with abandon, a style that was successful in the England of the 1820s; but when in 1821 he went to Paris, then the world's chess centre, he was beaten by both DESCHAPELLES and BOURDONNAIS. Subsequently he studied the game but he did not change his style. In 1822 he published a *A Treatise on the Game of Chess*, a popular book largely based on *Traité des Amateurs* (see VERDONI) and LOLLI but with a few contributions of his own. Although Cochrane came from an old Scottish family he led the London team in the famous correspondence match against Edinburgh, 1824–8. He persuaded his team to play the SCOTCH GAMBIT, but when London had obtained a fine position Cochrane left for India. Although the Londoners, led by LEWIS, failed to carry the attack, the Scotch Gambit became fashionable for more than 15 years, and other lively attacking openings were developed. Cochrane stayed in India until his retirement in 1869 except for one visit to England,

1841–3, when he played hundreds of friendly games against STAUNTON, who began by winning a large majority. Wilhelm STEINITZ knew both contestants and states that their last encounter was a match of 12 games, Staunton conceding pawn and move for the first six; and that Cochrane made an even score when receiving odds but won (+3=2−1) when playing on even terms.

John Cochrane should not be confused with James Cochrane (c.1770–1830), co-author of a book on the MUZIO GAMBIT (see GHULAM KASSIM GAMBIT).

Cochrane Attack, 1009 in the SCOTCH GAME, as played in 1841 by COCHRANE against STAUNTON and also against WALKER.

Cochrane Gambit, 1068 in the PETROFF DEFENCE, originated by COCHRANE in the 1840s. White sacrifices a knight for two pawns and a strong centre. White should not seek attack, according to STAUNTON, who played the gambit successfully, but should play a positional game advancing the PHALANX of pawns in the manner advocated by PHILIDOR. Should White establish two pawns on the fifth rank they would probably give sufficient compensation for the piece. In BRONSTEIN'S opinion this gambit is worth further investigation.

Cochrane–Shumov Defence, 977, an improvement on analysis by COCHRANE in a line in the SCOTCH GAMBIT made by Ilya Stepanovich Shumov (1819–81) and first published in *Chess Player's Chronicle*, 1850.

Cochrane Variation, 1133 in the KING'S GAMBIT Accepted. Black's sixth move, a refutation of the SALVIO GAMBIT, is rightly named after COCHRANE who published his analysis in 1822. The variation had occurred in a friendly game, Sarratt–Lewis, London, 1816; subsequently LEWIS disapproved of this move, not comprehending its real strength. Also 975 in the SCOTCH GAMBIT, played in games against STAUNTON and WALKER by Cochrane in 1841.

coffee houses, important chess resorts in the 18th and 19th centuries. In 1747 PHILIDOR played STAMMA at Slaughter's in St Martin's Lane, London, and from 1774 he frequented Parsloe's in St James's Street. In the same street was White's Chocolate House (later White's Club) where chess was often played for stakes. (Some betting slips from the 1740s survive.) These and other meeting places were, however, mostly patronized by the titled and wealthy. Coffee houses for the middling classes, as WALKER called them, flourished principally in the 19th century. In London there were Tom's in Cornhill, the Salopian at Charing Cross, Huttman's Garrick Chess Divan in Bedford Street, Gatti's in Adelaide Street, the Café Caro in Coleman Street, Kilpack's Divan in Covent Garden, and Starie's Philidorian Chess Rooms in Rathbone

Place. Gliddon's Divan, frequented by STAUNTON in the early 1840s, was described by contemporaries as 'like an Eastern tent, the drapery festooned up around you, and the views exhibited on all sides of mosques, and minarets, and palaces rising out of the water'. Soon, however, it was converted into an American bowling alley.

For most chessplayers the Divan meant Simpson's. In 1828 a Portuguese, Samuel Ries, opened the Divan in the Strand, and after five years gave it the more English sounding name of his head waiter. Simpson's was frequented regularly by all the greatest players of the time from its founding until 1903, when purchased by the Westminster Council to allow road widening. It reopened in 1904, but has had little to do with chess since then. Its chief rival, Purssell's in Cornhill, a restaurant, was demolished in 1894 and the players moved to Dr Butler's Head, a nearby hostelry.

The leading London resort in the 20th century was The Gambit in Budge Row. Opened in 1898, visited by most masters of the first half of the century, the location of the British team during the radio match with the USSR in 1946, it ended its days in 1958. In 60 years it was closed only once, for two days in September 1940 on account of damage in an air raid. Only men were allowed in The Gambit, although its owner for almost its entire existence was Edith Price, who won the last of her five British championship titles in 1948 at the age of 76. She also played twice for the Women's World Championship.

Public chess has been played in other types of premises in London such as the Mandrake, a racy Soho club, and taverns like the Ship and Turtle in Leadenhall Street and more recently the King's Head in Bayswater.

Other famous 19th-century chess cafés were: Amsterdam—Roode Leeuw; Berlin—Bauer, Belvedere, Kaiserhof, Kerkau, König; Geneva—Café de la Couronne; Leipzig—Hanisch; Madrid—Café du Levant; New York—International; Paris—Procope, and, most famous of all, the CAFÉ DE LA RÉGENCE; Riga—Reuter; Rome—Palazzo de' Cinque; St Petersburg—Dominik; Vienna—Central, Rabel.

coincidence, the unplanned duplication of chess ideas. There are many examples of identical games being played, in particular when an opening trap is involved. Judit POLGÁR was not the first person to receive a BRILLIANCY PRIZE for a game that had been played before, when she was so honoured at the 1988 Olympiad. Her game against Angelova was identical with Levchenkov–Eganian, USSR 1978.

Sometimes the coincidence is less complete.

Mikenas–Kashdan   Prague Olympiad 1931   Queen's Gambit Declined

1 d4 Nf6   2 c4 e6   3 Nc3 d5   4 Bg5 Nbd7   5 e3 Be7   6 Nf3 dxc4   7 Bxc4 a6   8 0-0 b5   9 Bd3 c5   10 Qe2 Bb7   11 Rfd1 Qb6   12 Rac1 0-0   13 Ne5 Rfe8   14 dxc5 Nxc5   15 Bxf6

Bxf6 16 Bxh7+ Kxh7 17 Qh5+ Kg8 18 Qxf7+ Kh7. In this position a draw was agreed.

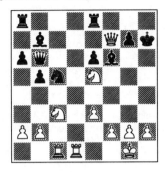

Janowski–Chajes New York 1916 Queen's Gambit Declined

1 d4 Nf6 2 Nf3 d5 3 c4 e6 4 Bg5 Be7 5 e3 Nbd7 6 Nc3 c6 7 Bd3 dxc4 8 Bxc4 b5 9 Bd3 a6 10 0-0 c5 11 Rc1 Bb7 12 Qe2 0-0 13 Rfd1 Qb6 14 Ne5 Rfe8 15 dxc5 Nxc5 16 Bxf6 Bxf6 17 Bxh7+ Kxh7 18 Qh5+ Kg8 19 Qxf7+ Kh7. This is the same position as that reached by Mikenas and Kashdan, but Janowski played on. 20 Nd7 Nxd7 21 Rxd7 Bc6 22 Ne4 Bxb2 23 Ng5+ Kh6 24 g4 g6 25 h4 Rh8 26 Qh7+ Black resigns.

Composition ideas may be repeated accidentally (see ANTICIPATION), or intentionally (PLAGIARISM).

#3

A problem by B. G. Laws, *Chess Monthly*, March 1893. The key is 1 Nd8.

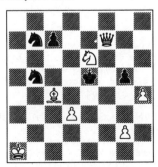

#3

P. H. Williams, *Morning Post*, 18 Dec. 1911. The key is the same and several variations are similar.

Often the standing of the composer is such that plagiarism is implausible, as in this example.

Coles, Richard Nevil (1907–82), English author, notably of biographies of Atkins, Burn, Sultan Khan, and (with KEENE) Staunton.

Colibri Opening, 1322, another name for the GROB OPENING chosen, perhaps, because the humming-bird hovers on the wing.

collaboration, now an acceptable practice in composition but not during play except in consultation games. At one time it was debated whether it was ethical for composers to collaborate and some tourney organizers disqualified joint work. Since there is no practical way of stopping it the argument fizzled out, and some of the finest problems and studies have come from partnerships. Many composers use computers to check their compositions for soundness, a form of collaboration. For the same practical reason there is an acceptance that players will seek help during an ADJOURNMENT, which is unquestionably against the spirit of chess. (See BEHAVIOUR for an account of what the laws say about a player's conduct.)

Colle, Edgard (1897–1932), Belgian champion six times between 1922 and 1929, skilled in combinative play. From 1922 to 1931 he averaged about four tournaments a year, many of them international, but he suffered frail health throughout his life, and his results were not consistent. His most notable wins were at Meran 1926, ahead of 13 players including SPIELMANN, KOSTIĆ, GRÜNFELD, and TARTAKOWER, and Scarborough 1930 (+6=5), ahead of MARÓCZY, RUBINSTEIN, and SULTAN KHAN. In stronger events he made only modest scores.

Colle–Marshall Hastings 1928–9 Colle System

1 d4 Nf6 2 Nf3 b6 3 e3 Bb7 4 Bd3 e6 5 Nbd2 c5 6 0-0 Nc6 7 c3 Rc8 8 dxc5 Bxc5 9 e4 Ng4 10 Qe2 Nce5 11 Nxe5 Nxe5 12 Bc2 Qh4 13 Nb3 Ng6 14 Nxc5 Rxc5 15 f4 Rh5 16 h3 0-0 17 Bd2 Rc5 18 Be3 Rcc8 19 f5 exf5 20 exf5 Ne5 21 f6 Rfe8 22 Rf4 Qg3 23 Qf2 Qxf2+ 24 Kxf2 g6 25 Rd1 Nc4 26 Bc1 d5 27 g4 Re5 28 Re1 Rxe1 29 Kxe1 Ne5 30 Kf2 Re8 31 Rd4 b5 32 Bf4 Nd7 33 g5 h6 34 h4 hxg5 35 hxg5 Nc5 36 Be3 Ne6 37 Rd1 Bc6 38 Re1 a5 39 Bd2

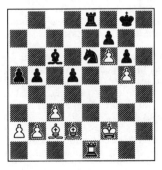

39 ... d4 40 cxd4 Nxd4 41 Rxe8+ Bxe8 (White has TWO BISHOPS) 42 Be4 b4 43 Bd5 Bb5 44 Ke3 Nc6 45 Ke4 Kf8 46 Be3 Ke8 47 Bc5 Nd8 48 Bb6 Nc6 49 b3 a4 50 Bc5 axb3 51 axb3 Nd8 52 Bxb4 Kd7 53 Kf4 Bd3 54 Ke3 Bf5 55 Bc3 Kd6 56 Bc4 Kc5 57 Bf1 Nc6 58 Be2 Bc2 59 b4+ Nxb4 60 Bxb4+ Kxb4 61 Kd4 Bb3 62 Bf3 Ba4 63 Be4 Be8 64 Kd5 Kc3 65 Kd6 Kd4 66 Ke7 Ba4 67 Bxg6 Ke5 68 Bxf7 Black resigns.

With the white pieces he frequently played the COLLE SYSTEM, which he handled with great virtuosity, and which often led to KING'S SIDE attacks. He died after an operation for a gastric ulcer.

Colle System, 1309, the opening moves, for White, Pd4, Nf3, Pe3, Nbd2, Pc3, and Bd3; White prepares an advance of the e-pawn thus opening the diagonal for the DARK BISHOP. Play frequently begins 1 d4 d5 2 Nf3 Nf6 3 e3 c5 (225), but Black has other ways of defending; for example, the game Ahues–Alekhine, San Remo 1930, opened 1 d4 Nf6 2 Nf3 b6 3 e3 Bb7 4 Nbd2 e6 5 Bd3 c5 6 c3.

The system made its first appearance in the 1890s when it was used by Black in the CHIGORIN VARIATION (148). Masters began to use the system for White around 1900, and in this form COLLE made it his speciality in the 1920s. His predilection has not been widely shared. See game under COLLE.

Collijn, Ludvig (1878–1939), Swedish chess administrator and patron. He ran tournaments over a period of 40 years, played a large part in organizing the Stockholm Olympiad in 1937, and was president of the Swedish Chess Association from its start in 1917 until his death. In 1918 he published a collection of games by ANDERSSEN, and in collaboration with his brother Gustaf (1880–1968) he produced many books of Scandinavian tournaments. Their most important work was *Lärobok*, a kind of Swedish Bilguer's HANDBUCH, which ran to four editions between 1898 and 1921 and earned them the nickname 'the Bilguer brothers'. The three parts of the book deal with general information, OPENINGS with illustrative games, and ENDGAMES, in that order. The second part of the last edition, occupying more than 400 pages and including 133 games, edited by RÉTI, RUBINSTEIN, and SPIELMANN, was consequently the most important source of openings information to be published in the 1920s.

Collijn Variation, three lines given by COLLIJN and his brother in the fourth edition of their *Lärobok*. They are 598 in the SCANDINAVIAN OPENING; 662 in the DANISH GAMBIT; and 581, the EXCHANGE VARIATION of the CARO–KANN DEFENCE.

Colman Variation, 958, a standard line, also known as the Bogoljubow Variation, in the TWO KNIGHTS DEFENCE. The English player Eugene Ernest Colman (1878–1964) discovered and analysed the variation while in a Japanese internment camp, 1942–5.

colour, white or black (although technically neither is a colour). The chessmen may be of any hue, but a colour distinction between the sides is desirable. Ivory sets are commonly white and red, or green and red. A presentation set given to MORPHY was silver and gold. However, the pieces are still referred to as white or black.

Since at least the 11th century the squares of the board have been of two contrasting shades and these too are often called white and black although if they are called light and dark there is less likelihood of confusion between pieces and squares.

colour-weakness, inability to gain effective control of squares of one colour, frequently associated with BISHOPS OF OPPOSITE COLOUR or a BAD BISHOP, and usually disadvantageous. (See HARRWITZ; SKEWER.)

column, (1) a FILE.

column, (2) see NEWSPAPER COLUMNS.

columnar notation, see TABULAR NOTATION.

combination, a sequence of forcing moves with a specific goal, and grounded in TACTICS. A SACRIFICE is likely to be present and BOTVINNIK, among others, says is always present. The purpose may be anything from a defensive resource to a mating attack, from a small POSITIONAL ADVANTAGE to a gain of material. Essential to most combinations, and a reason for their popularity, is surprise: the series of moves differs in form from the kind of continuation normally to be expected.

Combinations do not come from thin air. Usually a player will first have gained some kind of positional advantage, thus disorganizing the opponent. It is often said that when the advantage is marked the combinations will come of themselves. Sometimes a distinctive weakness, an unguarded piece, or an uncastled king is a signal for a combination. In games between grandmasters combinations, seen and avoided, may be overlooked by a beginner, playing through the game, who believes there are better moves, not seeing the combinative refutations. On the other hand, games between players of markedly different strengths often have a livelier appearance because the combinations come to the surface, the better player having seen further ahead.

combined piece, a piece that combines the powers of two or more different pieces. It may be moved at will in the manner of any one of its constituent parts. The queen, for example, combines the powers of the rook and bishop. Some other combined pieces are the AMAZON (R + B + N), the EMPRESS (R + N), the PRINCESS (B + N), and the GNU (N + CAMEL).

A problem (below) from the BONUS SOCIUS, late 13th century. The piece on h7 is a FERS (which can be moved one square diagonally) while the piece on e7 has the powers of an AUFIN (a $\sqrt{8}$ or 2,2, LEAPER) and a rook. White mates by moving this piece first to e6 (setting up a BLOCK) and then to g8. This is the

#2

earliest-known invention of a combined piece for use in a FAIRY PROBLEM. However, there is another way of uniting disparate moves into one piece, namely the change of powers on alternate moves, and this example is from a MS dated 1141. The piece on h1 moves as a knight on its first move, and as a FĪL on its second, knight on third, and so on, to make a tour of the board.

49	42	40	51	9	34	36	11
47	52	54	45	39	12	14	33
41	50	48	43	37	10	8	35
55	44	46	53	15	32	38	13
61	22	16	63	5	26	28	7
19	56	58	21	31	64	2	25
17	62	60	23	29	6	4	27
59	20	18	57	3	24	30	1

companion squares, see CONJUGATE SQUARES.

compensation, advantages which balance those held by the adversary. For example, one player might lose material but gain positional advantage as compensation.

competition, an event at one of three levels: (1) tournaments or matches; (2) exhibition, simultaneous, blindfold, or consultation games; (3) friendly contests. All may be played OVER-THE-BOARD, some by CORRESPONDENCE or TELECHESS. For problems and studies there are tourneys and solving competitions.

complete block problem, see BLOCK.

complete chess, see GREAT CHESS.

composition, a position other than one which arises during a game, usually but not necessarily composed for solving. The accompanying text may provide information for the student, STIPULATIONS for the solver, or a statement of the composer's

achievement. Compositions may be classified under the following six headings:

(1) PUZZLES. These are as ancient as chess itself and many do not require knowledge of the game. The KNIGHT'S TOUR, for example, is a mathematical puzzle and could pre-date CHATURANGA.

(2) DIDACTIC POSITIONS; (3) STUDIES; (4) PROBLEMS. From at least as far back as the 9th century (see MANṢŪBA) until the early 19th century these were grouped as if of one kind. In 1846 ALEXANDRE published a collection of 2020 positions consisting of 1217 orthodox problems, 136 studies and didactic positions, and 667 conditional problems and fairy problems; however, the compiler did not make this classification but mixed them all together. In the late 1830s a period of specialization began and before long each of these three kinds of composition gained a distinct identity.

(5) CONSTRUCTION TASKS; (6) RETROGRADE ANALYSIS. The first dates from 1849. Neither was developed to any great extent until the 20th century.

In 1961 the FIDE Permanent Commission for Chess Compositions began publication of the FIDE ALBUMS. These contain a selection of all kinds of composition except didactic positions.

Compromised Defence, 877 in the EVANS GAMBIT, a graphic and correct description of a line analysed by ANDERSSEN in *Schachzeitung*, 1851.

computers and chess. Under the delusion that skill at chess is evidence of high intelligence, the public has long been fascinated by the idea of chess-playing machines. (See AUTOMATON.) In 1864 Charles Babbage considered the use of a computer for this purpose, but suitable equipment was not available before the electronic age. The first computer program aimed at playing chess was developed in about 1944 in Germany by Konrad Zuse, but it was theoretical rather than practical, Zuse's purpose being to create a symbolic language suitable for logical rather than mathematical tasks. Around 1947 the English mathematician Alan Turing specified a chess program, but was unable to use a computer to run it, and instead simulated the operation by hand. In 1949 Claude Shannon of the USA presented a paper which became the basis for most subsequent research on the subject.

In the first instance computer scientists used chess as a model for decision-making processes, for investigating machine intelligence and what later came to be called expert systems (that is, a system that makes decisions at various critical moments based on criteria previously supplied by an expert on that topic). Only later, perhaps spurred by the scorn with which chessplayers greeted their earliest efforts, did some add total world supremacy to their list of objectives, a target unlikely to attract government or academic funding.

In 1958 a computer played chess correctly, i.e. in accordance with the laws, but the first serious program came in 1966 when Mac Hack became operational in the USA. The following year it played, unsuccessfully, in an ordinary tournament and at about the same time contests began to be held between computers. The first computer world championship was held at Stockholm in 1974 when 13 programs from eight countries took part. The winner, Kaissa, was from the USSR, but American programs triumphed at the next five gatherings, Toronto 1977, Linz 1980, New York 1983, Cologne 1986, and Alberta 1989. These contests are primarily scientific meetings, and, since 1980, have been run by The International Computer Chess Association, formed in 1977, which has published a quarterly journal since that date.

In parallel with, and an indispensable part of, the great advances being made in computer chess programs, there was a vast increase in the power of the machines themselves. Smaller, cheaper computers were being made for domestic use, some of which had chess programs. Other machines were dedicated solely to chess play. Within five years of the first of these appearing, in 1976, there was an abundant supply of machines capable of giving a good game to all but the best players, and ten years later commercial chess computers were available that played at grandmaster strength. The large computers, playing at a level close to that of CANDIDATES, were still clearly stronger than the domestic machines. In 1960 the challenge was to find a program capable of beating an ordinary player. By 1990 the challenge was to make it possible for a weak player to win occasionally against a computer set at its lowest level of play.

It appears to be only a matter of time before chess computers become invincible, but that does not mean that they will cease to be of any use. As well as providing an opportunity for practice, they will be able to analyse and probably annotate games, and can maintain large archives of previous games for inspection or comparison. At the other end of the skill spectrum, computers have become fine tools for novices. They do not allow illegal moves and may be asked for suggestions. By using the facility to retract, the beginner can try moves, learn why they are bad (if they are), and take them back, retrying until a good move is found. Some chess computers are sold specifically as teaching machines, and these have supporting coaching material.

After a program has been given the basic ability to play chess legally, the next task is to seek excellence. Despite its name, game theory is an earnest subject, with implications for the worlds of politics, commerce, and warfare. Its scientists call chess a finite, chance-free, two-person, zero-sum game, with perfect information, and so, in theory, capable of being played faultlessly. Zero-sum means that what is good for one player is bad to exactly the same amount for the other. Perfect information means that nothing is concealed from either player. However, the only way to play faultlessly is to analyse every position to exhaustion; and such is the richness of chess that the fastest com-

puters on earth, working in unison, would take many millions of years to scratch the surface.

In some ways computers are like beginners, but perfect ones. They consider all kinds of moves, foolish or clever, but at a speed beyond human comprehension, and without getting in a muddle. A powerful computer could examine more positions in one game than the average player does in a lifetime. To each move there are usually several possible replies. Analysing the branches, or tree-searching as it is called, can usually be carried only so far because of the exponentially increasing number of possibilities with each extra move. However, analysis to exhaustion, popularly known as 'brute force', does have its place in chess problem solving, and in analysis of the BASIC ENDGAME where every possibility must be examined.

Most chess computers have a problem-solving capability for direct mates, but there are special programs, such as the Alybadix suite which also solves selfmates, reflex mates, series mates, Circe, maximummers, and others. See BASIC ENDGAME for an account of those positions that have yielded up their secrets to database analysis by the computer. Again exhaustive analysis is used, but this time the direction is reversed. From all possible mating positions, moves are retracted until a full set of possible starting positions has been generated. In that way every starting position has a minimum 'move to win' number, and every correct forward move by the attacking side must be to a position that has a smaller number.

Given that brute force alone is not enough for playing chess, computers must employ other techniques. They have a substantial openings 'book' in their memories which they look up, as might a correspondence chess player. However, the most interesting facet of the work being done to improve chess programs is the development of techniques to improve the efficiency of tree-searches and the evaluation of terminal positions.

The play from this position in the second computer world championship illustrates both the cleverness and stupidity of programs. Black played 34 ... Re8, and five hundred spectators, including many masters, thought the program had failed. Subsequent testing revealed that it had rejected 34 ... Kg7 because of forced mate in five: 35 Qf8+ Kxf8 36

Bh6+ Kg8 (or 36 ... Bg7) 37 Rc8+ Qd8 38 Rxd8+ Re8 39 Rxe8. Any player who saw the mate would still play 34 ... Kg7 because the opponent might not find the refutation, whereas playing 37 ... Re8 is equivalent to resigning.

Until now all programs have worked on the principle that the opponent will always find the best move. This is essential when playing against another computer, but in any case there is no method of judging the probability of a human player failing to examine any particular move. The strongest human players look at the fewest CANDIDATE moves, but computers examine them all, sometimes with unexpected results.

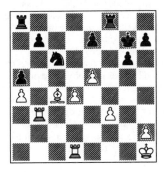

In this position the computer, Deep Thought, played 27 ... Ra7 and the audience laughed. However the player of the White pieces, KARPOV, said it was the best move. The next few moves of this game, played at Harvard University in 1990, demonstrate other aspects of computer chess. 28 Bd5 Rd8 29 Rb5 Ra6 30 Bc4 Ra7 31 Bd5 Ra6. Karpov saved time on the clock by repeating position, but Deep Thought did not. It recalculated every move as though a new position had arisen. 32 Rc5 Rd7 33 Kg2 Rb6 34 Bxc6 bxc6 35 Kf2 (35 Rxa5 Rb4 gives equality) 35 ... Rd5 36 Rxd5 cxd5 37 Rc1 Rb4 38 Ke3 Rxa4 (38 ... Rb3+ 39 Ke2 Rb4 probably draws, but Deep Thought believed it had the advantage) 39 Rc5 e6 40 Rc7+ Kg8 41 Re7 Ra3+ 42 Kf4 Rd3 43 Rxe6 Rxd4+ 44 Kg5 Kf7 45 Ra6 a4 (45 ... h6+ 46 Kxh6 Rh4+ 47 Kg5 Rh5+ draws, but the computer was looking for a win) 46 f4 h6+ 47 Kg4 Rc4? (Karpov agreed that 47 ... g5 probably draws) 48 h4 Rd4 49 Rf6+ Kg7 50 Ra6 Kf7 51 h5 (now the computer realized it stood worse) 51 ... gxh5+ 52 Kf5 Kg7 53 Ra7+ Kf8 54 e6 Re4 55 Rd7 Rc4 56 Rxd5 h4 57 Rd3 Ke7 58 Rd7+ Kf8 59 Rh7 h5 60 Ke5 h3 61 f5 Kg8 62 Rxh5 a3 63 Rxh3 a2 (another 'computer-type' move, as opposed to the 'human' 63 ... Ra4, although Black's game is lost anyway) 64 Ra3 Rc5+ 65 Kf6 Black resigns.

D. Levy, *Computer Chess Compendium* (1988) contains 31 of the most significant articles on the subject and hundreds of games; T. Harding, *The New Chess Computer Book* (1988) gives all the home computer user will want to know.

conditional continuation, a term used in CORRESPONDENCE CHESS: a player sending a move offers a subsequent move on condition that the opponent replies to the first in a specified manner. The offer of conditional moves is binding if accepted. For example, a player receiving an opening move, 1 e4, from White might reply, '1 ... d5. If 2 exd5 Nf6.' This can be carried too far. A player wishing to save time in a Sicilian Defence, after 1 e4 c5 2 Nf3 d6 3 d4 wrote '3 ... exd4 4 any Nf6 5 any g6 6 any Bg7' to which White replied '4 Qxd4 Nf6 5 Qxf6 g6 6 Qxh8—your last move (6 ... Bg7) is illegal'. A world champion of correspondence chess, Fritz Baumbach, once sent an 'if any' continuation and received a winning reply. He complained that he meant 'any sensible move', so his kind-hearted opponent agreed to a draw.

conditional problem, a problem using orthodox men but restricting their use in some way, e.g. mate to be given by a specific piece or pawn or on a certain square, or pieces might be FIDATED. Popular in medieval times, this type long remained so. In 1763 LOLLI included 22 in his collection of 100 positions, and large numbers were composed by KOCH, Julius Mendheim (c.1788–1836), and SILBERSCHMIDT, all from Germany, LEWIS and other early 19th-century composers including, belatedly, the English composer William Bone (1810–74). The fashion died out in the 1840s (see PROBLEM HISTORY). Today such compositions would be classed as FAIRY PROBLEMS. For examples, see MEDIEVAL PROBLEMS; PHILIDOR'S LEGACY.

congress, originally a gathering of the members of a chess body. It became increasingly common to hold a TOURNAMENT concurrently, and now the name is often used for an event comprising one or more tournaments without a business meeting. A FIDE congress is still primarily to settle the affairs of that body.

conjugate squares, usually a pair of squares occupied by kings in a pawn ending when the position is a ZUGZWANG. On rare occasions a duel is fought between opposite coloured pieces other than kings while the remaining men lie idle, and if a zugzwang occurs the duellists occupy conjugate squares. The OPPOSITION shows conjugate squares forming a regular pattern, and it is when an irregular pattern occurs that the term conjugate squares or irregular opposition is used.

A simple example is the TRÉBUCHET, in which the kings stand a knight's move apart. When there are several pairs of conjugate squares in a pawn ending the irregular pattern they form is specific to that pawn formation. These varying patterns are harder to discern than the recurring patterns of the regular opposition. Conjugate squares are also called companion, co-ordinate, related, or sister squares.

Inherent to this position are six conjugate pairs. These may be expressed as 'equations' defining the kings' positions, that of the white king being given first: a4 = b6; b3 or d3 = c5; c3 = a4 or d5; c2 = b5. Zugzwangs are marked z. White to play draws: 1 Kb3 Kc5z 2 Kc2 Kb5z 3 Kc3 Ka4z 4 Kc4 stalemate. Black to play loses: 1 . . . Ka6 2 Kb3 Kb5 3 Kc2z Kc5 (or 3 . . . Kc4 4 b3+, or 3 . . . Ka4 4 Kc3z Kb5 5 Kd4) 4 Kd3z Kd5 5 b3z. Pawn moves always change the pairs, in this case to a regular opposition pattern. Positions with more than half a dozen pairs are not common in practice.

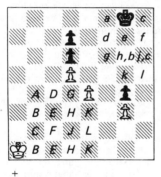

+

A study (VERSION) by the Englishman Charles Dealtry Locock, *British Chess Magazine*, 1892. Eighteen conjugate pairs are indicated by italic letters (the black king stands on a *b* square). Similar letters indicate the pairings, e.g. *B = b*, in this case representing four zugzwangs, b1 or b3 = g6 or g8. (Two unmarked pairs, c7 = e7 and c8 = e8 are not relevant to the play.) White wants to play K-d4 threatening e4-e5, or K-e3 threatening K-f4, and either would win unless Black could reply immediately . . . Kf6z or . . . Kg5z respectively. Thus the pairs *G = g* and *K = k* are identified.

By extension outwards, all the other pairs can be found. For example, if White plays Kd3, gaining access to both d4 and e3, Black needs to reply . . . Kg6z to gain access to f6 and g5; thus d3 = g6. Black to play could draw by 1 . . . Kg7 or 1 . . . Kh7, continuing 2 Kb2 Kh8z or Kh6z, or 2 Kb1 Kg6z. Holding the defensive (irregular) opposition, Black can always place White in zugzwang. White to play wins using the same method that follows from

holding the regular opposition: Black is held in zugzwang until White can outflank successfully. The key is 1 Kb1z. Two variations follow: 1 . . . Kg7 2 Kc1z Kg6 3 Kd1z Kg5 4 Kc2 (outflanking) 4 . . . Kh6 5 Kd2z Kh5 6 Kc3 (outflanking) 6 . . . Kg5 7 Kc4 (outflanking) 7 . . . Kg6 8 Kd3z; 1 . . . Kh8 2 Kb2z Kg8 3 Kb3z Kh8 4 Kc4 (outflanking) 4 . . . Kg7 5 Kc3z Kf7 6 Kd2 (outflanking) 6 . . . Kf6 7 Ke2 (outflanking) 7 . . . Kg6 8 Kd3z.

Locock's study, the first of its kind, made no immediate impact, but LASKER noted it, and in 1901 he constructed a conjugate square study which attracted wide interest. Many such studies followed. In the 1920s and 1930s attempts were made to establish a comprehensive classification of the many patterns that are possible in conjugate square positions. The results are unconvincing. For example, the Locock study is supposed to show the 'eight-square system' because the squares c4, d4, c3, d3, e3, c2, d2 and e2 are paired mirror-fashion with eight squares on the other side of the diagonal axis h2-b8. This is an interesting observation, but it accounts for fewer than half the conjugate pairs. To understand a set of such pairs, those that occur when the kings are close together should be discovered, and from this starting point other pairs can be derived.

=

A study by MANDLER, *Wiener Schachzeitung*, 1924, a rare example of conjugate squares occupied by pieces other than kings. The knight and bishop fight a duel while the kings and pawns stand by. If the black king is moved to c4 it is soon driven back by the bishop. For Black's knight there are five key dark squares, b2 and c5 which give checkmate, e5, g5, and f2 when mate cannot be prevented. The approach to these is by way of 15 light squares, b7, d7, f7, h7, e6, g6, c4, e4, g4, b3, d3, f3, h3, d1, or h1, and the bishop must prevent the knight from reaching any one of them. Zugzwangs arise because the bishop may be able to defend from only one square, e.g. with Nf6 the bishop must be on f5, and White, to play, cannot lose the move.

Inherently the position contains 32 zugzwangs. Of these 3 are not relevant to the solution: Nd8 = Bd5, Nf8 = Bf5, and Na5 = Bd5. The other

29 are listed below, and in all cases except the two marked by an asterisk White can defend only by zugzwang.

    Ne8 = Be6 or Be4
    Ne7 = Bh5*
    Ng7 = Bd5*
    Nd6 = Bd5
    Nf6 = Bf5
    Nh6 = Be6 or Bh5
    Nd5 = Bg4
    Nf5 = Bf3
    Nh5 = Be6 or Be4
    Nd4 = Bd5
    Nf4 = Bf5
    Nh4 = Be4 or Bh5
    Ne3 = Be2
    Ng3 = Bd5
    Nc2 = Bf3 or Bc4
    Nd2 = Bd5
    Ne2 = Be6
    Ng2 = Bg4
    Nc1 = Bc4
    Ne1 = Be2 or Be4
    Nf1 = Bf3 or Bc4
    Ng1 = Bg4

The different squares that may be occupied by the black knight lead to drawing positions that fall into three groups: 23 for which only a zugzwang serves; 2 (marked above with asterisks) for which White also has some non-zugzwang defences, e.g. with Ne7 White may defend by Be4 or Bf5; 11 for which there are no zugzwangs, although White must manœuvre the bishop with care, e.g. with Na1 White may defend by Bd1 (White to play Bb3 =) or by placing the bishop on the diagonal a2-g8.

The key is 1 Bh5z after which White can always hold Black in zugzwang if necessary, e.g. 1 ... Nd5 2 Bg4z, 1 ... Nf5 2 Bf3z, 1 ... Ng8 2 Bg4 (or Bg6) Nf6 3 Bf5z, or 1 ... Nc8 2 Bf3 (or Bf7) Nd6 3 Bd5z.

The information about conjugate squares contained in standard endgame books is sufficient for most practical purposes. Among specialist books are Rinaldo Bianchetti, *Contributo alla teoria dei finale di soli pedoni* (1925); Duchamp and Halberstadt, *L'Opposition et les cases conjuguées sont réconciliées* (1932); Walter Bähr, *Opposition und kritische Felder im Bauernendspiel* (1936).

connected pawn, a pawn that can guard or be guarded by a pawn on an adjoining file. The term is generally used in the plural to define a group of two or more such pawns. Because one connected pawn can protect the other they are usually easier to defend than if they were isolated, a factor which may be decisive in the endgame. Usually a more important consideration is their greater potential mobility. Central to PHILIDOR's teaching is the idea that connected pawns together have a dynamism greater than the sum of the parts, that such pawns may become a strategic (positional) force in themselves.

For example, after 1 e4 e5 2 Nf3 Nc6 3 Bc4 Bc5 4 c3 Nf6 5 d4 exd4 6 cxd4 Bb4 + 7 Bd2 Bxd2 + 8 Qxd2 White's connected pawns on d4 and e4 form a powerful force if unchallenged. Fortunately for Black, 8 ... d5 breaks up the connected pawns and equalizes the game.

consolidation, the stabilization of a 'loose' position. For example, manœuvres to gain material may leave pieces scattered; they are consolidated if they are brought back into play, their CO-OPERATION improved, as a preparation for the exploitation of the material advantage.

construction task, a position constructed to show a TASK for which the play is elementary or non-existent. The composer displays his wares: there is nothing for the solver to do. One kind of task would be to show the largest possible number of keys for, say, a two-mover; but most tasks require one SINGLE-MOVE to be made, by one or both sides, and these are called one-mover construction tasks, or ONE-MOVERS. Usually the idea is to show the largest or smallest number of moves of one type, e.g. checks or captures. The position may be legal or illegal, with or without OBTRUSIVE PIECES, with or without promotion in play. Conventionally, the orthodox board and men are used, but one-movers have been attempted in the fairy realm.

Known to the ancients, construction tasks were reintroduced in modern chess in the 19th century. Interest was stimulated by DAWSON in 1913 and again in 1938 with the publication of his book *Ultimate Themes*. He also introduced 'forced' forms in which every possible single-move must contribute to the task, e.g. if mate is the aim no move must fail to give mate. *The Problemist*, Nov. 1979, gives a résumé of construction task records at that time.

The diagram shows 27 men in a legal position, none guarded or attacked. At the FIDE Problem Commission meeting, Bournemouth 1989, solvers were asked to construct such a position using 26 men. The setter, BEASLEY, believed that to be the largest number possible. He and ten successful solvers subsequently devised this 27-man solution, which was dedicated to Dawson by the 'Bournemouth Solvers'.

consultation game, a game in which two or more players in a consultation take one side. Their opposition may also be a consultation team.

control, the mastery of a square such that if an enemy man moved there it might be captured advantageously. If play began 1 d4 d6 2 Nf3 White would control e5, winning a pawn should Black play 2 . . . e5. If White commenced 1 Nf3 Nf6 2 b3 d6 3 Bb2 the square e5 would not be controlled although it is attacked by two men and defended by one; Black could safely play 3 . . . e5. Thus effective control depends upon both number of men involved and their relative value.

A file, rank, or diagonal is controlled when a player's line-pieces attack all or most of the squares on that line and when the opponent cannot expediently defend by opposing a suitable line-piece. To control a line does not imply that all the squares on the line are separately controlled, only that the line piece has them under surveillance.

In the opening a player tries to gain control of the centre, which may mean no more than the control of the greater number of central squares. This is the same as gaining space in the centre, a synonymous term. Control of central squares is frequently but not necessarily advantageous.

control notation, a name used in some countries for the simplest method of describing a position. Commencing with White each man is named and its square identified. The squares may be named by STANDARD NOTATION or DESCRIPTIVE NOTATION, but the former is more commonly used. The SAAVEDRA study, for example, would be described as follows: White (or Wh.) Kb6, Pc6; Black (or Bl.) Ka1, Rd5. Control notation is best suited to positions with few men on the board. The alternative, FORSYTH NOTATION, is perhaps biased the other way.

conventional symbols are used as part of NOTATION, for ANNOTATIONS, or for a caption that accompanies the diagram of a COMPOSITION. Annotation symbols are the hardest to define, for an annotator may use them in a highly personal way. Sometimes there is a choice of symbols for one meaning and alternatives are shown in brackets.

Notation symbols, English language

K	king
Q	queen
R	rook
B	bishop
N (Kt, S)	knight
P	pawn
ch.	check
dbl.ch.	double check (rarely used)
dis.ch.	discovered check (rarely used)

Notation symbols, international

—	to, e.g. Ng1-f3, or N-KB3
x (:)	captures
0-0 (00)	castles king's side

0-0-0 (000)	castles queen's side
ep (e.p.)	en passant
+ (†)	check
# (‡)	checkmate
=	is promoted to
1–0 (1:0)	White won
0–1 (0:1)	Black won
½–½ (½:½)	the game was drawn

Annotation symbols, international

. . .	before a move, signifying it is to be made by Black
~	ad libitum
!	good move
!!	outstanding move
?	weak move
??	blunder
?!	move of doubtful value
!?	move of uncertain merit, but deserving attention
± (+ −)	White's position is distinctly better
± (+ =)	White's position is slightly better
=	the position is level
∓ (= +)	Black's position is slightly better
∓ (− +)	Black's position is distinctly better

Caption symbols, international

+	White to play and win
=	White to play and draw
*	set play is present
V	version, indicating that the original composition has been changed in some way
sol	solution
max	maximummer

(The symbols below are always followed by a number indicating length of solution, e.g. #2 means checkmate in two moves. White is to move first unless otherwise stated.)

#	mate
h#	helpmate (Black moves first)
hp	help-stalemate (Black moves first)
r#	reflex mate
rp	reflex stalemate
s#	selfmate
sh#	series helpmate (Black moves first)
shp	series help-stalemate (Black moves first)
sp	series stalemate
sr#	series reflex mate
srp	series reflex stalemate
ss#	series selfmate

cook, a composition term for an alternative key not intended by the composer, or a solution in fewer moves than stipulated; to show that a line of play in a game or in a composition is unsound. The term was first used in connection with chess by KLING and HORWITZ in their magazine *The Chess Player*, 1851, p. 40. 'Mr Alexander's [ALEXANDRE'S] collection of two thousand problems contains many faulty positions, and we shall now and then *cook* some of them, which may amuse . . . many of our readers.' On pages 118 and 126 the editors give six of Alexandre's problems and show that in all of them mate can be given in fewer than the stipulated number of moves.

It is not clear today whether the first use of the word was to imply an intention to 'do for' a problem by proving it unsound, or to take a raw idea and make something wholesome of it, to create a sound problem from an unsound one.

Cook, Eugene Beauharnais (1830–1915), the first American composer of note. He was also co-author of *American Chess Nuts* (1868), a collection of more than 2,400 positions, an overview of the early years of the problem art in America. His chess library of more than 3,000 items, at that time second in size (in USA) only to J. G. WHITE'S collection, was bequeathed to Princeton University where, as a student, he had composed his first problem. Among his several other hobbies was music—he played the violin—and he collected many volumes of PHILIDOR'S musical works. (See HENRY; MUTATE.)

Keidanz, *The Chess Compositions of E. B. Cook* (1927) contains about 650 positions.

#2

Composed in 1908, this problem was first published in 1927 (see book above). The key is 1 Rb1, with 14 variations.

Cook Variation, 1172 in the ALLGAIER GAMBIT, given by William Cook (1850–1917) in his *Synopsis of the Chess Openings* (1882).

Coons pairing system, a method of pairing players in SWISS SYSTEM tournaments devised by Everett Arthur Coons (1917–) and elaborated in *En Passant*, a Pittsburgh magazine, in the early 1950s. The competitors are divided into four groups, from I, the strongest, to IV, the weakest, according to GRADING. First round pairings are within each group. For the next two rounds everyone is paired, according to matching scores, with someone from another group: round two, I v. II, and III v. IV; round three, I v. III, and II v. IV. In subsequent rounds the usual Swiss system pairings are made.

Coons score, a tie-breaking method intended as a refinement of the NEUSTADTL SCORE. A Coons score is the sum of a proportion of each opponent's score based on the player's result against the opponent in question. The proportions are: win, 100%; draw, 50%; loss, 20%. For an example, see AUXILIARY SCORING METHOD.

co-operation, or co-ordination of pieces, the action of a player's pieces when they work together. The absence of co-operation is more noticeable than its presence, which may be regarded as normal. In master play, lack of co-operation is usually the consequence of an attack: the defender holds on at the price of a disorganized position. Sometimes, although gaining material advantage, the defender's men are scattered, leading to defeat. (See RAKING BISHOPS.)

O'Kelly–Donner Beverwijk 1963 Queen's Gambit Declined

1 c4 Nf6 2 Nc3 e6 3 Nf3 d5 4 d4 Be7 5 Bg5 0-0 6 e3 b6 7 cxd5 Nxd5 8 Bxe7 Qxe7 9 Nxd5 exd5 10 Bd3 c5 11 dxc5 bxc5 12 Qc2 g6 13 Rc1? Na6 14 a3 c4 15 Be2 Bf5 16 Qc3 Nc5 17 Nd4 Nd3+ 18 Bxd3 Bxd3 19 Nc6 Qe4 20 Qe5 Rfe8 21 Qxe4 dxe4 22 Rc3 a5 23 a4 Ra6 24 Nd4 Rb6 25 Nb5 Re5 26 Ra3 h5 27 h4 Rf5 28 g3 Kg7 29 Rh2

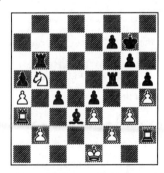

White holds everything for the time being, but his pieces lack co-operation, with fatal results. 29 ... Kf6 30 Kd2 Ke5 31 b3 Rbf6 32 Ke1 Kd5 33 Nd4 c3 34 Nxf5 Rxf5 35 Ra1 Kc5 36 Rd1 Rd5 37 f4 exf3 38 Rf2 Be2 White resigns.

co-ordinate notation, any NOTATION for which each rank and file has its own identification, enabling each square to be uniquely identified by its co-ordinates. The best known example is STANDARD NOTATION.

co-ordinate squares, see CONJUGATE SQUARES.

co-ordination of pieces, see CO-OPERATION.

Cordel Defence, 767, the CLASSICAL DEFENCE, and 809, two unrelated variations in the SPANISH OPENING named after the German author Oscar Cordel (1843–1913). The Classical Defence is in the GÖTTINGEN MS and, as JAENISCH noted in 1843, was long recommended by Italian players who naturally preferred such a development for the king's bishop.

Cordel Variation, 770, one of the many lines in the SPANISH OPENING examined by Cordel; 825 in the PONZIANI OPENING; 894 in the EVANS GAMBIT Accepted; 898 in the EVANS GAMBIT DECLINED; all from analysis by Cordel.

cordon, the boundary of an area of the board in which the defender's king is enclosed, a term used when describing the winning process for basic mates and some other endgames without pawns.

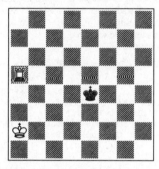

Black's king is confined to a space of 25 squares. White draws the cordon tighter, progressively reducing this space, as shown by the numbers in brackets.
1 ... Kd4 2 Kb3(22) Kd3 3 Ra4(17) Kd2 4 Rd4+ Ke2 5 Kc2(12) Ke3 6 Ra4 Ke2 7 Ra3(8) Ke1 8 Kd3 Kf2 9 Kd2(6) Kf1 10 Ke3 Kg2 11 Ke2(4) Kg1 12 Kf3 Kh2 13 Kf2(2) Kh1 14 Rh3.

Corkscrew Counter-gambit, 1048, BLACKBURNE'S joking description.

corner, specifically the squares a1, a8, h1, or h8, but often used to describe an area that also includes some adjoining squares.

correction, a problem term for certain effects created by alternative moves of a black piece or pieces (Black Correction) or of a white piece or pieces (White Correction). The following examples along with the accompanying problemists' jargon show the idea.

Black Correction
A problem by MANSFIELD (below), second prize, *Chess Correspondent*, 1947. The key is 1 Rh1, with the 'primary threat' hxg4#. To avoid this Black needs to move the Ng4 or the Bg6.

If the Ng4 makes a 'random' move (1 ... Nxe3, Nxf2, or Nf6) White plays 2 Be2#, the 'secondary threat'. Black could 'correct' the 'general error' of the random move by preventing the double check, 1 ... Ne5, a 'secondary black correction'. However, Black thus makes a 'secondary error' (obstruction of Ba1), and White answers 2 Ng7#.

#2

A random move by the Bg6 (e.g. Bxc2) permits 2 Be8#, another secondary threat. The secondary Black correction 1 ... Bf5 prevents the double check, but then 2 Nf4#. To prevent the double check *and* to immobilize the troublesome Ne6, Black can reply 1 ... Bf7, a 'tertiary black correction', but White replies 2 Qf5#.
(See also ANDERSSEN; VISSERMAN.)

The terms secondary and tertiary (and, perhaps, quaternary) are supposed to indicate degrees of complexity. A BLOCK problem may also show correction, the only difference being the absence of a primary threat. Black correction may be found in many 19th-century problems, but was first named and defined by HARLEY in 1935. There is, of course, no real correction, for Black is mated anyway, and more appropriate terms such as 'compensation' or 'continued defence' have been suggested.

White Correction
This is real correction: all but one of the random and corrected moves fail to solve the problem.

#2

A problem by AHUES, first prize, *Schweizerische Schachzeitung*, 1982. By moving the Bg6 White threatens Ng6#. A random move (e.g. Ba7?) is defeated by 1 ... Bb1. The following are secondary corrections: 1 Bf5? Bc7, 1 Be4? Rd6, 1 Bc2? Nd6. The key is 1 Bd3, avoiding the errors of the secondary corrections:

1 ... Bc7   2 Qxf6#
1 ... Rd6   2 Qe4#
1 ... Nd6   2 Qc1#.
(See also PETKOV.)

correspondence chess, TELECHESS in which moves are sent by mail (post or electronic). The memorizing of opening variations and also visualization are discounted, for books may be consulted and the men may be moved when a position is analysed. The slow pace may be alleviated by the offer of a CONDITIONAL CONTINUATION, binding if accepted.

Thomas HYDE refers to games being played in the 1600s between Venetian and Croatian merchants, who found the transmission of moves expensive. There may have been earlier games of this kind. However, the 'golden age' of correspondence chess was in the first half of the 19th century. Players from different cities and countries could not easily play together in any other way until travel facilities improved, after which over-the-board matches and then tournaments came into vogue.

By the end of the 20th century the strength of chess computers makes competitive correspondence play unsatisfactory, although for friendly play it retains its popularity.

The earliest known postal game, in 1804, was between players living at Breda and The Hague, about 40 miles (65 km) apart. The most important match was between the clubs of Edinburgh (which won +2=2−1) and London, 1824–8. Several newspapers published the moves, and for the first time a wide readership could study the games of contemporary players. An era of open games and attacking play began and the SCOTCH GAMBIT became one of the favoured weapons. The letters were carried a distance of about 400 miles (650 km) by mail coach, travelling night and day; at each of about 30 staging posts four horses stood ready, to be placed in the shafts within five minutes; breaks for three meals a day were restricted to 20 or 30 minutes; and the letters were delivered within three days, much as today. (By 1836 the journey time had been reduced to 42 hours 53 minutes.) The high cost of postage was, however, a deterrent. For example, each letter from London to Edinburgh cost 1s 1d, equivalent to several pounds today. Consequently most of the early games were played between groups of people who could share the cost. In 1834–6 the Paris Club defeated the Westminster Club (+2) and in 1842–6 Pest defeated Paris (+2), pointers to France's superiority in the 1830s and decline in the 1840s.

On 10 January 1840 Britain introduced a nationwide penny post and two months later WALKER reported a widespread increase in the number of correspondence games. Cheap postage soon followed in other countries. In the 1850s some magazines promoted tournaments, in 1870 the Caissa Correspondence Club, the first of its kind, was founded in England, and in 1888 *Monde Illustré* organized the first international tournament. Since 1917, when *The Chess Correspondent* was published

in USA, there have been numerous other periodicals devoted to this form of chess.

In December 1928 the Internationaler Fernschach Bund (IFSB) was founded in Germany; reconstituted after the Second World War as the International Correspondence Chess Association (ICCA), it became the International Correspondence Chess Federation (ICCF) in 1951 and was affiliated to FIDE in 1961. An agreement in 1968 confirmed that FIDE and ICCF would be jointly responsible for world correspondence championships of various kinds and for the awarding of FIDE titles. After a series of qualifying rounds the final of the first individual world championship tournament began in 1950. Such finals take about three or four years to complete. The German language monthly magazine *Fernschach*, founded in 1929, discontinued in 1939, and restarted in 1951, is the official organ of the ICCF. See BERLINER, LOLLI ATTACK, and PENROSE for games played by correspondence.

Egbert Meissenburg, *Die Geschichte des Fernschachspiels bis 1823* (1984); Bruno Bassi, *The History of Correspondence Chess up to 1839* (1965); T. D. Harding, *The Games of the World Correspondence Chess Championships I–X* (1987).

correspondence notation, a form of CO-ORDINATE NOTATION, recognized by FIDE, used for transmitting the moves of a correspondence game. The files are numbered 1 to 8 from the queen's flank to the king's flank, the ranks 1 to 8 from White's side of the board. Each square is described by two digits, the file number preceding the rank number. A move is shown by a four-digit number, the departure square preceding the arrival square. Thus, e2-e4 becomes 5254. Castling is represented by the king's move alone: for example 0-0 for White becomes 5171. The piece chosen on promotion is shown by a 5th digit ($1 = Q$, $2 = R$, $3 = B$, $4 = N$). There are no symbols for capture, check, or *en passant*. In another system used in Yugoslavia, promotion to a queen is shown as a normal move, e.g. 2728 = b7-b8 (Q). Underpromotion on the same square is shown thus: 2711 = b7-b8(R), 2721 = b7-b8(N), and 2731 = b7-b8(B).

The purpose of this notation is to avoid problems that arise in international chess when players might use different initial letters for the same piece, or even different alphabets. Originated by a German professor, J. W. D. Wildt of Göttingen, the notation was used a quarter of a century later by KOCH in his *Elementarbuch der Schachspielkunst* (1828) and is often named after him. In 1813 a version of it was used in the *Liverpool Mercury*. Ivan Timofeyevich Savenkov (1846–1914) supported it in 1877 in *Shakhmatny Vestnik* and so it bears his name in Russia.

Cotlar Variation, 11 ... Rd8 12 c4 Be6, an alternative to the BERNSTEIN VARIATION, 210, in the QUEEN'S GAMBIT Declined analysed by Ovsey Cotlar in *Caïssa*, Nov.–Dec. 1945. Cotlar, then living in

Argentina, was said to be a Russian who had won a tournament at Kiev in 1919 ahead of BOGOLJUBOW.

counterattack, (1) an attack mounted by the defender or by a player who is apparently defending.

counterattack, (2) a description of a kind of opening variation initiated by Black.

counter-gambit, an opening in which Black offers a gambit. It is only rarely a direct reply to a gambit, as in the ALBIN and FALKBEER COUNTER-GAMBITS, or a delayed response, as in the BRYAN, LÓPEZ-GIANUTIO, and WINAWER COUNTER-GAMBITS.

counterplay, active manœuvring by a player who is, or appears to be, on the defensive.

Counterthrust Variation, 415, a line in the KING'S INDIAN DEFENCE akin to the GRÜNFELD DEFENCE, 363.

country move, an irrelevant single-step advance of a rook's pawn to its third rank in the opening phase, e.g. 1 e4 e5 2 Nf3 Nc6 3 Bb5 Nf6 4 d3 d6 5 Bxc6+ bxc6 6 h3 (Anderssen–L. Paulsen, London 1862). When largely abandoned by masters country moves became the mark of an inexper-

ienced player, the name being used disparagingly (*cf.* PROVINCIAL OPENING). Wilhelm STEINITZ believed that early moves of the rook's pawn were invariably bad, that they would always weaken the pawn structure. This extreme view was not shared by the younger masters of the 1890s, and since then players have taken a pragmatic attitude, using their judgement to decide whether the move of a rook's pawn is advisable in a given situation.

coupe, a KNOCK-OUT tournament.

courier, UNORTHODOX CHESS going back at least to 1209, according to MURRAY, but not known to have been played outside Germany, where it long survived in the village of STRÖBECK and where, although it is no longer used, a courier board is still to be found in the main café.

The game is played on a 12 × 8 chequered board. The players face the long sides, each having, according to SELENUS, a light-coloured square on the right. Viewing the board from White's side the pieces are arranged on the first rank from left to right as follows: rook, knight, alfil, courier, MANN, king, fers, *Schleich*, courier, alfil, knight, rook. Twelve pawns are on the second rank. Black's array mirrors this. The *Schleich* is moved like a WAZIR, and the courier like a bishop. Usually each player began with the same four moves: the advance of the

The Chess Game by Lucas van Leyden (1494–1533)

pawns in front of the rooks and the fers to the fourth rank (only these three pawns could be moved two squares initially), and the 'joy-leap' of the fers to the square immediately behind its pawn. The king could neither leap nor castle. In an early 16th-century painting generally known as *The Chess Game*, Lucas van Leyden depicts a 12 × 8 board, a detail that some have supposed to be an example of artists' fallibility as social chroniclers; but Lucas had probably seen the courier board in use.

Cozio, Carlo Francesco (*c*.1715–*c*.1780), Italian count who wrote a four-part two-volume treatise on the game, *Il giuoco degli scacchi* (1766). The manuscript, in the library of Lothar SCHMID, is dated 1740, and there may have been an earlier edition. The first volume, parts one and two, contains 228 opening variations and more than 200 sub-variations, the largest number to appear in any book up to that time. The arrangement is not systematic, but the coverage is wide, and there are many lines of play not previously published: BALOGH DEFENCE, COZIO ATTACK, HANSTEIN GAMBIT, HUNGARIAN DEFENCE, LASKER VARIATION (1067), ROSSOLIMO VARIATION, and STEINITZ ATTACK. The second book consists of part three, dealing with different laws of chess used in Calabria, and part four, which contains a total of 201 endgames and middlegame positions, studies, and problems. For an article by ROYCROFT on part four, see *EG* no. 33, July 1973. Cozio's dates are conjectured from his re-investiture in 1736, presumably on coming of age, with the title of Count of Montiglio and Salabue to which he succeeded in 1725, and of his son's succession in 1780.

Cozio Attack, 1112 in the KING'S GAMBIT Accepted, given by COZIO in 1766.

Cozio Defence, 1102, a standard continuation in the KING'S GAMBIT Accepted given by LÓPEZ, and known also by other names such as Hanneken Defence, Lichtenhein Counterattack, Morphy Defence, and Prussian Defence; also 783 in the SPANISH OPENING, a variation first given by CARRERA, tried in recent times by LARSEN, and sometimes known as the Lucena–Cozio Variation, or Steinitz Variation. (See LEGALL'S TRAP.)

Cozio Defence Deferred, 690, the COZIO DEFENCE in the SPANISH OPENING played after 3 . . . a6, and sometimes called the Anderssen Variation.

Cozio Variation, 1106 and 1159, both in the KING'S GAMBIT Accepted, given by COZIO, but of no importance today.

Cracow Variation, 919 in the ITALIAN OPENING, played by Cracow Chess Club in a fixed opening correspondence tournament, 1909, and sometimes called the Bartmański Variation, after one of the players. The variation was not new, having been introduced in games played by John Lord at the London 1883 supporting tournament.

cramped position, a position in which the mobility of a player's men is restricted. A severe case often leads to a loss because the opponent's mobility can be correspondingly increased, with decisive effect. Slightly cramped positions, however, are usually defensible. This was understood and tested in practice by PAULSEN in the 1860s, when attacking play was regarded as the only correct strategy. While STEINITZ, LASKER, and most other world champions were expert at handling cramped positions, the skill has now become requisite for any leading player. The development of this ability influenced the development of chess strategy. (See SCHOOLS OF CHESS.)

critical move, see CRITICAL PLAY.

critical play, a problem term for play featuring the move of a line-piece (the critical move) across a CUTTING-POINT (which thus becomes the critical square) later occupied by a piece (which INTERFERES).

#3

A problem by the Bohemian composer Anton Nowotny (1827–71), *Leipziger Illustrierte Zeitung*, 1854. The solution is 1 Rbc2 (threatening 2 R2c4 ‡) 1 . . . Bxc2 (a critical move, crossing the critical square e4) 2 Nfe4 (the interference move, of a kind known as Nowotny Interference) and now 2 . . . Rxe4 3 Nf5 ‡, or 2 . . . Bxe4 3 Ne2 ‡.

Suppose it were Black's move after 1 Rc2 Bxc2. Black could play . . . Bg6, when interference on e4 is ineffective. Such a move across a cutting-point is called an anti-critical move.

See MANṢŪBA for a critical move problem using the laws of the old game. For the first known example in modern chess, see INDIAN THEME. See also DOUBLING THEMES; KUZOVKOV.

Critical play was examined thoroughly by KOHTZ and KOCKELKORN in *Das indische Problem* (1903).

critical square, see CRITICAL PLAY.

cross-check, a check in answer to a check. This may arise by interposing a man, by moving the king to discover check, or by capture of the checking piece. (Problem jargoneers call the last two, respectively, royal battery check and direct return capture check.) In the ending Q + P v. Q the threat of cross-checks by interposition is a common means of evading perpetual check; otherwise rare in play, cross-checks are sometimes featured in problems.

Crosskill, Alfred (1829–1904), English ENDGAME analyst, the son of an industrialist. After receiving a liberal education in England and Germany he worked in his father's business; later he became a proprietor of a foundry. Active in politics, and a rousing public speaker, he became mayor of his home town, Beverley, Yorkshire, from 1875 to 1878. In 1886 he retired from business and local politics to pursue his hobbies of literature, whist, and chess.

An outstanding analyst, he made two important contributions to endgame knowledge: a position that can be won only if the FIFTY-MOVE LAW is suspended, and *King and Queen against King and Rook*, a definitive work published under the pen-name Euclid in 1895. More than a century later, in 1985, Thompson solved by computer the endgame R + B v. R, thus incidentally validating Crosskill's analysis.

+

A study by Crosskill, *Chess Player's Magazine*, 1864. 1 Bd3 Re1 2 Bf5 Re3 3 Bd7 Kb8 4 Rg4 Rb3 5 Be6 Rb2 6 Bc4 Rh2 7 Rg8+ Ka7 8 Rg7+ Ka8 9 Bd3 Rh6+ 10 Kc7 Rf6 11 Rh7 Ka7 12 Re7 (Black is now in ZUGZWANG) 12...Rf8 13 Bb5 Rg8 14 Re1 Rg7+ 15 Bd7 Rg6 16 Be6 Rg7+ 17 Kc6 Rg6 18 Ra1+ Kb8 19 Rb1+ Ka7 20 Rb7+ Ka8 21 Re7 Rg2 22 Bf5 Rf2 23 Re5 Rf3 24 Be6 Kb8 25 Rb5+ Ka7 26 Ra5+ Kb8 27 Bd5 Rg3 28 Rb5+ Ka7 29 Rb7+ Ka8 30 Rh7 Rg6+ 31 Kc7+ Ka7 32 Bc4 Rg5 33 Kc6+ Kb8 34 Rh8+ Ka7 35 Bd5 Rg1 36 Rh7+ Kb8 37 Be4 Rc1+ 38 Kd6 Rc8 39 Rb7+ Ka8 40 Rf7+ Kb8 41 Bd5 Rc2 42 Rb7+ Kc8 43 Ra7 Kd8 44 Rf7 Re2 45 Rg7 Re1 46 Rb7 Rc1 47 Bb3 Rc3 48 Be6 Rd3+ 49 Bd5 Rc3 50 Rd7+ Kc8 51 Rf7 Rc6 52 Rb7+ Kc8 53 Rb4 Kd8 54 Bc4 Kc8 55 Be6+ Kd8 56 Rb8+ Rc8 57 Rxc8 mate.

cross-pin, the pinning of a piece that is itself pinning a man, a stratagem more often seen in composition than in play.

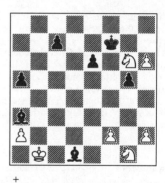

+

A study by KAMINER, second prize, *Trud*, 1935. 1 h7 Bh5 2 Nf4 gxf4 3 h8 = Q Bg6+ 4 Ka1 Be7 5 Nf3 Bf6+ 6 Ne5+ Ke7 7 Qh4! (cross-pin) 7...Bxh4 8 Nxg6+.
(See also BREDE THEME.)

crosstable, a table showing the result of every game in a tournament. The players may be arranged in alphabetical sequence, in result sequence, or in pairing sequence. Each has its advantages, but the last is least obvious. By using a crosstable in pairing sequence in conjunction with PAIRING TABLES it is possible to see in which round each game was played, and who had the white pieces. The result sequence is the most popular, as in the example, which shows the outcome of the double-round AVRO tournament held in the Netherlands, 1938. Each pair of figures shows the player's results against the opponent whose number appears at the head of the column, the left-hand figure being the first of the two rounds. (See GAIGE.)

	1	2	3	4	5	6	7	8	
1 Keres	x	1½	½½	½½	½½	1½	1½	½½	8½
2 Fine	0½	x	1½	11	10	10	½½	1½	8½
3 Botvinnik	½½	0½	x	1½	½0	1½	½1	½½	7½
4 Alekhine	½½	00	0½	x	1½	½½	½1	½1	7
5 Euwe	½½	01	½1	0½	x	0½	01	1½	7
6 Reshevsky	0½	01	0½	½½	1½	x	½½	1½	7
7 Capablanca	0½	½½	½0	½0	10	½½	x	½1	6
8 Flohr	½½	0½	½½	½0	0½	0½	½0	x	4½

Csom (pron. chom), István (1940–), Hungarian player and trainer, International Grandmaster (1973), national champion 1972 and, jointly, 1973. His best results were in the 1970s: Cleveland (Ohio) 1975, first; Kecskemét 1979, second (+7=7−1) equal with NOGUEIRAS, after FARAGÓ; Berlin 1979, first equal with SMYSLOV. In the 1980s he was first or equal first in various tournaments, notably Jarvenpaa 1985, New Delhi 1987, Silkeborg 1988, and Tel Aviv 1988–9. From 1968 he played in several Olympiads, notably in 1978, when Hungary won the gold medal ahead of the USSR.

Cunningham, Alexander (1654–1737), Scottish historian and scholar who gave his name to a gambit which dates back at least to GRECO.

Helped by the patronage of the Duke of Argyll, Cunningham achieved eminence as a diplomatist and from 1715 to 1720 was the British Minister to the Republic of Venice. The first attribution of the gambit to him is in an unpublished manuscript by Caze, dated Amsterdam, 1706.

Cunningham, Alexander (c.1655–1730), Scottish critic and scholar. Like the above he was patronized by a Whig politician; he lived for a while in The Hague and was an excellent chess-player. There was confusion about the identity of the 'gambit' Cunningham because of the close parallels of the two lives. At one time it was thought that they were the same person, but a letter in the *Scot's Magazine*, Oct. 1804, established they were two, the writer having examined the wills in Doctors' Commons. Then the gambit was attributed to the critic, an opinion not reversed until MURRAY published his findings in the *British Chess Magazine*, 1912.

Cunningham Gambit, 1121, a line in the KING'S GAMBIT Accepted that was evolved c.1706 by the Scottish historian Alexander CUNNINGHAM. After 4 Bc4 he advocated 4...Bh4+, probably a sound continuation, but superseded by 4...Nf6 as recommended by SCHLECHTER in the eighth edition of the HANDBUCH, 1912–16.

cutting point, a problem term for a square across which two or more line-pieces might need to be moved. This square is where their paths cross, and if it is occupied by another man the freedom of one or both pieces is impaired.

cutting-point themes, problem themes featuring interference on a CUTTING POINT.

#2

A problem by BLAKE, *Western Daily Mercury*, 1906. The key is 1 Qd2 threatening 2 Qxd4#. The R on a3 needs to defend g3 and e3, the B on e2 needs to defend b5 and c4, and their paths intersect on the cutting point d3.

1...Bd3	2 Qxh2#
1...Rd3	2 Be7#
1...Nbd3	2 Nc4#
1...Ncd3	2 Qxe2#
1...d3	2 Qe3#.

By-play 1...Qd6 2 Bxd4# and 1...Qxd7 2 Nxd7#. The first two variations, showing reciprocal interference by R and B, constitute Grimshaw interference, named after the English composer Walter Grimshaw (1832–90), who showed the idea in 1854. (See also ORGAN PIPES; RUSINEK.)

Similar reciprocal interference between R and B, accompanied by sacrifice on the cutting point, constitutes Nowotny interference; see BRISTOL CLEARANCE; CRITICAL PLAY.

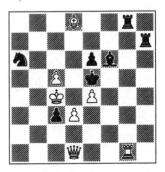

#4

A problem by the Polish composer Josef Plachutta (1827–83), *Leipziger Illustrierte Zeitung*, 1858. After the introductory play 1 Qf3 Nxc5 White continues by 2 Rg7, a sacrifice on the cutting point g7 (the R on h7 needs to guard c7, the R on g8 to guard g3).

| 2...Rhxg7 | 3 Qg3+ Rxg3 | 4 Bc7# |
| 2...Rgxg7 | 3 Bc7+ Rxc7 | 4 Qg3#. |

This is the Plachutta Theme. A year earlier LOYD had shown the same idea, and a version of his problem published in *The Illustrated London News*, Dec. 1857, was almost certainly known to Plachutta. (See also TROITZKY.)

In 1909 the American composer Otto B. Wurzburg (1875–1951) published a problem showing the same idea, but without sacrifice on the cutting point, and this became known as the Wurzburg–Plachutta theme. A year later the German composer Walther von Holzhausen (1876–1935) showed this theme on the diagonals, using Q and B, and this was called the Holzhausen theme, although new jargon was not required. (See KUZOVKOV.)

Unlike the Grimshaw and Nowotny interferences (using R and B), the Plachutta and its relations use like-moving pieces (R and R, or Q and B) and cannot be shown in two-movers.

All cutting-point themes can be preceded by critical play, which is an essential ingredient of the INDIAN THEME.

Cvitan, Ognjen (1961–), Yugoslav player, International Grandmaster (1987), World Junior Champion 1981, winner of tournaments at Prague 1987, Geneva 1988, and the strong Vršac 1989 (+3=11).

cyclic play, or cyclic shift, a problem term for the pattern formed by the contrast between moves played in one variation or phase and moves played in another. Suppose a, b, c represent black moves and A, B, C White moves; then the sequence aA, bB, cC in one phase and aB, bC, cA in another shows cyclic shift. A complete cycle would come about if another phase showed moves aC, bA, cB. Cyclic patterns may be shown in one or more phases, with moves by both sides or by one side. (See BAKCSI; GOUMONDY; LOBUSOV; VISSERMAN.)

The minimum requirement for the Lačný theme is three changed mates (or mating continuations) in two phases showing cyclic shift.

s#3

A self-mate by AVNER, first prize, Israel Ring tourney, 1981, showing four-fold cyclic shift, a Lačný theme in which the set play is contrasted with the post-key play. The set play (as if Black were to move first):

  1...Rxb3 2 Rd6+ Kf5 3 Ne3+ Rxe3#
  1...Rc2 2 Qc3+ bxc3 3 f8=Q+ Bxf8#
  1...Nxb3 2 Ne4+ Ke6 3 Nc5+ Nxc5#
  1...Nc2 2 Ra6+ Ke7 3 Qxb4+ Bxb4#
The key is 1 Qc2:
  1...Rb3 2 Qc3+ bxc3 3 f8=Q+ Bxf8#
  1...Rxc2 2 Ne4+ Ke6 3 Nc5+ Rxc5#
  1...Nb3 2 Ra6+ Ke7 3 Qc5+ Nxc5#
  1...Nxc2 2 Rd6+ Kf5 3 Ne3+ Nxe3#.
This theme was investigated by the Czech composer Ľudovít Lačný (1926–) in the 1950s. See MLADE-NOVIĆ for a 3-phase Lačný.

cylinder board, a rectangular board that is curved so that two opposite edges meet to form a cylinder; men may be moved across the joined edge. When a standard board is used the joining of the a- and h-files produces a vertical cylinder, the joining of the first and eighth ranks a horizontal cylinder. A form of ROUND CHESS, played on a board which is, in effect, a plane projection of a cylinder board, was known at least as early as the 10th century. The 8 × 8 cylinder board introduced by *Chess Amateur*

in 1922 was used for play in a tournament at San Francisco in 1924, but mostly for problems subsequently.

shp18

A SERIES-MOVER by the English composer Arnold John (Adam) Sobey (1925–), *The Problemist*, 1989. The omission of framing lines at the top and bottom of the diagram indicates a horizontal cylinder board. (The lines at the sides are omitted instead for a vertical cylinder board.) The man on h7 is a white WAZIR, the man on d2 a NIGHTRIDER. Black is to make 18 consecutive single-moves so that White can play only one move, giving stalemate. 1-5 e1=W, 6-9 Wf1-g1-g8-h8, 10 Wxh7, 11-14 Wh8-g8-g1-f1, 15-16 Kh8-h7, 17-18 Wf2-f3, and White moves the nightrider to b3, pinning the wazir, controlling h8 and h6, thus stalemating Black.
(See also ANCHOR RING.)

Czech Defence, 38 in the ENGLISH OPENING. By playing 6 d4 White can transpose into a GRÜNFELD DEFENCE. Also 88, a standard line in the SLAV DEFENCE sometimes called the Open Slav Defence.

Czech Variation, 281, a line similar to the BLOCK-ADE VARIATION, 52, of the BENONI DEFENCE, which PANOV claims to have introduced in 1937.

Czerniak Attack, 537, a name sometimes used for the LEVENFISH ATTACK in the SICILIAN DEFENCE because it may lead to a trap devised by Moshe Czerniak (1910–84), the first champion of Palestine (1936): 6...Bg7 7 e5 dxe5 8 fxe5 Nd5? 9 Bb5+ Kf8 10 0-0 Bxe5 11 Bh6+ Kg8 12 Nxd5 Qxd5 13 Nf5 Qc5+ 14 Be3 Qc7 15 Nh6+ Kg7 16 Rxf7 mate.

Czerniak Variation, 585, a line in the CARO–KANN DEFENCE played in the game Keres–Czerniak, Buenos Aires Olympiad 1939.

D

dabbaba, a LEAPER used in several versions of GREAT CHESS. The co-ordinates of its leap are 2,0, and the length of its move √4. Standing on d4, it attacks b4, d6, f4, and d2. The name was also used to describe pieces that moved in other ways. In the 10th century a dabbaba on a 10 × 10 board was moved like a MANN, in a 14th-century game like a bishop, and in an 18th-century game like an EM-PRESS. Dabbaba means sow, a movable structure to protect soldiers advancing upon a fort.

Dake, Arthur William (*né* Dakowski) (1910–), American player, honorary International Grand-master (1986), son of a Polish father and a Norwegian mother. Coming from Portland, Oregon, to New York in 1930 he won the Marshall Club championship, 1930–1, and thus obtained entry to the New York tournament, 1931. He fared badly in this event, but the experience sharpened his play, and at Pasadena 1932 he tied for third place with RESHEVSKY and H. STEINER, after ALEKHINE and KASHDAN. Dake never bettered this tournament performance, but he distinguished himself in three Olympiads (all won by the USA) in the last of which, Warsaw 1935, he made the best score at board four (+13=5). He largely gave up competitive chess in 1938, returning only for occasional events such as the 1945 US–USSR radio match.

Duke Alekhine   Pasadena 1932   Caro–Kann Defence
Panov–Botvinnik Attack

1 e4 c6 2 d4 d5 3 exd5 cxd5 4 c4 Nf6 5 Nc3 Nc6 6 Nf3 Be6 7 c5 g6 8 Bb5 Bg7 9 Ne5 Qc8 10 Qa4 Bd7 11 0-0 0-0 12 Bf4 a6 13 Bxc6 bxc6 14 Rfe1 Nh5 15 Bd2 Ra7 16 Re2 Be8 17 Rae1 f5 18 Nf3 Nf6 19 Rxe7 Rxe7 20 Rxe7 f4 21 Bxf4 Ne4 22 Be5 Bh6 23 Nxe4 dxe4

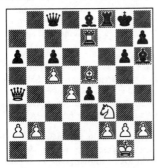

24 Ng5 Qf5 25 Qb3+ Bf7 26 Nxf7 Rxf7 27 Rxf7 Qxf7 28 Qb8+ Qf8 29 d5 e3 30 f4 Qxb8 31 Bxb8 Kf7 32 dxc6 Ke8 33 b4 g5 34 g3 gxf4 35 gxf4 Kd8 36 a4 Kc8 37 Bd6 Bg7 38 Kf1 Black resigns.

Damiano, Pedro (d. 1544), author of the first chess book to be published in Italy, *Questo libro e da imparare giocare a scachi et de le partite* (Rome, 1512). According to *Bibliotheca Lusitana* (1759) Damiano was an apothecary from Odemira in south-west Portugal. His book has 124 unnum-bered pages, 89 of which deal with problems and studies (all but one taken from other sources) with both Italian and Spanish text. Damiano suggests the game was invented by Xerxes which is why it was known in Spanish as Axedrez. He examines a few openings, noting that after 1 e4 e5 2 Nf3 the reply 2 ... Nc6 is best, 2 ... d6 is not good, and 2 ... f6 (the opening named after him) is worst. Besides advocating a CLASSICAL CENTRE he adds various maxims, e.g. 'If you have a good move look to see whether there is a better one' and 'With an advantage make equal exchanges.' The last chapter gives advice about BLINDFOLD CHESS.

Nearly 50 years elapsed before another textbook (by Ruy LÓPEZ) was published, and during that time Damiano's book achieved such wide popularity that seven editions were published in Rome and a French translation in Paris. English and German translations subsequently appeared. (See ANASTA-SIA'S MATE; OVERLOAD.)

Damiano Defence, 1051, a variation given by LUCENA and rightly condemned by DAMIANO as leading to a lost game.

Damiano–Steinitz Variation, 787, the NUREMBERG VARIATION of the SPANISH OPENING, given by DAMIANO, and played in games Tarrasch–Steinitz and Schlechter–Steinitz, both Nuremberg 1896.

Damiano Variation, 1069 in the PETROFF DEFENCE, given by DAMIANO and given a small revival in the 1970s.

Damljanović, Branko (1961–), Serbian player, International Grandmaster (1989). Finished equal first in the Yugoslav championship in 1989 but lost the play-off to KOŽUL. He was equal first in a tournament in India, at Kolhapur 1987, and later in the same year was equal first in a Swiss system tournament at Belgrade. In 1990 he was equal 12th in the interzonal tournament at Manila, failing by half a point to become a CANDIDATE.

dangerous diagonal, the diagonal e1–h4 for White or e8–h5 for Black. A beginner is often surprised by the arrival of the enemy queen on the h-file, attack-ing the f-pawn, giving check, or delivering mate. Grandmasters, too, may be surprised, as in the following game.

Nunn–Kiril Georgiev   Linares 1988   Caro–Kann Defence

1 e4 c6   2 d4 d5   3 Nd2 dxe4   4 Nxe4 Nd7   5 Ng5 h6?   6 Ne6 Qa5+   7 Bd2 Qb6   8 Bd3 fxe6?   9 Qh5+ Kd8   10 Ba5 and White won.

Danish Gambit, 660, analysed by many who lived in Denmark: in the 1830s by a jurist called Blankensteiner living in Jutland; by M. J. S. From, who played it in the Paris tournament of 1867; by LASA when he was Prussian Ambassador at Copenhagen (1865–78); and later by KRAUSE, SØRENSEN, and others. It is also known as the Nordic Gambit.

Danube Gambit, 413, a line in the ANTI-GRÜNFELD VARIATION, analysed by ADORJÁN of Budapest in 1967. The name was first used in the bulletin of the Amsterdam 1978 tournament with reference to the game Dzindzichashvili–Adorján, and is an analogy with the similar VOLGA GAMBIT (i.e. Benko Gambit).

Darga, Klaus Viktor (1934–), German player, International Grandmaster (1964), computer programmer. From 1953, when he tied for first place in the World Junior Championship (he lost on tie-break), Darga became a regular competitor in international tournaments. He won the West German championship in 1955 and 1961, and reached his best form in the late 1960s, notably at Winnipeg 1967 when he came first (+3=6) equal with LARSEN, ahead of KERES and SPASSKY. Afterwards he devoted himself to his profession and entered fewer tournaments. Darga played in ten Olympiads from 1954 to 1978. (See USELESS CHECK.)

dark bishop, a bishop, white or black, that is moved on the dark squares.

Dawson, Thomas Rayner (1889–1951), English composer, pioneer of both FAIRY PROBLEMS and RETROGRADE ANALYSIS. For fairy problems he invented new pieces: GRASSHOPPER (1912), NEUTRAL MAN (1912), and NIGHTRIDER (1925); he codified new rules such as the MAXIMUMMER (1913) and various kinds of SERIES-MOVERS; and he used unorthodox boards. In 1915 he wrote *Retrograde Analysis*, the first book on the subject, completing the project begun several years earlier by HUNDSDORFER.

From 1919 to 1930 Dawson conducted a column devoted to fairy chess in the *Chess Amateur*. In 1926 he was co-founder of the *Problemist*, which he edited for its first six years, and he founded and edited the *Problemist Fairy Supplement* (1931–6), continued as the *Fairy Chess Review* (1936–51). Besides conducting columns in several newspapers and periodicals, one of them daily, and one in the *Braille Chess Magazine*, Dawson edited the problem section of the *British Chess Magazine* from 1931 to 1951; he devised and published in its pages (1947–50) a systematic terminology for problem themes in the hope that it would supplant the extensive jargon then and now in use. Dawson wrote five books on fairy problems: *Caissa's Wild Roses* (1935); *C. M. Fox, His Problems* (1936); *Caissa's Wild Roses in Clusters* (1937); *Ultimate Themes* (1938); and *Caissa's Fairy Tales* (1947). Charles Masson Fox was a patron whose generosity made possible the publication of four of these books, and the two fairy problem magazines founded by Dawson. *Ultimate Themes* deals with TASKS, another of Dawson's favourite subjects. In 1973 all five books were republished in one volume, *Five Classics of Fairy Chess*.

Dawson found it difficult to understand the problemist's idea of beauty because it is not susceptible to precise definition. 'The artist talks of "quiet" moves, oblivious that they are White's most pulverizing attacks! This aesthetic folly, reverence, response, thrill, to vainglorious bombast runs throughout chess.' He was a rapid worker with about 6,500 compositions to his credit. Many of his orthodox problems are unmemorable, often composed to meet a need in one of his numerous theoretical writings. The problem given under PLUS-FLIGHTS, for example, was composed to fill just such a gap. His best work was in HELPMATES, fairy chess, and, above all, in retrograde analysis, which he considered the highest chess art.

His genius did not set him apart from his fellows; he would find time for casual visitors, and would explain his ideas to a tyro with patience, modesty, and kindness. Although he won many tourney prizes much of his work was designed to encourage others, to enlarge the small band of fairy problem devotees. He composed less for fame than to amuse himself, confessing to another composer: 'we do these things for ourselves alone.' A chemistry graduate, Dawson took a post in the rubber industry in 1922 and rose to be head of the Intelligence Division of the British Rubber Manufacturers, for which he founded, catalogued, and maintained a technical library. Unwell for the last years of his life, he died from a stroke. (See LOSING CHESS; PLUS-FLIGHTS; RETRACTOR; RETRO-OPPOSITION; RIFLE CHESS.)

K. Fabel and C. E. Kemp, *Schach ohne Grenzen* or *Chess Unlimited* (1969) is a survey, in German and English, of Dawson's contribution to the art of fairy problems; G. P. Jelliss, *Retro-Opposition* (1989), contains 136 problems with commentary by Dawson.

decentralize, to move a piece that attacks, guards, or occupies a central square so that it no longer does so. This is generally undesirable unless the centre is well secured, or unless decisive action can be taken elsewhere on the board.

decisive error, an error that would alter the result of the game if correct play were to follow. Thus a player might lose a drawn position or fail to win a won position.

decoy, to lure an enemy man from its defensive role: the man used for that purpose. The use of a flank pawn to decoy an enemy king commonly happens in the endgame; for an example see IVKOV. The sacrifice of a piece to divert the opponent's men in the middlegame is usually called a DIVERSIONARY SACRIFICE.

decoy themes, problem themes in which a DECOY deprives Black of an essential defensive resource.

#4

A problem by KOHTZ and KOCKELKORN, *Deutsches Wochenschach*, 1905. If 1 Qe2? (threatening 2 Bd3, 3 Qc2#) Black defends by 1 ... Bg5 2 Bd3 Bxe3. The solution is 1 Nd6 (the decoy) 1 ... Bxd6 2 Qe2 Bf4 3 exf4 (not 3 Bd3? Bxe3) Kxd4 4 Qe5#.

A defending piece (black B) is moved to another square (d6) from where it still defends against the primary threat, but the changed defence permits a different mate. The composers called this the Roman Theme in honour of Augusto Guglielmetti (1864–1936) of Rome, principal founder of the first Italian Chess Foundation. Decoy themes were known long before 1905, but publication of this example greatly stimulated further developments. (see MATTISON; VLADIMIROV.)

#3

A problem by the Lebanese composer Edgard J. Tchélébi (1928–63), first prize *Europe Échecs*, 1962. White's main threat is 1 g8 = N and 2 Ne7#, but Black defends satisfactorily by 1 . . . Bh4. The solution is 1 Rh8 (the decoy, threatening 2 g8 = Q, 3 Qe8#) 1 ... Rh4 (preparing for ... Qg4) 2 g8 = N Bxc5 3 Nd8#.

The black bishop's guard of e7 is changed permitting a 'new' mate, but here the change of guard is brought about by the move of another black man (the Rd4). This is called the Hamburg Theme.

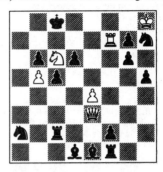

#3

A version of a problem by the German composer Friedrich Martin Palitzsch (1889–1932), *Deutsches Wochenschach*, 1919. If at once 1 Qa3? Black defends by 1 . . . Ba5. The solution is 1 Qg3 (a decoy threatening 2 Qxd6) 1 . . . Rd2 2 Qa3 Ba4 (the QB substitutes for the KB) 3 Qh3#.

One defence is substituted for another; this is the Dresden Theme, named after the composer's home city. (See also LOBUSOV.)

Composers have linked both Hamburg and Dresden Themes in one problem—in jargon the Elbe Theme, after the river that flows through both cities.

defence, (1) a move or moves played with the object of countering the opponent's threats. Defence may be passive (for an extreme case see FORTRESS) or active, when threats are answered by threats. More often than not masters prefer active defence, perhaps making some concessions to gain counterplay; examples from the opening phase are the BOLESLAVSKY VARIATION of the SICILIAN DEFENCE (Black concedes a HOLE at d5) and the MARSHALL COUNTERATTACK (Black sacrifices a pawn). A successful attacking game receives popular acclaim, but, as STEINITZ first observed, a well played defensive game is no less meritorious.

Composers use the word defence in a special sense: in a direct mate threat problem any move by Black that forestalls White's threat (using this word in its problem sense) is a defence.

defence, (2) a description of an opening, or an opening variation, initiated by Black. The name does not necessarily imply passive play: some defences are aggressive.

defensive centre, a centre consisting of a well defended centre pawn on its fourth rank. It is one of several kinds of PAWN CENTRE a player might choose in the opening phase. The best known example is the popular CLOSE VARIATION of the SPANISH OPENING in which Black defends a pawn on e5. A player who sets up such a centre gets a slightly cramped game, but he may have scope for a flank manœuvre, or, on occasion, the option of changing the central PAWN FORMATION. The soundness of the defensive centre was evident to STEINITZ, who sometimes used it when he had the white pieces, a new idea at the time.

A. Sokolov–Salov   Leningrad 1987   Spanish Opening
Barnes Defence

1 e4 e5 2 Nf3 Nc6 3 Bb5 g6 4 c3 a6 5 Ba4 d6 6 d4 Bd7 7 Bg5 f6 8 Be3 Nh6 9 h3 Nf7 10 0–0 Bg7 11 Nbd2 0–0 12 Re1 Qe7 13 Bc2 Ncd8 14 Nf1 Ne6 15 Qd2 Kh8 16 N3h2 Rg8 17 Ng3 h5 18 Ne2 Raf8 19 f4 Bh6 20 Nf3 (20 fxe5 maintains the equilibrium)

Black now breaks out of his slightly cramped position. 20 ... g5 21 fxg5 fxg5 22 Ng3 Nf4 23 dxe5 dxe5 24 Nf5 Bxf5 25 exf5 g4 26 hxg4 Rxg4 27 Bxf4 Bxf4 28 Qd5 Ng5 29 Kf1 Nxf3 30 Qxf3 Qg5 31 Qxb7 Bg3 32 Be4 Rh4 33 Ke2 Rd8 White resigns.

For other examples, see STEINITZ, VAGANYAN.

De Firmian, Nicholas Ernest (1957–), equal first, with BENJAMIN, in the US championship 1987, International Grandmaster (1985). He played for the USA in the Olympiads of 1984 and 1986.

D. Gurevich–de Firmian   Greenville 1983 US Championship   English Opening

1 Nf3 c5 2 c4 Nf6 3 Nc3 e6 4 g3 b6 5 Bg2 Bb7 6 0–0 Nc6 7 b3 Be7 8 Bb2 0–0 9 d4 Nxd4 10 Nxd4 Bxg2 11 Kxg2 cxd4 12 Qxd4 Qc7 13 Rad1 d6 14 f4 a6 15 a4 Rfd8 16 Rf3 d5 17 cxd5 exd5 18 b4 Qb7 19 g4 a5 20 g5 axb4 21 gxf6 Bc5 22 Qe5 bxc3 23 Bxc3 g6 24 Kg3

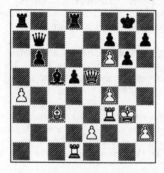

24 ... d4 25 Bxd4 Rd5 26 Qe3 Qd7 27 Bxc5 Rxd1 28 Bxb6 Re8 29 Qf2 h5 30 h3 Qxa4 31 Bc5 Re4 32 Be7 Qc4 33 Re3 h4+ 34 Kg4 Rg1+ 35 Qxg1 Rxf4+ 36 Kg5 Rf5+ White resigns.

Delmar Variation, 1024 in the PHILIDOR DEFENCE. Eugene Delmar (1841–1909) was not the first to play this move, but he did develop it as a SYSTEM in conjunction with the moves 6 Ng5 and 7 f4, e.g. Delmar–Hanham, New York 1889.

del Rio, Domenico Ercole (c.1718–c.1802), Italian author and lawyer, nicknamed the 'anonymous Modenese' after his only published chess book, *Sopra il giuoco degli scacchi osservazioni pratiche d'anonimo autore Modenese* (1750). Written in a more concentrated form than was usual at the time, this book of 110 pages was the basis of a more extensive work by LOLLI thirteen years later. Del Rio composed many problems that were fine for that period. Shortly before his death he completed another work. *La Guerra degli scacchi*, the manuscript of which is in the J. G. White collection in the Cleveland Library, Ohio. In 1984 Christopher B. Becker published the Italian text, with extensive translation and comments, under the title *The War of the Chessmen*. (See PROBLEM HISTORY; SCHOOLS OF CHESS.)

del Rio Attack, 1032, a line in the PHILIDOR DEFENCE, which DEL RIO, in his *La Guerra degli scacchi*, published only in 1984, claims to be a refutation of PHILIDOR'S analysis.

del Rio Variation, 646, also known as the Italian Defence, in the BISHOP'S OPENING.

demolish, to show that a composition is unsound and, perhaps, beyond repair. Thus, demolition, the demonstration that a composition is unsound.

demonstration board, a large chessboard mounted vertically. Chessmen in the shape of figurines may be attached, and games and positions shown to a large audience. Such boards are to be seen at many tournaments and matches. The first demonstration board, 4 ft (1.2 m) square, was designed by LÖWENTHAL in 1857 and used by him to illustrate his lectures. Today such boards are often electronic, activated by the players' board.

Denker, Arnold Sheldon (1914–), US champion 1944, honorary Grandmaster (1981). Denker was unfortunate in that he was perhaps at his best at a time when, because of war, little chess was being played, and American chess was dominated by FINE and RESHEVSKY.

derivative games, see KINDRED GAMES.

DERLD, 734, the 'Delayed Exchange Ruy López Deferred'. The line is also known as the Steenwijk Variation because it was played in that city in the

5th match game between EUWE and H. Kramer, 1940.

Deschapelles, Alexandre Louis Honoré Lebreton (1780–1847), reputedly the strongest player between the death of PHILIDOR and the time of BOURDONNAIS. He never met SARRATT, and he refused to meet the leading French players on even terms; but if he was not demonstrably the best player he was certainly the most colourful. In 1794, when his school at Brienne (where Napoleon had studied) was disbanded, he returned to Paris to discover that his aristocratic family had emigrated. He joined Napoleon's army, was left for dead at the siege of Mainz, fought again at Fleurus, was captured at Baylen and taken to Cadiz from where he made a clever escape. He lost his right hand (which caused him to be nicknamed Manchot) and was left with a sabre-scar from brow to chin. Among the first to be awarded the Cross of Honour, he tore it off when Napoleon crowned himself emperor.

He had a remarkable facility for games. Three months after learning the moves of Polish draughts (on a 10 × 10 board) he defeated the French champion; he played billiards pushing the cue with the stump of his right arm; and he boasted that he had learned all he needed to know about chess in three days. He first joined a chess club in 1798 and, not wanting to give his name because his parents were émigrés, he signed the register with the name of his dog Philiam. This became altered to William, leading to references to him as Guillaume le Breton. For a time he earned a living by playing at chess for stakes at the CAFÉ DE LA RÉGENCE. This lean time came to an end in 1812 when Marshal Ney made him superintendent of the tobacco monopoly at Strasburg, which brought him an income exceeding 40,000 fr. a year.

Following the battle of Waterloo he opposed the invasion by organizing a band of partisans who named him their general, but after this brief adventure he went back to the Café de la Régence, once again seeking a living from chess. A natural player, he despised book knowledge, and perhaps because he lacked it he played only at odds, conceding at least pawn and move to the strongest opponents. About 1820 he took Bourdonnais as a pupil. The two men could hardly have been more different: Deschapelles was delicate, irritable, slight, pale, abstemious, introverted, and a slow player; Bourdonnais was hearty, cheerful, ruddy, and a fast player.

In April 1821 Deschapelles played a triangular contest, conceding pawn and two to Bourdonnais and COCHRANE, who played level between themselves; Deschapelles defeated Cochrane (+6−1) but lost all seven games to Bourdonnais. Conceding pawn and move, Deschapelles lost a short match to LEWIS (=2−1) and, challenged by Cochrane to play even but to win two-thirds of the games, he lost that match too, blaming Cochrane's knowledge of openings.

A year or so later Deschapelles gave up chess and took to whist, rapidly becoming an expert and making more money than he could ever have made at the board. (Card players still refer to the Deschapelles coup, the lead of an unsupported high honour to establish an entry in partner's hand.) He was able to live comfortably in a pleasant villa with orchards, pheasants, and the most complete melon beds—he served ten varieties—in Paris. In the mid-1830s he renewed his interest in chess. Conceding pawn and two he played against SAINT-AMANT, drawing a match in 1836 (+1=1−1).

He was a stickler on matters of principle which, combined with his imperious manner and bad temper, frequently led him into duels which he happily fought left-handed. Arrested for being involved in the insurrection of June 1832—he had retained his republican beliefs—he wrote a pathetic letter to the King saying that he was too old, too infirm, and innocent. On his release he found that

The players' boards at this tournament (S.W.I.F.T., Brussels 1987) are connected by electric cables to computers which in turn are connected to demonstration boards. Each move is automatically reproduced on the board on the wall.

the Minister of the Interior had shown his letter around the whist club, exposing him to ridicule. Once, in the Café de la Régence, a waiter, sent to ask whether Deschapelles would play, took back a reply concerning stakes. 'Tell him my religion forbids me to play for money', to which Deschapelles responded, 'Mine forbids me to be absurd.'

His last days were spent writing unintelligible constitutions for Italy, Spain, Portugal, and various South American republics. Bedridden for the last 20 months of his life, he died of hydropsy, requesting in his will that no letter should be sent announcing his death, no newspaper should write about him, and that he should have a pauper's burial. Saint-Amant said: 'The only way to be on good terms with him without meanness or flattery is to see him seldom, never be under obligation to him, and to maintain a dignified reserve.'

Cochrane–Deschapelles St Cloud, 1821 (remove Black's f-pawn and begin with two single-moves by White)

1 e4 2 d4 Nc6 3 f4 d5 4 e5 Bf5 5 c3 e6 6 Bd3 Nh6 7 Ne? Qh4+ 8 g3 Qh3 9 Kd2 Bxd3 10 Kxd3 Qf5+ 11 Kd2 Ng4 12 Ke1 Qe4 13 Rg1 Nxh2 14 Nd2 Qd3 15 Kf2 Ng4+ 16 Ke1 Qe3 17 Nf1 Qf2+ 18 Kd2 Qf3 19 Kc2 Nf2 20 Qd2 Qe4+ 21 Kb3 Na5+ 22 Ka4 Nc4 23 Qe1 Qc2+ 24 b3

Here 24 ... a6 forces mate next move. 24 ... Nd3 25 Ne3 Nxe3 26 Qd2 Nb2+ 27 Kb5 c6+ 28 Ka5 Nec4+ 29

descriptive notation, a form of NOTATION sometimes called Anglo-Iberian or Anglo-American. This abbreviated form of a verbal description resembles the way in which a move would be described if notation did not exist. For example P-K4 (usually pronounced pawn to kay four) means pawn to king's fourth square. The heart of the system is the double identification of each square: one name is used by White, the other by Black.

The moves of the SPANISH OPENING would be written 1 P-K4 P-K4 2 N-KB3 N-QB3 3 B-N5 (there is no need to write 3 B-QN5 because only one bishop can be moved to N5). At one time the second moves might have been written 2 KN-B3 QN-B3; another bygone practice was to write, for example, 1 R-Ksq instead of R-K1; this survives in the occasional American R-K but is not recommended, as chess moves lend themselves to printer's errors. If two similar pieces can be moved to the

same square the departure square is given in parenthesis. Thus if a player has rooks on KN3 and QN2 and both could be moved to KN2 the description would be R(KN3)-N2 or R(QN2)-N2 or, perhaps, R/KN3-N2 or R/QN2-N2. If the intention is clear, part of the departure square description may be omitted, e.g. R(3)-N2. Care must be taken to describe the move in a way that fits no other move. For example, if White had knights on d3 and e3 and Black had pawns on c5, f5 and f4, then the move in STANDARD NOTATION, Nxf4, is precise. In descriptive notation NxP, NxBP and N(Q3)xBP are ambiguous: it would be necessary to write N(Q3)xKBP; NxP(B4) would suffice if it was clear whether (B4) means Black's B4 or White's B4.

Using this notation is like describing the location of a house in relationship to a landmark, 'the third house after the crossroads': the traveller needs to be moving in the right direction. Annotators have difficulty when discussing the importance of key squares, each of which has two names. There are a few ideas that are easier to discuss in general terms using descriptive notation, e.g. a FIANCHETTO can be described as P-N3 followed by B-N2. Even so, there was a marked drop in the use of descriptive notation in the 1970s.

Iberian and French usage has a different sequence. The hyphen is made redundant by giving first the name of the man, then the number of the square, and finally the name of the square. Using English initials for illustrative purposes, the Spanish Opening moves above are 1 P4K P4K 2 N3KB N3QB 3 B5N.

desperado, a piece, EN PRISE or trapped, that is used to inflict as much damage as possible before it is captured; a piece that is placed en prise when giving check, often so that its capture leads to stalemate.

Larsen–Lombardy   Reykjavik 1957   King's Indian
Sämisch Variation

1 d4 Nf6 2 c4 g6 3 Nc3 Bg7 4 e4 d6 5 f3 e5 6 d5 Nbd7
7 Bg5 0–0 8 Qd2 a6 9 0–0–0 Qe8 10 g4 Rb8 11 Nge2 b5
12 Ng3 bxc4 13 h4 Nb6 14 Kb1 c6 15 dxc6 Qxc6 16
Qxd6 Qb7 17 Rh2 Be6 18 h5 Ne8 19 Qe7 Nc7 20 Nf5
gxf5 21 gxf5 f6 22 Be3 Rfe8 23 Qc5 Bf7 24 Rg2 Kh8
25 Qxb6 Nb5 26 Nxb5 Qxb6 27 Bxb6 axb5 28 Bc7 Rb7
29 Rd7 Rc8

30 h6 Bxh6 31 Bxe5 (desperado) Rxd7 32 Bxf6+ Bg7
33 Rxg7 Rd6 34 Rxf7+ Kg8 35 Rg7+ Kf8 36 Rxh7
Rcc6 37 Be7+ Kg8 38 Bxd6 Kxh7 39 e5 Kh6 40 f4
Black resigns.

=

A MALYUTKA by HALBERSTADT, first prize, Réti
Memorial tourney, 1950. 1 Be1 Qe3 2 Bg3 (2 Bf2
loses) 2 . . . Qxg3(a) 3 Ra5+ Kb6 4 Ra6+ and
the rook, a desperado, gives perpetual check or its
capture leads to stalemate. Not 4 Rb5+?, e.g. 4 . . .
Kc6 5 Rb6+ Kc7 6 Rb7+ Kc8 and Black wins.
(a) or 2 . . . Qxc5 3 Bf2 or 2 . . . Kb6 3 Rc2 Qxg3
4 Rb2+ with perpetual check. (See also FRITZ;
KOROLKOV.)

Desprès Opening, 1327, named after Marcel
Desprès of France.

develop, to bring one's pieces into play during the
opening phase.

development, the process of developing the pieces
or the extent to which they are developed. To have
the better development is to have one's pieces more
effectively placed, always an advantage; to be ahead

in development is to have a greater number of
pieces in play, usually but not necessarily advantageous. Developing the pieces as fast as possible
was advocated by DEL RIO and many subsequent
writers; but securing the centre or establishing
strong points may be of more consequence, as, for
example, in the game given under CHANDLER.

De Vere, Cecil (1845?–75), pseudonym of Valentine
Brown, winner of the first official British championship tournament, organized by the British Chess
Association in 1866. He learned the game in London before 1858 and practised with BODEN and the
Irish player Francis Burden (1830–82). In the first
recorded mention of De Vere, *The Era,* 20 Dec.
1861, a report of a simultaneous display by PAULSEN
on 16 December, LÖWENTHAL was impressed by the
precocious skill of the '13-year-old' De Vere, implying that he was born in 1848.

De Vere played with unusual ease and rapidity,
never bothering to study the books. His features
were handsome (an Adonis, says MACDONNELL), his
manner pleasant, his conduct polite. He 'handled
the pieces gracefully, never "hovered" over them,
nor fiercely stamped them down upon the board . . .
nor exulted when he gained a victory . . . in short, he
was a highly chivalrous player.' So wrote STEINITZ,
who conceded odds in a match against De Vere and
was soundly beaten. (See PAWN AND MOVE.) De
Vere's charm brought him many friends.

At about the time that he won the national
championship his mother died, a loss he felt deeply,
'the only person who ever cared for me'. Receiving
a small legacy he gave up the job at Lloyds the
underwriters which Burden had obtained for him,
and never took another. He entered some strong
tournaments but always trailed just behind the
greatest half-dozen players of his time. His exceptional talent was accompanied by idleness and lack
of enthusiasm for a hard task. On the occasion of
the Dundee tournament of 1867 he took long walks
in the Scottish countryside with G. A. MacDonnell,
who writes that a 'black cloud' descended on De
Vere. It may have been the discovery that he had
tuberculosis; more probably he revealed to the
older man a deep-rooted despair, the cause perhaps
of his later addiction to alcohol.

In 1872 Boden handed over the chess column of
The Field to provide him with a small income; but
in 1873 the column was given to Steinitz on account
of De Vere's indolence and drunkenness. At the end
of November 1874 his illness took a turn for the
worse, he could hardly walk and ate little. His
friends paid to send him to Torquay for the sea air,
and there he died ten weeks later. He had failed to
nourish a natural genius, in respect of which,
according to Steinitz, De Vere was 'second to no
man, living or dead'.

Rosenthal–De Vere Paris 1867 French Defence Bourdonnais Attack

1 e4 e6 2 f4 d5 3 e5 c5 4 c3 Nc6 5 Bd3 c4 6 Bc2 Bc5 7
Nf3 Nh6 8 d4 cxd3 9 Qxd3 Qb6 10 b4 Bxb4 11 cxb4

Nxb4   12 Qe2 Bd7   13 Bd3 Ng4   14 Rf1 Rc8   15 Bd2 0–0
16 Bxb4

16 ... Rc1+ (ZWISCHENZUG)   17 Kd2 Rxf1   18 Qxf1
Qxb4+   19 Ke2 Qxf4   20 Qg1 Nxe5   21 Qe3 Nxd3   22
Kxd3 Qc4+   23 Kd2 Qb4+   24 Qc3 Qg4   25 Na3
Qxg2+   26 Ke3 e5   27 Nxe5 Re8   28 Re1 f6   29 Kd3
Bf5+   30 Kd4 fxe5+   31 Rxe5 Qg4+   32 Ke3 Qh3+
White resigns.

diagonal, a diagonal row of squares. Identification
is made by naming the squares at each end. The
diagonals a1–h8 and h1–a8 (known as the long
diagonals) and the seven- and six-square diagonals
are those most likely to be of strategic importance.

diagram, a pictorial representation of the board
and men. Conventionally, White plays up the page
and so, at one time, White was called south, Black
north; the king's side was east, the queen's, west.
Today this survives only in the opening names EAST
INDIAN DEFENCE and WEST INDIAN DEFENCE. Now the
men are printed as in the diagrams in this book but
in some medieval texts the black pieces were shown
'upside down', as if viewed from Black's side of the
board.

diagram blank, a printed diagram of the chessboard without any men.

dice, used long before chess for gambling purposes,
and perhaps even earlier for divination. It has been
conjectured, without supporting evidence, that a
forerunner of chess may have involved the use of
four-sided dice to determine which piece was to be
moved. There are equal grounds for the suggestion
that the first form of proto-chess was an oracular
ceremony involving dice and that these were discarded in order to create a game of skill.

dictionary or **encyclopedia of chess,** names used
interchangeably for books of various kinds. Three
encyclopedic works were published in the 1800s: J.
de la Torre, *Diccionario del juego del ajedrez* (Barcelona, 1837); ALEXANDRE, *Encyclopédie des échecs*
(Paris, 1837); and E. Carlo Usigli (1812–94), *Mis-
cellanea sul giuoco degli scacchi* (Naples, 1861). The
first contains the laws of chess based on PHILIDOR'S
book, definitions of chess terms (49 pp.) and illustrations of the chessboard, names of squares, stan-

dard notation, and a KNIGHT'S TOUR (4 pp.). The
second contains only opening variations. The third
is the nearest approach to a comprehensive encyclopedia.

A team of Russian experts, including KUBBEL and
LEVENFISH, wrote *Slovar shakhmatista* (Leningrad,
1929, 6,000 copies), and for the first time there were
entries for people and events. This lead, not followed by Sanchez Pérez, *Diccionario ilustrado de
ajedrez* (Madrid, 1934), was taken up again by B. J.
Horton, *Dictionary of Modern Chess* (New York,
1959), the first in English, and by all subsequent
authors.

Since then there have been works in English,
German, French, Italian, German, Portuguese,
Romanian, Polish, Danish, Czech, and Russian.
Among the more recent is *Szachy od A do Z* (1986–
7) by Litmanowicz and Gizycki, running to about
1,650 pages, and *Shakhmaty entsiklopedichesky slovar* (1990), a magnificent Soviet work edited by a
team co-ordinated by AVERBAKH.

Other types of book are *Oxford Encyclopedia of
Chess Games* (1981) by Levy and O'Connell, which
contains the scores of 3,773 games played between
1485 and 1866, and *Chess: the Records* (1986) by
Whyld, which gives the results of all major events.
(See also ENCYCLOPEDIA OF CHESS OPENINGS.)

didactic position, a position composed or from
play and used for instruction. The situation arising
after 7 Rc1 is played following the QUEEN'S GAMBIT
Declined, ORTHODOX DEFENCE (186) sometimes has
this name because it is used as the starting point of
much analysis. A didactic endgame is used to
demonstrate general principles and differs in this
respect from a study, which by its nature depends
upon the presence of a peculiar feature. However,
exceptional positions can be found that would not
be likely to occur in a game but for which the
analysis might reveal ideas useful to a player.

A study (after MANDLER, 1950) by the German
composer Rolf Richter (1944–88), second special
hon. mention, Chavchavadze Memorial tourney,
1987. 1 Kg3 Kc2   2 Kf4 Kc3   3 Ke5 Rg1   4 e4 Kc4
5 Kd6 Rd1+   6 Ke7 Kc5   7 e5 Kd5   8 g5 Rg1   9
e6 Ke5   10 Kf7 Kd6   11 e7 Rf1+   12 Ke8 Re1   13
g6 Rxe7+   14 Kf8 Ke6   15 g7 Rf7+   16 Kg8 Rf1
17 Kh8 Rh1+   18 Kg8 Kf6   19 Kf8 Ra1   20

g8 = N + drawn. Although the solution is unique (Black wins if at any stage White varies), a player might gain some understanding of the way to handle such endgames.

Diesen, Mark Carl (1957–), American player, World Junior Champion, 1976, since when he has abandoned chess.

Dijk (pron. dike), Nils Gustav Gerard van (1933–), Norwegian composer, International Master for Chess Compositions (1961), International Judge of Chess Compositions (1966), bank official. Born in Indonesia, he was interned in Java during the Second World War with his Dutch father and Norwegian mother, afterwards settling in Bergen. In 1951 he became interested in chess problems published in the local newspaper, becoming in time one of the world's leading composers of orthodox TWO- and THREE-MOVERS.

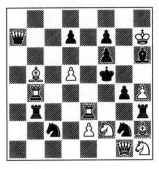

#3

A problem by van Dijk, first prize, *De Waarheid*, 1977. The key is 1 Bd6 threatening 2 Rf3 + and 3 e4 #.

1 . . . Rhxe3   2 Ng3 +
1 . . . Rbxe3   2 Bd3 +
1 . . . Qxe3   2 Bxd7 +
1 . . . Ngxe3   2 Qxg4 +
1 . . . Ncxe3   2 Qb1 +
1 . . . Bxe3   2 Rf4 +.

In the thematic variations White mates by Pe4, and the theme is ANNIHILATION that clears the e-file for the pawn, which plays like a line-piece on its first move.

Dilārām's mate, Firdewsī at-Tahīhal (b. 1453), a Turkish poet who took 40–50 years to write the world's longest poem (allegedly 890,000 verses containing all contemporary knowledge of history, philosophy, medicine, geometry, etc), completed a chess book in 1503 and decided to use in a story a famous 10th-century problem attributed to aṣ-ṣūlī. As it happens he copied the position incorrectly, adding an irrelevant black FERS on c3 and, more disastrously, moving the white knight to g5 and the rook on h4 to h5. A prince had wagered and lost his fortune to another prince during an intense chess session and in desperation offered as stake his

favourite wife, Dilārām (meaning heart's ease). When he seemed lost she called out 'O Shah, sacrifice both rooks and save Dilārām; advance your fīl and pawn and checkmate with your horse.'

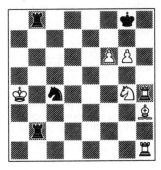

#5

The piece shown as a bishop is a FĪL (A). 1 Rh8 + Kxh8 2 Af5 + Kg8 3 Rh8 + Kxh8 4 g7 + Kg8 5 Nh6 mate.

The story has been told, sung, and embellished down the centuries. The problem, too, has had enduring popularity; more than 200 settings of it are known. A position using modern chessmen was given in a Persian manuscript dated 1796–8. This is a version of it.

#5

Mate in 5. 1 Rh8 +   2 Ng4 +   3 Rh8 +   4 g7 +   5 Nh6.

Dilworth Variation. 714 in the SPANISH OPENING. Played by Alphonse Goetz (real name Geoffroy-Dausay, 1865–1934) by correspondence in 1887, the line is sometimes named after Jan Kleczyński (1875–1939) of Poland who played it in a tournament held concurrently with the Olympic Games, 1924. The variation was revived by the English player Vernon Dilworth (1916–) in 1939 and played by him in the Irish Correspondence Championship 1941. Around 1944 a few leading Soviet players experimented with this variation; since then, in spite of Dilworth's persistent advocacy, it has gained only sporadic support at grandmaster level, most recently by YUSUPOV. Other 11th moves for Black can lead to the ALBIN VARIATION, the BAGUIO VARIATION, or the MACKENZIE VARIATION.

direct mate problem, a problem with the STIPULATIONS that White is to move first and to give checkmate in a given number of moves against any black defence.

discovered attack, an attack made by a LINE-PIECE when another piece or pawn has been moved out of the way.

discovered check, check given by a line-piece when another man has been moved out of the way. The line-piece checks without moving but the move made by the other man may create an additional threat, a form of DOUBLE ATTACK often leading to advantage. See, for example, SEE-SAW.

distant opposition, a kind of OPPOSITION in which the kings stand on the same file, rank, or diagonal with three or five squares between them.

Divan, see COFFEE HOUSES.

diversionary sacrifice, a DECOY offered as a sacrifice, especially a piece so offered in the middle game.

Menchik–Graf   14th Match game 1937   Queen's Gambit Declined

1 c4 e6 2 Nc3 d5 3 d4 Nf6 4 Nf3 Nbd7 5 e3 c6 6 Bd3 Be7 7 0-0-0 8 e4 dxe4 9 Nxe4 Nxe4 10 Bxe4 Nf6 11 Bc2 c5 12 dxc5 Qa5 13 Be3 Bxc5 14 Bd2 Qc7 15 Bc3 Be7 16 Qe2 b6 17 Ng5 g6 18 Qf3 Bb7 19 Qh3 h5 20 Rad1 Ng4

21 Rd7 Black resigns. If 21 . . . Qxd7, 22 Qxh5 forces mate. The immediate 21 Qxh5 only wins a pawn after 21 . . . Qxh2+

Dlugy, Maxim (1966–), Moscow-born US player, World Junior Champion 1985, International Grandmaster (1986). Dlugy was equal second (+4=4−1) in a strong tournament played in Manhattan in 1985.

Dobrescu, Emilian (1933–), International Judge of Chess Compositions (1958), International Grandmaster for Chess Compositions (1989), the leading study composer of Romania, and many times winner of the national composing championship. His work covers a wide range of ideas including POSITIONAL DRAW, ZUGZWANG, and SYSTEMATIC MOVEMENT; also a number of studies using Q v. R + B. He occasionally composed problems, especially in his early days.

E. Dobrescu and V. Nestorescu, *Studii de Sah* (1984), contains 140 compositions by Dobrescu, 71 by Nestorescu, and 12 joint compositions.

=

A study by Dobrescu, first prize, *Revista Romana de Sah*, 1980. 1 Qd4 Qf6 2 d8=Q+ Bxd8 3 Qc5+ Qe7 4 Ba3 Kg7 5 Qd4+ Qf6 6 Bb2 Kh6 7 Qe3+ Qg5 8 Bcl Kg7 9 Qd4+ Qf6 10 Bb2. A positional draw based on perpetual pinning.

Dokhoyan, Yuri Rafaelovich (1964–), Soviet player, International Grandmaster (1988), winner of two strong tournaments, Plovdiv 1988 (+5=6) and Wijk aan Zee (II tournament) 1989 (+6=3−2), as well as a lesser event at Bucharest 1986.

Dolmatov, Sergey Viktorovich (1959–), Russian player, International Grandmaster (1982), World Junior Champion 1978. He first played in the USSR championship in 1979, and on his sixth appearance in 1989 he was second (+6=5−4) equal with GELFAND, BELYAVSKY, and EINGORN, behind VAGANYAN. His best wins are Sochi 1988 (+3=7−1) and Clermont Ferrand 1989 (+3=7−1), shared with SAX, EHLVEST, and Renet, ahead of KORCHNOI, ANDERSSON, and RIBLI. He also won Barcelona 1983, Frunze 1983, Tallinn 1985, and, shared with Gelfand, Klaipeda 1988. His fifth place in the Manila 1990 interzonal made him a CANDIDATE, but, after a close-fought match in 1991, he lost to YUSUPOV in the tie-break play-off.

Gipslis–Dolmatov   Volgograd 1985   USSR Team Championship   Pirc Defence

1 e4 d6 2 d4 Nf6 3 Nc3 g6 4 f4 Bg7 5 Nf3 0-0 6 Bd3 Na6 7 0-0 c5 8 d5 Rb8 9 Qe2 Nc7 10 a4 a6 11 a5 b5 12 axb6 Rxb6 13 Na4 Rb8 14 c4 e6 15 e5 Ne8 16 exd6 Nxd6 17 Ne5 exd5 18 Nc6 Qh4 19 Nxb8 Bd4+ 20

Kh1 Re8 21 Qf3 dxc4 22 Nc6 Bg4 23 Nxd4 cxd3 24 Qc6 cxd4 25 Qxd6

25 ... Bf3 26 Be3 dxe3 27 gxf3 d2 28 Nc3 e2 29 Qxd2 exf1 = Q + 30 Rxf1 Rd8 31 Qe3 Nd5 32 Nxd5 Rxd5 33 Rc1 Qh3 34 Kg1 a5 35 Qc3 Qd7 36 Qc8+ Qxc8 37 Rxc8+ Kg7 38 Ra8 Rb5 39 b3 Rxb3 40 Rxa5 Rxf3 41 Ra4 Kf6 42 Kg2 Rd3 43 Ra5 Draw.

The game is a great credit to both players: Black for a sacrifice and counterattack when in an apparently lost position; White for his equally resourceful defence. Gipslis includes it in his book of best games.

Dombrovskis Theme, a problem theme: in two tries the intended mating moves, A, B, are forestalled by Black's replies a, b, respectively; in two variations of the solutions the black moves a, b, are answered by white moves A, B, respectively. The theme was first shown by the Latvian composer Alfrēds Dombrovskis (1923–) in the 1950s.

#2

A problem by KOVAČEVIĆ, first prize, Myllyniemi Jubilee tourney 1980.
1 Be4? (threatening 2 Nd6# (A)) Bd5 (a)
1 Ne3? (threatening 2 Bc4# (B)) Bd6 (b).
The key is 1 Qe8, threatening 2 c7#:
1 ... Bxd5 (a) 2 Nd6# (A)
1 ... Bd6 (b) 2 Bc4# (B).

domination, a study term indicating the direct or indirect control by White of all the squares to which a certain black piece can be moved or, according to KASPARYAN, to which it needs to be moved. The invention of the term is attributed to RINCK.

Kasparyan, *Domination in 2,545 Endgame Studies* (1980, rev. 1987), is a translation of a Russian work in two volumes (1972, 1974).

+

A study by the Soviet composer Alexei Sochniev, second hon. mention, Chavchavadze Memorial tourney 1989. 1 Rb6+ Kc1 2 Ra6 Rd5 3 Bc6 Re5 4 Nc3 a1 = Q 5 Rxa1+ Kc2 6 Ne2 Kb2 7 Nd4 Kxa1 8 Kf6. Black's rook has nowhere to go. See also KUBBEL and, for an example from play, KORCHNOI.

Donner, Johannes Hendrikus ('Jan Hein') (1927–88), International Grandmaster (1959). In 1954 he became the first player since 1919 to win the Dutch championship in front of EUWE. Donner also won the national title in 1957 and 1958, when Euwe did not compete. He is probably the only master to remember the date on which he learned the moves of chess: on 22 August 1941 he was taught them at school and returned home to find his father had been taken hostage by the Nazis.

Donner won or shared first prize at: Beverwijk 1958, equal with Euwe; Beverwijk 1963 (+9=6–2), ahead of BRONSTEIN; Amsterdam1965 (+4=5); Venice 1967 (+9=4), ahead of PETROSYAN. In a quadrangular tournament at Leiden 1970 he came second (+1=10–1), after SPASSKY, ahead of BOTVINNIK and LARSEN. From 1950 to 1978 Donner played in 12 Olympiads. In 1983 he was disabled by a stroke, and from hospital won the Henriëtte Roland Holst literary prize for his book *Na mijn dood geschreven* ('written after my death'). (See COOPERATION.)

Donner Variation, 401, a line in the KING'S INDIAN DEFENCE played by DONNER (and GELLER) in the 1950s.

Dorfman, Iosif Davidovich (1952–), Soviet player, International Grandmaster (1978). In his second USSR championship, 1976, he was fifth, and in 1977 he shared the title with GULKO, both scoring +4=11, ahead of PETROSYAN, POLUGAYEVSKY, and TAL. Since then his best tournament victories have been: Warsaw 1983 (+6=8); Lvov 1984 (+5=8), shared with VAGANYAN; Moscow 1985 (+6=7); Budapest 1988; Sarajevo 1988 (+5=10) (shared);

and Marseille 1989 (shared). He was second (+2=8), after ROMANISHIN at Debrecen 1990.

Velikov–Dorfman   Majorca (GMA) 1989   Zukertort Opening

1 Nf3 g6 2 g3 Bg7 3 d4 c5 4 c3 b6 5 dxc5 bxc5 6 Qd5 Nc6 7 Qxc5 Nf6 8 Bg2 Ba6 9 Nd4 Nxd4 10 Qxd4 0–0 11 Bxa8 Qxa8 12 f3 e5 13 Qd1 e4 14 Kf2 Re8 15 Re1 Qc6 16 Na3 Qe6 17 Nc2 Qh3 18 Kg1 Re5 19 Bf4 Rd5 20 Nd4 Rh5 21 g4 Nd5 22 Qb3 Nxf4 23 Qb8+

23 ... Bc8 24 Qxc8+ Bf8 25 Kf2 Re5 26 Ke3 exf3+ 27 Kxf4 d6 28 e4 f2 29 Nf3 fxe1=Q 30 Rxe1 h5 31 Nxe5 dxe5+ 32 Kg5 Kg7 33 Qd7 Qxg4+ White resigns, for if 34 Qxg4, Be7 is mate.

D'Orville, Peter August (1804–64), the most outstanding of those problemists who preceded the transitional period. (See PROBLEM HISTORY.) Even during this period 'to compose like D'Orville' was the highest praise a problemist could receive. His reputation rests on his slightly set direct mates, a form not entirely new, but better exploited by him than by his predecessors. His solutions contain moves, he says, that are unlikely to be chosen by players, thus problems became an art form unrelated to the game. He sought ECONOMY of force, and often provided pure mates. These problems are 'single-liners', for variations had yet to come into fashion. Although most of his problems are of an outmoded kind, e.g. conditional problems, even in these his composing skill surpasses that of those who came before him. In 1842 he published *Problèmes d'échecs, composés et dédiés aux amateurs de ce jeu*, a collection of 250 of his problems; an even larger number was published in ALEXANDRE'S collection four years later, but that includes several wrong attributions.

His family, long resident in the Bishopric of Cambrai, moved to Germany in the 16th century and were variously engaged in banking, manufacture, and trading. August was born and spent his childhood in St Petersburg. Later his father took over a snuff factory in Offenbach, and his family moved there. Representing the family business, August lived in Antwerp from 1836 to 1842, and during this period composed most of his problems. He lived his last years in Regensburg. (See PLAGIARISM.)

J. D. Beasley, *Some Problems by Auguste d'Orville* (1990), contains 38 problems, a biography, and an assessment of his work.

#5

Problem no. 147 in d'Orville's book. 1 Ne5 a5 2 Nc6 axb4 3 c4 b3 4 Nc2 bxc2 5 Bxc2#

Döry Defence, 356 and 429, pioneered by Ladislaus Döry, an Austrian Baron, in 1923, and played with some international success by KERES who won a small tournament at Vienna 1937 in which all games had to begin with this opening. In 1943 Döry was sentenced to death by the Nazis for sedition, but was released from prison by Allied troops in 1945.

double, (1) to make a pawn capture that creates DOUBLED PAWNS, or to induce or force an opponent to make such a capture. For example, after 1 e4 c6 2 d4 d5 3 Nc3 dxe4 4 Nxe4 Nf6 White could double Black's pawns by 5 Nxf6+; or after 1 e4 e6 2 d4 d5 3 Nc3 Nf6 4 Bg5 Bb4 5 e5 h6 6 Bd2 Bxc3 White could accept doubled pawns by 7 bxc3.

double, (2) to place two rooks so that they guard one another. To double rooks on an OPEN FILE or on the SEVENTH RANK, for example, usually leads to command of that file or rank. To place a queen and a bishop so that they guard one another might also be called doubling.

double attack, a simultaneous attack against two separate targets: these may be enemy men, or squares the enemy needs to defend. A double attack by one man against two is called a FORK. A double attack by two men could arise in several ways, e.g. from a DISCOVERED CHECK.

double bishop sacrifice, the sacrifice or offer of both bishops, one shortly after the other. In most instances the attacker has RAKING BISHOPS bearing down on the enemy king, and he commences by offering the GREEK GIFT. The first known example was in a game won by Lasker in 1889 (see BAUER).

Pachman–Neikirch   Portorož 1958   Queen's Gambit Declined Semi-Tarrasch Variation

1 c4 Nf6 2 Nc3 e6 3 Nf3 d5 4 d4 c5 5 cxd5 Nxd5 6 e3 Nc6 7 Bc4 Nxc3 8 bxc3 Be7 9 0–0 0–0 10 Qe2 b6 11

Rd1 cxd4 12 exd4 Na5 13 Bd3 Bb7 14 Bf4 Qd5 15 Rab1 Rac8 16 Rb5 Qd8 17 Ng5 Bxg5 18 Bxg5 Qd6

19 Bf6 Qf4 20 Be5 Qg5 21 f4 Qe7 22 Bxh7+ Kxh7 23 Qh5+ Kg8 24 Bxg7 f5 (declining the second bishop is no help) 25 Be5 Nc4? 26 Qg6+ Black resigns.

double check, check given by two pieces simultaneously. The defending king must be moved in reply, for which reason a double check can be a powerful tactical weapon. A double check always includes a DISCOVERED CHECK.

van den Bosch–Spielmann Match, Netherlands 1935 French Defence Tartakower Variation

1 e4 e6 2 d4 d5 3 Nc3 Nf6 4 Bg5 Be7 5 e5 Ne4 6 Bxe7 Qxe7 7 Nxe4 dxe4 8 Qe2 Nd7 9 0–0–0 f5 10 exf6 Nxf6 11 g3 0–0 12 Bg2 e5 13 Bxe4 Nxe4 14 Qxe4 Rxf2 15 Nf3 Qf7 16 Ng5 Bf5 17 Qxb7 Rxc2+ 18 Kb1

18 . . . Rc1+ (double check) 19 Kxc1 Qc4+ 20 Kd2 Qd3+ 21 Ke1 Qe3+ 22 Kf1 Rf8 White resigns.

doubled pawns, two pawns of the same colour on the same file. They may be weak because they are hard to defend or because they lessen the mobility of the pawn formation, perhaps creating HOLES; they may be strong because they guard important squares, an ADVANCE POINT perhaps, or indirectly, because an adjoining file can be used advantageously; or they may be of no account. Doubled pawns in front of the king may leave holes that assist the enemy attack, or the holes may be of little consequence. (See SPACE; STEINITZ.)

double fianchetto, two fianchettoes made by one player.

double-move chess, or Marseillais chess, an UNORTHODOX CHESS game described in *Le Soleil de Marseille*, 1925, by a Greek, Albert Fortis (1873–1926). He and a Norwegian, Ingval Rossow, who also lived in Marseilles, had popularized the game in 1922, but its invention is perhaps due to Johan de Queylar a few years earlier.

On each turn a player makes two single moves; a check may be given only on the second of these moves and must be evaded on the first move of the reply. In 1926, between rounds of a small tournament at Birmingham, ALEKHINE and other competitors amused themselves playing double-move chess. Playing triple-move chess Alekhine, declaring that the first player should always win, delivered SCHOLAR'S MATE: 1 e3 & Nf3 & Nc3, g5 & g4 & gxf3 2 Qxf3 & Bc4 & Qxf7.

Double Muzio Gambit, 1144. Besides the knight sacrifice that characterizes the MUZIO GAMBIT, White's LIGHT BISHOP is sacrificed. Although successful in Shumov–Beskrovny, St Petersburg, 1869, where play continued 8 . . . Kxf7 9 d4 Qxd4+ 10 Be3 Qf6 11 Qh5+ (Soviet analysis favours 11 Bxf4), it had a resounding defeat at New York 1889, Showalter–Taubenhaus, where the continuation was 9 . . . Qf5. Commenting that the line was 'really too bold for a tournament', STEINITZ observed that when COCHRANE used it in games where he gave odds of the queen's knight, the queen's rook was brought quickly into the attack.

double rook sacrifice, the sacrifice of both rooks as part of one operation. Unlike the DOUBLE BISHOP SACRIFICE, when the two bishops are usually thrown into the attack (active sacrifice), the rooks are usually left to be captured (passive sacrifice). The object, more often than not, is to decoy the enemy queen and put it temporarily out of play. The IMMORTAL GAME, the game under ORANG UTAN OPENING, and the game below, the earliest known example, are in that category. See DILĀRĀM'S MATE for an exception.

Dr Bowdler–H. S. Conway   London, 1788   Bishop's Opening

1 e4 e5 2 Bc4 Bc5 3 d3 c6 4 Qe2 d6 5 f4 exf4 6 Bxf4 Qb6 7 Qf3 Qxb2 8 Bxf7+ Kd7 9 Ne2 Qxa1 10 Kd2 Bb4+ 11 Nbc3 Bxc3+ 12 Nxc3 Qxh1 13 Qg4+ Kc7 14 Qxg7 Nd7 15 Qg3 b6 16 Nb5+ cxb5 17 Bxd6+ Kb7 18 Bd5+ Ka6 19 d4 b4 20 Bxb4 Kb5 21 c4+ Kxb4 22 Qb3+ Ka5 23 Qb5 mate.

Double Ruy López Opening, 835, a symmetrical line that can arise from either the FOUR KNIGHTS or the SPANISH OPENING (Ruy López). (See TWO BISHOPS.)

double threat, two threats made simultaneously, usually a DOUBLE ATTACK. This tactical device does not always bring the desired advantage. A game Tartakower–Capablanca, New York 1924, began 1 e4 e5 2 f4 exf4 3 Be2 d5 4 exd5 Nf6 5 c4 c6 6 d4 Bb4+ 7 Kf1 cxd5 8 Bxf4 dxc4 and White played 9 Bxb8, expecting to gain advantage from his active threat of 10 Qa4+, winning a piece, and the second, passive, threat of withdrawing his bishop. Black replied 9 . . . Nd5 and obtained the better game (e.g. 10 Bf4 Qf6).

doubling themes, three- or more-mover problem themes of the following kind: a line-piece is moved across a critical square; doubling takes place when another line-piece of the same colour and like movement is moved to this square; one line-piece guarded by the other (an essential feature) is moved again. The doubling may be on files, ranks, or diagonals. Pioneer problems showing Zepler Doubling and Turton Doubling follow.

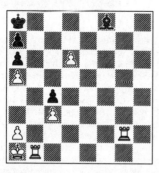

#3

A problem by ZEPLER, *Hamburgischer Correspondent*, 1929. 1 Rb4 Bg7 2 Rgb2 Bxc3 3 Rb8#. The piece moved first is moved again in the same direction as before.

#3

A version of a problem by TURTON, *Illustrated London News*, 1856. 1 Bh8 b4 2 Qg7 Ra8 3 Qxb2# (the version consists of the added Pb6, to avoid cooks). The second piece to be moved is moved again, in a direction opposite to that taken by the first piece to be moved. The actual doublings (the first two moves) in these two problems are geometrically identical, the difference subsisting only in the third moves.

In Turton's problem the weaker piece is moved first. Variations are the Brunner–Turton, when the

two pieces are of equal value (i.e. two rooks), and the Loyd–Turton, when the first piece to be moved is of greater value (i.e. Q followed by R or B).

See LOGICAL SCHOOL, and, for a rare example of doubling themes in play, RUBINSTEIN.

Dragon–Sämisch Variation, 533, a form of DRAGON VARIATION akin to the SÄMISCH VARIATION (396) of the KING'S INDIAN DEFENCE.

Dragon Variation, 476, 525, or 540 in the SICILIAN DEFENCE. These species of Dragon are characterized by the fianchetto of Black's DARK BISHOP and unmoved e-pawn.

The Dragon's traditional guise is 476, and its strength has spurred the invention of many 'anti-Dragon' variations; instead of 6 Be2 White may play the SOZIN, 469, or the RICHTER, 480, ATTACK, inducing Black to play 6 . . . e6. In 525 Black avoids these anti-Dragon attacks, but permits the LEVENFISH ATTACK, 537. In line 540 Black avoids or discourages these attacks at the cost of risking the MARÓCZY BIND, 541.

Originated in its present form by PAULSEN around 1880, the Dragon was frequently used by BIRD in the 1880s and gained general acceptance when played by PILLSBURY and other masters around 1900. The name may derive from the fancied resemblance of Black's pawn formation to the constellation Draco, but it also suggests fearsomeness: in particular White, fearing the power of Black's fianchettoed bishop, may seek to exchange it and thus 'extract the dragon's tooth'. (See EVANS, L.; IVKOV; KHALIFMAN; LUTIKOV; SOSONKO; TORRE, E.; UNZICKER; VASYUKOV.)

drama and chess, see THEATRE AND CHESS.

draughts, after chess the most popular board game in the West. It was probably invented in the south of France during the 12th century by placing backgammon pieces on a chessboard and moving them as in ALQUERQUE. Draughts has more affinity with some of the board games of Egypt and classical Greece and Rome than has chess.

Early in the history of draughts, or checkers, a rule was introduced making capture compulsory. To avoid the frequent draws found at the highest level as skills improved, a two-move restriction was imposed. Black's first move, and White's reply (Black moves first in draughts), are selected by ballot. At the beginning of the 18th century a version of draughts played on a 10×10 board appeared in Paris, and is now known as Polish draughts.

draw, a result which may come about by agreement between the players, by STALEMATE, by REPETITION OF POSITION, or under the FIFTY-MOVE LAW. In a competition the sequence for a player wishing to agree a draw is as follows: move, make offer, press opponent's clock. In settlement of a dispute an arbiter has authority to declare a game drawn. (See SCORING.)

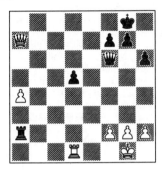

A position from a game Bernard–Adrian, French championship 1986. White played 1 a5 and offered a draw, which was accepted. He could have played 1 Qb8+ Kh7 2 Qb1+ winning a rook.

drawing master, one who draws many games and appears not to be striving for a win. Few great players have been drawing masters in this sense; usually their drawn games have come about after a hard struggle, or when no more than a draw is needed to secure their place in a match or tournament. The first grandmaster to be called a drawing master was SCHLECHTER, a description belied by his achievements.

With the intensive pressure of play at the highest professional level some players, for example ANDERSSON, conserve energy by never trying to force a win in an even position. If an advantage arises because the opponent has tried too hard, then these players will grind out the win remorselessly, but most of their games are drawn.

drawn position, a position that should be drawn if both sides play correctly. The term is used selectively, after the dust of battle has settled; otherwise, for example, the ARRAY could be so described.

Dresden Theme, see DECOY THEMES.

Dreyev, Alexei Sergeyevich (1969–), Russian player, World Under-16 Champion 1983 and 1984, European Junior Champion 1988, International Grandmaster (1989). He won a strong tournament, Moscow 1989 (+5=5−1), and in the same year made his debut in the USSR championship. At the interzonal, Manila 1990, he was equal fifth and became a CANDIDATE for the first time, but lost his match with ANAND in 1991.

dual, in a STUDY or DIRECT MATE PROBLEM an alternative for White's second or later move that fulfils the STIPULATIONS in a manner not intended by the composer. If there are two or more such moves they are still called duals. In some other kinds of problems, e.g. a helpmate, a dual might be an alternative move by White *or* Black. A serious dual is one that by-passes the composer's central idea so that the composition loses its point; generally this would be a dual in a main VARIATION. Lesser duals occur in SIDE VARIATIONS or BY-PLAY. In a composing TOURNEY an entry that is found to have a serious dual would usually be disqualified, while a lesser dual might be accepted. The Irish writer Patrick Thomas Duffy (1834–88) was the first to stigmatize a dual as a defect.

Duals are sometimes provided intentionally, and one kind of problem is that showing 'progressive duals'. A composer might show, say, five variations: in the first there are five possible mating moves, and one at a time these are eliminated so that in the last variation there is only one mating move.

dual-avoidance. In the main variations of a sound DIRECT MATE PROBLEM unwanted duals are avoided because a black move that permits one mate will prevent others. The term dual-avoidance is applied only when the main variations are linked by means of reciprocal, parallel, or other relationships. For example, in a two-mover THREAT PROBLEM (direct mate) Black may have two DEFENCES of a like kind, a and b; to each White appears to have two mating moves A and B both of a similar kind; in fact defence b allows mate A and prevents mate B whereas defence a allows mate B and prevents mate A; the mate in one variation is the 'avoided dual' in the other. Black's two defences should prevent the duals in a similar manner. (The parallels cannot be defined precisely.) For examples, see ELLERMAN and ZAPPAS. Dual-avoidance may also be shown in three or more variations (see STOCCHI THEME), and in problems other than direct mates.

Dubois, Serafino (1817–99). Italy's strongest player in the 1850s and 1860s. He met few masters from other countries. In 1845 WYVILL, visiting Rome, played many friendly games with Dubois, who won about two-thirds of them; in Paris ten years later he won about the same proportion of some 30 games played against RIVIÈRE. At the London tournament of 1862 Dubois shared fourth place with G. A. MACDONNELL after ANDERSSEN (the winner), L. PAULSEN, and OWEN, but was awarded fifth prize because he had won more games by default. Immediately the tournament ended he played and lost (+3=1−5) a match against STEINITZ, winner of the sixth prize. Dubois probably not such a strong player as the record suggests, for when he met Wyvill, Rivière, and Steinitz none was yet at his full strength. In April 1863 Dubois went from England to Holland, intending a long stay, but not liking the climate he returned to Rome, the city of his birth, about two years later. There he played to the Italian laws, which permitted free CASTLING, as he preferred, and his influence may have delayed Italy's falling into line with the castling law used elsewhere in Europe. Between 1868 and 1873 he wrote a three-volume work on the openings, giving variations with and without free castling; this book was soon forgotten, but his book of the Rome tournament, 1875, is of some historical interest: it was the first such event held in Italy.

Dubois–Réti Defence, 982 in the SCOTCH GAME, transposing into a standard variation of the TWO KNIGHTS DEFENCE.

Dubois Variation, 620 in the HAMPPE–MUZIO GAMBIT; 925 in the GIUOCO PIANISSIMO, as played by DUBOIS in Rome, 1850, when he out-manœuvred an Italian General.

Duchamp, Marcel (1887–1968), French chessplayer and renowned artist. A competitor in the world amateur championship of 1924, four French championships from 1924 to 1928, and four Olympiads from 1928 to 1933, Duchamp also played in several minor tournaments, notably sharing first prize with HALBERSTADT and J. J. O'Hanlon at Hyères 1928 and winning the championship of Paris in 1932. With Halberstadt he wrote *L'Opposition et les cases conjuguées sont réconciliées* (1932), published in a limited edition of 1,000 copies. His obsession for the game intensified as he grew older. Of his marriage in 1927 Man Ray writes: 'Duchamp spent most of the one week they lived together studying chess problems, and his bride, in desperate retalia-

tion, got up one night when he was asleep and glued the chess pieces to the board. They were divorced three months later.'

Duchamp used chess themes in several of his paintings and collages, and as the most highly esteemed artist to play chess at master level his comments on the game are of interest: 'Chess is a sport. A violent sport. This detracts from its most artistic connections. One intriguing aspect of the game that does not imply artistic connotations is the geometrical patterns and variations of the actual set-up of the pieces in the combinative, tactical, strategical and positional sense. It is a sad means of expression though—somewhat like religious art—it is not very gay. If it is anything, it is a struggle.'

Dudeney, Henry Ernest (1857–1930), England's 'king of puzzle-makers'. A keen player, Dudeney was also President of the Sussex Chess Problem Fraternity, from which the British Chess Problem Society grew. Although he composed no direct mate problems, many of his puzzles had a chess theme. A good solver, Dudeney won the prize offered by the New York Chess Association for the solution of the souvenir chess problem by LOYD, with whom he had much in common.

Dufresne, Jean (1829–93), German player and writer, a law student who became a journalist until defective hearing made him give up. He became an unsuccessful novelist, under the anagrammatic

Portrait of Chess Players (1911)
by Marcel Duchamp

pseudonym E. S. Freund, and more happily a chess writer. Several generations of Germans learned their chess from his *Kleines Lehrbuch des Schachspiels* (1881), of which numerous editions were published. His many other chess books include one on MORPHY which also ran to several editions, and a collection of prize-winning problems from early English composing tourneys. Although not a strong player, in 1854 he defeated Carl Mayet (1810–68) in a match (+7−5) but almost the only game of his to be remembered is a loss to ANDERSSEN in friendly play, the EVERGREEN GAME.

Duisburg Gambit, 119, the SCHARA-HENNIG GAMBIT.

Duke of Rutland's chess, see GREAT CHESS.

Dunst Opening, 8, the HEINRICHSEN OPENING. At one time its cause was advanced by Theodore Alexander Dunst (1907–85) of New York.

duplex, two problems in one; either White or Black can fulfil the stipulations, which are not necessarily the same for both sides. The earliest known example, composed by Giambattista Canterelli, 'nobleman from Corregio', is no. 26 in LOLLI's *100 positions*, 1763.

h#2 duplex

A problem by AVNER, first prize, *Die Schwalbe*, 1981. Black to play 1 Nxf4+ Nd5+ 2 Kd3 Nxf4#. White to play 1 Nxd7+ Nf6+ 2 Ke5 Nxd7#. A mixture of CROSS-CHECKS and UNPINS.

Durand, Philippe Ambroise (1799–1880), author of chess books, a French abbé who was professor of rhetoric at Falaise and then instructor of philosophy at Lisieux. After his retirement in 1860 he wrote three books in collaboration with PRETI, notably the two-volume *Stratégie raisonnée des fins de partie* (1871–3). This work was the first that was devoted exclusively to the practical ENDGAME, a phase which especially interested him. In particular he investigated the nature of the opposition and other kinds of CONJUGATE SQUARES, and he is credited with the invention of the term TRÉBUCHET.

Duras, Oldřich (1882–1957), Czech champion 1905, 1909, 1911, composer, International Grandmaster (1950), civil servant. During his prime, 1906–12, Duras played in 15 of the strongest 24 tournaments held in those seven years, and established himself as one of the best ten or twelve players in the world. His greatest achievement was at Vienna 1908 when he came first (+11=6−2) equal with MARÓCZY and SCHLECHTER, ahead of RUBINSTEIN. He also shared first prize with Schlechter at Prague 1908 (+11=5−3), and with Rubinstein at Breslau 1912 (+10=4−3); and he took second prizes at Nuremberg 1906 (+8=6−2), Vienna 1907 (+5=8), and Hamburg 1910 (+8=6−2). His last appearance in international play was at Mannheim 1914, the tournament broken off with the advent of the First World War. Unable afterwards to spare enough time from his professional duties to continue his tournament career, he successfully renewed his interest in the composition of studies and problems.

J. Louma, J. Podgorný, and E. Richter, *Oldřich Duras* (1954) is a biography with 200 games, 40 studies, and 50 problems, text in Czech.

Duras–Spielmann Vienna 1906–7 Scandinavian Opening

1 e4 d5 2 exd5 Qxd5 3 Nc3 Qa5 4 d4 Nf6 5 Nf3 Bg4 6 Be2 Nc6 7 Be3 0-0-0 8 Nd2 Bxe2 9 Qxe2 Qf5 10 Nb3 e6 11 a3 Bd6 12 0-0-0 Nd5 13 Na4 e5 14 dxe5 Bxe5? 15 Nac5 Nb6 16 a4 a5 17 g4 Qf6 18 c3 Rhe8 19 Nxb7 Rxd1+ 20 Rxd1 Bxc3 21 N7c5 Nb4 22 g5 Qe5 23 Nxa5 h5 24 bxc3 Qxc3+ 25 Kb1 Qxc5

26 Rd8+ Black resigns.

Duras Variation, 215, a sound line, sometimes called the Moscow Variation, in the QUEEN'S GAMBIT Declined; if 5 Bh4 Black can reply 5 . . . dxc4 or 5 . . . Bb4+ and 6 . . . dxc4, and White cannot respond with Pe2-e4. Another Queen's Gambit line, 189, introduced in the game Duras–Balla, Breslau 1912. Also 695 and 791, outmoded lines in the SPANISH OPENING, and 687, the KERES VARIATION and 751, the KHOLMOV VARIATION, in the same opening.

Durkin Opening, 2, played in over-the-board and correspondence games by Robert Durkin (1923–) of New Jersey, but rarely by anyone else.

Dutch Attack, 1312, a name occasionally applied to the BIRD OPENING.

Dutch Defence, 247, sometimes named after Elias STEIN, who lived in the Netherlands and first advocated the defence, and sometimes called the Rivière Opening. In the 19th century this was the only standard alternative to 1 . . . d5 as a response to 1 d4. After the advent of the HYPERMODERN movement in the 1920s many other defences gained popularity but the Dutch has retained its place in the masters' repertoire. Also 1302, where the 'Dutch' reply, 1 . . . f5, follows 1 Nf3. (See BROWNE; MORPHY; VIDMAR.)

Dutch Indian, 249, a defence combining the characteristic Indian and Dutch moves. Also 266, sometimes called the Modern Variation, in which White attacks the DUTCH DEFENCE by 'Indian' means, a fianchetto attack introduced by STEINITZ in his match against ZUKERTORT, 1872.

Dutch Variation, 90, a standard line in the SLAV DEFENCE, so named because of its use in the world championship, 1937, held in the Netherlands; 171, the BEEN AND KOOMEN VARIATION; 1207, an unexpected move in the FRENCH DEFENCE first played in a game Olland–te Kolsté, Utrecht 1906.

Duz-Khotimirsky, Fyodor Ivanovich (1879–1965), Russian player, International Master (1950). From 1900 to 1914 he competed in many Russian tournaments; he played abroad in only four major events, with indifferent results. His attacking style did not lend itself to consistent performance, but he gained a little fame on account of his occasional wins against even the strongest opponents. At the St Petersburg tournament of 1909 he won a special prize for defeating the joint winners, LASKER and RUBINSTEIN. After the First World War he entered the Soviet championship five times, sharing third place in 1923 and again in 1927, played without notable success in other national events and in the great Moscow international tournament of 1925. Duz-Khotimirsky also took an active part in the organization of Soviet chess, and was considered sufficiently important to have an autobiographical games collection published in 1953. He wrote 'Dus-Chotimirsky' when using the Roman alphabet.

Izbrannye party (1953) is an autobiographical collection of 57 annotated games.

dynamic factors, the MOBILITY elements, usually of a tactical kind, that might spring from a given position. These are taken into account when an EVALUATION OF POSITION is being made.

Dzindzichashvili, Roman Yakovlevich (1944–), Soviet-born player from Georgia, International Grandmaster (1977). He played in the USSR championships of 1971 and 1972, with indifferent results, and won the USSR First League tournament 1973 but did not play in the ensuing championship. In 1976 he emigrated to Israel and won the Hastings 1977–8 tournament (+7=7). Perhaps his best result came in the strong Tilburg 1978 tournament where he shared third place (+2=8−1) with HÜBNER and MILES, after PORTISCH and TIMMAN, and ahead of SPASSKY. In 1979 he moved to the USA and won the Swiss system Lone Pine tournament 1980. By 1983 he was accepted as American and played in the national championship, finishing equal first (+5=8) with CHRISTIANSEN and BROWNE. He again did well in 1989, sharing second place (+3=12) with GULKO and Rachels, after SEIRAWAN. In 1984 he turned in a fine performance on top board in the USA for the Olympiad at Thessaloniki, scoring 7½/11 on top board, but was not in the team for the next Olympiad in 1986. A colourful character, Dzindzichashvili is said to play chess only when he needs money to cover his poker losses.

Dzindzichashvili–Browne   New York 1984   King's Fianchetto Opening

1 g3 c5 2 Bg2 g6 3 Nf3 Bg7 4 c3 Nc6 5 d4 cxd4 6 cxd4 d5 7 Nc3 e6 8 0–0 Nge7 9 Bf4 0–0 10 Qd2 Nf5 11 e3 f6 12 h4 h6 13 g4 Nd6 14 g5 Ne4 15 Nxe4 dxe4 16 gxh6 exf3 17 hxg7 Kxg7 18 Bxf3 e5 19 Bg3 exd4 20 Rfd1 Ne5 21 Bg2 Bg4 22 exd4 Nf3+ 23 Bxf3 Bxf3 24 Rdc1 Rf7 25 Qd3 Bd5 26 h5 gxh5 27 Kh2 Qe8 28 Re1 Re7 29 Rg1 Be4

30 Bd6+ Kh7 31 Qg3 Rd7 32 Rae1 Qe6 33 Bb8 Qe8 34 Rxe4 Qxb8 35 Re5 fxe5 36 Qg6+ Kh8 37 Qh6+ Black resigns.

E

East Indian Defence, 434, an Indian Defence in which Black fianchettoes on the king's (east) wing, as opposed to the queen's (west) wing. This usually merges into the KING'S INDIAN DEFENCE (362).

Échecs amoureux, Les, or *Les Eschez amoureux*, a 14th-century French poem of 30,060 lines, of which 580 give a move-by-move description of a game between a lady and her suitor. The rules are those of SHAṬRANJ, and play begins with the short ASSIZE. The lady wins easily, her entranced opponent saying he does not mind whether she mates him or makes him bare. Around 1412 John Lydgate made an English translation, *Reson and sensuallyte*. There are prose versions for which CO-ORDINATE NOTATION was used with the files lettered a to h, as in STANDARD NOTATION, and the ranks i to q (excluding j) commencing from Black's side. Thus a1 becomes aq and h8 becomes hi. *Les Échecs amoureux* is probably the best example of the use of chess in romantic ALLEGORY, and it had many imitations.

echo, the imitation of a manœuvre, a stalemate, or a checkmate in a problem. This may occur with men of the same colour or of a different colour, concurrently (i.e. in variations) or consecutively. A chameleon echo is one that occurs on squares of a different colour. A SYSTEMATIC MOVEMENT may be regarded as a series of echoes.

See KASPARYAN (consecutive chameleon manœuvre); GANDEV (concurrent mates), MIRROR STALEMATE (concurrent chameleon stalemates).

economy, a composition term for the avoidance of superfluity. A position should contain as few pieces as are needed to show the idea (economy of force), and they should all take part to the best of their powers; there should be no waste of time in play; the idea should be shown clearly, unencumbered by complex SIDE VARIATIONS or merely ornamental BY-PLAY. Economy in all its aspects is one of the most important requirements of a composition by today's criteria. The term 'economy of force' was first used by the German composer Adolf Christian Bayersdorfer (1842-1901) in 1867.

Edge, Frederick Milns (1830–82), English journalist. Although not a chessplayer, Edge had a significant effect on chess history. He was in New York, a reporter for the London *Herald*, in 1857 when the first American congress took place. Appointed one of four assistant secretaries of that event, he was captivated by the chess world in general and by MORPHY'S play in particular. When Morphy's visit to England was announced, Edge, now back home, perceived for himself the role of public relations manager for Morphy and set to work preparing the ground. He introduced himself at the St George's and other London chess clubs, and at Simpson's Divan, as Secretary of the recent American Congress and made himself known to everyone of importance. However, the seeds of further trouble were sown when the officials of the congress did not send a document confirming his slightly exaggerated claim. He met some scepticism, felt humiliated, and strengthened his resolve to make Morphy the talk of the world.

Edge attached himself to Morphy when he arrived in England, and in many ways this was a useful partnership. Edge was ever busy, particularly writing letters, an activity which was distasteful to the indolent Morphy. Before Morphy left America he had set his sights on a match with STAUNTON, so Edge set to work promoting the event. Staunton was long out of first-class chess and in any case heavily engaged with his edition of Shakespeare, but no doubt he was flattered, and he did not decline at once. Morphy had entered the Birmingham tournament of 1858, and indeed its opening was delayed to ensure that he had arrived in England. Staunton decided to play there, too. Edge saw this as disastrous for his plans. If Morphy won, or even if Staunton beat him (and Morphy did sometimes lose when he first played a strong opponent), the public's enthusiasm for a match would be diminished. So Edge persuaded Morphy not to play.

The plot rebounded. Staunton lost to LÖWENTHAL, and realized that he could not get into shape to play Morphy while committed to his literary work, if at all. Morphy saw that Staunton was no longer a leading player, and was willing to let the matter drop, but the enraged Edge would have none of it. He began a campaign which unfairly blackened Staunton's reputation, and which still colours historical judgement.

Edge accompanied Morphy to Paris. After the brilliant success over HARRWITZ the next big trial was to be against ANDERSSEN, but Morphy was ill and wanted to go home. Edge set to work writing to all the chess clubs in Europe, and to Anderssen, asking them all to beg Morphy to stay, and in addition he obtained a medical certificate which he sent directly to Morphy's family. As a result Morphy remained in Paris until Anderssen could visit him during the Christmas school holiday. Meanwhile John Sybrandt went to Paris for the purpose of bringing back his brother-in-law, Morphy, and after his arrival Edge never saw his hero again.

Two months later, in March 1859, Edge wrote (in an unpublished letter), 'I have been a lover, a brother, a mother to you; I have made you an idol, a god . . .' That is exactly how Edge saw it. He had done everything within his power to make Morphy the famous person he had become. He had dealt with letters, even taking them from Morphy's pocket so as to ensure they received replies, and he cleared all obstacles from Morphy's path. He made Morphy dictate the scores of games to him, and sent them to all the leading chess columns and journals. Without his nagging, many Morphy games would have been forgotten. On the other hand, Morphy himself was not grateful to someone who was an irritation and yet indispensable. Perhaps the interplay between them had a bearing on Morphy's later mental problems.

G. H. Diggle, 'The Morphy–Edge Liaison', *British Chess Magazine*, 1964, pp. 261–5, is a perceptive study of this relationship; *Chess Notes*, 1983, no. 524, 1985, no. 1012, and 1985, no. 1030, give data on Edge.

education and chess. Many players advocate that the game should be taught at school. Some believe that broadening the base of the pyramid of players is likely to push up the top, others that chess has transferable skills and benefits character formation. Neither supposition has been proved true. Writing in 1803 PRATT called chess the gymnasium of the mind, a quotation variously attributed to Lenin, ANDERSSEN, and others. A month before his death CAPABLANCA restated this idea, '. . . chess ought to form part of the scholastic programme of all countries. Chess is in the intellectual order of things what sport is in the physical: an agreeable method of exercising part of the body which it is desired to develop.' Success at chess is aided by intelligence, logic, creative power, determination, and self-discipline, but where chess has been a compulsory subject at school there is no conclusive evidence that these qualities have been developed in a higher degree than would have followed if a different but academically relevant subject had been taught.

The game may bring social benefits for schoolchildren. They may learn to cope with the behavioural demands of winning or losing and to restrain impulsiveness (TOUCH AND MOVE LAW), while low academic achievers may be able to shine at the game. On the other hand there are negative aspects. After puberty, those girls who do not play as well as boys see themselves as worse because they are girls, which lowers their self-esteem. Educationalists therefore argue that the game should be taught only at pre-puberty. The ability of chess to engage interest and encourage concentration can lead to obsession.

Ehlvest, Jaan (1962–), Estonian player, European Junior Champion 1982–3, International Grandmaster (1987). He was a CANDIDATE in 1988 but was knocked out by YUSUPOV in the first match. His major successes in other events are: USSR championship 1987, equal third ($+7=7-3$) with EINGORN, after BELYAVSKY and SALOV; Vršac 1987, first equal ($+5=6$); Zagreb interzonal 1987, second ($+7=6-3$) equal with SEIRAWAN, after KORCHNOI; Belfort 1988, third ($+5=8-2$), after KASPAROV and KARPOV; Reykjavik 1988, fourth ($+5=9-3$) equal with HJARTARSON, after Kasparov, Belyavsky, and TAL; Reggio Emilia 1988–9, fourth ($+2=6-1$) equal with IVANCHUK, after M. GUREVICH, KIRIL GEORGIEV, and ANDERSSON; Rotterdam 1989 equal fifth ($+4=8-3$); Tallinn 1989 first equal ($+4=6$); Clermont Ferrand 1989, first ($+3=7-1$) equal with SAX, DOLMATOV, Korchnoi, and Renet; Belgrade 1989, second ($+3=7-1$) equal with TIMMAN, after Kasparov; Reggio Emilia 1989–90 ($+5=5$) first, ahead of Ivanchuk, RIBLI, and Andersson; Hanninge 1990 second ($+5=5-1$) equal with Karpov, behind Seirawan; Reggio Emilia 1991 second ($+1=11$) equal with POLUGAYEVSKY, behind Karpov.

Ehlvest–Kupreichik   USSR Championship 1987   Spanish Opening Close Defence

1 e4 e5   2 Nf3 Nc6   3 Bb5 a6   4 Ba4 Nf6   5 0–0 Be7   6 Re1 b5   7 Bb3 0–0   8 a4 b4   9 d4 d6   10 dxe5 Nxe5   11 Nbd2 Bb7   12 Nxe5 dxe5   13 Qf3 Kh8   14 g4 Bc5   15 Nc4

15 . . . Nxe4   16 Rxe4 f5   17 gxf5 Rxf5   18 Qxf5 Qd1+   19 Kg2 Rf8   20 Ne3 Qd8   21 Qxe5 Bd6   22 Qe6 Qh4   23 Ng4 h5   24 Kf1 Qh3+   25 Ke1 Qg2   26 Bd5 Bc8   27 Re5 Qg1+   28 Ke2 Bxe5   29 Qxe5 Bxg4+   30 f3 Qg2+   31 Kd3 Bf5+   32 Kc4 c6   33 Be4 Bxe4   34 Qxe4 Rxf3   35 Qe8+ Kh7   36 Qxh5+ Kg8   37 Qe8+ Rf8   38 Qe6+ Kh8   39 Kb3 Rf3+   40 Ka2 Rf6   41 Qc4 Black resigns.

eighth rank, the rank on which the opponent's pieces stand in the ARRAY.

eight officers puzzle, one of a group of puzzles in which the eight white pieces (officers), with or without black men, are to be placed on the board. Position 159 of KLING's *Chess Euclid* (1849) shows the eight white officers and the black king on their normal starting squares and gives the STIPULATIONS 'White having the move undertakes to command the 64 squares on the board in 14 moves, and mate only on the last.' The solution given, Black's moves all being forced, is 1 Qd6   2 Rh8   3 Bb2+   4 Qa6

5 Bh3 6 Ke2 7 Kd3 8 Bd4 9 Nd2 10 Ne2 11 Rg1 12 Nf4 13 Nd5 14 Be6 mate. Kling appears to have overlooked the fact that a piece does not command the square on which it stands, and so his solution is faulty, a6 being unguarded. In more modern times this kind of puzzle is given as a CONSTRUCTION TASK: place the 8 white pieces so that every square is commanded. There are 144 basic positions (by reflection and rotation 1,152 in all) in which White's pieces command 63 squares, but it is impossible to cover 64.

In *Boy's Own Paper*, 1884, the composer H. F. L. Meyer (1839–1928) demonstrated that the 64 squares can be covered by 7 pieces and 2 pawns. Two other eight officers tasks are placing the pieces so that they have the most, or the fewest, moves available to them. The answers are 100 and 10 respectively.

eight pawns game, see PAWNS GAME.

eight queens puzzle, a challenge first posed in *Schachzeitung*, 1848: eight queens are to be placed on the board so that none commands a square occupied by another (e.g. queens on a7, b2, c4, d1, e8, f5, g3, h6). By 1850 the mathematician Johann Karl Friedrich Gauss (1775–1855) and the astronomer Heinrich Schumacher (1780–1850) had found the 12 basic solutions which by rotation and reflection give a total of 92 solutions (not 96 because one solution is semi-symmetrical). Interest then shifted to the generalized version: the placing of n queens on a n^2 board, a puzzle that has an extensive literature of its own.

A different version is to place eight queens on a normal board so that they command the fewest squares, and to find the number of basic ways in which this can be done. The answers seem to be 53 and 6, but this has not been demonstrated mathematically (one answer: queens on a3, a4, a5, c1, c5, d1, e1, e3). Sixteen queens can be placed so that not more than two are on any rank, file, or diagonal.

eight rooks puzzle, a requirement to place eight rooks on a board so that none commands a square occupied by another, and to determine the number of ways this simple result can be achieved. The total number, including reflections and rotations, is

40,320. Another challenge is to determine the number of ways eight rooks can guard all 64 squares. The English puzzler George Peter Jelliss (1940–) has found 693,424, including rotation and reflection.

Eingorn, Viacheslav Semyenovich (1956–), Ukrainian player, International Grandmaster (1986), equal first in three strong tournaments, Bor 1985 (+ 5 = 8), Bor 1986 (+ 5 = 5 − 1), and Moscow 1986 (+ 5 = 6 − 2). In stronger events he was equal third (+ 5 = 11 − 1) in the USSR championship 1987, equal fifth (+ 3 = 13 − 1) in 1988, equal second (+ 4 = 9 − 2) in 1989; equal fourth (+ 3 = 6 − 1) at Tallinn 1989; first at Berlin 1990 (Swiss system, 548 players).

Eingorn–Gelfand   Debrecen 1989   Queen's Gambit Accepted

1 d4 Nf6 2 c4 e6 3 Nf3 d5 4 Nc3 dxc4 5 e4 Bb4 6 Bg5 c5 7 Bxc4 cxd4 8 Nxd4 Bxc3 + 9 bxc3 Qa5 10 Bb5 + Bd7 11 Bxf6 gxf6 12 Qb3 a6 13 Be2 Nc6 14 0–0 0–0–0 15 Rad1 Qc7

16 Qb2 Rfd8 17 Rd3 Ne7 18 Qc1 Ng6 19 Rg3 Kh8 20 Qh6 Rg8 21 f4 Qd6 22 e5 Qe7 23 exf6 Qxf6 24 Bd3 Rac8 25 f5 exf5 26 Bxf5 Bxf5 27 Rxf5 Qg7 28 Qd2 f6 29 Rh5 Qf7 30 Rgh3 Ne5 31 Qf4 Rg7 32 Nf5 Qd7 33 Nxg7 Black resigns.

Eisinger Variation, 908, a dubious line in the ITALIAN OPENING introduced during the Heidelberg 1933 tournament by the German player Max Eisinger (1909–89).

Ekström Variation, 154 in the QUEEN'S GAMBIT Declined, given by Folke Ekström (1906–) in an analytical study of the ANTI-MERAN GAMBIT published in *Boken om Schack* (1948); 725, played in the game Svensson–Ekström, Swedish Correspondence Championship, 1964

Elbe Theme, see DECOY THEMES.

Eliskases, Erich Gottlieb (1913–), International Grandmaster (1952). At the age of 16 he tied for first place in the Austrian championship, held in his home town, Innsbruck. Improving rapidly, he won a match against SPIELMANN in 1932 (+ 3 = 5 − 2), took second prize (+ 3 = 2), after E. STEINER, at Kecskemét 1933, and came first (+ 5 = 6) equal with

L. STEINER in the 18th Trebitsch Memorial tournament, 1935. His finest achievement was when he took first prize (+6=3) at the strong Noordwijk 1938 tournament, ahead of KERES and EUWE. Having realized that his style tended towards excessive caution, Eliskases decided to play more enterprisingly in this event. After the annexation of Austria by Germany he won four tournaments, each time by a clear margin: Bad Oeynhausen 1938 (+10=5), Bad Harzburg 1939 (+7=2), ahead of STÅHLBERG, and the German championships of 1938 and 1939. In 1939 he defeated BOGOLJUBOW in match play (+6=11−3).

In the notorious 'Nazi' articles of 1941 ALEKHINE dismissed the merit of a further match with CAPABLANCA for the world championship: '. . . this is hardly of the greatest utility to chess, for the title is not to be defended for long against younger power. On the contrary it would be of much greater service to the world chess community if for example Keres or Eliskases became the title-holder.' He then discussed their respective merits, noting that Keres has an attractive 'Morphy' style, but that of Eliskases is universal.

In 1941 Eliskases was thus projected as a possible world champion, but along with many other competitors in the 1939 Olympiad at Buenos Aires, he was stranded there when war broke out, and his international chess career virtually ceased. After a spell in Brazil he settled in Argentina, and played in many South American tournaments with fair success, notably at Mar del Plata 1948 when he came first (+9=8) ahead of Ståhlberg and NAJDORF. Eliskases had the distinction of playing for three different countries in Olympiads: Austria (1930, 1933, 1935); Germany (1939); and Argentina (1952, 1958, 1960, 1964). In 1935 he made the best third-board score (+12=6−1).

Spielmann–Eliskases   Semmering 1936 7th match game
Two Knights Defence Göring Variation

1 e4 e5 2 Nf3 Nc6 3 Bc4 Nf6 4 Ng5 d5 5 exd5 Na5 6 Bb5+ c6 7 dxc6 bxc6 8 Be2 h6 9 Nf3 e4 10 Ne5 Qc7 11 d4 exd3 12 Nxd3 Bd6 13 Na3 Ba6 14 g3 0–0 15 0–0 Rad8 16 Be3 Nd5 17 Bc5 Bxc5 18 Nxc5 Nc3

19 Nxa6 Qe5 20 Qe1 Nxe2+ 21 Kh1 Rfe8 22 Rd1 Qh5 23 h4 Qg4 24 Kh2 Nxg3 25 fxg3 Re2+ 26 Rf2 Rxf2+ 27 Qxf2 Qxd1 White resigns.

Eliskases Variation, 1231 in the FRENCH DEFENCE, introduced in the game Keres–Eliskases, Noordwijk 1938.

Ellerman, Arnoldo (1893–1969), one of the greatest composers of orthodox TWO-MOVERS, International Judge of Chess Compositions (1956), International Master for Chess Compositions, *honoris causa* (1959). His first successes were in association with the GOOD COMPANION CHESS PROBLEM CLUB, and he soon became one of its leading three composers. An exponent rather than an innovator, he exploited every changing fashion for some 50 years and became one of the most successful tourney competitors of his time. Born in Argentina of Dutch parents, he lived there all his life and was employed by the government as a chess journalist. In that capacity he edited *El Ajedrez Argentino*, a monthly magazine, and wrote several chess books, some about problems, some about the game, notably *1001 Problemas* (1945) and *Los Triunfos del Problemista Argentino Arnoldo Ellerman* (1956), a book containing 93 of his first-prize winners.

#2

A problem by Ellerman, first prize *BCM* tourney January–June 1946, showing DUAL-AVOIDANCE. The key is 1 Nc5 threatening 2 e3#.

1 . . . Rxf7   2 N5e6#
1 . . . Rf6   2 Be5#
1 . . . Rf5   2 N7e6#
1 . . . Rf3   2 Re4#
1 . . . Re4   2 Rd8#.

Elo, Arpad Emrick (1903–92), originator of the ELO RATING system, physicist. Born in Hungary as Árpád Imre Élö, he was ten years old when he emigrated to the USA. There he learnt chess in his teens, and eventually became professor of physics at Marquette University, Milwaukee. He competed in a number of tournaments in the USA and was champion or co-champion of Wisconsin nine times from 1935 to 1961. He spent 20 years developing, validating, and popularizing his rating system, which was accepted by FIDE in 1970 for international use. He then turned his attention to devising similar methods for golf.

Elo rating, or FIDE rating, the method of rating chessplayers used for all international tournaments and by many national bodies. It was taken from a scale previously used by the United States Chess Federation, based on the premisses that a rating of 2000 would be equivalent to scoring 50% in a US Open Championship and that no player's rating would be negative. The standard deviation is set at 200 points, and this span embraces those who are perceived as players of the same class. International Grandmasters are typically in the range 2500–2700 and world champions often higher. International Masters are mostly between 2300 and 2500. The scale is uniform across its range: a player at 1800 can expect to beat one at 1600 by the same margin (about 3:1) as a player at 2600 matched against one at 2400. Before their match in 1972 FISCHER and SPASSKY had ratings of 2785 and 2675 respectively, which suggested that Fischer would win 13:7. The actual result was 12½:7½ excluding the defaulted game, and so Fischer's rating went down slightly and Spassky's rose.

The calculations behind a change of rating, and the proof of the calculation, are too technical to be included here. There is no elementary algebraic formula, but the method of making the change is quite simple, the subtleties being concealed in two tables. Because a player can score only 100%, 50%, or 0% from one game, many games must be played before an Elo rating can be estimated with reasonable confidence. Statistics experts believe that 30 or more games are needed, but some organizations give ratings after 20 games. The FIDE TITLE system is founded on Elo rating, TOURNAMENT CATEGORY, and NORM.

The system works acceptably when used as intended, but has been criticized on some counts. For example, there is no mechanism for detecting any change in the overall 'value' of points, let alone correcting it, and this renders meaningless comparisons between players in different periods. An attempt was made by the Canadian player Nathan Joseph Divinsky (1925–), a professor of mathematics, to add further calculations to enable such comparisons to be made, but the statistical method has not satisfied everyone, and the resulting 'league table' has coincided with the opinion of few strong players.

Elo, *The Rating of Chessplayers, Past and Present* (1978); Beasley, *The Mathematics of Games* (1989); Keene & Divinsky, *Warriors of the Mind* (1989).

empress, an UNORTHODOX CHESS piece that combines the powers of rook and knight. Proposed by CARRERA in 1617, and called a champion by him, the piece has had many revivals. In an 18th-century Persian manuscript it was called a DABBABA, and in 1887 Benjamin R. Foster (1851–1926) of St Louis thought he was innovating when he introduced Chancellor Chess, using the piece. The name empress was given by Frank G. Maus (1879–1944), an inveterate experimenter.

encyclopedia of chess, see DICTIONARY.

Encyclopedia of Chess Openings, a five-volume set, virtually languageless, first published 1974–9 under the chief editorship of MATANOVIĆ. The commentary is by means of the usual CONVENTIONAL SYMBOLS, and about 30 special symbols, all of which are explained in many languages. Revised volumes are published from time to time. These books were the main resource of openings information for the serious player until electronic data bases took the field in the late 1980s.

endgame, the last phase of the game when there are few pieces on the board. Its beginning is not clearly demarcated. The character of the play differs somewhat from the middlegame. Mating attacks are less to be feared, so the kings may take an active part, and the pawns may be advanced with less danger to themselves or their kings. When there are few pawns STALEMATE, ZUGZWANG, and lack of sufficient mating force may entirely alter the character of play. (See BASIC ENDGAME.)

Generally, the ultimate but not necessarily immediate aim is to promote a pawn. Beginners often do not realize that the final phase is as important as the opening and middlegame. Sometimes a small advantage can be exploited only in the endgame, or there, as a last resort, a hard-pressed player might find salvation. Moreover, the endgame may be a creative phase in which wins may be wrested from a drawn position. Lack of skill may hinder a player's advancement: for example, three of the five losses sustained by BRONSTEIN in his drawn championship match with BOTVINNIK in 1951 were caused by weak endgame play.

The first work to be devoted wholly to the practical endgame was by DURAND and PRETI (1871–3). Subsequently standard treatises were written by BERGER in 1890 (revised by him in 1922), FINE in 1941, and AVERBAKH in 1956–62. An English translation of the greater part of Averbakh's work was published in seven volumes (1974–9), but a thoroughly revised Russian version, in five volumes, came out in 1980–4.

ending, an ENDGAME, or else a STUDY.

Endzelins, Lucius (1909–81), Estonian-born Australian who won the title of International Correspondence Chess Grandmaster (1959) by coming second, equal with SCHMID, in the 2nd World Correspondence Championship 1956–9, won by RAGOZIN. In over-the-board events he played for Latvia in the Olympiads of 1937 and 1939, and won the Australian championship in 1961.

enemy square, a square on the fifth rank or beyond, in the opponent's half of the board.

Englisch, Berthold (1851–97), Austrian player ranking about eighth in the world in the 1880s. He competed in eight international tournaments, from Leipzig 1877 to Frankfurt 1887, coming first at Leipzig 1879 and sharing first prize with BLACKBURNE and SCHWARZ at Wiesbaden 1880. In the strongest two tournaments of this period, Vienna 1882 and London 1883, he was seventh and equal fifth respectively. During the 1890s he played in a number of tournaments at Vienna, achieving the best result of his career in 1896 when he took first place in a quadruple-round tournament with SCHLECHTER, MARCO, and WEISS. Also in 1896 he drew a match with PILLSBURY, all five games being drawn. In 1897 he entered the Berlin tournament, fell ill, withdrew after 12 rounds, returned to Vienna, and died two weeks after the tournament ended.

Englisch–Chigorin London 1883 Sicilian Defence

1 e4 c5 2 Nc3 Nc6 3 Nf3 e6 4 Be2 Nge7 5 d4 cxd4 6 Nxd4 Ng6 7 0–0 Be7 8 Be3 0–0 9 f4 Bc5 10 Kh1 Bxd4 11 Bxd4 f5 12 Bc5 Rf7 13 e5 b6 14 Be3 Bb7 15 Nb5 Rb8 16 Nd6 Rf8 17 Nxb7 Rxb7 18 Bf3 Qe7 19 g3 Rc7 20 Qd2 Rfc8 21 c4 Nf8 22 b3 Nd8 23 Rfd1 Nf7 24 a4 Rd8 25 a5 bxa5 26 Qxa5 d6 27 exd6 Rxd6 28 Bxa7 Rxd1+ 29 Bxd1 e5 30 fxe5 Nxe5 31 Bd4 Nc6 32 Qd5+ Kh8 33 Bc3 Qe8 34 Bf3 Qc8 35 Re1 h6 36 Qd6 Kh7 37 Bd5 Ng6

38 Be6 Qb7 39 Bxf5 Ne7+ 40 Be4 Qxb3 41 Qd4 Nd5 42 Bxg6+ Kxg6 43 Qe4+ Kh5 44 Qf5+ g5 45 Qh3+ Kg6 46 Re6+ Kf7 47 Qf5+ Kg8 48 Re8+ mate.

Englisch Opening, 6, the ORANG UTAN OPENING. The line had a period of popularity in Vienna during the 1890s because of its adoption by ENGLISCH.

English Defence, 245, a defence frequently played by the Englishman Philip Norman Wallis (1906–73) and re-examined by several English players during the 1970s. It was used successfully by KORCHNOI in his world championship quarter-final match, 1977, against POLUGAYEVSKY.

English Knight's Opening, 813, the name sometimes given, outside England, to the PONZIANI OPENING, popular in England at the time of STAUNTON.

English Opening, 9, sometimes called the Sicilian Attack. Although mentioned by LUCENA this opening was rarely tried until 1843; then STAUNTON played it six times in his match against SAINT-AMANT.

Staunton writes in his *Chess-Player's Handbook* that 1 c4 'may be adopted with perfect security', adding that White would get a fine game if Black were to reply 1 . . . e5. After the demise of the English school, 1 c4 went out of fashion until the advent of the HYPERMODERN movement in the 1920s when TARTAKOWER remarked enthusiastically that it might well be the strongest of all openings. This view was not shared by others but 1 c4 has since become the third most popular opening move (after 1 e4 and 1 d4), and has been played in 20 per cent of all world championship games since 1935.

The English has variations peculiar to itself, but White often plays his d-pawn to d4, transposing to some other opening. This flexibility appeals to many players: they may steer a course of their own, or seek a transposition, choosing both the manner and the time. (See ACCUMULATION OF ADVANTAGES; ADORJÁN; DE FIRMIAN; SMALL CENTRE; STEINER, L.; ZUKERTORT.)

English Variation, 1305, a continuation in the ZUKERTORT OPENING that merges into the ENGLISH OPENING.

Englund Counterattack, 241, the CHARLICK GAMBIT; 1014, the QUEEN'S PAWN COUNTER-GAMBIT. Neither line is attributable to Englund.

Englund Gambit, 242, a version of the CHARLICK GAMBIT, 241, played by a Swede, Fritz Carl Anton Englund (1871–1933). In 1932 this gambit was tested, but not proven sound, in a small tournament held in Stockholm and won by STOLTZ.

enigma, a term used from the 1840s for a PROBLEM for which the position was given in CONTROL NOTATION. This may have been done so that serial numbering of diagrams should not be disturbed. Later in the 19th century enigma came to mean a chess PUZZLE as distinct from an orthodox problem.

en passant, a special method of capturing, available only to a pawn on its fifth rank: if an enemy pawn on an adjoining file is advanced two squares in one move, it can be captured as if it had been moved one square only. An *en passant* capture must be made immediately or not at all. The *en passant* rule dates from the 15th century, although it has been universally accepted only since 1880, when Italian players abandoned the PASSAR BATTAGLIA law. Its purpose was to prevent players using the relatively recent law (allowing a double-step first move of pawn) in order to evade capture by a pawn. Should the pawn evade capture by a piece by a double-step move, there is no penalty within the scope of the *en passant* laws.

After 1 e4 e5 2 Nf3 Nf6 3 d4 exd4 4 e5 Ne4 5 Qxd4 d5 White may capture *en passant* by removing Black's pawn at d5 from the board and moving the white pawn at e5 to d6. Such a capture is usually written exd6 ep, or simply exd6, indicating, as is customary, the arrival square of the capturing man. For RETROGRADE ANALYSIS, however, the form exd5 ep might be used to make it clear that the captured pawn's last move was from d7 to d5.

en prise, said of a man (other than a king) that is under attack, but usually only if its loss would be disadvantageous.

Éon de Beaumont, Charles Geneviève Louis Auguste André Timothée d' (1728–1810), French diplomat, lawyer, swordsman, lady-in-waiting, and part-time nun. A doctor of law, he dressed as a woman and in 1755, while on a secret mission for Louis XV, became confidante of the Empress Elizabeth of Russia. The following year he was back in St Petersburg as the diplomat brother of his former self. In 1763, following the peace treaty, he became minister-resident and later plenipotentiary for Louis XV at London. Madame de Pompadour resented d'Éon's influence and had the Count de Guerchy sent to London as ambassador. D'Éon complained to the courts that Guerchy was trying to kidnap him, and Guerchy responded with a libel suit. D'Éon, triumphant, continued to live extravagantly and became greatly in debt. At about this time sums totalling more than £120,000 were wagered as to his sex.

When Louis XV died in 1774 the author Beaumarchais was sent to London to negotiate with d'Éon to give up state papers and cease acting as ambassador. In return d'Éon was well paid and pensioned but had to agree to dress as a woman. In June 1777 the Chevalier d'Éon de Beaumont's name was listed as a subscriber to PHILIDOR'S new edition, but in July 1777 the high court, in a trial brought by a gambler, decided in d'Éon's absence that he was a woman. In August d'Éon turned up at Versailles in his old uniform of Captain of Dragoons whereupon the government immediately ordered him to dress as a woman, and as such he became lady-in-waiting to Marie Antoinette for two years. After that he entered a convent—perhaps more than one—before reappearing in London as a female fencer and chessplayer, good enough to beat Philidor in one of the latter's blindfold displays. His pension ceased after the French Revolution and in 1791 Christie's had a three-day sale of the books and manuscripts of 'Mademoiselle' d'Éon. In 1796 a fencing wound led to 'her' retirement. He spent the rest of his days in London, and not until he died was the truth about his sex established. The term 'eonism' has been adopted in psychiatry for male transvestism.

epaulet mate, a mate with two SELF-BLOCKS on the same file, rank, or diagonal, a termination sometimes shown in composition, but, as in play, its occurrence is rarely thematic. (See ORANG UTAN OPENING.)

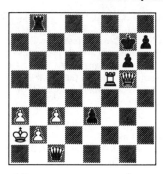

#7

A more-mover by LOLLI, no. 71 in his collection of 100 positions, 1763. 1 Qf6+ Kh6 2 Qh4+ Kg7 3 Qd4+ Kh6 4 Qf4+ Kg7 5 Qe5+ Kh6 6 Rh5+ gxh5 7 Qf6#.

equalize, to arrive at a position in which EQUILIBRIUM is established. The term is most often used to describe a situation in the opening when White's initiative has been reduced to insignificant proportions.

equihopper, a piece invented for use in FAIRY PROBLEMS by the British composer George Leathem (1881–1953) in 1938. An equihopper can be moved on queen-lines or as a $\sqrt{20}$, $\sqrt{40}$, or $\sqrt{52}$ LEAPER, always providing that there is a man of either colour at the mid-point of its move. On a normal board it has access to 16 squares of the same colour. As a leaper it cannot be obstructed, but it may be obstructed when moving on queen-lines. A non-stop equihopper cannot be obstructed at all.

equilibrium, or balance of position, the situation in a game when neither side has significant advantage. (See POSITION; THEORY; SCHOOLS OF CHESS.)

escape square, a square vacated to allow the king to escape from what might otherwise be checkmate. For example, a pawn in front of a castled king is commonly moved to prevent a BACK-RANK MATE. (Compare the composer's terms, FLIGHT and UNBLOCK.)

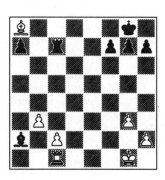

Black, to move, must take action regarding the trapped bishop. If 1 . . . Bxb3? 2 Rd1 Rc8 3 Bb7 Bxc2 4 Rd2 Rb8 and White wins a piece because of the threatened back-rank mate. Instead Black can make an escape square by 1 . . . g5 (sometimes called making a vent, or LUFT), and after 2 Bd5 a5 3 Bc4 a4 4 Ra1 axb3 5 cxb3 Rxc4 the game should be drawn.

Estrin, Yakov Borisovich (1923–87), Soviet player and author, International Correspondence Chess Grandmaster (1966), International Grandmaster (1984), lawyer. In over-the-board play Estrin's achievements were modest. He never qualified for the USSR championship, and his best victory was in a minor tournament, Leipzig 1976, but he excelled at postal play. Third, after RITTNER and ZAGOROVSKY, in the 6th World Correspondence Championship (1968–71), he won the 7th Championship (1972–5). He tied with Borisenko for the USSR correspondence championship 1960–2. A leading openings analyst, he collaborated with PANOV to write the fourth (1966) and later editions of *Kurs debyutov*, and was chief editor of *Malaya debyutnaya entsiklopediya* (1985) (a Soviet equivalent of MCO).

etymology. Nearly every European language derives its name for chess from the Arabic word for the king, *shah*. The main exceptions are Spanish and Portuguese which take their terms (*ajedrez* and *xadrez* respectively) directly from the Arabic name of the game—*ash-shaṭranj*. In Latin, the international language of the Middle Ages, the term *scacus* was used originally for the king, but as time passed it was used for any board game piece. Its plural, *scaci*, was used for the game of chess itself, and the Romance languages still use plural forms (e.g. *les échecs* (French), *gli scacchi* (Italian). Our word, chess, comes from earlier French forms, *escas*, *esches*.

'Euclid', the pen-name of CROSSKILL.

Euwe (pron. erwe, as in Derwent), Machgielis (1901–81), Dutch player, International Grandmaster (1950). International Arbiter (1951), World Champion 1935–7. He grew up in a home where his parents played chess. In 1921 he won the national championship (for the first of thirteen times), drew a match with MARÓCZY (+2=8−2), and played in his first strong international tournament, Vienna 1921, where he was second after SÄMISCH, in front of BREYER, GRÜNFELD, and TARTAKOWER. A student of mathematics at Amsterdam University, he graduated with honours in 1923, became a teacher of mathematics and mechanics in 1924, and gained a doctorate in 1926. Chess took second place to his profession, and he remained an amateur throughout his chess career.

For many years Max Euwe largely confined himself to small tournaments, and in one of them,

Wiesbaden 1925, he was first (+3=3), ahead of SPIELMANN and Sämisch. He narrowly lost matches to ALEKHINE (+2=5−3) during the Christmas vacation 1926–7, and against BOGOLJUBOW (+2=5−3), Easter 1928. This second match was only a few days after he had defeated COLLE (+5=1). In the summer of 1928 he won the second, and last, world amateur championship, played at The Hague.

In the early 1930s Euwe had several good tournament results: Hastings 1930–1, first (+6=2−1) ahead of CAPABLANCA; Bern 1932, second (+8=7), and Zurich 1934, second (+10=4−1), both times sharing the prize with FLOHR, after Alekhine; Hastings 1934–5, first (+4=5) equal with Flohr and THOMAS, ahead of Capablanca and BOTVINNIK. Euwe lost a match to Capablanca (=8−2) in 1931, drew with Flohr (+3=10−3) in 1932, and played in two training matches with Spielmann, winning +2=2 in 1932, but losing in 1935. In 1935 he defeated Alekhine (+9=13−8) in match play and became the world champion.

While holding the title Euwe competed in five tournaments, of which four were strong: Zandvoort 1936, second (+5=5−1), after FINE, ahead of KERES; Nottingham 1936, third (+7=5−2) equal with Fine and RESHEVSKY, half a point after Capablanca and Botvinnik, ahead of Alekhine and Flohr; Amsterdam 1936, first (+3=4) equal with Fine; and Bad Nauheim–Stuttgart–Garmisch 1937, first (+3=2−1), ahead of Alekhine. During this time he had scored two wins and a draw against Alekhine, yet in 1937 he was well beaten in the return title match.

Euwe in 1935

He won a tournament at Amsterdam–Hilversum–The Hague in 1939 (+4=6) ahead of Flohr, another at Budapest in 1940 (+4=1), and narrowly lost a match to Keres, 1939–40 (+5=3−6). During the German occupation Euwe's chess activities were mainly confined to the Netherlands, but he defeated Bogoljubow +5=3−2 at Carlsbad in 1941. When peace returned, Euwe achieved his finest tournament result, at Groningen 1946, when he took second place (+11=6−2), after Botvinnik, ahead of SMYSLOV, NAJDORF, SZABÓ, Flohr, and BOLESLAVSKY.

With the death of Alekhine in 1946 the world championship title was vacant. To deal with the matter FIDE delegates assembled in 1947, and at the same meeting the Soviet Union became a member. The delegates decided that Euwe, as the previous title-holder, and indeed the only ex-champion still alive, should become world champion pending the next contest. The next day the Soviet contingent arrived, having been delayed en route, had the decision annulled, and the title left vacant. Thus he would say wryly that he had been world champion for one day in 1947. In the world championship match tournament of 1948 Euwe, now in his forty-seventh year, fared badly, and although he continued playing until the end of his days he never equalled his earlier successes.

From 1957, when he gave up teaching, he held several appointments relating to the use of computers. From 1970 to 1978 Euwe was president of FIDE, succeeding ROGARD, and this period was one of the most active of his life. On behalf of FIDE he visited more than 100 countries at his own expense, and was largely responsible for the affiliation of more than 30 new member countries. He was supreme arbiter for the contentious championship matches of 1972 and 1978; his decisions there, and elsewhere, were often reviled, but he steadfastly pursued what he believed to be the best interests of the game, not fearing unpopularity.

A keen openings student, Euwe made improvements to many known variations; perhaps his most important contribution was the introduction of the SCHEVENINGEN VARIATION. 'He is', wrote KMOCH, 'logic personified, a genius of law and order . . . One would hardly call him an attacking player yet . . . he strides confidently into some extraordinarily complex variations.' Alekhine noted that Euwe was not an outstanding strategist, but a fine tactician who rarely made an unsound combination.

Euwe writes: 'Few people know that I had to repeat a year at secondary school, and this unpleasant experience may have had a decisive influence on the whole of my life. Convinced as I was of my own ability to pass through the school in the minimum five years, so that my failure was due to my own indolence, I felt I had failed in my duty to my parents and resolved to concentrate absolutely, in future, on whatever I should happen to take up.' His life was one of ceaseless activity; 'to be busy', he said, 'was to guarantee a good deal of one's health.' Besides chess, his family, and his

profession, he followed a wide range of other interests. In these circumstances his winning of the world title must be accounted a great sporting achievement.

Euwe wrote more books, many of them in collaboration with others, than any other great master, and they have been translated into many languages. Among those in English are *Strategy and Tactics* (1937), *From My Games* (1938), and *Meet the Masters* (1940). The best biography is *Max Euwe* by Münninghof, Euwe, and Welling (1976), which also includes 270 games. (See MINORITY ATTACK.)

Botvinnik–Euwe Hastings 1934–5 Caro–Kann Defence
Panov–Botvinnik Attack

1 c4 c6 2 e4 d5 3 exd5 cxd5 4 d4 Nf6 5 Nc3 Nc6 6 Bg5 e6 7 Nf3 dxc4 8 Bxc4 Be7 9 0–0–0 0–0–0 10 Rc1 a6 11 Bd3 h6 12 Be3 Nb4 13 Bb1 b5 14 Ne5 Bb7 15 Qd2 Re8 16 f4 Nbd5 17 Nxd5 Qxd5 18 f5 Bd6 19 fxe6 Rxe6 20 Bf5 Re7 21 Bh3 Bxe5 22 dxe5 Qxe5 23 Bf4 Qd5 24 Qxd5 Nxd5 25 Bd2 Rae8 26 b3 Re2 27 Rf2 Nf6 28 Ba5 Rxf2 29 Kxf2 Ne4+ 30 Kf1 Ng5 31 Bd7 Re7 32 Bf5 Re5 33 Bb1 Be4 34 Bxe4 Nxe4 35 Rc6 Rf5+ 36 Ke1

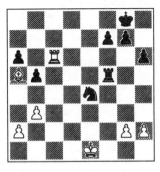

36 . . . Rf2 37 a4 Rxg2 38 Rxa6 bxa4 39 bxa4 Rxh2 40 Ra8+ Kh7 41 Bb6 Ra2 42 a5 h5 43 a6 h4 44 a7 h3 45 Bg1 Nf6 46 Kd1 Ng4 47 Re8 Rxa7 48 Bxh2 Rxa7 49 Bb8 Ra8 50 Rd8 Ne5 51 Bc7 Rxd8+ 52 Bxd8 Kg6 53 Ke2 Kf5 54 Ke3 Kg4 55 Bc7 Nf3 56 Kf2 f5 White resigns

Euwe Variation, 331 in the NIMZO-INDIAN DEFENCE, with the intention of replying to 6 Qc2 with 6 . . . Qf6; 351 in the QUEEN'S INDIAN DEFENCE, as played Euwe–Alatortsev, Leningrad 1934, but known earlier; 1191 in the FRENCH DEFENCE, instead of the usual 10 Ne2.

evaluation of position, an assessment of position to determine which side, if either, has the ADVANTAGE, and how the players should proceed. First the STATIC FACTORS are noted, then the DYNAMIC FACTORS examined, and finally a STRATEGY is chosen.

The static factors are those that can be seen without consideration of the moves that follow, the state of affairs on the board at a given moment: the balance of forces (see VALUE OF PIECES), advantage in SPACE or TIME, CONTROL of squares, lines, or parts of the board, pieces that are poorly situated (e.g. a BAD BISHOP), the PAWN CENTRE, ISOLATED, DOUBLED, or BACKWARD PAWNS, HANGING PAWNS, MAJORITIES, ADVANCE POINTS, HOLES, and other features of the PAWN FORMATION.

The relevance of these static factors is determined by consideration of the dynamic factors: the moves that might yet be played, the possible COMBINATIONS or MANŒUVRES that attack or defend certain pawns, squares, or parts of the board; in other words the tactical feasibility of various courses of action. There are no rules: dynamic factors are specific to any given position. The better the player the more precise and far-seeing will the examination be, the more relevant the lines examined and the wider their range. Examination might reveal no advantage when judged objectively, implying that EQUILIBRIUM is undisturbed, but the better player sees more deeply, and might thereby profit. Great masters usually assess the dynamic factors with equal skill, but on occasion slight differences lead to a decisive result. For example, both players see a series of, say, six moves, a manœuvre or a combination, but one of them makes a faulty assessment of the position that will then arise. This may be discovered after the first of the six moves has been played, and a new course chosen, but the position could be already compromised. Thus, as often as not, are games between the great masters won or lost.

The selection of a strategic plan (there is often more than one possibility) depends on its feasibility, as tested by examination of its dynamic factors. For example, a weak player, seeing an isolated pawn in the enemy camp, might decide without further ado to attack the pawn. A master would examine various lines of play to discover whether an attack would succeed, or, if the pawn cannot be gained, the opponent would be forced into a difficult situation: or another course of action might be chosen, bearing in mind that if the pawn is still there later it could then perhaps be profitably assailed.

A player's choice of plan might be wholly objective (or supposedly so), or subjective in varying degree: it is largely a matter of style. A LASKER would seek manœuvres, a RUBINSTEIN the perfect move; a TAL would look for combinations, a KARPOV for safe positional play; a CAPABLANCA or PETROSYAN would eye the distant endgame.

In over-the-board play there is not enough time for more than an occasional examination in detail, perhaps at a critical moment or between PHASES. For most of their moves masters rely on judgement and experience. For beginners the best use of evaluation lies in the study of their own games (especially losses) and those played by masters; but there is no substitute for practical play, the best way to acquire judgement.

Euwe, *Judgment and Planning in Chess* (1953); Kotov, *Think Like a Grandmaster* (1971).

Evans, Larry Melvyn (1932–   ), American player, International Grandmaster (1957). A successful player in many American and Canadian events, he won the US Open Championship four times—1951, 1952, 1954 (shared with POMAR), 1971 (shared with

BROWNE)—and shared first prize with Bisguier, ahead of RESHEVSKY, at New York 1955. His best achievements, however, were in the US championship: he came first in 1951, 1961–2, 1968 (+6=5), and 1980 (+5=5–2), equal with CHRISTIANSEN, who won the play-off, and Browne; and he came second to Bisguier in 1954, to FISCHER in 1963–4 (+6=3–2) and 1966 (+5=5–1), and to Browne in 1974. In 1952 he defended his title in a challenge match, crushing H. STEINER +8=4–2.

Not a frequent competitor overseas, Evans nevertheless came second (+8=4–1) equal with PETROSYAN after DONNER at Venice 1967, and represented his country in eight Olympiads from 1950 to 1976. In his one interzonal tournament, Amsterdam 1964, he made only a moderate score. He wrote *New Ideas in Chess* (1958), edited the tenth edition of *Modern Chess Openings* in 1965, and assisted in the preparation of Fischer's book *My 60 Memorable Games* (1969). In 1973 he began a syndicated chess column which appeared in papers such as the *Sunday Washington Post* and *Chicago Tribune*.

Evans–B. Zuckerman New York 1966–7 US Championship Sicilian Defence Dragon Variation

1 e4 c5 2 Nf3 d6 3 d4 cxd4 4 Nxd4 Nf6 5 Nc3 g6 6 Be3 Nc6 7 f3 Bg7 8 Qd2 0–0 9 0–0–0 Nxd4 10 Bxd4 Be6 11 Kb1 Qc7 12 h4 Rfc8 13 h5 Nxh5 14 Bxg7 Kxg7 15 g4 Nf6 16 Qh6+ Kg8

17 e5 dxe5 18 g5 Nh5 19 Bd3 e4 20 Rxh5 gxh5 21 Nxe4 Qf4 22 Nf6+ exf6 23 Bxh7+ Kh8 24 Bf5+ Kg8 25 Qh7+ Kf8 26 Qh8+ Ke7 27 gxf6+ mate.

Evans, William Davies (1790–1872), inventor of the EVANS GAMBIT, for about half a century one of the most popular attacking weapons (see SCHOOLS OF CHESS). He was born in Pembroke, Wales, went to sea at the age of 14, was employed by the Postal Department from about 1815, and rose to the rank of captain four years later. In 1824, soon after taking command of the first Royal Mail steam packet to sail from Milford Haven to Waterford, and while aboard, he invented his gambit. Evans was a keen player. He gathered a small chess circle in Waterford, and when on leave in England played chess in London, notably in 1826 when he showed his gambit to LEWIS and McDONNELL, and in 1838 when he played a long series of games with STAUNTON at the Westminster Chess Club. In January

1840 he was pensioned off on account of ill-health. He went to Greece, became captain of a steamer that sailed the Mediterranean and returned to London at the end of 1842. During the next 13 years there are several accounts of his presence in London, and then he settled abroad. He died and was buried in Ostend.

Evans claimed to have solved the THREE PAWNS PROBLEM, which, however, had already been solved by others. His claim to the invention of tri-coloured lighting for ships has not been verified independently, although he is known to have investigated the subject. For this invention he states that the Tsar of Russia gave him a gold chronometer, and that he also received money. For a more detailed life of Captain Evans see *British Chess Magazine,* 1928, pp. 6–18.

Evans Counter-gambit, 904, one of the oldest ways of declining the EVANS GAMBIT, but, despite its adoption by PILLSBURY at Nuremberg 1896, never a popular line.

Evans Gambit, 867 in the ITALIAN OPENING, named after W. D. EVANS who invented it in the 1820s. White gives up a pawn to gain rapid mobilization. The gambit was offered and accepted 22 times in the matches between BOURDONNAIS and McDONNELL, 1834, after which enthusiasm for the Evans was instant, widespread, and enduring. In his matches against CHIGORIN (1889, 1892) and GUNSBERG (1890–1), STEINITZ accepted the gambit 20 times. Soon after this the opening went out of fashion, although it is still used occasionally by some of the strongest grandmasters such as NUNN and TIMMAN. Countless lines of analysis have failed to show whether the gambit is sound. (See ANDERSSEN; CHIGORIN; EVERGREEN GAME; NEUMANN.)

Evans Gambit Declined, 896, usually regarded as safer than acceptance. However, White retains the initiative after 5 a4 a6 6 Nc3 Nf6 7 Nd5. It has been known as the Boden–Max Lange Variation.

Helms–Tenner, New York, 1942. 1 e4 e5 2 Nf3 Nc6 3 Bc4 Bc5 4 b4 Bb6 5 a4 a6 6 a5 Ba7 7 b5 axb5 8 Bxb5 Nf6 9 Ba3 Nxe4? 10 Qe2 Nxf2 11 Nxe5 Nd4 12 Nxd7+ Nxe2 13 Nf6 mate.

Evergreen Game, a name given by STEINITZ to the following FRIENDLY GAME, which has remained a favourite.

Anderssen–Dufresne Berlin, 1852 Evans Gambit

1 e4 e5 2 Nf3 Nc6 3 Bc4 Bc5 4 b4 Bxb4 5 c3 Ba5 6 d4 exd4 7 0–0 d3 8 Qb3 Qf6 9 e5 Qg6 10 Re1 Nge7 11 Ba3 b5 12 Qxb5 Rb8 13 Qa4 Bb6 14 Nbd2 Bb7 15 Ne4 Qf5 16 Bxd3 Qh5 17 Nf6+ gxf6 18 exf6 Rg8 19 Rad1 (a) Qxf3 (b) 20 Rxe7+ Nxe7 (c) 21 Qxd7+ Kxd7 22 Bf5+ Ke8 23 Bd7+ Kf8 24 Bxe7 mate (*Schachzeitung,* 1852)

(a) Analysis by I. Zaitsev (*64,* 1976) suggests that 19 Be4, recommended by many annotators, leads to a draw.

(b) Here 19 ... Rg4 (LIPKE, 1898) is preferable, and if 20 c4 Bd4 (I. Zaitsev).

(c) White wins after 20 ... Kd8 21 Rxd7+ Kc8 22 Rd8+ Kxd8 23 Bf5+ according to RUBINSTEIN, 1921.

everyday language and chess. Since medieval times the game has been used for a metaphor of life; both writers and players have been struck by the parallels. See, for example, JONES. Perhaps the best known example is in Fitzgerald's version of the *Rubáiyát of Omar Khayyám* (1859).

'Tis all a Chequer-board of Nights and Days
Where Destiny with Men for Pieces plays:
Hither and thither moves, and mates, and slays
And one by one back in the Closet lays.

A literal translation does not mention chess: 'We are playthings and heaven is the player—in very truth, not metaphorically: we play (our) little game of existence, (then) we fall back one by one into the box of non-existence.'

A few words have been derived from chess terms—exchequer (from the checkered board) and JEOPARDY. Hypermodern, defined by the *Oxford English Dictionary* as 'excessively modern', stems from its chess usage (see SCHOOLS OF CHESS) for developments in chess strategy in the early years of the 20th century. As indicated under TOURNAMENT, that word was first used in its modern sense in a chess context. The expression, *en passant,* when used in a general sense, appears to derive from normal French usage, although it may be surmised that familiarity with its chess connotation may have induced writers to choose it when English alternatives would be equally apt.

Figurative and other usages include: 'the widow's gambit was played, and she had not won the game.' Oliver Wendell Holmes in his novel *Elsie Venn* (1860), chapter 22; 'The Churchmen checked them often, but could never give the mate.' Selden, *Laws of England* (1649), I. xvi; 'It would be disgraceful indeed if a great country like Russia should run herself into such a stale-mate position.' *The Contemporary Review,* Sept. 1886. Stalemate, often used in the context of war and politics, is rarely an exact parallel: the impasse may be reversible.

The chessman most commonly referred to is the pawn, implying a minor figure or helpless person, the victim of fate. In 1991 a newspaper headline read 'The Pawns of Brindisi', referring to hapless refugees from Albania. In November 1990 an English judge gave two drug-pushers an eleven-year sentence, describing them as 'mere pawns'. They must have been relieved that they had not been promoted.

As an activity chess appears to have a good image, and this encourages PATRONAGE and also advertisers. Chessmen are often depicted as, for example, by a firm of furniture removers, Bishop's Move, which includes a chess bishop as the main feature of its logo. (Based in a cathedral city, the firm has indeed moved several bishops.)

Excelsior, a composition TASK: the advance of a pawn from its second to its eighth rank, preferably in consecutive moves. Having achieved this task in 1858, LOYD named it after either Longfellow's poem or the New York State motto.

+

A study by the English composer Hugh Francis Blandford (1917–81), first prize, *Springaren*, 1949. 1 Bd4+ Ka8 2 c4 Nd2 3 c5 Nb3 4 c6 Na5 5 c7 Nc6 6 c8=R+ (6 c8=Q+? Nb8+) 6 . . . Nb8+ 7 Kd6.
(See GRASSHOPPER.)

exchange, the capture of material by each player as part of the same combination or manœuvre but not necessarily on consecutive single-moves; to make such a capture. For example, after 1 e4 e5 2 Nf3 Nc6 3 d4 exd4 4 Bc4 Bc5 5 Ng5 Nh6 White can make a combination which exchanges two white pieces for two pieces and a pawn: 6 Nxf7 Nxf7 7 Bxf7+ Kxf7 8 Qh5+ g6 9 Qxc5. Informally, to exchange is often called to swap, or, particularly in the USA, to trade.

exchange, the, the capture of a rook by one player and a minor piece by the opponent. The player who captures the rook 'wins the exchange'. A player might win or lose the exchange for a pawn, i.e. a rook is exchanged for a minor piece and a pawn. Having a fondness for bishops, TARRASCH half-seriously suggested that to exchange one's knight for a bishop is to win the MINOR EXCHANGE.

Exchange Variation, usually a variation in which White exchanges a black centre pawn by capturing on d5 or e5, bringing about a FIXED CENTRE; 82 in the SLAV DEFENCE; 150, 158 (also called the Reshevsky Variation), 167, 175, 204 in the QUEEN's GAMBIT Declined (see CHRISTIANSEN; KASPAROV; LASKER, EM.; PAWN FORMATION; YUSUPOV); 581, sometimes called the Argentine, or Collijn Variation, in the CARO–KANN DEFENCE (see VELIMIROVIĆ); 1236, also known as the Morphy Variation, in the FRENCH DEFENCE (see ADVANCE POINT; BIRD; FIXED CENTRE; MIESES). Sometimes a line in which minor pieces are exchanged: 365 in the GRÜNFELD DEFENCE (see GELFAND; OUTPOST); 760, also known as the Lasker Variation, in the SPANISH OPENING; 854 in the THREE KNIGHTS OPENING.

Exchange Variation Deferred, 1198, the SVENONIUS VARIATION, that is, the Exchange Variation of the FRENCH DEFENCE played one move later than usual.

Exchange Variation Double Deferred, 734, DERLD, that is, the EXCHANGE VARIATION of the SPANISH OPENING deferred for two moves.

exhibition game, a game played in public for entertainment, as distinct from a match or tournament. In single combat a clock is often used and masters take such games seriously, having their reputations at stake. A SIMULTANEOUS DISPLAY is of less importance, and clocks are unlikely to be used if more than ten opponents face the master.

exposed king, a king with few or none of its own pawns and pieces nearby and, in consequence, exposed to attack.

Ezra, Abraham Ben Meir ibn (*c*.1092–*c*.1167), author of several Hebrew works on chess. He was born in Tudela, Spain, and worked as a philosopher, poet, and mathematician in Italy, France, England, and Egypt. He wrote the first chess poems in Hebrew, the most famous being the 'Song of Chess'. His works shed light on the laws of play in his time; they were the same as those of SHAṬRANJ except for the introduction of the FERS's leap, which suggests that this was the first modification of the laws made by medieval European players.

F

Fabel, Karl (1905–75), German composer, International Judge of Chess Compositions (1964), International Master for Chess Compositions (1967), expert in patents relating to the chemistry of plastics, civil judge. Although he composed many THREE- and MORE-MOVERS and some FAIRY PROBLEMS, he was best known as a leading exponent of the art of RETROGRADE ANALYSIS. An essay on the subject published in *Fairy Chess Review*, 1956–8, appeared in book form as *Introduction to Retrograde Analysis* (1973).

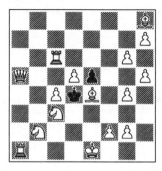

A problem by Fabel and the German composer Theodor Steudel (1928–), *Basler Nachrichten*, 1969. Mate in one. How many solutions?

White may play Pxe5 ep♯, for the only possible retro move is . . . Pe5, preceded by Rf6-c6+. Instead, White may play 1 Rd1♯. However, castling is illegal. White's 14 pawn captures, all from west to east, must have included Black's promoted a-pawn, so the white Ra1 must have been moved at some time.

Fahrni, Hans (1874–1939), Swiss player born in Prague. He won a match against SALWE in 1908 (+3=1−1) and achieved his best tournament performance in a quadruple-round event at Munich 1909, taking first prize (+6=4−2), ahead of TARTAKOWER, ALAPIN, and SPIELMANN. Skilled at fast play, Fahrni was the first master to meet 100 opponents in a simultaneous display; it took place in 1911 at Munich, where he lived for a time, and he scored +55=39−6 in seven and a half hours.

Fahrni Variation, 1263 in the ALEKHINE DEFENCE. Although proposed by FAHRNI in the early 1920s the line was little used until half a century later.

fairy mate, a checkmate in a FAIRY PROBLEM for which the special rules of that problem are deemed

to apply after the mating move, as if the king were to be captured. For example, in a MAXIMUMMER the position Wh: Ka1 Pa2, b2; Bl: Kf4, Rf1 shows a mate that is both normal and fairy; move the black king to e4 and the mate is normal but not fairy, for Black's 'post-mate' move . . . Rxa1 would not be the longest. In CHECKLESS CHESS the position Wh: Kb2, Pe3; Bl: Kd4, Be5 would be a fairy mate but not a normal mate.

fairy problem, or heterodox problem, any problem that is not an ORTHODOX PROBLEM. Broadly, there are two categories.

The first group comprises HELPMATES, SELFMATES, problems involving RETROGRADE ANALYSIS (including RETRACTORS), and stalemate problems in which, apart from the mating or stalemating STIPULATIONS, the laws of chess are observed. There is a growing tendency for these to be regarded as orthodox.

Secondly there are the problems using unorthodox men, rules, or boards. Typical men are BEROLINA PAWN, EQUIHOPPER, GRASSHOPPER, JOKER, KAMIKAZE PIECE, NIGHTRIDER, NEUTRAL MAN, ORPHAN, REFLECTING BISHOP, ROSE, ROYAL PIECE, various pieces once used in GREAT CHESS, many kinds of LEAPER, and the CHINESE FAMILY. For unorthodox rules see ALICE CHESS, CIRCE, IMITATOR, MADRASI, MAXIMUMMER, REFLEX CHESS, SERIESMOVER. Unusual boards include ANCHOR RING, CYLINDER BOARDS, GRID BOARDS, and boards with more or fewer squares than the normal 64.

When stipulations for fairy problems are made, then the normal laws are deemed to apply unless otherwise stated.

In the early 1900s BAIRD, discussing heterodox problems, referred to a chess fairyland. The Australian Henry Tate (1873–1926) suggested the term fairy chess in *The Australasian*, 20 June 1914, and this is widely used in preference to FIDE's official term, heterodox chess. (See PROBLEM; PROBLEM HISTORY.)

Kurt Smulders, *Sprookjesschaak* (1987).

Fajarowicz Variation, 291 in the BUDAPEST DEFENCE, named after S. Fajarowicz of Leipzig (hence sometimes called the Leipzig Variation), who introduced it against H. STEINER, Wiesbaden 1928. The line had, however, been discussed by the American analyst Stasch Mlotkowski (1881–1943), in the *British Chess Magazine*, 1919.

Falkbeer, Ernst Karl (1819–85), Austrian player, journalist. He left Vienna in the troubled year of

1848, travelled extensively in Germany, founded Austria's first chess magazine *Wiener Schachzeitung* in January 1855, and when it failed a few months later went to London. There, in match play, he met BIRD twice, losing in 1856 (+1−2) and winning in 1856–7 (+5=4−4). In his one tournament, Birmingham 1858, a knock-out event, he defeated SAINT-AMANT in the second round (+2−1) and lost to LÖWENTHAL in the fourth and final round (+1=4−3). From April 1857 to November 1859 he edited a chess column in the *Sunday Times*. Returning to Vienna in 1864 he continued his journalistic career which included the editorship of a chess column in *Neue Illustrirte Zeitung* from 1877 to 1885. He is chiefly remembered, however, for the enterprising COUNTER-GAMBIT named after him, the merits of which have been disputed ever since. (See SEA-CADET MATE.)

Falkbeer Counter-gambit, 1078, one of the two standard ways of declining the KING'S GAMBIT. The continuation 3 exd5 had been known since the time of POLERIO, and was generally considered to favour White after 3 . . . Qxd5, although PHILIDOR had pointed out that Black gets a satisfactory game by 3 . . . exf4. In the 1840s both FALKBEER and the Prague player Lederer investigated the reply 3 . . . e4. Falkbeer published an analysis of this move, now the usual continuation, in *Schachzeitung*, 1850.

Falkbeer Variation, 625. In *Schachzeitung*, 1857, FALKBEER recommended, but did not originate, this standard reply, sometimes called the Berlin Defence, to the VIENNA GAME.

family check, a FORK by a knight that simultaneously gives check and attacks a queen, and perhaps other men.

Agzamov–V. A. Chekhov   Potsdam 1985   Old Indian Defence

1 d4 Nf6 2 c4 d6 3 Nc3 Nbd7 4 e4 e5 5 Nf3 g6 6 Be2 Bg7 7 0–0 0–0 8 Qc2 c6 9 Rd1 Qe7 10 b4 exd4 11 Nxd4 Re8 12 f3 d5 13 exd5 cxd5 14 c5 a5 15 Ncb5 Nf8 16 Nd6 Rd8 17 bxa5 Rxa5 18 Bb2 Nh5 19 Nb3 Qe3+ 20 Kf1 Bxb2 21 Qxb2 Ra4 22 Rd3 Qg5?

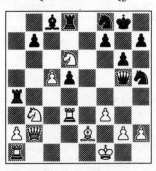

23 Qh8+ Kxh8 24 Nxf7+ (a family check) 24 . . . Kg7 25 Nxg5 Re8 26 Rd4 Rxd4 27 Nxd4 Nf4 28 Bb5 Re5 29 g3 Rxg5 30 gxf4 Rh5 31 Kg2 Rh4 32 Ne2 Ne6 33 Kg3 Rh5 34 c6 bxc6 35 Bxc6 Ba6 36 Nc3 Nd4? 37 Bd7

Ne2+ 38 Nxe2 Bxe2 39 Bg4 Rh6 40 Re1 Bc4 41 a4 g5 Black resigns.

In the chess column of the *Liverpool Weekly Courier*, 1886, the English player and problemist Oliver Harcourt Labone (1860–1925) claimed that the position r5k1/3q2Pp/p7/1p5Q/8/7P/1P4P1/5RK1 (Forsyth notation) had occurred in play, and that he had won by 1 Rf8+ Rxf8 2 Qxh7+ Kxh7 3 gxf8=N+, a typical family check.

Faragó, Iván (1946–), Hungarian player, International Grandmaster (1976), an economist who became a chess professional. In Hungarian championships he finished equal first (+2=7) in 1981 but the title went to PORTISCH on tie-break; in 1986 he won outright. His main victories in international events are: Halle 1978 (+5=8), a tie with KNAAK and UHLMANN; Kecskemét 1979 (+7=8); Svendborg 1981 (+6=3); Albena 1983; Budapest 1987 (+4=5).

Fedorowicz, John Peter (1958–), American player, International Grandmaster (1986). After coming last in the US championship of 1977, and again in 1981, his play gradually strengthened until, in 1987, he shared first place (+4=5) in the strong tournament at Cannes with GULKO, and won the Wijk aan Zee 'B' tournament 1990 (+7=4).

Fedorowicz–Norwood   London 1988 (Watson, Farley & Williams)   Modern Benoni

1 d4 Nf6 2 c4 c5 3 d5 e6 4 Nc3 exd5 5 cxd5 d6 6 Nf3 g6 7 Nd2 Nbd7 8 e4 Bg7 9 Be2 0–0 10 0–0 Re8 11 a4 Ne5 12 Ra3 g5 13 Qc2 a6 14 Nd1 b6 15 g3 g4 16 Qb1 Ra7 17 b4 Rae7 18 bxc5 bxc5 19 Rb3 Ned7 20 Ne3 Ne5 21 Rb8 Qc7

22 Rxc8 Qxc8 23 Nf5 Rd7 24 Bb2 Bf8 25 Qc1 h6 26 Nc4 Kh7 27 Bxe5 dxe5 28 Nb6 Qb7 29 Nxd7 Qxd7 30 Qc2 Qa7 31 Rb1 c4 32 Qxc4 Bc5 33 Kg2 a5 34 d6 Rd8 35 Ne7 Black resigns.

Fegatello Attack, 967 in the TWO KNIGHTS DEFENCE, an extensively analysed variation that favours White. It was known to the 16th-century Italian masters and the name is Italian for a piece of liver, perhaps implying that the sacrifice of White's knight is like a slice of liver used as bait in a trap.

fers, the medieval piece that supplanted the FIRZĀN and was in turn supplanted by the QUEEN. Besides having the same move as the firzān (one square diagonally in any direction) the fers had the power of leaping to a vacant square on its first move, with the choice of a $\sqrt{4}$ or a $\sqrt{8}$ leap, an innovation dating from the 12th century. (See EZRA.) For example, a previously unmoved fers at d1 could be moved to e2 or c2 or, even if surrounded by other men, to b1, b3, d3, f3, or f1. A fers created by promotion also had this power of leaping. For a brief period the names queen and fers were both in use for the old piece, the latter being reserved for a fers made by promotion. When draughts (checkers) was first played in England the game and the pieces were called ferses.

fianchetto (pron. f-yanketto), the development of a white bishop at g2 or b2 (less commonly at h3 or a3) or a black bishop at g7 or b7 (h6, a6); the concomitant pawn formation; to make such a development. Depending upon whether a king's or a queen's bishop is so developed the fianchetto is described as king's or queen's respectively. To move the knight's pawn to the fourth rank instead of the third is to make an extended fianchetto. The exchange of a bishop so developed may lead to a weakened fianchetto due to one or two HOLES left in the wake of the knight's pawn's advance. A player who develops both bishops this way makes a double fianchetto.

Strategic use of the fianchetto, pioneered by STAUNTON and PAULSEN, has since become the basis of many openings. The word is a diminutive of the Italian *fianco*, a flank. Francesco Piacenza, in his book *I Campeggiamenti degli scacchi* (Turin, 1683), describes flank openings as fianchetti. Modern usage dates from LOLLI, 1763, where he applied it, but only in the index, to 1 e4 b6 2 d4 Bb7.

Fianchetto Defence, 812, the BARNES DEFENCE to the SPANISH OPENING.

Fianchetto Defence Deferred, 759, the BARNES DEFENCE DEFERRED in the SPANISH OPENING.

Fianchetto Variation, 197 in the QUEEN'S GAMBIT Declined. The line might better be called the Flank Variation since Black's queen's bishop will not necessarily be developed away from the centre. (See SHOWALTER.)

fidated, or affidatus, immune from capture. In past times problemists sometimes specified that certain pieces or pawns were fidated, a STIPULATION often used to circumvent lack of composing skill or merely to deceive the solver.

FIDE, an acronym pronounced fee-day, the Fédération Internationale des Échecs. This is the French name for the international chess federation, founded in 1924 and now recognized as the world-wide governing body for most aspects of chess. The desire for such an organization is as old as international chess, and was a general ambition of STAUNTON, LASA, and others. No real progress was made until delegates from 15 countries met at Paris in 1924 and signed an agreement to establish FIDE. It started in a low key, but when a satisfactory formula for OLYMPIADS emerged, FIDE gained popularity, and its authority to control the LAWS was accepted. At the same time it launched a world championship for women. After ALEKHINE's death in 1946 the USSR joined FIDE, which then gained acceptance as the supreme body and took control of world titles for over-the-board chess. Most other forms of chess became linked with FIDE.

A combination of the demands of administering ELO RATING and the burgeoning of professional chess altered FIDE's financial status and increased the possibility of careers for officials. Inevitably the greater activity and higher stakes were conducive to the risk of friction, and the GRANDMASTERS' ASSOCIATION was set up to further the interests of the top professional players.

FIDE Albums, a series of books, each containing a selection of problems and studies composed during a given period and published on behalf of the FIDE Permanent Commission for Chess Compositions. Four volumes cover the years 1914–55 inclusive, and each subsequent volume covers a three-year period. The published compositions earn points for composers: 1 point for a problem, $1\frac{2}{3}$ points for a study, and a proportionate share for a joint composition. Since 1975 titles have been awarded on the basis of points scored.

Many thousands of problems and studies are submitted. For example, there were 6,575 entries for the 1980–2 Album, from which seven panels, each of three judges, selected 1,083 for publication.

FIDE Master (FM), the lowest-ranking FIDE title, inaugurated for over-the-board play in 1978, and for composition in 1990. Players qualify as for IGM and IM but at a reduced level, while composers need 12 points in FIDE ALBUMS.

FIDE Master for Chess Compositions, a title created by FIDE in 1990, based on points scored in FIDE ALBUMS, and ranking below the title of International Master for Chess Compositions.

FIDE titles. The following lifetime titles are awarded for performance, and are open to all: International Grandmaster, International Master, FIDE Master, International Correspondence Chess Grandmaster, International Correspondence Chess Master, International Grandmaster for Chess Compositions, International Master for Chess Compositions, FIDE Master for Chess Compositions, International Grandmaster for Solving, and International Master for Solving. In addition there are the titles International Woman Grandmaster, International Woman Master, and Woman FIDE Master.

The titles for play are normally awarded for an appropriate combination of ELO RATING and NORMS, but a few are gained by winning a competition which might be of uncertain quality. The requirements for correspondence chess are laid down by the International Correspondence Chess Federation, an independent body which co-operates with FIDE.

In addition to formal titles, which began in 1950, there are titles by implication from events such as the world championship.

field, see KING'S FIELD.

fifty-move law. If both players have made 50 moves without capturing a man or moving a pawn, a player whose turn it is to move may claim a draw except for six BASIC ENDGAMES for which the number of moves is extended to 75: these are Q v. B + B, Q v. N + N, B + B v. N, N + N v. P, Q + P one square from promotion v. Q, and R + B v. R. This law was enacted by FIDE in 1988 and superseded a mercifully short-lived 100-move law.

The first three of the six exceptions rarely occur in play. The last three occur more often, but the great majority of positions are either drawn or can be won in fewer than 50 moves. R + B v. R occurs most frequently, and wins in more than 50 moves are few, while many positions are drawn at the start. Not surprisingly, many players object to the imposition of a 75-move defensive task.

Generally, the occurrence of a 'long win' position is so improbable that some masters, among them KASPAROV, suggest that the old 50-move law would suffice for all endgames.

This position was analysed by the American computer expert Lewis Stiller and published in 1988. Against the best defence White needs 77 moves to win the black knight, but is allowed only 50.

1 Bg3 Nc4 2 Kd1 Ne3+ 3 Ke2 Nf5 4 Bf2 Ne7 5 Kf3 Nc6 6 Kg3 Nd4 7 Kg4 Nc6 8 Kh3 Nb4 9 Bb6 Nd3 10 Nc2 Nf2+ 11 Kg3 Ne4+ 12 Kf4 Nd2 13 Ne3 Kh2 14 Kg4 Nb3 15 Ba7 Nc1 16 Bd4 Nd3 17 Kh4 Nf2 18 Be5+ Kg1 19 Bc3 Ne4 20 Be1 Nf6 21 Kg5 Nd7 22 Kf4 Nc5 23 Kf3 Ne6 24 Bc3 Kh2 25 Kg4 Nd8 26 Be5+ Kg1 27 Kg3 Ne6 28 Bf6 Nc5 29 Bd4 Nb3 30 Ba7 Nd2 31 Nc4+ Kh1 32 Ne5 Nc4 33 Nd3 Nd6 34 Kh3 Nf7 35 Be3 Ne5 36 Nf4 Nc4 37 Bd4 Nd6 38 Nh5 Ne4 39 Be3 Nf2+ 40 Kg3 Ne4+ 41 Kf3 Nd6 42 Bf4 Nc4 43 Kf2 Na5 44 Nf6 Nb7 45 Kf3 Nd8 46 Bd6 Kg1 47 Ne4 Nc6 48 Nd2 Nd4+ 49 Ke4 Ne2 50 Ke3 Nc3 51 Be5 Na2 52 Kf3 Nb4 53 Kg3 Kh1

54 Bd4 Nc6 55 Bc5 Nd8 56 Ne4 Nb7 57 Bb4 Nd8 58 Ba5 Ne6 59 Bb6 Ng5 60 Nf2+ Kg1 61 Kf4 Nf7 62 Ng4+ Kg2 63 Ne3+ Kh3 64 Nf5 Kg2 65 Bc5 Nh8 66 Nd4 Kh3 67 Kf5 Kh4 68 Ne6 Kh5 69 Be3 Nf7 70 Ng7+ Kh4 71 Bf4 Nh8 72 Ne6 Nf7 73 Kg6 Nh8+ 74 Kg7 Kg4 75 Bh6 Kh5 76 Nf4+ Kg4 77 Kxh8

The law existed in SHAṬRANJ as a 70-move version, and since then the intention has always been the same, that is, to counter the obstinacy of one who continues playing in an unwinnable position. In 1561 Ruy LÓPEZ said that 50 moves was enough, but CARRERA thought this too generous and that 24 moves was right. On the other hand BOURDONNAIS argued for 60 moves. By the 19th century a request for a count could be made only in specific endgames (not always the same in the various sets of laws). The count began only when the claim was made and was not annulled by a capture or a pawn move. Anomalies could arise such as if the queen were captured near the end of a 50-move count in an endgame K + Q v. K + R the result would still be a draw if mate was not effected in the remainder of the 50 moves. The laws used at the London 1883 tournament stated that a pawn move or a capture annulled the count, but did not offer retrospective counting when the claim was first made.

figurines, pictorial representations of chessmen used by printers (and computers) for diagrams and, less often, for notation. The men are shown as follows, White preceding Black.

king	♔	♚
queen	♕	♛
bishop	♗	♝
knight	♘	♞
rook	♖	♜
pawn	♙	♟

These shapes are not quite universal and that of the bishop, in particular, may be quite different in foreign publications.

Notation with figurines first appeared in *Les Échecs simplifiés et approfondis* (1846) where the author, Count Robiano, calls it *notation parlante*. The Hungarians, whose vigorous tradition of chess literature is handicapped by their difficult language, and who therefore have special need of an internationally understood notation, first demonstrated the method, which became standard, in *Magyar Sakkujság* in 1897, and later adopted it in *Magyar Sakkvilág*. The first work to use it throughout was the tournament book of Ostend 1906. In 1947 the magazine *Chess*, attempting to find a format that could be used throughout the world, tried the double experiment of STANDARD NOTATION and figurines, but it was ill-received. In 1967 the almost language-less *Chess Informant*, better known as *Informator*, used this notation, and since then it has gained popularity.

fīl, a leaper used in SHAṬRANJ and placed in the array where the bishop now stands. The co-ordinates of the fīl's leap are 2,2 and the length of its move is $\sqrt{8}$. A fīl placed on f1 can be moved to d3 or h3 whether or not another man stands on e2 or g2. The weakest piece in the old game, the fīl (the medieval AUFIN) can be moved to only eight squares, e.g. the fīl on f1 can reach only b1, b5, d3, d7, f5, h3, or h7. Each of the four fīls has an exclusive set of eight squares available. The word fīl is derived from the Persian pīl, a translation of the Sanskrit *gaja*, elephant.

file, or column, a row of eight laterally adjoining squares between White's end of the board and Black's. Identification is by means of the file symbol, e.g. the third file from White's left is the c-file (STANDARD NOTATION) or the QB-file (DESCRIPTIVE NOTATION).

Filip, Miroslav (1928–), International Grandmaster (1955), International Arbiter (1978), champion of Czechoslovakia 1950 (shared), 1952, 1954. By sharing seventh place in the Göteborg interzonal, 1955, Filip became the first Czech CANDIDATE. After a second place (+9=6) in the European zonal tournament, Mariánské Lázně 1961, and a score of +8=12−2 to share fourth place in the Stockholm interzonal of 1962, he became a Candidate for the second time; but in the Candidates tournaments of 1956 and 1962 he ended at or near the bottom of the table. His best achievements in other international events were at Vienna 1961, second (+5=6) after AVERBAKH, and Mariánské Lázně 1960, equal first with L. PACHMAN. Filip played for his country in twelve consecutive Olympiads from 1952 to 1974.

Tal–Filip Curaçao 1962 Candidates tournament Sicilian Defence Paulsen Variation

1 e4 c5 2 Nf3 e6 3 d4 cxd4 4 Nxd4 a6 5 Nc3 Qc7 6 f4 b5 7 a3 Bb7 8 Qf3 Nf6 9 Bd3 Bc5 10 Nb3 Be7 11 0–0 0–0 12 Bd2 d6 13 g4 d5 14 e5 Nfd7 15 Qh3 g6 16 Nd4 Nc6 17 Nce2 Nxd4 18 Nxd4 Nc5 19 b4 Ne4 20 Be3 Rfe8 21 Rae1 Bf8 22 Nf3 a5 23 f5 exf5 24 gxf5

24 ... Rxe5 25 fxg6 hxg6 26 Nxe5 Qxe5 27 c3 axb4 28 Bd4 Bc8 29 Qg2 Qh5 30 Bxe4 dxe4 31 Qxe4 Qg5+ 32 Kh1 Be6 33 Be5 Rd8 34 h4 Qh5 35 Qf4 Rd3 36 Bf6 Qd5+ 37 Kg1 bxc3 38 Re4 Bc5+ 39 Kh2 Qa2+ White resigns.

finance, see PATRONAGE; PROFESSIONALISM.

Fine, Reuben (1914–93), American player and author, International Grandmaster (1950). From about 1936 to 1951, when he practically gave up competitive chess, Fine was among the strongest eight players in the world. He learned to play when 8 years old and became keen on the game at 15; at college he gave most of his time to chess, earned some money by playing all-comers in an amusement park, and graduated without difficulty. His early chess successes include match victories against DAKE in 1933 (+4=3−2) and HOROWITZ in 1934 (+4=5−1), and first prize (+6=3), ahead of FLOHR, at Hastings 1935–6.

Leaving the USA in June 1936, he made a remarkable European tour lasting 19 months. He played in 13 tournaments and won 8 of them, won a match against STÅHLBERG in 1937 (+4=2−2), made the highest second-board score (+9=5−1) at the Stockholm Olympiad 1937, was EUWE'S second in the nine-week world championship match of 1937, gave numerous simultaneous displays, had an operation for appendicitis, and found himself a Dutch bride. His tournament victories were: Zandvoort 1936 (+6=5), ahead of Euwe and KERES; Oslo 1936, ahead of Flohr; Amsterdam 1936 (+4=2−1), equal with Euwe, ahead of ALEKHINE; Stockholm 1937 (+7=2), ahead of Ståhlberg; Moscow 1937 (+4=2−1); Leningrad 1937 (+3=2); Margate 1937 (+6=3), equal with Keres, ahead of Alekhine; and Ostend 1937, equal with Keres and Grob. He played in the strongest two tournaments held during this period: Nottingham 1936, where he came third (+5=9) equal with Euwe and RESHEVSKY, half a point behind CAPABLANCA and BOTVINNIK, ahead of Alekhine and Flohr; and Semmering–Baden 1937, when he came second (+2=12) after Keres, ahead of Capablanca, Reshevsky, and Flohr. On his next visit to Europe, Fine played at AVRO 1938, the strongest tournament held up to that time, and came first (+6=5−3) equal with Keres.

Despite this brilliant record Fine never won the US championship. In 1936 he was equal third, in 1938 and 1940, second. Reshevsky won all three. In 1944, when Reshevsky was not playing, Fine was again second, this time behind DENKER, and never entered again.

After Alekhine died in March 1946 there was for a time no world champion. Fine later wrote: 'Inasmuch as Keres and I tied for first prize in the AVRO tournament, which was officially [?] designated . . . for the selection of the challenger . . . it seems to me only fair that Keres and Fine should be listed as co-champions for the period 1946–1948.' But FIDE thought differently, and organized a match tournament for the world championship, to be held in the spring of 1948. Fine was faced with a difficult choice. Having found chess unprofitable he had long been studying for a profession (psychoanalysis) and the tournament would have clashed with preparations for his final examinations. He declined to play, passed his exams, and set up a practice in Manhattan. No doubt this was the right decision, since he had passed his peak as a player, but later he fostered the idea that he had been prevented from playing. He scored his last important victory (+7=2), ahead of NAJDORF, at New York in December 1948 and a few weeks later these two drew a match (+2=4−2).

Fine edited the sixth and best edition of *Modern Chess Openings* (1939) and wrote *Basic Chess Endings* (1941), a classic from which a generation of players learned the ENDGAME, a phase in which Fine himself excelled. Among his other books is a biographical collection, *Lessons from my Games* (1958).

Fine–Lilienthal   Moscow 1937   Grünfeld Defence Russian Variation

1 d4 Nf6 2 c4 g6 3 Nc3 d5 4 Qb3 c6 5 Nf3 Bg7 6 e3 0–0 7 Bd2 e6 8 Bd3 Nbd7 9 0–0 Nb6 10 Rfd1 dxc4 11 Bxc4 Nxc4 12 Qxc4 Nd7 13 e4 Qc7 14 e5 Nb6 15 Qe2 f5 16 exf6 Rxf6 17 Ne4 Rf5 18 Bb4 Rd5 19 Ne5 Rd8 20 Rac1 Nd5 21 Ba3 Ne7 22 Qf3 Nd5 23 Qg3 Bh6 24 Rc2 Bf8 25 h4 Bxa3 26 Qxa3 Rf8 27 h5 Rf4 28 Re2 gxh5 29 Qg3+ Qg7

30 Rd3 h4 31 Qxg7+ Kxg7 32 g3 hxg3 33 Rxg3+ Kf8 34 f3 Nf6 35 Rh2 Rxe4 36 fxe4 Nxe4 37 Rg4 Nf6 38 Rf2 Black resigns.

Fine Variation, 349 in the QUEEN'S INDIAN DEFENCE, introduced into master chess in the game Fine–Landau, Ostend 1937, but sometimes known as the Chekhover–Rabinovich Variation after the two players who analysed it originally.

Fingerslip Variation, 1185 in the FRENCH DEFENCE. After ALEKHINE played it against FLOHR at the Nottingham tournament, 1936, he claimed it was a *lapsus manus* but it is more likely that he remembered the game Speijer–Alekhine, Hamburg 1910, where it was played. Subsequently the variation became popular and was used with great effect by KERES, among others.

first move, the single-move that begins the game, made by White in modern chess. At one time players drew for colour and again for the move; LUCENA advised players not getting the colour of their choice to give the board a quarter turn, putting a dark square to the near right corner. With the queen on its own colour it would thus stand on the same side as would the queen of the preferred

colour on a correctly placed board. In the Bourdonnais–McDonnell matches of 1834 each player had the same colour throughout, and the right to make the first move changed only after a game had been won. In the London 1851 tournament players had the same colour throughout any one match, but had the first move on alternate games.

Black was supposed to be a lucky colour and in 1835 WALKER suggested that, by way of compensation, White should have the first move, a practice that had become general by *c*.1870. In his column in *Bell's Life* Walker reversed the colours of games where necessary, so that White always moved first; this is now the custom when games from earlier times are published.

firzān, or firz, the piece used in SHAṬRANJ that was supplanted by the FERS (in turn supplanted by the queen). A firzān is moved one square diagonally in any direction and can be moved to only 32 squares of the board. A pawn reaching the eighth rank can be promoted only to a firzān. A player who promotes a pawn on the b-, d-, f-, or h-file obtains a firzān that can be moved on a different set of 32 squares. This could be important, as shown in the study by aṣ-ṣūlī given under MANṢŪBA. Firzān is derived from the Persian *ferzin*, a counsellor, which in turn stems from the Pahlavic *aparzan*, a reference to the tent of the commander-in-chief of the army.

Fischer, Robert James (1943–). International Grandmaster (1958), World Champion 1972–5. Born in Chicago, he was brought up in Brooklyn by his mother, a divorcée. At the age of six he acquired a chess set and soon became deeply absorbed in the game. Inattentive at school, unamenable to discipline, he absented himself from home for long hours playing chess. 'All I want to do, ever, is play chess.' What he learned of the world outside he gleaned incidentally from his mother, a teacher, and his older sister. Having access to an excellent chess library he read voraciously. At 14 he won both the US junior and senior championships; at 15 he became the youngest ever CANDIDATE by taking fifth place at the Portorož interzonal 1958. Early in 1959 he left school, believing he could learn nothing of value there. Scornful of everything outside himself and his chess, he understood little of what he scorned. Regarded as anti-social, resentful of all authority, he increasingly became alienated from his fellow-men. What he could do he would do for himself: 'If I win a tournament I win by myself. I do the playing, no-one helps me.' He rejected his mother's well-meant attempts to raise money on his behalf so that he might play abroad.

At Zurich 1959 he came third (+8=5−2) equal with KERES, after TAL and GLIGORIĆ; at the Candidates tournament, Bled–Zagreb–Belgrade 1959, he shared fifth place with Gligorić, after Tal, Keres, PETROSYAN, and SMYSLOV. At 16 he was able to earn his living from chess, and soon began to dress well, with suits tailored in London and New York. He also began a lifelong habit of dictating the conditions under which he would play, and was not backward in demanding appearance money. 'I add status to any tournament I attend', he remarked. In 1960 his mother left home on a peace march from California to Moscow, married on the way, and never came back. She had done what she could for her son, but they were fast drifting apart. Later he corresponded regularly with her when she settled in England.

Fischer's ambition was firmly set on the world championship, which he expected to win within a year or so. In 1961 he played a match with RESHEVSKY. The score stood at $+2=7-2$ when play was abandoned. Reshevsky wanted a change of schedule but Fischer would not accept the new one. Fischer played at Bled 1961, taking second place ($+8=11$) after Tal, ahead of Gligorić, Keres, Petrosyan, and GELLER, and at the interzonal, Stockholm 1962, where he took first place ($+13=9$), two and a half points ahead of the nearest rival. This excellent result may have caused him to overrate his prospects. Interzonals are qualifying events, and in this case his chief rivals needed only to finish among the first six.

After a poor start at the Candidates tournament, Curaçao 1962, Fischer played on with such determination that he finished in fourth place ($+8=12-7$) after Petrosyan, Keres, and Geller. Five of the eight competitors were from the USSR, and he believed, with some truth, that they had conspired against him. However, at 19, he was not yet good enough to win such an event. Always objective about his play, he was less self-critical regarding external factors. He complained about noise, a hidden camera, shiny chessmen, a movement in the audience, fidgety opponents, inadequate lighting, and so on; now it was a Russian plot. Besides his personal ambition to win the world championship, he came to believe it was his mission to defeat the Russians who had for so long dominated the game. He was convinced that Soviet deception had kept him from the title.

He blamed FIDE, too. If the world was against him he must learn to fend for himself, and for three years he played no international tournaments. However, he made one notable success, winning the US championship, 1963–4, with a CLEAN SCORE ($+11$). He attempted unsuccessfully to bypass FIDE and arrange a match directly with a Soviet player, perhaps even the world champion. In 1965 he agreed to play at Havana. Outflanking the State Department, who would not permit Americans to travel there, he sat in New York and played his games by teletype; he came second ($+12=6-3$) equal with Geller and IVKOV, half a point behind the winner, Smyslov. At Santa Monica 1966 Fischer welcomed the opportunity to compete against the best two Soviet players, and he came second ($+7=8-3$), half a point after Spassky, and ahead of Petrosyan. By winning ($+8=3$) the US championship 1966–7 (his eighth consecutive victory) Fischer qualified for the next interzonal, and he prepared by winning two international events in

1967, Monte Carlo ($+6=2-1$), and Skopje ($+12=3-2$). Almost all his special demands were met. He seemed set to win the Sousse interzonal, 1967, having established a comfortable lead after ten completed rounds, when he became involved in a dispute. He withdrew from the tournament, forgoing for another three years his chances of being champion.

Portisch–Fischer   Santa Monica 1966   Nimzo-Indian Defence Bronstein Variation

1 d4 Nf6 2 c4 e6 3 Nc3 Bb4 4 e3 b6 5 Ne2 Ba6 6 Ng3 Bxc3+ 7 bxc3 d5 8 Qf3 0–0 9 e4 dxe4 10 Nxe4 Nxe4 11 Qxe4 Qd7! 12 Ba3 Re8 13 Bd3 f5 14 Qxa8? Nc6 15 Qxe8+ Qxe8 16 0–0 Na5 17 Rae1 Bxc4 18 Bxc4 Nxc4 19 Bc1 c5 20 dxc5 bxc5 21 Bf4 h6 22 Re2 g5 23 Be5 Qd8 24 Rfe1 Kf7 25 h3 Qd5 26 Kh2 a6 27 Re4 Qd5 28 h4?

28 ... Ne3! 29 R1xe3 fxe3 30 Rxe3 Qxa2 31 Rf3+ Ke8 32 Bg7 Qc4 33 hxg5 hxg5 34 Rf8+ Kd7 35 Ra8 Kc6 White resigns.

After winning at Natanya 1968 ($+10=3$) and Vinkovci 1968 ($+9=4$) he withdrew from tournament play for a year and a half, devoting himself to study in order, he said, to plot his revenge. He received many invitations, but organizers were unable to meet his conditions. Many of these were met when he went to the Lugano Olympiad, 1968, where he hoped the Americans would defeat the Soviet team, but the lighting in the hall was not up to his requirements; refused permission to play all his games in a private room, he left abruptly. He came back in 1970 to play at Rovinj–Zagreb and took first prize ($+10=6-1$), and he was first again ($+13=4$) at Buenos Aires 1970.

Throughout the 1960s Fischer had been an inspiration to players, especially those outside the USSR, many of whom were anxious to see him win the world title. He had clearly been the world's best player in the second half of the decade, and he easily topped the official grading list issued by FIDE in 1970. He objected to the tournament conditions of the US championship 1969, which was also a zonal tournament, and by declining to play he failed to qualify for the next cycle of championship contests; but he was allowed to play in the Palma de Majorca interzonal 1970, when BENKO ceded his place. He won the tournament by the astonishing margin of three and a half points, the last of eight successive victories, if Sousse is discounted. His first Candidates match was against

TAIMANOV at Vancouver in 1971. When arguments about playing conditions reached an impasse, Fischer suddenly said, 'Let's play. I'm willing to play anywhere.' He played without a second. The result was astonishing—victory with a clean score of six wins. Even more astonishing was Fischer's result in the semi-final match against LARSEN, another clean score of six wins. Then he won the final match against Petrosyan (+5=3−1) in 1971, earning for himself the right to be challenger, and for SUETIN, Petrosyan's second, a box round the ears from Petrosyan's wife.

After extensive negotiations his world championship match against Spassky was scheduled to begin at Reykjavik on 2 July 1972. On that date Fischer was still in New York, wrangling from a distance with the organizers. This may have been brinkmanship, but Fischer may have feared the possibility of failure in the one task to which his life was dedicated. A postponement was granted. The English financier SLATER sent Fischer a telegram offering to double the prize fund, adding: 'If you aren't afraid of Spassky then I have removed the element of money.' Not liking the imputation of cowardice, and mollified by the extra money, Fischer suddenly declared 'it doesn't pay to be petty *like they are*' (our italics) and promptly flew to Iceland. Play began on 11 July 1972 and ended on 1 September with victory to Fischer. His score +7=11−3 includes one loss by default. No match in the history of the game received more worldwide publicity, and chessplaying was given a tremendous impetus everywhere. The first book of the match to be published, and there were many, sold more than 200,000 copies.

Fischer then withdrew from serious play. When challenged by KARPOV in 1975 he made numerous conditions; many of these were accepted but Fischer was adamant; *all* must be accepted. Despite intense lobbying, particularly from the USA, FIDE

Fischer waits for his opponent at the 1960 chess Olympiad

stood firm, Fischer declined to play, and Karpov was declared champion by default. Fischer needed to succeed at chess, his only resource apart from religion, and fear of defeat may have prompted his retirement.

Some believed that Fischer was always 'difficult', and were surprised in 1970 when he agreed to play for the Rest of the World in a match against the USSR. They were even more surprised when he played at second board, ceding first place to Larsen whose recent record was better than his; but Fischer wanted to see the Russians defeated, and he could accept logical argument as to his placing. (The USSR won the match by the narrowest possible margin; Fischer scored +2=2 against Petrosyan.) Most of his demands were sensible, and intended for the benefit of all, but Fischer was not equipped to persuade, or to respond to persuasion. In many ways he was a man of principle. He declined to lend his name for sponsorship because this would demean the game. Offered an enormous sum to appear at Las Vegas, where all he would have to do is sit around and play a few games, he declined, not wishing to be part of a side-show in a fun-fair. His championship match negotiations in 1972 were not directed at his opponent; when he realized that they might have upset Spassky he made a handsome apology.

Absorbed in the game and living alone, Fischer was not at ease in society, often getting a bad press as a consequence. He was probably more upset than most masters by noise and disturbances. For this reason he often laid down conditions under which he would play, but these were also intended to improve chess organization, an aim which had some success: playing conditions were improved; Candidates matches were substituted for Candidates tournaments; from 1975 world championship matches were decided by the winning of a given number of games, until the Karpov–Kasparov marathon of 1984 forced a return to a fixed-length match. A legacy of Fischer's success is the greater status of a world chess championship match in the eyes of the general public; and as a consequence the needs for detailed planning make a fixed length essential. After nearly twenty years as a recluse Fischer suddenly emerged in 1990 to promote a new idea for the TIMING OF MOVES, made possible by new technology. Every time a player makes a move one minute is added to the available time, thus avoiding the more extreme scrambles.

Fischer behaved well at the board. He never complained with the object of upsetting an opponent, and indeed sometimes his concern was for both players. His style was direct, vigorous, and relentlessly aggressive: in every game he strove his utmost to win, disdaining GRANDMASTER DRAWS. People flocked to see him play; his games were universally admired. Not satisfied merely to win a tournament, he needed to prove himself, to win by the largest possible margin. In 1969 he published *My 60 Memorable Games*, a classic of painstaking and objective analysis that modestly includes three of his losses. (See FIVE-MINUTE CHESS; POSITIONAL PLAY.)

Frank Brady, *Bobby Fischer* (1974), a revised and enlarged edition of *Profile of a Prodigy* (1965), contains an extensive biography and 90 games; R. G. Wade and K. J. O'Connell, *The Games of Robert J. Fischer* (1972) contains every traceable game (totalling 660) from serious play before the Spassky match.

Fischer Attack, 520, a standard line in the SICILIAN DEFENCE. When playing against this defence FISCHER liked to develop his bishop on the ITALIAN DIAGONAL, and so he sometimes played the SOZIN and LIPNITSKY ATTACKS (469, 504). Also 515, the ADAMS ATTACK, played three times in 1962 by Fischer.

Fischer Defence, 1120, a variation of the KING'S GAMBIT Accepted advocated by STAMMA in 1745 and by FISCHER ('a high-class waiting move') in the *American Chess Quarterly* in the early 1960s. Black reserves the option of defending his gambit pawn while avoiding the hazards of the KIESERITZKY and ALLGAIER GAMBITS. Compare BECKER DEFENCE, 1174, which is, perhaps, a less commendable way to achieve the same object.

Fischer System, 512, the POISONED PAWN VARIATION, not a true system, brought into prominence by FISCHER during his world championship match with SPASSKY in 1972.

Fischer Variation, 471 in the SICILIAN DEFENCE as played by FISCHER in his Candidates match with LARSEN in 1971. Fischer often played Pf2-f4 in the SOZIN VARIATION.

Fiske, Daniel Willard (1831–1904), American editor, writer, and bibliophile. Fiske was a man of great energy, perhaps inherited from his mother who learnt Italian at 79 and had a book of short stories published in her eighty-eighth year. As well as chess his interests included journalism, travel, librarianship, bibliography, teaching, civil service reform, the Egyptian alphabet (he wanted modern Arabic with a Roman alphabet to oust classical Arabic), and, most enduringly, Iceland. As a child he had been fascinated by tales of the early discovery of America by Vikings. Suspended from college, he went to Copenhagen and Uppsala to study Scandinavian languages, and in 1868 became professor of North European languages and librarian at the newly founded Cornell University. He collected an Icelandic library of 10,000 volumes, and after a lifetime's research wrote *Chess in Iceland and Icelandic Literature*, published posthumously in Florence (1905). He visited Iceland only once, in 1879. Fiske edited a chess column in the *New York Saturday Press* (1858–60), played in the first American Chess Congress 1857, compiled the tournament book, and edited *Chess Monthly* from its inception in 1857 to 1860, a few months before it

ceased publication. Paul MORPHY was co-editor, but his contribution was slight.

Fiske's wife, Jennie McGraw, died two years after the wedding leaving, as one of her bequests, $2 million to Cornell University, whose charter made the gift unacceptable. A legal wrangle ensued. Fiske resigned his professorship (1883) and moved to Villa Landor (the supposed setting of the *Decameron*) in Florence. There he made a Rhæto-Romanic library of 1,200 books, which he collected in six weeks, a Dante collecton of 7,000 books, and a Petrarch collection of 3,550 volumes. Travelling to meet a friend, he died at Frankfurt. He bequeathed his chess books to the Reykjavik library.

His brother William Orville Fiske (1835–1909), a musician and chess player, wrote the dance tunes 'Chess Polka' (1857) and 'Caissa Quickstep' (1859) and edited a chess column in the *Syracuse Daily Standard* (1857–9).

five-leaper, a $\sqrt{25}$ leaper invented for use in FAIRY PROBLEMS. On the normal board it always attacks four squares. If placed on a1 a five-leaper would attack a6 and f1 (for which the co-ordinates of its move are 5,0,) and d5 and e4 (for which the co-ordinates are 4,3,).

five-minute chess, a game for which each player has a total of five minutes. An illegal move loses if the offended player claims before moving, otherwise it stands. The game is drawn if: both flags fall before either player claims a win on time; a player has bare king, K + N v. K + Q, K + B v. K + Q, or K + B v. K + R and the opponent exceeds the time limit; the material is reduced to K v. K, K + N v. K, K + B v. K, or K + B v. K + B when the bishops are on squares of the same colour. These and other rules for five-minute chess (and ten-minute chess) were published by FIDE in 1976.

This speedy kind of chess (see LIGHTNING CHESS for others) first became popular in the early years of the 20th century. Then a student, CAPABLANCA played many games against LASKER at the Manhattan Chess Club. Capablanca won most of the lightning games but Lasker won the majority of the five-minute games, perhaps because there is time for deeper plans to be laid. Strongest of all five-minute events was a double-round tournament at Herceg-Novi in 1970. Outdistancing the field, FISCHER scored 19 points, followed by TAL 14½, KORCHNOI 14, PETROSYAN 13½, BRONSTEIN 13, HORT 12, MATULOVIĆ 10½, SMYSLOV 9½, RESHEVSKY 8½, UHLMANN 8, IVKOV 7½, and Ostojić 2.

Fast games are often marked by sharp tactical play, as in this example.

Korchnoi–Fischer Herceg-Novi 1970 Lightning Tournament King's Indian Defence Normal Variation

1 d4 Nf6 2 c4 g6 3 Nc3 Bg7 4 e4 d6 5 Be2 0–0 6 Nf3 e5 7 0–0 Nc6 8 d5 Ne7 9 Nd2 c5 10 a3 Ne8 11 b4 b6 12 Rb1 f5 13 f3 f4 14 a4 g5 15 a5 Rf6 16 bxc5 bxc5 17 Nb3 Rg6 18 Bd2 Nf6 19 Kh1 g4 20 fxg4 Nxg4 21 Rf3 Rh6 22 h3 Ng6 23 Kg1 Nf6 24 Be1

24 ... Nh8 25 Rd3 Nf7 26 Bf3 Ng5 27 Qe2 Rg6 28 Kf1 Nxh3 29 gxh3 Bxh3+ 30 Kf2 Ng4+ 31 Bxg4 Bxg4 White resigns. Black's threat to move his queen for the first time ends the game.

Once believed conducive to bad play, speed chess has become part of the training of masters, developing the ability to make quick judgements and decisions. Electronic timing devices have made such events easier to manage and less destructive of equipment.

fixed centre, a centre that consists of a pair of e- or d-pawns mutually blocked after an exchange of pawns on one or both adjoining files, e.g. 1 e4 e6 2 d4 d5 3 exd5 exd5, or 1 e4 c6 2 d4 d5 3 exd5 cxd5. In these exchange variations the play that follows usually consists of manœuvring with pieces. However, pawn play is possible and in either of the above variations White could continue 4 c4 which would enliven the game, although White might be left with an isolated pawn.

Winter–Alekhine   Nottingham 1936   French Defence Exchange Variation

1 e4 e6 2 d4 d5 3 exd5 exd5 4 Bd3 Nc6 5 Ne2 Bd6 6 c3 Qh4 7 Nd2 Bg4 8 Qc2 0–0–0 9 Nf1 g6 10 Be3 Nge7 11 0–0–0 Bf5 (Black exchanges his BAD BISHOP for White's 'good' bishop.) 12 Nfg3 Bxd3 13 Qxd3 h6 14 f4 Qg4 15 h3 Qd7 16 Rhf1 h5 17 Ng1 h4 18 N3e2 Nf5 19 Nf3 f6 (Black guards the ADVANCE POINT at e5.) 20 Nh2 Rde8 21 Bd2 Re6 22 Ng4 Rhe8 23 Rde1 R8e7 24 Kd1 Qe8 (Black TRIPLES on the open file) 25 Qf3 Na5 (threatening to occupy the advance point at c4) 26 b3

26 ... Nc4 27 Bc1 Nce3+ 28 Bxe3 Nxe3+ 29 Nxe3 Rxe3 30 Qf2 Qb5 31 Nc1 Rxc3 32 Rxe7 Bxe7 33 Qe1 Kd7 34 f5 Re3 35 Qf2 g5 36 Re1 Re4 37 Rxe4 dxe4 38 Kd2 Bd6 39 Kc2 Bf4 White resigns.

fixed opening, a prescribed opening for a competition. At Vienna 1903 and Abbazia 1912 the KING'S GAMBIT Accepted was prescribed, at Vienna 1904–5 the King's Gambit Declined; the winners were CHIGORIN, SPIELMANN, and SCHLECHTER respectively. At Budapest 1912 the players had to begin with the moves 1 d4 d5 2 c4 e6 3 Nc3 c5 4 cxd5 exd5 5 Nf3 Nc6 6 g3 Nf6 7 Bg2. (See also DÖRY DEFENCE; RICE GAMBIT; SARAGOSSA OPENING.) The purpose of such tournaments might be to evaluate an opening variation, although the choice of the King's Gambit may have been inspired by romantic notions of the supposed good old days. At club level fixed openings are commonly prescribed to provide an incentive to study. The most famous match with fixed openings, better known in Russia than elsewhere, was in 1890–1. Two games were played by telegraph between Chigorin in St Petersburg and the world champion STEINITZ in New York, and both were won by Chigorin. He selected the openings.

fixing a pawn, blocking a pawn so that it cannot be moved. Normally the term is used only when the pawn is chosen as an object of attack.

flag, a device fitted on each dial of a non-digital chess clock. Clocks are set so that the time limit is reached on the hour, and the flag, previously lifted by the minute hand, then falls. Before the introduction of the flag (1899) it was difficult to decide precisely when time was up, occasionally a matter of dispute. At New York in 1894 ALBIN successfully claimed a win against STEINITZ, who had three moves to make when the minute hand of his clock stood on the hour. The tournament controllers agreed that Steinitz had not exceeded the time limit, but considered that he was bound to do so because he could not make three moves in no time. Steinitz complained that he should have been allowed to try. Thus Albin won a lost game in a manner that most players then regarded as unsporting.

Flamberg, Aleksander (1880–1926), a leading Polish player just before the First World War, although overshadowed by his compatriots RUBINSTEIN, JANOWSKI, and perhaps ROTLEWI. In 1910 Flamberg won the Warsaw championship ahead of Rubinstein (whom he defeated). In the same year he won a match against BOGOLJUBOW (+4=1), and in 1913 he drew a match with DURAS (+1−1). In All-Russia tournaments he came second at St Petersburg 1911; fifth, ahead of ALEKHINE, at Vilnius 1912; and third (+11=4−2) at St Petersburg 1914. This last was the strongest of the three, and its purpose, apart from the awarding of the national championship title, was to determine who should play in the great St Petersburg tournament of that year (won by LASKER). Flamberg missed this opportunity by half a point, the difference between his score and that of the joint winners, Alekhine and NIMZOWITSCH.

Later that year he was again unfortunate. Playing in the Mannheim tournament, he was interned along with other Russian players when war commenced. He played in five tournaments arranged by the internees, and in one of them, a double-round event at Baden-Baden 1914, he was first ahead of Bogoljubow, RABINOVICH, and ROMANOVSKY. In 1916 Flamberg was allowed to return to Warsaw, but he played little further chess. He was second at Warsaw 1919, ahead of Rubinstein whom he again defeated, and in 1924 he successfully led Warsaw in a team match against Łódź, probably his last appearance in competitive chess.

flank, or wing, the squares on the a-, b- or c-files (the queen's flank) and the squares on the f-, g-, or h-files (the king's flank). Pawns on these six files are flank pawns.

flank opening, a general term for an opening in which neither of White's centre pawns is advanced to its fourth rank in the first few moves, but one of the flank pawns is.

Fleischmann, Leó (1881–1930), native of Budapest who used his Hungarian surname, Forgács, after 1904. During the years 1905 to 1913 Fleischmann won the Hungarian championship in 1907 and played in about a dozen international tournaments, notably Nuremberg 1906, Ostend 1906, Ostend Masters 1907, and Hamburg 1910. His best performance was at Nuremberg, tying with SCHLECHTER for third place, after MARSHALL and DURAS, ahead of CHIGORIN, TARRASCH, and VIDMAR. At Ostend in 1907 he took fifth place only one point behind the joint winners, BERNSTEIN and RUBINSTEIN. His best win was at the 'B' tournament, Barmen 1905. (The stronger 'A' tournament held concurrently was won by JANOWSKI and MARÓCZY.) In 1913 he gave up competitive chess.

Fleissig Gambit, 457, the MORRA GAMBIT, probably named after the Austrian player Max Fleissig (b. 1845).

Fleissig Variation, 989, the MEITNER VARIATION of the SCOTCH GAME, named after Bernhard Fleissig (1853–1931), the younger brother of Max.

flight, or flight square, a square to which a king could be moved, perhaps for its own safety. The term is used almost exclusively by composers although a flight is not uncommon in play, where it is known as an ESCAPE SQUARE. Flight squares may form patterns such as STAR-FLIGHTS and PLUS-FLIGHTS, which may be featured by composers.

float, a method that may facilitate pairings for the SWISS SYSTEM; to use such a method. If a sufficient number of qualified players with equal scores is not available, players from adjacent scoring groups may be floated up or down to balance numbers. The ups and downs of an individual player should also be balanced. To this end the tournament controller records the direction of every player's float and also the extent (in terms of points difference). If there is only one player with a specific score there will be a forced float, as distinct from a free float. Sometimes floating is taken to excess in order to match a player striving for a NORM with opponents having the necessary requirements.

Flohr, Salomon Mikhailovich (1908–83), International Grandmaster (1950), International Arbiter (1963), journalist, one of the best eight players in the world during the 1930s. He was born in Horodenka, now in the Ukraine, but then in a corner of Poland near to the borders of Czechoslovakia and Romania. The whole of his family, except his elder brother, was killed in a pogrom during the First World War, and shortly afterwards he moved to Czechoslovakia, where he became naturalized.

In the ten years from 1928 to 1937 Flohr played in 50 tournaments, national or international, shared or won first prize in 24 of them, and was lower than third on only four occasions. His best victories were: Sliač 1932 ($+6=7$), a tie with VIDMAR; Moscow 1935 ($+7=12$), a tie with BOTVINNIK, ahead of LASKER and CAPABLANCA; Poděbrady 1936 ($+10=6-1$), ahead of ALEKHINE; Kemeri 1937 ($+7=10$), a tie with PETROV and RESHEVSKY, ahead of Alekhine, KERES, and FINE. He also won some strong but small events, notably: Hastings 1931–2 ($+7=2$), ahead of KASHDAN and EUWE; Hastings 1933–4 ($+5=4$), ahead of Alekhine and LILIENTHAL; Hastings 1934–5 ($+4=5$), a tie with Euwe and THOMAS, ahead of Capablanca and Botvinnik; and Margate 1936 ($+6=3$), ahead of Capablanca. He drew matches against two of his closest rivals: Euwe, 1932 ($+3=10-3$), and Botvinnik, 1933 ($+2=8-2$). Playing for Czechoslovakia in five Olympiads, he twice made the best score on first board: 1935 ($+9=8$) and 1937 ($+9=7$).

In 1937 FIDE designated Flohr 'official' challenger for the world title. Alekhine accepted the challenge in 1938. The Bata shoe company agreed to sponsor Flohr but, at what might have been the high point of his career, political uncertainty prevented Bata from maintaining its support. Of Jewish birth, and anticipating the complete occupation of his country by anti-Semitic invaders, who had by October 1938 occupied a part, he was seeking a new home in the USSR, where he had spent a few months earlier in the year. In this worried frame of mind he played in the great AVRO tournament, November 1938, where the world's best eight players competed in a double-round contest. Keres and Fine shared first place, Flohr came last. To some extent Flohr restored his reputation when he won ($+8=8-1$), ahead of Reshevsky and Keres, a training tournament at Moscow and Leningrad in January 1939. Later in the year he won a tournament held at Kemeri and Riga ($+9=6$).

Around this time Flohr fled to Sweden and then to the USSR where he became naturalized in 1942. After the war he played in the interzonal

tournament at Saltsjöbaden 1948, scored
+3=15−1, and shared sixth place. In the double-
round CANDIDATES tournament, Budapest 1950,
Flohr again failed to defeat any of his strongest
rivals; he shared last place, after which he gave up
further world title ambitions. He entered the Soviet
championship nine times from 1944 to 1955, achieving his best position, fourth place, in 1944 and 1948.

Flohr's technique, especially in the ENDGAME, was
unsurpassed by his contemporaries. 'That rock of
safety and correctness', as TARTAKOWER once called
him, often depended on his high score against tail-
enders for his tournament victories. He was rarely
able to win against his equals: no wins against
Alekhine, Fine, or Reshevsky in the 12, 10, and 9
games respectively played between them, and no
wins against Botvinnik in the 17 games they played
outside their match. In contrast to his dour play, he
was a writer of considerable wit, popular as a
journalist, but too insubstantial for weightier tracts.
His books of the Petrosyan–Spassky matches of
1966 and 1969 are almost his only serious works,
but in collaboration with KOTOV he wrote *Sowje-
tisches Schach 1917–1935* (1960), a collection of 400
games by Soviet players of which nearly 100 are
annotated.

Flohr–Kashdan Folkestone Olympiad 1933 English
Opening Flohr–Mikenas Variation

1 c4 Nf6 2 Nc3 e6 3 e4 d5 4 e5 d4 5 exf6 dxc3 6 bxc3
Qxf6 7 d4 b6 8 Nf3 Bb7 9 Be2 Nd7 10 0-0 Bd6 11
Bg5 Qf5 12 Qa4 c6 13 c5 bxc5 14 dxc5 Qxc5 15 Rfd1
Be7

16 Rxd7 Kxd7 17 Be3 Qa3 18 Qd4+ Ke8 19 Qxg7 Rf8
20 Ng5 Rd8 21 Bh5 Bxg5 22 Bxg5 Rd5 23 c4 Rxg5 24
Qxg5 Kd7 25 Rd1+ Kc8 26 Bxf7 Kb8 27 Bxe6 Qxa2
28 Rd8+ Kc7 29 Qe7+ Kb6 30 c5+ Black resigns.

Flohr–Mikenas Variation, 40 (sometimes called the
Carls Variation) in the ENGLISH OPENING, played in
the game Flohr–Thomas, Hastings 1931–2, but
known earlier (e.g. Bogoljubow–Nimzowitsch,
London 1927). (See FLOHR.)

Flohr Variation, 33 and 44 in the ENGLISH OPENING,
the first recommended by ALEKHINE in 1926 as a
refutation of 2 Nf3, the second introduced by
NIMZOWITSCH and taken up successfully by FLOHR
in 1933; 72 in the QUEEN'S GAMBIT ACCEPTED, played
by Flohr against RESHEVSKY at Nottingham 1936

('seems to rehabilitate the entire line of defence'—
Alekhine); 376 and 379 in the GRÜNFELD DEFENCE;
466 in the SICILIAN DEFENCE, played by Flohr several
times at Nottingham and Moscow in 1936; 574 in
the CARO–KANN DEFENCE, an idea of OPOČENSKÝ's
played twice by Flohr at Moscow 1935; 1271 in the
ALEKHINE DEFENCE, used by Flohr when he had the
black pieces against BOTVINNIK at Moscow 1936
and Nottingham 1936.

Flohr–Zaitsev Variation, 747, the LENZERHEIDE
VARIATION of the SPANISH OPENING. Played in the
game Levenfish–Flohr, USSR championship 1947,
but LILIENTHAL had analysed this pawn sacrifice
previously.

FM, see FIDE MASTER.

focal play, a problem term for play featuring a line-
piece that cannot maintain its guard of two or more
squares. The piece may defend along one line (the
Anderssen Focal) or, more commonly, along two
lines. Both forms were known before 1850. The
term came into general use after the German composer Walther von Holzhausen (1876–1935) published his book *Brennpunktprobleme* in 1908.

#2

A problem by MANSFIELD, *Morning Post*, 1923. The
set play (what happens if Black moves first): 1 . . . R
on file 2 N1d2#, 1 . . . R on rank 2 Ng3#, the
black rook cannot maintain its guard of the two
focal points d2 and g3, and if 1 . . . d3 2 Qe7#.
The problem is a mutate (see BLOCK), i.e. the set
position is a block, and White, unable to maintain
it, sets up another block by means of the key 1 Qa6:

1 . . . R on file   2 Qe2#
1 . . . R on rank   2 Qg6#.

The R cannot maintain its guard of focal points at
e2 and g6, while if 1 . . . d3 2 Qe6#. The problem
also shows CHANGED PLAY.

Folkestone Variation, 123 in the QUEEN'S GAMBIT
Declined; it was used by the Swedish team at the
Folkestone Olympiad, 1933, and is sometimes
called the Swedish, or Stoltz, Variation. However,
it was first played in master chess in Schlechter–
Marco, Vienna 1907.

Foltys, Jan (1908–52), International Master (1950), a leading Czech player from 1936 until his death, national champion 1940 and, jointly, 1943. His international fame began when he came third after FLOHR and ALEKHINE at Poděbrady 1936, a performance he never bettered. He played second board for his country in the Olympiads of 1937 and 1939. During the Second World War he was again third in a strong event, this time after Alekhine and JUNGE at Prague 1942. Foltys's best victory was in a tournament at Karlovy Vary and Mariánské Lázně 1948. In 1951 he qualified for the interzonal tournament to be held at Saltsjöbaden 1952, but before it took place he died of leukaemia.

fool's mate, the shortest game ending in mate, e.g. 1 g4 e5 (or e6) 2 f3 (or f4) Qh4. There are eight possible ways of reaching this mate.

Forbes, Duncan (1798–1868), Scottish writer on chess history, professor of oriental languages. In 1854 and 1855 he wrote a series of articles in the *Illustrated London News*, collected and published as *Observations on the Origin and Progress of Chess* etc (1855). A greatly enlarged exposition of his theories was published in 1860 as *The History of Chess*. In his common-sense way he demolished the more fanciful claims regarding the origin of chess, but he used false evidence on which to base his own claim that the game is over 5,000 years old, and it is hard to believe that he was unaware of the error. 'The false prophet has taken us all in', said van der LINDE, who, with Albrecht Weber (1825–1901), discovered that the sources quoted by Forbes did not contain the attributed references. Later scholarship established that, in any case, these sources were at least 2,500 years younger than had been thought in Forbes's time. Regarded by his contemporaries as a monument to scholarship, Forbes's *History* is now ignored. 'He did not even make good use of the material known to him', wrote J. G. WHITE in 1898.

force, (1) the men of one colour (more rarely both colours) considered collectively; material.

force, (2) to play so that an opponent's choice of replies is severely limited. A forcing move is one that can be answered only by a forced move.

forced mate, a mate inflicted by FORCED MOVES.

forced move, originally a move to which there is no legal alternative, now a move to which there is no reasonable alternative. When annotators speak of a series of forced moves they usually mean only that the defender's moves are forced.

Forgács, see FLEISCHMANN.

Forgács Variation, 577, a line in the CARO–KANN first played in Forgács–Bernstein, St Petersburg 1909.

fork, a direct and simultaneous attack on two or more men by one man; to make such an attack. Any man may fork. The most commonly seen fork is by the knight: it attacks king and queen in FAMILY CHECK, two rooks in the game given under SCHMID, and two queens in the game given under PHILIDOR SACRIFICE. A fork by a pawn occurs after 1 e4 e5 2 Nf3 Nc6 3 Nc3 Bc5 4 Nxe5 Nxe5 5 d4. For a fork by a queen, see SHORT GAME.

Forsyth notation, a method of recording positions first published in the *Glasgow Weekly Herald*, 1883, the invention of its chess editor David Forsyth (1854–1909), a Scotsman who emigrated to New Zealand. The board is scanned rank by rank from a8 to h8, from a7 to h7, and so on; each man is shown by its initial, small letters for Black, capitals for White; blank squares are recorded by giving the total number of them between men; slanting lines (Forsyth originally suggested vertical lines) separate the ranks. For example 5q2/8/8/8/3k4/R7/3KP3/8 shows the position given under FORTRESS. Sometimes the numbers for adjoining unoccupied ranks are added together, e.g. 5q2/24/3k4/R7/3KP3/8. The *British Chess Magazine* advocated the abolition of dividing lines for ranks (5q29k4R10KP11), but they were soon reinstated as it was found that they reduced the likelihood and localized the effect of errors.

fortress, an unassailable stronghold for the defender's king, a means of drawing the game. This resource is featured in many studies by the Soviet composer Froim Markovich Simkhovich (1896–1945) who is believed to be the inventor of the term.

=

A position from MS 0.11.3 Escurial Library, Madrid. Dated *c*.1500, this is the earliest known fortress of the modern game. White plays 1 Rd3+ or 1 Rf3 after which the black king cannot invade White's territory, nor can the White king be winkled out. In all fortresses the defender must be able to mark time, so that the position cannot be broken up by means of a SQUEEZE or by ZUGZWANG. Here the white rook, having safe anchorage at d3 and f3, can be moved to and fro.

Some other fortresses of practical value in which Black draws against superior forces: White Ke8, Qh5; Black Kg8, Bg7, Ne5, by the German analyst Max A. K. S. Karstedt (1868–1945), *Deutsches Wochenschach*, 1903; White Kg4, Qa4; Black Kg7, Bf6, Bg6, LOLLI, 1763.

four-handed chess, an unorthodox game for four players, often paired to make two teams of two. The earliest version, dating from around AD 1030, has an ARRAY as in the diagram (the pieces shown as bishops are FĪLS). It was seen in India by an Arab scholar, al-Bērūnī, who reported that it was played with the aid of dice, and again this is the earliest reference to such an embellishment.

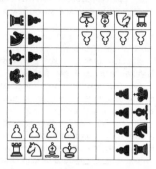

A Sanskrit tract, *Tithitattva*, of about AD 1500, describes a similar game, but this time with the fīl on a1 and rook on c1, and correspondingly for the other three sides. The ALFONSO MS of 1283 has a version in which the red men stand as follows: Ka1, Na2, Rb1, and fīl at b2, pawns a3 and b3 (promotion on the eighth rank), and on c2 and c1 (promotion on the h-file). The other players' men are placed similarly.

In modern times there have been many ideas for four-handed chess. The simplest use the normal board and men, each player of each pair making alternate moves without consultation. Another simple version uses two normal but distinguishable sets on two boards, side by side. The men may cross from board to board. To win, both kings of the opponents must be checkmated.

A normal board with the addition of a block of squares 8 × 2 on all four sides, to accommodate the full complement of 16 men for each of the four players, was introduced in 1779. Another version played in Russia at about the same time had a similarly enlarged board with a 4 × 4 addition in each corner, a total of 192 squares. The corner blocks formed citadels, each available only to one player.

Most proposals use modified boards. The best known is that described by George Hope Verney (1842–96) in *Four-handed Chess* (1881) and in more detail in *Chess Eccentricities* (1885). The popularity of this game, which uses an 8 × 8 board with blocks of 8 × 3 added to all four sides (192 squares in all) and two complete distinguishable sets, led to the formation of a club for four-handed chess which survived for more than half a century. The rules for all such games on enlarged boards mainly follow the laws of chess, with differences relating to the placing of the queens, the pawn's initial move, and castling. Other suggestions include a four-handed version of ROUND CHESS.

Four Knights Gambit, 861, another name for the BELGRADE GAMBIT in the SCOTCH GAME.

Four Knights Opening, 829, dating from the late 16th century. The knights are not always brought out in the sequence given.

Four Knights Variation, a self-explanatory name for 21 in the ENGLISH OPENING (see KORCHNOI); 692, the TARRASCH VARIATION in the SPANISH OPENING, a line that can arise from the FOUR KNIGHTS OPENING; 922 in the ITALIAN OPENING (see MASON); 941 in the TWO KNIGHTS DEFENCE.

Four Pawns Attack, 408 in the KING'S INDIAN DEFENCE (see BENKO), and 1260 in the ALEKHINE DEFENCE. In both of these variations White gains space by advancing pawns. They come under fire from Black, who hopes to show that their advance was premature.

Four Pawns Gambit, 642 in the BISHOP'S OPENING. Perhaps not seen since the 19th century, this is an extravagant example of the way in which pawns were once sacrificed merely to speed development.

fractional notation. This, like RUNNING NOTATION and TABULAR NOTATION, is a way of writing the moves and is not dependent on the notation proper for which it may be used. The black and white moves are written like a fraction, White's moves above the line. For example the moves of the SICILIAN DEFENCE would be written

$$1\frac{e4}{c5} \text{ or } 1\frac{\text{P–K4}}{\text{P–QB4}}.$$

This old form of presentation, perhaps based on the idea that a complete move requires activity from both players, is still used occasionally in books on the opening.

frame, a group of squares all of which are the same distance from an edge of the board; 28 squares form the outer frame, 20 the middle, 12 the inner.

Franco-Benoni Variation, 1182, the 'Benoni' move, Pc7-c5, in the FRENCH DEFENCE. The move, though not the name, was an idea of STAUNTON's played by him against WILLIAMS in London 1851.

Franco-Indian Defence, 243, so called because it may lead to the FRENCH DEFENCE, 1177, or to one of the INDIAN DEFENCES; it may, however, take a different course.

Franklin, Benjamin (1706–90), American states-man, printer, scientist, and persistent chess player. The first chess writing published in America was his 'Morals of Chess' in *Columbian Magazine*, Dec. 1786. This essay in praise of chess and prescribing a code of behaviour has been widely reprinted and translated. The American chess researcher Robert John McCrary has shown that part of the felicitous wording of the 'Morals' is taken from the preface to *An Introduction to the Game of Draughts* (1756) by William Payne, a preface rumoured to be the work of Dr Samuel Johnson.

Fraser, George Brunton (1831–1905), Scottish player and analyst. Many opening lines bear his name.

Fraser Attack, 873, an EVANS GAMBIT variation given by FRASER in *Chess Player's Chronicle*, 1855; 1006 in the SCOTCH GAME, analysed by Fraser in *Chess Player's Chronicle*, 1877.

Fraser Defence, 822, a line in the PONZIANI OPENING given by FRASER in *Era*, 1855. The following year in *Illustrated London News* he recommended, more justifiably, the same move after 5 dxe5, when he thought White's game indefensible; 1047, a GRECO COUNTER-GAMBIT variation suggested independently by Fraser and Hendrik Christopher Hege-lund Møller (1814–80) in 1873, but no longer regarded as sound.

Fraser–Minckwitz Variation, 615 in the VIENNA GAME. It was played by MINCKWITZ against STEINITZ at Baden-Baden 1870 and subjected to lengthy analysis by FRASER in *Chess Player's Chronicle*, 1879.

Fraser–Mortimer Attack, 874, a line in the FRASER ATTACK in the EVANS GAMBIT given by MORTIMER in a letter to the *Illustrated London News*, 1864.

Fraser Variation, 1111 in the KING'S GAMBIT Accepted, analysed by FRASER in *Chess World*, 1868.

free castling, see CASTLING.

free pawn, a PASSED PAWN.

French Defence, 1177, a standard reply to the KING'S PAWN OPENING. After the usual 2 d4 d5 White may play 3 exd5 (the EXCHANGE VARIATION, 1236) or 3 e5 (the NIMZOWITSCH VARIATION, 1238); but the most popular choice is the defence of the e-pawn by 3 Nd2 (TARRASCH VARIATION, 1230) or by 3 Nc3. After 3 Nc3 the principal lines are the passive RUBINSTEIN and BURN VARIATIONS (1196, 1213); the unfashionable STEINITZ VARIATION (1200); the solid CLASSICAL VARIATION, 1214; the aggressive CHAT-ARD–ALEKHINE ATTACK, 1221; and the counter-attacking WINAWER and McCUTCHEON VARIATIONS, 1184, 1205.

Known since the time of LUCENA, and once named after him, the French Defence was almost untried until the 19th century. In 1822 COCHRANE declared, contrary to the general opinion, that the 'King's Pawn One' gave Black a satisfactory game. The opening was given its modern name in 1834 when a Paris team, using this defence successfully, defeated London in a correspondence match. The Londoners could find nothing better than the Ex-change Variation which long remained fashionable. Around 1860 PAULSEN advocated 3 Nc3, greatly enlivening the opening, but few shared his opinion at the time. The French was first used, MOURET notes, to avoid the many gambits which became popular in the 1820s, and to block the ITALIAN DIAGONAL; later it was used to avoid the SPANISH OPENING. From the 1940s the French Defence became displaced by the SICILIAN DEFENCE as the leading response to 1 e4.

French Variation, 43 in the ENGLISH OPENING, so called because Black's moves are typical of the FRENCH DEFENCE.

Freund, E. S., the pen-name, an anagram of his surname, used by DUFRESNE when writing fiction (such as *Verloren Seelen*, 1860; *Die Tochter des Staatsanwalts*, 1866) and *Rätselschatz*, 1885.

Frič Opening, 1322, the name of the GROB OPENING in Czechoslovakia, the home of František Frič (pron. fritch) (1904–   ).

friendly game, or casual game, a game which is neither part of a competition nor an exhibition game. The term has no relevance to the mutual regard of the players nor to the aggressiveness of the moves played. Often no clocks are used; when they are, unorthodox time limits are sometimes found, such as a player being unable to use in excess of ten minutes more than the opponent. The two following games are among the most famous.

Morphy–Duke of Brunswick and Count Isouard, played in a box at the Paris Opéra, 1858   Philidor Defence

1 e4 e5   2 Nf3 d6   3 d4 Bg4   4 dxe5 Bxf3   5 Qxf3 dxe5   6 Bc4 Nf6   7 Qb3 Qe7   8 Nc3 c6   9 Bg5 b5?   10 Nxb5 cxb5   11 Bxb5+ Nbd7   12 0–0–0 Rd8   13 Rxd7 Rxd7   14 Rd1 Qe6   15 Bxd7+ Nxd7   16 Qb8+ Nxb8   17 Rd8 mate. (*The Field*, 4 Dec. 1858)

Capablanca–Fonarof   New York, 1918   Spanish Open-ing Steinitz Defence

1 e4 e5   2 Nf3 Nc6   3 d4 d6   4 Nc3 Nf6   5 Bb5 Bd7   6 0–0 Be7   7 Re1 exd4   8 Nxd4 Nxd4   9 Qxd4 Bxb5   10 Nxb5 0–0   11 Qc3 c6   12 Nd4 Nd7   13 Nf5 Bf6   14 Qg3 Ne5   15 Bf4 Qc7   16 Rad1 Rad8   17 Rxd6 Rxd6   18 Bxe5 Rd1   19 Rxd1 Bxe5   20 Nh6+ Kh8   21 Qxe5 Qxe5   22 Nxf7+ Black resigns. (*New York Evening Post*, 22 June 1918)

Friess Variation, 728. In *Deutsche Schachzeitung*, 1877, Hans Friess (d. 1888). a Rothenburg teacher, published analysis of this variation of the SPANISH OPENING.

fringe variation, a problem variation, not central to the composer's idea, that is added gratuitously, as distinct from by-play that stems inherently from the chosen setting. Such variations have long been out of fashion.

Fritz, Jindřich (1912–84), Czech composer best known for his studies, International Judge of Chess Compositions (1956), International Grandmaster for Chess Compositions (1975), lawyer. At first influenced by RINCK, he said that his eyes were opened in 1937 when he discovered the work of Soviet study composers. His several books include *Vybrané šachové problémy* (1979) which contains 50 problems and 252 studies composed by him.

+

A study by Fritz, first prize, *Szachy*, 1973. 1 Rd6+ Nf6 2 Rxf6+ Kg7 3 Rg6+ (a DESPERADO that forces Black's king to the d-file) 3 ... Kf8 4 Rg8+ Ke7 5 Re8+ Kd6 6 Re6+ Kc7 7 Rc6+ Kd8(d7) 8 Bf3 Bxf3 9 Rh6 h1=Q+ 10 Rxh1 Bxh1 11 0–0–0+ .

Fritz Variation, 964, line in the TWO KNIGHTS DEFENCE suggested by the German player Alexander Fritz (1857–1932) to SCHLECHTER who analysed it in *Deutsche Schachzeitung*, 1904. (See ANASTASIA'S MATE.)

From Defence, 1142, a dubious variation of the KING'S GAMBIT Accepted recommended by SALVIO and, later, by the diligent Danish analyst Martin Severin Janus From (1828–95).

From Gambit, 1316, first given by GRECO. Writing in *Schachzeitung*, 1862, SØRENSEN named this opening after his countryman, M. S. J. From.

Frydman, Paulin(o) (1905–82), International Master (1955). A leading Polish player during the 1930s, he was Warsaw champion in 1931, 1932, 1933, and 1936, and took second place in the Polish championship in 1926, and again (shared) in 1935. He entered several tournaments generally with modest results, but at Helsinki 1935 he had a triumph,

winning (+7=1), ahead of KERES and STÅHLBERG. From 1928 to 1939 he represented his country in seven Olympiads. After the last of them, Buenos Aires 1939, he was unable to return home, and decided to settle in Argentina. In his last important event, Buenos Aires 1941, a double-round tournament, he came third, three points behind the joint winners, NAJDORF and Ståhlberg.

Ftáčnik, Ľubomír (1957–), Czech champion 1981, 1982, 1983, and 1985, European Junior Champion 1976–7, International Grandmaster (1980). His major international tournament victories are: Cienfuegos 1980 (shared) (+7=5−1); Dortmund 1981 (shared) (+6=4−1); Esbjerg 1982 (+6=5); Trnava 1983 (+8=4−1); Trnava 1984 (shared) (+6=7); Altensteig 1987 (+5=6); Baden-Baden 1987 (Swiss); Trnava 1988 (+3=7); Haninge 1989 (+3=8); and the zonal, Stara Zagora 1990. In the ensuing interzonal, Manila 1990, he failed by half a point to qualify as a CANDIDATE.

Nunn–Ftáčnik Næstved 1985 Sicilian Defence Najdorf Variation

1 e4 c5 2 Nf3 d6 3 d4 Nf6 4 Nc3 cxd4 5 Nxd4 a6 6 Be3 e6 7 Qd2 b5 8 f3 Bb7 9 g4 h6 10 0–0–0 Nbd7 11 Bd3 b4 12 Nce2 d5 13 exd5 Nxd5 14 Nf4 Bd6 15 Nh5 Be5 16 Rhe1 (NUNN recommends 16 f4, e.g. 16 ... Nxe3 17 fxe5 Qg5 18 h4 Qxe5 19 Nxe6 etc.) 16 ... Qa5 17 Kb1

17 ... Nc3+ 18 bxc3 bxc3 19 Qc1 Bxd4 20 Bxd4 Bd5 21 a3 Rb8+ 22 Ka1 Rb2 23 Nxg7+ Kf8 24 Qxb2 cxb2+ 25 Bxb2 Rg8 26 Nh5 Bxf3 27 Be2 Bxg4 28 Ng3 Ke7 29 Ne4 Bf5 30 Nd6 Bxc2 31 Nc4 Qa4 32 Rd6 Rb8 33 Rf1 Rxb2 34 Kxb2 Qb3+ 35 Kc1 Qc3 36 Rxd7+ Kxd7 37 Rxf7+ Kd8 White resigns.

Fuderer, Andrija (1931–), Yugoslav player, International Master (1952), honorary Grandmaster (1990), research scientist. He had some moderate results in Yugoslavia (fourth at Bled 1950, second at Belgrade 1952) and finished first equal with PIRC and Rabar in the national championship in 1953, but lost the play-off. He played and scored well in the Olympiads of 1952, 1954, and 1958, but his best achievement was third equal with PACHMAN and SZABÓ, after KERES and SMYSLOV, at Hastings 1954–5. These results, supported by a brilliant attacking style, showed fair promise, but, putting his profession first, he ended his chess career around 1961. Thirty years later he made occasional appearances in club matches in Belgium, where he was then working.

Furman, Semyen Abramovich (1920–78), Soviet player, International Grandmaster (1966), Leningrad champion in 1954 and 1957. His best tournament win in international play was at Harrachov 1966, when he took first place ahead of TAIMANOV, HORT, and 15 other competitors, but a stronger performance was his third prize ($+6=8-1$), after KARPOV and TUKMAKOV, at Madrid 1973. Furman played in 14 USSR championships between 1948 and 1975, his best placings being: 1948 ($+9=4-5$) third; 1949 ($+9=5-5$) equal fifth; 1965 ($+8=7-4$) equal fourth. Furman rarely played in the West, but had one of his best in results at Bad Lauterberg 1977, third ($+5=8-2$), after Karpov and TIMMAN. This was to be his final event. In the USSR Furman was well known as a writer of chess articles and, above all, as a successful trainer of young players, most notably Karpov.

Semyen Furman (1988), in Russian, contains 115 games of which 86 are annotated, and other material such as a tribute from Karpov: 'Trainer, teacher, friend'.

Pietzsch–Furman   Harrachov 1966   Sicilian Defence
Rossolimo Variation

1 e4 c5 2 Nf3 Nc6 3 Bb5 g6 4 c3 Bg7 5 d4 Qb6 6 a4 cxd4 7 0–0 d3 8 Na3 Nf6 9 Nc4 Qc7 10 Qxd3 0–0 11 h3 d6 12 a5 Rd8 13 Bf4 e5 14 Bg5 Be6 15 a6 Ne7 16 axb7 Qxb7 17 Ba6 Qc7 18 Qe2 Rab8 19 Rfd1 Nh5 20 Na5 f6 21 Bc1 d5 22 exd5 Nxd5 23 Bc4 Kh8 24 g3 Rd6

25 Bxd5 Rxd5 26 Rxd5 Bxd5 27 g4 Nf4 28 Bxf4 exf4
29 Nd4

29 ... f5 30 gxf5 gxf5 31 Nxf5 Bxc3 32 bxc3 Rg8+ 33 Ng3 Qxc3 34 Qe1 Qd4 White resigns.

Furman–Taimanov Variation, 677, the WING VARIATION of the SPANISH OPENING.

Furman Variation, 69 in the QUEEN'S GAMBIT ACCEPTED. Beginning with 6 Qe2, FURMAN's plan is to play dxc5 (without allowing a queen exchange on d1) followed by Pe3-e4-e5.

Fyfe Gambit, 611 in the VIENNA GAME, an invention attributed to the Scottish player Peter Fyfe (1854–1940), first analysed in the chess column of the *Glasgow Weekly Herald*, 1883. Despite support from BLACKBURNE the gambit was rarely played.

G

Gaige, Jeremy (1927–), American chess archivist, journalist. In the 1960s Gaige realized that tournament results had not been well documented and set himself this Herculean task. He published *Chess Tournament Crosstables*, vol. I, 1851–1900 (1969), vol. II, 1901–1910 (1971), vol. III, 1911–1920 (1972), vol. IV, 1921–1930 (1974). These four volumes contain about 2,000 CROSSTABLES.

In parallel with his work on crosstables Gaige set out to record the basic data of those in the chess world, and in 1969 published *A Catalog of Chess-players and Problemists*, containing about 3,000 names with dates of birth and death. As his work became known and trusted, chess writers increasingly relied on Gaige's information, and also, in return, sent data to him. Later editions increased the number of subjects and the range of information, culminating in *Chess Personalia—A Biobibliography*, giving about 14,000 names with dates and places of birth and death as well as significant bibliographical references for each person. Meanwhile Gaige has continued his work on tournament tables and now has substantially more than 10,000 results. His scrupulously written works are a source of reference for chess journalists and writers all over the world.

gambit, an opening in which one player offers to give up MATERIAL, usually a pawn, sometimes a piece or more, in the expectation of gaining a POSITIONAL ADVANTAGE. Sometimes used loosely, especially in general literature, for any opening, the word is derived from the Italian *gambetta*, a wrestling term for tripping up the heels, and was first used in its chess sense by Ruy LÓPEZ in 1561.

Most, but not all, named gambits are offered by White. Only the QUEEN'S and KING'S GAMBITS were examined seriously before the 19th century. Then the number of gambits proliferated: analyses of the ALLGAIER and MUZIO GAMBITS appeared in 1819 and 1821 respectively; the EVANS GAMBIT was invented in 1824, and COCHRANE promoted the SCOTCH GAMBIT in the same year; in the 1840s JAENISCH examined the BISHOP'S and LESSER BISHOP'S GAMBITS, and KIESERITZKY the gambit named after him; BODEN and URUSOV made contributions. The gambit had become a powerful weapon. Around 1860 PAULSEN stated his belief that all gambits could be defended, backing his word in matches against KOLISCH and ANDERSSEN. The technique of defensive play continued to improve, and gambits, the invention of which has not ceased, are no longer regarded as more fearsome than any other openings.

gamesmanship, defined by its inventor, Stephen Potter, in *Gamesmanship* (1947) as 'the art of winning games without actually cheating'. His chess examples are directed towards the building of a reputation without winning a single game. Potter may well have seen a substantial paper, 'Chess Methods', by M. G. Sturm in *Chess*, Dec. 1946. Sturm writes: 'The most important part of the opening is to gain the white pieces . . . Place a black pawn in your left hand, and a white pawn in your right. Thrust both hands across the table, with your left slightly advanced. If your opponent is right-handed, which he probably is, he will almost invariably choose your left hand and the black pieces.'

In former times some players (such as LEWIS) maintained their prestige by refusing to play without giving odds. Others resorted to consultation games. The editor of *The Chess Player's Chronicle* wrote in 1856: 'Consultation Chess is *sui generis*, and should be played sparingly. Otherwise under its cover creep up those who dare not expose an undue reputation to a single-handed encounter. Thus men palm off their crusts for mutton.'

Without cheating (see MATULOVIĆ) or using BEHAVIOUR that could be penalized under the rules, there are ways of using gamesmanship to win.
(1) Player A is in difficulties and his (most dodges of this kind are made by men) opponent B has wandered away, perhaps looking at other games. From time to time he glances at his board and sees A deep in thought and looking distressed. After a long time he wanders by his board and sees to his horror that his clock has been ticking for an age and that A made his move when B was not looking.
(2) A sees that B is in time trouble and has stopped recording moves. A 'carelessly' writes one pair of moves twice. B sees from the upside-down score of A that the time check has been passed and slows down to make his next move only to find that he has lost on time, with still one more move to make.
(3) This is the reverse of the above. A finds a combination, but the critical move is immediately after the time check, when B will have ample time to find the best move. A omits one pair of moves from his score sheet. When the time check is reached B is unsure, seeing that A's score sheet shows one more move needed, and to be safe plays the extra move quickly.
(4) A makes a move setting a trap and immediately gives a slight twitch to lead B into thinking the trap was a mistake.

(5) A really does make a mistake, but seeing it as soon as made tries to look smug and make B suspect a trap.

There are many such ploys.

Gandev, Krasimir (1946–), Bulgarian problemist, International Master for Chess Compositions (1988), one of the world's foremost composers of fairy problems.

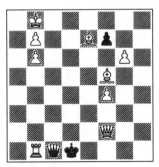

s#5 Circe

A CIRCE selfmate in five moves by Gandev, 4th prize, *Die Schwalbe*, 1980. After the key, 1 Ka8, there are two variations: 1 . . . fxg6 (Pg2) 2 Bg5 gxf5 (Bf1) 3 b8=N Qxb1 (Rh1) 4 Bb5+ Qxb5 (Bf1) 5 Bxb5+ (Qd8) Qxb8 (Ng1), or 1 . . . f6 2 Bc5 Qxc5 (Bc1) 3 Bb2+ Qc1 4 b8=B Qxb2 (Bc1) 5 Bxb2+ (Qd8) Qxb8 (Bc1).

Gaprindashvili, Nona Terentyevna (1941–), International Grandmaster (1978), Women's World Champion 1962–78. Her best results are tie for first place, with BALASHOV, PANNO, and Šahović, in the Swiss tournament at Lone Pine 1977; first equal with FARAGÓ and Winants, in the Wijk aan Zee 'B' tournament, 1987. She is Georgian.

García Gonzáles, Guillermo (1953–90), Cuban champion 1974, 1976, and 1983, International Grandmaster (1976). His first international success was first (+12=3−2) with ROMANISHIN at Cienfuegos 1977. In the mid-1980s he won several tournaments: Sagua la Grande 1984, Havana 1985, Havana 1986, Pontevedra 1986, Portugalete 1986 (+4−6), and Vigo 1986. He then reduced his chess activity. He died in a traffic accident.

García Palermo, Carlos H. (1953–), Argentinian player, International Grandmaster (1985) who won strong tournaments at Havana 1986 (+6=6−1) and Camagüey 1987 (+5=6−1) as well as two tournaments at Havana and another at Benasque in 1985.

Gavrikov, Victor Nikolayevich (1957–), International Grandmaster (1984). With M. GUREVICH and CHERNIN he was first in the USSR championship, 1985. Other tournaments, less strong than the Soviet championship, won by Gavrikov include

Tbilisi 1983 (+8=6−1), Leningrad 1984 (+7=6), Naleczów 1984 (+6=7), and, shared, Budapest 1989 (+4=6). In a Swiss system tournament at Biel in 1990 he was first in a field of 180 players.

Gavrikov–Dolmatov Irkutsk 1986 USSR Championship
1st League English Opening Symmetrical Defence

1 Nf3 Nf6 2 c4 c5 3 Nc3 e6 4 d4 cxd4 5 Nxd4 a6 6 g3 Qc7 7 Bg5 Be7 8 Rc1 d6 9 Bg2 0–0 10 0–0 Nbd7 11 h3 Re8 12 Qd2 Ne5 13 b3 Bd7 14 Rfd1 Rad8 15 e4 Bc8 16 Be3 Ned7 17 f4 b6 18 e5 dxe5 19 Nc6 Nh5 20 Nxd8 Rxd8 21 Qf2 exf4 22 gxf4 Bd6 23 Ne2 e5 24 fxe5 Bxe5

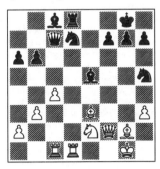

25 c5 bxc5 26 Bxc5 Re8 27 Bd6 Bxd6 28 Rxc7 Bxc7 29 Nd4 Bb6 30 Qh4 g6 31 Kh1 Ndf6 32 Nc6 Kg7 33 Re1 Black resigns.

GBR code, a method of representing numerically the forces present in a position, in order to classify for retrieval and comparison purposes. Four digits show the pieces, reading from left to right, queen, rook, bishop, knight; White's pieces are given the value 1, Black's 3, and the numbers for any one kind of piece are added together, giving a total in the range 0 to 8. The number 9 indicates something needing explanation, such as an extra piece arising from promotion. The four digits are followed by a decimal point and then two further digits indicating the number of pawns, first White's then Black's. Example 4578.36 = 1 white and 1 black queen (3 + 1), 2 white and 1 black rooks (1 + 1 + 3), 1 white and two black bishops (1 + 3 + 3), 2 white and 2 black knights (1 + 1 + 3 + 3), and 3 white and 6 black pawns. The kings are assumed, but some indexers enhance the system by giving the squares on which each king is placed.

The code is named after the initial letters of the English composers Richard Kenneth Guy (1916–), Hugh Francis Blandford (1917–81), and ROYCROFT, endgame study editors for the *British Chess Magazine*, 1948–51, 1951–72, and 1973–4 respectively. A similar numerical system, but requiring ten digits, was used by KOCH in 1813 and by BREDE in 1844. In the 1940s Guy and Blandford both contributed to a system using six digits, and in the 1970s Roycroft modified the allocation of digits to pieces so that the system became easier to memorize.

Gelbfuhs score, an obsolete AUXILIARY SCORING METHOD rendered complicated by its attempt to determine tournament placings in events in which not all competitors play the same number of games. Each defeated opponent's score is divided by the total number of games played by that opponent; for each opponent drawing, half the score is similarly divided. The sum of these fractions is a player's Gelbfuhs score. Adding fractions with slightly different denominators is irksome.

After the Vienna 1873 international tournament there were wrangles about placings, partly because unequal numbers of games were played. One of the contestants, Oscar Gelbfuhs (1852–77), an Austrian lawyer, then proposed his scoring method. A simpler version, the NEUSTADTL SCORE, which is applicable only when equal numbers of games are played, is now widely used for TIE-BREAKING.

Gelfand, Boris (1968–), International Grandmaster (1989), a Byelorussian who learned chess at the age of 4 and was a candidate master by the age of 11, when he was allocated to Kapengut for training. Having won the junior championship of the USSR in 1985 he decided to become a professional, but first had to complete two years' military service. On his return he became European junior champion 1987–8, and in the World Junior Championship in 1988 was equal first with IVANCHUK, Serper, and LAUTIER, to whom the title went on tie-break.

Gelfand–Ftáčnik Debrecen 1989 Grünfeld Defence Exchange Variation

1 d4 Nf6 2 c4 g6 3 Nc3 d5 4 cxd5 Nxd5 5 e4 Nxc3 6 bxc3 c5 7 Nf3 Bg7 8 Rb1 0–0 9 Be2 Nc6 10 d5 Ne5 11 Nxe5 Bxe5 12 Qd2 b6 13 f4 Bg7 14 c4 e5 15 0–0 f5 16 Bb2 Qd6 17 Qc3 Re8 18 Bd3 Re7 19 exf5 gxf5 20 fxe5 Bxe5 21 Qd2 Bxh2+ 22 Kh1 Be5 23 Qg5+ Qg6 24 Qxe7 Qh6+ 25 Kg1 Qe3+ 26 Kh1 Qh6+ 27 Kg1 Qe3+

28 Rf2 Bh2+ 29 Kxh2 Qxe7 30 Rf3 Qd6+ 31 Rg3+ Kf7 32 Rf1 h5 33 Bxf5 h4 34 Bg6+ Kg8 35 Bh7+ Kxh7 36 Rf7+ Kh6 37 Bc1+ Black resigns.

He won tournaments at Klaipeda and Vilnius also that year, but in 1989 he was first (+5 = 4 − 1) in the stronger Debrecen tournament, and in his first USSR championship was equal second (+4 = 9 − 2). In 1990 he competed in a top level tournament at Linares, and was second (+6 = 3 − 2), half a point behind KASPAROV. A few weeks later he was second (+6 = 5), half a point behind CHERNIN, at Dortmund. In the Manila inter-

zonal tournament June–July 1990 Gelfand became a CANDIDATE when he tied with Ivanchuk for first place. Kasparov said that he regarded these two as the only ones with a serious chance of contesting a title match, adding that he thought that Gelfand had the better chances because he was more consistent. In 1991 Gelfand defeated NIKOLIĆ +3 = 3 − 2 in the first round of Candidates' matches, but lost to SHORT in the second round.

Geller, Yefim Petrovich (1925–), Soviet player, International Grandmaster (1952), for more than 20 years among the world's best ten, six times a CANDIDATE, professional chessplayer. He played 23 times in the USSR championships, spanning 1949 to 1985. He came equal third (+10 = 5 − 4) in 1949, equal second (+10 = 3 − 4) in 1951, and third (+8 = 8 − 3) in 1952 before finally coming equal first (+10 = 4 − 5) in 1955 and defeating SMYSLOV (+1 = 6) in the play-off. He was the only player to lose five games in a Soviet championship and still win the title. Geller had other good results in this event: equal second 1960; equal third 1961; second 1966–7; equal third 1969; in 1979 he won outright (+6 = 11), but after that sank to the bottom end of the list.

In his first tournament abroad, Budapest 1952, he was second (+8 = 8 − 1), after KERES, ahead of BOTVINNIK and Smyslov, but for some time after that his international efforts were concentrated on the world championship: Neuhausen–Zurich Candidates tournament 1953, equal sixth (+8 = 13 − 7); Göteborg interzonal 1955, equal fifth (+7 = 10 − 3); Amsterdam Candidates tournament 1956, equal third (+6 = 7 − 5); Stockholm interzonal 1962, equal second (+10 = 10 − 2); Curaçao Candidates tournament 1962, second (+8 = 18 − 1) equal with Keres, half a point after PETROSYAN. This, Geller's nearest approach to the world title, seeded him into the 1965 Candidates' matches where he defeated Smyslov (+3 = 5) in the quarter-final but then lost to SPASSKY. In 1967 he was equal second (+8 = 12 − 1) in the Sousse interzonal, but in the quarter-final he again lost to Spassky; in the Palma de Majorca interzonal 1970 he scored +8 = 14 − 1, again shared second place, and was again knocked out in the quarter-final, this time by KORCHNOI.

His best wins in other events were: Kislovodsk 1966 (+6 = 5), ahead of STEIN; Wijk aan Zee 1969 (+7 = 7 − 1), equal with Botvinnik and ahead of Keres; Budapest 1973 (+6 = 9); Hilversum 1973 (+6 = 7 − 1), equal with SZABÓ; Teesside 1975 (+5 = 9), ahead of Smyslov; Moscow 1975 (+6 = 9), ahead of Spassky, Korchnoi, and Petrosyan; Wijk aan Zee 1977, a tie with Smyslov; Las Palmas 1980 (+6 = 5), equal with MILES and Petrosyan; and Dortmund 1989 (+4 = 7).

At the beginning of his career Geller was noted for his swift attacks and unusual combinative ideas, but he was 'weaker in positional battles and complicated endgames where . . . logic . . . and methodical playing are the main factors of success' (KOTOV).

Geller's tendency to risk everything for the attack led to defeats as well as victories. It worked better against some players than others; for example it paid off against Smyslov but failed against Korchnoi. In time he modified his style; his results became more consistent, and many of his best tournament successes came at a comparatively late stage of his career.

A leading openings expert of his time, Geller found many improvements in variations of the SPANISH OPENING, the KING'S INDIAN DEFENCE, and the SICILIAN DEFENCE. He retained his capacity for original and thorough analysis throughout his career, and was chosen to assist Spassky and KARPOV in their world championship matches of 1972 and 1975 respectively. His autobiographical *Za shakhmatnoi doskoi* (1962) was translated and enlarged as *Grandmaster Geller at the Chessboard* (1969, 1974), and a further Russian biography, *Grossmeister Geller* (1976), gives 64 annotated games, career results, many fragments of games, as well as much text. (See ZWISCHENZUG.)

Geller–Dreyev New York (Open) 1990 French Defence
Tarrasch Variation

1 e4 e6 2 d4 d5 3 Nd2 a6 4 Ngf3 c5 5 exd5 exd5 6 Be2 c4 7 0–0 Bd6 8 b3 b5 9 a4 Bb7 10 bxc4 bxc4

11 Bxc4 dxc4 12 Nxc4 Be7 13 Re1 Qc7 14 Rb1 Qxc4 15 Rxb7 Nc6 16 Nd2 Qxd4 17 Bb2 Qxa4 18 Re4 Qa2 19 Bxg7 0–0–0 20 Rb3 Bf6 21 Qg4+ Kc7 22 Qf4+ Kc8 23 Bxf6 Nxf6 24 Qxf6 Qxc2 25 Qf5+ Black resigns.

Geller Gambit, 98 in the SLAV DEFENCE, introduced into master play in the games Tolush–Smyslov, USSR championship 1947, and Tolush–Levenfish, Leningrad championship 1947, and thus sometimes called the Tolush–Geller Gambit. In 1948 GELLER used the gambit successfully against ZAGOROVSKY in the USSR team championship and retained the line in his repertoire for the next few years.

Geller Variation, 12, an aggressive defence in the ENGLISH OPENING which can also arise from the HROMÁDKA DEFENCE, as in D. Byrne–Geller, USA–USSR match 1955; 73 in the QUEEN'S GAMBIT ACCEPTED, as Geller–Kots, Ukraine championship 1958, when, after 7 . . . Nxe4, GELLER followed with 8 Qe2. Later, 8 d5 was preferred; 485 in the SICILIAN DEFENCE, introduced in Kotov–Geller, Candidates tournament 1953. Also 97, the SLAV GAMBIT.

Genoa Opening, 1322, the GROB OPENING. See SAN PIER D'ARENA OPENING for the origin of this name.

Georgadze, Tamaz Vasilyevich (1947–), Georgian player, International Grandmaster (1977), many times champion of Georgia. In the Tbilisi–Sukhumi tournament of 1977 he was first (+8=6−1) equal with KHOLMOV, and at Dortmund 1979 he was first outright (+6=5). He played in three consecutive Soviet championships, 1978, 1979, and 1980–1, finishing fourth on the first occasion. Since then his best results are: Hanover 1983, second (+7=7−1), after KARPOV; Costa del Sol 1986, first; Pontevedra 1986, first equal; and Salamanca 1989, first equal. In a Swiss system tournament at Lugano 1985, with 168 competitors, many of them grandmasters, he was equal second, just behind TUKMAKOV.

Georgiev, Kiril Dimitrov (1965–), Bulgarian champion 1984 (shared), 1986, and 1989, World Junior Champion 1983, International Grandmaster 1985. Among Georgiev's best results are first (+4=5−1) in the strong tournament at Terrassa in 1990; equal first (+4=7−1) in the strong Sarajevo 1986; equal second (+2=7) in the very strong Reggio Emilia 1988–9; equal third in two very strong events, Leningrad 1987 (+2=9−1) and Wijk aan Zee 1988 (+4=7−2).

Georgiev–Sax Reggio Emilia 1988–9 Sicilian Defence
Scheveningen Variation

1 e4 c5 2 Nf3 d6 3 d4 cxd4 4 Nxd4 Nf6 5 Nc3 e6 6 g4 h6 7 h4 Nc6 8 Rg1 h5 9 gxh5 Nxh5 10 Bg5 Nf6 11 Rg3 a6 12 Nxc6 bxc6 13 Qf3 Bd7 14 0–0–0 Be7

15 e5 dxe5 16 Ne4 Rb8 17 Bxf6 gxf6 18 Qg2 Rf8 19 Bc4 Qb6 20 Rb3 Qa7 21 Rbd3 Rb7 22 Qg7 f5 23 Nd6+ Bxd6 24 Rxd6 Qxf2 25 Bxe6 fxe6 26 Rxd7 Qf4+ 27 Kb1 Rxb2+ 28 Kxb2 Black resigns.

Gerbstman, see HERBSTMAN.

Gesta Romanorum, a MORALITY consisting of many tales compiled in England at the end of the 13th or beginning of the 14th century. About 165 MSS exist with between 100 and 200 tales, each ending with a moral. The first printing, in Latin, was around 1472. Subsequently Caxton's successor Wynkyn de Worde published an English translation. Although the stories name some real people they have no historical basis. One is about the Roman emperor Antonius who reflects, when playing chess, that the king is sometimes high, sometimes low. The moral is drawn that men should not be arrogant about their stations, for all chessmen are equal when put in the bag.

Gheorghiu, Florin (1944–), a university lecturer in foreign languages who, in 1965, became the first Romanian to gain the title of International Grandmaster. At the age of 16 he won the national championship, the first of ten times up to 1987. In 1963 he became World Junior Champion on tie-break, after all four games of a play-off match (against Janata) were drawn. An autobiographical best games collection, *Partide alese*, was published in Bucharest in 1980, but curiously it went as far as 1970 only, and most of Gheorghiu's best results came in the 1970s. Among them are: Varna 1971 ($+7=7-1$), second after VASYUKOV; Reykjavik 1972 ($+7=8$), first equal with HORT and ÓLAFSSON; Orense 1973 first ($+6=5$); Manila 1974 ($+5=7-2$), equal fourth with GLIGORIĆ after Vasyukov, PETROSYAN, and LARSEN; Novi Sad 1979 first ($+7=6$), ahead of GELLER and SVESHNIKOV; and Philadelphia 1979, a Swiss system event. In the interzonal tournament at Riga in 1979 Gheorghiu was equal fifth ($+7=7-3$), narrowly missing becoming a CANDIDATE. Whether it was disappointment at failing to reach the pinnacle of chess, or the relentless pressure by his government for him to earn foreign currency (most of his prize money went to the state), he began to acquire the reputation of one who could be approached to agree the outcome of a game to be played in the future. Young promise was never quite fulfilled.

Gheorghiu–Fischer Havana 1966 Olympiad Nimzo-Indian Defence Kmoch Variation

1 d4 Nf6 2 c4 e6 3 Nc3 Bb4 4 f3 d5 5 a3 Bxc3+ 6 bxc3 0–0 7 cxd5 exd5 8 e3 Nh5 9 Qc2 Re8 10 g4 Nf4 11 h4 c5 12 Kf2 Ng6 13 Bd3 Nc6 14 Ne2 Be6 15 g5 Rc8 16 h5 Nf8 17 g6 fxg6 18 hxg6 h6

19 Qb1 Na5 20 Nf4 c4 21 Bc2 Rc6 22 Ra2 Nd7 23 a4 Nf6 24 Ba3 Qd7 25 Rb2 b6 26 Rb5 Nb7 27 e4 dxe4 28 Bxe4 Rcc8 29 Re5 Bg4 30 Nd5 Rxe5 31 Nxf6+ gxf6 32 dxe5 Nc5 33 Bxc5 Qd2+ 34 Kg3 Bxf3 35 Bxf3 Rxc5 36 Qc1 Qxc1 37 Rxc1 Rxe5 38 Kf4 Kg7 39 Be4 h5 40 Rd1 Re7 41 Rd5 Kh6 42 Rd6 Kg7 43 Rc6 h4 44 Rxc4

h3 45 Kg3 Kh6 46 Bb1 Re3+ 47 Kh2 Re1 48 Bd3 Re3 49 Rh4+ Kg5 50 g7 Black resigns.

Ghulam Kassim Gambit, 1130 named after Ghulam Kassim (d. 1844) of Madras who, with James Cochrane (*c.*1770–1830), an Indian Civil Servant, published an analysis of the MUZIO GAMBIT in 1829—the first openings monograph. This variation, also known as the Koch Gambit and played by ATWOOD in the 18th century, is no longer regarded as sound.

Ghulam Kassim Variation, 921 in the ITALIAN GAME; 1008 in the SCOTCH GAME.

Gianutio Counter-gambit, 1124, an uncommon response in the KING'S GAMBIT Accepted perhaps owing more to POLERIO than GIANUTIO. Because it had just been revived by ALAPIN it was extensively tested during a FIXED OPENINGS tournament at Vienna 1903, where every game had to open with the King's Gambit. White won six games, three were drawn, and Black won the other two.

Gianutio (pron. janutsee-o) **della Mantia,** Orazio (16th cent.), author of *Libro nel quale si tratta della maniera di giuocar' à scacchi* (Turin, 1597), a slender volume (57 leaves) of great rarity. A translation by SARRATT was published in 1817. Gianutio throws light on the laws of chess then in use, describing the different forms of both the king's leap and free CASTLING. He drew from his experience (he was a strong player, according to PONZIANI) and from manuscript sources, but added little that was not already known to POLERIO and other masters of the time. This book, the first to be written by a player of the late 16th-century Italian school, was soon superseded by the more extensive treatises of SALVIO and CARRERA.

Gifford Variation, 1098 in the KING'S GAMBIT Accepted, introduced in the 1880s but receiving little attention until its adoption by CHIGORIN around 1900. It was an idea of the Paris-based player, H. W. Birkmyre Gifford who was, in 1873, the first official Dutch champion, a success he repeated in 1875. In his only outing into grandmaster chess, Paris 1878, Gifford was outclassed, but won a fine game from ANDERSSEN.

Gilbert, Ellen E. (1837–1900), American correspondence player. She had only local fame until the correspondence match between the USA and Britain in 1877–80 when the American manager caused much head-shaking by putting her against GOSSIP who was thought by some to be the strongest correspondence player known. She won her games, announcing mate in 21 moves in one game and mate in 35 in another. Gossip responded with unexpected gallantry and dedicated his *Theory of Chess Openings* (1879) to her. Mrs Gilbert (*née* Strong) was known as 'the Queen of Chess', a title commonly given to a woman who achieves a modest fame in this male-dominated game. She continued to play correspondence chess and announce long-range mates until her eyesight deteriorated.

Gilg, Karl (1901–81), International Master (1953). A Sudeten German, he played for Czechoslovakia in three Olympiads (1927, 1928, 1931), moved to Germany during the Second World War, and played for West Germany in the first European team championship, 1957. From 1926 to 1938 he entered several strong international tournaments, achieving only moderate results; but he won a few minor events, notably Trenčianské-Teplice 1937, when he was well ahead of a field that included BECKER and OPOČENSKÝ.

Gipslis, Aivars (1937–   ), International Grandmaster (1967), Latvian champion 1955, 1956, 1957, 1960, 1961, 1963, 1964, and 1966. He played in six USSR championships from 1958 to 1970, coming third (+6=12−2) equal with KORCHNOI and TAIMANOV, after STEIN and GELLER, in 1966–7. His best international tournament results were: Bad Liebenstein 1963, first (+6=9) equal with POLUGAYEVSKY; Pécs 1964, first (+6=9) equal with BOBOTSOV; Moscow 1967, second (+3=14) equal with Bobotsov, SMYSLOV, and TAL, after Stein, ahead of SPASSKY and PETROSYAN (his best performance); and Hradec Králové 1979–80, first (+6=5) equal with KARLSSON. Drink began to affect his performance, but he won a tournament at Jurmala in 1987. For many years from 1963 Gipslis edited the Latvian chess magazine *Sahs*. (See DOLMATOV.)

Aivar Gipslis (Moscow, 1987) includes career results, 51 annotated games and a further 39 without notes.

Osnos–Gipslis   Tbilisi 1966 USSR Championship
Bogoljubow Defence Grünfeld Variation

1 d4 Nf6 2 c4 e6 3 Nf3 Bb4+ 4 Nbd2 d5 5 e3 0–0 6 a3 Be7 7 Bd3 b6 8 0–0 c5 9 cxd5 exd5 10 b3 Ba6 11 Bxa6 Nxa6 12 Bb2 Rc8 13 Qe2 Nb8 14 Rfd1 Qc7 15 dxc5 bxc5 16 b4 Qb7 17 Rab1 c4 18 Bc3 Nbd7 19 Rbc1 Rfe8 20 Bd4 a5 21 bxa5

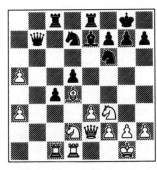

21 ... Qa8 22 Bc3 Bd8 23 Nb1 Nc5 24 Rc2 Nfe4 25 Nd4 g6 26 Ba1 Nd3 27 Qg4 h5 28 Qh3 Bf6 29 Nc3 Qxa5 30 Ncb5 Qa4 31 Rf1 Rb8 32 Nc7 Bxd4 33 Bxd4 Qxc2 34 Nxe8 Rb1 White resigns.

Gipslis Variation, 549 in the SICILIAN DEFENCE, played several times in the mid-1960s by GIPSLIS, but subsequently going out of fashion.

Giraffe, an unorthodox LEAPER that was used in some forms of GREAT CHESS. The co-ordinates of its leap are 1,4, and the length of its move $\sqrt{17}$. Placed on b2 a giraffe would attack a6, c6, f3, and f1.

Giuoco Pianissimo, 924, a restrained continuation of the ITALIAN OPENING (Giuoco Piano). This 'very quiet game' was named by ANDERSSEN. (See GUNSBERG; STEINITZ.)

Giuoco Pianissimo Deferred, 923, a move transposing into the variation above. (See KOSTIĆ.)

Giuoco Piano, 866, the ITALIAN OPENING. The name means 'quiet game' and until the 19th century was often applied to any opening that was not a gambit.

give-and-take key, a problem KEY that creates one or more FLIGHT squares for the black king and simultaneously deprives it of one or more flight squares.

Gledhill Attack, 1204, a FRENCH DEFENCE variation no longer considered effective. The English player Walter Gledhill (1854–1917) published his analysis, with comments by LASKER, in *British Chess Magazine*, 1901.

Gledhill Deferred Variation, 1200, the STEINITZ VARIATION of the FRENCH DEFENCE, in which the 'Gledhill' move, Qg4, is made two moves later than usual.

Gligorić, Svetozar (1923–   ), Yugoslav player, International Grandmaster (1951). Orphaned just before the war, he was taken into the home of the president of the Belgrade chess club, and they all fled to Montenegro on the German invasion. Gligorić saw about four months' active service with the partisans and was twice decorated for bravery. He first became widely known in chess circles in 1947 when he won a tournament at Warsaw two points ahead of BOLESLAVSKY, L. PACHMAN, and SMYSLOV who were busy watching each other. Since then he has played in more than seventy international tournaments and won or shared twenty first prizes. His best wins were shared: Dallas 1957 (+4=9−1) with RESHEVSKY; Sarajevo 1962 (+5=6) with PORTISCH; Belgrade 1969 (+6=8−1) with IVKOV, MATULOVIĆ, and POLUGAYEVSKY; and Sochi 1986 (+3=11) with VAGANYAN and BELYAVSKY. He won outright at Torremolinos 1961 (+6=5), Belgrade 1962 (+6=5), Reykjavik 1964 (+11=1−1), Montilla 1977 (+5=4), and many lesser events. Other fine results include: Zurich 1959 second (+9=4−2), after TAL, ahead of FISCHER and KERES; Bled 1961 equal third (+7=11−1) with Keres and PETROSYAN, after Tal and Fischer.

Gligorić played in seven interzonal tournaments and became a CANDIDATE three times. In 1952 he shared fifth place at the Saltsjöbaden interzonal, but was near the bottom in the ensuing Candidates tournament. In 1958 he took second place (+8 = 10 − 2) after Tal in the Portorož interzonal, and he shared fifth place with Fischer in the Candidates tournament the following year. In 1967 he came second (+7 = 14) equal with GELLER and KORCHNOI at Sousse, and then lost the Candidates quarter-final match to Tal.

The best Yugoslav player for about 20 years from 1951, Gligorić played in 19 Yugoslav championships from 1947 to 1965, winning or sharing the title 11 times. In 14 Olympiads (1950–74, 1978) he played on first board on all but one occasion (1954) and led his country to victory in 1950, when the Olympiad was held at Dubrovnik. At Munich in 1958 he made the best first-board score (+9 = 6).

His thoroughly professional style is based on systematic study and self-discipline. Early in his career he decided to play the KING'S INDIAN DEFENCE and the SICILIAN DEFENCE, both of which he studied intensively and to which he contributed many new ideas; his expert understanding of these defences materially aided his success. A diligent journalist and broadcaster, he has also written a number of books, the best-known being *Fischer v. Spassky* (1972); the English-language edition (of which 200,000 copies were sold) was on sale three days after the end of the match, and it has been claimed that, with the editions in other languages, this was the largest printing of any chess work.

Čiček & Ivkov, *Velemajstor Gligorić* (1973), is a biography, in Croatian, with 64 annotated games.

Gligorić–Kavalek   Skopje 1972 Olympiad   Modern Benoni

1 d4 Nf6 2 c4 c5 3 d5 e6 4 Nc3 exd5 5 cxd5 d6 6 e4 g6 7 Nf3 Bg7 8 Be2 0–0 9 0–0 Re8 10 Nd2 Nbd7 11 a4 Ne5 12 Qc2 Nh5 13 Bxh5 gxh5 14 Nd1 Qh4 15 Ne3 Ng4 16 Nxg4 hxg4 17 Nc4 Qf6 18 Bd2 Qg6 19 Bc3 Bxc3 20 bxc3 b6 21 Rfe1 Ba6 22 Nd2 Re5 23 f4 gxf3 24 Nxf3 Rh5 25 Qf2 Qf6 26 Re3 Re8 27 Rae1 Qf4

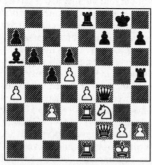

28 e5 dxe5 29 Re4 Qf6 30 Qg3+ Kh8 31 Nxe5 Rg8 32 Rg4 Rxg4 33 Nxg4 Qg6 34 c4 Rf5 35 Nh6 Rf6 36 Re8+ Kg7 37 Rg8+ Kxh6 38 Qh4+ Black resigns.

Gligorić Variation, 11 . . . Ng4 in response to the BLUMENFELD VARIATION (145) of the MERAN VARIA-TION of the QUEEN'S GAMBIT, an old line played in Blumenfeld–A. Rabinovich, Moscow Championship 1924. It was played from time to time, for example by SPIELMANN and TRIFUNOVIĆ; GLIGORIĆ met it first when it was played against him by BÖÖK at Saltsjöbaden 1948, but his analysis and adoption of the move led to its being named after him.

Also 749 in the SPANISH OPENING, played by Gligorić from 1974.

gnu, a COMBINED PIECE that has the powers of the knight and the CAMEL.

Goldin, Alexander Vladilenovich (1964–), Russian player, International Grandmaster (1989), winner of tournaments at Naleczów 1987, Vilnius 1988 (shared), and Trnava 1989, and second (+6 = 7) at Polanica Zdrój 1988.

Goldschmeding, Cornelis (1927–95), Dutch composer of orthodox problems, best known for his two-mover direct mates, International Judge of Chess Compositions (1958), International Grandmaster for Chess Compositions (1988).

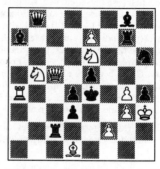

#2

A problem by Goldschmeding, first prize *Die Schwalbe*, 1981. The key is 1 Nbxd4 threatening 2 Bf3 ‡ :

1 . . . Re2   2 Qc6 ‡
1 . . . Rxf2   2 Nb5 ‡
1 . . . Rf7   2 Ng5 ‡
1 . . . Qf8   2 Nxc2 ‡ .

The try 1 Nexd4? is refuted by 1 . . . hxg3, while the try-play shows four changed mates: 1 . . . Re2? 2 Nc3 ‡ ; 1 . . . Rxf2? 2 Ne6 ‡ ; 1 . . . Rf7? 2 Nxc2 ‡ ; 1 . . . Qf8? 2 Nd6 ‡ .

Golombek, Harry (1911–95), English player and author, International Master (1950), International Arbiter (1954), honorary Grandmaster (1985). In 1945 Golombek became chess correspondent of *The Times*, a position he held until 1989. Also in 1945 he decided to become a professional chessplayer. He won the British championship three times (1947, 1949, 1955) and was equal first in 1959 but lost the play-off; he played in nine Olympiads from 1935 to 1962. An experienced arbiter and a good linguist, supervisor of many important tournaments and matches, he served for more than 30 years on the FIDE Commission that makes, amends, and arbitrates upon the laws and rules of chess. His many books, well over thirty, include *Capablanca's Hundred Best Games* (1947), *The World Chess Championship 1948* (1949), *Réti's Best Games of Chess* (1954), and *A History of Chess* (1976).

Good Companion Chess Problem Club, a club founded in 1913 by James Francis Magee (1867–1955) of Philadelphia. Good Companion was his translation of BONUS SOCIUS, the name of a medieval manuscript containing many problems. Club members usually met twice a month to take part in solving tourneys. Several special tourneys were arranged so that competitors the world over could participate, solving in their own localities. To obtain a plentiful supply of TWO-MOVERS for its solvers the club organized composing tourneys: for these and the fostering of new problem ideas the club became famous. Composers from many countries joined and in the 1920s there were about 600 members, the most distinguished of whom were ELLERMAN, GUIDELLI, and MANSFIELD. Ten times a year the club issued a magazine devoted wholly to problems. In 1924 both the club and the magazine foundered.

Hume & White, *The Good Companion Two-Mover* (1922), a collection of more than 900 problems.

Gorgiev, Tigran Borisovich (1910–76), Soviet study-composer from the Ukraine, International Judge of Chess Compositions (1956), International Master for Chess Compositions (1969), microbiologist. Until the late 1960s many of his best compositions showed ideas with great economy of material. Then, moving to the other extreme, he began composing GROTESQUES, a comical type of study that he made his own (White mates with minimum force against an army of black men). In 1959 he wrote *Izbrannye etyudy*, a selection of 156 of his studies, in Russian. A few studies in his later style are in *Shakhovy etyud na Ukraini* (1966), a book in Ukrainian, by Gorgiev and Bondarenko.

+

A miniature by Gorgiev, 2nd prize, *Shakhmaty*, 1929. 1 Bf6+ Kh7 2 Rg7+ Kh6 3 Rf7 Kg6 4 Rf8 Nc6 5 Bxd8 Kg7 6 Re8 Kf7 7 Rh8 Kg7 8 Bf6+! Kxf6 9 Rh6+.

Göring Attack, 871, an EVANS GAMBIT variation named after Carl Theodor Göring (1841–79) of Germany. He played it in the 1860s and the variation is attributed to him in analysis by MINCKWITZ published in *Schachzeitung*, 1871.

Göring Gambit, 972, a SCOTCH GAMBIT variation played by STAUNTON in the 1840s, first analysed in the Chicago *Sunday Leader* by PAULSEN against whose brother, Wilfried, Göring played the variation at Leipzig 1877. (See SEA-CADET MATE; SUETIN.)

Göring Variation, 954 in the TWO KNIGHTS DEFENCE. Already played by LASA in 1861 10 . . . Qc7 became preferred to 10 . . . Qd4 because of Göring's advocacy. Later, 10 . . . Bd6 superseded them both in popularity. (See ELISKASES.)

Gossip, George Hatfeild Dingley (1841–1907), player and author. Born in New York, he was brought up from an early age in England, where he lived until 1884. In 1883 Gossip shared fifth place in the London minor tournament, held concurrently with the master event (won by ZUKERTORT). After this modest achievement Gossip's play declined steadily, although he continued to believe he was a great master. He seemed destined for last place, which he took in tournaments at Breslau 1889, London 1889, Manchester 1890, London 1892, and New York 1893. In 1875, after several years' work, he completed *The Chess-Player's Manual*, a handsomely produced work with more than 800 of its 900 pages devoted to openings and illustrative games. In 1879 he produced *Theory of the Chess Openings*, a shorter work, more in the style of MCO, and it was sold out within six months. Both books were attacked, perhaps too severely, and Gossip did not hesitate to strike back. In the second edition of *Theory* (1891) he writes that he was faced with 'incessant opposition, disparagement, and non-recognition' in his attempts to get the new edition published. He was not at a loss when recommending himself to readers: 'Third Prize in the Melbourne Club Handicap Tourney, 1885' seemed to him an adequate testimonial. Clearly he was not popular, for his books were not significantly worse than the general run of the time, and they were better than, for example, those by BIRD (who was popular).

He had an unusual talent for making enemies. In his later years STEINITZ had the same problem but claimed at the end of his life that he had six chess friends. Gossip had none. Disliked in England, he travelled to Australia, the United States, and Canada, where he also became unpopular. Unwelcome in chess clubs, ignored by the chess press, he disappeared from the chess scene in the 1890s. Near the end he returned to England, the land of his childhood, there to die.

Göteborg Variation, 514 in the SICILIAN DEFENCE. Some restrict the name to 513, which originated on the occasion discussed under ARGENTINE VARIATION.

Göttingen manuscript, a Latin text of 33 leaves held in the University of Göttingen library, and comprising the earliest known work entirely devoted to modern chess. Twelve openings are described and 30 problems are given, one on a page. In 1922 the French chess scholar Victor Place (1865–1932) showed that this manuscript, another by LUCENA, and Lucena's book, had a great deal in common, and he concluded that the Göttingen manuscript was by Lucena. At one time a date of 1500–1505 had been conjectured for it, but Fritz Clemens Görschen (1911–81), writing in *Schach-Echo*, 1975, said that the manuscript was in the hands of King Alfonso V of Portugal when he visited France in the winter of 1474–5, and that it had been written in 1471. If this is correct then it could have been one of Lucena's sources.

Göttingen Variation, 1017, the LÓPEZ COUNTER-GAMBIT, already given in the GÖTTINGEN MANUSCRIPT.

Gottschall, Hermann von (1862–1933), German lawyer, player, and author, particularly of an excellent biography of ANDERSSEN, and editor of *Deutsche Schachzeitung*, 1887–97. He was the son of Rudolf von Gottschall (1823–1909), the German privy counsellor and poet who was a founder of the German chess federation.

Gottschall Variation, 991 in the SCOTCH GAME, an idea introduced *c*.1885 by GOTTSCHALL.

Goumondy, Claude (1946–), French problemist, International Judge of Chess Compositions (1984), International Grandmaster for Chess Compositions (1984), best known for his orthodox three-movers and helpmates.

#3

A problem by Goumondy, first prize, *Shahmat*, 1982. The key is 1 d4 threatening 2 Qb3 + .

1 . . . Nb6   2 Rc6 + Bxc6   3 Nc7 #
1 . . . Nxc7   2 Nxc7 + Bxc7   3 d5 #
1 . . . Nd2   2 d5 +   Bxd5   3 Nd4 #
1 . . . Nxd4   2 Nxd4 + Bxd4   3 Rc6 # .

The variations show CYCLIC PLAY (or cyclic shift) featuring a HALF-PIN on the e-file.

grading, a method of classifying players into categories, sometimes accompanied by TITLES. A RATING method is used to estimate the strength of a player, who is then put into a grade relative to that score. Rating systems may not be precise, and much fruitless argument can be avoided if players are lumped into broad categories; conflict is limited to those near their class boundaries. When the British Chess Federation began classification in the 1950s players were grouped in this way, but after the system became well-established, and the pioneering problems had been resolved, the ratings were given numerically.

Granda Zuñiga, Julio Ernesto (1967–), Peru's only International Grandmaster (1986), winner at Bayamo 1986, and, in the same year, equal first (+7=4−2) at the strong Havana tournament. In Spain in 1990 he won tournaments at León, Barcelona (+4=5), and Seville.

grandmaster, a chess exponent of the highest class. Since 1950, when FIDE introduced the formal title International Grandmaster, similar titles have been created for correspondence chess and for composition. A correspondent writing to *Bell's Life*, 18 Feb. 1838, refers to LEWIS as 'our past grandmaster', probably the first use of this term in connection with chess. Subsequently WALKER and others referred to PHILIDOR as a grandmaster, and a few other players were so entitled. The word gained wider currency in the early 20th century when tournaments were sometimes designated grandmaster events, e.g. Ostend 1907, San Sebastián 1912. At that time a grandmaster was someone who might sensibly be considered as a challenger for the world championship, but 80 years later some to whom the world champion could give odds bear that name. In 1991 there were almost as many grandmasters from Britain as there were from the whole world in 1950. (See also FIDE TITLES.)

grandmaster draw, a short game in which neither player strives to win and both agree to a draw. The term is misleading, for grandmasters are not more prone than others to play this way. Although such draws are unpopular with the public they are not necessarily to be criticized. A player who is well ahead of the field may decide to play safe in the closing rounds of a tournament, and his opponent may be satisfied to gain a half-point against the leader; or two players in a match may need a pause to recuperate. Attempts to prevent short draws by means of special rules have proved ineffective. One such rule specified that a draw should not be agreed until at least 30 moves had been made, but players intent upon drawing observed only the letter of the law. Organizers must share the blame when there are too many grandmaster draws in a tournament: it is within their power not to invite players known for their drawing proclivities.

Grandmasters' Association (GMA), a body established on 14 February 1987 with two main objectives. One was to initiate the WORLD CUP, and the other was to provide a power base from which grandmasters could negotiate with FIDE on such matters as improved schedules for the world championship cycle.

Grand Prix Attack, 450 in the SICILIAN DEFENCE, so called because of its popularity in the British weekend tournaments in which success earns points towards the Grand Prix awards. The aggressive nature of this line suits those who must play for a win at all costs, but it is not new, having been given by GRECO, and played fourteen times in the matches between McDONNELL and BOURDONNAIS in 1834. It is also known as the Hanham Variation or Vinken Variation.

grasshopper, a piece invented by DAWSON in 1913 for use in FAIRY PROBLEMS. It may be moved any distance along ranks, files, and diagonals to occupy, or capture on, a square immediately beyond an intervening man of either colour; it may not be moved unless it hops, nor may it hop over more than one man. The most popular of all fairy pieces, the grasshopper is represented by the symbol G or the figurine ♞.

#2

A problem by the English composer George Clarence Vincent Alvey (1890–1929), first prize, *Chess Amateur*, 1926, a tourney for problems using grasshoppers. The key is 1 c4 threatening 2 Qd5 ♯:

1 ... Gc3 (making a flight at f4) 2 Bb8 ♯
  (neither 2 Ne8 nor 2 Qe7 is legal)
1 ... Gxh8 2 Qe7 ♯
1 ... Gb3 2 Ne8 ♯ .

Grau Variation, 218, an unusual way of declining the QUEEN'S GAMBIT, played Fine–Grau, Stockholm

Olympiad 1937, but finding no permanent place in master chess.

Graz Variation, 678 in the SPANISH OPENING. Alois Fink (1910–) of Graz published analysis of this line in the *Österreichische Schachzeitung*, 1956, and the *Wiener Schach Nachrichten*, 1979.

great chess, a generic name for unorthodox games played on enlarged two-dimensional boards. For more than a thousand years such varieties have been proposed, but only COURIER gained lasting popularity. There have been other suggestions for enlarged boards: 10 × 8 (CARRERA, 1617); 9 × 9 (Chancellor Chess, B. R. Foster, 1887); 10 × 10 (complete or decimal chess, 9th century); 13 × 13; 14 × 14; 14 × 10 (Duke of Rutland's chess invented by the third Duke, d.1779); and 16 × 12 (CAPABLANCA's double chess, Julian Grant Hayward, 1916). Other shapes are 11 × 10 with an extra square at the right of the second rank and another to the left of the ninth rank (TIMUR's chess, 15th century); 10 × 10 with an extra square at each corner (citadel chess, 14th century); 8 × 8 plus 3 × 8 on all four sides; 8 × 8 plus 1 × 6 (extra files) on two sides; 8 × 8 plus 1 × 6 on all four sides (F. V. Morley, *My One Contribution to Chess,* 1947); 8 × 8 plus 1 × 4 (new files on both sides); or the same plus 1 × 2 to make yet two more files (Anatole Mouterde). Generally the oblong boards are placed so that there are more files than ranks. The odd squares in Timur's chess and citadel chess could be used to give a draw when occupied by a king. There are also games such as ALICE CHESS and KRIEGSPIEL that require two or more normal boards.

Some games like Capablanca's double chess use only the standard chessmen but usually new pieces are proposed. Frequently these were reinvented and given different names; conversely the same name was used for different types of piece. Some of the new pieces are: AMAZON (giraffe, prince, terror), DABBABA, EMPRESS (dabbaba, chancellor, champion, concubine, herald), PRINCESS (archbishop, cardinal, centaur, paymaster, police chief, rhinoceros), MANN (dabbaba), TALIA, LION (plane), WAZIR, and many kinds of LEAPER. On enlarged boards pawns are commonly allowed an initial advance of 1, 2, or 3 squares. Among the unorthodox pieces used for Timur's chess were the dabbaba, talia, wazir, and a 4,2, (√20) leaper. For the Duke of Rutland's chess 11 of the 14 pieces on the back rank were orthodox, another was a princess (called a counsellor), and two were 'crowned castles', each combining the powers of a rook and a *Mann.* Reading from a to n, each player's back rank array was as follows: R, crowned castle, N, N, B, B, Q, K, princess, B, B, N, crowned castle, R. Fourteen pawns occupying each player's second rank could be advanced 1, 2, or 3 squares on their first move.

Greco, Gioacchino (1600–c.1634), sometimes known as Il Calabrese as he was born near Cosenza in Calabria. At Rome in 1619 he compiled a manuscript on the openings for presentation to a patron, a practice he continued throughout his short life. In France he earned about 5,000 crowns from chess and in 1622 he went to England where he was robbed of this money while travelling to London. In England he began the practice of giving complete games to illustrate his opening variations. Although probably fictitious, the games were lively and entertaining. The first of his new-style manuscripts is in the Bodleian Library, the second in the British Library. He returned to Paris in 1624, went to Spain where he defeated all opponents at the court of Philip IV, accompanied a Spanish nobleman to the West Indies, and died there in or before 1634 leaving his fortune to the Jesuits. A selection of games from a lost English manuscript was published in London by Francis Beale in 1656 entitled *The Royall Game of Chesse-play*, 'Sometimes the recreation of the late King, with many of the Nobility. Illustrated with almost an hundred Gambetts. Being the study of Biochimo the famous Italian.' Another version, published in France 13 years later, was widely translated and appeared in at least 41 editions. One of them, a German edition by Moses Hirschel published in 1784, was reissued in facsimile in 1979. These books owed their popularity to the games which were included; Greco's openings were mostly those developed by Italian players of the 16th century but he is credited with the invention of the WING GAMBIT (445), a variation of the FALKBEER COUNTER-GAMBIT (3 cxd5 c6), and the FROM GAMBIT.

Beale's collection, the most important and interesting English-language chess book published up to that time, inspired the poet Lovelace to provide an epigraph:

> Sir, now unravelled is the Golden Fleece:
> Men that could only fool at fox and geese
> Are new made politicians by thy book,
> And both can judge and conquer with a look.
> The hidden fate of princes you unfold;
> Court, clergy, commons, by your law controlled;
> Strange, serious wantoning, all that they
> Blustered, and cluttered for, *you play*.

Greco Counter-gambit, 1044, later called the Latvian Counter-gambit, or Riga Gambit, said by POLERIO to have been the idea of his friend LEONARDO DI BONA. It was given in GRECO'S book, published in Paris, 1669. Advocated by DESCHAPELLES, it has since been tried by a few adventurous players such as the Swedish IM Jonny Hector (1964–).

Greco Gambit, 658 in the BISHOP'S OPENING, given by GRECO and still played; 1146, an unsound variation of the KING'S GAMBIT Accepted given by POLERIO, and sometimes called the Greco–Polerio Variation, or the Calabrian Gambit, after Greco's homeland.

Greco–Lolli Gambit, 1136, the WILD MUZIO GAMBIT.

Greco–Philidor Gambit, 1145, the PHILIDOR GAMBIT, given by GRECO.

Greco–Polerio Variation, 1146, another name for the GRECO GAMBIT.

Greco Variation, 915 in the ITALIAN OPENING, another line given first by POLERIO and then by GRECO.

Greek Defence, 443, the QUEEN'S FIANCHETTO DEFENCE, sometimes given this unsuitable name in the 19th century because it is to be found in GRECO.

Greek gift, the sacrifice of a bishop for the unmoved h-pawn of an opponent who has castled on the king's side. Often a prelude to a king's-side attack, it was first shown by POLERIO in the 16th century. Despite the classical advice not to accept Greek gifts, the defender usually has no better choice. The name probably stems from the occurrence of this sacrifice in GRECO's games, rather than from the Greek gift of a wooden horse to Troy.

Lilienthal–Najdorf Stockholm interzonal 1952 Nimzo-Indian Defence Sämisch Variation

1 d4 Nf6 2 c4 e6 3 Nc3 Bb4 4 a3 Bxc3+ 5 bxc3 c5 6 e3 Nc6 7 Bd3 b6 8 Ne2 0–0 9 e4 Ne8 10 0–0 d6 11 e5 dxe5 12 dxe5 Bb7 13 Bf4 f5 14 exf6 e5 15 fxg7 Rxf4 16 Nxf4 exf4

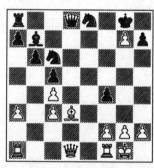

17 Bxh7+ Kxh7 18 Qh5+ Kxg7 19 Rad1 Qf6 20 Rd7+ Kf8 21 Rxb7 Nd8 22 Rd7 Nf7 23 Qd5 Rb8 24 Re1 f3 25 Re3 Black resigns.

(See also AVERBAKH; BAUER; POLUGAYEVSKY.)

Greenfeld, Alon (1964–), American-born Israeli, International Grandmaster (1989), with good results in two strong tournaments, first (+9=2−3) Beersheba 1988, and second (+6=6−1) Ljubljana–Rogaška Slatina 1989.

Green Variation, 1156, the KOLISCH DEFENCE of the KIESERITZKY GAMBIT. It was played by the English amateur Valentine Green (1831–77) in his match against STEINITZ 1863–4.

grid board, a board, used for FAIRY PROBLEMS, that is divided into groups of squares separated by grid-lines. Each man that is moved must cross one or more of these lines. When the English composer Walter Stead (1898–1976) invented the grid board in 1953 he proposed three vertical and three horizontal grid-lines dividing the normal board into 16 groups of four squares. Since then composers have used grids of other kinds, often making irregular patterns.

#2

A version of a problem by the English composer George Peter Jelliss (1940–), *Chessics*, 1977. The key is 1 Nd5.

1 . . . Ke6 or 1 . . . Re5 2 Qg6#
1 . . . Ke5 or 1 . . . Re6 2 Qf4#.

Grigoriev, Nikolai Dmitriyevich (1895–1938), Soviet player, analyst, and study composer, mathematics teacher. During the 1920s he won the Moscow championship three times in tournament play (1921, 1922, 1923–4), and again in 1929 by defeating PANOV in match play (+6=3−3). In 1923 he drew matches against NENAROKOV and Zubarev (both +5−5). His best result in six USSR championships (from 1920 to 1929) was fifth place in 1920. He was president of the committee for the three great Moscow international tournaments held between the two world wars, and was chess editor for *Izvestia* (1922–33) and in the editorial team of *Shakhmaty v SSSR* and *64*. He died after an operation for appendicitis.

Grigoriev is best known as an endgame analyst, one of the greatest of all time. He made significant and extensive contributions to endgame knowledge, specialized in pawn endings, of which he was the supreme master, and composed many studies, most of them having didactic content. When, in 1936, the French magazine *La Stratégie* promoted a tourney for studies with two pawns against one, he took 10 of the 12 awards.

I. A. Kan, *Shakhmatnoe tvorchestvo N. D. Grigor-*

ieva (2nd edn., 1954) is a comprehensive survey of Grigoriev's contribution to chess.

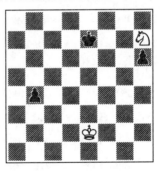

=

A MALYUTKA by Grigoriev, *Shakhmaty v SSSR*, 1932. 1 Kd3 Kf7 2 Kc4 Kg6 (2 . . . Kg7 3 Kxb4=) 3 Nf8+ Kf5 4 Nd7 h5 5 Nc5 h4 6 Nb3 h3 7 Nd2 h2 8 Nf1.

Grigoriev Variation, 528, an enterprising line in the SICILIAN DEFENCE favoured by GRIGORIEV; 531, the RICHTER VARIATION in a different Sicilian Defence line, recommended by Grigoriev. Also 1211 in the FRENCH DEFENCE, played by Grigoriev in the notorious 'five queens game'.

The game Grigoriev–Alekhine in the Moscow championship, 1915–16, went 1 e4 e6 2 d4 d5 3 Nc3 Nf6 4 Bg5 Bb4 5 e5 h6 6 exf6 hxg5 7 fxg7 Rg8 8 h4 gxh4 9 Qg4 Be7 10 g3 c5 11 0–0–0 Nc6 12 dxc5 Qa5 13 Kb1 e5 14 Qh5 Be6 15 Nxd5 Bxd5 16 Rxd5 Nb4 17 Rxe5 Qxa2+ 18 Kc1 0–0–0 19 Bd3 Qa1+ 20 Kd2 Qxb2 21 Ke3 Bf6 22 Qf5+ Kb8 23 Re4 Nxd3 24 cxd3 Bd4+ 25 Kf4 Qxf2+ 0:1. When ALEKHINE annotated the game in *Shakhmatny Vyestnik*, Feb. 1916, he said that had Grigoriev played 11 gxh4 he would have replied with 11 . . . cxd4, and he continued his analysis with 12 h5 dxc3 13 h6 cxb2 14 Rb1 Qa5+ 15 Ke2 Qxa2 16 h7 Qxb1 17 hxg8=Q+ Kd7 18 Qxf7 Qxc2+ 19 Kf3 Nc6 20 Qgxe6+ Kc7 21 Qf4+ Kb6 22 Qee3+ Bc5 23 g8=Q b1=Q 24 Rh6 Qxf1 25 Qb4+ Qb5 26 Qd8+ Ka6 27 Qea3+ and mate in two. Justifiably proud of this analysis, Alekhine published it in *My Best Games of Chess 1908–1923*, p. 69, as being the actual game played, and, lacking indication to the contrary, readers supposed that Alekhine had the white pieces.

Grimm Attack, 1108, KING'S GAMBIT variation named after the Hungarian player Vince Grimm (1800–72) who, with LÖWENTHAL and SZÉN, represented Pest in a famous correspondence match against Paris, 1842–5.

Grimshaw interference, see CUTTING-POINT THEMES.

Grin, the pen-name used by GULIAYEV.

Gringmuth notation, a code for use when transmitting moves by telegraph.

MA	NA	PA	RA	SA	TA	WA	ZA
ME	NE	PE	RE	SE	TE	WE	ZE
MI	NI	PI	RI	SI	TI	WI	ZI
MO	NO	PO	RO	SO	TO	WO	ZO
BO	CO	DO	FO	GO	HO	KO	LO
BI	CI	DI	FI	GI	HI	KI	LI
BE	CE	DE	FE	GE	HE	KE	LE
BA	CA	DA	FA	GA	HA	KA	LA

The move is indicated by a four-letter word comprising departure and arrival square designations. Castling is shown by the king's move only.

Dmitry Alexeyevich Gringmuth of St Petersburg saw that the UEDEMANN CODE had a serious flaw, so serious that it has never been used. The transposition of two letters, a common transmission fault, could give a plausible move. Gringmuth's notation, obviating this fault, has long since superseded all others, and is the official FIDE code, although commonly miscalled the Uedemann Code.

Gringmuth's notation had an unfortunate baptism. The match between the British Chess Club and the St Petersburg Chess Club, 1886–7, was played as a correspondence match, but the moves were sent by telegraph. The British Chess Club was fined by the umpire KOLISCH for repeatedly overstepping the time limit, and resigned with ill grace when both games were hopelessly lost.

Grob Opening, 1322, an old line analysed extensively by the Swiss player Henry Grob (1904–74) in his book *Angriff g2–g4* (1942). Among its other names are Ahlhausen, Brown, Colibri, Frič, Genoa, San Pier d'Arena, and Spike.

grotesque, a composition in which White operates with a small force against an army of black men.

+

A study by GORGIEV, fourth hon. mention, *Shakhmaty v SSSR*, 1967. 1 Nd4 Qa1 2 Nb5+ Kb2 3 Nd6 Rd1 4 Nc4+ Kc1 5 e8=N d5 6 Ned6 dxc4 7 Nxc4 Ra3 8 Ne5 and 9 Nd3#.

Gorgiev, gently mocking composers who take their work too seriously, intended such studies to be humorous; but he insisted on economy, that all the men should be necessary for the purpose of showing the idea.

The problemist BLÁTHY exploited the idea under the name 'dark doings'.

Gruber Variation, 965 in the TWO KNIGHTS DEFENCE, proposed in 1924 by the Viennese amateur Theodor Gruber.

Gruenfeld, Yehuda (1956–   ), Polish-born International Grandmaster (1980) who became champion of Israel in 1982 and played for Israel in the Olympiads of 1982 and 1984. In a zonal tournament at Luzern 1979 he was second (+4=2−1) to HÜBNER, but in the interzonal at Riga later in the year he achieved only a moderate result. He won the zonal tournament at Munich 1987 (+8=5−1) and finished in the middle at the ensuing interzonal tournament at Zagreb. His best tournament victories otherwise are: Biel 1980 (+7=3−1); New York 1981; Dortmund 1984. He is a deaf mute.

Grünfeld, Ernst Franz (1893–1962), Viennese player, International Grandmaster (1950), author. For a brief period in the 1920s he was one of the world's strongest eight or nine players. His best tournament victories were: Meran 1924 (+9=3−1), ahead of SPIELMANN and RUBINSTEIN; Budapest 1926, a tie with Monticelli, ahead of Rubinstein, RÉTI, and TARTAKOWER; Vienna (Trebitsch Memorial) 1928, a tie with Takács; and Ostrava 1933. Grünfeld took second place (+6=4−1) to ALEKHINE at Budapest 1921, and came third at Teplitz–Schönau 1922 (after Spielmann and Réti) and at Ostrava 1923 (after LASKER and Réti). He played for Austria in four Olympiads from 1927 to 1935.

Grünfeld was one of the leading experts of his time on openings, and this phase of the game so absorbed his interest that it sometimes seemed as if he derived the greatest satisfaction from those games in which he had demonstrated the soundness of his opening play. Although he played many of the openings that characterized the HYPERMODERN movement, and invented one of them himself, he was not adventurous in play, preferring a sound game and the avoidance of complex tactics. He was a contributor to the book of the Teplitz–Schönau 1922 tournament, wrote a book on the QUEEN'S GAMBIT in 1924, and a two-volume openings manual in 1950 and 1953.

Apšenieks–Grünfeld   Folkestone 1933 Olympiad
Queen's Gambit Declined Vienna Variation

1 c4 e6 2 Nf3 Nf6 3 d4 d5 4 Bg5 dxc4 5 e4 Bb4+ 6 Nc3 c5 7 e5 cxd4 8 exf6 gxf6 9 Qa4+ Nc6 10 0–0–0 Bxc3 11 Bh4

11 ... b5 12 Qxb5 Rb8 13 Qxc6+ Bd7 14 Qxc4 Bxb2+
15 Kc2 Qa5 16 Nxd4 Rb4 17 Bxf6 Rxc4+ 18 Bxc4
Qc3+ 19 Kb1 Ba3 20 Nc2 Qxf6 21 Nxa3 Ke7 22 Bb3
Qxf2 23 Nc4 Bc6 24 Rd2 Qf5+ 25 Ka1 Qf6+ 26 Nb2
Rg8 27 Rc1 Rxg2 28 Rxg2 Bxg2 29 a4 Qf4 30 Rc2 Be4
31 Rc4 Qxh2 White resigns.

Grünfeld Defence, 363, a popular variation of the
KING'S INDIAN DEFENCE named after the grandmaster who introduced it in the fourth game of his
match against BECKER, Vienna 1922. In the key
variation, 4 cxd5 Nxd5 5 e4 Nxc3 6 bxc3, Black
hopes to gain sufficient counterplay by attacking
White's CLASSICAL CENTRE (see BLOCKADE; FINE).
Ernst GRÜNFELD'S idea has been used in other
contexts; e.g. the KEMERI, 416, and COUNTERTHRUST,
415, VARIATIONS.

Grünfeld Gambit, 389, offering a pawn sacrifice in
the GRÜNFELD DEFENCE: 6 cxd5 Nxd5 7 Nxd5 Qxd5
8 Bxc7.

Grünfeld Variation, 195 in the QUEEN'S GAMBIT
Declined, introduced in the game Grünfeld–Maróczy, Vienna 1922: GRÜNFELD'S idea is that after an
eventual ... dxc4, White recaptures Bxc4 and meets
... b5 with Ba2; 337 in the BOGOLJUBOW DEFENCE,
as Grünfeld–Bogoljubow, Breslau 1925 (see GIPS-
LIS); 599 in the SCANDINAVIAN OPENING, recommended by Grünfeld in annotations to the Teplitz-
Schönau 1922 tournament book; 697, a pawn sacrifice in the SPANISH OPENING given in the same book.

Gufeld, Eduard Yefimovich (1936–), Ukrainian
player, International Grandmaster (1967), chess
journalist. A competitor in eight USSR championships from 1959 to 1972, he achieved his best result,
seventh (+ 6 = 10 − 3) equal with POLUGAYEVSKY, in
1963. His best international results are a second
place (+ 9 = 4 − 2), after ANDERSSON, at Camagüey
1974, first equal at Tbilisi 1974, first (+ 7 = 8) at
Tbilisi 1980, and first equal with GARCÍA GONZÁLES
at Havana 1985.

Eduard Gufeld (1985) is an autobiographical collection, in Russian, of 106 games.

Guidelli, Giorgio (1897–1924), Italian composer of
TWO-MOVERS, engineer. He began composing in
1913 and soon became one of the pioneers of the

two-mover renaissance which began around that
time. A leading member of the GOOD COMPANION
CHESS PROBLEM CLUB, he was proclaimed champion
composer of the club in 1917. Appropriately, he
came from a family descended from Guido
Novello, reputed author of the BONUS SOCIUS MS.
He won about 100 tourney awards in a career
prematurely ended by his death from pneumonia.
The Good Companion Two-Mover (1922) contains
more than 70 of his best problems.

Guimard Variation, 1232 in the FRENCH DEFENCE,
played often by the Argentinian grandmaster Carlos Enrique Guimard (1913–) in the 1940s, but it
had been used earlier, and is sometimes called the
Alapin Variation, or the Nimzowitsch Variation.

Guliayev, Alexander Pavlovich (1908–), Russian
composer of about 600 problems and studies, International Judge of Chess Compositions (1956), International Grandmaster for Chess Compositions
(1988), professor of technical science. A man with
an impish sense of humour, he uses the pen-name
Grin. He won first prizes in the Soviet composing
championship for two-movers in 1945–7, and for
three-movers in 1979–80.

#3

A problem by Guliayev, first prize, *Komsomolskoye
Znamya,* 1980. The key is 1 Qh1 threatening 2 Qg2.

1 ... Rg7	2 Rb3+ Kc4	3 Rf3#
1 ... Bxf5	2 Rf3+ Kxe4+	3 Rc3#
1 ... Nc3	2 Re2+ Kd3	3 Nf4#
1 ... Qa6	2 Kb2 ~	3 Rc3#.

White makes use of three BATTERIES while Black's
battery is rendered ineffective.

Gulko, Boris Frantsevich (1947–), German-born
Soviet player who later made his home in the USA,
International Grandmaster (1976), psychologist.
He played in eight Soviet championships, notably
coming second (+ 7 = 5 − 3) equal with ROMAN-
ISHIN, TAL, and VAGANYAN, after PETROSYAN, in
1975, and first (+ 4 = 11) in 1977, sharing the title
with DORFMAN after they drew the play-off match.
Other good performances include: Moscow championship 1974, first; Vilnius 1975, a zonal event,
first (+ 4 = 10 − 1) equal with BALASHOV, SAVON, and

TSESHKOVSKY; Cienfuegos 1976, first (+7=7); Nikšić 1978, first (+5=6) equal with TIMMAN.

At about this time Gulko decided to emigrate, an ambition that received much hostility from the state. His wife, *née* Anna M. Akhsharumova, was third in the USSR women's championship 1982, one point behind the winner, Ioseliani. However, the positions should have been reversed. Akhsharumova, who, on medical advice, gave up a protest fast just before the tournament, defeated Ioseliani, but by a blatant official fraud the point was taken from her and awarded to the loser.

During the protest years Gulko had few opportunities to play in tournaments, and none abroad, but he was equal first, with SMAGIN, at Barnaul 1984. In 1986 the family was allowed to emigrate and many good performances by Gulko followed: Marseille 1986, first (+4=4−1); Clichy 1986-7, first (+4=5); Biel 1987, first (+5=8−1); Cannes 1987, first (+5=3−1) equal with FEDOROWICZ; Amsterdam (OHRA) 1987, second (+4=4−2) equal with Timman and CHANDLER, after van der WIEL; Biel 1988, first (+3=8), equal with Ivan SOKOLOV, in front of TUKMAKOV and TORRE; Rome 1988, first equal with MARJANOVIĆ and SMYSLOV; Viña del Mar 1988, second (+2=3−1), behind LJUBOJEVIĆ; USA championship 1989, second (+4=10−1) equal with DZINDZICHASHVILI and Rachels, half a point behind SEIRAWAN; Linares 1990, his strongest event, sixth (+3=5−3) equal with YUSUPOV, behind KASPAROV, GELFAND, SALOV, IVANCHUK, and SHORT. In 1991 he was second (+3=7−2) equal with Vaganyan, after Ljubojević, at Reggio Emilia.

Gulko–Romanishin   Frunze 1985   King's Indian Defence

1 d4 Nf6 2 c4 g6 3 g3 Bg7 4 Bg2 d6 5 Nc3 0–0 6 e3 c6 7 Nge2 Be6 8 b3 Qc8 9 h3 Na6 10 Bb2 Bd7 11 g4 h6 12 f4 d5 13 0–0 h5 14 g5 Ne8 15 Kh2 dxc4 16 Ba3 Nd6 17 Bxd6 exd6 18 bxc4 Be6 19 Qa4 Re6 20 Rab1 Bd7 21 Ne4 Qc7 22 Qa3 Re6 23 N2c3 Rb8 24 d5 Re7 25 c5 Nxc5 26 Nxc5 dxc5 27 Qxc5 Ree8 28 d6 Qd8 29 e4 b6 30 Qa3 b5 31 e5 Qb6 32 Ne4 b4 33 Qg3 Bf5 34 Rbc1 Qa5 35 Nf6+ Bxf6 36 gxf6 Qxa2 37 Ra1 Qe6 38 Bxc6 Rec8 (38 . . . b3 offers more counter-play) 39 Qf3 b3 40 Bd5 Qd7 41 Bxb3

41 . . . Qb5 42 Ra3 a5 43 Rf2 Qb4 44 Qe3 a4 45 Bd5 Rc5 46 e6 Kh7 47 e7 Rc2 48 Rxc2 Bxc2 49 d7 Black resigns.

Gunsberg, Isidor Arthur (1854–1930), player and chess journalist. Born in Budapest (as Günzberg), he visited England when about nine years old and moved there permanently in 1876, later to become naturalized. He soon developed his talents in London, then the chess world's centre, and an opportunity to operate the automaton MEPHISTO led to his decision to become a chess professional at the age of 25. In 1881 he lost a match against BLACKBURNE, but he improved rapidly in the next few years. In July 1885 he decisively won a national tournament held in London, and a few weeks later surprised the chess world by winning the Hamburg international tournament ahead of half the world's best dozen players: Blackburne, ENGLISCH, MASON, TARRASCH, WEISS, and MACKENZIE. The following year he defeated BIRD (+5=3−1). In 1887 he beat Blackburne (+5=6−2) and shared first prize (+8−1) with BURN, ahead of Blackburne and ZUKERTORT, in the London tournament.

When the Sixth American Congress was held in New York in 1889, STEINITZ agreed to play a world championship match against the winner. Weiss and CHIGORIN tied for first prize; Steinitz had already played Chigorin, and Weiss was not interested in a match. Consequently Gunsberg, who was third, met Chigorin in a match, a stirring affair that ended in a draw (+9=5−9). Then Steinitz accepted Gunsberg's challenge. They played in New York and, after a hard struggle lasting seven weeks (1890–1), Gunsberg lost (+4=9−6). Subsequently he played in about a dozen strong tournaments, with no great success.

By now he was increasingly giving his time to other chess activities. A conscientious and punctual worker, he probably edited more chess columns than anyone else, and was one of the few who made an adequate, if sparse, livelihood from chess. In the *Daily Telegraph* during 1915 he published 104 problems, 15 of which were unsound (3 because of printer's errors). The *Evening News* accused Gunsberg of 'making blunders', to which he successfully responded with a libel action, an occasion for considerable levity in the High Court.

Gunsberg was also a competent tournament organizer, and was especially proud of his five-stage 36-player tournament at Ostend 1906. He wanted to give young players a chance, noting that there were many tournaments to which only the well-known masters were invited; at this tournament the careers of RUBINSTEIN (third), BERNSTEIN (equal fourth), and PERLIS (ninth), were fairly launched.

Mason–Gunsberg   New York 1889 (Best Game Prize)
Giuoco Pianissimo

1 e4 e5 2 Nf3 Nc6 3 Bc4 Bc5 4 d3 d6 5 Be3 Bb6 6 c3 Nf6 7 Nbd2 Qe7 8 a4 Be6 9 Bb5 Bxe3 10 fxe3 a6 11 Bxc6+ bxc6 12 Ba4 0–0 13 0–0 Ng4 14 Qe2 f5 15 exf5 Bxf5 16 e4 Bd7 17 Nc4 Nf6 18 Ne3 g6 19 c4? (White leaves a HOLE at d4 which gives access to the hole at b3.) 19 . . . Nh5 20 g3 Bh3 21 Rf2 Ng7 22 Qb2 Ne6 23 Re1 Rf7 24 Ree2 Raf8 25 Ne1 Nd4 26 Rd2 Qg5 27 N3g2 Bxg2 28 Kxg2 Qe3 29 Kf1

29 . . . Nb3 White resigns. If 30 Rde2 Rxf2+   31 Rxf2 Nd2+.

Gunsberg Counterattack, 849 in the FOUR KNIGHTS OPENING introduced at the London 1883 tournament in the game Ranken–Gunsberg.

Gunsberg Defence, 988 in the SCOTCH GAME, introduced by GUNSBERG in 1881 during his match with BLACKBURNE.

Gunsberg Variation, 830 in the FOUR KNIGHTS OPENING, a WAITING MOVE described by STEINITZ as having 'no other merit apart from its novelty', introduced by GUNSBERG in the first game of his match with BLACKBURNE, 1887.

Guretzky-Cornitz, Bernhard von (1838–73), German analyst, barrister. He composed MORE-MOVER problems and analysed the EVANS GAMBIT but is remembered for his detailed examination of the ending rook and pawn v. bishop (*Schachzeitung*, 1860 and 1863) and that of queen v. rook and pawn (*Neue Berliner Schachzeitung*, 1864).

Gurevich, Dmitry Borisovich (1956–), Moscow-born American, International Grandmaster (1983). He won two strong tournaments, New York 1983 (+6=4−1) and, shared, Jerusalem 1986.

Gurevich, Ilya Mark[ovich] (1972–), Soviet-born American who became World Junior Champion at Santiago de Chile, 1990.

Gurevich, Mikhail Naumovich (1959–), Soviet champion 1985, International Grandmaster (1986). First or equal first in many strong tournaments in the 1980s, including Sverdlovsk 1984, Jurmala 1985, Tbilisi 1985, Baku 1986, Havana 1986, Moscow 1987 (+6=5−2), Tallinn 1987 (+6=6−1), Bern 1989, Geneva 1989, Tel Aviv 1989 (+10=1). However, his best win was in the very strong Reggio Emilia 1988–9 (+4=5), and he was fifth (+2=6−2) at the same place 1989–90. In 1991 he emigrated to Belgium.

Gurevich–Georgadze   Tbilisi 1985   Queen's Gambit Declined Petrosyan Variation

1 d4 d5 2 c4 e6 3 Nc3 Be7 4 Nf3 Nf6 5 Bg5 h6 6 Bxf6 Bxf6 7 e3 0–0 8 Qc2 Na6 9 Qd2 b6 10 cxd5 exd5 11 Bb5 Bb7 12 Qe2 Nb8 13 0–0 a6 14 Ba4 Nc6 15 Rad1 b5 16 Bc2 Re8 17 Qd2 Ne7 18 Ne5 Nc8 19 Qd3 g6

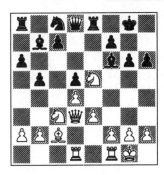

20 Nxf7 Kxf7 21 Qxg6+ Kf8 22 e4 dxe4 23 Bb3 Nd6 24 f3 e3 25 Ne4 e2 26 Qg8+ Ke7 27 Qh7+ Kf8 28 Nxd6 Bg7 29 Qg8+ Black resigns.

Gurgenidze, Bukhuty Ivanovich (1933–), Georgian player, International Grandmaster (1970), geologist, thirteen times Georgian champion between 1958 and 1986. He played in nine USSR championships between 1957 and 1985, peaking in 1958 when he was equal seventh. At his best during the 1960s, he shared first place with TAL in the Tbilisi tournament, 1969–70; both scored +7=7−1.

Gurgenidze, David Antonovich (1953–), Georgian study composer, Grandmaster for Chess Compositions (1990), winner of the 13th (1975–6) and 16th (1981–2) study composing championships of the USSR, engineer. A frequent prize-winner, he is among the youngest composers to be awarded the GM title. Endings with rooks and pawns are his speciality.

+

A MALYUTKA by Gurgenidze, first prize, *Shakhmaty v SSSR*, 1981, and also first prize in the 16th USSR composing championship. The try 1 Kb3? Rh5 2 g7 Rg5 draws because White's king will be unable to cross the barrier on its fifth rank. The solution shows a SYSTEMATIC MOVEMENT, unusual and perhaps unprecedented in a malyutka: 1 g7 Rb8 2 Rb7 (not 2 Rf7? Rg8=) 2 . . . Rc8 3 Kb3 Kg2 4 Rc7 Rd8 5 Kc4 Kg3 6 Rd7 Re8 7 Kd5 Kg4 8 Re7 Rg8 9 Ke6 Kg5 10 Kf7.

Gurgenidze Variation, 463 as Gurgenidze–Furman, USSR Championship 1967; 495, as Keres–B. I. Gurgenidze, USSR championship 1959, both in the SICILIAN DEFENCE; 580 in the CARO–KANN DEFENCE, played by GURGENIDZE in the 1970s after experimenting with 3 . . . b5 in the 1960s; 1277 in the ROBATSCH DEFENCE, as Klovan–Gurgenidze, Omsk 1965.

Gurvich, Abram Solomonovich (1897–1962), Soviet study composer, International Judge of Chess Compositions (1956), literary and dramatic critic. His first, and perhaps best, composing period was from 1925 to 1931. Shortly after the Second World War he returned to study composition and was awarded first prize in the sixth USSR composing championship, 1959–61. In the same year he published *Etyudy*, the first part consisting of 70 of his studies, the second part a long essay (121 pages) on the art of studies, accompanied by 69 examples.

+

A study by Gurvich, first prize, *Shakhmaty v SSSR*, 1955. 1 Rd2+ Kc8 2 Na7+ Kb8 3 Nc6+ Kc7 4 Nc2 Kxc6 5 Nd4+ Kb6 6 Rb2+ Ka7 7 Nc6+ Ka8 8 Rb6 Ra4 9 Kc1 or c2 Rxa3 10 Kb1! (ZUGZWANG) 10 . . . Ra4 11 Kb2 (zugzwang) 11 . . . Ra5 12 Nxa5 Nxa5 13 Rxa6+.

H

Haberditz Variation, 62 in the QUEEN'S GAMBIT ACCEPTED, as Grünfeld–Haberditz, Vienna 1946; 1233 in the FRENCH DEFENCE, tested in correspondence play *c*.1939 by the Viennese analyst Hans Haberditz (*c*.1901–57).

Hague Variation, 503, the NAJDORF VARIATION of the SICILIAN DEFENCE. At one time an attempt was made to restrict the name Najdorf Variation to those lines where Black later plays Pe7-e5, and to use Hague Variation for those where Pb7-b5 follows.

Halberstadt, Vitaly (1903–67), player, analyst, and composer, International Judge of Chess Compositions (1957). Born in Odessa, he spent most of his adult life in Paris, and became a naturalized French citizen. He won the championship of Paris in 1925, and played in other national tournaments; in one of these (Hyères 1926) he won a BRILLIANCY PRIZE for his game against JANOWSKI. He was also interested in the basic endgame, for which he made some original analysis, but he is best remembered for his studies. These often featured CONJUGATE SQUARES, about which he and DUCHAMP wrote a book in 1932, *L'Opposition et les cases conjuguées sont réconciliées.* In 1954 he made a collection of his own compositions and published these along with some work by other composers in his book *Curiosités tactiques.* (See DESPERADO.)

half-battery, a problemist's term for a situation in which a BATTERY would be created on a line if either of two pieces of the same colour were moved off the line.

half-centre, a PAWN CENTRE in which one side has a centre pawn on the fourth rank and the opponent has a pawn on the third rank of the adjacent centre file, the other two centre pawns having been exchanged. For example, after 1 e4 e5 2 Nf3 d6 3 d4 exd4 4 Nxd4, or 1 e4 e6 2 d4 d5 3 Nc3 dxe4 4 Nxe4 White has a half-centre. The traditional view, to which TARRASCH subscribed, is that possession of a half-centre brings advantage, subsisting in greater mobility and the centre pawn's attack on two squares in the enemy camp. Even in Tarrasch's time, however, it was known that the pawn on the fourth rank could become an object of attack. For example, after 1 e4 e5 2 Bc4 Nf6 3 d3 d5 4 exd5 Nxd5 Black has a half-centre, but White can con-

tinue 5 Nf3 Nc6 6 0–0 Be7 7 Re1 with a strong initiative arising from pressure on the king's pawn.

half-close game, see SEMI-CLOSE GAME.

Half Giuoco Piano, 936, the SEMI-ITALIAN OPENING.

half move, a term sometimes used for a SINGLE-MOVE or PLY. It is also to be found, with a different meaning, in joke puzzles. For example, (FORSYTH NOTATION) 8/8/4Q3/8/N7/3k4/8/R1K5. Mate in a half move. As there is no mate in one, how can there be a mate in half? The solution lies in the postulation that White has commenced castling queen's-side, has made half of the move by shifting the king, and will now move the rook to d1. There are other such fancies.

half-open file, a file on which only one player has a pawn or pawns. The opponent may seek advantage by using a rook to control such a file, said to be 'his' or 'her' file.

Taimanov–Kaidonov Belgrade 1988 Nimzowitsch Opening

1 Nf3 d5 2 b3 Nf6 3 Bb2 e6 4 c4 c5 5 e3 Nc6 6 cxd5 exd5 7 Bb5 Bd6 8 Ne5 0–0 9 Nxc6 (White hopes to exploit Black's WYVILL FORMATION, to which end 9 Bxc6 is better.) 9 . . . bxc6 10 Be2 Re8 11 0–0

11 . . . Rb8 (Black uses the half-open file to bring his queen's rook to an attacking position on the king's-side.) 12 d3 Rb4 13 Nd2 Rh4 14 g3 Ng4 15 Bxg4 Bxg4 16 f3 Rxh2 17 fxg4 Rxe3 18 Bf6 Rh3 19 Rf3 Rxg3+ 20 Kf1 gxf6 21 Rxg3 Bxg3 22 Nf3 Qd7 White resigns.

half-open game, see SEMI-OPEN GAME.

half-passed pawn, a pawn, on a HALF-OPEN FILE, that a player might advance with the support of another pawn and so gain a PASSED PAWN on that file. NIMZOWITSCH called the half-passed pawn a candidate, that is, a candidate for promotion.

White, with a half-passed pawn on c3, could obtain a passed pawn by 1 c4, although this would lead to a draw if Black were to reply 1 . . . Kd6. Instead White wins by 1 Ke3 Kd5 2 Kf4 Kd6 3 Ke4 Ke6 4 Kd4 Kd6 5 b4 and Black is in ZUGZWANG.

half-pin, a situation in which two men of the same colour are so placed on a line that if either were moved off the line the other would be pinned. The term, invented by MANSFIELD in 1915, is mostly used by composers although half-pins are not unusual in play. For example, after 1 d4 d5 2 c4 e6 3 Nc3 Nf6 4 Bg5 Nbd7 5 e3 c6 6 Nf3 Qa5 7 Nd2 there is a half-pin on the diagonal a5-e1. (See GOU-MONDY.)

Hamburg theme, see DECOY THEMES.

Hamilton-Russell, Frederick Gustavus (1867–1941), liberal patron and, in his last years, president of the British Chess Federation. In 1927 he donated a gold cup to FIDE to be the trophy for its international team tournaments which were just beginning and later became known as OLYMPIADS. The Hamilton-Russell cup is still awarded to the winning team.

Hamppe–Allgaier Gambit, 622, variation of the VIENNA GAME (once called the Hamppe Opening) that is akin to the ALLGAIER GAMBIT.

Hamppe–Muzio Gambit, 619, variation of the VIENNA GAME that has a similarity to the MUZIO GAMBIT.

Hamppe Opening, 608, the VIENNA GAME. Mentioned by PONZIANI and first analysed by JAENISCH in 1842, it was taken up a year or so later by the Swiss player Carl Hamppe (1814–76), a senior government official in Vienna.

Hamppe Variation, 609 in the VIENNA OPENING, a move effectively met by 3 . . . Bxf2+ .

Handbuch (German, handbook), the recognized abbreviation for Bilguer's *Handbuch des Schachspiels,* possibly the most influential chess-book for a period of 90 years. Commenced by Paul Rudolf von Bilguer (1815–40), the book was completed by a fellow member of the PLEIADES, von der LASA. The first edition in 1843 has xii + 376 + 124 pages of which the first 44 contain general rules and tips and then a chronological survey of writers, the next 332 pages give openings analysis, and book 2, the last 124 pages, covers endgames. The eighth and final edition, published in 11 parts between 1912 and 1916, has vi + 1,040 pages and uses smaller type. After 16 pages of general introduction there are 118 pages of history, 752 pages of openings analysis, 146 pages on the endgame, and a few pages of corrections. In the pages on openings there are 250 illustrative games. In 1921 MIESES published a 51-page *Ergänzungsheft* updating some opening variations, and in 1930 KMOCH published a *Nachtrag* of 232 pages all but two of which contain openings analysis. Most users of the *Handbuch,* especially those not familiar with the German language, think of it solely in the context of openings, in which respect its editorial judgement and typographical layout have not been surpassed.

Besides the first edition von der Lasa edited the next four (1852, 1858, 1864, 1874). The sixth edition (1880) by Constantin Schwede (1854–1917) was distinguished by a history derived from van der LINDE, the seventh (1891) by Emil SCHALLOPP (1843–1919) benefited from the assistance of BERGER and PAULSEN, and the final edition (1916–21) by SCHLECHTER included major contributions from Berger, Otto Gustav Koch (1849–1919), KOHTZ, SPIELMANN, TARRASCH, and TEICHMANN.

handicap, a method of compensating for the difference in skill between two chessplayers. Where the difference is substantial, one-sidedness hinders the development of the weaker player's ideas (they are forestalled) and blunts the edge of the stronger. In past times, when it was not easy to meet players of comparable strength, or stakes could not be obtained for a level game, many different handicapping ideas were devised. Most have become unfashionable, and perhaps unnecessary.

Handicaps may be classified into seven groups: material odds; special restrictions (such as PION COIFFÉ); weighting of results (such as counting a draw as a win for the weaker player); knowledge restrictions (such as RANDOMIZED CHESS); differential stakes; physical restrictions (such as blindfold play); differential time-limits.

The most popular form of handicap is material odds. The smallest commonly found is PAWN AND MOVE followed by PAWN AND TWO MOVES. Other frequently found odds are giving the exchange, knight, rook, or queen. All of these change the nature of the game. The weaker player has merely to seek exchanges and need not attempt creative play. The nature of the game is not changed if handicapping is by means of differential time-limits.

handicap tournament. The contestants give or receive handicaps according to their skills, perhaps measured by their RATING. In the 19th century

STEINITZ, ZUKERTORT, and other great masters played in handicap tournaments, but such events are now organized only at club level.

hanging centre, HANGING PAWNS on the centre files, especially when they form a CLASSICAL CENTRE. (See BLOCKADE; PAWN FORMATION.)

hanging pawns, a PAWN ISLAND consisting of a pair of UNITED PAWNS on HALF-OPEN FILES. The term, attributed to STEINITZ, is used only when at least one of the pawns is on one of the four central files. The pawn formation in the diagram shows hanging pawns on the c- and d-files, where they most commonly occur.

In themselves hanging pawns are neither strong nor weak. If they stand abreast on the fourth rank they attack four squares in the enemy's camp, perhaps restricting the opponent's mobility. Sometimes one of the pawns may advance to support an attack, as in the games given under CO-OPERATION and GIPSLIS. On the other hand, the hanging pawns may be hard to defend. They cannot be defended by other pawns, are subject to frontal attack on the half-open files, and may not be able to retain their unity if attacked by enemy pawns on adjoining files. In the game given under ATKINS the hanging pawns are broken up by flank attack.

Hanham Variation, 1022 in the PHILIDOR DEFENCE. At the New York 1889 tournament the American player James Moore Hanham (1840–1923) reintroduced the LORD VARIATION with a superior idea in mind: he had devised a way by which Black could defend the e-pawn and thus maintain a DEFENSIVE CENTRE. This variation, usually arising in the form of 1036, was endorsed by NIMZOWITSCH, and has become one of the main lines in the Philidor Defence. A similar idea is shown by 1075.

Also 450, the GRAND PRIX ATTACK; 659, the INDIAN OPENING; and 1181 in the FRENCH DEFENCE, given by LEWIS and tried by PAULSEN sometimes, notably against BLACKBURNE at London 1862 (see TOLUSH).

Hanneken Defence, 1102, the COZIO DEFENCE to the KING'S GAMBIT, analysed by the Prussian General Hermann von Hanneken (1810–86), in *Schachzeitung*, 1850.

Hanneken Variation, 976 in the SCOTCH GAME, an interesting gambit suggested by Hanneken.

Hansen, Curt (1964–), Danish champion 1983, 1984, 1985, World Junior Champion 1984, Nordic Champion 1983, European Junior Champion 1981–2, International Grandmaster (1985). Hansen's successes include victories at Esbjerg 1983 (+6=5), Gladsaxe 1983 (+4=4−1), Borganes 1985 (+6=4−1), and Vjestrup 1989 (+4=5). He was second (+4=6−1) at the strong Copenhagen 1985 tournament, and also at Wijk aan Zee 1991, this time shared with ADAMS, CHERNIN, and KHALIFMAN, after NUNN.

Hansen–Kir. Georgiev   World Junior Championship
Kiljava 1984   Queen's Gambit Declined Semi-Tarrasch Defence

1 d4 Nf6 2 Nf3 e6 3 c4 c5 4 Nc3 d5 5 cxd5 Nxd5 6 e3 Nc6 7 Bc4 cxd4 8 exd4 Be7 9 0–0 0–0 10 Re1 Nxc3 11 bxc3 b6 12 Bd3 Bb7 13 h4 Bf6 14 Ng5 g6 15 Qg4 h5 16 Qg3 Ne7 17 Ba3 Rc8

18 Nxe6 fxe6 19 Rxe6 Rc7 20 Rae1 Rf7 21 Bxg6 Rd7 22 Bxf7+ Kxf7 23 Rxf6+ Kxf6 24 Qe5+ Kf7 25 Qe6+ Kf8 26 Qf6+ Black resigns.

Hanstein Gambit, 1148 in the KING'S GAMBIT Accepted, a line given by COZIO. The Berlin player Wilhelm Hanstein (1811–50), founder of the magazine that became the *Deutsche Schachzeitung*, played the line. However, the earliest known game is Lasa–Hanstein.

Haring, Jacobus (1913–89), Dutch composer, International Judge of Chess Compositions (1964), International Master for Chess Compositions (1968), secretary of the Dutch Problem Society 1963–82, engineer. Inspired by MANSFIELD he became a leading composer of orthodox two-movers, a traditionalist rather than an innovator. He hoped his problems would appeal to players, and collaborated in writing a book, *Schaak . . ., maar raak!*, to this end. Conscious of impending death from cancer he was saddened by his failure to gain the title of International Grandmaster for Chess Compositions, for which he lacked a mere handful of FIDE ALBUM points. These points were earned in the *Album* for 1983–5, and he was awarded the title posthumously.

Bert Kieboom, *300 Schaakproblemem van Jac Haring* (1984).

#2

A problem by Haring, first prize *ex æquo, Due Alfieri*, 1980. Three thematic tries with promotion related to the solution are refuted thus: 1 d7? exf6, 1 dxe7? Rc8, and 1 fxe7? Rg7. The key is 1 f7:

1 ... exd6   2 fxg8 = Q #
1 ... R on file   2 f8 = N #
1 ... R on rank   2 Bg4 #.

Harkness system, an auxiliary scoring method also known as the MEDIAN SYSTEM. It was promoted by Kenneth Harkness (1898–1972), Scottish-born organizer of chess in the USA. The name has also been used for a Swiss system tournament pairing system proposed by Harkness in 1952, and also for a RATING method which was developed by Harkness during 1946–9, and used by the US Chess Federation from 1950 to 1960.

Harksen Gambit, 711 in the SPANISH OPENING, proposed by the Swedish player and composer Alfred Harksen (1886–1971) in *Deutsche Schachzeitung*, 1914.

Harley, Brian (1883–1955), English problem composer and author, an actuary by profession. A competent player, he devoted most of his later years to composition, with about 450 orthodox problems to his credit, and coined a few problem terms, including Black correction (see CORRECTION) and mutate. (See BLOCK.) He edited various chess columns, most enduringly in the *Observer* from 1919 until his death. There he published problems by the greatest composers of his time, and annotated many games in witty style, humorous in print as in life. His books have the popular touch, and his *Mate in Two Moves* (1931) and *Mate in Three Moves* (1943) inspired many would-be problemists. For players he wrote *Chess for the Fun of it* (1933) and *Chess and its Stars* (1936).

Harman Index, a collection of studies made by John Richard Harman (1905–86), British patent official and study enthusiast. Maintained and augmented by the English composer Brian David Stephenson (1954–   ), the index maintains more than 40,000 classified studies and is available to tourney judges seeking advice about ANTICIPATION.

Harrwitz, Daniel (1823–84), German from Breslau (Wroctaw) who was probably the world's best active player in the mid-1850s. 'The modern generation', said LASKER in 1932, 'fails to do justice to him. He was a great player.' In 1845 Harrwitz went to Paris where he was regarded as the equal of KIESERITZKY, and in 1846 they both went to London. There they took part in a triangular contest with STAUNTON; each played the other two, Staunton conceding odds of a rook, the others playing blindfold. Staunton defeated Kieseritzky, while Harrwitz, already an expert blindfold player, won both his games. In the same year Harrwitz lost a match to Staunton for 21 games up excluding draws: seven played level, seven at PAWN AND MOVE, seven at PAWN AND TWO MOVES. (Staunton conceded the odds.) Harrwitz scored −7, +6 = 1 − 1, and +3 − 4 respectively. It was his first big match, in which, curiously, he fared better with pawn and move than with pawn and two. Although Harrwitz was not yet at his full strength Staunton considered it his hardest match.

Visiting Breslau in 1848 Harrwitz met ANDERSSEN for the first time. He had been working in Berlin when Harrwitz first flourished. They played a match for 11 games up but when the score stood at five wins each they agreed to end the match. After Harrwitz lost the first game he took five days off to recuperate. To avoid revolutionary turmoil Harrwitz left his home town shortly afterwards and returned to London.

His next important match was in 1852 when he defeated WILLIAMS (+ 7 = 3). He also defeated Williams in matches in 1853, and in one of these, when he had suffered two losses, Harrwitz went to visit Hamburg before returning to finish the match. In the same year he played LÖWENTHAL for the first to win 11 games. When trailing badly (his score was + 2 = 1 − 7) Harrwitz took himself off to Brighton. Löwenthal had provided for such an eventuality in the conditions, and Harrwitz lost two games by default. Harrwitz returned, fought with great determination, and won (+11 = 12 − 10). There was much acrimony between rival supporters. One man hired an organ-grinder to play outside the window, knowing this would upset Löwenthal more than Harrwitz, and another, defying the non-smoking rule, blew thick cigar smoke into Löwenthal's face. The gentle Löwenthal was a surrogate for his chief supporter, Staunton. Harrwitz had challenged Staunton, but had been unable to agree terms, some blaming one party, some the other.

From January 1853 to June 1854 Harrwitz was proprietor and editor of the *British Chess Review*, an excellent periodical except perhaps for its bias against Staunton and his allies. ('To talk of the match between Messrs Löwenthal and Harrwitz, is just like speaking of the match between Mr Harrwitz and the Wandering Jew.') The English player Augustus Mongrédien (1807–88), who knew Harrwitz, wrote: 'He had the misfortune of being both contentious and witty—the former quality involving him in constant disputes, and the latter rendering these disputes both bitter and personal.' Staunton, of course, could well hold his own.

Soon Harrwitz departed for Paris to become professional at the CAFÉ DE LA RÉGENCE following Kieseritzky's death. Although physically unattractive, 'all head and brains' on a tiny body, he was a sparkling conversationalist, and popular at the Régence. At Manchester in 1857 he played in his only tournament and was knocked out in the first round by Anderssen. According to Löwenthal, Harrwitz subsequently played three games against Anderssen, winning them all. In 1858 Harrwitz was defeated by MORPHY ($+2=1-5$). His conduct during the match (he took more than one of his usual 'vacations') and the ill grace with which he faced defeat, combined with the adulation accorded to Morphy, lost Harrwitz the sympathy of the public and eventually cost him his job. Later he told friends that Morphy was by far the greatest player he had met. When KOLISCH came to Paris in 1859 Harrwitz played him a few games ($+1=1-2$) but was unable to recover his confidence. Receiving a modest inheritance after his father's death he retired to Bolzano in the Austrian Alps, emerging in 1878 to make a tour 'to see old friends and scenes of past glories once more before he died'. (See LOSE A MOVE; TRAP.)

Harrwitz–Morphy   First match game 1858   Queen's Gambit Declined Harrwitz Attack

1 d4 e6 2 c4 d5 3 Nc3 Nf6 4 Bf4 a6 5 e3 c5 6 Nf3 Nc6 7 a3 cxd4 8 exd4 dxc4 9 Bxc4 b5 10 Bd3 Bb7 11 0-0 Be7 12 Be5 0-0 13 Qe2 Nd5 14 Bg3 Kh8 15 Rfe1 Bf6 16 Qe4 g6 17 Nxd5 Qxd5 18 Qxd5 exd5 19 Ne5 Rad8 20 Nxc6 Bxc6 21 Rac1 Rc8 22 Bd6 Rg8 23 Be5 Kg7? 24 f4 Bd7 25 Kf2 h6 26 Ke3 Rxc1 27 Rxc1 Rc8 28 Rc5 Bxe5 29 fxe5 Be6 (Black has a COLOUR WEAKNESS; if he captures the rook on its outpost at c5 the white king advances by way of the dark squares.)

30 a4 bxa4 31 Bxa6 Rb8 32 Rb5 Rd8 33 Rb6 Ra8 34 Kd2 Bc8 35 Bxc8 Rxc8 36 Rb5 Ra8 37 Rxd5 a3 38 bxa3 Rxa3 39 Rc5 Kf8 40 Ke2 Ke7 41 d5 Kd7 42 Rc6 h5 43 Rf6 Ke7 44 d6+ Ke8 45 e6 fxe6 46 Rxe6+ Kf7 47 d7 Ra8 48 Rd6 Ke7 49 Rxg6 Kxd7 50 Rg5 Rh8 51 Kf3 Ke6 52 Kg3 h4+ 53 Kg4 h3 54 g3 Kf6 55 Rh5 Black resigns.

Harrwitz Attack, 170, a QUEEN'S GAMBIT Declined variation favoured by HARRWITZ and also by RUBINSTEIN, after whom it is sometimes named. Harrwitz played it successfully in matches, notably in 1853 against LÖWENTHAL and in 1858 against MORPHY, who considered the line so strong that he then avoided the Queen's Gambit, preferring the DUTCH DEFENCE, 247. In his world championship matches of 1978 and 1981 KORCHNOI employed the Harrwitz Attack in its current form, after 4 Nf3 Be7. See games under HARRWITZ, MACKENZIE, and PHILIDOR SACRIFICE.

Harrwitz Variation, 231, the MASON VARIATION which easily leads to the HARRWITZ ATTACK.

Hartong, Jan (1902–87), Dutch composer, specialist in orthodox TWO- and THREE-MOVERS, International Master for Chess Compositions, *honoris causa* (1959), director of an insurance company.

M. Niemeijer, *Jan Hartong* (1946).

#2

A TASK problem by Hartong, *British Chess Magazine*, 1952. The key is 1 hxg3, setting up a block. There are different mates for seven interferences of the black queen.

1 . . . b5	2 a8 = Q(B)#
1 . . . Nc3, c3	2 Re5#
1 . . . e5	2 Nf6#
1 . . . Nf2	2 Qg2#
1 . . . d2	2 Qe2#
1 . . . Nd2	2 Re1#
1 . . . Bb3	2 Bxb7#.

Hartston, William Roland (1947–), English player, International Master (1973), and author, editor of the column in the *Independent* from 1987. He was British champion in 1973 (after a play-off) and in 1975. In 1974 and again in 1980 he was equal first but unsuccessful in the play-offs. As well as achieving distinction as a television presenter and commentator on chess he has written many chess books, ranging from the light-hearted *How to Cheat at Chess* (1976) to the academic *Psychology of Chess* (with Peter Wason) (1983). Perhaps the one with the widest appeal is *The Kings of Chess* (1985), a lively study of the game's major figures.

Hārūn ar-Rashīd (*c.*763–809), 'Abbāsid caliph of Islam 786–809. Allegedly the first of his dynasty to play chess, 'he favoured good players and granted them pensions.' Under his caliphate the golden age of SHAṬRANJ began; court patronage continued, and early in the 9th century three grandmasters emerged: RABRAB, Abū 'n-Na 'ām, and Jābir al-Kūfī. In time they were followed by al-'ADLĪ, ar-RĀZĪ, aṣ-ṢŪLĪ, and other great players. Hārūn ar-Rashīd's court at Baghdad is idealized in *The Arabian Nights Entertainment*, sometimes called *The Thousand and One Nights*. This compilation of folk-tales was made some centuries after his death, and the chess passages it contains have no historical basis.

Hastings Variation, 216 in the QUEEN'S GAMBIT Declined, played in the game Buerger–Thomas, Hastings 1926–7.

Hauptturnier, German for premier tournament, and, like its English equivalent, usually the second level event after the master tournament. Soon after its founding in 1877 the Deutscher Schachbund began the practice of organizing a *Hauptturnier* at each of its congresses. The winner or sometimes the second-prize winner was subsequently entitled to play in a DSB master tournament. If he won at least a third of his games (the *Meisterdrittel*) in that event he gained the title of master.

Havel, Miroslav (1881–1958), pseudonym of the Czech composer Miroslav Košt'al, International Judge of Chess Compositions (1956), official in the Ministry of Railways. 'I endeavoured', he writes, 'to bring the Bohemian problem, as to its form, and especially economy of means, to its highest perfection.' He succeeded.

I. Mikan, *M. Havel: České granaty 1898–1958* (1975) contains 1,701 compositions by Havel.

#3

A problem by Havel, fourth prize, *Skakbladet*, 1924. The key is 1 Bf8 threatening 2 Rd1+, 3 Qb1‡.

1 ... Rxf8   2 Qg1+
1 ... Rf1   2 Qb3
1 ... Rd3   2 Bg7+.

Heathcote, Godfrey (1870–1952), English composer specializing in orthodox THREE- and MORE-MOVERS, lawyer, From the 1890s he and BLAKE were the two leading exponents of the so-called English style. (See PROBLEM HISTORY.)

Marble, Hume, and White, *Chess Idylls* (1918) contains 300 problems by Heathcote.

#4

A problem by Heathcote, *Westminster Gazette*, 1917. The key is 1 Bc2 and some MODEL MATES follow:

1 ... Bh3   2 b4+ Kd4   3 Qd5+ Nxd5 4 Nb5‡
1 ... Nd5   2 Qc6+ Kxc6 3 Ba4+ Kc5   4 Ne6‡
1 ... Bc6   2 Qd6+ Nxd6 3 Be3+ Kc4   4 b3‡
1 ... Kd4   2 Qf5 Bd5   3 Qxd5+ Nxd5 4 Ne6‡.

Heath Variation, 1072 in the KING'S GAMBIT Declined, a kind of EVANS GAMBIT ascribed by HARR-WITZ, when LÖWENTHAL played it against him (in their first match game, 1853), to the German player Schulder. Played also by MORPHY and KOLISCH, it was named after the English player and Scottish champion Christopher Barclay Heath (1877–1961), who published analysis in the *British Chess Magazine*, 1922–3.

heavy piece, see MAJOR PIECE.

hedgehog formation, two centre pawns abreast on the third rank, usually a defensive set-up as in the SCHEVENINGEN VARIATION. Such pawns guard four squares in the centre of the fourth rank, each pawn having two 'quills'.

Heinrichsen Opening, 8, noted with stern disapproval by Ruy LÓPEZ, played by BLACKBURNE at London 1883, and advocated by Arved Heinrichsen (1876–1900) of Lithuania; also known as Baltic, Dunst, Kotrč, or Queen's Knight Opening.

Hein Variation, 1101 in the KING'S GAMBIT Accepted, proposed by the German player R. Hein in *Neue Berliner Schachzeitung*, 1867.

Hellers, Erik Gustaf Ferdinand (1969–), Swedish player, International Grandmaster (1989), European Junior Champion 1984–5. He played for the

Swedish Olympiad team from 1988 and had his first major success at Budapest 1988, when he was first (+6=4−1). He was equal first at Malmö 1988–9.

helpmate, a type of problem invented by LANGE in 1854. Both sides conspire to get Black checkmated, a STIPULATION indicated by the symbol h‡. Black commences play and it is customary for each numbered move to consist of a black SINGLE-MOVE and the following white single-move, the reverse of the normal practice. A composer may choose TWIN or DUPLEX form, add set play (for which White moves first), or provide two or more solutions. Sometimes DUALS are added intentionally; these are called variations, and are indicated by a series of numbers; for example, for a helpmate in two, the numbers 1.1.2.1. indicate that two lines of play begin on the third single-move, i.e. on Black's second move.

h‡2 a) as diagram; b) remove Rb4

A pair of TWINS by MACLEOD, *Feenschach*, 1986.
  (a) 1 Qxd2 Re1   2 fxe1 = B Rc4‡
  (b) 1 Qxe2 Qe1   2 fxe1 = R Rc2‡.
For other examples, see DUPLEX, TWINS.

help problem, a problem for which the two sides conspire to meet the stipulations. Black usually moves first. (See HELPMATE; HELP-STALEMATE.)

help-stalemate, a problem similar to a helpmate except that the two sides conspire to stalemate the black king, a stipulation indicated by the symbol hp. Black moves first. For examples, see CHINESE FAMILY; CYLINDER BOARD.

Henneberger Variation, 188 in the QUEEN'S GAMBIT Declined, analysed, before the First World War, by Walter Henneberger (1883–1969) of Switzerland (and thus sometimes called the Swiss Variation). It received little attention until played eight times by ALEKHINE with the black pieces against CAPABLANCA in their championship match, Buenos Aires 1927 (and so providing another name for the line—the Argentine Variation). Henneberger did not originate the line which had, for example, been played by SHOWALTER in 1897 during his match with PILLSBURY. Also 857 in the FOUR KNIGHTS OPENING, analysed by Henneberger in *Schweizerische Schachzeitung*, 1919.

Hennig–Schara Gambit, 119, the SCHARA-HENNIG GAMBIT.

Henry, W. R., pseudonym of William Henry Russ (1833–66), pioneer American archivist. One of the first to recognize the importance of chess columns, he indexed them, compiled a manuscript collection of all problems published in America, and interested the American composer COOK in a joint effort to secure publication. Although the probability of success was small and there were no chances of financial gain, Henry worked on, assembled more than 4,000 problems, and wrote 'lifelets' of American composers with their portraits. He experimented with typefaces for diagrams and had 960 of the problems printed, spending $700. He established that a problem by C. H. STANLEY, *Spirit of the Times*, 1 Mar. 1845, was the first to be published in America. Henry did not live to see the publication of the book, *American Chess Nuts* (1868), by Cook, Henry, and Gilberg.

His end does not tally with the novelist's image of chessplayers as cold, calculating, and efficient. Having unofficially adopted an 11-year-old girl and paid for her upbringing, he proposed marriage when she was 21. She rejected his offer and one evening in Brooklyn he shot her four times in the head, jumped into the river to drown himself, found the tide out, climbed out, and shot himself twice in the head; muddy and freezing, he was arrested, interrogated, and taken to hospital. His injuries were not necessarily fatal, but he died ten days later, lacking the will to live. The woman survived.

heraldry, a subject much invaded by the use of chess pieces as symbols. The rook and knight are often used on coats of arms, parts of which may be chequered although rarely as an 8 × 8 square. Many families throughout Europe have the equivalent of rook as part of their name show such a device on one of their charges. Sometimes this takes the form of a medieval bifurcated rook rather than a castle tower, which has led to false conclusions about the nature of the charge. Some have argued that the use of chess pieces as heraldic devices indicates the widespread playing of chess among the nobility; but only the pieces that have a natural affinity with chivalry and its horses and castles are found frequently, and such chess pieces have been used by families with no special interest in the game.

Herbstman, Alexander Osipovich (1900–82), Soviet study composer, International Judge of Chess Compositions (1956), International Master for Chess Compositions (1959), professor of philology. He spent much of his childhood near Luzern where he learned chess, and in 1923, while studying in Moscow, he became interested in chess studies. One of his several books, *Izbrannye shakhmatny etyudy* (1964), contains 120 of his studies and a 60-page essay on study composition. In December 1979 he left the Soviet Union and, after a short period in Rome, settled in Sweden where he died.

+

A miniature by Herbstman, first prize, *Shakhmaty v SSSR*, 1945. 1 Nf3 Kh6 2 Bg8 Ne7+ 3 Ke6 Nxg8 4 Kf7 Kh7 5 Ng5+ Kh8 6 f3! Nh6+ 7 Kxg6 Ng8 8 Nf7#.

Herzfeld Defence, 1132, advanced by Sebastian Herzfeld (*c*.1824–1906), a Viennese physician, in about 1870 and analysed in detail by Adolf Csánk of Vienna, who called it the Vienna Defence, in *Chess Monthly*, Aug. 1889. It is sometimes styled the Steinitz Variation because in 1885 STEINITZ considered it the strongest way of meeting the SALVIO GAMBIT.

Herzog Defence, 587 in the CARO–KANN DEFENCE, as R. Pitschak–F. Herzog, Bad Liebwerda 1934.

heterodox chess, see UNORTHODOX CHESS.

heterodox problem, formal and rarely used term for FAIRY PROBLEM.

hexagonal chess, unorthodox play on a board formed from hexagons. The earliest version was suggested by the Viennese engineer Siegmund Wellisch in 1912. He chose a hexagonal board as the

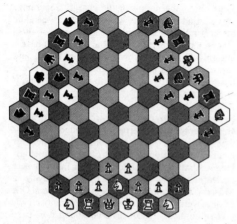

Hexagonal chess, 1912

most logical shape for THREE-HANDED CHESS, and 91 hexagons as the nearest equivalent, for three players, to the 64 squares used by two players in orthodox chess. So that no adjacent hexagons are of the same colour a third hue is needed, and he chose red. The diagram shows the array.

The king's move is to one of the six (or three or four) adjoining hexagons, the knight's move is to the nearest hexagon of the same colour (and so three knights are needed to cover the board), the rook's move is in straight lines through the sides of the hexagons. There are no bishops. The queen combines the moves of the rook and knight. The pawns are advanced through the sides of the hexagons to arrive or capture on one of the two hexagons lying ahead.

Forms of hexagonal chess using a board of overall quadrilateral shape have been devised, but the version that has had the most success in modern times is a two-handed game using a board similar to Wellisch's, the players sitting at opposite angles. It was introduced in 1949 by Wladyslaw Glinski (1920–91), a Polish-born Londoner. The forces differ from those of Wellisch in that each side has only two knights, but has three bishops and one extra pawn. The moves of the pieces, also different, are described in Glinski's book, *Rules of Hexagonal Chess* (1973).

Glinski's version achieved some popularity, and in 1976 the British Hexagonal Chess Federation was formed. A visit by Glinski to his homeland in 1978 generated much interest there and in 1980 an International Hexagonal Chess Federation was formed, the first world championship being held in 1987. Other than Britain, the countries showing the most interest are Poland, Hungary, Czechoslovakia, USSR, Yugoslavia, Italy, and the USA.

Heyde Variation, 634 in the VIENNA GAME recommended in *Deutsches Wochenschach*, 1890, in an article by the German-born player Albert Otto Heyde (1866–1920), founder of that periodical, who emigrated to the USA in 1902.

Hicken Variation, 900 in the EVANS GAMBIT DECLINED. The name was given in the 1870s after its use in Philadelphia by Folkert A. Hicken, who later became an Austrian vice-consul in Australia.

Hippopotamus Game, 671, a name given as a joke to the ALAPIN OPENING. In *Neue Berliner Schachzeitung*, 1868, a 'chess humoreske' by L. B. described a coffee-house game in which the local braggart played the writer. After 1 e4 e5 2 Ne2 Qh4 3 Nbc3 Nc6 4 g3 Qg5 5 d4 Nxd4 6 Bxg5 Nf3 mate, L. B. told his opponent, 'You must christen your exquisite opening with 2 Ne2 the Hippopotamus Game.' The author was probably the German writer Ludwig Immanuel von Bilow (1834–1903), whose *Schach-Struwwelpeter* (1883) displays the same kind of humour.

Hirschbach Variation, 899 in the EVANS GAMBIT, first given by the German player Hermann Hirschbach (1812–88) in the short-lived *Deutsche Schachzeitung*, 1847.

Hispano-Sicilian Variation, 462, the ROSSOLIMO VARIATION of the SICILIAN DEFENCE, in which the 'Spanish' move Bf1-b5 is played.

history of chess. The earliest evidence of a recognizable form of chess, CHATURANGA, is around AD 600. Before that, all is speculation. Board games have been played for about 6,000 years. Games in which chariots raced around boards may well have supplied the move of the rook. The various distinctive features of chess, many pieces with varied moves, pawn promotion, and the decisive significance of the king, may have been the work of one mind, or could have been developed piecemeal.

For the last hundred years the view has been developing that many games had their origin in divination ceremonies. Professor Joseph Needham, the Sinologist, believes that a quasi-astrological technique which evolved in China between the 1st and 6th centuries AD for determining the balance of Yin and Yang was converted for military divination purposes in India or China and probably formed the basis of chaturanga. By controlling the fall of objects on to a divination board the gods could communicate with men. At a later stage dice were added to determine the moves of the pieces and further reveal the celestial mind. Then someone was sacrilegious enough to convert this process to a game, perhaps eliminating the dice. The person who secularized the religious ceremony has, perhaps, the best claim to be the 'inventor' of chess.

Abundant MYTHS claim a single inventor of chess, but many of these may relate to other board games; for example, the 'grain of corn' legend could apply equally to ASHTĀPADA. It is possible that one person, using the religious ritual as a basis, created chaturanga at about AD 600 on the Ganges. Fa Xian, a Chinese Buddhist who wrote extensively about his long sojourn in India at the beginning of the 5th century, does not mention the game—an indication, perhaps, that it was not known then.

The first unmistakable reference to chess in all literature is in *Harschacharita* by the Indian court poet Bana, written between 625 and 640. Contemporary Chinese texts may also refer to chess. No authentic chess pieces earlier than the 7th century AD have been identified beyond question. Artefacts that are undoubtedly older have been excavated in the USSR, but if they are pieces at all they belong to a precursor of chess or to another game. Authentic chess pieces excavated in Italy have been dated as 2nd century AD; despite the integrity of the archaeologists who were concerned with the find, their dating is generally regarded with scepticism: were it proved correct the history of chess would need to be rewritten.

Chess flourished early in those countries in which Buddhism took root. The game may have been taken to China by Buddhists who travelled abroad to further their religion and to escape persecution at home. Their route would have been over the mountains north of the Indus, or through the Khyber Pass to join the caravan routes that came from the Caspian Sea. By about 800 the Chinese had developed a game in line with their own cultural background. (See CHINESE CHESS.) Through Korea chess reached Japan, and there, too, it was remodelled to suit the national temperament, taking the name SHOGI.

The westward movement of chaturanga is better documented. It reached Persia, where it became CHATRANG, around 625, and after the Arabian conquest, 638–51, was renamed SHAṬRANJ, a word which later found its way back to India as *sitringee*, a type of chequered carpet. An elaborate account of the arrival of chaturanga in Persia from India is to be found in a work of fiction, *Kārnāmak-ī-Artākshatr-ī-Pāpakān*, a Pahlavic romance once thought to have been written in the 7th century but later attributed to the 8th century. During the Golden Age of Islamic chess (8th to 10th centuries) play reached such a degree of excellence as to suggest to at least one grandmaster a greater antiquity for the game than is generally accepted. He believes that such skill could not have been developed in a mere three centuries.

Shaṭranj reached Western Europe by three paths: with the Moorish invaders of Spain in the 8th century, through the Islamic conquerors of Sicily shortly afterwards, and by way of the Byzantine Empire in the East. It was taken to Russia along at least three paths of which the earliest, in the 9th century, was probably the Caspian–Volga trade route. Byzantine Christians carried the game through the Balkans while the Vikings did the same from the Baltic, all long before the Mongolian conquest of 1223. By about 1000 the game was widely known throughout Europe.

Already in the Islamic period, problems (MANSŪBA) were popular, and MEDIEVAL PROBLEMS were part of the repertory of itinerant entertainers. (See PROBLEM HISTORY for an account of what has become almost an independent topic.) The earliest European references to chess show its popularity among religious orders, some of whose members made use of it in ALLEGORIES. The game was also found in courts and to some extent among soldiers and other nomadic groups.

Around 1475 took place the most significant of all changes during the recorded history of the game. (See LAWS, HISTORY OF.) The FERS was displaced by the queen, the AUFIN by the bishop, and the pace of the game was quickened. The power of the new pieces made time of greater importance: one indifferent move in the opening phase might subject a player to strong attack. The study of openings began. Previously the pawn could be promoted only to the lowly fers, now it could become a queen; and most of the endgame knowledge garnered in the preceding eight or nine hundred years became obsolete.

The new game originated in southern Europe, replacing the old game with remarkable speed although, as in medieval times, some of the laws varied from country to country. The earliest books on this new game by VICENT, LUCENA, DAMIANO, and Ruy LÓPEZ were all written in the Iberian peninsula. In the second half of the 16th century there was a swift advance in the status of the game when leading players in Italy were sponsored by wealthy, even royal, patrons. New openings were discovered, the art of attack made rapid progress. Masters kept secret notebooks of their discoveries, occasionally selling copies to those who could pay well. Many manuscripts by POLERIO, GRECO, and other players have survived.

Chess seems to have stagnated for about a century after Greco's death, but from the 1730s it was played in many of the numerous and fashionable COFFEE HOUSES, where a few professionals could make a livelihood from the increasing number of well-to-do habitués rather than relying on one rich patron. Some artists and academics supplemented their meagre or erratic incomes in this way. A market was created for chess books which began to appear with regularity. In the long run the most important of them was PHILIDOR'S *Analysis* (1749). Until he wrote this book POSITIONAL PLAY (strategy), so dominant in the old game, had received scant attention. His ideas were attacked by rival authors and the concept of SCHOOLS OF CHESS developed. Until 1800 chessplayers were isolated geographically, but soon those in cities formed clubs, and matches between clubs in different cities were arranged by the only practical means, CORRES-PONDENCE CHESS. Players were increasingly drawn from the middle classes, the fashion for the game having declined among the aristocracy since the 1780s. Paris was the leading centre, its most famous resort the CAFÉ DE LA RÉGENCE, its most famous player BOURDONNAIS; his series of matches with McDONNELL in 1834 was the most important chess event of the 1830s.

A swift advance began in the 1840s, its momentum lasting until the present day, as NEWSPAPER COLUMNS and chess PERIODICALS grew in number, and ORGANIZATION developed. With the publication of Bilguer's HANDBUCH and a book by JAENISCH, the technique of opening play began to make rapid strides. International MATCHES between individual players took place, notably the contest between STAUNTON and SAINT-AMANT in 1843, protagonists of England and France respectively. Staunton's positional play showed notable developments, and with his victory England took over the leadership of the chess world from France.

Staunton advocated standards for LAWS, NOTATION, the shape of the CHESSMEN, and the TIMING OF MOVES. He organized the first international TOURNAMENT, London 1851. Although ANDERSSEN won, heralding a period when German players led the world, London remained the chess centre until the 1870s, still the only place in which a professional could make a living. Meanwhile, in 1858, MORPHY came to Europe, defeated several leading players within the space of a few months, returned home and retired. His success generated a wide enthusiasm for the game.

By 1872 STEINITZ, a native of Prague, had become the world's best player. (See WORLD CHAMPION-SHIP.) He brought new standards into chess analysis and harmonized the theory of the game, thus resolving the issues that had been disputed by the various schools of chess. (The later use of this phrase relates to style rather than fundamental approach.) At about this time a form of snobbish-ness developed which led to acrimony between amateurs and professionals, a distinction seldom made in chess. Professionals began to find London uncongenial and, with few exceptions, mediocrity prevailed. When Steinitz emigrated to USA in 1883 Britain ceased to have a major influence on world chess.

International chess life comprises an increasing number of tournaments and matches, including those for the world title. National organizations grew slowly, but in 1924 the creation of FIDE, now the international governing body, became possible. FIDE organized the first OLYMPIAD and the first women's world championship in 1927, established international laws, took charge of the world cham-pionship in 1947 (previously run on a free enter-prise basis), conferred FIDE TITLES from 1950, adopted international RATING in 1970, and estab-lished STANDARD NOTATION in 1981. The period of FIDE consolidation coincided with the rise of the USSR to the summit of world chess, an achieve-ment based on political and social motives.

Since the middle of the 20th century chess has become a truly international game, played on every continent and at every social level. Careers in management or administration now provide oppor-tunities for enthusiasts who choose not to be com-petitors.

For further reading MURRAY'S *A History of Chess*, the standard work, is indispensable. He also wrote *A Short History of Chess* (1963). The most straightforward and comprehensive account is *Zur Geschichte und Literatur des Schachspiels* (1897) by von der LASA. Other useful books are *Chess: the History of a Game* (1985) by Richard Eales, *Chess in Old Russia* (1979) by LINDER, and *Schach: eine Kulturgeschichte* (1986) by Joachim Petzold.

history of problems, see PROBLEM HISTORY.

Hjartarson, Jóhann (1963–   ), Icelandic champion 1980, 1984, International Grandmaster (1985). After winning at Reykjavik 1984 and Gjovik 1985 (both +5=6), he had three victories in stronger tournaments, Szirák 1987 (+9=7−1), Aureyri, and Munich, both 1988, and both +5=6. Moving up into the highest level, his positions were lower, but results equally good: equal fourth Reykjavik 1988 (+5=9−3), equal third Tilburg 1988 (+3=8−3), and sixth Belgrade 1989 (+2=7−2). He stepped in at the last minute to fill a vacancy at Tilburg, breaking off his honeymoon to do so.

Hjartarson–Korchnoi Candidates match 1988 Spanish Opening Open Defence

1 e4 e5 2 Nf3 Nc6 3 Bb5 a6 4 Ba4 Nf6 5 0–0 Nxe4 6 d4 b5 7 Bb3 d5 8 dxe5 Be6 9 c3 Be7 10 Nbd2 Nc5 11 Bc2 Bg4 12 Re1 Qd7 13 Nf1 Rd8 14 Ne3 Bh5 15 b4 Ne6 16 Nf5 d4 17 Be4 Bg6 18 g4 h5 19 h3 Kf8 20 a4 hxg4 21 hxg4 Qe8 22 axb5 axb5

23 Ra6 Nb8 24 Rxe6 fxe6 25 Nxe7 Bxe4 26 Rxe4 dxc3 27 Ng6+ Kg8 28 Rd4 Rxd4 29 Qxd4 Rh3 30 Ng5 Rh6 31 Nf4 Nc6 32 Qxc3 Qd8 33 Nf3 Nxb4 34 Bd2 Qa8 35 Kg2 Nc6 36 g5 b4 37 Qc5 Rh7 38 Nxe6 g6 39 Qd5 Kh8 40 Ned4 Qc8 41 e6 Nxd4 42 Nxd4 c5 43 Bf4 Ra7 44 Nc6 Black resigns.

Hodgson, Julian Michael (1963–), English player, International Grandmaster (1988). Equal first at Wijk aan Zee 'B' tournament 1985 and Kecskemét 1988. British Champion 1991.

Hoffer, né **Hofenreich,** Lipót (1842–1913), chess journalist and administrator. A Jew from Budapest, Hoffer moved to Vienna in 1860 and henceforth used the German version of his forename, Leopold. Shortly afterwards he went to Paris, where he seems to have realized that his ability at chess failed to match his ambition. He was assistant manager at the Paris tournament 1867. When the Franco-Prussian war broke out in 1870 he arrived penniless in London, knowing very little English. Wilhelm STEINITZ, who had met him at the Paris tournament, protected and fed him until he was able to provide for himself. Moved more by social snobbery than gratitude Hoffer later became a bitter enemy of Steinitz, and their verbal warfare makes astonishing reading in a more restrained age. In 1882 he succeeded Steinitz as editor of the important chess column in *The Field,* a post he held for the rest of his life. Steinitz, whose excellent contributions to *The Field* had made the weekly column famous, justifiably castigated Hoffer for the poor quality of his ANNOTATIONS. Hoffer's magazine *Chess Monthly* ran from 1879 to 1896 and was enhanced by ZUKERTORT'S co-operation until 1888. Hoffer had a large powerful-looking head, ill-complemented by a slight body and deformed feet; his fiery temper and obsequiousness to the rich and powerful made him unpopular, but he was respected for his hard work as administrator, referee, and journalist.

hole, a square on a player's third rank or beyond that cannot be guarded by a pawn. A player who has a hole in his or her half of the board may be at a disadvantage if the opponent can occupy the hole with a piece; otherwise the hole may be of little consequence. The term was invented by STEINITZ in 1886; he believed that a player who has a hole on the third or fourth rank always finds it a serious weakness, and that even a hole on the fifth rank is disadvantageous. This view has gradually been modified, and in the latter half of the 20th century masters have been willing to accept holes if they gain compensating mobility. For example, after 1 e4 c5 2 Nf3 Nc6 3 d4 cxd4 4 Nxd4 Nf6 5 Nc3 d6 6 Be2 e5 7 Nb3 Black has a hole at d5 (fourth rank), but the consensus is that Black has a defensible game. A hole on a player's third rank, however, often proves too great a handicap. For examples, see GUNSBERG, LASA, MILES, and STEINITZ, in which the losers have holes on d4, f4, f6, and c4 respectively.

Holloway Defence, 1141, an inferior line for Black in the MUZIO GAMBIT, given by LEWIS and named after Alfred Holloway (1837–1905), secretary of the Bristol Chess Club, who later emigrated to Australia. The name was bestowed by George H. Selkirk (of the Bristol Club) in his *Book of Chess* (1868).

Holzhausen Attack, 933 in the ITALIAN OPENING, given in *Deutsche Schachzeitung,* 1900, by the German player and problemist Walther von Holzhausen (1876–1935). His idea is that the obvious reply 10 . . . Qc5 is met by 11 Bxf7+ and only by the best play can Black escape with a draw.

Holzhausen Theme, see CUTTING-POINT THEMES.

horizontal line, a RANK.

Horny Defence, 1173, a refutation, published in *Anweisung das Schachspiel* (1824), of ALLGAIER'S analysis of the gambit named after him. Johann Horny, author of this book, was an actor in the Hesse Electoral Royal Theatre.

Horowitz, Israel Albert (1907–73), International Master (1950), International Arbiter (1951), a leading US player during the 1930s, chess author, US Open Champion 1936, 1938, and 1943. In 1941 he challenged RESHEVSKY for the US championship and lost a hard-fought match (=13–3). Horowitz showed his best form in OLYMPIADS, playing in 1931, 1935, and 1937 (all won by USA), and in 1950, making a total score of +29=19–3. He was proprietor and editor of *Chess Review,* for many years the leading American chess magazine, from 1933 (soon after it was founded by KASHDAN) until 1969 when it was merged with *Chess Life* to become *Chess Life and Review.* Horowitz wrote more than 20 books, usually in collaboration. He was not always generous to his co-authors; for example, after the death of F. J. Wellmuth, compiler of *The Golden Treasury of Chess*, Horowitz added a few games and brought out further editions under his own name. Perhaps his most interesting book, written in collaboration with P. L. Rothenberg, is *The Personality of Chess* (1963), reprinted with the misleading title *The Complete Book of Chess* (1969).

In a lightning tournament Horowitz once gave odds of queen, rook, bishop and knight, and won.

Horrwitz bishops, jargon for RAKING BISHOPS used by NIMZOWITSCH in the original version of his book *My System*. No one knows whether he meant HORWITZ, HARRWITZ, or someone else. In the English version, however, the translator wrote Horwitz bishops in later editions.

Hort, Vlastimil (1944–), International Grandmaster (1965), the strongest Czech player of his generation, national champion 1970, 1971, 1972, 1975, and 1977. A frequent competitor, he has played in more than 90 international tournaments, winning or sharing 23 first prizes. His best wins are: Mariánské Lázně 1965 (+7=8), equal with KERES; Skopje 1969 (+7=8), equal with MATULOVIĆ ahead of SMYSLOV; Havana 1971 (+8=7), ahead of GELLER; Luhačovice 1971 (+8=7); Leipzig 1973 (+6=9); Slanchev Breag 1974 (+7=8); Vinkovci 1976 (+8=5−2), equal with SAX; Banja Luka 1976 (+5=10); Amsterdam 1979 (+5=8), equal with Sax; Dortmund 1982 (+6=5), ahead of ROMANISHIN and PSAKHIS; and Biel 1984 (+6=4−1), equal with HÜBNER.

Hort shared second prize in a number of very strong tournaments: Rovinj–Zagreb 1970 (+5=12), equal with GLIGORIĆ, KORCHNOI, and Smyslov, after FISCHER; Wijk aan Zee 1975 (+6=8−1), after PORTISCH; Ljubljana–Portorož 1977 (+5=8), equal with SAVON after LARSEN; Bad Kissingen 1981 (+4=4−2), equal with SEIRAWAN after Korchnoi; Reggio Emilia 1986-7 (+1=10), equal with CHERNIN, Smyslov, and Spassky after RIBLI. He also shared second place (+9=7−3) with POLUGAYEVSKY, after MECKING, at Manila 1976, his fourth interzonal, and became a CANDIDATE. He lost to SPASSKY in the quarter-final.

Besides representing Czechoslovakia in many OLYMPIADS from 1960, Hort played fourth board for the Rest of the World in the match against USSR in 1970, and scored +1=3 against Polugayevsky. A big man with an acute sense of humour, Hort is also a pessimist, and in 1985 he left his homeland and settled for a while in Germany. With JANSA he wrote *The Best Move* (1980), containing 230 instructive positions, but differences in political outlook ended their friendship.

Browne–Hort   Wijk aan Zee 1975   Pirc Defence

1 e4 d6 2 d4 Nf6 3 Nc3 g6 4 Nf3 Bg7 5 Be2 0–0 6 0–0 c6 7 a4 a5 8 Be3 Ng4 9 Bg5 h6 10 Bh4 Na6 11 Re1 Nb4 12 Bc4 g5 13 Bg3 Nf6 14 Nd2 d5 15 Bb3 Bg4 16 f3 Bh5 17 Be5 Qb6 18 Kh1 Rfd8 19 Qe2 Rac8 20 Rad1 Bg6 21 Qf1 Rd7 22 f4 gxf4 23 Qxf4

23 ... Nxc2 24 Bxc2 Qxb2 25 Bxf6 exf6 26 Qe3 Qxc2 27 Rc1 Qb2 28 Nxd5 Re8 29 Nc4 Qa2 30 Re2 Qxe2 31 Qxe2 cxd5 32 Nb6 Rdd8 33 Qb5 Bxe4 34 Qxa5 f5 35 Qd2 Re6 36 a5 Rg6 37 Rg1 Bf8 38 Na4 Rc8 39 Nc3 Bb4 40 Qb2 Rxc3 White resigns.

Hort–Antoshin Variation, 267 in the DUTCH DEFENCE. According to TAIMANOV this line was originated by HORT around 1960 (e.g. Fuchs–Hort, Halle 1960) and developed by ANTOSHIN soon afterwards.

Hort Variation, 16 in the ENGLISH OPENING, as Quinteros–Hort, Vinkovci 1972.

Horwitz, Bernhard (1808–85), player and composer born in Germany but domiciled in England from 1845. He studied art in Berlin where he gained chess experience as one of the PLEIADES. In England he earned money by playing and teaching chess and by portraiture, especially of children, although he would have preferred to succeed at landscape painting. The greatest players of the time defeated him in match play, but he won against BIRD in 1851 (+7=4−3); it was the year of the great London tournament in which Horwitz defeated Bird in the first round and was then knocked out by STAUNTON. In the following year KLING opened his chess and coffee rooms in Oxford Street and assisted Horwitz by appointing him chess professional 'in daily attendance'. Kling was also the driving force behind their joint editorship of a magazine, *The Chess Player* (1851-3), and a book, *Chess Studies* (1851). Horwitz is chiefly remembered for this pioneering book which contains 208 studies and DIDACTIC POSITIONS, with an analysis of the MUZIO GAMBIT added, perhaps, to increase sales. In 1857 he was appointed professional at the Manchester Chess Club and through his influence BLACKBURNE learned much about the endgame. Horwitz retained his interest in this phase and crowned his composing career by winning first prize in the world's first study-composing tourney, an international event organized by LÖWENTHAL in 1862.

Eight years after Kling's death Horwitz published *Chess Studies and End-Games* (1884). It contains 427 positions including all those in *Chess Studies* and more than 50 other studies composed with Kling's collaboration, and to conceal their origin Horwitz prepared the entire manuscript by hand. From cover to cover he never mentioned Kling. (This ingratitude was remedied in the posthumous edition of 1889.) (See BODEN'S MATE; KLING.)

Horwitz Attack, 1002 in the SCOTCH GAME, played by HORWITZ in his match with STAUNTON in 1846. In his *Chess-Player's Handbook* (1847), Staunton expressed the view that Horwitz's move rehabilitated 4 Nxd4 which had been under a cloud following the popularity of the PULLING COUNTER-ATTACK, 1001.

Howell Attack, 723 in the SPANISH OPENING, named after the American Clarence Seaman Howell (1881–1936), whose analysis appeared in the *British Chess Magazine*, 1922. The variation was played four times in the world championship match tournament, 1948, and as a result was called the Moscow Attack or the Keres Variation.

Hromádka Defence, 278, sometimes called the Loose Gambit, or Benoni Deferred. It was introduced by the Czech master Karel Hromádka (1887–1956) in the Piešt'any tournament, 1922. The play that follows often leads to the MODERN BENONI.

Hrubý, Vincenz (1856–1917), Czech-born player whose best results, including match wins against ENGLISCH, in 1882 (+3=1−1), and ALBIN, in 1891 (+5=1−3), were obtained when he was living in Vienna. He was a schoolteacher in Trieste.

Hübner, Robert (1948–), International Grandmaster (1970), the strongest German player in the second half of the 20th century, papyrologist. At 18 he was joint winner of the West German championship, at 19 he was first (+7=8) at Büsum 1968, and at 21 he became a CANDIDATE, having scored +10−10−3 to share second place with GELLER and LARSEN, after FISCHER, at the Palma de Majorca interzonal, 1970. He played PETROSYAN in the quarter-final, drew six games, lost the seventh, and resigned the match on account of stress aggravated by street noises. (Petrosyan turned off his hearing aid.)

At the Skopje Olympiad, 1972, Hübner made the best first-board score (+12=6) and followed that with several good tournament results: Houston 1974, first; Biel interzonal 1976, equal fifth (+6=11−2); Tilburg 1977 and 1978, both very strong tournaments in which Hübner scored +3=6−2 to share third place; Munich 1979, first equal with ANDERSSON, BALASHOV, and SPASSKY; and Rio de Janeiro interzonal 1979, first (+7=9−1) equal with PORTISCH and Petrosyan. Again a Candidate, Hübner beat ADORJÁN (+2=7−1) and Portisch (+2=9), then met KORCHNOI in the final. When trailing +2=3−3 with two games adjourned he withdrew, finding the stress unacceptable.

As a finalist in this match series Hübner automatically became a Candidate in the next championship cycle, but lost the quarter-final to SMYSLOV

on tie-break when the scores were +1=12−1. Meanwhile he had been second (+4=5−3) equal with Korchnoi, after Andersson, at Johannesburg 1981, and first (+6=4), ahead of Korchnoi, at Chicago 1982. His best results since then are: Biel 1984, first (+6=4−1) equal with HORT; Linares 1985, first (+4=6−1) equal with LJUBOJEVIĆ; Tilburg 1985, first (+4=9−1) equal with MILES and Korchnoi; Solingen 1986, first (+7=3−1); Munich 1988, second (+3=8) after HJARTARSON. In 1990 he was fifth at the interzonal, Manila, and became a Candidate for the fourth time. Later in the same year, once more in the German Olympiad team, he made the highest rating performance (2720) of all the competitors. In the candidates match at Sarajevo 1991 he was defeated by TIMMAN.

M. van Fondern and P. Kleine, *Dr Robert Hübner—60 seiner schönsten Partien* (1981).

Hübner–Ivanchuk   Novi Sad 1990 Olympiad   Pirc Defence

1 e4 d6 2 d4 Nf6 3 Nc3 g6 4 Nf3 Bg7 5 Be2 0–0 6 0–0 Bg4 7 Be3 Nc6 8 Qd2 e5 9 d5 Ne7 10 Rad1 Ne8 11 Ng5 Bxe2 12 Nxe2 h6 13 Nh3 Kh7 14 f4 exf4 15 Rxf4 Ng8 16 Rdf1 Qe7 17 Bd4 Be5 18 R4f3 Nef6 19 Nf2 Nd7 20 Nd3 Bxd4+ 21 Nxd4 Ndf6 22 Qb4 Qxe4 23 Rxf6 Nxf6 24 Rxf6 Qxd5

25 Nf5 gxf5 26 Qh4 Kg8 27 Rxh6 f6 28 Qh5 Black resigns.

Hübner Variation, 318 in the NIMZO-INDIAN DEFENCE as Najdorf–Hübner, Wijk aan Zee 1971. The idea is to follow with Pd7–d6 and leave White with DOUBLED PAWNS.

Hug, Werner (1952–), Swiss champion, 1975, and winner of the World Junior Championship in 1971. He has not become a great player.

Hume, George (1862–1936), Scottish problemist who settled in England. For about 20 years he edited the books of the Christmas Series for A. C. WHITE, often receiving material that was, says White, 'in the most sketchy form, incomplete in all directions'. These books have become collectors' items, and they include *Changing Fashions* (1925), containing 150 of Hume's own problems.

After retirement he took over A. C. White's extensive problem collection (weighing 'about half a ton') and known subsequently as the White–Hume Collection. He attempted to keep this up to date, for the purpose of checking ANTICIPATIONS, spending eight hours a day on the task. After his death the collection was broken up and parcelled out to others.

Hundsdorfer, Wolfgang August Eduard (1879–1951), German problemist, a pioneer in the field of RETROGRADE ANALYSIS in the early years of the 20th century. He wrote part of *Retrograde Analysis* (1915), but before publication he gave up chess activities altogether, as far as is known. The book was completed by DAWSON. (See PERPETUAL RETROGRESSION.)

Hungarian Defence, 937, a move given by COZIO which took its name from a correspondence game between Paris and Pest, 1842–5. Also 1156, the KOLISCH DEFENCE to the KING'S GAMBIT Accepted.

Hungarian Variation, 381 in the GRÜNFELD DEFENCE, played in the game Portisch–Adorján, Budapest 1970, and by other Hungarian players at that time; 563 in the SICILIAN DEFENCE, played by BENKO in the 1950s and sometimes called the Accelerated Fianchetto Variation (see RIBLI); 542 in the same opening, the CHEKHOVER VARIATION.

Hunt Opening, 6, the ORANG UTAN OPENING, practised by the Canadian-born English doctor Joseph William Hunt (1851–1920).

Husák, Karel (1925–), Czech player who shared second place with HÝBL after BERLINER in the 5th World Correspondence Championship, 1965–8, a performance that earned him the title of International Correspondence Chess Grandmaster (1968).

Hutton pairing, a method of matching many teams while demanding only one game from each player. Devised in 1921 by a Scottish clergyman, George Dickson Hutton (1866–1929), this pairing method has since been used regularly for correspondence team events and for matches where many teams assemble for a single day—hence the alternative name, jamboree pairing. The players in each team are ranked in order of strength, and each player meets someone with a similar ranking. When the number of teams is one more than the number of boards, each team meets every other team on one board, an ideal arrangement; but organizers have tables enabling them to cope with any numbers of teams or boards. A similar technique, but with every team meeting every other team on two boards (or on one board for two points in the event of odd numbers), is called the Crépeaux System, possibly after the former French champion, Robert Crépeaux (1900–94).

Hýbl, Jaroslav (1928–), Czech player, International Correspondence Chess Grandmaster (1968), a postal player whose best achievement was second place shared with HUSÁK after BERLINER in the 5th World Correspondence Championship, 1965–8.

Hyde, Thomas (1636–1703), English author of the first scholarly attempt to unravel the origins of chess, professor of Hebrew and Arabic at Oxford, Bodley's librarian, archdeacon of Gloucester. One of the first Europeans to gain a knowledge of Chinese, he was interpreter of oriental languages for Charles II, James II, and William III. His *Historia sahiludii* (1689) and *Historia nerdiludi* (1694) are usually found together as *De ludis orientalibus* (1694). The first of these examines the earliest traces of chess and reaches the conclusion that it was invented in India and thence taken to Iran and Arabia. Written in Latin, with large verbatim extracts in other languages and alphabets, it was reprinted in 1767 as the second volume of Hyde's collected works.

hypermodern, TARTAKOWER'S name for a movement that flourished in the 1920s brought about in reaction to TARRASCH'S formalistic teachings. The founder is generally considered to be NIMZOWITSCH. He, ALEKHINE, BOGOLJUBOW, GRÜNFELD, and RÉTI re-examined the main problem of the opening phase: how to control or dispute control of the centre. Many openings and opening variations introduced by them have since become standard play. (See SCHOOLS OF CHESS.)

I

IBCA, the International Braille Chess Association, see BLIND, CHESS FOR THE.

ICCA, the International Correspondence Chess Association, see CORRESPONDENCE CHESS.

ICCF, the International Correspondence Chess Federation, see CORRESPONDENCE CHESS.

ICF, the International Chess Federation, the English name for the FIDE, now seldom used.

ideal mate, a PURE MATE in which all the men on the board take part, a termination sometimes featured by composers.

+

A problem by BAZLOV, first prize *ex æquo, New Statesman,* 1975. 1 Nf3+ Ke4 2 Rc3 Ng4+ 3 Ke6 b1=N 4 Rb3 Kf4 5 Ng1 Nd2 6 Rd3 Ne4 7 Nh3#.
(See also CHÉRON; KLING; KOROLKOV.)

ideal stalemate, a STALEMATE in which all the men on the board take part, in which no square in the king's field is attacked by more than one enemy man, and in which men acting as self-blocks are not under attack unless necessarily pinned. For examples, see MIRROR STALEMATE; SOMOV-NASIMOVICH.

IGM, INTERNATIONAL GRANDMASTER, a title awarded by FIDE.

illegal move, a move of a piece or pawn in a manner that is not permitted by the laws. If a player makes such a move and this is discovered during the game, even after adjournment, the position must be reinstated as it was before the move was made and play continued in accordance with the TOUCH AND MOVE LAW. If reinstatement is impossible the game is annulled and a fresh one played. (Article 8 of the laws of chess.) If the illegal move is discovered after the game has ended there is no remedy.

This position arose between two grandmasters, Motwani–Chandler, British zonal, Blackpool 1990, both players in time-trouble. The game went 30 Nxg7+ Rxf4. White, seeing that 31 gxf4 Rg8 pinned the knight, resigned. Then, both players saw that 30 . . . Rxf4 was an illegal move, but the game had ended with the resignation, which had to stand.

In the 19th century some writers used the term 'false move' when a man was moved contrary to the laws, such as moving a knight like a bishop.

illegal position, (1) a position, in a game, that should not have arisen. Article 8 of the laws of chess lays down the following procedure: if the board has been placed incorrectly (i.e. h1 is a dark square) the position must be transferred to a correctly placed board and the play continued; if after men have been accidentally displaced, or after adjournment, the position is incorrectly set up, the position shall be reinstated and play continued; if the array has been incorrectly set, or if the position cannot be reconstructed after the men have been accidentally displaced, the game is annulled and a fresh one commenced. These remedies are to be applied only if the illegal position is discovered during play. During a tournament in London 1989 a game Wilder–K. Arkell commenced 1 e4 c6 2 d4 d5 3 Nc3 g6 4 Nf3 Bg4 5 h3 Bxf3 6 Qxf3 dxe4 7 Nxe4 Qxd4. At this point the players, disturbed by sunshine reflecting from the board, moved to a different part of the room, and play continued 8 Bd2 Nf6 9 Nxf6+ Qxf6 10 Qb3 Qe6+ 11 Qxe6 fxe6 12 Bc3 Rg8 13 g3 Bg7 14 Bxg7 Rxg7 15 Bh3 and the game was drawn after 51 moves. Only later was it discovered that during the relocation White's h-pawn had been re-set on h2.

illegal position, (2) a composed position that could not have arisen from the ARRAY by legal means, e.g. a position containing white pawns at a2, a3, and b2. Such positions are forbidden in studies (by definition) and in many kinds of problem (by convention). A composer may state that one side is to play although the position could have arisen only if it were the other side's turn to play, an illegal situation known as RETRO-STALEMATE. To determine whether a position is legal may require RETROGRADE ANALYSIS.

Illescas Cordoba, Miguel (1965–), Spanish player, International Grandmaster (1988), who performed well in the exceptionally strong tournament at Linares 1988 (+1=9−1) when he was equal sixth; at Barcelona 1990 he was second (+3−6) after GRANDA.

Ilyin-Genevsky, Alexander Fyodorovich (1894–1941), Soviet player. Expelled from school at the age of 17 because of his radical ideas, Ilyin was sent to Geneva to complete his education. After winning the championship of Geneva in 1914 he added the town's name to his own. He returned to Russia, fought in the First World War and, suffering from shell-shock, found that he had forgotten how to play chess, and had to re-learn the game.

Ilyin-Genevsky organized the 'First All-Russia Chess Olympiad', later called the first USSR championship, 1920, and played in nine of the first ten USSR championships, 1920–37. He was champion of Leningrad in 1925 (equal with LEVENFISH, RABINOVICH, and ROMANOVSKY), 1926, and 1929, and winner of the first Trades Unions championship of the USSR, 1927. An energetic organizer, he was editor of *Shakhmatny Listok*, 1925–30. An interesting account of his early life was translated into English as *Notes of a Soviet Chessmaster* (1986), to which 49 of his games have been added. Fleeing the siege of Leningrad, he was the only person killed when the barge was bombed.

Ilyin-Genevsky Variation, 253, a standard line, sometimes called the Old Dutch, in the DUTCH DEFENCE which first became popular in the 1920s, an alternative to the Stonewall Defence, 251 (see STONEWALL); 1262 in the ALEKHINE DEFENCE, analysed in 1927 by Nikolai Tikhonovich Sorokin (1900–84) and played in the Leningrad championship 1936 in the game Ilyin-Genevsky–Levenfish.

IM, INTERNATIONAL MASTER, a title awarded by FIDE.

imitator, a 'piece', invented for use in FAIRY PROBLEMS, that cannot check, obstruct, capture, or be captured; belonging to neither White nor Black, it imitates in length and direction all moves made by other men, and its move has the same limitations and requirements as that of the man being imitated. Moves that cannot be imitated cannot be made. Castling is regarded as two moves, first the king, then the rook. A man may be moved to or beyond a square occupied by an imitator, for the imitation is

simultaneous. Like a shadow, the imitator cannot be moved independently, and might better be called a fairy stipulation than a piece. The Dutch composer Theodorus Cornelis Louis Kok (1906–), using the pseudonym GJ (= Gerrit Jansen), invented the imitator in 1939.

#2

A problem (after J. E. H. Creed) by the British composer BEASLEY, *The Problemist*, 1989. The piece on g2 is an imitator. The key is 1 Bb6(If1). This is not check because the imitator cannot now be moved to the north-west.

   1 . . . Nc3(Id2)   2 Kb4(Ie1)#
   1 . . . Nf4(Ig3)+   2 Kb5(Ih3)#
   1 . . . Ng3(Ih2)   2 Ka4(Ih1)#
   1 . . . Nd4(Ie3)+   2 Bxd4(Ig1)#.

Immortal Game, a name given by FALKBEER in 1855 to the following FRIENDLY GAME.

Anderssen–Kieseritzky   London, 1851   Bishop's Gambit

1 e4 e5 2 f4 exf4 3 Bc4 Qh4+ 4 Kf1 b5 5 Bxb5 Nf6 6 Nf3 Qh6 7 d3 Nh5 8 Nh4 Qg5? 9 Nf5 c6 10 g4 Nf6 11 Rg1 cxb5 12 h4 Qg6 13 h5 Qg5 14 Qf3 Ng8 15 Bxf4 Qf6 16 Nc3 Bc5 17 Nd5!? Qxb2

Having already sacrificed a bishop, ANDERSSEN now makes a DOUBLE ROOK SACRIFICE. 18 Bd6 Bxg1 (instead, 18 . . . Qxa1 + 19 Ke2 Qb2 is better) 19 e5 Qxa1 + 20 Ke2 Black resigns (*La Régence*, July 1851). Later sources give a possible continuation, 20 . . . Na6 21 Nxg7+ Kd8 22 Qf6+ Nxf6 23 Be7 mate. White also wins after 20 . . . Ba6 21 Nc7+ Kd8 22 Nxa6.

Immortal Problem, see BAYER.

incomplete block, see BLOCK.

Indian Defence, 275, a name given in 1924 to this variation, hitherto called simply Irregular Opening, by TARTAKOWER in his book *Indisch*. In the first half of the 19th century MOHESCHUNDER had defended against 1 d4 by 1 . . . Nf6 and followed with a king's or queen's FIANCHETTO, a development that may properly be called 'Indian'. Players of the HYPERMODERN movement often and systematically began the game this way. As well as leading to the KING'S INDIAN DEFENCE, QUEEN'S INDIAN DEFENCE, NIMZO-INDIAN DEFENCE, OLD INDIAN DEFENCE, GRÜNFELD DEFENCE, and so on, the reply 1 . . . Nf6 can lead to many openings that are in no sense 'Indian'.

Indian Opening, 659, a name used in the second half of the 19th century when Valentine Green (1831–77), who had recently returned from India, played this in the London tournament of 1862, and elsewhere. It was played at New York 1889 by Hanham, and sometimes bears his name.

In modern times the term is used occasionally when White opens with a move characteristic of an INDIAN DEFENCE but with a move in hand.

Indian Theme, the name of a famous PROBLEM theme: a LINE-PIECE is moved across a critical square (see CRITICAL PLAY), another piece of the same colour is moved to this square, creating a BATTERY, and may then be moved again to unmask the piece that was moved first.

#3

A version of a problem by LOVEDAY, *Chess Player's Chronicle*, 1845. 1 Bc1 (a critical move) 1 . . . b4 2 Rd2 (White places his rook on the critical square creating a battery) 2 . . . Kf4 3 Rd4 mate. The interference move (2 Rd2) releases Black from a stalemate situation, a common but not essential ingredient of the theme. In the original problem there was an extra black pawn on b6 and mate in four was stipulated. There were nine KEYS and many DUALS, but the problem was not considered unsound since the composer's intentions cannot be circumvented: White can fulfil the stipulations only by means of the 'Indian' manœuvre. (See OUDOT.)

Although CRITICAL PLAY had been shown in the old game (see MANṢŪBA), this is the first known example in a problem of the modern game, and its publication marked the beginning of the so-called transitional period (SEE PROBLEM HISTORY).

Ingo classification, SEE RATING.

initial array, SEE ARRAY.

initiative, the power to make threats. To have the initiative is to be able to make threats that are more effective than those the opponent can make, thus dictating the course of the game. When play commences, White, having the first move, has the initiative; its value may become insignificant as play continues and Black is then said to have EQUALIZED. To maintain the initiative White must often follow well-analysed paths, but may prefer to avoid these, choosing a quiet opening and forfeiting the initiative in order to set Black an unfamiliar task. Sometimes Black acts aggressively, forcing White to play sharply to retain the initiative. For example, after 1 e4 Nf6 White must either passively guard the e-pawn, or advance it with attendant risk; as TARTAKOWER remarked of this opening, 'White has his initiative to defend.'

The struggle for initiative continues throughout the game. Some players concede material, or accept other disadvantages, rather than give up the initiative: they rightly suppose that mistakes are more likely to be made by a defender than by an attacker, and that errors in defence are more likely to be fatal. Others like to gain material and are prepared to play defensively, ceding the initiative, if only for a time. The choice centres on personal style.

Innocent Morality, an allegory written in the middle of the 13th century, probably by a British friar, John of Waleys. It appears in one manuscript of his works and the Latin of all the known manuscripts has an English character. The *Innocent Morality* also appears in a manuscript collection of the sermons of Pope Innocent III, but does not accord with his exalted view of the clergy. 'The alphins [AUFINS] are the various prelates of the church, Pope, Archbishop, and their subordinate bishops, who rise to their Sees not so much by divine inspiration as by royal power, interest, entreaties, and ready money. These alphins move and take obliquely three points, for almost every prelate's mind is perverted by love, hatred, or bribery, not to reprehend the guilty, or bark against the vicious, but rather to absolve them of their sins: so that those who should have extirpated vice are in consequence of their own covetousness become promoters of vice and advocates of the Devil.' The morality was published *c.*1470 as part of *Summa collationum* by Joh. Gallensis, and this is the earliest known printed reference to chess.

interfere, to place a man so that a line-piece on one side of that man cannot attack squares on the other side. On an otherwise empty board, place a queen at a1 and a man at a7, using men of either colour; the man at a7 interferes with the queen by preventing its being moved to a8. Thus, interference, the action of interfering.

International Arbiter, a title created by FIDE in 1951 and awarded to candidates who have suitable experience of conducting tournaments and matches. An arbiter should have detailed knowledge of the laws and rules and be able to speak one language (English, French, German, Russian, or Spanish) other than his own.

International Correspondence Chess Grandmaster, a title created by FIDE in 1953, second only to that of world correspondence champion.

International Correspondence Chess Master, a FIDE title ranking below that of International Correspondence Chess Grandmaster, first awarded in 1953.

International Grandmaster (IGM), the highest official title (other than world champion) for OVER-THE-BOARD play, first awarded by FIDE in 1950. One way of qualifying is to achieve a specific number of GM NORMS in tournament play. The standard for these has been raised more than once, but owing to the inbuilt inflationary bias in ELO RATING the number of qualifiers increases geometrically. Lower titles are International Master and FIDE Master.

International Grandmaster for Chess Compositions, the highest FIDE title for composers, first awarded to KASPARYAN, LOSHINSKY, MANSFIELD, and VISSERMAN in 1972. Composers qualify for this title when a sufficient number of their compositions have been published in FIDE ALBUMS.

International Judge of Chess Compositions, a title created by FIDE in 1956 and awarded to those who have judged composing tourneys to the satisfaction of a committee appointed by the Permanent FIDE Commission for Chess Compositions.

International Master (IM), a title for OVER-THE-BOARD play instituted by FIDE in 1950. The most common method of qualifying is by reaching the required number of IM NORMS in tournaments. (Compare INTERNATIONAL GRANDMASTER; FIDE MASTER.)

International Master for Chess Compositions. Created by FIDE in 1959, ranking below INTERNATIONAL GRANDMASTER FOR CHESS COMPOSITIONS, this title was first awarded *honoris causa* to CHÉRON, ELLERMAN, HARTONG, HERBSTMAN, Kipping, and MANSFIELD. Subsequently the IM title was awarded on the basis of points scored in the FIDE ALBUMS.

international solving titles, master and grandmaster, were inaugurated in 1982, and are awarded according to results obtained in the world championships for solving problems and studies.

International Woman Master (IWM). Restricted to women players, this title, first awarded by FIDE in 1950, ranks below that of WOMAN GRANDMASTER (WGM).

interpose, to move a man so that it interferes with the action of a line-piece of the opposite colour. For example, after 1 d4 e6 2 c4 Bb4+ White interposes by moving a man to c3 or d2.

Interzonal Tournament, a FIDE qualifying tournament for the world championship, open to those who qualify in a ZONAL TOURNAMENT or who have been seeded by FIDE. Successful competitors become CANDIDATES. Eight interzonal tournaments were held at approximately three-year intervals from 1948 to 1970. Two parallel interzonals were held in 1973, 1976, and 1979, and three in 1982, 1985, and 1987. In 1990 a single Swiss system tournament of 64 players was introduced.

introductory play, a composer's term for play that leads to but is not an essential part of the central idea or theme of a composition. For examples see ORGAN PIPES, and the problem by Plachutta given under CUTTING-POINT THEMES. No longer fashionable in problems, introductory play remains a common feature in studies.

Inverted Grünfeld Variation, 1301, in which White follows the plan of the GRÜNFELD DEFENCE.

Inverted Hanham Opening, 1011, so called because White sets up a DEFENSIVE CENTRE similar to that set up by Black in the HANHAM VARIATION, 1022, of the PHILIDOR DEFENCE.

Inverted Hungarian Opening, 1010, so called because White's king's bishop is placed as Black's would be in the HUNGARIAN DEFENCE, 937.

Iordansky Attack, 952, enterprising variation of the TWO KNIGHTS DEFENCE analysed by the Moscow player Peter Konstantinovich Iordansky (1891–1937), champion of Moscow in 1913 and of the Red Army and Navy in 1927.

IQP, a popular abbreviation for the ISOLATED QUEEN'S PAWN.

Irish Gambit, 1012, the CHICAGO GAMBIT. On his death bed the anonymous inventor was asked what subtlety lay behind his gambit (so the tale runs), and his last words were: 'I hadn't seen the king's pawn was defended.'

irregular opening, in the early 19th century any opening that did not begin 1 e4 e5 or 1 d4 d5. However, JAENISCH said, 'As this distinction is purely arbitrary, and unfounded on principle, we cannot ourselves adopt it. We distinguish all the openings as "correct", or else as "incorrect" or "hazardous".' Since then many so-called irregular openings have become standard play. These and many other openings have acquired names and the term 'irregular opening' has gradually fallen into disuse.

isolani, NIMZOWITSCH'S jargon for the ISOLATED QUEEN'S PAWN.

isolated pawn. A pawn is isolated when there are no pawns of the same colour on adjoining files. If attacked it may be a weakness, for it must be defended by pieces which then assume a passive role; if the square in front of such a pawn is not occupied by an enemy pawn then that square is a HOLE, sometimes a source of weakness. On the other hand an isolated pawn may confer advantage: it guards ADVANCE POINTS on adjoining files; if supported by pieces it might be moved forward to disrupt the opponent's game. (See ISOLATED QUEEN'S PAWN.) If passed and far from the scene of action an isolated pawn could be used as a DECOY. (See OUTSIDE PASSED PAWN.)

isolated queen's pawn (IQP), an isolated pawn on the d-file. Positions with an IQP commonly occur, and the argument as to whether the pawn is weak, as STEINITZ believed, or strong, as TARRASCH thought, has continued long after the passing of these two great masters. Devoting a chapter of *My System* to this question, NIMZOWITSCH believed that a player should learn how to manœuvre both with and against such a pawn. In general its strength is felt in the middlegame, its weakness in the endgame. A player who has an IQP gains freer piece play and, in consequence, prospects of an attack. The files that adjoin the pawn and the ADVANCE POINTS it guards may be occupied; sometimes the pawn may be advanced to break through in the centre. Even if the pawn is blocked an attack may be developed. In the endgame the isolated queen's pawn, although disadvantageous, is not alone a fatal weakness. In world championship matches both SPASSKY (v. PETROSYAN 1969) and KORCHNOI (v. KARPOV 1978) accepted an isolated queen's pawn in five and six games respectively, and they lost none of these games.

Flohr–Capablanca   Moscow 1935   Queen's Gambit Declined

1 d4 d5 2 c4 e6 3 Nc3 Nf6 4 Nf3 Nbd7 5 Bg5 Be7 6 e3 0–0 7 Qc2 c5 8 cxd5 Nxd5 9 Bxe7 Qxe7 10 Nxd5 exd5 11 Bd3 cxd4 12 Nxd4 Qb4+ 13 Qd2 Nc5 14 Bb5 Qxd2+ 15 Kxd2 a6 16 Bd3 Be6 17 Rac1 Rfc8 18 Rc2 Nxd3 19 Kxd3 Rxc2 20 Kxc2 Kf8 21 Kd2 Rc8 22 Rc1 Rxc1 23 Kxc1 Ke7

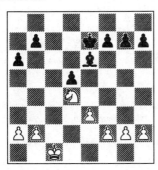

24 Kd2 Kd6 25 Kc3 b6 26 f4 Bd7 27 Nf3 f6 28 Kd4 a5 29 Nd2 Bc8 30 Nb1 Be6 31 Nc3 Kc6 32 a3 h6 33 g3 h5 34 b4 axb4 35 axb4 Kd6 36 b5 g6 37 Na4 Kc7 38 Nc3 Kd6 39 f5 gxf5 40 Ne2 Bd7 41 Nf4 Be8 42 Nxd5 Bxb5 43 Nxb6 Bc6 44 Nc4+ Ke6 45 Nb2 Bb5 46 Nd1 Be2 47 Nf2 Bf1 48 Nd3 Bxd3 49 Kxd3 Ke5 50 Ke2 Ke4 (ZUGZWANG) 51 h3 Kd5 52 Kf3 Ke5 (zugzwang) draw agreed.

The defence in this endgame brought to a head a change in the evaluation of the IQP: previously regarded as an undesirable weakness, it became acceptable, conferring in itself neither advantage nor disadvantage.

Italian bishop, a bishop on the ITALIAN DIAGONAL.

Italian Defence, 646, the DEL RIO VARIATION of the ITALIAN OPENING.

Italian diagonal, the diagonal a2-g8 for White, a7-g1 for Black, so named because in the ITALIAN OPENING both players move their king's bishops to this diagonal. This was regarded as the best possible development for these bishops until the SPANISH OPENING began to gain ground in the 1850s. Each bishop bears down upon the opposing f-pawn and may assist in a king's side attack. For examples, see BAGIROV and KAMSKY. Also, in the game given under BOLBOCHÁN the White bishop on this diagonal plays an essential part in the opening manœuvres.

After about a century during which the Bishop Opening 1 e4 e5 2 Bc4 was rarely played, it was revived successfully by LARSEN, NUNN, and a few others. At about the same time FISCHER popularized this development (Bf1-c4) in several variations of the SICILIAN DEFENCE.

Italian Opening, 866, often called the Giuoco Piano (Quiet Game). The main line, 4 c3 Nf6 5 d4 exd4 6 cxd4 Bb4+ leads to an even game; an interesting alternative for White is the EVANS GAMBIT, 867. The opening remained popular from the time of LUCENA until the second half of the 19th century. To the Modenese masters it was the best of all possible openings and to those who liked attacking play it was the gateway to the Evans Gambit. From about 1850 the SPANISH OPENING, 673, gradually became more popular; however, the Italian Opening was played in the world championship matches of 1889, 1890, 1892, 1894, 1896, and 1981. (See BARDELEBEN.)

Italian Variation, 712, sometimes called the Viennese Variation, in the SPANISH OPENING. The black bishop moves to the ITALIAN DIAGONAL; 858 or, more commonly, 941 in the FOUR KNIGHTS OPENING, where the white bishop occupies the Italian Diagonal (see MASON); 1054 in the PETROFF DEFENCE, similarly.

Ivanchuk, Vasily (1969–), Ukrainian player, International Grandmaster (1988), European Junior Champion 1986-7. After being first in strong tournaments at Tallinn 1986, Lvov 1987

(+6=11), and Debrecen 1988, Ivanchuk performed well at the premier level: equal fifth (+5=9−3) in the 1988 USSR championship; equal fourth (+3=4−2) at Reggio Emilia 1988–9; first at Linares 1989 (+5=5) ahead of KARPOV, LJUBOJEVIĆ, SHORT, and TIMMAN; first at Yerevan 1989 (+7=3−1) in front of LPUTYAN; equal first (+5=8−1) with POLUGAYEVSKY at Biel 1989; second at Reggio Emilia 1989–90 (+3=7), after EHLVEST; and fourth at Linares 1990 (+3=7−1). Playing for the USSR team in the WORLD TEAM CHAMPIONSHIP at Luzern in 1989, he scored 6½ from 7 games.

In 1990 he tied for first place, with GELFAND, in the interzonal tournament at Manila, and became a CANDIDATE. In January 1991 he won his first Candidates match (+4=1) against YUDASIN. A few weeks later he won, +6=7, one of the strongest tournaments of modern times, Linares 1991, ahead of KASPAROV, BELYAVSKY, SPEELMAN, YUSUPOV, and Karpov, inflicting defeats on the world champion and his predecessor.

In August 1991 Ivanchuk lost his second-round Candidates match. In the quick-play tie breaker Yusupov won a fine game, and the second game was drawn.

Although blessed with great energy and ability, Ivanchuk is also moody and emotional. Losing his temper, he has been known to sweep the pieces from the board during a tournament. Seen by some as an anti-hero, he says, 'What's the good of setting goals when their achievement is never in one's own hands?'

Malanyuk–Ivanchuk   USSR Championship 1988
Nimzo-Indian Defence Kmoch Variation

1 d4 Nf6 2 c4 e6 3 Nc3 Bb4 4 f3 d5 5 a3 Be7 6 e4 dxe4 7 fxe4 e5 8 d5 Ng4 9 Nf3 Bc5 10 b4 Bf2+ 11 Ke2 c5 12 Nb5 a6 13 Qa4

13 ... axb5 14 Qxa8 Bd4 15 Nxd4 cxd4 16 Qxb8 0–0 17 Ke1 Qh4+ 18 g3 Qf6 19 Bf4 g5 20 c5 exf4 21 Qd6 Qg7 22 Bd3 Ne5 23 Kd2 f3 24 Bxb5 g4 25 Qe7 Ng6 26 Qg5 h6 27 Qh5 d3 28 Bxd3 Re8 29 h3 Re5 30 hxg4 Rxh5 31 gxh5 Ne5 32 Rae1 Qg5+ 33 Kc2 f2 34 Rd1 Qe3 White resigns.

Ivanović, Božidar (1946–), Yugoslav champion 1973 and 1981, equal first in 1983 but lost the play-off, International Grandmaster (1977), winner of

tournaments at Bar 1977, Priština 1988, and Tarrasa 1989.

Ivkov, Borislav (1933–), Yugoslav player, International Grandmaster (1955), journalist. He began auspiciously by winning the first FIDE World Junior Championship, 1951. His adult career brought him several shared first prizes, including: Beverwijk 1961 (+7=1−1), with LARSEN; Belgrade 1964 (+7=9−1), with KORCHNOI and SPASSKY; Zagreb 1965 (+9=9−1), with UHLMANN, ahead of PETROSYAN (then world champion), PORTISCH, BRONSTEIN, and Larsen; Sarajevo 1967 (+6=9), with STEIN; Belgrade 1969 (+7=6−2), with POLUGAYEVSKY, GLIGORIĆ, and MATULOVIĆ, ahead of BOTVINNIK and GELLER; Amsterdam 1974 (+5=10), with JANSA and TUKMAKOV, ahead of Geller. He won outright (+7=6) at Havana 1985. Ivkov played in interzonal tournaments of 1964, 1967, 1970, 1973, and 1979, usually scoring well, and qualifying as a CANDIDATE in 1964, only to lose to Larsen in the quarter-final, 1965.

Yugoslav champion in 1958 (with Gligorić), 1963 (with Udovčić), and 1972, Ivkov represented his country in many Olympiads from 1956 to 1980, notably making the best score at fourth board (+11=5) in 1962, and at second board (+7=6) in 1970.

Ivkov–Taimanov   Yugoslavia–USSR match 1956   Sicilian Defence Rauzer Variation

1 e4 c5 2 Nf3 Nc6 3 d4 cxd4 4 Nxd4 Nf6 5 Nc3 d6 6 Bg5 e6 7 Qd2 Be7 8 0–0–0 0–0 9 f4 Nxd4 10 Qxd4 h6 11 Bh4 Qa5 12 e5 dxe5 13 Qxe5 Qxe5 14 fxe5 Nd5 15 Bxe7 Nxe7 16 Bd3 Bd7 17 Bh7+ Kxh7 18 Rxd7 Nc6 19 Rxb7 Nxe5

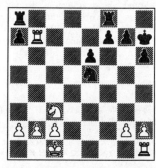

20 Re1 f6 21 Re3 Rfb8 22 Rc7 Rc8 23 Nb5 Rab8 24 Ra3 a5 25 Rxc8 Rxc8 26 Nd4 Nc4 27 Rc3 e5 28 b3 Nd6 29 Rxc8 Nxc8 30 Nc6 a4 31 bxa4 Kg6 32 a5 Kf7 33 a6 Ke6 34 a7 Nb6 35 Nb4 Kd6 36 c4 Kc5 37 Nd5 Na8 38 Ne3 Kb6 39 Nf5 Kxa7 40 Nxg7 Nb6 41 g4 Nxc4 42 Nf5 e4 43 Nxh6 Ne5 44 h4 Kb6 45 h5 Kc5 46 Kd2 Kd5 47 Nf5 Nf3+ 48 Ke2 Ng5 49 h6 Black resigns.

Ivkov Variation, 509 in the SICILIAN DEFENCE, as in the game Ivkov–Petrosyan, Bled 1961.

IWM, see INTERNATIONAL WOMAN MASTER.

J

j'adoube, the usual warning given, when adjusting a piece or pawn, by a player whose turn it is to move. The obsolete French verb, used in the days of chivalry, corresponds to the English 'dub'. The TOUCH AND MOVE LAW requires a statement of intention to be given in such cases, although the exact form is not specified. Weak players often try to give respectability to the retraction of a move by using this phrase after the event, and such inexcusable behaviour has been known even at the highest level. At the Sousse interzonal 1967, Grandmaster MATULOVIĆ, playing BILEK, withdrew a losing move saying 'Ich spreche j'adoube'; this ruse went unpunished, but he earned the nickname J'adoubović.

There are no specific laws restricting the adjustment of men by the player who is not on the move, but an arbiter could impose a penalty if such action appeared to be distracting the other player.

Jaenisch (pron. yanish), Carl Friedrich Andreyevich (1813–72), player and author. Born in Vyborg, then in Finland, he was educated first in Moscow and then in St Petersburg, where he became an assistant professor of mechanics. Commissioned in the Engineers, he rose to the rank of major, but in 1838 he began to write a book on openings and two years later left the army 'because he loved chess so much'. To further his research he travelled to Warsaw and Germany where he collaborated with PETROFF and LASA, the best two analysts of the time. After four years' labour he produced his major work, *Analyse nouvelle des ouvertures du jeu des échecs* (1842–3). A single-volume English version by WALKER, *Chess Preceptor*, was published in 1847. (For some of its original contents, see BIRD DEFENCE, BISHOP'S GAMBIT, JAENISCH COUNTERATTACK, JAENISCH VARIATION, LESSER BISHOP'S GAMBIT, NIMZOWITSCH DEFENCE, PETROFF DEFENCE, PONZIANI DEFENCE, and VIENNA GAME.) With this book and Bilguer's HANDBUCH (1843), the development of modern opening play began.

Tutored by Petroff, Jaenisch became a competent but not great player. He made one attempt to play in a tournament (London 1851) but arrived too late and had to content himself with a match against STAUNTON, which he lost (+2=1−7). (See KNIGHT'S TOUR.)

Jaenisch Counterattack, 1034, sometimes called the Nimzowitsch Variation, in the PHILIDOR DEFENCE. Black's 3 . . . Ng8-f6 (JAENISCH, 1842) has stood the test of time, and is often used as a means by which Black may transpose to the HANHAM VARIATION, 1022; 821 in the PONZIANI OPENING, declared by Jaenisch in 1842 to be better than PONZIANI'S 3 . . . f5.

Jaenisch Gambit, 10 in the ENGLISH OPENING, considered risky by JAENISCH, who attributed it to SALVIO; 784 and 691, the SCHLIEMANN DEFENCE and SCHLIEMANN DEFENCE DEFERRED, usually named in Russia and Germany after Jaenisch who, however, considered the BERLIN DEFENCE to be best.

Jaenisch Variation, 652, considered by JAENISCH to be the only sound reply to the CALABRIAN COUNTERGAMBIT; 892 in the EVANS GAMBIT, a line which, in Jaenisch's opinion, proved the inferiority of 5 . . . Bc5; 1018 in the PHILIDOR DEFENCE, given by Jaenisch in 1843; 1104, a standard defence to the BISHOP'S GAMBIT originated by Jaenisch but sometimes named after BOGOLJUBOW, who played it against SPIELMANN at Carlsbad 1923; 1165 in the KIESERITZKY GAMBIT. Also 1114, the LESSER BISHOP'S GAMBIT.

Jaffe Variation, 555 in the SICILIAN DEFENCE, introduced at Carlsbad 1911 by the Russian-born American, Charles Jaffe (c.1879–1941).

jamboree pairing, see HUTTON PAIRING.

Janošević (pron. yanoshevitch), Dragoljub (1923–). International Grandmaster (1965), chess journalist, a Yugoslav player who won first prize (+7=8) at Vršac 1969 ahead of BENKO.

Janowski (pron. yanofsky), Dawid Markelowicz (1868–1927), Polish-born player who settled in Paris around 1890. He began his professional career in 1894, and achieved his best results within the space of eight years: Vienna 1898, third (+22=7−7), after TARRASCH and PILLSBURY, ahead of CHIGORIN and MARÓCZY; London 1899, second (+15=4−7) equal with Maróczy and Pillsbury, after LASKER but ahead of Chigorin; Monte Carlo 1901, first (+10=3−2), ahead of SCHLECHTER and Chigorin; Vienna 1902, first equal with WOLF; Monte Carlo 1902, third (+14=4−4), after Maróczy and Pillsbury, ahead of Schlechter and Tarrasch; Hanover 1902, first (+11=5−1), ahead of Pillsbury; Cambridge Springs 1904, second (+10=2−3) equal with Lasker, after MARSHALL, ahead of Schlechter; Ostend 1905, second (+15=6−5) equal with Tarrasch, after Maróczy, ahead of Schlechter; Barmen 1905, first

(+9=3−3) equal with Maróczy, ahead of Schlechter.

Janowski played many matches, notably three, backed by a wealthy patron, Leo Nardus (1860–c.1940), against Lasker, one of which was for the world championship. The first, May 1909, was drawn (+2−2); in the second, October 1909, Janowski was heavily defeated (+1=2−7); and in the third, for the title, he was crushed (=3−8). Janowski, playing in the Mannheim 1914 tournament when war began, was after a short internment permitted to travel to Switzerland. The Russian consul in Geneva issued him with a passport, and in December 1915 he went to the USA, scraping a livelihood there for nine years before returning to Paris. In December 1926 he travelled to Hyères to play in a tournament, but died of tuberculosis before it began. A fund was raised to meet his funeral expenses, for he was penniless.

Marshall, who knew Janowski well, writes: 'He had little foibles about the kind of game he liked—his weakness for the two bishops was notorious—and he could follow the wrong path with more determination than any man I met! He was also something of a dandy and quite vain about his appearance.' In Janowski's formative years (1890–4) play rarely went beyond the MIDDLEGAME and his brilliant play in this phase sufficed to earn him, for a short time, a place in the world's leading half-dozen players; but he neither played for the ENDGAME nor played it well, a failing that precluded his becoming a serious contender for the world championship. When Janowski was shown that the loss of a particular game was caused by lack of endgame knowledge his answer, writes CAPABLANCA, was always the same: 'I detest the endgame. A well-played game should be practically decided in the middlegame.' Janowski was addicted to gambling at casinos, and his games show a similar tendency. He played intuitively, always to win, and usually created interesting positions, not always to his advantage; and although he played in many BRILLIANCY PRIZE games he achieved the unusual distinction of losing as many as he won. (See COINCIDENCE.)

S. B. Voronkov and D. G. Plisetsky, *David Yanovsky* (1987), in Russian, containing an excellent biography and 175 games, is the only book about him.

Bogoljubow–Janowski New York 1924 Queen's Gambit Accepted

1 d4 d5 2 Nf3 Nf6 3 c4 dxc4 4 e3 e6 5 Bxc4 c5 6 Nc3 Nc6 7 0–0 Be7 8 Qe2 0–0 9 Rd1 Qc7 10 a3 a6 11 dxc5 Bxc5 12 b4 Be7 13 Bb2 Bd7 14 Rac1 Rac8 15 Bd3 Rfd8 16 Ne4 Nxe4 17 Bxe4 Be8 18 Nd4 Qb6 19 Qf3 Ne5 (A positional sacrifice: Black loses a pawn, but gains TWO BISHOPS and the freer game.) 20 Bxh7+ Kxh7 21 Qh5+ Kg8 22 Qxe5 Bf6 23 Qh5 Ba4 24 Re1 Qd6 25 h3 Bc2 26 Qf3 b5 27 Qe2 Ba4 28 Qf3 Rc4 (After this move Black's rooks dominate the open file. Alekhine recommends 29 Rxc4.) 29 ... Rdc8 30 Rb1 e5 31 Ne2 Bc2 32 Rbc1 Be4 33 Qg4 Bb7 34 Rxc4 Rxc4 35 f4 Qd2 36 Qg3 Re4 37 Bc3 Qd5 38 Bxe5

38 ... Rxe3 39 Qg4 Bxe5 40 fxe5 Rxe5 41 Kh2 Qd2 42 Qg3 f6 43 h4 Bd5 44 Qf2 Bc4 White resigns.

Janowski–Larsen Variation, 75, sometimes known as the Modern Variation, in the QUEEN'S GAMBIT ACCEPTED, from the game Marshall–Janowski, St Petersburg 1914, and played by LARSEN in 1958.

Janowski Variation, 114 in the ALBIN COUNTER-GAMBIT, first played in the game Bernstein–Janowski, Barmen 1905; 116 in the QUEEN'S GAMBIT Declined, introduced by JANOWSKI in a match against SHOWALTER in 1899 (see MINORITY ATTACK); 201 in the same opening, a dubious move played in the game Capablanca–Janowski, New York 1924, and thus sometimes called the New York Variation; 838 in the FOUR KNIGHTS OPENING, played Janowski–Pillsbury, Paris 1900 and called 'Janowski's favourite move' by TARTAKOWER; 1210 in the FRENCH DEFENCE, as Janowski–Burn, Ostend 1907.

Also 203, the BOTVINNIK VARIATION in the Queen's Gambit Declined, as in the game Janowski–Goetz which decided the championship of the CAFÉ DE LA RÉGENCE in 1896; 1237, the ALAPIN VARIATION of the French Defence, which can transpose into 1210, above.

Jansa, Vlastimil (1942–), International Grandmaster (1974), Czech champion in 1964 (after a play-off), 1974, and, jointly with HORT, 1984. A player in many Olympiads since 1964, his chief tournament victories are: Amsterdam 1974 (+7=6−2), equal with IVKOV and TUKMAKOV; Trnava 1982; Kragujevac 1984, equal with Padevsky; Borganes 1985 (+5=6), equal with HANSEN; Prague zonal 1985, equal with PINTÉR and ŞUBA; Gausdal, August 1987, a Swiss with 50 players.

Japanese chess, see SHOGI.

jeopardy, in medieval times a chess position that seemed in the balance, the kind of position that appears today in newspapers and chess magazines as a mental exercise for the reader, the forerunner of the problem. The word is derived from the Old French *jeu parti*, literally a divided game of uncertain issue; in English this was corrupted in various ways, e.g. juperty, and eventually disappeared from chess to pass into general usage with its current meaning.

Jerome Gambit, 930, an unsound gambit suitable only for social chess. It appeared first in *American Chess Journal*, 1876, recommended by Alonzo Wheeler Jerome (1834–1902) of Paxton, Illinois.

Johner, Paul F. (1887–1938), Swiss player and musician who in his later years settled in Berlin, where he died. In two minor tournaments, Copenhagen 1916 and Berlin 1917, he won and shared first prize respectively; but his best win was in a double-round quadrangular tournament at Berlin, Feb. to Mar. 1924, when he came ahead of RUBINSTEIN, TEICH-MANN, and MIESES. He won or shared the Swiss Championship six times from 1907 to 1932, on two occasions (1908, 1928) sharing the title with his brother Hans (1889–1975).

Joker, a man, used for FAIRY PROBLEMS, invented by the German composer Otto Georg Edgar Dehler (1887–1948) in 1939; it takes the powers of the last man (or one of them in the event of castling) moved by the adverse side. When imitating a king, however, it does not suffer royal limitations and might, for example, be moved to a square adjoining that occupied by the opposing king.

\#2

A problem by the British composer John Edward Hodgson Creed (1904–74), *Fairy Chess Review*, 1944. The J represents a white joker. There are GRASSHOPPERS on a1, c2, f6, and g4. A special condition: for the first move White may choose to move the joker like any one of Black's men. The key is 1 Jf5 threatening 2 Qd2#.

1 ... Kd3   2 Qxd6#
1 ... Kd5   2 Nc3#
1 ... B~+   2 Je4#
1 ... Rxb4   2 Qe5#.

Jones, Sir William (1746–94), author of CAÏSSA. A man of astonishing achievements, his upbringing was largely the work of his mother, for when he was three he lost his father, an eminent mathematician. In 1763, inspired by VIDA, he composed *Caïssa*, and the following year persuaded a native of Aleppo

(perhaps STAMMA) to join him at Oxford and coach him in Arabic. By 1768 he had achieved such a reputation that he was asked to translate a Persian manuscript, the life of Nadir Shah, into French for the king of Denmark. The translation, which occupied him for a year, was published in 1770. His only reward was a diploma making him a member of the Royal Society of Copenhagen. He continued to work on the languages of southern Europe and the Middle East until 1774, when he was called to the bar.

He worked diligently at law, and used his linguistic skills to translate a tract on the Muslim laws of inheritance. He wanted to become a judge in India, and although his support for the American revolution damaged his prospects he achieved his ambition in 1783. On arrival in Calcutta he began a study of Sanskrit that ultimately led him to detect there the origin of many western languages and initiate the science of comparative linguistics. He founded the Asiatic Society of Bengal in 1784, and in 1790 its magazine published his paper 'On the Indian game of chess'.

In 1768 he wrote, in Latin, a letter to Charles Rewicki, a Polish diplomat. 'When I reflect on our constitution, I seem as it were to contemplate a game of chess, a recreation in which we both delight. For we have a king whose dignity we strenuously defend, but whose power is very limited; the knights, and bishops, and other pieces, have some kind of resemblance to the order of nobility, who are employed in war, and in the management of public affairs; but the principal strength is in the pawns or people; if they are firmly united they are sure of victory, but if divided and separated, the battle is lost. The motions of all as in the game of chess, are regulated by fixed laws.' (See STAMMA; VIDA.)

Jordansky Attack, see IORDANSKY ATTACK, 952.

Jubair, Sa'id bin (665–714), a Black African who allegedly took up chess to make himself ineligible for an appointment as a judge, which he thought would fit ill with his religious beliefs. (Under Muslim law chess was disapproved of, though not forbidden, and regarded as incompatible with judgeship.) He became the greatest BLINDFOLD CHESS player known and the first to turn his back on the boards in contrast to the contemporary custom of feeling the pieces. Jubair was condemned for his part in a revolt, and his executioner is said to have dreamed that God would kill him once for every man he had killed, but 70 times for the death of Jubair.

He is not to be confused with Jābir al-Kūfī, one of the great players of the early 9th century.

judgement of position, an EVALUATION OF POSITION or an assessment of DYNAMIC FACTORS.

Junge, Klaus (1924–45), born in Chile of German parents who moved to Hamburg in the 1930s, believing their three sons would be better educated in Germany. Junge competed successfully in several tournaments during the early years of the Second World War, and at 17 shared first place with P. SCHMIDT in the German championship of 1941, but lost the play-off. Improving at a phenomenal pace, he came first (+7=3−1) equal with ALEKHINE at Prague 1942. Only BOTVINNIK and SZABÓ had previously shown such playing strength at the age of 18, but this was Junge's last tournament. An officer in the German army, and the last of the three brothers to die in the war, he was killed in action on 17 April 1945, just three weeks before fighting in Europe ended.

Budrich and Schulte, *Das war Klaus Junge* (1956) contains a biography and games.

Lehmann–Junge   Rostock 1942   Queen's Gambit Declined Semi-Slav Defence

1 d4 d5 2 c4 e6 3 Nc3 c6 4 Nf3 Nf6 5 Bg5 dxc4 6 e4 b5 7 e5 h6 8 Bh4 g5 9 Nxg5 hxg5 10 Bxg5 Nbd7 11 Qf3 Bb7 12 Be2 Rg8 13 h4 Qb6 14 exf6 c5 15 d5 b4 16 Bxc4 bxc3

17 dxe6 cxb2 18 Rb1 Rxg5 19 exf7+ Kd8 20 Qc3 Rxg2 21 Rxb2 Qc7 22 Rh3 Rg1+ 23 Ke2 Bg2 24 Rg3 Bf1+ 25 Kd1 Qd6+ 26 Rd2 Qxg3 27 fxg3 Bd3+ mate.

Junge Variation, 137, an alternative to the ABRAHAMS VARIATION in the QUEEN'S GAMBIT Declined introduced in the game Lachmann–Junge, German championship 1941.

K

K, the English language symbol for the king. Thus K-side, meaning KING'S-SIDE.

Kagan, Bernhard (1866–1932), Polish-born player and publisher. As a young man he moved to Berlin and became an amateur publisher; shortly before the First World War, when his business in cigars declined, he became more dependent on chess publishing. In 1921 he launched *Kagans neueste Schachnachrichten*, a rich but chaotic periodical which ran until his death. It had multiple numbers, supplements, special issues, and so on, so that Kagan could publish whatever he liked when it suited him. The whole of the 1924 volume, for example, was published in 1923, so Kagan published special issues 1 to 9/10 in 1924. In a period when inflation presented unusual difficulties Kagan financed many tournaments and sustained German chess activities.

Kalandadze, Velimir Iosifovich (1935–), prolific study composer from Georgia, International Master for Chess Compositions (1984), engineer. Like his compatriot D. GURGENIDZE, his speciality is studies with rooks and pawns, a field previously thought to be barren.

+

A study by Kalandadze, first prize *ex æquo, Shakhmaty v SSSR*, 1979. 1 Kh3 Rh4+ 2 Kxh4 Rb1 3 Ra2+ Kxa2 4 Rc2+ Rb2 5 Rc1 Rb1 6 Rh1 Rxh1 7 h8=Q Rg1 8 Qa8+ Kb2 9 Qh1! Rxh1 10 b7.

kamikaze piece, a piece used for FAIRY PROBLEMS (e.g. a kamikaze knight) that makes non-capturing moves in the normal way, but upon capturing is removed from the board along with the captured man. This fairy piece was invented by LAWS in 1928, but was not named until its rebirth in 1963. The

Japanese word *kamikaze* (divine wind), the name of a typhoon that destroyed an invading Mongol fleet in 1281, was used to describe the suicide pilots of the Second World War. (For kamikaze Circe, see CIRCE.)

Kaminer, Sergey Mikhailovich (1908–38), Soviet study composer, chemical engineer. A perfectionist, he won tourney awards for a high proportion of his published studies. (See CROSS-PIN.) In October or November 1937, a few months before he disappeared, Kaminer handed a notebook containing all his work on studies to BOTVINNIK for safe-keeping because he had a feeling that his compositions would otherwise be lost. 'His presentiment turned out to be correct', wrote Botvinnik, who revealed the existence of the notebook in the 1950s after Stalin's death. Some years later Kaminer was 'posthumously reinstated', but a great composer had been cut off in his prime.

R. M. Kofman, *Izbrannye etyudy S. Kaminera i M. Liburkina* (1981) includes 75 of his studies.

Kamsky, Gata (1974–), Siberian-born player, International Grandmaster (1990). He went to the USA in March 1989 to play in the New York Open Tournament, and stayed there with his father, who claimed that their Tartar origins would hinder a future chess career in the USSR. As a result of a series of exceptional results in tournaments run on the Swiss system, he shot to number 8 on the world grading list in June 1990. Not having made a NORM in an all-play-all, he still had no title, but a rise of more than 300 Elo points in one year is without parallel. His 51st position in the interzonal tournament at Manila 1990, a bitter disappointment, but still a fine achievement for one so young, was soon followed by victory at the highest level, Tilburg 1990 (+5=7–2), equal with IVANCHUK, ahead of GELFAND and SHORT. After a victory (+6=4–1) at New Delhi 1990, shared with ANAND, there was another set-back when he took last place at the super-tournament at Linares 1991.

The similarities and differences between the upbringings of Kamsky and the POLGÁR sisters provide rich material for psychologists. The Polgárs were taught at home by their parents, both teachers. They had a wide education and became outstanding chessplayers with little help from the official chess body in Hungary. Kamsky's mother left home when he was small, and he was nurtured by his father, Rustam, a boxer. 'Any child can become a world champion. He has to work a lot, and someone has to work with him. The coach has to put his soul into it. To give up his social life,' says Rustam, who certainly put his soul into it. He meant world champion at anything, and chose chess for Gata because his son's poor eyesight made sports unsuitable. Dominating Gata physically and psychologically, Rustam took him out of school at 13 and subjected him to a 14-hour-a-day regime of chess study, with a 35-minute jog to build up chess endurance; he was allowed no hobbies, no friends. Although his opponents have described him as pleasant, they found that any conversation with him was taken over by his father—a symptom of his suspicion of potential rivals. Rustam, feeling that the American players were conspiring against them, obtained sponsorship from a French commercial organization. Invited to play on board 3 for the USA in the 1990 Olympiad, Gata refused: 'first board or not at all'. In 1991 he reinforced this claim by winning the USA championship.

Andersson–Kamsky   Tilburg 1990   King's Indian Defence London System

1 Nf3 Nf6 2 d4 g6 3 Bf4 Bg7 4 e3 d6 5 h3 0-0 6 c4 c6 7 Nc3 Nbd7 8 Be2 a6 9 0-0 b5 10 Rc1 Bb7 11 Nd2 bxc4 12 Nxc4 c5 13 d5 Nb6 14 e4 Nxc4 15 Bxc4 a5 16 Re1 Ba6 17 Bxa6 Rxa6 18 e5 Nd7 19 exd6 exd6 20 b3 Ne5 21 Rc2 Rb6 22 Na4 Rb4 23 Bxe5 dxe5 24 Rc4 Qd6 25 a3 Rxc4 26 bxc4 e4 27 Qd2 f5 28 Nc3 Bd4 29 Nb5 Qe5 30 Qxa5 f4 31 Qc7

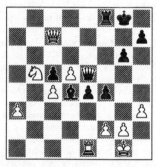

31 ... Bxf2+ 32 Kxf2 Qb2+ 33 Re2 e3+ 34 Kf3 Qc1 White lost on time, but the threat of 35 ... Qf1+ is unanswerable.

Kan, Ilya Abramovich (1909–78), International Master (1950), International Arbiter (1956), lawyer. Kan, BELAVENETS, BOTVINNIK, MAKOGONOV, and RAGOZIN were the leaders of the first generation to learn their chess and make their mark under the Soviet regime. All except Botvinnik were overtaken by the tide of younger players that was to bring about the Soviet hegemony after the Second World War, and in the 1950s Kan turned his attention to chess organization and writing about the game. He played in ten USSR championships but never bettered his first result, third in 1929. In 1936 he shared the championship of Moscow with ALATORTSEV. Other tournament successes include: Leningrad 1936, third; Moscow 1937, second (+3=3–1),

after FINE; Sverdlovsk 1943, third equal with SMYSLOV; Moscow 1948, first equal with AVERBAKH.

Kan Variation, 1188 in the FRENCH DEFENCE, introduced in Lasker–Kan, Moscow 1936; 545, the PAULSEN VARIATION of the SICILIAN DEFENCE; 897, the EVANS GAMBIT DECLINED, SHOWALTER VARIATION, as Kan–Botvinnik, Odessa 1929.

Kaplan, Julio (1950–), winner of the World Junior Championship 1967, a success accompanied by the title of International Master. Born in Argentina, he settled in Puerto Rico with his family when he was 13, and played for his adopted country in a few Olympiads from 1966. At Los Angeles 1974 he shared second prize with GHEORGHIU, after GLIGORIĆ, but after that devoted his time increasingly to his work as a computer programmer.

Kaplanek Variation, 1154 in the KIESERITZKY GAMBIT, suggested by the Viennese player Karl Kaplanek (1855–1935) and tested by FALKBEER in 1882.

Karlsbad Variation, see CARLSBAD VARIATION.

Karlsson, Lars Carl-Gustaf (1955–), Swedish player, International Grandmaster (1982). His tournament victories include Malmö 1979, Hradec Králové 1979–80 (+6=5), equal with GIPSLIS, Esbjerg 1981 (+7=3–1), Niš 1981, Eksjö 1982 (+5=6), Helsinki 1983 (+7=3–1), Hastings 1983–4 (+5=7–1), equal with SPEELMAN, Copenhagen 1988 (+4=5), and Oslo 1988.

Karpov, Anatoly Yevgenyevich (1951–), Russian player, International Grandmaster (1970), World Champion 1975–85. Born in Zlatoust, a small town in the Urals, he was taught the moves of chess when he was 4, and became a competent player by the age of 13 without having read any chess books. He was then accepted as a student in a correspondence chess school organized by the Trades Unions Sports Society. During school holidays he made visits to Moscow where BOTVINNIK, head of the tuition courses, gave personal lessons, and to Riga where he met FURMAN, whose advice on openings he sought for many years.

At the age of 15 he became one of the youngest Soviet players ever to gain the title of National Master, and at 16 he won the European Junior Championship 1967–8. At Leningrad University he read economics and studied English and Spanish: over the years his command of spoken English has become quite good. After winning the World Junior Championship in 1969, three points ahead of his nearest rival, he made his run-up to the world championship with astonishing speed. In seven strong tournaments from 1970 to 1973 he shared first prize three times: Moscow 1971 (+5=12), with STEIN, ahead of SMYSLOV, PETROSYAN, TAL, and SPASSKY; Hastings 1971–2 (+8=6–1), with KORCHNOI; and San Antonio 1972 (+7=7–1), with Petrosyan and PORTISCH. At the Leningrad interzonal 1973 he came first ($+10=7$) equal with Korchnoi, and in 1974 he defeated three other CANDIDATES in match play: POLUGAYEVSKY ($+3=5$), Spassky ($+4=6-1$), and Korchnoi ($+3=19-2$). Karpov was now the official challenger, but the title-holder, FISCHER, declined to play and FIDE declared Karpov the world champion in April 1975, a few days before his 24th birthday.

If, through no fault of his own, Karpov's right to the title seemed blemished for lack of a match, he made amends by setting up a fine tournament record in the next two years, winning seven first prizes: Portorož–Ljubljana 1975 ($+7=8$); Amsterdam 1976 ($+2=4$); Skopje 1976 ($+10=5$); Montilla 1976 ($+5=4$); USSR championship 1976 ($+8=8-1$); Bad Lauterberg 1977 ($+9=6$); and Las Palmas 1977 ($+12=3$). After a comparative failure at Leningrad 1977 ($+5=10-2$) to share fourth place, Karpov came first in strong tournaments at Tilburg 1977 ($+5=6$) and Bugojno 1978 ($+6=8-1$, shared with Spassky). Later in the year he met his first challenger, Korchnoi, and successfully defended his title ($+6=21-5$) in a hard and unusually long match at Baguio in the Philippines.

From then until 1981 he played in ten tournaments, winning or sharing first place nine times, notably in seven very strong events: Montreal 1979 ($+7=10-1$) shared with Tal; Waddinxveen 1979 ($+4=2$); Tilburg 1979 ($+4=7$); Bad Kissingen 1980 ($+3=3$); Bugojno 1980 ($+5=6$); Tilburg 1980 ($+5=5-1$); and Moscow 1981 ($+5=8$). At the age of 30 Karpov's tournament achievements already surpassed those of any other player.

In the autumn of 1981 he again defeated Korchnoi ($+6=10-2$), and in 1982 he resumed his successful tournament career, scoring $+5=7-1$ to

Karpov in 1982

tie with ANDERSSON for first place at London, winning outright ($+5=5-1$) at Tilburg, and taking first place ($+3=8-1$, including one win by default) equal with Andersson in Turin. In 1983 he won the USSR championship ($+5=9-1$) for the second time, Hanover ($+8=6-1$), and the strong Tilburg tournament ($+3=8$), followed by victories in 1984 at London ($+6=6-1$) and Oslo ($+3=6$).

At the end of the same year, 1984, Karpov began the defence of his title against a new challenger, KASPAROV, and there followed one of the most baffling and controversial episodes in chess history. The match was for the first to win 6 games. When leading $+4=5$, Karpov appears to have made a decision to win the match without loss. Kasparov, written off at this stage by the analysts, seems to have set upon a course of attrition. Karpov's stamina was in question (it is noticeable that he prefers tournaments with relatively few games), and Kasparov was undoubtedly in more robust physical shape. There followed 17 draws and then Karpov won again, and victory was within sight. After four more draws, $+5=26$, Kasparov won at last. After another 14 draws, there were two wins in quick succession by the challenger. At $+5=40-3$ CAMPOMANES, President of FIDE, stopped the match. The contest lasted five months and it was obvious to spectators that both players, but particularly Karpov, were exhausted, although they denied it. Each claims that the termination was against his wish, and that it favoured the opponent.

After winning a double-round tournament at Amsterdam 1985 ($+4=6$) Karpov again faced Kasparov in the rescheduled match. The organizers avoided the administrative difficulties of a 'timeless' event by limiting the match to 24 games. Kasparov demonstrated how much he had improved during the previous confrontation by winning the first game, and eventually the match. Karpov had the privilege of an automatic return match, and after two tournament victories in 1986, Brussels ($+7=4$) and Bugojno ($+4=9-1$), he played, for the first time, as challenger for the world title, and lost.

In 1987 Karpov was first ($+2=4$) equal with TIMMAN at Amsterdam, and first ($+5=4$) at Bilbao. Also in that year, as a consequence of delays in the previous cycle and other changes, it was already time for the next world championship match. Karpov, having defeated A. Y. SOKOLOV in the Candidates final, was again the challenger, and this time drew the match $+4=16-4$. During the next three years he had further tournament successes including victories at: Brussels 1988 ($+7=8-1$), Moscow 1988 ($+6=11$, USSR championship, tied with Kasparov), Tilburg 1988 ($+7=7$), Wijk aan Zee 1988 ($+6=6-1$), Skellefteå 1989 ($+4=11$), Biel 1990 ($+5=9$). A world championship match was again due, Karpov was again the challenger, having defeated Timman in the Candidates final, and again he lost. In five title matches between 1985 and 1990 the two Ks had played 144 games, with the total result, from Karpov's viewpoint, $+19=104-21$. Karpov appeared unshaken by this match loss and won the very strong tournament at Reggio Emilia 1991, but perhaps a delayed reaction was the cause of a lack-lustre performance at the even stronger Linares 1991 event a few weeks later. In August 1991 he defeated ANAND ($+2=5-1$) in a Candidates match, but in 1992 he lost the semi-final match against SHORT.

Small, with slightly protruding eyes and chestnut hair, Karpov has an almost childlike expression when relaxed, but his appearance conceals a man of determination and strength. To be champion, he says, 'requires more than simply being a strong player; one has to be a strong human being as well'. At the board he shows little emotion: to his opponent he seems cold and detached. Away from the board he is polite and diplomatic. His style is positional, modelled on that of CAPABLANCA, whom he admires. 'Let us say that a game may be continued in two ways: one of them is a beautiful tactical blow that gives rise to variations that don't yield to precise calculations; the other is clear positional pressure that leads to an endgame with microscopic chances of victory . . . I would choose [the latter] without thinking twice. If the opponent offers keen play I don't object; but in such cases I get less satisfaction, even if I win, than from a game conducted according to all the rules of strategy with its ruthless logic.' Like others who play the board, not the man, he writes '*the* opponent'. (See CLOSE GAME; OUTPOST.)

A. Karpov, *Sto pobednikh party* (1984) contains, as the name implies, 100 annotated games, and also seven bare game scores added while the manuscript was at the printers; D. Levy, *Karpov's Collected Games* (1975) contains 530 games, many of them annotated; K. J. O'Connell and D. Levy, *Anatoly Karpov's Games as World Champion 1975–1977* (1978) contains more than 200 games.

Hjartarson–Karpov Seattle 1989 Candidates match, 3rd game Spanish Opening

1 e4 e5 2 Nf3 Nc6 3 Bb5 a6 4 Ba4 Nf6 5 0–0 Be7 6 Re1 b5 7 Bb3 d6 8 c3 0–0 9 h3 Bb7 10 d4 Re8 11 Nbd2 Bf8 12 a3 h6 13 Bc2 Nb8 14 b4 Nbd7 15 Bb2 a5 16 Bd3 c6 17 Nb3 axb4 18 cxb4 exd4 19 Nfxd4 c5 20 bxc5 dxc5 21 Nxb5 Nxe4 22 Qc2 Ndf6 23 Nc3

23 . . . Ng5 24 Bb5 Rxe1+ 25 Rxe1 Qc7 26 Bf1 Qc6 27 Re3 Bd6 28 h4 Ne6 29 Nd1 Ng4 30 Rxe6 Bh2+ 31 Kh1 Qxe6 32 f3 Qe1 White resigns.

Karpov Variation, 1273, a line in the ALEKHINE DEFENCE analysed by O'KELLY but brought to a fine pitch by KARPOV, who played it against VAGANYAN in 1969 during the match to decide who would be the Soviet representative in the World Junior Championship that year, and then in the championship itself and elsewhere.

Kashdan, Isaac (1905–85), International Grandmaster (1954), International Arbiter (1960), the best player in the United States, and one of the best half-dozen players in the world in the early 1930s. He became well known after the Hague Olympiad 1928, when he made the highest first-board score ($+12=2-1$). In 1930, after defeating L. STEINER in match play ($+5=1$), Kashdan played in the Hamburg Olympiad and prolonged his stay in Europe to compete in three tournaments: Berlin (Aug.), first ($+5-1$); Stockholm (Oct.), first ($+4=1-1$), ahead of BOGOLJUBOW, STOLTZ, and STÅHLBERG; and Frankfurt, second ($+7=4$), after NIMZOWITSCH. Subsequently his best tournament results were: New York 1931, second ($+6=5$), after CAPABLANCA; Hastings 1931–2, second ($+6=3$), after FLOHR, ahead of EUWE and SULTAN KHAN; London 1932, third ($+5=5-1$) equal with Sultan Khan, after ALEKHINE and Flohr, ahead of TARTAKOWER and MARÓCZY; and Pasadena 1932, second ($+5=5-1$), after Alekhine, ahead of RESHEVSKY and FINE. In 1933 Kashdan founded the *Chess Review*, a magazine which he soon handed over to HOROWITZ, and wrote a book of the Folkestone Olympiad in which he had played.

Around this time Alekhine remarked that Kashdan might be the next world champion, but, finding a full-time chess career unprofitable, Kashdan became an insurance salesman, thus limiting his further chess ambitions. In his fifth and last Olympiad, Stockholm 1937, he made the best third-board score ($+13=2-1$). In the Olympiads Kashdan always played on a higher board than MARSHALL, the titular US champion, and always achieved better results. Obviously they should have played a match for the US championship, and a victory would have assisted Kashdan financially, but Marshall demanded a prize fund of $5,000, and only $900 was raised. After Marshall at last relinquished his claim to be US champion (1936) Kashdan entered several championship tournaments, but the title which had been his due was no longer within his grasp. In 1942 he almost won. He was in the lead, but declined offers of congratulations, for if Reshevsky could draw a LOST POSITION in the final round there would be a play-off match. Reshevsky's opponent blundered, and after holding his own at first, Kashdan lost the play-off ($+2=3-6$). In the US Open Championship he shared first prize in 1938 and won outright in 1947. He was chess editor of the *Los Angeles Times* from 1955, after he moved to California where he became a leading chess organizer and columnist.

Kashdan–Flohr   Hamburg Olympiad 1930   Nimzowitsch Defence

1 e4 Nc6 2 d4 d5 3 e5 Bf5 4 c3 e6 5 Ne2 Nge7 6 Ng3
Bg6 7 Bd3 Qd7 8 Qf3 b6 9 Nd2 Na5 10 h4 Bxd3 11
Qxd3 c5 12 b4 cxb4 13 cxb4 Nc4 14 h5 Rc8 15 h6 g6
16 Nf3 Nf5 17 a3 Qa4 18 Rb1 a5 19 Ne2 axb4 20 g4
bxa3 21 gxf5 gxf5 22 Rg1 b5 23 Nd2 Nxd2 24 Bxd2 b4
25 Rg3 Rc4 26 Nc1 Qa7 27 Nb3 Qc7 28 Ke2 Kd7 29
Rbg1 Rc2 30 Rg8 Rxg8 31 Rxg8 Be7 32 Qb5+ Qc6 33
Qb8 Qa6+ 34 Kd1 Rc8 35 Rxc8 Qxc8 36 Qxc8+ Kxc8
37 Kc2 Kb7 38 Nc1 Kc6 39 Kb3 Kb5 40 Na2 Bh4 41
Be1 f6 42 Nxb4 fxe5 43 dxe5 Bg5 44 Nc2 Kc6 45
Nd4+ Kd7

46 Kxa3 Bxh6 47 Kb3 Bf4 48 Nf3 h5 49 Bc3 Bh6 50
Bb4 Bg7 51 Bd6 Bh6 52 Kc3 Bg7 53 Kd3 Bh6 54 Ke2
Bc1 55 Kf1 Bb2 56 Bc5 Kc6 57 Bd4 Bc1 58 Kg2 Bf4
59 Be3 Bxe3 60 fxe3 d4 61 exd4 Kd5 62 Kg3 Ke4 63
Ng5+ Kxd4 64 Kf4 Kd5 65 Nf3 Kc4 66 Kg5 Kd5 67
Kf6 f4 68 Nh4 Ke4 69 Kxe6 f3 70 Nxf3 Kxf3 71 Kf5
h4 72 e6 h3 73 e7 h2 74 e8=Q Kg2 75 Kg4 Black
resigns.

Kasparov, Garry (1963–), Armenian-Jewish
player from Baku, International Grandmaster
(1980), World Champion from 1985. He was originally called Harry Weinstein but when he was a
child his father died and the authorities, deciding
that he should have a more suitable name, called
him Kasparov, a Russified version of his mother's
maiden name, Kasparyan. Increasingly, as he
became known outside the USSR, he was addressed
as Garry, many westerners supposing that his name
was a Russian version of Gary.

At first he trained under BAGIROV and then, like
KARPOV, by means of a correspondence course
supervised by BOTVINNIK; but Kasparov's hero is
ALEKHINE and not, like Karpov's, CAPABLANCA. At
the age of 12, much the youngest competitor,
Kasparov won the USSR junior (under 18) championship, undefeated, and repeated the success the
following year, this time conceding only a single
draw. When he won the Sokolsky Memorial tournament at Minsk 1978, in front of Kupreichik and
16 others, it was clear that a great player had
arrived. In 1979 he won his first international
tournament, Banja Luka (+8=7); in 1980 he won
the Baku tournament (+8=7), completing on his
birthday (13 April) the score necessary for his
Grandmaster title, and five months later he won the
World Junior Championship, without loss.

The strongest 17-year-old since FISCHER, his tournament successes in the next few years placed him
at the top, above Karpov, in the world ranking lists:
Moscow 1981, second (+3=9−1) equal with
POLUGAYEVSKY and SMYSLOV, after Karpov; USSR
championship, Frunze, first (+10=5−2) equal
with PSAKHIS; Bugojno 1982, first +6=7; Moscow
1982, interzonal, first (+6=7), becoming a CANDI-
DATE; Nikšić 1983, first (+9=4−1). After Candidates matches in which he defeated BELYAVSKY
(+4=4−1) and KORCHNOI (+4=6−1) in 1983,
and Smyslov (+4=9) in 1984, he became challenger for the world championship. See KARPOV for
an account of the aborted match of 1984–5.

The replayed match with Karpov in 1985 was
won by Kasparov (+5=15−3) after a match that
was fought hard until the end, Karpov losing the
last game trying at all costs to win. Almost immediately the two were in contest again, Karpov exercising his right to a return match, in 1986. Again
Kasparov pulled through (+5=14−4), and although the scores were close, Karpov had the
psychological disadvantage of never having been in
the lead.

Owing to some hitches in the schedule, Kasparov's next defence of his title was due in 1987, but
meanwhile he won two very strong tournaments,
Brussels (OHRA) 1986 (+6=3−1) and Brussels
(SWIFT) 1987 (+6=5), equal with LJUBOJEVIĆ.
When the world championship Candidates matches
concluded Karpov was again the challenger. The
match, in 1987, ended +4=16−4, many observers
believing that neither player had performed up to
his previous level.

By now Kasparov was entering only the highest
level of tournament, with impressive results:
Amsterdam 1988, first (+6=6); Belfort 1988, first
(+9=5−1); USSR championship 1988, first

Kasparov in 1990

(+6=11) shared with Karpov; Reykjavik 1988, first (+6=10−1); Barcelona 1989, first (+7=8−1) equal with Ljubojević; Skellefteå 1989, first (+4=11) equal with Karpov; Tilburg 1989, first (+10=4); Belgrade 1989, first (+8=3); Linares 1990, first (+6=4−1).

Kasparov–Andersson   Reykjavik 1988 World Cup
Queen's Gambit Declined Exchange Variation

1 d4 Nf6 2 c4 e6 3 Nc3 d5 4 cxd5 exd5 5 Bg5 c6 6 Qc2 Be7 7 e3 Nbd7 8 Bd3 Nh5 9 Bxe7 Qxe7 10 Nge2 g6 11 0–0–0 Nb6 12 Ng3 Ng7 13 Kb1 Bd7 14 Rc1 0–0–0 15 Na4 Nxa4 16 Qxa4 Kb8 17 Rc3 b6 18 Ba6 Ne6 19 Rhc1 Rhe8 20 Qb3 Qd6 21 Nf1 Ka8 22 Nd2 Nc7 23 Bf1 Ne6 24 g3 Rc8 25 Bg2 Rc7 26 h4 Rd8 27 Nf3 Bc8

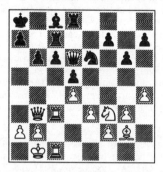

28 Qa4 c5 29 Ng5 Nxg5 30 hxg5 Bb7 31 dxc5 bxc5 32 Qf4 Qxf4 33 gxf4 d4 34 Rxc5 Rxc5 35 Bxb7+ Kxb7 36 Rxc5 dxe3 37 fxe3 Re8 38 Re5 Rxe5 39 fxe5 Kc6 40 Kc2 Kd5 41 b4 Kxe5 42 a4 f6 43 gxf6 Kxf6 44 b5 Black resigns.

Kasparov–Karpov World Championship, Lyons 1990
20th game   Spanish Opening Lenzerheide Variation

1 e4 e5 2 Nf3 Nc6 3 Bb5 a6 4 Ba4 Nf6 5 0–0 Be7 6 Re1 b5 7 Bb3 d6 8 c3 0–0 9 h3 Bb7 10 d4 Re8 11 Nbd2 Bf8 12 a4 h6 13 Bc2 exd4 14 cxd4 Nb4 15 Bb1 c5 16 d5 Nd7 17 Ra3 f5 18 Rae3 Nf6 19 Nh2 Kh8 20 b3 bxa4 21 bxa4 c4 22 Bb2 fxe4 23 Nxe4 Nfxd5 24 Rg3 Re6 25 Ng4 Qe8 26 Nxh6 c3 27 Nf5 cxb2 28 Qg4 Bc8 29 Qh4+ Rh6 30 Nxh6 gxh6

31 Kh2 Qe5 32 Ng5 Qf6 33 Re8 Bf5 34 Qxh6+ Qxh6 35 Nf7+ Kh7 36 Bxf5+ Qg6 37 Bxg6+ Kg7 38 Rxa8 Be7 39 Rb8 a5 40 Be4+ Kxf7 41 Bxd5+ Black resigns.

At the end of 1990 it was, as expected, Karpov again who emerged as challenger for the title, but the holder triumphed +4=17−3. Just as their styles of play form a marked contrast, so do their

personalities. Where Karpov is quiet and reserved, Kasparov is ebullient and outspoken. Karpov looks delicate and cautious, Kasparov looks tough and reckless. They have spurred each other to greater heights. (See KAVALEK.)

Kasparov, *Ispitanie vremenem* (1985) contains autobiography, games, photographs, and analysis.

Kasparyan, Henrikh Moiseyevich (1910–95), player, composer, analyst, author, International Master (1950), International Judge of Chess Compositions (1956), International Grandmaster for Chess Compositions (1972), railway engineer. He received all three titles at their inception. A native of Tbilisi, he was champion of Armenia ten times and a competitor in four USSR championships from 1931 to 1947. In match play he defeated CHEKHOVER, another player and composer, in 1936 (+6=7−4). His playing career might have been advanced had he moved to Moscow, but he preferred to live in Yerevan. His published endgame analyses include an article on rook endings in *Shakhmaty v SSSR*, 1946.

A composer of problems from the age of 15, he turned to studies a few years later with such success that he became widely regarded as the greatest composer of his time. He won the first (1945–7), fourth (1953–5), fifth (1956–8), eighth (1965–6, shared), ninth (1967–8), and tenth (1969–70) study composing championships of the USSR. His many books on the subject are authoritative: *2,500 Finales* (1963), a two-volume work published in Buenos Aires; *Domination in 2,545 Endgame Studies* (2nd edn., 1987), an English translation of his two volumes on domination first published in Russian in 1972 and 1974; *555 Etyudov-miniatyur* (1975); *Positsionnaya nichaya* (2nd edn., 1977); *Razvitiye etyudnikh ideyi* (1979); *Sila peshki* (1980); *Zamechatelny etyudy* (1982); *Tainy etyudista* (1984); *Sbornik etyudov i party* (1987); *Etyudy, staty analizy* (1988).

G. Akopyan, *Volshebnik shakhmat* (1981) is a biography with many games and studies,

+

A study by Kasparyan, first prize, Grzeban Jubilee 1983. The solution begins 1 Qd4+ Kxc7 2 Qa7+

Kd8 3 Rd6+ and there are two main variations showing UNPINS and a chameleon ECHO:

3 ... Kc8 4 Rc6+ Kd8 5 Qxa2 g1 = Q 6 Qa5+ Ke8 7 Qe5+ Kf7 8 Qc7+ Kg8 9 Qb8+ Kg7 10 Qb7+ Kh8 11 Rc8+ Qg8 12 Rxg8+ Kxg8 13 Qxh1 and wins.

3 ... Ke8 4 Qxa2 g1 = Q+ 5 Kb8 f3 (or 5 ... Qg4 6 Qa5) 6 Qe6+ Kf8 7 Qc8+ Kg7 8 Qc7+ Kh8 9 Rd8+ Qg8 10 Rxg8+ Kxg8 11 Qxh2 and wins.

Kaufmann, Arthur (1872–c.1940), Viennese player who in two short spells showed that he was of grandmaster calibre. All his games were played in Vienna. His first playing period was from 1892 to 1898. In 1893 he drew a match with MARCO (+5−5), and his best tournament results at this time were a third place, equal with SCHLECHTER, after SCHWARZ and Marco in 1893–4, a second to Marco in 1896, and a second to Marco, ahead of Schlechter, in 1897–8. He then almost disappeared from the chess scene until 1913 when he finished last in a tournament. A tall, slim, conceited man, Kaufmann was spurred to his best achievements by this setback. In Trebitsch Memorial tournaments he came second in 1914 (+9=4−1), half a point behind Schlechter (whom he defeated), and 2½ points ahead of the third-prize winners, RÉTI and SPIELMANN; in 1915 he came third, after Schlechter and Réti. He then defeated Réti in match play (+4=1−1). In 1916 he competed with Schlechter and VIDMAR in a three-sided match-tournament, each playing a total of twelve games. Although Kaufmann came last he scored only one point less than the winner, Schlechter. In the same year Kaufmann defeated TARTAKOWER (+2=2) and virtually retired from chess.

Kaufmann Variation, 631 in the VIENNA GAME, played frequently by KAUFMANN at the beginning of the century; 790, a strong line for White in the SPANISH OPENING; 1062 in the PETROFF DEFENCE.

Kavalek, Lubomir (1943–), International Grandmaster (1965), professional player and journalist from Prague who emigrated to Germany in 1968, settled in Washington DC two years later, and became a US citizen. A student of journalism, communications, and Russian literature, he also found time to develop his chess talents and when 19 years old, in 1962, won the Czech championship. He was first (+8=5−2), ahead of BRONSTEIN, at Amsterdam 1968, and in the same year won the Czech championship again, ahead of HORT, SMEJ-KAL, FILIP, and L. PACHMAN.

During the 1970s Kavalek was one of the most active and successful tournament competitors from the USA, taking first prizes at Caracas 1970 (+10=6−1), Bauang 1973 (+6=3), and Solingen 1974 (+7=6−1, a tie with POLUGAYEVSKY). In other strong tournaments he often took a high place: Manila 1973, third (+8=6−1), after LARSEN and LJUBOJEVIĆ; Wijk aan Zee 1975, fourth (+3=12); Manila interzonal 1976, seventh; Mont-

real 1977, second (+4=5), after GLIGORIĆ; Tilburg 1977, third (+1=10) equal with Hort, HÜBNER, and TIMMAN, after KARPOV and MILES; Bochum 1981, first (+9=6), ahead of Hort. Kavalek finished equal first in the US championship in 1972, but because it was a zonal event there was a play-off which he lost. He was equal first again in 1973, and this time co-champion. In 1978 he won outright. He played twice for Czechoslovakia in Olympiads (1964, 1966), and for the USA from 1972 to 1986. In the 1980s he turned his attention to organizing tournaments and promoting the GRANDMASTERS' ASSOCIATION.

In 1990 Kavalek published a book of the GMA's first World Cup, 1988–9, containing all 1,600 games and a perceptive text, sometimes surprisingly revealing. For example, writing about KASPAROV he says 'When the truth is inconvenient for him he has been known to resort to "fables", and to become angry when they are revealed for what they are'.

Timman–Kavalek   Amsterdam 1975   Sicilian Defence Najdorf Variation

1 e4 c5 2 Nf3 d6 3 d4 cxd4 4 Nxd4 Nf6 5 Nc3 a6 6 Bg5 e6 7 f4 Be7 8 Qf3 Qc7 9 0-0-0 Nbd7 10 Bd3 h6 11 Qh3 Nb6 12 Bh4 e5 13 Nf5 g6 14 Nxe7 Bxh3 15 Bxf6 Be6 16 f5 Rf8 17 Bb5+ Bd7 18 Ned5 Nxd5 19 Nxd5 Qa5 20 Bxd7+ Kxd7 21 a4 Qc5 22 b4 Qc6 23 a5 gxf5 24 exf5

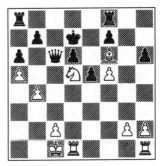

24 ... Rg8 25 Nb6+ Ke8 26 g3 Rg4 27 Rhe1 Rb8 28 Bxe5 dxe5 29 Rxe5+ Kf8 30 Nd7+ Kg7 31 f6+ Kh7 32 Nxb8 Qc3 33 Rdd5 Rd4 White resigns.

Kazantsev, Alexander Petrovich (1906–), Soviet composer, International Judge of Chess Compositions (1956), International Master for Chess Compositions (1975), engineer and science fiction writer. For one of his 70-odd studies he won the silver medal in the third FIDE composing tourney, 1960. He also composed a few problems. In 1975 he published *Dar Kaissy* (2nd edn, 1983), science fiction woven around chess positions, including many studies.

The following study, notable for the SELF-BLOCKS created on h1 and g1, was provisionally awarded first prize in the Golden Fleece tourney, 1986, but was disqualified because Kazantsev had already published an earlier version. Indeed, he had spent many years seeking the best setting for this idea, first conceived in the 1950s.

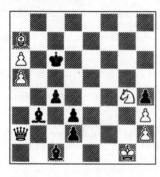

=

1 Qa1 d1=Q+ 2 Kg2 Qd2+ 3 Bf2 Bb2 4 a7 Kb7 5 a6+ Ka8 6 Qh1 Qd1 7 Bg1 Qe2+ 8 Nf2. Black dares not relieve this PIN-STALEMATE, e.g. 8 ... Qe1? 9 Kf3 d2 10 Kf4+.

Kecskemét Variation, 682, 733, or 756 in the SPANISH OPENING, the same position arising from different sequences. It was first played in the game L. Steiner–Alekhine, Kecskemét 1927.

Keeble, John Frederick (1855–1939), problemist and chronicler who lived in Norwich all his life. He edited the chess column of the *Norwich Mercury* from 1902 to 1912, contributed many significant articles elsewhere, investigated a number of chess questions, and established the burial place of several great players and arranged the tending of their graves. He lived at only two addresses for 73 years, worked for the railway company for 53 years, and was a member of the Norfolk and Norwich chess club for 61 consecutive years. Winner of the club championship in 1884, he did not compete again until 1933 and then won it three years in succession.

Keene, Raymond Dennis (1948–   ), English player and author, International Grandmaster (1976), International Arbiter (1981), British champion 1971. From 1966 to 1980 he played in eight Olympiads, and his title was earned by his performance in two of them: Nice 1974 (+7=6−2) and Haifa 1976 (+4=6). His best tournament victory was at Dortmund 1980. Increasingly he turned his attention to writing and organizing. A diligent and fluent author, he has written more than 50 chess books and claims to be able to write one over a weekend if necessary. An early book, much admired, *Aron Nimzowitsch: a Reappraisal* (1974), was revised and translated into Russian (1986). He also wrote *Leonid Stein* (1976) and, with R. N. Coles, *Howard Staunton* (1975). The style of play of the three subjects is cognate with that of Keene himself. A more recent work, *Warriors of the Mind* (1989), written with the Canadian professor of mathematics Nathan Divinsky, sets out to select the best 64 players of all time. Although the statistical underpinning has met with limited acceptance, the bio-

graphies and games give a good view of most of the world's best players. Keene became chess editor of *The Times* in 1989, after GOLOMBEK'S retirement, and he has a column in the *Spectator*.

By a combination of enthusiasm and shrewdness, Keene has attracted substantial sponsorship and has proved himself capable of efficient and rapid organization of chess events. The arrangements for the London half of the 1986 world championship match were largely his doing. In 1984 a match USSR v. Rest of the World was scheduled to be played in Belgrade. Two weeks before its start date CAMPOMANES telephoned Keene to say that the plans had fallen through. Within a few days Keene had found sponsorship and a venue in London, and the match went ahead on time. 'A magnificent organizational achievement at such short notice', wrote NUNN.

Keidanski–Urusov Attack, 655, the URUSOV GAMBIT. *Deutsches Wochenschach*, 1889, gave a detailed analysis, in the style of the HANDBUCH, of the Urusov Gambit. The author, Hermann Keidanski (1865–c.1938), used the name Keidanz in USA, where he spent much of his later life.

Keidanz Variation, 944 in the TWO KNIGHTS DEFENCE. Keidanz (*né* Keidanski) published his analysis in the German-language newspaper *Bahn frei* of New York and it was reprinted in the January 1905 issue of *Wiener Schachzeitung*.

Keller, Michael (1949–   ), German problemist, one of the best three-mover composers of his time, International Master for Chess Compositions (1984). (See RECIPROCAL PLAY.)

#2

A problem by Keller, first prize, *Schakend Nederland*, 1980. The set play: 1 ... f5 2 f4#; 1 ... Qf5 2 Nc6#. The key is 1 Nd4, threatening 2 Qe6#.

1 ... f5   2 Nf3#
1 ... Qf5   2 Ndc6#
1 ... Rb8   2 f4#
1 ... Ng~   2 Nbc6#.

This is the Rukhlis Theme (see CHANGED PLAY). In relation to the set play the first two variations show changed mates, the second two mate transference.

Kemeri Variation, 416 in the GRÜNFELD DEFENCE, sometimes called the Neo-Grünfeld variation. The line was played in the 1920s but owes its name to the game Alekhine–Mikenas, Kemeri 1937. Black's 7th move was the innovation which set him on the path to victory, but because the characteristic move is White's early Pg2-g3, 392 and 370 are also occasionally called Kemeri Variation.

Kempelen, Farkas (1734–1804), a Hungarian more commonly known by the German version of his name, Wolfgang von Kempelen. He invented the first AUTOMATON, and was extremely proud of the mechanism which controlled its arm and which later became of importance in prosthetics. He was less proud of having invented the first great cabinet illusion for which he is chiefly remembered. (See TURK.) A councillor at the Austro-Hungarian court and a man of considerable ingenuity, Kempelen invented an extensively practised method of embossed printing for the blind and carried out research into mechanical speech which was studied by the pioneers of telecommunication. He designed the hydraulic system that operated the fountains at Schönbrunn, and a canal system to link Budapest with the Adriatic at Rijeka (Fiume). For his services to the state he was made a Baron.

Kennedy, Hugh Alexander (1809–78), English player and author. In one of his stories, 'Some Reminiscences in the Life of Augustus Fitzsnob, Esq.', inspired by Thackeray's *Book of Snobs* (1848), Kennedy describes a chess game played by Napoleon against Count Bertrand, and used one of his own games, played against OWEN, to give weight to his piece of fiction. This Kennedy–Owen game has since been printed many times as a genuine Napoleon game. (See SZÉN.)

Keres, Paul (1916–75), International Grandmaster (1950), International Judge of Chess Compositions (1957), for about 25 years from 1936 among the world's best eight players, on occasion ranking second. Born in Narva, Estonia, and having few opportunities in his youth to meet other players, he engaged instead in several hundred games by correspondence; by this means he acquired enough skill to win the national over-the-board championship in 1934–5, a feat he repeated three times in the next ten years. Estonia, having found herself a star, decided to compete in the Olympiad at Warsaw 1935. Keres scored more wins than any other topboard player, and surprised the chess world with both his success and the brilliance of his play. (He also led an Estonian team in 1937, and again in 1939 when his country won the bronze medal.)

Keres soon proved that his results at Warsaw were no accident. He shared first prize with ALEKHINE (+4=5) at Bad Nauheim 1935, and with FINE (+6=3), ahead of Alekhine, at Margate 1937. Keres writes that, because of one or two comparative failures around this time, he began to play in a more solid manner, taking fewer risks. He then took first prize (+6=6−2), ahead of Fine, CAPABLANCA, RESHEVSKY, and FLOHR, at Semmering-Baden 1937, the strongest tournament of the year. Widely regarded, not least by Alekhine, as a possible future world champion, Keres was invited to play in the AVRO tournament 1938, a gathering of the world's best eight players and the strongest tournament held up to that time. Playing even more solidly, Keres scored +3=11 to share first prize with Fine. In the same year he drew a match with STÅHLBERG (+2=4−2). Soon after Keres won at Margate (+6=3), ahead of Capablanca and Flohr, the Second World War began and hopes of a world championship for him or anyone else faded.

While Estonia and the Netherlands were still at peace Keres defeated EUWE (+6=3−5) in match play, 1939–40. Six months later Estonia was annexed by the USSR and Keres, now a Soviet citizen, played in the USSR championship of 1940, and at Leningrad–Moscow 1941, the so-called 'absolute championship' of the Soviet Union, in which he took second place (+6=10−3), after BOTVINNIK, ahead of SMYSLOV and BOLESLAVSKY. Shortly afterwards Estonia was invaded and Keres found himself under German rule. He played in several tournaments, notably two strong events at Salzburg, taking second place (+4=4−2) after Alekhine in 1942, and sharing first prize with him (+5=5) in 1943. Later that year he played at Madrid and then made his way to Sweden. When the war in Europe ended he returned home, but not before making a deal with the Soviet authorities. In return for promising not to interfere with Botvinnik's challenge to Alekhine, he would be 'forgiven' for playing in German tournaments. In 1947, at his second attempt, Keres won the USSR championship (+10=8−1).

For some years he concentrated his efforts on world championship events. Seven times a CANDIDATE, he was never a challenger, a distinction he often failed to achieve by the narrowest of margins. His first attempt came in the world championship match tournament of 1948 for which the Candidates were selected by FIDE. Keres came third (+8=5−7) equal with Reshevsky, after Botvinnik and Smyslov. Keres then played in all five Candidates tournaments: Budapest 1950, fourth (+3=12−2); Neuhausen–Zurich 1953, second (+8=16−6) equal with Reshevsky, after Smyslov; Amsterdam 1956, second (+3=14−1), after Smyslov; Bled–Zagreb–Belgrade 1959, second (+15=7−6), after TAL; and Curaçao 1962, second (+9=16−2) equal with GELLER, half a point after PETROSYAN. In a play-off to determine a challenger (should the champion, Botvinnik, retire without playing) Keres defeated Geller (+2=5−1). Seeded as a Candidate in 1965 Keres lost the quarter-final match to SPASSKY.

During these years Keres won a match against UNZICKER in 1956 (+4=4), won the USSR championship in 1950 (+8=7−2) and 1951 (+9=6−2), and won or shared first prize in six strong international tournaments: Budapest 1952

(+10=5−2), ahead of Geller, Botvinnik, and Smyslov; Hastings 1954–5 (+6=2−1), equal with Smyslov; Zurich 1961 (+7=4), ahead of Petrosyan; Los Angeles 1963 (+6=5−3), equal with Petrosyan; Beverwijk 1964 (+8=7); and Mariánské Lázně 1965 (+7=8), equal with HORT. In seven consecutive Olympiads from 1952 to 1964 Keres made the best score at third or fourth board on four occasions and a total score of +52=32−3. In 1975 he won a tournament at Tallinn (+6=9). Returning home from a trip to Canada, where he won the Swiss system Open Championship, the last of more than 200 tournaments, he died of a heart attack. 'The greatest loss to chess since the death of Alekhine', said Botvinnik.

Euwe–Keres Match 1939–40 5th game Nimzo-Indian Defence Classical Variation

1 d4 Nf6 2 c4 e6 3 Nc3 Bb4 4 Qc2 0–0 5 Bg5 h6 6 Bh4 Nc6 7 e3 Re8 8 Bd3 e5 9 d5 e4 10 dxc6 exd3 11 Qxd3 dxc6 12 Qxd8 Bxc3+ 13 Qd2 Bxd2+ 14 Kxd2 Ne4+ 15 Ke2 Be6 16 Rc1 g5 17 Bg3 Rad8 18 Nf3 c5 19 Rhd1 Rxd1 20 Kxd1

20 ... g4 21 Ng1 Rd8+ 22 Ke1 Rd2 23 f3 Rxg2 24 fxe4 Rxg1+ 25 Kd2 Rxc1 26 Kxc1 Bxc4 27 b3 Bd3 28 Bxc7 h5 29 Kd2 Bb1 30 Kc3 h4 31 a4 Bxe4 32 Kc4 b6 33 a5 bxa5 34 Kxc5 Bc2 35 Kb5 Bxb3 36 Kxa5 Kg7 37 Ka6 Kg6 38 e4 g3 39 hxg3 h3 40 g4 Kg5 White resigns.

Keres had played in eight of the strongest tournaments held during his adult lifetime, winning or sharing one first prize, five second, one third, and one fourth. He had won or shared 19 first prizes and 7 second prizes in other strong international events, and won the Soviet championship three times. Rarely has a player, other than a world champion, had such a fine record, and the sobriquet 'crown prince of chess' used in his lifetime was well earned. He also composed problems and studies.

Apparently relaxed when playing, he moved the men quietly, never displaying ill-temper. His charm and tact made him friends everywhere, not least in English-speaking countries (he spoke the language fluently). In 1962 he was elected Estonian Sportsman of the Year, a testimony to both his achievements and his popularity. From 1937 Keres gradually changed his style, and although he was remembered for his brilliant tactics, both before and after this change, his style became wholly classical: he chose clear-cut lines of play, simplified

so that only the essential features of the position remained, and eschewed tactical play unless the consequences were foreseeable. He preferred well-established openings and never lost his liking for the open play that characterized his early games. Faced with new opening schemes he showed 'slight uncertainty', wrote Botvinnik, adding that Keres had 'a tendency to fade somewhat at decisive moments in the struggle . . . when his mood was spoiled he played well below his capabilities'.

Varnusz, *Paul Keres' Best Games* (1987, 1990), a two-volume work, includes a brief biography, career results, and more than 400 games.

Keres Defence, 244. Known since the 1840s, this defence was played by BUCKLE in his 4th match game against LÖWENTHAL, 1851. What is now the standard reply, 3 Bd2, was recommended by STAUNTON. (See MAKOGONOV.)

Keres Gambit, 1092, sometimes called the Mason Gambit, in the KING'S GAMBIT Accepted. In 1928 Carlos TORRE advocated the line, which he called the Requena Gambit, and that may have led to its adoption by KERES in correspondence play.

Keres–Panov Variation, 524, a KERES VARIATION of the SICILIAN DEFENCE.

Keres Variation. An excellent openings analyst, KERES originated several important lines, and strengthened many variations by his analysis and praxis: 20 in the ENGLISH OPENING; 31 in the same opening, known from a game Euwe–Bogoljubow, Mährisch-Ostrau 1923, popularized by Keres in the 1950s, but LASKER used a similar idea at St Petersburg 1909; 301 and 321 in the NIMZO-INDIAN DEFENCE, the second being played in Ståhlberg–Keres, Bad Nauheim 1936; 388 in the GRÜNFELD DEFENCE, as Pachman–Keres, Moscow 1947; 400 in the KING'S INDIAN DEFENCE played by Keres in the 1960s; 459 in the SICILIAN DEFENCE; 486 also in the Sicilian Defence, played instead of the usual 9 Qd2 with the idea of mobilizing the queen on the third rank; 498, the WING GAMBIT DEFERRED; 524 in the same opening, a sound attacking line played Keres–Bogoljubow, Salzburg 1943, and sometimes called the Keres–Panov or Panov Variation.

There are several Keres lines in the SPANISH OPENING; 687 (sometimes called the Duras Variation), successfully played in the game Keres–Alekhine, Margate 1937; 723, the HOWELL ATTACK; 745, first played in the game Thomas–Stoltz, Warsaw Olympiad 1935; 11 . . . Nd7, an alternative to the CHIGORIN VARIATION (746), introduced by Soviet players around 1944; 761, a line played by Lasker in the 1890s, but known earlier.

Also 1084 in the FALKBEER COUNTER-GAMBIT, from the correspondence game Keres–Malmgren, 1933–4; 1274 in the ALEKHINE DEFENCE, as in Keres–Jansa, Budapest 1970; 1288 in the RÉTI OPENING, introduced in Geller–Keres, USSR Spartakiad 1963; and 29, the BREMEN VARIATION of the ENGLISH OPENING.

Kevitz Defence, 42 in the ENGLISH OPENING.

Kevitz–Trajković Defence, 288, inspired by NIMZOWITSCH, played by Carlos TORRE against SÄMISCH, Baden-Baden 1925, by the American Alexander Kevitz (1902–81), and by the Yugoslav Mihailo Trajković (1922–), around 1950. It is sometimes called the van Geet Opening.

Marshall–C. Torre, friendly game played on board SS *Antonia* in 1925, en route for Baden-Baden.

1 d4 Nf6 2 c4 Nc6 3 d5 Ne5 4 b3 e6 5 Bb2 Bb4+ 6 Nd2 Ne4 7 Bc1 Qf6 White resigns.

key, the first SINGLE-MOVE of a problem's solution, supposedly a clue to the post-key play. The word key may also be used for the first single-move of a study's solution, although less appropriately when there is introductory play, which is often designed to conceal the composer's main ideas.

Keym Werner (1942–), German problemist, a leading composer of fairy problems, International Judge of Chess Compositions (1985). For an example of his work, see LAST MOVE PROBLEM.

Khalifman, Alexander Valeryevich (1966–), Soviet player, International Grandmaster (1990). He has progressed steadily towards the highest level. Playing in four USSR championships between 1986 and 1990, he had his best result, equal fifth, in the last of these. His best all-play-all win was at Dordrecht 1988 (+6=3), but he won the strong New York Open 1990, a Swiss system event, and by the end of that year was equal tenth on the world rating list. This show of strength helped towards his recruitment for a Frankfurt club in the BUNDESLIGA for 1990–1, and he became a resident of Germany. He was first (+3=5−1) equal with ADAMS and Piket at Groningen 1990, and equal second (+4=8−1), level with Adams, CHERNIN, and HANSEN, after NUNN, at Wijk aan Zee 1991.

Kuzmin–Khalifman Leningrad 1990 USSR Championship Sicilian Defence

1 e4 c5 2 Nf3 d6 3 d4 cxd4 4 Nxd4 Nf6 5 Nc3 Nc6 6 Be2 g6 7 0–0 Bg7 8 Nb3 0–0 9 Bg5 Be6 10 Kh1 Na5 11 f4 Nc4 12 f5 Nxb2 13 Qe1 Bd7 14 Qh4 Na4 15 Nxa4 Bxa4 16 Nd4 Rc8 17 Bd3 Bd7 18 Rab1 Qc7 19 Rf3 Qc5 20 Ne2 Qa5 21 Rh3 h5 22 Nf4 Qxa2 23 Rf1

23 . . . Rxc2 24 Nxh5 Nxh5 25 g4 f6 26 Be3 Qb3 27 Bxc2 Qxc2 28 gxh5 Bc6 29 Rg3 g5 30 Qg4 Qxe4+ 31 Qxe4 Bxe4+ 32 Kg1 Kf7 33 Rg4 Bd3 34 Rf2 Rh8 35 Bxa7 Rxh5 36 Bb6 d5 37 Rb4 Be4 38 Bc5 g4 39 Rxb7 Bf8 40 Rf4 Rg5 41 Kf2 Bxf5 42 Ra4 Rh5 43 Kg2 Be4+ 44 Kg3 f5 White resigns.

Kholmov, Ratmir Dmitriyevich (1925–), Soviet player, International Grandmaster (1960), ten times Lithuanian champion or co-champion 1949–61. His lively style, characterized by intuitive combinative skill, brought him several victories in international tournaments, notably at Kecskemét 1962 (+7=8), Havana 1968 (+10=4), and Budapest 1976 (+7=7−1); and he shared first prize (+6=5) with SMYSLOV at Moscow 1960, (+8=6−1) with TAL at Dubna 1973, and (+7=8) with GEORGADZE at Tbilisi–Sukhumi 1977. A competitor in 16 USSR championships from 1948 to 1972, Kholmov had good results on several occasions: 1957 sixth (+6=13−2), 1959 equal fourth (+7=10−2), 1962 fourth (+9=8−2), and 1963 first (+6=12−1) equal with STEIN, who won the play-off, and SPASSKY. In 1987 he was still performing well enough to win the Moscow championship. In 1982 he published *Ratmir Kholmov,* a book (in Russian) containing 63 annotated games and details of his chess career up to 1970.

Matulović–Kholmov Kislovodsk 1966 Spanish Opening Close Defence

1 e4 e5 2 Nf3 Nc6 3 Bb5 a6 4 Ba4 Nf6 5 0–0 Be7 6 Re1 b5 7 Bb3 0–0 8 a4 Bb7 9 d3 d6 10 Bd2 Qd7 11 Nc3 Nd4 12 Nxd4 exd4 13 Ne2 c5 14 Ng3 Rfe8 15 h3 Qc7 16 axb5 axb5 17 Rxa8 Bxa8 18 Nf5 c4 19 dxc4 bxc4 20 Ba4 Rb8 21 Bf4 Bf8 22 Qxd4 Qa5 23 Ra1 Nxe4 24 Ne3 Rb4 25 b3 c3 26 Nc4 Qf5 27 Bd7 Qxf4 28 Rxa8

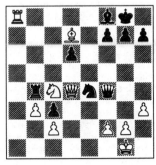

28 . . . Rxb3 29 cxb3 c2 30 Ra1 c1=Q+ 31 Rxc1 Qxc1+ 32 Kh2 d5 33 Qxd5 Qf4+ 34 Kg1 Qxf2+ 35 Kh2 Qf4+ 36 Kh1 Ng3+ 37 Kg1 Ne2+ 38 Kh1 Qf1+ White resigns.

Kholmov Variation, 751, also known as the Duras Variation, in the SPANISH OPENING, introduced by CHIGORIN in a game against SCHLECHTER, Cambridge Springs 1904.

kibitzer, an onlooker, especially one free with advice. This American term stems via Yiddish from *Kiebitz* (German), a peewit.

Kiel Variation, 604, line in the CENTRE COUNTER GAME that is ineffective if White avoids the trap 5 Qa4+ N8c6 6 d5? when Black could reply 6 . . . b5 7 Qxb5 Nc2+ 8 Kd1 Bd7 9 dxc6 Bf5+ .

Kieseritzky, Lionel Adalbert Bagration Felix (1806–53), player and editor of mixed Polish and German descent, born in Dorpat (now Tartu). He was supposed to follow his father as an advocate, but instead he became a teacher of mathematics. Increasingly devoted to chess, he sailed to France in 1839, just in time to meet BOURDONNAIS, who struggled to give him knight odds. Installed in the CAFÉ DE LA RÉGENCE, Kieseritzky gave lessons for five francs an hour or played a game for the same fee. He had a thorough knowledge of openings, a receptive memory, and a rich imagination. His strength was shown most favourably when giving great odds to weak players: against masters he was less convincing. Kieseritzky's best match achievement was the defeat of HORWITZ (+7 = 1 − 4) at London in 1846, although he is chiefly remembered for the loss, in friendly play, of the 'IMMORTAL GAME', when he made his final visit to London, in 1851. The purpose of that visit was to play in the London tournament, but he was knocked out in the first round by the eventual winner, ANDERSSEN, who also defeated him in the all-play-all tournament that began a few days later. Kieseritzky was an accomplished blindfold performer, and an energetic player of off-hand games. Against the German–American master Schulten in 1850 he scored +107 = 10 − 34.

Kieseritzky brought out a magazine, *La Régence*, 1849–51, but the use of an obscure notation of his own devising limited its success. A similar failure to communicate also hampered his chess lessons, which were given in a mixture of mathematical and musical notation (he was a skilful musician). He invented a three-dimensional form of chess, but had no support for it. His pale, spongy complexion, unattractive appearance, and sharp tongue, made him a difficult man to like. When he died none would contribute to save him from a pauper's funeral and none stood by the grave.

Kieseritzky Attack, 960, TWO KNIGHTS DEFENCE variation originally noted by LANGE in *Magdeburger Schachzeitung*, 1849. Sometimes called the Morphy Variation.

Kieseritzky Counter-gambit, 1094 or 1105, the BRYAN COUNTER-GAMBIT in the KING'S GAMBIT Accepted. (See IMMORTAL GAME.)

Kieseritzky Gambit, 1151 in the KING'S GAMBIT Accepted. In the 1840s KIESERITZKY did much to popularize this line, which dates from POLERIO, 1590, and was analysed by SALVIO, 1604, and PHILIDOR, 1749. White seeks to demonstrate that the defence of the gambit pawn by 3 . . . g5 weakens Black's king's-side pawn formation. This positional aim, suggested first by Philidor and later by RUBIN-

STEIN, contrasts with the combinative ideas that normally attach to the ALLGAIER and MUZIO GAMBITS. Black's best replies are the BERLIN and PAULSEN DEFENCES (1160, 1163).

Kieseritzky–Pillsbury Variation, 893, the STONEWARE DEFENCE.

Kieseritzky Variation, 670 in the CENTRE GAME, given by KIESERITZKY in his magazine *La Régence* in 1849. Also 1055, the BODEN–KIESERITZKY GAMBIT; 1164, STOCKWHIP VARIATION.

kindred games, games with the same ancestry as chess. They fall into three classes.

Firstly there are regional variations which came into being as the game or its precursor spread around the world, a process that began at least as far back as the 7th century AD. All these games were standard in their regions and most bear an easily recognized relationship to the international game, which could itself be considered to be a European regional variation. Some, notably CHINESE CHESS and SHOGI, are markedly different. Chinese chess may well have been the first to branch from, if it does not antedate, the early Indian game.

Secondly there are derivative games, such as the many forms of GREAT CHESS. Such games, often the invention of one person and rarely popular, are usually classed as UNORTHODOX CHESS. Most of them were devised for light diversion, but a few are intended to improve the standard game.

Thirdly there are games invented chiefly and sometimes exclusively for use in FAIRY PROBLEMS.

king, the most important but not the strongest piece, represented by the symbol K or by the figurine ♚. It can be moved orthogonally or diagonally to any adjoining square that is not attacked

by an enemy man, and has one special move, CASTLING. In a corner the king attacks three squares, elsewhere on the edge five squares, away from the edge eight squares. In the ARRAY White's king stands on e1, Black's on e8.

Usually the tallest piece and frequently bearing a crown, the king has always been the most important piece because its safety is the decisive issue of the game. Theoretically the only way to win is to make it impossible for the opponent's king to evade capture, but the king is never taken; the game ends by CHECKMATE when capture on the next move is inevitable. (See also STALEMATE.)

The king's basic move has never changed. In the 13th century, however, the king was permitted, once in a game, to make a leap, and from this move castling was developed. The name is a translation of the Persian *shah*.

king hunt, a series of moves in which a player chases a king around the board, with checkmate as the aim.

Chandler–Ribli Bundesliga 1985 Sicilian Defence Najdorf Variation

1 e4 c5 2 Nf3 d6 3 d4 cxd4 4 Nxd4 Nf6 5 Nc3 a6 6 Be3 e6 7 Qd2 b5 8 f3 Bb7 9 0–0–0 Nbd7 10 g4 h6 11 Bd3 Ne5 12 Kb1 g5 13 h4 gxh4 14 g5 hxg5 15 Bxg5 Be7 16 Bxh4 Nxd3 17 Qxd3 b4 18 Nxe6 fxe6 19 e5 bxc3 20 exf6 Qb6 21 Qxc3 Rc8 22 Qd3 Qb5

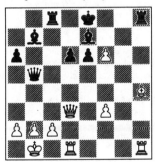

23 Qg6+ Kd7 24 fxe7 Qf5 25 e8=Q+ Rhxe8 26 Qg7+ Kc6 27 Rd3 Ba8 28 Rc3+ Kb5 29 Qd7+ Bc6 30 a4+ Ka5 31 Rxc6 Qxf3 32 Be1+ Black resigns.

For other examples, see LARSEN; TAL; VAGANYAN. For an unsuccessful hunt, see EHLVEST.

King's Bishop Counter-gambit, 1094 or 1105, the BRYAN COUNTER-GAMBIT.

King's Fianchetto Defence, 46 in the ENGLISH OPENING, likely to transpose to a KING'S INDIAN DEFENCE (see MATANOVIĆ). Also 1276, the ROBATSCH DEFENCE.

King's Fianchetto Opening, 1318, 1 g3, a move that leaves open the possibility of transposition to a standard opening. The move, dating from LUCENA, has also been called the Rat Opening and, more recently, the Benko Opening. (See AZMAIPARASHVILI; DZINDZICHASHVILI; MILES.)

king's field, a composer's term for all the squares adjacent to the one on which the king stands. Depending on its position, the field consists of 3, 5, or 8 squares. It is incorrect to include the square on which the king stands as part of the field.

King's Gambit, 1070, one of the oldest openings, given in a manuscript attributed to LUCENA. White uses the f-pawn to exert pressure on the centre, and, perhaps, to open the f-file for the king's rook. By means of the CLASSICAL DEFENCE, 1071, or the FALKBEER COUNTER-GAMBIT, 1078, Black may decline the gambit. Acceptance, 1091, is more usual, after which the KING'S KNIGHT GAMBIT, 1116, is the most popular continuation although not demonstrably better than the BISHOP'S GAMBIT, 1093, or the LESSER BISHOP'S GAMBIT, 1114.

The most commonly played openings during the 18th century seem to have been the ITALIAN OPENING, the BISHOP'S OPENING, and the King's Gambit Accepted; yet contemporary writers, with the exception of PHILIDOR, considered the gambit unsound. Doubtless its lively possibilities were attractive, and it remained popular well into the 19th century. In his *Chess-Player's Manual* (1883) GOSSIP gives 238 pages of variations without arriving at any firm conclusions as to the merits of this gambit. Out of fashion since the 1890s, it is still played occasionally by masters such as KORCHNOI and HJARTARSON: their aims are strategic, as advised by Philidor, rather than tactical.

King's Indian Defence, 362, also called, on rare occasions, East Indian Defence. Black delays a decision about central pawns, giving White a free hand in the centre for a while. The opening has two main groups. In the GRÜNFELD DEFENCE, 363, and the kindred COUNTERTHRUST and KEMERI VARIATIONS (415, 416) Black plays Pd7-d5; if this pawn is exchanged White may set up a CLASSICAL CENTRE which Black then attacks. In the traditional lines which form the other group, Black plays Pd7-d6 and usually sets up a centre by Pe7-e5. An alternative, developed in the 1950s, is the YUGOSLAV VARIATION, 387, 417, in which Black plays Pc7-c5. Two well-known lines are the FOUR PAWNS ATTACK and the SÄMISCH VARIATION. There are many other lines which do not fit neatly into these categories.

The traditional form of the King's Indian, pioneered by PAULSEN *c*.1879 and played by BLACKBURNE and CHIGORIN, was considered inferior for a long time; in 1939 FINE could write that it had practically disappeared from master-play. From this fate it was rescued, mainly by the efforts of BRONSTEIN and BOLESLAVSKY, to become one of the most popular defences of the 1950s. By contrast, the group of Grünfeld-type defences has remained popular since its inception in the 1920s.

(See GULKO; KAMSKY; PANOV; POSITIONAL SACRIFICE; SMEJKAL; YATES; ZAITSEV.)

King's Knight Gambit, 1116 in the KING'S GAMBIT Accepted. Many early writers supposed that Black could obtain the advantage by 3 . . . g5, defending the gambit pawn, as given in a manuscript attributed to LUCENA; only PHILIDOR pointed out that White might gain positional compensation on account of his central pawn MAJORITY and Black's awkwardly placed king's-side pawns. Understanding this, 20th-century players have tended to avoid the complicated play following 3 . . . g5, preferring the ABBAZIA DEFENCE, 1117, or the modern form of the CUNNINGHAM GAMBIT, 3 . . . Be7 4 Bc4 Nf6. All that can be said about 3 . . . g5, which has not been adequately tested in modern times, is that the QUAADE, HANSTEIN, ROSENTRETER, and KIESERITZKY GAMBITS are supposed to offer White better chances than the MCDONNELL, GHULAM KASSIM, SALVIO, PHILIDOR, and ALLGAIER GAMBITS.

King's Knight Opening, 672, given by LUCENA.

king's leap, see KING.

King's Pawn Opening, or Royal Opening, 441, any opening that begins 1 e4.

king's-side, or K-side, an area of the board consisting of all the squares on the h-, g-, and f-files including on occasion the squares on the e-file.

king's-side castling, castling on the king's side, represented by the symbol 0-0.

Kirov Ivanov, Nino (1945–), International Grandmaster (1975), Bulgarian champion 1978 (after a play-off). He played in the Olympiads of 1974 and 1984, and had his best tournament victories at Vršac 1975, first equal with Bukić, and at Skopje 1987, first in a field of 130 players.

Kleczyński Variation, 714, the DILWORTH VARIATION.

Klein, Ernst Ludwig (1910–90), Viennese-born British player and author, winner of the British championship in 1951. A shrewd writer, he could have become a great coach had it not been for his prickly temperament. (See TECHNIQUE; WEAKNESS.)

Klein Variation, 1039 in the PHILIDOR DEFENCE, played in a correspondence game in 1912, C. Behting–Nimzowitsch, when White won quickly.

Klett, Maximilian Philipp Friedrich von (1833–1910), German composer specializing in orthodox THREE- and MORE-MOVERS, army officer. He was the 'Bach of the problem art' wrote Adolf Bayersdorfer (1842–1901), who, like his contemporaries, rightly regarded Klett as the leading exponent of the so-called Old German Style. (See PROBLEM HISTORY.) His most creative period began around 1860 and culminated in the publication in 1878 of his book *Ph. Klett's Schachprobleme*, containing 113 of his problems.

J. D. Beasley, *A Selection of Chess Problems by Philipp Klett* (1979).

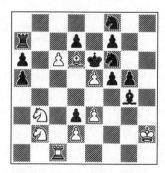

#4

A problem by Klett, *Deutsche Schachzeitung*, 1875. The solution begins 1 Na4 Kd5 2 Rb1!
2 . . . Kxc6   3 Nb6 Kb7   4 Nxa5#
2 . . . Kc4   3 Nb6+ Kb5   4 Nd4#
2 . . . Ke4   3 Nc3+ Kf3   4 Rf1#.

Kling, Josef (1811–76), composer and pioneer endgame analyst. Born in Mainz, where he became an organist, Kling moved to Paris in 1834 and settled in London three years later. He was the principal architect of a definitive analysis of the endgame R + B v. R, which was in *Le Palamède*, 1836, and in STAUNTON'S *Chess-Player's Handbook* (1847). Kling published his *Chess Euclid* in 1849, containing more than 200 of his problems, but he achieved greater fame as co-author, with HORWITZ, of *Chess Studies* (1851), a classic that launched the art of study composition. From 1851 to 1853 these two edited *The Chess Player*, a weekly magazine which contains many joint compositions, and which chronicles the events of the time. In 1852 Kling established his 'Chess and Coffee Rooms' in New Oxford Street, and materially assisted Horwitz by appointing him resident professional. (See EIGHT OFFICERS PUZZLE; PROMOTION; TRIANGULATION.)

+

A study by Kling and Horwitz, *Chess Studies* (1851). 1 Bb5+ Kf8 2 Bd6+ Kg8 3 Bc4+ Kh7 4 Bf1 Kh6 5 Bf4+ Kh5 6 Kf5 Kh4 7 Bh6 Kg3 8 Be3 Kh2 9 Kf4 Kh1 10 Kf3 Bh2 11 Bg2+ Kg1 12 Bxf2, an IDEAL MATE.

Kling and Horwitz Counterattack, 1140 in the KING'S GAMBIT Accepted, first published in the book by these two players, *Chess Studies* (1851).

Klyatskin Defence, 561, the NIMZOWITSCH VARIATION of the SICILIAN DEFENCE. Mikhail Gertsovich Klyatskin (1897–1926), a Polish-born Muscovite, published analysis of the French Defence, Alekhine Defence, and the Sicilian Defence.

Kmoch, Johann Joseph (1894–1973), better known as Hans Kmoch, International Master (1950), International Arbiter (1951). A Viennese player and writer of Czech parentage, he emigrated to the Netherlands in the 1930s and then to the USA where he settled in 1947. He showed enough skill as a youth to win a club championship, but when asked to align himself to a political party as a condition of continuing membership he left the club and gave up the game for about ten years. During this period his hobby was writing articles, many of them humorous. After the First World War he made writing his profession, and resumed his interest in chess.

He shared first place in a HAUPTTURNIER organized by the Austrian chess association, Vienna 1921, began his international career the following year, and achieved his best performance at Debrecen 1925 when he came first (+9=2−2), ahead of TARTAKOWER and GRÜNFELD. Kmoch played for Austria in the Olympiads of 1927, 1930, and 1931. He is chiefly remembered for his annotations, articles, and books, including a supplement in 1930 to Bilguer's HANDBUCH, *Die Kunst der Verteidigung* (1927), and useful biographies of EUWE and RUBINSTEIN. Another of his well-known books is *Pawn Power in Chess* (1959), in which he coined dozens of unnecessary and often ugly jargon words. For example, he writes of a pawn move made by Black, 'The conversion of the *duo* into a *leuco-bound chain* creates a *bad ram* and enhances the *melanpenia* of Black's position', meaning that Black further restricts his bad bishop.

Kmoch Variation, 163 in the QUEEN'S GAMBIT Declined; 313, the NOA VARIATION and 328, both in the NIMZO-INDIAN DEFENCE (see GHEORGHIU; IVANCHUK); 1026 in the PHILIDOR DEFENCE; 1266, sometimes called the Capablanca Variation, in the ALEKHINE DEFENCE. Some of these appeared in the supplement to the HANDBUCH, written by KMOCH and published in 1930.

Knaak, Rainer Fritz Albert (1953–), International Grandmaster (1975), East German champion in 1974, 1978, 1982, and 1984, co-champion with UHLMANN in 1983, and equal first with Uhlmann, who gained the title, in 1973. In international tournaments he was first (+6=7) at Leipzig 1983, equal first with Malich and SMEJKAL at Leipzig 1977, and (+7=4−2) with FARAGÓ and Uhlmann at Halle 1978. He was also equal first at Cienfuegos 1984, Varna 1985, Leipzig 1986, and Dortmund 1990, and took second prize (+7=7−1) after TAL

at Halle 1974, and (+7=3−1) after Sturua at Trnava 1980.

Knaak–Christiansen Thessaloniki 1988 Olympiad Nimzo-Indian Defence Rubinstein Variation

1 d4 Nf6 2 c4 e6 3 Nc3 Bb4 4 e3 c5 5 Bd3 Nc6 6 Ne2 cxd4 7 exd4 d5 8 cxd5 Nxd5 9 a3 Be7 10 Bc2 0–0 11 Qd3 g6 12 h4 e5 13 dxe5 Nxc3 14 Qxc3 Bg4 15 f3 Rc8 16 fxg4 Nxe5 17 Qb3 Bxh4+ 18 g3 Rxc2 19 Qxc2 Nd3+ 20 Kf1 Qd5

21 Ng1 Re8 22 Bh6 Bxg3 23 Rd1 Qxh1 24 Qxd3 Qh2 25 Qe2 Qxe2+ 26 Nxe2 Be5 27 b4 b5 28 Rd7 Ra8 29 Nd4 a6 30 Nc6 Bf6 31 g5 Bb2 32 Ne7+ Kh8 33 Nd5 a5 34 bxa5 Black resigns.

knight, MINOR PIECE represented by the figurine ♘. Because it has the same initial letter as the king it is customary in notation to use the initial N or, less frequently now, Kt. For compositions, however, the symbol S (for *Springer*, the German word for this piece) is often used because N is the symbol for a fairy piece, the NIGHTRIDER.

The knight is a LEAPER with a move of fixed length from one corner to the diagonally opposite corner of a rectangle three squares by two. It has no fixed route, only a departure and an arrival square. A knight at e5 always attacks d3, c4, c6, d7, f7, g6, g4, and f3 regardless of the position of other men on the board. Its power is greater when it is centralized. On the outer FRAME it attacks 2, 3, or 4 squares, on the middle frame 4 or 6 squares, elsewhere 8 squares. In the array White's knights are on b1 and g1, Black's on b8 and g8. Those on b1 and b8 are called queen's knights, those on g1 and g8, king's knights. They are the only pieces that can

be moved in the opening before any pawns have been moved.

As far as is known the knight's move has been the same since chess began. In many countries its name is linked with the cavalry, which it originally represented, but the German *Springer* means leaper or jumper, and a few other countries use words with a similar meaning.

A knight is the only piece that cannot LOSE THE MOVE; it can be moved from b5 to b6, for example, in an odd number of moves, but never in an even number.

A ZUGZWANG given by SALVIO in 1604. Black to play loses: 1 ... Kc8 2 Nf3 Kc7 3 Nd4 Kc8 4 Nb5 and White can extricate his king. White to play draws: 1 Nf3 Kc8 2 Nd4 Kc7 3 Nb5+ Kc8 4 Nd6+ Kc7. Unable to lose the move, the knight can never attack c7 or c8 without giving check.

knight ending, an endgame with kings, knights or a knight, and one or more pawns. (See BOGOLJU-BOW.)

knight player, a player who would expect to receive odds of a knight from a first-class opponent. This way of classifying players, common in the 19th century, is now obsolete.

knight's tour, the tour of a knight over an otherwise empty board visiting each square once only. There are countless ways of achieving this, and about 8,000,000 ways of performing the more restricted version known as a re-entrant tour, in which the knight, on its 64th move, could arrive back at its starting square. There are 2,032 ways of

38	35	62	25	60	23	10	7
63	26	37	34	11	8	59	22
36	39	28	61	24	57	6	9
27	64	33	40	5	12	21	58
50	29	4	13	48	41	56	19
1	14	49	32	53	20	47	44
30	51	16	3	42	45	18	55
15	2	31	52	17	54	43	46

making a knight's tour version of a MAGIC SQUARE, based on the squares being numbered in sequence of moves. The total for each rank and each file is 260, but it is impossible to make each long diagonal add up to 260 as well. They make 256 and 264 in this example, first published by JAENISCH in 1862.

An exercise that has little to do with chess, the knight's tour has long been widely popular. It is even possible that the tour antedates chess and that the knight's move was derived *from* the tour. Mathematicians have formulae for making tours on boards of various sizes, or for producing tours that trace distinctive patterns.

Knight Variation, 576 in the CARO–KANN DEFENCE.

knight wheel, a problem TASK: a knight standing in the CENTRAL ZONE is moved in each of the eight possible directions, each move leading to a different mating continuation. There are two kinds: black knight wheel and white knight wheel. The moves may be shown in the solution, the SET PLAY, or the TRY-PLAY. The term is also used to describe an incomplete wheel, as in the example by REHM, in which a knight's moves show seven 'spokes' of a wheel.

knock-out tournament, a tournament in which players are paired for each round, the losers being eliminated, a system commonly used in the 1850s and 1860s. Sixteen players competed in the world's first international tournament, London 1851, each round consisting of short matches. All important tournaments from London 1862 to the Curaçao CANDIDATES tournament 1962 were played on the ALL-PLAY-ALL basis. Five of the eight players at Curaçao came from the USSR and there was criticism that an all-play-all event gave them an unfair advantage. In 1965 and subsequently FIDE, anxious that justice should be seen to be done, arranged a series of matches, in effect a knock-out tournament, to decide which of eight Candidates should be challenger.

Knorre Variation, 708, a dubious line in the SPANISH OPENING played in the 1870s by the Russian-born astronomer Victor Knorre (1840–1919); 955 in the TWO KNIGHTS DEFENCE, recommended by Knorre.

Koch, Johann Friedrich Wilhelm (1759–1833), German author of *Die Schachspielkunst* (1801), *Codex der Schachspielkunst* (1813–14), *Elementarbuch der Schachspielkunst* (1828) and *Sechshundert Schachspielaufgaben* (1834). In his 1828 book he used CORRESPONDENCE NOTATION, and in his 1813 book he used a system for classifying endgames. While this differs from the GBR CODE, it shows the benefit to be derived from such a classification.

Koch Gambit, 1130, the GHULAM KASSIM GAMBIT, given by KOCH in his *Elementarbuch der Schachspielkunst* (1828). He attributed the invention of this opening to a Lt. Col. Donop, one-time Prussian commandant of Brussels, but it was known earlier, in the 18th century.

Koch notation, see CORRESPONDENCE NOTATION.

Koch Variation, 556 in the SICILIAN DEFENCE, played in the game B. Koch–Elstner, Berlin 1932, but originated in 1928 by Wilhelm Schönmann (1889–1970), who represented Germany in the Olympiad that year. It is also known as the Ahues Variation.

Kockelkorn, Carl (1843–1914), German player and composer. Although he was strong enough to win the West German Chess Association's tournament in 1876, he is remembered only for his composing partnership with KOHTZ that lasted the whole of his adult life. He 'always remained the fine artist . . . his chief duty was to polish and advise', writes WEENINK, but the exact part played by each of these inseparable friends will never be known. (See DECOY THEMES; PROBLEM HISTORY.)

Kofman, Rafael Moiseyevich (1909–88), Soviet problemist, born in Izmail, Romania, when it was part of Russia, International Judge of Chess Compositions (1956), International Master for Chess Compositions (1973). A member of the Red Army, he was captured by the Nazis, but his knowledge of Romanian saved him from being executed as a Jew. He wrote, sometimes with co-authors, half-a-dozen books on composition, the earliest being *Sovietskaya shakhmatnaya kompozitsiya* (1937) and the last, in 1985, a collection of compositions by five Soviet composers. In 1960, at a time when he lost his job because of his contacts abroad, he published a collection of LOYD's compositions.

Kohtz, Johannes (1843–1918), German composer, chess historian, director of a railway company. Most of his problems were composed in collaboration with his lifelong friend KOCKELKORN. They chiefly composed orthodox THREE- and MORE-MOVERS, and in 1875 they published *101 ausgewählte Schachaufgaben*. Of greater consequence was the publication of their book *Das indische Problem* (1903), a comprehensive examination of CRITICAL PLAY. This heralded a major change of direction in the art of problem composition. (See PROBLEM HISTORY.) In 1911 they published a four-mover and added the motto *Eine Schwalbe macht noch keinen Sommer* (one swallow does not make a summer), indicating that further problems by them were not necessarily to be expected. These two pioneers were commemorated in 1924 when the German problem association, Schwalbe, Vereinigung von Problemfreunden, and its magazine *Die Schwalbe* were founded. (See DECOY THEMES. The problem under KLETT was dedicated to them.)

Kohtz wrote on the game's pre-history in 1910 and collaborated with Otto Gustav Koch (1849–1910) to write a historical introduction for the eighth edition of Bilguer's HANDBUCH.

Kolisch, Ignác (1837–89), one of the world's leading players from 1859 to 1867, remembered for his lively attacking games. Born in Pressburg (Bratislava) of a well-to-do Jewish family, he studied in Milan and then Vienna where, at the age of 19, he was regarded as the best chessplayer. He became secretary to Grigory Alexandrovich Kushelev-Bezborodko (1832–70), a banker who was president of the St Petersburg Chess Club. From 1859 they travelled Europe together, and Kolisch played matches against leading players in Paris, London, and St Petersburg. He defeated HARRWITZ ($+2=1-1$), HORWITZ ($+3-1$), BARNES ($+10-1$), Ilya S. Shumov (1819–81) ($+6-2$), and ROSENTHAL ($+7-1$). He drew with OWEN ($+4-4$), ANDERSSEN ($+5=1-5$), and URUSOV ($+2-2$), and lost to Anderssen ($+3=2-4$) and PAULSEN ($+6=18-7$). While playing Paulsen in London he stayed with Mr Strode, owner of 'Chislehurst', later the residence of Napoleon III. According to HOFFER, Strode, liking Kolisch's company, offered to pay him £5 for every match game he did not lose, the outcome being an exceptional number of drawn games.

In February 1863 Kolisch left his employment and went from London to Paris. There he met MORPHY, who broke his promise to play a match. From 1864 to 1867 he indulged in financial speculation, spending six months of 1866 in Sardinia. He was able to give valuable advice to the Paris branch of the Rothschild family, to whom he had been introduced in 1859; he was later rewarded for it.

Somewhat annoyed that he had not been consulted about the organization of the Paris tournament of 1867, Kolisch nevertheless attended as a visitor. Persuaded to play, he won first prize ($+20-2$) ahead of STEINITZ, WINAWER, and NEUMANN, his finest chess performance. Steinitz recalls that Kolisch at once sold his prize, a Sèvres vase valued at 4,000 fr., and one account suggests he invested the proceeds in property speculation. Kolisch was a businessman first, chessplayer second. 'A young man with mustachios, shortsighted eyes, and a swaggering mien', Kolisch possessed undoubted charm, and seemed adept at finding influential friends wherever he went. In 1871 Rothschilds helped to set him up as a banker in Vienna; he became well established within two years, a millionaire by 1880, and was created a baron the following year. Soon afterwards he bought a newspaper, the *Wiener Allgemeine Zeitung*, in which he wrote editorials under a pen-name. He indulged in friendly play and remained a generous patron of chess until his death.

Kolisch played in the attacking manner prevalent in the 1860s, a style superseded among the leading masters during the 1870s. From 1872 to 1874 a Viennese team headed by Kolisch played a famous correspondence match of two games against a London team headed by Steinitz. London triumphed, Steinitz remarking that with these two games modern chess began.

S. Jonasson, *Ignaz von Kolisch, Schackmästare och Mecenat* (1968) contains 60 games and a biography in Swedish.

Kolisch Defence, 1156 in the KING'S GAMBIT Accepted, given in the HANDBUCH, 1843, played by SZÉN in the 1830s. It is also known as the Green Variation, or Hungarian Defence.

Koltanowski, George (1903–), International Master (1950), International Arbiter (1960), honorary Grandmaster (1988), winner of the Belgian Chess Federation championship in 1923, 1927, 1930, and 1936, chess journalist. Leaving Europe towards the end of 1938 he toured Central and North America giving simultaneous displays, some of them blindfold, and soon after the Second World War began he settled in the USA. He played in three Olympiads, twice for Belgium (1927, 1928) and once for the USA (1952). His tournament results were modest, although he won some minor events.

Koltanowski is best known as a journalist, arbiter, and blindfold chess expert. He made radio broadcasts and educational films on chess, wrote more than a dozen books on the game, and supervised many tournaments. Playing blindfold he often gave several displays in a week, without apparent strain; at Edinburgh in 1937 he set up a world blindfold record, playing 34 boards simultaneously and scoring $+24=10$ in $13\frac{1}{2}$ hours.

In San Francisco Koltanowski played 56 consecutive blindfold games, at 10 seconds a move, in 1960. He won 50 and drew 6 in 9 hours. One opponent flew from Pittsburgh for the event only to blunder on his 4th move, which Koltanowski kindly attributes to travel fatigue. The game went 1 e4 e5 2 Nf3 Nf6 3 Nxe5 Nxe4 4 Qe2 Nd6 5 Nc6+ Black resigns.

Kondratiyev Variation, 1186 in the FRENCH DEFENCE, an idea of the Soviet player Pavel Evseyevich Kondratiyev (1924–84).

Konstantinopolsky Opening, 1013, introduced to master play in the game Konstantinopolsky–Ragozin, team championship, Moscow 1956.

Koomen Variation, 138 in the QUEEN'S GAMBIT Declined, an alternative to the ABRAHAMS VARIATION introduced by the Dutch player Wim Koomen (1910–88) in the early 1940s.

Kopayev Variation, 685, line in the SPANISH OPENING which came to notice when it was examined by Kopayev and played by PANOV, after whom it is sometimes named, in the 1940s. It had, however, been played by SZABÓ in 1935. Nikolai Antonovich Kopayev (1914–78) was an accomplished analyst of both endgames and openings. (See KROGIUS.)

Kopnin, Alexei Grigoriyevich (1918–91), International Judge of Chess Compositions (1959), International Master for Chess Compositions (1975), Soviet composer noted mainly for problems. He was also a skilled analyst of basic endgames thus, on occasion, finding ideas for his studies.

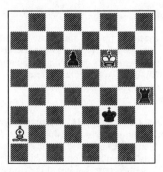

= a) as diagram b) Ba2–b3

Twin studies by Kopnin, *Shakhmaty v SSSR*, 1985.
(a) Try: 1 Ke6? Rh6+ 2 Kd5 Kf4 3 Bc4 Rg6 4 Bb3 Rg3 5 Bc4 Rc3 6 Ba6 Rb3 7 Bf1 Rb1 8 Be2 Rb6 9 Bd3 Rb8 10 Bh7 Rd8 11 Bc2 Kg5 12 Ke6 d5, and Black wins.
Solution: 1 Ke7 Rd4 2 Ke6 Ke4 3 Bb3 (ZUGZWANG) 3 ... Rd2 4 Ba4 d5 5 Bc6=.
(b) Try: 1 Ke7? Rd4 2 Ke6 Ke4 and White, in zugzwang, loses, e.g. 3 Bc2+ Ke3 4 Bb3 Rb4 5 Bc2 Rb6 6 Kd5 Rb2 7 Bh7 Rd2+ 8 K~ d5.
Solution: 1 Ke6 Rh6+ 2 Kd5 Ke3 3 Ba4 Rh4 4 Bc6 Rd4+ 5 Ke6=.
The try in one study is the key in the other.

Korányi, Attila (1934–), Hungarian composer, International Judge of Chess Compositions (1984), International Master for Chess Compositions (1988). Editor of the study section of *Magyar Sakkélet* from 1980.

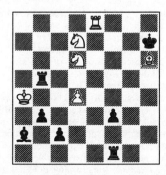

+

A study by Korányi, second prize, Bán Memorial Tourney 1982. 1 Rg8 b2 2 Nf6+ Kxh6 3 d5 Rb4+ 4 Ka5 Rb5+ 5 Ka6 Rb6+ 6 Kxb6 b1=Q+ 7 Ka7 Qb7+ 8 Kxb7 Bxd5+ 9 Nxd5 Rb1+ 10 Ka6 Ra1+ 11 Kb5 Rb1+ 12 Ka4 Ra1+ 13 Kb3 c1=N+ 14 Kc4 Ra6 15 Nf5+ Kh7 16 Rg1 Ne2 17 Rg7+ Kh8 18 Nde7 f2 19 Rg2 Ra4+ 20 Kb3 Nd4+ 21 Kxa4 Nxf5 22 Rh2+ Kg7 23 Nxf5+ and wins.

Korchnoi, Viktor Lvovich (1931–), International Grandmaster (1956), one of the world's leading players from 1960 for about 30 years, ranking third after FISCHER and SPASSKY from about 1967 to 1975, second to KARPOV from 1975 to 1980. In Leningrad, his native city, he learned the game at the age of six. He suffered hardship during the siege of Leningrad (1941–3) and, advised that he was too frail for the rigours of a chess career, took to eating porridge daily, which, he believes, strengthened his constitution. Certainly he became one of the toughest and most tenacious players of his time. Soon after gaining the Soviet master title (1951) he became a chess professional but found time to complete his history degree at Leningrad university in 1959.

From 1954 to 1990 Korchnoi played in about 70 strong international tournaments other than world championship events, winning or sharing 40 first prizes and coming below third only seven times. Many of his best wins in strong tournaments were in the 1960s: Budapest 1961 ($+9=5-1$), ahead of BRONSTEIN; Yerevan 1965 ($+6=7$), ahead of PETROSYAN; Budva 1967 ($+5=6$), ahead of TAL; Wijk aan Zee 1968 ($+10=4-1$), ahead of Tal; Palma de Majorca 1968 ($+11=6$), three points clear of a field that included Spassky and Petrosyan. Rarely content to draw a game, he made some exceptionally high scores in weaker tournaments, notably first prize ($+14=1$), five and a half points ahead of the second-prize winner, at Gyula 1965. In national events his results were good, if less consistent. He won the Leningrad championship in 1955, 1957 (shared), and 1964. In 16 appearances in the USSR championship he won four times: 1960 ($+12=4-3$), 1962 ($+10=8-1$), 1964–5 ($+11=8$), and 1970 ($+12=8-1$). From 1960 to 1974 he played in six Olympiads, scoring $+50=31-3$ (one of the losses was by default).

Korchnoi's world championship endeavours began in 1962 when he scored $+9=10-3$ to share fourth place in the Stockholm interzonal; thus qualified he competed in the CANDIDATES tournament later in the year, taking fifth place. In 1967 he scored $+10=8-3$ to share second place in the Sousse interzonal, defeated RESHEVSKY ($+3=5$) in the quarter-final, Tal ($+2=7-1$) in the semi-final, and then lost to Spassky. In the Candidates matches of 1971 Korchnoi defeated GELLER ($+4=3-1$), then lost to Petrosyan. In 1973 he was first ($+11=5-1$) equal with Karpov in the Leningrad interzonal, won matches against MECKING ($+3=9-1$) and Petrosyan, who withdrew when the score was $+3=1-1$, and then, in 1974, lost narrowly to Karpov ($+2=19-3$). In effect the last was a world championship match, because Karpov was awarded the title when Fischer declined to play.

An outspoken and lively man, Korchnoi was often disciplined or criticized by the authorities. Feeling that his career was in jeopardy he left the Soviet Union in 1976 and for many years was the target of much official hostility. He lived in the Netherlands at first, and won the Dutch championship in 1977, but shortly afterwards made Switzerland his home. He won the Swiss championship in 1982, 1984, and 1985, and played for his new country in Olympiads from 1978 onwards.

At an age when most masters begin to lose their strength, Korchnoi became perhaps an even tougher opponent after his break with the USSR. As with others, for example GULKO, the increased self-confidence and release of frustrated energy resulted in success over the board. In the Candidates matches of 1977 Korchnoi defeated Petrosyan ($+2=9-1$), POLUGAYEVSKY ($+5=7-1$), and Spassky ($+7=7-4$) to become challenger. Facing the full resources of Soviet chess he narrowly lost to Karpov ($+5=21-6$) in the title match, 1978.

There followed victories in several very strong tournaments: South Africa 1979 ($+6=5-1$); Buenos Aires (July) 1979 ($+8=5$), shared with LJUBOJEVIĆ; London 1980 ($+5=7-1$), shared with ANDERSSON and MILES; Bad Kissingen 1981 ($+8=2$); and success in Candidates matches, 1980, against Petrosyan ($+3=9-2$), Polugayevsky ($+3=9-2$), and HÜBNER ($+3=3-2$, Hübner retiring). Against Karpov in Merano 1981, Korchnoi's challenge for the title was less convincing than it had been in 1978. Seeded as a Candidate in the next cycle, he defeated PORTISCH ($+4=4-1$) in the quarter-final, 1983, but then lost badly to the new star, KASPAROV.

For the next cycle FIDE resurrected a Candidates' tournament, Montpellier 1985, but Korchnoi, who was ill, failed badly there, despite intervening victories: Wijk aan Zee 1984 (with BELYAVSKY); Sarajevo 1984 (with TIMMAN); Titograd 1984 (with Velimirović); Tilburg 1985 (with Miles and Hübner). Now in his fifties, Korchnoi continued to hold his own against the best of the rising stars: Brussels 1985, first ($+9=4$); Vienna 1986 (Swiss system), first equal with Belyavsky, ahead of Karpov, FTÁČNIK, NUNN, Spassky; Brussels (SWIFT) 1986, second ($+5=4-2$), behind Karpov; Brussels (OHRA) 1986, second, behind Kasparov; Wijk aan Zee 1987, first ($+7=5-1$) with SHORT; Beersheba 1987, first ($+6=5$) equal with SPEELMAN; Zagreb 1987, first ($+8=6-2$), ahead of EHLVEST and SEIRAWAN. This last event was an interzonal, and so, yet again, Korchnoi was a candidate. FIDE had decided that the tournament formula was not good, and reverted to match play. Drawn against HJARTARSON in 1988, the scheduled six games were inconclusive ($+2=2-2$), but Korchnoi lost the second of the extra two games. Undeterred, Korchnoi continued to perform well at the highest level: Amsterdam (OHRA) 1988, first ($+3=6-1$); Clermont Ferrand 1989, first ($+4=5-2$) equal with SAX, DOLMATOV, Ehlvest, and Renet; Amsterdam (OHRA) 1989, second ($+3=5-2$) with Speelman, after Belyavsky; Tilburg 1989, second ($+4=9-1$), after Kasparov, ahead of Ljubojević and Sax; Beersheba 1990. At the interzonal tournament, Manila 1990, Korchnoi again qualified as a Candidate, and in 1991 defeated his first opponent, Sax ($+2=7-1$) but then lost to Timman.

Korchnoi's style is characterized by his willingness to fight every game with determination. An expert in defensive play, he writes: 'If a player believes in miracles he can sometimes perform them.' He rarely makes a GRANDMASTER DRAW and on one occasion rebuked those who used the term, which he regarded as a slight on the greatest players. He is versatile, able to play any kind of position in any phase of the game, and to exploit the different methods of different opponents—characteristics like those of LASKER, whom he greatly admires. An English translation of his autobiography, *Chess is My Life* (1977), contains 75 of his games.

D. Levy and K. J. O'Connell, *Korchnoi's Chess Games* (1979) contains 1,700 games, tournament tables and match results.

Korchnoi–Árnason   Beersheba 1987   English Opening
Four Knights Variation

1 c4 e5 2 Nc3 Nf6 3 Nf3 Nc6 4 g3 d5 5 cxd5 Nxd5 6 Bg2 Nb6 7 0–0 Be7 8 b3 0–0 9 Bb2 Re8 10 Rc1 Bg4 11 d3 Bf8 12 Nd2 Qd7 13 Re1 Rab8 14 Nce4 Nd4 15 Nc5 Qc8 (15 . . . Bxc5 equalizes) 16 Nf3 Nd7 17 Nxd4 Bxc5 18 Nf3 Bb6 19 Rc4 Be6 20 Rh4 f6 21 d4 g5 22 Rh6 Kg7 23 dxe5 Kxh6 24 exf6 Rg8 25 Qd2 Kh5 26 h3 Nc5 27 g4+ Bxg4 28 hxg4+ Qxg4 29 Ne5 Qh4 30 Qc2 Ne4 31 Qxe4 Bxf2+ 32 Kf1 Qxe4 33 Bxe4 Bxe1 34 Kxe1 Rbd8 35 f7 Rgf8 36 Ba3 Rxf7 37 Nxf7 Rd4 38 Bxb7 g4 39 Ne5 Kh4 40 e3 Black resigns.

The final position shows DOMINATION.

Korchnoi Variation, 36 in the ENGLISH OPENING, played by KORCHNOI in the 10th game of his match with MECKING in 1974; 330 in the NIMZO-INDIAN DEFENCE, introduced in the game Korchnoi–Nedeljković, Baden bei Wien 1957; 454 in the SICILIAN DEFENCE, introduced by Korchnoi in his 5th match game with SPASSKY in 1968; 1264 in the ALEKHINE DEFENCE, played Geller–Korchnoi, USSR championship 1960.

korkser chess, a form of UNORTHODOX CHESS which survived long in rural areas. There are no standard rules. Frequently occurring differences from the standard game are that each side has two consecutive moves to start the game, castling is not permitted if the king has been checked, a pawn may be promoted only to a piece already captured, and 'check to the queen' must be announced. Players who follow these obsolete rules may still be found, and the term is derisory.

Korolkov, Vladimir Alexandrovich (1907–87), Soviet composer, International Judge of Chess Compositions (1956), International Grandmaster for Chess Compositions (1975), electrical engineer. Although he composed problems he is better known for his studies, for which he often discovered bold new ideas sometimes requiring a complex structure of many pieces and pawns. Such compositions have been called 'chess skyscrapers'. He won the unofficial USSR study composing championship in 1929, shared the second official one (1947–8) with LIBURKIN, and won the seventh (1962–4) outright. He published 108 of his studies in *Izbrannye etyudy* (1958). With CHEKHOVER he wrote *Izbrannye etyudy A. A. Troitskogo* (1959), and in 1969 he published *Shakhmatist ulybayetsya,* a children's book with stories woven round problems and studies.

+

A miniature by Korolkov, after J. Selman, first prize *Lelo* (a Soviet sports magazine), 1951. 1 f7 Ra6+ 2 Ba3 Rxa3+ 3 Kb2 Ra2+ 4 Kc1 (not 4 Kxa2? Be6+ = . To avoid the DESPERADO White's king is moved to the king's-side by way of the dark squares.) 4 . . . Ra1+ 5 Kd2 Ra2+ 6 Ke3 Ra3+ 7 Kf4 Ra4+ 8 Kg5 Rg4+ 9 Kh6 Rg8 10 Ne7 Be6 11 fxg8 = Q(R)+ Bxg8 12 Ng6, an IDEAL MATE.

Kosenkov, Vsevolod Tikhonovich (1930–   ), International Correspondence Chess Grandmaster (1979), Russian player who took third place after SLOTH and ZAGOROVSKY in the 8th World Correspondence Chess Championship, 1975–9.

Košťal, see HAVEL.

Kostić, Boris (1887–1963), International Grandmaster (1950), a Serbian who was a professional player for most of his life. He learned chess at the age of 16 and obtained practice at Vienna and Budapest while he was a student. An excellent linguist, he began travelling in 1910 when he went to live in Cologne, where he defeated MARSHALL (+1=2) and LEONHARDT (+3=1−1) in match play. Moving on to South America in 1913 and from there to the USA, where he visited almost every state, he earned a livelihood by playing matches against local champions and giving displays. His speciality was simultaneous blindfold chess, and on one occasion, at New York in 1916, he scored + 19 = 1 in about six hours, chatting freely with the spectators at the same time.

Kostić settled for a time in Gary, Indiana, where the school friend who taught him chess found him a job in a bank. His tournament career in the USA included New York 1916, Chicago 1918 (where he won the Western championship), and New York 1918, when he came second after CAPABLANCA. At Havana in the spring of 1919 he played a match with Capablanca and lost every one of the five games, a result that ended his ambition for the highest honours, but did not crush his spirit. A month or so later Kostić returned to Europe and continued his travels, which included a world tour from 1924 to 1926 when he played in China, India, and many other countries. He played for Yugoslavia in four Olympiads from 1927 to 1937, usually turning up on the eve of departure in a threadbare jacket and worn-out shoes, and being rewarded with new clothes. His best tournament victories were Trenčianské Teplice 1928 (+6=4−1) and Ljubljana 1938, ahead of SZABÓ and TARTAKOWER. Kostić made his last bow in a veterans' tournament, Zurich 1962; he tied for first prize with Grob, at 58 the youngest competitor. A man of great vigour and robust health, he scratched his foot and died of blood poisoning.

Nimzowitsch–Kostić Göteborg 1920 Giuoco Pianissimo Deferred

1 e4 e5 2 Nf3 Nc6 3 Bc4 Bc5 4 Nc3 Nf6 5 d3 d6 6 Bg5 h6 7 Bxf6 Qxf6 8 Nd5 Qd8 9 c3 0–0 10 b4 Bb6 11 a4 a6 12 b5 Ne7 13 Nxb6 cxb6 14 bxa6 bxa6 15 0–0 Ng6 16 Kh1 Kh8 17 Bd5 Rb8 18 Qd2 Nf4 19 c4 (ceding Black a STRONG SQUARE at c5) 19 . . . f5 20 Ng1 Ne6 21 Ne2 Nc5 22 Qc2 fxe4 23 Bxe4 Nxe4 24 dxe4 Be6 25 Ra3 Rc8 26 Rc3 Qc7 27 a5 bxa5 28 f3 Qc5 29 Rc1 Rb8 30 Ng3 Rb4 31 Nf1 Rfb8 32 Ne3 Rb2 33 Qd1

33 . . . Bd7 34 Rd3 a4 35 Nc2 R8b6 36 Na3 R2b3 37 Nb1 Be6 38 Rdc3 Qd4 39 Qxd4 exd4 40 Rxb3 Rxb3 41 Kg1 Bxc4 42 Rxc4 Rxb1+ 43 Kf2 a3 44 Ra4 Rb2+ White resigns.

Kotov, Alexander Alexandrovich (1913–81), International Grandmaster (1950), International Arbiter (1951). Kotov made his name when playing in his first USSR championship, Leningrad 1939. He and BOTVINNIK jointly held the lead when they met in the last round, and the crowds that gathered to watch the DEMONSTRATION BOARD outside the playing hall brought traffic to a halt. Kotov lost, and took second prize. Already he was known for his ability to develop powerful attacks against the enemy king, the chief characteristic of his style.

During the Second World War he worked as an engineer in a factory at Moscow. He won the city championship 1941, and came third (+10=1−4) equal with LILIENTHAL after SMYSLOV in the Moscow tournament 1942. His best tournament results came soon after the war: Pärnu 1947, second (+6=6−1), after KERES; interzonal tournament Saltsjöbaden 1948, fourth (+5=13−1); USSR championship 1948, first equal with BRONSTEIN—they shared the title; USSR championship 1949, fifth (+8=7−4) equal with Boleslavsky and FURMAN; Candidates tournament, Budapest 1950, sixth (+5=7−6); interzonal Saltsjöbaden 1952, first (+13=7), three points ahead of the field; Candidates tournament, Neuhausen–Zurich 1953, sixth (+8=12−8).

Kotov–Bronstein Moscow 1944 13th USSR Championship Old Indian Defence

1 d4 Nf6 2 c4 d6 3 Nc3 e5 4 Nf3 Nbd7 5 g3 g6 6 Bg2 Bg7 7 0–0 0–0 8 e4 c6 9 Be3 Ng4 10 Bg5 f6 11 Bc1 f5 12 Bg5 Qe8 13 dxe5 dxe5 14 exf5 gxf5 15 Re1 e4 16 Nh4 Nge5 17 f4 h6

18 Nxf5 Rxf5 19 Nxe4 Qf8 20 Nd6 Rxg5 21 fxg5 hxg5 22 Rf1 Qe7 23 Nf5 Qc5+ 24 Kh1 Nf6 25 Nxg7 Neg4 26 Rxf6 Kxg7 27 Rf1 Be6 28 Qe2 Re8 29 h3 Ne3 30 b4 Qe5 31 Rae1 Black resigns.

Kotov became one of the world's best ten players by these achievements, but even before the last of them, he had begun to change the direction of his career, writing books and articles on the game, and taking part in organization. For a few years he continued to play, competing in the national championship for the ninth and last time in 1958. He wrote a comprehensive two-volume work *Shakhmatnoe nasledie Alekhine* (1953–8) containing a biography and 372 games, and made a shorter version with 75 games, published in English as *Alexander Alekhine* (1975). His *Tainy myshleniya shakhmatista* (1970) was published in English as *Think Like a Grandmaster* (1971) and he wrote two less successful sequels, *Play Like a Grandmaster* (1978) and *Train Like a Grandmaster* (1981). Kotov was co-author, with Yudovich, of *Sovetskaya shakhmatnaya shkola* (1951); the second edition

(1955) was revised and translated into many languages, in English as *The Soviet School of Chess* (1958). The same authors produced a completely new work, *The Soviet Chess School* (1982). Kotov also wrote a chess novel, *White and Black*, which was made into a play, and a collection of 118 of his own games, *Izbrannye party* (1962). A further collection, *Alexander Kotov*, appeared in 1984 after his death.

Kotov–Robatsch Defence, 438. As in the ROBATSCH DEFENCE, 1276, there are many possibilities of transposition to other openings. This defence was played by BIRD in a match against FALKBEER in 1856.

Kotov syndrome, a process described in KOTOV's book *Think Like a Grandmaster* (1971). After a lengthy but inconclusive evaluation of likely moves the player, suddenly conscious of time passing, plays quickly, without analysis, a last-minute inspiration. The response to Kotov's description revealed that the process, often disastrous, is universal.

Kotrč–Mieses Gambit, 596 in the SCANDINAVIAN OPENING, analysed by the two players after whom it is named, and by J. E. Hall. Occasionally it is called the Leonhardt Gambit.

Kotrč Opening (pron. kot-urch), 8, the HEINRICHSEN OPENING, given by Jan Kotrč (1862–1943), editor and publisher of the Czech magazine *České Listy*, who said it was analysed by English players.

Kovačević, Marjan (1957–), Yugoslav composer whose work includes problems of all kinds, International Master for Chess Compositions (1983), International Judge of Chess Compositions (1989). (See DOMBROVSKIS THEME.) A leading problem solver, he is one of the few who hold the title of International Solving Grandmaster, awarded to him in 1988.

Kovačević, Vladimir (Vlado) (1942–), Croatian player, International Grandmaster (1976), electronics engineer. He won all-play-all tournaments at Maribor 1980 (+8=4−1), Tuzla 1981, Vinkovci 1982 (+9=2−2), Stara Pazova 1988, and Vinkovci 1989, and was second at Sarajevo 1982 (+10=4−1), after BELYAVSKY, and again at Hastings 1982–3 (+7=3−3), after VAGANYAN. He played for his country in the Olympiads of 1982 and 1984. In SWISS SYSTEM events he was equal first at Bela Crkva 1982 (162 players), and outright first at Šibenik 1987 (178 players). He wrote an account of the first 30 years of the Yugoslav team championship, *30 godina kupa maršala Tita* (1988).

Kožul, Zdenko (1966–), Yugoslav champion 1989 and 1990, each time after a play-off with DAMLJANOVIĆ, International Grandmaster (1989). In 1989 Kožul was first in two other tournaments, Marseille and Ptuj. A good player of lightning chess, he was second in a rapid play tournament at

Murcia 1990, behind TUKMAKOV and in front of 118 others including 98 grandmasters.

Kralin, Nikolai Ivanovich (1944–), Russian composer, International Master for Chess Compositions (1988), electrical engineer. He composes problems but is better known for his studies. He won the 14th (1977–8) study composing championship of the USSR, and shared the win in the 17th (1983–4).

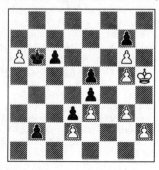

=

A study by Kralin, second prize, *Shakhmaty v SSSR*, 1980. This was a theme tourney in which the competitors were required to show TEMPO-PLAY. 1 a7 Kxa7 2 g4 b1=N 3 h3! (a TEMPO-MOVE) 3 ... Nc3 4 h4 (Black, in ZUGZWANG, must now move the king, which has no good square.).4 ... Kb7 5 dxc3 d2 6 c4 d1=Q 7 c5 Qd4 8 exd4 e3 9 d5 e2 10 d6 e1=N 11 d7 Nd3 12 d8=N+ (White promotes with check.) 12 ... K~ 13 Ne6 Nf4+ 14 Nxf4 exf4 stalemate.

Krause, Orla Hermann (1867–1935), Danish analyst. Much of Krause's working life as a doctor was at a hospital in Oringe, on the main Danish island, Zealand, from where he sent analysis to the German chess magazines. He represented his country in the Olympiad at London in 1927. In addition to the openings that bear his name, see DANISH GAMBIT and PANOV–BOTVINNIK ATTACK.

Krause Gambit, 1113, the VILLEMSON GAMBIT.

Krause–Panov System, 583 in the CARO–KANN OPENING, the PANOV–BOTVINNIK ATTACK, which was first analysed by KRAUSE.

Krause Variation, 94 in the SLAV DEFENCE, an unclear sacrifice proposed by KRAUSE around 1926. In his book *Traité complet d'échecs* (1927) CHÉRON endorsed the line and later introduced it into master play at the Hague Olympiad, 1928, in the game Przepiórka–Chéron, which concluded 9 fxe4 Nxe4 10 Qf3 Qxd4 11 Qxf7+ Kd8 12 Qxg7 Bxc3+ 13 bxc3 Qf2+ and White resigns.

Also 165 in the QUEEN'S GAMBIT Declined, and 223 in the same opening, analysed by Krause in *Wiener Schachzeitung*, 1928 and 1929, and sometimes called the Accelerated Tarrasch; 584, the

BOTVINNIK VARIATION of the CARO–KANN DEFENCE, suggested by Krause in *Deutsches Wochenschach*, 1911; 860 in the SCOTCH FOUR KNIGHTS GAME, extolled by Krause in *Deutsches Wochenschach*, 1912, although it had already been played in the game Nimzowitsch–Leonhardt, Ostend 1907; 918 in the ITALIAN OPENING, Krause, *Deutsches Wochenschach*, 1911; 950 in the TWO KNIGHTS DEFENCE; 1028, Krause, *Deutsches Wochenschach*, 1912; 1063 in the PETROFF DEFENCE, given by Krause in 1895, and examined by SCHLECHTER in *Deutsche Schachzeitung*, 1900.

Krejcik Variation (pron. cry-chick), 274, a bizarre response to the DUTCH DEFENCE. The Austrian player Josef Emil Krejcik (1885–1957) was highly imaginative in both play and composition. If GRÜN-FELD'S 2 g3 is good, then perhaps Krejcik's 2 g4, suggested in the early 1920s, is better! Also 1252 in the ALEKHINE DEFENCE, with the idea that 2 . . . Nxe4 can be answered by 3 Bxf7 +; even so, Black has the better chances after 3 . . . Kxf7 4 Qh5 + Kg8.

Krénosz Variation, 115 in the ALBIN COUNTER-GAMBIT, played with the Black pieces by the Hungarian player Ferenc Krénosz (1906–72) against SZABÓ, Budapest 1939.

kriegspiel, an unorthodox game invented by the English player Henry Michael Temple (1862–1928). Each opponent uses a separate set without seeing or being told the other's moves. On a third board, out of sight of the players, an umpire copies the play, preventing illegal moves by saying 'You may not', and providing limited information to help the players guess or deduce the position of their opponent's men. The umpire announces that a move has been made, and, if it is a capture, names the square but not the capturing man. Check is called in one of five ways: 'from a knight', 'on the rank', 'on the file', 'on the long diagonal', 'on the short diagonal'. The diagonals are described as seen from the checked king's point of view. The only question a player may ask is 'Any?', meaning are any pawn captures possible; if the answer is yes, at least one must be tried. For games and advice on play see *British Chess Magazine*, 1944, pp. 6, 52, 105, 153, or Alexander's *A Book of Chess* (1973), pp. 110–12.

The game, entertaining for players, umpire, and spectators alike, was introduced into the Knight Lights Club in the City of London by Temple in 1898. In the Netherlands it is known by the English name 'Can I?' Using electronics, it will be possible for players, perhaps in widely separated locations, to play kriegspiel with a computer as umpire.

The name, German for 'war game', was used in the 18th and 19th centuries for a military simulation training game, usually spelt *Kriegsspiel*, and also for some UNORTHODOX CHESS games. Typically these were played on an 11 × 11 board with pieces bearing military titles such as a battery, a piece that could be moved one, two, or three squares like a queen, and could capture a man without necessarily occupying the square on which the man had been placed.

Krikheli, Iosef Mikhailovich (1931–88), a leading Soviet composer, International Grandmaster for Chess Compositions (1984), mathematician. His work extended to more than 500 problems and about 50 studies; he is, perhaps, best remembered for problems of the LOGICAL SCHOOL and helpmates. He won the 15th USSR composing championship for more-movers (1979–80). At a congress of composers at Sukhumi he died suddenly of a heart attack while playing blitz chess. (See SERIES-MOVER.)

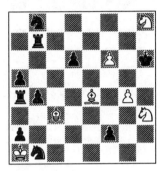

#8

A problem by Krikheli, first prize, *Probleemblad*, 1970. Two thematic tries 1 Be5? (refuted by 1 . . . f1 = Q) and 1 Bd4? (refuted by 1 . . . Ra3) recur in the solution: 1 Bg6 Rb5 2 Bd3 Rb7 3 Bd4 f1 = N 4 Bg6 Rb5 5 Be4 Rb7 6 Be5 dxe5 7 Bg6 ∼ 8 g5 #.

Krogius, Nikolai Vladimirovich (1930–), Soviet player, International Grandmaster (1964), co-champion (with ARONIN) in 1952 of the RSFSR (Russian Federation), psychologist. Krogius was less successful in his seven USSR championship attempts than he was in international tournament play. He won first prizes at Sochi 1964 (+7=8), ahead of SPASSKY, at Sochi 1967 (+5=10), shared with SHAMKOVICH, SIMAGIN, Spassky, and ZAITSEV, and at Varna 1969 (+8=7), ahead of HORT. Other good results were Budapest 1965, fourth (+5=10), after POLUGAYEVSKY, TAIMANOV, and SZABÓ; Sochi 1966, third (+5=10) equal with MATULOVIĆ, after KORCHNOI and Polugayevsky; and Sochi 1973, third (+3=12) equal with SMEJKAL, after TAL and Spassky. Krogius wrote several books on the psychology of chess, advising the chess masters how they should prepare themselves for competitive play, and a chance to test his theories came when he was appointed to assist Spassky in the world championship match of 1972. Spassky lost.

Krogius–Lutikov   27th USSR Championship 1960
Spanish Opening Siesta Variation

1 e4 e5 2 Nf3 Nc6 3 Bb5 a6 4 Ba4 d6 5 c3 f5 6 exf5 Bxf5 7 0–0 Bd3 8 Qb3 Rb8 9 Re1 e4 10 Nd4 Ne7 11 c4 Kd7 12 Ne6 Qe8 13 Nf4 b5 14 cxb5 axb5 15 Qe6 + Kd8 16 Nxd3 exd3 17 Bd1 Qg6 18 Qh3 h5 19 Nc3 Qf5 20 Qe3 g6 21 Ne4 Ne5 22 Ng3 Qf7 23 Bb3 Qh7 24 f4 Bh6 25 Qe4 Nd7 26 Qxd3 Bxf4 27 Ne2 Be5 28 Qh3

Nf5 29 d4 Bf6 30 Bd2 Re8 31 Kh1 Nb6 32 Qd3 Nc4
33 Bxc4 bxc4 34 Qxc4 g5 35 Nc3 Rf8 36 Nd5 Qf7

37 Re7 Qxe7 38 Nxe7 Bxe7 39 Rc1 Ke8 40 Qxc7 Kf7
41 g4 hxg4 42 Rf1 Kg6 43 Rxf5 Kxf5 44 Qxe7 Rbe8 and
Black resigns.

Krylenko, Nikolai Vasilyevich (1885–1938), Commissar for War in the first Bolshevik government, and later Commissar for Justice in the USSR. Krylenko may have done more than anyone else to popularize chess. As chairman of the chess section of the All-Union Council for Physical Recreation he was largely responsible for persuading the Soviet government to sponsor the game and to organize the Moscow international tournaments of 1925, 1935, and 1936. Such powerful support, from one of the most feared and reviled men in Europe, ensured mass interest and led directly to the later strength of Soviet chess. Although only a first category player, he edited *64* from 1924, wrote a book on the Moscow tournament of 1935, and, with P. F. Nikiforov, a book on chess and draughts organization (1932).

Krylenko, widely held to be responsible for Stalin's purges, himself disappeared in one of them and was executed, only to be rehabilitated after Stalin's death.

Kubbel, Karl Artur Leonid (1892–1942), Soviet composer, chemical engineer. He and the PLATOV brothers, following in the wake of TROITZKY, initiated a period of Russian supremacy in the art of study-composing; he laid down his 'golden rule' of economy: 'to squeeze out of the material all its hidden possibilities'. In particular, at a time when the stipulation 'White to play and win' predominated, Kubbel investigated the possibilities of White's obtaining a draw by self-stalemate. His output includes many more problems than studies. He considered himself 'in the first place a problemist'; but he is better remembered for his pioneering work in study composing. He published two collections of these studies, *150 shakhmatnykh etyudov* (1925) and *250 izbrannikh etyudov* (1938).

A Baltic German by birth, he decided some time after the revolution to use the forenames Leonid Ivanovich, although he continued on occasion to retain the initials K. A. L. He had two brothers who were also composers, and they too Russianized

their names: Arvid I. Kubbel (1889–1938) and Yevgeny I. Kubbel (1894–1942). The eldest competed in the national championships of 1920 and 1923, but committed the crime of sending his compositions to the foreign bourgeois press and was executed by the secret police. The other two died in the siege of Leningrad.

T. G. Whitworth, *Leonid Kubbel's Chess Endgame Studies* (1984) contains more than 300 examples; Ya. G. Vladimirov and Yu. G. Fokin, *Leonid Kubbel* (1984) contains about 450 problems and 250 studies (in Russian).

=

A study by K. A. L. Kubbel, first prize, *Magyar Sakkvilág*, 1929. 1 Nd7+ Kd6 2 Bf4+ Kxd7 3 Bg4+ Ke8 4 Bh5 Qxh5 5 Nf6+ Kf7 6 Nxh5 Kg6 7 Bg3! Nxg3 8 Nf4+ K~ 9 Nd3 Nc4+ 10 Kb3 Na5+ 11 Kc2=. Black's bishop is trapped, its escape blocked by the black knights.

Kudrin, Sergey (1959–), Russian-born player who has lived in the USA since 1978, International Grandmaster (1984). All of his first places in major tournaments have been shared—Beersheba 1984, Torremolinos 1985, London 1988 (+4=4−1), and Salamanca 1989. He was equal second (+5=2−2) at Marseille 1987.

Kupreichik, Viktor Davidovich (1949–91), Byelorussian player, International Grandmaster (1980), journalist. In his first three USSR championships (1969, 1974, 1976) he came last; according to one critic he showed undoubted talent, and needed only 'discipline and care'. After making good this deficiency he was equal fifth in 1979 and equal sixth in 1980–1, but his three later appearances were less satisfactory. He has had several good wins in international tournaments: Wijk aan Zee (masters) 1977 (+9=1−1); Kirovakan 1978 (+8=6−1), a tie with VAGANYAN; Reykjavik 1980 (+5=7), ahead of BROWNE and MILES; Plovdiv 1980 (+6=5); Medina del Campo 1980 (+4=5); Hastings 1981–2 (+6=6−1), ahead of ANDERSSON; Sverdlovsk 1984, equal with PSAKHIS, M. GUREVICH, and GAV-

RIKOV; Zenica 1985; Winnipeg 1986 (Swiss system), tie with YUSUPOV, ahead of H. ÓLAFSSON, HJARTAR-SON, and 48 other players; Malmö 1987–8, shared with BELYAVSKY; Val Maubée 1989, with Shirov; Rimavská Sobota 1990.

Gavrikov–Kupreichik USSR Championship 1985
Semi-Slav Defence Botvinnik Variation

1 d4 d5 2 c4 e6 3 Nf3 Nf6 4 Nc3 c6 5 Bg5 dxc4 6 e4 b5 7 e5 h6 8 Bh4 g5 9 Nxg5 hxg5 10 Bxg5 Be7 11 exf6 Bxf6 12 Bxf6 Qxf6 13 g3 Na6 14 Bg2 Bb7 15 Ne4 Qe7 16 0–0 0–0–0 17 a4 Kb8 18 Qd2 Nb4 19 Qf4+ Qc7 20 Qxc7+ Kxc7 21 Ng5 Rhf8 22 axb5 cxb5 23 Rxa7 Nc6 24 Bxc6 Kxc6 25 Nf3 Kb6 26 Rfa1

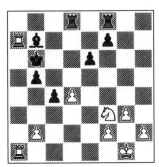

26 ... e5 27 Nxe5 Rxd4 28 h4 Rfd8 29 Nxf7 Rd1+ 30 Kh2 Rxa1 31 Rxa1 Rf8 32 Nd6 Rxf2+ 33 Kh3 Bg2+ 34 Kg4 Kc5 35 Nf5 Be4 36 Ne3 Kd4 37 Nd1 Bf3+ 38 Kg5 Rd2 39 Nc3 Rxb2 40 Kf4 Kxc3 41 Kxf3 Rh2 42 Kg4 White resigns.

Kupreichik Variation, 669 in the CENTRE GAME played in Kupreichik–Estrin, Leningrad 1965.

Kurajica, Bojan (1947–), Yugoslav player, International Grandmaster (1974), World Junior Champion 1965. In his youth he divided his time between chess and weight-lifting, as well as graduating in philology at Zagreb. His best results are: Sombor 1968, first, with HORT and IVKOV; San Felíu de Guixols 1974, first, with Sigurjónsson; Solingen 1974, third, with SPASSKY, after POLUGAYEVSKY and KAVALEK; Wijk aan Zee 1976, third, with TAL, after LJUBOJEVIĆ and F. ÓLAFSSON; Wijk aan Zee 1977, fourth (+4=6−1), behind GELLER, SOSONKO, and TIMMAN. He played for Yugoslavia in the 1980 and 1984 Olympiads and was runner-up in the national championship in 1984.

Kuzmin, Gennady Pavlovich (1946–), Russian player, International Grandmaster (1973). In nine USSR championships between 1965 and 1981 his best place was in 1973, equal second (+5=11−1) shared with KARPOV and KORCHNOI, after SPASSKY. At Baku 1977 he won the First League tournament (+6=11), and at Kherson 1989 he shared first place with Novikov in the semi-final of the national

championship. In other events his best achievements are: Hastings 1973–4, first equal with SZABÓ, TAL, and TIMMAN; Lvov 1978, third (+3=10−1) equal with ROMANISHIN and TSESHKOVSKY, after BALASHOV and VAGANYAN; and Dortmund 1981, first (+5=6) equal with SPEELMAN and FTÁČNIK.

Kuzmin–Lein Baku 1972 40th USSR Championship
Spanish Opening Berlin Defence

1 e4 e5 2 Nf3 Nc6 3 Bb5 Nf6 4 d3 d6 5 0–0 Be7 6 Re1 0–0 7 Nbd2 a6 8 Bxc6 bxc6 9 d4 Nd7 10 Nc4 f6 11 Na5 Nb8 12 c3 Qd7 13 Nh4 g6 14 Nf3 Rf7 15 b4 Bf8 16 Bb2 Qe8 17 c4 Bg7 18 Qb3 exd4 19 c5 Nd7 20 Nxd4 dxc5 21 Ne6 c4 22 Nxg7 Kxg7 23 Nxc4 Qe6 24 Qc3 Kg8 25 e5 f5 26 Rad1 Bb7

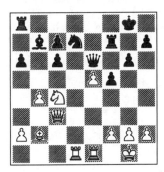

27 Nd6 cxd6 28 Rxd6 Nf8 29 Rxe6 Nxe6 30 Rd1 Re8 31 Rd6 Rc7 32 Qc4 Kf7 33 Qh4 Black resigns.

Kuznetsov, Alexander Petrovich (1913–82), composer from Moscow, International Judge of Chess Compositions (1966), International Master for Chess Compositions (1974). His output consisted of about 300 studies and 130 problems. His best work in the field of studies was often composed jointly with others; when on his own, he sometimes devised unusual ideas, perhaps shown at the expense of form, a style some call romantic.

+

A study by Kuznetsov, *64 shakhmatnoye obozrenie* (1982), reminiscent of a MANṢŪBA. 1 Qf1+ Kg3 2 Bf4+ Kxf4 3 Qxf2+ Ke5 4 Qh2+ f4 5 e3 Qh8+ 6 Kg4 Qxh2 7 b8=Q+ d6 8 Qxb2+

Qxb2 9 d4+ Qxd4 10 exf4#.

Kuzovkov, Alexander Sergeyevich (1953–), problemist from the Soviet Far East specializing in orthodox direct mate problems, International Master for Chess Compositions (1989), civil engineer. In the 16th USSR composing championship (1981–2) he was first in the three-mover section and also in the more-mover section.

(see diagram)

A more-mover by Kuzovkov, first prize, *Probleemblad*, 1982. The key is 1 Qc3, the threat is 2 Nb3 with 3 Qd3+ to follow. To make a flight at f5 Black must place a piece on f4, the critical square, e.g. 2 . . . Qf4 3 Qe5+, or 2 . . . Bf4 3 Nd2+. The main variations show CRITICAL PLAY, and the so-called Holzhausen Theme (see CUTTING-POINT THEMES).

1 . . . Qc1(a)   2 Nxe6 Qf4   3 Qe5+

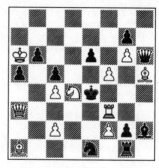

#4

		2 . . . Bf4	3 Ng5+
1 . . . Bb8(a)	2 Ne2 Qf4	3 Ng3+	
		2 . . . Bf4	3 Qe3+.

(a) these moves are anti-critical in respect to 2 Nb3? but critical in respect to the replies 2 Nxe6 and 2 Ne2 respectively.

L

La Bourdonnais, see BOURDONNAIS.

Lačný theme, see CYCLIC PLAY.

ladder competition, a continuous event in many chess clubs. Players are ranked and listed and any player is entitled to challenge a higher rated player, exchanging places on the ladder if successful. Clubs vary in their rules concerning challenges. In some only the person immediately above may be challenged, in others it is either of the next two above, or the next highest available. There are no fixed dates or numbers of games.

In the problem world, ladders take a different form. Points are awarded for each problem solved. On reaching a predetermined figure a competitor is said to have ascended the ladder, may receive a prize as well as the glory, and begins again with no score.

al-Lajlāj, Abu'l-Faraj bin al-Muzaffar bin Sa'-īd (d. *c*.970), pupil of aṣ-ṣūlī and author of an important chess work. This book is no longer extant but manuscripts containing some of its contents have survived and in *A History of Chess* MURRAY shows all that he could find of the openings systems given by Lajlāj. (See TA'BI'A.) Pareja in his *La fase araba del gioco degli scacchi* (Rome, 1953) believed there were two separate players known as al-Lajlāj (the stammerer); but Murray thought that Abū'l-Faraj Muḥammad bin 'Obaidallāh al-Lajlāj was a variation in the names of the same man.

Landau Variation, 106 in the SLAV DEFENCE, introduced in the game Landau–Euwe, Amsterdam 1936; 316, the RUBINSTEIN VARIATION of the NIMZO-INDIAN DEFENCE. Salo Landau (1903–43) was a Polish Jew who settled in the Netherlands during the First World War and died in the concentration camp at Auschwitz, Poland, during the Second. He was seen as the best Dutch player after EUWE in the 1930s.

Landstrasse Gambit, 1286, the RÉTI OPENING. The opening that RÉTI made widely known was analysed first by Alfred Emil Wolf (1900–23), champion of Vienna and son of S. R. Wolf. The name comes from the Viennese Landstrasse Schachbund, in which Wolf played.

Lange, Max (1832–99), German all-rounder: player, analyst, problemist, administrator, author, and inventor of the HELPMATE. Lange was elected secretary of the German chess federation in 1894,

and blighted a lifetime of service to chess by losing the game scores of the tournaments at Leipzig 1894 and Cologne 1898. With ANDERSSEN he edited *Schachzeitung* (later *Deutsche Schachzeitung*) in 1858 and 1859, with others from 1860 to 1863, and alone in 1864. A number of opening lines are associated with him, in particular the MAX LANGE ATTACK. (See BERTIN; KIEṢERITZKY ATTACK.)

Lange Attack, see MAX LANGE ATTACK.

Lange Variation, 902, standard line in the EVANS GAMBIT DECLINED, recommended by LANGE in 1865.

Lapienis, Donatas Petras (1936–), Lithuanian, International Correspondence Chess Grandmaster (1979) and the world's highest rated correspondence player in 1990.

Lärobok Variation, 1037 in the PHILIDOR DEFENCE given, but not recommended, in the 4th edition of the famous Swedish handbook edited by COLLIJN.

Larsen, Jørgen Bent (1935–), Danish player, International Grandmaster (1956), among the world's best ten for about 15 years. Born in a small village in north-west Jutland, he learned the moves at the age of six. He was not specially talented as a youth, but when, at the age of 17, he moved to Copenhagen to study civil engineering, he improved. He won the Danish championship in 1954 and every time he entered up to 1964. Competing next in 1989 he narrowly lost the tie-break match. He represented Denmark for the first of many times, on top board, at the 1954 Olympiad. At the next Olympiad, Moscow 1956, Larsen made the best score on board 1 ($+11=6-1$), was promoted to grandmaster, and was recognized by the Soviet bloc as the first of the younger players to offer a serious challenge to them.

He had completed two years of his studies, but the press of tournament engagements persuaded him to become a full-time chess professional, earning a living from play and journalism. His first notable successes were in two strong tournaments at Beverwijk: first equal with PETROSYAN in 1960, and first ($+7=1-1$) equal with IVKOV in 1961. After two years of detested military service Larsen returned to the more congenial miniature battlefield. At the interzonal tournament, Amsterdam 1964, he was first ($+13=8-2$) equal with SMYSLOV, SPASSKY, and TAL. In the Candidates matches that followed in 1965 he defeated Ivkov ($+4=3-1$) but lost to Tal in the semi-final. Again a victor in the interzonal, Sousse 1967 (+13=5−3), one and a half points ahead of his nearest rival, Larsen won his first match, 1968, against PORTISCH (+3=5−2), but lost to Spassky. At the Palma de Majorca interzonal 1970, Larsen was second (+9=12−2) equal with HÜBNER and GELLER, after FISCHER. He won the first match in 1971 (+4=3−2) against UHLMANN, but was whitewashed by Fischer. At Biel 1976 Larsen won (+8=9−2) his third interzonal, a record equalled only by Tal, but lost the first Candidates match.

From 1958 to 1990 Larsen played in more than 60 strong tournaments, apart from interzonals, and won or shared 24 first and 10 second prizes. From August 1967 to March 1970 he achieved an extraordinary record in 9 consecutive major events, failing to win first prize only once, at Palma de Majorca 1968, when he came second (+11=4−2) equal with Spassky, after KORCHNOI. His victories additional to the Sousse interzonal are: Havana 1967 (+11=8), ahead of TAIMANOV and Smyslov; Winnipeg 1967 (+4=4−1), shared with DARGA, ahead of KERES and Spassky; Palma de Majorca 1967 (+11=4−2), ahead of BOTVINNIK, Smyslov, and Portisch; Monte Carlo 1968 (+7=5−1), ahead of Botvinnik, Smyslov, and HORT; Büsum 1969 (+8=6−1); Palma de Majorca 1969 (+10=4−3), ahead of Petrosyan, Korchnoi, and Spassky; and Lugano 1970 (+7=5−2).

Since that time his best tournament wins are: Teesside 1972 (+8=6−1); Hastings 1972–3 (+10=3−2); Manila 1973 (+11=3−1); Orense 1975 (+10=3−2); Ljubljana–Portorož 1977 (+7=5−1); Buenos Aires 1979 (+9=4), three points ahead of a field that included Spassky and Petrosyan; Buenos Aires 1980 (+8=3−2), ahead of TIMMAN, LJUBOJEVIĆ, and KARPOV; Naestved 1985 (+4=5−2), with Vaganyan and BROWNE; Reykjavik 1985 (+5=6); London (Williams, Watson & Farley) 1989 (+7=5−1); London (W. W. & F.) 1990 (+6=6−1); New York 1990 (W. W. & F.) (+5=3−1).

Larsen is no DRAWING MASTER. He plays to win and as a consequence sometimes loses, but in most tournaments this approach has brought him more wins than losses. Because of his lively play he is in demand among tournament organizers, and although his play may have weakened a shade with the passing years, his aggression has not. At the beginning of a game he avoids well-trodden paths and he has successfully revived many old and forgotten opening variations. He writes: 'I do not deliberately play openings that are obviously bad. I emphasise the surprise element, and in some cases this makes me play a variation without being convinced that it is correct.' He is not reckless, however. When opportunity serves he can play a solid positional game, and he is also a good ENDGAME player. (See DESPERADO.)

His autobiographical collection, *Larsen's Selected Games of Chess 1948–69* (1970), has appeared in several languages; E. Brøndum, *Bent Larsen—the*

Fighter (1978) contains 75 games from the period 1966–77; an instructional book, *Skak Skole* (1975), was published in 1982 as *Larsen's Good Move Guide*.

Larsen–Chandler   Hastings 1987–8   Réti Opening

1 Nf3 d5 2 c4 d4 3 g3 g6 4 Bg2 Bg7 5 d3 e5 6 0–0 Ne7 7 b4 0–0 8 Nbd2 a5 9 b5 c5 10 bxc6 Nexc6 11 Ba3 Nb4 12 Qb3 N8a6 13 Bxb4 axb4 14 a3 bxa3 15 Qxa3 Re8 16 Rfb1 f5 17 Ne1 Nc7 18 Bd5+ Kh8

19 Qxa8 Nxa8 20 Rxa8 Bh6 21 Ndf3 Qe7 22 Bxb7 Bd7 23 Rxe8+ Bxe8 24 Bd5 Qd6 25 Rb7 g5 26 h4 gxh4 27 Nxh4 Bd7 28 Nef3 f4 29 Be4 fxg3 30 fxg3 Be3+ 31 Kg2 Bg4 32 Rxh7+ Kg8 33 Rb7 Qa6 34 Nxe5 Be6 35 Re7 Kf8 36 Nhg6+ Kg8 37 Rxe6 Qa2 38 Re8+ Kg7 39 Re7+ Kh6 40 Ng4+ Kh5 41 Re5+ Bg5 42 Nf4+ Kxg4 43 Bf3+ mate.

Larsen Opening, 5, the QUEEN'S FIANCHETTO OPENING, which LARSEN sometimes calls the Baby Orang Utan.

Larsen Variation, 369 in the GRÜNFELD DEFENCE, played by LARSEN in the 1960s; Black's 8th move deters White from playing 9 h4 because of the reply 9 . . . Qg4. Also 406 in the KING'S INDIAN DEFENCE, as in the game Sultan Khan–Flohr, Prague Olympiad 1931; 1020 in the PHILIDOR DEFENCE, played Tal–Larsen, 2nd match game 1969; 1269 in the ALEKHINE DEFENCE, played in the game R. P. Michell–Réti, Margate 1923.

Lasa, Tassilo von Heydebrand und der (1818–99), German player, author, chess historian, diplomat. Usually known as von der Lasa, the baron was involved in the developments that made Germany the leading chess nation of the second half of the 19th century. He was a member of the Berlin PLEIADES, a short-lived group of seven players who promoted the first German chess magazine, *Schachzeitung* (later *Deutsche Schachzeitung*), and the *Handbuch des Schachspiels* (1843). The editor of the book, BILGUER, died early in the project, which was then completed by Lasa, who revised and edited the next four editions, up to 1873, while retaining Bilguer's name in the title.

Lasa never competed in tournaments or formal matches, but his play shows him to have been among the best of his time. In 1846 he played seven games against LÖWENTHAL, winning most of them;

on two occasions he won the majority of a series of games played against STAUNTON, at Berlin in 1844 and at Brussels in 1853; and *The Chess Player*, 29 Nov. 1851, published a report that, playing a series of games against ANDERSSEN, Lasa was leading by ten games to five.

Although he may have preferred friendly play, the main obstacle to his participation in organized chess events was his career. He was posted around Europe, and to Brazil, perhaps his most difficult appointment being that of Prussian Ambassador at Copenhagen immediately after the German–Danish war. His postings gave him the opportunity to examine rare manuscripts and books, and in 1887, seven years after his retirement, he travelled round the world, including India and Australia, adding to his chess library. His collection of about 2,300 titles, one of the best of the period, remains intact. He contributed more than 90 articles to chess periodicals, over more than 40 years. The most important of his books, *Zur Geschichte und Literatur des Schachspiels* (1897), still perhaps the clearest account of the game's development in Europe from medieval times, is written with the wisdom that permeates all his works.

N. Divinsky, 'The Mighty Baron', *British Chess Magazine*, 1985, pp. 226–32, examines Lasa's playing strength.

Staunton–Lasa   First of a series of games 1853   Two Knights Defence

1 e4 e5 2 Nf3 Nc6 3 Bc4 Nf6 4 Nc3 Bb4 5 0–0 0–0 6 d3 d6 7 Bg5 Bxc3 8 bxc3 Be6 9 Bb3 a5 10 a4 h6 11 Bh4 Bxb3 12 cxb3 Qe7 13 Ne1 g5 14 Bg3 Rad8 15 h4 d5 16 hxg5 hxg5 17 Qf3 d4 18 c4 Kg7 19 Qf5 Nh5 20 Nf3 f6 21 Qg4 Rh8 22 Nh4 Kf7 23 Nf5 Qe6 24 Bh2 Rdg8 25 Qd1 Nf4 26 g3 Nh3+ 27 Kg2 Ne7 28 g4 Rh7 29 Rh1 Rgh8 30 Qd2 Qb6 31 Qc2 Ng6

. (Black has a decisive advantage: the HOLE at f4 is of more consequence than the hole at f5.) 32 Kf3 Nhf4 33 c5 (White begins an ingenious but not quite adequate counterattack on the queen's side.) 33 . . . Qa6 34 Bxf4 Rxh1 35 Rxh1 Rxh1 36 Bd2 Nf4 37 Bxf4 gxf4 38 Kg2 Rh7 39 b4 axb4 40 Qb3+ Qe6 41 Qxb4 Kg6 42 Qxb7 Kg5 43 a5 (Black wins also after 43 Kf3 Rh3+ 44 Kg2 Kxg4) 43 . . . Kxg4 44 a6 f3+ 45 Kg1 Qa2 46 Ne3+ dxe3 47 Qc8+ Kh4 White resigns.

Lasker, Edward (1885–1981), German-born American player and author, International Master

(1963), International Arbiter (1956), engineer. After winning several national tournaments in the USA, Lasker challenged MARSHALL for the US championship, losing narrowly (+4=9−5) in a match of 18 games in 1923. While still living in Germany he wrote in 1911 *Schachstrategie*, an English version, *Chess Strategy*, appearing in 1915, after the author's emigration. For the first time a competent teaching method was used to explain the whole game and, revised from time to time, the book remained popular for many years. Of his other books, the autobiographical *Chess Secrets I Learned from the Masters* (1951) is more entertaining than factual.

Lasker, Emanuel (1868–1941), German player, world champion 1894–1921. He was born in Berlinchen in Brandenburg (now Barlinek, Poland) where his father held a minor post in the synagogue. While on a visit to Berlin when he was eleven years old his elder brother, Berthold, taught him the moves of chess, and Emanuel was immediately fascinated by the game. He was sent away to school, where he showed a remarkable talent for mathematics, and after passing his school finals he returned to Berlin in March 1888. Dividing his time between university studies and chess, he improved so much at the game that he gained the German master title in the HAUPTTURNIER at Breslau 1889.

After returning to Berlin he defeated BARDELEBEN (+2=1−1) and MIESES (+5=3) and at Liverpool in 1890 he defeated BIRD (+7=3−2). His first important tournament success was in a small but strong event at London 1892, first (+5=3), half a point ahead of BLACKBURNE. These two then played a match, and when Lasker won decisively (+6=4) he began to think of the possibility of becoming world champion. He challenged TARRASCH who declined to play, suggesting that Lasker should first win a major tournament.

Lasker then took the bold step of going to the USA where he might meet the title-holder, STEINITZ. Within two years, during which his successes included the defeat of the American champion SHOWALTER (+6=1−2), he succeeded in obtaining a match with Steinitz. He emerged victorious (+10=4−5) in May 1894, but the chess world was not unduly impressed with his defeat of a man 32 years his senior: he had yet to prove himself. The world's greatest players competed at Hastings 1895 where Lasker, convalescent from a near-fatal illness, took third place (+14=3−4) after PILLSBURY and CHIGORIN, ahead of Tarrasch and Steinitz. Lasker's chess was still improving and he established beyond doubt his position as the world's best player by winning four successive major tournaments: St Petersburg 1895–6, a four-master match tournament (+8=7−3), ahead of Steinitz, Pillsbury, and Chigorin; Nuremberg 1896 (+12=3−3), ahead of MARÓCZY, Pillsbury, Tarrasch, Steinitz, and Chigorin; London 1899 (+18=7−1), 4½ points ahead of JANOWSKI, Maróczy, and Pillsbury who shared second prize; and

Paris 1900 ($+14=1-1$), ahead of Pillsbury and Maróczy. During this period he also defeated Steinitz in a return match 1896–7 ($+10=5-2$). Nor had he neglected his mathematics. Two years at Heidelberg University 1897–9, a thesis presented at Erlangen University in 1900, and he gained his doctorate.

After nearly four years without hard practice he entered Cambridge Springs 1904 and came second ($+9=4-2$) equal with Janowski, two points behind MARSHALL. For the next few years Lasker settled in the United States, and during this period he accepted challenges from Tarrasch and Maróczy, two of his strongest three rivals, but nothing came of them. (His other rival, Pillsbury, died in 1906.) In 1907 Lasker played a championship match against Marshall and won easily ($+8=7$). Returning to Germany in 1908 he played and defeated Tarrasch ($+8=5-3$).

At St Petersburg 1909 Lasker and RUBINSTEIN set a cracking pace, scoring $+13=3-2$ and $+12=5-1$ respectively to share first place. The third-prize winners were DURAS and SPIELMANN, $3\frac{1}{2}$ points behind. Later that year Lasker played two exhibition matches against JANOWSKI, drawing the first ($+2-2$) and winning the second ($+7=2-1$), and early in 1910 he met SCHLECHTER in a match of ten games. A hard-fought struggle ended in a tie ($+1=8-1$), the arbiter declaring that Lasker was still champion. (For an account of the match, see SCHLECHTER.) A few months later Lasker defeated Janowski ($+8=3$), his fourth championship match in a four-year period. Subsequently he was challenged by both CAPABLANCA and Rubinstein, his closest rivals, but negotiations came to nothing.

In 1911 Lasker married Martha Cohn, the widow of an industrialist, and gained financial security.

Lasker at the outset of his career

However, he continued to work at chess, his next tournament being St Petersburg 1914, a historic event because Capablanca, now clearly favoured as a challenger, met Lasker for the first time in a formal tournament. In the first stage, an all-play-all contest of eleven players, Capablanca scored 8, Lasker $6\frac{1}{2}$. These two, along with ALEKHINE, Marshall, and Tarrasch, then competed in a double-round all-play-all second stage. In this Lasker made the astonishing score of six wins and two draws to take first prize ($+10=7-1$), half a point ahead of Capablanca, both well ahead of the field. A match between them seemed probable, but the First World War intervened.

The war may have extended Lasker's tenure of the title beyond its natural span, but he could still play world-class chess, as he demonstrated in a small but strong tournament at Berlin 1918 when he came first ($+3=3$), ahead of Rubinstein, Schlechter, and Tarrasch. Nevertheless Lasker was defeated by Capablanca in their match of 1921. Freedom from the burden of holding the title seemed to give Lasker a new zest, and he won tournaments at Ostrava 1923 ($+8=5$) and at New York 1924 ($+13=6-1$), ahead of Capablanca and Alekhine. These two achievements, astonishing for a man of his age, were his last tournament victories.

From 1895 to 1924 he had played in ten major tournaments, winning or sharing eight first prizes, one second, and one third. His 78 per cent score in these events ($+119=46-18$), spread over 30 years, was easily the best record of the time. He played in five more tournaments: Moscow 1925, second ($+10=8-2$) after BOGOLJUBOW, ahead of Capablanca; Zurich 1934, fifth ($+9=2-4$); Moscow 1935, third ($+6=13$), after BOTVINNIK and FLOHR, ahead of Capablanca; Moscow 1936, sixth; and Nottingham 1936 ($+6=5-3$) to share seventh place. He played in the last four from necessity. As a result of the persecution of Jews he and his wife were driven out of Germany in 1933 and their property confiscated. In England from 1933, the USSR from 1935, he went finally to the USA in 1937, and there he died.

A fine tactician, an expert in manœuvring, Lasker was also one of the greatest defensive players. In the opening phase he did not intentionally seek inferior positions, a common misconception fostered by RÉTI. He liked to leave the beaten track and was not concerned that this sometimes left him with a slight disadvantage, providing the position offered scope for his talent. He believed that such positions were defensible and he had the skill to back his belief. Sceptical of all dogma, he played positions as they arose and according to their nature or his opponent's predilections. He intentionally avoided making long-term plans, believing them to be undesirable; games rarely unfold in a logical way, and holding to a fixed idea might impair a player's judgement. His head ruled his heart, and Lasker owed much to his great strength of character. He entered few tournaments, but concentrated hard in every game in every event.

More successfully than his contemporaries he learned how to cope with his own errors. He knew that in a series of games he would sooner or later make a mistake. When this happened he was prepared, remaining calm, and immediately seeking the best course in a changed situation. Lasker could make a mistake 'and smile, knowing that perfection is not granted to mortal man', writes FINE.

Lasker wrote several books. His first, *Common Sense in Chess* (1896), based on a series of lectures, ran to more than 30 editions or translations. *Lehrbuch des Schachspiels* (1926), rewritten by him in English as *Lasker's Manual of Chess* (1927), describes his approach to the game, gives a sympathetic testimony to Steinitz, and offers an explanation of the THEORY of the game, attributed to Steinitz. He wrote one tournament book (St Petersburg 1909), and edited four short-lived chess magazines. An educated man with an enquiring mind, Lasker also wrote on other subjects. He published several mathematical papers and his thesis on geometrical calculus remains relevant in the computer age. He wrote books on philosophy, drawing analogies with chess. These are not without interest but philosophers noted that he constructed no logical system. He recognized this himself, and in his book *Struggle* (1907) he suggested that more experienced hands should build on his ideas. He also wrote books on bridge—he was an international player in the early 1930s—and on other games. His last book, *The Community of the Future* (1940), a sociological study, sets forward his ideas for the creation of non-competitive educational self-help co-operatives.

'A gentleman of culture, pleasing manners, and becoming modesty', wrote HOFFER in 1890, adding that Lasker did not wish to become a professional, but would always maintain an interest in the game. Fate decreed otherwise. Lasker earned his living by chess for most of his life, but he never spent all his time on the game, nor let it dominate his life. He was greatly affected by Steinitz's impoverishment, and demanded high fees whenever he played, believing a champion should be properly rewarded. Popular among the rank and file whom he met on his many simultaneous tours, he would have preferred to gain financial support in small donations rather than from patronage; but he became disillusioned when such attempts repeatedly failed. Because of his high demands, he appeared infrequently in major events, but he gave good value for money. In his prime he never played for a draw. For appearing at St Petersburg 1914 he was paid 4,000 roubles. 'I do not find this too much for one who plays like this . . . for the inspired games he played in this tournament', writes Tarrasch. (See BACKWARD PAWN; BAUER.)

F. Reinfeld and R. Fine, *Dr Lasker's Chess Career* (1935), reprinted as *Lasker's Greatest Games 1889–1914* (1965); J. Gilchrist and K. Whyld, *Lasker I* (1955), *Lasker II* (1957), *Lasker III* (1957), contain a total of 1,142 unannotated games.

Alekhine–Lasker   New York 1924   Queen's Gambit Declined Exchange Variation

1 d4 d5 2 c4 e6 3 Nf3 Nf6 4 Nc3 Nbd7 5 cxd5 exd5 6 Bf4 c6 7 e3 Nh5 8 Bd3 Nxf4 9 exf4 Bd6 10 g3 0–0 11 0–0 Re8 12 Qc2 Nf8 13 Nd1 f6 14 Ne3 Be6 15 Nh4 Bc7 16 b4 Bb6 17 Nf3 Bf7 18 b5 (a premature MINORITY ATTACK) 18 . . . Bh5 19 g4 Bf7 20 bxc6 Rc8 21 Qb2 bxc6 22 f5 Qd6 23 Ng2 Bc7 24 Rfe1 h5 25 h3 Nh7 26 Rxe8+ Rxe8 27 Re1 Rb8 28 Qc1

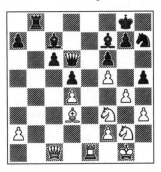

28 . . . Ng5 29 Ne5 fxe5 30 Qxg5 e4 31 f6 g6 32 f4 hxg4 33 Be2 gxh3 34 Bh5 Rb2 35 Nh4 Qxf4 36 Qxf4 Bxf4 White resigns.

Lasker Defence, 886, played in the game Chigorin–Lasker, St Petersburg 1895–6, and usually regarded as the most solid way of defending the EVANS GAMBIT Accepted. The defence was first played by BOURDONNAIS, in his 26th match game against McDONNELL, 1834.

Lasker Gambit, 263 in the STAUNTON GAMBIT, a line which came to attention after the game Lasker–Pillsbury, Paris 1900, although it had been played in Martinez–Mason, Philadelphia 1876. Also the similar 264.

Lasker–Pelikán Variation, 488, the PELIKÁN VARIATION of the SICILIAN DEFENCE.

Lasker Trap, 111 in the ALBIN COUNTER-GAMBIT; if 6 Bxb4 exf2+ 7 Ke2 fxg1 = N +, and Black wins, a trap first pointed out by DUBOIS in 1872.

Lasker Variation, 89 in the SLAV DEFENCE, as played in Verlinsky–Lasker, Moscow 1925, following analysis by a Canadian, Georges Maréchal (hence the occasional name, Maréchal Variation); 184, sometimes called the Atkins Variation, in the QUEEN'S GAMBIT Declined, played three times by LASKER in his match against MARSHALL in 1907, or 207, the same line played two moves later; 600 in the SCANDINAVIAN OPENING, with the idea of playing Pg2-g4, Ne5, and Nc4, suggested by Lasker in his book of the 1909 St Petersburg tournament; 12 Nbd2 Nc6 (RUBINSTEIN VARIATION) in the SPANISH OPENING, a pawn sacrifice (13 . . . cxd4 14 cxd4 Nxd4 15 Nxd4 exd4) arising out of the CHIGORIN VARIATION (746) and introduced Lasker–Tarrasch, 3rd match game 1908; 786 in the SCHLIEMANN DEFENCE to the Spanish, recommended by

Lasker in *Lasker's Chess Magazine*, 1904; 1067 in the PETROFF DEFENCE, attributed to COZIO; 1208 in the FRENCH DEFENCE, played in the 4th game of Lasker's match against MARSHALL in 1907; 1256 in the ALEKHINE DEFENCE, sometimes called the Advance Variation, the Pursuit Variation, or the Two Pawns Attack, introduced by Lasker in a simultaneous display, 1927; 1314 in the BIRD OPENING, from a game Bird–Lasker 1892, although the line had been played earlier.

Also 760, the EXCHANGE VARIATION of the SPANISH OPENING, played in tournaments more than a dozen times by Lasker; 881, the ALAPIN VARIATION of the EVANS GAMBIT, frequently leading to the LASKER DEFENCE; 985 the LOYD–LASKER VARIATION of the SCOTCH GAME; 1196, the RUBINSTEIN VARIATION of the French Defence, used by Lasker in the world championship match of 1894, and in the match in 1907 against Marshall, who played the French in every game where he was Black.

last move problem. The solver examines a composed position, and by means of RETROGRADE ANALYSIS tries to discover the last SINGLE-MOVE that must have been played, as if the position had arisen in a game. The laws of the game are deemed to apply unless other laws are stated or implied. The STIPULATIONS may or may not state which side made the last move.

Last move?

A last move problem by KEYM, *Feenschach*, 1977. Pc7-c6 was played long ago, so White moved last. Black's KB was captured on f8, and Black's KR on its back row, from h8-d8. White's rooks on d8 and e8 were created by promotion; this implies captures on c7 and d8 of a black piece created by promotion of the a-pawn, a black Q, and two black Ns. As the retractions Ra8 × Rb8, Pc7 × Rb8, and Pc7 × Q(B,N) = R would all lead back to illegal positions, White's last move must have been Pa7 × Rb8 = R.

latent pawn, an 18th–century proposal. If a player advances a pawn to the eighth rank before losing a piece, the pawn remains dead but is immediately promoted to the first piece lost. For an example of this, see PROMOTION. The latent pawn is not to be confused with the dummy pawn, a pawn on the eighth rank which, at its owner's request, remains a pawn. Neither version is to be found outside the realms of FAIRY PROBLEMS.

Latvian Counter-gambit, 1044, the GRECO COUNTER-GAMBIT. It was studied by players from Riga, in particular by Karl Behting (1867–1943) whose analysis appeared in *St Petersburger Zeitung*, 1909, and by APŠENIEKS who played it frequently, e.g. in the 1930 Olympiad.

Lau, Ralf (1959–), German champion 1987 (shared with HORT), International Grandmaster (1986). First at Budapest 1986 and equal first Budapest 1985, his best results are two shared second places in very strong tournaments at Manhattan 1985 and Solingen 1986.

Lautier, Joël (1973–), Canadian-born Frenchman, Junior World Champion 1988, International Grandmaster (1990), and, in 1990, the first Frenchman to reach the interzonal stage of the world championship. He played on first board for France in the 1990 Olympiad at Novi Sad. He was taught chess at the age of 3 by his Japanese mother.

laws, or laws of chess. Internationally accepted laws, now drawn up by the FIDE Rules Commission, consist of 19 articles of which the first 10 apply to chess at all levels while the remainder are concerned with competitive play at a formal level (see RULES).

The first five articles define chess.

Art. 1 states that the game is between two opponents and defines the BOARD and its correct placing, and the terms FILE, RANK, and DIAGONAL.

Art. 2 enumerates the men, shows their FIGURINES and gives the ARRAY.

Arts. 3 and 4 say that White has the initial move and define a move.

Art. 5 gives the moves of each man.

Art. 6 defines the completion of a move.

Art. 7 is the TOUCH AND MOVE LAW.

Art. 8 gives the procedure to follow if an ILLEGAL MOVE is made or if an ILLEGAL POSITION arises.

Art. 9 defines CHECK and CHECKMATE.

Art. 10 states that a game is won by checkmate or if the opponent RESIGNS, and gives the five ways by which a game may be drawn: by agreement, by STALEMATE, by REPETITION OF POSITION, under the FIFTY-MOVE LAW, or if the forces on the board are insufficient for either side to mate.

laws, history of. The fundamental laws, such as the ARRAY, how the CHESSMEN move, and CHECKMATE, have remained unchanged in essentials since the beginning of the game, although the FERS has been displaced by the queen and the ALFIL by the bishop. There is a more turbulent record for a second group of laws covering auxiliary aspects of play (CASTLING, EN PASSANT, FIFTY-MOVE LAW, PASSAR BATTAGLIA, PROMOTION, REPETITION OF POSITION, STALEMATE). A third group has developed but changed little in intent; it embraces what might be called conventions, such as the orientation of the board, FIRST MOVE, TOUCH AND MOVE LAW, J'ADOUBE, ILLEGAL MOVES, what a spectator may or may not do, what to do if it is discovered that a king has been in check for some moves, penalties, and BEHAVIOUR.

As clubs arose, so did the need for formal laws. Commonly it was agreed that PHILIDOR, SARRATT, or WALKER, for example, would be followed. None of these authorities included the essential basic conditions, perhaps because their laws were published in explanatory textbooks. Leading clubs sometimes published their own sets of laws—The Hague in 1803, London in 1807, Paris in 1836, and St Petersburg in 1854. This last was produced by JAENISCH, one of the three great workers for a unified code. At the time of the London 1851 tournament, STAUNTON called for a 'Constituent Assembly for Remodelling the Laws of Chess'. The other leading activist, LASA, published his proposals in *Schachzeitung*, 1854. Staunton's proposals, first published in the *Illustrated London News* and *Chess Praxis*, both in 1860, became generally accepted in English-speaking countries, but the incompatible laws of the British Chess Association were used at London 1862 and elsewhere. Other tournament organizers offered their own versions or used those published first by the British Chess Company in 1894. German-speaking countries usually followed BERGER'S yearbook or the latest edition of Bilguer's HANDBUCH.

One of the earliest tasks undertaken by FIDE was to produce an international code. The first editions, 1929, 1952, 1955, and 1966 (with intervening amendments) were written in French. Each country had its own translation, and so the British version was not identical with the American one, for example. Since 1974 the laws have been published in English in the first instance. Many countries, such as the USSR, continued to use their own set of laws for internal competitions; in 1984 FIDE abandoned hope of publishing a set of laws that would be universally accepted, and brought out a new code designed for events under FIDE's control. For the first time, the FIDE laws relate only to chess at the highest level. There is no section that could be detached and used as an authority for those millions playing informally.

Obsolete or fictitious laws may still be found in ill-written primers and games encyclopedias, or may be supplied with cheap sets, a situation aggravated by the decision made in 1984 by FIDE.

Laws, Benjamin Glover (1861–1931), English problemist, composer of more than 1,000 problems, first president of the British Chess Problem Society. However, he is best remembered as an editor. After the death of ZUKERTORT in 1888 he was recruited by HOFFER to deal with problems for *Chess Monthly*, which he did for the remaining eight years of that journal's life. In 1898 he became problem editor for *The British Chess Magazine*, and remained so until

his death. More than any one man, writes DAWSON, Laws created the English School (see PROBLEM HISTORY; see also COINCIDENCE; KAMIKAZE PIECE; REFLEX CHESS; SHORTHAND).

leaper, a piece that is moved a fixed distance in a single leap and that cannot be obstructed on its way. Using the distance between the centres of two laterally adjoining squares as a unit of measurement, the leaper's move may be defined by the length of its move, or by the co-ordinates of its leap. For example, the knight is a leaper that is moved a distance of $\sqrt{5}$ squares for which the co-ordinates are 1 and 2. Because the length of move cannot be varied a leaper cannot LOSE THE MOVE on a normal board.

Some other leapers are: the FĪL ($\sqrt{8}$ or 2,2) used in the old game; the DABBABA ($\sqrt{4}$ or 2,0), the CAMEL ($\sqrt{10}$ or 3,1), and the GIRAFFE ($\sqrt{17}$ or 4,1), used in Islamic unorthodox chess; the ZEBRA ($\sqrt{13}$ or 3,2), the FIVE-LEAPER ($\sqrt{25}$), and the ROOT 50 LEAPER, invented for use in FAIRY PROBLEMS. Each of the last two has two sets of co-ordinates: for the five-leaper 4,3 and 5,0; for the $\sqrt{50}$ leaper 5,5 and 7,1. A GNU combines the powers of knight and camel, moving at will in the manner of either piece.

legal, in accordance with the laws of chess. Composers commonly use the word to describe positions that could have arisen from the array.

Legall de Kermeur (1702–92), champion player of the CAFÉ DE LA RÉGENCE and PHILIDOR's teacher. He was described as 'a thin, pale, old gentleman, who had sat in the same seat in the Café, and worn the same green coat for a number of years . . . While he played at chess he took snuff in such profusion that his chitterling frill was literally saturated with strong particles of the powder . . . He was in the habit of enlivening the company during the progress of a game by a variety of remarks which everybody admired for their brilliance.' He is said to have originated the unorthodox PAWNS GAME. For the only known game played by him see Legall's mate (below).

Legall's mate, a checkmate similar to the following prototype.

Legall–St Brie   Paris, 1750   Bishop's Opening

1 e4 e5 2 Bc4 d6 3 Nf3 Bg4 4 Nc3 g6? 5 Nxe5 Bxd1 6 Bxf7+ Ke7 7 Nd5. The SEA-CADET MATE is another version.

Legall's trap, an opening trap that may be compared to LEGALL'S MATE. A knight captures on K5 (e5 for White, e4 for Black) thus leaving a queen EN PRISE to a bishop. This trap has ensnared CAPABLANCA, CHIGORIN, TARRASCH, and many other victims including this one in a correspondence game played in Australia during 1938.

D. G. Benjafield–C. J. Wippell.   Spanish Opening.

1 e4 e5 2 Nf3 Nc6 3 Bb5 Nge7 4 Nc3 a6 5 Ba4 b5 6 Bb3 h6 7 d4 d6 8 a4 b4 9 Nd5 Bg4

10 Nxe5 Bxd1 (a blunder, but hard to resist) 11 Nf6+ gxf6 12 Bxf7 mate. After 10 ... Nxe5 11 f3 Nxf3+ 12 gxf3 Bh3 White has a clear advantage.

Lein, Anatoly Yakovlevich (1931–), Soviet-born player, International Grandmaster (1968), mathematician. His best achievement in the USSR championship was at Tbilisi 1967, the third of his seven attempts, when he took sixth place (+7=9−4). In the early 1970s he began to win strong events including the Moscow championship in 1971 and four international tournaments: Moscow 1970 (+8=1−2), a shared victory; Cienfuegos 1972 (+9=10); Novi Sad 1972 (+9=6); and Novi Sad 1973 (+9=6). In 1976 Lein emigrated to the USA, since when his best results have been: first place in the Swiss system US Open Championship 1976 (shared with another ex-Soviet player, SHAMKO-VICH); a shared third place, after KORCHNOI and LJUBOJEVIĆ, São Paulo 1979; first Brisbane 1979; equal first with SEIRAWAN at Grand Manan 1984; and first (+7=5−1) at Vestmannaeyjar 1985.

Lein–Benjamin   Estes Park 1986 US Championship
Queen's Indian Defence

1 d4 Nf6 2 Nf3 e6 3 c4 b6 4 Nc3 Bb4 5 Bg5 h6 6 Bh4 Bxc3+ 7 bxc3 Bb7 8 Nd2 d6 9 f3 Nbd7 10 e4 g5 11 Bf2 Nh5 12 g3 f5 13 Bd3 Qf6 14 Qe2 0–0 15 h4 Ng7 16 Rh2 c5 17 hxg5 Qxg5 18 Rh3 cxd4 19 cxd4 fxe4 20 Nxe4 Qa5+ 21 Kf1 h5 22 Kg1 d5 23 cxd5 Qxd5 24 Rf1 Nf6 25 Rh4 Rac8 26 Rf4 Nxe4 27 fxe4 Qd6 28 Be3 Rxf4 29 Rxf4 Rc3 30 Bc4 b5 31 Bb3 a5 32 Qd2 Qb4 33 d5 a4 34 d6 axb3 35 d7 b2 36 d8=Q+ Kh7

37 Rf7 b1=Q+ 38 Kf2 Q1xe4 39 Rxg7+ Kxg7 40 Q2d7+ Black resigns.

Leipzig Variation, 291, the FAJAROWICZ VARIATION, much played in the city where its creator lived.

Lemberg Gambit, 1299, the TENNISON GAMBIT, revived in 1917 by WAGNER of Lvov (German name, Lemberg).

Lengfellner System, an openings approach of which 235 is one example; the plan, whether White or Black, is to move the d- and e-pawns one square forward, in either order. Lengfellner, a Berlin physician, financed a match between Alexei Selezniev (1888–1967) and BARDELEBEN in 1920 to test the line (won by Selezniev +2=4), although one of the purposes of the system is to enable a player without book knowledge to open a game securely.

length of game is customarily measured by the number of moves made by White. If the FIFTY-MOVE LAW were applied throughout then the longest possible game would last 5,949 moves (A. F. H. Britten, 1956), but the various exceptions made to that law since then call for periodical adjustments. In practice the average length of a game is from 35 to 40 moves, and games rarely exceed 100 moves. The longest game played in a world championship match was the 5th game between KORCHNOI (White) and Karpov in 1978, which ended in STALEMATE on the 124th move; in master chess a game I. Nikolić–Arsović, Belgrade 1989, ended in a draw on Black's 269th move.

Leningrad System, a DUTCH DEFENCE which is played on the lines of a KING'S INDIAN DEFENCE, as in 256 for example. The line, which gives greater mobility for Black's bishops than is found in most Dutch Defence variations, was pioneered by three men from Leningrad, the players Nikolai Georgyevich Kopylov (1919–), Yevgeny Filipovich Kuzminikh (1911–), and professor of history Kirill Vinogradov, and made popular by KORCHNOI.

Leningrad Variation, 270 and 271, examples of the LENINGRAD SYSTEM in the DUTCH DEFENCE; 333 in the NIMZO-INDIAN DEFENCE, a line (also known as the Réti Variation) played by ALEKHINE and others and restored by SPASSKY (after whom it is sometimes named), KORCHNOI, and Vladimir Grigoriyevich Zak (1913–), all from Leningrad; 1235 in the FRENCH DEFENCE, as played in the Leningrad championship 1949 (in this case, the name is not commonly used in Russia).

Lenzerheide Variation, 747 in the SPANISH OPENING, a line first played in the game Schlechter–Bardeleben, Coburg 1904, revived in the 1940s as the Flohr–Zaitsev or Zaitsev Variation, and taken up during the 1956 Clare Benedict team tournament at Lenzerheide. It was played several times in the 1990 world championship match, Kasparov–Karpov. (See KARPOV; SAX.)

leo, a fairy piece that is moved like a LION for capturing moves and like a queen for non-capturing moves. A member of the so-called CHINESE FAMILY, this piece was devised by the British soldier Major J. Akenhead in 1947.

Leonardo di Bona, Giovanni (1542–87), Neapolitan lawyer and one of the strongest players of his time. Known as *Il puttino* (the bairn) because of his slight build, he toured the Iberian Peninsula and Italy successfully, meeting the strongest opposition including Ruy LÓPEZ. Unfortunately most of what we know about Leonardo comes from SALVIO's chess romance *Il Puttino* (Naples, 1634), in which it is difficult to disentangle fact and fiction.

Leonhardt, Paul Saladin (1877–1934), player, journalist. Born in Poznań, Leonhardt became keen on chess while studying at Leipzig, and subsequently spent most of his life in Germany. His best results were in 1907 when he was first (+3=5), ahead of MARÓCZY and SCHLECHTER, in a double-round tournament at Copenhagen, and won third prize (+9=9−2), after RUBINSTEIN and Maróczy, in the Carlsbad tournament. In match play he defeated NIMZOWITSCH (+4−1) at Hamburg in 1911. Leonhardt is also remembered as an analyst of openings, especially the SPANISH OPENING, about which he wrote a monograph, *Zur spanischen Partie* (1913). He died of a heart attack while playing a game at the Königsberg chess club.

Leonhardt–Tarrasch Hamburg 1910 First Brilliancy Prize
Three Knights Opening

1 e4 e5 2 Nf3 Nc6 3 Nc3 Bb4 4 Nd5 Ba5 5 Bc4 d6 6 0–0 Nf6 7 d3 h6? 8 c3 Nxd5 9 exd5 Ne7 10 d4 exd4 11 Qa4+ c6 12 dxc6 bxc6 13 Nxd4 Bd7 14 Re1 Kf8 15 Bf4 Bc7 16 Qa3 Nc8 17 Re3 Kg8 18 Rae1 d5 19 Bxc7 Qxc7

20 Re8+ Bxe8 21 Rxe8+ Kh7 22 Bd3+ f5 23 Rxh8+ Kxh8 24 Qf8+ Kh7 25 Bxf5+ g6 26 Bxg6+ Black resigns.

Leonhardt Attack or **Leonhardt–Sozin Attack,** 469, the SOZIN ATTACK in the SICILIAN DEFENCE, analysed by LEONHARDT in 1910.

Leonhardt Gambit, 596, the KOTRČ–MIESES GAMBIT instigated by LEONHARDT in the game Leonhardt–Mieses, Prague 1908.

Leonhardt Variation, 470 in the SICILIAN DEFENCE, analysed by LEONHARDT in 1910; 740 in the SPANISH OPENING; 818 in the PONZIANI OPENING, analysed by Leonhardt in COLLIJN's *Lärobok*, 1911; 868 in the EVANS GAMBIT Accepted, for which he published analysis in *Deutsches Wochenschach*, 1906; 968 in the FEGATELLO ATTACK, given by Leonhardt in *Tidskrift för Schack*, 1907; 1218, a TARRASCH VARIATION in the FRENCH DEFENCE endorsed by Leonhardt.

Lepuschütz, Hans (1910–84), Austrian composer, International Judge of Chess Compositions (1957), International Master for Chess Compositions (1966), a leading specialist in MORE-MOVERS. His work often shows strategical ideas in a clear way, ending in MODEL MATE.

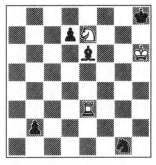

\#5

A problem by Lepuschütz, second prize, *Freie Presse*, 1967. 1 Ra3 Bd5 2 Rc3 Bc6 3 Rg3 Bd5 4 Rg8+ Bxg8 5 Ng6 mate. 1 Rc3? d6!; 1 Rg3? b1 = Q.

Lerner, Konstantin Zaivelevich (1950–), Ukrainian player, International Grandmaster (1986). His best results are first or equal first at Polanica Zdrój 1985 (+8=5−2), Moscow 1986 (+5=6−2), Polanica Zdrój 1986 (+5=7), Tallinn 1986, Genoa 1989, and second (+7=9−1) in the USSR championship 1984.

Lesser Bishop's Gambit, 1114 in the KING'S GAMBIT Accepted, a line in which 3 Be2 takes the bishop less far than c4 (the BISHOP'S GAMBIT). This gambit was originated in 1842 by JAENISCH, after whom it is sometimes named, and pioneered by BIRD in the 1880s. Occasionally it is called after TARTAKOWER who played it four times at the New York tournament, 1924. Although rarely played, this gambit is not less favourable to White than the Bishop's Gambit or the KING'S KNIGHT GAMBIT.

Lesser Giuoco Piano, 936, another name for the SEMI-ITALIAN OPENING.

Levenfish, Grigory Yakovlevich (1889–1961), International Grandmaster (1950), a leading Russian player (although born in Poland) of the generation that learned the game before the revolution, and led Soviet chess in the 1920s and 1930s, engineer in the glass industry. After winning the St Petersburg championship in 1909, Levenfish played in several local events and one tournament abroad, Carlsbad 1911. He won the Leningrad championship in 1922, 1924, and 1925 (shared), and had an excellent record in the USSR championship tournaments: 1920 third, 1923 second, 1924 equal third, 1925 second, 1933 equal third, 1934–5 co-champion, 1937 champion. (Five attempts at the title during the next ten years were less successful.) In match play he drew with BOTVINNIK in 1937 ($+5=3-5$) and defeated ALATORTSEV in 1940 ($+5=7-2$); and in the Leningrad–Moscow training tournament 1939 he shared third place after FLOHR and RESHEVSKY.

Rook Endings (1971) is the English translation of a book he and SMYSLOV published in 1957; *Izbrannye party i vospominanya* (1967) contains 79 annotated games, and reminiscences.

Botvinnik–Levenfish   2nd match game 1937   Queen's Gambit Declined Slav Defence

1 d4 d5 2 c4 c6 3 Nc3 Nf6 4 e3 g6 5 Nf3 Bg7 6 Bd3 0–0 7 0–0 e6 8 b3 Nbd7 9 Qe2 Re8 10 Bb2 b6 11 Rad1 Bb7 12 Ne5 Nxe5 13 dxe5 Nd7 14 f4 Qe7 15 cxd5 exd5 16 e4 d4 17 Nb1 c5 18 Nd2

18 ... g5 19 g3 gxf4 20 gxf4 Kh8 21 Nc4 Rg8 22 Kh1 f6 23 Nd6 fxe5 24 Nxb7 exf4 25 e5 Bxe5 26 b4 Nf6 27 Qf3 Ng4 28 Rd2 Rab8 29 Be4 d3 30 Qxd3 Rxb7 31 Bxb7 Qxb7+ 32 Qf3 Qxf3+ 33 Rxf3 Bxb2 34 Rxb2 Ne5 35 Rf1 Nd3 36 Rg2 c4 37 Rc2 b5 38 a3 f3 39 Rd2 Rg2 40 Rxg2 fxg2+ 41 Kxg2 c3 42 Kf3 c2 The game was adjourned here and Botvinnik resigned without resumption.

Levenfish Attack, 537, a popular way, developed by LEVENFISH in the 1930s, of meeting the DRAGON VARIATION. Sometimes called the Czerniak Attack.

Levenfish Variation, 132, a recommendation by LEVENFISH made in the Russian Yearbook, 1937, in which he gave a 53-page analysis of the QUEEN'S GAMBIT; 383, line in the GRÜNFELD DEFENCE abandoned because of the reply 8 e5; 884, a colourful but possibly unsound sacrifice in the EVANS GAMBIT.

Levitsky Variation, 233, as in Levitsky–Rubinstein, Vilna 1912 (where the Russian master Stepan

Mikhailovich Levitsky (1876–1924) finished third, just behind RUBINSTEIN and BERNSTEIN, and ahead of NIMZOWITSCH, ALEKHINE, LEVENFISH, and others); 56, the RICHTER ATTACK, where the characteristic move is played later.

Levy, David Neil Lawrence (1945–), English player who, as an IM, represented Scotland in the Olympiads. He is better known as an author and expert on computer chess.

Lewis, William (1787–1870), English player and author. Leaving his native Birmingham as a young man, he worked for a time with a merchant in London. He learned much of his chess from SARRATT, a debt that was not repaid. Around 1819 he was operator of the TURK, meeting all-comers successfully. With COCHRANE he visited Paris in 1821 and, receiving odds of pawn and move from DESCHAPELLES, defeated him in a short match ($+1=2$). Lewis had already begun to write and of the more useful books he published around this time were translations of GRECO and CARRERA which appeared in 1819 and 1822 respectively. Although he considered Sarratt's *A Treatise on the Game of Chess* (1808) a poorly written book, Lewis brought out a second edition in 1822 in direct competition with Sarratt's own (and superior) revision, published in 1821 by his impoverished widow. (In 1843 many contributed to a fund for Mrs Sarratt in her old age. Lewis's name is not on the subscription list.) In 1825 BOURDONNAIS visited England. Lewis recalled that they played about 70 games, and according to WALKER seven of them constituted a match which Lewis lost ($+2-5$).

With no significant playing achievement to his credit Lewis acquired such a high reputation that a correspondent writing to the weekly magazine *Bell's Life* in 1838 was moved to call him GRAND-MASTER. From 1825 he preserved this reputation by the simplest means: he declined to play on even terms. In the same year he opened a club where he gave lessons. Walker and MCDONNELL were among his pupils. Speculating unwisely on a piano-making patent, Lewis went bankrupt in 1827, and the club closed. After three precarious years of teaching chess (rich patrons were becoming fewer) Lewis became actuary of the Family Endowment Society and enjoyed financial security for the rest of his life.

Circumstances now made it possible for him to concentrate on his writing, and he published his most important two works: *Series of Progressive Lessons* (1831) and *Second Series of Lessons* (1832), both republished with various revisions. Lewis continued to write but gradually withdrew from other chess activities. His last notable connection with chess was as stakeholder for the Morphy–Löwenthal match of 1858.

Lewis's *Lessons* contain extensive analyses of many opening variations, examined in the privacy of his study but not subjected to the rigours of competitive play. Subsequent writers, notably LASA, were influenced by these books, but the content, adequate for the 1830s, was obsolescent. Around 1840 writers no longer worked in isolation (a circumstance Lewis found unavoidable) and new positional ideas were being shaped. Because Lewis failed to assimilate these, his judgements were faulty, and his voluminous *Treatise on the Game of Chess* (1844) was out of date when published. (See SCHOOLS OF CHESS.) Industrious rather than inventive, he made only one innovation, the LEWIS COUNTER-GAMBIT; but it had no practical value in 1844, for simpler defences had already been discovered. Lewis's work commands respect, but he is more aptly described as the last and one of the best of the 'old' writers rather than the first of the new, a description more fitting for JAENISCH and the authors of Bilguer's HANDBUCH.

Lewis chessmen, perhaps the best known of antique chessmen. They are carved from walrus ivory in Scandinavian style of the 12th century. Similar carvings were made in Iceland and Britain at the same time so the source cannot be positively identified. Nor has their age been scientifically verified: they could have been made as late as the 17th century. The pawns are abstract and look like decorated tombstones. The pieces are all different in some way, the tallest being 10.5 cm. All have human representations with facial expressions varying from gloom to anger. Some of the rooks show men biting their shields in the manner of berserkers. None looks happy.

Until their discovery in 1831 the chessmen were hidden in an underground structure the size and shape of an oven on the Isle of Lewis in the Outer Hebrides. No one knows how they came to be there. Sixty-seven of them, purchased for £84, have been in the British Museum since 1831, and a further eleven are in the National Museum of Antiquities in Scotland. If other pieces were found their discovery was not made known. A belt, buckle, and 14 plain draughtsmen were also in the hoard.

Michael Taylor, *The Lewis Chessmen* (1978).

Lewis Counter-gambit, 644, an aggressive defence to the PHILIDOR VARIATION of the BISHOP'S OPENING, launched by LEWIS in 1834 with 21 pages of analysis. Although probably sound it was not much played, for other and simpler defences became available around this time.

L'Hermet Variation, 667 in the CENTRE GAME, a move with some surprise value; 801, sometimes called the Mackenzie Variation, in the SPANISH OPENING, a temporary sacrifice whose main strength again lies in surprising the opponent. Neither line was originated by the German player Rudolf l'Hermet (1859–1945), who edited for many years the chess column of his local paper, the *Magdeburgische Zeitung*, in which he gave analysis of these variations.

Liberzon, Vladimir Mikhailovich (1937–), Soviet-born player, International Grandmaster (1965). He played in five USSR championships from 1960 to 1970 making his best result, a fourth place, in 1968. His tournament achievements around this time include a fourth place ($+4=8-1$) at Yerevan 1965, a score of $+7=8$ to share first prize with UHLMANN at Zinnowitz 1967, and a second place ($+5=10$), after PORTISCH, ahead of VASYUKOV and STEIN, at Amsterdam 1969. In 1973 he emigrated to Israel, won the national championship 1973–4, and played for his adopted country in several Olympiads from 1974 to 1980. His tournament wins include Beersheba 1976 (shared), Natanya 1977 (shared), Venice 1974, Lone Pine 1975, and Lone Pine 1979 (shared). The last two were strong Swiss system events.

libraries. Three outstanding collections exist in libraries open to the public. The J. G. WHITE collection in Cleveland, Ohio, and the van der Linde–Niemeijer collection in the Royal Library at The Hague are of comparable size and have no rivals. The Anderson Chess Collection in Melbourne, Australia, donated by M. V. ANDERSON, is probably

King, knight, and queen: examples of the chessmen found on the Isle of Lewis

the largest chess library in the southern hemisphere. The chess library of Grandmaster Lothar SCHMID is the largest and finest in private hands, with more than 15,000 items.

Liburkin, Mark Savelyevich (1910–53), Soviet study composer, study editor of *Shakhmaty v SSSR*, 1945–53, accountant. He shared with KOROLKOV the second USSR study-composing championship (1947–8) and won the third (1949–52) outright. His studies are original and of a high standard. (See MIRROR STALEMATE.)

Bouwmeester and Spinhoven, *De magische schaak-figuren* (1976) contains 278 studies, 83 of them by Liburkin; R. M. Kofman, *Izbrannye etyudy S. Kaminera i M. Liburkina* (1981), includes 126 of his studies.

Lichtenhein Counterattack, 1102, the COZIO DEFENCE to the KING'S GAMBIT Accepted, adopted by the German–American player Theodor Lichtenhein (1829–74).

Lichtenhein Defence, 1056 in the PETROFF DEFENCE, played in the game Morphy–Lichtenhein, New York 1857.

light bishop, a bishop that is moved on the light squares.

lightning chess, or rapid transit chess, games played much more quickly than the usual time limit demands. The term generally means games for which there is a fixed time-limit for each move, but it is sometimes also used to describe FIVE-MINUTE CHESS, which is perhaps more popular now. When each move is timed, an electronic timer is often used to ensure precision. The player must move immediately on hearing the signal, neither sooner nor later. There are no official rules, but organizers usually apply the FIDE Five-Minute Chess rules where appropriate.

An early reference to lightning chess was in 1897, when a London club organized a tournament in which players were allowed 30 seconds a move. In 1935 a tournament was played at The Hague in which different time limits were used for each batch of six moves, to allow for the natural requirements of the phases. The first 6 moves were at 15 seconds each, then 30, 45, 60, 40, 30, and finally 20 for moves 37 onwards. However, most events are at a standard 10 seconds per move. The word blitz (German for lightning), sometimes used, should not be confused with blitzkrieg, a form of UNORTHODOX CHESS.

light piece, a MINOR PIECE.

Lilienthal, Andor (1911–), International Grandmaster (1950). Born in Moscow of Hungarian parents, he was taken to Hungary at the age of two. In the early 1930s he made three notable tournament achievements: Stubnianské Teplice 1930, first (+8=2−2), ahead of PIRC and FLOHR; Hastings

1933–4, second (+5=3−1) equal with ALEKHINE; and Újpest 1934, first (+7=8), ahead of Pirc and Flohr. Playing for Hungary in three Olympiads, 1933, 1935, and 1937, he made the best second-board score (+11=8) on the second occasion.

In 1935 Lilienthal emigrated to the Soviet Union, where he took a post as chess trainer to the trades unions, and later that year he played three matches, drawing with ALATORTSEV (+4=4−4), defeating BELAVENETS (+3=5) and Yudovich (+1=1). Playing *hors concours*, he came first in the RSFSR (Russian Federation) championship of 1938. In 1939 he became a Soviet citizen, and at the Leningrad–Moscow training tournament the same year was third equal with LEVENFISH, after Flohr and RESHEVSKY. He played eight times in the USSR championship, his best result being in 1940 when he was first (+8=11) equal with BONDAREVSKY, ahead of KERES and BOTVINNIK. Other important successes are: Moscow championship 1942, third (+9=3−3) equal with KOTOV, after SMYSLOV and BOLESLAVSKY; Baku 1944, first (+6=4−1); Pärnu 1947, third after Keres and Kotov; Moscow Central Chess Club 1962, third equal, after AVERBAKH and VASYUKOV. In 1952 he defeated RAGOZIN +4=5−1 in match play. After 1965 he retired from master play, and in 1976 he returned to Hungary. (See also GREEK GIFT.)

Életem, a sakk (Budapest, 1985) is an autobiography and more than 150 annotated games; *Andre Liliental* (Moscow, 1989) is a Russian book covering the ground in more limited fashion.

Lilienthal–Stein   Kiev 1957   King's Indian Defence Sämisch Variation

1 d4 Nf6 2 c4 g6 3 Nc3 Bg7 4 e4 d6 5 f3 e5 6 Nge2 0–0 7 d5 c5 8 Bg5 a6 9 Qd2 Bd7 10 g4 b5 11 Ng3 bxc4 12 h4 Ra7 13 h5 Qa5

14 Nf5 Bxf5 15 gxf5 Nxh5 16 Rxh5 f6 17 fxg6 fxg5 18 Bh3 Rxf3 19 Be6+ Kf8 20 gxh7 Bh8 21 0–0–0 Rb7 22 Rxg5 Rg7 23 Rxg7 Bxg7 24 Rh1 Bh8 25 Qh6+ Ke7 26 Qg5+ Rf6 27 Rh6 Qd8 28 Rg6 Black resigns.

Lilienthal Variation, 156 in the SEMI-SLAV DEFENCE, introduced in the game Lilienthal–Botvinnik, USSR championship 1944.

Linde, Antonius van der (1833–97), Dutch chess historian, born Antonie van der Linden. A theologian and philosopher (his doctoral thesis was on Spinoza), he possessed great energy for research, a penetrating mind, and an acid pen. In 1870 he published his demolition of the popular Dutch legend that it was not Gutenberg, but L. J. Coster (born, like van der Linde, in Haarlem) who was the father of printing. As a consequence he became the unpopular participant in a literary war, and when real war broke out, the Franco–Prussian, he found himself even more at odds with the middle and upper classes, whose sympathies were with France. He went to Berlin in 1871 and, except for a spell in Arnhem 1874–6, lived in Germany for the rest of his days.

His *Geschichte und Litteratur des Schachspiels* (Berlin, 1874, two vols.), *Quellenstudien zur Geschichte des Schachspiels* (Berlin, 1881), and *Das erste Jartausend* [sic] *der Schachlitteratur* (Berlin, 1881) are sufficiently important to have been reprinted a century later (1979, 1968, and 1978). The most valuable of his other chess books are *De schaakpartijen van Gioachino Greco* (Nijmegen, 1865) and *Das Schachspiel des XVI. Jahrhunderts* (Berlin, 1874).

Van der Linde was the first chess historian to clear the myths about the origin of the game and to establish the game's early history. He had followed FORBES until he discovered that the British writer was dating as 3000 BC a text published in AD 1500, and constructing a whole theory based on that dating. Believing that Forbes had deliberately lied, Linde was furious, and his *Geschichte*, nearly finished, was then entirely rewritten on the basis of facts which van der Linde verified. (See BONUS SOCIUS.)

C. M. Bijl, *Antonius van der Linde* (1976), is a biography, bibliography, and games collection.

Linder, Isaak Maxovich (1920–), Russian chess historian, author of several books about the creativity of 19th-century Russian players as well as studies of the earliest traces of chess in what became the USSR. Only one of his books has been translated into English, *Chess in Old Russia* (1979). With his son Vladimir he wrote *Capablanca v Rossy* (1988), a detailed account of the champion's visits to Russia, and *Das Schachgenie Capablanca* (1988), an account of his whole career.

Lindgren, Bo Waldemar (1927–), Swedish composer, International Judge of Chess Compositions (1966), International Grandmaster for Chess Compositions (1980), writer and publicist. His father, Frithiof Lindgren (1897–1957), was also a well-known problemist. His own work includes THREE- and MORE-MOVERS, often in the BOHEMIAN style, SELFMATES, HELPMATES, and other types classified as FAIRY PROBLEMS. In 1978 he published *Maskrosor*, containing 207 problems and 6 studies composed by him.

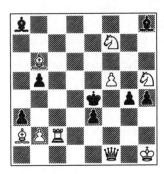

#2

A problem by Lindgren, *Dagens Nyheter*, 1982. The try 1 Bb1? is refuted only by 1 ... a2. The key is 1 Qb1 threatening 2 Rf2#.

    1 ... Kd3+   2 Rg2#
    1 ... Kxf5+   2 Rc6#
    1 ... Kf3   2 Ng5#
    1 ... e2   2 Rc3#.

line, all the squares on any one FILE, RANK, or DIAGONAL. In FAIRY PROBLEMS lines of other kinds are also used (see for example NIGHTRIDER and ROSE). Also, another name for an opening VARIATION.

line clearance, see BRISTOL CLEARANCE; ANNIHILATION.

line-piece, a piece that can be moved any distance along a line; the squares thus traversed must be unoccupied but the square to which such a piece is moved may be occupied by an enemy man which is thus captured and removed from the board. Orthodox line-pieces are the queen, rook, and bishop. Some line-pieces used for UNORTHODOX CHESS, KINDRED GAMES, or FAIRY PROBLEMS are the ROSE which is moved on an octagonal line, the LEO, PAO, and VAO which are moved as line-pieces only for non-capturing moves, and the NIGHTRIDER.

line vacation, the removal of a man from a line so that a LINE-PIECE of the same colour is no longer obstructed on that line. Only composers use the term, although the manœuvre is not uncommon in play.

lion, a piece that was used in several forms of GREAT CHESS. The lion may be moved any distance along ranks, files, and diagonals to occupy or capture on a square any distance beyond an intervening man of either colour. Like the grasshopper it cannot be moved unless it hops and it cannot hop over two men.

Lipke, Paul (1870–1955), German player, lawyer. In a national tournament, Kiel 1893, he took third prize after BARDELEBEN and WALBRODT.

Subsequently he entered two strong international tournaments: Leipzig 1894, second (+11 = 4 − 2), after TARRASCH, whom he defeated, ahead of TEICH-MANN, BLACKBURNE, and Walbrodt; Vienna 1898, eighth equal with MARÓCZY in a field of 19. A player of GRANDMASTER strength, he never entered the lists again. In his time he was renowned as a blindfold player.

Lipnitsky Attack, 504 in the SICILIAN DEFENCE, named after the Ukrainian player Isaak Oskarovich Lipnitsky (1923–59). Other names are Paulsen Variation and Sozin–Najdorf Variation.

Lipnitsky Variation, 706 in the SPANISH OPENING, played Minckwitz–Vitzthum, Leipzig 1870, and never regarded as fully satisfactory because of the continuation 8 dxe5 Nxe4 9 h3.

Lipschütz, Samuel (1863–1905), Hungarian player who emigrated to the USA in 1880, working first as a printer and then in insurance. In 1892 he won the US championship by defeating SHOWALTER in match play (+7 = 7 − 1). Three years later Showalter won a return match. Lipschütz played in two international tournaments (London 1886 and New York 1889) and in several national events, notably tying with STEINITZ for the New York State championship of 1897, and coming first (+7 = 2 − 1) ahead of MARSHALL and Showalter in the Manhattan Chess Club championship 1900, his last and probably his best result. Lipschütz was of GRAND-MASTER class and might have achieved more had he not suffered from a disease of the lungs. He travelled to Hamburg for treatment and died after an operation. His 122-page addendum to Gossip's *Chess-Player's Manual* (1888) helped to make this one of the standard opening books of the time.

Lipschütz–Napier   Thousand Islands 1897   Spanish Opening

1 e4 e5 2 Nf3 Nc6 3 Bb5 a6 4 Ba4 Nf6 5 d4 exd4 6 0–0 Be7 7 e5 Ne4 8 Nxd4 Nxd4 9 Qxd4 Nc5 10 Bb3 Nxb3 11 axb3 0–0 12 Bf4 d6 13 exd6 Bxd6 14 Bxd6 Qxd6 15 Qxd6 cxd6 16 c4 Bf5 17 Nc3 Bc2 18 Ra3 b5 19 Nd5 bxc4 20 bxc4 Rfb8 21 b4 Be4 22 Nc7 Ra7

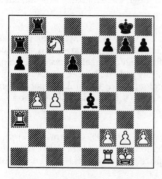

23 Nb5 axb5 24 Rxa7 bxc4 25 f3 Bf5 26 Rfa1 Kf8 27 Ra8 Rxa8 28 Rxa8+ Ke7 29 Kf2 c3 30 Ra7+ Ke6 31 Rc7 c2 32 b5 Bd3 33 b6 Black resigns.

liquidation, see SIMPLIFICATION.

Lisitsin, Georgy Mikhailovich (1909–72), Soviet player, International Master (1950), winner of the Leningrad championship 1939, joint winner 1933–4 and 1947. He shared first prize with CHEKHOVER in the Trades Unions championship tournament, Moscow 1936, tying a play-off match +1 = 10 − 1. He played in ten USSR championships from 1931 to 1956, sharing third prize in 1933 and fourth in 1954. His best book is *Strategiya i taktika shakhmat* (1958).

Lisitsin Gambit, 1303, enterprising and probably sound gambit played in the game Lisitsin–Botvinnik, Leningrad Masters tournament 1933.

Lisitsin Variation, 650, an improvement by LISITSIN to a line in the BISHOP'S OPENING first published in *Sovremenny debyut* by LEVENFISH, 1940.

literature and chess. The best four English language works of fiction in which chess is central are relatively recent. Nabokov used the pen name V. Sirin for *Zaschita Luzhina* (1930), written in Russian but published in Berlin. A French translation, *La Course du Fou*, appeared in 1934 but despite an enthusiastic review by ZNOSKO-BOROVSKY an English version, *The Defence*, was not published until 1964. Stefan Zweig, a Viennese who became British, wrote his short *Schachnovelle* in Petropolis, Brazil, a few weeks before his suicide there; published in 1942 and translated as *The Royal Game* (1944), this novel was described by John Fowles as 'one of the most powerful ever based on the imagery of a game'. *Master Prim* (1968) by James Whitfield Ellison is an account of an uncouth young American chess genius and like *The Dragon Variation* (1969) by Anthony Glyn includes genuine game scores.

Writers have found LIVING CHESS an enduring attraction. In 1467 Francesco Colonna wrote in Italian *Hypnerotomachia Poliphili* which has been called the *Finnegans Wake* of the 15th century; published in 1499 with woodcuts thought by some to be the work of Raphael, this beautiful book describes a chess ballet and was adapted and expanded by Rabelais in the posthumous fifth book of *Gargantua*. A similar chess ball in *Melincourt* (1817) by Thomas Love Peacock finds a bizarre echo in 'A quiet game of chess' (1948), a short story by Maurice Richardson in his series about Engelbrecht, the surrealist sportsman. A more orthodox living display is described in E. M. Forster's 'Chess in Cracow'.

Among the great authors who have dealt with chess are Chaucer, Boccaccio, Goethe, TOLSTOY, Dostoevsky, and George Eliot. A. C. WHITE edited

Eliot's works and declared that of all English novelists she had the greatest intellectual sympathy for chess. (Unlike Ouida, who in *Strathmore* (1865) wrote of 'a pretty young woman castling her adversary's queen'.) Turgenev was a strong player losing only $+1=2-3$ against the Polish professional Ladislas Maczuski (1838–98) at the CAFÉ DE LA RÉGENCE in 1861. During a game with the 15-year-old Tolstoy, Turgenev recalled his Paris days, 'They called me *Le chevalier du pion*. I am fond of pawns ... '

Chess is found in a wide range of fiction including the *Arabian Nights' Entertainment* and Lewis Carroll's *Through the Looking Glass, and what Alice found there* (1872). Among the many detective stories are S. S. van Dine's *The Bishop Murder Case* (1929), Edouard Pape's *La Variante XVIII dans le Gambit Camoulogène* (s.a.), and Rex Stout's *Gambit* (1962). Ian Fleming's *From Russia with Love* (1957) has a tense chess scene, and there is even a pornographic novel, which only thinly disguises living masters, *The Pushers* (1968), published under the pen-name Kenneth Harding. Short stories abound. 'Moxon's Master' (1893) by Ambrose Bierce anticipates the chess computer by 80 years while 'Three Sailors Gambit' by Lord Dunsany has a supernatural theme.

Chess is found in even greater profusion, if not richness, in poetry. Many of the early examples are in ALLEGORIES but perhaps the best-known allusion occurs in Fitzgerald's version of 'The Rubáiyát of Omar Khayyám':

Impotent Pieces of the Game He plays
Upon the Chequer-board of Nights and Days;
Hither and thither moves, and checks, and slays,
And one by one back in the Closet lays.

This is from his second translation of 1868 (for the 1859 version see EVERYDAY LANGUAGE AND CHESS). Some of the many other translations have included two other quatrains which mention chess. From the 12th century are EZRA's poem and two sections of the *Carmina Burana*. Many poems have been composed for an occasion. Méry wrote 'Une Revanche de Waterloo' based on a Bourdonnais–McDonnell game and provoked a reply in the form of verse from A. C. S. d'Arblay. A political poem, 'The queen and her pawns against the king and his pieces', was published in 1828. The goddess CAÏSSA was created in poetry (1763).

Among the many poets who have used chess imagery are Dante, Skelton, Spenser, Donne, Abraham Cowley, Pope, Cowper, Byron, Keats, Tennyson, Browning, Yeats, Masefield, T. S. Eliot, and Graves. Ho Chi Minh, in the interval between being a London chef and the Viet Cong leader, wrote a chess poem which includes the line 'At times a pawn leads all to victory'. Modern poems centred on chess include: Ezra Pound, 'The Game of Chess' (1915), Vladimir Mayakovsky, 'Nagruzhka na Makushku' (1928), Louis MacNeice, 'Chess' (c.1938), Patricia Beer, 'Checkmate' (1959), Eliza-

beth Jennings, 'A Game of Chess' (1961). A poem by the Argentinian Jorge Luis Borges translated as 'Chess' (1968) begins:

In their serious corner, the players
move the gradual pieces. The board
detains them until dawn in its hard
compass: the hatred of two colours.

Alfred de Musset, told that mate with two knights was impossible, composed this problem published in *La Régence*, 1849.

#3

White mates in three beginning 1 Rd7 Nxd7 2 Nc6.

There are many anthologies of chess quotations from literature, the best known of them by TWISS. Andrew Waterman's *The Poetry of Chess* (1981) excludes prose quotations.

literature of chess. 'The words "chess literature", by the way, are applied to those text-books reproducing openings and games in notation, which look, for all the world, like lists of the numbers of motor cars and which convey absolutely nothing to the uninitiated', wrote a reviewer in the *Florence Italian Gazette*, 1912. What chess books lack in literary distinction they make up for in numbers. In his *History of Chess* (1913), MURRAY expressed a commonly held opinion: 'The game possesses a literature which in content probably exceeds that of all other games combined.' He estimated the total number of books, magazines, and newspaper columns to be about 5,000 at that time. In 1949 B. H. Wood suggested in the *Illustrated London News* chess column, which he edited, that the total number was about 20,000. Since then there has been a steady annual increase in the number of chess publications. No one knows the total figure. There is no complete list, and if there were the question of definition would need to be resolved. The largest single list published is the J. G. WHITE catalogue of 1964. Of the 12,000 cards reproduced more than 600 are various editions of Omar Khayyám. Is this one chess book, or 600? Is it a chess book at all? Chess was not mentioned in the original text, but was introduced by the translator.

The first chess books to be published were versions of CESSOLE's morality; the first practical chess books of the modern game were by LUCENA and VICENT in the 1490s, followed by DAMIANO (1512) and Ruy LÓPEZ (1561). Early chess books had editions of between 50 and 300 copies, about one hundredth of an average issue today. The largest print runs of chess books were in the USSR, sometimes reaching two or three hundred thousand.

The category containing the most titles and the biggest editions is primers. It also embraces the highest proportion of ill-written works, and POLU-GAYEVSKY's dictum that 90 per cent of chess books are not worth opening has particular relevance here. The most important works for practising players are tournament and match books, the prime source of most information. Books and monographs on openings are popular, and as they are thought to become out of date quickly there is a steady supply of new titles. Another popular category is that of games collections, in particular biographical ones of great players; many of the recommended titles in the *Companion* are of this kind.

'What refuge is there for the victim who is oppressed with the feeling that there are a thousand new books he ought to read, while life is only long enough for him to attempt to read a hundred?' Oliver Wendell Holmes sen.

living chess, chess played with human beings taking the part of chessmen and moving on a giant board, a diversion recorded at least as early as the 15th century. Most commonly such chess is intended as a spectacle or pageant and a rehearsed game or problem is used. In 1891 a Club of Living Chess was formed in Dublin with the purpose of giving living chess displays for suitable charities, and in 1892 one of its members, Dr Ephraim McDowell Cosgrave, wrote what is probably the only book on the subject, *Chess with Living Pieces*. Sometimes a real game is played between two masters with the moves reproduced by the living pieces like a huge DEMONSTRATION BOARD. Legend has it that a master playing such a game was much attracted to the actress representing his queen. Fearing she might disappear, he avoided an exchange at all costs, eventually losing the game, for his opponent, realizing the situation, drove the hapless queen round the board. Rushing keenly to his queen, the loser invited her to dinner: exhausted, she declined. (See MAROSTICA.)

Ljubojević (pron. lioobo-yevich), Ljubomir (1950–), International Grandmaster (1971), the

Living chess: a game played on London's South Bank during the Festival of Britain, 1951, between Rossolimo and Broadbent

leading Yugoslav player from 1974 until the late 1980s, when he was overtaken by Predrag NIKOLIĆ. Often among the world's best dozen during this period, Ljubojević was ranked third after KARPOV and KASPAROV in 1983. His early tournament achievements include a first place (+ 7 = 8) equal with PANNO, ahead of PORTISCH and LARSEN, at Palma de Majorca 1971, and a second place (+ 9 = 5 − 1), after Larsen, at Manila 1973. Playing in his first Olympiad, Skopje 1972, Ljubojević made the best third-board score (+ 13 = 5 − 1). (He was a regular member of subsequent Olympiad teams.) In May 1974 he was severely injured in a car accident and during the convalescence he reappraised his style.

Subsequently he achieved more consistent results, among them several excellent tournament victories: Las Palmas 1975 (+ 8 = 6), ahead of TAL; Manila 1975 (+ 4 = 6), ahead of POLUGAYEVSKY and Larsen; Wijk aan Zee 1976 (+ 5 = 5 − 1), ahead of Tal; Titovo Užice 1978 (+ 8 = 4 − 1); São Paulo 1979 (+ 7 = 6), equal with KORCHNOI; Buenos Aires 1979 (+ 8 = 5), equal with Korchnoi; Brasilia 1981 (+ 5 = 5); Linares 1985 (+ 4 = 6 − 1), equal with HÜBNER; Reggio Emilia 1985–6 (+ 4 = 6 − 1), equal with ANDERSSON and ROMANISHIN; Amsterdam 1986 (+ 3 = 7); Belgrade 1987 (+ 5 = 6), ahead of TIMMAN, BELYAVSKY, P. Nikolić, and Korchnoi; Brussels 1987 (+ 6 = 5), equal with Kasparov, ahead of Karpov; Viña del Mar 1988 (+ 3 = 2 − 1); Barcelona 1989 (+ 6 = 10), equal with Kasparov. At Reggio Emilia 1991 he was first (+ 3 = 8 − 1), ahead of VAGANYAN and GULKO. In 1979 he defeated GLIGORIĆ in match play (+ 4 = 3 − 3).

Despite these fine results, and others only slightly less outstanding, Ljubojević has never become a CANDIDATE. He plays the openings in original and sometimes hazardous fashion, but with great tactical skill, a style that is interesting although it may have contributed to his uneven results. Bursting with energy, he converses rapidly and forcefully in several languages.

Ljubojević–Korchnoi   Linares 1985   French Defence, Winawer Variation

1 e4 e6 2 d4 d5 3 Nc3 Bb4 4 e5 c5 5 a3 Bxc3 + 6 bxc3 Ne7 7 Qg4 0–0 8 Nf3 Nbc6 9 Bd3 f5 10 exf6 Rxf6 11 Bg5 Rf7 12 Qh5 g6 13 Qh4 c4 14 Be2 Qa5 15 Bd2 Nf5 16 Qg5 Bd7 17 g4 Nd6 18 h4 Ne4 19 Qe3 Ra f8 (v. KOVAČEVIĆ recommends 19 ... e5) 20 h5 gxh5 21 Rxh5 Rg7 22 Ng5 Be8 23 Nxe6 Bxh5 24 Nxg7 Bg6 25 Nf5 Qc7 26 0–0–0 Qa5 27 Kb2 Rf6 28 Bf3 Ne5 29 Bxe4

29 ... dxe4 (if 29 ... Rb6 + 30 Ka2 Qb5 31 Bxd5 + Kf8 32 Qh6 + Ke8 33 Bc6 + Rxc6 34 Qe3) 30 dxe5 Rb6 + 31 Ka2 Qb5 32 Qxb6 axb6 33 Bf4 Qa5 34 Rd8 + Kf7 35 Nd4 e3 36 e6 + Kf6 37 fxe3 Bxc2 38 Rf8 + Ke7 39 Rf7 + Kd8 40 Bd6 Bb1 + 41 Kb2 Black resigns.

Lobron, Eric (1960–   ), German player, born in the USA, International Grandmaster (1982). His results have been uneven, but he has won tournaments at: Biel 1981 (+ 8 = 5), equal with HORT; Ramat-Hasharon 1982 (+ 6 = 5), ahead of LIBERZON; Manila 1982 (+ 6 = 2 − 1), equal with POLUGAYEVSKY; New York 1983 (+ 6 = 7 − 1); Manhattan 1985 (+ 4 = 5); Biel 1986 (+ 4 = 6 − 1), shared with Polugayevsky; Ter Apel 1987 (shared); and Lyons 1988 (+ 5 = 3 − 1) shared with AGDESTEIN. West German champion in 1980 and 1984, he played in the German Olympiad teams of 1980, 1982, and 1984.

Lobusov, Andrei Yakovlevich (1951–   ), Russian problem composer in all orthodox genres, and selfmates, International Judge of Chess Compositions (1987), International Master for Chess Compositions (1988). He won the 14th USSR composing championship for three-movers (1979–80). His writings include perceptive surveys of contemporary compositions in the pages of *Shakhmaty v SSSR.*

#3

A problem by Lobusov, first prize, *Tidskrift för Schack,* 1980. The key is 1 Nf5 threatening 2 Rxc4 +.

1 ... Qb4   2 Re3 + Nxe3   3 Nd6 #
1 ... Qd4   2 Nd6 + Nxd6   3 Qxe5 #
1 ... Bb4   2 Qxe5 + Nxe5   3 Nd2 #
1 ... Bd4   2 Nd2 + Nxd2   3 Re3 #.

This is the so-called Dresden Theme (see DECOY THEMES), in which the variations show CYCLIC PLAY.

Locock Gambit, 1042 in the PHILIDOR DEFENCE, named after the English player Charles Dealtry Locock (1862–1946). The gambit is probably sound; 4 ... Be7 instead of 4 ... h6 is better for Black.

Łódź Variation, 122, the SCHLECHTER VARIATION of the QUEEN'S GAMBIT Declined.

Logical School, a school of problem composition pioneered by German composers in the 1920s, derived from the work of KOHTZ and KOCKELKORN earlier in the century. The word 'logical' refers to the close relationship between the TRY-PLAY and the solution. In the try-play a defensive manœuvre (by Black) succeeds, but when repeated in the solution the same manœuvre fails. Reciprocal relationships are possible: Black's defensive resource in the try-play might, say, depend on a clearance by ANNIHILATION, and this is circumvented in the solution by a similar clearance, this time by White. Logical problems, normally MORE-MOVERS, should show 'economy of aim', i.e. White's manœuvres should serve only the single aim—there should be no side effects. The solution is usually a single line of play, but there might be closely linked variations, e.g. the two 'legs' of a Plachutta Theme (see CUTTING-POINT THEMES).

Most problem themes originated as resources for White. In an article 'Black is Beautiful' (*The Problemist*, July 1980) REHM shows how logical problems offer opportunities of modifying themes as defensive resources for Black, which greatly adds interest to the play. Logical ideas can be shown in a study, when try-play may begin after introductory play. (See MATTISON.)

#5

A more-mover by ZEPLER, *British Chess Magazine*, 1940. 1 Kf1 is a try (1 Rd∼ fails similarly) 1 ... Qa8! (not 1 ... Rb8? 2 Rg2∼ 3 Rg8+ Qxg8 4 fxg8+ Rxg8 5 Nf7#) 2 Rg2 Rb8, a Loyd–Turton DOUBLING THEME rendering 3 Rg8+ ineffective.

The solution is 1 Ke1 Qa8 2 Rg2 Rb8 3 f8=Q+ Rxf8 4 Rg8+ Rxg8 5 Nf7#.

(See also KRIKHELI.)

Lolli, Giambatista (1698–1769), a native of Nonántola, near Modena, who with DEL RIO and PONZIANI formed the so-called Modenese school, author of a treatise *Osservazioni teorico-pratiche sopra il giuoco degli scacchi* (1763). Its 632 large pages include, in the form of a letter, del Rio's broadside against PHILIDOR. (See SCHOOLS OF CHESS.)

The first part of Lolli's book contains the openings given in Del Rio's earlier book, and the second part contains new variations provided by Del Rio. To the bare lines of play given by his master, whom he never contradicts, Lolli has added, with Del Rio's approval, extensive annotations. The openings coverage is not wide-ranging compared, for example, with COZIO's book published three years later. More than 40 per cent of the two parts deals with the ITALIAN OPENING.

The third part of the book, in which Lolli comes into his own, consists of the best examination of the ENDGAME given up to that time, and 100 positions (studies and problems). Besides important analysis of the endgame R + B v. B he discovered in the endgame Q v. B + B a FORTRESS, which, according to computer research by Thompson in 1985, appears to be the only known drawn position in this endgame. Lolli's book was popular and his problems were frequently used by other authors, including Heinse (see ANASTASIA'S MATE), and in the earliest newspaper columns. In 1817 a book containing the 100 positions was published in Verona: the solutions were printed in STANDARD NOTATION, its first use in Italy. (See EPAULET MATE.)

Lolli Attack, 966 in the TWO KNIGHTS DEFENCE. Long thought to favour White, the attack has come under a cloud following a postal game finishing in 1990 and played in Czechoslovakia. Black's 10th move was a THEORETICAL NOVELTY. Kalvach–Drtina: 1 e4 e5 2 Nf3 Nc6 3 Bc4 Nf6 4 Ng5 d5 5 exd5 Nxd5 6 d4 Bb4+ 7 c3 Be7 8 Nxf7 Kxf7 9 Qf3+ Ke6 10 Qe4 b5 11 Bxb5 Bb7 12 f4 g6 13 fxe5 Rf8 14 Qg4+ Rf5 15 Bd3 Nxd4 16 Rf1 Ne3 17 Bxe3 Nf3+ 18 gxf3 Qxd3 19 Qd4 Bh4+ 20 Qxh4 Qxe3+ White resigns.

Lolli Variation, 1007, LOLLI's response to the SCOTCH GAME. He considered this safer than 3 ... exd4, a view not widely shared today.

Loman Defence, 948, variation in the MAX LANGE ATTACK named after the Dutch champion Rudolf Johannes Loman (1861–1932), a musician who spent much of his adult life in England.

Lombardy, William James (1937–). American player, International Grandmaster (1960). World Junior Champion at Toronto 1957 (he won every game he played in the tournament), three years later Lombardy led the USA team to victory ahead of the USSR in the student teams Olympiad, held in Leningrad. In this event his personal score, +10=2, included the defeat of SPASSKY. In 1963 and 1965 Lombardy won the SWISS SYSTEM US Open Championships. His decision to enter the priesthood in 1963 necessarily limited his chess ambition, but he played in five more Olympiads from 1968 to 1978 (seven in total), acted as FISCHER'S second in the world championship match 1972, and competed in a few international tournaments. He was equal first at Caracas 1982. In two stronger events he shared third prize: Monte Carlo 1969, with HORT (both scored +3 = 8), after SMYSLOV and PORTISCH; Reykjavik 1978, with Hort, LARSEN, and ÓLAFSSON, after BROWNE and MILES.

Petursson–Lombardy   Neskaupstadhur 1984   King's Indian Defence Sämisch Variation

1 d4 Nf6 2 c4 g6 3 Nc3 Bg7 4 e4 d6 5 f3 c6 6 Bd3 a6 7 Nge2 b5 8 0–0–0 0–0 9 Be3 bxc4 10 Bxc4 d5 11 Bb3 dxe4 12 fxe4 a5 13 Kh1 Ba6 14 Rf3 a4 15 Nxa4 Nxe4 16 Nac3 Nd6 17 Ng3 Bc4 18 Bc2 Be6 19 Qc1 Nd7 20 Bh6 Nf6 21 Qf4 Ra5 22 Re1 Nb5 23 Bxg7 Kxg7 24 d5 cxd5 25 Nxb5 Rxb5 26 b3 Qa5 27 Ref1 Qxa2 28 Bb1 Qb2 29 Qg5 h6 30 Qe3 d4 31 Qe1 Rxb3 32 R3f2 Qc3 33 Qd1 Bg4 34 Qc1 Qxc1 35 Rxc1 Rc3 36 Re1 d3 37 Rd2 Rd8 38 h3 Be6 39 Kh2 h5 40 Nf1 Rd4 41 Re3 Bf5 42 Ng3 Ne4 43 Rdxd3 Nxg3 White resigns.

Lommer, Harold Maurice (1904–80), International Judge of Chess Compositions (1958), International Arbiter (1962), International Master for Chess Compositions (1974), the greatest British study composer. Born in Islington of German parentage, he moved to Switzerland when he was four and returned to England 18 years later. Inspired in his youth by the SAAVEDRA study, he became the leading specialist in promotion TASKS and in 1933 was the first to show ALLUMWANDLUNG in a study, which RINCK had declared was impossible. Lommer also showed in studies six consecutive promotions to rooks (1935) and a MINIMAL with concurrent promotions to queen, bishop, and knight.

+

A study by Lommer, *Sunday Times*, 1933. After 1 gxh7+ four variations show allumwandlung:

1 ... Qxh7   2 exf8 = Q #
1 ... Kh8   2 exf8 = R+ (not 2 exf8 = Q+ Kxh7 3 exf5 Re3+, a DESPERADO)
1 ... Kg7   2 exf8 = B+
1 ... Kxh7   2 exf8 = N+.

In 1938 Lommer and the English player Maurice A. Sutherland (d. 1954), who backed the project, published *1,234 Modern End-game Studies*. In 1975

Lommer compiled a sequel, *1,357 End-game Studies*. These two collections, catholic in taste, made by a composer who was above all an artist, have become standard works. Besides his studies, the best of which are in these books, he composed FAIRY PROBLEMS.

After the Second World War he became proprietor of a Soho club where players and composers often met; in 1949 the club organized a small international tournament, won by BERNSTEIN. Lommer retired in 1961 and went to live in Valencia, where he died.

London rules, a set of 21 rules proposed by CAPABLANCA in 1922, under which world champions would meet challengers.

The main provisions are: a match for the first to win six games; playing sessions to last five hours; time-limit to be 40 moves in 2½ hours; the champion must defend his title within one year of receiving a challenge from a recognized master; the champion to decide the date of the match; the champion is not obliged to accept a challenge for a purse of less than $10,000, of which 20% is paid to the title-holder, the rest being divided 60% to the winner, 40% to the loser; the contestants must accept the highest bid. This last condition could determine where the match is to be held. At that time there were no internationally agreed laws of play and clause 20 of the rules specifies that the British Chess Code, with slight modifications, is to be used.

These rules were presented on the occasion of the London tournament of 1922, and a players' declaration (later clause 22) was added: 'We, the undersigned, agree to abide by the above conditions proposed by Señor J. R. Capablanca, and we hereby declare that these rules and no others should govern all future championship contests, and that should any one of us at any time become world's champion, we will be ready to defend the championship under the above conditions.' This was signed by ALEKHINE, BOGOLJUBOW, MARÓCZY, RÉTI, RUBINSTEIN, TARTAKOWER, and VIDMAR.

Previously, the champion made the rules, often to the disadvantage of the challenger, and when Capablanca finally brought LASKER to the board, in 1921, he had to raise $25,000. Capablanca's rules were widely held to be fair to both contestants, as he intended. Under these terms he accepted challenges from Rubinstein, NIMZOWITSCH, and Alekhine, in that order. The first two could not raise the stakes; in 1927 he himself was largely responsible for raising the stake money for his match with Alekhine, which he lost.

The new champion evaded a return match, choosing to meet less worthy opponents. His second 'peripatetic' match against Bogoljubow was played in various cities for about £50 a game (the BCF refused his offer to play in England, believing the challenge not to be genuine). In accepting challengers of his choice, Alekhine kept to the letter of the rules. These did not forbid stakes of less than $10,000, nor did they provide that a challenger grant a re-match, or even meet his strongest rivals. Throughout the 1930s there were many arguments as to which of the two greatest players was the stronger, but no one doubted that Capablanca would have been a worthy challenger.

Both the spirit of the London rules and many of its provisions were incorporated in the rules used after FIDE took control of the championship in 1948.

London Variation, 435, a line in the KING'S INDIAN DEFENCE played several times at the London tournament 1922. In the usual continuation, 4 ... c5 5 e3 d6 6 c3, White's first six moves constitute the London System. Lacking aggression, it never became popular for White. (See KAMSKY.)

Also 1289, an opening in which the moves of the London System are played by Black, who thus achieves harmonious development. Introduced in the game Réti–Lasker, New York 1924, it soon became a standard defence to the RÉTI OPENING. The first four moves (up to 4 ... Bf5) are sometimes called the New York variation.

long castling, QUEEN'S-SIDE CASTLING.

long diagonal, a diagonal that extends from a corner square, i.e. a1–h8 or h1–a8.

long-range piece, in orthodox chess the queen, the rook, and the bishop.

long-range problem, or many-mover, a problem in which mate is to be given, or some other aim achieved, in a large number of moves. Usually, White repeats many times a manœuvre that gains or LOSES THE MOVE.

#127

A MINIMAL by BLÁTHY, *Magyar Sakkvilág*, 1930. After 1 Qe1 + Rc1 2 Qd2 Rc2, Black plays Rc1–c2 or Rc2–c1 unless otherwise indicated: 3–16 Qd1 +, xd3 +, d1 +, d2, e1 +, e4 +, xh1 +, e4 +, e1 +, d2,

d1 +, d3 +, f1 +, xf5 +, 17 Qe4 h2‾ 18–21 Qe1 +, d2, d1 +, d3 +, 22 Qe4 h1 ~ 23–28 Qxh1 +, e4 +, e1 +, d2, d1 +, d3 + 29 Qe4 h3 30–34 Qe1 +, d2, d1 +, d3 +, e4 and so on to 121–122 Qxh1 +, h7 + 123 Qe4 Bb3 124–126 Qe1 +, d2, d1 + 127 Qxb3 #.

This TASK record for a minimal direct mate with a legal position and no OBTRUSIVE PIECES stood for 25 years. Then the Austrian composer Josef Halumbirek (1891–1968) made a version by changing Q to d4, Pd3 to a7, Nf5 to f1, # 130 (*Schach*, 1955), a new task record, as yet unbeaten; but the credit for discovering the matrix belongs to Bláthy.

Long Whip Variation, 1164, see STOCKWHIP VARIATION.

Loose Gambit, 278, the HROMÁDKA DEFENCE. The German player Walter Loose gave more than 4 pages to it in his book *Deutsche Nachkriegstheorie* (1947).

López Counter-gambit, 1017, an unsound line in the PHILIDOR DEFENCE, given in the GÖTTINGEN MANUSCRIPT and sometimes called the Göttingen Variation.

López Defence, 1107, the CLASSICAL DEFENCE to the BISHOP'S GAMBIT.

López de Segura, Ruy (pron. Rue-y Lopeth) (*c.*1530–*c.*1580), Spanish priest from Zafra, Badajoz, who was a leading player of his day. He studied DAMIANO's book and wrote his *Libro de la invención liberal y arte del juego del Axedrez* (Alcalá, 1561) as a response. He lost matches against LEONARDO DI BONA and Paolo BOI at Madrid, 1574–5. It was the first documented chess competition, and marked a decline in López's standing.

His book is in four parts. The first deals with the history and usefulness of chess and the laws current in Spain, where a player could still win by bare king or stalemate and where the fifty-move law was in force. In part two the author introduces the word 'gambit' and gives some openings not previously published: the KING'S GAMBIT, some lines in the BISHOP'S OPENING, and the STEINITZ DEFENCE to the SPANISH OPENING. The last two parts contain criticism of games published by Damiano. The book makes 'little advance', writes PONZIANI, who considered López 'an unfruitful genius and devoid of enthusiasm'. Much greater advances were soon to follow, LASA writing that to turn from López to POLERIO is 'to step from darkness into light'. López treats Damiano ungenerously, as if jealous of his predecessor's successful book. After 1 e4 e5 2 Nf3 Damiano indicated that 2 ... Nc6 was Black's best move (the consensus of posterity); López considered Black's second move inferior because White could continue 3 Bb5 (subsequently named the Ruy López or the Spanish Opening), although the variations he gives do not show advantage to White.

López Gambit, 647 in the BISHOP'S OPENING if White follows up with Pf2–f4.

López–Gianutio Counter-gambit, 1100, a risky defence in the KING'S GAMBIT Accepted.

López Opening, 673, another name for the SPANISH OPENING.

Lord Variation, 1022 in the PHILIDOR DEFENCE, later revived as the HANHAM VARIATION. It was introduced in the 1860s by the English player John Lord.

lose a move, an inexact term usually meaning to lose a tempo (below) but sometimes meaning to LOSE THE MOVE, an incorrect usage. In his *Chess History and Reminiscences* BIRD tells the following tale of 19th-century gamesmanship. 'Harrwitz, not quite so small as Gunsberg, seemed sinking to the ground, but the story that he once disappeared overawed by Staunton's style and manner of moving, and was, after a search, found under the table, is a mere canard of Staunton's which need not be too confidently accepted. Staunton pretended sometimes not to see Harrwitz, and would look around the room and even under the chairs for him when he was sitting at his elbow, which greatly annoyed Harrwitz, who … was not slow to retaliate. In a game one day, Staunton materially damaged his prospects … and testily complained "I have lost a move". Harrwitz told the waiter to stop his work, and search the room until he found Staunton's lost move, and his manner of saying it caused a degree of merriment by no means pleasing to the English Champion.'

lose a tempo, to play in *n* moves what could have been played in *n − 1* moves. Throughout the game a player almost always endeavours to gain time, and a loss of one or more tempi is often disadvantageous, but exceptions are not unusual. For example, after 1 e4 e6 2 c4 several grandmasters have played 2 … e5, transposing into a king's pawn game where White's c-pawn is ill-placed. A player may lose a tempo at any stage of a game, but can LOSE THE MOVE only in the endgame. (See TIME, 1.)

lose on time, to lose the game because the stipulated number of moves has not been completed within the allotted time.

lose the exchange, to lose a rook for a MINOR PIECE.

lose the move, to play as follows: a player whose turn it is to move manoeuvres so that an identical or similar position occurs with the opponent to move. The other player is thus placed in ZUGZWANG or subjected to a SQUEEZE. Losing the move, a manoeuvre that arises only in the endgame, may be achieved by moving the king (TRIANGULATION), a pawn (a TEMPO-MOVE), or a line-piece (a WAITING MOVE). For an example, see aş-ṢŪLĪ.

Loshinsky, Lev Ilyich (1913–76), Soviet high-school teacher widely regarded as the greatest of all problem composers. In 1956 he was elected International Judge of Chess Compositions, and when, in 1972, the title of International Grandmaster for Chess Compositions was introduced, he was one of only four to receive it. Winner of an exceptionally large number of tourney awards, he was especially famous for his orthodox THREE-MOVERS. In the USSR composing championships he won the three-mover section of the first nine, which took place from 1945 to 1968, the second (1947–8), third (1949–52), fourth (1953–5), and sixth (1959–61) TWO-MOVER sections, and the eighth (1965–6) MORE-MOVER section. 'What he did', writes MATTHEWS, 'was to do very much better and carry very much further things that were being done to some extent already. The result was a standard of composition never previously attained.' (See PICKANINNY.)

Vladimirov, Kofman, and Umnov, *Grossmeister shakhmatnoi kompositsy* (1980) contains a biography of Loshinsky and more than 500 of his problems.

losing chess, a form of UNORTHODOX CHESS known in former centuries by its Spanish name *ganapierde*. Both players must capture if they can, but if more than one capture is possible they may exercise choice. There is neither check nor checkmate, kings may be captured and may be moved into check. A pawn may be promoted to a king. To lose all one's men or to be stalemated wins the game.

+

A study in losing chess by DAWSON, *Deutsches Wochenschach*, 1925, shows ASYMMETRY. 1 **Rb2**

Bxb2 2 Rh8 Bxh8 3 e4 B~ 4 e5. After 1 Rh2? all
of White's men cannot be lost.

Periodically losing chess becomes fashionable, a
diversion from the serious business of tournament
play. In the following game White's first move,
surprisingly, is a decisive error. 1 d4? e5 2 dxe5
Qg5 3 Bxg5 (3 Qxd7 Bxd7 is no better) 3 ... Kd8
4 Bxd8 a6 5 Bxc7 Ra7 6 Bxb8 b6 7 Bxa7 a5 8
Bxb6 g6 9 Bxa5 Bb4 10 Bxb4 Ne7 11 Bxe7 Rf8
12 Bxf8 h6 13 Bxh6 g5 14 Bxg5 f6 15 Qxd7 Bxd7
16 Bxf6 Bh3.

loss. In ordinary play a loss arises from resigning or
being checkmated, but in competitive play it can be
imposed for exceeding the time limit, or, less commonly, for misbehaving. This last category includes
arriving later than a specified period after the time
set for start of play, making an indecipherable or
illegal sealed move, and refusing to comply with the
rulings of the arbiter.

lost position, a position that one side will lose if
played correctly by both contestants.

Louma Variation, 474 in the SICILIAN DEFENCE,
named after the Czech player Josef Louma (1898–
1955), whose idea was to aim for control of the
square d5 after 7 ... bxc6 8 0–0 Be7 9 Qd3.

Loveday, Henry Augustus (1815–48), originator of
the INDIAN THEME. (See also PROBLEM HISTORY.) He
was born at Barrackpur, India, and came to England when his father, a general, retired in 1824.
Around 1838, when he graduated from Cambridge,
he played a few games with STAUNTON 'without
disadvantage to either side'. Soon afterwards he
returned to India and in August 1844, while serving
as chaplain at St James's Church, Delhi, sent his
famous problem to Staunton, accompanied by a
letter signed 'Shagird'. This Persian or Turkish
word means 'student', and was the name assumed
by Loveday for his published games in the *Delhi
Gazette* and for the few problems he composed.
Although Staunton revealed Loveday's identity
more than once, he may also have played a joke by
referring to him, truthfully but misleadingly, as a
native of India. Many problemists thought Shagird
was an indigenous Indian, a belief that persisted
until 1920 when KEEBLE published his researches in
the *British Chess Magazine*. When the Indian problem was published Loveday was already suffering
from the liver disease that caused his death.

Löwenborg Attack, 995 in the SCOTCH GAME, proposed in the 1920s by the Swedish champion (1917)
Otto Löwenborg (1888–1969), and played Spielmann–Yates, Semmering 1926.

Löwenthal, János Jakab (1810–76), one of the best
half-dozen players of the 1850s. The son of a

Budapest merchant, Löwenthal improved his play,
especially in the ENDGAME, by practice with SZÉN,
and first became widely known as a member of the
correspondence team that defeated Paris, 1842–5.
In 1846 he travelled in Europe, defeating many
players, but losing more games than he won when
he played LASA in Vienna. Löwenthal served Kos-
suth's revolutionary government in a civilian capacity, and when the regime was overthrown in 1849
he fled to New York, arriving almost penniless,
with the intention of travelling west and settling on
the land. Educated, cultured, elegantly dressed, he
could hardly have thought of a less suitable plan.
Fortunately chessplayers, especially STANLEY, came
to his aid and he began a professional chess career
by establishing a cigar divan in Cincinnati.

About a year later his customers paid his fare to
the London International Tournament of 1851.
There he was knocked out in the first round by
WILLIAMS. Although he subsequently gained his
revenge in a match (+ 7 = 4 – 5), he felt too embarrassed to return to the USA, where so much had
been expected of him. He sought to remain in
London, and STAUNTON, who sympathized with his
plight as a political refugee, obtained for him the
secretaryship of the St George's Chess Club at £100
a year. Löwenthal settled in England and became
naturalized in 1866, taking the forename John. (He
is usually known, however, by the German form,
Johann.) He worked hard teaching chess (he
invented the DEMONSTRATION BOARD), organizing
chess events (including the world's second international tournament, London 1862), and editing
chess columns, the best known being in *The Era*
from 1854 to 1867. He edited the *Chess Player's
Magazine* from 1863 to 1867, and for many years,
first as manager and then as secretary, served the
British Chess Association. He was also active in the
masonic movement.

Löwenthal's somewhat nervous temperament
was not well suited to serious play. In 1851 he lost a
short match to BUCKLE; and he had the worse of a
series of games with ANDERSSEN. In 1853 he narrowly lost a long match against HARRWITZ; in 1858
he lost to MORPHY, although he gained substantial
opening advantage in most of the games. Löwenthal's best performance was at the Birmingham
tournament 1858. He won first prize (£63) after
scoring victories over Staunton (+ 2), OWEN
(+ 2 = 1), and FALKBEER (+ 3 = 4 – 1) in successive
rounds. The greatest openings expert of his time, he
often failed to make the most of the advantages he
gained. Staunton remarked: 'The Hungarian plays
the openings remarkably well — but when he gets
into the middle game he plays like a rook player',
adding after a pause, 'By George, sirs, he *is* a rook
player.'

Löwenthal wrote *The Chess Congress of 1862*
(1863), a substantial work of 630 pages which also
covers events from 1840 to the onset of the congress. he also wrote *Morphy's Games of Chess*
(1860)—the only collection that was made with

Morphy's assistance. Courteous, honest, self-effac-ing, with 'a sense of propriety', Löwenthal was well liked. He 'tried to please everybody' and attempted the almost impossible feat of maintaining a friend-ship with both Staunton and the many other fac-tions in London chess. Eventually he fell out with Staunton over the trifling matter of who won most friendly games when they played together in the winter of 1851–2. When Löwenthal fell ill in 1874 a fund of £100, subscribed by Lord Randolph Churchill, WYVILL, COCHRANE, and many other chess friends, provided for his retirement at St Leonards-on-Sea where he died and was buried. He left all he had 'to promote the interests of English chess'. The Löwenthal Cup, of solid silver, was purchased by his executors. First awarded in indi-vidual competition, the cup has been the annual trophy of the champion county in England since 1922. For a more detailed account of Löwenthal's life see *British Chess Magazine*, 1926, pp. 345–8, and 1976, pp. 308–14.

Löwenthal Variation, 468, the BOURDONNAIS VARIATION of the SICILIAN DEFENCE.

Loyd, Sam[uel] (1841–1911), the most famous Am-erican composer. He improved upon the ideas of his contemporaries (e.g. EXCELSIOR task; Turton doubling (see DOUBLING THEMES)) and contributed many ideas of his own (e.g. PLACHUTTA THEME; ORGAN PIPES). (For some examples of his work see ANNIHILATION; RETROGRADE ANALYSIS; SHORTEST GAME PROBLEM.) He composed quickly and often did not bother to polish his work; but his problems, designed for the solver, always contained some pointed and original idea. More than any other composer he made problems popular when com-posers such as KLETT were making them so difficult that few could solve them.

In 1867 he travelled to Europe. He played in the Paris tournament that year, with little success, and went to Germany where he met KOHTZ and other German composers who were impressed with his clear presentation of ideas, although many years were to pass before they were to adopt such ideas themselves. (See PROBLEM HISTORY.)

From early childhood Loyd had been fascinated by conjuring, sleight-of-hand, ventriloquism, and puzzles of all kinds, and he practised all these diversions. At the age of 27, after trying his hand at various trades, he found his true vocation: invent-ing puzzles. They were often used by advertisers, and he called himself an advertising agent; others called him the puzzle king. His multifarious inven-tions were collected by his son, Sam Loyd jun., in *Cyclopedia of Puzzles* (1914). *Mathematical Puzzles of Sam Loyd* (1958) and *More Mathematical Puz-zles of Sam Loyd* (1960) contain selections made by Martin Gardner.

Loyd gave up composing chess problems for eight years while he established his business, and

recommenced in 1876. Two years later he published *Chess Strategy*, a book containing about 500 of his problems and a somewhat incoherent text. Inter-preted and rewritten by A. C. WHITE, who added biographical material and about 200 problems, it appeared as *Sam Loyd and his Chess Problems* (1913). Reprinted in 1962, this book forms an excellent introduction for the uninitiated who wish to enter the problem world.

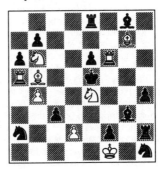

#3

A problem by Loyd that won first prize in the *Checkmate* novelty tourney 1903. The key is 1 Ke2 and he called the problem the 'STEINITZ GAMBIT' because this move is often made in that gambit. If 1 ... f1 = Q+ 2 Ke3, or if 1 ... f1 = N+ 2 Rf2+. Loyd's aim, typically light-hearted, was to provide a key that allowed Black a double check. This kind of problem earned him the sobriquet 'showman of the problem world'. He would have liked that description.

Loyd–Lasker Variation, 985 in the SCOTCH GAME, played by LOYD (and ROUSSEAU) at Paris 1867, and by LASKER at St Petersburg 1909. Often it is called simply the Lasker Variation.

Loyd–Turton Theme, see DOUBLING THEMES.

Lputyan, Smbat Gariginovich (1958–), Armenian player, International Grandmaster (1984). He was first or equal first in many strong tournaments—Tashkent 1984, Sarajevo 1985 (+6=9), Irkutsk 1986, Hastings 1986–7, Dortmund 1988 (+5=6), Uzhgorod 1988, Yerevan 1988 (+8=4–1), Alten-steig 1989 (+5=4–1), and second (+4=7) at the very strong tournament at Yerevan 1989.

Lucena, Luis Ramirez (15th–16th cent.), author of the oldest surviving book dealing with practical play. *Repetición de amores e arte de axedrez con cl iuegos de partido* was published almost certainly in 1497, and was the work of a young student in Salamanca. At the time the word *repetición* meant a discourse prepared according to strict scholarly standards, and the work may have been submitted towards a degree; on the other hand the word may be satirical, for the main theme of the book is a biting attack on the rising awareness of feminism. Love and chess may not seem like related topics, but to Lucena they were both miniature warfare.

The son of an ambassador, Lucena had travelled widely in Italy, France, and Spain, and the openings he gave were, he said, the ones the best players used. There are eleven openings, with analysis that contains elementary errors. 'It looks as though Lucena had written his book in a great hurry, directly he had learned something of the new game', writes MURRAY, and indeed it seems to be a careless compilation. His account was written at a time when the new game was superseding the old, and the 150 positions are partly of the old game and partly of the new; among them is the so-called PHILIDOR'S LEGACY, but not the LUCENA POSITION.

The GÖTTINGEN MANUSCRIPT and another contemporary tract appear to be by the same author, but it is not known how much, if at all, Lucena was indebted to VICENT or any other writer. Fewer than a dozen copies of the book, some incomplete, are extant. Unknown to most subsequent writers until the middle of the 19th century, the book had little or no direct influence. (See PROBLEM HISTORY.)

Lucena–Cozio Variation, 783, the COZIO DEFENCE to the SPANISH OPENING, given by LUCENA who considered that Black has equality after 5 c3 d5.

Lucena Defence, 1177, the FRENCH DEFENCE, at one time called after LUCENA, who gave it. Its modern name came into use in the middle of the 19th century.

Lucena position, a key position in the ending K + R + P v. K + R. It is not in LUCENA's book, but was first published in 1634 by SALVIO who attributes it to Scipione Genovino.

White wins by 1 Rf4 Rh1 2 Re4+ Kd7 3 Kf7 Rf1+ 4 Kg6 Rg1+ 5 Kh6 Rh1+ 6 Kg5 Rg1+ 7 Rg4. Three hundred years later NIMZOWITSCH described the white rook's manœuvre as building a bridge (under which the king may shelter).

ludus latrunculorum (Latin 'the mercenaries' game') a board game widely played in classical Roman and Greek times. The exact rules are not known but it was played on a squared board, most commonly one of 8×8 squares. When literary scholars translate the Latin they frequently and incorrectly suppose the game to be an ancestor of chess or draughts.

luft, an abbreviation for the German word *Luftloch*, literally an air-hole, an ESCAPE SQUARE. The word has been used by English-speaking players, especially in the first half of the 20th century when German was the international language of chess.

Lukács, Péter (1950–), Hungarian champion 1980, International Grandmaster (1986). First or equal first at Helsinki 1983, Vrnjačka Banja 1985, Havana (II) 1986, Polanica Zdrój 1986, Budapest 1987, Gdynia 1987.

Lundin Variation, 146 in the QUEEN'S GAMBIT Declined, named after the game R. Lindqvist–Lundin, Stockholm championship 1931, but already played in Eliskases–Canal, Budapest 1922, and sometimes called the Bogoljubow Variation, or the Neo-Meran Variation; also 394 in the GRÜNFELD DEFENCE, recommended in 1933 by the Swedish grandmaster Erik Ruben Lundin (1904–88) after a match against SPIELMANN in which Lundin won a game when Spielmann played 6 … Bg7 instead.

Lundqvist, Åke (1913–), Swedish player, International Grandmaster of Correspondence Chess (1962). He was Swedish correspondence chess champion in 1945, and in the World Correspondence Championships was third after O'KELLY and Dubinin in the 3rd, 1959–62, having been fourth in the previous competition. He competed again in the following championship, finishing eighth.

lust to expand, NIMZOWITSCH's graphic term for what he regarded as a BLOCKED PAWN's desire to advance. He had observed how often it happens that such a pawn is advanced advantageously after it is freed.

Lutikov, Anatoly Stepanovich (1933–89), Soviet player, International Grandmaster (1974), RSFSR (Russian Federation) champion 1955 and 1959. At Alma-Ata 1968–9, in his sixth and penultimate attempt to win the USSR championship, he took third place after POLUGAYEVSKY and ZAITSEV. In international play his best tournament wins were at Leipzig 1973 (+7=7−1, to tie with HORT) and Albena 1976 (+7=5). Other good results were Kislovodsk 1966, third (+5=4−2) equal with KHOLMOV, after GELLER and STEIN, and Beverwijk 1967, second (+6=9), after SPASSKY.

Lutikov–Averbakh   27th USSR Championship 1960
Sicilian Defence Richter Attack

1 e4 c5 2 Nf3 d6 3 d4 cxd4 4 Nxd4 Nf6 5 Nc3 Nc6 6 Bg5 a6 7 Qd2 Bd7 8 f4 b5 9 a3 e6 10 Nf3 Qc7 11 Be2

Rd8 12 Bxf6 gxf6 13 0–0 Bh6 14 Kh1 Ne7 15 Qd4 Bg7 16 f5 0–0 17 Qf2 Qc5 18 Qg3 Kh8 19 Bd3 e5 20 Rae1 a5 21 Nd1 Bc6 22 Qh4 Ng8 23 Ne3 Qa7 24 Ng4 Rb8 25 Nd2 Rfd8 26 Rf3 Qe7 27 Rh3 h6 28 Nf1 Qf8 29 Ng3 d5

(see diagram)

30 Nh5 dxe4 31 Bf1 e3 32 Rg3 Rd4 33 Qh3 e2 34 Bxe2 Re4 35 Nf2 Qc5 36 Nxe4 Bxe4 37 Rxg7 Qf2 38 Qg3 Bxg2+ 39 Qxg2 Qxe1+ 40 Bf1 Black resigns.

Lutikov Variation, 742 in the SPANISH OPENING.

M

McCutcheon Variation, 1205, a line in the FRENCH DEFENCE played by John Lindsay McCutcheon (1857–1905) of Pittsburgh against STEINITZ in a simultaneous display at New York in 1885. After the usual continuation, 5 e5 h6 6 Bd2 Bxc3 7 bxc3 Ne4 8 Qg4, White has attacking chances on the king's-side while Black has prospects on the other side of the board. This aggressive defence, fashionable around 1905, remains in use although less popular than the WINAWER VARIATION which has similar strategic characteristics.

McDonnell, Alexander (1798–1835), the best player in England around 1830. Born in Belfast, the son of a doctor, he spent some years in the West Indies and later worked in London as secretary of the Committee of West Indies Merchants. In the 1820s he took chess lessons from LEWIS, who soon found that he could not successfully offer odds of pawn and move to his pupil. Challenged to play even, Lewis declined, fearing for his reputation. From June to October 1834 McDonnell played six matches against BOURDONNAIS. Of the 85 games that are known to have been played, McDonnell won 27, drew 13, and lost 45. His lack of experience against strong opponents was a serious handicap as was the fact that he seldom played level games. Even when playing blindfold he would give knight odds to players as strong as Worrall.

On occasion McDonnell's combinative play could be brilliant and imaginative, but his opening play (based on Lewis's teaching) and his technique were inferior. He is described as 'quiet, reserved, outwardly imperturbable' with 'an insular sense of decorum', quite different from the extrovert Frenchman. Whereas Bourdonnais played fast and with ease, McDonnell concentrated at length upon his moves and retired from a playing session exhausted, sometimes 'walking his room the greater part of the night in a dreadful state of excitement'. His contemporaries believed that this long period of stress hastened his death from Bright's disease. The games were regarded as the finest ever played, and were first published in England where they greatly stimulated interest in chess.

Unlike his great rival, McDonnell died wealthy. Besides chess he was interested in political economy, on which he wrote half a dozen books or pamphlets.

Bourdonnais–McDonnell   50th match game   Queen's Gambit Accepted

1 d4 d5   2 c4 dxc4   3 e4 e5   4 d5 f5   5 Nc3 Nf6   6 Bxc4 Bc5   7 Nf3 Qe7   8 Bg5 Bxf2+   9 Kf1? Bb6   10 Qe2 f4   11 Rd1 Bg4   12 d6 cxd6   13 Nd5

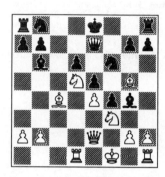

13 ... Nxd5   14 Bxe7 Ne3+   15 Ke1 Kxe7   16 Qd3 Rd8 17 Rd2 (ANDERSSEN suggests 17 Bd5) 17...Nc6   18 b3 Ba5 19 a3 Rac8   20 Rg1 b5   21 Bxb5 Bxf3   22 gxf3 Nd4   23 Bc4 Nxf3+   24 Kf2 Nxd2   25 Rxg7+ Kf6   26 Rf7+ Kg6 27 Rb7 Ndxc4   28 bxc4 Rxc4   29 Qb1 Bb6   30 Kf3 Rc3 31 Qa2 Nc4+   32 Kg4 Rg8   33 Rxb6 axb6   34 Kh4 Kf6 35 Qe2 Rg6   36 Qh5 Ne3 White resigns.

MacDonnell, George Allcock (1830–99), Irish-born player and author. In 1854 he was ordained in the Anglican church at Dublin where he served until 1857 when he obtained a curacy in London. In the following 20 years he played in about a dozen tournaments. He achieved two notable results: Dundee 1867, third equal with DE VERE, after NEUMANN and STEINITZ, ahead of BLACKBURNE; and London 1872, third equal with De Vere and ZUKERTORT, after Steinitz and Blackburne, but placed fourth after a triangular play-off. MacDonnell is better remembered for his lively chess column under the pen-name 'Mars' in the *Illustrated Sporting and Dramatic News* and for two books, *Chess Life and Pictures* (1883) and *The Knights and Kings of Chess* (1894), both containing picturesque accounts of contemporary players.

A genial man, fond of company, full of anecdotes and imitations of STAUNTON and other leading players, MacDonnell, 'the king's jester of chess', was popular among London players. If given to flights of fancy when he took up his pen he was nevertheless a sincere friend and a man of principle. After fulfilling a promise to perform a marriage ceremony for a divorced church-goer in January 1872 he was dismissed, and suffered four years of hardship before he could obtain another curacy. (In July 1872 when he played in the London tournament he adopted the pseudonym 'Hiber'.) In 1887 he was granted a living at Bisbrooke near Uppingham and then gave up first-class competitive play partly, perhaps, because of ill-health. He died after a long illness.

McDonnell Attack, 1109 or 1110 in the KING'S GAMBIT Accepted. This appears to have been prepared by McDONNELL for his match with BOURDONNAIS in 1834, when he played the BISHOP'S GAMBIT in five games and lost them all. He never tried this new attack which, to this day, is considered one of the best at White's disposal. The alternative name, Max Lange Attack, is rarely used because of possible confusion with the more famous line.

McDonnell Defence, 893, the STONE–WARE DEFENCE to the EVANS GAMBIT.

McDonnell Double Gambit, 641 in the BISHOP'S OPENING, introduced by McDONNELL in the 24th game of his matches against BOURDONNAIS in 1834.

McDonnell Gambit, 1129 in the KING'S GAMBIT Accepted, successfully introduced by McDONNELL in the first game of his third match against BOURDONNAIS. This alternative to the MUZIO GAMBIT, 1138, is regarded as a less effective choice, but it has not been tested thoroughly.

Mackenzie, Arthur Ford (1861–1905), composer of Scottish descent, a schoolteacher in Jamaica. He composed orthodox TWO- and THREE-MOVERS and published some of his work in *Chess: its Poetry and Prose* (1887). His life might have passed unremarkably had not illness brought the loss of his sight in the early months of 1896. After a period of despair he found he could still compose, and soon his problems were even better than before. Moreover, he began to move away from the conventional style of his time. In particular the growing popularity of the two-mover and its further development owed much to his influence. (See BLOCK; OBTRUSIVE PIECE; PROBLEM HISTORY.)

A. C. White, *Chess Lyrics* (1905), contains 282 problems by Mackenzie.

Mackenzie, George Henry (1837–91), a Scot who was one of the world's best half-dozen players in the 1880s. After leaving school in 1853 Mackenzie went to France and Germany, and tried his hand in business for about three years. Already keen on chess, he began to study the game seriously during this period. Finding office work uncongenial, he bought a commission in the King's Royal Rifle Corps and served in Ireland, where he met MACDONNELL, and for a brief time (1857–8) in India. He resigned his commission in 1861 and went to London to gain chess experience.

In the summer of 1862 he lost a match to MacDonnell (+4=2−7), but made such progress that he won the return match (+6=2−3). Mackenzie, who, wrote STEINITZ, 'combined uprightness with good temper and suavity of disposition and manners', had become one of the strongest two or three British-born players. In 1863 he went to the USA and enlisted in the Northern army. After 15 weeks as a private he became a captain in a Black

infantry regiment, from which he was discharged a few months later, allegedly for desertion and impressment. He rejoined the army in the autumn of 1864 to fight with distinction in three battles, after which he was arrested (for his earlier desertion) and imprisoned. After his release in May 1865 he settled in New York and devoted most of his time to chess. From then until 1880 Mackenzie contested 13 tournaments and 7 matches in the USA. He won all of them (except one drawn match) and was rightly regarded as the best player in the USA. All his opponents in these tournaments were American, apart from BIRD at New York 1876.

Mackenzie's early games were played in attacking style. 'New ideas made no impression on him until he had competed several times in European tournaments,' wrote Steinitz. The first of his trips from America to Europe was in 1878 when he played at Paris and, as in other strong events— Vienna 1882. London 1883, Hamburg 1885, he took a high place. He drew a match with BURN (+4=2−4) in 1886. The 'new ideas' had apparently been absorbed by 1887 when he made his outstanding performance at Frankfurt; first (+13=4−3), one and a half points ahead of BLACKBURNE and WEISS, who shared second place. Except for Steinitz and CHIGORIN, most of the world's best players, including TARRASCH, were competing.

In the 1880s Mackenzie developed tuberculosis. Notwithstanding his poor condition he shared third place with Bird, after Tarrasch and Blackburne, at Manchester 1890, his last tournament. When he returned to America his illness became so severe that he felt he had become too much of a burden to others. He died of an overdose of morphine which, according to Steinitz, was taken intentionally.

Burn–Mackenzie Frankfurt a/M 1887 Queen's Gambit Declined Harrwitz Attack

1 d4 e6 2 c4 d5 3 Nc3 Nf6 4 Bf4 Bd6 5 Bg3 b6 6 e3 Bb7 7 Nf3 0–0 8 Rc1 a6 9 cxd5 exd5 10 Bd3 Re8 11 Bh4 Nbd7 12 Ng5 Nf8 13 Qf3 Ng6 14 Bxg6 hxg6 15 Nh3 Be7 16 Bxf6 Bxf6 17 0–0 g5 18 Kh1 Rc8 19 Ng1 g6 20 Nge2 Kg7 21 Qg3 Qe7 22 Rc2 c5 23 Rfc1

23 ... cxd4 24 Nxd5 (not 24 exd4 when 24 ... Bxd4 cannot be met by 25 Nxd4 because of the threat of a BACK-RANK MATE) 24 ... Rxc2 25 Nxe7 Rxe2 26 h4 Rxe7 27 hxg5 Be5 28 Qh4 dxe3 29 f3 Rd2 30 Re1 e2 31 f4 Bxb2 32 f5 gxf5 33 g6 Rd1 34 Qxe7 Rxe1+ 35 Kh2 Kxg6

36 Qd6+ Kh7 37 Qg3 Rd1 38 Qh4+ Kg8 39 Qg3+ Bg7 White resigns.

Mackenzie Variation, 11 ... f5 12 Nb3 Bb6 13 Nb3d4 Nxd4 14 Nxd4 Bxd4 15 cxd4 f4 16 f3 Ng3, an alternative to the DILWORTH VARIATION (714) in the SPANISH OPENING, from the game B. Fleissig–Mackenzie, Vienna 1882. Also 801, the L'HERMET VARIATION.

Macleod, Norman Alasdair (1927–91), Scottish composer, International Judge of Chess Compositions (1980), International Master for Chess Compositions (1984). His work includes both orthodox and fairy problems, notably helpmates. At the age of 15, soon after learning the game, he came across HARLEY'S *Mate in Two Moves* and began composing, 'the most rewarding hobby anyone can have'. Continuing also to play, he represented his country at the Munich Olympiad, 1958. A civil servant from 1946, he served in the British Foreign Office from 1951 until his retirement in 1983. (See HELPMATE.)

MacLópez, 971, the RELFSSON GAMBIT. Noting that the characteristic move of the SPANISH OPENING (the Ruy López), Bf1–b5, is made in the SCOTCH GAMBIT, BLACKBURNE invented the facetious name.

Madrasi, a kind of fairy problem invented by the Indian Abdul Jabbar Karwatkar (1937–) in 1979, and named after his home town: any man, except a king, that is attacked by a similar enemy man becomes paralysed, losing all powers except that of paralysing. With orthodox men the paralysing is reciprocal but this is not always so with fairy men. For example, with white grasshopper at a1, white pawn at a6, black grasshopper at a7, Black's grasshopper is paralysed, White's is not.

#4 Madrasi

A BABSON TASK by the Indian composer Narayan Shankar Ram (1961–), *Feenschach*, 1983. Both rooks are already paralysed. The key is 1 Bc7.

1 ... f1 = Q   2 g8 = Q Qf5   3 Qge6
1 ... f1 = R   2 g8 = R Re1 +   3 Rg1
1 ... f1 = B   2 g8 = B Bc4   3 Kf8
1 ... f1 = N   2 g8 = N Nf~   3 Ne7.

A variant is King Madrasi (or Madrasi Rex Inclusive), in which the kings may stand on adjacent squares paralysing one another.

magazines, SEE PERIODICALS.

magic square, a mathematical puzzle: a series of consecutive numbers, often commencing with the number 1, is to be arranged to form a square so that, in chess terms, the numbers on each rank, file, or long diagonal add up to the same total. On an 8×8 magic square the common total is 260. This kind of exercise probably antedated the invention of chess, and BIDEV believed that magic squares could have been used to determine the moves of the chessmen, a thesis he expounded in *Šah simbol kosmosa* (1972), from which this example comes.

1	2	62	61	60	59	7	8
9	10	54	53	52	51	15	16
48	47	19	20	21	22	42	41
40	39	27	28	29	30	34	33
32	31	35	36	37	38	26	25
24	23	43	44	45	46	18	17
49	50	14	13	12	11	55	56
57	58	6	5	4	3	63	64

This square is related to the moves of the SHAṬRANJ men. Obviously a rook's rank or file, anywhere on the board, totals 260. The ALFIL ($\sqrt{8}$ leaper) could reach only eight squares (e.g. c1, g1, a3, e3, c5, g5, a7, e7), and no two alfils could meet. Each of these four sets of eight squares totals 260. A FERS, with its move of one square diagonally, placed on any square on the first rank and crossing the board moving first left, then right (or vice versa), and so on, covers squares summing to 260. A king placed on e1 or e8 and crossing the board by moving e1–e2–d3–d4–e5–e6–d7–d8, or e1–e2–f3–f4–e5–e6–f7–f8, or the similar moves from e8, again touches squares totalling 260. The same happens if a knight zig-zags across the board from its array position (b1–d2–b3–d4–b5–d6–b7–d8 or g1–e2–g3–e4–g5–e6–g7–e8 or b8–d7–b6–d5–b4–d3–b2–d1 or g8–e7–g6–e5–g4–e3–g2–e1). The eight squares commanded by a knight on c3, f3, c6 or f6 also add to the magic total. A magic square for a KNIGHT'S TOUR appears to be impossible, but this has not been proven mathematically.

maidens game, SEE MUST-CAPTURE CHESS.

majority, or pawn majority, a number of pawns opposed by a smaller number (a minority) on a localized part of the board. Majorities, like other characteristics of the pawn formation, influence the strategy of the game.

Situations commonly occur in which both players have castled on the king's-side and there are pawn majorities on each flank, White having one, Black the other. The king's-side majority could be advanced to attack the enemy king's position. Because of this possibility, such a majority was once thought to be inherently favourable, a view that persisted until the 1840s.

As players began to develop the game's strategy they realized that such attacks were unlikely to succeed against correct defence, that a majority on the queen's-side could be just as effective as one on the king's-side, and was sometimes preferable. During the greater part of his career STEINITZ consistently sought queen's-side majorities. (For games in which a queen's-side majority is decisively advantageous see KUPREICHIK and SOKOLOV; for a game in which a king's-side attack with pieces succeeds while the opponent's majority on the other side is being moved slowly forward, see OPPOSITE FLANK ATTACK.)

Majorities also play their part when the kings are not both castled on the king's side; and wherever they stand, a player may profit from a central majority which, with rare exceptions, confers greater mobility. (See GULKO and PSAKHIS for examples.) A majority is ineffective if the pawns lack mobility. This may happen if they are doubled, isolated, or backward pawns, or if the opponent is able to mount a successful MINORITY ATTACK. (See ALEKHINE; AVERBAKH; IVKOV; SHOWALTER.)

major piece, the queen or rook. Either can force mate when there are no other men but kings on the board.

Makarychev, Sergei Yurievich (1953–), Russian player, International Grandmaster (1976). He was equal second at Amsterdam Grandmasters' 1975, half a point behind the winner, LJUBOJEVIĆ, joint champion of Moscow in 1976, equal second (+ 3 = 5 − 1) at Oslo 1984, and first (+ 6 = 8) at Frunze 1985.

Makogonov, Vladimir Andreyevich (1904–93), Soviet player, International Master (1950), mathematics teacher. He played in eight USSR championships from 1927 to 1947, twice taking or sharing fourth place (1937, 1939), and obtaining good results in three strong tournaments: equal third at Leningrad–Moscow 1939; second (+ 6 = 6 − 2), after BOTVINNIK, at Sverdlovsk 1943; equal second with MIKENAS, after FLOHR, at Baku 1944. Makogonov made several contributions to openings knowledge, notably in the variation of the KING'S INDIAN DEFENCE named after him, and in the TARTAKOWER VARIATION of the QUEEN'S GAMBIT Declined.

His brother Mikhail (1900–43) competed in the USSR championship of 1929.

Makogonov–Keres Leningrad–Moscow 1939 Queen's Pawn Opening Keres Defence

1 d4 e6 2 c4 Bb4+ 3 Nc3 f5 4 Qb3 Qe7 5 a3 Bxc3+ 6

Qxc3 Nf6 7 g3 d6 8 Nf3 b6 9 Bg2 Bb7 10 0–0 0–0 11 b4 Nbd7 12 Bb2 c5 13 Rfd1 Ne4 14 Qb3 Ndf6 15 dxc5 bxc5 16 Nd2 Rab8 17 f3 Nxd2 18 Rxd2 Ba8 19 Qe3 f4 20 Qd3 fxg3 21 hxg3 Rfd8 22 Qe3 cxb4 23 axb4 Rxb4 24 Rxa7 Rb7 25 Ra6 Rc7 26 Ba3 e5 27 Bh3 Ne8

28 c5 Rc6 29 cxd6 Nxd6 30 Rxd6 Rcxd6 31 Bxd6 Qb7 32 Be6+ Kh8 33 Qb6 Re8 34 Bxe5 Qe7 35 Ra7 Black resigns.

Makogonov Variation, 373, a variation in the GRÜNFELD DEFENCE introduced by MAKOGONOV in 1951; 410 in the KING'S INDIAN DEFENCE.

Makovetz, Gyula (1860–1903), Hungarian player who edited Hungary's first chess magazine, *Budapesti Sakkszemle,* from its inception in 1889 to 1893, and edited a chess column in the Budapest paper *Pesti Napló.* In tournament play he met strong opposition only twice: Graz 1890, when he came first (+ 4 = 2), ahead of BAUER, LASKER (whom he defeated), and MARCO; and Dresden 1892, when he shared second place with the Bohemian player Moritz Porges (1858–1909), after TARRASCH, ahead of Marco, WALBRODT, and BARDELEBEN. He defeated CHAROUSEK in match play, 1893, + 2 = 2 − 1.

Malanyuk, Vladimir Pavlovich (1957–), Ukrainian player, International Grandmaster (1988). First or equal first at Minsk (First League) 1985, Minsk (Sokolov Memorial) 1985, Lvov 1986, Frunze 1987, Budapest 1989, and equal 2–3 in the stronger tournament at Tallinn 1987.

Malkin Variation, 721 in the SPANISH OPENING, named after a Russian-born engineer, Isidor Israel Malkin, who spent his adult life in Berlin and there, in the years around the First World War, earned a reputation as an openings expert. His booklet on the Spanish Opening (Close Defence) appeared in 1914, but another book, *Die neuen Wege der Schachtheorie,* was not published, although extracts from it were given in *Deutsche Schachzeitung.* This variation was in *Kagan's neueste Schachnachrichten,* 1921, no. 2.

Malmgren, Harald Valdemar (1904–57), Swedish player who specialized in postal play from 1928. He was awarded the title of International Correspondence Chess Grandmaster in 1953 for his achievement in the first World Correspondence Championship when he came second equal with NAPOLITANO after PURDY. The final took place from 1950 to 1953. Following an accident, Malmgren spent 13 months of this time in plaster and was able to devote most of his convalescence to the task.

malyutka, a Russian word for a composition in which there are five or fewer men (including kings) on the board. (Compare WENIGSTEINER; MEREDITH.)

man, a piece or pawn.

Mandler, Arthur (1891–1971), Czech composer, International Judge of Chess Compositions (1956), International Master for Chess Compositions (1966). A fine endgame analyst, he was a master of studies with didactic content, in the 'natural' style advocated and practised by his close friend RÉTI, whose studies were collected and published by Mandler in 1931. (See CONJUGATE SQUARES; DIDACTIC POSITION.)

+

A MALYUTKA by Mandler, *Národní Osvobození*, 1938. 1 Kd6 (1 Kxb7? Kb3 = ; 1 Kb6? Kb3 =) 1 ... Ka3 (1 ... b5 2 Kc5; 1 ... Kb3 2 f4) 2 Kc5 Ka4 3 f4 b5 4 f5 b4 5 Kc4 b3 6 Kc3 Ka3 7 f6 b2 8 f7 b1 = Q 9 f8 = Q + .

Mandler, *Sbírka šachových skladeb* (1970) contains some 300 of his problems; *Studie* (1970), a companion volume, has more than 200 studies.

Manhattan Defence, 173 or 182, also known as the Westphalia or American Defence, a variation of the QUEEN'S GAMBIT Declined played at New York 1927, a tournament held in Manhattan; but the defence was known long before, having occurred, for example, in the tournament game Ed. Lasker–Capablanca, New York 1915. White's 5th move can be either 5 e3 or 5 Nf3. (See BOGOLJUBOW.)

Mann, the German name for a piece used in COURIER. A *Mann* may be moved one square in any direction, like a king with no royal characteristics. The Arabian historian al-Mas'ūdi, writing *c*.950, mentions a piece with similar powers of movement

which was used in a form of GREAT CHESS and called a DABBABA.

Mannheim Variation, 66 in the QUEEN'S GAMBIT ACCEPTED, introduced by BOGOLJUBOW in his 23rd game against ALEKHINE in 1934, during the part of their match played at Mannheim.

manœuvre, a tactical operation designed to improve a player's position; to make such an operation; to jockey for position. A manœuvre is neither a COMBINATION (for the elements of surprise and sacrifice are lacking) nor a sustained attack, but threats of a tactical kind are often present. Manœuvring is the normal way to proceed when direct methods are not feasible; thus, writes EUWE, a player seeks to build upon small advantages. Most games include some manœuvring, however short. Writing extensively on the subject, NIMZOWITSCH points out that evenly balanced positions frequently have some distinctive features that could form a basis for manœuvring. Normally manœuvres are specific to the position, but some, especially in the endgame, have become standardized. See MIESES and RAZUVAYEV for manœuvres to reposition a queen and a bishop respectively.

Nimzowitsch–Rubinstein Dresden 1926 English Opening Symmetrical Variation

1 c4 c5 2 Nf3 Nf6 3 Nc3 d5 4 cxd5 Nxd5 5 e4 Nb4 6 Bc4 e6 7 0–0 N8c6 8 d3 Nd4 9 Nxd4 cxd4 10 Ne2 a6 11 Ng3 Bd6 12 f4 0–0 13 Qf3 Kh8 14 Bd2 f5 15 Rae1 Nc6 16 Re2 Qc7 17 exf5 exf5 18 Nh1 Bd7 19 Nf2 Rae8 20 Rfe1 Rxe2 21 Rxe2 Nd8 22 Nh3 Bc6 23 Qh5 g6 24 Qh4 Kg7 25 Qf2 Bc5 26 b4 Bb6 27 Qh4 Re8 28 Re5 Nf7 29 Bxf7 Qxf7 30 Ng5 Qg8 31 Rxe8 Bxe8

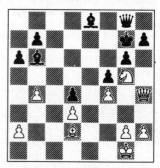

32 Qe1 Bc6 33 Qe7 + Kh8 34 b5 Qg7 35 Qxg7 + Kxg7 36 bxc6 bxc6 37 Nf3 c5 38 Ne5 Bc7 39 Nc4 Kf7 40 g3 Bd8 41 Ba5 Be7 42 Bc7 Ke6 43 Nb6 h6 44 h4 g5 45 h5 g4 46 Be5 Black resigns.

Having completed development in this game, White begins manœuvring with 18 Nh1, with the immediate object of improving the knight's position. After about a dozen moves White's advantage is clear, and a tactical phase begins.

Mansfield, Comins (1896–1984), English TWO-MOVER composer, widely regarded in his time as the greatest in his field. During the life of the GOOD

COMPANION CHESS PROBLEM CLUB (1913–24) he was one of the pioneers who gave new life to the two-mover. The ideas then introduced have since become traditional, and Mansfield adhered to them, continuing to gain successes although not always following the latest trend. In 1942 he wrote *Adventures in Composition*, an excellent guide to the art of composing. He was awarded the title of International Judge of Chess Compositions in 1957; for eight years from 1963 he was president of the FIDE Commission for Chess Compositions; in 1972 he was one of the first four to be awarded the title of International Grandmaster for Chess Compositions. (See CORRECTION; FOCAL PLAY.)

manṣūba (pl. manṣūbāt), an Arabic term for a composed middlegame or endgame position that is set for instruction (its primary purpose) or for solving. The student is told what end to achieve, but is not required to accomplish this task in a set number of moves. Composing, at its best in the 9th and 10th centuries, continued until the 1700s in those parts of the world where SHAṬRANJ was played.

About 1,600 manṣūbāt, mainly from Persian and Arabic sources dating from about 1140 to 1795, were examined by MURRAY, and he identified 553 distinctly different positions. These were published in his *History of Chess* (1913). He believed that about 200 were composed before AD 1000. In modern terms his collection might be regarded as 246 problems, 66 conditional problems, and 241 endgames. Strictly defined, however, they are all studies or didactic positions. The largest extant collection of manṣūbāt, compiled by ABU 'L-FATH, was not known to Murray, who might otherwise have added many more examples.

The positions may contain OBTRUSIVE PIECES (FIR-ZĀNS) and illegal pawn formations, but the FĪLS were always placed on squares they could have reached in a game. The rooks were the only line-pieces, and few of the line-themes of the modern problem could be shown. All but about 24 of the solutions consist entirely of checks, and in more than half of the positions Black threatens instant mate. Both characteristics were designed to avoid COOKS. Extra men are often added to provide a game-like position, and ECONOMY of force is rarely evident. Lengthy KING HUNTS were popular. The weakness of the firzān and fīl suit this kind of play: they may act as SELF-BLOCKS yet not interfere with the chase; or they may guard FLIGHTS yet not support alternative solutions. The Arabs appreciated SACRIFICE, especially in the early stages of the solution, and mating the king on the most improbable square, or with the weakest piece, the fīl. About 100 manṣūbāt end with PURE MATES and about half of these are MODEL MATES. For manṣūbāt in modern dress, see BAYER, KUZNETSOV, STAMMA.

In the following diagrams the firzān (F), which can be moved one square diagonally, is shown as a queen, and the fīl (A), a 2,2 (√8) LEAPER, is shown as a bishop.

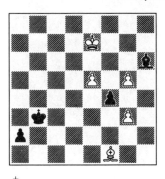

+

A study attributed to aṣ-ṢŪLĪ showing how a potential COLOUR-WEAKNESS may be avoided. 1 g4 Af8 2 g6 Ah6 3 g5 Af8 4 g7 and a white pawn captures the fīl, is promoted to a dark firzān on d8, f8, or h8, and White wins by BARE KING. After tries 1 gxf4? Axf4 or 1 g6? fxg3 White cannot gain sufficient control of the dark squares.

+

A study from a manuscript dated 1257. A knight and firzān usually draw against a knight, but here White can force an exchange and win by bare king. 1 Kc7 Na6+ 2 Kb7 Kb5 3 Na3+ Ka5 4 Nc4+ Kb5 5 Nd6+ Ka5 6 Fc3 Nc5+ 7 Kc6 Ne6 8 Nb7+ Ka4 9 Nc5+.

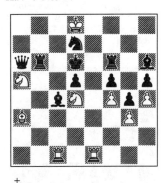

+

A problem attributed to al-'ADLĪ. 1 Re6+ (a sacrifice to make a self-block) 1 ... Axe6 2 Rc6+ Rxc6 3 Nb5+ (to decoy Black's firzān) 3 ... Fxb5 4 Nb7.

+

A position from a manuscript dated 1140. 1 Rxf8 Kxf8 2 Kf6 Rf1+ 3 Ff5 Rg1 4 g7+ Rxg7 (CRITICAL PLAY) 5 Fg6, a win by bare king after 5 ... Rg8 6 fxg8=F, or 5 ... Rxg6 6 Kxg6.

For another example, see DILĀRĀM'S MATE.

+

This and the following two manşūbāt are from an undated Persian manuscript. Here White has the inferior forces but can win by stalemate. 1 Ae3 Fh2+ 2 Kf2 Fg1+ 3 Axg1 Kh2 4 Ae3 Kh1 5 Kg3 g1=F 6 Ag5 Fh2+ 7 Kf2 (White triangulates to lose the move.) 7 ... Fg1+ 8 Kf3 Fh2 9 Ae3 Fg1 10 Kg3 Fh2+ 11 Kf2 Fg1+ 12 Axg1 Kh2 13 Ae3 Kh1 14 Kg3 h2 15 Kf2 (f3, h3).

+

White cannot play quietly because Black threatens mate in 3. 1 Rb8+ (SQUARE VACATION that creates a self-block) 1 ... Nxb8 (leaving b4 unguarded) 2 Nb6+ Kb7 3 Nd5+ Kc6 4 Rb6+ Kxd5 5 Nxb4+ Ke4 6 f3+ Kxf3 7 Rf6+ Ke2 8 Rf2+ Kd1 9 Rd2+ Ke1 (after 9 ... Kc1 white mates in three) 10 Nxd3+ Kf1 11 Rd1+ Ke2 12 Re1+ Kf3 13 Rf1+ Ke4 14 Rf4+ Kd5 15 Nb4+ Ke6 16 Rf6+ Kd7 17 Rd6+ Kc7 18 Nd5+ Kb7 19 Rb6+ Ka8 20 Nc7. White's king is mated on the square from which its journey began.

+

The HALF-BATTERY on the e-file gives a clue to the solution: 1 Rc7+ Ke8 2 Nxf6+ gxf6 3 Re7+ (a DECOY) 3 ... Kxe7 4 Ac5+ K~ 5 Re7.

H. J. R. Murray, *A History of Chess* (1913); A. van der Linde, *Quellenstudien zur Geschichte des Schachspiels* (1881), much used by Murray, was reprinted in 1968.

manuscripts, the only source of much chess history from the period before printing. Some are discussed under ALFONSO; BONUS SOCIUS; CESSOLE; CIVIS BONONIAE; ÉCHECS AMOUREUX; GESTA ROMANORUM; GÖTTINGEN MANUSCRIPT; INNOCENT MORALITY; VIDA.

many-mover, another name for a LONG-RANGE PROBLEM.

mao, the problemist's name for the mǎ (meaning horse), a piece used in CHINESE CHESS. The mao's move is similar to that of the knight, but it is not a LEAPER: it is moved by way of the laterally adjoining squares. For example, a mao at e5 could capture on, or be moved to, c4 or c6 only if d5 were unoccupied.

Marco, Georg (1863–1923), player from Czernowitz who settled in Vienna, journalist. He won several Viennese tournaments in the 1890s, on one occasion, in 1895, coming ahead of SCHLECHTER. His cautious style, 'keeping the draw in hand', was not conducive to success in strong tournaments, in which his best results were fourth places at Dresden

1892 and Cambridge Springs 1904 (+ 5 = 8 − 2), and fifth prize at Munich 1900. In match play he drew with KAUFMANN in 1893 (+ 5 − 5), with Schlechter in 1893 (= 10) and 1894 (+ 4 = 3 − 4), and he defeated ALBIN in 1901 (+ 4 = 4 − 2).

Marco was 'a man of considerable stature and fine muscular appearance ... jokingly called "the strongest chess-player in the world" ... always bubbling over with fun and cracking jokes with any and all ...', but he was serious both in his efforts to secure better rewards for professional players, and in his literary work. He wrote with humour and style, and is chiefly remembered for his authoritative annotations in the *Wiener Schachzeitung* which he edited jointly in 1898 and 1899 and then solely until 1916, and for his tournament books: Vienna 1903, Ostend 1906, Carlsbad 1907 (in collaboration with Schlechter), Vienna 1908, and Baden-bei-Wien 1914.

Marco–Gunsberg   Monte Carlo 1901   Spanish Opening
Berlin Defence

1 e4 e5 2 Nf3 Nc6 3 Bb5 Nf6 4 Nc3 Bc5 5 Nxe5 Nxe5
6 d4 Bd6 7 f4 Nc6 8 e5 Bb4 9 exf6 Qxf6 10 d5 Nd4
11 Bd3 Bc5 12 Ne4 Qe7

13 0–0 Nxc2+ 14 Kh1 Nxa1 15 Re1 Kd8 16 Bd2 Bd4
17 d6 cxd6 18 Bb4 Qe6 19 Qxa1 a5 20 Bxd6 Re8
21 Qc1 Bb6 22 Re2 Qd5 23 Ng5 Rxe2 24 Bxe2 Ke8
25 Ba3 f6 26 Bh5+ g6 27 Qe1+ Kd8 28 Bf3 Qd4
29 Qe7+ Kc7 30 Ne6+ Black resigns.

Maréchal Variation, 89, the LASKER VARIATION of the SLAV DEFENCE, analysed by Georges Maréchal of Canada.

Margate Variation, 482 in the SICILIAN DEFENCE, from the game Alekhine–Foltys, Margate 1937.

Marienbad Variation, 426, a form of QUEEN'S INDIAN DEFENCE, introduced by NIMZOWITSCH in a match in 1923 and played by him against RUBINSTEIN at Marienbad 1925; 447 in the SICILIAN DEFENCE, played in the game Spielmann–Sämisch in the same event.

Marini Variation, 22 in the ENGLISH OPENING, by the Argentinian player Luis Marini (1912–), with the same ideas as lie behind Pa7–a6 in the SICILIAN DEFENCE, of which this is a reversed form.

Mariotti Variation, 239 in the PIRC DEFENCE, an old line (e.g. Schmid–Udovčić, Venice 1953) revived in the late 1970s by the Italian grandmaster Sergio Mariotti (1946–).

Marjanović, Slavoljub (1955–), Yugoslav champion 1985, International Grandmaster (1978). His major tournament wins are: Belgrade 1979 (+ 8 = 5), two points ahead of the field; Bor 1983 (+ 6 = 7); and Rome 1988. In stronger tournaments he was fifth (+ 6 = 6 − 3) at Bled–Portorož 1979. He was in his country's team at Olympiads in 1980 and 1984.

Maróczy (pron. marotzy), Géza (1870–1951), Hungarian player, International Grandmaster (1950). After LASKER, then world champion, Maróczy was the most successful player in the first few years of the 20th century. He learned chess as a schoolboy, but read his first book (in Magyar) and developed his game while studying in Zurich. He did not complete his engineering course, and became a technician at a waterworks. After winning the amateur championship at Hastings 1895 he defeated CHAROUSEK (+ 6 = 6 − 2) later that year, and achieved a grandmaster performance in his first major tournament when he came second (+ 8 = 9 − 1) after Lasker, ahead of TARRASCH and PILLSBURY, at Nuremberg 1896. During the next three years Maróczy changed his employment to mathematics teacher, and had indifferent results in two tournaments.

Between 1899 and 1908 Maróczy competed in 15 tournaments, only once coming lower than third. His best results in the first part of this period are: London 1899, second (+ 12 = 10 − 4) equal with JANOWSKI and Pillsbury, after Lasker; Paris 1900, third (+ 11 = 2 − 3 and four draws not counted) equal with MARSHALL, after Lasker and Pillsbury; Munich 1900, first (+ 10 − 4 − 1) equal with Pillsbury and SCHLECHTER, but placed third after a play-off (gaining a prize, however, for having won the greatest number of games); Monte Carlo 1902, first (+ 13 = 9 − 2), ahead of Pillsbury; Monte Carlo 1903, second (+ 15 = 8 − 3), after Tarrasch, ahead of Pillsbury and Schlechter; Monte Carlo 1904, first (+ 5 = 5), ahead of Schlechter; Barmen 1905, first (+ 7 = 7 − 1) equal with Janowski, and ahead of Marshall, BERNSTEIN, and Schlechter; and Ostend 1905, first (+ 16 = 7 − 3), a point and a half ahead of a field that included Janowski, Tarrasch, and Schlechter.

The time had come for Maróczy to make his challenge for the world championship, and in April 1906 he and Lasker signed an agreement to play a match for the first to win eight games (draws not counting), the match to take place six months later in Vienna, Cuba, and New York. In August a revolution broke out in Cuba, the Vienna Chess Club became dissatisfied because not all the games would be played there, and the match fell through. Negotiations for title matches commonly bring ill-feeling between the rivals; Maróczy remained friendly with Lasker, but the opportunity for a match never came again. He continued to achieve good results, among them a second prize (+10=9−1) at Carlsbad 1907, and first (+10=8−1) equal with DURAS and Schlechter at Vienna 1908; but when it became clear that his bid for the championship was over he played less often, and less successfully.

During the First World War he suffered privation. Afterwards he lived for a time in the Netherlands, England (where he coached MENCHIK), and the USA, returning to Hungary in 1927. His last big win was at Carlsbad 1923, when he scored +7=9−1 to tie with ALEKHINE and BOGOLJUBOW. He continued tournament play until 1947, and played for Hungary in the Olympiads of 1927, 1930, and 1933.

Although he won a few BRILLIANCY PRIZES Maróczy's style was positional rather than combinative, and he showed exceptional talent for the ENDGAME. He was gentle and unusually self-effacing for a grandmaster. Widely respected, he was controller for the Alekhine–Euwe matches of 1935 and 1937. His writings were mostly in Magyar, but his book *Paul Morphy* (1909) was written in German and translated into Russian in 1929.

The second volume of the series on Hungarian chess history, *Magyar sakktörténet*, is a detailed and thorough biography and collection of Maróczy's games up to 1908; A. Földeák, *Géza Maróczy—Leben und Lehren* (1971) contains a biography and 66 games or game positions.

Maróczy–Canal Carlsbad 1929 Second Brilliancy Prize
ex æquo Sicilian Defence Scheveningen Variation

1 e4 c5 2 Nf3 e6 3 d4 cxd4 4 Nxd4 Nf6 5 Nc3 d6 6 Be2 Be7 7 0–0 0–0 8 Kh1 Nc6 9 Be3 Qc7 10 f4 Rd8 11 Bf3 a6 12 Qe1 Na5 13 Rd1 Nc4 14 Bc1 Rb8 15 g4 d5 16 exd5 Nxd5 17 Nxd5 exd5 18 Qg3 b5 19 Qg2 Bb7 20 h4 Bc5 21 c3 b4 22 cxb4 Bxb4 23 b3 Nb6 24 f5 Re8 25 g5 Bc3

26 g6 (the beginning of a decisive attack) 26 ... Bxd4 27 Rxd4 hxg6 28 fxg6 f6 29 Bf4 Qc5 30 Rfd1 Re5 31 Bxe5 fxe5 32 Rxd5 Qe7 33 Rxe5 Qxe5 34 Bxb7 Qh5 35 Rd4 Re8 36 Qe4 Qb5 37 Bd5+ Kh8 38 Qf3 Nxd5 39 Rxd5 Re1+ 40 Kg2 Qe2+ 41 Qxe2 Rxe2+ 42 Kf3 Re8 43 Rd6 Ra8 44 b4 Kg8 45 a3 Black resigns.

Maróczy Attack, 573, a dubious line in the CARO–

KANN DEFENCE recommended by MARÓCZY in annotations to the game Chajes–Réti, Carlsbad 1923.

Maróczy Bind, 494 or 541. White's PAWN FORMATION in these variations of the SICILIAN DEFENCE was once thought to bestow a powerful or even decisive advantage. In the 1980s masters discovered improvements for Black, but at club level the belief remained that White is likely to gain an enduring edge.

Maróczy Variation, 13 Qb1 in the CLASSICAL VARIATION (200) of the QUEEN'S GAMBIT Declined; 461 and 564 in the SICILIAN DEFENCE, which resemble the MARÓCZY BIND; 522 in the STEMGAME of the SCHEVENINGEN VARIATION in the same opening, Maróczy–Euwe, Scheveningen 1923; 840 in the FOUR KNIGHTS OPENING, as Maróczy–Bogoljubow, London 1922; 855 in the same opening, as Maróczy–Euwe, London 1922; 962 in the TWO KNIGHTS DEFENCE recommended by MARÓCZY in an annotation to game 83 of his book *Paul Morphy* (1925); 1064 in the PETROFF DEFENCE, as Maróczy–Pillsbury, Monte Carlo 1902; 1187 in the FRENCH DEFENCE, as Maróczy–Seitz, Györ 1924; 1222 in the same defence, highly recommended by Maróczy in his book *Die französische Partie* (1927), where he notes that TEICHMANN had condemned the move in an annotation in *British Chess Magazine*, 1899; 1253 in the ALEKHINE DEFENCE, played regularly by Maróczy in the early 1920s, e.g. Maróczy–Marco, Hague 1921.

Marostica, a town in north Italy between Venice and Lake Garda where, since 1954, there has been a biennial game of LIVING CHESS performed in honour of a legendary game played in 1454 for the hand of a lady. The same game is used each time, and the event is a tourist attraction. One of the best restaurants there is named 'alla Scacchiera' (at the chessboard).

'Mars', the *nom de guerre* of G. A. MACDONNELL.

Marseillais chess, SEE DOUBLE-MOVE CHESS.

Marshall, Frank James (1877–1944), American player who ranked among the world's best ten for about 20 years from 1904. Born in New York, he was taken to Montreal when he was eight, learned chess when he was ten, returned to New York in 1896, and soon became a professional player. His style was combinative and he sought open positions from which he might launch an attack. Early in 1904, or sooner, he realized the limitations of his style. Combinative play remained his preference, and he was proud of his reputation for SWINDLES, but he acquired some positional skills, improved his endgame and defensive play, and studied the openings. He was self-confident, could judge well his opponent's capabilities, and made a fair success of his tournament career.

He won three strong tournaments: Cambridge

Springs 1904 (+11=4), two points ahead of LASKER and JANOWSKI; Nuremberg 1906 (+9=7), ahead of DURAS and SCHLECHTER; and Havana 1913 (+8=5−1), ahead of CAPABLANCA. The best of his other results are: Paris 1900, third (+11=2−3) equal with MARÓCZY, after Lasker and PILLSBURY; Monte Carlo 1904, third (+4=5−1), after Maróczy and Schlechter; San Sebastián 1911, fourth (+4=9−1), after Capablanca, RUBINSTEIN, and VIDMAR, ahead of Schlechter and TARRASCH; New York 1915, second (+10=4), after Capablanca; and London 1927, third (+4=7), after NIMZOWITSCH and TARTAKOWER.

Marshall liked the rough and tumble of tournament play, and had neither the style nor the temperament for long and hard-fought matches. He became a benchmark for the world champion and his rivals and was soundly beaten by Tarrasch in 1905, Lasker in 1907, and Capablanca in 1909, who were more concerned with each other than with Marshall. In several of his many other matches he had notable victories: against TEICHMANN, 1902 (+2=3); Janowski, 1905 (+8=4−5) and 1912 (+6=2−2); MIESES, 1908 (+5=1−4); LEONHARDT, 1911 (+2=4−1); and Duras, 1913 (+3=1−1).

In 1909 Marshall, after defeating SHOWALTER in a match (+7=3−2), claimed the US championship, a title he defended only once, when he defeated Edward LASKER in 1923 (+5=9−4). Other challengers could not raise the stake money and in 1935, under pressure 'from coast to coast', the directors of the National Chess Federation voted unanimously to organize tournaments for the championship. Marshall relinquished the title, and his club donated a suitable trophy. (The first US championship tournament, won by RESHEVSKY, was held in 1936.) Marshall played for and captained the US team in five Olympiads, 1930, 1931, 1933, 1935, and 1937, making the best second-board score in 1933 (+14−6), and bringing home the gold medal four times.

In 1942 this 'pre-occupied old gentleman who looks like a Shakespearean actor, smokes strong cigars, and takes a chess board to bed with him so that he can record any plays he thinks up' published *My Fifty Years of Chess* (ghosted by REINFELD). The book contains 140 of his games and a brief autobiography, and was reprinted as *Marshall's Best Games of Chess* (1960). His only interests were chess and family life, to both of which he was devoted: his only weakness a liking for drink, he was too professional a player to let it interfere with serious play.

Although he was the leading American player after Pillsbury's death in 1906 until KASHDAN's rise to fame around 1930, Marshall had many hard times as a chess professional. Fortunately his unaffected and outgoing personality brought him many friends, and with their help he opened 'Marshall's Chess Divan' in 1915. From it the famous Marshall Chess Club sprang, and in 1931 the members purchased a house in Manhattan, providing both club rooms and a secure home. Returning home late one night Marshall collapsed and died in the

street. His wife continued to run the chess club until her death in 1971.

Nimzowitsch–Marshall Bad Kissingen 1928 Brilliancy Prize Queen's Indian Defence

1 d4 Nf6 2 c4 b6 3 Nc3 Bb7 4 Bg5 e6 5 Qc2 h6 6 Bh4 Be7 7 e4 0-0 8 e5 Nd5 9 Bg3 Nb4 10 Qb3 d5 11 exd6 Bxd6 12 0-0-0 N8c6 13 Bxd6 Qxd6 14 a3

14 ... Nxd4 15 Rxd4 Qxd4 16 axb4 Qxf2 17 Qd1 Rfd8 18 Qe2 Qf4+ 19 Kc2 a5 20 bxa5 Rxa5 21 Nf3 Ra1 22 Kb3 b5 23 Qe5 bxc4+ 24 Kb4 Qc1 25 Nb5 c5+ White resigns.

Marshall Attack, 1074, standard line in the KING'S GAMBIT Declined, introduced in the game Marshall–E. Cohn, Carlsbad 1907.

Marshall Counterattack, 754 in the SPANISH OPENING. Black gives up a pawn for a strong attack, a sacrifice introduced to master play by MARSHALL in the New York tournament 1918. However, the move had been played in 1893 by four Cubans in consultation, in a game with WALBRODT played in Havana. Marshall's opponent, CAPABLANCA, met this PREPARED VARIATION with equanimity, perhaps knowing the Cuban game, and won, a result that put this line out of business for about 20 years. Since the 1940s improvements for Black have been found but no final verdict on the soundness of the variation has been made.

Marshall Defence, 219, a dubious variation in the QUEEN'S GAMBIT Declined which MARSHALL tried in the mid-1920s until the game Alekhine–Marshall, Baden-Baden 1925, discouraged him.

Marshall Gambit, 121 and 135 in the QUEEN'S GAMBIT Declined. The first was introduced by MARSHALL at Monte Carlo 1904, while the second, a sound way of avoiding the MERAN VARIATION, is as the game Marshall–Schlechter, Monte Carlo 1902.

Also 601 in the SCANDINAVIAN OPENING, an old line given in the first edition of the HANDBUCH (1843). Marshall played it at Carlsbad 1907, but it had not fallen out of use; BLACKBURNE was among those who had used it regularly, and it sometimes bears his name.

Marshall Trap, 1066 in the PETROFF DEFENCE. White should play 10 Nc3.

Marshall Variation, 560, line in the SICILIAN DEFENCE given by JAENISCH; 851 in the SPANISH FOUR KNIGHTS GAME, introduced in Maróczy–Marshall, Monte Carlo 1904; 1065 in the PETROFF DEFENCE, an old line played, for instance, by STAUNTON in the London 1851 tournament, but used by MARSHALL throughout his life, alert to the possibility of the MARSHALL TRAP; 1195, FRENCH DEFENCE variation of dubious merit, played at Amsterdam 1851; 152, STONEWALL Variation.

Also 11 ... 0–0–0 12 Nxe6 fxe6 13 g4 Qe5 14 fxg7 Rhg8 15 Bh6, an alternative to the RUBIN-STEIN VARIATION (946), and probably White's best way to continue the MAX LANGE ATTACK. Before the Hamburg 1910 tournament TARRASCH had made a characteristic assertion to the effect that the Max Lange Attack favoured Black. Marshall spent months testing his PREPARED VARIATION, sprang it on Tarrasch, and won a memorable victory. Years passed before players were again willing to meet this attack.

Marwitz, Jan Hendrik (1915–91), Dutch study composer. He was by no means prolific, but the few studies that he produced are of high quality. With the endgame editor of *Tijdschrift v.d. KNSB*, Cornelis Jan de Feijter (1907–88), he wrote *De Eindspelstudie* (1948), a thorough introduction to the subject, with 100 illustrative examples.

Black to move, White draws

A study by Marwitz, first prize, de Feijter Jubilee tourney 1981. 1 ... Bd2+ 2 Kxd2 Rd5+ 3 Ke3 Re5+ 4 Kd4 Re4+ 5 Kc5 Nxb7+ (5 ... Rxb7 6 Bf3) 6 Kb6 Ra5 7 Bb5+ Kf8 8 Rf1+ Kg7 9 Rb1 Re5 10 g6 Rg5 11 Rb4 (11 Rb2? Nd6 or 11 Rb3? Nc5) 11 ... Re5 12 Rb1 =. A POSITIONAL DRAW: Black's pieces cannot be freed.

Mason, James (1849–1905), one of the world's best half-dozen players in the early 1880s, journalist. He was born in Kilkenny, Ireland, and adopted the name James Mason (his original name is unknown) when he and his family emigrated to the USA in 1861. He became a boot-black in New York, frequenting a Hungarian café where he learned chess. Coming to the notice of J. Gordon Bennett of the *New York Herald*, he was given a job in the newspaper's offices, a start in life that both suited

his literary aspirations and gave him the chance to study chess. In 1876 he made his mark, winning first prize at the fourth American Congress, Philadelphia, and in the *New York Clipper* tournament, as well as defeating the visiting master BIRD in match play (+ 11 = 4 − 4).

Settling in England in 1878 he drew a match with POTTER (+ 5 = 11 − 5) in 1879. At Vienna 1882, the strongest (and longest) tournament held up to that time, he took third prize (+ 17 = 12 − 5), behind the joint winners STEINITZ and WINAWER. This was his finest achievement, but he had other good tournament results: London 1883 (won by ZUKERTORT), equal fifth; Nuremberg 1883, third after Winawer and BLACKBURNE; Hamburg 1885, second equal with Blackburne, ENGLISCH, TARRASCH, and WEISS, after GUNSBERG; Manchester 1890 (won by Tarrasch), equal fifth; and Belfast 1892, first equal with Blackburne. Fond of drink, Mason is alleged to have lost many games when in a 'hilarious condition'. 'A jolly good fellow first and a chess-player afterwards', he never fulfilled the promise of his first years in England. Instead he wrote books on the game, in excellent style, notably two popular textbooks, *The Principles of Chess in Theory and Practice* (1894) and *The Art of Chess* (1895); both ran to several editions. Another of his books, *Social Chess* (1900), contains many short and brilliant games.

Mason–Janowski   Monte Carlo 1901   Italian Opening
Four Knights Variation

1 e4 e5 2 Nf3 Nc6 3 Bc4 Bc5 4 Nc3 Nf6 5 d3 d6 6 Be3 Bb6 7 Qe2 0–0 8 h3 Nd4 9 Qd2 Ne6 10 Bb3 c6 11 Ne2 Qc7 12 g4 a5 13 a4 Nc5 14 Bxc5 Bxc5 15 Ng3 Be6 16 Ba2 d5 17 g5 Nd7 18 Nh4 Qb6 19 c3 g6 20 Rh2 f6 21 Nf3 f5 22 exd5 cxd5 23 d4 exd4 24 Nxd4 Ne5 25 Nge2 Nc4 26 Bxc4 dxc4 27 0–0 Bd7 28 Qc2 Rae8 29 h4 Bd6 30 Rhh1 Re4 31 h5 Qd8 32 Rdg1 Rg4 33 Qd2 Rxg1+ 34 Rxg1 Qe7 35 hxg6 hxg6 36 Nf4 Bxf4 37 Qxf4 Re8 38 Rh1 Bxa4 39 Qh4 Qe5

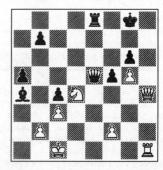

40 Nf3 Qd6 (to avoid mate in three Black must give up a pawn and piece) 41 Qxc4+ Kg7 42 Qxa4 Re4 43 Qd1 Qc7 44 Nd4 a4 45 f3 Re7 46 Qxa4 Qf4+ 47 Kb1 Qxg5 48 Qa8 Black resigns.

Mason Gambit, 1092, the KERES GAMBIT in the KING'S GAMBIT Accepted, played unsuccessfully by MASON against ROSENTHAL in the Paris tournament 1878.

Mason Variation, 231 in the QUEEN'S PAWN OPEN-ING, an old line given in the GÖTTINGEN MS and played regularly by MASON in the 1880s. Sometimes named after HARRWITZ or RUBINSTEIN, who also tried the variation.

master, generally a strong player. Since the middle of the 20th century the title has increasingly become incorporated into formal titles and is less frequently used otherwise. (See FIDE MASTER; INTERNATIONAL MASTER; NATIONAL MASTER.)

Matanović, Aleksandar (1930–), Yugoslav player, International Grandmaster (1955), journa-list. National champion in 1962 (shared), 1969, and 1978 (after a play-off). He played for Yugoslavia in 11 Olympiads (1954–72, 1978) scoring 83% (+8=4) on fourth board in 1970. In four inter-zonals (1952, 1958, 1967, 1976) he made only moderate results, the best of them his seventh place at Portorož in 1958. His best international wins are: Zevenaar 1961 (+7=8); Titovo Užice 1966 (+6=8−1), a tie with SUETIN; and Bad Pyrmont 1970, shared. At Houston 1974 he was second (+5=6), after HÜBNER.

Matanović might have had greater success in play had he concentrated his efforts, but he was also involved in the publication of chess literature. He is the founder (1966) and editor-in-chief of *Chess Informant*, a multilingual twice-yearly (until 1991, thence three-times a year) publication with world-wide circulation. Many other books have sprung from the team set up to publish *Informator*, as it is more commonly known. Among them are the EN-CYCLOPEDIA OF CHESS OPENINGS, in five volumes, first edition published 1974 to 1979, the *Encyclo-pedia of Chess Endings*, five volumes (the first four appeared 1982 to 1989), and the single-volume *Encyclopedia of Chess Middlegames* (1980), all with Matanović as editor-in-chief. (See QUADRANT.)

Golombek–Matanović Opatija 1953 English Open-ing King's Fianchetto Defence

1 c4 Nf6 2 Nc3 g6 3 g3 Bg7 4 Bg2 0–0 5 Nf3 c5 6 0–0 Nc6 7 d4 d6 8 dxc5 dxc5 9 Be3 Qa5 10 Qc1 Rd8 11 Nd2 Nd4 12 Bxd4 cxd4 13 Nb3 Qb4 14 Nd5 Nxd5 15 Bxd5 e6 16 Bg2 Bd7 17 Rd1 Ba4 18 Qd2 Qb6 19 c5 Qa6 20 Qb4 Rab8 21 Rd2 b6

22 Nxd4 (22 c6 Bf8) 22 … bxc5 23 Qxc5 Rbc8 24 Nc6

Rxd2 25 Ne7+ Kh8 26 Qxc8+ Qxc8 27 Nxc8 Bxb2 28 Re1 Rd7 29 e3 Ba3 30 Rb1 Rc7 31 Rb8 Kg7 32 Bb7 Rc1+ 33 Kg2 Rb1 34 Kh3 Bc5 White resigns.

match, a contest between two individuals, or a TEAM MATCH. Individual matches from as far back as the 9th century are on record, but the first OVER-THE-BOARD matches of consequence to the game as played today were those between McDONNELL and BOURDONNAIS in 1834 when, almost a new depar-ture at the time, 85 game scores were recorded.

A decade later STAUNTON achieved his supremacy solely by match play, and the first WORLD CHAM-PIONSHIP contest in 1886 was also a match. The chess public has shown that it prefers to have a match play rather than tournament play champion-ship, although a WORLD CUP winner other than the reigning world champion might gain support.

In the 19th century, when travel was more diffi-cult than it is now, non-championship match play between the great players was frequent. After the middle of the 20th century the pressure of the tournament programme led to the grandmasters limiting their match appearances to CANDIDATES matches, but then increased need for sponsorship led to a change. Short matches between two top grandmasters can be arranged easily, given appro-priate financial backing. (See CLEAN SCORE.)

Feenstra Kuiper, *Hundert Jahre Schachzweikämpfe* (1967).

match tournament, a tournament in which players meet each other a predetermined number of times, giving the event the character of match play. There is no defined lower limit, but a double-round tour-nament would not be regarded as a match tourna-ment. The early knock-out tournaments were played as a series of matches for the best of so many games, but these were not match tournaments. There have been few attempts to arrange ALL-PLAY-ALL tournaments as 'best of x games' between each player. The result when this was tried in the Vienna international tournament 1873 was neither satisfac-tory nor popular.

mate, see CHECKMATE.

material, all the men on the board except the kings. To have a material advantage is to have the greater total VALUE OF PIECES.

mate transference, see CHANGED PLAY.

mathematics. See COMPUTERS; ELO RATING; KNIGHT'S TOUR; LENGTH OF GAME; MAGIC SQUARES; MYTHS; OPENINGS, NUMBER OF POSSIBLE.

mating net, an arrangement of men around a king in such a way that it will be checkmated. The term is usually applied to positions where the defending king is not mated by a series of FORCED MOVES.

(Polugayevsky–Nezhmetdinov, Sochi 1958) After 24 ... Rxf4 25 Rxh2 White's king is in a mating net. The game ended 25 ... Rf3+ 26 Kd4 Bg7 27 a4 c5+ 28 dxc6 bxc6 29 Bd3 Nexd3+ 30 Kc4 d5+ 31 exd5 cxd5+ 32 Kb5 Rb8+ 33 Ka5 Nc6+ White resigns.

Matthews, Robin Charles Oliver (1927–), British composer, International Judge of Chess Compositions (1957), International Master for Chess Compositions (1962), economist, appointed Master of Clare College, Cambridge, in 1975. Matthews has specialized in orthodox THREE-MOVERS and is among the world's leaders in this field. He won first prize in the World Composing Tournament 1984–8.

#3

A problem by Matthews, second prize, *The Problemist*, 1978. The key is 1 Nc6, threatening 2 Kd7:

1 ... Rg1   2 Rg6+
1 ... Rf1   2 Rf6+
1 ... Rf2   2 Bf4
1 ... Rg2   2 Bg3
1 ... Ra2   2 Bb8

Mattison, Herman (1894–1932), Latvian player and study composer, known in Latvia as Matisons. In 1924 he won his country's first championship tournament and, later that year, ahead of COLLE and EUWE, the first world amateur championship, arranged in connection with the Olympic Games at Paris. In the second and last amateur championship, organized by FIDE at The Hague in 1928, he

took third prize after Euwe and PRZEPIÓRKA, ahead of BECKER. Mattison composed many studies, for which he is perhaps better known, and was also a strong endgame player. He played first board for Latvia at the Prague Olympiad 1931, and two of his victims were ALEKHINE and RUBINSTEIN whom he defeated in the endgame phase.

+

A version of a study by Mattison, first prize, *Shakhmatny Listok*, 1927. 1 Nf7+ Kg8 2 a7 Re8 3 Nd6 Rd8 4 Nf5 (Roman DECOY THEME: if 4 b6? Bd4 5 Nc8 Rxc8 6 b7 Rc1+ =) 4 ... Bf8 5 b6 Bc5 6 Ne7+ Kf8 7 Nc8 Rxc8 8 b7. This is a correction, by V. Vlasenko in *Shakhmaty v SSSR*, 1986. Mattison's position had the white king on e1 and the black rook on b6, making the solution unclear.

T. G. Whitworth, *Mattison's Chess Endgame Studies* (1987) gives 60 of these, all that could be found, and six games.

Matulović, Milan (1935–), Yugoslav player, International Grandmaster (1965). He won or shared first prizes at Belgrade 1963 (+4=7) and again in 1965, and came third (+6=8−1) equal with KROGIUS, after KORCHNOI and POLUGAYEVSKY, at Sochi 1966. In 1967 he came second (+11=4−2) equal with GELLER, half a point behind FISCHER, in the Skopje–Kruševo–Ohrid tournament, and he played in the Sousse interzonal in which, after a little cheating (see J'ADOUBE), he came ninth. Matulović obtained three tournament victories in 1969, probably his best year: Skopje (+8=6−1), a tie with HORT ahead of SMYSLOV; Athens (+10=6−1), ahead of Hort and HÜBNER; and Belgrade (+6=8−1), shared with GLIGORIĆ, IVKOV, and Polugayevsky, ahead of Geller and BOTVINNIK. Subsequently he won or shared first prizes at Sarajevo 1971, Majdanpek 1976, Helsinki 1981 (+6=4−1), Vrnjačka Banja 1985, and Vrnjačka Banja 1986. National champion in 1965 and again in 1967 (+7=10), he played for his country in five consecutive Olympiads from 1964 to 1972. He likes sharp play, and has made some contributions to openings knowledge, notably in variations such as the MORRA GAMBIT, one of his specialities, but his endgame skill is suspect. Although a non-smoker and teetotal, his anti-social behaviour leads to his being invited to few tournaments.

Polugayevsky–Matulović USSR–Yugoslavia match 1964
English Opening Symmetrical Variation

1 Nf3 c5 2 c4 Nf6 3 Nc3 g6 4 d4 Bg7 5 d5 d6 6 g3 0–0
7 Bg2 Na6 8 0–0 Nc7 9 Bf4 b5 10 cxb5 Rb8 11 a4 a6
12 bxa6 Rxb2 13 a7 Bb7 14 Ne1 Rb6 15 Nc2 Qa8 16 e4
Nd7 17 Ra3 Ba6 18 Re1 Qxa7 19 Bd2 Ne5 20 Nb5
Bxb5 21 axb5 Qb7 22 Bf1 Nxb5 23 Ra5 Ra8 24
Rxa8+ Qxa8 25 f4 Nd7 26 Bh3 Rb7 27 Ne3 Nd4 28
Nc4 Nb6 29 Nxb6 Rxb6 30 e5

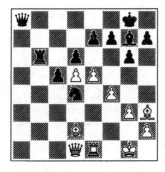

30 ... Qxd5 31 Bg2 Qb3 32 Qg4 Qe6 33 Qd1 dxe5 34
fxe5 h5 35 Qa4 h4 36 gxh4 Rb2 37 Bg5 Qf5 38 Qa8+
Kh7 39 Qe4 Qf2+ 40 Kh1 Nf3 White resigns.

Matulović Gambit, 457, the MORRA GAMBIT, tried
on occasion by MATULOVIĆ.

maximummer, a kind of FAIRY PROBLEM invented
by DAWSON in 1913. Black must make the geometrically longest move, or one of them if there is a
choice, a STIPULATION indicated by the abbreviation
'max'. The unit of measurement is the distance
between the centres of two orthogonally adjoining
squares. For example, a move from a1 to a8
measures 7 ($\sqrt{49}$) and is shorter than a move from
a1 to f6 ($\sqrt{50}$). The measurements of castling are
$\sqrt{16}$ (king's-side) and $\sqrt{25}$ (queen's-side). Unless
otherwise stipulated, both check and mate are
normal (i.e. not fairy) and the White king may not
be moved into check.

s#8 max

A version by DAWSON of a problem by PAULY, *Chess
Amateur,* Dec. 1920. White forces Black to give

mate: 1 h6 Qa3 2 b4 Qh3+ 3 Kf7 Qc8 4 g4 Qc1
5 Kg8 Qxh6 6 g5 Qa6 7 Kh8 Qf1 8 b5 Qf8#.

The moves of the black queen form an eight-
pointed star. Here Black's notional capture Qf8xh8
is not the longest move and so the mate is not fairy.
Other kinds of maximummer in which a fairy mate
is required are rarely seen.

Max Lange, see LANGE.

Max Lange Attack, 945. This attack can arise from
several openings: TWO KNIGHTS DEFENCE, PETROFF
DEFENCE, SCOTCH GAMBIT, BISHOP'S OPENING, CENTRE
GAME, ITALIAN OPENING. The attack was suggested
by LANGE in 1854, and always bears both of his
names. Lange also recommended 1109, a deferred
version of the McDONNELL ATTACK (1110) which is
sometimes called the Max Lange Attack.

Max Lange Defence, 610 in the VIENNA GAME. This
line did not originate with LANGE, but it was
endorsed by him in his book *Kritik der Eröffnungen*
(1855).

Mayet Defence, 895 in the EVANS GAMBIT, played in
the game Anderssen–Mayet 1867. Carl Mayet
(1810–68), a member of the Berlin PLEIADES and
cousin of Hanstein, another member, wrote the
section on the SPANISH OPENING in the first edition
of the HANDBUCH. Sometimes the line is called the
Anderssen Variation.

MCO, a popular abbreviation for *Modern Chess
Openings.* Written by the English players Richard
Clewin Griffith (1872–1955) and John Herbert
White (1880–1920), the book first appeared in 1911.
The second edition, 1913, with additional lines and
the names of the players, was reprinted in 1916.
Further editions appeared in 1925, 1932, and the
best, written by FINE, in 1939. Popular among
English-speaking players, it was never as authoritative as Bilguer's HANDBUCH, which was becoming
outdated by the 1930s, but it could be carried in the
pocket. Editions published after the Second World
War, from the seventh in 1946 to the thirteenth in
1990, no longer have that merit. In an attempt to
cope as well as possible within a single volume with
the increasing number of opening variations the
number (and size) of pages has grown from 190 in
the 1st edition to 390 in the 7th and 727 in the 13th.
This last is the first to use standard notation and
would have been about 150 pages bigger had descriptive notation been retained.

Meadow Hay Opening, 3, the WARE OPENING,
thought to have a rustic character.

Mecking, Henrique da Costa (1952–), International Grandmaster (1972), a Brazilian player
who was ranked in the world's first ten from 1976 to
1980. After winning the national championship at
the age of 13 he began to devote most of his life to
chess; at 15 he again won the Brazilian champion-

ship, but of greater importance was his victory (+3=3) in the final of a zonal tournament at Buenos Aires, and participation in the Sousse interzonal 1967, where he shared eleventh place. He was no more successful in his next interzonal, Palma de Majorca 1970, but three years later he took first place (+7=10) in the Petropolis interzonal. In 1974 he lost his first CANDIDATES match to KORCHNOI. In this match Mecking obtained excellent middlegame positions but lacked the experience to make the most of the advantages he gained. Again he won (+8=10−1) an interzonal, Manila 1976, and again he lost the quarter-final match, this time to POLUGAYEVSKY. The next interzonal, on his home ground, Rio de Janeiro 1979, turned out to be his swan song. After two rounds he withdrew on medical grounds, and suspended his chess career.

Apart from events in the world championship cycle Mecking played in few international tournaments, his best results being: Vršac 1971, first (+8=7), ahead of PORTISCH; Las Palmas 1975 (+7=6−1), equal second with ANDERSSON and TAL, after LJUBOJEVIĆ; Manila 1975 (+3=6−1), equal second with Polugayevsky, LARSEN, and PFLEGER, after Ljubojević.

An intensely nervous player, Mecking found it difficult to hold up under stress. He became convinced that he was terminally ill. In the 1980s, believing his life to have been saved by divine intervention, he commenced training for the priesthood. In 1991 he made a return to first-class chess when he played a match with NIKOLIĆ, losing one game and drawing the other five.

Filguth, *Mequinho o perfil de um gênio* (1983) contains 90 games, several interviews, crosstables of all major events, and many photographs.

Mecking–Ljubojević Vršac 1971 Sicilian Defence Close Variation

1 e4 c5 2 Nf3 d6 3 Nc3 a6 4 g3 b5 5 Bg2 Bb7 6 d3 g6 7 0–0 Bg7 8 Nh4 b4 9 Ne2 Nc6 10 f4 Nf6 11 h3 e5 12 f5 d5 13 Bg5 dxe4 14 Bxe4 c4 15 Bg2 cxd3 16 Qxd3 Qxd3 17 cxd3 Nd7 18 Rac1 Rc8 19 fxg6 hxg6 20 Bd5 Rf8 21 Be4 f5 22 Bxc6 Rxc6 23 Rxc6 Bxc6 24 Nxg6 Rf7

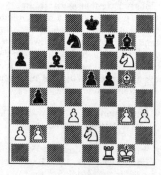

25 Nd4 exd4 26 Re1+ Ne5 27 Nxe5 Bxe5 28 Rxe5+ Kd7 29 h4 Bb5 30 Rd5+ Ke6 31 Rxd4 Rc7 32 h5 Rc2 33 h6 Kf7 34 Rd6 Black resigns.

median system, a tie-breaking method for use in SWISS SYSTEM tournaments. Each player's SOLKOFF SCORE (the sum of opponents' scores) has the top and bottom components removed. Some organizers remove the highest and lowest pairs of opponents' scores in events of nine to twelve rounds and the three at each end for events of more than twelve rounds.

medieval chess. The game spread across Europe from the 8th to the 10th centuries and was played according to the laws of SHAṬRANJ, as confirmed by the Einsiedeln MS, *c.*1100, the earliest European text to mention chess. Several changes took place subsequently: the leap of the FERS mentioned in EZRA's 12th-century poem; the king's leap (see CASTLING), described by CESSOLE, and the pawn's double-move given in the ALFONSO MS, both in the 13th century; the law that stalemate was a drawn game, given in the Cracow MS, 1422; and the EN PASSANT law, first noted in the 15th century.

These innovations were not universal and there were many local variants. For example, in Germany only the a-, d-, e-, and h-pawns could make a double move. Prior to the introduction of this double move the tedium of the opening phase could be relieved in several countries by the short ASSIZE. The Lombard assize allowed no win by BARE KING. In some regions a player having one fers on the board could not promote a pawn. (Nowhere could a player promote to any piece other than a fers.) The chequered board was introduced before 1100, its adoption probably accelerated by the contemporary invention of DRAUGHTS for which chequering was particularly useful. (A 10 × 5 chequered board was adapted for accounting purposes, and the revenue department of Normandy and England was called the Eschecker, later spelt exchequer.)

Neither textbooks nor scores of games from medieval times have survived, and perhaps none ever existed. A few poems describe the moves of the men and, on occasion, give elementary advice. When players from different regions met they were obliged to discuss the laws before play began, for there were many different assizes. This must have greatly hindered the development of the game. The players of Lombardy were reputedly the best, but in the absence of evidence it may be doubted that they matched the skills of their Islamic predecessors. However, they were pioneers of the problem art (see MEDIEVAL PROBLEMS). At one time the Church was opposed to chess-playing, probably because of the frequent use of stakes. Some edicts were issued, notably one by Cardinal Damiani in 1061 forbidding the clergy to play. (Despite this lapse he was later canonized.) By the 13th century this prohibition had been eased or forgotten.

Played by kings and the nobility, regarded as a knightly accomplishment, used symbolically in MORALITIES, chess is frequently mentioned in literary sources, notably in romances. A knight Gavin plays Charlemagne for stakes, the knight offering his life, the king his wife and the realm of France. Charlemagne loses with bad grace. Gavin discreetly refuses the queen's hand but accepts the town of Lyon which, as it happens, is in the hands of the Saracens. Such tales have little factual basis. Historians believe that the game of chess was unknown in the court of Charlemagne. Some accounts of kings playing chess when they should be attending to matters of state, and of hostages playing while awaiting execution may be more realistic, as may the many accounts of violence when men or boards were used as weapons. Totally unreal but utterly splendid is Merlin's magic board, with pieces of gold and silver, which plays without human help.

medieval problems. Islamic problems, or MANṢŪ-BĀT, were almost certainly known in Europe before AD 1000, but the first European reference to chess problems was during the reign of Richard I (1189–99), when Giraldus Cambrensis (Gerald of Wales) wrote *Gemma Ecclesiastica*. He expresses contempt for juperties (problems) as compared with the game, and notes with regret that problems have become fashionable. Evidently problem collections existed at that time and these would have included *manṣūbāt*; whether European problems were also included is a matter of conjecture.

Of the 30 or more surviving medieval European collections, the earliest date from the second half of the 13th century, when problems of European origin seem to have become well established. The largest collections, some of them beautifully illuminated, are the BONUS SOCIUS and the CIVIS BONO-NIAE, both from Lombardy, and three 14th-century manuscripts from Picardy which, although based on the Bonus Socius MS, contain many problems not from that source. The earliest-known English sources are the Cotton MS (1273), the King's Library MS, and a manuscript in Trinity College Library, Cambridge; two, if not all three, were written by Benedictine monks from Dorset. (See also ALFONSO MANUSCRIPT.)

The rules were those of SHAṬRANJ, with one important change: the FIRZĀN, now to be called the FERS, had the added power of a leap on its first move. The FĪL took the name AUFIN. On the diagrams below the fers (F) is depicted as a queen, the aufin (A) as a bishop.

European composers set out to baffle the solver rather than provide instruction. Their compositions contained illegal positions of all kinds, and a variety of STIPULATIONS, and were sometimes intentionally made without solutions. Less competent but more inventive than their Arab predecessors, European composers introduced the SELFMATE, the SERIES-MOVER, ECONOMY of force, hidden keys, VARIATION play, and the stipulation that mate is to be given in a stated number of moves. Problems were sometimes set for a wager, but whether this practice was widespread is uncertain.

When the modern game took over (c.1475) medieval problems became out of date and were

gradually forgotten; but a new word, JEOPARDY, had been added to the language.

+

A position from the King's Library MS, still given in textbooks, and showing the final phase of the endgame K + N + N v. K + RP after one of the knights has been sacrificed. There are two solutions: 1 Nf6 Kh1 2 Ne4 Kh2 3 Nd2 Kh1 4 Nf1 h2 5 Ng3, or 1 Ng7 Kh1 2 Nf5 Kh2 3 Ne3 Kh1 4 Nf1 h2 5 Ng3.

#2

This and the next two problems are from the Bonus Socius MS. Here White has three ways of mating in one move, but is required to mate in two moves 'exactly', a common stipulation. The key is 1 Rd1, with three variations: 1 ... Rxe6+ 2 Nf6, 1 ... Ra5 2 Ng5, 1 ... Axf4 2 Rd8.

#4

White is to give mate with the aufin. 1 Rb2 a1 = F 2 Ra2+ Fa3 (the fers's leap) 3 Axa3 Ka7 4 Ac5. The play is sometimes said to show the INDIAN THEME, but there is no CRITICAL PLAY.

+

Aufin and knight cannot normally force mate against a lone king, but as this rare example of medieval endgame analysis shows, mate is sometimes possible if the defender has a pawn. 1 Nc7 Kg8 2 Ne6 Kh7 3 Kg5 Kh8 4 Kh6 Kg8 5 Kg6 Kh8 6 Kf7 Kh7 7 Ng7 Kh6 8 Kf6 Kh7 9 Nf5 Kh8 10 Ke7 Kg8 11 Ke8 Kh8 12 Kf8 Kh7 13 Kf7 Kh8 14 Nh6 Kh7 15 Ng8 Kh8 16 Ad3 Kh7 17 Af5+ Kh8 18 Ne7 b1 = F 19 Ng6. Similar play for the endgame K + N + N v. K + P was rediscovered in the 18th century.

(See COMBINED PIECE; PROBLEM HISTORY.)

H. J. R. Murray, *A History of Chess* (1913).

Medinese victory, a win by leaving the opponent with a BARE KING, even when the immediate reply leaves the winner in the same condition. This was the law in the city of Medina and also in early Indian chess. In Persian and Islamic chess generally such a termination would be a draw: in order to win at least one man as well as the king had to be kept for at least one move after baring the opponent's king.

Meitner Variation, 989 in the SCOTCH GAME, named after STEINITZ's college friend Philipp Meitner (1838–1910) of Vienna. The line is sometimes named after Bernhard Fleissig who also played it in the 1880s.

men, see CHESSMEN.

Menchik, Vera Frančevna (1906–44), Women's World Champion from 1927 until her death. Daughter of a Czech father and an English mother, Menchik was born in Moscow, learned chess when she was nine, settled in England around 1921, and took lessons from MARÓCZY a year or so later. In 1927 FIDE organized both the first Olympiad and the first world championship for women. These two events were run concurrently, except in 1928, until the Second World War began in 1939. Menchik

won the women's tournament every time: London 1927 (+10=1); Hamburg 1930 (+6=1−1); Prague 1931 (+8); Folkestone 1933 (+14); Warsaw 1935 (+9); Stockholm 1937 (+14); and Buenos Aires 1939 (+17=2). She also beat her chief rival, the German-born Sonja Graf (1914–65), in a title-match at Semmering 1937 (+9=5−2) (they had played an informal match at Rotterdam 1934 won by Menchik +3−1). She played in her first championship tournament as a Russian, in the next five as a Czech, and the last as a Briton (having married the English chess organizer Rufus Henry Streatfeild Stevenson (1878–1943) in 1937).

In international tournaments which did not exclude men she usually ended in the bottom half of the table; one of her best results was at Maribor 1934 when she was third, after PIRC and L. STEINER, ahead of SPIELMANN. In 1942 she defeated MIESES in match play (+4=5−1) but, to spare the veteran's feelings, the outcome was given no publicity. A chess professional, she wrote articles for *Social Chess Quarterly* and *Chess*, gave lessons, lectures, and displays, and was appointed manager of the National Chess Centre in 1939. A year later it was totally destroyed in an air raid. Menchik herself, along with her sister Olga (also a player), and their mother were killed in a bombing raid.

Her style was positional and she had a sound understanding of the endgame. On occasion she defeated in tournament play some of the greatest masters, notably EUWE, RESHEVSKY, and SULTAN KHAN. Men she defeated were said to belong to the Vera Menchik club. When the women's chess Olympiads began in 1957, the trophy for the winning team was called the Vera Menchik Cup. (See DIVERSIONARY SACRIFICE.)

E. I. Bykova (herself a world champion), *Vera Menchik* (1954), contains 93 annotated games and a biography, in Russian; J. Kalendovský, *Klub Very Menčikové* (1986), has 94 annotated games and a biography, in Czech.

Mephisto, the best of the so-called chess AUTOMATONS. Unlike the TURK and AJEEB it had no man concealed within but was operated from another room by electro-mechanical means. The builder was an Alsatian, Charles Godfrey Gümpel (c.1835–1921), who moved to London in his early years. He made surgical appliances and had many patents to his credit including one for steering ships by electricity. He was a supporter of homoeopathy and wrote many pamphlets on topics such as natural immunity against cholera or the prevention of sudden death from internal causes. Mephisto was first shown in 1878 and later that year won a handicap tournament in London. Although it entered no more competitions, Mephisto was shown regularly for about ten years, even having its own club in London at one time. The usual operator was GUNSBERG, but when Mephisto went to Paris in 1889 it was worked by TAUBENHAUS. Subsequently the machine was dismantled. No one succeeded in discovering how the automaton was operated but it was compared favourably with the pneumatically-operated whist-playing android exhibited by the great illusionist Maskelyne. This was Psycho, a head and chest mounted on a glass pillar, obviously incapable of hiding the smallest child.

K. Whyld, 'The English Devil', *British Chess Magazine*, July 1977.

Mephisto–Chigorin London, 1883 Hamppe–Allgaier Gambit

1 e4 e5 2 Nc3 Nc6 3 f4 exf4 4 Nf3 g5 5 h4 g4 6 Ng5 h6 7 Nxf7 Kxf7 8 d4 f3 9 gxf3 Be7 10 Bc4+ Kg7 11 Be3 Bxh4+ 12 Kd2 d5 13 exd5 Na5 14 Bd3 Be7 15 fxg4 Nf6 16 Bxh6+ Rxh6 17 g5 Rxh1 18 Qxh1 Qh8 19 gxf6+ Bxf6 20 Rg1+ Kf7 21 Qe4 Qh6+ 22 Kd1 Bd7 23 b4 Re8 24 Qg6+ Qxg6 25 Bxg6+ Kf8 26 Bxe8 Bxe8 27 Rf1 Ke7 28 d6+ cxd6 29 Nd5+ Kd8 30 Nxf6 Black resigns.

Meran Variation, 142, one of the main variations of the SEMI-SLAV DEFENCE to the QUEEN'S GAMBIT Declined. Black delays acceptance of the gambit pawn until a more favourable moment, and seeks active play on the queen's-side, making an extended fianchetto for the light bishop which then bears down on the central squares. The idea was tried in Schlechter–Perlis, Ostend 1906, and Capablanca–Bernstein, Moscow 1914, and a similar plan was used in the 17th match game, Steinitz–Lasker 1897, for example, but the variation came into fashion only after its adoption by RUBINSTEIN and TARTAKOWER during the Meran tournament 1924.

Meredith, a problem in which there are from 8 to 12 men including the kings on the board. The name originated in 1915 when the GOOD COMPANION CHESS PROBLEM CLUB organized a composing tourney for such problems in honour of the American composer William Meredith (1835–1903).

Mephisto in London, 1882

merry-go-round, a POSITIONAL DRAW in which a king is driven round a circuit of squares.

=

A study by the Czech composer František Josef Prokop (1901–73), third prize, Moscow International Tournament, 1925. 1 Nf8+ Kh8 2 Ng6+ Qxg6 3 f8=Q+ Kh7 4 Bb1! Bc3+ (if 4 ... Qxb1 5 Qf5+ Qxf5, a MIRROR STALEMATE) 5 Ke3 Bd4+ 6 Kd2 Be3+ (6... Qxb1 7 Qh8 + Kg6 8 Qh7 +, another mirror stalemate) 7 Kc3 Bd2+ 8 Kd4.

Mestel, Andrew Jonathan (1957–), English player, British champion 1976, 1983, and 1988, World Under-18 Champion 1974, International Grandmaster (1982). In the 1976 British championship he made a record by winning 9 successive games. Mestel's opportunities for master play are infrequent—he is a lecturer at a University; he scored perhaps his best success at London 1977 when he was second (+ 4 = 4 – 1) equal with QUINTEROS and STEAN, after HORT, and he has played several times in the English Olympiad team since 1976. Mestel, also an outstanding solver of chess problems, has represented his country in world team solving championships, and was awarded the title of International Solving Master in 1986.

Mestel Variation, 909 in the ITALIAN OPENING, as Mestel–Doyle, Dublin 1975.

Metger, Johannes (1851–1926), German player and analyst who has an opening variation named after him. (See AUXILIARY SCORING METHODS.)

Metger Variation, 841 in the FOUR KNIGHTS OPENING, sometimes aptly called the Metger Unpin Variation, introduced in the game Bardeleben–Metger, Kiel 1893, with the idea of following with Nc6–d8–e6 unless White exchanges on c6.

middlegame, the phase of the game that follows the opening. The change from one to the other, generally beginning between the 11th and 20th moves, is often imperceptible, with no clear demarcation. Nobody, said ALEKHINE, has been able to define exactly when the middlegame begins and ends.

Mieses, Jacques (1865–1954), German-born player and author, International Grandmaster (1950), International Arbiter (1951). He never assimilated the positional ideas of STEINITZ and TARRASCH, preferring to set up a game with the direct object of attacking the enemy king, a style that brought him a public following and many BRILLIANCY PRIZES, but few successes in high-level play. His best result was in the first Trebitsch Memorial tournament, Vienna 1907, first (+9=2−2), ahead of DURAS, MARÓCZY, and SCHLECHTER. Later in the year he shared third place with NIMZOWITSCH, after BERNSTEIN and RUBINSTEIN, in a 28-round tournament at Ostend. He played 25 matches, mostly short, and won six of them, including a defeat of Schlechter in 1909 (+2=1).

Mieses reported chess events, edited chess columns, and wrote several books. In 1921 he published a supplement to the eighth edition of Bilguer's HANDBUCH, and he revised several editions of DUFRESNE's popular *Lehrbuch des Schachspiels*. He also organized chess events, including the tournament at San Sebastián in 1911, where he insisted that competitors were paid for travel and board, a practice that later became normal at that level. After living in Germany for 73 years he escaped the Nazi persecution of Jews by seeking refuge in England. A courteous and dignified old gentleman, still upright in bearing, he became widely liked in his adopted country. Soon after naturalization he became the first British player to be awarded the International Grandmaster title.

A generation earlier, his uncle Samuel Mieses (1841–84) was a player of master strength.

Mieses–Mason   Monte Carlo 1901   French Defence Exchange Variation

1 e4 e6   2 d4 d5   3 exd5 exd5   4 Be3 Nf6   5 Bd3 Bd6   6 Nc3 c6   7 Qd2 Qe7   8 0–0–0 Na6   9 Re1 Be6   10 Bg5 h6   11 Bh4 g5   12 Bg3 Nc7   13 Nf3 Nd7   14 Ne5 (note ADVANCE POINT)   14 ... Bxe5   15 Bxe5 Nxe5   16 Rxe5 0–0–0   17 Na4 b6   18 h4 f6   19 Re3 Qd6   20 b4 Kb7   21 Qc3 Qf4   22 Kb1 gxh4   23 Ka1 Bd7   24 Rb1 Ne6   25 Ba6+ Kc7   26 Nc5 Nxc5   27 bxc5 Rb8   28 Rf3 Qg5

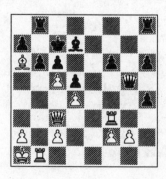

29 Qe1 Qg4 30 Rd1 Rbe8 31 Qh1 Kd8 32 Qh2 bxc5 33 Qd6 Qe6 34 Qxc5 Bc8 35 Bxc8 Qxc8 36 Rxf6 Re6 37 Rf7 Ke8 38 Qxa7 Rf8 39 Rb7 Black resigns.

Mieses Opening, 47, played by BODEN in the 1850s and by MIESES in his match against TEICHMANN, 1910; in Spain it is called the Valencia Opening.

Mieses Variation, 637 in the VIENNA GAME. Although not its originator, MIESES played this line more frequently than did any other master; 1000 in the SCOTCH GAME, played in his match with TARRASCH in 1916 by Mieses who gave credit to the Berlin player Thalheim. However, BLACKBURNE had played it in a simultaneous exhibition in 1881, and so it is sometimes called the Blackburne–Mieses Attack.

Mikenas, Vladas Ionovich (1910–92), Estonian-born player who settled in Lithuania in 1931, and won its championship in 1945, 1947, 1948, 1964, and 1968, International Master (1950), International Arbiter (1968), International Correspondence Chess Master (1971), journalist. He played for Lithuania in five Olympiads from 1931 to 1939, won the Baltic championship in 1945 and 1965, and competed in ten USSR championships between 1940 and 1970, his best result being equal fifth, in 1944. Notable achievements in international tournaments are: Kemeri–Riga 1939, fourth, after FLOHR, STÅHLBERG, and SZABÓ, ahead of BOGOLJUBOW and PETROV; Lublin 1971, first equal with Luben Dimitrov Spasov (1943–) of Bulgaria. On three occasions, 1941, 1945, and 1946, he played *hors concours* in the Georgian championship, finishing third, first, and second respectively. (See COINCIDENCE; SACRIFICE.)

Vladas Mikenas (1987) is an autobiographical collection (in Russian) containing 69 annotated games and an account of his chess career.

Mikenas Variation, 285, a sharp attacking line in the MODERN BENONI espoused by MIKENAS from the mid-1950s; 1257 in the ALEKHINE DEFENCE, played in a 1948 match game Nezhmetdinov–Mikenas. Also 283, the PAWN STORM VARIATION, which may lead to 285.

Mikhailov, Alexey Ivanovich (1936–), Russian player, International Correspondence Chess Grandmaster (1983), building engineer. In the 9th World Correspondence Championship, ending in 1983, he was second equal with BAUMBACH. In the 11th championship, ending in 1989, he was again equal second, this time with NESIS and after Baumbach. All three had the same score, but Baumbach won by NEUSTADTL SCORE.

Mikhalchishin, Adrian Bogdanovich (1954–), Ukrainian player, International Grandmaster (1978), physicist. He played in four USSR championships between 1978 and 1985, reaching his highest position, fourth, in 1984 when the event was held in Lvov, his home town. He was equal first with VAGANYAN at Rome 1987; equal first at Vrnjačka Banja 1978; and second at Hastings 1985–6.

Miles, Anthony John (1955–), English-born player, International Grandmaster (1976). While an undergraduate he entered and won by a margin of one and a half points the World Junior Championship, Manila 1974. The following year his university, Sheffield, awarded him an honorary MA degree for his chess achievements, and he left without completing his studies, to become a chess professional. The successes came quickly; London 1975, first (+6=3−1); Amsterdam 1976, first equal with KORCHNOI; Amsterdam 1977, first (+7=7−1); Biel 1977, first (+8=6−1); Tilburg 1977, second (+5=4−2), after KARPOV, ahead of HORT and HÜBNER; Tilburg 1978, third (+4=4−3) equal with DZINDZICHASHVILI and Hübner, after PORTISCH and TIMMAN; London 1980, first (+6=5−2) equal with ANDERSSON and Korchnoi; Las Palmas 1980, first (+6=5) equal with GELLER and PETROSYAN; Baden-Baden 1981, first (+6=7) equal with RIBLI, ahead of Korchnoi; Porz Köln 1981–2, second (+8=1−2), behind TAL, ahead of Hort; Biel 1983, first (+5=6), shared with NUNN; Tilburg 1984, first (+5=6), ahead of BELYAVSKY, Ribli, and Hübner; Portorož–Ljubljana 1985, first (+4=6−1) equal with Portisch and Ribli; and Tilburg 1985, first (+6=5−3) equal with Hübner and Korchnoi.

Around this time Miles began to feel the strain of ten years at the top. He was the first British player of modern times who could be seen as a possible challenger for the world title, and in the late 1970s he was well clear of his British rivals. However, largely inspired by Miles's success, a new generation, led by SHORT, was in pursuit, and by the mid-1980s Miles was no longer top board in the Olympiad side. Successes became fewer, his marriage ended, and his confidence was weakened. Determined to make a new start, he transferred his allegiance to the USA in 1987, and immediately shared first place with GULKO, who won the play-off, in the US Open Championship.

The move was not a lasting success. Miles had indifferent results and was not selected for the US Olympiad team in 1988. He had maintained a home in Germany and commuted to play in the BUNDESLIGA, and by 1990 he was spending an increasing proportion of his time in Europe. His confidence began to return, and with it more victories. He was first in two Swiss system events, Rome 1990, ahead of BAREYEV, CHERNIN, SMYSLOV etc, and Bad Wörishofen 1990 (shared), and at Biel 1990 was equal third (+3=9−2) after Karpov and Andersson.

Miles–Andersson Las Palmas 1980 King's Fianchetto Opening

1 g3 c5 2 Bg2 Nc6 3 Nf3 g6 4 c3 Bg7 5 d4 cxd4 6 cxd4 d5 7 Nc3 e6 8 Bf4 Nge7 9 Qd2 0–0 10 Bh6 Bxh6 11 Qxh6 Nf5 12 Qd2 b6 13 Rd1 Ba6 14 h4 Na5 15 g4 Nd6 16 h5 Qf6 17 hxg6 fxg6 18 Qh6 Rf7 19 g5 Qg7

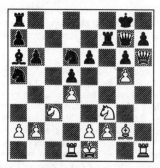

20 Ne5 Qxh6 21 Rxh6 Rff8 22 Nd7 Rf7 23 Nf6+ Kh8 24 Bh3 Bc8 25 Kd2 Rg7 26 f4 Rb8 27 Rh1 Nac4+ 28 Kd3 Rbb7 29 b3 Na3 30 e4 dxe4+ 31 Ncxe4 Nxe4 32 Kxe4 Nb5 33 Ke5 Rbe7 34 Bf1 Black resigns.

Miles Variation, 343 in the QUEEN'S INDIAN DEFENCE played regularly by MILES in the late 1970s.

Milner-Barry Gambit, 1241, a line in the FRENCH DEFENCE proposed by the British player Sir Stuart Milner-Barry (1906–95) and tried in both correspondence and over-the-board play. If Black takes the pawn, 10 . . . Qxe5, White gets a fierce attack by 11 Re1 Qd6 (else 12 Nxd5) 12 Nb5.

Milner-Barry Variation, 311, sometimes called the Zurich, or Swiss, Variation, a line in the NIMZO-INDIAN DEFENCE introduced by Milner-Barry in the Premier Reserves tournament, Hastings 1928–9. The line became more widely known when it was played at Zurich 1934. Also 1079 in the FALKBEER COUNTER-GAMBIT, an ancient line revived effectively at Margate 1937 by Milner-Barry.

Minckwitz, Johannes (1843–1901), German player and writer, merchant. He edited *Deutsche Schachzeitung*, 1865–76 and 1879–86, and also some important chess columns such as that in the *Leipziger Illustrierte Zeitung*. As a player his results were modest, his best being a second place at Barmen 1869, after ANDERSSEN, ahead of ZUKERTORT, and a first place shared with WEISS and SCHWARZ at Graz 1880 (Schwarz winning the play-off). Minckwitz wrote a few chess books, among them *Humor im Schachspiel* (1885), but his life ended tragically: while mentally unbalanced he threw himself under a tram, lost both arms, and died five days later.

Minckwitz Variation, 810 in the SPANISH OPENING, much played by MINCKWITZ around 1865. The line was later abandoned in favour of 6 Qe2.

miniature, a composition with seven or fewer men including the kings; a SHORT GAME or a BREVITY.

minimal, a composition in which the side that has to give mate, or to win, has only one man besides the king; a composition in which the side that has to draw has only a king. For examples, see ABDURAHMANOVIĆ; LONG-RANGE PROBLEM; SAAVEDRA.

minor exchange, the exchange of a knight for a bishop, a term invented by TARRASCH who said that a player whose knight is exchanged gains the minor exchange. He preferred bishops to knights, but whether the bishop is the stronger piece depends upon the PAWN FORMATION. The bishop might be stronger in open positions, although the knight often holds its own if it can gain a foothold in the CENTRAL ZONE. The knight may be stronger in a blocked position and may be decisively advantageous if opposed by a BAD BISHOP. See KUPREICHIK for a game in which a bishop dominates.

minority, a number of pawns opposed by a larger number (a MAJORITY) on a localized part of the board.

minority attack, an attack by a minority (of pawns) against a majority, with the aim of creating pawn weaknesses in the opponent's position. Such an attack, desirable only for certain pawn formations, is commonly associated with the EXCHANGE VARIATION of the QUEEN'S GAMBIT Declined. After PILLSBURY had pioneered such an attack, STEINITZ played it successfully against Lee at London 1899. With his customary lack of insight, HOFFER, annotator of the tournament book, wrote, 'the plan of attacking ... practically four pawns with two should not succeed.'

The usual form occurs after 1 d4 d5 2 c4 e6 3 Nc3 Nf6 4 Bg5 Nbd7 5 cxd5 exd5 and, in due course, White advances the b-pawn to b5. The attack takes time, and normally Black can take steps to render it ineffective; for an example, see LASKER. In the following game the attack takes a slightly different path. See also the game under OPPOSITION.

Euwe–Alekhine Zurich 1934 Queen's Gambit Declined Janowski Variation

1 c4 e6 2 d4 d5 3 Nc3 a6 4 cxd5 exd5 5 Bf4 Nf6 6 e3 Bd6 7 Bxd6 Qxd6 8 Bd3 Nc6 9 Nge2 0-0 10 a3 Ne7 11 Qc2 b6 12 b4 Bb7 13 0-0 Rfe8 14 Ng3 Ng6 15 Rfc1 Nh4 16 Nce2 c6 17 Rab1 Re7 18 a4 Rae8

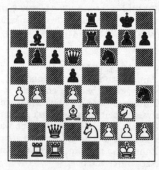

19 a5 (this minority attack leaves Black with a BACKWARD PAWN at c6) 19 . . . b5 20 Nf4 Rc7 21 Qc5 Qd7 22 Re1 Ng6 23 Bf5 Qd8 24 Nd3 Bc8 25 Rbc1 Ne7 26 Bxc8 Nxc8 27 Ne5 Re6 28 e4 Nxe4 29 Nxe4 dxe4 30 Rxe4 f6 31 Nf7 Qe8 32 Rxe6 Qxe6 33 Nd8 Qe4 34 Nxc6 h6 35 d5 Qd3 36 h3 Qd2 37 g3 Kh8 38 Kg2 Qd3 39 Re1 Kh7

40 Re3 Qd2 41 Re8 Qd3 42 Qd4 Qc4 43 Qe4+ Qxe4+
44 Rxe4 Kg8 45 Nb8 Kf7 46 Nxa6 Rd7 47 Rd4 Ne7
48 d6 Nf5 49 Rd5 Nxd6 50 Nc5 Rd8 51 Ne4 Nb7 52 a6
Ke6 53 Rxd8 Black resigns.

minor piece, the bishop or the knight. The endgames K + B v. K, and K + N v. K are drawn.

minus score, one in which the losses exceed the
wins, thus, less than 50 per cent.

mirror mate, a mate in which eight squares adjoining the king's position are unoccupied.

mirror stalemate, a stalemate in which eight
squares adjoining the king's position are unoccupied. (See MERRY-GO-ROUND.)

=

A study by LIBURKIN, first prize, *Shakhmaty v
SSSR*, 1946. After 1 Rg5 Bd6 2 Ke1 two variations show ideal mirror stalemates, the one a chameleon echo of the other:
2 ... Ke3 3 Kd1 Ra1 + 4 Kc2 Rxh1 5 Re5 +
Bxe5
2 ... Ra1 + 3 Kf2 Rxh1 4 Rd5 + Bxd5.

Miss in Baulk Variation, 905 in the ITALIAN OPEN-
ING, a line in which the white king moves to safety.
The name is a billiards term for a stroke that
concedes a penalty point but severely limits the
opponent's attacking possibilities.

Mladenović, Miodrag (1964–), Yugoslav problemist. A successful composer from his teens, he
works in both orthodox and fairy fields.

r#2

A problem by Mladenović, first prize, *The Problemist*, 1982. Either player must give mate if able to
do so. The set play (what could happen if Black
moves first):
1 ... Qd1   2 g5
1 ... Qf1   2 c5
1 ... Qxh1   2 c3.
The try 1 Rxd4 threatening 2 Ke4 is refuted by 1 ...
Ng5, but
1 ... Qd1?   2 c5
1 ... Qf1?   2 g3
1 ... Qxh1?   2 g5.
The key is 1 Rxf4 threatening 2 Ke4:
1 ... Qd1   2 c3
1 ... Qf1   2 g5
1 ... Qxh1   2 c5.
This is the Lačný Theme (see CHANGED PLAY).

mobility, freedom of movement for the pieces and
pawns. A player's principal aim at any stage of the
game is to obtain greater mobility, the normal
prerequisite for an attack. The player whose pieces
have the greater mobility may combine them more
easily or regroup them more quickly (see POSI-
TIONAL PLAY; SPACE). Greater mobility for pawns (a
more flexible or more elastic pawn formation), as
PHILIDOR showed, can also be advantageous.

Sultan Khan–Capablanca   Hastings 1930–31   Queen's
Indian Defence

1 Nf3 Nf6 2 d4 b6 3 c4 Bb7 4 Nc3 e6 5 a3 d5 6 cxd5
exd5 7 Bg5 Be7 8 e3 0–0 9 Bd3 Ne4 10 Bf4 Nd7 11
Qc2 f5 (an out-of-character move by CAPABLANCA, who
apparently underrates his opponent) 12 Nb5 Bd6 (DURAS
suggests 12 ... a6) 13 Nxd6 cxd6 14 h4 Rc8 15 Qb3 Qe7
16 Nd2 Ndf6 17 Nxe4 fxe4 18 Be2 Rc6 19 g4 Rfc8 20
g5 Ne8 21 Bg4 Rc1 + 22 Kd2 R8c2 + 23 Qxc2 Rxc2 +
24 Kxc2 Qc7 + 25 Kd2 Qc4 26 Be2 Qb3 27 Rab1 Kf7
28 Rhc1 Ke7 29 Rc3 Qa4 30 b4 Qd7 31 Rbc1 a6 32
Rg1 Qh3 33 Rgc1 Qd7

White's pieces all have mobility. He manœuvres to limit the
scope of Black's only active piece, the queen. 34 h5 Kd8
35 R1c2 Qh3 36 Kc1 Qh4 37 Kb2 Qh3 38 Rc1 Qh4 39
R3c2 Qh3 40 a4 Qh4 41 Ka3 Qh3 42 Bg3 Qf5 43 Bh4
g6 44 h6 Qd7 45 b5 a5 46 Bg3 Qf5 47 Bf4 Qh3 48 Kb2
Qg2 49 Kb1 (White gains time on the clock) 49 ... Qh3
50 Ka1 Qg2 51 Kb2 Qh3 52 Rg1 Bc8 (otherwise the
black queen will be denied all freedom after 53 Bg4) 53
Rc6 Qh4 54 Rgc1 Bg4 55 Bf1 Qh5 56 Re1 Qh1 57

Rec1 Qh5 58 Kc3 Qh4 59 Bg3 Qxg5 (Black's harassment yields a pawn, but not in time to save the game.) 60 Kd2 Qf5 61 Rxb6 Ke7 62 Rb7+ Ke6 63 b6 Nf6 64 Bb5 Qf3 65 Rb8 Black resigns.

model mate, a PURE MATE in which all the attacker's men, with the possible exception of king and pawns, take part. In BOHEMIAN problems model mates are always required, but otherwise they are less frequently seen. In the *Southern Weekly News*, Sept. 1902, BERNARD suggested the term as a substitute for 'pure and economical mate'. (Compare IDEAL MATE.)

Modena, an Italian town near Bologna. It was long ruled by the Este family who built up a fine library and encouraged chess. In the 18th century DEL RIO, LOLLI, and PONZIANI lived there. (See SCHOOLS OF CHESS.)

Modern Benoni, 282, one of the most popular variations of those that have the characteristics of the BENONI DEFENCE, 50. Played by Hromádka in the 1930s, favoured by TAL, after whom it is sometimes called, in the 1950s, it is now standard play, usually continued by the fianchetto of Black's dark bishop. (See BAGIROV; FEDOROWICZ; GLIGORIĆ; ÓLAFSSON, H.)

Modern Bishop's Opening, 943, a form of the BISHOP'S OPENING which received attention in the 1980s from NUNN, KARPOV, SPASSKY, DOLMATOV, PSAKHIS, and others. It can be reached by other sequences of moves.

Modern Defence, 1276, the ROBATSCH DEFENCE. At one time the name was used for 1117, the ABBAZIA DEFENCE.

Modern Paulsen, 521, a variation of the SICILIAN DEFENCE developed by TARTAKOWER in the 1920s, often characterized by the development of Black's queen on c7. Also sometimes used for 503, the NAJDORF VARIATION. The 'old' PAULSEN VARIATION is 545.

Modern Variation, a name doomed to cause reflections on mortality. It is used for 1049 in the GRECO COUNTER-GAMBIT, as played in 1881 in a correspondence game Charlick–Mann, perhaps the inspiration for BLACKBURNE who used the line in a simultaneous display in Australia in 1885; 1118 in the KING'S GAMBIT Accepted, played, for example, Schlechter–Swiderski and other games at the Vienna Gambit tournament 1903. Also 75, the JANOWSKI–LARSEN VARIATION; 147, the WADE VARIATION; 266, the DUTCH INDIAN; 468, the BOURDONNAIS VARIATION.

Moheschunder Bannerjee, also known as 'The Brahmin', an Indian player, born perhaps between 1780 and 1800 who lived into the second half of the 19th century. His fame spread to Calcutta and a member of the chess club there went to Moheschunder's village in order to play him. That encounter is documented in a letter to *Chess Player's Chronicle*, 1850, pp. 318–19. Although Moheschunder barely knew European rules, never having been further than 20 miles from his home, he soundly beat the visitor. Taken to Calcutta, Moheschunder received a drubbing from COCHRANE, but nevertheless created such a good impression that he was engaged as club professional to the Calcutta Club, of which Cochrane was president. Practice with European rules soon increased his strength and in 1852 he played a match on even terms with Cochrane, losing $+9=3-13$.

Cochrane clearly regarded Moheschunder as his strongest opponent in India, and left a manuscript collection of the games they played. The English player Valentine Green (1831–77) also played 'the Brahmin' in India around 1860, and, on returning to London, said that the Indian was superior to even the best European players. (See INDIAN DEFENCE; PIRC–ROBATSCH SYSTEM.)

Møller Attack, 913, standard line in the ITALIAN OPENING analysed in *Tidsskrift for Skak*, 1898, by the Danish player Jørgen Møller (1873–1944). Black is prevented from playing Pd7–d5, a move that often frees Black's game in this opening.

Møller Defence, 702 in the SPANISH OPENING, an old line revived by Møller, whose analysis was published in *Tidsskrift for Skak*, 1903.

Mongrédien Variation, 1279, played twice in the London 1862 tournament by Augustus Mongrédien (1807–88), the London-born son of a refugee from the French revolution. Mongrédien (his descendants dropped the accent) was president of both London and Liverpool chess clubs at the same time, a measure of his popularity.

Monticelli Trap, 335 in the BOGOLJUBOW VARIATION that may also occur by transposition from the CAPABLANCA VARIATION of the QUEEN'S INDIAN DEFENCE. White threatens mate by 10 Ng5, and wins the exchange after 10 ... Qxg5 11 Bxb7. The STEMGAME is Monticelli–Prokeš, Budapest 1926. Mario Monticelli (1902–95), a journalist, was Italian champion in 1930, 1934, and 1939.

moralities, ALLEGORIES with an uplifting message. The most important of these is by CESSOLE; see also GESTA ROMANORUM and INNOCENT MORALITY. Whatever benefits moralities brought to the public, they brought two in particular to chess; they helped to make the game more widely known and they contributed to the breakdown of ecclesiastical prejudice against the game. On the other hand moralities were sometimes inaccurate about the method of play, being more concerned with making the pieces display the required quality, and fictions, later regarded as historical fact, were created. For example, Cessole gave each pawn a different name, which led to the false belief that pawns at that time were separately identified.

more-mover, a problem that requires four or more moves for its solution by the side fulfilling the stipulations, and the same number or one fewer by the other side.

Morgado, Juan Sebastián (1947–), Argentinian player and journalist, International Correspondence Chess Grandmaster (1983). In the tenth World Correspondence Championship, ending in 1984, he was second behind PALCIAUSKAS.

Morovic Fernández, Iván Eduardo (1963–), Chilean champion 1981, International Grandmaster (1986), shared first place at Las Palmas 1987 (+4=5).

Morphy, Paul Charles (1837–84), American player who defeated three of Europe's leading masters in 1858 and then retired from the game. Born in New Orleans of Creole descent, Morphy developed exceptional talent at an early age. From the age of 8, encouraged by his family, he played hundreds of games against the best players of New Orleans. At 13 he could beat them all, and was already one of the best players in America. For a time he applied himself to his studies, receiving the degree of LL B in 1857 while still too young to practise. Later that year he won a national tournament at New York.

Morphy went to Europe in 1858 and startled the chess world by beating LÖWENTHAL (+9=2−3), HARRWITZ (+5=1−2), and ANDERSSEN (+7=2−2) within the space of six months, proving to himself and his contemporaries that he was

Morphy, a portrait made by Winslow Homer in 1859

the best player in the world. Morphy went to Europe well versed in openings knowledge, to which he made no significant addition; when outside the bounds of his knowledge he played the opening no better than others. In both tactical skill and technique, however, he outdistanced all rivals. Anderssen and Löwenthal frequently gained strong advantages against him, but they rarely won these games. Morphy could win his WON POSITIONS, and he often drew LOST POSITIONS. His technique, not equalled until the 1870s, produced many games in clean-cut style that have not lost their appeal. After the opening Morphy usually commenced an attack, as was the style of the time, but there were a few remarkable exceptions. His third, fourth, and fifth match games against Harrwitz were among the best he played, foreshadowing the POSITIONAL PLAY of a later age.

When Morphy returned to New York he was fêted, the first American to achieve world supremacy in any sphere. He was so idolized that even today there are those who find it difficult to appraise him. Perhaps the pithiest verdict lies in the phrase 'the pride and sorrow of chess'. Until 1859 all was pride, afterwards all was sorrow. For a year he wrote a chess column in the *New York Ledger*, for which he was paid $3,000. He was assisted by another player who, along with the editor, found Morphy 'incorrigibly lazy'.

Morphy seemed incapable of work, and did nothing for the rest of his life. George Putnam, before he became a publisher, met Morphy in 1863 and writes: '. . . he had given up his chess and was not making a success at the Bar. It appeared that he had not been able to convince himself that the cause of the Confederacy was well founded or that Louisiana had a right to secede. He had, therefore, not gone to the front with men of his own age and standing. On the other hand he had no intention of taking up arms against his State. He remained, therefore, between the two great war parties, sympathising with neither and exposed to the loneliness that must always come to the "in-between" man. He ought under the circumstances to have carried himself off to Paris or elsewhere.' Increasingly withdrawn from society, he suffered in his last years from delusions of persecution. He was looked after by his mother and younger sister until he died of a stroke while taking a bath.

Morphy did not give up chess because of disenchantment with the conduct of some European players, as is supposed by a few who base their opinions on EDGE'S mischievous book. Before he went abroad he had decided to give up the game on his return. He was, after all, only playing until, at the age of 21, he could practise law, and he shared his family's belief that chess was no fit occupation for a grown man. He was, however, conscious of the 'chess fever' (his own phrase) that assailed him from time to time. He kept in touch with chess affairs during his long retirement. He visited Paris in 1863 and 1867, where he played privately and met KOLISCH, PETROFF, and other players; but he avoided the chess haunts, not wishing to meet professionals. Anderssen, in a letter to von der LASA (31 Dec. 1859), refers to Morphy's need to prove himself at chess: 'Morphy ... treats chess with the earnestness and conscientiousness of an artist. With us, the exertion that a game requires is only a matter of distraction, and lasts only as long as the game gives us pleasure; with him, it is a sacred duty. Never is a game of chess a mere pastime for him, but always a problem worthy of his steel, always a work of vocation, always as if an act by which he fulfils part of his mission.' When Morphy gave up chess, he lost that sense of mission.

Short and slimly built, with a pale, unbearded face, delicate white hands, and feet 'preternaturally small', Morphy could have passed for a woman. His dress was immaculate, his manners impeccable, his nature uncommunicative and introverted. His memory was exceptional: he could recite verbatim most of the Civil Code of Louisiana, and he could recall innumerable games of chess. (See EDGE; FRIENDLY GAME; STAUNTON.)

Maróczy, *Paul Morphy—Sammlung der von ihm gespielten Partien mit ausführlichen Erläuterungen* (1909), reprinted in 1979 with a foreword by Korchnoi; P. W. Sergeant, *Morphy's Games of Chess* (1915, reprinted 1957); D. Lawson, *Paul Morphy, the Pride and Sorrow of Chess* (1976), is an extensive collection of biographical data, mostly from 19th-century sources; F. P. Keyes, *The Chess Players* (1960), a novel with extensive bibliography.

Harrwitz–Morphy   3rd match game 1858   Dutch
Defence

1 d4 f5 2 c4 e6 3 Nc3 Nf6 4 Bg5 Bb4 5 Qb3 c5 6 d5 e5 7 e3 0–0 8 Bd3 d6 9 Ne2 h6 10 Bxf6 Qxf6 11 a3 Bxc3+ 12 Qxc3 Qg6 13 0–0 Nd7 14 b4 b6 15 f3 h5 16 Bc2 Bb7 17 Ba4 Qf7 18 Bxd7 (This and White's next move give Black a queen's-side advantage, which he exploits impeccably: MARÓCZY recommends 18 Bc6.) 18 ... Qxd7 19 bxc5 bxc5 20 f4 e4 21 Rab1 Ba6 22 Rfc1 Qa4 23 Ng3 h4 24 Nf1 Rab8 25 Nd2 Rb6 26 Rxb6 axb6 27 Qb3 Qxb3 28 Nxb3 b5 29 Na5 Ra8 30 cxb5 Bxb5 31 Nb7 Ra6 32 Rc3 Kf8 33 Nd8 Bd7 34 Rb3 Ke7 35 Rb8 c4 36 Kf2 c3 37 Ke2 Rxa3 38 Nc6+ Bxc6 39 dxc6 c2 40 Kd2

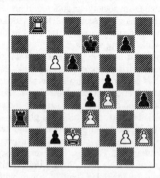

40 ... Rc3 41 Kc1 Rxc6 42 Rb3 Kf6 43 Ra3 g5 44 g3 hxg3 45 hxg3 gxf4 46 gxf4 Kg6 47 Ra5 Rc5 48 Ra6

Rc3 49 Rxd6+ Kh5 50 Rd2 Kg4 51 Rg2+ Kf3 52 Rg5 Rc5 53 Rh5 Kxe3 54 Rh4 Kf3 White resigns.

Morphy Attack, 870, the most popular continuation from the NORMAL POSITION of the EVANS GAMBIT. Probably the first master to use the line consistently was BLACKBURNE, but it had been played earlier by BOURDONNAIS in his 84th match game against McDONNELL, 1834.

Morphy Defence, 674 in the SPANISH OPENING. This move, 3 ... a6, first given by DEL RIO, played by STANLEY in his match against ROUSSEAU in 1845 and by LÖWENTHAL against MORPHY in 1858, became popular after its adoption by Morphy. In 1889 STEINITZ wrote, 'on principle this [move] ought to be disadvantageous as it drives the bishop where it wants to go.' His view has not prevailed. More than a dozen other replies have been tried on Black's third move, but 3 ... a6 is played more often than all of them put together.

Also 1083, RUBINSTEIN VARIATION of the FALKBEER COUNTER-GAMBIT; 1095, BLEDOW VARIATION; 1102, COZIO DEFENCE.

Morphy Gambit, 1082 in the FALKBEER COUNTER-GAMBIT, played by MORPHY in 1857 in a friendly game against J. R. Schulten at New York. Also 457, the MORRA GAMBIT, which Morphy came close to playing in two minor games.

Morphy Variation, 1096 in the BISHOP'S GAMBIT, played by MORPHY in his match against Mongrédien in Paris 1859, and again in an off-hand game against J. Budzinsky played at about the same time. Also 456, the SICILIAN CENTRE GAME; 960, the KIESERITZKY ATTACK; 1236, the EXCHANGE VARIATION of the FRENCH DEFENCE, invariably played by Morphy.

Also 1153, the CAMPBELL VARIATION of the KING'S GAMBIT Accepted, named after Morphy's uncle and chess instructor Ernest Morphy (1807–74).

Morra Gambit, 457 or 465 in the SICILIAN DEFENCE, a line that recurs from time to time, having been played by BLACKBURNE in 1870, for example. It was advocated in the 1940s by the French player Pierre Morra (1900–69) and is also called the Fleissig, Matulović, Morphy, Rivadavia, or Smith–Morra Gambit.

Mortimer, James (1833–1911), American player, journalist, playwright. Employed in the US Diplomatic Service from 1855 to 1860, he was based in Paris, and for his work the Emperor Napoleon III awarded him the Cross of the Legion of Honour. He remained in Paris as a journalist until 1870 when (like the Emperor) he settled in England. There he became proprietor of a London newspaper, *Figaro*, to which first LÖWENTHAL (1872–6) and then STEINITZ (1876–82) contributed an excellent chess column. The paper ceased publication when Mortimer went to prison rather than reveal the identity of a contributor whose work resulted in a libel action. Mortimer was successful as a playwright, with more than 30 London productions to his name. While reporting Spain's first international tournament, at San Sebastián, he caught pneumonia and died.

Mortimer Defence, 793, a weak reply to the SPANISH OPENING, perhaps leading to the simple MORTIMER TRAP.

Mortimer Trap, 794 in the SPANISH OPENING. Black wins a piece: 5 Bc4 Qa5+, or 5 Nc4 d6 (not 5 ... cxb5 6 Nd6 mate) 6 Ba4 b5.

Moscow Attack, 723, the HOWELL ATTACK.

Moscow Variation, 215, the DURAS VARIATION of the QUEEN'S GAMBIT Declined, from the games Bogoljubow–Marshall and Duz-Khotimirsky–Bohatirchuk, Moscow 1925; 499 (also known as Nimzowitsch Variation, Rossolimo Attack, and Venice Attack) and 538 (sometimes called Rauzer Variation or Riumin Variation; see ROMANISHIN), two sound attacking lines in the SICILIAN DEFENCE, unrelated to one another, both developed in the 1930s; 1290, the TORRE VARIATION, as Réti–Torre, Moscow 1925.

Motzko Attack, 715 in the SPANISH OPENING, tested by Motzko in correspondence play, 1903–4, and played in the game Breyer–Spielmann, Piešt'any 1912. Franz Motzko, a citizen of Trzynietz (now Cieszyn) edited a chess column in the local paper, *Silesia,* as well as in the Viennese newspaper *Reichspost* before the dissolution of the Austro-Hungarian Empire.

Mouret, Jacques-François (*c.*1787–1837), French player. A great-nephew of PHILIDOR and pupil of DESCHAPELLES, he became chess tutor of the future king, Louis-Philippe. 'He was a clever fellow, sharp, gay, lively, amusing, and had studied seriously the theory of chess, by which he made his living. His talent redeemed a little the rudeness of his manner and a certain licentiousness which he indulged in. He used to be in a continual state of semi-intoxication', wrote Delannoy.

Mouret was one of the most successful operators of the TURK. Of more than 300 games in which he gave odds of a pawn and move, he lost only 6 while inside the AUTOMATON, and a collection of 50 of the best of these games was published in 1820. In 1834, to meet his need for drink, he wrote an explanation of the secret of the Turk in the *Magasin Pittoresque,* the only one of the many operators to betray his VOWS.

mousetrap theme, see SWITCHBACK.

move, (1) the transfer of a man to another and vacant square; the transfer of a man to a square occupied by an enemy man which is then removed from the board (a CAPTURE); CASTLING, the only move where two men are transferred; an EN PASSANT capture; PROMOTION: to make a move, i.e. to make a SINGLE-MOVE.

A move is completed when the player's hand no longer touches either the man that has been moved (for castling this means the rook) or the substituted piece in the case of promotion. For control purposes the move is not completed until the player's clock is stopped, unless mate, stalemate, or agreement has already ended the game. A player moving a piece and then picking it up again before releasing it is bound by the TOUCH AND MOVE LAW.

The moves of games, studies, and orthodox problems are counted by the number of white moves. In this sense a move means two single-moves, or a single move by White. A game of 40 moves consists of 40 single-moves by White, and 39 or 40 single-moves by Black. The SCORE OF GAME is a record of the moves.

move, (2) the turn to play. For example, a player may say 'It is White's move' or 'White has the move'. See LOSE THE MOVE.

mover, as part of the description of a problem, an informal way of saying '-move chess problem', e.g. a 'two-mover' is a 'two-move chess problem'.

Mujannah Opening, 1313. The name is a modern application of one used in TA'BI'A and is defined by openings expert Hugh Edward Myers (1930–) as an opening in which White plays pawns to both f4 and c4 before playing pawns to e4 or d4, 'no matter how long it takes'. Move order is not critical. (See games under STAUNTON and WILLIAMS.)

Müller Gambit, or **Müller–Schultze Gambit,** 863, see SCHULTZE–MÜLLER GAMBIT.

Murey, Ya'acov (1941–), Moscow-born Israeli who lives in France, International Grandmaster (1987). He has two shared second places in strong tournaments, Marseille 1987 and Royan 1989 (both +5=2−2).

Murey Variation, 340 in the QUEEN'S INDIAN DEFENCE, conceived by MUREY in 1986. He showed it to LAUTIER, who achieved the grandmaster title with its help.

Murray, Harold James Ruthven (1868–1955), foremost chess historian, school inspector. His *History of Chess* (1913), perhaps the most important chess book in English, was the result of about 14 years of research inspired by LASA and grounded on van der LINDE's work. During that period Murray contributed 35 articles to the *British Chess Magazine,* some of which outlined his discoveries.

Most of the 900-page *History* is concerned with the evolution of modern chess from its oriental precursor up to the early 18th century. In the last two chapters, which trace the game's development from PHILIDOR to the 20th century, he was somewhat handicapped, lacking an understanding of chess strategy. He learned Arabic so that he could read important manuscripts, and, in addition to his own circle, he was able to solicit help from colleagues of his father, Sir James A. H. Murray, editor-in-chief of the *Oxford English Dictionary*. He was also aided by J. G. WHITE, with both advice and the loan of rare books from the Cleveland collection, and by many others. His book includes an authoritative account of both MANṢŪBĀT and MEDIEVAL PROBLEMS. (See also HISTORY OF CHESS.) In 1952 he published a companion volume, *A History of Board Games other than Chess*.

While the scholarship of his chess book has never been questioned it is inaccessible to the average chessplayer. Aware of this problem, Murray wrote a briefer work, approaching the topic in a more popular way. The manuscript, written many years earlier, lay unfinished at his death and was completed and published in 1963 as *A Short History of Chess*. He also left the manuscript of a history of draughts. (See CIVIS BONONIAE.)

Murshed, Niaz (1966–), champion of Bangladesh in 1979, at the age of 12 years and 10 months, and several times subsequently, International Grandmaster (1987), the first from his country. He played on first board for Bangladesh in the 1984 Olympiad, and in tournament play was second at Calcutta 1986 and equal first at Calicut 1988.

music and chess. Some great players have been first-class musicians, like TAIMANOV. Conversely Adolf Brodsky (1851–1929), a first-class chessplayer, gave the first performance of Tchaikovsky's violin concerto after its dedicatee declared it unplayable, and later became conductor of the Hallé Orchestra. Robert Schumann said that music might be compared to chess. The queen, having supreme power, might symbolize melody, but with the king, as representative of harmony, there would rest the final issue. Mendelssohn, also, was a strong player.

Those who have reached the top in both fields include PHILIDOR, who played chess and composed music, and Rudolf Heinrich Willmers (1821–78), who played music and composed chess problems. While playing Schumann's 'Carnival' in a piano recital in Copenhagen, Willmers stopped suddenly, wrote on his cuff, and then continued. He explained afterwards that he had been struggling for a week to solve a difficult problem when the solution came to him in a flash. 'I had to jot it down to get it out of my head and let me concentrate entirely on my playing.'

Many songs or minor compositions celebrate chess occasions or bear chess-related titles, but the only major works other than ballet (see THEATRE AND CHESS) appear to be *Échecs au roi* by the Czechborn composer Bohuslav Martinů (1890–1959) and an opera, *Das Schachturnier* (*Le tournoi aux échecs*), by Eberwein. The publisher's serial number indicates that the overture dates from 1819, many years before the first chess tournament. It is not known if this work was ever completed or performed.

must-capture chess, an unorthodox game in which a capture must be made if possible, although a player may choose which capture to make if there is an option; otherwise the normal laws of chess are observed. This game is described in the ALFONSO MS (1283), where it is called the forced game, or, supposedly having been invented by girls from Morocco (which suggests an Islamic origin), *juego de Doncellas*; hence, in English, the maidens' game.

In 1946 the American composer Mannis Charosh (1906–) devised 'series must-capture chess', a modification of the maidens' game. If a capturing man can make a further capture it must do so, and continue to do so if possible. Thus several consecutive single-move captures can be made on a player's turn to move.

mutate, see BLOCK. Mutates were so named by HARLEY in 1919, long after the earliest known example was composed by E. B. COOK in 1868.

Muzio d'Alessandro, 17th-century Neapolitan who happened to see the Sicilian player Geronimo Cascio play an interesting opening (with Italian castling, Rf1 and Kh1), and passed on the information to SALVIO. Misunderstanding Salvio's text, SARRATT thought that Muzio had played the line, and named it after him.

Muzio Gambit, 1138, variation of the KING'S GAMBIT in which White sacrifices a knight for a strong attack, mistakenly named after MUZIO. Mentioned by POLERIO, after whom it is sometimes named, the gambit was examined by SARRATT who published a valuable analysis in his posthumous *New Treatise* (1821). The continuation 5 ... gxf3 6 Qxf3 Qf6 7 e5 Qxe5 8 d3 Bh6 9 Nc3 Ne7 10 Bd2 Nbc6 11 Rae1 was regarded as favouring White until 1858 when 'W.S.' of Milwaukee discovered an adequate reply, 11 ... Qf5, a move introduced to master play in the 6th match game Kolisch–Paulsen, 1861, which ended 12 Nd5 Kd8 13 Bc3 Rg8 14 Bf6 Bg5 15 Rxe7 Bxf6 16 Re4 Bg5 17 g4 Qg6 18 h4 Bxh4 19 Qxf4 d6 20 Qxf7 Qxf7 21 Rxf7 Ne5 22 Rxh7 Nxc4 23 Rxc4 c6 24 Nc7 Rb8 25 Rf4 Be7 26 Rff7 Kxc7 27 Rxe7+ Kb6 28 Rhg7 Rxg7 29 Rxg7 Be6 30 Rg6 Bxa2 31 Rxd6 Rg8 32 Kf2 Rxg4 33 Ke2 Rg2+ 34 Kd1 Bb1 35 c3 Rxb2 White resigns.

Myllyniemi, Arvo Matti (1930–87), the leading Finnish problem composer of his time, International Judge of Chess Compositions (1958), International Master for Chess Compositions (1976). A composer of most kinds of problems, he published *Toteutuneita oivalluksia* (1980) containing 300 of his compositions.

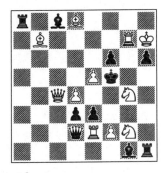

#2

A problem by Myllyniemi, first prize, *Satakunnan Tehtavakerho* theme tourney 1982, showing CHANGED PLAY. The set play (Black moves first):

1 ... fxe5   2 Qf7#
1 ... Ra4   2 Qxc8#
1 ... Qb4   2 N4xe3#
1 ... exf2   2 Be4#
1 ... Bh2   2 Nxh6#.

The key is 1 d5, threatening 2 Qf4#:

1 ... fxe5   2 Rf7#
1 ... Ra4   2 Bxc8#
1 ... Qb4   2 N2xe3#
1 ... exf2   2 Qe4#
1 ... Bh2   2 Nh4#.

mysterious rook move, the move of a rook to a file that is blocked by a pawn of the same colour, thus anticipating an exchange of pawns that might open that file. This is a form of preventive action (PRO-PHYLAXIS) named by NIMZOWITSCH, but known long before his time. The term is often misused to describe any unexpected rook's move. (See BLACK-BURNE.)

Kupchik–Capablanca Lake Hopatcong 1926 Queen's Indian Defence

1 d4 Nf6 2 Nf3 e6 3 e3 b6 4 Bd3 Bb7 5 0-0 Ne4 6 Nbd2 f5 7 c3 Be7 8 Qc2 d5 9 Ne5 0-0 10 f3 Nxd2 11 Bxd2 Nd7 12 Nxd7 Qxd7 13 Rae1 c5 14 Qd1 Rf6 15 Qe2 Raf8 16 Bb5 Qc7 17 f4 c4 18 Kh1 Bd6 19 Rf3 h5 20 Ref1

20 ... Rh6 A mysterious rook move to deter White from playing Pg4 (preceded by Ph3). 21 Be1 g6 22 Bh4 Kf7 23 Qe1 a6 24 Ba4 b5 25 Bd1 Bc6 26 Rh3 (White continues his attack against an unassailable position, and soon retreats with fatal loss of time.) 26 ... a5 27 Bg5 Rhh8 28 Qh4 b4 29 Qe1 Rb8 30 Rhf3 a4 31 R3f2 a3 32 b3 cxb3 33 Bxb3 Bb5 34 Rg1 Qxc3 35 Qxc3 bxc3 36 Rc2 Rhc8 37 Bh4 Bd3 38 Rcc1 Rxb3 39 axb3 a2 White resigns.

myths in chess largely concern the origin of the game. One of the most popular tales, almost certainly in its main point antedating any form of proto-chess, is of a Brahmin, Sissa, who invented the game to teach his despotic ruler that the monarch cannot win without the help of his subjects. The grateful ruler asks Sissa what reward he wants, to which the reply is a grain of corn for the first square of the board, two for the second, four for the third, eight for the fourth, and so on. Irritated by such a trifling request the ruler tries to persuade Sissa to accept something more valuable, but when this offer is declined he orders the grain to be given. The answer to this calculation, often given to school-children, is $2^{64} - 1$, or 18,445,744,073,709,551,515 grains, equivalent to more than 5,000 years' production at present levels for the whole world. (Dante, *Paradiso*, xxviii, 92–3, conceives of an even greater number when he refers to the Hierarchy of Angels: 'They numbered myriads more than the entire Progressive doubling of the chess squares.')

Other mythical inventors of the game are Shem, King Solomon, the princely brothers Lydus and Tyrrhenus (to take their minds from starvation), Hermes, Aristotle, Semiramis, Zenobia, Attalus, Palamedes (who invented many excellent things including three meals a day), Xerxes, Shatrenscha (a Persian astronomer), Ulysses, Diomedes, and Adam, the first man. There are also demonstrably untrue claims for groups of people: the Greeks, Romans, Babylonians, Scythians, Egyptians, Castilians, Irish, Welsh, and South American Indians.

Reasons for the game's invention fall into groups. The military category includes teaching the art of war (which the game mimics), stimulating bored troops, or relaxing those overtaxed. Another theme is that chess was invented as a tactful way of breaking to a queen the news of her son's death in battle, or his death at the hand of his brother in accordance with the laws of warfare (as shown by the laws of chess), or simply to soothe the queen in her bereavement. Another tale suggests that the Hindus invented chess to upstage the Persians, who were excessively proud of having invented backgammon; and there are many accounts that chess was devised to demonstrate the preferred virtues, or as a bloodless substitute for war.

N

N, a symbol for the knight, often used because it is simpler than Kt and less likely to be confused with K, the symbol for the king.

Nadareishvili, Gia Antonovich (1921–91), Soviet composer, International Judge of Chess Compositions (1960), International Grandmaster for Chess Compositions (1980), neurologist at Tbilisi. He won the twelfth (1973–4) USSR study-composing championship and gained awards in many other tourneys. He also wrote many books. *Izbrannye etyudy* (1970), contains about 230 studies, 100 by the author; *Shakhmatny etyud v Gruzin* (1975) is a collection of studies by Georgian composers; *Izbrannye shakhmatny etyudy* (1976) contains 125 studies by the author and an appendix on the endgame queen against one or two pieces; *Etyudy glazami grossmeisterov* (1982) contains 312 studies by many composers with comments by 43 famous players; *V poiskahk krasoty* (1986) has 204 studies by the author and sundry essays and photographs. There is also a collection of his studies in Georgian, published in 1965.

+

A study by Nadareishvili, first prize, *64 shakhmatnoe obozrenie*, 1981. 1 b8=Q Raf1+ 2 Ke2 Re1+ 3 Kd2 Rd1+ 4 Kc2 Rc1+ 5 Kb2 Rb1+ 6 Ka2(a3) Ra1+ 7 Kb3 Rgb1+ 8 Kc2 Rc1+ 9 Kd2 Rd1+ 10 Ke2 Re1+ 11 Kf2 Rf1+ 12 Kg2 Rg1+ 13 Kh3 Rh1+ 14 Qh2 Rxh2+ 15 Kxh2 Ra2+ 16 Kg1 Ra1+ 17 Kf2 Ra2+ 18 Ke1 Ra1+ 19 Kd2 Ra2+ 20 Kc1 Kc3 21 Kb1 Ra6 22 b7 Rb6+ 23 Kc1 Rf6 24 Kd1 Kd3 25 Ke1 Re6+ 26 Kf1 Rf6+ 27 Kg2 Ke2 28 b8=Q Rf2+ 29 Kh3 Rf3+ 30 Qg3. A theme of perpetual check avoidance.

Najdorf (pron. nie-dorf), Miguel (1910–), International Grandmaster (1950), a Polish-born player who sought asylum in Argentina in 1939, became naturalized five years later, and changed his forename from Mieczyslaw to Miguel. His best international results were: Hungarian championship 1936, first (+10=4−1), playing *hors concours*, equal with L. STEINER; Buenos Aires 1941, first (+9=4−1) equal with STÅHLBERG; Groningen 1946, fourth (+6 = 11 − 2) with SZABO, after BOTVINNIK, EUWE, and SMYSLOV; Prague 1946, first (+9=3−1); Buenos Aires 1947, second (+4=5−1), after Ståhlberg, ahead of Euwe; Amsterdam 1950, first (+ 11 = 8), ahead of RESHEVSKY and Ståhlberg; Bled 1950, first (+8=5−1); Havana 1962, first (+14=5−2), ahead of POLUGAYEVSKY, SPASSKY, GLIGORIĆ, and Smyslov; Los Angeles 1963, third (+3=9−2) equal with ÓLAFSSON, after KERES and PETROSYAN; Mar del Plata 1965, first (+10=5), one and a half points ahead of STEIN; Reykjavik 1976, third (+7=7−1) equal with TUKMAKOV, after Ólafsson and TIMMAN. In 1949 Najdorf drew matches against FINE (+2=4−2) and TRIFUNOVIĆ (+1=10−1); later he lost two matches against Reshevsky.

When Fine withdrew from the world championship of 1948 FIDE declined to substitute Najdorf who, as one of the world's best ten players at that time, had a strong claim to the vacant place. Later in the year he played in the first interzonal tournament at Saltsjöbaden, scoring +6=9−4 and sharing sixth place. In the two great CANDIDATES tournaments he came fifth (+3=12−3) at Budapest 1950, and sixth (+5=19−4) equal with GELLER and KOTOV at Neuhausen–Zurich 1953. His last title attempt was in the Göteborg interzonal of 1955, but he failed to qualify as a Candidate.

Najdorf played for Poland in the Olympiads of 1935, 1937, and 1939, and for Argentina in eleven Olympiads from 1950 to 1976. In 1950 and 1952 he made the best scores at first board, +8=6 and +11=3−2 respectively. He won the championship of Argentina in 1949, 1951, 1955, 1960, 1964, 1967, and 1975.

He was a brilliant MIDDLEGAME player, and it is in this phase that most games are won; but at the highest level his skill in the opening and ENDGAME phases did not match that of his leading contemporaries, and he won no strong tournament.

R. Castelli, *Najdorf, juego y gano* (1968), contains 110 games.

Najdorf–Keres Buenos Aires 1939 Queen's Gambit Declined Slav Defence

1 d4 d5 2 c4 c6 3 e3 Nf6 4 Nf3 g6 5 Bd3 Bg7 6 0–0 0–0 7 Nc3 dxc4 8 Bxc4 Nbd7 9 Qe2 Ne8 10 Bb3 e5 11

Nxe5 Nxe5 12 dxe5 Bxe5 13 f4 Bg7 14 e4 Be6 15 Bxe6
fxe6 16 e5 Nc7 17 Be3 Nd5 18 Ne4 b6 19 Rad1 Qe7
20 g3 Rad8 21 a3 Nc7 22 Rd6 c5

23 f5 exf5 24 Bg5 Qxe5 25 Bxd8 Ne6 26 Bf6 Black
resigns.

Najdorf Variation, 503, popular line in the SICILIAN
DEFENCE. The original idea was to answer 6 Be2 by
6 . . . e5, supposedly an improvement on the BOLE-
SLAVSKY VARIATION. White has several other op-
tions on the sixth move, to some of which Black
would not find the reply 6 . . . e5 expedient. Even so,
NAJDORF'S 5 . . . a6 is a useful move for the defence.
He played and advocated his variation from
around 1947, but it had been played previously,
notably Bogoljubow–Canal, Carlsbad 1929, by
OPOČENSKÝ on several occasions, and by KOTOV and
other masters, and has been called the Argentine
Variation, the Hague Variation, and the Modern
Paulsen. (See ANAND; BELYAVSKY; FTÁČNIK; KAVA-
LEK; KING HUNT; PARMA; SAVON; STEAN; TAL.)

Napier, William Ewart (1881–1952), English-born
player whose family emigrated to the USA when he
was five years old and moved to Brooklyn in 1895.
There he learned his chess, achieving several local
successes including a tie with Eugene Delmar
(1841–1909) for second place, after PILLSBURY and
ahead of MARSHALL, in the New York State championship 1901. Later that year he returned to
England to study music and mostly studied chess
instead. In each of the three major tournaments in
which he competed, Monte Carlo 1902, Hanover
1902, and Cambridge Springs 1904, he won a
BRILLIANCY PRIZE; and in the first British Chess
Federation championship 1904 he tied with ATKINS
for first place, gaining the title after a play-off
(+1=3). In 1905 Napier drew a match with MIESES
(+4=2−4), lost to TEICHMANN (+1=4−5), and
then returned to New York. Soon afterwards he
gave up first-class competitive chess, became a
naturalized US citizen (1908), and moved to Pennsylvania to make his career in the Scranton Life
Assurance Company (of which he became vice-
president). He married PILLSBURY's niece, and
brought up a family of two daughters. For some
time he edited a chess column in the *Pittsburgh*

Dispatch, and otherwise maintained his interest in
the game. From 1932 he lived in New York, Philadelphia, and Washington where he enjoyed club
chess.

Napolitano, Mario (1910–95), Italian player, International Correspondence Chess Grandmaster
(1953), local government officer. Although he
played in several minor over-the-board tournaments with some success, and in the Olympiads of
1935 and 1937, he is better known for his achievements in postal chess: winner of the Italian championship, 1941 and 1947, and in particular, second
equal with MALMGREN after PURDY in the first
World Correspondence Championship 1950–3.

national master, a title awarded by a national
organization for performance in events under its
control, and sometimes confined to citizens of the
host country. There are no internationally imposed
requirements. Both the method of qualifying and
the standard of performance vary between countries. Such awards were first made regularly in
Germany. (See HAUPTTURNIER.) From the 1950s,
when FIDE introduced its international titles and
when rating methods were developed, the practice
of awarding national titles became widespread.

national tournament, an event for which entry is
restricted to nationals of one country. The most
important are for the title of national champion,
although stronger entries may be attracted to
events offering richer prizes. The leading chess
countries hold many chess tournaments throughout
the year: although entry is not always restricted
they may become in effect, through lack of foreign
entrants, national tournaments, and are often so
called. Since 1939 the strongest national tournaments have taken place in the USSR, where the
championship can be as strong as an INTERZONAL
TOURNAMENT. An exceptionally strong tournament,
Leningrad–Moscow 1941, the unique 'absolute
championship of the USSR', was won by BOTVIN-
NIK.

Nei, Iivo (1931–), Estonian player, International
Master (1964), director of the Tallinn chess school.
He played in four Soviet championships (1960,
1963, 1966–7, and 1967) making moderate scores.
At his best in the 1960s, he came first (+9=5−1)
equal with KERES, ahead of PORTISCH, IVKOV, and
LARSEN, at Beverwijk 1964, and second (+5=8)
equal with Keres, after STEIN, at Tallinn 1969. Nei
won the Estonian championship 8 times between
1951 and 1974.

Nenarokov, Vladimir Ivanovich (1880–1953), Russian player, International Master (1950). He won
the Moscow championship in 1900, 1908, 1922 and
1924, on the last two occasions by defeating the

holder, GRIGORIEV, in match play ($+6=2-3$ and $+6=4-4$). Nenarokov drew a match with TARTAKOWER in 1905 ($+2-2$), defeated DUZ-KHOTIMIRSKY in 1907 ($+5=1-3$), and in 1908 won all three games of a match against the 16-year-old ALEKHINE, a result carefully ignored by the latter when compiling his career record.

Nenarokov Variation, 24 in the ENGLISH OPENING, as Botvinnik–Nenarokov, Leningrad championship 1933; 716, a little-played line in the SPANISH OPENING.

Neo-Catalan Opening, 1296, a sequence of moves, sometimes called the Blümich Variation, that often leads to the Catalan System (see CATALAN OPENING). (See RÉTI.)

Neo-Grünfeld Variation, 416, better called the KEMERI VARIATION.

Neo-Meran Variation, 146, the LUNDIN VARIATION.

Neo-orthodox Variation, 205 in the QUEEN'S GAMBIT Declined, a line favoured by TARTAKOWER. (See SACRIFICE.)

Nesis, Gennady Yefimovich (1947–), Russian player, International Correspondence Chess Grandmaster (1985), chess journalist, electronics engineer. In the 11th World Correspondence Championship, which ended in 1989, he was second equal with MIKHAILOV, after BAUMBACH. All three had the same score, but Baumbach had the best NEUSTADTL SCORE.

Neumann, Gustav Richard Ludwig (1838–81), player from Germany who was among the best half-dozen in the world around 1870. With ANDERSSEN he was co-editor of the *Neue Berliner Schachzeitung* from its inception in 1864 to 1867, and during these years the two of them met in many friendly encounters (more than 70 of the games are known). Also at this time he had a remarkable CLEAN SCORE, although only in a strong club event: he won a tournament of the Berlin *Schachgesellschaft* with a score of $+34$. In 1867 Neumann took fourth place, after KOLISCH, STEINITZ, and WINAWER, in the Paris tournament, won matches against Winawer ($+3$) and ROSENTHAL ($+5=6$), and achieved first prize, ahead of Steinitz, in the Dundee tournament. He remained in Paris for more than two years, ostensibly studying physics and chemistry, suffered a breakdown in December 1869, recovered, went back to Germany, and shared third prize with BLACKBURNE, after Anderssen and Steinitz, in the tournament at Baden-Baden. Neumann's last tournament was a minor event at Altona in 1872 in which he took second place after Anderssen. For the rest of his life he suffered severe mental illness which was attributed to a head injury sustained as a boy.

Winawer–Neumann   Baden-Baden 1870   Evans Gambit

1 e4 e5 2 Nf3 Nc6 3 Bc4 Bc5 4 b4 Bxb4 5 c3 Ba5 6 d4 exd4 7 0–0 Bb6 8 cxd4 d6 9 d5 Nce7 10 e5 Ng6 11 Bb2 N8e7 12 Bb5+ Bd7 13 exd6 cxd6 14 Bxd7+ Qxd7 15 Bxg7 Rg8 16 Bf6 0–0–0 17 Na3 Kb8 18 Re1

18 ... Nf4 19 Ng5 Nfxd5 20 Bxe7 Nxe7 21 Ne4 d5 22 Nf6 Qh3 23 Nxg8 Rxg8 24 g3 Bxf2+ 25 Kh1 Rxg3
White resigns.

Neumann Defence, 1152, a line in the KING'S GAMBIT Accepted introduced by NEUMANN around 1870, leading to a game with about level chances.

Neustadtl score, an AUXILIARY SCORING METHOD for all-play-all tournaments, now widely used for tie-breaking and, taking the names of two of its opponents, usually called the SONNEBORN–BERGER SCORE. Hermann Neustadtl (1862–1909), a Viennese doctor originally from Prague, suggested this scoring method in a letter published in *Chess Monthly* in 1882: the sum of the normal score of the opponents a player defeated is added to half the sum of the normal scores of those who drew.

Neustadtl made no mention of the earlier GELBFUHS SCORE, which is based on the same principles. His method is simpler, and gives the same placings if the competitors have all played the same number of games. Both methods were intended to supplant the normal scoring (1 for a win, $\frac{1}{2}$ for a draw, 0 for a loss). Neustadtl scoring was used to determine placings in the winter tournament of the Liverpool Chess Club 1882–3, but it was called the Gelbfuhs Atomic System. Some thought the initials appropriate, but others were impressed because 'the law of constant proportion' was in harmony with 'the law of reciprocal proportion'. A few other tournaments were played on the same basis, but Neustadtl scoring soon fell out of use for its original purpose, to be revived much later, under the wrong name, as a means of tie-breaking.

neutral man, a man invented by DAWSON in 1912 for use in FAIRY PROBLEMS, indicated by the added symbol 'n'. A neutral piece or pawn may be regarded as being of either colour according to the preference of the player whose turn it is to move. A neutral pawn that is promoted becomes a neutral piece.

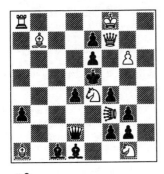

#2

A problem by the French composer Yves Cheylan (1938–), *Die Schwalbe*, 1980. The man on f3 is a neutral queen. After the key, 1 g7, White threatens Qh5 mate when Black could not get out of check by nQxQh5 (acting as a black queen) because the nQ could instantly revert to its white role. Black must therefore move the nQ:

1 ... nQe3   2 Qxf4# (the White Q is guarded
                      by the nQ)
1 ... nQd3   2 Bxd4#
1 ... nQc3   2 Ra5# (Black cannot interpose,
                      nQc5)
1 ... nQb3   2 Qxe6#.

newspaper columns and chess columns in periodicals have been an important part of chess development. The first chess column began in the *Liverpool Mercury* in 1813, and the first in a weekly publication, *The Lancet*, in 1823, although a game had been given in 1822. The earliest on the Continent were *Der Berliner Staffete* from 1828, the Russian *Illustratsiya* from 1845, and the Dutch *Asmodée* from 1847; and in America the New York *Spirit of the Times* from 1845, written by STANLEY. By the end of the century more than a thousand periodicals had included a chess column at one time or another, and at the peak more than one hundred columns were active at the same time in Britain alone.

Altogether there have been well over 5,000 columns. Many are trivial, containing only a stale problem from some other source and serving only to deter potential players. Others have provided both original material from the catchment area and important items from exchanges. A few have been of exceptional importance. The development of STEINITZ's ideas first took place in the pages of two London journals, *The Field* and *Figaro*, and in the *New York Weekly Tribune*. Among the best in Britain today are the *Guardian*, edited by BARDEN from 1956, the *Independent*, edited by HARTSTON since 1987, and *The Times*, edited by KEENE since 1986. One of the best European columns is in the Yugoslav daily *Politika*.

New York Variation, 201, the JANOWSKI VARIATION.

Niemeijer, Meindert (1902–87), Dutch bibliophile, problem composer, and author, International Judge of Chess Compositions (1958), International Master for Chess Compositions (1975), lawyer and banker. In 1948 he gave his collection of 7,000 chess books to the Royal Dutch Library to be added to the 846 books of van der LINDE bought by the library in 1876. *Bibliotheca Van der Linde–Niemeijeriana; Catalogue of the chess collection in the Royal Library, The Hague* (1955) lists 6,493 titles, some of which embrace many volumes; all the British Chess Federation Yearbooks, for example, are under one number in the catalogue. *Bibliotheca Van der Linde–Niemeijeriana aucta et de novo descripta* (1974), written in English, elaborates on the bibliography and history sections with details of 407 books, monographs, or periodicals. In addition 893 articles or extracts from books and periodicals are listed. Niemeijer published some 30 books on problems as well as three works on bibliography and one on the rook in heraldry. He made a collection of more than 50,000 Dutch topographical picture postcards, one of his several interests outside chess.

nightrider, a LINE-PIECE invented by W. S. Andrews in 1907 and first used in FAIRY PROBLEMS in 1925 by DAWSON, who named it (perhaps after Nightrider Street, adjacent to the place where he attended problemists' meetings). It is represented by the symbol N or by the figurine ♘. (For players N means knight, but problemists use S as a symbol for that piece.) The nightrider can make, in one move, one knight's move or more in a straight line. On an otherwise empty board a nightrider at a1 could be moved to c2, e3, or g4, or, on another line, to b3, c5 or d7; it can be obstructed only by men on those squares where it touches down on its journey. (Compare ROSE.)

Nikolić, Predrag (1960–), International Grandmaster (1983), Yugoslav champion 1980 and 1984. In 1990 a shared fifth place at the Manila interzonal made him a CANDIDATE, but in 1991 he lost the Candidates match with GELFAND after a two-game rapid-play tie-breaker. His other major successes are: Sarajevo 1982, third (+7=7−1), after BELYAVSKY and V. KOVAČEVIĆ; Sochi 1982, second (+5=9−1), after TAL; Sarajevo 1983, first (+7=7−1); Vršac 1983, first (+7=4−2) equal with TARJAN and AGZAMOV; Novi Sad 1984, first (+4=7); Bor 1986, first (+5=5−1) equal with EINGORN and Watson; Havana 1987, first (+4=4); Sarajevo 1987, first (+6=5), in front of POLUGAYEVSKY and VAGANYAN; Tilburg 1987, Second (+3=9−2) equal with HÜBNER and KORCHNOI, behind TIMMAN; Ljubljana–Rogaška Slatina 1989, first (+7=5−1); Wijk aan Zee 1989, first (+4=7−2) equal with ANAND, SAX, and RIBLI; Hastings 1989–90, second (+3=9−2), after DOLMATOV. In 1991 he defeated MECKING (+1=5) when the Brazilian made a return to chess after a long absence.

Nikolić–Braga   Thessaloniki 1988 Olympiad   Hromádka Defence Petrosyan System

1 d4 Nf6 2 c4 c5 3 d5 e5 4 Nc3 d6 5 e4 Be7 6 g3 Na6 7 Bg2 Nc7 8 f4 exf4 9 Bxf4 Nd7 10 Nf3 g5 11 Be3 g4 12 Nd2 Ne5 13 Qe2 Bd7 14 Bf4 Bf6 15 h3 h5 16 hxg4 hxg4 17 Rxh8+ Bxh8 18 0-0-0 Qf6 19 Rh1 0-0-0

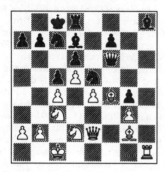

20 Rh6 Ng6 21 e5 dxe5 22 Be3 Qg7 23 Rh5 Na6 24 Nde4 Qf8 25 Qf2 b6 26 Qxf7 Qxf7 27 Nd6+ Kc7 28 Nxf7 Rf8 29 Nxh8 Rxh8 30 Rg5 Rh2 31 Be4 Black resigns.

Nimzo-English Variation, 45, the NIMZOWITSCH VARIATION of the ENGLISH OPENING.

Nimzo-Indian Defence, 298. By pinning White's knight on c3 Black controls e4, preventing an enlarged white pawn centre (Pe2–e4) while retaining options for the advance of the black pawns. For example, Black might play 4 ... Pd7–d5 (after 4 e3), or 5 ... Pc7–c5 (exploiting the WYVILL FORMATION after 4 a3 Bxc3+ 5 bxc3), or 6 ... Pe6–e5 (after 4 Qc2 Nc6 5 Nf3 d6 6 Bd2).

The defence was tried by ENGLISCH at Vienna 1882, by BLACKBURNE in 1883 ('Not much good comes of this' he wrote), and was pioneered by NIMZOWITSCH around 1914. The most popular reply for White is the RUBINSTEIN VARIATION, 316 (4 e3). Other well-known lines are the KMOCH, SÄMISCH, CLASSICAL, LENINGRAD, and SPIELMANN VARIATIONS (4 f3, 4 a3, 4 Qc2, 4 Bg5, and 4 Qb3 respectively). The name is a contraction of Nimzowitsch–Indian.

Nimzowitsch, Aaron (1886–1935). As a player he ranked third in the world after CAPABLANCA and ALEKHINE (LASKER having temporarily retired) from about 1925 to 1930; as an innovator he founded the HYPERMODERN movement (see SCHOOLS OF CHESS); as a writer of instructional books he was unrivalled in his time. Born in Riga of Jewish parents, he learnt the moves when he was eight, and began to take the game seriously about ten years later, when he should have been studying mathematics. He first made his mark by sharing third place, half a point behind the winners, BERNSTEIN and RUBINSTEIN, in the Ostend Masters tournament of 1907, and

improved to win third prize, after SCHLECHTER and DURAS, at Hamburg 1910, and to share second prize (+8=8−3) with SPIELMANN, half a point behind Rubinstein, at San Sebastián 1912. He participated without success, for his style was not fully developed, in the great St Petersburg tournament of 1914, but then his chess career was interrupted by the war and its aftermath.

Around 1920 he was able to leave Latvia. His name, originally of four syllables (Ni-em-zo-witsch, meaning 'from Germany'), was spelled without an 'e' on his travel documents; overjoyed at having a passport at all, he accepted the new name. He began to rebuild his chess career, first in Sweden, and from 1922 in Copenhagen, where he lived for the rest of his life in one small rented room. During that time Nimzowitsch played in 22 strong tournaments, winning or sharing eight first, six second, and three third prizes. He regarded his win (+8=1) at Dresden 1926, one and a half points ahead of Alekhine, as his best performance. Other notable victories were Copenhagen 1923 (+6=4); Marienbad 1925 (+ 8 = 6 − 1), a tie with ,Rubinstein; Hanover 1926 (+ 6 = 1) ahead of Rubinstein; London (Oct.) 1927 (+ 7 = 2 − 2); Bad Niendorf 1927 (+ 4 = 3), a tie with TARTAKOWER; Berlin (Feb.) 1928 (+ 8 = 4 − 1); Carlsbad 1929 (+ 10 = 10 − 1), ahead of Capablanca; and Frankfurt 1930 (+ 9 = 1 − 1). His most notable second places were a tournament at Berlin in October 1928, when he scored + 4 = 6 − 2, a point-and-half after Capablanca, and at San Remo 1930 (+ 8 = 5 − 2) behind Alekhine.

Nimzowitsch–Rubinstein   Berlin *Tageblatt* 1928   Nimzowitsch Opening

1 Nf3 d5 2 b3 Bf5 3 Bb2 e6 4 g3 h6 5 Bg2 Nd7 6 0-0 Ngf6 7 d3 Be7 8 e3 0-0 9 Qe2 c6 10 Kh1 a5 11 a4 Nc5 12 Nd4 Bh7 13 f4 Nfd7 14 Nd2 Qc7 15 e4 dxe4 16 Nxe4 Nxe4 17 dxe4 e5 18 Nf3 exf4 19 gxf4 Rfe8 20 e5 Nc5 21 Nd4 Ne6 22 Rad1 Nxd4 23 Bxd4 Bf5 24 Be4 Bxe4+ 25 Qxe4 Rad8

26 e6 Bf8 27 Be5 Qc8 28 f5 fxe6 29 f6 Rxd1 30 f7+ Kh8 31 Rxd1 Rd8 32 Qg6 Black resigns.

Nimzowitsch is said to have described himself on his visiting cards as the crown prince of chess. In 1926 his challenge for a world title match was accepted by Capablanca, but Nimzowitsch was unable to raise the stake money. Alekhine, who became champion in 1927, preferred to play two matches against BOGOLJUBOW; Nimzowitsch had a good claim to be considered, but, egotistic, highly strung, irritable, over-sensitive to criticism, and almost pathologically suspicious, he failed to find support. Although he had long suffered from heart trouble, his early death was unexpected; taken ill suddenly at the end of 1934, he lay bedridden for three months before dying of pneumonia.

Nimzowitsch contributed more to the game than most of his contemporaries. He traces the beginning of the hypermodern movement back to 1904 when he first met TARRASCH, who criticized his play adversely, an incident Nimzowitsch never forgot. From that moment he began to re-examine the formalistic teachings of Tarrasch, to which the hypermodern movement was, in large measure, a reaction. Seeking a new approach to the problem of controlling the centre, Nimzowitsch re-examined many openings ideas that had been used by the 19th-century masters, CHIGORIN, PAULSEN, STEINITZ, and WINAWER, and which were regarded by Tarrasch as 'unorthodox'. Besides the openings that Nimzowitsch revived (e.g. the WINAWER VARIATION), the NIMZO-INDIAN DEFENCE, and other openings named after him, he introduced the QUEEN'S INDIAN DEFENCE and the MARIENBAD VARIATION.

Nimzowitsch wrote three important books: *Die Blockade* (1925), translated into English as *Blockade* (1980); *Mein System* (1925), translated into many languages, with an English version called *My System* (1929); and *Die Praxis meines Systems* (1929), published in an English translation as *Chess Praxis* (1936), a book that contains 109 of his games. *My System* is the most important. The title is misleading, for only part of the book deals with a system of play; it may have been chosen as an echo of a popular book of the same name dealing with body-building. The suggestion that the old-established procedures of PROPHYLAXIS and OVERPROTECTION will, of themselves, lead to advantage depends upon whether there is any square of sufficient importance to overprotect, or whether the opponent has any threats worth preventing. There are positions where some other course of action is more appropriate. Generally Nimzowitsch does not explain how one's game should be built up, or how a player might aim for positions of a certain kind; instead he discusses how to deal with such positions should they arise. This practical advice, copiously illustrated, is of more use to a student than generalizations, often negative, about how to set up his game. He makes few dogmatic assertions; for example, he does not say that an ISOLATED PAWN is necessarily weak or strong, but shows how to play with and against such a pawn. Notwithstanding the author's claim, few, if any, of the STRATAGEMS or MANŒUVRES he describes were originated by him; but his exposition is brilliant, effective, and entertaining. He coined a number of terms, among them BUILDING A BRIDGE (a manœuvre shown in the 17th century); PROPHYLAXIS (previously exemplified by PHILIDOR); ISOLANI (well understood by Steinitz); and MYSTERIOUS ROOK MOVE (a manœuvre antedating the author's birth). (See MANŒUVRE.)

R. D. Keene, *Aron Nimzowitsch: a Reappraisal* (1974), was revised and translated into Russian in 1986.

Nimzowitsch Attack, 414 in the KING'S INDIAN DEFENCE, introduced by NIMZOWITSCH in the 1920s and used by ALEKHINE in matches against EUWE (1927) and BOGOLJUBOW (1929) but now out of fashion; 777 in the SPANISH OPENING, which began its rise to popularity after Nimzowitsch–Capablanca, St Petersburg 1914, and perhaps contributed to the virtual disappearance of this form of the STEINITZ DEFENCE from the repertoire.

Nimzowitsch Defence, 593. Known since the 16th century, used regularly by the German player Eduard Fischer (1831–97), this opening was reintroduced by NIMZOWITSCH. After 2 d4 he favoured the continuation 2 . . . d5 as played by him against DURAS at Ostend 1907. (See KASHDAN; POSITIONAL SACRIFICE.)

Nimzowitsch Opening, 1284. After 1 Nf3 White plays 2 b3 in response to any Black move other than 1 . . . e5. The opening had been recommended by CHIGORIN but is rightly named on account of its successful use by NIMZOWITSCH. (See HALF-OPEN FILE; PIRC.)

Nimzowitsch Queen's Pawn Defence, 53, a response to 1 d4 intended to induce 2 d5, and sometimes known as the Orenburg Defence. The idea, attributed to BOGOLJUBOW, derives from the analogous variation, 561, of the SICILIAN DEFENCE introduced by NIMZOWITSCH in 1911. (Compare NIMZOWITSCH DEFENCE.)

Nimzowitsch Variation, 27, 32, and 45 in the ENGLISH OPENING, the first a NIMZOWITSCH favourite, the second played by Nimzowitsch, RUBINSTEIN, and RÉTI in the 1920s, and sometimes called the Alekhine System, although neither name is appropriate, the third (also known as Nimzo-English Variation) so called because of its affinity with the NIMZO-INDIAN DEFENCE; 261 in the STAUNTON GAMBIT, played in Brinckmann–Nimzowitsch, Copenhagen 1924; 286 in the HROMÁDKA DEFENCE, as Nimzowitsch–Marshall, New York 1927; 336 in the BOGOLJUBOW DEFENCE, introduced in Vidmar–Nimzowitsch, Semmering 1926; 344 in the QUEEN'S INDIAN DEFENCE, from Grünfeld–Nimzowitsch, Breslau 1925 (see SOKOLOV); 467 and 561 in the SICILIAN DEFENCE, the first a dubious line introduced in Rubinstein–Nimzowitsch, Carlsbad 1923, and so also known as the Carlsbad Variation, the second, sometimes called the Rubinstein, or Klyatskin Defence, and a precursor to the ALEKHINE DEFENCE

(1248), from Spielmann–Nimzowitsch, San Sebastián 1911.

Also 1023 in the PHILIDOR DEFENCE, as Nimzowitsch–Marco, Göteborg 1920; 1050 in the GRECO COUNTER-GAMBIT, as Nimzowitsch–Behting, Riga 1919 ('even if all the rest of the world play here [6 Nc3], I yet hold my move [Ne3] to be more correct' said Nimzowitsch in *My System*); 1080 and 1081 in the FALKBEER COUNTER-GAMBIT, the first given by GRECO, the second recommended by STAUNTON and practised by BIRD (see PILLSBURY); 1238 in the FRENCH DEFENCE, sometimes called the Advance Variation, or the Close Variation, given by BERTIN, played by Staunton in his second match game against POPERT in 1840, and by PAULSEN, and successfully rehabilitated by Nimzowitsch, who frequently continued with 1243.

Also 41, the SICILIAN VARIATION of the English Opening; 449, the CLOSE VARIATION of the Sicilian Defence; 499, the MOSCOW VARIATION of the Sicilian Defence; 578, the BRONSTEIN–LARSEN VARIATION of the CARO–KANN DEFENCE, as Leonhardt–Nimzowitsch, Carlsbad 1911; 836, the PAULSEN VARIATION of the FOUR KNIGHTS OPENING; 1034, the JAENISCH COUNTERATTACK in the Philidor Defence; 1184, the WINAWER VARIATION of the French Defence; 1232, the GUIMARD VARIATION in the same opening.

NN, an abbreviation of the Latin *nomina* (names) used when the names of players are not known, the chessplayer's counterpart of the poet Anon. The most plausible alternative explanation is that the letters should be written N.N. for *nescio nomen,* a Latin phrase meaning 'name unknown'.

Noah's Ark Trap, specifically 689 in the SPANISH OPENING, generally any variation in which a white bishop on b3 is trapped by black pawns. White's error in 689 is 8 Qxd4. In the book of the New York 1924 tournament (p. 17) ALEKHINE carelessly recommended this variation as a means of obtaining a quick draw; his advice was followed by E. STEINER who, playing CAPABLANCA in the Budapest tournament 1929, fell into the ancient trap. Some suggest that the black pawns on a6, b5, c5, d6 resemble the shape of an ark, others that the trap is 'as old as the Ark'.

Noa Variation, 313 in the NIMZO-INDIAN DEFENCE, also known as the Capablanca or Kmoch Variation; it was played regularly by the Hungarian Josef Noa (1856–1903), who, however, reached the position after 1 d4 d5 2 c4 e6 3 Nc3 Bb4 4 Qc2 Nf6.

Nogueiras Santiago, José de Jesús (1959–), International Grandmaster (1979), Cuban champion 1978, 1984 (shared), 1991. He won tournaments at Cienfuegos 1984 and Havana 1984 (+4=8−1), was second (+5=9), after TIMMAN, at Taxco 1985,

and fourth (+3=9−1), after SHORT, KORCHNOI, and ANDERSSON, at Wijk aan Zee 1987. He competed in the CANDIDATES tournament at Montpellier 1985, with dismal results.

Hjartarson–Nogueiras   Belfort 1988   French Defence
Winawer Variation

1 e4 e6 2 d4 d5 3 Nc3 Bb4 4 e5 Ne7 5 a3 Bxc3+ 6 bxc3 c5 7 Qg4 Qc7 8 Qxg7 Rg8 9 Qxh7 cxd4 10 Ne2 Nbc6 11 f4 Bd7 12 Qd3 dxc3 13 Qxc3 Nf5 14 Rb1 0–0–0 15 Rg1 d4 16 Qd3 Na5 17 g4 Ba4 18 c3

18 ... Bc2 19 Qxc2 d3 20 Qa2 Qc5 21 Rg2 Ne3 22 Bxe3 Qxe3 23 Rg3 d2+ 24 Kd1 Qf2 25 Kc2 d1=Q+ 26 Rxd1 Rxd1 27 Kxd1 Qxf1+ 28 Kd2 b5 29 Ke3 Nc4+ 30 Ke4 Qf2 White resigns.

Nordic Gambit, 660, the DANISH GAMBIT.

norm, a percentage score relevant to a specific TOURNAMENT CATEGORY. For example, in a single-round ALL-PLAY-ALL tournament of 16 players a score of 57% (8½ out of 15) would be a GM norm in a category 13 tournament, an IM norm in a category 7 tournament, and a WGM norm in a category 1 tournament. In tournaments conducted according to the regulations laid down by FIDE a sufficient number of norms may qualify for a FIDE TITLE.

Normal Position, 126 in the TARRASCH DEFENCE to the QUEEN'S GAMBIT Declined; from here the analysts begin their variations with the implication that the preceding moves (after 3 ... c5) are the best for both sides. Also 869 in the EVANS GAMBIT, the starting point for innumerable analyses in the 19th century.

Normal Variation, name given to what is, at some time, the most common line in a specific opening. Examples are 293 in the BUDAPEST DEFENCE; 403 in the KING'S INDIAN DEFENCE (see FIVE-MINUTE CHESS); 588 in the PANOV–BOTVINNIK ATTACK; 927 in the GIUOCO PIANISSIMO.

notation, a convention for recording the moves of a game; a way of recording a position, for which see CONTROL NOTATION and FORSYTH NOTATION. Nothing has contributed more to the advancement of chess knowledge than acceptable notations for describing moves. They do for chess what the writing of notes does for music, and both written versions are called scores. A notation system must do four things, but the method used for any one of the four does not necessarily restrict the options for the other three. It must identify (1) the move number, (2) the man moved, (3) the departure and arrival square (full notation) or just the arrival square (abbreviated notation), and (4) provide a system for recording exceptional moves such as castling.

(1) Move number
The same method is used in all notations. Move 1 is the first move by White and also the first move by Black, and so on. If White mates on the twentieth move it is still numbered 20 although Black makes no reply. When White concedes defeat after a black move, a move number often precedes the word 'resigns'; resignation is not a move, but the number is used to make clear that it is White who has resigned. A move made by one player is called a SINGLE-MOVE, or, in computer terminology, a PLY, and not a HALF-MOVE, a name sometimes used in trick puzzles.

(2) The man moved
When both departure and arrival squares are named it is not essential to give the identity of the man; CORRESPONDENCE and GRINGMUTH NOTATIONS do not do so. Usually the man is identified by its initial letter, although in some printed works FIGUR-INES are used. In English K is used for king and Kt, or increasingly often N, for knight. In Russian, too, these two pieces share the same initial, but there K is knight and Kp king. (In the Cyrillic alphabet 'p' corresponds to 'r'.) Frequently the initial 'P' for pawn is omitted, the rest of the move sufficing. All other methods are obsolete. For example, STAMMA used the file letter on which the piece stood in the ARRAY.

(3) The squares
There are two basic methods, descriptive, or unique. They may be compared to methods of identifying a house; 'third on the left after the bridge' (descriptive), or '6 High Street' (unique). As in this example, DESCRIPTIVE NOTATION has to allow for approach from the opposite direction ('or third on the right before the bridge'), and so each square has two names, e.g. K3 for White is K6 for Black. The universal STANDARD NOTATION, using letters for files and numbers for ranks, is the obvious example of a unique labelling method. Forms of co-ordinate notation have been used in Arab countries since the 9th century and in Europe since the 13th century, some using numbers for files and letters for ranks, or all letters, or all numbers, and beginning from different corners. Correspondence notation uses numbers for both files and ranks. The only system currently in use that uniquely identifies squares without the use of co-ordinates is Gringmuth

notation. At one time Italian authors numbered the squares 1 to 64 (scanning from h1 to a1, h2 to a2 and so on, much as in draughts notation).

(4) Other moves
There are CONVENTIONAL SYMBOLS for use in describing castling (0–0 or 0–0–0, as used in the third edition of Allgaier's *Neue theoretisch-praktische Anweisung*, 1811). Although not necessary, they may be used for other purposes, e.g. checks and captures. Miron James Hazeltine (1824–1907), editor of the *New York Clipper* chess column from 1855 to 1905, introduced the dash, e.g. P–K4 instead of P to K4, but WALKER had already shown in his collection of more than a thousand games, published in 1844, that neither is necessary and PK4 is enough.
The layout of the moves on the page in RUNNING NOTATION or TABULAR NOTATION, either of which may use FRACTIONAL NOTATION, does not depend on the basic notation method used.

Nottingham Variation, 526 in the SICILIAN DEFENCE, from the game Alekhine–Botvinnik, Nottingham 1936.

Nowotny interference, see CRITICAL PLAY; CUTTING-POINT THEMES.

numeric[al] notation, a notation for which the moves are described only by numbers. See CORRESPONDENCE NOTATION for a specific example, and NOTATION for a general discussion.

Nunn, John Denis Martin (1955–   ), English player, European Junior Champion 1974–5, International Grandmaster (1978), British champion 1980 after a play-off (the year before he was equal first but missed on tie-break). He went to Oxford at the unusually young age of 15, graduated in 1973, and gained his doctorate in 1978. He remained at Oxford as a mathematics lecturer until 1981, when he became a professional player. He had by then achieved several good results in international tournaments: Budapest 1978, first; Hastings 1979–80, first (+5=10) equal with ANDERSSON; Baden-bei-Wien 1980, third (+5=10), after SPASSKY and BELYAVSKY; Helsinki 1981, first (+5=6) equal with MATULOVIĆ; and Wiesbaden 1981, first (+6=3).
Among his best tournament results as a professional are: Wijk aan Zee 1982, first (+5=7−1) equal with BALASHOV, ahead of TAL, HÜBNER, and TIMMAN; Helsinki 1983, second (+5=6), after KARLSSON; Biel 1983, first (+5=6) equal with MILES; Brighton 1983, first (+5=4); Gjovik 1983, first (+3=6), shared with BROWNE and ADORJÁN; Wijk aan Zee 1985, second (+4=8−1) equal with Belyavsky, after Timman; Brussels (OHRA) 1986, third (+3=4−3) equal with Hübner, after KASPAROV and KORCHNOI; Amsterdam (OHRA) 1988,

second +2=7−1, after Korchnoi; Wijk aan Zee 1990, first (+5=6−2), ahead of PORTISCH and Andersson; Wijk aan Zee 1991, first (+5=7−1), ahead of ADAMS, CHERNIN, HANSEN, and KHALIFMAN.

Nunn has been in the English Olympiad team since 1976. He won the prize for best performance on second board (10/11) in 1984, and on a rest day won the problem-solving championship. Possessing a remarkably quick SIGHT OF THE BOARD, he is an expert solver. He made the second highest individual score in the world team solving championship, 1978, and won the solving championship of Great Britain in 1981, 1984, and 1992. In 1991 he earned the title of International Solving Master. (See DANGEROUS DIAGONAL; TEMPO-MOVE.)

Nunn–Gheorghiu Biel 1983 Sicilian Defence Paulsen Variation

1 e4 c5 2 Nf3 e6 3 d4 cxd4 4 Nxd4 a6 5 Bd3 Nf6 6 0-0 d6 7 c4 b6 8 Nc3 Bb7 9 f4 Be7 10 Kh1 0-0 11 Qe2 Nc6 12 Nxc6 Bxc6 13 b3 Qc7 14 Bb2 Rad8 15 Rae1 Bb7 16 Bb1 Nd7 17 Qh5 Rfe8 18 Re3 Nf6 19 Qh3 g6 20 f5 Bc8 21 Rg3 Kg7 22 Qh4 Rf8 23 Bc1 Rde8 24 e5 (Instead of winning the exchange White begins a decisive attack, aided by his RAKING BISHOPS.) 24 ... dxe5 25 Qh6+ Kh8 26 Rh3 Rg8 27 Bg5 Rg7 28 Bxf6 Bxf6 29 Ne4 Qd8 30 fxg6 Be7

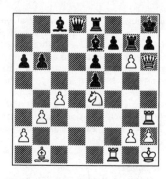

31 Qxh7+ Rxh7 32 Rxh7+ Kg8 33 gxf7+ Kxh7 34 fxe8=Q Black resigns.

Nuremberg Variation, 787, a rare response, occasionally called the Damiano–Steinitz Variation, in the SPANISH OPENING, played Schlechter–Steinitz, Nuremberg 1896.

Nyholm Attack, 795, variation in the SPANISH OPENING named after the Swedish player Gustaf Nyholm (1880–1957), but known before his time.

O

obstruct, to place a man on a particular square so that another man of the same colour cannot be moved to that square; loosely, to interfere. In the ARRAY all men except the knights and pawns are obstructed.

obstruction, the action of obstructing; the man that causes another man to be obstructed.

obtrusive piece, a composer's description of a piece in a legal position that must have been created by promotion. The term is not used for pieces so created during the play.

#3

A. F. Mackenzie, *Jamaica Gleaner*, 1891 White mates in three by 1 Ba7 Kxa7 2 c8 = R. The bishop is obtrusive, for Black's last move must have been ... Ka7–a8 and White's before that Pb7–b8 = B + . (See ORTHODOX PROBLEM.)

O'Connell, Kevin J. (1949–), English author and computer expert.

odds, games at, see HANDICAP.

Ōim, Tõnu (1941–), Estonian player, International Correspondence Chess Grandmaster (1981), winner (+ 10 = 6) of the 9th World Correspondence Championship 1977–83. He was born in Tallinn, where he works in the P. Keres Chesshouse and for the Estonian Sports Committee.

O'Kelly de Galway, Albéric (1911–80), Belgian professional player, International Grandmaster (1956), International Correspondence Chess Grandmaster (1962) International Arbiter (1962). A frequent competitor in tournaments he made his best over-the-board victory at Dortmund 1951, but winning the third World Correspondence Cham-

pionship 1959–62 was probably his best achievement. Between 1937 and 1959 he won the Belgian championship outright on seven occasions and shared it a further three times; and he played for his country in eight Olympiads between 1937 and 1968. In his later years he gave more of his time to chess organization, and was chief arbiter for the world championship matches of 1966 and 1969. A good linguist and a prolific author, he wrote many articles and books, often in languages other than French.

O'Kelly Variation, 460 in the SICILIAN DEFENCE, first made popular by TARTAKOWER in his match with RÉTI in 1920, and re-examined by O'KELLY in the 1950s.

Ólafsson, Fridrik (1935–), International Grandmaster (1958), the strongest Icelandic player up to his time. He learned chess at the age of 8, won the national championship for the first of seven times when he was 17, won the Nordic championship at 18, and became widely known at the age of 20 when he shared first prize with KORCHNOI at Hastings 1955–6. In the Portorož interzonal tournament 1958 he came fifth equal with FISCHER and qualified for the CANDIDATES tournament of 1959. In this event lack of top-level experience told against him: consistently in time-trouble, he took the penultimate place. Around this time he completed his law studies and obtained a post in the Ministry of Justice.

During the next few years his best results were: Los Angeles 1963, third (+ 4 = 7 − 3) equal with NAJDORF, after KERES and PETROSYAN, ahead of RESHEVSKY and GLIGORIĆ; Lugano 1970, second (+ 5 = 7 − 2), after LARSEN, ahead of Gligorić; Wijk aan Zee 1971, second (+ 6 = 7 − 2) equal with IVKOV, Gligorić, and Petrosyan, after Korchnoi; Reykjavik 1972, first (+ 8 = 6 − 1) equal with GHEORGHIU and HORT, ahead of STEIN; and Las Palmas 1974, second (+ 7 = 6 − 2) equal with BELYAVSKY, after LJUBOJEVIĆ and ahead of POLUGAYEVSKY.

In 1974 Ólafsson gave up his government post to become a professional player, and at Wijk aan Zee 1976 achieved his best tournament result, first (+ 4 = 7) equal with Ljubojević, ahead of TAL. At Reykjavik later in the year he scored + 7 = 8 and shared first prize with TIMMAN. He played in several Olympiads from 1952, notably making the best first-board score (+ 10 = 8) at Varna in 1962. His few matches include a crushing defeat (+ 4 = 2) of PILNIK in 1955. In 1978 Ólafsson was elected president of FIDE for a term of four years, in succession to EUWE. After his failure to be re-elected in 1982 he became less involved with chess and was appointed secretary to the Icelandic parliament.

Ólafsson–Larsen   Reykjavik 1978   Alekhine Defence

1 e4 Nf6 2 e5 Nd5 3 d4 d6 4 Nf3 g6 5 Bc4 Nb6 6 Bb3 Bg7 7 Ng5 d5 8 0–0 Nc6 9 c3 Bf5 10 g4 Bxb1 11 Qf3 0–0 12 Rxb1 Qd7 13 Bc2 Nd8 14 Qh3 h6 15 f4 hxg5 16 f5 Ne6 17 fxe6 Qxe6 18 Bxg5 c5 19 Kh1 cxd4 20 cxd4 Rfc8

21 Bf5 gxf5 22 gxf5 Qc6 23 Rg1 Qc2 24 Rbe1 Kf8 25 f6
Black resigns.

Ólafsson, Helgi (1956–   ), Icelandic Champion 1978, 1981, International Grandmaster (1985). First at Neskaupstadhur 1984, equal first (+6= 4−1) at Gjovik 1985, and equal second (+5= 4−2) at the strong Copenhagen 1985 tournament. (See PHILIDOR SACRIFICE.)

H. Ólafsson–Lobron   Reykjavik (open) 1984   Modern Benoni

1 d4 Nf6 2 c4 e6 3 Nf3 c5 4 d5 exd5 5 cxd5 d6 6 Nc3 g6 7 Bf4 a6 8 a4 Bg7 9 e4 0–0 10 Be2 Bg4 11 0–0 Bxf3 12 Bxf3 Ne8 13 Qb3 b6 14 Nb1 Nd7 15 Na3 Qf6 16 Bg3 h5 17 h3 Qxb2 18 Rab1 Qf6 19 Rfe1 Qe7 20 Be2 Be5 21 Nc4 Bd4 22 Nxb6 Nxb6 23 Qxb6 h4 24 Bh2 Qxe4 25 Bxa6 Qc2 26 Kh1 Nf6 27 Bxd6 Rfe8 28 Bb5 Rxe1+ 29 Rxe1 Qd2 30 Rf1 Ne4 31 Qc7 Bxf2 32 Bf4 Qxd5 33 Qc6 Rd8 34 Qxd5 Rxd5 35 Rc1 g5 36 Bc6 Rd8 37 Be5 Be3 38 Rb1 Nf2+ 39 Kh2 g4 40 g3

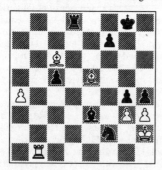

40 ... Rd2 41 Rb8+ Kh7 42 Rb2 hxg3+ 43 Kxg3 Bf4+ 44 Kxf4 Nd3+ 45 Ke3 Nxb2 46 Be4+ Kg8 47 Kxd2 Nc4+ 48 Kc3 Nxe5 49 hxg4 Black resigns. The OUTSIDE PASSED PAWN decides the endgame.

Ólafsson Variation, 322 in the NIMZO-INDIAN DEFENCE introduced by F. ÓLAFSSON in a game against NAJDORF, Hollywood 1963.

Old Dutch, 253, the ILYIN-GENEVSKY VARIATION.

old game, a term used in this book for the forms of chess (SHAṬRANJ, MEDIEVAL CHESS) practised in Europe before the revolution which transformed the game c.1475. (See HISTORY OF CHESS.)

Old Indian Attack, 1297, a REVERSE OPENING, taking its name by analogy with the OLD INDIAN DEFENCE.

Old Indian Defence, 289, distinguished from the KING'S INDIAN DEFENCE by the development of Black's bishop on e7 after Pe7–e5. This defence was played by TARRASCH when facing SCHLECHTER at Monte Carlo 1902, and other grandmasters tried it shortly afterwards. One of them was CHIGORIN, who used the line successfully in the last few years of his life, and it is sometimes called the Chigorin Indian, particularly in Russian literature where the King's Indian is called the Old Indian, and the Queen's Indian is called the New Indian. (See BERNSTEIN; FAMILY CHECK; KOTOV; VAGANYAN.)

The name is sometimes given to 234, the PILLSBURY DEFENCE, which may become an Indian defence.

Old Variation, 814, the now obsolete treatment of the PONZIANI OPENING played in the days when seizing the ITALIAN DIAGONAL was a major strategy.

Old Zurich Variation, 312, one of the early lines in the history of the MILNER-BARRY VARIATION (311) dating from before the Zurich 1934 tournament which gave rise to its alternative name.

Olympiad, the popular name for the FIDE World Team Championship. Attempts to link chess with the Olympic Games were made at Stockholm in 1912 (ALEKHINE's first tournament victory outside Russia) and at Paris in 1924, but the chess world has never been anxious to distinguish amateurs from professionals. Official Olympiads, for the HAMILTON-RUSSELL cup, began with London 1927. Teams of four, five, or six players chosen without regard to professional status play over four boards. Olympiads were held on eight occasions before the Second World War, and have since been held every other year from 1950. These have been unconnected with the Olympic Games, but in 1936 the German Chess Federation, not then a member of FIDE, arranged a contest of national teams over eight boards in Munich to complement the Berlin Olympic Games. In 1976 a politically inspired 'counter-Olympiad' of no chess significance was held in Tripoli (Libya). Since 1957 there have been Olympiads restricted to women (for the Vera MENCHIK cup) and there are similar events restricted to blind players.

Árpád Földeák, *Chess Olympiads 1927–1968* (1979); Averbakh and Turov, *Shakhmatnye Olimpiadi* (1974); Turov, *Pyat Shakhmatnikh Olimpiad* (1984).

one-mover, a kind of CONSTRUCTION TASK; a problem for which one SINGLE-MOVE or a single-move by each side fulfils the STIPULATIONS. A one-mover problem might contain many tries and, although not difficult to solve, it could be used to test a player's SIGHT OF THE BOARD. The solving task is harder if RETROGRADE ANALYSIS is needed to reveal the solution.

#1

A problem by PLAKSIN, second hon. mention, *Die Schwalbe*, 1978. The solver must discover who is to move.

The four missing men on each side were all captured by pawns. The black a-pawn has captured four White pieces, two of which were created by promotion. White's e-pawn and h-pawn have each captured a piece, and two white pawns have captured a piece on f7, en route to promotion.

Suppose White begins the retractions: RETRO (i.e. moves in backward order) 1 Ba4–b5 d3xNe2 2 Nf4–e2 c4xNd3 3 Ne6–f4 b5xNc4 4 Nf8–e6 a6xNb5 5 f7–f8 = N a7–a6 6 g6xf7; and Black can make further retractions with the uncaptured piece at f7, White can retract another promotion to N, Black can retreat Pf7–f6, and further disentanglement can lead back to the array. Thus it is Black's move in the set position, 1 ... e2–e1 = Q#.

Should Black begin the retraction RETRO-STALE-MATE would occur after five moves: lacking an uncaptured piece at f7, Black would have no more legal retractions.

For another example, see FABEL.

open board, a board showing a position in which there are many open lines. In play this comes about after the exchange of several pawns, especially those on the four central files. An open board favours the LINE-PIECES, so that a bishop is likely to be stronger than a knight.

Open Defence, 707 in the SPANISH OPENING, a literal description to distinguish it from the CLOSE DEFENCE, 732. The usual continuation is 6 d4 b5 7 Bb3 d5 8 dxe5 Be6; Black's pieces get into play at the expense of some disarray of the queen's-side pawns. The defence sometimes bears the name of TARRASCH who championed it, believing that Black's mobility outweighs the defects in pawn formation. Most masters have taken the contrary view. (See BOLESLAVSKY; HJARTARSON.)

open file, a file on which there are no pawns. A player may seek advantage by placing a rook on an open file, and if the rook cannot be challenged by an enemy rook it is said to control or command that file. This is likely to be advantageous if it can be moved forward to make threats along one of the ranks, especially the seventh rank. The queen, too, might take possession of a file. A player's control might be strengthened by the doubling or tripling of major pieces on an open file.

open game, (1) a game that begins 1 e4 e5. These moves sometimes lead to a CLOSE GAME.

open game, (2) a game in which pawn exchanges open DIAGONALS, FILES, and perhaps RANKS for use by the LINE-PIECES, as distinct from a CLOSE-GAME, when the range of these pieces is restricted.

1 e4 e5 2 Nf3 Nc6 3 d4 exd4 4 Nxd4 Nf6 5 Nc3 Bb4 6 Nxc6 bxc6 7 Bd3 d5 8 exd5 cxd5, an open game in both senses.

1 e4 e5 2 Nf3 Nc6 3 Bc4 Be7 4 d4 d6 5 d5 Nb8 6 Bd3 Nf6 7 c4 0–0, a close game.

1 d4 d5 (a CLOSE OPENING) 2 c4 dxc4 3 e3 e5 4 Bxc4 exd4 5 exd4 Bb4+ 6 Nc3 Nf6, an open game.

opening, the first phase of the game, commencing from the ARRAY. The slow pace of the old game permitted much variety in the sequence of the early moves, but when the modern game began (*c.*1475) moves needed to be played in precise order, and the study of openings began. Progress was slow because openings are developed by an empirical process of trial and error. What is called opening theory is exactly the opposite: it is the outcome of experience.

Apart from a leap towards the end of the 16th century there was little advance until the 19th; then players from different cities and countries began to pool their knowledge, and a distinct improvement may be found in JAENISCH's book and Bilguer's HANDBUCH, both published in the early 1840s. Since then knowledge and understanding of the openings has grown steadily. There have been many innovators but their ideas gained acceptance only when developed and tested in play, the work of many hands.

For a long time players planned from the first move to attack the enemy king. During the 1870s such attacking play became the 'ultimate but not the first object of the game' (STEINITZ) and opening play was directed towards objectives of a general kind, broadly the achievement of greater mobility by means of development and control of the centre.

Specific objectives are determined later. The most popular first moves are 1 e4 and 1 d4, fashion at various times preferring one or the other. Then follow 1 c4 and 1 Nf3 in that order. Of the games played for the world championship, from the outset in 1886 up to 1990, the most popular first move for White was 1 d4 (364), followed by 1 e4 (275), 1 c4 (94), 1 Nf3 (55), and a solitary 1 g3. Of the 27 replies made by Black, the most common were, in response to 1 d4, 1 ... d5 (168) and 1 ... Nf6 (172), and to 1 e4, 1 ... e5 (158).

Beginners soon find it necessary to have some knowledge of the openings and may decide to know a little of everything or a good deal about a limited repertoire, a difference in approach found even at master level. Some labour diligently at openings monographs or manuals. Others prefer to play through a large number of games in which the chosen opening is played, a time-honoured way to gain an understanding of the underlying ideas.

For the master a different approach is needed. A sound understanding of opening principles can be taken for granted, but there is a relentless search for THEORETICAL NOVELTIES, to be used or avoided. At a level where the necessary technique to capitalize on an advantage can be assumed, games are frequently decided by the comparative state of the player's knowledge of openings. Hundreds of international tournament games are played each week, and masters must strive to keep in touch with them.

Every game, unless it replicates an earlier one, departs at some stage from 'theory', but such departures are only significant as theoretical novelties if they call for a new EVALUATION OF POSITION. Many leading players use a computer database to help them detect new moves, but computers cannot yet make an evaluation that would be acceptable to a grandmaster.

openings literature. Early writers included model openings in their works, but the first author to attempt a comprehensive survey of openings known at the time and to tabulate them was ALEXANDRE with his *Encyclopédie* (1837); JAENISCH produced the first openings analyses on modern lines in his *Analyse nouvelle des ouvertures* (1842–3); and the merits of these books were combined in Bilguer's HANDBUCH (1843). Although it was less systematic, STAUNTON'S *Handbook* (1847) became the standard reference work in English-speaking countries, but as time passed a demand arose for more up-to-date works in English, an example of which is Freeborough and Ranken's *Chess Openings* (1889) which had four editions up to 1910. The various editions of *Modern Chess Openings* (MCO) from 1911, the eighth and last edition of Bilguer's *Handbuch* (1916–21), and the fourth edition of COLLIJN'S *Lärobok* (1921) were the popular reference sources for strong players between the two world wars.

Openings books can be prepared by diligent examination of all games played by masters and near-masters. This was done by Mordecai Morgan in his *Chess Digest* (1901–5), four large volumes the last of which gives game-scores well into the

A plate from Kenny's *Practical Grammar* (1818) showing the board after 1 e4 e5 2 Bc4 Bc5 3 c3 Nf6 4 d4 exd4 5 cxd4 Bb6 6 Nc3 0–0 7 Nge2 c6 8 Bd3

middlegame, and all giving original sources of publication. Such books usually assess the merit of an opening according to the result of the game, and give little guidance of value. The skills of a grandmaster are needed to evaluate an opening line on its own merit. Works of this kind include *Lärobok*, Bilguer's *Handbuch*, and EUWE'S *De theorie der schaakopeningen* (1937–9). Published in Dutch, translated into other languages, Euwe's book consisted of 12 volumes, an indication of the growth of openings knowledge. The ENCYCLOPEDIA OF CHESS OPENINGS needs five volumes, and at the time of writing there are typically about 50 monographs on particular opening variations, or sub-variations, in print at any one time.

openings nomenclature. Before an adequate system of NOTATION was introduced, the use of a name for an opening was more convenient than a lengthy description of the moves. Increasingly from the 1840s openings were examined and new lines of play evolved. These were named after players or analysts, after towns or countries, or after a tournament in which, perhaps, the line was played. A name would rarely describe the characteristics of an opening or variation. Naming is often haphazard. The DAMIANO DEFENCE is named after the man who proved its weakness, the MUZIO GAMBIT after the man who saw it played. A player whose name is used is neither necessarily nor frequently the originator, but is more likely to be the one who introduced it to master play, studied it deeply, or made it popular. The most used general terms are Variation, Gambit, Defence, Opening, and Attack; less common are Counter-gambit, Counterattack, Game, and System. Some are used exclusively to define lines of play introduced by one side: a Defence, for example, is always defined by a black move; but these terms are not otherwise used consistently and they afford no basis for classification.

By the early 20th century names began to be seen as a reflection of national, ethnic, or personal pride, and there were competing and sometimes incompatible naming methods. One opening line may have many names; conversely, one name may describe different lines. Weak players may produce valuable innovations in the opening, but the real skill comes in proving the worth of an innovation by analysis, play, or both, a task for experts.

In 1932 FIDE set up a commission to produce a standard set of names, but the result, published in the following year, was largely ignored. Another attempt was made in 1965 through *FIDE Revue*, but since then there has been a movement away from the use of proper names for all but the basic openings and towards systematic classification to help indexing and retrieval. (See, for example, RABAR CLASSIFICATION.)

The moves that constitute some hundreds of named openings and variations are given in Appendix I.

Open Slav Defence, 88, the CZECH DEFENCE to the QUEEN'S GAMBIT.

openings, number of possible. Those ways of starting a game which become part of opening practice form a small proportion of those legally possible. White has a choice of 20 first moves. Black the same number of replies, making 400 different possible positions after one move each. In 1895 C. Flye St Marie calculated that 71,852 different legal positions were possible after two moves by each player. This figure is geometrically correct but in 1946 DAWSON showed that White might have the option of an EN PASSANT capture in 232 of these positions, depending on which of about 200,000 different playing sequences were chosen. From a chess point of view, therefore, 72,084 different positions are possible.

After three moves each, more than 9,000,000 positions are possible. To arrive at every one of the possible positions after four moves each at the rate of one position a minute day and night would take a player 600,000 years. There are 2×10^{43} possible different legal positions on a chess-board, and it has been estimated that the number of distinct 40-move games is 25×10^{115}, far greater than the estimated number of electrons in the universe (10^{79}). (For another astronomical figure, see MYTHS.)

open tournament, a tournament that, nominally at least, has no restriction on entry. Thus the open championship of a country may be won by a non-resident. In practice entry to an open tournament may depend on a minimum level of proven ability.

Opočenský, Karel (1892–1975), Czech player, International Master (1950), International Arbiter (1951), national champion 1927 (after a play-off), 1929, 1938, and 1944, co-champion 1943, civil servant. A member of the Czech team in the 1931, 1933, 1935, and 1939 Olympiads, he made the best fourth-board score ($+10=3$) at Folkestone 1933. His best tournament achievement was at Bad Stuben (Štubňianské Teplice) 1930, when he shared third place with FLOHR and GILG, after LILIENTHAL and PIRC. In later life he took an active part in organization, serving on several FIDE committees, and he was chief arbiter for the world championship matches of 1951 and 1954. Among his literary activities he was editor-in-chief of *FIDE Revue* for its first two years, 1953–4.

Opočenský Gambit, 279, ALEKHINE'S name for the BENKO GAMBIT, bestowed after OPOČENSKÝ had played it against STÅHLBERG, Poděbrady 1936.

Opočenský Opening, 437, also known as the Trompowsky Opening, played by JANOWSKI in the 1920s, by OPOČENSKÝ in the 1930s, by his countryman HORT in the 1970s, and by MILES in the 1980s.

Opočenský Variation, 350 in the QUEEN'S INDIAN DEFENCE, as Opočenský–Keres, Buenos Aires Olympiad 1939; 374 in the GRÜNFELD DEFENCE, as Opočenský–Pachman, Prague 1947; 505 in the

SICILIAN DEFENCE, played Lokvenc–Opočenský, Prague 1943, and taken up by NAJDORF.

opponent, specifically, one who does not have the move; generally, the adversary of an identified player.

opposite coloured bishops, see BISHOPS OF OPPOSITE COLOUR.

opposite flank attacks, attacks by White on one side of the board and by Black on the other side. The attacks may be by pieces, by pawns, or both. The kings may be uncastled, or castled on the same or different flanks. An attack may be in front of a castled king, or on the far side. The game is often an exciting race to see who gets there first. Generally, a burgeoning attack on the flank is best met by counterattack in the centre, and it is when this is impracticable that opposite flank attacks occur.

Pillsbury–Tarrasch   Hastings 1895   Queen's Gambit Declined Pillsbury Variation

1 d4 d5 2 c4 e6 3 Nc3 Nf6 4 Bg5 Be7 5 Nf3 Nbd7 6 Rc1 0–0 7 e3 b6 8 cxd5 exd5 9 Bd3 Bb7 10 0–0 c5 11 Re1 c4 12 Bb1 a6 13 Ne5 b5 14 f4 Re8 15 Qf3 Nf8 16 Ne2 Ne4 17 Bxe7 Rxe7 18 Bxe4 dxe4 19 Qg3 f6 20 Ng4 Kh8 21 f5 Qd7 22 Rf1 Rd8 23 Rf4 Qd6 24 Qh4 Rde8 25 Nc3 Bd5 26 Nf2 Qc6 27 Rf1 b4 28 Ne2 Qa4 29 Ng4 Nd7 30 R4f2 Kg8 (30 ... Qxa2? 31 Nf4 Bf7 32 Ng6+) 31 Nc1 c3 32 b3 Qc6 33 h3 a5 34 Nh2 a4 35 g4 axb3 36 axb3 Ra8 37 g5 Ra3 38 Ng4 Bxb3 39 Rg2 Kh8 40 gxf6 gxf6 41 Nxb3 Rxb3 42 Nh6 Rg7 43 Rxg7 Kxg7

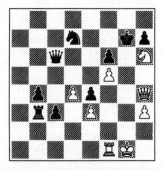

44 Qg3+ Kxh6 45 Kh1 Qd5 46 Rg1 Qxf5 47 Qh4+ Qh5 48 Qf4+ Qg5 49 Rxg5 fxg5 50 Qd6+ Kh5 51 Qxd7 c2 52 Qxh7+ mate.

For other examples, see BALASHOV; LJUBOJEVIĆ.

opposition, a special relationship between the positions of the kings, partly depending on the distance between them. The unit of measurement is the distance between the centres of two laterally adjoining squares. The kings stand in opposition when (a) the position is a ZUGZWANG and (b) the co-ordinates of the distance between the kings consist of even numbers as follows: 2,0, direct opposition; 4,0, distant opposition; 6,0, long-distant opposition; 2,2, ($\sqrt{8}$), or 4,4, ($\sqrt{32}$) or 6,6, ($\sqrt{72}$), diagonal opposition; 2,4, ($\sqrt{20}$), or 2,6, ($\sqrt{40}$), or 4,6, ($\sqrt{52}$), oblique opposition. The opposition may also be

called vertical for kings standing on the same file, or horizontal for kings on the same rank. (Zugzwang is an essential constituent; yet the term opposition is often misused to describe any situation in which kings stand as close as possible on the same rank or file. See PSEUDO-OPPOSITION.) When the kings stand in opposition the player who does not have the move is said, loosely, to have the opposition; to create such a position is to take the opposition; to draw the game by maintaining the opposition is to have the defensive opposition.

The kings stand in vertical direct opposition. White to play draws: 1 Ke5 Ke7z (z symbolizes zugzwang) 2 Kd5 Kd7z 3 Kc5 Kc7z 4 b5 (unable to advance the king, White advances the pawn instead) 4 ... Kb7 5 b6 Kb8 6 Kc6 Kc8z 7 b7+ Kb8z. Black to play loses: 1 ... Ke7 2 Ke5z Kd7 3 Kd5z Kc7 4 Kc5z Kb7 5 Kb5z Ka7 6 Kc6 (White makes an outflanking manœuvre.) 6 ... Kb8 7 b5 Ka7 8 Kc7 Ka8 9 Kb6 Kb8 10 Ka6 Ka8 11 b6z Kb8 12 b7z. It is an inherent characteristic of this pawn formation (a single white pawn at b4) that six zugzwangs are possible; these occur with the white king on a5, b5, c5, d5, e5, or f5 and the black king at a7, b7, c7, d7, e7, or f7 respectively. These relationships may be shown as a5 = a7, b5 = b7, and so on, each 'equation' representing a pair of squares known as CONJUGATE SQUARES, a term implying the reciprocal relationship common to all zugzwangs.

This example shows the practical possibilities. The player who has the opposition may outflank the enemy king, or may prevent a similar outflanking by the opponent.

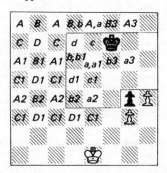

Here the pawn formation contains 27 conjugate pairs showing the opposition in one form or another (16 direct, 5 distant, 4 diagonal, 2 oblique). Italic letters and numbers indicate these pairs, upper case for White, lower case for Black. For example, if White's king is on a C1 square and Black's on a c1 square the kings stand in opposition. With one exception (W. Kh8, B. Kh5), White wins if the white king crosses the line on the diagram (into Black's territory) before the h-pawn is moved. This cannot be done, so the position is drawn.

1 Kd2 Ke6 2 Ke3 Ke5z 3 Kd3 (the advance 3 h5 also draws) 3 ... Kd5z 4 Kc3 Ke5z (Black takes the diagonal opposition) 5 Kb3 Kd5z 6 Ka3 Ke5z (Black takes the oblique opposition) 7 Ka4 Ke4z (Black takes the horizontal distant opposition) 8 Ka5 Ke5z 9 Kb6 Kd6z. By maintaining the defensive opposition Black can keep out White's king.

The italic letters reveal the regular pattern of conjugate squares that characterizes the opposition. Notionally there are four interlocking groups of squares (marked a, b, c, and d) and if both kings stand on squares of one group their positions are correlated. In practice this is true only to a limited extent, because the theoretical pattern is modified by the pawn formation. Here, for example, a black king at e6 (an a square) would stand in opposition to a white king at a6, c6, a8, or e8 (A squares), but if the White king were to stand on other A squares (e.g. c4) the position would not be a zugzwang.

The kings stand in vertical long-distant opposition. Twenty conjugate pairs are possible, all forms of vertical opposition on the c–, d–, e–, f–, or g-file. White to play draws: 1 Kf1 Kf7z 2 Ke1 Ke7z 3 Kd1 Kd7z 4 Kc2 Kc6z (vertical direct opposition) 5 Kc3 Kc5z (direct opposition) 6 Kd2 Kd6z 7 Kd3 Kd5z, and Black maintains the defensive opposition. Black to play loses: 1 ... Kf7 2 Kf1z Ke7 3 Ke1z Kd7 4 Kd1z Kc7 5 Ke2 (outflanking) 5 ... Kd6 6 Kd2z Ke6 7 Kc3 (outflanking) 7 ... Kd5 8 Kd3z Kc5 9 Ke4 (outflanking) 9 ... Kc6 10 Kd4 Kd6 11 Kc4 Kc6 12 a4z Kb6 13 Kd5, and White will gain Black's pawn.

Opposition at a distance is not common in play, but direct opposition is of consequence in many pawn endings.

Compare CONJUGATE SQUARES, when the distance between the kings usually contains at least one odd-numbered co-ordinate. Some authorities regard the opposition as a special case of conjugate squares. Others regard conjugate squares as a special form of opposition which they designate irregular opposition.

Belyavsky–P. Nikolić   Belgrade 1987   Bogoljubow
Indian

1 d4 Nf6 2 c4 e6 3 Nf3 Bb4+ 4 Bd2 Bxd2+ 5 Qxd2 0–0 6 Nc3 d5 7 e3 Qe7 8 cxd5 exd5 9 Bd3 c6 10 Qc2 Re8 11 Ne5 Nbd7 12 Nxd7 Bxd7 13 0–0 Qd6 14 h3 Re7 15 b4 Rae8 16 b5 (a MINORITY ATTACK) 16 ... c5 17 dxc5 Qxc5 18 Rfd1 Re5 19 Rac1 Qb4 20 Bf1 Rg5 21 Rd4 Qa3 22 Nb1 Qe7 23 Kh1 Bf5 24 Qb2 Bxb1 25 Qxb1 Ne4 26 Rc2 Rf5 27 Qe1 h5 28 Kg1 Qe6 29 Bd3 Rg5 30 h4 Re5 31 Qd1 Nf6 32 Be2 g6 33 a4 Rc8 34 Bf3 Rxc2 35 Qxc2 Kh7 36 g3 Qd6 37 Kg2 a6 38 bxa6 bxa6 39 a5 Qa3 40 Qc7 Re7 41 Qb6 Re6 42 Qb7 Kg7 43 Bxd5 Nxd5 44 Qxd5 Rf6 45 Rf4 Rxf4 46 gxf4 Qc1 47 f5 Qc7 48 Qd4+ f6 49 Qd5 gxf5 50 Qxf5 Qb7+ 51 e4 Qf7 52 Qc8 Qg6+ 53 Kf3 Qg1 54 Qc7+ Kf8 55 Qd6+ Kf7 56 Qc7+ Ke8 57 Qf4 Kf7 58 Ke2 Qb1 59 Qf5 Kg7 60 Qd7+ Kg6 61 Qd5 Kg7 62 Qf5 Qc2+ 63 Kf1 Qd1+ 64 Kg2 Qe2 65 Qf3 Qb5 66 e5 Qxe5 67 Qg3+ Kf7 68 Qxe5 fxe5

69 Kf3 Ke7 70 Ke4 Ke6 71 f3 (a TEMPO-MOVE) 71 ... Kf6 72 f4 exf4 73 Kxf4 Black resigns. White wins only because he has the opposition.

Orang Utan Opening, 6, dating from the 19th century, and also called the Englisch, Hunt, Polish, or Sokolsky Opening. During the New York tournament, 1924, TARTAKOWER visited the zoo and was so impressed by Suzan, an orang utan, that he decided to dedicate his next game to her. On the following day he played 1 b4 against MARÓCZY. The opening had been studied and practised by the Moscow mathematician Nikolai Vasilyevich Bugayev (1837–1903), whose analysis was published in *Shakhmatnoye Obozreniye* just before his death.

B. Fleissig–Schlechter   Friendly game Vienna, 1893
Orang Utan Opening

1 b4 e6 2 Bb2 Nf6 3 a3 c5 4 b5 d5 5 d4 Qa5+ 6 Nc3 Ne4 7 Qd3 cxd4 8 Qxd4 Bc5 9 Qxg7 Bxf2+ 10 Kd1 d4 11 Qxh8+ Ke7 12 Qxc8 dxc3 13 Bc1 Nd7 14 Qxa8 Qxb5 15 Bf4 Qd5+ 16 Kc1 Be3+ 17 Bxe3 Nf2 18 Bxf2 Qd2+ 19 Kb1 Qd1+ 20 Ka2 Qxc2, an EPAULET MATE.

Orenburg Defence, 53, the NIMZOWITSCH QUEEN'S PAWN DEFENCE, analysed in the 1920s by Utretsky and Argunov from the Russian city of Orenburg.

organization, the formal structure of chess-playing, developed with the railways as travel became more practical in the middle of the 19th century. Chess clubs were increasingly common at the beginning of the century and the first organization beyond that level was the Yorkshire Chess Association, formed in 1841. Soon its membership extended and in 1844 its annual meeting was in Nottingham. In 1852 it became the Northern and Midlands Counties Chess Association, and in 1857, as it enlarged, simply the Chess Association. In 1862 its title changed to British Chess Association, although the name had been used informally for some years. The BCA had a fitful existence, became dormant, was revived in 1885, and expired around 1892. In 1865 North Yorkshire and Durham Chess Association was formed, to become the Yorkshire Chess Association in 1867 and the Counties Chess Association in 1870. The CCA was more provincial and initially more aligned to amateur chess than its rival, the BCA, but had a similar mixed success and faded away around 1893, although nominally it was associated with Craigside tournaments until 1901. A Scottish Chess Association was founded in 1884, Irish in 1885, and South Wales in 1888. The Metropolitan Chess Clubs Competition, 1887, became the London Chess League in 1893 and with the Southern Counties Chess Union (SCCU), 1892, Midlands CCU, 1897, and Northern CCU, 1899, became the basis of the British Chess Federation (BCF).

A West German chess federation was formed in 1861 followed by a North German in 1868 and a Central German in 1871, and they developed into the Deutscher Schachbund of 1877. Other national organizations were being formed at the time—Netherlands in 1873, Bohemia in 1886, for example. In the USA a number of short-lived national associations were formed, often in conjunction with a master tournament. By 1888 seven State associations existed and they formed a USCA, but that too disappeared. The Western Chess Association was founded in 1900. An offshoot was the National Chess Federation (1926). In 1934 the WCA enlarged to become the American Chess Federation which in 1939 merged with the NCF to form the USCF. An All-Russian chess federation was not formed until 1914 despite efforts by JAENISCH and CHIGORIN, and the same year saw the first unsuccessful attempt to create an international body, an attempt stifled by war. Ten years later FIDE began operations, although it was a feeble infant at first.

In addition to organizations set up to further the aims of over-the-board players, there are local, national or international bodies to look after the interests of juniors, correspondence chess players, problemists, study devotees, collectors of sets, philatelists, professional players, blind players, arbiters, and chess journalists.

organ pipes, a problem idea originated by LOYD in 1857 and named by the German architect Georg Schnitzler. Two black rooks and two black bishops are aligned on a file or on a rank, and in the main variations each bishop interferes with each rook, and vice versa.

#3

The pioneer problem by Loyd, *Chess Monthly*, 1857. After the INTRODUCTORY PLAY 1 Rd4+ exd4 White plays 2 Qc5, setting up a BLOCK. This is a CUTTING-POINT THEME showing Grimshaw interference.

    2 ... Bg7 or Bg6 3 Qg5#
    2 ... Rg7 or Rf6 3 Qxd4#
    2 ... Rf7 or Rg6 3 Nh5#
    2 ... Bf7 or Bf6 3 Qf5#.

By-play 2 ... Be5 3 Qc1#. After 2 ... Rg7 there is a dual, 3 Qd6#.

Orléans, Charles d' (1391–1465), French prince, poet, and chessplayer, father of Louis XII of France. At an early age he married the widow of Richard II of England. Taken prisoner by the English at the battle of Agincourt (1415), he was ransomed 25 years later. He greatly enjoyed his captivity, writing poetry of distinction, hunting, and playing chess—a theme in many of his poems, including one on the death of his wife. The first verse, given here (in medieval French), plays on the double meaning of *dame*, lady and chess queen:

J'ay aux eschecs joué devant Amours,
Pour passer temps, avecques Faulx Dangier;
Et seurement me suy gardé tousjours
Sans riens perdre jusques au derrenier
Que Fortune lui est venu aidier
Et par Meschief, que maudite soit elle,
A ma dame prise soudainement:
Parquoy suy mat, je le voy clerement
Se je ne fais une dame nouvelle.

orphan, a FAIRY PROBLEM piece invented by the American composer David Leo Brown (1945–) in 1971. It stands immobilized and powerless unless attacked, in which event it assumes the powers of the attacking man or men. The orphan transfers these powers to orphans of the opposite colour if it attacks them, creating a kind of chain reaction.

Orphans are shown as circles

1 Nf6+ cannot be played because White's own king would then be in check.

orthodox chess, the game played in accordance with the laws, as distinct from the many variants of the game known collectively as UNORTHODOX CHESS.

Orthodox Defence, 186 in the QUEEN'S GAMBIT Declined, a name originally given by TARRASCH to show contempt for its timidity, as contrasted with the TARRASCH DEFENCE, 118, which he considered the only correct line. The most favoured continuations for White are 7 Qc2 and 7 Rc1. (See ATKINS.)

orthodox problem, traditionally a DIRECT MATE PROBLEM consisting of a legal position and play that conforms to the laws. In 1968, however, the FIDE Problem Commission, meeting at Arcachon, declared that HELPMATES and SELFMATES should also be regarded as orthodox when, except for the special mating requirements, the laws of the game are observed. Castling is permitted unless its illegality can be proved. A composer must not use more men of any kind than the number in the ARRAY. Another convention concerns OBTRUSIVE PIECES; some tourney judges object to these and some take a more lenient view, but few approve the use of an obtrusive piece if the composer's idea could be shown otherwise. Many problems that require RETROGRADE ANALYSIS to demonstrate the correctness of the KEY (e.g. an EN PASSANT capture) must by definition conform to the laws if the normal board and men are used; yet they are not classified as orthodox problems. (See also PROBLEM.)
J. M. Rice, *An ABC of Chess Problems* (1970).

o-t-b, abbreviation for OVER-THE-BOARD, usually printed in lower case letters.

Oudot, Jean (1926–74), French problemist and author, International Judge of Chess Compositions (1959), problem editor of *Europe Échecs* from 1959 until his death, mathematics teacher. He composed all types of problems, but is chiefly remembered for his fairies.

#4

A problem by Oudot, first prize, *L'Echiquier de France*, 1957. The key is 1 a5 and there are two continuations, each showing the INDIAN THEME.
1 ... Nc5   2 Rxc5 a6   3 Be5 Kg5 4 Bf6#
1 ... Nb8(c7)   2 Bxb8(c7) a6   3 Re5 Kg3 4 Re4#.

outpost, a square on the fifth, sixth, or seventh rank that is guarded by a pawn but cannot be attacked by an enemy pawn, especially such a square on an open file. One player's outpost is the opponent's HOLE. Possession of an outpost is likely to be advantageous if it can be occupied by pieces, a salient in enemy territory.

Karpov–Kasparov   Lyon 1990 World Championship
17th match game   Grünfeld Defence Exchange Variation

1 d4 Nf6 2 c4 g6 3 Nc3 d5 4 cxd5 Nxd5 5 e4 Nxc3 6 bxc3 Bg7 7 Be3 c5 8 Qd2 0-0 9 Nf3 Bg4 10 Ng5 cxd4 11 cxd4 Nc6 12 h3 Bd7 13 Rb1 Rc8 14 Nf3 Na5 15 Bd3 Be6 16 0-0 Bc4 17 Rfd1 b5 18 Bg5 a6 19 Rbc1 Bxd3 20 Rxc8 Qxc8 21 Qxd3 Re8 22 Rc1 Qb7 23 d5 Nc4 24 Nd2 Nxd2 25 Bxd2 Rc8

26 Rc6 (White occupies the outpost, a means of gaining control of the open file. The offer of a pawn cannot be accepted because of the BACK-RANK MATE.) 26 ... Be5 27 Bc3 Bb8 28 Qd4 f6 29 Ba5 Bd6 30 Qc3 Re8 31 a3 Kg7 32 g3 Be5 33 Qc5 h5 34 Bc7 Ba1 35 Bf4 Qd7 36 Rc7 Qd8 37 d6 g5 38 d7 Rf8 39 Bd2 Be5 40 Rb7 Black resigns.

For other examples, see ADAMS; HARRWITZ; JANOWSKI; SCHLECHTER; TAL.

outside passed pawn, or remote passed pawn, a PASSED PAWN on the flank that is furthest from the enemy king or from other pawns on the board. In a pawn ending an outside passed pawn might decoy the enemy king, leaving the defender's other pawns open to attack. The decoy may also be effective in other kinds of endgames, or in other phases of the game. In the middlegame, however, an outside passed pawn may sometimes become a weakness, because it is hard to defend. (See ÓLAFSSON, H.)

Overbrook Press, see ALTSCHUL.

overload, to burden (a piece or pawn) with too many defensive tasks. A player who has an overloaded man commonly has to give ground.

(no White king given)

One of Damiano's *subtilita*, i.e. examples which might be of use to players. The black queen, defending both h7 and f7, is overloaded, and White wins by 1 Qxh7+ Qxh7 2 Nf7 mate. In problems, overloading is called FOCAL PLAY.

overprotection, a term used by NIMZOWITSCH to describe a long-established general principle: a player controlling the centre, or some other strategically important point, should strengthen and consolidate this control.

over-the-board, a description of a game in which the players meet across the board, as distinct from CORRESPONDENCE CHESS, for example.

Owen, John (1827–1901). English player, vicar of Hooton, Cheshire, from 1862 to 1900. In 1858, playing under the pseudonym 'Alter', he lost (=2−5) a match against MORPHY, who conceded pawn and move. (This poor result was attributed by HOFFER to Owen's just having married.) Subsequently Owen played better. He drew a match with KOLISCH in 1860 (+4−4) and at the London tournament of 1862 took third prize, after ANDERSSEN (whom he defeated) and PAULSEN, ahead of DUBOIS, G. A. MACDONNELL, STEINITZ, and BLACKBURNE. From 1857 to 1898 Owen played in more than a dozen tournaments, all of them in Great Britain. He liked close openings and often played the QUEEN'S FIANCHETTO DEFENCE, sometimes named after him, and the LARSEN OPENING.

Owen Defence, 443, the QUEEN'S FIANCHETTO DEFENCE, which OWEN played frequently in the 19th century. He often defended any opening by 1 . . . b6 or 1 . . . g6 and as often began a game by 1 b3 or 1 g3.

P

Pachl, Franz (1951–), German problemist, International Judge of Chess Compositions (1988), International Master for Chess Compositions (1989). His speciality is direct-mate two-movers and helpmates. Another of his hobbies is mini-golf, at which he was German champion in 1977.

#2

A problem by Pachl, first prize, *The Problemist*, 1980, showing the Zagoruiko Theme (see CHANGED PLAY). The key is 1 Qb4 threatening 2 Bxe5#:

1 ... exd5   2 Bf5#
1 ... exd4   2 Qxd4#.

There are three tries:

1 e8 = Q? (refuted by 1 ... Nf8):
1 ... exd5?   2 Rf4#
1 ... exd4?   2 Qxe6#
1 Qe1? (refuted by 1 ... Ng5):
1 ... exd5?   2 Nf5#
1 ... exd4?   2 Rf4#
1 Qa8? (refuted by 1 ... Nf6):
1 ... exd5?   2 Qxd5#
1 ... exd4?   2 Re5#.

Pachman, Luděk (1924–), Czech-born player, national champion seven times from 1946 to 1966, International Grandmaster (1954), brother of Vladimír PACHMAN. He won three zonal tournaments and competed in four successive interzonal tournaments: Saltsjöbaden 1948, Saltsjöbaden 1952, Göteborg 1955, and Portorož 1958. He came nearest to being a CANDIDATE on the last occasion, when he was seventh and the first six qualified. He won minor tournaments at Mar del Plata 1959 (shared with NAJDORF), Sarajevo 1960, Mariánské Lázně 1960, Graz 1961, and Athens 1968 (+7=8). His best tournament achievement was at Havana 1963, when he came second (+11=10) equal with GELLER and TAL, half a point behind KORCHNOI. Pachman

represented his country in all eight Olympiads from 1952 to 1966, playing at first board except in 1956 when he went down one place.

An unquestioning Communist from his youth, Pachman re-examined his position in the light of the consequences of the 'Prague spring' of 1968, and became implacably hostile to his former beliefs. As a result he was imprisoned twice (1969–70, 1972). Describing his political life in *Checkmate in Prague* (1975) he relates that he intentionally jumped head first from his bed on to the floor of his cell, which caused permanent injury to his head and spine. In 1972, obtaining permission to leave Czechoslovakia, he became a chess professional in West Germany, and added a second 'n' to his surname. For some years he was boycotted by the Communist bloc, but at the Manila interzonal 1976 he had a simultaneous disaster and triumph: he shared last place, but forced recognition from his enemies, who were obliged to meet him in play. Later that year he played in the Olympiad for his adopted country, West Germany, and in 1978 he won its championship.

Ståhlberg–Pachman   Amsterdam Olympiad 1954
Queen's Gambit Declined Slav Defence

1 d4 d5 2 c4 c6 3 Nf3 Nf6 4 Nc3 dxc4 5 a4 Bf5 6 e3 e6
7 Bxc4 Bb4 8 0–0 Nbd7 9 Qe2 0–0 10 e4 Bg6 11 Bd3 h6
12 Bf4 Qe7 13 Na2 Ba5 14 b4 Bd8 15 Rab1 Rc8 16
Ne5 Bh7 17 Nc4 Bc7 18 Bxc7 Rxc7 19 Nc3 Nb6 20
Nxh6 axb6 21 e5 Nd5 22 Bxh7+ Kxh7 23 Nxd5 cxd5
24 Qb5 Rc6 25 g3 Qc7 26 a5

26 ... Kg8 27 axb6 Rxb6 28 Qa5 Rc6 29 Qxc7 Rxc7 30
Rfd1 Rc4 (decisive use of OUTPOST) 31 Ra1 Rfc8 32
Rdb1 Rxd4 33 Ra7 Rb8 34 b5 Re4 35 Rc1 d4 36 Rd1
Rxe5 37 Rxd4 Rxb5 38 Rd7 g5 39 Kg2 h5 40 Ra4 Kg7
41 h4 g4 42 Ra7 Kg6 43 Rc7 Rb2 44 Re7 Rb5 White
resigned during the adjournment.

The first of Pachman's writings to become popular were his earliest books on openings, published in Prague in 1948, and later translated into English.

His three-volume *Strategie moderního šachu* (1948–50) and his two-volume *Taktika moderního šachu* (1962) followed a similar course, but the English versions were abridged. *Modern Chess Strategy* (1963) was condensed into one volume, and *Modern Chess Tactics* (1970) was a shortened version of the first of the two volumes on the subject. *Meine 100 besten Partien und meine Probleme* was published in 1978. (See DOUBLE BISHOP SACRIFICE.)

Pachman, Vladimír (1918–84), Czech composer, International Judge of Chess Compositions (1956), International Grandmaster for Chess Compositions (1975). Besides orthodox THREE- and MORE-MOVERS he also composed studies, and is one of the few who have achieved success in both fields. He was the brother of Luděk PACHMAN and the great-nephew of the Czech problemist Josef Cumpe (1868–1943), whose influence he acknowledged; but his style is highly individual: he neither slavishly followed Czech tradition nor cared for current fashions.

+

A study by Pachman, third prize, *The Problemist*, 1982–3. 1 Ng5 Rf5 2 Ne4+ Kf3 3 Nd2+ Kxe3 4 Ra3+ d3 5 Ra4 c4 6 Rxc4 Re5 7 Ra4 (TEMPO-PLAY by White's rook forces the advance of the black a-pawn.) 7 ... Re6 8 Rb4 a6 9 Rc4 Re5 10 Ra4 Re6 11 Rb4 a5 12 Ra4. Black, in ZUG-ZWANG, loses the exchange.

V. Pachman, *Vybrané šachové skladby* (1972, 2nd edn., 1979), contains 427 compositions.

Pachman Variation, 372 in the KING'S INDIAN DEFENCE.

Padevsky, Nikola Bochev (1933–), Bulgarian champion 1954, 1955, 1962, and 1964, International Grandmaster (1964), lawyer.

painting and chess, see ART AND CHESS.

pairing, arranging opponents in a tournament. For an ALL-PLAY-ALL event PAIRING TABLES are used, the players drawing by lot for number. A SWISS SYSTEM tournament presents greater problems. There are three basic rules for pairing in such a competition:

no two players should meet more than once; as far as possible players should be drawn against opponents with the same score; and each player should have a balanced number of games with white and black pieces. These conditions imply that the pairing for a round can be made only after all games from preceding rounds have been completed. This is not always possible and various ways have been devised to make suitable pairings when some games remain unfinished. Some organizers interpret Swiss system pairing requirements liberally, in order for example to ensure that a local player meets a sufficient number of rated players and thus has the opportunity of achieving a NORM.

B. M. Kažić, *The Chess Competitor's Handbook* (1980).

pairing tables. These are used to pair opponents for each round of an ALL-PLAY-ALL tournament. In *Deutsche Schachzeitung*, 1886, pp. 134–7, Richard Schurig (1825–96) published tables for tournaments with from three to 24 players, allowing for the bye where applicable. These tables have been used ever since. The rounds do not have to be played in the sequence given. For example, in the Hastings international tournament of 1895 the round number was drawn from a hat each morning to discourage preparation. With scant regard for chess history FIDE calls Schurig's creation 'Berger tables' because BERGER gave them, duly acknowledged, in his two *Schachjahrbücher* (1892–3 and 1899–1900).

Palciauskas, Victor (1941–), Lithuanian-born player, who moved to the USA at the age of eight, International Grandmaster for Correspondence Chess (1983), World Correspondence Chess Champion 1984, professor of geophysics.

Panno, Oscar Roberto (1935–), the strongest Argentine-born player up to his time, International Grandmaster (1955), civil engineer. After tying with PARMA for first place in the World Junior Championship 1953, he won the title on tie-break, and in the same year won the Argentine championship. In 1955 he qualified as a CANDIDATE by taking third place (+9=8−3) in the Göteborg interzonal. In the consequent Candidates tournament, Amsterdam 1956, he shared eighth place, his nearest approach to the world title.

Unsuccessful in the interzonal of 1958, Panno largely gave up competitive chess for about ten years while he attended to his profession. Then he came first in three strong tournaments: Buenos Aires 1968 (+8=2−1), ahead of NAJDORF; Palma de Majorca 1971 (+7=8), a tie with LJUBOJEVIĆ, ahead of PORTISCH and LARSEN; and Palma de Majorca 1972 (+6=8−1), a tie with KORCHNOI and SMEJKAL, ahead of Ljubojević and POLU-GAYEVSKY. Other good results in the 1970s include Buenos Aires 1977, second (+6=4) after SANGUI-NETI; Buenos Aires 1978, second (+4=9) equal with SMYSLOV and VAGANYAN, after ANDERSSON; and in a Swiss system event, Lone Pine 1976, he shared second place with eight other grandmasters, half a point behind PETROSYAN. In the Argentine championship, 1975, he had the same score as Najdorf, but lost on tie-break. However, he was outright winner again in 1985. Panno played in several Olympiads from 1954, making the best second-board score (+ 10 = 8) at Havana 1966.

Panno–Hort   Havana 1966 Olympiad   King's Indian Defence Zinnowitz Variation

1 c4 Nf6 2 Nc3 g6 3 e4 d6 4 d4 Bg7 5 Be2 0–0 6 Bg5 c5 7 d5 e5 8 g4 a6 9 a4 h6 10 Bd2 Qd7 11 h3 Kh7 12 Nf3 Qe7 13 a5 Nbd7 14 Be3 Rb8 15 Nd2 Ne8 16 h4 f5 17 gxf5 gxf5 18 exf5 Nef6 19 Nde4 Nxe4 20 Nxe4 Nf6

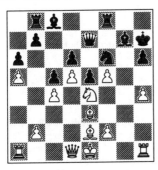

21 Ng5+ hxg5 22 hxg5+ Kg8 23 gxf6 Qxf6 24 Qd2 e4 25 Rg1 Bxf5 26 Bg5 Qd4 27 Be7 Bh7 28 Qxd4 cxd4 29 Bxd6 d3 30 Be5 Black resigns.

Panno System, 423 in the KING'S INDIAN DEFENCE, played with the aim of building up an attack on the white pawn at c4, no longer to be defended by a bishop.

Panno Variation, 419 in the KING'S INDIAN DEFENCE, introduced to master play by PANNO around 1955.

Panov, Vasily Nikolayevich (1906–73), Soviet player and author, International Master (1950), journalist. He won the Moscow championship in 1929, competed in six USSR championships from 1929 to 1948 with modest results, and achieved his best tournament win (+ 10 = 6 − 1) at Kiev 1938. Panov is remembered, however, for his openings investigations, his reporting as chess correspondent of *Izvestia* 1942–65, and for his many books. He wrote, in Russian, a beginner's book, several manuals of the game, a book of the Moscow tournament of 1956, biographies with games of ALEKHINE and CAPABLANCA, and *Kurs debyutov* (1957), an excellent general guide to the openings which ran to many editions, and was Russia's best-selling book on the subject. (See ESTRIN.)

V. Panov, *Sorok let za shakhmatnoi doskoi* (1966), an autobiography with 50 games; Ya. B. Estrin, *Vasily Panov* (1986), 80 games and extensive additional material.

Kotov–Panov   Moscow Championship 1936   King's Indian Defence

1 d4 Nf6 2 Nf3 g6 3 c4 Bg7 4 Nc3 0–0 5 g3 d6 6 Bg2 Nc6 7 d5 Nb8 8 0–0 e5 9 e4 Nbd7 10 Qc2 a5 11 a3 Nc5 12 Be3 Ng4 13 Bxc5 dxc5 14 h3 Nh6 15 Rab1 Re8 16 Nd2 f5 17 b4 Bf8 18 Na2 Nf7 19 Kh2 f4 20 Nb3 axb4 21 axb4 cxb4 22 c5

22 ... Ng5 23 Rfd1 f3 24 h4 Nxe4 25 Bxf3 Rxa2 26 Qxa2 Nc3 27 Qd2 Qf6 28 Bg2 e4 29 Rbc1 Nxd1 30 Rxd1 Qc3 31 Qe3 Bf5 32 Kg1 Qxe3 33 fxe3 Bh6 34 Re1 Re5 35 Bf1 c6 36 dxc6 bxc6 37 Bc4+ Kf8 38 Kf2 Bg4 39 Kg1 Ke7 40 Kg2 Rf5 41 Be2 Bxe2 42 Rxe2 Rd5 43 Kf2 Rd3 44 Na5 Kd7 45 Nc4 Ke6 46 g4 Kd5 47 Nb2 Ra3 48 Rd2+ Kxc5 49 g5 Bg7 White resigns.

Panov–Botvinnik Attack, 583. Analysed in *Deutsches Wochenschach* in 1911 by KRAUSE, recommended by SCHLECHTER, and re-examined by PANOV in 1930, this variation of the CARO–KANN DEFENCE became popular after BOTVINNIK played it in his first and ninth match games against FLOHR, 1933. The name Krause–Panov System is sometimes given. (See DAKE; EUWE.)

Panov Variation, 656 in the BISHOP'S OPENING, suggested by PANOV *c.*1960; 12 Nbd2 Bb7, a possible continuation of the CHIGORIN VARIATION (746) in the SPANISH OPENING, first played Verlinsky–Panov, Moscow 1944, with the idea of playing Pd6–d5 and opening the centre in due course; 1272 in the ALEKHINE DEFENCE, played Rubinstein–Spielmann, Moscow 1925, and brought back into fashion by Panov–Mikenas, Moscow Championship 1943. Also 524, the KERES VARIATION in the SICILIAN DEFENCE; 584, the BOTVINNIK VARIATION of the CARO–KANN DEFENCE; 685, the KOPAYEV VARIATION.

pao, a piece used in CHINESE CHESS. When not capturing it is moved like a rook; captures are possible only when the man to be taken lies beyond an intervening man, of either colour, on the same rank or file. On an otherwise empty board, place a white pao at c3, a man of either colour at c5, and a black man at c6 or c7 or c8. The pao can be moved as far as a3, h3, c1 or c4; it does not threaten (or guard) the piece at c5, but can capture the man that lies beyond. For the pao's kin, see CHINESE FAMILY.

Paoli Variation, 959 in the TWO KNIGHTS DEFENCE, an unexpected move, devised by Enrico Paoli (1908–   ), aimed to sustain pressure on the squares e4 and f5. Although an IM, Paoli's fame lies in his endgame studies.

Paris Defence, 936, the SEMI-ITALIAN OPENING, which has similar ideas to the PHILIDOR DEFENCE.

Paris Gambit, 1325, sometimes called the Amar Gambit, an interesting sacrifice.

Parisian Opening, 58, the VERESOV VARIATION under its TARTAKOWER disguise.

Paris Opening, 1324, probably so named by TAR-TAKOWER, who, however, also called it the Amar Opening. It has also been styled the Sanz Opening.

Parma, Bruno (1941–), World Junior Champion 1961, International Grandmaster (1963), journalist. A leading Yugoslav player for many years, he was a member of his country's team in many Olympiads from 1962, his defensive skill being maximized by adroit team selection. He won or shared first place in four strong international tournaments: Bucharest 1968 (+5=7); Sarajevo 1970, equal with LJUBO-JEVIĆ; Natanya 1971, equal with KAVALEK; and Vršac 1973, equal with TRINGOV. Parma also had good results at Amsterdam 1965, a second place (+3=6) after DONNER, and at Zagreb 1965, fourth (+5=14), shared with PORTISCH, after IVKOV, UHL-MANN, and PETROSYAN, and ahead of BRONSTEIN and LARSEN.

Parma–Balashov   Moscow 1971   Sicilian Defence
Najdorf Variation

1 e4 c5   2 Nf3 d6 . 3 d4 cxd4   4 Nxd4 Nf6   5 Nc3 a6   6 Bg5 e6   7 f4 Qc7   8 Qf3 b5   9 Bxf6 gxf6   10 e5 Qb7   11 Ne4 fxe5   12 fxe5 dxe5

13 Bd3 f5   14 Nxe6 fxe4   15 Bxe4 Qb6   16 Nxf8 Rxf8   17 Qh5+ Rf7   18 Qxe5+ Be6   19 0–0–0 Raa7   20 Rd6 Qe3+   21 Kb1 Rae7   22 Rxe6 Black resigns.

Páros, György (1910–75), Hungarian composer who used his original surname, Schlégl, up to 1932. International Judge of Chess Compositions (1956), International Grandmaster for Chess Compositions (1975), doctor of law. He began as a successful composer of orthodox TWO-MOVERS; later he became the world's foremost composer of HELP-MATES. (See TWINS.)

#2

A problem by Páros, *Magyar Sakkvilág*, 1931. The key is 1 Rb4 threatening 2 Qd7#:

1 ... Rg4   2 Nxf5#
1 ... Rf3   2 Qxe4#
1 ... Ref4   2 e3#
1 ... Rff4   2 dxe4#.

partial retrograde analysis, or PRA, RETROGRADE ANALYSIS that reveals two or more hypotheses about the history of a position; these establish the legality of two or more forward lines of play so that if any one line is legal the others are not.

#2 PRA

A problem by the English composer William Langstaff (1897–1974), *Chess Amateur*, 1922. Two solutions are possible: 1 Ke6 (assuming Black has moved K or R) 1 ...~   2 Rd8#; 1 h5xg6 ep (assuming Black has not moved K or R) 1 ... 0–0 2 h6–h7#. There is no means of discovering which solution is 'correct'. This is a 2-choice PRA problem. Examples of 5-choice PRA have been composed, usually involving complex retrograde analysis.

In 1859 LOYD toyed with partial analysis, but it was the publication of a fine example by the Danish composer Umro Niels Høeg (1876–1951) in *Deutsches Wochenschach*, 1907, that led to the investigation of many new ideas in this field.

partie, a French word meaning 'game' once commonly used in English, now an affectation. In her otherwise well-researched novel *The Chess Players* Frances Parkinson Keyes describes the Morphy–Mongrédien match of 1859: 'The first game ... resulted in a draw; in the second Paul scored seven parties one after another; and the third slipped from his opponent's grasp after a ten-hour struggle.' This curious gaffe may have arisen from unclear reports of the match, which MORPHY won $(+7 = 1 - 0)$.

passar battaglia, an Italian phrase meaning 'dodging the fight' and referring to the absence of an EN PASSANT law: a pawn on its fifth rank was unable to capture an enemy pawn passing by on an adjoining file. The option of advancing a pawn two squares forward on its first move was probably a 13th-century innovation and *passar battaglia* would then have been the normal practice. Even after the *en passant* capture was introduced, probably in the 15th century, there were some curious exceptions: both DAMIANO and Ruy LÓPEZ state that such a capture could not be made if it brought about a DISCOVERED CHECK. The *passar battaglia* law survived in several parts of Europe for a long time, finally disappearing in 1880 when the Italians revised their laws.

passed pawn. A pawn is passed when no enemy pawns on the same or an adjoining file stand on the ranks ahead. Only a piece can prevent the advance of such a pawn. (See BELYAVSKY; YUSUPOV.)

pat, French for stalemate, and indicated in problem STIPULATIONS by the letter p. However, the Italian word *patta* simply means a draw.

patents, in the chess world, fall mainly into two categories, clocks and self-writing boards. The first granted British patent relating to chess, taken out in 1884 by Amandus Schierwater of Liverpool, was for a carriage clock with two knobs on the top and three small additional dials. One dial shows the number of moves played and whose turn it is, the others show time taken by each player. One of the most recent inventions is also a clock, this time the idea of FISCHER (see TIMING OF MOVES).

Perhaps the earliest Russian chess patent, around 1871 by F. E. Brandt of St Petersburg, was a self-writing chessboard, the Scaccograph, operated by batteries driving electro-magnets. Although this objective was not realized in an acceptable form until the electronic revolution of the 1980s, the number of earlier attempts reveal the perceived need. In 1884 M. Hours-Humbert, a Besançon lawyer, and around 1887 Dr Wurtemberger of Zurich made boards like Brandt's. In 1903 Lala Raja Babu, Superintendent of the Palace Games Department of the Maharaja of Patiala, was granted a British patent for a mechanically driven board 'thereby doing away with the necessity of a referee or the assistance of a third party to write down the moves ...' Unlike the earlier models it printed the moves in descriptive notation, and controlled the time-pieces. In 1929 DURAS and J. Simunek obtained a German patent for a device that recorded the departure and arrival squares, and as late as 1945 Arthur W. Fey of Pennsylvania spent more than $1,000 on patents and materials for a board that did no more than the Scaccograph.

The first German patent was in the next most popular area for inventions, unorthodox chess. It

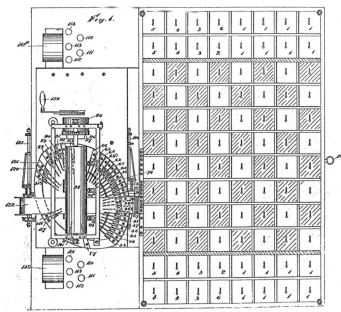

One of the technical drawings accompanying a patent registered in 1903 by Lala Raja Babu for the design of a chessboard that would automatically record the moves

was granted in 1881 to A. Krause for a board with triangular 'squares'. In 1868 a provisional British patent was issued to a Mr Owen for magnetic pieces, but it was never taken up. Other ideas include travelling sets using a cork board and men with sharp points on the base, boards with rubber rings on each square to secure the men, and a board with a disc under each square which can be rotated to show the man occupying it, obviating the need for a set. Other patents relate to pocket sets, diagrams, chess stationery, sets in which the pieces stack within the larger men, and even the boxes.

patronage, in chess as elsewhere, gives status to the game, and often provides financial sponsorship as well. From its earliest days chess has been associated with rulers, giving it a superior image, but with the increase in PROFESSIONALISM there is a need for money as well as glory. The great players cannot copyright their creations, the game scores, so they need income from other sources. Increasingly this has come from patronage, individual or corporate. A Cuban sugar tycoon gave $25,000 towards the costs of the world championship match in 1921. The Nottingham 1936 tournament was underwritten by J. N. Derbyshire, the world championship match of 1972 would not have happened without the financial injection from SLATER. More often a company sponsors a tournament with which its name is associated, a public relations exercise which works well if the public regards chess as prestigious and its players as role models. In the BUNDESLIGA some chess teams are backed financially by the main clubs of which they form part. A recent development is the sponsorship of an individual player by a company, as for example in the case of KAMSKY who has been supported to the extent of 1,000,000 francs by a French property company. (See BENEDICT; PIATIGORSKY; SLATER; ROTHSCHILD.)

patzer, a weak player, from the German *Patzer*, one who bungles or botches.

Paulsen, Louis (1833–91), one of the great chess theoreticians, and a player ranking among the world's best half-dozen in the 1860s and 1870s. Born in Nassengrund, Germany, of a chess-playing family, he learned the game young but showed no special enthusiasm for it at this time. In 1854 he joined his brother Ernst's tobacco business in Iowa, USA. Louis entered America's first important tournament, New York 1857, and took second place after MORPHY. Then he began to take chess seriously, although he remained an amateur throughout his life. He built up a reputation as a blindfold expert, achieving the unprecedented feat of playing fifteen opponents simultaneously (although his usual number was ten), and he studied '. . .with such zeal that I don't like to lose five minutes of time'. For two years he tried in vain to arrange a match with Morphy, and in the autumn of 1860 he returned home to work in the family agricultural business. (It included a distillery; Paulsen himself

was a lifelong teetotaller and non-smoker.)

His best tournament results were: Bristol 1861, first, ahead of KOLISCH; London 1862, second to ANDERSSEN; Hamburg 1869, second to Anderssen after a play-off; Leipzig 1877, first ($+9-2$), ahead of Anderssen, ZUKERTORT, and WINAWER; Frankfurt 1878, first; and Leipzig 1879, second, after ENGLISCH. Paulsen's style was better suited to match play, at which he was undefeated. He drew with Anderssen in 1862 ($+3=2-3$) and led Kolisch ($+7=18-6$) in an unfinished match, 1861. He defeated NEUMANN in 1864 ($+5=3-2$), Anderssen in 1876 ($+5=1-4$) and again in 1877 ($+5=1-3$), and SCHWARZ in 1879 ($+5-2$). His last tournament was at Breslau 1889 when he shared fourth place — no mean achievement, for he was already suffering from the diabetes that caused his death.

Quiet and unassuming, Paulsen was a thinker rather than a doer. 'He is extremely diffident', wrote STAUNTON, 'rarely speaking unless spoken to.' Paulsen discovered a larger number of opening ideas than any of his contemporaries. For the attack he contributed to the SCOTCH GAME, the GÖRING GAMBIT, the PAULSEN ATTACK, the PAULSEN VARIATIONS of the Vienna Game and of the FOUR KNIGHTS OPENING. For the defence he discovered the BOLESLAVSKY VARIATION, the PAULSEN DEFENCE of the KIESERITZKY GAMBIT, and the Paulsen Variation of the SICILIAN DEFENCE. He introduced the PIRC DEFENCE, and improved Black's chances in the MUZIO GAMBIT and in several lines of the Sicilian Defence. His contributions were not confined to an odd move or random improvements: he also invented whole systems of play. He introduced 3 Nc3 (after 1 e4 e6 2 d4 d5) in the FRENCH DEFENCE, a move that revitalized White's prospects when no one else could think of anything better than 3 exd5, and he experimented with 3 e5, later adopted by NIMZOWITSCH. From the NORMAL POSITION of the EVANS GAMBIT he developed a defensive system that is still regarded as the best, and he introduced the FIANCHETTO in many openings. The architect of the Sicilian Defence, he invented the DRAGON VARIATION, which remains popular, and he pioneered the KING'S INDIAN DEFENCE, still a much-played defence to the QUEEN'S PAWN OPENING. He also worked out a defensive system against the then popular ANDERSSEN VARIATION of the SPANISH OPENING, a set-up successfully adopted by STEINITZ in the thirteenth game of his match with Anderssen in 1866.

Of even greater consequence was Paulsen's influence on the THEORY of the game: how play should be conducted. Around 1860 most players sought direct attack, and they often obtained considerable advantage when they had the first move. Much openings analysis was centred on White's attacking possibilities, and most of Paulsen's ideas were improvements for Black. The first great master of defence, he believed that sound defences were always possible, that Black could maintain the equilibrium, that attacks by White would then fail; and on this understanding the theory of play attributed to Steinitz was founded.

In his games Paulsen's defensive notions often encouraged premature attacks. He would sometimes move pieces *backwards*; surely, his contemporaries thought, this must be wrong. The first to realize that advantage might subsist in the possession of the TWO BISHOPS, he would withdraw them to safe squares even if he thereby aggravated his defensive difficulties. He was the great sceptic of his time. Like LASKER after him, he was aware of the need to re-examine all long-held assumptions. When Morphy offered to concede odds of pawn and move, Paulsen's reply, that he wished to consider whether such odds might favour Black, was treated with derision; but it was not an unreasonable view, especially considering Morphy's attacking skill, which might benefit materially by possession of the HALF-OPEN FILE.

Paulsen wrote no books, and none has been written that explains adequately his theoretical contributions. H. Paulussen, *Louis Paulsen* (1982), is a valuable collection of material on the whole Paulsen family, but two-thirds of the book relates to the subtitle, *Das Schachspiel in Lippe 1900–1981*, a topic of limited interest; *Weltgeschichte des Schachs: Morphy und Paulsen* (1967) contains 113 of Paulsen's games. (See MUZIO GAMBIT.)

Paulsen–Zukertort   Leipzig 1877   Four Knights Opening Classical Defence

1 e4 e5 2 Nf3 Nc6 3 Nc3 Nf6 4 Bb5 Bc5 5 0–0 d6 6 d4 exd4 7 Nxd4 Bd7 8 Nf5 0–0 9 Bg5 Bxf5 10 exf5 Nd4 11 Bd3 d5 12 Bxf6 gxf6 13 Na4 Qd6 14 Nxc5 Qxc5 15 Qg4+ Kh8 16 Qh4 Rg8 17 Qxf6+ Rg7 18 c3 Nc6 19 Rae1 Rag8

20 Re3 Qd6 21 Qxd6 Rxg2+ 22 Kh1 cxd6 23 f6 Ne5 24 Bxh7 Ng4 25 Bxg8 Nxe3 26 Bxf7 Black resigns.

Paulsen–Alapin Attack, 696, the WORMALD VARIATION.

Paulsen Attack, 632, sometimes called the American Attack or Steinitz Variation in the VIENNA GAMBIT, as Paulsen–Blackburne, Breslau 1889, but the move had been first played in master chess four months earlier, by LIPSCHÜTZ at New York 1889; 665, a CENTRE GAME variation given by STAMMA and named after PAULSEN's brother Wilfried (1828–1901); 987, a SCOTCH GAME line sometimes called the Blackburne Variation, as Paulsen–Anderssen, Leipzig 1877; 1019 in the PHILIDOR DEFENCE, with

the idea of continuing 5 ... Qxd5 6 Qe2+; 1103 in the BISHOP'S GAMBIT, from the 11th game of Paulsen's match with KOLISCH, played in London in 1861, although the move is to be found in Schulten–Morphy, New York 1857; 1240 in the FRENCH DEFENCE, the most favoured continuation of the NIMZOWITSCH VARIATION, as in the first game of Paulsen's match against SCHWARZ in 1879.

Paulsen–Bird Variation, 876, the PAULSEN VARIATION in the EVANS GAMBIT.

Paulsen Defence, 1163, one of the best ways of meeting the KIESERITZKY GAMBIT, mentioned by GRECO, played by PAULSEN in the 1860s.

Paulsen Variation, 545. Probably originated by ANDERSSEN, who played it in his third match game against Suhle in 1859, this line, occasionally called the Kan Variation, brought the SICILIAN DEFENCE back into circulation after a temporary eclipse induced by fear of the SZÉN VARIATION. (See FILIP; NUNN.)

Also 557 in the Sicilian Defence, from the first match game Anderssen–Paulsen, 1876 (see ANDERSSEN; POSITIONAL PLAY); 624 in the VIENNA GAME, played five times by PAULSEN in the Vienna 1873 tournament; 775 in the SPANISH OPENING, as Anderssen–Paulsen, Leipzig 1877; 836, a line in the FOUR KNIGHTS OPENING introduced by Paulsen in the 1870s, and later favoured by NIMZOWITSCH after whom it is sometimes named; 876, successfully played by Paulsen against KOLISCH in the Bristol tournament 1861, and now a standard defence, occasionally known as the Paulsen–Bird Variation, in the EVANS GAMBIT; 878 in the same opening, this time from W. Paulsen in the early 1860s; 997 in the SCOTCH GAME, as Paulsen–Minckwitz, Brunswick 1880; 1143 in the MUZIO GAMBIT, from the 6th match game Kolisch–Paulsen 1861; 1183 in the FRENCH DEFENCE, another novelty from the match against Kolisch in 1861.

Also 504, the LIPNITSKY ATTACK in the SICILIAN DEFENCE; 979, the ANDERSSEN COUNTERATTACK in the SCOTCH GAMBIT; 990, the BLACKBURNE ATTACK; 1157, the POLERIO DEFENCE.

Pauly, Wolfgang (1876–1934), composer of German birth who settled in Romania at the age of five, and came to be regarded as the greatest problemist of his adopted country. He is best known for his FAIRY PROBLEMS, for which he was an early enthusiast, and his MORE-MOVERS; but he liked to explore all aspects of problem composition, and among other things acquired a reputation for TWINS. He assisted A. C. WHITE with a few Christmas Series books, notably *Asymmetry* (1927). As a young man he tried his hand at mathematics and astronomy, and he is credited with the discovery of a comet (1898 VII); later he became an actuary. (See MAXIMUMMER.)

Pavlov Variation, 903 in the EVANS GAMBIT

Declined, an idea of the Soviet player Dmitry Nikolayevich Pavlov (1870–1942), although it had been considered by the American analyst Stasch Mlotkowski (1881–1943) in *British Chess Magazine*, 1917.

pawn, the chessman of smallest size and value represented by the symbol P or the figurine ♙. A pawn can be moved neither sideways nor backwards but only forwards on its file, one or two squares on its first move, one square at a time subsequently. When a capture is made by a pawn it is moved one square diagonally forward and not in any other way. So that a pawn making its first move cannot evade capture by a pawn on an adjoining file the EN PASSANT law was introduced. Place a white pawn on e2 and a black pawn on f4 and if White plays Pe2–e4 Black may capture *en passant*: the pawn at f4 is placed on e3 (fxe3 ep) and the pawn at e4 is removed from the board. When a pawn is moved to the eighth rank it must immediately and as part of the same move be replaced by a queen, rook, bishop, or knight of the same colour, a procedure known as promotion. At the start of the game each player has eight pawns, one on each square of his second rank, and they are named by the files on which they stand. The a-pawn (standard notation) is the queen's rook's pawn or QRP (descriptive notation). The description may change: if an a-pawn makes a capture it becomes a b-pawn. The rook's pawn (on the a- or h-file) attacks one square, the others two.

The pawn is the only chessman that cannot capture in the same direction as it can be moved, and its path may be blocked by an enemy man; the man of least value, the pawn can threaten pieces, usually forcing them to withdraw; these characteristics, its slow pace, its inability to retreat (to correct a rash advance), and the possibility of promotion are the basis of most of the game's strategy: the pawn formation dictates the course of play. (See SCHOOLS OF CHESS.) On account of improved technique the loss of a pawn is regarded more seriously than in former times and TARTAKOWER could write in the 1920s, 'Never lose a pawn and you will never lose a game.' Beginners often ignore this advice in order to lock their pieces in combat.

The name derives from the Anglo-French word *poun* and ultimately from a direct translation of the

Arabic word *baidaq*, a foot soldier. In the old game the pawn could be promoted only to a FIRZĀN or FERS. Neither in SHAṬRANJ nor in early European chess could the pawn be advanced two squares on its first move, an innovation that apparently dates from the 13th century.

pawn and move, a handicap that consists of playing Black and removing the pawn at f7 before start of play. These were the time-honoured odds frequently offered by PHILIDOR, DESCHAPELLES, and other leading masters of the past. They rarely played even. The last player able to hold most of the best players of his time at these odds was BOURDONNAIS, who died in 1840 'pawn and move better than any English player'. In 1860 MORPHY offered pawn and move to any player in the world. None of his strongest rivals responded, nor is it likely that he could have defeated them on these terms, so far had the standard of play improved by this time. The last important match at pawn and move, offered by STEINITZ to DE VERE, took place in London, 1865–6. De Vere won (+ 7 = 2 − 3).

De Vere–Steinitz   4th match game 1865   (remove Black's f-pawn)

1 d4 Nf6 2 Nc3 e6 3 e4 Bb4 4 Bg5 h6 5 Bxf6 Qxf6 6 e5 Qf7 7 Bd3 0–0 8 Nf3 Nc6 9 0–0 Be7 10 Ne4 b6 11 c3 Bb7 12 Bc2 Bd8 13 Qd3 g6 14 Rae1 Kg7 15 Ng3 Ne7 16 Nh5+ Kh8 17 Nf6 Nf5 18 g4 Bxf6 19 gxf5 gxf5 20 exf6 Rg8+ 21 Kh1 Qh5 22 Bd1 Rg4 23 Rg1 Rag8 24 c4 Be4 25 Qe3 R8g5

Black threatens 26 ... Qxh2+ 27 Kxh2 Rh5+ 28 Nh4 Rgxh4+ 29 Kg3 f4+ 30 Qxf4 Rh3+ 31 Kg4 R5h4 mate. 26 Qxe4 fxe4 27 Nxg5 Rxg1+ 28 Rxg1 Qg6 29 f7 Qf6 30 Bh5 hxg5 31 Rxg5 Qxg5 32 f8=Q+ Kh7 33 Qf7+ Kh6 34 Bd1 Qd2 35 Qh5+ Kg7 36 Qg4+ Kf8 37 Kg2 Qxd4 38 h4 Qxc4 39 h5 Qxa2 40 Qf4+ Kg8 41 Qg5+ Kf7 42 Qg6+ Ke7 43 Qg7+ Black resigns.

pawn and two moves, or pawn and two, a handicap consisting of playing Black, removing the f-pawn before start of play, and allowing White to commence with two moves instead of one. These are severe odds and some masters prefer to offer a knight instead. The most important match at pawn and two took place in 1821. For many years DESCHAPELLES had been champion of the CAFÉ DE LA RÉGENCE, and reputedly the best player in France. Challenged by his pupil BOURDONNAIS, he agreed to a match of seven games at pawn and two. He lost them all. In 1846 STAUNTON defeated HARRWITZ (+12 = 1 − 9). He conceded odds in some of the games with the following curious results:

even	+7 = 0 − 0
pawn and move	+1 = 1 − 6
pawn and two	+4 = 0 − 3.

Atwood–Verdoni London, 1796 (remove Black's f-pawn)

1 e4 ... 2 d4 e6 3 Bd3 c5 4 d5 d6 5 c4 e5 6 f4 exf4 7 Bxf4 Qf6 8 Qd2 Bg4 9 h3 Bh5 10 Nc3 h6 11 Nce2 g5 12 Be3 Bg7 13 Rb1 Nd7 14 g4 Bg6 15 Ng3 Ne5 16 Qe2 Ne7 17 Nf5 Bxf5 18 exf5 0–0–0 19 b4 b6 20 bxc5 dxc5 21 Nf3 Rhe8 22 Kf2 N7c6 23 Nxe5 Nxe5 24 Qc2 Rd7 25 Rhe1 Rde7 26 Qb3 Qd6 27 Bf1

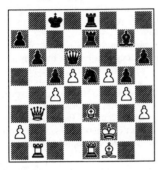

27 ... Nxg4+ 28 hxg4 Rxe3 29 Rxe3 Bd4 30 Rbe1 Qf4+ 31 Kg2 Bxe3 and Black won. See game under DESCHAPELLES.

pawn centre, pawns occupying the CENTRAL ZONE, especially the CENTRE PAWNS. To give up the centre is to exchange so that one is left without a centre pawn on the fourth rank while the opponent has one or two so placed. Players commonly advance one or both of the centre pawns to form a pawn centre, hoping as a consequence to gain SPACE and MOBILITY, and the form the centre takes influences the strategy of the game. Sometimes a player defers setting up a pawn centre until ready to give it the full support of the pieces, an idea pioneered by STAUNTON. There are many kinds of pawn centre, including a BLOCKED CENTRE, a CLASSICAL CENTRE, a DEFENSIVE CENTRE, a FIXED CENTRE, a HALF-CENTRE, and a SMALL CENTRE. (See SCHOOLS OF CHESS.)

pawn chain, specifically, united pawns aligned on a diagonal; generally, the pawns that form, in effect, a player's front line. A player's pieces may be developed outside the pawn chain (in front of the pawns), or behind the pawn-chain (at the rear of the pawns).

pawn configuration, see PAWN FORMATION.

pawn ending, an endgame with kings and a pawn or pawns only. (See KASPAROV.)

pawn formation, the situation of the pawns of one or both colours, on all or part of the board. A flexible or elastic pawn formation is one in which there are options of advancing the pawns in several different ways. It is often inadvisable, or even impossible, to move some of the pawns; in consequence the pawn formation tends to be static, or to change slowly. In closed or partly closed situations it forms a matrix that determines both the mobility of the pieces and the strategy of the game.

There are two principal ways in which the pawns influence the play: their mobility or lack of it, and the squares which they can or cannot guard. A single pawn that is blocked has little mobility; it cannot control the square to which it would advance. Two or more UNITED PAWNS, however, may become a force in themselves, for one may support the advance of another. Thus the principal characteristic of the pawn formation concerns the collective mobility of the pawns. (Significantly, players do not speak of a piece formation: the prospects of each piece may be considered separately.)

Flexible pawn formations tend to increase mobility, which may be decreased by ISOLATED, DOUBLED, or BACKWARD PAWNS. An overall assessment, however, must take account of many other factors.

This position may arise after 1 e4 e5 2 Nf3 Nc6 3 d4 exd4 4 Nxd4 Nf6 5 Nxc6 bxc6 6 Bd3 d5 7 exd5 cxd5 8 Bb5+ Bd7 9 Bxd7+ Qxd7 10 0–0 Be7. Does the advantage lie with Black, who has a pawn in the centre, or with White, with fewer PAWN ISLANDS? This question cannot be answered. An exhibition game between TARTAKOWER (White) and CAPABLANCA, 1914, continued 11 Nd2 0–0 12 b3 Rfe8 13 Bb2 Rad8 14 Nf3 Ne4 15 Qd3 Bc5 16 Rad1 Re6 17 c4 (This attack, although correct in principle, appears to be mistimed.) 17 ... Rd6 18 Rde1 f5 19 Bd4 Bxd4 20 Nxd4 Qf7 21 Nb5 R6d7 22 Rc1 dxc4 23 Qxc4 Qxc4 24 bxc4 c6 25 Na3 Rd2 and Black won the endgame. By 17 c4 White attacks Black's pawns, but after 20 ... Qf7 it becomes apparent that Black is attacking White's pawns. Such transformations are not uncommon. Assessment of a pawn formation always depends on a keen perception of the tactical possibilities, the so-called dynamic factors.

Botvinnik–Petrosyan World Championship 1963, 18th match game Queen's Gambit Declined Exchange Variation

1 d4 d5 2 c4 e6 3 Nc3 Be7 4 cxd5 exd5 5 Bf4 c6 6 e3 Bf5 7 g4 Be6 8 h3 Nf6 9 Nf3 Nbd7 10 Bd3 Nb6 11

Qc2 Nc4 12 Kf1 Nd6 13 Nd2 Qc8 14 Kg2 Nd7 15 f3 g6
16 Rac1 Nb6 17 b3 Qd7 18 Ne2 Ndc8 19 a4 a5 20 Bg3
Bd6 21 Nf4 Ne7 22 Nf1 h5 23 Be2 h4 24 Bh2 g5
25 Nd3 Qc7 26 Qd2 Nd7 27 Bg1 Ng6 28 Bh2 Ne7 29
Bd1 b6 30 Kg1 f6 31 e4 Bxh2+ 32 Qxh2 Qxh2+ 33
Rxh2 Rd8 34 Kf2 Kf7 35 Ke3 Rhe8 36 Rd2 Kg7 37
Kf2 dxe4 38 fxe4 Nf8 39 Ne1 Nfg6 40 Ng2 Rd7 41 Bc2
Bf7 42 Nfe3

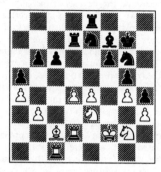

White has a CLASSICAL CENTRE, and supposes these pawns
to be strongly placed. Black induces one of them to
advance, blocks them both with knights, and shows that
White's HANGING CENTRE is a source of weakness. 42 ... c5
43 d5 Ne5 44 Rf1 Bg6 45 Ke1 Nc8 46 Rdf2 Rf7 47
Kd2 Nd6 48 Nf5+ Bxf5 49 exf5 c4 50 Rb1 b5 51 b4
c3+ 52 Kxc3 Rc7+ 53 Kd2 Nec4+ 54 Kd1 Na3 55
Rb2 Ndc4 56 Ra2 axb4 57 axb5 Nxb5 58 Ra6 Nc3+
59 Kc1 Nxd5 60 Ba4 Rec8 61 Ne1 Nf4 White resigns.

pawn island, a group of pawns of one colour
separated by at least one file from any others of the
same kind. For example, after 1 e4 c6 2 d4 d5 3
Nc3 dxe4 4 Nxe4 Nf6 5 Nxf6+ gxf6 White has
two pawn islands, Black three. As PHILIDOR pointed
out, the fewer the pawn islands the more likely are
the pawns to be mobile and easy to defend, considerations of greater consequence in the endgame
than in the middlegame. One of the aims of the
MINORITY ATTACK is to saddle the opponent with
more pawn islands. Generally, however, the possession of fewer islands is not of itself decisive.

pawn majority, see MAJORITY.

pawn minority, see MINORITY.

pawn promotion, see PROMOTION.

pawn race, a race for promotion between rival
pawns. See SVESHNIKOV for an example.

pawns game, an unorthodox game said to have
been invented by LEGALL. White places from seven
to nine extra pawns anywhere on the third or fourth
rank and plays without the queen, or adds three or
four extra pawns and plays with only one rook.

pawn skeleton the general structure of the pawns
as the game emerges from the opening phase. The
term is apt, for the pawns are the backbone of the
game and shape its character.

pawn snatching, capturing pawns at the cost of
position—fiddling while Rome burns. See, for example, the game given under BOLBOCHÁN, in which
his opponent grabs a centre pawn and is unable to
complete his development. (See also POISONED
PAWN.)

Pawn Storm Variation, 283, graphic name for a
line in the HROMÁDKA DEFENCE which may lead to
the MIKENAS VARIATION and so sometimes bears that
name.

pawn weakness, a pawn or pawns that are hard to
defend or that lack mobility. A square that cannot
be guarded by a pawn, and is hard to defend as a
consequence, might also be called a pawn weakness, or more precisely a weakness in the PAWN
FORMATION.

There may be weakness in ISOLATED, BACKWARD,
DOUBLED, or HANGING PAWNS, but they are equally
likely to be of no account, or even a source of
strength. The situation of the pieces and the DYNA-
MIC FACTORS (SEE EVALUATION OF POSITION) determine whether any characteristic of the pawn formation is weak or otherwise. Examination may reveal
that an apparent pawn weakness is merely notional;
if it cannot be attacked it is not a weakness. Masters
sometimes permit apparent weaknesses in their own
camp while they pursue other aims, an imbalance
characteristic of creative play.

A player can more easily improve the position of
a piece than that of a pawn, which cannot be moved
backwards. Therefore, some pawn weaknesses are
called permanent. However, a pawn that is
obstructed and apparently helpless may gain mobility later.

Many beginner's books give negative advice
about the pawns, recommending, for example, that
one should avoid being left with an isolated pawn.
Instead players should, on occasion, be willing to
accept such a pawn: they will improve their understanding of pawn formations and be better able to
judge when the possession of such a pawn could be
advantageous. Players afraid of isolated pawns
should take up some other game.

Pelikán Variation, 488 in the SICILIAN DEFENCE,
named after the Czech-born Argentinian Jiří
Pelikán (1906–84); the line had been played
in Tarrasch–Mieses, Nuremberg 1888, and
Schlechter–Lasker, match 1910 (hence the common
name, Lasker–Pelikán Variation), but was largely
forgotten until strengthened by Pelikán in the
1950s. (See SHORT.) Also 1179 in the FRENCH
DEFENCE, as Pelikán–Ståhlberg and Pelikán–Vuko-
vić, Buenos Aires 1947.

pendulum draw, a POSITIONAL DRAW in which the
final moves of the main variation consist of moving
a piece to and fro. There is no precise definition, but
the piece should swing over a reasonable distance,
and the end should not be perpetual check.

21 Nh7 Be5 22 Qxh6 Re6 23 Nxf6+ Rxf6 24 Bxf6 Bxf6 25 Re3 Be5 26 Rh3 Qe7 27 Rh5 f5 28 Qg6+ Qg7 29 Qe6+ Qf7 30 Qc8+ Qf8 31 Qxc7 Bg7 32 Rxf5 Qe8 33 Rg5 Qf8 34 Rxa5 cxb2 35 Ra7 Black resigns.

=

A study by the Romanian composer Virgil Nestorescu (1929–), second place, match, Romania–Bulgaria, 1975. 1 Re6 Nd6 2 Rxd6 Bc4+ 3 Kb6 Bf2+ 4 Kc6 Bxd5+ 5 Kxd5 h3 6 Kc6 Ne7+ 7 Kb5 h2 8 Ka6 Kc7 9 Rd1 Bg1 10 Rd8 Ba7 11 Rd1 Bg1 12 Rd8 Ba7.

Penrose, Jonathan (1933–), the leading English player during the 1960s, International Master (1961), International Correspondence Chess Grandmaster (1983), lecturer in psychology. Early in his chess career Penrose decided to remain an amateur and as a consequence played in few international tournaments. He won the British championship from 1958 to 1963 and from 1966 to 1969, ten times in all (a record). He played in nine Olympiads from 1952 to 1974, notably scoring +10=5 on first board at Lugano 1968, a result bettered only by the world champion, PETROSYAN. In the early 1970s he further restricted his chess because the stress of over-the-board play adversely affected his health. He turned to correspondence play, was the highest rated postal player in the world 1987–9, and led the British team to victory in the 9th Correspondence Olympiad.

Penrose–B. Vukcević (Yugoslavia) 9th Correspondence Olympiad 1982–5 Spanish Opening Planinc Variation

1 e4 e5 2 Nf3 Nc6 3 Bb5 a6 4 Ba4 Nf6 5 0–0 b5 6 Bb3 Bb7 7 Re1 Bc5 8 c3 d6 9 d4 Bb6 10 Bg5 h6 11 Bh4 0–0 12 a4 exd4 13 axb5 axb5 14 Rxa8 Bxa8 15 cxd4 Re8 16 Nc3 g5 17 Qd2 Na5 18 Bc2 b4 19 Nxg5 bxc3 20 Qf4 Bxd4

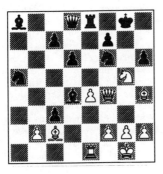

periodicals, or chess magazines, began with *Le Palamède*, Paris, 1836. The editor, BOURDONNAIS, said that although he had 263 subscribers, 120 would have been sufficient. When he died in 1840 the magazine lapsed, but a second series, also published in Paris, ran from December 1841 to 1847. The earliest British magazine, *The Philidorian*, was started by WALKER in December 1837 but had only six monthly issues. Garrick's Chess Divan (see COFFEE HOUSES) offered its habitués a single-sheet serial, *Curious Chess Problems*, the first to be devoted solely to that aspect of chess, from January 1840. A few weeks later a sister publication, *Games of Chess*, was launched. At the end of August 1840 the two were merged into *The Palamede*, which seems to have ended in September 1841.

The first important periodical in English, *The Chess Player's Chronicle*, sprang from the *British Miscellany* in 1841, was edited by STAUNTON until 1854, and continued in various guises until 1902; the final ten years or so were fitful. The German periodical *Schachzeitung* first appeared in 1846, became the *Deutsche Schachzeitung* in 1872 and, except for the years 1945–9, carried on until December 1988. The *British Chess Magazine*, founded in 1881 and still active, has the longest unbroken run. The Soviet bi-monthly *64* has sold the most copies of an issue, 100,000. Among the more famous serials are *La Stratégie* (France), 1867–1940, founded by PRETI; STEINITZ'S *International Chess Magazine* (USA), 1885–91; the official Dutch magazine, originally *Tijdschrift van den Nederlandschen Schaakbond* but the name has changed since then, 1893– ; *Wiener Schachzeitung* (Austria), 1898–1916, 1923–38, 1948–9, noted for its first period when MARCO was editor; *Shakhmaty v SSSR* (USSR), under that name 1931–91; *Chess* (England) 1935– ; *Shakhmatny Byulletin* (USSR), 1955–90; *Chess Informant* (Yugoslavia), 1966– ; and *New in Chess* (Netherlands) 1984–

There have been perhaps 2,000 chess serials, mostly short-lived. Some aim at a restricted group such as a club or a special aspect of chess. *The British Correspondence Chess Association Magazine*, 1906–20, *Raumschach* (1909) (three-dimensional chess), *Chess Reader*, 1955–66 (bibliography), *EG* 1965– (endgame), *ICCA Journal* 1977– (computer chess), *GSM-Zeitschrift* 1977– (chess-related postage stamps), and *The Chess Collector* 1988– (chess sets) were each the first in its field.

Perkonoja, Pauli Kalervo (1941–), Finnish study composer, International Master for Chess Compositions (1969), International Judge of Chess Compositions (1972). He is better known for his remarkable solving skill, and in 1982, the year of its inception, he alone was awarded the title of International Solving Grandmaster.

Perlis, Julius (1880–1913), Viennese player, born in a part of Russia that is now Polish, lawyer. Perlis first came into prominence when he took ninth place among 36 competitors at Ostend 1906, a tournament organized for the purpose of finding new talent. He played in strong tournaments at Vienna 1908, St Petersburg 1909, and Carlsbad 1911, scoring modestly. Still improving, he achieved his best result at San Sebastián 1912, when he came fifth after RUBINSTEIN, NIMZOWITSCH, SPIELMANN, and TARRASCH, ahead of DURAS, SCHLECHTER, and TEICHMANN. Perlis never reached his peak. A keen mountaineer, he set out alone for an Alpine climb on a misty September morning and was found dead two days later.

perpetual check, an unstoppable series of checks usually instigated to avoid loss of the game. Although not defined as a draw in the LAWS, perpetual check must lead eventually to a draw by three-fold repetition of position, or under the FIFTY-MOVE LAW, if not by agreement sooner. See the game under REPETITION OF POSITION.

perpetual retrogression, a retro-analytical series of illegal positions: moves can be retracted in perpetuity, but none leads back to the ARRAY.

#5

The pioneer problem by HUNDSDORFER, *Münchener Neueste Nachrichten,* 1908. Black's last move was Pc7–c5 and the preceding move by White 1 ... Rc6–b6. The solution begins 1 bxc6 ep Bxb6 2 Qe5 dxe5 3 Bxe5. The solver is required to discover by means of RETROGRADE ANALYSIS why Black's last move must have been 1 ... Pc7–c5.

Black has made five captures with the f-pawn and one with the a-pawn, and has promoted the h-pawn to a dark bishop after capturing the other missing white man at g1. The black d-pawn was moved long ago to release the light bishop. The only other last move which could have been made is an advance of the c-pawn.

The following retro-variations (retracted moves in backward order) show why Black's c-pawn cannot have been moved from c6: 1 ... c6–c5 2 Bc7–

b8 Bb8–a7 3 Bd8–c7, and now 3 ... c7–c6 leaves White's dark bishop illegally placed, 3 ... Bc7–b8 leaves White in RETRO-STALEMATE (i.e. having no last move), while 3 ... Qa7–a8 or 3 ... Ba7–b8 leads to the endless shuffling of the dark bishop and the black queen in their little cage: i.e. perpetual retrogression.

Peruvian Variation, 172, the VENICE VARIATION, played by the Peruvian player CANAL.

Petkov, Petko Andonov (1942–), Bulgarian composer, International Grandmaster for Chess Compositions (1984), International Judge of Chess Compositions (1989). He is able to compose TWO- and THREE-MOVERS of high quality but is better known for problems of a less orthodox kind, having been especially successful with SELFMATES.

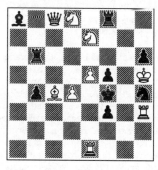

#2

A problem by Petkov, *Shakhmatna Misl,* 1981. The key is 1 Bf7 threatening 2 Qc1 ‡.

   1 ... Ng2   2 Qxf5 ‡
   1 ... Rc6   2 Nd5 ‡
   1 ... Bc6   2 Ne6 ‡.

The Nowotny interference (see CUTTING POINT THEMES) is echoed in the try 1 Qc6? (1 ... Rxc6 2 Nd5 ‡, 1 ... Bxc6 2 Ne6 ‡), but is refuted by 1 ... Rxd8. The key shows white CORRECTION: the other tries are 1 Bd5? Rc6; 1 Be6? Bc6; 1 B~? Ng2.

Petkov, *Izbrani shakhmatni zadachi* (1982) contains 222 problems.

Petroff, Alexander Dmitryevich (1794–1867), the best Russian player of his time. He learned the moves when he was 4 years old, improved his game at St Petersburg, where he lived from the age of 10, and became the best player of the city before he was 20. His maternal grandfather, Ivan A. Sokolov, a senator, used his influence to get his grandson on the Commission of Requests, which examined all petitions to the Tsar. In 1840, at the invitation of Field Marshal Prince Paskevich of Poland, Petroff went to Warsaw as Under-secretary of State.

Petroff won matches against JAENISCH in the 1840s, URUSOV in 1853 (+2=2) and 1859 (+13=1–7), and Ilya S. Shumov (1819–91) in

1862 ($+4-2$), but he never played the leading masters of Western Europe. An able analyst, he assisted Jaenisch in the development of the Petroff Defence and other opening variations. Petroff did not fully retire until 1863. He then made a trip to Dieppe, where he happened to meet a London Chess Club player, D. M. Salter. As a result they played over 200 games at odds of pawn and two moves. Salter described him as tall, with a broad forehead and large grey eyes, adding that 'goodness and sagacity dwelt on his face'.

Besides his nickname 'the Russian Bourdonnais' Petroff was also called 'the Northern Philidor', but not simply on account of the coincidence of initials; Petroff's *Shakhmatnaya igra* (1824) owes much to PHILIDOR. This handbook, of which 300 copies were printed, consists of five parts, published in two volumes: I, beginner's advice and definitions; II, laws, a few short games, and 289 maxims for players, form the first volume, in DESCRIPTIVE NOTATION. The second volume, in STANDARD NOTATION, comprises III, the openings and fictitious games from Philidor's book; IV, other openings; V, endgames, puzzles, and problems. Largely a compilation from earlier writers, Petroff's book had little influence on the development of the game. He also wrote a series of articles, 'Scenes from a Chessplayer's life' (1844), translated many times (e.g. *Le Palamède*, 1845), and also a draughts primer.

I. M. Linder, *Alexander Dmitryevich Petrov* (1952, 2nd edn, 1955) is a biography with games and bibliography.

Petroff Defence, 1052, also called the Russian Defence. Although dating from LUCENA, this defence was not thought satisfactory for Black until JAENISCH published an extensive analysis in the French magazine *Le Palamède*, April 1842. After 3 Nxe5 PETROFF discovered the true worth of 3 ... d6, a move attributed to COZIO; Petroff and Jaenisch examined this move thoroughly, and it supplanted the older moves 3 ... Nxe4 (Lucena) and 3 ... Qe7 (Ruy LÓPEZ). Jaenisch implies that Petroff was the abler analyst, and the name seems appropriate. The defence served its turn in the 1840s (to avoid the SCOTCH GAMBIT) and in the 1850s (to avoid the SPANISH OPENING). It first occurred in a world championship match in 1969, played by PETROSYAN, and has been played by other grandmasters such as SMYSLOV, KARPOV, and YUSUPOV, but has never achieved wide popularity. (See SPACE; THEORETICAL NOVELTY; WEISS.)

Petroff Gambit, 648 in the BISHOP'S OPENING, but can arise from the PHILIDOR DEFENCE. Attributed to PETROFF by JAENISCH, who thought that acceptance favours Black.

Petrosyan, Tigran Vartanovich (1929–84), Soviet player, International Grandmaster (1952), World Champion 1963–9. He was born in Tbilisi of Armenian parents. They taught him draughts and backgammon when he was 4, and he believed these games were excellent preparation for chess, which he learned a few years later. His parents died when he was 16, and, needing to help the rest of the family, he took over his father's job as a caretaker of an officers' home. He found consolation in chess, and soon began to win junior events and local championships. In 1946 he went on his own to live at Yerevan, having been touched by the enthusiasm of Armenian supporters when he went there to play, and won the Armenian championship in 1946 and 1948. In 1949 he moved to Moscow, where in 1951 he won the city championship, and came second ($+8=7-2$) equal with GELLER after KERES in the USSR championship, his third attempt. In the Saltsjöbaden interzonal 1952 he was second ($+7=13$) equal wth TAIMANOV, after KOTOV. The youngest of 15 CANDIDATES, he took fifth place ($+6=18-4$) at Neuhausen–Zurich 1953, one of the strongest four tournaments held up to that time. These achievements placed him among the world's best seven or eight players.

As if he had come too far too fast, his career seemed to pause. In his next interzonal, Göteborg 1955, he came fourth ($+5=15$) and qualified for another outstanding Candidates tournament, Amsterdam 1956, in which he scored $+3=13-2$ and shared third place. There was almost a repeat performance in the next championship cycle: he shared third place in the Portorož interzonal 1958, and came third ($+7=17-4$) in the following Candidates tournament. Petrosyan was, however, making advances on the home front. He won the Moscow championship of 1956 and had outstanding results in four consecutive strong USSR championships: 1958, second ($+5=12$), after TAL; 1959, first ($+8=11$); 1960, second ($+10=7-2$) equal with Geller, after KORCHNOI; and 1961, first ($+9=9-1$). At the Stockholm interzonal 1962 he scored $+8=14$, shared second place, and became a Candidate for the fourth time; then, at Curaçao 1962 he took first place ($+8=19$) and at last became challenger.

His world championship match against BOTVINNIK took place in 1963, and after a struggle lasting two months Petrosyan won the title ($+5=15-2$). He paid tribute to BOLESLAVSKY's 'invaluable help' as trainer and second. During his championship years Petrosyan competed in seven strong international tournaments; he played as a champion should at Los Angeles 1963, scoring $+4=9-1$ to tie with Keres for first prize, but his only other first place was at Buenos Aires 1964, when he scored $+8=9$ and again shared the victory with Keres. In 1966 he met his first challenger, SPASSKY. By winning ($+4=17-3$), Petrosyan became the first world champion since STEINITZ to defeat his closest rival in match play. In 1968 he won the Moscow championship ($+6=9$) for the third time, and successfully presented to Yerevan University his M.Phil. dissertation, 'Chess Logic', widely said to have cost him more money than time. Meeting Spassky again, in 1969, Petrosyan lost a match that ended on his fortieth birthday (17 June); later that

year he again won the USSR championship
(+ 6 = 16), after a play-off in which he defeated
POLUGAYEVSKY (+ 2 = 3 − 1).

Petrosyan was selected as Candidate for the next
two championship cycles, and he had no difficulty
qualifying subsequently; but he was less successful
in the Candidates matches: in 1971 he defeated
HÜBNER (+ 1 = 6) and Korchnoi (+ 1 = 9) but lost to
FISCHER; in 1974 he defeated PORTISCH (+ 3 = 8 − 2)
then lost to Korchnoi; and in 1977 and 1980 he lost
to Korchnoi in the quarter-final matches.

His best achievements after 1969 were: San Antonio 1972, first (+ 6 = 9) equal with KARPOV and
Portisch; Amsterdam 1973, first (+ 6 = 8 − 1) equal
with PLANINC; Manila 1974, second (+ 5 = 9), after
VASYUKOV; Milan 1975, second (+ 2 = 9) equal with
Karpov and LJUBOJEVIĆ, after Portisch; Biel interzonal 1976, second (+ 6 = 12 − 1) equal with Portisch and Tal, after LARSEN; Tallinn 1979, first
(+ 8 = 8); Rio de Janeiro interzonal 1979, first
(+ 6 = 11) equal with Hübner and Portisch; Las
Palmas 1980, first (+ 6 = 5) equal with Geller and
MILES; and Tilburg 1981, second (+ 3 = 8), after
BELYAVSKY.

Petrosyan played frequently for Soviet teams,
usually with excellent results: in ten Olympiads
from 1958 to 1978 he won prizes for the highest
score six times, and made a remarkable total for the
ten events + 79 = 50 − 1. His performances in the
USSR championship are also notable for their
consistency. After his fledgling appearances in 1949

and 1950 he was (in some cases shared): first in
1959, 1961, 1969, and 1975; second in 1951, 1958,
1960, and 1973; third 1955, 1976, and 1977; fourth
1954. His only 'failures' were in 1957 (equal
seventh) and 1983 (equal sixth).

Influenced by NIMZOWITSCH's works, Petrosyan's
style was largely characterized by PROPHYLAXIS: the
anticipation of any plan his opponent might devise.
He preferred non-committal play, gradually
improving the position of his men, and keeping his
options open so that he could strike at the right
moment. In the opening phase he did not strive
unduly for the initiative, seeking scope for manœuvre rather than sharp play. Like all great masters
he could play any kind of game should the need
arise, but his preference was for a close game in
which gain of space and control of key squares are
more important than time. His considerable endgame skill was the necessary concomitant. His
cautious and deeply positional style was not widely
appreciated, or even understood, by those below
master level. He drew many games, partly because
of the 'negative' characteristics of his style, but also
because, on occasion, he showed a lack of fighting
spirit. Draws may be of little account in a match, or
even in a match-tournament of leading masters (e.g.
the Curaçao Candidates tournament), but the loss
of half a point is of greater significance in other
events. From 1952 to 1984 he played in more than
50 strong international tournaments, and,
unusually for a leading master, won more second

Petrosyan playing at the Alekhine Memorial Tournament, Moscow, 1971

prizes (17) than first prizes (16). A few weeks before his death from cancer he had to withdraw from the USSR team to play the Rest of the World.

Petrosyan was chief editor of the monthly *Shakhmatnaya Moskva* from 1963 to 1966, and the weekly paper *64* from 1968 to 1977. Allegedly this last post was taken from him as punishment for losing to the 'renegade' Korchnoi, but indolence was the more probable factor. (See BLOCKED CENTRE; PAWN FORMATION; TWO BISHOPS.)

Strategiya nadezhnosti (1985) contains a biography and career results, 100 annotated games, and a further 31 games without notes; E. Shekhtman, *The Games of Tigran Petrosian* (1991, 2 vols), is a collection of more than 2,000 games.

Hübner–Petrosyan   Candidates match 1971 7th game
Sicilian Defence Scheveningen Variation

1 e4 c5 2 Nf3 d6 3 Nc3 e6 4 d4 cxd4 5 Nxd4 Nf6 6 Be3 Be7 7 f4 Nc6 8 Qf3 e5 9 Nxc6 bxc6 10 fxe5 dxe5 11 Bc4 0-0 12 h3 Be6 13 Bxe6 fxe6 14 Qe2 Rb8 15 0-0 Rxb2 16 Rab1 Rb4 17 Qa6 Qc7 18 a3 Rxb1 19 Rxb1 Ra8 20 a4 h6 21 a5 Kh7 22 Qb7

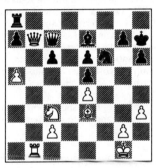

22 ... Qxa5 23 Qxa8 Qxc3 24 Qxa7 Nxe4 25 Rf1 Bh4 26 Rf7 Bf6 27 Kh2 Qxc2 28 Qd7 Qb3 29 Bf2 Qd5 30 Qa7 Qd2 31 Qe3 Qc2 32 Be1 c5 33 h4 c4 34 Rc7 Qd3 35 Qf3 Qb1 36 Qe3 Nd6 37 Qd2 Nf5 38 Rxc4 e4 39 Qc2 Qxe1 40 Rxe4 Be5+ White resigns.

Petrosyan System, 280, a treatment of the HROMÁDKA DEFENCE, usually leading to the CZECH VARIATION, employed by PETROSYAN in the 9th game of his match with SPASSKY in 1969. (See BERLINER; BLOCKED CENTRE; NIKOLIĆ.)

Petrosyan Variation, 157, sometimes called the Alatortsev Variation, in the QUEEN'S GAMBIT Declined, played by GUNSBERG in 1904 and three times by PETROSYAN in his world championship match, 1963 (see M. GUREVICH); 339 in the QUEEN'S INDIAN DEFENCE, favoured by Petrosyan in the 1960s and by KASPAROV in the 1980s (see BENJAMIN; SALOV); 399, a line in the KING'S INDIAN DEFENCE known since the 1920s but much used by Petrosyan in conjunction with 8 Bg5, if permitted by Black's response (see STEIN); 1194 in the FRENCH DEFENCE, an unusual move played in Sakharov–Petrosyan, Tbilisi 1956,

and Ólafsson–Petrosyan, Bled 1961.

Petrov, Vladimir (1908–43), Latvian player, champion of Riga 1926, 1932, and 1936, winner of national championship tournaments in 1930 (with a clean score), 1934 (shared with APŠENIEKS), and 1937. He entered several strong tournaments during the 1930s, usually with moderate results but with one outstanding achievement, at Kemeri 1937, when he came first (+9=6−2) equal with FLOHR and RESHEVSKY, ahead of ALEKHINE, KERES, and FINE. At Łódź 1938 he scored +6=7−2, and shared third place after PIRC and TARTAKOWER. He made the best third-board score (+9=5−2) at the Prague Olympiad 1931, and while he was playing in his seventh and last Olympiad, Buenos Aires 1939, war began. He returned home, his country was annexed (June 1940), and he became a Soviet citizen. Subsequently he came tenth in the USSR championship 1940, and second (+7=1−2) after RAGOZIN at Sverdlovsk 1942. He died in a prison camp at Vorkuta.

Petrović, Nenad (1907–89), Yugoslav composer, International Judge of Chess Compositions (1956), International Grandmaster for Chess Compositions (1975), civil engineer. His compositions include problems of all kinds: ORTHODOX, retro-analytical, HELPMATE, SELFMATE, MAXIMUMMER, and others, with an emphasis on TASKS. He held important posts in the problem world: President of the FIDE Commission for Chess Compositions 1958–64; editor, 1951–81, of *Problem*, a journal reporting the Commission's affairs; and editor of FIDE ALBUMS up to the volume for 1980–2 (published in 1988). In 1949 he wrote *Šahovski Problem*, a complete and authoritative treatise on chess problems.

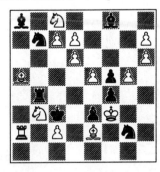

S#2

A selfmate showing ALLUMWANDLUNG doubled, second prize, Pongrácz Memorial Tourney 1980. Tries: 1 d8 = R? Be7, 1 d8 = B(Q)? Bxh6, 1 d8 = N? Sc5 (xa5, xd6)+, 1 h8 = B(Q)? Bxd6, 1 h8 = R? Bg7.

The key is 1 h8 = N:

1 ... Be7	2 dxe7
1 ... Bxh6	2 gxh6
1 ... Bxd6	2 exd6
1 ... Bg7	2 hxg7

Pétursson, Margeir (1960–), Icelandic champion 1987, 1988, International Grandmaster (1986). He was equal first at Smederevska Palanka 1984, Gausdal 1985, and Aosta 1990 (Swiss system, 110 players).

Pfleger, Helmut (1943–), German player, International Grandmaster (1975), physician. His first notable success was in 1965, when he tied with UNZICKER for first place in the national championship: they shared the title. Later tournament achievements include: Montilla 1973, first (+4=4−1) equal with KAVALEK, and Manila 1975, second (+4=4−2) equal with LARSEN, MECKING, and POLUGAYEVSKY, after LJUBOJEVIĆ. In the first of his six Olympiad appearances up to 1982, Tel Aviv 1964, Pfleger made the best fourth-board score (+10=5).

For some time his duties at the hospital restricted his available time for chess, but he was able to make a study on the effect of chess on health, and also to begin a career as a TV commentator.

phalanx, a group of united pawns. The term, a misnomer, is generally used only when the pawns are being advanced. See WILLIAMS.

phase. Conventionally, a game may have three consecutive phases: OPENING, MIDDLEGAME, and ENDGAME, in that order. The change from middlegame to endgame is marked by a few exchanges. The change from opening to middlegame can rarely be defined precisely; the most difficult part of the game, this change usually takes several moves, and might be called the transitional phase.

A problem may have several phases, concurrent but never consecutive. The solution (KEY and POST-KEY PLAY) is a phase; if the composer intended that there should be more than one SOLUTION, then each would be a phase. Other phases, not necessarily present, are concerned with what might happen rather than with what does happen. The SET PLAY (what would happen, in a DIRECT MATE PROBLEM, if Black were to move first) is a phase; each THEMATIC TRY (an attempted solution that fails) and its following TRY-PLAY is a phase; DUALS are part of the phase in which they occur.

phearse, an occasional spelling of FERS.

philately and chess. The first postage stamp depicting a chess motif was issued in Bulgaria, 1947, to commemorate the Balkan Games in which teams of chessplayers competed. Since then more than fifty countries have issued a total of about five hundred perforate stamps. Most celebrate a chess event or player, and the subjects include portraits and chess positions. The first portrayal of a great master (CAPABLANCA) is on four of a set of Cuban stamps, 1951; two are based on a portrait by a Cuban artist, E. Valderrama, and two are from a photograph taken in 1941. Another of the set of seven stamps shows the final position of the last game of the world championship match, 1921. An earlier stamp (Yugoslavia, 1950) shows incorrectly a position from the game Capablanca–Lasker, New York 1924.

Various countries have shown portraits of other world champions and leading players. In 1979 the

A first day cover from 2 April 1966, issued to commemorate an international chess festival held at Le Havre. The stamp, showing a knight and the symbols for king and queen, was the first one from France devoted to chess.

Republic of Mali issued a set intended to depict four great masters: besides ALEKHINE, BOGOLJUBOW, and JANOWSKI there is Willi Schlage (1887–1940) a player with only a local reputation in Germany. Chess has also been featured on labels since 1938 and on first day covers, one of which (Cuba 1966) shows an incorrect version of a study by LASKER and Capablanca. About 2,500 different postmarks refer to chess. The first, in 1923, was used by the Post Office at Borstendorf, a village south-east of Chemnitz, to advertise the local manufacture of chess sets. The earliest postmark linked to a chess event was in Kecskemét in 1927. A postmark used in PIRAN, 1958, celebrated the world's first great meeting of composers.

P. C. Burnett, *Chess on Stamps* (1972), is an illustrated record of chess stamps, 1947–71; J. Sutcliffe and H. Ulfströmer, *Checkmate* (5 vols., 1975–80), is a comprehensive treatise with English text; an international society based in Germany, the Gemeinschaft für Schachmotivsammler (GSM), publishes a continuing series of leaflets, *Schach auf Briefmarken*, covering all stamps issued since 1947.

Philidor, François-André Danican (1726–95), reputedly the best chessplayer of his time, author of the most influential book on the modern game, composer of music. The family name, previously Danican (originally Duncan; his Scottish ancestors settled in Normandy), was changed to Philidor in the 17th century, allegedly after Louis XIII, hearing Michel Danican play the hautbois, exclaimed 'J'ai trouvé un second Filidori' (a reference to an Italian court musician). However, no traces have been found of Filidori, and an alternative theory is that the name is a French version of the Gaelic 'Filidheach', meaning 'of the bardic clan'. François-André's father André (c.1647–1730), keeper of the king's music library, made an extensive collection of contemporary and old music scores that might otherwise have been lost to posterity, and introduced the *Concert spirituel* (public concert) in 1725.

François-André (he later discarded the François) showed early talent for music, entering the choir of the Chapel-Royal, Versailles, at the unusually young age of 6. His first chess experience (as described by his eldest son) came when he was 10. During spells of inactivity some of the 80 court musicians would play chess on a long table with six inlaid boards. The young Philidor offered to play an old musician whose opponent was absent. The old man laughingly agreed, but his good humour vanished when he began to lose. The boy gave checkmate and ran from the room, fearing the consequences of his opponent's wounded pride.

From about the age of 14 when his choral duties lessened, his voice having broken, Philidor spent much of his time on chess, often in the CAFÉ DE LA RÉGENCE, and he tended to neglect his studies. Instructed by LEGALL, the leading French chessplayer, Philidor became as proficient as his teacher in about three years. Legall, who had once played a blindfold game and had found the strain excessive, asked Philidor whether he could play this way. Philidor replied that he thought he could, for he had often played games in his head while in bed at night. After an easy success with a single game, he played in public two games blindfold simultaneously. He also acquired considerable skill at Polish draughts (on a 10 × 10 board).

Towards the end of 1745 Philidor went to Rotterdam. He was not an instrumentalist himself, but he was to assist in presenting 12 concerts starring a 13-year-old girl, Lanza, who played the harpsichord, and the virtuoso violinist, Geminiani. The girl died, the concerts were cancelled, and Philidor was stranded in the Netherlands without money. The opportunity to play chess abroad, which may have influenced his decision to travel, became a necessity; and he earned his living by teaching and playing chess and draughts, chiefly among army officers at The Hague. In 1747 he went to London where Sir Abraham Janssen (d.1765), perhaps the strongest player in England, introduced him to STAMMA and others who met for chess in a private room of Slaughter's coffee-house. There Philidor played a match with Stamma, giving odds of the draw (see HANDICAP) and backing himself five to four. Philidor won eight games, drew one (which counted as a loss), and lost one. He also beat Janssen (+4−1).

In 1748 Philidor wrote his famous book. He was then at Aix-la-Chapelle, where he met the fourth Earl of Sandwich (there to sign the famous treaty on behalf of England) upon whose advice he travelled to Eindhoven, the Duke of Cumberland's headquarters. Despite his Scottish blood Philidor had no qualms in soliciting, only two years after Culloden, the patronage of the Duke. Forty-five army officers ordered 119 of the 127 subscribed copies, the Duke taking 50 of them. In 1749 *L'analyze des échecs* was published in London. The first edition of 433 copies was followed by two reprints the same year, and an English edition in 1750. More

An engraving of Philidor

than 100 versions, in many languages, have appeared.

For the first time an author explained with detailed annotations how the middlegame should be played; for the first time the strategy of the game as a whole was described; for the first time concepts of the BLOCKADE, PROPHYLAXIS, POSITIONAL SACRIFICE, and MOBILITY of the PAWN FORMATION were laid down. Philidor's famous comment, 'Les pions sont l'âme du jeu' (in the English edition '... the Pawns; they are the very Life of the Game'), is often misunderstood. He believed that ignorance of correct pawn play was the biggest weakness of his contemporaries. Some thought he was saying that pawns are more important than pieces; others, that everything should be subordinated to the aim of promoting pawns. (See SCHOOLS OF CHESS.) Philidor was also the first writer to examine a BASIC END-GAME (R + B v. R) in depth, although that was almost his only contribution to this phase of the game. Already regarded as the strongest player in France, the Netherlands, and England, his chess reputation was consolidated by the book. He was received in fashionable society, attending, for example, the weekly chess dinners given by the French Ambassador, the Duke of Mirepoix.

In 1751 Philidor left England for Prussia, playing before King Frederick at Potsdam. He took his mistress there, and 'because of her had some difficulty with several officers ... as a result of which he had to depart unexpectedly'. He played three blindfold games simultaneously at Berlin, winning them all, visited several courts, and returned to England, where he stayed until November 1754.

Back in France after nine years' absence Philidor gave more of his attention to musical composition, although he found time in 1755 to play his last match against Legall when, says TWISS, the student beat his master. In 1760 he married a singer, Angélique-Henriette-Elisabeth Richer (1736–1809), the good-humoured and lively daughter of a musician. The surviving correspondence suggests that the marriage, which produced seven children, was a happy one. He was said to be an amiable man, completely devoid of wit. His wife's brother came early one morning to find the Philidors in bed. 'What's this, sister,' he shouted, 'I find you in bed with M. Philidor.' 'But that's my wife', replied the bewildered man. An embarrassed admirer once tried to excuse Philidor's boring conversation by saying, 'That man has no common sense — it is all genius.' He was fidgety at the chess-board, his legs rarely still.

In 1771 and 1773 Philidor made brief trips to London to play at the Salopian Coffee-house near Charing Cross. In 1774 English chess enthusiasts founded Parsloe's chess club, with a distinguished membership limited to 100. A fund was raised to enable Philidor to spend from February to May at the club, visits which continued for some 20 years. Here he gave lessons for a crown each, and here, in May 1782, he gave the first of his famous blindfold displays to the London public. The achievement,

not the result ($= 1 - 1$), was considered astonishing. The following year he bettered his performance ($+ 2 = 1$): 'A wonder of such magnitude ... as could not be credited, without repeated experience of the fact' (*The World*, 28 May 1783). He gave at least ten such displays, the last in 1795. In 1777 he published a second edition of his book, and in 1790 a third, dedicated to his friend and patron Count BRÜHL.

The Daily Picayune, a New Orleans newspaper, once described the Golden Age of chess as starting with Philidor and ending with MORPHY, adding that one could only guess what either might have accomplished had he turned his remarkable faculties to 'useful purposes'. If music be considered useful, then in the case of Philidor we do know. In parallel with his chess career he was a music composer of comparable brilliance and originality. Philidor's contemporaries found it difficult to believe he could excel in two fields, and in the *Public Advertiser* of 9 December 1753 he took space to deny the rumour that he was not the author of certain music, adding 'the art of music has been at all times his constant study and application, and chess only his diversion'.

When he was 11 Philidor had a motet performed before Louis XV, who gave the composer five louis d'or. While in England he set to music Congreve's 'Ode to Music'; Handel, present at its first performance, gave it qualified approval. *Carmen Seculaire* (1779), *Te Deum* (1786), and *Ode Anglaise* (1788) (to celebrate one of George III's periods of sanity) are his major concert works, but it was as a composer of *opéra bouffe* (comic opera) that Philidor excelled. He wrote 25 such works, four of them with collaborators (including J. J. Rousseau). He has been rated above Grétry, and his *Tom Jones* (1765) was called the finest work in the theatre. He was the first to use *air descriptif* (*Le Maréchalferrant*, 1761), the unaccompanied vocal quartet (*Tom Jones*), and a duet of two independent and seemingly incongruous melodies. After a performance of *Le Sorcier* in 1764 he was called by the audience, the first composer to be so distinguished in Paris. *Ernelinda, Princess of Norway* (1766), a grand opera with ballet, so pleased Louis XV that he gave Philidor a pension of 25 louis d'or from his privy purse. His music was largely ignored in England. Diderot wrote, 'I'm not surprised that in England all doors are closed to a great musician and open to a famous chess-player'; but Philidor's gains from chess subsidized his compositions, for which he was poorly paid.

Royal patronage eventually brought misfortune to Philidor. In December 1792 he left France for England, never to return. Following the revolution the playing of his music (and with it part of his income) ceased abruptly, for political rather than musical reasons. After his 'chess season' in 1793 he was unable to return to France and his family (at least during the lifetime of another Café de la Régence chessplayer, Robespierre). He tried to have his name removed from the list of *émigrés*, but succeeded only when he was dying. Depressed because he would not see his wife again, suffering from ill-health, and short of funds, he made his last home at 10 Ryder Street, near St James's Church, Piccadilly, from which he was buried on 3 September 1795, three days after his death. (The actual burial ground is behind St James's chapel, Hampstead Road.)

The Comédie-Française gave a benefit concert for his widow, who was in financial difficulties. The City of Paris had a terracotta bust made by Pajou, who added a well-intentioned inscription:

Avoir ton âme et ton génie,
Par les mains de Pajou voir son buste sculpté,
C'est selon moi le sort le plus digne d'envie:
C'est être deux fois sûr de l'immortalité.

In 1840 the city authorities, no longer sharing this view, disposed of the bust. A letter in the *Chess Player's Chronicle*, 1841, stated that a portrait of Philidor by Gainsborough was in the possession of a Mr Holford, but it has never been traced.

Philidor left no literary works on music and for many years his compositions were rarely heard. *Le Maréchal-ferrant* was performed in Dreux, his birthplace, in 1926 to celebrate the composer's bicentenary, and *Blaise le Savetier* was revived in 1976 for a 250th anniversary celebration in London. With the renewal of interest in period music his works are occasionally recorded or broadcast. No scores survive of the games Philidor played in his prime, but ATWOOD recorded 68 games from his last years, all blindfold or at odds. His influence on the strategy of chess, however, is pervasive, although only fully recognized since the mid-20th century. (See PAWN AND TWO MOVES; POSITIONAL SACRIFICE.)

G. Allen, *The Life of Philidor* (1863) reproduced in facsimile, 1971.

Brühl–Philidor   London, 1783 (Philidor blindfold)
Bishop's Opening

1 e4 e5 2 Bc4 c6 3 Qe2 d6 4 c3 f5 (Here and later Black consistently aims for a strong central pawn formation.) 5 d3 Nf6 6 exf5 Bxf5 7 d4 e4 8 Bg5 d5 9 Bb3 Bd6 10 Nd2 Nbd7 11 h3 h6 12 Be3 Qe7 13 f4 h5 (PROPHYLAXIS, holding back White's king's-side pawns) 14 c4 a6 15 cxd5 cxd5 16 Qf2 0–0 17 Ne2 b5 18 0–0 Nb6 19 Ng3 g6 20 Rac1 Nc4 21 Nxf5 gxf5 22 Qg3+ Qg7 23 Qxg7+ Kxg7 24 Bxc4 bxc4 25 g3 Rab8 26 b3 Ba3 27 Rc2 cxb3 28 axb3 Rfc8 29 Rxc8 Rxc8 30 Ra1 Bb4 31 Rxa6 Rc3 32 Kf2 Rd3 33 Ra2 Bxd2 34 Rxd2 Rxb3 35 Rc2

35 ... h4 (Thus White's pawns are broken up while Black's remain connected.) 36 Rc7+ Kg6 37 gxh4 Nh5 38 Rd7 Nxf4 39 Bxf4 Rf3+ 40 Kg2 Rxf4 41 Rxd5 Rf3 42 Rd8 Rd3 43 d5 f4 44 d6 Rd2+ 45 Kf1 Kf7 46 h5 e3 47 h6 f3 White resigns.

Philidor Counterattack, 649, dating back to LUCENA. White's usual reply, 3 d4, owes more to PHILIDOR, who insisted on its necessity.

Philidor Counter-gambit, 1030, recommended by its inventor, PHILIDOR, as best play for Black in the PHILIDOR DEFENCE, but no longer regarded as sound.

Philidor Defence, 1015, defence to the KING'S KNIGHT OPENING noted by LUCENA and recommended by Ruy LÓPEZ. Its strongest advocate was PHILIDOR: he disliked blocking his pawns with knights and considered 2 ... d6 better than 2 ... Nc6, a preference not shared by subsequent generations. (See BODEN'S MATE; FRIENDLY GAME; POSITIONAL SACRIFICE). Also 1160, the BERLIN DEFENCE in the KIESERITZKY GAMBIT, recommended by Philidor.

Philidor Gambit, 1145, variation of the KING'S GAMBIT Accepted, given by SALVIO and recommended by PHILIDOR, but less popular than the main alternative, the HANSTEIN GAMBIT (1148). Mentioned by GRECO, it sometimes bears the name Greco–Philidor Gambit.

Philidor sacrifice, the sacrifice of a minor piece for one or two pawns when, by doing so, one's own pawns (usually united) gain compensating mobility, a tactic practised and recommended by Philidor. In the opening variation 1 e4 e5 2 Nf3 Nf6 3 Nxe5 d6 4 Nxf7 Kxf7 White has prospects of advancing pawns in the centre and on the king's-side. Some authorities suggest that two united pawns are as good as a minor piece if they are established abreast on the fifth rank.

Christiansen–H. Ólafsson   USA–Nordic match Reykjavik 1986   Queen's Gambit Declined Harrwitz Attack

1 d4 Nf6 2 c4 e6 3 Nf3 d5 4 Nc3 Be7 5 Bf4 0–0 6 e3 c5 7 dxc5 Bxc5 8 a3 Nc6 9 b4 Be7 10 Qc2 Bd7 11 Be2 Rc8 12 0–0 dxc4 13 Rad1 Qe8 14 Rd2 a5 15 b5

15 ... Nb4 16 axb4 axb4 17 Ne4 b3 18 Nxf6+ Bxf6 19 Qb1 c3 20 Rxd7 Qxd7 21 Qxb3 c2 22 e4 Rc3 23 Qa4

Rfc8   24 Bc1 h6   25 e5 Be7   26 Qg4 Kh8   27 Qh5 Ba3   28
Qg4 Bxc1   29 Rxc1 Rb3   30 Qe4 Rb1   31 Rxb1 c1 = Q +
32 Ne1 Qcd2   33 Bd3 g6   34 h4 Qd5   35 Qg4 Qxe5   36
Nf3 (forking two queens)   36 ... Qef4   37 Qxf4 Qxf4   38
Bf1 Rc1   39 g3 Rxf1 +   White resigns.

See also AGDESTEIN and BLACKBURNE. In the game
given under RAGOZIN, Black sacrifices the exchange
twice in order to make a decisive pawn advance.

Philidor's legacy, the name for one kind of SMOTH-
ERED MATE.

A position from LUCENA c.1497. White mates in five
without capturing any black men: 1 Qe6+ Kh8   2
Nf7+ Kg8   3 Nh6+ Kh8   4 Qg8+ Rxg8   5 Nf7
mate. From time to time in master play the possibility of checkmates of this kind influence the
course of the game.
  Beale, in his *Royall Game of Chesse-Play* (London, 1656), gives the following game by GRECO: 1 e4
e5   2 Nf3 Nc6   3 Bc4 Bc5   4 0–0 Nf6   5 Re1 0–0   6
c3 Re8   7 d4 exd4   8 e5 Ng4   9 cxd4 Nxd4   10
Nxd4 Qh4   11 Nf3 Qxf2+   12 Kh1 Qg1+   13 N
or Rxg1 Nf2, a kind of checkmating finish that is
also not uncommon.
  These checkmates are not especially connected
with Philidor. The name derives from *An Introduction to the History and Study of Chess* (Cheltenham,
1804), by Thomas Pruen. The book includes Philidor's text and, among other matter, a position
which Pruen calls 'A Clever Legacy'. In Hoyle's
Treatise on Chess (1808) it had become 'Philidor's
Legacy'.

Philidor Variation, 643, sometimes called the Classical Attack, in the BISHOP'S OPENING, given by Ruy
LÓPEZ, and advocated by PHILIDOR as the proper
way to build a PAWN CENTRE. The variation had an
extraordinarily long run during which STAMMA's
continuation, 3 ... Nf6   4 d4 exd4   5 e5 d5, was
thought to favour White. Eventually improvements
for Black were found: 6 exf6 dxc4   7 Qh5 0–0
(PRATT, 1825); 6 Bb3 Ne4   7 cxd4 Qh4 (CALVI,
1842). Also 455 and 565, Philidor's replies to the
SICILIAN DEFENCE.

philosophy and chess. The earliest book treating
this topic directly is *The Philosophy of Chess* by
William Cluley (1857). In essence it tackled two
questions: is there a generalized theory of chess?

and is chess a paradigm of life? Cluley, who appears
to have left no mark on the chess world, advanced
views that were to become commonplace, but must
have been unpalatable to many of his contemporaries (see SCHOOLS OF CHESS). 'The means of defence
are necessarily as good and as strong as those of
attack.' 'We ought not to aim at an advantage, or
expect a victory otherwise than through an opponent's blunders.' 'A drawn game is, at first, the only
legitimate pursuit, and ... checkmate is primarily
to be regarded as an accident and not as a necessity.' Many, before and since, but all chessplayers,
have argued that playing chess is invaluable for
teaching lessons that are transferable to life itself.
Cluley suggested that playing chess was more bene-
ficial than learning mathematics, and quoted
Bishop Warburton's objections: 'In making a man
conversant with studies in which *certainty* is the
result, [mathematics] unfit him (or at least do not
prepare him) for sifting and balancing (what alone
he will have to do in the world) probabilities; there
being no worse practical men than those who
require more evidence than is necessary.' Cluley
also said, without using these words, that while
chess might theoretically be deterministic, perfection of play was impossible, and so it was, in effect,
probabilistic, and therefore more like the larger
canvas of life.
  In the years since Cluley's book the world of
philosophy has changed as much as has the world
of chess. Wittgenstein, perhaps the most influential
philosopher of the twentieth century, frequently
used chess analogies to illuminate his theories
about language.
  Other philosophical echoes are found in LASKER'S
Struggle (1907), and in the view, advanced by BIDEV
and others, that chess originated from a religious
ceremony, and so has a natural link with philosophy.

Piatigorsky, Gregor (1903–76), famous Russian-
born cellist who with his chess-playing wife Jacque-
line (*née* Rothschild) gave (through the Piatigorsky
Foundation) a cup for a triennial tournament to
include two grandmasters from the USA, two from
the USSR, and four from other countries. Two
tournaments were held: Los Angeles 1963, won by
KERES and PETROSYAN; and Santa Monica 1966,
won by SPASSKY. They were the strongest tournaments to be held in the USA since New York 1927.
For the second event there was a prize fund of
$20,000 and the number of competitors was
increased to ten.

pickaninny, a problem TASK: a black pawn (other
than a rook's pawn) on its second rank is moved, in
different variations, in each of the four possible
ways (two forward moves, two captures) and each
of these moves is answered by a different white
move. First shown by SHINKMAN in 1885, the task
was named by Frank Janet (*né* Elias Silberstein)
(1875–1957) in 1914. (Compare ALBINO.)

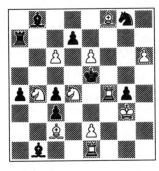

#3

A problem by CHEPIZHNY and LOSHINSKY, first prize, *Thèmes 64*, 1966. After the key, 1 h7, the variations show both a pickaninny (with Pd7) and an albino (with Pe2).

1 ... dxc6 2 Nbxd6+ Kd5 3 e4 #
1 ... d6 2 Rf5+ Kxd4 3 e3 #
1 ... d5 2 Nd3+ cxd3 3 exd3 #
1 ... dxe6 2 Nf3+ gxf3 3 exf3 #.

piece, specifically, a queen, rook, bishop, knight, or king—a pawn is not a piece; more generally used for any chessman.

Pierce Gambit, 621, VIENNA GAMBIT variation analysed by the English player William Timbrell Pierce (1839–1922) in the *British Chess Magazine*, Jan. 1886. (W. T. Pierce also deserves credit for his attempt to introduce STANDARD NOTATION as early as 1878, when he used it in the *Brighton Herald*.)

Pigusov, Yevgeny Anisimovich (1961–), Russian player, International Grandmaster (1987), first or equal first at Bayamo 1985 (+5=6), Havana (II) 1986, and the strong Sochi 1987 (+4=10).

Pillsbury, Harry Nelson (1872–1906), American player, one of the best three or four in the world from 1895 to 1903. As a youth he went to Boston to study for a commercial career, but spent much of his time playing whist, draughts, and chess. In April 1893, less than five years after learning the moves, he beat the visiting master WALBRODT (+2=1), and a month or so later began his professional career with some chess engagements in Philadelphia. As well as chess journalism and acting as the hidden player in the automaton AJEEB, Pillsbury specialized in simultaneous blindfold displays. On occasion he would play both chess and draughts blindfold, and take a hand of whist at the same time. Courteous, amiable, with an outgoing personality and unassuming manner, he was a favourite guest in many chess clubs.

In 1895 he sailed to Europe and played in the Hastings tournament, one of the strongest events held up to that time. Pillsbury, normally gregarious, declined to stay in a hotel where he might meet other masters: 'I want to be quiet; I mean to win this tournament.' Although most of the leading masters were playing, LASKER, TARRASCH, CHIGORIN, STEINITZ, and many others, the 22-year-old Pillsbury was first (+15=3−3). No player had previously won his first major tournament, and the achievement has since been equalled only by CAPABLANCA. Alfred Emery (1865–c.1940), a chessplayer and journalist who was present, writes that Pillsbury's 'best combinations were made with apparently little trouble. An inveterate smoker, often consuming a dozen cigars without pause, he would, when working out some particular combination, send a cloud of smoke among the pieces. Then, tilting his chair like an American rocker, he would sum up, as it seemed, the wider progress of the game, himself often the coolest of the company.'

Pillsbury next played in the St Petersburg four-master match tournament 1895–6. He scored well against Lasker (+2=3−1) and Chigorin (+3=1−2), but so badly against Steinitz (=2−4) that he took only third prize. At Nuremberg 1896 Pillsbury was unwell (from syphilis contracted at St Petersburg), but he fought hard, scored +10=4−4, and shared third place with Tarrasch, after Lasker and MARÓCZY. He ended his first visit to Europe by taking third prize after Chigorin and CHAROUSEK at Budapest 1896.

Back home, he played two matches against SHOWALTER, the first gaining and the second retaining the US championship: 1897, +10=3−8; 1898, +7=2−3. Four strong tournaments followed: Vienna 1898, first (+24=7−5) equal with Tarrasch, who won the play-off match; London 1899, second (+14=8−5) equal with Maróczy and JANOWSKI, after Lasker; Paris 1900, second (+12=1−3), after Lasker; Munich 1900, first (+9=6) equal with Maróczy and SCHLECHTER. In 1901 he married in Philadelphia and made his home there.

At Hanover 1902 he took second prize (+10=4−3) after Janowski. During this tournament Pillsbury played the toughest ever simultaneous blindfold display. He scored +3=11−7 against 21 opponents, all of whom were competing in the HAUPTTURNIER for the master title. Contrary to warnings that he was jeopardizing his prospects in the tournament by this display, his results improved. In two tournaments at Monte Carlo, Pillsbury came second in 1902 (+14=6−4), after Maróczy, and third in 1903 (+14=9−3), after Tarrasch and Maróczy. He played in the King's Gambit tournament, Vienna 1903, but came only fourth; he was not allowed to use his favourite openings, the QUEEN'S GAMBIT and the SPANISH OPENING, to which he contributed many original ideas. In his last tournament, Cambridge Springs 1904, he failed, for the first time in an important event, to win a high prize. The terminal stage of his illness had begun.

Against Lasker, then world champion, Pillsbury made a better score (+4=4−4) in strong tournaments than any of his contemporaries. His play was vigorous and combinative, and although he sometimes lost through overplaying his hand, his style was maturing. Had he not died so young he might well have rivalled Lasker's supremacy. (See OP-POSITE FLANK ATTACKS.)

Chigorin–Pillsbury   Vienna 1898   Falkbeer Counter-Gambit Nimzowitsch Variation

1 e4 e5   2 f4 d5   3 exd5 e4   4 Bb5+ c6   5 dxc6 bxc6   6 Bc4 Nf6   7 d4 Bd6   8 Ne2 0–0   9 0–0 c5   10 d5 Nbd7   11 Bb3

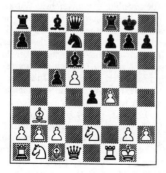

11 ... c4   12 Bxc4 Bc5+   13 Kh1 Nb6   14 Bb3 Ng4   15 Qe1 Nxd5   16 h3 Nde3   17 Bxe3 Nxe3   18 Nbc3 Nxf1   19 Nxe4 Bb6   20 Qxf1 Bb7   21 N2c3 Qh4   22 Nd5 Rae8   23 Ng5 h6   24 Nf3 Qg3   25 Ne5 Be3   26 Nd3 Re4   27 Qf3 Qxf3   28 gxf3 Ree8   29 Kg2 Bd4   30 c3 Bxd5   31 Bxd5 Re2+   32 Kg3 Rd2   33 cxd4 Rxd3   34 Rc1 Rxd4   35 Rc5 Rd8   36 Bc4 Rd2   37 b4 g6   38 b5 Kg7   39 a4 h5   40 a5 h4+ White resigns.

Pillsbury Attack, 191 in the QUEEN'S GAMBIT Declined as played by PILLSBURY in his first international game, against TARRASCH at Hastings 1895. A great exponent of the Queen's Gambit in the days before it became fashionable, Pillsbury, in positions like this, aimed to play his knight to e5 and Pf2–f4, along with 0–0, a formation sometimes called 'the Pillsbury set position'.

Pillsbury Defence, 234, an old opening, given by CARRERA, occasionally called the Old Indian Defence, usually a prelude to the PIRC DEFENCE (237) (see BREVITY). Also 812, the BARNES DEFENCE to the SPANISH OPENING, played Lasker–Pillsbury, New York 1893.

Pillsbury Variation, 164, or 133 by a different sequence, in the SEMI-TARRASCH VARIATION of the QUEEN'S GAMBIT Declined, as Pillsbury–Lasker, St Petersburg 1895–6 and also Cambridge Springs 1904 (see OPPOSITE FLANK ATTACKS); 803 in the SPANISH OPENING introduced in Pillsbury–Lasker, St Petersburg 1895–6 (on Christmas Day); 804 in the same opening, Pillsbury–Lasker, London 1899; 845 in the FOUR KNIGHTS OPENING, played successfully in the game Chigorin–Pillsbury, St Petersburg 1895–6, but discarded on account of the reply 8 Nh4 introduced by TARRASCH in 1904. Also 176, the CAMBRIDGE SPRINGS DEFENCE.

Pilnik, Hermann (1914–81), professional player, International Grandmaster (1952). Born in Germany,

he settled in Argentina around 1930, won the national championship in 1942, 1945, and 1958, and played for his adopted country in five Olympiads from 1950 to 1958. At Mar del Plata 1942 he scored +12=2−3 to share second prize with STÅHLBERG, after NAJDORF. His best victories were Mar del Plata 1944, a score of +9=6 to tie with Najdorf, ahead of Ståhlberg, and Belgrade 1952, both being minor tournaments. Pilnik became a CANDIDATE after sharing seventh place in the interzonal tournament Göteborg 1955, but he fared badly in the Candidates tournament that followed. He travelled extensively and lived for varying periods in several countries, eventually settling in Venezuela. There he taught chess in the Caracas Military Academy, and there he died. (See BLOCK-ADE.)

Pilnik Variation, 743 in the SPANISH OPENING also known as the Teichmann Variation because of games by Teichmann at Carlsbad 1911, but it was played by BURN in 1904. (See TEICHMANN.)

pin, a situation in which a LINE-PIECE (the pinning man) holds down an enemy man (the pinned man); to bring about such a situation.

There are two kinds of pin: (1) pins against the king, the only kind recognized by composers. For example 1 d4 Nf6   2 c4 e6   3 Nc3 Bb4, and White's knight at c3 (the pinned man) cannot be moved; or 1 d4 e6   2 c4 Bb4+   3 Bd2, when the pinned man at d2 is not wholly immobilized but it cannot be moved from the diagonal e1–a5. (2) pins against men other than the king, e.g. 1 e4 e5   2 Nf3 d6   3 d4 Bg4 when White's knight at f3 can be moved only by allowing the queen to come under attack.

Of the basic elements that make up the tactical content of the game the pin is one of the most powerful.

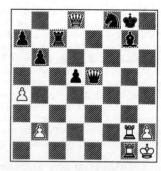

In this position, reached in a game Klinger–Blatný, Bad Wörishofen 1988, Black's knight and bishop are pinned to the king. Klinger played 1 Qb8, pinning the rook to Black's queen. If now 1 ... Re7 then 2 Qxe5 Rxe5   3 Rxg7+, so Blatný played 2 ... Qe7 but resigned after 3 Rxg7+ Qxg7   4 Qxc7 because his queen is now pinned to the king.

pin-mate, a composer's term for a checkmate that

depends upon the pinning of one or more of the defender's men.

pin-stalemate, a composer's term for a stalemate that depends upon the pinning of one or more men.

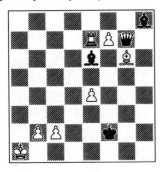

=

A study by SOMOV-NASIMOVICH, *64*, 1939. 1 e5 Qxe5 2 f8=Q+ Kg1 3 c3 Qe1+ 4 Bb1 Qxc3 5 Rg7+ Bxg7 6 Qf1+ Kxf1 7 Bd3+ Ke1 8 bxc3 Kd2 9 Bc2 Kc1 10 Bb3 Bxb3 stalemate.
For another example, see KAZANTSEV.

Pintér, József (1953–), International Grandmaster (1982), champion of Hungary 1978 and 1979, member of the Olympiad team from 1980. His best results are: Rome 1979, first; Plovdiv 1979, first (+6=5); Rome 1982, first (+5=4) equal with KORCHNOI; Copenhagen 1985, first (+6=5); Prague (zonal) 1985, equal first with JANSA and ŞUBA; Szirák 1985, first (+6=5−2) equal with TUKMAKOV; Szirák 1986, second (+5=6−2), after PSAKHIS; Warsaw 1987, first (+6=3−2); Beersheba 1988, second (+8=3−3) equal with Korchnoi, after GREENFELD; Dortmund 1988, second, equal with King, after LPUTYAN; Budapest 1989, first equal; León 1989, first equal with Zsuzsa POLGÁR.

Portisch–Pintér   Hungarian Championship 1984
Queen's Gambit Declined Semi-Tarrasch Defence

1 d4 Nf6 2 c4 e6 3 Nf3 d5 4 Nc3 c5 5 cxd5 Nxd5 6 e4 Nxc3 7 bxc3 cxd4 8 cxd4 Nc6 9 Bc4 b5 10 Be2 Bb4+ 11 Bd2 Qa5 12 Bxb4 Qxb4+ 13 Qd2 Bb7 14 a3 Qxd2+ 15 Kxd2 a6 16 a4 b4 17 a5 Rd8 18 Ke3 f5 19 exf5 exf5 20 Bc4 Ke7 21 d5

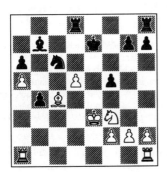

21 ... Kf6 22 dxc6 Rhe8+ 23 Kf4 Re4+ 24 Kg3 Bc8 25 Rac1 Rg4+ 26 Kh3 f4 27 Ne5? (after 27 Bxa6 Black has nothing better than perpetual check) 27 ... Kg5 28 Nf7+ Kh5 29 Be2 Rd3+ 30 g3 f3 31 Rc5+ Rg5+ 32 g4+ Bxg4+ 33 Kg3 fxe2+ White resigns.

Pin Variation, the most graphic of the names for 554 in the SICILIAN DEFENCE, the others being Sicilian Counterattack and Tartakower Variation.

pion coiffé, or capped pawn, a handicap that consists of undertaking that the mating move shall be made by a specific pawn, appropriately capped or marked at the start of the game, and to deem the game lost if this cannot be achieved. The pawn may not be promoted, a ruling that only partly settled centuries-old arguments. About 70 endgames in which mate is to be given by a capped pawn were analysed by CARRERA, who noted for example that with K+P+Q v. K mate can be forced with any pawn other than one on a centre file. He and later writers, including STAUNTON, considered that the handicap of *pion coiffé* was about equal to giving the odds of a queen.

In 1856 Thomas Loyd (1830–1914) capped his g-pawn (the usual one) against his brother, Sam LOYD, then about 14 years old.

1 Nc3 d5 2 e4 e6 3 d4 Bb4 4 e5 f6 5 Bf4 fxe5 6 Qh5+ g6 7 Qxe5 Bxc3+ 8 bxc3 Nf6 9 Bd3 Nc6 10 Qg5 Qe7 11 h3 Qf7 12 Ne2 h6 13 Qg3 Nh5 14 Qe3 0–0 15 Bxh6 Re8 16 Qg5 Ne7 17 Ng3 Nxg3 18 fxg3 Nf5 19 0–0 Qh7 20 Bxf5 exf5 21 Rf4 Bd7 22 Raf1 Bb5 23 R1f2 Re1+ 24 Kh2 Bd7 25 g4 Re4 26 gxf5 Rxf4 27 Rxf4 Re8 28 fxg6 Qe7 29 Qh5 Qe6 30 g7 Qd6 31 Qf7+ Kh7 32 g8=Q+ Kxh6 33 Qgh7+ (Qfh7+, mate, wins for Black) 33 ... Kg5 34 Qhg7+ Qg6 35 Rg4+ Kh5 36 Rg5+ Kh4 37 Rh5+ Kxh5 38 Qgxg6+ Kh4 39 g3 Thomas mates with capped pawn.

Piran Codex. In 1958 the FIDE Commission for Chess Compositions met at Piran, a small coastal resort in Yugoslavia. With the help and advice of many others, standards for the composition of problems and studies were established. Known as the Piran Codex, these standards were published in *Problem*, Jan. 1959, and have since been amended a few times. The Committee also decided to begin publication of the FIDE ALBUMS. Composers from many countries attended; this gathering, the first of its kind, became an annual event, hosted in turn by different countries.

Pirc (pron. peerts), Vasja (1907–80), Yugoslav player, International Grandmaster (1953), International Arbiter (1973), national champion in 1936, 1937, and 1953, co-champion in 1935 and 1948, historian. His best results in strong international tournaments were in the 1930s: Budapest 1934, second (+7=7−1), half a point behind LILIENTHAL, one and a half points above FLOHR; Łódź 1938, first (+8=7), ahead of TARTAKOWER, PETROV, STÅHLBERG, and ELISKASES; Bad Harzburg 1938, first (+4=5), ahead of BOGOLJUBOW and Eliskases; and Noordwijk 1938, third (+3=5−1), after Eliskases and KERES, ahead of EUWE, Bogoljubow, SPIELMANN, and Tartakower. In 1949 Pirc drew a match with Euwe ($+2=6-2$). He was a prolific author, and is remembered for his openings inventions, some of which bear his name. The Pirc Defence (or Pirc–Robatsch System), long regarded as dubious, became standard play during his lifetime.

Nimzowitsch–Pirc   Bled 1931   Nimzowitsch Opening

1 Nf3 Nf6 2 c4 c6 3 b3 d5 4 Bb2 e6 5 Qc2 Bd6 6 Nc3 0–0 7 e3 a6 8 d4 Nbd7 9 Be2 Qe7 10 0–0 Re8 11 Rad1 dxc4 12 Bxc4 b5 13 Bd3 Bb7 14 Ne4 Nxe4 15 Bxe4 f5 16 Bd3 c5 17 e4 cxd4 18 Bxd4 e5 19 Bb2 Nc5 20 Nd2 Rad8 21 exf5

21 ... e4 22 f6 gxf6 23 Be2 Nd3 24 Bxd3 exd3 25 Qb1 Qg7 26 g3 Qg6 27 Bd4 Re2 28 Bb6 Bxg3 White resigns.

Pirc Defence, 237, line played by PAULSEN at Nuremberg 1883 and Breslau 1889, and revived by PIRC in the 1940s; also known as the Antal, or Ufimtsev Defence, or Yugoslav Variation. It can arise from other sequences, e.g. 606. Compare the ROBATSCH DEFENCE and the PIRC–ROBATSCH SYSTEM. (See DOLMATOV; HORT; HÜBNER.)

Pirc Defence Deferred, 1280, reaching, by a different route, a similar position to 237, White having developed the other knight.

Pirc–Robatsch System, combination of the PIRC and ROBATSCH DEFENCES, sometimes called the Modern Defence, although played regularly in the 1860s by MOHESCHUNDER. White can move both his centre pawns to the fourth rank. Black plays Pd6, Pg6, Bg7, and Nf6, not necessarily in that order, and may later strike at the centre by Pe7–e5 or in some other way. The system became popular in the 1960s in answer to 1 e4, but can also be played after 1 d4 when transposition to other openings, e.g. the KING'S INDIAN DEFENCE, may be at White's disposal.

Pirc Variation, 143, a variation in the QUEEN'S GAMBIT Declined played in the game Grünfeld–Soultanbéieff, Folkestone Olympiad, 1933; 310 in the NIMZO-INDIAN DEFENCE, credited to both KERES and PIRC, although it was played by MARSHALL at London in 1927.

Plachutta theme, see CUTTING-POINT THEMES.

plagiarism, the deliberate copying of another's game or composition. Games are sometimes repeated by coincidence, but occasionally almost unknown players have laid claim to games played by grandmasters. Composers commonly suffer on account of ANTICIPATION, when an idea has been used before although the setting may not have been identical. Plagiarism is rare, its exposure swift.

#2

A problem by D'ORVILLE, no. 34 in his book *Problèmes d'échecs* (1842). The solution is 1 Qg8 + .

#2

A problem from *Problems and Puzzles* (1943) by Francis Percival Wenman (1891–1972), the problem world's most notorious plagiarist. Of the 70 problems in this book at least 40 owe their origin to other composers. In this example Wenman moved the position one file and rotated the board ninety degrees, a common trick in pawnless positions. The solution is 1 Qa6 + . This kind of problem has never been in fashion in the twentieth century.

Plaksin, Nikita Mikhailovich (1931–), Russian composer, International Judge of Chess Compositions (1989), hydrodynamics engineer. Of his generation he is the leading specialist in RETROGRADE ANALYSIS. He published 100 such compositions in 1965, and another 50, all based on the FIFTY-MOVE LAW, in *Problem* 188–193, 1979. (See ONE-MOVER.)

Planinc (pron. planints), Albin (1944–), Yugoslav player, International Grandmaster (1972). An imaginative player, always seeking new ideas, he is capable of a win, or a loss, against almost anyone. His best tournament victories are at Ljubljana 1969 ($+7=7-1$), ahead of GLIGORIĆ, UNZICKER, BYRNE, MATANOVIĆ, and GHEORGHIU, and at Amsterdam 1973, when he scored $+7=6-2$ to tie with PETROSYAN, ahead of KAVALEK and SPASSKY. A few weeks after his triumph at Ljubljana, Planinc was 15th out of 16 in a tournament at Zagreb.

Planinc Variation, 699 in the SPANISH OPENING, played regularly by PLANINC, but it was not his creation, being an organic part of the ARCHANGELSK VARIATION. (See PENROSE.)

Platov, Vasily Nikolayevich (1881–1952), Soviet composer, epidemiologist. With TROITZKY and KUBBEL he pioneered study composing in Russia. He came from Latvia where, in the 1890s, the art was being actively encouraged in the columns of the *Rigaer Tageblatt* and the *Baltische Schachblätter.* He was study editor of *Shakhmatnoe obozreny* (1909–10), *Shakhmaty* (1922–9), and *64* (1925–32). Many of his studies were composed with his brother Mikhail N. Platov (1883–1938), a collaboration that ended abruptly in 1937 when Mikhail, an engineer, made a derogatory remark about Stalin at a production meeting and, as a result, was sentenced to work in the north where he died within a year. The brothers published two collections of their joint or individual compositions: *Sammlung der Endspielstudien* (1914) and *Sbornik shakhmatnykh etyudov* (1928), containing 153 and 200 studies respectively. (See STAIRCASE MOVEMENT.)

player, specifically, the contestant whose turn it is to play; generally, either contestant, or anyone who plays.

play-off. Sometimes it is essential to eliminate one or more players from those with an equal score, for example in an event which is part of the world championship cycle and from which only a fixed number of players can go forward, or when a prize is not divisible. Commonly a statistical TIE-BREAKING method is used, but if the issue is deemed important enough a play-off match is held, at least in the first instance, and perhaps at a faster rate of play.

Pleiades, an influential though ephemeral (1837–43) group of Berlin players of whom the most important were von der LASA and BLEDOW. The name is derived from seven of the twelve daughters of Pleione fathered by Atlas in Greek mythology, and is commonly used for any group of seven. Depending on conditions, between six and nine of the many stars in the constellation named after the Pleiades are visible to the naked eye.

plus, an advantage. (See CONVENTIONAL SYMBOLS for some ways in which this might be indicated.)

plus-flights, the four FLIGHTS laterally adjoining the square occupied by a king that does not stand on the edge of the board. (Compare STAR-FLIGHTS.)

#3

A problem by DAWSON, *The Problemist*, 1941. The key is 1 Ne7.

1 ... Ke5 or e3   2 Rc4 K~   3 Re4#
1 ... Kd4 or f4   2 Re2 K~   3 Re4#.

plus score, a score of more than 50 per cent in a tournament. Lower scores, although positive, are sometimes called minus scores.

ply, term used by computer programmers for the range of any SINGLE-MOVE. Thus a five-ply analysis from the ARRAY would look as far as White's third move.

pocket knight chess, an unorthodox game in which before play commences both players remove a knight from the array (usually the queen's knight) and at any time during the game may place this 'pocket' knight anywhere on the board in substitution for a move. At the beginning of the 20th century this game was popular in continental Europe where it was known as tombola chess. In kleptomaniac chess some piece other than a knight is pocketed.

pocket set, a set designed to be folded and carried in a pocket. Unlike a TRAVELLING SET it is two dimensional: the men lie flat on the squares as they would appear in a diagram. Perhaps the first such set was devised by Peter Mark Roget (1779–1869) of *Thesaurus* fame. In 1845 he registered the design of 'The Economic Chess Board, provided with a complete set of chess men, adapted for playing games in carriages, or out of doors, and for folding up and carrying in the pocket, without disturbing the game.' The set was sold for some years by Longman & Co. 'in a neat foolscap octavo case, price 2s.6d.' Many pocket sets are of leather with durable plastic men, but an independent demand arose from correspondence players who wanted to leave the position of their game set up to avoid both tedium and oversight. Cheaper cardboard sets were produced to help those with many games active at the same time. Pocket sets with multiple boards were produced in the 1920s, one popular set being known as Leporello, after Don Juan's valet.

Poděbrady Variation, 481 in the SICILIAN DEFENCE, played by ALEKHINE in the Poděbrady tournament, 1936.

poetry and chess, see LITERATURE AND CHESS.

Pogosyants, Ernest Levonovich (1935–90), Soviet composer, International Grandmaster for Chess Compositions (1988), mathematics teacher. A prolific composer, he constructed about 6,000 problems and studies, 984 of them in one year (1984). His title was awarded mainly on account of his studies; many are lightweight, but they are always piquant.

He is described by VLADIMIROV as highly energetic, inventive, full of wit, constantly writing sketches and aphorisms; also as enjoying life to the full despite illness, loss of sight, and poverty in his last years, when he eked out a living on the small fees paid by newspapers for his compositions.

poisoned pawn, an unmoved pawn, conventionally on the knight's file, whose capture subjects the capturer to a strong attack. This is a form of PAWN SNATCHING, and the capture usually involves a loss of time. For examples, see BROWNE; SPIELMANN COUNTERATTACK; YUSUPOV.

Poisoned Pawn Variation, 512, complicated line in the SICILIAN DEFENCE which caught the public's imagination during the world championship match between SPASSKY and FISCHER in 1972, and consequently sometimes miscalled the Fischer System. Whether the acceptance of the pawn, 8 . . . Qxb2, is sound or otherwise is not certain. However, masters are usually willing to make the offer: see BELYAVSKY.

Polerio, Giulio Cesare (*c*.1550–*c*.1610), leading Italian player, from Lanciano in the Abruzzi. In 1574

An early pocket set, designed by De la Rue. White is at the top.

he followed LEONARDO DI BONA to Spain where they defeated Ruy LÓPEZ and CERON in match play before travelling together to Portugal. Many of Polerio's manuscripts exist and show him to have been a judicious recorder of the important opening variations of his time: TWO KNIGHTS DEFENCE and FEGATELLO ATTACK; SCOTCH GAMBIT; CENTRE GAME; FALKBEER COUNTER-GAMBIT; SALVIO GAMBIT and variations; MUZIO GAMBIT and WILD MUZIO GAMBIT; and variations of KING'S GAMBIT Accepted and the ITALIAN OPENING. Contemporary manuscripts of unknown authorship, some of which may have been written by Polerio, include other new openings: GRECO COUNTER-GAMBIT; CALABRIAN COUNTER-GAMBIT; BODEN–KIESERITZKY GAMBIT; THREE KNIGHTS and FOUR KNIGHTS OPENINGS; KIESERITZKY GAMBIT; SICILIAN DEFENCE; CARO–KANN DEFENCE; NIMZOWITSCH DEFENCE (1 e4 Nc6); QUEEN'S FIANCHETTO and ROBATSCH DEFENCES; and SLAV DEFENCE.

Van der Linde, *Das Schachspiel des XVI. Jahrhunderts* (1874) fully analyses Polerio's manuscripts.

Polerio Defence, 969 in the TWO KNIGHTS DEFENCE, one of the moves suggested here by POLERIO in 1594. 1157 in the KIESERITZKY GAMBIT, also known as the Paulsen Variation, or the Salvio–Polerio Defence, is also in a Polerio manuscript, but may be the idea of a contemporary, Giovanni Domenico.

Polerio Gambit, 1113, the VILLEMSON GAMBIT given by POLERIO, with a different theme. After 1 e4 e5 2 f4 exf4 3 d4 Qh4+ 4 g3 fxg3 White makes a king's leap, 5 Kg2, which was then a permissible alternative to CASTLING.

Polerio Variation, 1045 in the GRECO COUNTER-GAMBIT, attributed to LEONARDO by POLERIO.

Polgár, Judit (1976–), International Grandmaster (1991), youngest and strongest of the three Hungarian sisters. From 1 January 1990 she was the highest rated woman player in the world. In 1988 she was equal first with her sister Zsuzsa (below) at Egilsstadhir, and in 1990 won the Under-14 World Championship. She was first equal with TUKMAKOV at Amsterdam 1990, a Swiss system event with 24 strong players.

In December 1991 Polgár won the Hungarian Super-Championship (+3=6), ahead of ADORJÁN and SAX. In doing so she also earned her third Grandmaster NORM, and so, at the age of 15 years and 5 months qualified to become the youngest Grandmaster up to that date, a month younger than FISCHER was when he reached that level. She may also be the first woman to have won a national championship, in this case a strong one, open to players of either sex.

J. Polgár–Knaak Germany 1990 Television Tournament
French Defence

1 e4 e6 2 d4 d5 3 Nc3 Bb4 4 e5 c5 5 a3 Bxc3+ 6 bxc3 Ne7 7 Qg4 Qc7 8 Bd3 cxd4 9 Ne2 Qxe5 10 Bf4 Qf6 11 Bg5 Qe5 12 cxd4 h5 13 Qh4 Qc7 14 Bf4 Qa5+ 15 Bd2

Qd8 16 g4 e5 17 dxe5 Bxg4 18 Rg1 Qd7 19 f3 Be6 20 Nd4 Nbc6 21 Nxc6 Nxc6 22 Rxg7 Qc7

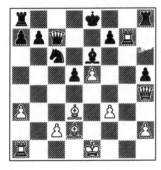

23 f4 Nxe5 24 fxe5 Qxe5+ 25 Kf2 Qxg7 26 Rg1 Qb2 27 Bb4 f6 28 Re1 0–0–0 29 Rxe6 Kb8 30 Qxf6 Qa2 31 Qd4 Rc8 32 Bd2 Ka8 33 Be3 Rxc2+ 34 Bxc2 Qxc2+ 35 Ke1 Qb1+ 36 Kd2 Qa2+ 37 Kd1 Qb1+ 38 Ke2 Qc2+ 39 Bd2 Rf8 40 Qxd5 Black lost on time.

Polgár, Zsofia (1974–), International Master (1990), middle of the three Hungarian sisters, and often said to be the weakest of the three. However in February 1989 she won a tournament in Rome, run on the Swiss system, scoring 8 wins and conceding a draw, in a favourable position, in the last round. Experts considered this, a rating performance of more than 2900, to be matched only by FISCHER or KASPAROV at their best.

Polgár, Zsuzsa (1969–), International Grandmaster (1991) the senior of the three sisters, who, with Idilkó Mádl (1969–), won the gold medal for Hungary in the Women's Olympiad in 1988 (the first time that the USSR had failed), and again in 1990. She was equal first with her sister Judit (above) at Egilsstadhir 1988; equal first at León 1989; equal second (+3=6) at Royan 1988; and third (+2=7) at Pamplona 1989–90, behind YUDASIN and KORCHNOI.

The Polgár sisters were educated at home although, unlike KAMSKY, they have not been restricted to chess in their upbringing. Indeed they have a wide range of knowledge, and have had to prove this to the disgruntled Hungarian authorities who preferred that they should attend school. The family also attracted the anger of the Hungarian chess association when they refused to play in single-sex events. When the girls came near the top of the women's ranking lists FIDE responded by increasing the rating of all women except the Polgárs by 100 points, a temporary set-back. Traditionalists were disturbed when it became clear that the women's world champion was no longer the strongest female player.

Polish Defence, originally 49, later including 424; in each case Black plays Pb7–b5. The first of these lines was launched by WAGNER against Kuhn in the tenth Swiss Correspondence Championship, 1913. Wagner published his analysis in *Deutsches*

Wochenschach, 1914. He was then living in Stanislau, Poland, now Ivano-Frankovsk in the Ukraine. (See C. TORRE.)

Polish Gambit, see BLACKMAR–DIEMER GAMBIT.

Polish Opening, 6, one of the several names for the ORANG UTAN OPENING.

Pollock Defence, 765, an uncommon line in the SPANISH OPENING, used by the English master William Henry Krause Pollock (1859–96) against LASKER and BURN. Writing in the *Baltimore News* about the ALAPIN DEFENCE (766), Pollock said, 'It is even worse than my move, if only because less ridiculous.'

Pollock Variation, 1220, ineffective line, sometimes called the Argentine Variation, in the FRENCH DEFENCE, also used by WALBRODT at Hastings, 1895.

Polugagayevsky, Lev Abramovich (1934–95), Soviet player, International Grandmaster (1962), one of the world's best ten players during the 1970s. He played in nearly 40 strong tournaments from 1960 to mid-1981, winning or sharing 18 first and 10 second prizes. His best wins up to 1972 were: Mar del Plata 1962 (+8=7), ahead of SMYSLOV and NAJDORF; Sochi 1963 (+6=5), ahead of Smyslov; Budapest 1965 (+7=8), equal with SZABÓ and TAIMANOV; Beverwijk 1966 (+8=7); Amsterdam 1970 (+8=7), equal with SPASSKY; Mar del Plata 1971 (+11=4); Skopje 1971 (+9=6); Amsterdam 1972 (+9=6); and Kislovodsk 1972 (+9=4–1). Also during these years Polugayevsky shared first place in three consecutive USSR championships: Kharkov 1967, played on the Swiss system, when he and TAL became joint champions; Alma-Ata 1968–9 (+7=11–1), when he won the play-off against ZAITSEV; and Moscow 1969 (+7=14–1), when he lost the play-off with PETROSYAN.

Playing in his second interzonal, Petropolis 1973, Polugayevsky scored +7=9–1 to share second place with GELLER and PORTISCH. Successful in the play-off, he became a CANDIDATE only to lose to KARPOV in the quarter-final. Next he had three fine tournament results: Solingen 1974 (+7=6–1), equal with KAVALEK, ahead of Spassky; Sochi 1974 (+7=8); and Budapest 1975 (+7=7–1), equal with RIBLI, ahead of Portisch. At the Manila interzonal 1976 he again became a Candidate, scoring +7=11–1 and sharing second place with HORT, after MECKING. Polugayevsky defeated Mecking (+1=11) in the quarter-final match, but then lost to KORCHNOI. At Wijk aan Zee 1979, Polugayevsky was first (+4=7), and later that year became a candidate for the third time by taking second place (+8=7–2) in the Riga interzonal. After defeating Tal (+3=5), he lost to Korchnoi in the semi-final.

Although his hopes of becoming world champion were now effectively over, Polugayevsky continued to produce good tournament results: Moscow 1981, second $(+2=11)$ equal with KASPAROV and Smyslov, after Karpov; Bugojno 1982, second $(+4=8-1)$ equal with LJUBOJEVIĆ, after Kasparov; London 1984, second $(+4=8-1)$ equal with CHANDLER, after Karpov; Biel 1986, first $(+4=6-1)$ equal with LOBRON; Sarajevo 1987, second $(+4=6-1)$ equal with VAGANYAN, after NIKOLIĆ; Haninge 1988, first $(+6=4-1)$, in front of ANDERSSON; Biel 1989, first $(+5=8-1)$ equal with IVANCHUK; Reggio Emilia 1991, second $(+2=10)$ equal with EHLVEST, behind Karpov.

Polugayevsky wrote *Rozhdeniye varianta* (1977); *Grandmaster Preparation* (1981) is an English translation with revisions and added material. An excellent book for those aspiring to succeed in competitive chess, it includes many of the author's games. A measure of the care he devotes to writing is given by this comment: 'Ninety per cent of all chess books you can open at page one and then immediately close again for ever. Sometimes you see books that have been written in one month. I don't like that. You should take at least two years for a book, or not do it at all.'

Ya. V. Damsky, *Grossmeister Polugayevsky* (1982) contains a biography and 60 games annotated in Russian.

Polugayevsky–E. Torre   London 1984   Slav Defence Wiesbaden Variation

1 d4 d5 2 c4 c6 3 Nf3 Nf6 4 Nc3 dxc4 5 a4 Bf5 6 e3 e6
7 Bxc4 Bb4 8 0–0–0 0–0 9 Qe2 Nbd7 10 e4 Bg6 11 Bd3
Bh5 12 Bf4 Re8 13 e5 Nd5 14 Nxd5 cxd5 15 h3 Be7
16 Rfc1 a6 17 Rc3 Bxf3 18 Qxf3 Nb8

19 Bxh7+ Kxh7 20 Qh5+ Kg8 21 Rg3 g6 22 Rxg6+
fxg6 23 Qxg6+ Kh8 24 Qh6+ Kg8 25 Qxe6+ Kh8 26
Qh6+ Kg8 27 Qg6+ Kh8 28 Qh5+ Kg8 29 Bh6 Bf8
30 Qg6+ Kh8 31 Bxf8 Rxf8 32 Qh6+ Kg8 33 Ra3
Black resigns.

Polugayevsky Variation, 510 in the SICILIAN DEFENCE. It is the subject of a detailed account by POLUGAYEVSKY, 'Birth of a Variation', in his *Grandmaster Preparation*. The move was not new, but Polugayevsky used it in an original way.

Pomar, Arturo (1931–), Spanish professional player, International Grandmaster (1962). Hailed as a child prodigy, he was 11 years old when he played in his first international tournament, Madrid 1943. Although he barely avoided last place, he

defeated SÄMISCH, but the promise of these early years was never quite fulfilled. He shared first place with GLIGORIĆ, DONNER, and PORTISCH at Madrid 1960, a zonal event, but at the interzonal, Stockholm 1962, he shared eleventh place among 23 contestants. Pomar won the Spanish championship in 1946, 1950, 1957, 1958, 1959, 1962, and 1966, and played for his country in 10 Olympiads between 1958 and 1976. His best results in international tournaments are: Torremolinos 1961, first $(+7=3-1)$ equal with Gligorić; Málaga 1964, first $(+7=3-1)$, ahead of Portisch; Palma de Majorca 1966, second $(+8=6-1)$, after TAL, ahead of Portisch; and Málaga 1971, first $(+8=6)$.

Ponziani, Domenico Lorenzo (1719–96), priest, and law lecturer from Modena in Italy, author of an important chess treatise. He was identified as the anonymous Modenese because the first edition of his book *Il giuoco incomparabile degli scacchi* was published in 1769 without the author's name appearing. In 1820 an English naval officer J. B. Smith, using the pen-name J. S. Bingham, translated it into English as *The Incomparable Game of Chess* by Ercole DEL RIO, although Ponziani had already given his name in the second edition, 1782. This edition is the best practical guide written by the Modenese masters. He takes a broader view of strategy and gives a more comprehensive range of opening variations including the VIENNA GAME and the gambit and counter-gambit named after him. (See BLOCKADE; SCHOOLS OF CHESS.)

Ponziani Counter-gambit, 823 in the PONZIANI OPENING. The Modenese author published his analysis of this sound defence in 1782. The ROUSSEAU GAMBIT, 939, which has some resemblance, is sometimes given this name.

Ponziani Gambit, 654, sometimes called the Calvi Variation, in the BISHOP'S OPENING. After 3 ... exd4 White should play 4 Nf3, the URUSOV GAMBIT, and not 4 e5, rightly condemned by JAENISCH.

Ponziani Opening, 813, mentioned by LUCENA. It was liked by STAUNTON, and for that reason sometimes called the English Knight's, or Staunton Opening. Also 54, the CHIGORIN VARIATION, given by PONZIANI, and also known as the Richter Variation.

Popert, H. W. (*fl.*1830–44), player from Hamburg who was regarded as one of the strongest players of his day. He spent some years in London around 1840, and gave lessons to STANLEY. In 1840 he played a match against STAUNTON and lost by the odd game. Shortly afterwards he suffered a stroke and his chess ability fell abruptly. He was, wrote KENNEDY, 'obliged ... to receive the knight from players to whom he had formerly rendered pawn and two'. The change did not diminish his keenness for the game. Around the beginning of 1844 he collapsed in the Strand and was taken into Simpson's Divan 'with lack-lustre eyes'. Shortly afterwards he returned to Hamburg where he died, probably later in the same year. (See NIMZOWITSCH VARIATION.)

Popović, Petar (1959–), Yugoslav player, International Grandmaster (1981), winner at Pécs 1980 (+ 8 = 4 − 11), equal with Flesch; Novi Sad 1981 (+ 6 = 4 − 1), shared with Bjelajac; Bor 1985 (+ 6 = 6 − 1), shared with EINGORN; Djakarta 1986, equal with Ardiansyah; Pucarevo zonal 1987 (+ 5 = 4), equal with BARLOV; and Zenica 1989.

Popović–Kr. Georgiev Thessaloniki 1988 Olympiad
Sicilian Defence Scheveningen Variation

1 e4 c5 2 Nf3 d6 3 d4 cxd4 4 Nxd4 Nf6 5 Nc3 e6 6 g4 a6 7 g5 Nfd7 8 Be3 b5 9 a3 Bb7 10 h4 Be7 11 Qg4 Nc6 12 0-0-0 Nce5 13 Qg2 Rc8 14 f4 Nc4 15 Bxc4 Rxc4 16 f5 Nc5 17 g6 hxg6 18 fxg6 Rxc3 19 gxf7+ Kxf7 20 bxc3 Qa5 21 h5 Rxh5 22 Rxh5 Qxa3+ 23 Kb1 Na4

24 Rf1 + Bf6 25 Rxf6+ Kg8 26 Rh8 + Black resigns.

Portisch, Lajos (1937–), Hungarian player, International Grandmaster (1961), one of the world's best ten players in the 1970s. Chess being played often in his family (his brother Ferenc (1939–) is an International Master), he learned it at an early age. Lajos made no sudden leap forward but progressed steadily over the years. He first made his name in 1958 when he won the Hungarian championship (for the first of ten such victories) and a tournament at Balatonfüred.

A good indication of Portisch's place in chess history is that he has been a CANDIDATE eight times, an outstanding achievement, but has never looked likely to emerge as challenger for the world championship: Amsterdam interzonal 1964, eighth (after winning a play-off against RESHEVSKY + 2 = 1), then a loss to TAL in the quarter-final; Sousse interzonal 1967, fifth (+ 8 = 11 − 2), followed by a loss to LARSEN; Petropolis 1973, second (+ 7 = 9 − 1) equal with GELLER and POLUGAYEVSKY, and after success in the play-off, defeat by PETROSYAN; Biel 1976, second (+ 9 = 6 − 4) equal with Petrosyan and Tal, a win against Larsen (+ 5 = 3 − 2), then a loss to SPASSKY in the semi-final match; Rio de Janeiro 1979, first (+ 9 = 5 − 3), a victory on tie-break over Spassky (+ 1 = 12 − 1) because he won with black pieces, and a defeat by HÜBNER in the semi-final; Toluca 1982, first (+ 6 = 5 − 2) equal with TORRE,

followed by a loss to KORCHNOI; Tunis interzonal 1985, third, followed by failure in the Montpellier Candidates tournament; and Szirák 1987, third (+ 8 = 8 − 1) equal with NUNN (whom he defeated + 2 = 4 in a tie-break match), after HJARTARSON and SALOV, followed by a win over VAGANYAN (+ 1 = 5) and then a loss to TIMMAN in the semi-final.

Apart from national championships and interzonals, Portisch played in about 75 strong tournaments from 1958 to 1990, winning or sharing 20 first prizes, the best being: Beverwijk 1965 (+ 7 = 7 − 1), equal with Geller; Skopje–Ohrid 1968 (+ 11 = 7 − 1), ahead of Geller and Polugayevsky; Monte Carlo 1969 (+ 6 = 4 − 1), equal with SMYSLOV; Amsterdam 1969 (+ 8 = 7); Wijk aan Zee 1972 (+ 6 = 9); San Antonio 1972 (+ 6 = 9), equal with KARPOV and Petrosyan; Wijk aan Zee 1975 (+ 6 = 9); Wijk aan Zee 1978 (+ 5 = 6), ahead of Korchnoi; Tilburg 1978 (+ 4 = 6 − 1), ahead of Hübner; Reggio Emilia 1984–5 (+ 4 = 5 − 2); Portorož 1985 (+ 4 = 6 − 1), equal with MILES and RIBLI; and Sarajevo 1986 (+ 4 = 7 − 1), equal with Kir. GEORGIEV and PSAKHIS. He represented his country in many Olympiads from 1956, notably in 1978 when he scored + 8 = 4 − 2 on first board and Hungary won the gold medal, ahead of the USSR. Portisch, playing on board three for the Rest of the World against USSR in 1970, defeated Korchnoi + 1 = 3.

Portisch owes his success partly to perseverance and will to win. Quiet and undemonstrative, he is liked by other masters for his sportsmanship; when he loses he blames only himself. Unfortunately his games have not become widely appreciated; his positional style, characterized by quiet manœuvring—he has been called the Hungarian Petrosyan—is effective but unspectacular.

E. Varnusz, *Selected Games of Lajos Portisch* (1979), contains 90 games.

Portisch–Timman Montpellier 1985 Candidates tournament Queen's Indian Defence

1 d4 Nf6 2 c4 e6 3 Nf3 b6 4 e3 Bb7 5 Bd3 Bb4+ 6 Nbd2 0-0 7 a3 Bxd2+ 8 Qxd2 c5 9 b4 d6 10 Bb2 Nbd7 11 0-0 Rc8 12 dxc5 bxc5 13 b5 e5 14 Bf5 g6 15 Bc2 Nb6 16 Qe2 Ne4 17 a4 Qe7 18 a5 Nd7 19 Rad1 Rcd8 20 Nd2 f5 21 Rfe1 Ndf6 22 f3 Ng5 23 Qf2 Ne6 24 f4 Ne4 25 Nxe4 fxe4 26 Qg3 exf4 27 exf4 Rxf4 28 Bc1 Rh4

29 Rd5 e3 30 Bxe3 Rxc4 31 Bg5 Qd7 32 Rd2 Nxg5 33

Bb3 Ne4 34 Bxc4+ Kh8 35 Qh4 Re8 36 Rf2 Qg7 37 Rf7 Qd4+ 38 Kh1 h5 39 Qf4 g5 40 Rf8+ Rxf8 41 Qxf8+ Kh7 42 Bg8+ Black resigns.

position, the disposition of pieces and pawns, of one or both colours, at any stage of the game or as set in a composition. (See ARRAY for the position at the start of play.) If the strengths of the white and black men are compared and neither side has an overall advantage, the position is said to be level. Otherwise one side is said to have the better position, the other the worse. Sometimes both sides have advantages but neither has an overall advantage, and although a draw would be a proper outcome the complex nature of the position makes such a result less predictable; an annotator might say there were chances for both sides, or, baffled by a highly complex situation, that the position was unclear.

The term 'balance of position', now generally called the EQUILIBRIUM, was used by STEINITZ when discussing the theory attributed to him.

positional advantage, any advantage other than a material advantage, e.g. a gain in TIME, SPACE or MOBILITY, or possession of the better PAWN FORMATION.

positional draw, a study term for an impasse other than stalemate, usually characterized by a repetition of moves. Neither side can make progress and neither can safely deviate. Typically positional advantage is exactly counterbalanced by material advantage. A common example is PERPETUAL CHECK. See also examples given under FORTRESS, in which one side has the positional advantage of a stronghold.

=

A problem by the Soviet composer Leonard Ilyich Katsnelson (1936–), second place, 10th Soviet team championship, 1979. 1 b8 = Q Qxb8 2 f8 = Q Qxf8 3 h8 = Q Bc3 4 Qf6! Qd6 5 Qd4 Qa6 6 Qd3 Qb5 7 Qe2 Qc4 8 Qd3 Qb5 9 Qe2. A rare example of reciprocal queen-offers without checks.

(See also DOBRESCU; MARWITZ; MERRY-GO-ROUND; PENDULUM DRAW; RUSINEK.)

H. M. Kasparyan, *Positsionnaya nichya* (2nd edn., 1977).

positional play, MANŒUVRES made with the aim of improving a player's position, as distinct from combinative play leading to mate or gain of material. A positional combination is a combination made with the same end in view: such combinations, often short and perhaps better described as tactical interludes, and more often threatened than realized, are common features of positional play. The distinction between positional and tactical play is not clear-cut: all good moves have a strategic purpose and most contain tactical elements. A combination largely consists of forced and forcing moves with a specific aim, and the few variations may be calculated precisely. In positional play, however, the player to move may have a choice of several sound continuations, and a precise assessment of the numerous lines of play that might occur is not feasible. As a consequence positional aims are of a general kind, e.g. the gain of mobility.

All masters make use of positional play with the ultimate aim of making a decisive attack, i.e. a combination, or obtaining a won endgame. So-called combinative players will seek an early opportunity for an attack. Positional players usually abjure early attacks, preferring not to commit themselves too soon and seeking improvement of position instead.

Fischer–Petrosyan Buenos Aires 1971 7th match game, final Candidates match Sicilian Defence Paulsen Variation

1 e4 c5 2 Nf3 e6 3 d4 cxd4 4 Nxd4 a6 5 Bd3 Nc6 6 Nxc6 bxc6 7 0–0 d5 8 c4 Nf6 9 cxd5 cxd5 10 exd5 exd5 11 Nc3 Be7

The material is level. White has a small advantage in time, insofar as Black's fourth move has proved ineffective: indeed, his a-pawn would be better placed at a7. White has fewer pawn islands while Black's two isolated pawns are not easy to defend.

12 Qa4+

After the reply 12 ... Bd7 (probably best) White plays 13 Qd4, with a good initiative.

    12 ...   Qd7

Black offers a sacrifice for a strong counterattack: 13 Bb5 axb5 14 Qxa8 0–0 12 Qa5 d4 13 Nxb5 Bb7.

    13 Re1

White changes plan: this positional move forces Black to exchange queens with loss of time.

    13 ...   Qxa4
    14 Nxa4   Be6

| 15 Be3 | 0–0 |
| 16 Bc5 | |

White forces the exchange of Black's 'good' bishop, ceding his gain in time for a more permanent advantage.

16 ...	Rfe8
17 Bxe7	Rxe7
18 b4	

Not 18 Nc5 a5.

18 ...	Kf8
19 Nc5	Bc8
20 f3	

Making room for the king to advance on the dark squares.

| 20 ... | Rea7 |

Byrne suggests 20 ... Rxe1+ 21 Rxe1 Ne8. This holds everything for the time being, but Black still has a difficult game.

| 21 Re5 | Bd7 |
| 22 Nxd7+ | |

Less complicated than 22 a4. White's bishop is stronger than Black's knight in this position.

| 22 ... | Rxd7 |
| 23 Rc1 | Rd6 |

Otherwise White plays 24 Rc6.

| 24 Rc7 | Nd7 |

After this Black is soon brought to a standstill. An alternative is 24 ... Ne8.

| 25 Re2 | g6 |
| 26 Kf2 | |

White brings up his king for the final assault.

| 26 ... | h5 |

If 26 ... Re8 27 Rxe8+ Kxe8 28 Ra7 Rb6 29 a3 Nb8, White's king marches up to c5 by way of the dark squares.

27 f4	h4
28 Kf3	f5
29 Ke3	d4+
30 Kd2	Nb6

To prevent 31 Bc4. There is no adequate defence.

31 Ree7	Nd5
32 Rf7+	Ke8
33 Rb7	Nxf4
34 Bc4	Black resigns.

positional sacrifice, a sacrifice of material for positional advantage, as distinct from a sacrifice that leads directly to a mating combination or gain of material. The first to give serious attention to positional sacrifice was PHILIDOR, who used this fictitious game as a model.

1 e4 e5 2 Nf3 d6 3 Bc4 f5 4 d3 c6 5 exf5 Bxf5 6 Bg5 Nf6 7 Nbd2 d5 8 Bb3 Bd6 9 Qe2 Qe7 10 0–0 Nbd7 11 Nh4 Qe6 12 Nxf5 Qxf5 13 Bxf6 gxf6 14 f4 Qg6 15 fxe5 fxe5 16 Rf3 h5 17 Raf1 0–0–0 18 c4

Of Black's next move (18 ... e4) Philidor writes: 'Here is a Move as difficult to comprehend, as it is to be well ... explained ... it is best to push your King's Pawn upon his Rook, and sacrifice it; because then your Adversary (by taking it, as he cannot well do otherwise) openeth a free passage to your Queen's Pawn, which you are to advance immediately, and sustain in case of need with your other Pawns, in order to make a Queen with it, or draw some other considerable Advantage by it to win the Game. It is true that his Queen's Pawn (now become his King's) appears to have the same Advantage of having no opposition from your pawns to make a Queen; however, the Difference is great, because his pawn being entirely separated from his Camarades, will always be in danger of being snatch'd away in his Road by a Multitude of your Pieces all at War against it. But to know well how to make use of these Moves at proper times, one must already be a good Player.' Philidor here refers to Black's better PAWN FORMATION. Subsequently he exemplifies another advantage: the freeing of Black's minor pieces and the confining of White's. From the diagram the game proceeded 18 ... e4 19 dxe4 d4 20 Bc2 Ne5 21 Rf6 Qg7 22 Qf2 Ng4 23 Qf5+ Kb8 24 Rxd6 Rxd6 25 Qf4 Qe5 26 Qxe5 Nxe5 27 Rf5 Ng4 28 c5 Rg6 29 Nc4 Ne3 30 Nxe3 dxe3 31 Rf3 Rd8 32 Rxe3 Rd2 White resigns.

The distinction between a positional sacrifice and any other kind is somewhat fuzzy. Many sacrifices contain a considerable tactical element but do not permit an exact calculation of all the consequences. In the following game White sacrifices a queen for two minor pieces and two pawns, leaving Black with a badly placed queen and queen's rook and without the right to castle. A competent master might make this sacrifice without further calculation, judging that such a position must be advantageous.

Smagin–Šahović   Biel 1990   Nimzowitsch Defence

1 e4 Nc6 2 d4 d5 3 e5 Bf5 4 c3 e6 5 Nd2 f6 6 f4 fxe5 7 fxe5 Nh6 8 Ndf3 Nf7 9 Ne2 Be7 10 Ng3 Bg4 11 Bd3 Ng5

12 Nxg5 Bxd1 13 Nxe6 Qb8 14 Nxg7+ Kd8 15 Kxd1 b5 16 Ne6+ Kc8 17 Nf5 Bf8 18 Rf1 Kb7 19 Bh6 Bxh6 20 Nc5+ Kc8 21 Nxh6 Ne7 22 Be2 Ng6 23 Nf7 Black resigns.

Duz-Khotimirsky–Capablanca   Moscow 1925   King's Indian Defence

1 Nf3 Nf6 2 d4 g6 3 e3 Bg7 4 Bd3 0–0 5 0–0 d6 6 e4 Nbd7 7 h3 c5 8 c3 e5 9 dxe5 dxe5 10 a4 Qc7 11 Na3

11 ... c4 (a positional sacrifice to gain a lead in development) 12 Nxc4 Nc5 13 Qe2 Nxd3 14 Qxd3 Rd8 15 Qe2 Be6 16 Na3 h6 17 Re1 a6 18 Qc2 Bd7 19 Be3 Bc6 20 Nd2 b5 21 axb5 axb5 22 f3 Nh5 23 Rad1 Bf8 24 Nab1 Bd7 25 Nf1 Nf4 26 Ng3 b4 27 Ne2 g5 28 Nc1 Rdc8 29 c4 b3 (a positional sacrifice to keep White's pieces tied up) 30 Nxb3 Ba4 31 N1d2? Bb4 32 g3 Ne6 33 Qd3 Rd8 34 Qe2 Rab8 35 Rf1 Bxd2 36 Nxd2 Bxd1 37 Qxd1 Rxb2 38 Qc1 Ra2 39 Rf2 Rd3 40 Nf1 Raa3 41 f4 Rac3 42 Qe1 exf4 43 gxf4 Nxf4 44 Bxf4 gxf4 45 Qe2 f3 46 Qa2 Rc1 47 Rxf3 Rxf3 48 Qg2+ Rg3 White resigns.

For some examples, see ALEKHINE; BOLBOCHÁN; SCHLECHTER; SVESHNIKOV.

postage stamps, see PHILATELY AND CHESS.

postal chess, see CORRESPONDENCE CHESS.

post-key play, or actual play, play that follows the KEY of a problem. In a DIRECT MATE PROBLEM and most other kinds of problem the key and the post-key play together form the solution.

post mortem, examination of a game soon after it has ended. Players often crowd the board throwing in their comments. Although such analysis is frequently superficial it is sometimes used as a basis for published annotations that remain unchallenged for years.

Potter, William Norwood (1840–95), a leading English player of the 1870s, barrister's clerk. He met strong opposition in only one tournament, London 1876, when he took third place after BLACKBURNE and ZUKERTORT. In match play he lost to Zukertort in 1875 (+2=8−4) and drew with MASON in 1879 (+5=11−5). Potter was editor of the *London Chess Magazine* (1874–6) and wrote for the *Westminster Papers* and *Land and Water*, contributing annotations of a high standard to all three journals. He played a part in the development of new ideas attributed to STEINITZ, with whom he established a firm friendship and to whom he may have shown the ideas of the English School (see SCHOOLS OF CHESS). In 1872 the London Chess Club, represented by Blackburne, HORWITZ, LÖWENTHAL, Potter, Steinitz, and WISKER, began a correspondence match of two games against a Viennese team led by KOLISCH for stakes of £100 a side. (The moves were sent by telegraph and confirmed by letter.) Unable

to accept the ideas of Potter and Steinitz, the rest of the London team soon withdrew, leaving these two to play on. They won the match. Subsequently Steinitz declared that 'modern chess' began with these two games.

Potter Variation, 879 in the EVANS GAMBIT, given by POTTER in his column in *Land and Water*; 983, introduced in the 1870s, and possibly White's best continuation in this form of the SCOTCH GAME.

Prague Variation, 125 in the QUEEN'S GAMBIT Declined, played in the Prague tournament, 1908.

Pratt, Peter (*c*.1770–*c*.1835), a member of the London Chess Club who wrote *Theory of Chess* (1799) and, more successfully, *Studies of Chess* (1803). This later work was reissued, with occasional revision, seven times up to 1825. Its chief merit is that it contains the whole of PHILIDOR; its chief defect, that it also contains a good deal of Pratt. He was not a strong player (in 1817 LEWIS gave him the odds of a knight in a match) but he was ever seeking improvements to the game. For example, he opposed the idea that a pawn could be promoted to a piece that would give a player a second queen, a third rook or knight, or a second bishop of the same colour. He proposed that in such a situation the pawn should become a Hydra, a piece having a double knight's move. However, Pratt had some distinction. He would play blindfold chess with a friend, calling out his moves in rhyming couplets. (See EDUCATION AND CHESS; PHILIDOR VARIATION; VALUE OF PIECES.)

Pratt Variation, 645 in the BISHOP'S OPENING, given by PRATT in the 1825 edition of his book based on PHILIDOR'S work.

premature attack, an attack that is launched before a player has an advantage of some kind. Against correct defence the attacker will have to retreat with loss of time, or will find the attacking pieces misplaced. For an example, see the game under ANTOSHIN in which Black breaks through in the centre, often the best way to meet a premature attack.

Beginners, anxious to cross swords as soon as possible, often attack prematurely. No doubt this is part of the learning experience; one can only advise that, at least, they develop all their pieces first.

Van den Bosch–Kramer   Leeuwarden 1941   Queen's Bishop Game

1 d4 Nf6 2 Nf3 g6 3 Nc3 d5 4 Bf4 c6 5 Qd2 Bg7 6 Bh6 0–0 7 h4 Bf5 8 0–0–0 Bxh6 9 Qxh6 Ng4 10 Qd2 Nxf2 11 e4 Nxh1 12 Qh6 f6 13 exf5 Qe8 14 h5 gxh5 15 Ne4 Nd7 16 Bc4 dxc4 17 Rxh1 Qf7 18 Rh3 Kh8 19 Nh4 Rg8 20 Ng6+ Rxg6 21 fxg6 Qxg6 22 Qe3 Qxg2 23 Rxh5 Rg8 24 Nf2 Qf1+ White resigns. His attack is broken and his material deficiency is fatal.

prepared variation, a line of play in the opening prepared before a game commences. The line might be from a textbook or recent tournament play or might be devised by a player. An unwary opponent might allow this line to be played, otherwise it could be set aside for a future occasion. Preparation is as old as the game but is no substitute for talent. For example, in the first important matches of the modern game, in 1834, McDONNELL prepared some BISHOP'S GAMBIT variations but his opponent BOURDONNAIS swept them aside with ease. For another débâcle of this kind, see ARGENTINE VARIATION. These failures are no argument against preparation, which is necessary in greater or lesser degree at all levels of play. Anxious to do especially well at San Remo 1930, ALEKHINE made extensive preparation for each and every opponent. He would probably have won the tournament without such labour but not, perhaps, by such a decisive margin. Ever increasing numbers of new ideas in the opening are being evolved, and the pace of change continues to accelerate. At grandmaster level it is not sufficient to know what others played a few months before but rather what they played in the last one or two weeks. Masters have become wary of prepared variations as is often shown in their opening play; they may be less concerned to play the 'best' move than to avoid the possibility of a prepared line, imagined or real. In the world championship match of 1972 FISCHER, conscious of the inventive capability of his Soviet opponent's back-up teams, successfully varied his opening play throughout the match, even to the extent of using openings that he had never played before. (See THEORETICAL NOVELTY.)

Preti, Jean-Louis (1798–1881), Italian-born musician and chess writer who had to flee his homeland in 1826 because of his involvement in a political conspiracy. After 18 years in Bordeaux he moved to Paris and there, in 1867, started *La Stratégie,* a monthly magazine which he edited until 1875. His son Numa Preti (1841–1908) succeeded him and was followed by Henri Delaire (1860–1941), who was editor from 1908 until the magazine ceased publication in 1940. J. L. Preti was co-author with DURAND of *Stratégie raisonnée des fins de partie* (1871–3).

Primitive Pillsbury, 166, the original continuation of the PILLSBURY VARIATION, 164, later superseded by 6 Nxd4.

princess, an unorthodox piece that combines the powers of the bishop and knight. A piece with similar powers, used in some forms of GREAT CHESS, was called a centaur by CARRERA in 1617 and a WAZIR according to an 18th-century Persian manuscript.

Prins Variation, 382 in the GRÜNFELD DEFENCE played in the game Kmoch–Prins, Amsterdam 1940.

problem, a composition accompanied by stipulations, provided for the solver, stating that one side is to give mate, or achieve some other aim, in a set number of moves, and usually stating or implying which side is to move first.

As a consequence of the stipulations the strategy of the game ceases to be relevant. On the other hand problemists can achieve tactical effects that would be unlikely to occur in play. They may place the men where they choose and construct positions that would not happen in play, because the disparity in forces would have induced resignation long before, and, most importantly, they need not prevent solutions that take more than the stipulated number of moves. Besides ORTHODOX PROBLEMS there are FAIRY PROBLEMS using boards, men, and rules foreign to the game. In these several ways problems have become separated from play to an extent not paralleled in any other game. For example, the chess equivalent of a bridge problem would be a STUDY, not a problem.

The composer endeavours to create a SOUND problem, one that can be solved only in the manner intended, without COOKS or DUALS. The idea, or at least its setting, should be original, avoiding ANTICIPATION. The relative importance of variety (see VARIATION; PHASE), ECONOMY, and solving difficulty depends on fashion or taste.

Numerous different themes and patterns may be used, among them BREDE THEME, BRISTOL CLEARANCE, CHANGED PLAY, CORRECTION, CRITICAL PLAY, CUTTING-POINT THEMES, CYCLIC PLAY, DECOY THEMES, DOMBROVSKIS THEME, DOUBLING THEMES, DUAL AVOIDANCE, FOCAL PLAY, INDIAN THEME, KNIGHT WHEEL, RECIPROCAL PLAY, SCHIFFMAN DEFENCE, SIERS RÖSSEL THEME. There are TASKS of various kinds, e.g. ALBINO, ALLUMWANDLUNG, BABSON TASK, PICKANINNY. Besides DIRECT MATE PROBLEMS there are other forms such as HELPMATE, HELPSTALEMATE, SELFMATE, SELF-STALEMATE, REFLEX CHESS, SERIES-MOVER. (See also BOHEMIAN; LOGICAL SCHOOL.)

Problemists have developed an extensive jargon running to several hundred words, much of it not fully understood by themselves. Fortunately problems can be, and are, enjoyed without knowledge of this arcane language.

For the caption abbreviations used with diagrams, see CONVENTIONAL SYMBOLS. (See also PROBLEM HISTORY.)

problem history. Problems originated in medieval Europe. Composers were aware of the earlier MANṢŪBĀT, which used such tactical devices as BATTERIES, DECOYS, HALF-BATTERIES, interference (see INTERFERE), SELF-BLOCKS, and SQUARE VACATION. The principal European innovation was the requirement to give mate in a set number of moves, and if this could not be done the problem was regarded as unsound. (A manṣūba is unsound only if the composer's intentions can be circumvented, the length of the solution being of no consequence.) Europeans were original in other ways. They used non-checking KEYS more often, sometimes adding VARIATIONS, and were inclined to seek greater ECONOMY of material; they toyed with FAIRY PROBLEMS and invented the SELF-MATE and the SERIES-MOVER. In short, they were more creative although they lacked their predecessors' constructional skill. For examples, see MEDIEVAL PROBLEMS, and for an extensive collection see MURRAY'S *A History of Chess*.

All these problems became obsolete when the new game was introduced, *c*.1475. There seems to have been little interest in the art until STAMMA published his 100 positions (modern manṣūbāt, not problems) in 1737. This collection, often reprinted, stimulated the masters of MODENA, who reintroduced the stipulation to give mate in a set number of moves. Most of their problems show a beleaguered and defenceless black king, a surplus of black men, most of them mere bystanders, and a solution consisting entirely or mostly of checks.

#5

A typical DEL RIO problem, no. 49 in LOLLI's collection. 1 Rf8+, 2 Bh6+, 3 Rg8, 4 Rh5+, 5 g5#. On rare occasions del Rio composed with greater economy of force: White Ke3, Rd7, Bf3, Nf4, Black Kf5, mate in 4. 1 Rd6 Ke5, 2 Rg6, 3 Be4+, 4 Nd3#. This has one key. Compare LUCENA: White Kd4, Rh7, Bf1, Nd5, Black Kd6, mate in 3. 1 Bd3, Be2, Bh3, Bb5, Ba6, Rg7, Re7, or Ra7.

In 1763 Lolli published 100 positions (actually 105) consisting of 58 ORTHODOX PROBLEMS, 22 CONDITIONAL PROBLEMS, 5 selfmates, and 20 endgames, representing a good overview of the art up to this time. Neither he nor PONZIANI (who gave only three of his own problems) composed as well as del Rio. Lolli's best problem (see EPAULET MATE) was based on a game which was drawn by perpetual check, the winning continuation a subsequent discovery.

The composers who followed were mainly German or English, and conditional problems formed a substantial part of their work. The English composer LEWIS made conscious attempts to use fewer non-checking moves. (These are often called quiet moves, but they are the most forcing moves available, and only appear to be quiet.) Orthodox problems up to the 1830s might best be described as STRATAGEMS, forcing lines with little scope for defence, the black king supinely awaiting its doom. Indeed, the English version (1817) of Montigny's

collection is called *Stratagems of Chess*; the introduction states '...these situations are in reality so many problems ...' This may be the first use of the word problem applied to a chess position, a usage subsequently popularized by Lewis.

The first composer to break with tradition was D'ORVILLE. Economy of white force—all pieces taking part in the play—had long been understood. D'Orville sought economy of black force, abandoning the idea of constructing a game-like position, and he provided MODEL MATES, rare before his time. Thus, after a long period of mere stratagems and tricks, often using special stipulations, problems emerged as an art form. However, D'Orville also composed many problems of an older kind.

Another innovator was BREDE. Before his time black men were either inactive or merely used to threaten instant mate so that the solution was necessarily a series of checks. Brede sometimes gave freedom to the black men, so that they could hinder White from mating in a set number of moves. Different kinds of hindrance would lead to different mating continuations, i.e. variations.

#4

Problem no. 23 in Brede's collection of 1844. The apparently quiet key is 1 Qh4, and now:

1 ... Rxh4 (or 1 ... f6, Bf6) 2 Nc6 a6 3 Rxa6+ Bxa6 4 Rb8#
1 ... Rd6 2 Nc6 Bxc6 3 Qd8+ Rxd8 4 Bxc6#
1 ... a6 2 Nxa6 Rxh4 3 Rxb7 Rxe4 4 Nxc5#
1 ... Bxe4+ 2 Qxe4+ Kb8 3 Na6+ Kc8 4 Qe8#.

Unfortunately there is no solution after 1 ... Be5, for if 2 Na6, f6, but the problem shows the kind of variety that Brede sought to achieve. He also composed a two-mover showing six distinct mates, an unprecedented achievement.

In the 1840s there was a surge of interest in problems, perhaps because these could be regularly published in NEWSPAPER COLUMNS or PERIODICALS, or because of the increasing number of chess enthusiasts, or for both reasons. In 1846 ALEXANDRE published his problem encyclopedia, an attempt to bring together all known problems of the modern game up to that time. So great were the changes taking place that his book was almost immediately out of date.

For more than the first three and a half centuries of the modern game problemists largely failed to see the possibilities of the new line-pieces (Q,B). Then, in 1845, STAUNTON published the INDIAN THEME problem featuring CRITICAL PLAY. This stimulated the imagination of problemists, who soon invented other kinds of line-themes such as CUTTING-POINT THEMES, DOUBLING THEMES, BRISTOL CLEARANCE, developed other ideas including DECOY THEMES, FOCAL PLAY, and introduced TASKS such as ALBINO, EXCELSIOR. The years 1845 to 1861, in which the content of problems was so greatly enriched, is sometimes called the transitional period. The introduction of TOURNEYS in the 1850s also encouraged composers.

In the second half of the nineteenth century there were differing ideas as to the form a problem should take. The BOHEMIAN style, as now, emphasized model mates and minimum force, using few, if any, white pawns. The founder, the Czech composer Antonín König (1836–1911), apparently took his inspiration from John BROWN, who, like D'Orville, sought artistic form.

#3

A problem by the Czech composer Antonín Kvíčala (1847–1908), *Svetozor* 1869. Three model mates follow the key 1 Rc3:

   1 ... Rxa2 2 Re3+ Kf4 3 Nd5#
           2 ...   Kd4 3 Nf5#
   1 ... Rd2   2 Qe6+ Kxe6 3 Re3#.

For the so-called Old German School BERGER published a code of standards in *Deutsche Schachzeitung*, 1884–5. Problems were to be three- or more-movers, difficult to solve, with several variations, some of which lead to model mates; the pawn formation should seem natural, as if it might have arisen in play; as far as possible White's moves should not seem to be forceful. To a Bohemian composer the smattering of white pawns to cover outlying flights would seem crude, as would the permissive attitude towards introductory play (merely for the purpose of making the problem harder to solve). The requirement of a game-like position was retrogressive. Nevertheless some fine examples were composed. For an example, see KLETT.

In America LOYD, the most innovative 19th-century composer, made problems of quite a different kind. His aim was to puzzle and amuse, and he was possibly the greatest popularizer of his time. Neither solving difficulty nor variations were sought as ends in themselves. Unhampered by the need to provide model mates, he was able to develop a wide range of ideas. Ingenious rather than complex, he showed these ideas in sharply pointed form. A younger American, SHINKMAN, composed problems of all kinds, including fairy problems and selfmates.

In England composers sought neatness of construction, pleasing settings, good key moves (for all of which they evolved their own criteria), and the avoidance of lesser duals—in short, their concern was with form, although content was not disregarded. The leading exponents were HEATHCOTE and BLAKE, who came to the fore in the 1890s.

Most composers supposed that the different styles of the late 19th century would merge, but the changes that began in the new century resembled a renaissance rather than a fusion. As regards three- and more-movers the principal founders of the so-called New German style were KOHTZ and KOCKELKORN, who published their famous book *Das indische Problem* in 1903. They drew their inspiration from the transitional period, in particular from the Indian Problem. Problems were to show themes, and to show them in the clearest manner; other considerations became less important. Model mates survive in the Bohemian style; although valued when they occur they are rarely practicable with complex themes, which usually need many white pieces. The manner of achieving the mate was to be of more importance than the mating position. These ideas were nearer to those of Loyd, whom the authors praise, than to those of Berger's code. Although only critical play is examined in *Das indische Problem*, the authors and other composers soon demonstrated that many themes could be used in accordance with the new criteria. Despite Berger's dogged opposition, the New German Style soon ousted the Old. One development was the LOGICAL SCHOOL.

The two-mover, somewhat neglected previously, also received a new infusion of life, unity being achieved by the provision of variations that related to one another. In 1904 A. F. MACKENZIE was able to show a CROSS-CHECK in three variations. Soon composers began to feature HALF-PIN, UNPINS, batteries, half-batteries, interference, and other tactical elements, sometimes using one of them in several ways. From 1913 to 1924 these developments were encouraged by the GOOD COMPANION CHESS PROBLEM CLUB. The content of the two-mover was further enriched by CORRECTION and DUAL-AVOIDANCE, also by themes in which different PHASES are linked to one another by patterns of some kind, e.g. CHANGED PLAY, CYCLIC PLAY, DOMBROVSKIS THEME. Three-movers also gained; besides featuring critical play (not possible in a two-mover), many complex ideas can be devised.

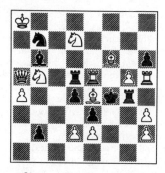

#3

A problem by G. F. ANDERSON and the American Vincent Lanius Eaton (1915–62), *British Chess Magazine*, 1953. The key is 1 Bb1 and in six variations Black voluntarily forgoes the possibility of check by a rook on a5, g8, or d8.

    1 ... Bxa5   2 Nxd4
    1 ... Nxa5   2 Nd6
    1 ... Bc5 or 1 ... Ba7   2 Nc7
    1 ... Nc5   2 Nc3
    1 ... Nd8   2 gxh6
    1 ... Nd6   2 Nf8.

The collaborators, who spent 300 hours composing this highly complex problem, tried to show in as many variations as possible a theme called check-prevention. Other variations begin 1 ... Bc7 2 Rxd5, 1 ... Rxb5 2 Rf5+, 1 ... Rc5 2 Nxc5, 1 ... d3 2 Qb4+, 1 ... Rg1 2 Rh4+, and 1 ... hxg5 2 Rhxg5.

The new century also brought about greater concern for economy of force, to which end MEREDITH tourneys were introduced in 1914. Attitudes towards by-play changed: sometimes minor duals are permitted in preference to their prevention by adding material; sometimes, as in many problems by MANSFIELD, the by-play itself becomes of added interest; sometimes by-play is avoided altogether, as in the problems given under IMITATOR and ROOT-50 LEAPER. Introductory play and FRINGE VARIATIONS went out of fashion at the beginning of the 20th century.

Around 1912 a few devotees led by DAWSON investigated RETROGRADE ANALYSIS and fairy problems (which then included selfmates and HELPMATES). Dawson regarded retrograde analysis, an exercise in deductive reasoning fathered by Loyd, as the highest chess art. He stimulated interest in helpmates (a form invented by LANGE in 1854). These and other kinds of FAIRY PROBLEM were his speciality. From 1919, in the pages of the *Chess Amateur*, he conducted the first long-running column devoted to fairy problems, and through his influence they became established abroad. Dawson valued fairy problems more highly than the orthodox kind because of their unlimited scope. Their acceptance, long opposed, became widespread many years after his death.

Many orthodox problem themes have been extensively explored. Composers seeking originality tend towards greater complexity, perhaps using phase-related notions such as the Dombrovskis Theme, one of several so-called pattern themes. One result is the development of obscure jargon, a barrier between the composer and many solvers.

problem, orthodox, see ORTHODOX PROBLEM.

professionalism, the art of surviving on an income derived from chess. In medieval times a few sharpers may have included chess problems in their armoury, but few lived solely by chess until the 18th century. Chessboards were provided by many COFFEE-HOUSES, and some players attempted to earn a living playing visitors for small stakes. Those with enough of a reputation would also give lessons, or be backed to play a match when, if successful, they would receive part of the purse. In the 19th century players were able to supplement these earnings with prize money from tournaments and by giving simultaneous displays.

Although the number of professional players had greatly increased by the late 20th century their economic situation was much the same as it was a century earlier, except that the best players receive appearance money regardless of results. Not many can afford to marry and raise families, or live in anything like luxury, but a few at the top can now become wealthy, and this goal sustains those on the lower levels. The reasons for the increased numbers are perhaps two-fold. Economic conditions have reduced the number of career opportunities for bright young people, leading some with exceptional chess ability to consider becoming professional, at least for a few years. Secondly, there has been an increase in the number of SPONSORS.

Perhaps only in London was the chess professional looked down upon socially in the 19th century. This attitude was a factor in STEINITZ'S decision to leave England.

progressive chess, an unorthodox game in which White makes the first move, Black makes two SINGLE-MOVES in reply, White then makes three single-moves, Black four, and so on. Check may be given only on the last of a series of single-moves and must be evaded on the first move of the following series. The French expert on unorthodox games Joseph Boyer (1895–1961), who suggested the name progressive chess, said it was known in France as Scotch chess because ZNOSKO-BOROVSKY said that he had seen it played when he visited Scotland in 1947. The game is also called *Blitzkrieg* (lightning war) because of the short, devastating nature of the play. When there are several single-moves to be played the search for a mating continuation catches some of the flavour of a problem. The following correspondence game was played between J. Boyer (White) and A. Verse in 1957: 1 d4 d5 & Nc6   2 Bg5 & Bxe7 & Bxd8 Bg4 & Bxe2 & Bxd1 & Rxd8   3 Ba6 & Bxb7 & Nc3 & Nxd5 & Bxc6+   Rd7 & Bxc2 & Bb3 & Bxd5 & Bxc6 &

Bb4+ 4 Ke2 & Rc1 & Rxc6 & Kf3 & Rxc7 & Rxa7 & g4. White has played so that his opponent cannot promote a pawn but he is checkmated: 4 ... Bd2 & Rxd4 & Rxg4 & h5 & Ne7 & Nc6 & Nd4.

prohibition chess, see CHECKLESS CHESS.

Prokeš (pron. pro-kesh), Ladislav (1884–1966), Czech player and composer, International Judge of Chess Compositions (1956). Although a strong player who represented his country in three Olympiads (1927, 1928, 1930) and won the championship of Prague in 1928, he is better known for his studies. When his tournament days were practically over (1929) he began to give more of his time to composing, and his best studies came in the later years of his life. He specialized in piquant MINIATURES and is sometimes regarded as the player's composer because the positions he set seemed to be of a kind that might occur in play. In 1951 he published *Kniha šahových studii*, containing 623 of his compositions.

+

A study by Prokeš, *Le Monde des échecs*, 1946. 1 e4 Kf2 2 Nd5 Kf3 3 Nc3 Ke3 4 Ka2! Kd3 5 Kb3 (ZUGZWANG) 5 ... Kd4 6 Kb4 (zugzwang) 6 ... Kd3 7 Kc5 Kxc3 8 e5.

promoted piece, the informal term for a piece that has been created by PROMOTION.

promotion, the exchange of a pawn that has reached the eighth rank, as a part of the same move, for a queen, rook, bishop, or knight of the same colour. Thus a player might have two or more queens, or three or more rooks, bishops, or knights. To exchange for any other man, e.g. one of a different colour, or a king, or to remain a pawn is to make an ILLEGAL MOVE. To promote to a queen is to queen; to any other piece is called UNDERPROMOTION. (In informal games a player wishing to promote when no spare queen is available may use an upturned rook, or any other device, instead.) The current law on promotion is essentially the same as that used by STAUNTON for the first international tournament, London 1851.

Promotion dates from the earliest times. In SHAṬRANJ and MEDIEVAL CHESS a pawn could be promoted only to a FERS, a weak piece. When the modern game was introduced (*c*.1475) some argued that the acceptance of a plurality of queens was tantamount to condoning adultery. Others, restricting their logic to chess, said that it should not be possible to have more power than the initial forces.

The first original chess work in German, written in 1728, stated that a promoted pawn could be exchanged only for a piece that had already been captured, and if none was available it had to remain dormant, a latent pawn, on the eighth rank until a capture took place. At the end of the 18th century ALLGAIER demonstrated the absurdity of such a law. The diagram shows a version of the position he gave.

White has not lost a piece, so the pawn that has captured on h8 is latent. After 1 Ne4xd6+ Black cannot capture the knight because that would convert the pawn on h8 to a knight and the black king would remain in check. If 1 ... Kf8 or 1 ... Kf6 then 2 Qh6 is mate, because 2 ... Nxh6 is again self-check. If 1 ... Kg6 2 Nh4+ (immune) Kg7 3 Qxe5+ Nf6 4 Qxf6+ Kg8 5 Qf8 mate, White's queen being immune throughout, as also after 2 ... Kf6 3 Qxe5 mate.

By the 19th century the effect of promotion in the medieval game, the giving of minimal advantage, was forgotten, and it was thought that promotion should give the maximum possible advantage. It was claimed that in some cases the best move would be to remain as a dummy pawn, and KLING composed a position to show this.

After 1 bxa8 = Q (or any other piece) White is mated by 1 . . . gxh3 and 2 . . . h2, but if the pawn on a8 remains a dummy, then 1 . . . gxh3 is stalemate. A law allowing this was adopted by the British Chess Association in 1862, and STEINITZ spoke in its favour in 1889. Until modern times the St Petersburg laws were perhaps the only ones to state that the promoted piece must be of the same colour as the pawn, and some problemists took advantage of the oversight. In a rule given by LUCENA a queen arising from promotion also had the power of a knight on its first move.

promotion square, the more correct but rarely used name for the QUEENING SQUARE.

prophylaxis, a word used by NIMZOWITSCH to describe a strategic idea first exemplified by PHILIDOR: the anticipation, prevention, or determent of the opponent's threats.

In almost every game there are some prophylactic moves by one or both sides, and the use of the term is often limited to preventive moves, especially with pawns, that might seem remarkable in some way, as in the game given under MYSTERIOUS ROOK MOVE.

Some players are especially skilled at manœuvring behind the lines, preparing to meet any breakthrough contemplated by the opponent. One such player was PETROSYAN. (See PHILIDOR.)

protected passed pawn, a passed pawn that is protected by another pawn.

In the endgame a player's king may be hampered by the need to keep it within the square of the pawn (see QUADRANT). Giving the position White Kd3, Pa4, Pb5; Black Ke5, Pa5, Pg5, FINE (1941) indicates that White wins because the black g-pawn cannot be defended. With other pieces on the board, however, a protected passed pawn is rarely in itself a decisive factor. (See ANNOUNCED MATE.)

Averbakh–Panov, Moscow championship 1950. Black has a BAD BISHOP for which the protected passed pawn on e5 is insufficient compensation. The game ended 1 Kf3 Kf7 2 Kg4 Be7 3 Kf5 Bf8 4 Nf6 h6 5 gxh6 Bxh6 6 Ne4 Bf8 7 h6 Bxh6 8 Nxd6+ Ke7 9 Ne4 Be3 10 d6+ Kd7 11 Kxe5 Black resigns.

Polugayevsky–Smyslov   Moscow 1960   Slav Defence Schlechter Variation

1 d4 d5   2 Nf3 Nf6   3 c4 c6   4 e3 g6   5 Nc3 Bg7   6 Bd3 0–0   7 0–0 Bg4   8 h3 Bxf3   9 Qxf3 e6   10 Rd1 Nbd7   11 e4 e5   12 exd5 exd4   13 dxc6 Ne5   14 Qe2 Nxd3   15 Rxd3 bxc6   16 Bg5 Qa5   17 Bxf6 Bxf6   18 Ne4 Bg7   19 Qf3 Rab8   20 b3 Rfe8   21 Ng3 c5

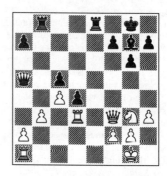

The passed pawn hinders the CO-OPERATION of White's pieces, and takes part in the final combination, but Black's control of the open file is probably of greater significance. 22 Ne4 Rb6   23 g4 Rbe6   24 Ng3 Qa3   25 Rd2 a5   26 Rad1 Bh6   27 Rc2 Qb4   28 Kg2 Bg5   29 Rd3 Bh4   30 Nf1 Kg7   31 Rcd2 Qb8   32 Ng3 Rf6   33 Qd1 Qb7+   34 Kh2 Qc7   35 Kg2 Qc6+   36 Kh2 Bxg3+   (Black exchanges the bad bishop)   37 Rxg3 Qe4   38 Rgd3 Re5   39 Rc2 h5   40 Rcd2 hxg4   41 hxg4 g5   42 Rh3 Ree6   43 Qc2 Qf4+   44 Rg3 Re1   45 Kg2 Re3 White resigns.

protection, the defence of a piece or a pawn so that if it were captured the capturing piece could in turn be taken, a move known as recapture. A king cannot be protected in this sense, only sheltered.

Provincial Opening, 831, so called because of White's COUNTRY MOVES (4 a3, 5 h3).

Prussian Defence, 940, the TWO KNIGHTS DEFENCE, the subject of a monograph, published in 1839, by the Prussian player BILGUER; 1102, the COZIO DEFENCE to the KING'S GAMBIT, analysed by von Hanneken of Prussia.

Przepiórka (pron. pshe-purer-ka), Dawid (1880–1940), Polish player and composer. He was active in tournament play from 1904 to 1931, and achieved his best result in a small but strong event at Munich, December 1926, when he came first (+4=1), ahead of BOGOLJUBOW and SPIELMANN. An amateur, on one occasion requesting a medal instead of prize money, he took second place to EUWE in the world's second and last amateur championship in 1928. Przepiórka played in two Olympiads: 1930, the only occasion on which the Polish team took the gold medal, and 1931. A chess all-rounder, he composed problems (especially MORE-MOVERS) and studies, edited chess columns, and contributed to the Polish magazine *Świat Szachowy.* Also a patriot, he sold his house to finance the Polish team's trip to the Buenos Aires Olympiad 1939. His name means quail, a fair description of his bird-like appearance. During the Second World War the occupying Germans arrested those present at a forbidden meeting of the Warsaw chess circle. The Jews, including Przepiórka, were sent to concentration camps and killed.

Weenink *David Przepiórka, a master of strategy* (1932), contains 126 compositions by Przepiórka.

Psakhis, Lev Borisovich (1958–), Russian-born Israeli player, International Grandmaster (1982). He was co-champion of the USSR twice in succession, at Vilnius 1980–1, scoring $+8=5-4$ to tie with BELYAVSKY, and at Frunze 1981, scoring $+9=7-1$ to tie with KASPAROV. Four further attempts between 1983 and 1987 were less successful.

His best results in international events are: Sarajevo 1981, first ($+7=8$); Dortmund 1982, third ($+5=5-1$), after HORT and ROMANISHIN; Yerevan zonal 1982, second ($+6=8-1$); Cienfuegos 1983, first ($+8=3$); Sochi 1985, equal second ($+5=8-1$), after SVESHNIKOV; Sarajevo 1986, first ($+3=9$) equal with Kir. GEORGIEV and PORTISCH; Szirák 1986, first ($+6=6-1$); Yerevan 1986, first equal with Romanishin; Jurmala 1987, first equal with GIPSLIS and RAZUVAYEV; Moscow 1988, first ($+3=6-1$); Yerevan 1988, second ($+6=7$), after LPUTYAN; Tel Aviv 1990, first ($+5=6$). In a Swiss system tournament at Bela Crkva 1987, Psakhis was equal second among 236 competitors.

Kir. Georgiev–Psakhis   Sarajevo 1986   French Defence Winawer Variation

1 d4 e6 2 e4 d5 3 Nc3 Bb4 4 a3 Bxc3+ 5 bxc3 dxe4 6 Qg4 Nf6 7 Qxg7 Rg8 8 Qh6 Nbd7 9 Ne2 c5 10 g3 b6 11 Bg2 Bb7 12 0–0 Qe7 13 a4 Ng4 14 Qf4 f5 15 a5 Ndf6 16 c4 cxd4 17 Ba3 Qd7 18 h3 e5 19 Qc1

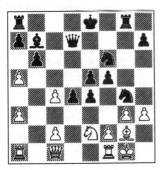

19 ... f4 20 Nxf4 Nxf2 21 Nh5 Nxh5 22 Qh6 Nxg3 23 Rxf2 0–0–0 24 a6 Ba8 25 Kh2 Rg6 26 Qf8 e3 27 Bxa8 exf2 28 Qxf2 Qf5 29 Qxf5+ Nxf5 30 Be4 Ne3 31 c5 (31 Bxg6 hxg6 also favours Black) 31 ... b5 32 c6 Rf6 33 Rg1 Nf1+ 34 Kh1 Nd2 35 Bxh7 Nc4 36 Bb4 Rxc6 37 Ra1 Ne3 38 Be4 Nxc2 39 Bxc6 Nxa1 40 Bb7+ Kb8 41 Kg2 Nc2 42 Be7 Rd7 43 Bf6 Ne3+ 44 Kg3 Nc4 White resigns.

pseudo-opposition, a position that is not a ZUGZWANG but in which the kings appear to stand in direct opposition.

Annotators often and incorrectly use the term opposition for this kind of position, but a draw comes about whoever has the move, with correct play, e.g. 1 ... Kb6 2 Kb4 Kc6 3 Kc4 Kd6 4 Kb5 Kd7 5 Kc5 Ke6 6 Kc6 Ke7 7 Kd5 Kf6 8 Kd6 Kf7 9 Kxe5 and Black takes the 'real' opposition 9 ... Ke7 = .

To win such positions the white king needs to stand opposite the black king on the edge, so that mate may be threatened; but the kings are not in opposition, for White wins regardless of who has the move.

pseudo-sacrifice, a sacrifice in appearance only, as in the example of STRATAGEM.

psychology and chess. The word 'psychology' has a popular meaning which is at odds with its scientific meaning. When Miles responded to Karpov's 1 e4 with 1 ... a6 (see ST GEORGE DEFENCE) he might have said that it was a psychological move. By playing what is regarded as an inferior defence, he was almost insulting the then world champion. This might have two obvious effects. Karpov could be rattled and lose his concentration, and should he fail to 'punish' the weak move and emerge from the opening with a clear advantage, he might feel that he had failed. This kind of scheming could more properly be called GAMESMANSHIP.

Psychology is the study of normal behaviour. Is there a set of characteristics that are found consistently in great players? What are the thought processes of grandmasters, and would an understanding of them be applicable in other areas? At what rate does chess skill rise and fall? These are typical questions a psychologist asks.

The first psychological study of chessplayers was made in the 1890s by the French scientist Alfred Binet. He became interested in blindfold chess and interviewed and tested a number of experts. In a résumé published in 1893 he wrote, 'The blindfold game contains everything: power of concentration, scholarship, memory, visual imagery, not to mention strategic talent, patience, courage, and many other faculties. If one could see what goes on in a chess player's head, one would find a stirring world of sensations, images, movements, passions, and an ever changing panorama of states of consciousness.' The following year he published *Psychologie des grands calculateurs et joueurs d'échecs* (reprinted 1981), believing there was a link between skill at mental arithmetic and blindfold chess.

During the Moscow 1925 tournament three Soviet psychologists, Dyakov, Petrovsky, and Rudik, carried out tests on several of the players in an effort to determine the factors likely to lead to chess success. Their paper, *Psikhologiya shakhmatnoy igry*, published in Moscow the following year, could isolate only their exceptional will to win. Modern psychologists, for the most part, accept that chess skill is *sui generis*. If there is such a thing as intelligence, chess ability is no measure of it.

The next significant paper on the psychology of chess was less fortunate. In 1931 Ernest Jones published 'The Problem of Paul Morphy' in the *International Journal of Psycho-analysis*. Couched in Freudian terms, the paper says: 'it is plain that the unconscious motive actuating the players is . . . one of father-murder [and] the most potent assistance is afforded by the mother (= queen). It is perhaps worth noting that the mathematical quality of the game gives it a peculiarly anal-sadistic nature.' The same approach is to be found in 'Psychoanalytic Observations on Chess and Chess Masters' in the journal *Psychoanalysis* in 1956, but whilst Jones hardly played chess at all the author of this last paper could have been a world championship contender. It is by FINE, and was reprinted in book form as *The Psychology of the Chess Player* (1967).

In the late 1930s and early 1940s Adrian de Groot (1914–) carried out tests to analyse the thought processes of chess masters. Himself a strong player, he was on friendly terms with those who co-operated with him. His doctoral thesis was published in 1946 as *Het denken van den schaker*, but became better known as part of the English-language *Thought and Choice in Chess* (1965). Interesting though the experiment is, it appears to prove only that the players were generating a verbal rationalization for moves which were played on criteria incapable of such expression. The weakest players carry out the most analysis. Once PETROSYAN remarked that he knew he was off form if the move that first suggested itself to him was not the

right one, but of course he could not say how that move sprang from his mind.

Scientists working on chess computer programs have also tried to replicate the thought processes of the great players, but their initial successes were based on doing what a beginner does, that is, examining as many lines as possible, but doing it to a depth and with an efficiency beyond human scope. Nobody knows how to program instinct. On the other hand there are endgames in which computer programs can find winning methods which have yet to be explained by human logic.

N. Krogius, *Psychology in Chess* (1976); W. R. Hartston and P. C. Wason, *The Psychology of Chess* (1983); D. H. Holding, *The Psychology of Chess Skill* (1985); J. Dextreit and N. Engel, *Jeu d'échecs et sciences humaines* (1981).

Pulling Counterattack, 1001 in the SCOTCH GAME; in reply White usually sacrifices a pawn to gain positional advantage. Although STEINITZ played this variation with fair success, most later masters have considered Black's defensive task too difficult. The variation was originated in the 1830s by Wellington Pulling (1812–66), a strong English player with a flair for blindfold displays, and first published in WALKER'S *Treatise on Chess* (1841).

Purdy, Cecil John Seddon (1906–79), Australian player and author, International Master (1951), International Correspondence Chess Grandmaster (1953), winner (+9=3−1) of the first World Correspondence Chess Championship, 1950–3. He won the national (over-the-board) championship on four occasions from 1934 to 1951, but is better remembered for his lifelong devotion to the cause of chess in Australia. He founded the *Australasian Chess Review* and edited it from 1929 through two changes of name (*Check!* in 1945, *Chess World* in 1946) until 1967 when it ceased publication. Of his several books the most amusing is *Among These Mates* (1939), written under the pseudonym 'Chielamangus'. His interest in all aspects of the game led him on one occasion to visit the Hebrides seeking background material for a television play about the LEWIS CHESSMEN.

Both Purdy's father-in-law Spencer Crakanthorp (1885–1936) and his son John Spencer Purdy (1935–) have been champions of Australia.

pure mate, or clean mate, a checkmate that meets the following criteria: unoccupied squares in the KING'S FIELD are attacked once only; pieces that function as SELF-BLOCKS are not under attack unless necessarily pinned; and the mating move is not a double check unless this is necessary to prevent the defender from interposing a man or capturing a checking piece. Pure mates are of interest to composers rather than players, and their occurrence in a game is usually incidental.

Steinkühler–Blackburne Friendly game Manchester, 1863
Italian Opening

1 e4 e5 2 Nf3 Nc6 3 Bc4 Bc5 4 c3 Nf6 5 d4 exd4 6 cxd4 Bb4+ 7 Bd2 Bxd2+ 8 Nfxd2? Nxd4 9 0–0 d6 10 Nb3 Nxb3 11 Qxb3 0–0 12 Re1 Nh5 13 e5 Qg5 14 exd6 Nf4 15 Bxf7+ Kh8 16 g3 cxd6 17 Nc3 Nh3+ 18 Kg2 Qf6 19 Bd5 Qxf2+ 20 Kh1

20 ... Qg1+ 21 Rxg1 Nf2+ 22 Kg2 Bh3, a pure mate. There are self-blocks on g1, h2, and g3; five other squares in the king's field are attacked once only: f1 by a bishop, h1 and h3 by a knight, f2 and f3 by a rook.

Pursuit Variation, 1256, the LASKER VARIATION of the ALEKHINE DEFENCE in which White continues to chase the knight.

puzzles, generally, problems using chess pieces or boards but not invoking the king's royal powers. The best known is probably the KNIGHT'S TOUR. Many such puzzles are mathematical. For example, how many ways may a standard set and board be used to set up the ARRAY correctly? The answer is 208,089,907,200. This is by DUDENEY, England's 'king of puzzle makers'. Another Dudeney puzzle: place as many pieces as possible on the board so that no two pieces of the same kind attack or guard one another, ignoring the presence of other kinds of pieces. His solution (FORSYTH NOTATION): BBBBQRBB/1NRN1N1Q/NRNQN1NB/QN1NRN1B/B1N1N1QR/BQ1N1NRN/N1NRNQN1/RBQNBBBN, a total of 8 queens, 8 rooks, 14 bishops and 21 knights.

Mathematical puzzles may have originated in India and almost certainly antedated the invention of chess. One of the oldest chess MYTHS, that of the Brahmin Sissa, called for mathematical understanding. Early Arabian players called puzzles Mikhāriq and often included them in their collections of MANṢŪBĀT. For example, place a diagonal row of pawns from a1 to h8 and a knight on g6, the knight to capture all eight pawns (which do not move). It can be done, but not easily, in 15 moves. If both long diagonals are filled with pawns they can be captured in 30 moves.

Lord Dunsany (1878–1957) invented what he called a 32-mover. Using a Staunton set, build up a pyramid using only 8 men to form the base. (See also EIGHT OFFICERS PUZZLE; EIGHT QUEENS PUZZLE; EIGHT ROOKS PUZZLE.)

Q

Q, the English language symbol for the queen. Thus Q-side, the queen's-side.

QGD, a common abbreviation for QUEEN'S GAMBIT Declined.

Quaade Gambit, 1128 in the KING'S GAMBIT Accepted, advocated by a Dutch sea-captain, D. L. Quaade, in 1882 but known earlier. The analysis was elaborated in the pages of *Deutsche Schachzeitung* by the German lawyer Carl Friedrich Schmid (1840–97). Compare ROSENTRETER GAMBIT, 1149.

quadrant, sometimes called quadrangle (SARRATT) or square of the pawn, a term used to define the relationship between the position of a king and that of an enemy pawn which might be a candidate for PROMOTION. The quadrant is formed by taking as many squares along the pawn's rank as there are on the file in front of it and forming an imaginary square.

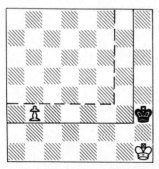

The advance of a pawn cannot be prevented by the opposite side's king if the king cannot be brought within the quadrant, which becomes smaller as the pawn advances. The diagram shows two quadrants marked with a bold line for a pawn at b2 or b3 and a broken line for a pawn at b4, Black to play draws by 1 ... Kg3 or 1 ... Kg4. White to play wins by 1 b4 because the black king cannot get within the quadrant.

The position below, the last throes of a game Bisguier–Matanović, Munich Olympiad 1958, shows the way in which the quadrant often settles a game. After 68 Ke7 a2 69 f6 a1=Q 70 f7 Qe5+ 71 Kd8 Qd5+ 72 Ke7 Qxh5 White resigns. If 73 f8=Q Qc5+ 74 Ke8 Qxf8+ etc, and if 73 Kf6 then 73 ... Qxf7+ wins brutally.

See the study under RÉTI.

queen, (1) a major piece represented by the symbol Q or the figurine ♛. It is a LINE-PIECE that may be moved along the ranks and files like the rook and along the diagonals like the bishop. On an otherwise empty board the queen attacks an odd number of squares in the range 21 to 27 depending on its position. In the ARRAY the queens stand on d1 and d8.

Now the strongest piece, the queen was one of the weakest until the new game was introduced c.1475. The most influential of the changes then made was the added power given to the new queen, a piece the Italians called *rabioso* (furious). The game with the new moves, *scacchi alla rabioso*, has given some readers the plausible but wrong idea that the name was adopted because chessplayers were inclined to madness. The use of the word queen was early and widespread, but the origin of the name is enigmatic. The Arabic *firz* or FIRZĀN (counsellor) was never translated into a European

language although the piece was adopted in various forms, changing its gender from masculine to feminine. Long before the modern game was introduced this ancestor of the queen was called *dame* and is still so called in France. Chessplayers may have borrowed the word from the game of draughts which the French to this day call *jeu de dames*. The transition from *dame* to queen would be natural, a desire to pair the central pieces.

queen, (2) to promote (a pawn) to a queen; used loosely for promotion to any piece.

queen ending, an endgame with kings, queens, or a queen, and usually one or more pawns.

queening square, the square on which a pawn is promoted, or on which one side is aiming to promote a pawn. Players, who rarely consider UNDERPROMOTION, seldom use the more correct term, promotion square.

Queen's Bishop Game, 229, sometimes called the Romi Opening, or Rubinstein Variation, but an old opening played many times by BLACKBURNE in the 1890s. (See RESHEVSKY; YUDASIN.)

Queen's Fianchetto Defence, 443, a 16th-century invention sometimes called the Owen Defence, or, for no good reason, the Greek Defence. See also 1279.

Queen's Fianchetto Opening, 5, sometimes called the Larsen Opening. It was given by LUCENA, played regularly by OWEN, and often used by STAUNTON and MORPHY when giving odds of the queen's knight.

Queen's Gambit, 59. On declining the gambit Black has a wide range of choices, principally the SLAV, SEMI-SLAV, and ORTHODOX DEFENCES (in which White might choose an EXCHANGE VARIATION), and the TARRASCH DEFENCE. Some other lines for Black are the MANHATTAN, CAMBRIDGE SPRINGS, and LASKER DEFENCES, the SEMI-TARRASCH, and TARTA-KOWER VARIATIONS.

Mentioned first by LUCENA, the opening was recommended by STAMMA, after whose home town, Aleppo, it is sometimes named. In 1834 BOURDON-NAIS played it 16 times against McDONNELL with outstanding success ($+12=3-1$). Even so, the gambit was not widely used until the end of the 19th century, after which its popularity grew to a peak in the 1920s and 1930s. In the world championship match, 1927, all but 2 of the 34 games began with this opening. (See BÖNSCH; COINCIDENCE; CO-OPERATION; DIVERSIONARY SACRIFICE; ISOLATED QUEEN'S PAWN; SIMPLIFICATION; TRAP; TUKMAKOV.)

Queen's Gambit Accepted, 60, considered bad for Black from the time of LUCENA until the 1930s, when it became an established part of a master's repertoire. (See BOLBOCHÁN; EINGORN; JANOWSKI; McDONNELL; SPIELMANN; STEMGAME.)

Queen's Indian Defence, 277 (also known as Sämisch Defence), 338, 425, or 1307. This owes much to NIMZOWITSCH'S advocacy and is complementary to the NIMZO-INDIAN DEFENCE, to be played when White plays Ng1–f3 before or instead of Nb1–c3. The struggle concerns control of the square e4: with the N at f6 and the B at b7 Black maintains a grip on the square, withholding, for the time being, the advance of a pawn to its fourth rank. The usual form of the opening is 338. Increasingly rarely it is called the West Indian Defence. (See BENJAMIN; LEIN; MARSHALL; MOBILITY; MYSTERIOUS ROOK MOVE; PORTISCH; RAKING BISHOPS; SALOV; SEIRAWAN; SULTAN KHAN; WYVILL FORMATION.)

Queen's Knight Opening, 608, the VIENNA GAME, or 8, the HEINRICHSEN OPENING.

Queen's Pawn Counter-gambit, 1014, a line of doubtful merit, first mentioned by ASPERLING, and sometimes called the Englund Counterattack.

Queen's Pawn Opening, 48. The term is often used more narrowly to describe those openings that begin 1 d4 d5, and in which White does not play an early Pc2–c4.

queen's-side, an area of the board consisting of all the squares on the a-, b-, and c-files including, on occasion, those on the d-file.

queen's-side castling, castling on the queen's-side, represented by the symbol 0–0–0.

queen's-side majority, a MAJORITY of pawns on the queen's side.

quick play, synonymous with ALLEGRO, and perhaps more commonly used in England.

Quinteros, Miguel Angel (1947–), professional player from Argentina, International Grandmaster (1973). At the age of 18 he became the youngest player to win his nation's championship (1966), a title he next won in 1980. From 1970 he played regularly for Argentina in the Olympiads. His best results in tournament play are: Torremolinos 1973, first equal with BENKO; Bauang 1973, second ($+6=1-2$) equal with IVKOV, after KAVALEK; Lanzarote 1974, first ($+6=6-1$); Orense 1975, fourth ($+7=6-2$) equal with GHEORGHIU, after LARSEN, LJUBOJEVIĆ, and ANDERSSON; London 1977, second ($+4=4-1$) equal with MESTEL and STEAN, after HORT; Morón 1982, a zonal tournament, first ($+10=4-1$); New York 1983, second ($+5=5-1$).

R

Rabar Classification, a method of indexing openings introduced in *Chess Informant,* 1966, and gradually gaining wider acceptance until it was inexplicably abandoned in 1981. The Yugoslav player and author Braslav Rabar (1919–73) tried to devise a method related to the practical needs of play and opening study, without seeking to bolster obsolescent jargon.

B. Rabar, *Classification of Chess Openings* (1971).

Rabelais Variation, 161, TARTAKOWER'S whimsical name for the SEMI-TARRASCH VARIATION, which he also dubbed 'the nameless variation'.

Rabinovich, Ilya Leontyevich (1891–1942), sometimes called E. (Elias) Rabinovich, a leading Soviet player between the two world wars, chess author, schoolteacher. In 1914 he travelled to Germany to play in a HAUPTTURNIER at Mannheim; the First World War commenced and he was interned for about three years. The internees arranged several chess tournaments, and of these he won the sixth (1916) and tied for first place in the seventh (1917), both times ahead of BOGOLJUBOW.

After the war Rabinovich won a match against ROMANOVSKY in 1920 (+5=2−1), won or shared the Leningrad championship four times (1920, 1925, 1928, 1940), and entered the USSR championship nine times from 1920 to 1939, becoming joint champion with LEVENFISH in 1934. He suffered from malnutrition during the siege of Leningrad and died shortly afterwards.

In 1927 Rabinovich published (4,000 copies) the first original book in the Russian language devoted exclusively to the endgame. In 1938 a second edition of 7,000 copies was published, and this was translated into Dutch and published in three parts: *Toreneindspelen* (1942), *Paard- en lopereindspelen* (1948), and *Pionneneindspelen* (1950).

Rabinovich Variation, 700 in the SPANISH OPENING, given in *Shakhmaty* by RABINOVICH shortly before his death. Also 584, the BOTVINNIK VARIATION of the CARO–KANN DEFENCE, advocated by the Moscow champion (1926), Abram Isaakovich Rabinovich (1878–1943).

Rabrab Khata'ī, strong 9th-century player whose name indicates that he was from Cathay. The first name is uncertain and is sometimes given as Zairab or Zabzab. He was famed as an ENDGAME analyst, notably for his pioneering work on the endgame rook against knight, in particular the classic position White Kb5, Rh1; Black Ka7, Nb7, which, as he demonstrated, White should win. (This position and similar ones were examined in modern times by BERGER, MANDLER, and others; a definitive analysis by computer was made in 1970.)

radio chess, games for which the moves are transmitted by radio. All early games were played at sea, a circumstance that suited the primitive equipment then available. In June 1902 games were played between SS *Campania* and SS *Philadelphia* over distances up to 160 miles on the Atlantic Ocean, the first of many such encounters. The first radio match of any consequence was played in March 1941 between clubs in Moscow and Leningrad. In September 1945 the USSR defeated the USA (15½:4½), the first important sporting event to follow the Second World War and one that marked the beginning of Soviet chess supremacy. In 1946 the USSR beat England (18:6), Australia beat France (5½:4½), and Spain beat Argentina (8:7).

Other forms of radio chess include matches played between a master in the studio and listeners, and games between teams of masters in the studio, each team's consultations being broadcast but kept secret from the other team.

Radulov, Ivan Georgiev (1939–), Bulgarian player, International Grandmaster (1972), civil engineer. He was national champion 1971, 1975, 1977, and 1980–1, the last three after play-offs. He won three strong international tournaments: Forssa–Helsinki 1972 (+8=6−1); Montilla 1974 (+2=7); and Montilla 1975 (+3=6), a tie with POLUGAYEVSKY. Since then he has not reached the same level, but in 1985 he was equal second among 214 competitors in a Swiss system tournament at Budapest. He has been in the Bulgarian Olympiad team since 1968.

Ragozin, Viacheslav Vasilyevich (1908–62), Soviet player, International Grandmaster (1950), International Arbiter (1951), International Correspondence Chess Grandmaster (1959), building engineer. One of the first generation to learn chess under the Soviet regime, Ragozin came to the fore in the late 1930s, notably achieving three good tournament results: Leningrad championship 1936, first; USSR championship 1937, second equal with Konstantinopolsky, after LEVENFISH; and Leningrad–Moscow 1939, third equal with Levenfish, LILIENTHAL, and MAKOGONOV, after FLOHR and RESHEVSKY, ahead of KERES. After winning the Sverdlovsk 1942 tournament (+8=2) and the Leningrad championship of 1945, Ragozin achieved his best result in over-the-board play at the strong Moscow 1947 tournament, second (+ 8 = 5 − 2), half a point after BOTVINNIK, ahead of BOLESLAVSKY, SMYSLOV, and Keres. A new wave of Soviet players now overtook his generation, only Botvinnik surviving this challenge. Turning to postal chess Ragozin won the second World Correspondence Championship, 1956–8 (+ 9 = 4 − 1).

In 1936 Ragozin became Botvinnik's sparring partner, and for many years they practised and analysed together; thus Ragozin contributed significantly to Botvinnik's successes. Ragozin's literary output included the editorship of the monthly magazine *Shakhmaty v SSSR* for many years, and an excellent book on the Botvinnik–TAL world championship match of 1960. He died while compiling *Izbrannye party Ragozina*, a collection of 74 of his games, published in 1964. Twenty years later *Vyacheslav Ragozin*, edited by M. M. Yudovich, containing 100 games, 89 of which are annotated, was published. (See PHILIDOR SACRIFICE.)

Lilienthal–Ragozin   Moscow 1935   Nimzo-Indian Defence Sämisch Variation

1 d4 Nf6 2 c4 e6 3 Nc3 Bb4 4 a3 Bxc3 + 5 bxc3 c5 6 f3 d5 7 e3 0–0 8 cxd5 exd5 9 Bd3 Nc6 10 Ne2 Re8 11 0–0 a6 12 Qe1 b5 13 Qf2 Be6 14 h3 Ra7 15 Bd2 Qb6 16 Rfb1 Rae7 17 a4 c4 18 Bc2 Bc8 19 Ng3 h5 20 Ne2 Nd8 21 Ra2 Bd7 22 axb5 axb5 23 Rba1 Bc8 24 Rb2 Bd7 25 Qh4 Ne6 26 Kh1 Nf8 27 Ng3

27 ... Rxe3 28 Bxe3 Rxe3 29 Nxh5 Nxh5 30 Qxh5 Bc6 31 Qg5 Rxc3 32 Qd2 Rxc2 33 Rxc2 Ne6 34 Rd1 b4 35 Rb2 b3 36 Qc3 Nc7 37 Re2 Qa7 38 Qb4 Nb5 39 Re7 Qa3 40 Qe1 c3 41 Re8 + Bxe8 42 Qxe8 + Kh7 43 Qxf7 Qa8 44 Re1 Nd6 45 Qc7 c2 46 Qxd6 b2 47 Qf4 Qc6 White resigns.

Ragozin Variation, 160 in the QUEEN'S GAMBIT Declined, and 320 in the NIMZO-INDIAN DEFENCE. The first variation can lead to the second, and in each of them RAGOZIN'S aim is to enable the Black e-pawn to advance Pe6–e5. Also 364, the RUSSIAN VARIATION of the GRÜNFELD DEFENCE.

raking bishops, a player's light and dark bishops placed so that they command adjacent diagonals along which they attack the opponent's position from a distance. Possession of such bishops is often advantageous. (See also BAUER; KARPOV; NUNN; RAZUVAYEV.)

Bellón–Belyavsky   Haifa 1989   European Team Championship Queen's Indian Defence

1 d4 Nf6 2 c4 e6 3 Nf3 b6 4 e3 Bb7 5 Bd3 Be7 6 0–0 0–0 7 b3 c5 8 Bb2 cxd4 9 exd4 d5 10 Ne5 Nc6 11 Nxc6 Bxc6 12 Nd2 Qd6 13 Rc1 Rac8 14 Qe2 Qf4 15 g3 Qh6 16 f4 dxc4 17 bxc4 Rfd8 18 Nf3 Ng4 19 h4 Bb7 20 Ng5 Nf6 21 f5 e5 22 d5 Nh5

23 f6 (White completes the process of opening lines for both his bishops to bear down on the black king's position.) 23 ... gxf6 24 Bxh7 + Kf8 25 Qf3 b5 26 Be4 Bd6 27 cxb5 Kg7 28 Nh3 Rg8 29 g4 Nf4 30 Nxf4 exf4 31 g5 Qxh4 32 Bxf6 + (The raking bishops break through, after which Black's king obstructs the CO-OPERATION of his pieces.) 32 ... Kf8 33 Rxc8 + Bxc8 34 Rc1 Bd7 35 Qf2 Rxg5 + 36 Bxg5 Qxg5 + 37 Qg2 Qh6 38 Qh2 Qg7 + 39 Kh1 Qd4 40 Bf3 Qe3 41 Qh8 + Ke7 42 Qh4 + Black resigns.

randomized chess, a form of UNORTHODOX CHESS designed to discount knowledge of the openings. The pawns are placed as in the ARRAY and behind them the pieces are placed in unorthodox fashion. Commonly a symmetrical arrangement is made as follows: White places any piece on a1, Black places a similar piece on a8 and selects a piece for b8 which White matches on b1, and so on. Each player must have a light and a dark bishop. Thus, 2880 arrays are possible. The players must agree about castling rules before play commences.

In screen chess, sometimes called battle chess, the white and black arrays are not intentionally mirrored. A screen is temporarily placed across the board while the players set up their own pieces as they fancy, in ignorance of the opposition. Thus 8,294,400 different arrays are possible. When revived in the 1970s it was called baseline chess. (In England during the First World War KRIEGSPIEL was called screen chess to avoid the use of German words.)

The demand for this form of chess arose when openings became the subject of systematic study, but, curiously, a classifier of openings, ALEXANDRE, was one of the first to experiment with randomized chess. In 1921 the Swiss composer Erich Brunner (1885–1938) revived the idea, which sometimes bears his name.

rank, or horizontal line, a row of eight laterally adjoining squares from side to side of the board. A rank is customarily defined by its relationship to the player. From White's point of view the white pieces in the ARRAY are on the first rank and the black pieces on the EIGHTH RANK, which corresponds with the rank numbers in STANDARD NOTATION. However, from Black's point of view the white pieces are on the eighth rank and the black ones on the first rank.

Major pieces can manœuvre as effectively on the ranks as on the files. Rooks are especially well placed on the SEVENTH RANK.

Ranken, Charles Edward (1828–1905), English player and author, editor for a time of the *Chess Player's Chronicle*, the first president of the Oxford University Chess Club. His name is associated with an opening line. (See STAUNTON.)

Ranken Variation, 833, a good line for White in the FOUR KNIGHTS OPENING, analysed in the *Chess Player's Chronicle*, 1879, by RANKEN.

rapid chess, FIDE's term for games in which each player must play the whole game inside 30 minutes. In 1987 an unpopular decision was made by FIDE to use the term 'active chess' and to award titles, Grandmaster in Active Chess, etc, based on a separate rating list. This seemed to imply that the major titles were awarded for inactive chess, and the change to 'rapid chess' was made in 1989. (See also ALLEGRO.)

rapid transit chess, a term used in the USA for LIGHTNING CHESS, named after the New York city transport system.

Rashkovsky, Naum Nikolayevich (1946–), Russian player, International Grandmaster (1980). From 1972 to 1987 he competed in seven USSR championships, only once (1986) finishing in the top half of the table. In 1982 he was, with BRONSTEIN, joint champion of Moscow. His only victory in an international tournament was at Sochi 1979.

rating, a method of estimating playing strength. Its purpose might be the selection of players for a team or tournament, the awarding of titles, pairing of opponents in a SWISS SYSTEM tournament, allocation of players in a competition with several tournaments, provision of a facility for offering awards to players of different strengths within the same tournament, or simply the assessment of the relative strength of players who have not met. An early example was the custom of classing players by the handicap they would receive from a first-class player, an empirical method that did not always prove reliable in alien environments. Towards the end of the 19th century various writers tried to assess the relative strength of leading masters, and partly because the exercise was restricted to master events of about equal strength, the ranking lists were close to general opinion.

Unlike athletes, whose results can be measured against standards such as time or distance, chess-

players can be measured only against each other. The basis of all modern systems gives each player a rating derived from the opponents' ratings and the scores made against them. There is some affinity with AUXILIARY SCORING METHODS. 'The measurement of the rating of an individual might well be compared with the measurement of a cork bobbing up and down on the surface of agitated water with a yardstick tied to a rope which is swaying in the wind', said ELO in 1962.

The first modern type of rating system was used by the Correspondence Chess League of America in 1939. The Soviet player Andrey Andreyevich Khachaturov (1917–) proposed a similar system in *Shakhmaty v SSSR* in 1946, but the one that made an impact on international chess was the Ingo system, launched in 1948 and named by its designer, Anton Hösslinger (1875–1959), after his home town, Ingolstadt in Bavaria. In 1950 the United States Chess Federation adopted a different system and shortly afterwards the British Chess Federation introduced a grading system designed by CLARKE.

In 1960 a new USCF method was introduced by a committee chaired by Elo, later to become the official FIDE rating system, and known either by that name or as ELO RATING. All the modern methods give similar results if players are in the same class but only Elo rating appears to be dependable when there are great differences in playing strength.

Clarke (*British Chess Magazine*, 1953, 1960, 1973) and Elo (*Chess Life*, 1962, 1964) applied modern rating methods retrospectively to the middle of the 19th century, but both were adamant that it is meaningless to use rating to compare players of different eras. It is like comparing soccer teams fifty years apart by their positions in their tables. One mathematician who has tried to make such a comparison is Divinsky (see ELO RATING).

A. E. Elo, *The Rating of Chessplayers* (1978); J. D. Beasley, *The Mathematics of Games* (1989); R. W. B. Clarke, 'Rating Systems', in *British Chess Magazine*, 1969.

Rat Opening, 1318, a joking description of the KING'S FIANCHETTO OPENING. Manley, a London publican who frequented Purssell's coffee-house around 1880, was partial to it. He explained that when meeting strong players he liked to keep his pieces close to home, for if he placed them in the open his opponents took them off.

Rauzer, Vsevolod Alfredovich (1908–41), leading Soviet player during the 1930s. His best playing achievement was at Leningrad 1936, when he shared first prize with CHEKHOVER ahead of KAN, Konstantinopolsky, RAGOZIN, ALATORTSEV, and Riumin. He achieved only moderate results in six USSR championships from 1927 to 1937, after the last of which a serious illness ended his playing career. A student of openings, he is remembered for the two well-known variations named after him.

Rauzer Variation, 187 in the QUEEN'S GAMBIT Declined, an old line (Steinitz–Pillsbury, Nuremberg 1896) much analysed by RAUZER in the 1930s; 484 in the SICILIAN DEFENCE, Rauzer's line in the RICHTER ATTACK (see IVKOV; SOSONKO); 536, also in the Sicilian Defence, not by Rauzer, but having some similarities to 484 and 538; 12 Nbd2 Nc6 (RUBINSTEIN VARIATION) 13 dxc5 dxc5 14 a4, a possible continuation from the CHIGORIN VARIATION (746) of the SPANISH OPENING: the general idea is shown by the game Rauzer–Riumin, Leningrad 1936; 1192 in the FRENCH DEFENCE, as Rauzer–Alatortsev, USSR championship 1933. Also 538, the MOSCOW VARIATION of the Sicilian Defence.

ar-Rāzī (*fl*.850), native of Ray, near Tehran, one of the five ʿālīyat (grandmasters) of the 9th century, and the greatest of them according to aş-ŞŪLĪ. Around the middle of the century ar-Rāzī defeated al-ʿADLĪ in the presence of the Caliph. He wrote *Kitāb ash-shaṭranj*, a book giving openings, positions for study (MANṢŪBĀT), and advice. For example, he recommends that one should not play while eating or when the mind is occupied by other matters. Seen and used by aş-Şūlī, the book was later lost.

Razuvayev, Yuri Sergeyevich (1945–), Soviet player and trainer, International Grandmaster (1976). His victories in international tournaments include: Dubna, 1979, shared; Polanica Zdrój 1979; Keszthely 1979; Dormund 1985, shared; Jurmala 1987, shared; Moscow 1988, shared; and Nový Smokovec 1990. At Cienfuegos 1976 he was second (+6=8) equal with Sigurjónsson, half a point after GULKO. In six USSR championships between 1972 and 1985 he failed to find the top half of the result table. In 1984 he took eighth board for the USSR against the Rest of the World, and drew all four games with HÜBNER.

Razuvayev–Levitt Reykjavik (Open) 1990 Slav Defence Alapin Variation

1 d4 d5 2 c4 c6 3 Nc3 Nf6 4 Nf3 dxc4 5 a4 Bf5 6 e3 e6 7 Bxc4 Bb4 8 0–0 Nbd7 9 Qe2 Bg6 10 e4 Bxc3 11 bxc3 Nxe4 12 Ba3 Qc7 13 Nd2 Nxd2 14 Qxd2 0–0–0

15 Be7 Rde8 16 Bh4 f6 17 a5 Rhf8 18 Bg3 e5 19 f4 Qd6 20 fxe5 fxe5 21 Rxf8 Qxf8 22 a6 b6 23 Rd1 Qd6 24 Be2 h5 25 Bf3 Kc7 26 h4 Bf7 27 Kh2 g6 28 c4 Kc8 29 Qc2 Qf6 30 c5 b5 31 d5 Bxd5 32 Bxd5 cxd5 33 Rxd5 Re6 34 Qd3 Nb8 35 Qxb5 Rxa6 36 Rxe5 Black resigns.

recapture, the capture of a man that has made a capture, usually as an immediate reply and on the same square, sometimes a move or so later and perhaps on another square; to make such a move.

reciprocal play, a problem term: a pattern formed by moves played in one VARIATION or PHASE contrasted with those played in another. For example, Grimshaw Interference (see CUTTING-POINT THEMES) may show reciprocal play occurring in the same phase: piece A interferes with piece B in one variation, and piece B interferes with piece A in another. However, the term is more commonly used to describe forms of CHANGED PLAY.

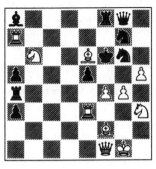

#3

A problem by KELLER, first prize, *Probleemblad*, 1980. The set play (what happens if Black moves first):

1 ... Qxe6 2 Bh4+ Nxh4 3 fxe5#
1 ... Nxe6 2 fxe5+ Nxe5 3 Bh4#.

The key is 1 Qa6, threatening Nd5+ and the mating variations show a reversal of the mating continuations as contrasted with the set play.

1 ... Qxe6 2 fxe5+ Nxe5 3 Bh4#
                Qxe5 3 Nd5#
1 ... Nxe6 2 Bh4+ Nxh4 3 fxe5#
                Ng5 3 Nd5#.

recording moves, see SCORE OF GAME.

Ree, Hans (1944–), Dutch player and writer, International Grandmaster (1980), national champion 1967, 1969, 1971, and 1982, twice joint European Junior Champion, 1964–5 and 1965–6. Ree first attracted attention in 1966 when he took first prize ahead of LARSEN and DONNER at a small tournament at Ter Apel, in the Netherlands. He was then a student of mathematics and philosophy, but decided a few years later to become a chess professional. Among his successes are a match victory against Donner (+2=5−1) in 1971; a first place shared with SPASSKY in the Swiss system

Canadian Open Championship, Vancouver 1971 (the title was awarded to Spassky on tie-break); first at Graz 1979; first equal with UNZICKER at the second level Amsterdam 1980 tournament; and first (+ 2 = 3) equal with van der WIEL and LOBRON at Ter Apel 1987. He has played in several Olympiads since 1966.

reflecting bishop, a piece, for use in FAIRY PROB-LEMS, invented by the American composer Gilbert Dobbs (1867–1941) in 1937. It is moved like an ordinary bishop but may also be bounced off the edges. For example, a reflecting bishop on c3 can travel in one move, if unobstructed, by way of a5, d8, h4, and e1 back to c3; if on the long diagonal it can bounce out of the corner, although such a move would usually be pointless.

reflex chess, an unorthodox game invented by the Englishmen William Geary (1839–1923) and LAWS in 1881. Both players try to get themselves check-mated, but either must give mate on the move if this becomes possible. Players usually begin the game by advancing their kings in suicidal fashion.

Reflex mate problems are denoted by the symbol r#; for examples, see MLADENOVIĆ; REHM. Stale-mate instead of checkmate may be the aim, a stipulation denoted by the symbol rp; for an ex-ample, see ABDURAHMANOVIĆ.

refute, to prove analysis unsound, commonly used in connection with opening variations.

Rehm, Hans-Peter (1942–), German composer, International Judge of Chess Compositions (1971), International Grandmaster for Chess Composi-tions (1984), joint editor of *Die Schwalbe* 1969–74, mathematics lecturer at Karslruhe University. The leading composer of his country, he specializes in more-movers, notably of the LOGICAL SCHOOL, and fairy problems. A talented pianist, he has given public performances.

r#3

A REFLEX CHESS problem by Rehm, the composer's VERSION of a problem that won third prize, *Thèmes 64*, 1982. The key is 1 h8 = B threatening (after 2 Ng8 +) 3 Bxb2 when Black must play 3 ... Qxb2#. The same mating finish occurs in the variations, in

which the Nf6 is moved to different squares (des-cribing a KNIGHT WHEEL) in order to avoid a situation in which White might be forced to give mate.

1 ... Nxb1	2 Nd5 +
1 ... Nb3	2 Nd7 +
1 ... Ndxc4	2 Ne8 +
1 ... Nf3	2 Nh7 +
1 ... Ndf1	2 Nxh5 +
1 ... g3	2 Ng4 + .

Reinfeld, Fred (1910–64), a New Yorker who was the world's most prolific chess writer, with more than 100 titles to his name. In his early works he attempted to add to chess knowledge, but soon realized that he could make a better career by writing for the larger market created by weaker players. His readers liked his clear style, and his publishers liked his reliability. He was a good but not great player, twice New York State champion, for example, and capable of beating the best on a good day. (See MARSHALL; RESHEVSKY.)

Rejfíř, Josef (1908–62), seven times a member of the Czech Olympiad team between 1928 and 1958. His work as a scientist kept him out of chess for 20 years. He won the Premier Reserves tournament at Hastings 1931–2 and again 1932–3.

related squares, see CONJUGATE SQUARES.

Relfsson Gambit, 971 in the SCOTCH GAMBIT, also called the MacLópez, an old line named after the Swedish master Torsten Relfsson (1871–1944).

Rellstab Variation, 11 ... Nxe5 (SOZIN VARIATION) 12 Nxe5 axb5 13 0–0, arising from the BLUMEN-FELD VARIATION (145) of the MERAN VARIATION, the subject of analysis by the German master Ludwig Adolf Friedrich Hans Rellstab (1904–83) in *Ranne-forths Schachkalender 1932*. Played Vajda–Rosselli, Nice 1931, it is sometimes called the Vajda–Rell-stab Variation. Later the STÅHLBERG VARIATION was preferred to this pawn sacrifice. Also 1041 in the PHILIDOR DEFENCE, introduced in the game Rell-stab–Tylor, Hastings Reserves 1929–30.

remis, obsolete French word, sometimes used in English, for a draw. In France itself the most common expression is *nulle*.

remistod, the death of chess by draws (*Tod*, Ger-man for death), predicted by LASKER around 1918 and by CAPABLANCA ten years later.

Both champions made their prophecies when past their prime, and both suggested ways to give the game new life. Lasker favoured the abolition of castling, Capablanca experimented with unortho-dox games on enlarged boards. Because the re-sources of chess are for practical purposes unlim-ited or because of a human tendency to make errors, or for both reasons, death by draws has not occurred.

remote passed pawn, see OUTSIDE PASSED PAWN.

repetition of position, the popular name for the claim of a draw when a position has occurred for the third time with the same contestant to play, or will so occur after a declared and binding move by a player whose turn it is to play. The position is considered to be the same if men of the same kind and colour occupy the same squares, and if they possess all the same powers including the right to castle or to capture EN PASSANT.

Early statements of this law, for example in LASA's proposals of 1854, postulated the repetition of moves, or series of moves, without specifying how often these might be repeated. Only much later was this law redefined as applying to all positions, no matter how widely separated.

In his first encounter with the world champion, ALEKHINE was happy to seek a draw.

Alekhine–Lasker   Moscow, March 1914, Exhibition Game   Scotch Game

1 e4 e5 2 Nf3 Nc6 3 d4 exd4 4 Nxd4 Nf6 5 Nc3 Bb4 6 Nxc6 bxc6 7 Bd3 d5 8 exd5 cxd5 9 0–0 0–0 10 Bg5 Be6 11 Qf3 Be7 12 Rfe1 h6 13 Bxh6 gxh6 14 Rxe6 fxe6 15 Qg3+ Kh8 16 Qg6 draw agreed. Black cannot avoid draw by repetition, e.g. 16 ... Qe8 17 Qxh6+ Kg8 18 Qg5+ Kh8 19 Qh6+

The first time these players met in a tournament, at St Petersburg a few months later, the game again ended in a draw by repetition of position.

Players sometimes repeat the position not to draw, but in order to gain time on the clock, as for example in the game under TUKMAKOV. There have been instances, even at the highest level, of players miscounting, and getting unwanted draws.

Reshevsky, Samuel Herman (1911–92), International Grandmaster (1950), from 1935 to 1953 ranked among the best eight in the world, at best among the first three. During these years he played in 14 major tournaments, winning half of them and only once coming lower than third. The sixth child in a Jewish family, Reshevsky was born in Poland, where he learned the game at the age of 4 and soon became the strongest of all child prodigies. He toured Poland when he was 6, giving simultaneous displays against 20 or more players and rarely losing a game, made similar tours in Europe, and arrived with his family to settle in the USA a few weeks before his ninth birthday. Two years of travelling in America giving displays which drew large audiences (and enriched his parents) were followed by his first tournament, in October 1922. He won one game, against JANOWSKI. A few months later his parents were charged with 'improper guardianship'; the case was dismissed, but a guardian was appointed to prevent 'undue' exploitation. Hitherto his education had been largely limited to Talmudic studies; at the age of 12, after some private tuition, he began to attend an ordinary school. In 1931 he chose accountancy for his subject, and in 1934 he completed his studies at Chicago University; but his life was devoted to chess.

In 1935, having played in half a dozen tournaments in the USA, Reshevsky commenced his career at grandmaster level by winning first prize (+6=3) ahead of CAPABLANCA at Margate, subsequently achieving several excellent performances: Nottingham 1936, third (+7=5−2) equal with EUWE and FINE, after BOTVINNIK and Capablanca, ahead of ALEKHINE and FLOHR; Kemeri 1937, first (+10=4−3) equal with Flohr and PETROV, ahead of Alekhine and KERES; Semmering Baden 1937, third (+4=7−3) equal with Capablanca, after Keres and Fine; Hastings 1937–8, first (+5=4); AVRO 1938, fourth (+3=8−3) equal with Euwe and Alekhine. Reshevsky won four consecutive US championship tournaments: 1936 (+10=3−2), 1938 (+10=6), 1940 (+10=6) and 1942. He twice defended his title in match play, against HOROWITZ (+3=13) in 1941 and against KASHDAN (+6=3−2) in 1942.

A deeply religious man, married with one son and two daughters, Reshevsky felt that chess was playing too large a part in his life; in 1944 he decided to give more time to his family, to advance his career in accountancy, and to play chess less often, although he won the US open championship that year. In 1945 he won a pan-American championship at Los Angeles (+9=3) and in 1946 he again won the US championship. Without further hard practice he played in the world championship match tournament of 1948, scoring +6=9−5 to share third place with Keres, after Botvinnik and SMYSLOV. In this event he was granted a new and special concession: that he need not play between sunset on Friday and sunset on Saturday. He believed that his previously having played on the Jewish sabbath was a sin, his father's recent death a punishment. In 1950, in the prime of his chess career, Reshevsky wanted to play in the CANDIDATES tournament to be held in Budapest. The State Department refused to let him travel there, thus depriving him of his best chance to become a challenger for the world title. He prepared himself for the next championship cycle by tournament and match play, and was second (+9=10) after NAJDORF at Amsterdam 1950, first (+6=4−1) at New York 1951, and defeated GLIGORIĆ in 1952 (+2=7−1), Najdorf in 1952 (+8=6−4) and 1953 (+5=9−4). In the Candidates tournament of 1953 he came second (+8=16−4) equal with BRONSTEIN and Keres, after Smyslov. Reshevsky, who took his family with him, was handicapped by the lack of a back-up team of the kind available to most of the other competitors; perhaps he considered such a team, or even a second, unnecessary.

He continued to play in strong tournaments, averaging about one a year, winning at Dallas 1957 (+5=7−2) equal with Gligorić, Buenos Aires 1960 (+8=1−1) equal with KORCHNOI, Natanya 1969 (+7=6), and his sixth US championship in 1969 (+5=6). In match play he defeated BENKO in 1960 (+3=5−2), and when he met FISCHER in 1961 he was awarded the stakes after the match was broken off, the score standing $+2=7-2$. In 1967 he shared sixth place at the Sousse interzonal; after a drawn play-off he was placed sixth on tie-break, but lost to Korchnoi in the quarter-final. Gradually his playing strength declined, but into his old age he continued participating in ever weaker events.

The games of Reshevsky's prime are characterized by solid rather than fashionable openings, and a dour positional style. For the first 20 moves he would take most of the time allotted for the first 40, believing it important to build a sound position, so that further moves could be played rapidly if necessary. He published *Reshevsky on Chess* (1948), containing 110 of his games, and *How Chess Games are Won* (1962), containing another 60. The first book was ghosted by REINFELD, the second he wrote himself.

Keres–Reshevsky Kemeri 1937 Queen's Bishop Game

1 d4 d5 2 Nf3 Nf6 3 Bf4 c5 4 e3 Nc6 5 c3 Bg4 6 Nbd2 e6 7 Qa4 Bxf3 8 Nxf3 Qb6 9 Rb1 Be7 10 Bd3 0-0 11 0-0 Rfd8 12 Bg3 Rac8 13 Ne5 Nh5 14 Qc2 g6 15 Nxc6 Qxc6 16 Be5 f6

17 Bg3 Nxg3 18 hxg3 Kg7 19 g4 e5 20 Qe2 Qe6 21 Rbe1 Rc7 22 f3 Rh8 23 Bc2 Qb6 24 dxe5 fxe5 25 b3 c4 26 Qd2 Rd8 27 Kh1 cxb3 28 Bxb3 Qa5 29 Rc1 d4 30 exd4 exd4 31 Rfd1 dxc3 32 Qe3 Rxd1+ 33 Rxd1 Qg5 34 Qd4+ Kh6 35 Qf2 Qh4+ 36 Qxh4+ Bxh4 37 Kh2 Bg5 38 Bc2 Re7 39 Rd3 Bd2 40 Kg3 Re2 White resigns

Reshevsky Variation, 326 in the NIMZO-INDIAN DEFENCE, played several times by RESHEVSKY at AVRO 1938, but the line is much older (e.g. Rubinstein–Yates, Bad Kissingen 1928). Also 158, the EXCHANGE VARIATION of the QUEEN'S GAMBIT Declined, another line popular with Reshevsky but not pioneered by him.

resign, to concede defeat without playing on to the checkmate. Weak players seldom resign because frequent blunders swing the advantage, and stalemate is common resource. At a competent level it is considered discourteous to play on in a clearly lost position if the opponent is not under time pressure, but if an adjournment is imminent, play often continues to that point to allow time to confirm the player's fears. Occasionally masters resign in drawn positions or, more rarely, in won positions.

A position reached in a game Négesy–Honfi, Budapest 1955. Black played 1 ... Qxa2+ and White resigned. Both players saw that the knight was needed on c3 to prevent ... Rd1 mate. However, after 2 Nxa2 Rd1+ White can now defend by 3 Nc1, with an easy win.

result table, see CROSSTABLE.

Réti, Richard (1889–1929), player, author, and composer. Born in Bazin, Hungary (now Pezinok, Czechoslovakia), he studied mathematics and physics at Vienna, where he gained excellent chess practice, and shortly before the First World War became a chess professional. He earned his living partly by writing chess columns: *Becsi Magyar Ujsag; Morgenzeitung* (Ostrava); *Algemeen Handelsblad* (Amsterdam); *Berliner Börsen-Courier; Berliner Bilden-Courier.* He also gave displays, in particular BLINDFOLD CHESS at which he was expert. At São Paulo in 1925 he played 29 such games simultaneously, then a record.

There were few tournaments during the war, but Réti's play improved steadily, and from 1918 until his death he played in about 25 strong tournaments, obtaining several good results: Kaschau (now Košice) 1918, first ($+9=2$), ahead of VIDMAR and SCHLECHTER; Göteborg 1920, first ($+7=5-1$), ahead of RUBINSTEIN and BOGOLJUBOW; Teplice-Šanov 1922, first ($+8=2-3$) equal with SPIELMANN, ahead of GRÜNFELD and Rubinstein; Ostrava 1923, second ($+7=5-1$), after LASKER, ahead of Grünfeld, Bogoljubow, and Rubinstein; Bad Homborg 1927, second ($+5=3-2$), after Bogoljubow; and Brno 1928, first ($+6=2-1$) equal with SÄMISCH. Réti won the Czech championship in 1925, and played for Czechoslovakia in the Olympiad of 1927, making the highest first-board score ($+9=5-1$). He did not shine in match play, but in 1920 he defeated EUWE $+3-1$ and BREYER $+4=1$.

Despite the significance of his playing achievements Réti is better remembered for his contribution to the HYPERMODERN movement (see SCHOOLS OF CHESS), and for his book *Die neuen Ideen im Schachspiel* (1922); it deals with chess strategy, Réti's favourite subject, and the history of its development up to and including hypermodern play. A substantially different version was translated into English as *Modern Ideas in Chess* (1923).

Lacking adequate resources, Réti was unaware that some positional ideas were known earlier than he supposed, and he fails to mention, for example, the contributions made by STAUNTON, PAULSEN, and CHIGORIN. Nevertheless, this pioneer work is a classic of chess literature.

He died of scarlet fever before completing *Die Meister des Schachbretts*. Published the year after his death, this book contains biographical notes concerning 23 masters from the time of ANDERSSEN, and games played by them, with annotations explaining the strategy. An English translation, *Masters of the Chessboard*, was published in New York, 1932, and a different version, *Masters of the Chess Board*, in London, 1933. (See SMALL CENTRE.)

Réti–Bogoljubow New York 1924 First Brilliancy Prize Neo-Catalan Opening

1 Nf3 Nf6 2 c4 e6 3 g3 d5 4 Bg2 Bd6 5 0-0 0-0 6 b3 Re8 7 Bb2 Nbd7 8 d4 c6 9 Nbd2 Ne4 10 Nxe4 dxe4 11 Ne5 f5 12 f3 exf3 13 Bxf3 Qc7 14 Nxd7 Bxd7 15 e4 e5 16 c5 Bf8 17 Qc2 exd4 18 exf5 Rad8 19 Bh5 Re5 20 Bxd4 Rxf5 21 Rxf5 Bxf5 22 Qxf5 Rxd4 23 Rf1 Rd8 24 Bf7+ Kh8

25 Be8 Black resigns after this INTERFERENCE move which threatens a BACK-RANK MATE.

A cultured and educated man, Réti regarded chess as an art, and his books reveal the hand of an artist. Fittingly, he composed studies, and they compare with the best. He sought simple and natural-looking positions that would appeal to players.

A study by Réti, *Deutschösterreichische Tages-Zeitung*, 1921. White achieves the apparently im-

possible task of stopping Black's pawn: 1 Kg7 h4 2 Kf6 Kb6 (otherwise White promotes his pawn) 3 Ke5 Kxc6 4 Kf4.

J. Kalendovský, *Richard Réti, šachový myslitel* (Prague, 1989) contains 200 annotated games, 56 studies, extensive extracts from chess columns, and a full translation into Czech (a language which Réti did not speak) of *Die neuen Ideen*.

Réti Gambit Accepted, 1287, sound but unpopular.

Réti Opening, 1286, also called the Landstrasse Gambit. It may transpose, for example, to the CATALAN OPENING. If instead White maintains a SMALL CENTRE, fianchettoes both bishops, and castles on the king's-side, the play is a Réti System. White endeavours to control the central squares directly or indirectly with pieces, withholding the advance of centre pawns to the fourth rank until Black's intentions are known. Meanwhile White remains poised to attack any enemy pawn centre that might be set up. The opening was first played in a game A. E. Wolf–Teich, in the Landstrasse Schachbund, 1923, and by RÉTI against GRÜNFELD at Margate 1923, exactly a month later. (See BALASHOV; LARSEN; SHORT GAME; SPRAGGETT.)

Réti Variation, 127 in the QUEEN'S GAMBIT Declined, played in the game Réti–Tarrasch, Piešt'any 1922; 547 in the SICILIAN DEFENCE, as Réti–Tartakower, Mannheim 1914; 820 in the PONZIANI OPENING, from Tartakower–Réti, Berlin February 1928; 1073 and 1085 in the KING'S GAMBIT Declined, the first as analysed by Réti in *Magyar sakkvilág*, 1918 (continuing 7 ... Nc6 8 b4 Bb6 9 Qb3), and the second as Réti–Tarrasch, Göteborg 1920. Also 333, the LENINGRAD VARIATION of the NIMZO-INDIAN DEFENCE, played Réti–Marshall, Brno 1928; 1178, the SPIELMANN ATTACK in the FRENCH DEFENCE, as Réti–Maróczy, Göteborg 1920.

retractor, a problem in which some moves are retracted and from the changed position forward moves are played. The side that retracts the last SINGLE-MOVE begins the forward play.

A problem by DAWSON, second hon. mention, *The Problemist*, 1937. White and Black retract a move each, then Black makes a forward move and White mates.

After an UNCAPTURE by White, Nd5xNe3, and an uncapture by Black, Nf5xNe3, the position is: White Ka1, Na3, d5, e3; Black Ke5, Ne6, e4, f5. Black plays 1 ... Nf5–d4 and White replies 2 Na3–c4#. Both sides conspire to fulfil the stipulations, and this is called a help-retractor, an idea dating from the nineteenth century.

In the 1920s composers began to prefer defensive retractors in which Black tries to prevent White from fulfilling the stipulations. Two kinds were named after the Romanian composer Zeno Proca (1906–36) and the Danish composer Umro Niels Høeg (1876–1951) respectively. White begins and ends the retractions, playing the stipulated number of moves indicated by a minus sign. Usually, White then plays one forward move (+1) giving mate. In the Proca retractor the side retracting a move decides which man, if any, has been uncaptured; in Høeg retractors, however, when one side makes a retraction the other side chooses which man, if any, may have been uncaptured. Emphasis is on the retractions, the discovery of which may involve retrograde analysis.

#−4+1 Proca

A Proca retractor by the German composer Wolfgang Dittmann (1933–), fourth prize, *Die Schwalbe*, 1980. Thirteen men have been captured by black pawns; therefore Black cannot uncapture with a piece; and an uncapture by a pawn does not defeat the stipulations. The retractions (in backwards order) are 1 Rb4–b7 Qc4–e6 (Black blocks the rank, otherwise White retracts Rh4–b4 and mates by Rxh7) 2 Rb3–b4 Nc3–a4 3 Rb5–b3 Nd5–c3 4 Rb8–b5, and 1 Rxg8#.

retro, a problemist's term indicating that the following moves are given in backward order.

retrograde analysis, or retro-analysis, discovery of the play that would lead to a given position, a subject of interest to composers. The object may be to discover whether a position is LEGAL, whose turn it is to play, the last move or moves that have been played (see LAST MOVE PROBLEM), whether certain moves can be retracted (see RETRACTOR), whether castling is illegal, or whether the last move to have been played permits an EN PASSANT capture. So-

called problems with *en passant* keys, but lacking retro-analytical proof, were constructed in the 1840s: these are PUZZLES, not problems. In the 1850s a few simple retro-analytical problems were composed, but there was little advance until LOYD made his Souvenir problem in 1894. It was the republication of this, in *Deutsche Schachzeitung*, 1907, that led to an extensive development of the art of retrograde analysis, notably by DAWSON, the Danish composer Umro Niels Høeg (1876–1951), HUNDSDORFER, and TROITZKY; subsequently CERIANI, FABEL, PLAKSIN, KEYM, and CAILLAUD were among those who became expert in this field.

#4

The Souvenir problem composed by Loyd for the occasion of the New York Chess Association's annual meeting, 1894. All the missing men were captured by pawns, by White on e3, d4, c5, b6, a7 and b3, by Black on g6 and f4. Black's last move cannot have been made by any of his pieces (none has a square to have come from) nor by his pawns at f4, e6, or b6 (the first because this pawn came from g5, the others because the bishops came out long before). Therefore Black's last move was made by the pawn at f5. This pawn cannot have come from f6, for then White would have been in RETROSTALEMATE (pieces are locked in, pawns at a7, b4, and g5 came from b6, a2, and g4 respectively, and the pawn at b3 moved long ago to release the dark bishop. Thus it is proved that Black's last move was Pf7–f5, and White's before that, Rf6–g6. The key is gxf6 ep+, and mate follows 1 ... Kf5 2 Rg5+. The interest for solvers in all such problems lies in unravelling the past: the solution is often mundane. (See also ONE-MOVER; PARTIAL RETROGRADE ANALYSIS; PERPETUAL RETROGRESSION; RETRO-OPPOSITION.)

T. R. Dawson and W. Hundsdorfer, *Retrograde Analysis* (1915); K. Fabel, *Introduction to Retrograde Analysis* (1973).

The term is used in a different sense by computer analysts working on endgame databases. Here the final position for a particular ending is the starting point, earlier positions being derived by analysing backwards.

retro-opposition, a situation arising in RETRO-GRADE ANALYSIS in which a white and a black man both need to occupy the same square, and as they cannot do so at the same time a WAITING MOVE is needed to resolve the dilemma. (If no waiting move is available then one side is in RETRO-STALEMATE.)

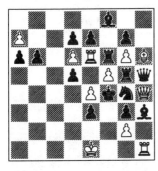

#1

A problem by DAWSON, *L'Italia Scacchistica*, 1919. White is to give mate, and the choice is between Rf1 and 0–0. The missing black man (a knight) was captured by White's h-pawn, and the five missing white men were captured by Black's a-, b-, c-, f-, and h-pawns.

All this happened long ago, and the only way to unravel the position is to retract the following moves (given in backward order): 1 ... Rf7–f6   2 Rf6–e6 Ke5–f4   3 K or Rh1 makes a waiting move (there is no alternative) 3 ... Kd4–e5   4 Re6–f6 etc. In effect, castling is illegal because the rooks at e6 and f6 cannot occupy f6 at the same time. They are, as it were, out of phase, a situation remedied by the waiting move. The solution is, therefore, 1 Rf1 ‡.

T. R. Dawson, *Retro-Opposition and other Retro-analytical Chess Problems* (1989). Edited by G. P. Jelliss.

retro-stalemate, a description of a composed position that would be legal if one side were to have the move but is illegal because the composer states or implies that the other side has the move. For example, the position, White Ka1, Pa2, Black Kc2, would be illegal if a composer stated that Black is to play; and White, who could not have played last, is said to stand in retro-stalemate. When a legal position is subjected to retrograde analysis in which one variation leads back to retro-stalemate, then this is proof that one of the retracted moves is illegal.

Positions may be set up in which neither side can have moved last, e.g. Wh: Kb1, Ba2; Bl: Kg8. This is an impossible position that could not arise in play.

Reverse Alekhine, 1319, a little-tried response to 1 g3 e5.

Reverse Benoni, 1294, the WING BLUMENFELD.

Reverse Grünfeld, name used occasionally for the CATALAN OPENING and some variations of the RÉTI OPENING.

reverse opening, an opening in which White commences with a series of moves more commonly used by Black.

Reverse Pirc, 1320 in response to the KING'S FIANCHETTO OPENING.

Rey Ardid Variation, 124 in the QUEEN'S GAMBIT Declined, introduced, in a correspondence game in 1935, by the Spanish master Ramón Rey Ardid (1903–88).

Reynolds Variation, 144, sound attack against the MERAN VARIATION of the QUEEN'S GAMBIT Declined, introduced by the English player Arthur Reynolds (1910–43), who published his analysis in *Chess*, May 1939.

Ribli, Zoltán (1951–   ), Hungarian champion 1973, 1974 (+9=6), and (with SAX) 1977 (+8=9), International Grandmaster (1973). European junior champion (with VAGANYAN and Maeder) in 1968–9, and alone in 1970–1, Ribli achieved his first success in a strong tournament at the age of 20, first equal with SUETIN at Kecskemét 1972. Several good results followed: Budapest 1975, first (+6=9) equal with POLUGAYEVSKY, ahead of PORTISCH; Amsterdam 1978, second (+6=5−2), after TIMMAN, ahead of HORT; and Bled–Portorož 1979, second (+6=8−1) equal with LARSEN, after Timman. In the interzonal Riga 1979, Ribli scored +7=8−2 and tied with ADORJÁN for third place, after TAL and Polugayevsky. Only three players from this event went forward as CANDIDATES and Ribli failed to qualify when NEUSTADTL SCORES were applied for tie-breaking. Three noteworthy first prizes followed: Mexico 1980 (+8=4), Baden-Baden 1981 (+6=7), shared with MILES, and the interzonal Las Palmas 1982 (+5=8). Ribli now became a Candidate for the first time, but after defeating E. TORRE (+3=6−1) in the quarter-final he lost to SMYSLOV. The following year, 1983, Ribli was second (+4=9) after ANDERSSON at Wijk aan Zee. Other major successes are: Bugojno 1984, second (+3=10), behind Timman; Tilburg 1984, second (+3=7−1) equal with BELYAVSKY, HÜBNER, and TUKMAKOV, after MILES; Portorož–Ljubljana 1985, first (+3=8) equal with Portisch and Miles; Dortmund 1986, first (+5=6); Reggio Emilia 1986–7, first (+2=9); Wijk aan Zee 1989, first (+3=9−1) shared with ANAND, NIKOLIĆ, and Sax; Reggio Emilia 1989–90, third (+1=9) equal with Andersson, behind EHLVEST and IVANCHUK.

Andersson–Ribli   Debrecen 1970   Sicilian Defence
Hungarian Variation

1 e4 c5   2 Nf3 g6   3 d4 cxd4   4 Nxd4 Nc6   5 Nc3 Bg7   6 Be3 Nf6   7 Bc4 d6   8 f3 0–0   9 Bb3 a6   10 0–0 Na5   11 f4 Nxb3   12 axb3 b5   13 Qf3 Bb7   14 f5 Rc8   15 Nd5 Rc5   16 Rae1 Nxd5   17 exd5 Rxd5   18 Qg4 Bc8   19 Qe4

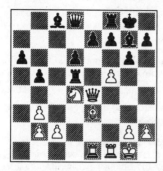

19 ... Rxd4 20 Bxd4 Bxf5 21 Qh4 Bxd4+ 22 Qxd4
Bxc2 23 Re3 e5 24 Qa7 e4 25 Qd4 Qd7 26 Rc3 Bd3 27
Rfc1 Qe6 28 Rc6 Rd8 29 Qb6 Rd7 30 Rc8+ Kg7 31
Qd4+ Qe5 32 Qe3 b4 33 Ra8 f5 34 g3 Rf7 35 Ra7
Rxa7 36 Qxa7+ Kh6 37 Qe3+ g5 38 h4 f4 39 hxg5+
Kxg5 40 gxf4+ Qxf4 41 Qxf4+ Kxf4 42 Kf2 e3+ 43
Ke1 d5 44 Rc8 Bf5 45 Rb8 a5 White resigns.

Rice Gambit, 1161 in the KING'S GAMBIT Accepted,
a grotesque monument to a rich man's vanity. Isaac
Leopold Rice (1850–1915), a German-born American industrialist, financed many tournaments restricted to this gambit, and gave prizes for other
games in which it was used. White's sacrifice of the
knight is neither good nor necessary. Extensive
analysis has failed to find sufficient compensation,
but in any case Black has several good ways of
avoiding the gambit. After Rice died, masters
wasted no more time on the gambit.

Richardson, Keith Bevan (1942–   ), English player,
International Correspondence Chess Grandmaster
(1975), bank manager. Around 1961 Richardson
decided that over-the-board play, which had
brought him some success as a junior, would interfere with his professional career, and he took to
postal chess instead. His best performances in this
field were two equal third places in the World
Correspondence Championship: the 7th, ending
1975, equal with ZAGOROVSKY, after ESTRIN and
BOEY; the 10th, ending 1984, equal with SANAKOYEV,
after PALCIAUSKAS and MORGADO.

Richardson Attack, 889, a variation of the EVANS
GAMBIT. It was introduced by the New York player
Philip Richardson (1841–1920) and published by
MASON in the *Dubuque Chess Journal,* 1873.

Richter, Kurt Paul Otto Joseph (1900–69), German
player and author, International Master (1950). His
most successful year was 1935, when he won the
German championship at Aachen and shared first
place with BOGOLJUBOW at Berlin. During the
Second World War he was chess columnist for the
Deutsche Allgemeine Zeitung, and when peace came
he largely gave up play to concentrate on writing.
He was a major contributor to *Deutsche Schachzeitung* in the post-war years, and his books include
Kurzgeschichten um Schachfiguren (1947) and *Hohe*

Schule der Schachtaktik (1952). He wrote, in fine
style, about the kind of brilliant tactics that are
found in his own play. The several opening lines
that are named after Richter are all attacking lines
for White that he played and analysed.

A. Brinckmann, *Kurt Richters beste Partien* (2nd
edn, 1961) contains 98 annotated games; Golz and
Keres, *Schönheit der Kombinationen* (1972) contains
a selection of Richter's writings, and examples of
his play; the English translation is entitled *Chess
Combination as a Fine Art* (1976).

Richter–Brinckmann   Aachen 1935   French Defence
Rubinstein Variation

1 d4 d5 2 Nc3 e6 3 e4 dxe4 4 Nxe4 Nd7 5 Nf3 Ngf6 6
Bg5 Be7 7 Nxf6+ Bxf6 8 Qd2 b6 9 Bb5 Bxg5 10 Nxg5
Bb7 11 0–0–0 h6

12 d5 e5 (if 12 ... Bxd5 13 c4 Qxg5 14 Bxd7+ Kxd7 15
f4; or 12 ... Qxg5 13 Qxg5 hxg5 14 dxe6 fxe6 15 Rxd7)
13 Ne6 fxe6 14 dxe6 0–0 15 Qxd7 Qg5+ 16 Kb1 Rae8
17 Qxc7 Re7 18 Rd7 Qxg2 19 Rc1 Rc8 20 Rd8+ Black
resigns.

Richter Attack, 56, a line in the QUEEN'S PAWN
OPENING dating back to Popiel–Marco, Vienna
1890, and subsequently played by MARSHALL,
BREYER and TARTAKOWER. The English player John
Herbert White (1880–1920), who favoured this
opening, published analysis in the first edition of
MCO (1911). Later it was taken up by RICHTER and
by Gavril Nikolayevich Veresov (1912–79), who
played it in the final of the USSR championship,
1940, and after whom it is sometimes named. These
two differed in their strategic aims, as can be seen
by comparing the Veresov Variation (58) and the
Richter Variation (57). Sometimes known as the
Betbeder or Levitsky Variation.

Also 480 in the SICILIAN DEFENCE, introduced by
the Berlin masters Berthold Koch (1899–1988) and
Richter in the early 1930s, with the idea of preventing Black from playing the DRAGON VARIATION. The
line has remained popular. (See LUTIKOV; E. TORRE;
UNZICKER.)

Richter Variation, 57, RICHTER'S treatment of the
RICHTER ATTACK, aimed at central control; 483,
Richter's original continuation in the Richter Attack of the SICILIAN DEFENCE, found wanting after
7 ... dxe5 8 Qf3 Be7; 531, sometimes called the

Grigoriev Variation, in the DRAGON VARIATION of the same opening, as Richter–Petrov, Bad Harzburg 1938; 727 in the SPANISH OPENING, from the game Richter–Eliskases, Bad Nauheim 1935; 1229, sometimes called the Anderssen Attack, in the FRENCH DEFENCE, played regularly since the 1870s, but by no one more than Richter in the 1930s. The name is occasionally given to the CHIGORIN VARIATION, 54, which may lead to 57.

rider, a term sometimes used by FAIRY PROBLEM composers for a LINE-PIECE.

Riemann, Fritz (1859–1932), Polish-born German player, town councillor at Erfurt. When a student at Breslau, Riemann practised with ANDERSSEN and took lessons from him. From 1879 to 1888 Riemann played in several national and three international tournaments, all in Germany. He achieved his best result at Leipzig 1888 when he scored +5=1−1 to share first prize with BARDELEBEN, ahead of TARRASCH. Although Riemann's play showed promise he then gave up competitive play for reasons of health. In 1925, when he was probably the last surviving pupil of Anderssen, he published *Schacherinnerungen des jüngsten Anderssen-Schülers.*

rifle chess, an UNORTHODOX CHESS game invented in 1921 by the American explorer William Buehler Seabrook (1886–1945). A capturing man remains stationary, shooting its target off the board without occupying the vacant square, an action that counts as a move. Captures can be made in no other way, and only one at a time.

#2

A problem by DAWSON, *Fairy Chess Review,* 1947. The solution is 1 Qa2, and black can only play 1 ... b6 or 1 ... b5 because the capture 1 ... bxa6 is check. Then 2 Qd5 #. Note that 1 Kg4, for example, is not stalemate because the reply 1 ... bxa6 is possible, but neither does it lead to mate next move. If White's king is placed on h2 and queen on g1 the solution becomes 1 Qa1 Pb6/5 2 Qh1 mate.

Riga Gambit, 1044, the GRECO COUNTER-GAMBIT.

Riga Variation, 729. Named from a correspondence game, Berlin–Riga 1906–7, this line was abandoned after CAPABLANCA showed an advantage for White in a tournament game against Ed. LASKER, New York 1915.

Rinck, Henri (1870–1952). Rinck and TROITZKY are rightly regarded as the principal founders of modern study composing. Born in Lyon of a prosperous French family with brewing interests, Rinck specialized in the refining of oils; 'for the better prosecution of his work' he moved to Spain around 1900. There he began composing and there he spent most of his life. He was both immodest about his own work and jealous of Troitzky's reputation, and when he found that fewer of his than of Troitzky's studies had been included in Sutherland and Lommer's *1234 Modern End-game Studies* he sulked for a long time; but most judges would regard Troitzky as the more creative. By the 1930s Rinck was outclassed by younger composers with more varied repertoires.

Rinck published collections of his studies, each book including the whole of its predecessors: 150 in 1909 (2nd edn, 1913), 300 in 1919, 700 in 1927, and finally *1414 Fins de parties* (dated 1950, published in 1952), a daunting and unwinnowed 800 pages containing all his compositions. (At his request a copy was buried with him, under his arm.) More than 500 studies are pawnless, a field in which stratagems are few, so there is much repetition. For example, there are more than 130 examples of the endgame two rooks v. two minor pieces. In collaboration with the Belgian analyst Louis Malpas (1893–1973) he wrote *Dame contre tour et cavalier* (1947), an excellent analysis of this endgame.

+

A MALYUTKA by Rinck, first prize, *La Stratégie,* 1912–14. 1 Qc5 Ke6 2 Bc8+ Kf7 3 Bf5 Qb3 4 Qc7+ Kf8 5 Qd8+ Kf7 6 Bg6+ Kg7 7 Qe7+ Kg8 8 Kh6 Qh3+ 9 Bh5.

Rio de Janeiro Variation, 805, a discovery that gave the BERLIN DEFENCE of the SPANISH OPENING a new though brief lease of life. The variation was played in a telegraph game Buenos Aires–Rio de Janeiro, 1903, and named after the home of its originator, João Caldas Vianna (1862–1931). For obvious reasons it is sometimes called the Brazilian System, or Caldas Vianna Variation.

rithmomachy, a game in vogue from the 11th to the 17th centuries, variously known as Arithmomachia (battle of numbers), Arithmetic Chess, or Philosopher's Game (*Iudus philosophorum*). It is played on an 8 × 16 board between two players, odds and evens. Each side has eight round men, eight triangles and eight square men. Four round men are numbered 2, 4, 6, and 8 for evens, and 3, 5, 7, and 9 for odds, and the other four round men are marked with the squares of those numbers. The remaining men bear larger numbers formed by addition, multiplication and so on. Each shape of piece has a different move. One of the squares on each side is formed by making a pyramid of squares, triangles, and rounds, and this is sometimes called a king, because the first phase of the game is to capture the enemy pyramid. There are then three 'triumphs' based on arrangements of numbers. Captures are made in various ways, all demanding calculation.

The game appears to have been played only in western Europe, and by the educated classes. It has recently experienced a small revival of interest, and one writer has speculated that it was used as a medieval teaching aid.

J. Stigter, *Rithmomachia, the Philosopher's Game: a reference list* (1985).

Rittner, Horst Robert (1930–), German player, International Correspondence Chess Grandmaster (1961), winner (+10=5) of the sixth World Correspondence Championship, 1968–71. Rittner also won the Ragozin memorial correspondence tournament, 1963–6, ahead of O'KELLY, ESTRIN, and SIMAGIN. He was editor of the German magazine *Schach*, 1966–90.

Riumin Variation, 346 in the QUEEN'S INDIAN DEFENCE, analysed by Nikolai Nikolayevich Riumin (1908–42), ALATORTSEV, and LILIENTHAL. Also 538, the MOSCOW VARIATION of the SICILIAN DEFENCE.

Rivadavia Gambit, 457, the MORRA GAMBIT in its Argentinian disguise. There are many chess clubs on the Calle Rivadavia, Buenos Aires.

Rivière, Jules Arnous de (1830–1905), the strongest French player for about 20 years from the late 1850s. Originally Arnous-Rivière, he awarded himself the noble 'de'. His father was French, his mother English. He played in the Paris international tournament of 1867, taking sixth place well behind the world's leaders but ahead of ROSENTHAL. Rivière also played in a few minor tournaments in Paris. In 1855 he was defeated by DUBOIS in a long series of games; in 1860 he won against BARNES (+5−2); in 1867 he beat LÖWENTHAL (+2); and in 1883 he narrowly lost a match against CHIGORIN (+4=1−5). Rivière edited several chess columns, published books on

billiards and roulette, and invented many new games including one with two-coloured dominoes. He is also remembered for some casual games with MORPHY, played privately in 1863.

Rivière Opening, 247, the DUTCH DEFENCE.

Rivière Variation, 1162 in the KING'S GAMBIT Accepted, superseded by the move 6 . . . Nxe4.

Robatsch Defence, 1276, also known as the King's Fianchetto Defence, the Modern Defence, or the Ujtelky Defence. Known since the 16th century this defence was rarely played until the middle of the 20th century, when it was used by the Austrian grandmaster (and orchidologist) Karl Robatsch (1928–). Play usually leads to the PIRC–ROBATSCH SYSTEM although other options are open to Black, as, for example, the GURGENIDZE VARIATION, 1277.

Rodríguez, Amador Céspedes (1957–), Cuban Champion 1984, 1988, International Grandmaster (1977). He was first or equal first at Cienfuegos 1984, Caracas 1985, Bayamo 1987, Pančevo 1987 (+7=5), Holguin 1989, and Torre del Mar 1990 (Swiss system, 84 players).

Rogard, Bror Axel Folke Per (*né* Rosengren) (1899–1973), Swedish chess organizer, International Arbiter (1951), lawyer. In 1949 he succeeded RUEB as president of FIDE, holding the post until 1970 when he, in turn, was succeeded by EUWE.

Rogers, Ian (1960–), Australian champion 1979–80, 1985–6, Commonwealth champion 1983, International Grandmaster (1985). First or equal first at Nuovo 1984, Kragujevac 1985, Wijk aan Zee (II) 1985, Calcutta 1988, and then first in two stronger tournaments at Groningen, 1988 (+5=3−1) and 1989 (+4=5).

Rohde, Michael Arthur (1959–), American player, International Grandmaster (1988). Equal first at San Francisco 1987.

Romanishin, Oleg Mikhailovich (1952–), Ukrainian player, International Grandmaster (1976). With an aggressive style ('draws make me angry') he has had several notable tournament victories: Odessa 1974 (First League tournament) (+9=6−2); Novi Sad 1975 (+9=6); Yerevan 1976 (+8=5−2); Hastings 1976–7 (+10=3−1); Leningrad 1977 (+8=7−2) to tie with TAL, ahead of SMYSLOV and KARPOV; Polanica Zdrój 1980 (+7=6); Lvov 1981 (+6=6−1), equal with Tal; Jurmala 1983 (+9=4); Moscow 1985 (+5=6), in front of VAGANYAN and TUKMAKOV; Reggio Emilia 1985–6 (+3=8), equal with ANDERSSON and LJUBOJEVIĆ; Yerevan 1986; Berlin 1990, shared with BALASHOV; and Debrecen 1990 (+3=7). In nine appearances in the USSR championship between 1974 and 1983 his best place was in 1975, second (+ 7 = 5 − 3) shared with GULKO, Tal, and Vaganyan, behind PETROSYAN. In 1990 he won two Swiss system events, Győr (116 players), and Šibenik (60 players). At Reggio Emilia 1991 he was fourth (+ 2 = 8 − 2) equal with YEPESHIN and BELYAVSKY, after Ljubojević, Gulko, and Vaganyan.

Romanishin–Tukmakov   Yerevan 1976   Sicilian Defence Moscow Variation

1 e4 c5 2 Nf3 d6 3 Bb5+ Bd7 4 c4 Nc6 5 Nc3 Nf6 6 0–0 g6 7 d3 Bg7 8 Bg5 h6 9 Be3 0–0 10 h3 e5 11 Nh2 Nh5 12 Nd5 Be6 13 Qd2 Kh7 14 g4 Nf4 15 Bxf4 exf4 16 Bxc6 bxc6 17 Nxf4 Rb8 18 Rab1 Qg5 19 Nf3 Qf6 20 Kg2 Rxb2 21 Rxb2 Qxb2 22 Qxb2 Bxb2 23 Rb1 Rb8 24 Nxe6 fxe6 25 Ne1 Rb6

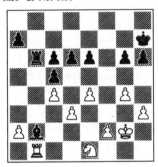

26 f4 Kg7 27 Nc2 Kf6 28 h4 e5 29 g5+ Ke6 30 f5+ gxf5 31 gxh6 Kf7 32 exf5 Kg8 33 Kf3 Kh7 34 Ke4 Kxh6 35 Rg1 Bc3 36 f6 d5+ 37 Kf5 Black resigns.

Romanishin Variation, 26 in the ENGLISH OPENING, played, but not originated, by ROMANISHIN in the 1970s; 819 in the PONZIANI OPENING, as Sax–Romanishin, Tilburg 1979; 984 in the SCOTCH GAME.

Romanovsky, Peter Arsenyevich (1892–1964), International Master (1950), International Arbiter (1951). He learned his chess in St Petersburg, won the Polytechnic Institute championship in 1913, and went to Mannheim in 1914 to seek his master title in the HAUPTTURNIER. When the war began he and other Russian players were interned. Subsequently he became one of the leading Soviet players. A frequent competitor in the Leningrad championship, he came first only once, when he shared the title in 1925 with ILYIN-GENEVSKY, LEVENFISH, and RABINOVICH. Curiously, Romanovsky was more successful in USSR championships: second to ALEKHINE in 1920; champion in 1923; second to BOGOLJUBOW in 1924; and joint champion, with BOHATIRCHUK, in 1927. His best international achievement was at Leningrad 1934 when he shared second place with Riumin, after BOTVINNIK, ahead of EUWE. About this time Romanovsky began to give more time to teaching and to writing books and articles about the game. In 1934 he became the first Soviet chessplayer to be awarded the title of Honoured Master of Sport. In 1942 he won the city championship of Ivanovo with

a CLEAN SCORE (+ 10). Both of his brothers, Alexander (1880–1943) and Yevgeny (1884–1942), played chess.

I. Z. Romanov, *Petr Romanovsky* (1984) contains a biography, 114 games of which 86 are annotated, compositions, and career results.

Yates–Romanovsky   Moscow 1925   Spanish Opening Close Defence

1 e4 e5 2 Nf3 Nc6 3 Bb5 a6 4 Ba4 Nf6 5 0–0 Be7 6 Re1 d6 7 c3 0–0 8 d4 Bd7 9 Nbd2 exd4 10 cxd4 Nb4 11 Bxd7 Qxd7 12 Nf1 c5 13 b3 d5 14 a3 Nc6 15 Ne5

15 ... Qd8 16 Nxc6 bxc6 17 e5 Ne4 18 Ne3 f5 19 f3 cxd4 20 Qxd4 Nc5 21 Qd1 f4 22 b4 fxe3 23 bxc5 d4 24 Qd3 Bxc5 25 Bb2 Rb8 26 Re2 Qd5 27 Bc1 Rb3 28 Qd1 d3 29 Rxe3 d2 White resigns.

Romanovsky Variation, 302 in the NIMZO-INDIAN DEFENCE recommended by ROMANOVSKY.

Roman Theme, see DECOY THEMES.

Romantic Attack, 1246, the BOURDONNAIS ATTACK basking in one of TARTAKOWER's guises.

Romi Opening, 229, the QUEEN'S BISHOP GAME.

Romi Variation, 141, line in the QUEEN'S GAMBIT Declined favoured by the Italian player Massimiliano Romi (né Romih) (1893–1979), but known before his time, having been played, for example, in the game Vidmar–Marshall, Carlsbad 1911.

rook, the major piece represented by the letter R or the figurine ♖, a LINE-PIECE that is moved along ranks and files. On an otherwise empty board it

attacks 14 squares. (For a special rook's move, see CASTLING.) In the array White's rooks stand on a1 and h1, Black's on a8 and h8.

Until the new queen's move was introduced in the 15th century the rook was the most powerful piece and a player attacking it was expected to call check-rook. The name comes from the Sanskrit *ratha*, a chariot, through Persian and Arabic *rukh*. Most European languages adapted the word by homophony through the Italian *rocco*, tower, which was thus translated. The only language other than English that uses a direct transliteration is Icelandic, with *hrókur*. In English-speaking countries non-players sometimes call it a castle, but all speak of castling. Except for that move the powers of the rook have been unchanged throughout the known history of chess.

rook ending, an endgame with kings, rooks (or a rook), and with or without pawns.

rook player, a player who would expect to receive odds of a rook from a first-class opponent, a classification sometimes used in the 19th century for weak players.

Rook's Pawn Gambit, 1176, the STAMMA GAMBIT.

root 50 ($\sqrt{50}$) leaper. Invented for use in FAIRY PROBLEMS, this LEAPER is moved a distance of $\sqrt{50}$ squares, and the co-ordinates of its leap are 5,5, or 7,1.

#4

A problem by the English composer Christopher Cedric Lytton (*né* Sells) (1939–), *The Problemist*, 1980. The man at c8 is a white $\sqrt{50}$ leaper. The key is 1 Kb8, setting up a BLOCK. Black's knight must be moved, in each case allowing one of three possible mates while preventing the other two.

1 ... Ng6   2-4 $\sqrt{50}$ – d1–e8–f1
1 ... Nf3   2-4 $\sqrt{50}$ – h3–a4–h5
1 ... Nf5(g2) 2-4 $\sqrt{50}$ – b1–a8–h7.

rose, a line-piece invented by the French composer Robert Meignant (1924–) in 1968 and used in FAIRY PROBLEMS; it is moved like a NIGHTRIDER but on an octagonal path. For example, on an otherwise empty board a rose at a4 could be moved by

way of b6, d7, f6, g4, f2, d1, b2 to a4, its starting point; it could also be moved on this path anticlockwise; or it could be moved on the paths a4–b6–a8, a4–c5–d7, a4–c5–e4–f2, a4–c3–e4–f6–e8, and a4–c3–d1.

Rosenthal, Samuel (1837–1902), Polish-born player who settled in Paris in 1864 to become a journalist and chess teacher. He played in six important matches, losing them all except one (a defeat of WISKER in 1871, +3=4−2), and he entered about six tournaments. At Vienna 1873 he took fourth place after STEINITZ, BLACKBURNE, and ANDERSSEN ahead of PAULSEN. Rosenthal's best performance, however, was his eighth place at London 1883, when nearly all the world's best players were among the competitors. He then gave up serious play in favour of writing articles, editing chess columns, and teaching. Steinitz wrote that Rosenthal was the only chess professional of his time who earned a good living, averaging 20,000 fr. annually for the last 30 years of his life. In 1898 he sued one of his students when his contract was terminated; the Tribunal at Seine awarded him 15,000 fr. arrears of pay but not the 25,000 he claimed in addition for loss of earnings.

Rosenthal Variation, 799 in the SPANISH OPENING, played by ROSENTHAL against ZUKERTORT in their 1880 match, but previously played by MORPHY against PAULSEN; 865 in the THREE KNIGHTS OPENING, as Rosenthal–Steinitz, London 1883; 1003 in the SCOTCH GAMBIT, as Wisker–Rosenthal, 4th match game, 1870; 1158, the SALVIO DEFENCE to the KIESERITZKY GAMBIT.

Rosentreter Defence, 934 in the ITALIAN OPENING, from the game Rosentreter–Höfer, Berlin 1899.

Rosentreter Gambit, 1149, old variation of the KING'S GAMBIT Accepted, advocated in 1882 by the German army captain Adolf Rosentreter (1844–1920). This gambit, like the QUAADE GAMBIT, would be unsound but for the following curious variation: 4 ... g4 5 Ne5 (SØRENSEN GAMBIT) 5 ... Qh4+ 6 g3 fxg3 7 Qxg4 g2+? 8 Qxh4 gxh1=Q. Unexpectedly, White's attack is more than sufficient compensation for the sacrifice. Also 1113, the VILLEMSON GAMBIT.

Rossolimo, Nicolas (1910–75), International Grandmaster (1953). Born in Kiev, he settled with his Russian mother in Paris in 1929, his Greek father having emigrated to the USA some years earlier. Rossolimo took a job as a taxi-driver. His best tournament achievements were at Paris 1938, when he came second (+6=3−1), half a point after CAPABLANCA, and at Paris 1939, first (+9=5), ahead of TARTAKOWER. For a few years after the Second World War he became more active in tournament play, notably winning the French championship in 1948 and achieving some fair results in small tournaments at Hastings: 1948–9, first; 1949–50, second after SZABÓ ahead of EUWE; and 1950–1, second equal with O'KELLY after UNZICKER. In 1953 he joined his father in the USA. There he drove a taxi, gave chess lessons, and also earned money, perhaps, from the sales of a record of Russian folk-songs. In the Swiss system US Open Championship 1955 he came first equal with RESHEVSKY and, favoured by the tie-break, took the first prize, a Buick car. He lived for varying periods in France, always returning to the USA, where he died three days after being found with head injuries at the bottom of a flight of stairs. Rossolimo played in five Olympiads: for France in 1950 and 1972, for the USA in 1958, 1960, and 1966.

Rossolimo Attack, 499, the MOSCOW VARIATION of the SICILIAN DEFENCE, a cousin of the ROSSOLIMO VARIATION.

Rossolimo Variation, 462 (sometimes called the Hispano–Sicilian Variation) in the SICILIAN DEFENCE, given by COZIO, played by BIRD and WILLIAMS at the London tournament 1851, by WINAWER against STEINITZ at Paris 1867, favoured by NIMZOWITSCH, and reintroduced by ROSSOLIMO around 1940. (See FURMAN; SVESHNIKOV.)

Rothschild, Albert (1844–1911), chess patron, financier. Baron Rothschild was a member of the Viennese branch of the famous banking family and played daily in the Vienna Chess Club where he was regarded as a strong player. As a boy he had STEINITZ as a tutor and he loved the tactical brilliance which then characterized Steinitz's play. Rothschild funded many BRILLIANCY PRIZES.

Rotlewi, Gersz (1889–1920), Polish player. His career at master level began in the winter of 1907–8. In matches he lost to SALWE in 1909 ($+5=3-8$) and defeated him in 1911 ($+3=6-1$); in the All-Russia tournament, St Petersburg 1909, he came second to ALEKHINE; and at Carlsbad 1911 he came fourth after TEICHMANN, RUBINSTEIN, and SCHLECHTER, ahead of MARSHALL, NIMZOWITSCH, VIDMAR, Alekhine, and DURAS. The promise of Rotlewi's rapid progress and his 'refreshing and energetic play' was not fulfilled; struck by a serious nervous illness, he never played again.

round, (1) a set of games, normally scheduled to begin on the same day, that forms a discrete stage of a tournament. For example, in an ALL-PLAY-ALL tournament of eight players there will be seven rounds each consisting of four games. After the four games of the first round have been completed (or perhaps adjourned) the players will be paired with different opponents and the second round will commence.

round, (2) a complete set of rounds, using this word in the sense of round (1). A tournament in which each player meets every other player once is a single-round tournament. In a double-round tournament each player meets every other player twice, in a treble-round tournament three times, and so on. Tournaments above double-round are often known as MATCH TOURNAMENTS. Ideally a different word should be used to distinguish the two kinds of round and to eliminate such remarks as 'in the third round of the second round . . . '.

round chess, UNORTHODOX CHESS played on a round board. Such games have a venerable history dating at least from the 10th century as evidenced by Islamic manuscripts. A version known as zatrikion or Byzantine chess, because it was popular in the capital of the Eastern Roman Empire, used a board of four concentric rings each divided into 16 spaces. Each of the ranks, which are arranged like spokes in a wheel, contains four spaces. For the array a player's men are placed on adjoining ranks: on the first, four pawns; on the second, a rook on the perimeter then knight, FĪL, and king; on the third, a similar arrangement with FIRZĀN instead of king; and on the fourth, four pawns. The opponent's men are similarly placed mirror fashion on the other side of the circle. Unlike SHAṬRANJ, pawns are not promoted, a firzān may capture a firzān, a fīl may capture a fīl. Another version, sometimes called circular chess, has a similar board except that the vacant centre is divided into four quarter circles, known as citadels. At the start the king and firzān are on the perimeter and if a player can move his king into a citadel he cannot lose. Zatrikion had a brief revival in England, Germany, and India around the beginning of the 19th century. George Hope Verney (1842–96), an assiduous experimenter with unorthodox games, devised three- and four-handed forms of round chess with 4×24 and 4×32 spaces respectively, and published these in his book *Chess Eccentricities* (1885).

The modern equivalent of a round board, used only by composers, is called a CYLINDER BOARD. The game described in the ALFONSO MS as Los Escaques is an astronomical game played on a circular board, and has no connection with chess despite its name.

round-robin, an American term for an ALL-PLAY-ALL tournament, although there is no logical connection.

Rousseau, Eugène (c.1810–c.1870), French player, bank cashier, who worked for a time in New Orleans. After beating J. W. Schulten (d.1875) in two matches, 1841 and 1843, he was thought to be one of the strongest players in the USA and in 1845 played STANLEY for $1,000, perhaps the first national championship anywhere. He lost ($+8=8-15$). The match may have had another consequence, for Ernest Morphy was Rousseau's second, and his nephew Paul is known to have attended the match. It may have been the spark that inspired MORPHY. Rousseau was undoubtedly the strongest player in New Orleans before Morphy's arrival, but his reputation there as one of Europe's strongest players seems open to question. In 1850, on a visit to New Orleans, LÖWENTHAL beat him 5–0 in off-hand games, and in the tournament at Paris 1867 he finished next to last, scoring 3 wins and 19 losses. One of those wins, the last game he played there, was against WINAWER who was thereby put out of the running for first prize. (See BODEN VARIATION; MORPHY; ROUSSEAU GAMBIT; STAKES.)

Rousseau Gambit, 939, a dubious gambit which stems from PONZIANI, hence the alternative name, Ponziani Counter-gambit. It was tried unsuccessfully by ROUSSEAU in 1845 when he met STANLEY in match play.

Royal Opening, 441, an old name for the KING'S PAWN OPENING.

royal piece, a FAIRY PROBLEM piece that retains its normal powers of moving but must respond to being attacked as would a king, and can be mated or stalemated, which is often the stipulated aim. Usually the side that has a royal piece does not have a normal king.

Roycroft, Arthur John (1929–), English study composer and author, International Judge of Chess Compositions (1959), computer systems analyst. In 1965 he founded *EG* which became the world's first long-running periodical devoted wholly to studies and endgames. This he published and edited until 1991, a total of 102 issues in 6 volumes, a magazine of record. His *Test Tube Chess* (1972), the best English-language guide to the art of studies, was revised and republished as *The Chess Endgame Study* (1981). Studies are commonly classified by the GBR CODE of which he was co-inventor.

Ruban Variation, 398 in the KING'S INDIAN DEFENCE, a line from the Leningrad player Vadim Ruban (1964–).

Rubinstein, Akiba (or Akiva) (1882–1961), International Grandmaster (1950), one of the world's best four players from about 1907 to 1922. The youngest of twelve children, he was born at Stawiski, a Polish border town then in Russia. At the age of 16 he learned chess, and the rest of his life was devoted to the game. Around 1901 he moved to Łódź where he met SALWE, with whom he played matches, drawing the first (+5=4−5) and winning the second (+5=2−3). In 1905 Rubinstein shared first prize in the Barmen HAUPTTURNIER, his master career began, and he soon had excellent performances in major tournaments: Carlsbad 1907, first (+12=6−2), ahead of MARÓCZY; Łódź 1908, first (+6=7−3); St Petersburg 1909, first (+12=5−1) equal with LASKER; San Sebastián 1911, second (+4=10) after CAPABLANCA, ahead of SCHLECHTER and TARRASCH; Carlsbad 1911, second (+12=10−3) equal with Schlechter, after TEICHMANN. During these years Rubinstein also won an All-Russia tournament, Łódź 1907–8, and matches against MARSHALL in 1908 (+4=1−3), MIESES in 1909 (+5=2−3), and FLAMBERG in 1910 (+4=1).

In 1912 Rubinstein won four major events: San Sebastián (+8=9−2), ahead of Schlechter; Piešt'any (+12=4−1), ahead of Schlechter; Breslau (+9=6−2), a tie with DURAS; and Vilnius, where he defeated ALEKHINE twice; he also won a minor tournament at Warsaw. Because of these five victories 1912 was called the Rubinstein year. His tournament record for the six years 1907 to 1912 was better than that of any other master; at one time or another he had met the best ten or eleven players, and he had a MINUS SCORE against only Maróczy. Rubinstein now challenged Lasker to a match for the world championship, and after long negotiations this was scheduled for the autumn of 1914. Before the required finance ($2,500) had been raised the great St Petersburg tournament of 1914 took place. Rubinstein failed badly, while Lasker won narrowly ahead of Capablanca with the rest of the field far behind. Rubinstein's chances of a match faded and then, with the outbreak of the First World War, disappeared.

Recommencing his career in 1918, he defeated Schlechter in match play (+2=3−1). Besides Lasker and Capablanca, he had to contend with two new aspirants to the world title, Alekhine and BOGOLJUBOW. He defeated Bogoljubow in 1920 (+5=3−4), was first (+7=2−3) ahead of Bogoljubow at Triberg 1921, and first (+9=5) ahead of Alekhine and Bogoljubow at Vienna 1922. This last win and his shared win at St Petersburg 1909 were his two greatest achievements. Rubinstein challenged Capablanca, who had won the title in 1921, and agreed terms, but funds were not forthcoming. He was now 40, and just as his prospects before the war had been overshadowed by those of Capablanca, so they were now dimmed by those of Alekhine.

Rubinstein's subsequent achievements in 20 international tournaments included only two victories: Marienbad 1925 (+9=14−2), shared with NIMZOWITSCH, and Rogaška–Slatina 1929 (+9=5−1). Other prizes included a second (+10=9−1) after Alekhine at Baden-Baden 1925, a third (+6=1−2) at Dresden 1926, a second after Capablanca at Budapest 1929, and a third (+9=2−4) after Alekhine and Nimzowitsch at San Remo 1930. Rubinstein played for Poland in the Olympiads of 1930 and 1931. In 1930, when his country won the gold medal, he played in every match and his 88.2% score of +13=4 is the best result ever made at first board. (Higher percentage scores subsequently were made against hand-picked opponents.) Rubinstein retired in 1932 after a lifetime of professional chess that brought him little reward. A fund was raised on his behalf in 1933. He retained an interest in the game, analysed openings, played friendly games, and coached O'KELLY and other players.

Rubinstein was a great student of the openings, expecially of his favourite QUEEN'S GAMBIT, and a fine endgame player, perhaps the greatest rook ending expert of his time. In play he was a perfectionist: a game was to be constructed carefully, move by move, and was not to him a fight. His best games were in irreproachable style; but he did not like to be thrown off course, and in consequence he sometimes failed in the middlegame, even against players well below his strength.

A lifelong shyness became almost pathological in his later years. After making a move he would withdraw to a corner of the room, as though feeling his very presence gave offence. His confidence was undermined, more than that of most masters, by the loss of a game. His great successes in 1912 and 1922, stimulated by hopes of a championship match, were followed, when the hopes faded, by dismal failures: sixth equal at St Petersburg 1914, twelfth at Carlsbad 1923, and tenth at Ostrava 1923.

Rubinstein was co-editor of COLLIJN's *Lärobok*, but he was a lazy writer and left no literary work other than annotations, always of a high quality, in periodicals. In 1933 KMOCH published *Rubinstein gewinnt!*, a selection of 100 games. In the same year that it was reprinted, 1941, an English translation, *Rubinstein's Chess Masterpieces*, appeared. (See TIME (1).)

Razuvayev and Murakhvery, *Akiba Rubinstein* (1980), is a biography in Russian, with 120 games.

Rubinstein-Hromádka Ostrava 1923 First brilliancy prize
King's Gambit Declined Classical Defence

1 e4 e5 2 f4 Bc5 3 Nf3 d6 4 Nc3 Nf6 5 Bc4 Nc6 6 d3 Bg4 7 h3 Bxf3 8 Qxf3 Nd4 9 Qg3 Qe7 10 fxe5 dxe5 11 Kd1 c6 12 a4 Rg8 13 Rf1 h6 14 Ne2 0–0–0 15 Nxd4 Bxd4 16 c3 Bb6 17 a5 Bc7 18 Be3 Kb8 19 Kc2 Ka8 20 Rf3 Nd5 21 Bg1 Nf4 22 Qf2 Bb8 23 g3 Nxh3 24 Rxf7 Qd6

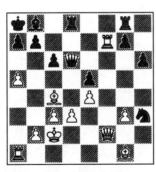

25 Qb6 Rd7 26 Bc5 Rxf7 27 Bxd6 Rf2+ 28 Qxf2 Nxf2 29 Bc5 Black resigns. White's play shows Turton Doubling (21 Bg1, 22 Qf2, and 25 Qb6) and Zepler Doubling (20 Rf3, 22 Qf2, and 24 Rxf7) (see DOUBLING THEMES).

Rubinstein Attack, 193, variation of the QUEEN'S GAMBIT Declined, successfully played by RUBINSTEIN around 1908, and now a standard line; 122, the SCHLECHTER VARIATION.

Rubinstein Counter-gambit, 562 in the SICILIAN DEFENCE. If 7 dxc5 Bxc5 8 Qxd5, 8 ... Qb6 gives Black a dynamic advantage as compensation for the lost pawn. The idea may have been originated by KRAUSE, and was revived by LARSEN in 1959.

Rubinstein Defence, 561, the NIMZOWITSCH VARIATION of the SICILIAN DEFENCE, much played by RUBINSTEIN, e.g. Alapin–Rubinstein, Vilna 1912.

Rubinstein Variation, 37, an ENGLISH OPENING line that can also arise in the SYMMETRICAL DEFENCE; 70 in the QUEEN'S GAMBIT ACCEPTED, as Rubinstein–Tartakower, Marienbad 1925. Four lines in the QUEEN'S GAMBIT Declined: 151, sometimes called the Anti-Meran Variation, played Rubinstein–Vidmar, San Remo 1930; 179 in the CAMBRIDGE SPRINGS DEFENCE, given by RUBINSTEIN in COLLIJN's *Lärobok* but known earlier (e.g. Swiderski–Marco, Coburg 1904); 13 dxe5 Nxe5 14 Nxe5 Qxe5 15 f4, reached from the CLASSICAL VARIATION (200) and sometimes called the Capablanca Variation, as Rubinstein–Lasker, living pieces game, Berlin, 1924 (but seen already in Treybal–Hromádka, Piešt'any 1922); 202, proposed by von SCHEVE and sometimes known as the Argentine Variation, akin to the RUBINSTEIN ATTACK (193).

Also 227 in the QUEEN'S PAWN OPENING, as Rubinstein–Maróczy, The Hague 1921; 229, the QUEEN'S BISHOP GAME, played, for example, Rubinstein–Perlis, Ostend 1906, but known earlier; 231, the MASON VARIATION, similar to 229; 248 in the DUTCH DEFENCE, an old line, e.g. played by WILLIAMS at London 1851; 297 in the BUDAPEST DEFENCE, played several times by Rubinstein at the Berlin, April 1918, tournament (see SMOTHERED MATE); 316, sometimes called the Landau Variation, introduced in Rubinstein–Alekhine, St Petersburg 1914, the most commonly played fourth move in the NIMZO-INDIAN DEFENCE (see KNAAK); 348 in the QUEEN'S INDIAN DEFENCE; 354, an interesting pawn sacrifice in the BLUMENFELD VARIATION, introduced in the game Rubinstein–Tartakower, Teplice–Šanov 1922.

Further, 582 in the CARO–KANN DEFENCE, recommended by Rubinstein in the fourth edition of the *Lärobok*; 681 in the SPANISH OPENING, popular with STEINITZ; 703, the RUSSIAN DEFENCE in the same opening; 704, which follows the previous line, recommended by Rubinstein in the *Lärobok*; 12 Nbd2 Nc6, a possible continuation from the CHIGORIN VARIATION (746), again in the Spanish Opening, perhaps leading to the RAUZER VARIATION; 853 in the FOUR KNIGHTS OPENING, played by MARSHALL, TEICHMANN, and SCHLECHTER around 1903, but named on account of its successful use by Rubinstein in 1912; 946 in the TWO KNIGHTS DEFENCE, another old line re-examined by Rubinstein in the *Lärobok* (other possible lines here are the MARSHALL VARIATION and the ZEMCH VARIATION); 1083, also known as the Morphy Defence and played by Steinitz, LASKER, and PILLSBURY, in the FALKBEER COUNTER-GAMBIT.

Also two lines in the FRENCH DEFENCE: 1196, sometimes called the Lasker Variation, from the game Maróczy–Rubinstein, Carlsbad 1907, but no longer a popular line (see RICHTER), Rubinstein himself later preferring the BURN VARIATION (1213); 1216, a recommendation by Rubinstein.

Rubtsova, Olga Nikolayevna (1909–), Soviet player, Women's World Champion 1956–8,

Rudenko, Lyudmila Vladimirovna (1904–86), Soviet player, Women's World Champion 1950–3.

Rudenko, Valentin Fyodorovich (1938–), Ukrainian composer, International Judge of Chess Compositions (1960), International Grandmaster for Chess Compositions (1980), educationalist. Working largely in the field of orthodox DIRECT MATE PROBLEMS, he became the leading Soviet composer, a worthy successor to LOSHINSKY. In the eleventh (1971–2), twelfth (1973–4), and thirteenth (1975–6) USSR composing championships he won both the TWO- and THREE-MOVER sections, and in the twelfth he also won the MORE-MOVER section; he also won the two-mover section in the fifteenth championship (1979–80) and the three-mover section in the seventeenth (1983–4).

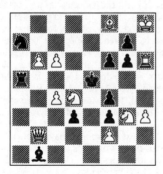

#4

A more-mover by Rudenko, second prize, Loshinsky Memorial Tourney 1982. The set play (Black moves first):
1 ... f5 2 Nxf3+ Ke6 3 Ng5#
1 ... g5 2 Ndf5+ Ke6 3 Nxg7#.
The key is 1 Qd2 threatening 2 Qxf4+ and Rh4+. The set play defences are answered differently, with model pin-mates:
1 ... f5 2 Bxg7+ Kd6 3 Qb4+ Rc5 4 Ngxf5#
1 ... g5 2 Nxf3+ Ke6 3 Qe1+ Re5 4 Nxg5#.

Rueb, Alexander (1882–1959), Dutch lawyer and diplomat who became the first President of FIDE (1924–49). An International Judge of Chess Compositions (1951), Rueb had a deep knowledge of studies, which was demonstrated in his five-volume work *De Schaakstudie* (Gouda, 1949–55) and the companion *Bronnen van de Schaakstudie*, also five volumes and published at the same time. Besides a historical survey these books include many studies classified according to a system invented by the author.

Rukhlis Theme, see CHANGED PLAY; CHEPIZHNY.

rule of square, see QUADRANT.

rules, conventions for playing competitive chess, as distinct from the LAWS which are inherent in the game. Until 1984 the Laws and the Rules were given separately, but then FIDE amalgamated them. The rules for sighted players meeting OVER-THE-BOARD now appear in the Laws.
Art. 11 requires each player to keep a SCORE OF THE GAME.
Art. 12 deals with TIMING OF MOVES.
Arts. 13 and 14 are concerned with ADJOURNMENT procedures.
Art. 15 specifies what BEHAVIOUR is prohibited.
Art. 16 lays down the duties of the arbiter.
Art. 17 says that a winner scores one, a loser zero, and a drawn game earns half a point for each player.
Art. 18 gives the procedure for requesting clarification of the Laws.
Art. 19 claims validity for the Laws.
Art. 10 specifies when a game is completed, and some of its provisions bear upon Arts. 12, 13 and 14, and also late arrival by either or both players.

running notation, notation written continuously along a line. It takes up less space than alternatives such as TABULAR NOTATION.

Rusinek, Jan (1950–), Polish study composer, International Judge of Chess Compositions (1983), International Master for Chess Compositions (1984), mathematician. In 1971, almost at the start of his composing career, he won five first prizes, and since then has won many more. His ideas are original, his technique consummate. His achievements are likely to rival those of his greatest predecessors. He was study editor of *Szachy* from 1979 until the magazine closed in 1990.

=

A study by Rusinek, first prize, *Shakhmaty v SSSR*,

1975. 1 Bc6+ Kf8 2 Rxf3 Re1 3 Ne2 (SQUARE VACATION) 3 ... Rxe2 4 Rd3 d1=Q 5 Rxd1 Rd2 6 Re1 Be2 7 Rg1 Bg4 8 Re1 Re2 9 Rd1 Bd2 10 Ra1 Ba5 11 Rd1 Rd2 12 Re1. A POSITIONAL DRAW based on Grimshaw interference (see CUT-TING-POINT THEMES).

Russ, see HENRY.

Russell Collection, a large reference source of original letters, photographs, scoresheets, historical memorabilia, and the like, related to chess. In the late 1970s the publisher Hanon William Russell (1947–) began the collection, housed in Milford, Connecticut, with a view to furthering chess research and preserving documents and other items of historical importance.

Russian Defence, 703, variation of the SPANISH OPENING favoured by CHIGORIN in the 1890s (with the continuation 6 d4 Nd7) and later by RUBINSTEIN, who was classed as Russian at the time, and after whom it is sometimes named (although it is occasionally known as the Steinitz Variation instead). Also another name for 1052, the PETROFF DEFENCE.

Russian Three Knights Variation, 1053 in the PETROFF DEFENCE.

Russian Variation, 209 in the orthodox QUEEN'S GAMBIT Declined, as Ståhlberg–Lasker, Moscow 1936; two similar lines in the GRÜNFELD DEFENCE, 364 (also known as Botvinnik Variation, Ragozin Variation, Soviet Variation, or Yugoslav Variation) and 380 (also known as Yugoslav Variation); and another Grünfeld Defence line, 378, the THREE KNIGHTS VARIATION.

Rutherford code, a telegraphic code devised by the English player Sir William Watson Rutherford (1853–1927) in 1880 and first used in matches between Liverpool and Calcutta. Its purpose was to enable moves in two games to be sent as a single Latin word (numbers or ciphers were not accepted by the Post Office), and is estimated to have saved more than 75 per cent of the potential cost.

Having selected the moves, coding is in two stages. Working to a plan, every possible move is counted until the chosen move is reached, the position in the sequence giving a number that identifies the move. Two numbers, of one or two digits each, represent the moves of each game. The first number is multiplied by 60 and the second number added to the product, preceding zeroes being added if necessary to the total to give a four-digit number.

To convert the four digits to a word, the thousands and hundreds digits, which will be in the range 00 to 39, are represented by 40 Latin roots given in a table, the tens by 10 prefixes, and the units by 10 suffixes. Thus 2231 is broken down: 22 = rog, 3 = de, 1 = as = derogas.

Decoding is the reverse process. Rutherford believed that there would never be more than 50 legal moves in any position.

After regulations were altered to allow ciphers to be transmitted, the simpler GRINGMUTH NOTATION became the popular choice.

Ruy López Opening, 673, alternative name in some countries for the SPANISH OPENING.

Ryan Opening, 442, the ST GEORGE DEFENCE, used sometimes by the American player John S. Ryan (c.1849–c.1914).

S

S, a symbol for the knight (German *Springer*) often used by composers.

Saavedra, Fernando (1847–1922), monk who served in many countries including Australia and whose claim to chess fame is based on the discovery while he was in Scotland of a single move. Born in Seville, he was buried in the churchyard of the Brothers of the Passion at Mount Argos.

+

G. E. Barbier (1844–95), Scottish champion in 1886, published this position in the *Glasgow Weekly Citizen*, May 1895. White's first move is 1 c7, and in April 1895 he had given the position after this move claiming that Black to play could draw by 1 ... Rd6+   2 Kb5 Rd5+   3 Kb4 Rd4+   4 Kb3 Rd3+   5 Kc2 Rd4   6 c8=Q? Rc4+   7 Qxc4 stalemate. Saavedra discovered that, instead of 6 c8=Q, White could win by 6 c8=R (if 6 ... Ra4 7 Kb3), and thus the most famous of all chess studies was created, one that inspired other composers, among them LIBURKIN and LOMMER.

sacrifice, a move that gives up material to gain positional or tactical advantage; to make such a move. Occasionally a player makes a POSITIONAL SACRIFICE but more frequently compensation is of a tactical kind, usually the prospect of an attack on the enemy king; and it is this kind of attack that gives chess its unique appeal; any number of men may be given up if mate can be achieved. A speculative or unsound sacrifice is one that should not lead to gain, but many players are startled by an opponent's sacrifice and as a consequence fail to discover the best defence. According to SPIELMANN, a master of attack, a sacrifice does not need to be sound in all variations, only that it should surprise an opponent and that the correct defence should be hard to find.

Sacrificial attacks remain popular in play, and are commonly a feature of BRILLIANCY PRIZE games. Such attacks are also shown in MANṢŪBĀT, in the modern manṣūbāt of STAMMA, and in many early problems; for an example see BAYER. Although no longer fashionable among problemists, sacrifice is still to be found in STUDIES. One example is that given under POGOSYANTS. (See ORANG UTAN OPENING.)

Mikenas–Lebedev   Tbilisi 1941   Georgian championship (*hors concours*)   Queen's Gambit Declined Neo-orthodox Variation

1 d4 Nf6   2 c4 e6   3 Nc3 d5   4 Bg5 Be7   5 e3 h6   6 Bh4 0–0   7 Rc1 c6   8 Bd3 Nbd7   9 Nf3 dxc4   10 Bxc4 Nd5   11 Bg3 Nxc3   12 bxc3 c5   13 0–0 a6   14 Bd3 Nf6   15 Ne5 Bd6   16 Bh4 Be7   17 Bb1 Qe8   18 dxc5 g5   19 Bg3 Bxc5

20 f4 Bxe3+   21 Kh1 Bxc1   22 fxg5 Bxg5   23 Rxf6 Kg7   24 Qd3 h5   25 h4 Kxf6   26 Ng4+ hxg4   27 Be5+ Kxe5   28 Qd4 mate.

Saint-Amant, Pierre Charles Fournier de (1800–72), the leading French player after the death of BOURDONNAIS (1840). His business career went from clerk to actor, wine merchant, and later explorer. He learned chess from Wilhelm Schlumberger (*c*.1800–38) who later went to America as the TURK's operator. Playing regularly at the CAFÉ DE LA RÉGENCE, Saint-Amant improved so much that in 1834 he was made leader of the Paris team that defeated the Westminster Club in a famous correspondence match. His happiness at the Café was sometimes marred by his energetic wife: resenting the time he gave to the game she would tap on the window with her umbrella to summon him home. In December 1841 Saint-Amant revived *Le Palamède*, a monthly chess magazine which ran until the end of 1847. On visits to London in 1843 he played several matches, notably defeating the rising STAUNTON (+3=1−2) for a stake of one guinea. This event led to a demand for a return match which was won by Staunton just before Christmas in the same year. Subsequently Saint-Amant played less often, but he was a frequent and popular visitor to chess gatherings in France and England. His last serious game was in 1870 when, visiting London, he turned out and won for the Westminster Club, the same club that his team had played against at the start of his career as a master. Having retired to Algeria in 1861, he died there after a fall from his carriage.

Saint George chessmen, the standard pattern of chessmen in Britain until superseded by STAUNTON CHESSMEN in the 1850s. The Saint George chessmen were relatively cheap to make, for all could be turned on a lathe, but it was not always obvious which piece was which. The more expensive sets had a carved horse's head on the knight. The sets were made in France alongside the Régence pattern which was the standard set used there.

St George Defence, 442, given this name by British enthusiasts after MILES defeated world champion KARPOV at Skara 1980 playing the line, but previously known as the Ryan Opening.

St Petersburg Variation, 713, also known as the Vienna Variation, and the similar 720 in the SPANISH OPENING, both common in the 19th century. (See BACKWARD PAWN.)

Salov, Valery Borisovich (1964–), Polish-born Russian player, World Under-16 Champion 1980, European Junior Champion 1983–4, International Grandmaster (1986). He was equal first ($+7=8-2$) with BELYAVSKY in the USSR championship 1987, but lost the play-off. Also in 1987 he was first ($+9=7-1$) equal with HJARTARSON in the interzonal tournament at Szirák, and so became a CANDIDATE, only to lose to TIMMAN. In the 1988 Soviet championship, a stronger event than in 1987, he was third ($+6=8-3$) equal with YUSUPOV, behind KASPAROV and KARPOV. At the interzonal, Manila 1990, Salov had to withdraw after seven rounds because of illness.

Other successes in very strong or top tournaments include equal third ($+4=5-3$) Leningrad 1987, second ($+4=12$) Brussels 1988, third ($+2=2-2$) Amsterdam 1989, third ($+7=6-3$) Barcelona 1989, equal fifth ($+5=6-4$) Rotterdam

Two versions of the Saint George set (*l. to r.*) pawn, rook, knight, bishop, queen, king

1989, and third (+4=6–1) Linares 1990. (See DEFENSIVE CENTRE.) He moved to Spain in 1991.

Vyzhmanavin–Salov Irkutsk 1986 USSR Championship 1st League Queen's Indian Defence Petrosyan Variation

1 d4 Nf6 2 c4 e6 3 Nf3 b6 4 a3 Ba6 5 Qc2 Bb7 6 Nc3 c5 7 e4 cxd4 8 Nxd4 Bc5 9 Nb3 Nc6 10 Nxc5 bxc5 11 Bd3 d6 12 0–0 0–0 13 Bg5 h6 14 Bh4 g5 15 Bg3 e5 16 Qd1 a5 17 Rb1 Rb8 18 Re1 Kg7 19 f3 Bc8 20 Bf2 Be6 21 Bf1 Rb7 22 Nb5 Nd4 23 b4 axb4 24 axb4 Nxb5 25 cxb5 c4 26 b6 Qb8 27 Re2 Re8 28 Rd2

28 ... c3 29 Rc2 Rxb6 30 Bxb6 Qxb6+ 31 Kh1 d5 32 exd5 Nxd5 33 Qd3 Qd4 34 Rcc1 Ne3 35 Qxd4 exd4 36 Ba6 Rd8 37 Bd3 Bc4 38 Bxc4 Nxc4 39 Kg1 Nd2 40 Ra1 Nb3 White resigns.

Salvio, Alessandro (c.1575–c.1640), Neapolitan author and doctor of law who was one of the leading players and perhaps the best analyst of his time. Salvio founded a chess club in Naples, a centre of Italian chess, an 'academy' for the study of the game and the dissemination of its practice. In 1604 he published *Trattato dell'inventione et arte liberale del gioco degli scacchi*, a great improvement on GIANUTIO's book written seven years earlier, and the first comprehensive work to reveal the advances made by the great Italian players of the late 16th century since the time of LÓPEZ. Most of Salvio's openings were previously known to these players, some of whom he met and played, but some lines in the KING'S GAMBIT may have been his own. (See FROM DEFENCE; PHILIDOR GAMBIT; ROSENTHAL VARIATION; STOCKWHIP VARIATION.) For 13 years, until CARRERA wrote his book, Salvio's work held the field as the only authoritative and contemporary guide.

Apparently he had a jealous temperament and an inflexible mind that brooked no contradiction. In 1634 he published *Il Puttino, altramente detto il cavaliero errante*, a colourful account of the life of LEONARDO DI BONA, and he attached a reprint of his *Trattato*. Despite the lapse of 30 years he saw little need to alter his original text, but he added a virulent attack on the 'presumptuous' Carrera (see ABRAHAMS VARIATION). Salvio also wrote *La Scaccaide* (1612), a chess tragedy in verse; Carrera notes that the poetry is 'not very elegant'.

Salvio applied his legal training to an aspect of the game not covered by FIDE laws: what should happen if a dispute between players should lead to the murder of one of them by the other? Citing parallel cases, Salvio argued that as the players had been engaged in a lawful activity (which some forms of gambling were not) the crime should be treated as 'casual homicide' rather than 'deliberate homicide', a more serious offence. (See KNIGHT; LUCENA POSITION.)

Salvio Defence, 1158, also known as the Rosenthal Variation, a line in the KIESERITZKY GAMBIT given by SALVIO in 1634.

Salvio Gambit, 1131, unsound form of the KING'S GAMBIT Accepted mentioned by POLERIO and published by SALVIO in his 1634 edition, where he said that he had recently found it in a Portuguese book. That book has not been traced, but van der LINDE believed it to have been the work of Santa Maria, after whom the line is sometimes named. The gambit's last appearance in master chess was in 1866.

Salvio–Polerio Defence, 1157, the POLERIO DEFENCE, given by SALVIO in his 1604 edition where he attributed it to Giovanni Domenico of Arminio.

Salwe, Georg Henryk (1862–1920), Polish player, manufacturer. He learned chess when he was about 20 years old, but played in his first major tournament (Kiev 1903, won by CHIGORIN) when he was 40. For some time, however, he had been the strongest player in Łódź, where he nurtured a generation of strong Polish players. At St Petersburg 1906 he won the fourth All-Russia tournament, ahead of RUBINSTEIN. Shortly afterwards he lost a match to Chigorin (+5=3–7), who challenged him for the title of Russian champion.

Salwe began his international career at Ostend 1906, the event organized by GUNSBERG to bring forward new talent; there were 36 competitors, and Salwe shared twelfth place. In the next six years he played in 11 international tournaments, with fair results. He played in many matches: against Rubinstein he drew (+5=4–5) in 1903, but lost in 1904 and 1907; against MIESES he won in 1905 (+2–1); against ROTLEWI he won in 1909 (+8=3–5) and lost in 1911: and he lost to both MARSHALL and FAHRNI in 1908, and to DURAS and BOGOLJUBOW in 1913. After playing in his last international tournament (Piešt'any 1912), Salwe entered a few national events, the last in January 1914. He gave up competitive chess in his fifty-second year.

Sämisch, Friedrich (1896–1975), German player, International Grandmaster (1950), first a bookbinder then a professional player. His most notable match victory was against RÉTI in 1922 (+4=3–1) and his best tournament achievement was at Baden-Baden 1925, when he came third (+10=7–3), after ALEKHINE and RUBINSTEIN, ahead of BOGOLJUBOW, MARSHALL, TARTAKOWER, GRÜNFELD, and NIMZOWITSCH. A frequent competitor in tournaments, Sämisch won or shared first place in four master events: Dortmund 1928 (+5=3), ahead of Réti and Bogoljubow; Brno 1928 (+5=4), a tie with Réti; Swinemünde 1930 (+6=2−1), ahead of FLOHR; and Berlin 1930, a tie. At Berlin (Sept.) 1928 he came second (+6=4−1) after Bogoljubow. In his later years Sämisch was unable to manage his clock; he lost more games on time than any other master, and in one tournament, Linköping 1969, he lost all 13 games this way. In serious play he could not bring himself to make a decision without first examining every possibility, yet he could play fast chess well: in his sixty-first year he won two LIGHTNING CHESS tournaments, a good illustration in support of KARPOV's opinion that handling time pressure is not correlated with skill at lightning chess.

Sämisch–Grünfeld Carlsbad 1929 First Brilliancy Prize
Nimzo-Indian Defence Sämisch Variation

1 d4 Nf6 2 c4 e6 3 Nc3 Bb4 4 a3 Bxc3+ 5 bxc3 d6 6 f3 0–0 7 e4 e5 8 Bd3 Nc6 9 Ne2 Nd7 10 0–0 b6 11 Be3 Ba6 12 Ng3 Na5 13 Qe2 Qe8 14 f4 f6 15 Rf3 Kh8 16 Raf1 Qf7 17 fxe5 dxe5 18 d5 Nb7 19 Nf5 Nd6 20 Rh3 g6 21 Nh6 Qg7 22 g4 g5 23 Rh5 Nc5 24 Bxc5 bxc5 25 Rf3 Qe7 26 Rfh3 (26 h4 is better) 26 ... Bc8 27 Qf2 Ne8 28 Rf3 Ng7 29 Rhh3 Bd7? (29 ... Ne8 offers best chances) 30 Rhg3 Be8 31 h4 gxh4 32 Rg2 h3 33 Rxh3 Bg6 34 Rf3 Rab8 35 Qh4 Rb3 36 Rgf2 Rxc3 37 g5 Ne8 38 gxf6 Qd8 39 Ng4 Rxd3 40 Rxd3 Bxe4 41 Re3 Nd6 42 Nxe5 Bf5 43 Rxf5 Nxf5 44 Ng6+ Kg8

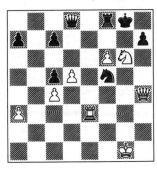

45 Re7 Rf7 46 Rxf7 Kxf7 47 Ne5+ Kf8 48 Qxh7 Black resigns.

Sämisch Attack, 1254 in the ALEKHINE DEFENCE, played Sämisch–Alekhine, Budapest 1921.

Sämisch Defence, 277, the QUEEN'S INDIAN DEFENCE.

Sämisch Variation, 91 in the SLAV DEFENCE, as Sämisch–Alekhine, four-player tournament 1937; 168 in the QUEEN'S GAMBIT Declined, played in the game Sämisch–Bogoljubow, Budapest 1921, and popular with ALEKHINE for some years; 299 and 396, standard lines in the NIMZO-INDIAN (see GREEK GIFT; RAGOZIN; SÄMISCH) and KING'S INDIAN DEFENCES (see BYRNE; DESPERADO; LILIENTHAL; LOMBARDY) respectively, advocated and practised by SÄMISCH, perhaps his most important contribution to the game.

Sanakoyev, Grigory Konstantinovich (1935–), Russian correspondence player, International Correspondence Chess Grandmaster (1984), research scientist (lubricating materials). In the 10th World Correspondence Championship, which ended in 1984, he was third, equal with RICHARDSON, behind PALCIAUSKAS and MORGADO.

Sanders–Alapin Defence, 887, variation in the EVANS GAMBIT given by Thomas Cooke Sanders (1843–c.1887) of Oxford, in the *Chess Player's Chronicle* 1871, and re-examined by ALAPIN in *Schachfreund*, 1898.

sandglass, device once used for the TIMING OF MOVES. Two sandglasses were used. One, for the player to move, was upright while the other was on its side. When a move was made the upright sandglass was laid on its side and the other raised, sometimes the wrong way up. Unlike CLOCKS, sandglasses were free from mechanical breakdown and their standing or resting position could be seen at a glance, but they could be set for only a fixed period. A time-limit of, say, 40 moves in two-and-a-half hours followed by 16 moves in one hour could not be accommodated. First used in the Anderssen–Kolisch match of 1861, they were superseded by clocks in the 1880s.

Sanguineti, Raúl. (1933–), Argentine player, International Grandmaster (1982). He won the national championship seven times from 1956 to 1974 and played in many South American tournaments, notably taking first prize (+7=3) at Buenos Aires 1977. Apart from two interzonals, Portorož 1958 and Biel 1976, he competed in few European tournaments. A competitor in several OLYMPIADS from 1956, he made the best score (+7=4) of those playing first reserve at Moscow 1956.

San Pier d'Arena Opening, 1322, the GROB OPENING. The name, given by TARTAKOWER, comes from a suburb of Genoa, where he gave a simultaneous display in 1930 and was shown the opening by the Italian player Luigi Penco (1895–1955).

San Remo Variation, 305 and 315, two lines in the NIMZO-INDIAN DEFENCE linked only because they were both played at the San Remo tournament of 1930 (by NIMZOWITSCH and ALEKHINE respectively).

San Sebastián Variation, 162 in the QUEEN'S GAMBIT Declined.

sans voir, see BLINDFOLD CHESS.

Santasiere's Folly, 1285, a relative of the ORANG UTAN OPENING (6). At Portsmouth 1923, already assured of first prize, ALEKHINE played this opening against Drewitt. Later it was taken up by Anthony Edward Santasiere (1904–77), a colourful American player, who tried it against KASHDAN in the US championship, 1938, and subsequently published analysis in the *Chess Correspondent*.

Sanz Opening, 1324, the PARIS OPENING, reputedly used *c*.1930 by the Spanish player José Sanz (1907–69).

Saragossa Opening, 7, an 18th-century opening which became popular in the Saragossa chess club, Spain, in 1919. A member, José Juncosa (1887–1972), published analysis in *Revista del Club Argentino*, 1920. The line was tested in a FIXED OPENING tournament at Mannheim 1922.

Sarratt, Jacob Henry (1772–1819), civil servant, reputedly the best player in England from around 1805 until his death. He developed his game by practice with VERDONI, and with a strong French player, Hippolyte de Bourblanc (d.1813), with whom he had a friendship dating from 1798. Sarratt's first important contribution to the game was in connection with the LAWS OF CHESS. He persuaded the London club, founded in 1807, to accept that a game ending in stalemate should be regarded as a draw, and not as a win for the player who is stalemated. There were scant opportunities to become a chess professional during the lifetimes of PHILIDOR and Verdoni, but after the latter's death in 1804 he became a professional at the Salopian coffee-house at Charing Cross, London.

In 1808 Sarratt wrote his *Treatise on the Game of Chess*, largely a compilation from the Modenese masters. In it he advocated that players should seek direct attack upon the enemy king, a style that dominated the game until the 1870s. (See SCHOOLS OF CHESS.) An Oxford surgeon, William Tuckwell, wrote that he learned chess 'from the famous Sarratt, the great chess teacher, whose fee was a guinea a lesson'. In 1822, after he had met both DESCHAPELLES and BOURDONNAIS, LEWIS wrote that Sarratt was a better player than Bourdonnais, and was, indeed, the most finished player he had ever met.

Sarratt translated the works of several early writers on the game, making them known for the first time to English readers. *The Works of Damiano, Ruy-Lopez, and Salvio* (1813) and *The Works of Gianutio and Gustavus Selenus* (1817) have been criticized as being too compressed, but they are serviceable. He died impoverished on 6 November 1819, after a long illness during which he was unable to teach. Instead he wrote *A New Treatise on the Game of Chess*, published posthumously in 1821. This is the first book to include a comprehensive beginner's section. In more than 200 pages Sarratt teaches by means of questions and answers. Another feature is a 98-page analysis of the MUZIO GAMBIT.

A tall, lean, yet muscular man, sociable and talkative, he seems in his younger days to have had interests of a different kind, among them prize-fighting and the breeding of fighting dogs. Apparently a Londoner, he met his first wife in Jersey, marrying at the age of 18; but he was soon back in London where he met Philidor. His first wife died in

1802, and in 1804 he married a Drury Lane singer, Elisabeth Camilla Dufour, also from Jersey. 'It would be difficult to find a more accomplished, a more amiable, or a happier couple than Mr and Mrs Sarratt' (Mary Julia Young, *Memoirs of Mrs Crouch*, 1806). Hazlitt, who met Sarratt around 1812, wrote: 'He was a great reader, but had not the least taste. Indeed, the violence of his memory tyrannised over and destroyed all powers of selection. He could repeat passages of Ossian by heart, without knowing the best passage from the worst.'

Sarratt's early publications were *History of Man* (1802); translations of two Gothic novels, *The Three Monks!!!* (1803), from the French of Elisabeth Guérnard, and *Koenigsmark the Robber* (1803), from the German of R. E. Raspe; *A New Picture of London* (1803), an excellent guide that ran to several editions, the last in 1814. When war broke out with France in 1803 Sarratt became, for a short period, a lieutenant in the Royal York Maryle-Bone Volunteers and published *Life of Buonaparte*, a propaganda booklet detailing Napoleon's alleged war crimes, and warning of the desolation that would follow if he were to invade. Mrs Sarratt too was a writer; she contributed tales to various journals, and published *Aurora or the Mysterious Beauty* (1803), a translation of a French novel. She survived her husband until 1846, ending her days giving chess lessons to the aristocracy in Paris. In 1843 Louis-Philippe and many players from England and France subscribed to a fund on her behalf.

Saul, Arthur, author of *The famous game of Chesseplay* (1614), the earliest original book in the English language. It was reprinted a further six or seven times, including a revised version by J. Barbier, issued in 1640, presumably after the death of Saul. Possibly the author was the Saul who graduated from Oxford in 1549, became a religious exile under Queen Mary, and prebendary of Bedminster and Radcliffe in 1559. (See STALEMATE.)

Savon, Vladimir Andreyevich (1940–), Soviet player, International Grandmaster (1973). His best results are: Debrecen 1970, first equal with BILEK; USSR championship 1971, first (+9=12), one and a half points ahead of a field that included TAL, SMYSLOV, and KARPOV; Sukhumi 1972, second (+8=5−2), after Tal; Vilnius zonal 1975, first (+4=10−1) equal with GULKO; and Ljubljana–Portorož 1977, second (+6=6−1) equal with HORT, after LARSEN. Altogether Savon played in ten Soviet championships between 1961 and 1974 with undistinguished outcome except for the year in which he won, and the following year, 1972, when he was equal third.

Savon–Polugayevsky   Leningrad 1971 39th USSR Championship   Sicilian Defence Najdorf Variation

1 e4 c5 2 Nf3 d6 3 d4 cxd4 4 Nxd4 Nf6 5 Nc3 a6 6 Be2 e6 7 f4 Be7 8 0–0 0–0 9 Be3 Qc7 10 a4 Nc6 11 Nb3 b6

12 Bd3 Bb7 13 Qf3 Nb4 14 Nd4 g6 15 Rad1 e5 16 Nde2 d5 17 fxe5 dxe4 18 Nxe4 Qxe5

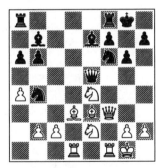

19 Qxf6 Nxd3 20 Bd4 Bxf6 21 Nxf6+ Kg7 22 Nd7 Qxd4+ 23 Nxd4 Nxb2 24 Rb1 Rfd8 25 Ne5 Rxd4 26 Rxf7+ Kh6 27 Rxb7 Nxa4 28 Rb3 Rd1+ 29 Kf2 Rd2+ 30 Kg3 Nc5 31 Ng4+ Kg5 32 Re7 Rxg2+ 33 Kxg2 Nxb3 34 Kg3 Kf5 35 Re5+ mate.

Sax, Gyula (1951–), Hungarian player, International Grandmaster (1974), national champion 1976 and (jointly with RIBLI) 1977, European Junior Champion 1971–2, regular member of the Hungarian Olympiad team from 1972 onwards. In 1974 he won tournaments at Campiglio, ahead of HORT, and Vrnjačka Banja, ahead of TAIMANOV. The best of his subsequent achievements are: Rovinj–Zagreb 1975, first (+5=7−1); Vinkovci 1976, first (+7=7−1) equal with Hort, ahead of POLU-GAYEVSKY; Las Palmas 1978, first (+7=7−1) equal with TUKMAKOV; Amsterdam 1979, first (+6=6−1) equal with Hort; Tilburg 1979, fourth (+2=8−1), after KARPOV, ROMANISHIN, and PORT-ISCH, ahead of SPASSKY; Vršac 1981, first (+8=7), ahead of PETROSYAN; Smederevska Palanka 1982, first (+6=7); Rome 1986, first (+3=6) equal with ANDERSSON; Warsaw zonal 1987, first (+4−7); Subotica interzonal 1987, first (+7=7−1) equal with SHORT and SPEELMAN.

This last event made Sax a CANDIDATE for the first time, but he lost his match with Short. Further tournament successes are: Adelaide 1986–7 (Swiss system), first (+10−1) from an entry of 262 players; Seville 1987 (Swiss), second equal, from 210 competitors; Wijk aan Zee 1989, first (+4=7−2) equal with ANAND, Ribli, and NIKOLIĆ; Clermont Ferrand 1989, first (+3=7−1) equal with DOLMATOV, EHLVEST, KORCHNOI, and Renet; Tilburg 1989, third (+2=10−2) equal with LJUBO-JEVIĆ, behind KASPAROV and Korchnoi. In 1990 he was equal fifth at the Manila interzonal, and became a Candidate again, but lost his match with Korchnoi in 1991.

Sax–Bánas Balatonberény 1984 Spanish Opening Lenzerheide Variation

1 e4 e5 2 Nf3 Nc6 3 Bb5 a6 4 Ba4 Nf6 5 0–0 Be7 6 Re1 b5 7 Bb3 d6 8 c3 0–0 9 h3 Bb7 10 d4 Re8 11 a4 h6 12 Nbd2 Bf8 13 Bc2 exd4 14 cxd4 Nb4 15 Bb1 bxa4 16 Rxa4 a5 17 Ra3 Ra6 18 Nh2 Qa8 19 Rae3 Qa7 20 e5 Nfd5 21 Rg3 dxe5 22 dxe5 Rae6 23 Ne4 Kh8 24 Nf3 Qb6 25 Nfg5 hxg5 26 Nxg5 g6

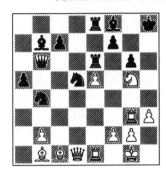

27 Qh5+ Black resigns.

Scacchia ludus, see VIDA.

Scandinavian Marshall Gambit, 603, a line in the SCANDINAVIAN OPENING suggested by LASKER in an annotation in the book of the St Petersburg 1909 tournament; STEINITZ preferred 4 d4 cxd5 5 c5, but 5 Nc3 transposes to the CARO–KANN DEFENCE. The line was played in the middle of the 19th century by LASA and LANGE.

Scandinavian Opening, 595, a defence first given by LUCENA and much analysed by Scandinavian players in the 19th century. It is also known as the Centre Counter Game. (See DURAS.)

Scandinavian Variation, 1249 in the ALEKHINE DEFENCE, a line which has the character of the SCANDINAVIAN OPENING. Also 1117, the ABBAZIA DEFENCE, which has a more distant resemblance to the Scandinavian Opening.

Schallopp, Emil (1843–1919), German player and author, head of the shorthand department of the Reichstag. A popular and regular participant in international tournaments, especially in the 1880s, Schallopp never won an important event, but at Wiesbaden 1880 he was fourth, after BLACKBURNE, ENGLISCH, and SCHWARZ, and ahead of MASON, BIRD, WINAWER, PAULSEN, and nine others. At Nottingham 1886 he was second to BURN, and won the best game prize for his game with ZUKERTORT. He is remembered today for his literary output, in particular the 7th edition of the HANDBUCH (1891).

Schallopp Defence, 1126 in the KING'S GAMBIT Accepted, played Thorold–Schallopp, Hereford 1885, but popular with the Russian player Ilya Stepanovich Shumov (1819–81) much earlier. For example, a game Jaenisch–Shumov, in this line, was in the *Illustrated London News*, 20 April 1857.

Schara–Hennig Gambit, or Hennig–Schara Gambit, or von Hennig–Schara Gambit, 119 in the QUEEN'S GAMBIT Declined. Anton Schara of Vienna often played the line, really a counter-gambit, in 1918–20, and in 1925 Leo Godai published analysis in the Austrian *Arbeiter-Schachzeitung*. The

German player Heinrich von Hennig introduced the variation to master play in the HAUPTTURNIER at Duisburg 1929, and so it is sometimes named after that city.

Scheve, Theodor von (1851–1922), German player. From the 1880s he had fair results in many national tournaments and he played at Frankfurt 1887, Dresden 1892, and Leipzig 1894. In his fourth international tournament, Monte Carlo 1901, in his fiftieth year, he achieved his best result: third equal with CHIGORIN, after JANOWSKI and SCHLECHTER. He also played at Monte Carlo 1902, Berlin 1907, and Ostend 1907.

Scheveningen pairing system, a system that consists of dividing the competitors into two groups of an equal number of players and pairing each player in one group with every player in the other. No one meets a player from his own group. This system was used in a tournament played at Scheveningen in 1923, the idea being that ten Dutch players could thus face ten foreign masters.

Only the intention, that of giving selected players experience against strong opposition, distinguishes this system from that used in a TEAM MATCH with similar pairings.

Scheveningen Variation, 475, line in the SICILIAN DEFENCE that has been commonly used since the Scheveningen tournament of 1923, when it was played in the game Maróczy–Euwe. Its essential characteristic is Black's SMALL CENTRE, a pawn formation that was not new in 1923 but was consistent with the spirit of the HYPERMODERN movement. Subsequently 518 also came to be regarded as the Scheveningen Variation and in this, its most popular form, Black reserves the option of developing the queen's knight at c6 or d7. Similar play can arise from 508. (See GEORGIEV; MARÓCZY; PETROSYAN; POPOVIĆ.)

Schiffers, Emanuel Stepanovich (1850–1904), for many years the second player in Russia after CHIGORIN: both lived in St Petersburg, the birthplace of Russian chess. When in 1873 the two first met, Chigorin received the odds of a knight, but they were of about the same strength in 1878, when Schiffers won the second of two matches (+7=1−6). Schiffers played in eight major tournaments abroad from Frankfurt 1887 to Cologne 1898, achieving his best result, sixth prize, at the great Hastings tournament of 1895. At Rostov-on-Don in 1896 Schiffers lost a match against STEINITZ (+4=1−6).

Schiffers was known in his time as Russia's great chess teacher; from 1889 he gave public lectures on the game in many cities, the first to be given in Russia, and at the end of his life he wrote a textbook, *Samouchitel shakhmatnoi igry*, which was published in 1906. After five reprintings it was revised and republished by NENAROKOV in 1926. Tall, well built, and distinguished-looking, Schiffers

earned his livelihood largely by giving private chess lessons.

Schiffman defence, a problem term for the following manœuvre: to prevent a threatened mate by discovered check Black moves a man so that it becomes pinned (a SELF-PIN); should White attempt to carry out the threat this man becomes unpinned and can prevent mate; however, because this man is pinned White can mate in another way (a PIN-MATE). This manœuvre was considered by MANS-FIELD one of the most interesting that could be used in a two-mover.

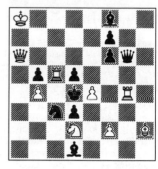

#2

A problem by Schiffman that won second prize in the British Chess Federation tourney, 1928. The key 1 Bg1 threatens 2 f4 mate; three moves that prevent this lead to pin-mates.

1 ... Qxe4   2 Qxf6
1 ... Nxe4   2 Qa1
1 ... dxe4   2 f3.

The name commemorates Israel Abramovich Schiffman (1903–30), who wrote a paper on the subject in 1928. A native of Odessa, he went to Germany to complete his education. There he contracted a lung illness at the age of 21 and having time on his hands while in a sanatorium he began to compose problems. Soon afterwards he moved to Romania where he died of influenza a few years later. During six years of composing he won about 60 tourney awards, mostly for orthodox TWO-MOVERS.

Schlechter, Carl (1874–1918), Viennese player who from 1900 until his death ranked at best fourth, at worst seventh, in the world. He was one of the few grandmasters who also composed problems. He learned the moves around 1890, and soon gave up his studies to devote himself to chess, becoming good enough to draw matches against MARCO (1892, =10, and 1894, +4=3−4), JANOWSKI (1896, +2=3−2), and ALAPIN (1899, +1=4−1), and to score well in a number of international events. From 1900 to 1908 he had several excellent tournament results: Munich 1900, first (+9=6) equal with MARÓCZY and PILLSBURY; Monte Carlo 1901, second (+9=6−2), after Janowski; Monte

Carlo 1903, fourth (+ 12 = 10 − 4), after TARRASCH, Maróczy, and Pillsbury; Monte Carlo 1904, second (+ 4 = 6), half a point after Maróczy; Vienna 1905 (Austro-Hungarian championship), first; Ostend 1906, first (+ 4 = 4), ahead of Maróczy and RUBIN-STEIN in the final stages, and first overall; Ostend Grandmasters 1907, second (+ 7 = 10 − 3), after Tarrasch; Vienna 1908, first (+ 9 = 10) equal with DURAS and Maróczy, ahead of Rubinstein; Prague 1908, first (+ 9 = 9 − 1) equal with Duras, ahead of Rubinstein and Maróczy. In match play he defeated Janowski in 1902 (+ 6 = 3 − 1).

In 1910 Schlechter challenged LASKER for the world title. A 30-game championship match was agreed, but it was whittled down to 10 for lack of funds. The conditions of the abbreviated match were not published, and it is not known whether the title was in the balance. After nine games Schlechter led + 1 = 8 and he made great efforts to win the last game. He lost, and the match was drawn. Meanwhile the public had decided that it was a championship match, *de facto* if not *de jure*, and the referee, perhaps bowing to this view, declared that Lasker had retained his title. The games of this match, full of fight, are unusually interesting.

Schlechter's later achievements include first prize at Hamburg 1910 (+ 8 = 7 − 1), a share of second place (+ 13 = 8 − 4) with Rubinstein, after TEICH-MANN, at Carlsbad 1911, a drawn match with Tarrasch in 1911 (+ 3 = 10 − 3), and first prize (+ 6 = 8) at Vienna 1915. Before and during the First World War Schlechter edited the eighth, last, and best edition of Bilguer's HANDBUCH (1912–16), a classic of more than 1,000 large pages. Schlechter himself made many contributions to openings knowledge, apart from those variations named after him. During the last months of 1918 his health declined rapidly, and at Budapest, soon after completing a chess engagement, he died of pneumonia.

In developing his style, Schlechter followed the precepts of STEINITZ, to build up the game by seeking positional advantage, and not to attack until an advantage had been obtained. In the early part of his career, when this method often led to drawn games, he became known as a 'drawing master', an inappropriate description of his mature style. Aware that Schlechter often made fine combinations, and had BRILLIANCY PRIZES to his credit, BURN writes that Schlechter 'was a master in two distinct and antagonistic styles'. However, Schlechter's combinative play, sound or otherwise, often stemmed from the Steinitzian imperative: a player who has the advantage *must* attack. In this respect Schlechter was not a cautious player who merely sought to hold the draw in hand.

Slight of build, bright-eyed, courteous, and placid, Schlechter might have been more successful but for his good nature. In his match with Lasker, his decision to play for a win in the last round was sportsmanlike (perhaps necessary if, as rumoured, he had to lead by two games to claim the title) but unrealistic. A tougher man would have been satisfied to win the match by drawing the last game,

making his mark in the record book, and leaving the chess world to decide who was champion, or to arrange a full-sized match. In the tenth round of the Ostend Grandmaster tournament 1907, Schlechter obtained a big advantage against Tarrasch, who suddenly 'felt ill' (a very old gambit); Schlechter agreed to a draw, eventually taking second place half a point behind Tarrasch. (See ORANG UTAN OPENING.)

Spielmann, *Karl Schlechter* (1924) contains a selection of Schlechter's games with Swedish text. Verkhovsky, *Karl Schlechter* (1984) is a biography and selection of games, text in Russian.

Nimzowitsch–Schlechter   Hamburg 1910   English Opening Sicilian Variation

1 c4 e5 2 g3 Nf6 3 Bg2 Be7 4 Nc3 0–0 5 Nf3 Nc6 6 0–0 d6 7 b3 Re8 8 Bb2 Bd7 9 d4 exd4 10 Nxd4 Bf8 11 e3 Bg4 12 Nxc6 bxc6 13 Qc2 Bd7 14 Ne2 Ng4 15 Nd4

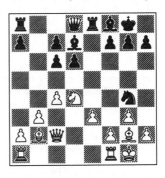

15 ... c5 (a POSITIONAL SACRIFICE) 16 Bxa8 Qxa8 17 Nf5 Ne5 18 Bxe5 Rxe5 19 Nh4 Bh3 20 Rfe1 Re4 21 f3 Re8 22 Qf2 Bd7 23 Re2 g6 24 Rf1 Bg7 25 Qe1 a5 26 Ng2 a4 27 b4 cxb4 28 Qxb4 Rb8 29 Qa3 Qa6 30 Rc2 Be6 31 Qd3 d5 32 Nf4 dxc4 33 Qe2 a3 (securing an OUTPOST at b2) 34 Rd1 h5 35 Rdd2 Rb2 36 Kg2 Qc6 37 Rxb2 axb2 38 Rxb2 Bxb2 39 Qxb2 c3 40 Qc2 Bc4 41 Kf2 Ba6 42 e4 Qb6+ 43 Kg2 Qb2 White resigns.

Schlechter Attack, 949 in the MAX LANGE, an old line played, for example, by PAULSEN in 1862.

Schlechter Defence, 661, standard variation of the DANISH GAMBIT recommended by SCHLECHTER in *Deutsche Schachzeitung*, 1914; 709 in the SPANISH OPENING, played by Schlechter in his world championship match against LASKER in 1910, a move that took away the favoured status of 8 a4; 1167 in the ALLGAIER GAMBIT, analysed by Schlechter in *Deutsche Schachzeitung*, 1899, where he gives credit to R. Gebhardt and LIPKE for revealing its merits.

Schlechter Variation, 100, 108, 371, or 375, combination of KING'S INDIAN and SLAV DEFENCES, played by ALAPIN against TARRASCH at Nuremberg 1896, by SCHLECHTER in his match with LASKER, 1910, and now a standard line (see LEVENFISH; NAJDORF; PROTECTED PASSED PAWN); 122 in the QUEEN'S GAMBIT Declined, sometimes called the Łódź Variation, or Rubinstein Attack, introduced in the game Schlechter–Duz-Khotimirsky, Prague 1908, and usually regarded as the best way for White to attack the TARRASCH DEFENCE. The variation was tested in a FIXED OPENINGS tournament, Budapest 1912.

Also 696, the WORMALD VARIATION; 827 in the THREE KNIGHTS OPENING, as Forgács–Schlechter, San Sebastián 1912; 1025 in the PHILIDOR DEFENCE, as Schlechter–Alekhine, Hamburg 1910.

Schliemann Defence, 784 in the SPANISH OPENING, originated by JAENISCH in 1847 and sometimes called after him. Many years later the defence was named after the German lawyer Adolf Karl Wilhelm Schliemann (1817–72) although the line he practised in the 1860s was a variation of the CORDEL DEFENCE (3 ... Bc5 4 c3 f5). By playing 3 ... f5 Black weakens the ITALIAN DIAGONAL, a2–g8, but as that is not occupied by White's LIGHT BISHOP Jaenisch felt that his move might be practicable. His defence, although somewhat risky, has attracted the attention of SPASSKY and LJUBOJEVIĆ, among others, while his idea has born fruit in the SIESTA VARIATION, 684.

Schliemann Defence Deferred, 691, sometimes called the Jaenisch Gambit. Compare the SCHLIE-MANN DEFENCE. Deferment offers Black no advantage.

Schmid, Lothar Maximilian Lorenz (1928–), German player, International Grandmaster (1959), International Grandmaster of Correspondence Chess (1959), International Arbiter (1975), publisher. He won several minor events including the Clare Benedict tournament, Zurich 1954, when he came ahead of EUWE, but his best playing achievement came in 1968 when the chess club of his home town, Bamberg, celebrated its centenary by organizing a tournament of eight leading German players and eight foreign masters. Schmid scored +6=8−1 and shared second place with PETROSYAN (then world champion), after KERES, ahead of UNZICKER and IVKOV. Schmid played for Germany in eleven Olympiads from 1950 to 1974, and in many other team events.

Schmid is also active in chess organization, notably having been chief arbiter for the world championship matches of 1972, 1978, and 1986, a task requiring great tact and patience. At one time he played correspondence chess: he won the Dyckhoff Memorial tournament (1954–6) with the remarkable score of 13 wins and 2 draws, and took second place (+9=3−2) equal with ENDZELINS after RAGOZIN in the second World Correspondence Chess Championship, 1956–8. A collector of chess books and paraphernalia, he has the largest private chess library in the world.

Kavalek–Schmid Nice Olympiad 1974 Alekhine Defence

1 e4 Nf6 2 e5 Nd5 3 d4 d6 4 Nf3 Bg4 5 Be2 e6 6 0–0 Be7 7 c4 Nb6 8 h3 Bh5 9 Nc3 0–0 10 Be3 d5 11 c5 Bxf3 12 Bxf3 Nc4 13 Bf4 b6 14 b3 Na5 15 Rc1 bxc5

16 dxc5 Nac6 17 Re1 Bg5

18 Nxd5 exd5 19 Bxg5 Qxg5 20 Bxd5 Kh8 21 Rc4 a5 22 e6 fxe6 23 Rxe6 Nd8 24 f4 Qg3 25 Re7 Ra6 26 Rxc7 Ne6 27 Re7 Nxf4 28 Qf3 Nxh3+ 29 Kh1 Qxf3 30 Bxf3 Rh6 31 Rc3 Nc6 32 Rc7 Nd4 33 gxh3 Nb5 White resigns.

Schmidt, Paul Felix (1916–84), Estonian-born player. International Master (1950). He was born in the same place, Narva, and in the same year as KERES and they became rivals. In 1936 a match between them was drawn (+3=1−3) and a year later Schmidt won first prize (+5=1−1), ahead of FLOHR, Keres, and STÅHLBERG, in a tournament at Pärnu. After graduating at Tallinn in 1938 Schmidt went to Germany, and there he won the German Open Championship in 1941 after a play-off with JUNGE (+3=1) and competed in several other tournaments, notably coming first (+8=1−2) equal with ALEKHINE, Cracow–Warsaw 1941. He studied at Heidelberg after the Second World War, specialized in chemistry, and gained his Ph.D. in natural sciences in 1951. A year later he emigrated to the USA, pursued a career in industry, and gave up competitive chess.

Schmidt Attack, 824, variation in the PONZIANI OPENING recommended in *Deutsche Schachzeitung,* 1879, by Eugen von Schmidt (1821–1905), an Estonian author and psychologist who settled in Moscow.

Schmidt Variation, 993, standard line in the SCOTCH GAME recommended by E. von Schmidt in *Schachzeitung,* 1865, and occasionally called the Zukertort–Berger variation.

Schmid Variation, 51 in the BENONI DEFENCE; 1268 in the ALEKHINE DEFENCE, a line first recommended by GRÜNFELD, played in the game Ghiţescu–Schmid, Varna 1962.

Schofman Variation, 451 in the GRAND PRIX ATTACK of the SICILIAN DEFENCE, a line which came to attention in the 1970s.

scholar's mate, a mate given by a queen when it captures an opponent's unmoved f-pawn early in the game, e.g. 1 e4 e5 2 Qh5 Nc6 3 Bc4 d6 4 Qxf7 mate. Arthur SAUL, in *The Famous Game of Chesse-play* (1614), said 'it is a schollers mate, but there is no man of judgement in Chesse-play will take such a mate; it may be called also a treacherous mate; for otherwise it were unpossible a King should be delivered into the hands of his enemyes, without the losse of some men, unlesse the ... Kings power would make sleepe a defence for treason, and so suffer their King to be taken before they would take any knowledge thereof.'

schools of chess. The word 'school' is understood to mean a group of players who share a common view regarding the strategy of the (modern) game.

The school of Philidor
In 1749 PHILIDOR published his *L'analyze des échecs*. Before this time many writers had given useful hints on play, but he was the first to discuss, in detail, the strategy of the game as a whole and the first to appreciate that play of the pieces and pawns is closely interrelated throughout the game. For four fictitious games and ten BACK GAMES he gives copious middlegame annotations showing how the pawn formation relates to, and largely shapes, the strategy. He believed that maintaining mobility of the pawn formation was the most important positional (strategic) factor, and he discussed ISOLATED, DOUBLED, and BACKWARD PAWNS, and PAWN ISLANDS, indicating that the strength or weakness of such features depends on whether they improve or impair the mobility of the pawns. Pieces should not obstruct the pawns but should support them from the rear. He warns of the premature advance of pawns that may subsequently lack adequate support, and he discusses HOLES, BLOCKADE, PROPHYLAXIS, and POSITIONAL SACRIFICE.

The openings Philidor chose all began 1 e4 e5 and were not the best for his purpose. Whatever opening is used (and more suitable ones had yet to be developed) it is not always feasible to set up a game in which pawn play predominates in the manner shown in his illustrative games. These often end with a phalanx of pawns penetrating deep into the enemy rank, and Philidor must have known that such a BREAKTHROUGH was unlikely in practice. (See, however, GULKO and PHILIDOR SACRIFICE.) Nevertheless, his idea of maintaining a flexible pawn formation, so that manœuvres with pawns would be supported by pieces from the rear, subsequently became common in close openings. For some examples, see BARCZA, KAMSKY, and SPACE (Petrosyan game). Philidor's ideas are often shown by his play. Choosing a Sicilian Defence against Bowdler, in a blindfold simultaneous game in 1783, he set up a pawn formation which might be considered the precursor of the STAUNTON SYSTEM: 1 e4 c5 2 Bc4 e6 3 Qe2 Nc6 4 c3 a6 5 a4 b6 6 f4 d6 7 Nf3 Nge7 8 Ba2 g6 9 d3 Bg7.

The fictitious games in Philidor's book were criticized by DEL RIO on two main grounds: that the defence is often made to play weak moves in the openings, and that after 1 e4 e5 Philidor considered 2 Nf3 inferior. In the second edition of his book (1777) Philidor states, as if it were obvious, that the weak moves were given intentionally so that he might show 'how the pawns should be played in a variety of different situations'. He admits that it is sometimes better to develop the king's knight in front of the f-pawn, but adds that if possible this pawn is better left free to extend or support the pawn centre. He does not otherwise recant, but as if to prove his point adds another 16 games and back games in further demonstration of his ideas.

For 90 years Philidor was both widely praised and largely misunderstood. His ideas bore fruit in the English school of the 1840s, an advance soon forgotten. After a further lapse of time NIMZO-WITSCH could write in his famous book *Mein System* (1925): 'In the last resort position play is nothing other than a fight between mobility (of the pawn-mass) on the one side and efforts to restrain this on the other ... In the case of a mobile pawn-mass we must therefore look for collective and not individual mobility.' Since then Philidor has increasingly gained recognition as the first of the fathers of modern chess strategy.

The Modenese school
The ideas of the Modenese school are contained in the works of del Rio, LOLLI, and PONZIANI, all of whom lived in Modena. In 1750 del Rio published a textbook. Harking back to the play of the Italian masters of the 16th century, he advised his readers to play in what he supposed to be the old Italian style, and to begin the game with the ITALIAN OPENING. In 1763 the opening variations of this book, and some new lines added by del Rio, were published by Lolli, who added a commentary. Meanwhile del Rio had read Philidor's book. Convinced that the Frenchman's ideas were wrong, and incensed that he had ignored the Italian Opening, del Rio wrote a chapter for Lolli's book (pp. 365–8) in criticism of Philidor. In detail some of his comments were just, in a wider sense, irrelevant. Del Rio was analysing opening play while Philidor was concerned with strategy, for which his didactic games were well chosen.

In contrast to Philidor, who believed that a player should build up a solid position for the middlegame, preparing for a pawn advance if this became feasible, the Modenese stated that 'the aim of the first moves should be to develop the pieces in the shortest time possible'. This was good advice when playing the open game they advocated.

In 1769 Ponziani wrote his treatise. In the revised version (1782) he remarks that although Philidor overstated the realm of the pawn his middlegame annotations were those of a perspicacious and enlightened player. The Modenese idea of fast development followed by attack is the best for the open game; some positions are suitable for pawn play; the style of either school might be appropriate according to circumstance. This, a fair assessment, was apparently endorsed by del Rio, who thus moderated his earlier views.

Playing for direct attack on the enemy king, as advocated by the Modenese school, dominated the game until the 1840s and strongly influenced chess playing until the end of the 1860s. This phase in the development of chess strategy was both natural and necessary, and during this period much was learnt about how direct attacks should be conducted and also how they should be prevented or repulsed.

The English school

Already in the 1840s books by JAENISCH and von der LASA were revealing a few positional (strategic) ideas that anticipated the school of STEINITZ; but the startling change made by the English school took a different path. Founded by STAUNTON in the 1840s, the school gained many followers on account of his practical successes. Play in the early stages was not directed at the enemy king. The ground was to be prepared, the gaining of central control and key points was to be sought, and sustained attacks followed only after some strategic advantage had been obtained. To this end Staunton pioneered the use of FLANK OPENINGS, the FIANCHETTO, and the SMALL CENTRE. He also invented the STAUNTON SYSTEM, in which the pieces are developed behind the pawns to support their later advance. Staunton never wrote about these ideas and it can only be conjectured whence they sprang. Distrustful of all authority except his own, Staunton may well have rejected the views of contemporary writers; and perhaps he nourished his imagination, not by reading badly edited versions of Philidor's book, but from a study of the original texts.

Among his followers were HORWITZ, WILLIAMS, WYVILL, and on occasion ANDERSSEN and HARRWITZ, but after Staunton had practically retired from serious play (1853) the ideas of his school were neglected. The age of attack had yet to run its full course.

The school of Steinitz

Around 1860 PAULSEN, a pioneer of defensive play, came to believe that many of the king's-side attacks of his time succeeded only because the defender played incorrectly, and it was the development of defensive technique that, in time, ended the so-called romantic age of direct attack. A new theory of the game developed, that a player should not commence a sustained attack without previously obtaining an advantage of some kind that would 'justify' such an attack.

When Steinitz came to understand this he was faced with new problems: the need to develop defensive technique, and how 'some kind of advantage' might be gained. He rejected the current view that attack was more 'honourable' than defence, a view that hampered some of his contemporaries who gave little thought to the art of defence. He developed his accumulation theory, the gathering of small advantages, to be followed by the invasion

of enemy territory only when a sufficient overall advantage had been gained. The kinds of advantage Steinitz sought were already known: weaknesses of various kinds in the pawn formation, the exploitation of holes and advance points, the better placement of pieces, and so on. He specialized in the exploitation of a QUEEN'S-SIDE MAJORITY when both kings are castled on the king's-side, and, prompted by Paulsen, he developed and refined the appropriate technique for handling the TWO BISHOPS.

The new school began in 1872–3. Steinitz's games at Vienna 1873, in which he manœuvres on both sides of the board in his search for advantage, contrast sharply with the violent attacks that characterize the games of his match with Anderssen in 1866. Steinitz had definite ideas about the two most important aspects of positional play: control of the centre, and concern for the pawn formation. Formal development of all the pieces should take second place to control of important squares, as BERTIN implies in his fifth rule. He would concede a HALF-CENTRE, providing he had no pawn weaknesses, or would accept a DEFENSIVE CENTRE. Both possibilities became acceptable because of the improvements he made in defensive technique. He took especial care with pawn play, eventually reaching a somewhat extreme view: a player should make no pawn moves other than those necessary for development; the unmoved pawns would retain a kind of passive mobility, the greatest number of options would be available, and no pawn weaknesses would be created.

Thus Steinitz was not a 'pawn player' in the manner of Philidor, and many of his successors, including CAPABLANCA, were also 'piece players'. To this extent the views of the Modenese players, still valid for many kinds of position, survived. Above all, Steinitz developed the techniques necessary for handling these many positional factors. In the *International Chess Magazine*, 1885, p. 98, he writes: 'The assault against the king's side forms the exception whereas in former days it was made the rule. Generally at the outset the attack is directed chiefly towards the centre or the queen's wing ... The indiscriminate king's side attack has been superseded by strategical manœuvres, marches and counter-marches for gaining and accumulating small advantages on any part of the board.'

Apart from Paulsen, his precursor, Steinitz had few followers in the 1870s, the most notable, perhaps, being BURN; but by the 1890s the great majority of active masters had been influenced in varying degrees by the tenets of the new school. Some of Steinitz's ideas, however, were not widely accepted. One of those who understood that the defensive potential of a cramped position was an inherent characteristic of the game was LASKER, and he became, like Steinitz, the greatest defensive player of his time. Respecting Steinitz, and sharing some of his views, CHIGORIN believed, in particular, in the defensive centre, and his investigations established the lasting popularity of the CLOSE DEFENCE to the SPANISH OPENING.

The next great teacher, TARRASCH, followed Steinitz in many respects, notably as regards the queen's-side majority. Above all Tarrasch believed that mobility was the dominant strategic factor, that Steinitz had overrated the importance of so-called pawn weaknesses, that a player who lacked mobility would be unable to exploit them. This was a useful corrective, but Tarrasch's view of the game was in some senses narrow, even dogmatic. Because ceding a half-centre or maintaining a defensive centre would seem to imply a loss of mobility, he rejected such central formations. The period 1900–14 is called by EUWE the years of 'technique and routine', when the new ideas were being 'worked out and refined'. These years were dominated by Tarrasch's views. For various reasons, those like Capablanca, Lasker, and NIMZOWITSCH, who understood Steinitz better, kept their own counsel.

The Hypermodern movement
The leading theorists of this movement, which flourished in the 1920s, were BREYER, Nimzowitsch, and RÉTI. Nimzowitsch, the founder, was also the most consistent practitioner. Most other masters used hypermodern methods as an occasional addition to their armoury. The movement was largely a reaction from the rigid views held by Tarrasch, and was principally concerned with the problem of the opening and control of the centre. The middlegame continued to be played in the manner advocated by Steinitz, although the revival of the flank openings led to middlegames not unlike those of the English school.

The principles of Steinitz were applied to the very first moves of the game, hitherto taken for granted. After 1 e4 e5 2 Nf3 Nc6 3 Bb5 the pawn at e5 becomes an object of attack, forcing Black to play defensively. Also after 1 d4 d5 2 c4 Black's d-pawn becomes an object of attack. Should Black thus set up a centre pawn as a target? What else should Black play? The answer lay in Steinitz's concept that all pawn moves carry the seed of a pawn weakness. If White plays 1 d4 then the square e4 is weakened to the extent that it cannot be defended by White's d-pawn. Black should therefore try to control e4, but without setting up a target by 1 ... d5. One way of doing this is to play the DUTCH DEFENCE (1 ... f5), which was revived by TARTAKOWER and ALEKHINE. Another way is to control e4 with pieces, the basis of the QUEEN'S INDIAN DEFENCE and the NIMZO-INDIAN DEFENCE, both pioneered by Nimzowitsch. After 1 e4 Black could reply 1 ... c5 (the SICILIAN DEFENCE), for the pawn at c5 is an unlikely target. If it would be wrong for Black to set up a centre pawn as a target, would this also be wrong for White? Réti answered the question by elaborating the Réti System: the centre was to be dominated by pieces rather than pawns. (The Staunton System, a precedent, may have been unknown to Réti.) If it were wrong to place a centre pawn on the fourth rank at the start of a game, then it might be right to induce the opponent to do so. Philidor warned of the danger of setting up a pawn

centre too soon, and the practical expression of such a danger is seen in the GRÜNFELD DEFENCE. In the ALEKHINE DEFENCE Black immediately attacks White's pawn at e4, so that White must either play supinely, or set up an advanced pawn centre that gives Black a target in the play that follows. The Sicilian Defence was re-investigated: Black does not aim to play Pd5, but to set up a small centre, as in the DRAGON VARIATION (invented by Paulsen) and the SCHEVENINGEN VARIATION. The flank opening, 1 c4 (ENGLISH OPENING), was revived, Tartakower declaring it to be the opening of the future. For many openings the fianchetto was used, a development that has remained fashionable.

The hypermodern movement led to increasing interest in flank openings for White, but more significant, and equally permanent, was the introduction of many new defences for Black. No longer was it believed that any reply to 1 e4 other than 1 ... e5, or any reply to 1 d4 other than 1 ... d5, was necessarily inferior.

The Soviet hegemony
The centre of world chess moved to the Soviet Union in the 1940s. An early development was the emphasis placed on mobility. Tarrasch believed that a player who had greater mobility could play so that pawn 'weaknesses' would not come under fire. This idea was restated. A weakness is not a weakness if it cannot be attacked. On this view some new opening variations were introduced. In the BOLESLAVSKY VARIATION of the Sicilian Defence, Black leaves a hole on d5. (See WEAKNESS.) In the traditional form of the KING'S INDIAN DEFENCE, BOLESLAVSKY and BRONSTEIN pioneered a move for Black (... c6) that 'weakens' the square d6 but revitalizes the defence. Black's pawns retain their mobility across the board, an impressive vindication of Philidor's ideas. These and many other innovations were designed to offer Black counter-play, but not without slight risk. For the same reason, and with comparable risk, Tarrasch had advocated the TARRASCH DEFENCE to the QUEEN'S GAMBIT. A player with a different style, SMYSLOV, introduced the SMYSLOV VARIATION (386) of the Grünfeld Defence, a line of play that would not have been out of place in the repertoire of a hypermodern player. The former world champion KARPOV plays in a style not unlike that of Capablanca, whose play, according to Lasker, was the highest development of Steinitz's ideas. On the other hand, KORCHNOI's play has been compared to that of Lasker, and KASPAROV's to that of Alekhine.

Soviet players have made many contributions to the game. Like other players of the period they have built on the work of their predecessors, borrowing ideas from many sources. They claim to have a national 'school' based on the games and teachings of Chigorin, but the time for schools has passed. The manner in which a master plays depends less upon geography than on personal style.

Schultze–Müller Gambit, or Müller–Schultze Gambit, or Schultze Gambit, 863 in the FOUR KNIGHTS OPENING. The opening was popular in the mid-1870s among the strong players of Leipzig, who gave it its humorous name. The line is better than its cousin, the CHICAGO GAMBIT, 1012, because White obtains some lead in development as well as a pawn for the knight after 4 . . . Nxe5 5 d4 Ng6 6 e5 Ng8.

Schultz Variation, 1147 in the KING'S GAMBIT Accepted, given in *Schachzeitung*, 1858, attributed to Georg Schultz of Hanover, and used by ANDERSSEN in the 1860s.

Schwartz Defence, 61, a dubious variation in the QUEEN'S GAMBIT ACCEPTED published in *Le Palamède*, 1842, and attributed to Wilhelm Schwartz (1816–1912) of Livonia.

Schwarz, Adolf (1836–1910), Hungarian-born player who settled in Vienna in 1872, merchant. He was active in tournament play for about ten years from 1873, and achieved his best result at Wiesbaden 1880 when he shared first place with BLACKBURNE and ENGLISCH. In match play Schwarz defeated MINCKWITZ in 1878 (+3=4−2), WINAWER in 1880 (+3−1), and ALBIN in 1897

(+2=1−1). At Graz 1880, where he shared first prize with Minckwitz and WEISS, his nephew Jacques Schwarz (c.1856–1921) also played; the only game Jacques won was against his uncle.

score of game, a record of the moves of a game. Article 11 of the LAWS requires each player to keep a record of the game in STANDARD NOTATION, as the game proceeds. Players with less than five minutes before a time control may defer writing until after the allotted time. If both players have to complete their score sheets after the control then the clocks may be stopped. A player refusing to keep a score sheet as specified loses.

score sheet, a form, usually printed, on which the moves of a game have been or may be written.

scoring. A player usually scores 1 for a win, ½ for a draw, and 0 for a loss. Modern competitive play began in the early years of the 19th century when draws were customarily ignored. A match would be won by the player who first scored an agreed number of wins or who scored the most wins when a set number of games was played. With the advent of ALL-PLAY-ALL tournaments draws became of more consequence. At the London international tournament of 1862 drawn games were annulled

Two score sheets from the chess Olympiad at Munich in 1958. One, in descriptive notation, is in the handwriting of Campomanes, the other is in that of Botvinnik (opponent's name, given in Russian, is Donner).

and the contestants were required to play another game. Similar rules were used in some other tournaments that followed, but gradually fashion changed and draws were counted as half a point. Drawn games remained unpopular with the chess public and at the end of the century a few scoring systems were devised to discourage draws. At Paris 1900, for example, a draw counted as a quarter of a point for each player and a second game was played to determine the allocation of a further half point. The fashion for such devices soon passed. Draws apart, critics have regarded the basic scoring system as too crude and many AUXILIARY SCORING METHODS have been devised to meet a variety of needs.

Scotch chess, see PROGRESSIVE CHESS.

Scotch Four Knights Game, 859, 994, a combination of the SCOTCH GAME and the FOUR KNIGHTS OPENING, arising from either.

Scotch Gambit, 974, the most-played variation of the SCOTCH GAME during its heyday. The Gambit may be older than the Game; around 1590 POLERIO recommended 'a new opening in order to vary play occasionally': 1 e4 e5 2 d4 exd4 3 Bc4 Nc6 4 Nf3. The gambit may also arise as 928 in the ITALIAN OPENING.

Scotch Game, 970. Noted briefly by DEL RIO in 1750, this opening was taken up by COCHRANE who recommended its use by the London Chess Club in a correspondence match against Edinburgh Chess Club, 1824–8. Seeing the effectiveness of the opening the Edinburgh players used it too, won the match, and gave the opening its name. The Scotch Game, usually in its gambit form (above), remained popular for more than twenty years, and JAENISCH could write in 1843 that it was the strongest of all openings. Since the 1850s most players have preferred the SPANISH OPENING, 673. (See PAWN FORMATION.)

Maczuski–Kolisch Paris, 1864

1 e4 e5 2 Nf3 Nc6 3 d4 exd4 4 Nxd4 Qh4 5 Nc3 Bb4 6 Qd3 Nf6 7 Nxc6 dxc6 8 Bd2 Bxc3 9 Bxc3 Nxe4 10 Qd4 Qe7 11 0-0-0 Qg5+ 12 f4 Qxf4+ 13 Bd2 Qg4 14 Qd8+ Kxd8 15 Bg5+ Ke8 16 Rd8 mate. The final combination was echoed 56 years later in a game Réti–Tartakower.

screen chess, see RANDOMIZED CHESS.

Sea-Cadet mate, a version of LEGALL'S MATE which was arranged as a display of living chess in Act II of *Der Seekadet,* an operetta by Genée and Zell (1876): 1 e4 e5 2 Nf3 Nc6 3 d4 exd4 4 c3 dxc3 5 Nxc3 d6 6 Bc4 Bg4 7 0-0 Ne5 8 Nxe5 Bxd1 9 Bxf7+ Ke7 10 Nd5 mate. The moves of this game, conducted on stage by Queen Maria Franziska of Portugal, are those of a friendly game won by FALKBEER at Vienna in 1847. The operetta was performed during the international tournament held at Barmen in 1905.

sealed move, a move written down and sealed in an envelope when a game is adjourned, a practice introduced at the Paris tournament, 1878. The move is binding on the player and not known to the opponent. Either player analysing during the adjournment must do so as if it were the opponent's turn to play. The practice of sealing moves is normal in all individual competitions, but may be relaxed for team events during brief adjournments such as tea breaks.

Article 13 of FIDE's rules gives the procedure for sealing a move. The player must record the move unambiguously, place both scoresheets in the envelope and seal it, and then stop the clock. If a move is made on the board, in error, it must be sealed. The envelope bears the names of the players, the position before the sealed move, time used by each player, the name of the player who sealed and the move number.

Article 14 covers the more dangerous area of unsealing the move. The position before the sealed move is set up on the board and the clocks adjusted. The sealed move is made on the board and the clock started. If the player who sealed is not present a reply may be temporarily sealed. If the players agree a draw, or one resigns during the break and then it emerges that the sealed move was invalid the draw or resignation still stands.

Article 10 says that a game is lost by a player who seals a move 'the real significance of which is impossible to establish' or an illegal move.

second, a player's attendant in a match or tournament. Originally he dealt with administration, secured fair play, held the stakes, and so on. In the world championship match Lasker–Tarrasch 1908, ALAPIN and WOLF assisted in the preparation of opening analysis. From the middle of the 20th century seconds have also assisted with adjournment analysis and have sometimes acted as trainers. Some players have been helped in these ways by a team of seconds, and this has become normal for world championships. Having a large number of helpers, however, is less effective than is generally supposed. In the fifth game of his quarter-final Candidates match against FISCHER in 1971 TAIMANOV, shown a plethora of variations at the last minute, was so confused that he made one of the worst blunders of his career shortly after resumption of play. Some players have been doubtful about their seconds, suspecting them of revealing prepared analysis to the other side, and some feel that a second may perform a disservice by focusing the player's attention on a line which would otherwise be rejected as inferior.

see-saw, or windmill, a combination consisting of two line-pieces giving a series of consecutive checks in matched pairs and so that every other check is a discovered check by means of which, on occasion, material may be gained.

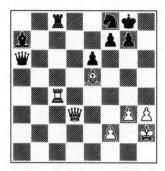

White wins this apparently lost position by means of a see-saw: 1 Rg4 Qxd3 2 Rxg7+ Kh8 3 Rxf7+ Kg8 4 Rg7+ Kh8 5 Rxa7+ Kg8 6 Rg7+ Kh8 7 Rd7+ Kg8 8 Rxd3. (See ALBURT.)

Seirawan, Yasser (1960–), American player, World Junior Champion 1979, International Grandmaster (1980). Born in Damascus, he was about two years old when he, his Syrian father, and English mother moved to England, and in 1967 the family emigrated to USA. Seirawan's early tournament results include: Wijk aan Zee 1980, first (+7=6) equal with BROWNE ahead of KORCHNOI and TIMMAN; Bad Kissingen 1981, second (+5=2−3) equal with HORT, after Korchnoi; Las Palmas 1981, third (+4=4−2) equal with Korchnoi, after Timman and LARSEN; US championship 1981, first (+4=10) equal with Browne; Mar del Plata 1982, third (+5=5−3) equal with KARPOV and POLUGAYEVSKY, after Timman and PORTISCH; London 1982, third (+6=4−3), after ANDERSSON and Karpov; and Grand Manan 1984, first equal with LEIN.

In 1985 Seirawan was second (+7=9−1), after VAGANYAN, at the Biel interzonal and became a CANDIDATE, only to be eliminated in the Montpellier Candidates tournament later in the year. As some compensation, he won the US championship at Estes Park (+6=9) in 1986. In 1987 he was equal second (+8=4−4) with EHLVEST, after Korchnoi, and once more became a Candidate. Again he was eliminated, this time in match play, by Speelman in 1988, and again he was first (+5=9−1) in the US championship in the ensuing year, at Long Beach 1989. (However, this time it was a three-way tie.) Seirawan's more recent results include: Skellefteå 1989, third (+3=11−1) equal with SALOV and SHORT, after KARPOV and KASPAROV; Haninge 1990, first (+6=5), in front of Karpov and Ehlvest; Jacksonville 1990, first in front of Browne, YUDASIN, and 257 other players (Swiss system). Also in 1990 he defeated Timman in match play +3=2−1.

Seirawan–Dzindzichashvili   US Championship 1984
Queen's Indian Defence

1 d4 Nf6 2 c4 e6 3 Nf3 b6 4 Nc3 Bb7 5 Bf4 Bb4 6 Qb3 Ba5 7 e3 Ne4 8 Bd3 Bxc3+ 9 bxc3 d6 (9 ... 0–0 is

preferable) 10 Qc2 f5

11 d5 exd5 12 cxd5 Bxd5 13 Nd4 g6 14 f3 Nc5 15 e4 fxe4 16 fxe4 Bb7 17 0–0 0–0 18 Bc4+ d5 19 exd5 Bxd5 20 Qe2 Qd7 21 Bh6 Black resigns. If 21 ... Rxf1+ 22 Rxf1 Nc6 23 Qf3.

Selenus, Gustavus (1579–1666), author of *Das Schach- oder König-spiel* (Leipzig, 1616), the first German instructor for chessplayers. In part a translation of an Italian version of Ruy LÓPEZ, the book is important as a source of information about both the laws of chess then current in Germany, and also COURIER. There is an appendix on RITHMOMACHY. The use of a chess notation in which the squares were numbered 1 to 64 limited the book's appeal.

Gustavus is an anagram of Avgustus, and Selenus refers to the Greek goddess of the moon, and hence to the Latin *luna*. The author's real name was Duke Augustus of Lüneburg, later Duke of Brunswick (an ancestor of one of MORPHY's opponents — see FRIENDLY GAME). A man of astonishing achievements, he entered the University of Rostock at the age of 14, soon gave an oration lasting nearly an hour, and was made Rector shortly afterwards. A year later he moved to Tübingen and was again made Rector. After two years he went to the Academy of Strasburg, where his brother Franz was Dean. From 1598 to 1604 he travelled almost continuously: he went to Padua, Florence, Naples, Sicily, Malta, and all the main courts of Germany in his first spell. By way of Belgium, he went to attend the coronation of James I of England in 1603, and then to the court of Henri IV of France.

Founder of the famous Bibliotheca Augusta in Wolfenbüttel, he personally collected and financed rich additions from Germany, France, Spain, Italy, and Belgium. As Duke of Brunswick he was regarded as a good and wise ruler. He negotiated with the Kaiser for the removal of occupation troops from Wolfenbüttel, which he made his residence, rebuilding the old town and castle.

self-block, an obstruction in the KING'S FIELD by a man of the same colour. The term is more frequently used by composers than by players.

selfmate, formerly sui-mate, a problem in which White moves first and forces Black to give mate, a stipulation indicated by the symbol s‡ (s‡). The idea dates from medieval times. (See BAKCSI; CYCLIC

PLAY; GANDEV; MAXIMUMMER; SERIES-MOVER; PETRO-VIĆ.)

self-pin, a composer's term for a move that places a man so that it becomes pinned in the composer's sense of the word, i.e. pinned against a king.

self-stalemate, the stalemate of a player's own king sought intentionally, sometimes a defensive resource in the BASIC ENDGAME (see STALEMATE), sometimes featured in studies (see BRON; HALBERSTADT; KAZANTSEV; KRALIN; MIRROR STALEMATE; PIN-STALEMATE).

Semi-Benoni, 52, the BLOCKADE VARIATION of the BENONI DEFENCE.

semi-close game, an opening in which White commences 1 d4 and Black does not reply 1 ... d5.

Semi-Duras Variation, 782 in the SPANISH OPENING, arising from the STEINITZ DEFENCE. Compare the KERES VARIATION, 687, in the STEINITZ DEFENCE DEFERRED.

Semi-Italian Opening, 936, also known as the Half Giuoco Piano, Lesser Giuoco Piano, or Paris Defence. Black plays 3 ... d6 instead of 3 ... Bc5, leading to play not unlike that in the HUNGARIAN DEFENCE.

Semi-Meran, any other move in the position where 6 ... dxc4 introduces the MERAN VARIATION, 142.

semi-open game, an opening in which White plays 1 e4 and Black does not reply 1 ... e5.

Semi-Slav Defence, 134 in the QUEEN'S GAMBIT Declined. In this case, unlike some other 'semi' openings, the full Slav is played with the added move Pe7–e6. Black threatens to capture and defend, temporarily or otherwise, the gambit pawn, thus gaining active play on the queen's-side (as, for example, in the ABRAHAMS VARIATION, 136). White may forestall this threat by playing Pe2–e3 which, however, shuts in his DARK BISHOP. Black may regard this as sufficient gain and play the CHIGORIN or BOGOLJUBOW VARIATION (148, 149), aiming to free his game by the advance of the e- or c-pawn. On the other hand, and more commonly, Black chooses the combative MERAN VARIATION (142). White may forestall this by playing, for example, the ANTI-MERAN GAMBIT or the MARSHALL GAMBIT (153, 135).

The Semi-Slav, mentioned by SALVIO, was almost ignored until promoted by CHIGORIN and ALAPIN in the 1890s, and popular acceptance came only in the 1920s. (See G. F. ANDERSON; BOTVINNIK; JUNGE; KUPREICHIK; TRIFUNOVIĆ.)

Semi-Tarrasch Variation, 161, rarely known by the fanciful name Rabelais Variation, in the QUEEN'S GAMBIT Declined, a line that at one time often transposed to the main line of the TARRASCH DEFENCE, 118, in which Black defends an ISOLATED QUEEN'S PAWN. The unfortunate prefix was added when masters found that the continuation 5 cxd5 Nxd5 led to a game with characteristics different from those of the Tarrasch Defence, for Black is not saddled with an isolated pawn. Black might continue 6 e4 Nxc3 7 bxc3, when White has a CLASSICAL CENTRE and Black is poised for counter-attack, a situation analogous to that in the EXCHANGE VARIATION (365) of the GRÜNFELD DEFENCE. The first known occurrence of the Semi-Tarrasch Variation was in the 38th game of the Bourdonnais–McDonnell matches, 1834. (See DOUBLE BISHOP SACRIFICE; HANSEN; PINTÉR.)

Semmering Variation, 103 in the QUEEN'S GAMBIT Declined, a line that became popular at the Semmering tournament in 1926.

Sergeant, Philip Walsingham (1872–1952), English author of biographical games collections for CHAROUSEK, MORPHY, and PILLSBURY as well as other works of importance such as *A Century of British Chess* (1934) and *Championship Chess* (1938).

series-mover, a FAIRY PROBLEM in which one or both sides make a series of SINGLE-MOVES while the other side does not move. The side making the series may not move the king into check, and may give check only on the last move of a series. A rule forbidding RETRO-STALEMATE (as if it were at any stage of the series the other side's turn to play) is sometimes imposed.

In a series helpmate (sh#) or a series helpstalemate (shp) Black begins play, and after the stipulated number of moves has been made White chooses a move that gives mate or stalemate. In a series selfmate (ss#) or a series self-stalemate (ssp) White begins play, and at the end of the series Black is forced to give mate or stalemate. Also in a series reflex problem (sr# or srp) White begins play. Duals must be avoided, i.e. the moves of a series should meet the STIPULATIONS only if played in the sequence intended by the composer. The seriesmover, dating from medieval times, was actively promoted by DAWSON, among others, and has been used for some unorthodox games.

ss#24

A series self-mate with ALLUMWANDLUNG, by KRIK-HELI, first prize, *The Problemist*, 1980. White plays 1–5 g8 = N, 6 h8 = Q, 7–8 Qh6xc6, 9–11 h8 = R, 12 Rh5, 13–14 Ne4, 15 Nc5, 16–17 Kd5–d6, 18 Rd5, 19–22 h8 = B, 23 Be5, 24 Qb6 + and Black is forced to play Rxb6#.

(See also CYLINDER BOARD.)

set play, or apparent play, a line of play, provided intentionally by a composer, that could occur if Black were to move first in a DIRECT MATE PROBLEM or if White were to move first in a HELPMATE. In a direct mate problem, set play would permit the STIPULATIONS to be met if White's first move were to be passed up. In a direct mate two-mover, for example, set play consists of a black move answered by a white mating move.

If a position is a BLOCK there is set play for every black move. More commonly there is set play for a few black moves, or there is none. A composer sometimes constructs a problem in which two or more lines of set play are contrasted with two or more variations of the solution, a form of CHANGED PLAY.

seventh rank, the opponent's second rank, on which pawns stand in the ARRAY. For White this is the rank a7–h7 in STANDARD NOTATION, for Black it is a2–h2. A rook is often well placed on the seventh rank from where it can attack pawns laterally if they have not been moved and from the rear otherwise. Rooks doubled on the seventh rank usually bring decisive advantage.

seventh rank absolute, a term coined by NIMZO-WITSCH for the situation in which control by a rook or rooks of the SEVENTH RANK confines the enemy king to the first rank.

Speelman–Nogueiras Barcelona 1988 World Cup Tournament   French Defence Tarrasch Variation

1 e4 e6   2 d4 d5   3 Nd2 c5   4 exd5 Qxd5   5 Ngf3 cxd4   6 Bc4 Qd6   7 0–0 Nf6   8 Nb3 Nc6   9 Nbxd4 Nxd4   10 Nxd4 a6   11 Re1 Qc7   12 Qe2 Bc5   13 c3 0–0   14 Bg5 Bxd4   15 cxd4 Nd5   16 Rac1 Qb6   17 Qg4 f5   18 Qf3 Qxd4   19 Bxd5 exd5   20 Rc7 f4   21 Ree7 Bf5   22 Qc3 Qxc3   23 bxc3 Rae8   24 Rxg7 + Kh8

25 h4 Bg6   26 f3 b5   27 Ra7 Re1 +   28 Kh2 Re6   29 Rgc7 Kg8   30 Bh6 Rf5   31 Rg7 + Kh8   32 Bg5 Rf8   33 h5 Bb1 34 Rgd7 Kg8   35 Bh4 Re2   36 h6 Re6   37 Rg7 + Kh8

38 Bf2 Rxh6 +   39 Kg1 Black resigns.

shame mate, a term, now obsolete, used in Iceland to describe an inferior way of losing. Among the mates considered disgraceful were those given by a pawn, and those given to a king on a corner square, or in the centre of the board or, worst of all, to an unmoved king.

Shamkovich, Leonid Alexandrovich (1923–), Russian-born player, International Grandmaster (1965). He won the RSFSR (Russian Federation) championship in 1954 and 1956, and competed in the USSR championship six times from 1954 to 1972, sharing fifth place on his fourth attempt in 1964. His best international results were: Moscow 1962, equal third, after AVERBAKH and VASYUKOV; Mariánské Lázně 1965, third (+ 6 = 9), after HORT and KERES; and Sochi 1967, first (+ 6 = 8 − 1) equal with KROGIUS, SIMAGIN, SPASSKY, and ZAITSEV. In 1975 Shamkovich emigrated to Israel where he won the Open Championship. In the following year he won the US Open Championship, having moved, by way of Canada, to the USA where he settled. He shared first place at New York 1977, and in 1986–7 he shared fifth place out of 78 competitors in a strong Swiss system tournament at Holon, Tel Aviv, but his appearances in tournaments were becoming less frequent.

Shamkovich Variation, 385, the SIMAGIN VARIATION of the GRÜNFELD DEFENCE.

shaṭranj, the version of the old game used in Islamic countries for more than a thousand years. The array was similar to that of the modern game but in place of the queen each player had a FIRZĀN (F), and in the place of each bishop a FĪL (A). Pawns could be moved only one square at a time (which slowed the opening phase) and could be promoted only to firzāns. There was no such move as castling. A player could win by checkmate or BARE KING, or by stalemating the opponent. The relative value of the pieces as given by aṣ-ṢŪLĪ may be compared with the modern pieces, the figures in brackets representing the queen and bishop:

	shaṭranj	modern
rook	5	5
knight	$3\frac{1}{3}$	3
firzān	$1\frac{2}{3}$	(9)
fīl	$1\frac{1}{4}$	$(3\frac{1}{4})$
KP or QP	$1\frac{1}{4}$	
BP or NP	$\frac{5}{6}$–1	1
RP	$\frac{5}{8}$	

Because of the comparative weakness of the old pieces, attacks on the enemy king were infrequent, and the game largely consisted of positional manœuvring. The four fīls could neither attack nor guard one another; the firzāns were also moved on paths that never crossed. As a consequence these pieces were not easily exchanged, and throughout the game play was dominated by the strength or weakness of squares these pieces could or could not control, a situation paralleled in the modern game, but in a less intricate form, only when there are bishops of opposite colour.

BLACK

1:0	0:2	1:1	0:1	1:0	0:2	1:1	0:1
1:1	1:0	0:1	2:0	1:1	1:0	0:1	2:0
1:1	0:1	1:0	0:2	1:1	0:1	1:0	0:2
0:1	2:0	1:1	1:0	0:1	2:0	1:1	1:0
1:0	0:2	1:1	0:1	1:0	0:2	1:1	0:1
1:1	1:0	0:1	2:0	1:1	1:0	0:1	2:0
1:1	0:1	1:0	0:2	1:1	0:1	1:0	0:2
0:1	2:0	1:1	1:0	0:1	2:0	1:1	1:0

WHITE

The diagram shows how the white and black fīls and firzāns might command the different squares of the board. For example, d7 is marked 2:0, indicating that White can attack this square twice (with firzān and light fīl) while it cannot be attacked by Black's fīls and firzān. The players' strongest squares are on the odd-numbered ranks. There are strong squares for White at b5 and f5, for Black at b4 and f4. Those on the f-file are considered more important, partly because masters preferred to attack on the king's-side. White has a strong square at d3, Black at d6, on which a blockade might be held against attack on the d-file, or by which the firzān might travel on its way to the enemy ranks. Each player can use diagonals (e.g. for White b1–h7 and h1–a8), along which the firzān and perhaps the king might advance unhindered by the enemy fīls or firzān. There are potential safe holes in the enemy camp (e.g. for White b7, d7, f7, and h7) and if a firzān guarded by a pawn occupies such a hole it can be removed only by the sacrifice of a knight or rook.

In the middlegame each player may try to

A game of shaṭranj: miniature from a medieval Persian manuscript, *A Treatise on Chess*

advance the firzān to such a hole, and to prevent the opponent from doing likewise. The king's fīl is considered more valuable than the queen's because it can support the firzān. A player with a rook on the SEVENTH RANK will find it at least as strong as it would be in the modern game; if on the d- or f-file, it cannot be attacked by the enemy fīls or firzān. (See game below.)

To prevent the intrusion of enemy pieces, a player must look to his pawns. For example, White might establish a pawn at e3 guarding the weak squares d4 and f4, or a pawn at g5 or c5 guarded by his dark fīl, so that the enemy firzān cannot easily be moved up the board. An isolated pawn on the fourth rank might be hard to defend. On the other hand, an isolated pawn on the fifth rank that can be guarded by a fīl might be a source of strength, perhaps spearheading an attack. The greater importance of pawns in the old game is indicated by aṣ-Ṣūlī's varying evaluation according to the file on which they stand. The pawns are used as a fighting force to a greater extent than in the modern game. A player could move them forward without endangering the king, which might well support their advance.

The strongest openings are flank openings, when a player tries to advance pawns so that they may occupy or control strong points that lie on the flanks. The pawns are moved up first, the pieces developed at the rear. The linking of the rooks, often achieved on the first rank in modern chess, usually takes place on the second rank, after the pawns have been advanced. (See TA'BI'A for some typical opening systems.) It would rarely profit a player to seek attack at the expense of his pawn formation; he might gain material but then be unable to win the endgame.

It is no easy task to win by bare king. The opponent's fīls and firzān, moving on a different set of squares from the player's, must be exchanged or captured. In the modern game there are, in effect, five different kinds of piece other than the king (Q, R, N, Bs dark and light); in the old game there were eight, including four kinds of fīl and two kinds of firzān. In consequence, there are many different kinds of endgame, most of them posing the same problem: how to force exchanges. This the pawns may help to achieve, controlling squares to which the opponent's fīl or firzān might be moved, or by promotion to a firzān that could challenge the enemy firzān. A fīl, the weakest piece, may well be exchanged for a pawn; in the middlegame such an exchange might be the prelude to a mobilization of a phalanx of pawns.

A reconstructed 10th-century game: 1 ... f6 (Black commences play and prepares for a mujannaḥ—see TA'BI'A) 2 f3 f5   3 f4 Nf6   4 Nf3 c6   5 e3 c5   6 Ah3 g6   7 Nh4 (an idle attack on f5) 7 ... e6   8 b3 Fe7 (Black seeks a chance to bring the king's rook quickly into play, and defers completion of the opening system.) 9 Fe2 Ah6   10 g3 Kf7   11 Nf3 Rd8   12 Ne5+ (a pointless check) 12 ... Kg8   13 Nd3 d6   14 Nf2 Nc6   15 d3 b6   16 e4 fxe4   17 dxe4

d5   18 Fd3 (White sets up a blockade on d3 which Black outflanks by a neat combination.) 18 ... c4! 19 bxc4 dxc4   20 Fxc4 Aa6   21 Fd3 Rac8   22 Nc3 Nb4   23 Na4 Rxc2!   24 Af1.

The position (but not the preceding moves) was given by aṣ-Ṣūlī, and probably arose in one of his games against a comparatively weak player (White). It is unlikely that ABŪ 'L FATḤ is correct in saying that this game was played before the invention of ta'bī'āt. Black plays 24 ... Ac4 and wins. A number of manuscripts give an abundance of variations, including the following: 25 Nh3 Nxe4   26 a3 Re2+   27 Kd1 (27 ... Fxe2   28 Nc2 mate) 27 ... Nxd3   28 Fxd3 Rxd3 mate; or 25 Nd1 Nxe4   26 N1c3 (26 Fxc2 Nxc2 mate, or 26 Fxe4 Re2 mate) 26 ... Rxd3   27 Axd3 Nxd3+   28 Kf1 Rf2+   29 Kg1 Nd2   30 ~ Nf3 mate.

The great players were called 'ālīyāt (sing. 'ālīya). Abū 'n-Na 'ām, Jābir al-Kūfī, RABRAB, al-'ADLĪ, and ar-RĀZĪ flourished in the 9th century, aṣ-Ṣūlī and al-LAJLĀJ in the 10th. Several wrote books, of which none has survived, but information from these books may be found in manuscripts dating from the 12th century.

The Golden Age of Islamic chess, which lasted more than 150 years, began during the rule (786–809) of HĀRŪN AR-RASHĪD, fourth Caliph of the 'Abbasīd dynasty. The court continued to patronize the game, for which some rulers showed excessive fondness. Caliph al-Ma'mūn, a son of Hārūn ar-Rashīd, lamented his poor play. 'Strange that I, who rule the world from the Indus in the East to Andalusia in the West, cannot manage 32 chessmen.' In 866 al-Mu'tazz was playing shaṭranj when a messenger brought in the head of his predecessor, Caliph al-Musta'īn; al-Mu'tazz would pay no attention to this gruesome proof of his successful bid for power until he had finished his game. His son, of the same name (d. 908), one of the poets whose works were edited by aṣ-Ṣūlī, wrote the following.

> O thou whose cynic sneers express
> The censure of our favourite chess,
> Know that its skill is science' self,
> Its play distraction from distress;
> It soothes the anxious lover's care,
> It weans the drunkard from excess;
> It counsels warriors in their art,
> When dangers threat, and perils press;
> And yields us, when we need them most,
> Companions in our loneliness.

The translation is by Nathaniel Bland (1803–65) and is to be found in his paper on Persian Chess (1847).

Shinkman, William Anthony (1847–1933), one of the greatest two American composers of the 19th century, and more prolific and thorough in his work than the other, LOYD. He composed more than 3,000 problems, excelling at every kind. While European composers were largely concerned with DIRECT MATE orthodox problems, Shinkman developed the SELFMATE and several new ideas. His was the principal influence that kindled DAWSON's interest in FAIRY PROBLEMS. Shinkman was taken from Bohemia to the USA at the age of six, in due course becoming an insurance agent, a property agent, and, in 1893, City Clerk of Grand Rapids, Michigan, where he lived throughout his adult life, and to which he owed his nickname 'the wizard of Grand Rapids'.

#2

A problem by Shinkman, *Illustrated American*, 1890. 1 Qe6 (setting up a BLOCK) 1...Kb4 2 c5#. A curiosity: the mating move opens BATTERIES on three lines simultaneously. Other variations are 1...Kc6 2 Qc8#; 1...N~ 2 Qxd6#; 1...d5 2 Qb6#; 1...Kxd4 2 Bb6#; 1...Rb4 2 Qd5#.

A. C. White, *The Golden Argosy* (1929) contains 600 problems by Shinkman.

Shirov, Alexey Dmitryevich (1972–), Latvian-born player of Russian descent, World Cadet (under-16) Champion 1988, International Grandmaster 1990. He had shared victories at Val Maubée 1989 and Daugavpils 1990 and won outright (+5=4) at Stockholm 1990. A qualifier for the interzonal at Manila 1990, he missed becoming a CANDIDATE by half a point.

Shirov–Smejkal   Bundesliga 1992   Grünfeld Defence
Exchange Variation

1 d4 Nf6 2 c4 g6 3 Nc3 d5 4 cxd5 Nxd5 5 e4 Nxc3 6 bxc3 Bg7 7 Bb5+ c6 8 Ba4 0–0 9 Ne2 e5 10 0–0 Nd7 11 Ba3 Re8 12 Bb3 Nb6 13 f4 exd4 14 f5 gxf5 15 Ng3 dxc3 16 Qh5 Nc4 17 Rad1 Qb6+ 18 Kh1 Qb5 19 Nxf5 Bxf5 20 Rxf5 Ne5 21 Bxf7+ Nxf7 22 Qxf7+ Black resigns.

shogi, the 'Generals Game', is Japanese chess. Believed to be derived from two forms of chess received from China or Korea, one AD *c*.800 and the other between about 1000 and 1200, it has, nevertheless, substantial differences from the chess games found there. The 9 × 9 board is unchequered. The pieces (shogi includes pawns in the term) move on squares (not points) and are all of the same colour, the side to which they belong being indicated by the direction in which they point. The captured pieces change sides: the captor holds them 'in hand' and may, with some limitations, 'drop' them on the board at any time in lieu of making a move. The object of the game is to checkmate or capture the opposing king.

Each player has twenty pieces arranged at start of play as follows: first rank — lance, knight, silver, gold, king, gold, silver, knight, lance; second rank — a bishop on the second file from the left, a rook on the second file from the right (viewed from each player's own side); third rank — nine pawns. The full names of gold, silver, are gold general, silver general, while one side's king is jewelled general, the other side's, king general — hence the name Generals Game.

The moves of the pieces are: king, like a chess king (but no castling); gold, like a king but not to the two squares diagonally to its rear; silver, one square directly forward or one square in any diagonal direction; knight, like a chess knight (a LEAPER) but only to the one of the two squares that lie most nearly straight ahead; lance, like a rook, but only forward on its file; pawn, directly forward one square (also captures this way).

Promotion is entirely different from that in chess. A player may, optionally, promote any piece, other than king or gold, when moved into, within, or out of the furthest three ranks. Pawns, lances, knights, and silvers promote to golds; rooks and bishops add the powers of the king to their own, becoming COMBINED PIECES. The name of a piece is marked on

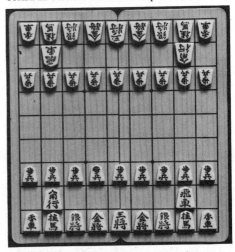

Shogi, the initial array shown on a pocket set

one face, and its promoted version on the reverse. A captured piece can be dropped only in its unpromoted form.

The special features of dropping and promotion may have influenced the design of the men which are all the same shape; thin, flat, and five-sided, with one pointed end.

Because pawns directly facing each other are mutually *en prise*, and pawn chains and blocked pawn positions do not arise, strategy differs from that in the international game. The continual reappearance of captured pieces prevents the occurrence of endgames of the type found in the international game, and draws are uncommon.

Shogi is one of the most popular regional variations. There are versions on smaller or larger boards, going up to one of 25 × 25 squares with 177 pieces on each side, but like unorthodox versions of international chess their appeal is limited and sometimes short-lived.

J. Fairbairn, *Shogi for Beginners* (1983); T. Aono, *Better Moves for Better Shogi* (1983).

Short, Nigel David (1965–   ), up to his time the strongest English player of the 20th century, International Grandmaster (1984). In 1980 he was second to KASPAROV in the World Junior Championship, and in 1982 he gave up academic studies to concentrate on chess. His best results include: Amsterdam 1982 (Swiss system), first equal with HORT; Baku 1983, first; Esbjerg 1984, first (+5=5−1); London 1986, second (+4=8−1); Solingen 1986, second (+6=3−2) equal with LAU, after HÜBNER; Wijk aan Zee 1986, first (+6=7), in front of LJUBOJEVIĆ and van der WIEL; Reykjavik 1987, first (+6=4−1), in front of TAL, TIMMAN, KORCHNOI, PORTISCH, and POLUGAYEVSKY; Subotica interzonal 1987, first (+7=7−1) equal with SAX and SPEELMAN; Wijk aan Zee 1987, first (+6=7) shared with Korchnoi; Hastings 1987–8, first (+4=10); Amsterdam 1988, an outstandingly strong event, first (+3=2−1) in front of KARPOV and Ljubojević; Tilburg 1988, second (+4=9−1), after Karpov; Hastings 1988–9, first (+4=8−1), ahead of Korchnoi; Amsterdam 1989, second (+3=2−1), after Timman, in front of SALOV; Skellefteå 1989, equal third (+4=9−2) with Salov and SEIRAWAN. behind Kasparov and Karpov.

In 1985 Short became the first British player to qualify as a CANDIDATE, but at the Montpellier Candidates tournament he failed to progress to the quarter-finals. For the next cycle, the Candidates tournament was abolished in favour of four tiers of matches. Again a Candidate, Short coasted home in his first match against Sax, winning the first two games followed by three draws. In the quarter-final he was paired against his compatriot Speelman, and lost. The following year, 1991, was one of considerable success for Short. In the Candidates cycle he had his revenge when he defeated Speelman +3=4−2. Then, in the Euwe Memorial tournament at Amsterdam, he was equal first (+3=6) with SALOV in front of Karpov, Kasparov, Korchnoi and Timman. Next he defeated GELFAND +4=2−2 in the quarter-final of the Candidates matches. At the end of the year a unique English super-championship was held sponsored by the bankers Duncan Lawrie. Eight players met in a knock-out. Short won, defeating ADAMS +3=2−1 in the last round. These achievements led the readers of *Europe Échecs* to vote Short the player of 1991. Kasparov came second. In 1992 Short defeated Karpov +4=4−2 and thereby qualified to meet Timman in the Candidates final. (See SKEWER.)

Short–Sax   Candidates match 1988   Sicilian Defence Pelikán Variation

1 e4 c5 2 Nf3 Nc6 3 d4 cxd4 4 Nxd4 Nf6 5 Nc3 e5 6 Ndb5 d6 7 Bg5 a6 8 Na3 b5 9 Bxf6 gxf6 10 Nd5 f5 11 Bd3 Be6 12 Qh5 Bg7 13 0–0 f4 14 c4 bxc4 15 Bxc4 0–0 16 Rac1 Ne7 17 Rfd1 Rc8 18 Nxe7+ Qxe7 19 Rc3 Kh8 20 b3 f5 21 Rh3 h6 22 Bxe6 Qxe6 23 Rhd3 Rcd8 24 Qe2 fxe4 25 Qxe4 f3 26 Nc1 Rf1 27 Qd5 Qg4 28 Rxf3 Rxf3 29 Qxf3 Qxf3 30 gxf3 d5

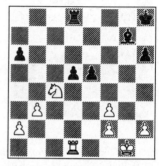

31 Kf1 Bf6 32 Nb6 d4 33 Ke2 Bg5 34 Nc4 Bf4 35 h3 Rg8 36 b4 Rg2 37 a4 Kg7 38 b5 axb5 39 axb5 Kf6 40 b6 Ke6 41 b7 Rg8 42 Rb1 Rb8 43 Rb5 Kd7 44 Na5 Kc7 45 Kd3 Kd6 46 h4 Kc7 47 Rb2 Bh2 48 Ke4 Bf4 49 Rc2+ Kd7 50 Kd3 Bh2 51 Rc1 Bf4 52 Rg1 Kd6 53 Kc4 Black resigns.

short castling, KING'S-SIDE CASTLING.

shortest game problem, or synthetic game problem. There are two kinds: to commence from the ARRAY and to achieve a given TASK in the fewest number of moves, or to construct the shortest game leading to a given position.

In 1866 LOYD set an example of the first kind, to discover the shortest game ending in stalemate: 1 e3 a5 2 Qh5 Ra6 3 Qxa5 h5 4 Qxc7 Rah6 5 h4 f6 6 Qxd7+ Kf7 7 Qxb7 Qd3 8 Qxb8 Qh7 9 Qxc8 Kg6 10 Qe6 stalemate.

For an example of the second kind, place White's f-pawn on f3 and the other 31 men as in the array. The solver is to find the shortest game leading to this position with White to play. As Black cannot LOSE THE MOVE White must do so, and one of the many solutions is 1 f3 Nc6 2 Kf2 Nb8 3 Kg3 Nc6 4 Kh4 Nb8 5 Kh3 Nc6 6 Kg3 Nb8 7 Kf2 Nc6 8 Ke1 Nb8.

short game, a game completed in a small number of moves, say 20 or fewer, sometimes known as a BREVITY or a MINIATURE. Here are two examples. Agzamov–Veremeichik, USSR Junior Championship 1968. 1 d4 Nf6 2 Nf3 c5 3 Bf4 cxd4 4 Nxd4 e5 White resigns. Zaichik–Zhikuralidze, Georgian championship 1976, 1 Nf3 d5 2 c4 Nf6 3 g3 Bf5 4 cxd5 Nxd5 5 e4 Black resigns. Both losers overlooked the effect of a check from a queen on the a-file.

shorthand. Although suggestions for chess shorthand have been made frequently, for the most part these were methods of abbreviating a notation that was currently in use. Attempts to introduce genuine stenography were first made by Eugène Vignon in *Le Palamède*, 1845. C. B. Boitel-Gill, in the *British Chess Magazine*, 1897, proposed the use of Pitman shorthand characters, and other variations have been suggested. The problem composer and author LAWS, who throughout his business life used shorthand, was of the opinion that it had little place in chess.

short-range pieces, the knight and the king.

Showalter, Jackson Whipps (1860–1935), American player known as the Kentucky Lion after his birthplace and his mane of hair, but also perhaps on account of his playing strength; teacher. Successful in several national tournaments from 1888 to 1894, Showalter also played at New York 1889, America's first international tournament, and, on four visits to Europe, in six major events abroad, the last in Munich 1900. In tournaments at Cincinnati 1888, St Louis 1890, and Lexington 1891 Showalter won the US championship, which from then until 1936 was decided by match play. He lost the title to LIPSCHÜTZ in 1892, regained it from him in 1895 (+7=3−4), and lost it to PILLSBURY in 1897. This last match was expected to be an easy triumph for Pillsbury, and scores of +7−0 in his favour were forecast. After 19 games the score was tied with 8 wins each, and then Pillsbury won two games in succession, and with it, the match. Showalter's supporters were so impressed with the loser's performance that they bought him a bicycle.

Showalter played in many other matches in the 1890s, notably against JANOWSKI in 1899, defeating him in two friendly matches, and then in a formal match for a stake of $250 a side (+4=2−1). In 1900 Showalter took second place (+6=2−2), after Lipschütz, ahead of MARSHALL, in the Manhattan Club championship. He then practically retired from play, but returned periodically, and usually out of practice. In 1904 he was fifth at Cambridge Springs; in 1909 he lost a match to Marshall; from 1915 to 1918 he played three matches and entered four Western championship tournaments, winning the first, Excelsior 1915; and he made isolated appearances in 1922 and 1926. Showalter made a few useful contributions to open-

ings knowledge, the most famous of which is the CAPABLANCA FREEING MANŒUVRE. A genial man, he was much liked by his contemporaries; STEINITZ, not an easy man to befriend in his later years, remarked that Showalter was one of only six men 'from whom I would accept a cigar'.

Pillsbury–Showalter   13th match game 1897   Queen's Gambit Declined Fianchetto Variation

1 d4 d5 2 c4 e6 3 Nc3 Nf6 4 Bg5 Be7 5 e3 Nbd7 6 Rc1 0–0 7 Nf3 c6 8 Bd3 dxc4 9 Bxc4 b5 10 Bd3 a6 11 0–0 c5 12 Ne4 c4 13 Nxf6+ Nxf6 14 Bb1 Bb7 15 Ne5 Ne4 16 Bxe7 Qxe7 17 f3 Nd6 18 Qc2 g6 19 Qd2 f6 20 Ng4 Nf7 21 e4 Rad8 22 Qe3 h5 23 Nf2 Kg7 24 Nh3 Qd6 25 Rcd1 Qb6 26 Rfe1 Rd7 27 e5 fxe5 28 Ng5 Nxg5 29 Qxg5 Rf6 30 Qxe5 Rd5

31 Qe4 e5 32 Kh1 exd4 33 Qe8 Rd8 34 Qe7+ Rf7 35 Qe5+ Qf6 36 a4 d3 37 axb5 axb5 38 Kg1 Qxe5 39 Rxe5 Rd5 40 Re3 Rfd7 41 Kf2 Kf6 42 Rde1 R5d6 43 h4 b4 44 Rc1 Ba6 45 Ba2 Rc7 46 Bb1 c3 47 bxc3 bxc3 48 Bxd3 Rxd3 49 Rxd3 Bxd3 50 Ke3 Bf5 51 Kd4 c2 52 Ke3 Rd7 53 g4 Rd1 White resigns.

Showalter–Capablanca System, 198, the CAPABLANCA FREEING MANŒUVRE which had been tried earlier by SHOWALTER.

Showalter Variation, 779 in the STEINITZ DEFENCE to the SPANISH OPENING, played by SHOWALTER in the second game of his match against LASKER in 1892; 800 in the BERLIN DEFENCE to the Spanish Opening, played by Showalter in his match with PILLSBURY in 1897; 897, also known as the Kan, Smyslov, or Sokolsky Variation, a line in the EVANS GAMBIT DECLINED, analysed by Showalter in *American Chess Magazine*, Sept. 1897.

Shteinsapir Variation, 885, the SOKOLSKY VARIATION, first played in the game Shteinsapir–Romanovsky, Leningrad 1937.

Sicilian Attack, 9, the ENGLISH OPENING. An attempt was made in the 1920s to class 1 c4 e5 as Sicilian Attack, and to reserve the name English Opening for other responses to 1 c4, but the idea is largely forgotten.

Sicilian Centre Game, 456, sometimes called the Morphy Variation. White plays the usual CENTRE GAME move, 2 d4, in response to the SICILIAN DEFENCE.

Sicilian Counterattack, 554, the PIN VARIATION.

Sicilian Defence, 444, 1 e4 c5, an opening with lines of play both more numerous and harder to evaluate than those of any other opening. Defences to 1 e4 other than 1 ... e5 may owe their adoption to Black's desire to avoid the SPANISH OPENING, but this is least true of the Sicilian: it stands in its own right, a defence offering Black a wide range of options.

White may attack with the CLOSE VARIATION, 449, the ROSSOLIMO VARIATION, 462, or the MOSCOW VARIATION, 499, but the most popular choice is 2 Nf3, and whether Black replies 2 ... d6, 2 ... Nc6, or 2 ... e6 play continues 3 d4 cxd4 4 Nxd4. Now White stands slightly better in the centre, sometimes extended by Pf2–f4, while Black has prospects on the queen's-side and may profit there by using the half-open c-file. The main lines are: the DRAGON VARIATION with its associated 'anti-Dragon' attacks (after 2 ... Nc6 or 2 ... d6); the SCHEVENINGEN VARIATION (after 2 ... d6 or 2 ... e6); the NAJDORF VARIATION (after 2 ... d6); the PAULSEN, SZÉN, and BASTRIKOV VARIATIONS (after 2 ... e6). Other well-known lines are the BOLESLAVSKY, PELIKÁN, and BOURDONNAIS VARIATIONS, in which Black plays Pe7–e5, and the NIMZOWITSCH VARIATION, 561.

The Sicilian Defence was named by SARRATT after the homeland of CARRERA, who in 1617 first published this opening. 'A very good [opening] to try the strength of an adversary with whose skill you are unacquainted', wrote PHILIDOR in 1777, but it was generally regarded as inferior until BOURDONNAIS, in his matches with McDONNELL, 1834, demonstrated that the continuation 2 f4 e6 3 Nf3 d5 4 e5, recommended by the books, gave Black a satisfactory game. In the 1840s JAENISCH, STAUNTON, and the authors of the HANDBUCH stated that 1 ... c5 was the best answer to 1 e4 'as it renders the formation of a centre impracticable for White, and prevents every attack'. From the 1850s both ANDERSSEN and PAULSEN played the Sicilian, but notwithstanding the practice and precepts of the experts, the Defence achieved little popularity in the 19th century. This was the romantic age of chess, when MORPHY, whose genius flowered less in the close game, could speak of 'disabusing the public mind of that pernicious fondness for the Sicilian Defence'. However, it gained ground slowly in the 20th century, and by the 1950s it had become the favoured defence to 1 e4. (See ARGENTINE VARIATION; MECKING; TSESHKOVSKY.)

Sicilian Gambit, 559 in the SICILIAN DEFENCE. White sacrifices a pawn for a speedy development, e.g. 7 ... Bxc3 8 bxc3 Nxe4 9 Bd3 d5 10 Ba3.

Sicilian Variation, 14 in the ENGLISH OPENING, a reversed SICILIAN DEFENCE; 41 (sometimes called the Nimzowitsch Variation), also in the English Opening, in which both sides have played the equivalent of a Sicilian Defence. (See SCHLECHTER; STOLTZ; UHLMANN.)

side variation, a study variation that is not central to the composer's idea.

Siers Rössel theme, or Siers battery, a theme named after the German composer Theodor Siers (1910–91), who published a collection of KNIGHT WHEEL problems in 1948, *Rösselsprünge im Schachproblem*. In the main variations a knight discovers check on the second move and gives mate on the third. Sometimes both knights do this.

#3

A problem by V. RUDENKO, first place USSR team championship, 1982. The key is 1 Qf2, and the first four variations show SWITCHBACKS.

1 ... Bd6   2 N6xd5+ Ke4   3 Nf6#
1 ... e5   2 Nxd7+ Ke4   3 Nf6#
1 ... Bxd4   2 N4xd5+ Kg6   3 Nf4#
1 ... d6   2 Nxe6+ Kg6   3 Nf4#
1 ... ~   2 Nd3+ Kg6   3 Ne5#.

Siesta Defence, 680, the STEINITZ DEFENCE DEFERRED, which may lead to the SIESTA VARIATION.

Siesta Variation, 684. Played by von SCHEVE at Dresden 1892 and by MARSHALL some years later, this line in the SPANISH OPENING became popular after CAPABLANCA played it at Budapest 1928, a tournament held at the Siesta sanatorium. (See KROGIUS.)

sight of the board, the ability to make an evaluation of position with reference to the speed with which this can be done. A rapid sight of the board is always an asset, especially when a player is in time-trouble; but this faculty is given only to the talented and developed only by experience. Three great masters who outdistanced their contemporaries in this respect were MORPHY, CAPABLANCA, and FISCHER.

sign of the cross, a popular theme in stories centred on chess. Typically, the devil is playing a man for his soul, but as he is making the winning move the pieces make a cruciform pattern, and the prince of darkness disappears in a cloud of brimstone.

This, one of many similar positions, is, appropriately, by Gümpel, the inventor of MEPHISTO, *Bulletin du Cercle Philidor*, 1905. 1 Rxg7+ Kf6 2 Qxc6+ Rxc6 3 Rxc6+ Qd6 4 Rxd6+ cxd6 5 Nc7 d5 6 Nxd5+ Ke6 7 Re7+ and zap!

Silberschmidt, Hirsch Hermann (1801–66), German author of two chess books, 1826 and 1829, dedicated to his patron, the Duke of Brunswick who was to become immortalized in the chess world by his loss to MORPHY at the Paris Opéra. Silberschmidt's good fortune at having such a powerful patron turned sour when the hated Duke was driven into exile. Accused of being the Duke's agent, Silberschmidt was jailed from 1830 to 1844. Whilst in prison he was visited by LEWIS. A King's Gambit variation bears his name. (See ABBAZIA DEFENCE.)

Silberschmidt Variation, 1135 in the KING'S GAMBIT Accepted. Examining SALVIO's analysis (which begins 7 d4 f3), SILBERSCHMIDT found improvements that give Black a decisive advantage; these were published in *Das Gambit oder Angriff und Verteidigung gegen Gambitzüge* (1829).

Simagin, Vladimir Pavlovich (1919–68), Soviet player, International Grandmaster (1962), International Correspondence Chess Master (1966), trainer, who died of a heart attack while playing in a tournament at Kislovodsk. In the Moscow championship he was: 1946, second (+8 =6 −1), after BRONSTEIN; 1947, first, after a play-off; 1953, second equal with LILIENTHAL, after Bronstein; 1956, second to PETROSYAN after a play-off; 1958, second to VASYUKOV; 1959, first, ahead of LIBERZON and Bronstein. Simagin was less successful in the seven USSR championships he entered from 1951 to 1965. His best international results are: Sarajevo 1963, second equal with GLIGORIĆ, IVKOV, and UHLMANN, half a point after PORTISCH; and Sochi 1967, first (+6 =8 −1) equal with KROGIUS, SHAMKOVICH, SPASSKY, and ZAITSEV.

A careful analyst and writer, Simagin discovered several interesting lines of play in the opening phase, some of which have been named after him. He was also a formidable correspondence player, being second in the 1st USSR Correspondence Championship 1948–51, winner of the 6th, 1963–4, and second in the 7th, 1965–6.

Simagin, *Luchshie party* (1963), a collection of 64 games; S. B. Voronkov, *Vladimir Simagin* (1981), is a biography with result tables and 94 annotated games, in Russian.

Simagin Improved Variation, 367 in the GRÜNFELD DEFENCE, thought to be an improvement on the SIMAGIN VARIATION, 366.

Simagin Variation, 327 in the NIMZO-INDIAN DEFENCE; 366 and 385, sometimes known as the Shamkovich Variation, in the GRÜNFELD DEFENCE; 422 in the KING'S INDIAN DEFENCE; 496 in the SICILIAN DEFENCE, as in Suetin–Simagin, Tula 1950; 511, also in the Sicilian Defence; 750 in the SPANISH OPENING, from the game Simagin–Estrin, Moscow championship, 1961.

simplification, the exchange of a number of pieces or, on rare occasions, pawns. Calling this liquidation, EUWE suggests four main categories:
(1) A player wishes to force a draw. Trying too hard to force exchanges, however, often leads to a loss of time, as in the game below.
(2) When on the defensive, a player may seek exchanges to lessen the force of the attack. This time-honoured advice, given in almost every textbook, is not often easy to follow.
(3) A player with an advantage may exchange to obtain a clear-cut position that offers the opponent little chance of counter-play. For an example, see ACCUMULATION OF ADVANTAGE.
(4) Masters who have a special talent for handling simplified positions may seek them intentionally.

Alatortsev–Capablanca Moscow 1935 Queen's Gambit Declined

1 d4 Nf6 2 c4 e6 3 Nc3 d5 4 Bg5 Be7 5 e3 0–0 6 cxd5 Nxd5 7 Bxe7 Qxe7 8 Nf3 Nxc3 9 bxc3 b6 10 Be2 Bb7 11 0–0 c5 12 Ne5 Nc6 13 Nxc6 Bxc6 14 Bf3 Rac8 15 a4 cxd4 16 cxd4 g6 17 Bxc6 Rxc6 18 Qd3 Qb7 19 Rfb1 Rfc8 20 h3 a6 21 Qa3 Rc2 22 Qd6

22 ... Rxf2 23 Qg3 Re2 White resigns.

simultaneous display, a number of games played concurrently by one player (usually) against many. The master walks around the inside of an area, surrounded by tables and chess sets, with the opponents on the outside. Each participant must move when the master arrives at the board, neither sooner nor later. However, if clocks are used players move when ready so that on every board the clock could be ticking against the exhibitor. Such clock simultaneous displays, usually at about 20 moves an hour, are greatly demanding on the master, who rarely takes on more than ten opponents in this manner. In a leapfrog display two masters circulate, making alternate moves on each board, giving themselves entertainment in the form of trying to guess their partner's intentions. However, the usual simultaneous display is more a trial of the master's physical condition than of chess skill. In Cologne in 1984 HORT played 663 games in 33 hours, in groups of 60 to 120 at a time, scoring more than 80 per cent and losing 3 kilos.

In a typical display the master faces between 20 and 40 opponents and plays simply, seizing upon errors, but confident that superior endgame technique, if needed, will suffice. As games end the remaining players, usually in increasingly difficult positions, find the master coming round more rapidly, and few have the skill to survive. There are two types of replacement display, such as that by Hort. Either a set number of games are played and then new players appear at every board or, more often, as one game ends a new player takes over that board.

single-move, a move by White *or* a move by Black. This term makes a useful distinction, for the word 'move' is frequently used to mean a move by White *and* a move by Black. Computer scientists use the word 'ply' for a single-move.

sister squares, an alternative name, coined by BERNARD, for CONJUGATE SQUARES.

Sitzfleisch (German 'buttocks', fig. 'perseverance'), undue procrastination or extreme persistence during play. In the middle of the 19th century some players became notorious for the slowness of their play, a situation largely remedied by the introduction of the TIME-LIMIT. In club matches, however, when unfinished games are adjudicated, some players who have enough time on their clocks sit out the game, hoping the adjudicator will find resources they themselves cannot find.

Six Pawns Attack, 409, variation in the KING'S INDIAN DEFENCE recommended by a German specialist in unusual openings, Heinz Gerhart Gunderam (1904–   ).

skewer, a common stratagem; a line-piece attacks a man which is moved out of the way (line vacation) thus enabling the line-piece to capture another man that lies beyond; to capture (a man) in this way. The term was invented by a Liverpool schoolteacher, Edgar Pennell (1902–85), in 1937.

The position White Kg2, Ra8, Pa7; Black Kg7, Ra1 is drawn. White's king cannot defend the pawn and free the rook because it is driven away by

checks. Black's king cannot attack the pawn. If it is moved on to the sixth rank White checks with the rook and promotes on the following move, but to move it along the seventh rank loses by means of a skewer; 1 ... Kf7? 2 Rh8 Rxa7 3 Rh7+.

Short–Vaganyan   Barcelona 1989 World Cup   French Defence Winawer Variation

1 e4 e6   2 d4 d5   3 Nc3 Bb4   4 e5 c5   5 a3 Ba5   6 dxc5 Bxc3+   7 bxc3 Qc7   8 Nf3 Nd7   9 Bb5 Qxc5   10 a4 a6   11 Bxd7+ Bxd7   12 0–0 Qxc3   13 Bd2 Qc4   14 Rb1 Qc7   15 c4 Ne7   16 Bb4 Bc6   17 cxd5 Bxd5   18 Bd6 Qd7   19 Rc1 Rc8   20 Ng5 Rxc1   21 Qxc1 Nf5   22 Ba3 f6   23 exf6 gxf6   24 Qc3 Rg8   25 Qxf6 h6   26 Re1 hxg5   27 Qxf5 Kd8   28 Qe5 Kc8   29 Bc5 Qg7   30 Qg3 Qc7   31 Qa3 Kd7   32 Be3 Qd6   33 Qb2 Kc8   34 Qd4 Kd7   35 Rd1 Ke7   36 h3 Kf7   37 Rc1 Qd8   38 Qg4 Bc6   39 Rc5 Bd5   40 Qh5+ Rg6   41 Bd4 e5   42 Bxe5 Be4   43 Rc7+ Ke6   44 Bg3 Qd4   45 Qg4+ Kf6   46 Qc8 Rg7   47 Qf8+ Kg6   48 Rxg7+ Qxg7   49 Qe8+ Kf5   50 Qc8+ Kf6   51 Be5+ Black resigns.

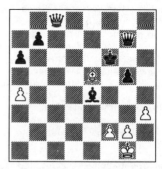

After 51 ... Kxe5   52 Qc3+ Black succumbs to a skewer.

skittles, casual or FRIENDLY GAME or games, played fast and without a clock.

Slater, James Derrick (1929–   ), British chess patron, financier, children's author. Slater achieved wide fame in the chess world on the occasion of the Fischer–Spassky world championship match of 1972: FISCHER showed reluctance to play and apparently decided to do so when Slater added £50,000 to the prize fund. Slater has also made contributions to many other chess causes and in 1973 set up the Slater Foundation, a charitable trust which, among other activities, pays for the coaching of young players. Leonard BARDEN advises the trust on chess matters. In the 1970s, partly owing to this patronage, junior players in Britain became as strong as those in any other country.

M. Chandler and R. Keene, *The English Chess Explosion* (1981), charts the progress of some of these young British players.

Slav Defence, 78 or, by transposition, 1293, one of the principal defences to the QUEEN'S GAMBIT. Black's second move carries the threat, after due preparation, of capturing and holding (by Pb7–b5) the gambit pawn. This threat is rarely carried out, but White must take appropriate precautions, enabling Black's queen's bishop to be developed satisfactorily, either on the king's-side, as in the CZECH DEFENCE, 88, or on the queen's-side, as in the ALEKHINE VARIATION, 96, e.g. 5 ... b5 6 a4 b4 7 Na2 Ba6. A sound line for White is the EXCHANGE VARIATION, 82; Black may avoid this by playing Pe7–e6 before Pc7–c6, reaching the SEMI-SLAV DEFENCE, 134.

Mentioned by POLERIO c.1590, and promoted by CHIGORIN, the Slav Defence, as distinct from the Semi-Slav Defence, first became popular in the 1930s when it was played repeatedly in all ALEKHINE's matches with BOGOLJUBOW and EUWE. (See BONDAREVSKY; CANAL; LEVENFISH; NAJDORF; PACHMAN.)

Slav Gambit, 97, a QUEEN'S GAMBIT Declined variation in which Black can hold the gambit pawn (5 ... b5) but White gains a compensating attack. The line was analysed by TOLUSH and BONDAREVSKY in 1947, and played by GELLER many times subsequently. Consequently it is sometimes called the Tolush–Geller Gambit, or the Geller Variation.

Sloth (pron. slot), Jørn (1944–), International Correspondence Chess Grandmaster (1978), teacher of mathematics and Russian, the first Dane to win a world championship at chess. He showed youthful talent by sharing first place at an international junior event (later known as the European Junior Championship) at Groningen 1964. Playing in the 8th World Correspondence Championship (1975–80) he scored +8=6 to share first place with ZAGOROVSKY. The NEUSTADTL SCORE for tie-breaking was invoked, and Sloth declared world champion. Subsequent attempts to gain an International Master title in over-the-board play were fruitless.

Smagin, Sergey Borisovich (1958–), Russian player, International Grandmaster (1987), first or equal first at Barnaul 1984, Tashkent 1984, Dresden 1985, Naleczów 1985, Novi Sad 1986, Sochi (+5=8−1) 1987, Trnava 1987, Zenica 1987, Berlin (+4=5) 1988. (See POSITIONAL SACRIFICE.)

small centre, a centre in which a player advances neither centre pawn beyond the third rank in the opening phase. The small centre for Black, usually a defensive formation, has long been known, and is a characteristic of some openings, e.g. the SCHEVENINGEN VARIATION.

As a strategic weapon for White the small centre was pioneered by STAUNTON—see his game under that heading. Many years later players of the HYPERMODERN movement revived Staunton's idea which is, briefly, to advance the centre pawns later when they are assured of strong support. On rare occasions these pawns are never moved again, play taking place on the flanks. (See NIMZOWITSCH.)

Réti-Capablanca   New York 1924   English Opening

1 Nf3 Nf6 2 c4 g6 3 b4 Bg7 4 Bb2 0–0 5 g3 b6 6 Bg2 Bb7 7 0–0 d6 8 d3 Nbd7 9 Nbd2 e5 10 Qc2 Re8 11 Rfd1 a5 12 a3 h6 13 Nf1 c5 14 b5 Nf8 15 e3 Qc7

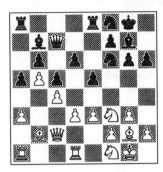

16 d4 Be4 17 Qc3 exd4 18 exd4 N6d7? (18 ... Ne6 gives Black a good game) 19 Qd2 cxd4 20 Bxd4 Qxc4 21 Bxg7 Kxg7 22 Qb2+ Kg8 23 Rxd6 Qc5 24 Rad1 Ra7 25 Ne3 Qh5 26 Nd4 Bxg2 27 Kxg2 Qe5 28 Nc4 Qc5 29 Nc6 Rc7 30 Ne3 Ne5 31 R1d5 Black resigns.

Smejkal, Jan (1946–), Czech champion 1973, 1979, and 1986, International Grandmaster (1972). A sporting opponent who plays to win, Smejkal competes regularly, with fair success. The best of his early victories are: Polanica Zdrój 1970 (+8=7); Smederevska Palanka 1971 (+7=8); Polanica Zdrój 1972; and Palma de Majorca 1972 (+6=8−1), equal with KORCHNOI and PANNO, ahead of POLUGAYEVSKY and LJUBOJEVIĆ. In the interzonal at Leningrad 1973 he was equal fourth (+9=4−4), but only the first three became CANDIDATES. Although not successful in the interzonals of 1976 and 1979, Smejkal had good results elsewhere: Wijk aan Zee 1975, third (+5=9−1), after PORTISCH and HORT, ahead of HÜBNER and GELLER; Novi Sad 1976, first (+9=5−1), ahead of Hort—Smejkal's best achievement up to this time; Vršac 1977, first (+7=7−1); Amsterdam 1979, third (+6=5−2) equal with ANDERSSON, after Hort and SAX; Trenčianské-Teplice 1979, first (+8=4−2), ahead of Hort; Vršac 1981, second (+8=6−1), after Sax; Baden-Baden 1985, first; and Bahrain 1990, first. From 1968 Smejkal played regularly in the Olympiads.

Smejkal–Geller   Siegen Olympiad 1970   King's Indian Defence

1 c4 g6 2 Nf3 Bg7 3 d4 Nf6 4 g3 0–0 5 Bg2 d6 6 0–0 Nbd7 7 Nc3 e5 8 e4 c6 9 Be3 Qa5 10 h3 Qb4 11 Qe2 exd4 12 a3 Qa5 13 Nxd4 Nb6 14 Rfd1 Re8

15 Ndb5 Nxc4 16 Qxc4 Be6 17 Qe2 cxb5 18 Nxb5 Bb3
19 Rd4 d5 20 exd5 Nxd5 21 Rxd5 Bxd5 22 Bxd5 Rad8
23 Qc4 Rxd5 24 Qxd5 a6 25 Qxb7 axb5 26 Rd1 Bxb2
27 Rd7 Qa8 28 Qxb5 Bxa3 29 Ra7 Black resigns.

Smith–Morra Gambit, 457, the MORRA GAMBIT, practised by the American player Kenneth Ray Smith (1930–   ).

smothered mate, a mate given by a knight to a king surrounded by its own men or, using the term loosely, surrounded by men of either colour. One example is PHILIDOR'S LEGACY. In master play such a finish is unlikely, although it may be threatened on occasion. A game Kumaran–Graham, Barnsdale Country Club Young Masters tournament 1989, went 1 d4 Nf6 2 c4 e5 3 dxe5 Ng4 4 Bf4 Bb4+ 5 Nd2 Nc6 6 Ngf3 Qe7 7 a3 Ngxe5 8 axb4 Nd3 mate. (For another example, see OVERLOAD.)

+

A study by the Soviet composer A. S. Seletsky, first prize, *Shakhmaty v SSSR*, 1933. 1 Qg5 Ke6+ 2 Kg1 Kxd7 3 Nc5+ Kc8 4 Ba6+ Kb8 5 Qg3+ Ka8 6 Bb7+ Bxb7 7 Nd7 Qd8 8 Qb8+ Qxb8 9 Nb6 mate. The variation 3 ... Kd6 4 Qg3+ Kd5 5 Bc4+ Kxc4 6 Qb3+ Kxc5 7 Qa3+ K~ 8 Qxf8 offers Black longer resistance. In 1933 it was believed that White should win, but this was not proved until 1985 (see BASIC ENDGAME).

Smyslov, Vasily Vasiliyevich (1921–   ), International Grandmaster (1950), World Champion 1957-8. He learned the game at the age of six, studied chess books in his father's library, and was inspired shortly before his 14th birthday by the presence in Moscow of two past champions, CAPABLANCA and LASKER. Smyslov's play then improved rapidly. In January 1938 he won the All-Union boys' championship, and later that year he came first equal with BELAVENETS in the Moscow city championship. At about this time he began studies in the Moscow Institute of Aviation. In 1940, on the first of his 19 appearances in the competition, he came third (+8=10) in the USSR championship. This qualified him for the even stronger Leningrad–Moscow match tournament 1941, where he came third (+4=12−4), after BOTVINNIK and KERES. Smyslov followed this by winning (+10=4−1) the Moscow championship in 1942, taking second place (+8=5−3) after Botvinnik in the USSR championship of 1944, and again winning the Moscow championship 1944-5, two points ahead of RAGOZIN in second place.

Although ALEKHINE, who watched events in the Soviet Union, hoping yet to revisit his homeland, had already noted Smyslov's talents, he was relatively unknown outside the USSR until he twice defeated RESHEVSKY in the famous USSR v. USA radio match of 1945, and took third place (+7=11−1) after Botvinnik and EUWE at Groningen 1946. This tournament, the first big event after the Second World War, was a kind of practice run for the world's best players, and Smyslov's result influenced his selection for the world championship match tournament of 1948. There he came second (+6=10−4), after Botvinnik, ahead of Keres, Reshevsky, and Euwe. In 1949 he came first (+9=8−2) equal with BRONSTEIN in the USSR championship, and in the Budapest CANDIDATES tournament 1950 he came third (+5=10−3) after Bronstein and BOLESLAVSKY.

In the next Candidates tournament, Neuhausen–Zurich 1953, Smyslov made his greatest tournament achievement, first place (+9=18−1), two points ahead of his nearest rivals. However, Botvinnik retained the world champion title when the challenge match of 1954 was drawn (+7=10−7). After a fine victory (+10=9) at Zagreb 1955, Smyslov won the Amsterdam Candidates tournament 1956 (+6=11−1), again by a clear margin, 1½ points ahead of the nearest player. He shared first with Botvinnik at the Alekhine Memorial tournament, Moscow 1956 (+7=8), and, challenger for the second time, defeated Botvinnik (+6=13−3) to become world champion.

Smyslov's reign was short, little over a year. In the return match of 1958 he lost the title (+5=11−7) and, although a Candidate in 1959, 1964, and 1982, he never again became challenger. The FIDE championship rules then in force led to his being champion for one year only; yet retrospective grading shows him ahead of Botvinnik from about 1950 to 1957, and first in the world for the second half of this period.

He was certainly one of the great champions. During more than 30 years following his loss of the title he scored many international tournament achievements. The best of these are: Moscow 1960, first (+6=5); Moscow 1963, first (+8=7), the first of a run of eight successive victories; Havana 1965, first (+13=5−3); Monte Carlo 1969, first (+5=6) equal with PORTISCH; Moscow 1971, third (+4=13), after KARPOV and STEIN; Teesside 1975, second (+4=9−1), after GELLER; Buenos Aires 1978, second (+4=9) equal with PANNO and VAGANYAN, after ANDERSSON; Moscow 1981, second (+3=9−1) equal with KASPAROV and POLUGAYEVSKY, after Karpov. At the Las Palmas interzonal, 1982, Smyslov took second place (+6=5−2), a remarkable achievement: at 61 he became the oldest player ever to qualify as a Candidate. The quarter-final match with HÜBNER was drawn (+1=12−1), but Smyslov was awarded victory on the spin of a roulette wheel, the agreed method of tie-breaking. He then defeated RIBLI (+3=7−1), but lost to Kasparov in the final.

Apart from world championship events Smyslov played in about 60 strong international all-play-all tournaments from 1939 to 1990, winning or sharing 25 first prizes, and rarely finishing below fourth place. A loyal team member, he competed for his country on many occasions, including nine Olympiads in which he scored +69=42−2 in all.

Smyslov learned much about chess from his father, a strong player, and says that in his youth he was most influenced by the books of TARRASCH and NIMZOWITSCH, masters with disparate approaches to the game. Smyslov's style is positional, and certainly less direct than Tarrasch's way of playing. Occasionally Smyslov hesitates during the combinative phase that follows the gain of a strategic advantage, not caring to involve himself in the calculation of precise variations, although this is well within his capacity. Such a stress-free approach may explain his ability to win tournaments in his old age. Above all he excels at the endgame, and he rightly attributes his victory over Botvinnik in 1957 to his skill in this phase.

Tall, slow-moving, good-natured, cheerful, with

a placid disposition, Smyslov chooses his words carefully, rarely disparaging others. He makes few enemies and few close friends. His other abiding interest besides chess is singing: in 1950 he narrowly failed when being auditioned for the Bolshoi Opera. While making his greatest tournament achievement (Neuhausen–Zurich 1953) he found time to sing operatic extracts on Swiss radio, and some years later, playing a hard game of LIVING CHESS against Botvinnik, Smyslov sang to the audience of thousands during the interval. This love of music explains the title of Smyslov's autobiography, *V poiskakh harmonii* (1979)—'in search of harmony'. An enlarged and modified English version is *125 Selected Games* (1983). (See PROTECTED PASSED PAWN; WEAKNESS.)

Portisch–Smyslov Moscow 1967 Nimzo-Indian Defence Smyslov Variation

1 d4 Nf6 2 c4 e6 3 Nc3 Bb4 4 e3 c5 5 Nf3 0–0 6 Bd3 d5 7 0–0 dxc4 8 Bxc4 Qe7 9 a3 Ba5 10 Qc2 Bd7 11 Bd3 Rc8 12 Bd2 cxd4 13 exd4 h6 14 Rfe1 Qd8 15 Qc1 Qf8 16 Ne5 Nc6 17 Nxd7 Nxd7 18 Re4 f5 19 Re1 Nxd4 20 Qd1 Nf6 21 Be3 e5 22 Qa4 Bb6 23 Bxd4 exd4 24 Ne2 Ne4 25 Nf4 Rc6 26 g3 Qf7 27 Bb1 Kh8 28 Ba2 Qf6 29 Bd5

29 ... d3 30 Bxc6 Bxf2+ 31 Kh1 Qxc6 32 Qxc6 bxc6 33 Red1 d2 34 Kg2 Bd4 35 Rab1 Rb8 36 Ne2 Bxb2 37 Kf3 Rb3+ 38 Kf4 Nd6 39 Rxd2 g5+ mate.

Smyslov Defence, 39 in the ENGLISH OPENING, played by SMYSLOV in his world championship match against BOTVINNIK in 1958, although it was known earlier.

Smyslov Variation, 18 and 30, two sound defences to the ENGLISH OPENING; 71 in the QUEEN'S GAMBIT ACCEPTED, played Smyslov–Petrosyan, Candidates Tournament 1959; 76 in the same opening, as Golombek–Smyslov, Budapest 1952; 86 in the SLAV DEFENCE, an old line played by Balogh in 1921; 325 in the NIMZO-INDIAN DEFENCE, from Portisch–Smyslov, Moscow 1967 (see SMYSLOV); 377 in the GRÜNFELD DEFENCE, favoured by Smyslov in the 1950s, and 386, a similar variation; 411, also in the Grünfeld Defence, suggested by ALATORTSEV and developed by Smyslov, who played it in the world championship matches of 1948 and 1958; 453 in the SICILIAN DEFENCE, a trap from Smyslov–Sajtar,

Smyslov at the time he was world champion

Moscow–Prague match 1946 (if 7 . . . Nxe2 8 Nxe2 Bxb2 9 Rb1 Qa5+ 10 Bd2 Qxa2 11 Rxb2 Qxb2 12 Bc3!); 752 in the SPANISH OPENING, with the idea of Be7–f8 to follow, introduced by Smyslov in 1961. Also 897, the SHOWALTER VARIATION of the EVANS GAMBIT.

Sokolov, Andrey Yuriyevich (1963–), World Junior Champion 1982, USSR Champion 1984 (+8=9), International Grandmaster (1984). The strongest tournament won by Sokolov is Montpellier Candidates 1985 (+5=8−2), a victory he shared with VAGANYAN and YUSUPOV. The following year he defeated Vaganyan (+4=4) and Yusupov (+4=7−3) in Candidates matches, but in the final, 1987, was outclassed by KARPOV. Other good results at the highest level include equal second (+1=13) Bugojno 1986, equal fourth (+3=10−2) Belfort 1986, equal fifth (+3=10−2) Rotterdam 1989, and, in a Swiss system event with 98 players, Moscow 1990, first.

Korchnoi–Sokolov Montpellier 1985 Candidates Tournament Queen's Indian Defence Nimzowitsch Variation

1 d4 Nf6 2 c4 e6 3 Nf3 b6 4 g3 Ba6 5 Nbd2 Bb7 6 Bg2 Be7 7 0–0 0–0 8 Qc2 d5 9 cxd5 exd5 10 Ne5 c5 11 Ndf3 Na6 12 Bh3 Ne4 13 Be3 Bd6 14 a3 Qe7 15 Rfd1 c4 16 Nh4 g6 17 Nef3 Bc8 18 Bxc8 Raxc8 19 Ng2 Nb8 20 Bf4 b5 21 h4 Nd7 22 Ne3 Qe6 23 Ng2 Rfe8 24 e3 Bf8 25 Nh2 Qh3 26 Nf1 Qe6 27 f3 Nef6 28 g4 a5 29 Ng3 Nb6 30 Re1 Qc6 31 h5 b4 32 axb4 axb4 33 Nh4 b3 34 Qb1 Nfd7 35 hxg6 hxg6 36 Ne2 Qf6 37 g5 Qe6 38 Kg2 Bb4 39 Rh1 Bd2 40 Qg1 Kg7 41 Qh2 Rh8 42 e4 c3 43 bxc3 b2 44 Rab1

44 . . . dxe4 45 Bxd2 exf3+ 46 Kxf3 Nc4 47 Nf4 Qc6+ 48 d5 Qa4 49 Rxb2 Nxb2 50 Be3 Ne5+ 51 Kg3 Qb3 52 Ne2 Qxd5 53 Bd4 Rh5 54 Kf4 Rxh4+ White resigns. If 55 Qxh4 Qf3+ 56 Kxe5 Nc4 mate.

Sokolov, Ivan (1968–), Yugoslav champion 1988, International Grandmaster (1987). He was equal first at Portorož 1987 and the strong Biel 1988, and third (+4=8−2) at the stronger Biel 1989.

Sokolsky Opening, 6, the ORANG UTAN OPENING. The Soviet player Alexei Pavlovich Sokolsky (1908–69) made it the subject of a monograph, *Debyut 1 b2–b4* (1963). He wrote a general openings manual, *Shakhmatny debyut* (1960), where he advocated many novelties.

Sokolsky Variation, 359 in the CATALAN OPENING, as Novotelnov–Sokolsky, Moscow 1947; 368 in the GRÜNFELD DEFENCE The idea originated with the game Sokolsky–Tolush, Omsk 1944, but there the moves 11 . . . Bg4 12 f3 were omitted. Also 500 in the SICILIAN DEFENCE; 885, attack in the EVANS GAMBIT Accepted suggested by ALAPIN in 1903, advocated by Sokolsky, and sometimes called the Shteinsapir Variation; 897, the SHOWALTER VARIATION in the same opening; 1040 in the PHILIDOR DEFENCE, as Sokolsky–Ilyin-Genevsky, match game, Leningrad 1937.

Soldatenkov Variation, 1077 in the KING'S GAMBIT Declined, a line given by LÓPEZ in 1561 but not taken seriously until played at Carlsbad 1907 by MARSHALL. The idea came from Vasily V. Soldatenkov, a Russian military attaché of the Tsarist times.

Solkoff score, an AUXILIARY SCORING METHOD used for tie-breaking in SWISS SYSTEM tournaments, and sometimes known as 'sum of opponents' scores' which is what it is. The tied player with the higher total takes the higher place. Ephraim Solkoff (1908–), an American engineer, devised this scoring method in 1949 after disappointment with his placing in a weekend tournament. Had this way of gauging the strength of the opposition been used the tie would have been broken in his favour.

solution, play that meets the STIPULATIONS of a composition and, in problems involving RETROGRADE ANALYSIS, proof that this play is LEGAL. A problem-solver may also be expected to discover SET PLAY or THEMATIC TRIES, if any; these are sometimes called part of the solution but they should be called PHASES of the problem.

solving tourney, a competition for the solving of studies or problems. In 1977 FIDE inaugurated a world chess solving contest, to be held annually; teams representing their countries are required to solve studies and problems. Since 1982, the individual making the best score has been awarded the title of World Solving Champion for the year. Other solving titles (grandmaster, master) were introduced in 1982.

Somov-Nasimovich, Yevgeny Nikolayevich (1910–42), Soviet study composer, publisher's reader. He began composing at the age of 16, but the promise he showed during the 1930s was cut short by his death in the Second World War. (See PIN STALEMATE.)

Sonneborn–Berger score, a long forgotten AUXILIARY SCORING METHOD, although the name has erroneously been transferred to the commonly used NEUSTADTL SCORE. In 1886 a London bank clerk, William Sonneborn (1843–1906), wrote to *Chess*

Monthly saying that the GELBFUHS SCORE was defective because it did not take into account the quality of the player's own results. He proposed that a player's total score, expressed as a fraction of the number of games played, should be squared and then added to his Gelbfuhs total. A year later BERGER wrote to *Deutsche Schachzeitung* proposing to alter the Neustadtl Score for the same reason and in the same manner but not using fractions. When Berger discovered that he had been anticipated by Sonneborn, the only difference in their proposals being the way of dealing with fractions, he suggested their method should be called Sonneborn–Berger. They were united in their hostility to the Neustadtl score which ironically now bears their names.

In 1891 Sonneborn again wrote to *Chess Monthly* saying that in addition to the quality of won games the quality of lost games should be taken into account; these should be calculated in the same way as won games and then the two components should be added and the won game component calculated on a percentage of the sum; this percentage is then to be applied to the total number of games played to give the final score. Whatever its merit, this method of scoring, too complicated for acceptance by the chess public, was never used.

Sørensen, Søren Anton (1840–96), Danish player and analyst, colonel in the army. Some opening lines bear his name. (See DANISH GAMBIT; FROM GAMBIT.)

Sørensen Defence, 663, a simple and reliable way of declining the DANISH GAMBIT, played in the game From–Winawer, Paris 1867.

Sørensen Gambit, 1150 in the KING'S GAMBIT Accepted.

Sosonko, Gennady Borisovich (1943–), International Grandmaster (1976). Born in Siberia, Sosonko moved to Leningrad in 1944, studied the economic geography of the capitalist countries at university, and subsequently became one of KORCHNOI's sparring partners. Sosonko played in the USSR championship in 1967, one of 126 players in the unique experiment with the Swiss system, but was only equal 27th. Not one of the supreme Soviet players, he was allowed to emigrate to Israel in 1972. He soon moved to the Netherlands where, as a professional player, he won the national championship in 1973 and, shared with TIMMAN, 1978. His best results are: Wijk aan Zee 1977, first (+5=6) equal with GELLER; Tilburg 1979, fifth (+3=5−3) equal with LARSEN, SPASSKY, and Timman; Tilburg 1980, fourth (+1=10) equal with Spassky; Tilburg 1982, third (+4=5−2) equal with ANDERSSON; Tilburg 1983, fourth (+2=8−1) equal with VAGANYAN. His best win was at Wijk aan Zee 1981 (+4=8), shared with Timman.

Timman–Sosonko   Match 1984, 1st game   Sicilian Defence

1 e4 c5 2 Nf3 d6 3 d4 cxd4 4 Nxd4 Nf6 5 Nc3 Nc6 6 Bg5 e6 7 Qd2 Be7 8 0–0–0 Nxd4 9 Qxd4 Qa5 10 f4 Qa5 11 Bc4 Bd7 12 e5 dxe5 13 fxe5 Bc6 14 h4 Rfd8 15 Qf4 Nh5 16 Qg4 Bxg5+ 17 Qxg5 g6 18 Rhf1 Rxd1+ 19 Rxd1 Qc5 20 g4 h6 21 Qxh6 Qxc4 22 gxh5 Qxh4 23 Rg1 Rd8 24 Ne2 Bf3 25 Qf4 Qxf4+ 26 Nxf4 Rd4 27 Nd3 Bxh5 28 Kd2 Re4 29 Rg2 Kg7 30 b4 b6 31 a4 Bg4 32 a5 bxa5 33 bxa5 Bf5 White resigns.

Soultanbéieff Variation, 87 in the SLAV DEFENCE, introduced in a correspondence game, Macht–Soultanbéieff, 1931–2. The Russian-born Victor Ivanovich Soultanbéieff (1895–1972) fled at the end of 1920 and a year later sought asylum in Belgium, where he remained for the rest of his life.

sound. If analysis determines that a COMBINATION cannot be faulted it is said to be sound. Players endeavour to play sound openings, but these are less susceptible to precise analysis and a VARIATION may be regarded as sound at one time and not at another. A composition is said to be sound when the STIPULATIONS can be met and there are no COOKS.

Soviet Variation, 364, the RUSSIAN VARIATION of the GRÜNFELD DEFENCE.

Sozin Attack, 469 (also called the Sozin–Velimirović Attack), variation in the SICILIAN DEFENCE played Blackburne–Paulsen, Vienna 1882, and analysed in the early years of this century by LEONHARDT, after whom it is sometimes named. It was examined by the Russian player, Veniamin Innokentevich Sozin (1896–1956), re-introduced in the game Sozin–Rokhlin, Odessa 1929, and became popular from the 1950s.

Sozin–Najdorf Attack, 504, the LIPNITSKY ATTACK in the SICILIAN DEFENCE in which the SOZIN ATTACK move, 6 Bc4, is played in the NAJDORF VARIATION.

Sozin Variation, 11 ... Nxe5 in response to the BLUMENFELD VARIATION (145) of the QUEEN'S GAMBIT Declined, introduced by Sozin in 1925, and standard play since; 1038 in the PHILIDOR DEFENCE, played Konstantinopolsky–Duz-Khotimirsky, Kiev 1938, and recommended by Sozin.

Sozin–Velimirović Attack, 469, the SOZIN ATTACK.

space, the area of the board. To gain an advantage in space is to achieve the possibility of moving one's men to more squares than are available to the opponent's men. Not all the squares 'gained' need to be controlled—they may simply be inaccessible to the opponent's men. Normally, to gain space is to gain MOBILITY, and the terms are frequently synonymous. Whether such an advantage is significant will depend on other factors, and cannot be determined merely by counting squares. In the opening a player tries to gain space in the centre, and if successful can exploit this in the middlegame.

In the endgame there are few pieces to use space, or be cramped by the lack of it, and space becomes less important, or relevant only to localized parts of the board.

Tarrasch–Marco   Vienna 1898   Petroff Defence

1 e4 e5   2 Nf3 Nf6   3 Nxe5 d6   4 Nf3 Nxe4   5 d4 Be7   6 Bd3 Nf6   7 0–0 0–0   8 h3 Be6   9 c4 c6   10 Ng5 Na6   11 Nc3 Nc7   12 f4 h6   13 Nf3

White has an advantage in space. The better to exploit this he avoids exchanges. 13 ... Qc8   14 Qc2 Rb8   15 f5 Bd7   16 Bf4 b5   17 b3 c5   18 d5 (White declines the offered pawn, preferring to leave Black's position cramped.) 18 ... b4   19 Ne2 a5   20 g4 Nh7   21 h4 Qd8   22 Bg3 a4   23 Kh1 Ra8   24 Rae1 Ne8   25 Nf4 Bf6 (Numerically, the players each control about the same number of squares, but Black's space on the queen's-side cannot be used profitably. White's mobility, however, is significantly greater, making a combination possible.) 26 Ne6 axb3   27 axb3 Qb6   28 Nxf8 Kxf8   29 g5 hxg5   30 hxg5 Nxg5   31 Qh2 Kg8   32 Nxg5 Bxg5   33 f6 g6   34 Bxg6 Black resigns.

Fischer–Petrosyan   World Championship semi-final 1971 5th match game   Petroff Defence

1 e4 e5   2 Nf3 Nf6   3 Nxe5 d6   4 Nf3 Nxe4   5 d4 Nf6   6 Bd3 Be7   7 h3 0–0   8 0–0 c6   9 Re1 Nbd7   10 Bf4 Re8   11 c4 Nf8   12 Nc3 a6

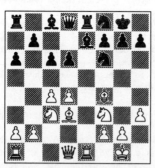

White has a small advantage in space and mobility. 13 Qb3 (Either 13 Qc2 or 13 d5 is better.) 13 ... Ne6   14 Bh2 Bf8   15 Re2 b5 (Black undermines White's central space advantage) 16 Qc2 Bb7   17 Rae1 g6   18 b4 (threatening Pc5) 18 ... bxc4   19 Bxc4 Nc7   20 Bb3 Rxe2   21 Rxe2 Ncd5   22 a3 a5   23 Nxd5 cxd5 (Black now has a central space advantage and soon gains sufficient mobility for his pieces.) 24 b5 a4   25 Ba2 Qb6   26 Qb1 Ra5 (NAJDORF suggests 26 ... Bh6)   27 Rb2 Ne4   28 Bf4 Nc3   29 Qc2 Rxb5 (29 ... Nxb5 leads to the better endgame for Black,

but it is hardly sufficient to win.) 30 Rxb5 Nxb5   31 Qxa4 Qa6   32 Qxa6 Bxa6   33 Be3 Nxa3   34 Bxd5 Bc4   35 Bc6 Nc2   36 Bd2 Be2   37 Be4 Bxf3   38 Bxc2 Drawn.

space chess, see THREE-DIMENSIONAL CHESS.

Spanish Four Knights Game, 832, FOUR KNIGHTS OPENING in which White plays the characteristic Spanish move Bf1–b5

Spanish Opening, 673, sometimes called the López, or Ruy López Opening, the most famous of all openings. White puts pressure on the centre. Black's e-pawn is not yet seriously endangered but sooner or later it must be defended or compensation obtained for its loss. Black cannot easily strike back in the centre by Pd7–d5, the usual freeing manoeuvre; indeed, any move by the d-pawn at an early stage would leave the knight on c6 pinned and immobilized. White's grip on the game has spurred the invention of many defences, some of which have been analysed to the 20th move and beyond.

The most popular choice, the CLOSE DEFENCE, 732, gives Black the option of a solid defensive game (737–752) or the MARSHALL COUNTERATTACK, 754, a pawn sacrifice to gain a powerful initiative, by no means a CLOSE GAME. The next most popular choice, the STEINITZ DEFENCE DEFERRED, 680, again offers the second player the option of an aggressive counterattack, the SIESTA VARIATION, 684. In the OPEN DEFENCE, 707, the counter-thrust Pd7–d5 is achieved at the cost of some disarray in Black's pawn formation. In all of these defences Black plays 3 ... a6, and must be prepared to meet the EXCHANGE VARIATION, 760. Without 3 ... a6 Black usually plays the BERLIN DEFENCE, 788, which may transpose into the STEINITZ DEFENCE; neither is popular.

The Spanish Opening, mentioned in the GÖTTINGEN MS, was recommended by Ruy LÓPEZ and named after his homeland. However, the opening was rarely played before the mid-1840s, when players began to understand its strategic significance. Soon the Spanish was one of the most feared openings. In an effort to improve Black's chances STEINITZ tried many experiments, without notable success, but his pioneering efforts pointed the way, and in the early years of the 20th century the Close Defence was developed by CHIGORIN and other leading masters. Although this defence has shorn the Spanish Opening of much of its terror, White retains an initiative for longer than in any other opening. (See LIPSCHÜTZ.)

Spasov, Vasily Vasiliev (1971–   ), Bulgarian player, International Grandmaster (1990). At the World Junior Championship held at Tunja, Colombia, in 1989 he was first equal with the Polish entrant, Gdanski, and won the title on tie-break. In 1990, again on a tie-break, he won the Bulgarian championship, and, at the end of the year, represented his country in the Olympiad at Novi Sad.

Spassky, Boris Vasiliyevich (1937–), International Grandmaster (1955), World Junior Champion 1955, World Champion 1969–72. Born in Leningrad, he learned chess in the Urals, where he lived during the Second World War. Meanwhile his parents divorced and he returned after the war to live with his mother, sister (later to be USSR women's draughts champion), and elder brother. Joining the chess section of the Palace of Pioneers in 1947, he spent about five hours a day on chess, trained at first by Vladimir Grigorievich Zak (1913–) and from 1951 by TOLUSH. At university he dropped mathematics for journalism ('I am not a journalist by spirit') in order to have more time for chess and outdoor sports (he could exceed his own height in the high jump). He believes that he wasted five years by studying, but he also developed a wide range of interests outside chess.

In 1955 Spassky made the first of his eleven appearances in the USSR championship, sharing third place ($+7=9-3$), and at the Göteborg interzonal qualified as a CANDIDATE. In the following year he came first ($+7=9-1$) equal with TAIMANOV (who won the play-off) and AVERBAKH, in the USSR championship, and third ($+3=13-2$) equal with BRONSTEIN, GELLER, PETROSYAN, and SZABÓ, after SMYSLOV and KERES, in the Candidates tournament at Amsterdam. In 1959 he came second ($+8=9-2$) equal with TAL, after Petrosyan, in the USSR championship, and first ($+4=6-1$), shared with Bronstein and Smyslov, in the international tournament at the Moscow Central Chess Club.

Notwithstanding these achievements Spassky relates that at this time he had no thoughts about the world championship. He noted with dismay the extreme dedication needed for continuing success. A pressing problem was the breakdown of his young marriage. 'We were like bishops of opposite colour', he remarked, and in 1961 he was divorced. Nor had he been able to make a satisfactory relationship with Tolush, his trainer. 'I had no one to turn to at this time except my mother.' He respected Tolush who had shown him that, besides strategy, chess had something extra, 'attacks, sacrifices, creative ideas', but he needed a friend. He found one in BONDAREVSKY, who became his trainer in 1961 and whose encouragement was the foundation of Spassky's later successes. His climb to the top began with five excellent firsts: USSR championship, Baku 1961 ($+10=9-1$); USSR championship, Leningrad 1963 ($+5=14$), equal with STEIN (who won the play-off) and KHOLMOV; Belgrade 1964 ($+9=8$); Moscow zonal tournament 1964 ($+4=6-2$), ahead of Stein, KORCHNOI, and Geller; Amsterdam interzonal 1964 ($+13=8-2$), equal with LARSEN, Smyslov, and Tal. A Candidate for the second time, Spassky defeated Keres ($+4=4-2$), Geller ($+3=5$), and Tal ($+4=6-1$) to become challenger. He lost the match against Petrosyan in 1966 by the narrowest of margins ($+3=17-4$).

At Santa Monica in the same year Spassky again won a top-level tournament ($+5=13$), ahead of FISCHER, Larsen, and Petrosyan. Victories at Beverwijk 1967 ($+7=8$) and Sochi 1967 ($+5=10$) were followed by a series of Candidates matches in which he defeated Geller ($+3=5$), Larsen ($+4=3-1$), and Korchnoi ($+4=5-1$); and in 1969 he defeated Petrosyan ($+6=13-4$) to become world champion.

A posed photograph taken at the Lloyds Bank tournament, London 1984. Spassky, on the right, faces Short, the world's youngest grandmaster at the time. Looking on is 12-year old Adams, soon to become the world's youngest grandmaster himself.

Spassky–Keres Candidates match 1965 5th game Spanish Opening Close Defence

1 e4 e5 2 Nf3 Nc6 3 Bb5 a6 4 Ba4 Nf6 5 0–0 Be7 6 Re1 b5 7 Bb3 d6 8 c3 0–0 9 h3 Na5 10 Bc2 c5 11 d4 Qc7 12 Nbd2 Bd7 13 Nf1 cxd4 14 cxd4 Rac8 15 Ne3 Rfe8 16 b3 exd4 17 Nxd4 Bf8 18 Bb2 Qd8 19 Ndf5 Bxf5 20 Nxf5 g6 21 Ne3 Bg7 22 Qd2 Nb7

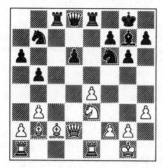

23 b4 Qe7 24 f3 Qf8 25 Bb3 Nd8 26 Rad1 Rc6 27 Rc1 Qe7 28 Kh2 Qd7 29 Nd5 Nxd5 30 Bxd5 Rxc1 31 Rxc1 Qe7 32 Bxg7 Kxg7 33 Qc3+ Kg8 34 f4 Ne6 35 g3 Ng7 36 Qc7 Qf6 37 Rc2 Rf8 38 Qb6 g5 39 fxg5 Qxg5 40 Qxa6 Qe5 41 Qxb5 Ne6 42 Qf1 Kg7 43 Qf5 Keres sealed 43 . . . Qxf5 but resigned during the adjournment.

Naturally polite, with a friendly disposition, Spassky liked to meet people and became one of the most popular of all champions. Of athletic build, 'the most handsome champion since Capablanca', he charmed the ladies, too. (He had re-married in 1966.) His style of play, which has been compared to ALEKHINE'S, was, BOTVINNIK said, universal: he played every kind of game, and his games were often characterized by lively tactics. In 1970 he had two fine victories, Leiden (+2=10) and Amsterdam (+8=7), equal with POLUGAYEVSKY. In the 1972 world championship match, however, he could not withstand Fischer's fierce onslaught: although he fought valiantly to the end, he lost the title. In spite of his outward calm, his poker face at the board, he felt keenly the heavy responsibility of defending his country's prestige.

Faced with hostility in his homeland as a consequence of losing his title he responded by again winning the USSR championship in 1973 (+7=9−1). A Candidate in 1974, he defeated BYRNE (+3=3) and then lost to KARPOV in the semi-final. His second marriage having ended in divorce, he married a French diplomat in 1975 and went to live in Paris, retaining his Soviet citizenship. A Candidate for the fifth time in 1977, he defeated HORT (+2=13−1) and PORTISCH (+4=9−2) but lost the final match to Korchnoi.

His play may have lost some of its sparkle, and his natural laziness inclined him to accept peaceful draws, but he remained a player of the highest class. In 1980 he drew (+1=12−1) a Candidates match with Portisch but was eliminated because Portisch's victory was with the Black pieces while his was with White. In tournaments he was at Bugojno 1978,

first (+6=8−1) equal with Karpov; Baden 1980, first (+6=9) equal with BELYAVSKY; Linares 1983, first (+3=7); Brussels 1985, second (+8=5), after Korchnoi; Reggio Emilia 1986–7, second (+1=10) shared with CHERNIN, Hort, and Smyslov, after RIBLI; Wellington 1988, first (+5=5) shared with CHANDLER.

Spassky played for the USSR in seven Olympiads from 1962 to 1978, and for France from 1984.

B Cafferty, *Spassky's 100 Best Games* (1972) also contains a biography.

Spassky Variation, 575 in the CARO–KANN DEFENCE, introduced in Chajes–Réti, Carlsbad 1923. In a game against LIBERZON in the 1960 USSR championship, SPASSKY followed the same plan. Earlier players such as CHAROUSEK and LASKER played 8 Bd3.

Also 421 in the KING'S INDIAN DEFENCE, as Donner–Spassky, Göteborg 1955; 333, the LENINGRAD VARIATION of the NIMZO-INDIAN DEFENCE.

Speckmann, Werner (1913–), German composer and author, International Judge of Chess Compositions (1959), International Master for Chess Compositions (1967), magistrate. He specializes in orthodox two- and three-movers, and especially in miniatures and WENIGSTEINERS. His book *Strategie im Schachproblem* (1958) includes 242 of his miniatures, while *Das logische Schachproblem* (1965) is a significant examination of more-movers. He has also composed a few studies, and among his many other books is *Meisterwerke der Endspielkunst*, devoted to the works of GURVICH. Speckmann was problem editor of *Deutsche Schachzeitung* from 1963 until the magazine folded in 1988.

#6

A problem by Speckmann, second prize, *Schach*, 1981. After the key 1 Ne6 (not 1 Nd5? Kh3) two variations lead to chameleon echo mates: 1 . . . Kh3 2 Ng5+ Kg2 3 Ne4 Bf5 4 Qxf5 Kh2 5 Qf2+, or 1 . . . d3 2 Ng5 Kh5 3 Nf7 Kg6 4 Ne5+ Kg7 5 Qf7+.

speed chess, sometimes used synonymously with ALLEGRO, but often with the time limit reduced from thirty minutes to twenty-five minutes for each player, a reduction that has been found to produce games more suitable for television programmes. Occasionally the term is used to describe games limited to five or ten minutes for each player.

Speelman, Jonathan Simon (1956–), British champion 1978, 1985, and 1986, International Grandmaster (1980). He had a number of good results in the early 1980s: London 1980, fourth (+5=5−3) equal with SOSONKO, after MILES, ANDERSSON, and KORCHNOI; Maribor 1980, second (+6=7); Dortmund 1981, first (+5=6) equal with FTÁČNIK and KUZMIN; Hastings 1981–2, second equal with SMYSLOV, after KUPREICHIK; London 1982, fourth (+2=10−1) equal with LJUBOJEVIĆ, TIMMAN, and PORTISCH, after Andersson and KARPOV; and Hastings 1983–4, first (+5=7−1) equal with KARLSSON. His play became even more impressive after a long-standing eye problem had been treated; Hastings 1986–7, first equal with CHANDLER, LARSEN, and LPUTYAN; Bath zonal 1987, first (+8=2); Beersheba 1987, first (+6=5) equal with Korchnoi; Subotica interzonal 1987, first (+7=7−1) equal with SAX and SHORT, ahead of TAL and RIBLI.

This last performance made Speelman a CANDIDATE, and after winning matches in 1988 against SEIRAWAN (+3=2) and Short (+2=3), he went down to Timman in the semi-final in 1989. Meanwhile his tournament successes continued: Hastings 1987–8, second (+4=9−1), behind Short; Amsterdam (OHRA) 1989, second (+1=9) equal with Korchnoi, after BELYAVSKY; Linares 1991, fourth with YUSUPOV, after IVANCHUK, KASPAROV, and Belyavsky. Seeded through to the 1991 Candidates cycle, Speelman was knocked out by Short. He played in every Olympiad 1980–90. An excellent analyst, Speelman has written several books, among them *Analysing the Endgame* (1988). (See BREVITY; SEVENTH RANK ABSOLUTE.)

Psakhis–Speelman   Hastings 1987–8 Brilliancy Prize
Queen's Gambit Accepted

1 d4 d5 2 c4 dxc4 3 Nf3 c5 4 d5 e6 5 Nc3 exd5 6 Qxd5 Qxd5 7 Nxd5 Bd6 8 Nd2 Ne7 9 Nxc4 Nxd5 (Black cedes the two bishops, but gains in development, soon commanding the open file.) 10 Nxd6+ Ke7 11 Nxc8+ Rxc8 12 g3 Nc6 13 Bg2 Rd8 14 Bg5+ f6 15 Bd2 Rd6 16 0–0 Rad8 17 Rfc1 b6 18 Kf1 a5 19 Be1 g6 20 Rab1 Ndb4 21 a3

21 ... Na2 22 Rc4 Nd4 23 b3 (if 23 Ra1 Nb3 24 Rxa2 Rd1) 23 ... Nb5 24 Rb2 Nac3 25 a4 Nd1 26 Rb1 Na3 27 Rcc1 Nxb1 28 Rxb1 f5 29 Bb7 g5 30 Ba6 f4 31 Bd3 Rxd3 32 exd3 Rxd3 33 Ke2 Rd5 34 gxf4 gxf4 35 Rc1 Nb2 36 Bc3 Nd3 37 Rg1 Nb4 38 Rg7+ Kf8 39 Bb2 Rd3 White resigns.

Spence, Jack Lee (1926–78), American lawyer who rescued many tournaments from oblivion by publishing duplicated books containing their games. He was twice champion of Nebraska (where he lived all his life), but it is for his books, approaching 100 in number, that he is remembered.

Spielmann, Rudolf (1883–1942), Viennese professional player who spent most of his adult life in Germany until, as a Jew, he fled from the Nazis, and spent the last three years of his life in Sweden. He played in more than 100 tournaments and more than 50 matches.

At St Petersburg 1909 he shared third place with DURAS, after LASKER and RUBINSTEIN. He won the Abbazia tournament 1912, in which everyone had to play the KING'S GAMBIT Accepted, and was called the last knight of the King's Gambit by TARTAKOWER. In the same year Spielmann came second (+8=8−3) equal with NIMZOWITSCH, after Rubinstein, at San Sebastián. After the First World War, during which Spielmann served in the Austrian army, his first major success was Stockholm 1919, first (+6=3−3) in a quadrangular contest with BOGOLJUBOW, RÉTI, and Rubinstein. In 1922 he was second (+11=7) equal with ALEKHINE, after Bogoljubow, at Piešťany, and first (+6=6−1) equal with Réti, ahead of Rubinstein, at Teplice-Šanov.

Spielmann was not a follower of the HYPERMODERN movement that was so popular at the time. He sought an open game, preferring direct attack against the enemy king. With a reputation as one of the world's best masters of attack, he admitted that his combinative play was often intuitive, not fully calculated. If this approach let him down he tended to lose confidence, and a fine tournament success could be followed by dismal failure. He attempted to eliminate the defects of his style, improving his judgement of attacking possibilities, his endgame skill, and his technique, with some success, and in the late 1920s he could be ranked among the world's top ten. During this period he had outstanding results in three major tournaments: Semmering 1926, first (+10=6−1), ahead of Alekhine, VIDMAR, Nimzowitsch, and Rubinstein; Berlin (Oct.) 1928, third (+3=7−2), after CAPABLANCA and Nimzowitsch; Carlsbad 1929, second (+11=7−3) equal with Capablanca, whom he defeated, after Nimzowitsch, ahead of Rubinstein, EUWE, Vidmar, and Bogoljubow. His later results were less impressive.

Spielmann's match career included many victories against strong opponents: LEONHARDT 1906 (+6=5−4); Nimzowitsch 1908 (+4=1−1); MIESES 1910 (+5=2−1); Réti 1910 (+4=1) and 1921 (+3=3); Tartakower 1910 (+3=2−1) and 1921 (+3=1−2); STÅHLBERG 1930 (+4=1−1);

STOLTZ 1930 (+3=1−2) and 1932 (+4=1−1); PIRC 1931 (+3=6−1); Bogoljubow 1932 (+4=2−3); and Euwe 1935 (a training match, +4=4−2).

In contrast to the aggressiveness of his play Spielmann was a man of mild temperament and friendly disposition, although a great complainer. He regarded the game as an art, the beauty subsisting in SACRIFICE and combinative play. The best of his few books, *Richtig opfern!* (1935), was translated as *The Art of Sacrifice* and published in the same year. He contributed to the last edition of Bilguer's HANDBUCH and was a co-author of the last edition of COLLIJN's *Lärobok*. (See DOUBLE CHECK.)

J. L. Spence, *The Chess Career of Rudolph Spielmann* (3 vols., 1969–74), contains 242 games.

Spielmann–Grünfeld Teplice-Šanov 1922 Bishop's Gambit

1 e4 e5 2 f4 exf4 3 Bc4 Nc6 4 Nf3 g5 5 0–0 d6 6 d4 Bg7 7 c3 h6 8 g3 g4 9 Nh4 f3 10 Nd2 Bf6 11 Ndxf3 gxf3 12 Qxf3 Rh7 13 Ng6 Rg7 14 Nf4 Bg4 15 Qg2 Bg5 16 h3 Bd7 17 Nh5 Rh7 18 e5 dxe5 19 Qe4 f5

20 Rxf5 Bxf5 21 Qxf5 Re7 22 Bxg5 hxg5 23 Rf1 Qd6 24 Bxg8 exd4 25 Qf8+ Kd7 26 Qxa8 Qc5 27 Nf6+ Kd6 28 Qf8 Qe5 29 Kg2 d3 30 Rf2 Qe1 31 Qh6 Black resigns.

Spielmann Attack, 1178, also known as the Réti Variation, an unusual response to the FRENCH DEFENCE suggested by KIESERITZKY c.1848, introduced by Mongrédien at London 1862, and played in Spielmann–Müller, Vienna 1928, and Spielmann–Grau, San Remo 1930, as well as Réti–Maróczy, Göteborg 1920.

Spielmann Counterattack, 586 in the CARO–KANN DEFENCE, played with disastrous results in the game Botvinnik–Spielmann, Moscow 1935: 1 c4 c6 2 e4 d5 3 exd5 cxd5 4 d4 Nf6 5 Nc3 Nc6 6 Bg5 Qb6 7 cxd5 Qxb2 8 Rc1 Nb4 9 Na4 Qxa2 10 Bc4 Bg4 11 Nf3 Bxf3 12 gxf3 Black resigns.

Spielmann Variation, 304, also known as the Alekhine Variation, in the NIMZO-INDIAN DEFENCE, played three times by SPIELMANN at the Carlsbad tournament, 1929; but known since the game Grünfeld–Sämisch, Vienna 1922; 308, five moves further

in the same variation, the original idea behind Spielmann's 304.

Also 352, the BLUMENFELD VARIATION, and 355, which may arise from it and was played in the game Kmoch–Spielmann, Semmering 1926; 569 in the CARO–KANN DEFENCE, a move that received no support until played by LUTIKOV in the 1960 USSR championship (3 ... d4 4 Bc4 Nf6 5 e5); 629 in the VIENNA GAME, dating from Mason–Bardeleben, Nuremberg 1896; 834 in the SPANISH FOUR KNIGHTS GAME, as Schlechter–Spielmann, Breslau 1912, but an earlier example is Bardeleben–Zukertort, Leipzig 1877; 1225 in the FRENCH DEFENCE, as Bogoljubow–Spielmann, Vienna 1922; 1251 in the ALEKHINE DEFENCE, from the third match game Spielmann–Landau 1933, anticipated by Mieses–Colle, Frankfurt 1930.

Spike Opening, 1322, graphic name for the GROB OPENING.

spite check, a check given as a means of delaying the checkmate of the player's king or decisive loss of material, and usually having no other purpose. However, on occasion, a SWINDLE may lurk within. (See ATKINS; FTÁČNIK; VAGANYAN.)

sponsor, see PATRONAGE.

spot, an American slang term for giving odds, as in 'to spot someone a pawn'.

Spraggett, Kevin Berry (1954–), Canadian champion 1984, Commonwealth champion 1984 (shared with CHANDLER) and 1985 (shared with Thipsay), International Grandmaster (1985).

Spraggett–Yusupov Candidates match 1989 2nd game Réti Opening

1 Nf3 d5 2 g3 Nf6 3 Bg2 Bf5 4 c4 e6 5 0–0 Be7 6 b3 0–0 7 Bb2 h6 8 d3 Bh7 9 Nbd2 Nc6 10 a3 a5 11 cxd5 exd5 12 Qc2 Nd7 13 Bh3 Re8 14 Rfe1 Nf8 15 Rac1 Ne6 16 Qb1 Bf6 17 Qa1 Bxb2 18 Qxb2 Qd6 19 Rb1 Nc5 20 Bf1 Bf5 21 Rec1 Na6 22 Rc2 Re7 23 Rbc1 Rae8 24 e3 Bh7 25 Nb1 Rd8 26 Be2 d4 27 e4 f5 28 exf5 Bxf5 29 Bf1 Qd7 30 Nbd2 Rf8

31 Rxc6 bxc6 32 Nxd4 Nb8 33 Nxf5 Qxf5 34 Ne4 Nd7 35 Rxc6 Ne5 36 Rc5 Nf3+ 37 Kh1 Qg6 38 Rxa5 Qb6 39 b4 Nxh2 40 Qb3+ Kh7 41 Kxh2 Rxf2+ 42 Bg2 Rf8

43 Rc5 Kh8 44 a4 Qg6 45 a5 Qg4 46 Qc2 c6 47 a6 Rb8
48 Rxc6 Qh5+ 49 Kg1 Rxb4 50 Rc8+ Kh7 51 d4 Qf5
52 g4 Qg6 53 Nf6+ gxf6 54 Rh8+ Black resigns.

He created some surprise when, in the Taxco interzonal 1985, he qualified as a CANDIDATE, but in the ensuing tournament at Montpellier he finished last. In the next cycle he again qualified. This time the Candidates tournament had been abolished, and in 1988 he met SOKOLOV. After a level match (+1=6−1) the tie-break was resolved by 15-minute games. The first was drawn, Spraggett won the second and then met YUSUPOV in the quarter-finals in 1989. Again the fixed length match was drawn (+1=6−1), but Spraggett lost the quick-play tie-breaker. Outside the world championship events he has had few major successes, a victory at Quebec 1986 being one of them.

spurious games, games that are partly or wholly unauthentic. Many have been invented for teaching purposes, such as those in GRECO's manuscripts or PHILIDOR's books. There are several instances of genuine games being falsely attributed to famous persons, and at least three such games are said to have been played by Napoleon (see KENNEDY; TURK). Players who no longer have a chance of winning a prize sometimes concoct a game to create some sort of record or to show brilliant ideas, and they play out the moves when they meet in a tournament. This is such an example from the Portuguese Junior Championship 1978. José Silva–João Rafael.

1 a3 h6 2 b3 g6 3 c3 f6 4 d3 e6 5 e3 d6 6 f3 c6
7 g3 b6 8 h3 a6 9 a4 b5 10 a5 b4 11 c4 d5 12 c5
d4 13 e4 f5 14 e5 f4 15 g4 h5 16 g5 h4 17 Nc3
dxc3 18 Ra3 bxa3 19 b4 Nf6 20 exf6 Rh6 21
gxh6 g5 22 b5 g4 23 b6 g3 24 d4 c5 25 Bb5 axb5
26 d5 Bg4 27 hxg4 e4 28 d6 e3 29 Qd5 cxd5 30
Ne2 d4 31 Nxd4 Be7 32 dxe7 Qxe7 33 Bb2 Qe4
34 fxe4 cxb2 35 a6 b4 36 Nc2 b3 37 Ke2 bxc2
38 Rd1 Nd7 39 g5 Rc8 40 g6 Rc7 41 bxc7 Nb6
42 cxb6 h3 43 Rd7 Kxd7 44 Kd3 Ke6 45 e5 Kf5
46 Kc4 Ke4 47 Kc5 Kd3 48 Kd6 Kd2 49 Kd7
Kd1 50 Kd8 f3 51 g7 g2 52 h7 a2 53 f7 h2 54
b7 f2 55 a7 e2 56 e6 Kd2 57 e7 Kd1 58 a8=R
h1=R 59 b8=N g1=N 60 c8=B f1=B 61
e8=Q e1=Q 62 f8=B c1=B 63 g8=N b1=N
64 h8=R a1=R Draw agreed.

More justifiably, games for LIVING CHESS displays are usually pre-arranged: the spectators expect fast play, and the actors need to be trained.

Sometimes a player alters a game score to make the finish more interesting. Doubtless believing in artistic licence, ALEKHINE altered several of his games in this way. His conduct regarding the famous five queens game (see GRIGORIEV VARIATION) is more reprehensible.

A few players have published games they falsely claim to have won against a leading master. Such fraudsters may have analysed with masters and selected variations which they claim were victories. Thus Frederick Horace Deacon (1830–75) claimed wins against both MORPHY and STEINITZ. Prince Dadian of Mongrelia was probably the worst offender. He published many short and brilliant games against masters, paying them handsomely. After CHIGORIN declined to collaborate in such a fraud he was refused entry to the Monte Carlo tournament, 1903, for which Dadian was the sponsor. (See RICE GAMBIT for another example of misused patronage.)

Claims that a study has occurred in play are almost certainly untrue. The chances of this happening are infinitesimal. Editors of chess columns and popular works share the guilt for this kind of plagiarism: they like to say that a clever finish is from a game to attract readers who would not bother to examine a composition as such. A composer or player may discover an amusing piece of play that lacks the merit of a good study, and may publish it as a real game ending. See, for example, Labone's endgame under FAMILY CHECK.

This position, published in *Teplitz-Schönauer Anzeiger*, Oct. 1921, was said to be the finish of a game played in Berlin. After 1 Rxa6+ Kxa6 2 Kxh8 h5 White resigned, when an on-looking master pointed out the draw by 3 Kg7 (see the study under RÉTI, published anonymously a month earlier in *Deutschösterreichische Tages-Zeitung*). Whoever perpetrated this plagiarism had little talent. By placing the white rook on a7 instead of a5 only 1 Rxa6+ draws for White, whereas in the diagram position White wins by 1 Kxh8.

The following game, famous on account of its brilliant finish with many threats of BACK-RANK MATES, was allegedly played between E. Z. Adams

(White) and C. TORRE at New Orleans in 1920, and was published in the *American Chess Bulletin*, 1925. Philidor Defence.

1 e4 e5 2 Nf3 d6 3 d4 exd4 4 Qxd4 Nc6 5 Bb5 Bd7 6 Bxc6 Bxc6 7 Nc3 Nf6 8 0–0 Be7 9 Nd5 Bxd5 10 exd5 0–0 11 Bg5 c6 12 c4 cxd5 13 cxd5 Re8 14 Rfe1 a5 15 Re2 Rc8 16 Rae1 Qd7 17 Bxf6 Bxf6

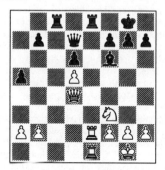

18 Qg4 Qb5 19 Qc4 Qd7 20 Qc7 Qb5 21 a4 Qxa4 22 Re4 Qb5 23 Qxb7 Black resigns. Research by BRANDRETH in 1982 strongly suggests that this was a spurious game, an invention by Torre who nominated his teacher and friend, Edwin Ziegler Adams (1885–1944), the winner. (See PLAGIARISM.)

square, see BOARD.

square of the pawn, see QUADRANT.

square vacation, a composition term: the removal of a man from a square, usually so that it may be occupied by another man. (See RUSINEK.)

#3

A problem by VUKCEVICH, first prize, *The Problemist*, 1981. The key is 1 Bb6, threatening 2 Qg6 with the idea of vacating a square for White's e-pawn or for the knight at c3.

1 ... Rf5   2 Qf4
1 ... Nf5   2 Qh4
1 ... e5   2 Qf5.

squeeze, a term used in this book for a position in which one player (but not both) would be at a disadvantage if under the obligation to move. This is distinct from what (in this book) is called a ZUGZWANG (or by some authorities, a reciprocal zugzwang). For example, the position White Kc7, Be2, Pb6; Black Kc5, Bc8 is a squeeze. If Black has to move, the pawn is soon promoted; but White, having to move, is at no disadvantage, for a WAITING MOVE (e.g. Bd3) maintains the squeeze, and White still wins. (If the position were moved two files to the east, Black, too, would have waiting moves, and the game would be drawn.)

For practical purposes zugzwangs and squeezes occur only in the endgame; both are characterized by the absence of direct threats, both are abnormal in the sense that for the greater part of a game players want to gain rather than lose time.

A position given by BERGER (1890). Only Black, who is in a squeeze, is at a disadvantage on account of having to move. Were it White's turn to play then 1 Qd8+ Kb7 2 Qd5+ Kb8 3 Qd7 LOSES THE MOVE. The object of the squeeze is to force Black to move the rook from its safe position. Black to move, 1 ... Rh6 (1 ... Ka8 2 Qc8+ Rb8 3 Qc6+ Rb7 4 Kd6 and White wins the pawn or checkmates.) 2 Qe8+ Kb7 3 Qe7+ Ka6 4 Qg7 Re6 5 Qd7 Rb6 (White now loses the move to set up another squeeze, again forcing the rook to move away.) 6 Qc8+ Ka5 7 Qc7 Ka6 8 Qd7 (the squeeze) 8 ... Rb2 9 Qd3+ Kb7 10 Qf3+ Kc8 11 Qf8+ Kb7 12 Qg7+ and wins.

Ståhlberg, Anders Gideon Tom (1908–67), International Grandmaster (1950), International Arbiter (1951), Swedish player who ranked among the world's best ten for a few years around 1950. In the 1930s he had two good match victories, against SPIELMANN in 1933 (+3=4−1) and against NIMZOWITSCH in 1934 (+4=2−2), and two good tournament results: Dresden 1936, third (+4=3−2) equal with MARÓCZY, after ALEKHINE and Engels; and Stockholm 1937, second (+4=5) after FINE. In 1938 he drew a match against KERES (+2=4−2). From 1929 to 1939 Ståhlberg held the Swedish championship continuously, and played for his country in seven Olympiads. After the last of these, Buenos Aires 1939, when war had begun in Europe, he remained in Argentina, where he achieved three notable tournament wins: Mar del Plata 1941 (+9=8), ahead of NAJDORF and ELISKASES; Buenos

Aires 1941, a double-round event ($+9=4-1$) tied with Najdorf; and Buenos Aires 1947 ($+6=4$), ahead of Najdorf, Eliskases, and EUWE.

In 1948 Ståhlberg returned to Europe, and in the next five years he achieved several good results in tournament play: Saltsjöbaden 1948, an interzonal, sixth ($+4=13-2$) equal, to become a CANDIDATE; Budapest 1950, a great Candidates event, seventh; Amsterdam 1950, third ($+9=9-1$), after Najdorf and RESHEVSKY; Budapest 1952, third ($+7=8-2$) equal with BOTVINNIK and SMYSLOV, after Keres and GELLER; and the interzonal at Saltsjöbaden 1952, equal fifth, again qualifying as a Candidate. He made only a modest score in the Candidates tournament of 1953; in his mid-forties, he was now overtaken by a new generation of strong players. However, he continued to play in Olympiads (1952 to 1966) and other international events, and was chief arbiter in five world championship matches (1957–63). In Leningrad to take part in a tournament, he collapsed and died before play began.

A linguist, a man of wide interests, Ståhlberg liked good living, and he also liked other games, such as contract bridge at which he excelled. His most popular book *Schack och schackmästare* (1937) was revised in 1952 and translated into English as *Chess and Chessmasters* (1955). He also wrote an autobiographical collection, *I kamp med världseliten* (1958), which includes 53 of his games.

Ståhlberg–Petrosyan   Budapest 1952   Benko Gambit
1 d4 Nf6 2 Nf3 c5 3 d5 b5 4 Bg5 Qa5+ 5 c3 Ne4 6 Nbd2 Nxg5 7 Nxg5 h6 8 Nf3 d6 9 e4 Nd7 10 a4 bxa4 11 Rxa4 Qc7 12 Qa1 Nb6 13 Bb5+ Bd7 14 Bxd7+ Qxd7 15 Ra6 Nc8 16 0–0 e5 17 dxe6 fxe6 18 Nh4 Kf7 19 f4 Qd8 20 Nhf3 Qe8 21 f5 exf5 22 Qa2+ Qe6

23 Ne5+ Ke7 24 Nc6+ Kd7 25 Qa4 Ke8 26 exf5 Qe3+ 27 Kh1 Black resigns.

Ståhlberg Variation, 11 ... Nxe5 (SOZIN VARIATION) 12 Nxe5 axb5 13 Qf3, from the BLUMENFELD VARIATION (145) of the MERAN VARIATION, originated by Luis Alberto Gulla of Uruguay, who published a game in *El Ajedrez Americano*, 1928. Used by STÅHLBERG in his 5th match game against SPIELMANN in 1933, the line became popular after the game Capablanca–Levenfish, Moscow 1935.
Also 306 in the NIMZO-INDIAN DEFENCE, first played in Winter–Sultan Khan, Hastings 1930–1; 1217 in the FRENCH DEFENCE as in the game Besruchko–Ståhlberg, Kemeri 1939.

staircase movement, a manœuvre in which a queen, rook, or king is moved in a diagonal direction by means of short orthogonal moves.

+

A study by M. Platov, *Vechernyaya Moskva*, 1927. 1 Nb6+ Ka7 2 Nc8+ Qxc8 3 Bg1+ Ka8 4 Kd4+ (the staircase movement begins here) 4 ... Ka7 5 Ke4+ Ka8 6 Ke3+ Ka7 7 Kf3+ Ka8 8 Kf2+ Ka7 9 Ke1+. (See the first game under ALEKHINE.)

stakes. In the 18th and 19th centuries chess, like many competitive events, was a vehicle for gambling. Wagers were placed, and matches were usually played for stakes raised by sponsors, the victor receiving part, perhaps half, of the winnings. When STANLEY played ROUSSEAU in 1845, in a match that is seen as perhaps the first national championship, the stakes were $1,000. In 1843 STAUNTON played SAINT-AMANT for stakes of £100. In 1858 MORPHY defeated LÖWENTHAL, then struggling to earn a living at chess, and used the £100 he had won to furnish Löwenthal's house. Most of STEINITZ's matches were played for stakes, and he gave stake-odds of 4:3, probably raising his own money, against BIRD in 1866. That the winner should take all became unacceptable as the number of professional players increased, and in all important matches since 1886 the losers have received some payment.

stale, an old word for stalemate; to give or to undergo stalemate. 'They stand at a stay: Like a Stale at Chesse, where is no Mate, but yet the game cannot Stirre' (Bacon, *Essayes*, 1625).

stalemate, a position in which a player whose turn it is to move is neither in check nor able to make a move; to put a player in such a position. Stalemate ends the game, which is then drawn. (Neither player can subsequently lose on time.)

In practice stalemate occurs only in the endgame, a drawing resource for the defender. (See BISHOP OF THE WRONG COLOUR for one of the best-known examples.) The following positions, given in FORSYTH NOTATION, show some of the basic endgames which are drawn by stalemate regardless of whose turn it is to play:

K7/2k5/P7/40. 1 a7 Kc8, or 1 Ka7 Kc8 2 Kb6 Kb8
3 a7 + Ka8 4 Ka6.
k7/1p1K4/1P6/40. 1 Kc8 or 1 Kc7. Add a white
bishop and the position is still drawn.
k7/B2K4/1P6/40. (Paulsen–Metger, Nuremberg
1888) 1 Kc6 or 1 Kc7, or 1 Bb8 Kxb8 2 Kc6 Kc8
3 b7 + Kb8 4 Kb6.
8/4K1k1/6Pp/7P/32. (Najdorf–Kotov, Saltsjöbaden interzonal 1948) 1 Ke6 Kh8 2 Kf6 Kg8 3 g7
Kh7 4 Kf7.

Belyavsky–Christiansen Reggio Emilia 1987–8 Catalan
Opening

1 d4 Nf6 2 c4 e6 3 g3 Bb4+ 4 Bd2 Qe7 5 Bg2 Bxd2+
6 Qxd2 d6 7 Nc3 0–0 8 Nf3 e5 9 0–0 Re8 10 e4 Bg4 11
d5 Bxf3 12 Bxf3 Nbd7 13 b4 a5 14 a3 Ra6 15 Nb5 Nb6
16 Rac1 axb4 17 axb4 Qd7 18 Qd3 Ra4 19 Qb3 Rea8
20 Rfd1 h5 21 h4 g6 22 Rb1 Ng4 23 Be2 Qe7 24 Rbc1
c6 25 dxc6 bxc6 26 c5 dxc5 27 bxc5 Nd7 28 Nd6 Ndf6
29 Bc4 Nxf2 30 Kxf2 Ra3 31 Bxf7+ Kg7 32 Qe6 Ra2+
33 Kg1 R8a3 34 Ne8+ Kh6 35 Nxf6 Rxg3+ 36 Kh1

36 ... Qxf7 37 Rd7 Qxf6 38 Qxf6 Rh2 + Draw agreed.
White (who could have won by 38 Rh7 +) takes care to
avoid perpetual check but overlooks the stalemate after 39
Kxh2 Rg2 +.

Stalemate often comes as a surprise, and is a
familiar theme for study composers; for examples,
see DESPERADO; KAZANTSEV; KRALIN; MIRROR STALE-
MATE; PIN-STALEMATE.

Attitudes towards stalemate have varied over the
centuries. In some eastern countries it is not
allowed, and it cannot occur in SHOGI. It was said by
LUCENA to be an inferior win for the player giving it.
In 1614 SAUL said, 'You shall understand a stale is a
lost game by him that giveth it, and no question to
be made further ther-of', for he regarded it as a
dishonourable thing to give. Despite PHILIDOR'S
efforts this remained the rule in England until,
under SARRATT's influence, it was given as a draw in
the London Chess Club laws of 1807, which
remained for half a century the *de facto* standard.

Stamma, Phillip (*fl.* mid-1700s), chessplayer from
Aleppo, possibly of Greek origin. In Paris he published *Essai sur le jeu des échecs* (1737), a book
containing 100 problems. Unable to make a livelihood in France, he travelled to London where he
played chess at the fashionable Slaughter's coffee-
house. Influential friends, notably Lord Harr-

ington, previously BERTIN'S patron, secured him the
appointment of Interpreter of Oriental Languages,
by Royal Warrant dated 14 August 1739 and signed
by George II, a post carrying the salary of £80 a
year. In 1745 he published *The Noble Game of
Chess*, dedicated to Lord Harrington, and containing the same 100 problems plus 74 opening variations. Still in London in 1747, he played and lost a
match against PHILIDOR; these two also played the
Duke of Rutland's Chess (see GREAT CHESS) at
which Philidor again proved the better player.
Stamma's subsequent whereabouts are not known.
He may have travelled to Oxford around 1764, for
JONES mentioned that at this time he invited a
Syrian from London to teach him Arabic.

Of the game Stamma writes: 'If you bring out
your pieces too soon, before you have opened their
Road, they will confine your *Pawns*, and croud
your Game ... in general it is best to bring out your
Pieces under the Protection of your *Pawns* ...'. He
advocates both the QUEEN'S GAMBIT and the BIRD
ATTACK. He gives a few interesting facts about the
old game with which he was familiar in his youth,
and from which, perhaps, he derived his positional
approach to the game. His were the first books of
the modern game in which a version of STANDARD
NOTATION was used.

Stamma's 100 problems are not problems in the
modern sense, for there is no requirement to solve
them in a given number of moves. They owe
nothing to European problem tradition, and are
best described as MANṢŪBĀT. They have been
reprinted many times, most recently in 1979,
usually with the added stipulations of 'mate in *n*
moves'. In this form many were cooked, and
Stamma thus unfairly criticized. (See PROBLEM HIS-
TORY.)

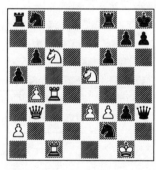

+

A position that is no. 2 of Stamma's 100. White is to
play and win. 1 Rh4 Qxh4 2 Qg8+ Kxg8 3
Ne7+ Kh8 4 Nf7+ Rxf7 5 Rc8+ and mates. If
1 ... Qf5, 2 e4 Qg5 (2 ... Nh3+ 3 Kg2 Nf4+ 4
Rxf4 Qxf4 5 Qg8+ etc.) 3 Qg8+ etc.

Stamma Gambit, 1176, a method of playing the
KING'S GAMBIT Accepted, recommended by STAMMA
in 1745 but supported by no master. It is sometimes

called the Calvi Variation, or Rook's Pawn Gambit.

standard notation, a method of recording the moves of the game, sometimes known as CO-ORDINATE NOTATION (of which it is an example), algebraic notation (a foolish name; algebra is not involved), or, more rarely, continental notation. The FILES are identified alphabetically, RANKS numerically, and each square is uniquely named by its file letter and rank number, in that order.

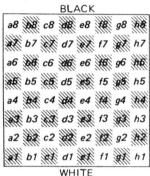

On account of its clarity and brevity standard notation has become established internationally. Players must record their games in this notation to meet the LAWS published by FIDE. There are two main versions: full, in which both departure and arrival squares are given; abbreviated, in which the departure square is named only when essential. In the former the moves of the KING'S KNIGHT GAMBIT are written 1 e2–e4 e7–e5 2 f2–f4 e5xf4 3 Ng1–f3, in the latter, 1 e4 e5 2 f4 exf4 3 Nf3.

In both versions the symbols for the pieces are given, but not the symbol for pawn. In abbreviated notation, checks (+) and capture signs (x or :) may be omitted; they are given in this book. Information about the departure square is necessary if two pieces of the same kind could be moved to the arrival square. If a player with knights on a2 and b5 plays Nc3 this will be either Nac3 or Nbc3, if the knights are on a2 and a4 the move will be N2c3 or N4c3. For EN PASSANT captures the arrival square is given as usual. After 1 d4 c5 2 d5 e5 White can capture *en passant* 3 dxe6 ep (or 3 d5xe6 ep, or 3 de6). (In the specialized field of RETROGRADE ANALYSIS this is shown as 3 dxe5 because, in going backwards, the captured piece needs to be replaced.) The symbol for a pawn is sometimes given in annotations, e.g. Pe4 instead of e4, to make clear that a move and not a square is intended.

Standard notation is international. Countries such as Russia which have a Cyrillic alphabet also use the Latin alphabet for this purpose. There are minor differences of usage. Where Russian books give Cf1:c4 or C:c4, Germans give Lf1–c4: or Lc4: and English give Bf1xc4 or Bxc4. (See NOTATION.)

Stanley, Charles Henry (1819–1901), player from Brighton in England who gave a powerful impetus

to chess in America. He took lessons from POPERT, and in 1841, receiving pawn and two moves, defeated STAUNTON in match play (+ 3 = 1 − 2). About two years later Stanley moved to the USA where he defeated the strongest players in New York and launched America's first chess column in *The Spirit of the Times* (1 March 1845–4 Oct. 1848). The column contains the first chess problem to be published in America.

In 1845 Stanley defeated ROUSSEAU (+ 15 = 8 − 8) in a match for a stake of $1,000, then a record sum. Among those who attended was MORPHY, and the match may well have inspired his interest in the game. The following year Stanley published *Thirty-one Games at Chess,* America's first book of a match, became secretary of the New York chess club, and founded the *American Chess Magazine* (1846–7). This and *The Chess Palladium and Mathematical Sphinx* share the distinction of being the first chess journals in USA. He edited a chess column in *The Albion* (1848–56) and through this he met and assisted LÖWENTHAL, a penniless refugee, in 1849. Matches with Löwenthal in 1850 and SAINT-AMANT in 1852 were drawn (+ 3 − 3, + 4 − 4). A minor problemist, originator of one kind of FOCAL PLAY, Stanley promoted America's first composing tourney in 1855.

In the same year he became involved in a diplomatic incident. The British were attempting to recruit Americans as soldiers to serve in the Crimean War, an activity illegal in the USA. Dapper, demonstrative, sociable, 'fond of puns but otherwise an entertaining conversationalist', Stanley had a weakness for drink, which made him even more loquacious. After some hard drinking he revealed information to an American agent, linking the illegal recruitment with the British consular staff in which Stanley had a function. The result was a diplomatic breach between the two countries, but despite his indiscretion he stayed in the USA.

When Morphy arrived in New York for the tournament of 1857 Stanley was considered to be the American champion, but after the tournament he lost a match to Morphy (+ 1 − 4) although receiving odds of pawn and move. In honour of the younger man Stanley, who had married in 1850, named his daughter Pauline, and in 1859 he brought out a book, *Morphy's Match Games.* The admiration was not mutual: Morphy sent his winnings from the match to Mrs Stanley who was in some need. 'Stanley would have drunk it all up', said a friend.

In 1859 Stanley published *The Chess Player's Instructor* which was reprinted twice in the same year, and again in 1880 as *De Witt's American Chess Manual.* Around 1860 he returned to England, where he edited a chess column in the *Manchester Weekly Express and Guardian* (1860–2). During his 17-year absence the standard of play had greatly improved in Europe and he failed to make any impression in either match or tournament play. In 1862 he returned to the USA where, in 1868, he lost a short match against G. H. MACKENZIE

(+1−2) after which he disappeared from the chess scene, an incurable alcoholic. The last 20 years of his life were spent in institutions on Ward's Island and in the Bronx.

Stanley Variation, 676, the CARO VARIATION in the SPANISH OPENING, played twice by STANLEY in his match with ROUSSEAU in 1845.

star-flights, the four flight-squares diagonally adjoining the square occupied by a king that does not stand on the edge of the board. (Compare PLUS-FLIGHTS.)

#2

A problem by ALAIKOV, second prize, *Shakhmatny Misl*, 1982. The key is 1 Rh2+, and star-flights follow.

```
1 ... Kd1    2 Nxc3#
1 ... Kf3    2 Bh5#
1 ... Kxf1   2 Bc4#
1 ... Kd3    2 Qd8#.
```

The TRY-PLAY shows the ALBINO task with star-flight refutations.

```
1 dxc3+?   Kd1
1 d3+?     Kf3
1 dxe3+?   Kxf1
1 d4+?     Kd3.
```

static factors, those characteristics of a position that can be seen without consideration of the moves that might follow. (See EVALUATION OF POSITION.)

Staunton, Howard (1810–74), the world's leading player in the 1840s, founder of a SCHOOL OF CHESS, promoter of the world's first international chess tournament, chess columnist and author, Shakespearian scholar. Nothing is known for certain about Staunton's life before 1836, when his name appears as a subscriber to William Greenwood Walker's *Games at Chess, actually played in London, by the late Alexander McDonnell Esq.* Staunton states that he was born in Westmorland in the spring of 1810, that his father's name was William, that he acted with Edmund Kean, taking the part of Lorenzo in *The Merchant of Venice*, that he spent some time at Oxford (but not at the university), and that he came to London around 1836. Other

sources suggest that as a young man he inherited a small legacy, married, and soon spent the money. He is supposed to have been brought up by his mother, his father having left home or died.

Staunton never contradicted the rumour that he was the natural son of the fifth Earl of Carlisle, a relationship that might account for his forename, for the Earl's family name was Howard, but the story is almost certainly untrue. (Edmund Kean claimed to be the son of the Duke of Norfolk, also a member of the Howard family.) In all probability Howard Staunton was not his real name. A contemporary, Charles Tomlinson (1808–97), writes: 'Rumour ... assigned a different name to our hero [Staunton] when he first appeared as an actor and next as a chess amateur.'

At the unusually late age of 26, Staunton became ambitious to succeed at chess. A keen patriot, his motivation may in part have sprung from a desire to avenge MCDONNELL'S defeat at the hands of a Frenchman. A ROOK PLAYER in 1836 (his own assessment), Staunton rose to the top in a mere seven years. In 1838 he played a long series of games with W. D. EVANS, and a match with ALEXANDRE in which he suffered 'mortifying defeat' during the early sittings; but he continued to study and practise with great determination. In 1840 he was strong enough to defeat POPERT, then living in London. In the same year he began writing about the game. A short-lived column in the *New Court Gazette* began in May and ended in December because, says WALKER, there were 'complaints of an overdose'. He was more successful in his work for *British Miscellany*, which in 1841 became the *Chess Player's Chronicle*, England's first successful chess magazine, edited by Staunton until 1854.

Throughout 1842 COCHRANE, then on leave from India, played several hundred games with Staunton, a valuable experience for them both. In 1843 the leading French player, SAINT-AMANT, visited London and defeated Staunton in a short contest (+3=1−2), an event that attracted little attention. Later that year the two masters met in a historic encounter, lasting from 14 November to 20 December, fought before large audiences in the famous CAFÉ DE LA RÉGENCE. Staunton's decisive victory (+11=4−6) marked the end of French chess supremacy, an end that was sudden, complete, and long-lasting. From then until the 1870s London became the world's chess centre.

In October 1844 Staunton travelled to Paris for a return match, but the day before play could begin he became dangerously ill with pneumonia, and the match was cancelled. Unwell for some months afterwards, he never fully recovered; his heart was permanently weakened. In February 1845 he began the most important of his journalistic tasks, one that continued until his death, namely the conduct of the world's most influential chess column, in the *Illustrated London News*. Each week he dealt with a hundred or more letters; each week he published one or more problems, the best of the time. In 1845 he conceded odds of pawn and two moves and defeated several of his countrymen; in 1846 he won two matches playing level, against HORWITZ (+14=3−7) and HARRWITZ (+7). In 1847 Staunton published his most famous chess book, the *Chess-Player's Handbook*, from which many generations of English-speaking players learned the rudiments of the game and which is still in print, nearly a century and a half later. He published the *Chess-Player's Companion* in 1849.

In 1851 Staunton organized the world's first international tournament as an adjunct to the Great Exhibition in London. He also played in it, an unwise decision for one burdened with the chore of organization at the same time. After defeating Horwitz (+4=1−2) in the second round, he lost to ANDERSSEN, the eventual winner. Moreover, he was defeated by WILLIAMS, his erstwhile disciple, in the play-off for places. Later that year, after defeating JAENISCH (+7=1−2), Staunton scored +6=1−4 against Williams, but lost the match because he had conceded his opponent three games' start. In 1852 Staunton published *The Chess Tournament*, an excellent account of this first international gathering. Subsequently he unsuccessfully attempted to arrange a match with Anderssen, but for all practical purposes he retired from serious play at this time.

Among his many chess activities Staunton had long sought standardization of the LAWS OF CHESS and, as England's representative, he crossed to Brussels in 1853 to discuss the laws with LASA, the leading German chess authority. Little progress was made at that time, but the laws adopted by FIDE in 1929 are substantially in accordance with Staunton's view. The trip was also the occasion of an

Staunton

informal match, broken off when the score stood +5=3−4 in Lasa's favour. Staunton took the match seriously, successfully requesting his English friends to send him their latest analyses of the opening.

Staunton had married in 1849 and, recognizing his new responsibilities, he now sought an occupation less hazardous than that of a chessplayer. In 1856, putting to use his knowledge of Elizabethan and Shakespearian drama, he obtained a contract to prepare an annotated edition of Shakespeare's plays. This was published in monthly instalments from November 1857 to May 1860, a work that 'combined commonsense with exhaustive research'. (In 1860 the monthly parts, ready for binding in three volumes, were reissued; in 1864 a four-volume reprint, without the illustrations by Sir John Gilbert, was published; in 1979 the original version was published in one volume.) Staunton, who performed this task to a tight schedule, was unable to accept a challenge from MORPHY in 1858: his publishers would accept no breach of contract. After the proposal for a match was frustrated EDGE stirred up a quarrel, casting Staunton as the villain. Morphy, perhaps unwisely, signed some letters drafted by Edge, while Staunton, continuously importuned by Edge, was once driven to make a true but impolitely worded comment about Morphy. Generally these two great masters behaved honourably, each holding the other in high regard; but Edge's insinuations unfairly blackened Staunton's reputation.

Subsequently Staunton wrote several books, among them *Chess Praxis* (1860), which includes 168 pages devoted to Morphy's games, and *Great Schools of England* (1865), revised with many additions in 1869. In the last two years of his life he wrote 19 articles for *The Athenaeum* on 'Unsuspected Corruptions of Shakespeare's Texts'. Working on another chess book he was seized by a heart attack, and died in his library chair.

Staunton was no one's pupil; what he learned about chess he learned by himself. For the most part he played the usual openings of his time, but he introduced several positional concepts. Some of these had been touched upon by PHILIDOR, others were his own: the use of the FIANCHETTO for strategic ends, the development of FLANK OPENINGS specially suited to pawn play. He may be regarded as the precursor of the HYPERMODERN movement, and the STAUNTON SYSTEM the precursor of the RÉTI OPENING. In his *Chess-Player's Companion* Staunton remarks that after 1 e4 e5 Black's game is embarrassed from the start, a remark anticipating by more than half a century BREYER's ideas about this opening. In 1964 FISCHER wrote: 'Staunton was the most profound opening analyst of all time. He was more theorist than player but none the less he was the strongest player of his day. Playing over his games I discovered that they are completely modern. Where Morphy and Steinitz rejected the fianchetto, Staunton embraced it. In addition he understood all those positional concepts which modern players hold so dear, and thus with Steinitz must be considered the first modern player.' (See SCHOOLS OF CHESS.)

Tall, erect, broad-shouldered, with a leonine head, Staunton stood out among his fellows, walking 'like a king'. He dressed elegantly, even ostentatiously, a taste derived, perhaps, from his background as an actor. G. A. MACDONNELL describes him '... wearing a lavender zephyr outside his frock coat. His appearance was slightly gaudy, his vest being an embroidered satin, and his scarf gold-sprigged with a double pin thrust in, the heads of which were connected by a glittering chain ...'. A great raconteur, an excellent mimic who could entertain by his portrayals of Edmund Kean, Thackeray, and other celebrities he had met, he liked to hold the stage, 'caring for no man's anecdotes but his own'. He could neither understand nor tolerate the acceptance of mediocrity, the failure of others to give of their best. A man of determined opinions, he expressed them pontifically, brooking little opposition. Always outspoken, he often behaved, writes POTTER, 'with gross unfairness towards those whom he disliked, or from whom he suffered defeat, or whom he imagined to stand between himself and the sun'; 'nevertheless', he continues, 'there was nothing weak about him and he had a backbone that was never curved with fear of anyone.' Widely disliked, Staunton was widely admired, a choice that would have been his preference. Reminiscing in 1897, RANKEN wrote: 'With great defects he had many virtues; there was nothing mean, cringing, or small in his nature, and, taking all in all, England never had a more worthy chess representative than Howard Staunton.'

R. D. Keene and R. N. Coles, *Howard Staunton the English World Chess Champion* (1975), contains biography, 78 games, and 20 parts of games.

Staunton–Williams 8th match game 1851 Bird Opening

In this game White makes a SMALL CENTRE, completes his development, and only then decides how best to advance his pawns, a hypermodern strategy that anticipates the Réti Opening.

1 f4 e6 2 e3 f5 3 g3 Nf6 4 Bg2 d5 5 Nf3 c5 6 b3 Nc6 7 0–0 Bd6 8 Bb2 0–0 9 Qe2 Bc7 10 Na3 a6 11 Rad1 b5 12 c4 bxc4 13 bxc4 Rb8 14 Bxf6 Qxf6 15 cxd5 exd5 16 d4 c4 17 Ne5 Nb4

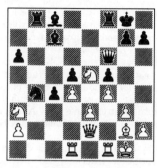

18 Naxc4 dxc4 19 a3 Bxe5 20 dxe5 Qf7 21 axb4 Rxb4 22 Rd6 Bb7 23 e6 Qc7 24 Rd7 Qc8 25 Qd1 Bc6 26 Bxc6 Qxc6 27 Qd4 Rf6 28 Rd6 Qb5 29 Rd8+ Rf8 30 Rxf8+ Kxf8 31 Qd6+ Ke8 32 Rd1 Black resigns.

Staunton chessmen, the standard pattern of chessmen whose design, influenced by earlier sets bearing similar features, was registered by Nathaniel Cook in March 1849. Only men of this general style are allowed in FIDE events. The design of the knight was inspired by the Parthenon frieze in the British Museum. The manufacturing rights were bought by John Jacques and in September 1849 the sets were advertised, made in ivory or wood, and STAUNTON began to recommend the sets in the *Illustrated London News*. Each set was accompanied by a *New Treatise*, written by Staunton, and the box bore a label bearing his signature 'to secure the Public against Fraudulent Imitation'. Some of the expensive ivory sets had a manuscript signature, but most were in facsimile. The design became popular on account of the pleasing proportions of the men, their stability, the ease with which each man could be identified, and not least Staunton's advocacy. Each set that was sold brought him a fee.

M. Mark, *British Chess Sets* (1986).

Staunton set, (*l. to r.*) pawn, rook, knight, bishop, queen, king

Staunton Defence, 50, the BENONI DEFENCE, played twice against STAUNTON by SAINT-AMANT in their second match of 1843.

Staunton Gambit, 258, vigorous response to the DUTCH DEFENCE, played by STAUNTON against HORWITZ in 1847.

Tartakower–Mieses   Baden-Baden 1925

1 d4 f5   2 e4 fxe4   3 Nc3 Nf6   4 g4 d5   5 g5 Ng8   6 f3 exf3
7 Qxf3 e6   8 Bd3 g6   9 Nge2 Qe7   10 Bf4 c6   11 Be5 Bg7
12 Qg3 Na6   13 0–0 Bd7   14 Bd6 Qd8   15 Qf4 Black resigns.

Staunton Opening, 813, the PONZIANI OPENING.

Staunton System, series of moves devised by STAUNTON: for White, Pc4, Nc3, Pg3, Bg2, Pe3, Nge2, 0–0; or for Black, Pc5, Nc6, Pg6, Bg7, Pe6, Nge7, 0–0. In either case a queen's-side fianchetto might follow. After his retirement the system was neglected for a long time, perhaps because players disliked the HOLES in the pawn formation (for White, f3 and d3; for Black, f6 and d6).

In the 1920s, when players were less afraid of holes, NIMZOWITSCH reintroduced the Staunton System for Black: 1 e4 c5   2 Nc3 Nc6   3 g3 g6   4 Bg2 Bg7   5 Nge2 e6   6 d3 Nge7, and this variation soon became standard play. Since the middle of the 20th century masters have occasionally used the system when playing the white pieces.

steamroller, a group of united pawns that advance and drive back in disarray the enemy pieces in their path.

Stean, Michael Frank (1953–), English player, International Grandmaster (1977). In 1974 he was equal first in the British championship, but lost the play-off. In the same year, at Nice, in the first of five Olympiad appearances up to 1982, he won the BRILLIANCY PRIZE for his game against BROWNE (see below). After that he made several good performances: Montilla 1976, equal second with KAVALEK and Ricardo Calvo (1943–), after KARPOV; Montilla 1977, third (+3=6), after GLIGORIĆ and Kavalek, ahead of BYRNE, TAIMANOV, and ANDERSSON; London 1977, second (+4=4−1) equal with MESTEL and QUINTEROS, after HORT; Vršac 1979, first (+8=5−1); Smederevska Palanka 1980, first (+7=6); Beersheba 1982, first.

Stean was one of KORCHNOI'S seconds in the world championship cycles of 1977–8 and 1980–1, and the two became loyal friends. In particular Stean provided help with the openings, a subject on which he has extensive knowledge. He published *Simple Chess* (1978), a guide to the understanding of positional ideas. In the mid-1980s Stean became less active at chess and concentrated on a career in finance. However, he retained his column in the *Observer*, and continued to follow events.

Stean–Browne   Nice 1974 Olympiad   Sicilian Defence Najdorf Variation

1 e4 c5   2 Nf3 d6   3 d4 cxd4   4 Nxd4 Nf6   5 Nc3 a6   6 Bg5 Nbd7   7 Bc4 e6   8 0–0 h6   9 Bxf6 Nxf6   10 Bb3 b6   11 f4 Bb7   12 Qd3 Be7

13 Nxe6 fxe6   14 Bxe6 b5   15 e5 Qb6+   16 Kh1 dxe5   17 Qg6+ Kd8   18 Qf7 Qc5   19 fxe5 Bxg2+   20 Kxg2 Rf8   21 Rad1+ Kc7   22 Qxg7 Rg8   23 exf6 Rxg7+   24 fxg7 Bd6   25 Rf7+ Kc6   26 Bd5+ Kb6   27 Bxa8 Qg5+   28 Kh1 Be5   29 b4 a5   30 Rb7+ Kc6   31 g8=Q Qxg8   32 Rb8+ Black resigns.

Steenwijk Variation, 734, the DERLD.

Stein, Elias (1748–1812), Alsatian who settled in The Hague when young and became chess tutor to the sons of William V, the last Stadtholder of Holland. One son became King of Holland, the other an Austrian Field-Marshal. It was chiefly for these pupils that Stein wrote *Nouvel Essai sur le jeu des échecs, avec des réflexions militaires relatives à ce jeu*, published in 1789. The eighteenth opening in the book carries a note that if the opponent opens by pushing his queen's pawn two squares, you cannot do better than to push the king's bishop's pawn two squares (1 d4 f5), the line that became known as the DUTCH DEFENCE. Two further editions of Stein's book appeared in the 19th century, and there were two translations into Dutch, both of which had later editions.

Stein's pupil Friedrich Wilhelm von Mauvillon (1774–1851) said of him that he 'departed from this world an unconquered chess-player'; but he never met the great French, Italian, or English players of his day.

Stein, Leonid Zakharovich (1934–73), Ukrainian player, Soviet champion 1963, 1965, and 1966–7, International Grandmaster (1962), factory worker and, later, chess professional. He made slow progress at the start of his chess career. Besides working as a fitter he attended evening classes to improve his education, leaving little time to study chess; but he improved steadily. In his first USSR championship, Moscow 1962, he came third (+8=8−3) equal with GELLER, after PETROSYAN and KORCHNOI, and since this was a zonal tournament, he qualified for the interzonal at Stockholm 1962, where he finished sixth (+9=9−4) with GLIGORIĆ and BENKO. He would then have become a CANDIDATE had he been from any other country, but at that time FIDE limited the number of players from each country, a rule that effectively only applied to the USSR.

At his third attempt Stein gained the USSR championship in 1963 (+6=12−1), winning a play-off with SPASSKY and KHOLMOV. In 1964 he was second (+2=9−1) equal wth BRONSTEIN, after Spassky at Moscow 1964, a zonal tournament of such strength that Geller was last. Again, in the interzonal, Amsterdam 1964, his fifth place (+12=9−2) would have made a Candidate of a player from any other country. Stein continued to produce excellent results: Yerevan 1965, second (+5=7−1) equal with Petrosyan (then world champion) after Korchnoi; USSR championship, Tallinn 1965, first (+10=8−1) ahead of POLU-GAYEVSKY and KERES; Kislovodsk 1966, second (+7=1−3) after Geller, ahead of TAL; USSR championship, Tbilisi 1966–7, first (+8=10−2), ahead of Korchnoi; Sarajevo 1967, first (+7=7−1) equal with IVKOV; Moscow 1967, first (+6=10−1) ahead of SMYSLOV and Tal.

Now he had another shot at the interzonal, Sousse 1967, and this time there was no 'nation-ality' rule. However, he had a relatively bad tourna-ment, finished equal sixth with RESHEVSKY and HORT, and had to play-off for the one place. Hort and Stein each won one game, but Reshevsky drew all eight of his, and qualified by tie-break. Stein was not down-hearted: Kecskemét 1968, first (+9=6), two and a half points ahead of the field; Tallinn 1969, first (+8=5), ahead of Keres; Moscow 1971, first (+5=12) equal with KARPOV, ahead of Smy-slov, Petrosyan, Tal, Spassky, and Korchnoi; Zagreb 1972, first (+6=7); Kislovodsk 1972 second (+6=8), after Polugayevsky; and Las Pal-mas 1973, first equal with Petrosyan.

Widely expected to become a Candidate at the Rio de Janeiro interzonal 1973, he looked forward eagerly: 'You will be surprised . . . my whole life will take another course . . . then I'll really start to play chess.' But a few weeks before the start of play he collapsed and died.

Stein's style, often called romantic, embraced an intuitive approach to combinative play, and his games were widely appreciated by the chess public. (At Yerevan 1965 the organizers awarded him a special prize 'for ingenuity'.)

R. D. Keene, *Leonid Stein—Master of Attack*, containing a biography and 78 games, was re-issued in 1988; E. Ye. Gufeld and Ye. M. Lazarev, *Leonid Stein* (1980), is a Russian collection of 50 annotated games, part-games, career results, and much bio-graphical material.

Gligorić–Stein   Moscow 1967   King's Indian Defence
Petrosyan Variation

1 d4 Nf6 2 c4 g6 3 Nc3 Bg7 4 e4 d6 5 Nf3 0–0 6 Be2 e5
7 d5 a5 8 0–0 Na6 9 Bg5 h6 10 Bh4 g5 11 Bg3 Nh5
12 Nd2 Nf4 13 Bg4 Nc5 14 f3 c6 15 Qc2 cxd5 16 cxd5
b5 17 a4 bxa4 18 Nc4 h5 19 Bxc8 Rxc8 20 Nxa4 Qc7
21 Ne3 Qa7 22 Bf2 Ncd3 23 Qd2 Nxf2 24 Rxf2 g4 25
Nf5 gxf3 26 Kh1

26 . . . Qxf2 27 Qxf2 fxg2+ 28 Qxg2 Nxg2 29 Kxg2
Rc2+ 30 Kf3 Rb8 31 Ke3 Rb3+ 32 Nc3 Rbxb2 33
Ra3 Rxh2 34 Kd3 Rh3+ 35 Ne3 Bh6 36 Nd1 Rb1
White resigns.

Stein Defence, 247, the DUTCH DEFENCE.

Steiner, Endre or Andreas (1901–44), Hungarian player. His best results in tournaments are: Trenč-ianské Teplice 1928, second after KOSTIĆ, ahead of SPIELMANN, GRÜNFELD, and RÉTI; Kecskemét 1933, first (+4=1), ahead of ELISKASES and CANAL; Kemeri 1937, sixth (+9=4−4). He achieved excel-lent results in five Olympiads: 1927, 1928, 1931, 1933, and 1937. In 1927 he made the best score (+6=5−2) on board four; in 1928 he made the best score (+10=3−3) at board two; and in 1937 he was awarded a special prize for the highest score on any board (+12=5−1).

His father Bernát (1874–1944) and brother Lajos (below) were also well-known players.

Steiner, Herman (1905–55), Hungarian-born Am-erican professional player, organizer and colum-nist, at one time known as H. Stoner, International Master (1950). Steiner played for the USA in four Olympiads, 1928, 1930, 1931, and 1950, on the last occasion being captain of the victorious team. While in Europe for the 1931 event he played in a few tournaments and in one of them, Berlin 1931, he was first (+3=1−1), ahead of SÄMISCH and L. STEINER. Otherwise his best international result was at Pasadena 1932, when he was equal third with DAKE and RESHEVSKY, after ALEKHINE and KASHDAN, in front of FINE. Steiner shared the US open cham-pionship in 1942, won it outright in 1946, and won the US championship, 'the goal of his ambitions', in 1948. He died suddenly from a heart attack despite the immediate attention of a doctor.

Steiner's work for the cause of American chess on the West Coast was of greater significance than his playing achievements. He moved from New York to Hollywood in 1932, worked ceaselessly for the promotion of chess, and was editor of a chess column in the *Los Angeles Times* from 1932 until his death. Among his many activities, he founded the Hollywood Chess Group which was patronized by screen actors such as Humphrey Bogart, company that suited his 'picturesque and friendly' personality.

Steiner, Lajos (1903–75), Hungarian champion 1931 and 1936, Australian champion 1945, 1946, 1946–7, 1952–3, 1958–9, International Master (1950), brother of Endre STEINER. Trained as a mechanical engineer, he later became a professional chessplayer. His first notable achievement was at Kecskemét 1927, a two-stage tournament. He won the preliminary section (+7=2) ahead of NIMZO-WITSCH; after adding his results in the final section he came equal to Nimzowitsch in second place, half a point behind ALEKHINE. Steiner's best victories came in the mid-1930s: a match defeat of LILIEN-THAL (+3=2−1) in 1935; Trebitsch Memorial tournament, Vienna 1935, first (+6=4−1), shared with ELISKASES, ahead of SPIELMANN and GRÜNFELD. Steiner played for Hungary in the Olympiads of 1931, 1933, and 1935, on the last occasion at first board.

On a tour through the Far East he was first in the Australian championship of 1936–7, playing *hors concours*. He settled in Australia in 1939, and married Edna Kingston, the country's leading woman player. In 1948, after ten years without international practice, he visited Europe and played in a few tournaments, writing a book, *Kings of Chess 1948* (1949), describing his experiences. He took third prize after FOLTYS and BARCZA at Karlovy Vary–Mariánské Lázně , but was unsuccessful in the interzonal tournament.

Eliskases–Steiner Budapest 1933 Hungarian Championship English Opening

1 c4 Nf5 2 Nc3 e5 3 Nf3 Nc6 4 e3 Bb4 5 Nd5 e4 6 Nxb4 Nxb4 7 Nd4 0–0 8 Be2 d5 9 a3 Nd3+ 10 Bxd3 exd3 11 c5 Ne4 12 b4 Qg5 13 g3 Bh3 14 f3

14 ... f5 15 Qb3 f4 16 exf4 Rae8 17 fxg5 Nxc5+ 18 Kd1 Nxb3 19 Nxb3 Bg2 20 Nd4 Bxh1 21 f4 Re4 22 Bb2 Rfe8 White resigns.

Steiner Variation, three variations attributable to Endre STEINER: 1029 in the PHILIDOR DEFENCE, as E. Steiner–Brinckmann, Budapest 1929; 1180 in the FRENCH DEFENCE, played by Steiner, for example against TARTAKOWER at Budapest 1929, but also by

many others previously, such as Edward Löwe (1794–1880) in the London 1851 tournament; 1255 in the ALEKHINE DEFENCE, as E. Steiner–Pikler, Hungarian championship, 1931. However, his brother Lajos also played it against the same opponent, in the same event. This line is also known as the Weenink Attack.

From Herman STEINER, 292 in the BUDAPEST DEFENCE, as H. Steiner–Fajarowicz, Wiesbaden 1928. Also three variations due to Lajos STEINER: 95 in the SLAV DEFENCE, as Najdorf–L. Steiner, Saltsjö-baden 1948; 332 in the NIMZO-INDIAN DEFENCE; 1255 in the Alekhine Defence (see above).

Steinitz, Wilhelm (1836–1900), World Champion 1886–94. Born into a large family in Prague, he went to Vienna as a young man and attempted to earn a living as a journalist. After winning the Vienna championship 1861–2 he played in his first international tournament, London 1862 (won by ANDERSSEN). Steinitz took sixth place, and immediately afterwards defeated DUBOIS, the fifth-prize winner, in match play (+5=1−3). He became a professional, and settled in London where he won several matches, notably against BLACKBURNE in 1862–3 (+7=2−1), Anderssen in 1866 (+8−6), and BIRD in 1866 (+7=5−5). The match against Anderssen, largely characterized by gambits and fine tactical play, was conducted in a sportsmanlike manner by both players. Aware that Anderssen, an amateur, might be under pressure to return to Breslau (as he had been when he played MORPHY and PAULSEN), Steinitz turned up punctually for every game, even on the day his daughter was born. His attacking style showed few signs of the positional play he developed later. 'It was the style predominating in his time ... In this style he continued to play for a number of years, not differing in this respect from any of his contemporaries' (Em. LASKER). At Baden-Baden 1870 Steinitz came second, half a point after Anderssen, but ahead of Blackburne, NEUMANN, Paulsen, and WINAWER. At London 1872 he was first (+ 7) and a nonscoring draw that was replayed, ahead of Blackburne and ZUKERTORT, and in September 1872 he decisively beat Zukertort in match play (+ 7 = 4 − 1). At this time LOWENTHAL wrote: 'Mr Steinitz may be fairly regarded as the present occupant of the exceptional position formerly held by Mr Morphy', and BURN wrote that Steinitz was 'now probably the strongest living player'.

Steinitz had achieved this pre-eminence by means of superior tactical skill, yet within a year his style changed dramatically, and in his next tournament, Vienna 1873, most of his play was positional. He scored + 18 = 5 − 2 while Blackburne, playing 30 games, lost 7 of them; but, in accordance with the unusual scoring rules, these two were adjudged to have tied. Steinitz won the play-off (+2). (Including these two games, Steinitz ended the tournament with 16 consecutive wins in which Paulsen, Anderssen, and Blackburne were each defeated twice.)

Answering a correspondent's enquiry regarding the world's best player, Steinitz wrote: '... probably little difference exists between several first-class players ... *Pro tem.*, Steinitz, who has not yet lost any set match on even terms, and who has come out victorious in the last two international tournaments, London 1872 and Vienna 1873, could claim the title of champion' (*The Field*, 18 July 1874). In the nine years following the Vienna tournament he played serious chess only once, in 1876, when he made a CLEAN SCORE (+7) in a match against Blackburne.

Steinitz in 1891

Steinitz then played in the strongest two tournaments held up to that time: Vienna 1882, first (+20=8−6) equal with Winawer (a play-off was drawn, +1−1), ahead of MASON, MACKENZIE, Zukertort, and Blackburne; London 1883, second (+19−7), after Zukertort, ahead of Blackburne, CHIGORIN, Mackenzie, Mason, and Winawer. James G. Cunningham (1838–1905) wrote of Steinitz as he saw him then: 'He is a man of great physical vigour, and possesses a well-preserved constitution. Everything about him denoted power rather than grace, strength rather than beauty. His stature was short but form massive, his chest broad, his bearing sturdy. [His features were] rugged in outline, and his face the face of a man of action rather than a man of thought ... with bright tawny locks, round face, a crushed-up nose ... broad forehead, deep-set eyes, and a rough shaggy beard of the bright tawny hue, the whole balanced squarely on a thick neck, that again on a short massive body' (*British Chess Magazine*, Jan. 1892).

In 1883, 'after 20 years as a foreigner' in England, Steinitz emigrated to the United States and eventually took American nationality.

Zukertort's success in the London tournament of 1883 caused some to claim he was the world's best player, notwithstanding his crushing defeat at the hands of Steinitz in 1872, and a second match was played in 1886, in the cities of New York, St Louis, and New Orleans. They agreed that the first to win ten games should be declared world champion, but that if each won nine the title would not be awarded. Steinitz, at 49 the older by six years, won (+10=5−5), a victory he owned to superior strategy and greater stamina. Subsequently he defended his title against Chigorin in 1889 (+10=1−6), GUNSBERG in 1890–1 (+6=9−4), and Chigorin in 1892 (+10=5−8). The games of these four matches are full of interest, both tactical and strategic. In 1894 Steinitz, aged 58, hero of an unbroken series of 24 match victories since 1862, lost his title to the 25-year-old Lasker in a match of 19 games.

Steinitz had been the best player in the world for about 20 years, standing higher than any other champion above his contemporaries, had kept the world championship until his 59th year, and until this time had achieved a better tournament record than anyone else. Not content to rest upon his laurels, he strove to regain his pre-eminence. Rhoda Bowles (1861–1931), chess editor of *Womanhood*, met Steinitz during the Hastings 1895 tournament. 'Oh, Madam Bowles what shall I do?' he said, 'I have just lost my game to Lasker, and that is my fourth successive loss, I shall never win again ... I am utterly broken down.' The next day she pinned a buttonhole to his coat saying she had come to turn his luck. 'The change in his look was startling; from a haggard expression he developed an eager look of desire for his opponent.' For the ensuing game, see BARDELEBEN.

At St Petersburg 1895–6, a quadrangular match-tournament, he took second place (+7=5−6), after Lasker, ahead of PILLSBURY and Chigorin, but in a return match with Lasker, 1896–7, he was soundly beaten. An added burden was failing health. Heart trouble (mitral stenosis), ultimately fatal, was linked with periods of irrationality, the first of them being immediately after the return match. Most of the world's best players competed at Vienna 1898; Steinitz came fourth, a fine achievement in the circumstances. He fought hard in every game, as he had fought throughout his career; even his drawn games averaged 54 moves. Less than a year after his last tournament, London 1899, he died in poverty.

Like most champions, Steinitz selected and developed other people's opening ideas; his few innovations include the DUTCH INDIAN. From 1873 he made many useful experiments in an effort to find a satisfactory defence to the SPANISH OPENING. The improved defences established after his death rest on his practical trials. In the middlegame Steinitz was especially interested in 'weaknesses' in the pawn structure, isolated pawns, doubled pawns, and HOLES, the so-called permanent features. He advised great care before making any pawn moves other than those needed to open the game, lest, as play progressed, a hole be created (the term was his invention). Such restrained pawn play probably reached its highest development in the games of CAPABLANCA. Steinitz's play influenced many other players, especially those such as NIMZOWITSCH who, questioning the dictates of TARRASCH, came to the forefront some years after Steinitz's death. For his important contribution to positional play, see THEORY and SCHOOLS OF CHESS.

Steinitz is often said to have been morose and irritable. This accusation may have been partly true of his last few years when he was, financially and physically, a broken man, but in the 1860s he was called pleasant, well-tempered, and a man who took defeat with a smile. Other accounts describe him as a kind friend who helped many players, notably the ungrateful HOFFER who arrived in England as a penniless immigrant. He disliked pretentiousness and falsehood, and could write scathingly in condemnation, as when Zukertort decided overnight that he was a doctor of medicine. In chess politics he was inevitably drawn into disputes, which he entered with his usual fighting spirit, so that he was sometimes called quarrelsome, but few considered how often he was in the right. He disliked the importunities of journalists, in consequence often getting a bad press.

Steinitz made important literary contributions. He edited chess columns in the London *Figaro* from 1876 to 1882; *Ashore or Afloat*, 1883; *New York Tribune*, 1890–3; *New York Herald* from 1893; but the most important was *The Field*, 1873–82. His annotations in these columns were an outstanding improvement on what had gone before. (*The Field* column was lost to him as a result of manœuvres made while he was away at the Vienna tournament, and was taken over by Hoffer, a good reporter but poor analyst, whose miserable annotations inflamed Steinitz.) He was proprietor and editor of the *International Chess Magazine* (1885–91), one of the best and most interesting magazines, now a collector's item. He wrote a book of the New York International tournament of 1889, annotating every one of the 432 games. In Part I of his *Modern Chess Instructor* (1889) he analyses some openings, and writes a long introduction explaining some of his chess theories. The work was never completed, although he published Part II section 1 in 1895.

C. Devidé, *A Memorial to William Steinitz* (1901), contains 73 games, and was reprinted with an additional six games as *William Steinitz, Selected Games* (1974); L. Bachmann, *Schachmeister Steinitz* (1910–21), four volumes, reprinted in two volumes (1980), contains a biography and about 1,000 games; D. Hooper, *Weltgeschichte des Schachs: Steinitz* (1968), contains 575 games including all that could be found from his serious match and tournament play; J. Hannak, *Der*

Michel Angelo des Schachspiels (1936), is an interesting but unreliable biography, with no games.

Lasker–Steinitz   World Championship 1894 17th match game   Giuoco Pianissimo

1 e4 e5 2 Nf3 Nc6 3 Bc4 Bc5 4 d3 Nf6 5 Nc3 d6 6 Be3 Bb6 7 Qd2 Na5 8 Bb5+ c6 9 Ba4 Bxe3 10 fxe3 b5 11 Bb3 Qb6 12 0–0 Ng4 13 Rae1 f6 (Black sets up an unbreakable DEFENSIVE CENTRE.) 14 h3 Nh6 15 Ne2 Nxb3 16 axb3 0–0 (Steinitz hopes to gain advantage on account of White's being saddled with DOUBLED PAWNS on the b- and e-files.) 17 Ng3 a5 18 d4 (After this fruitless attack on the centre, White's pawn at e4 becomes hard to defend.) 18 ... Nf7 19 Qf2 Ra7 20 Rd1 a4 21 b4 Qc7 22 Ne1 c5 23 Qd2 Be6 24 d5 Bd7 25 Ra1 cxb4 26 Qxb4 Rc8 27 Qd2 Qc4 28 Rf2 Ng5 29 Qd3 Rac7 30 h4 Nf7 31 Qxc4 Rxc4 32 Rd2 g6 33 Kf2 Nd8 34 b3 R4c7 35 Rdd1 Nb7 36 Rdb1 Kf7 37 Ke2 Ra8 38 Kd2 Na5 39 Kd3 h5 40 Ra2 Raa7 41 b4 Nc4 42 Nf3 Ra8 43 Nd2 Nb6 44 Rf1 Rac8 45 Nb1 Ke7 46 c3 Nc4 47 Raf2

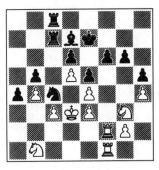

47 ... Na3 48 Ne2 Nxb1 49 Rxb1 Bg4 50 Rc1 Rc4 51 Rc2 f5 White resigns. The fall of White's e-pawn is followed by that of his d-pawn, e.g. 52 Ng3 fxe4+ 53 Kd2 Bd7 54 Rc1 Be8 55 Ne2 Bf7.

Steinitz Attack, 1057, a standard line in the PETROFF DEFENCE suggested by PETROFF and recommended by STEINITZ, who played it against BLACKBURNE in their match of 1862–3 and throughout his career; 1245, variation in the FRENCH DEFENCE given by COZIO and played six times (+4=1−1) by Steinitz at the Vienna tournament of 1882. Also 694, the ANDERSSEN VARIATION of the SPANISH OPENING.

Steinitz Counter-gambit, 232, a kind of QUEEN'S GAMBIT reversed, played in the game Mason–Steinitz, London 1883.

Steinitz Defence, 776 in the SPANISH OPENING, practised by STEINITZ in the 1890s. His idea was to disturb Black's pawn formation as little as possible and, perhaps, to maintain the pawn at e5. The latter object is seldom achieved: for example, to avoid the TARRASCH TRAP, 780, Black must play 7 ... exd4, still, however, with a playable game. Masters usually arrive at the Steinitz Defence by transposition, e.g. 3 ... Nf6 4 0–0 d6, thus avoiding the continuation 3 ... d6 4 d4 Bd7 5 Nc3 Nf6 6 Bxc6 Bxc6 7 Qd3 when White threatens to gain advantage by castling on the queen's-side. This defence, which stems from Ruy LÓPEZ, has never been popular, for Black gets a passive position with few chances of counter-play. It has been played by LASKER, CAPABLANCA, and SMYSLOV; like Steinitz, these champions were all expert defensive players. (See FRIENDLY GAME.)

Also 931 in the ITALIAN OPENING, from the game Dubois–Steinitz, London 1862. White's 7th move is inferior.

Steinitz Defence Deferred, 680, occasionally called the Siesta Defence, in the SPANISH OPENING. Black's aims are the same as in the STEINITZ DEFENCE, but more easy to achieve. The pawn on e5 can often be maintained because an immediate attack on the centre by 5 d4 could lead White into the NOAH'S ARK TRAP, 689. (See WALBRODT.)

Steinitz Gambit, 614 in the VIENNA GAME, introduced successfully in the game Steinitz–Neumann, Dundee 1867; 1113, the VILLEMSON GAMBIT.

Steinitz Variation, 74 in the QUEEN'S GAMBIT ACCEPTED, as in the 9th game of the first world championship match in 1886, Zukertort–Steinitz, and also Pillsbury–Steinitz, St Petersburg 1895–6. In each case the position was reached by transposition, for STEINITZ did not like accepting the gambit on the second move. His idea was to exploit White's ISOLATED QUEEN'S PAWN.

Also 566 in the SICILIAN DEFENCE, tried by Steinitz in his 12th match game against ANDERSSEN in 1866 but played only rarely, e.g. by TARTAKOWER, after whom it is sometimes named; 571 in the CARO–KANN DEFENCE, suggested but not played by Steinitz; 635, Steinitz's usual play in this VIENNA GAME continuation; 817, a defence to the PONZIANI OPENING introduced in the game Wisker–Steinitz, handicap tournament, London 1869; 864 in the THREE KNIGHTS OPENING, played Paulsen–Steinitz, Baden-Baden 1870, and frequently thereafter by Steinitz; 872 and 890 in the EVANS GAMBIT, the first from Steinitz–Hodges, simultaneous display, New York 1890, the second played in all nine games where Steinitz was Black in his match with CHIGORIN in 1889.

Further, 912 in the ITALIAN OPENING, played twice by Steinitz in 1896 during his return match with LASKER; 956 in the TWO KNIGHTS DEFENCE, recommended by Steinitz in his *Modern Chess Instructor*, where he also supported 1005 in the SCOTCH GAME; 1016 in the PHILIDOR DEFENCE, as Steinitz–MacDonnell, Dublin 1865; 1059 in the PETROFF DEFENCE, recommended by PETROFF, supported by Steinitz, and revived by FISCHER in 1962; 1099, sometimes called the Winawer Variation, in the BISHOP'S GAMBIT, played by Steinitz six times in master events during 1898; 1200, sometimes called the Gledhill Deferred Variation, in the FRENCH DEFENCE, played a few times by Steinitz from 1873; 1219, also in the French Defence, played only once (1866) by Steinitz in serious play; 1242 in the same opening, as Steinitz–Showalter, Vienna 1898.

Finally, a group for which the name Steinitz Defence is the less common choice: 632, the PAULSEN ATTACK in the VIENNA GAME; 703, the RUSSIAN DEFENCE, and 783, the COZIO DEFENCE, in the SPANISH OPENING; 1132, the HERZFELD DEFENCE to the SALVIO GAMBIT.

Stein Opening, 1312, the BIRD OPENING.

stemgame, a game that initiates a specific opening variation.

Blackburne–Fleissig   Vienna 1873   Queen's Gambit Accepted

1 d4 d5 2 c4 dxc4 3 Nf3 b5 4 a4 c6 5 e3 Bd7 6 Ne5 e6 7 axb5 cxb5 8 Qf3 Black resigns. This was the stemgame for 3 Nf3, a new move that has since become standard play.

Stevenson, Vera Menchik, see MENCHIK.

stipulation, an instruction, usually plural, for the solving of a composition, e.g. 'White to play and draw', or 'White to play and mate in two moves'. These and some other commonly used stipulations are often represented by CONVENTIONAL SYMBOLS.

Stocchi theme, named after the Italian composer Ottavio Stocchi (1906–64), this problem theme shows at least three different self-blocks on one flight square, answered by three different mates, in a manner showing DUAL-AVOIDANCE. Suppose, in the example given here, Black, in answer to the key, were to place a FIDATED 'dummy' on f3, then White could mate in three different ways. In each of three main variations all but one of these mates is prevented by Black, thus duals are avoided: the black moves 'separate' the mates, as problemists say. See BREDE for a problem in which the dummy test would leave White without a single mating move.

In short, the Stocchi theme shows black moves that actively prevent all but one of the threatened mates, while in the Brede problem the self-blocking moves permit a mate by default, as it were.

\#2

A problem by CAILLAUD, second prize *ex æquo*, *Thèmes 64*, 1981. The tries, 1 Nd3? gxf3, 1 Nd5? Kxf3, 1 Ne6? Qxf3, and 1 Ng6? Nxf3, together with the key, 1 Nh5, form part of a KNIGHT WHEEL. The thematic mates (Qb1, Qe7, Qh7) are separated after the captures on f3:

1 ... gxf3   2 Qb1 ‡ (not Qe7 + ?, Qh7 + ?)
1 ... Qxf3   2 Qe7 ‡ (not Qh7 + ?, Qb1 + ?)
1 ... Nxf3   2 Qh7 ‡ (not Qb1 + ?, Qe7 + ?).
By-play: 1 ... Kxf3   2 Ne5 ‡, 1 ... Rf2 2 Re3 ‡.

Stockholm Variation, 393 in the GRÜNFELD
DEFENCE, played in the Vienna 1922 tournament but
attracting little attention before the match between
Lundin and SPIELMANN, played at Stockholm in
1933.

Stockwhip Variation, 1164, outmoded line in the
KING'S GAMBIT Accepted, given by CARRERA. The
name, rarely used in English-speaking countries, is
a translation of its German name, *Lange Peitsche*,
sometimes rendered more directly as Long Whip.
Its other name, Kieseritzky Variation, is even less
common.

Stoltz, Gösta (1904–63), International Grandmaster (1954), Swedish player noted for his brilliant
combinative play, car mechanic and, periodically,
chess professional. From 1927 he played in many
chess events, including nine Olympiads (1927–37,
1952, 1954), producing some fine games, but rarely
playing with the consistency needed for success in
strong tournaments. He had fair results in two
small tournaments: Stockholm 1930, second
(+3 = 2 − 1) equal with BOGOLJUBOW, after KASH-
DAN, ahead of STÅHLBERG and SPIELMANN; and
Göteborg 1931, equal first with FLOHR and Lundin,
ahead of Ståhlberg and SÄMISCH. His best achievement was at Munich 1941, first (+10 = 4 − 1), one
and a half points ahead of a field that included
ALEKHINE and Bogoljubow. In 1931 he played two
matches against Flohr, winning the first
(+3 = 3 − 2) but losing the second.

Stoltz–H. Steiner Saltsjöbaden 1952 First beauty prize
English Opening Sicilian Variation

1 c4 e5 2 Nc3 d6 3 g3 f5 4 Bg2 Nf6 5 d4 Be7 6 e3 0–0
7 Nge2 Kh8 8 Qc2 Qe8 9 b3 Nc6 10 Ba3 exd4 11 exd4
f4 12 0–0–0 Nh5 13 Be4 g6 14 Nd5 Qd8 15 Bb2 f3 16
Nef4 Bg5 17 Bxg6 hxg6 18 Qxg6 Ng7 19 h4 Bxf4 + 20
gxf4 Bf5 21 Qh6 + Bh7 22 Ne3 Rf6 23 Qg5 Rg6

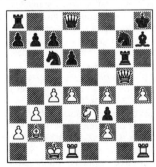

24 d5 Rxg5 25 hxg5 Ne7 26 Ng4 Qc8 27 g6 Qxg4 28
Rxh7 + Kg8 29 Rxg7 + Kf8 30 Rf7 + Ke8 31 Re1
Qxg6 32 Rexe7 + Kd8 33 Bf6 Qxf6 34 Rxf6 Black
exceeded the time limit.

After the Second World War Stoltz won the
national championship three times (1951, 1952, and
1953), was Nordic champion, with BÖÖK, in 1947,
and played in the interzonal tournaments of 1948
and 1952. His results were increasingly affected by
alcoholism, but flashes of his old skill remained,
and at Saltsjöbaden interzonal 1952 he won the
BRILLIANCY PRIZE for the game above.

Stoltz Variation, 128 in the QUEEN'S GAMBIT Declined, TARRASCH DEFENCE, played by STOLTZ in a
consultation game in 1944; 140, a way of avoiding
the MERAN VARIATION introduced in the game
Stoltz–Lindberg, Härnösand 1935. Also 123, the
FOLKESTONE VARIATION, for which Stoltz was largely
responsible.

stonewall, name of a pawn formation: for White,
pawns on d4, e3, and f4; or for Black, pawns on d5,
e6, and f5. The name is descriptive of the central
bastion that Black builds up to obstruct White's
attack, as in the Stonewall Defence (251 in the
DUTCH DEFENCE) and the Stonewall Variations, (104
and 152 also called the Marshall Variation), in the
QUEEN'S GAMBIT Declined. The Stonewall Attack
(220) is paradoxically named. White sets up the
typical pawn formation with the idea of securing
the centre before attacking on the king's-side.

Stone–Ware Defence, 893, sometimes called the
Kieseritzky–Pillsbury Variation or McDonnell
Defence. Played by MCDONNELL in his 53rd match
game against BOURDONNAIS in 1834, the variation
was reintroduced by the Boston (USA) players
Henry Nathan Stone (1823–1909) and Preston
Ware (1821–90) around 1888.

stratagem, a short tactical manœuvre of a type that
occurs frequently. For example, after 1 e4 e5 2
Nc3 Nf6 3 Bc4 Black may play 3 ... Nxe4 4 Nxe4
d5, a stratagem that arises in various forms. (See
MARCO.)

strategy, the planning and conduct of the long-
term objectives in a game. Moves directed primarily
towards this end are commonly referred to as
POSITIONAL PLAY, as distinct from combinative play
(tactics). In its widest sense, strategy embraces all
that happens on the board. Tactics should accord
with strategic ends, and moves chosen to further a
long-term plan should be examined to determine
their tactical feasibility. 'Strategy', wrote EUWE,
'requires *thought*, tactics requires *observation*.' The
thinking is modified, move by move, as the position
changes.

Contrary to popular belief, masters do not make
preconceived plans that unfold as the game proceeds
from start to finish. In the opening phase the players
strive for an advantage in SPACE, TIME, and
MOBILITY, objectives of a general kind. A game of
MANŒUVRE might follow when a master seeks a
'network of options', as HARTSTON puts it, maintaining flexibility until a definite plan of action (usually
tactical) presents itself. Asked by his opponent,

BRONSTEIN, why, at one point in their game, he had not played a natural pawn advance, Hartston replied that he had rejected the move because he could not see the right plan that would follow. 'Wrong', said Bronstein, 'there are no plans in chess, only moves.'

Strategy as understood by players, who use the word in its normal sense, has no place in problems. Composers use the word to describe certain kinds of play, all of which a player would define as tactics.

Ströbeck, a small village on the western edge of Halberstadt in Germany. There are irreconcilable legends about the history of chess in Ströbeck, some suggesting that the game was popular there as far back as 1004. One story is that those who could play chess were given tax relief. In 1616 SELENUS first drew attention to the village when he wrote of the chess skill of the inhabitants and the strong tradition of COURIER which he found there. In 1651 the Elector of Brandenburg gave the village a combined chess and courier board and two sets, one ivory and one of silver.

When LEWIS visited the village in 1831 he noted that courier was dying out, and added that the silver set was lost, 'having been lent to the Dean and Chapter at Halberstadt, who forgot to return them'. At that time there were rules of chess peculiar to Ströbeck. Games began with a kind of TA'BI'A, both sides advancing a-, d-, and h-pawns two squares and moving their queens two squares forward. No other pawn could advance two squares and castling was not allowed. When a pawn reached the eighth rank it was not promoted at once, but was immune from capture there. To achieve promotion the pawn had to make, not necessarily consecutively, three backward moves of two squares. Although called a 'joy leap' this move could be made only if the intervening square was empty. The retreating pawn had no powers. Thus, a pawn reaching a8 would move to a6, a4, and on reaching a2 become a queen or other piece. Lewis pointed out that this could lead to unexpected draws. If White has a king on d6 and pawns on e5 and e6, while Black has a bare king on h8, the game must be a draw because after the pawn moves to e8 it cannot get back to e2 as the other white pawn must obstruct it. According to Silberschmidt (see SILBERSCHMIDT VARIATION) the locals demanded a stake from strangers, who often fell foul of the local rules. Lewis doubted whether any of the inhabitants could have defeated a first-class player who conceded odds of a knight.

Another tradition in Ströbeck is a LIVING CHESS display. In 1940 a film, designed to further Nazi propaganda, was made of this event. The copy in the village archives was removed by Anglo-American troops in 1945 and the historic costumes were destroyed during the war. In the first half of the twentieth century there was a falling away in chess interest among the inhabitants, and it was not always possible to provide living chessmen who knew how to play. Since then, new costumes have been made, and chess was made a compulsory subject at school in 1952. The 'local rules' have been dropped.

F. Wegener, 'Schach in Ströbeck', *Der Harz*, 1985, no. 13/14 pp. 75–96.

strong square, a square on a player's fourth rank or beyond that can be used effectively by that player's pieces. This square will be safe from attack by enemy pawns, such an attack being either impossible or inadvisable. An ADVANCE POINT, for example, is likely to be a strong square. (See KOSTIĆ.)

study, a legal position, usually composed and rarely from play, that is accompanied by the stipulations for the solver that one side (conventionally White) is to win or force a draw, these stipulations being indicated by the symbols + and = respectively. Unless otherwise stated, White plays first. According to the PIRAN CODEX there should be uniqueness of solution (i.e. each time White plays only one move fulfils the stipulations) against Black's best defence. Perhaps this should read 'what appears to be Black's best defence'. The composer intends this line of play to be the main variation and it often ends with a tactical denouement adding piquancy. The unique main play distinguishes the study from a DIDACTIC POSITION, although there is occasionally an overlap. The solution might be regarded as a correctly played finish to a fictitious game, but this analogy should not be taken too far. Neither the set position nor the tactical play of the solution is likely to be of a kind that might occur in play. Composers do not seek game-like solutions: on the contrary, they seek rare exceptions to the normal expectation. White, always in difficulties, wins when this seems impossible, or draws when the position seems hopelessly lost.

Composers have shown CUTTING-POINT THEMES, DECOY THEMES, and a few other ideas pioneered by problemists, but there are many problem themes that cannot be shown in studies. In other ways, however, study composers have greater scope: they seek aims other than mate or stalemate, they are not limited to a set number of moves, and they may add introductory play, often of interest in itself. They are expected to seek ECONOMY, as in compositions of any kind. For some study ideas, see DESPERADO, DOMINATION, ECHO, IDEAL MATE, IDEAL STALEMATE, SYSTEMATIC MOVEMENT, TEMPO-PLAY. Sometimes SACRIFICE of a large number of men, as in MANṢŪBĀT, is also featured.

Study composition reached a high level during the great days of Islamic chess in the 9th and 10th centuries. (See MANṢŪBA, aṣ-ṢŪLĪ.) Subsequently the art lay neglected almost until the 19th century. In 1851 KLING and HORWITZ published a pioneer work, *Chess Studies; or Endings of Games*, containing 208 positions, a mix of studies (the authors established this term) and didactic positions, all intended for instruction. In the 1890s a distinct advance was made, principally by TROITZKY and the Latvian Jānis Zēvers (aka Sehwers) (1868–1940), soon followed by RINCK, then KUBBEL and the PLATOV brothers. Soviet composers have since dominated the field.

The first large collection, *A Thousand End-Games* (1910–11), was made by the Englishman Creassey Edward Cecil Tattersall (1877–1957); he inserted many didactic positions, but neglected to cite source of original publication, now a standard practice. From 1939 authoritative collections have been made by LOMMER and KASPARYAN. (See HARMAN INDEX; ROYCROFT.)

A. J. Roycroft, *Test Tube Chess* (1972), republished as *The Chess Endgame Study* (1981).

Şuba, Mihai (1947–), Romanian-born British player, International Grandmaster (1978), mathematician and computer analyst. Şuba was Romanian champion 1980, 1981, and 1986, and played for his native land in the Olympiads from 1978 to 1986. His best international tournament results are: Las Palmas interzonal 1982, third ($+6=4-3$), after RIBLI and SMYSLOV, ahead of PETROSYAN and TUKMAKOV; Dortmund 1983, first ($+6=4-1$), ahead of HORT and CHANDLER; Prague zonal 1985, first equal with JANSA and PINTÉR; Beersheba 1986, first; Timişoara 1987, first equal. In 1988, during the political convulsions in Romania, Şuba moved to England; and he represented his new country in the 1989 European team championship. After that he restricted his chess activities in order to refresh his professional skills at university.

Süchting Variation, 84 in the SLAV DEFENCE, from the game Schlechter–Süchting, Carlsbad 1911.

sudden death, a way of resolving a tie by playing an extra game or games, perhaps with ever tighter time limits, until one side wins.

Suetin, Alexey Stepanovich (1926–), Russian player and author, International Grandmaster (1965). He played in ten USSR championships from 1950 to 1967, at his best sharing fourth place in 1963 ($+8=7-4$) and 1965 ($+6=11-2$). 'To gain a tournament first', he writes, 'mastery is not enough; you must dare, take risks', adding that a competitor should be prepared for complex games from the outset, and even if unsuccessful will be warmed up for the following rounds. This approach brought him several victories: Sarajevo 1965 ($+6=9$), ahead of MATULOVIĆ and POLUGAYEVSKY; Copenhagen 1965 ($+8=6-1$), shared with GLIGORIĆ and TAIMANOV, ahead of LARSEN; Titovo Užice 1966 ($+5=10$), shared with MATANOVIĆ, ahead of Gligorić; Havana 1969 ($+8=6-1$), shared with KORCHNOI; Brno 1976, the first Czech Open Championship, a tie with HORT, who won the title on tie-break; Lublin 1976 ($+6=7$); Dubna 1979, shared with RAZUVAYEV, Šahović, and I. A. Zaitsev. At Havana 1968 Suetin came second

($+9=5$) equal with STEIN, after KHOLMOV. A late success came when he won the Hastings Challengers tournament 1990–1. Suetin's books deal with MIDDLEGAME strategy, and the openings.

Alexey Suetin (Moscow, 1987) is a biography with more than 100 games or part-games.

Klovan–Suetin Minsk 1962 Latvia–Byelorussia Scotch Game Göring Gambit

1 e4 e5 2 Nf3 Nc6 3 d4 exd4 4 c3 dxc3 5 Bc4 cxb2 6 Bxb2 Bb4+ 7 Nc3 Nf6 8 Qc2 d6 9 0–0–0 0–0 10 e5 Ng4 11 h4 Ncxe5 12 Nd5 Bc5 13 Ng5 g6 14 Ne4 Bf5 15 f4

15 ... c6 16 fxe5 cxd5 17 Bxd5 Rc8 18 Kb1 Ne3 19 Qe2 Qb6 20 Ka1 Bxe4 21 Bxe4 Nxd1 22 Rxd1 dxe5 23 Bxe5 Rfe8 24 Bb2 Rcd8 25 Rxd8 Rxd8 White resigns.

Suetin Variation, 741 in the SPANISH OPENING, favoured by SUETIN in the 1960s. White intends to support the advance of the b-pawn, e.g. 9 ... Na5 10 Bc2 c5 11 d4 Qc7 12 b4.

Suhle Variation, 979, the ANDERSSEN COUNTER-ATTACK.

sui-mate, an obsolete name for SELFMATE, first used by the American player Napoleon Marache (1815–75) in *Chess Palladium and Mathematical Sphinx*, 1846.

aş-Şūlī, Abū-Bakr Muhammad ben Yaḥyā (854–946), the strongest player of his time, composer, and author of the first book describing a systematic way of playing SHAṬRANJ. For more than 600 years the highest praise an Arab could bestow on a chessplayer was to say that he played like aş-Şūlī. His family came from Jurjan, bordering the Caspian Sea, and his name indicates a Sulian (Turkish) background.

He came to prominence during the reign of al-Muktafī, caliph of Baghdad from 902 to 908, in whose presence he played a match against the court player al-Māwardī. When aş-Şūlī won, the caliph dismissed the loser with a pun: 'your rosewater [*māward*] has turned to urine'. Acquiring a high reputation as a scholar, biographer, and historian, aş-Şūlī remained in the court of the next two caliphs. A good conversationalist with a genial manner, he had wide knowledge. His large collection of books made him the butt of a satirical poem: 'Of all men, aṣ-Ṣūlī possesses the most learning—in his library. If we ask him for an explanation on a point of science he answers, "Boy! Bring here such and such a packet of science".' He wrote many history books and two textbooks on chess. In 940 he made an indiscreet political comment and had to flee from Baghdad. He died at Basra in reduced circumstances, leaving behind one outstanding pupil, al-LAJLĀJ.

aṣ-Ṣūlī's principal contribution to the strategy of shaṭranj was his advocacy of flank openings (see TA'BI'A). Besides composing MANṢŪBĀT he was an excellent ENDGAME analyst and player. (See DILARAM'S MATE; MANṢŪBĀT; TA'BI'A.)

+

The pieces shown as queens on the diagram are FIRZĀNS, which may be moved one square diagonally in any direction. Of this position, with White to play, aṣ-Ṣūlī writes 'This is very old, yet neither al-'ADLĪ nor anyone else has said whether it is drawn or can be won. There is no one on earth who has solved it unless he was taught by me.' White wins by BARE KING, i.e. capturing the black firzān without permitting the black king to capture the white fers in reply. For example 1 Ka2? Kc4 2 Kxa1 Kxc3 is a draw.

The computer-generated solution that follows was obtained by BEASLEY. There are many duals (shown in brackets), but none win in fewer than 20 moves. Black defends by maintaining the same relationship between the kings' positions as that between the firzāns' positions. White wins by driving the black king towards one of the far boundaries, when the edge of the board prevents Black from maintaining this balance.

1 Kb4 Kd6 2 Kc4 Ke6 3 Kd4 Kf6(a) 4 Kd5(Ke4) 4 ... Kf7 5 Ke5(Fd2) 5 ... Kg7 6 Ke6(Kf5, Fb4, Fd2) 6 ... Kf8(b) 7 Kd6(Kf5, Kf6, Fb4, Fd2) 7 ... Ke8 8 Kc6(Ke5, Fd2) 8 ... Kd8 9 Kb6(Kd5, Fd2) 9 ... Kc8(c) 10 Kc5 (Fd2) 10 ... Kd7 11 Kb5(Fd2) 11 ... Kc7(d) 12 Kc4(Fd2) 12 ... Kd6 13 Kb4(Fd2) 13 ... Ke5(e) 14 Ka3 Kd5 15 Kb3(f) 15 ... Kc5 16 Kc2(Fd2) 16 ... K~ 17 Fd2 K~ 18 Fc1 K~ 19 Kb1 K~ 20 Kxa1.

(a) After 3 ... Kf5 4 Fb4 the relationship between the firzāns is changed. Black, whose king cannot mimic this relationship by 4 ... Ke7, loses after 4 ... Ke6 5 Kd3 Ke5 6 Kc4 Kd6 7 Kc3 Kd5 8 Kc2 Kc4 9 Fa3 (ZUGZWANG) 9 ... Kb5 10 Kb1 Ka4 11 Ka2 (zugzwang) 11 ... K~ 12 Kxa1.

(b) Black disturbs the balance and is not permitted to regain it subsequently; but after 6 ... Kg8 7 Kf6 Kh8 a position given by ABŪ 'L-FATH is reached, and White wins by Kg6 or Kf7, e.g. 8 Kg6 Kg8 9 Fd2 Kf8 10 Fc1 Ke7 11–15 Kg6–b1 K~ 16 Kxa1.

(c) 9 ... Ke8/e7 10 Ka5 Kd7 11 Kb5 transposes.

(d) 11 ... Ke7/e6 12 Ka4 Kd6 13 Kb4 transposes.

(e) 13 ... Kc6 14 Fd2 Kd5 15 Kc3 Ke4 16 Kb3, and now 16 ... Kd3 17 Fc1 (zugzwang), or 16 ... Kd4 17 Kc2, or 16 ... Kf3 17 Ka2. 13 ... Ke6 14 Ka3 Kd5 15 Kb3 transposes.

(f) The starting position with Black to play: the result of a 15-move manœuvre by the white king in order to LOSE THE MOVE.

The first known publication to show the correct winning method was by AVERBAKH in 1986. Noting the extraordinary king chase, to the far edge and back, he writes: 'It is a creation of genius.'

In aṣ-Ṣūlī's text the Black king is on e4, with Black to move, but any move other than the immediate 1 ... Kd5 loses quickly.

Sultan Khan (1905–66), perhaps the greatest natural player of modern times. Born in the Punjab, he learned Indian chess when he was nine. In the Indian game of his time the pieces were moved as in international chess, but the laws of promotion and stalemate were different, and a pawn could not be advanced two squares on its first move. The game opened slowly, with emphasis on positional play rather than tactics, and not surprisingly Sultan Khan became a positional player. He was taken into the household of Sir Umar Hayat Khan, and learned the international game in 1926. Two years later he won the All-India championship, and in the spring of 1929 his patron and master took him to London. Within a few months he won the British championship, going back to India shortly afterwards.

Returning to Europe in May 1930, Sultan Khan began a career that included defeats of many leading players. His best results are: Liège 1930, second to TARTAKOWER; Hastings 1930–1, third (+5=2−2), after EUWE and CAPABLANCA; Hastings 1931–2, fourth; Bern 1932, fourth (+10=2−3); London 1932, third (+6=3−2) equal with KASHDAN, after ALEKHINE and FLOHR. Sultan Khan won the British championship again in 1932 and 1933, and played first board for the British Chess Federation in the Olympiads of 1930, 1931, and 1933. In match play he defeated Tartakower (+4=5−3) in 1931, and lost to Flohr (+1=3−2) in 1932. At the end of 1933 he returned with his master to India, and his chess career was over. He had no regrets. Another servant in the household, Fatima (who had won the British Ladies Championship in 1933), said that Sultan felt that he had been freed from prison. He suffered from bouts of malaria and, in the English climate, from continual colds and throat infections, often turning up to play with his neck swathed in bandages. When Sir Umar died in 1944 Sultan Khan was left a small farmstead near his birthplace, and there he lived out his days. He would not coach his children in chess, his eldest son, Ather Sultan, recalls, but told them that they should do something more useful with their lives.

A striking figure, of dark complexion, with a lean face and broad forehead, his black hair often hidden under a turban, he sat at the board impassively, showing no emotion in positions good or bad. He did not believe that he possessed any special skill, rather that the player applying the greater concentration should win. When Sultan Khan first travelled to Europe his English was so rudimentary that he needed an interpreter. Unable to read or write, he never studied any books on the game, and he was put into the hands of trainers who were also his rivals in play. He never mastered openings which, by nature empirical, cannot be learned by the application of common sense alone. Under these adverse circumstances, and having known international chess for a mere seven years, only half of which was spent in Europe, Sultan Khan nevertheless had few peers in the MIDDLEGAME, was among the world's best two or three ENDGAME players, and one of the world's best ten players. This achievement brought admiration from Capablanca who called him a genius, an accolade he rarely bestowed. (See MOBILITY.)

R. N. Coles, *Mir Sultan Khan* (rev. edn., 1977) contains 64 games.

Soultanbéieff–Sultan Khan Liège 1930 Queen's Indian Defence

1 d4 Nf6 2 Nf3 b6 3 c4 e6 4 g3 Bb7 5 Bg2 Bb4+ 6 Bd2 Bxd2+ 7 Nbxd2 0–0 8 0–0 c5 9 Qc2 Nc6 10 dxc5 bxc5 11 e4 Qc7 12 Rfe1 d6 13 Racl h6 14 a3 Nd7 15 Qc3 a5 16 Nh4 g5 17 Qe3 Qd8 18 Nf3 Qe7 19 h3 Rab8 20 b3 Ba8 21 Nb1 Nde5 22 a4 Nxf3+ 23 Bxf3 Nd4 24 Bd1

24 ... f5 25 exf5 Rxf5 26 Rc3 Rbf8 27 Rf1 Rf3 28 Bxf3 Rxf3 White resigns.

sum of progressive scores, an AUXILIARY SCORING METHOD used for tie-breaking in SWISS SYSTEM tournaments. The aggregate scores made by a player after each round are added together. For example,

a player whose progressive scores read 1,2,3,3,3 (=12) would be placed above a player whose progressive scores read 0,0,1,2,3 (=6). This popular and simple way of resolving ties is based on the supposition that a player who scores more points in the early rounds will have been pitted against stronger opposition.

Suttles Variation, 1281 in the ROBATSCH DEFENCE, as Jiminez–Suttles, Palma de Majorca 1970.

Svenonius Variation, 837 in the FOUR KNIGHTS OPENING; 1076 in the KING'S GAMBIT Declined; 1198, sometimes called the Exchange Variation Deferred, in the FRENCH DEFENCE. The Swedish analyst Ludwig Oskar Svenonius (1853–1926) contributed many articles on the openings to *Deutsches Wochenschach*.

Sveshnikov, Yevgeny Ellinovich (1950–), Russian player, International Grandmaster (1977). He qualified for and played in his first USSR championship when he was 17, and in 1978, at his fifth of eight attempts, he tied for fifth place. His tournament firsts include: Sochi 1976 (+5=10), equal with POLUGAYEVSKY, ahead of GELLER; Le Havre 1977 (+8=7); Cienfuegos 1979 (+9=4); Sochi 1983 (+6=6−2), shared with Vaiser; Hastings 1984–5; Sochi 1985 (+6=7−1); Moscow 1989. He had a good score also at Novi Sad 1979 (+6=6−1), equal second with Geller, after GHEORGHIU.

Timman–Sveshnikov Wijk aan Zee 1981 Sicilian Defence Rossolimo Variation

1 e4 c5 2 Nf3 Nc6 3 Bb5 e6 4 0–0 Nge7 5 c3 d5 6 exd5 Qxd5 7 d4 cxd4 8 c4 Qd6 9 Nxd4 Bd7 10 Nxc6 Nxc6 11 Nc3 a6 12 Ba4 Qxd1 13 Rxd1 Ne5 14 b3 Bb4 15 Bb2 f6 16 Bxd7+ Nxd7 17 Ne4 0–0–0 18 c5 Kb8 19 Bd4 e5 20 Be3 f5 21 a3 Bxa3 22 Ng5

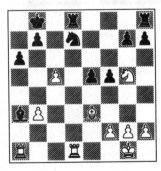

22 ... Nxc5 23 Rf1 f4 24 Bxc5 Bxc5 25 Nf7 g5 26 Racl Bd4 27 Nxh8 Rxh8 28 Rfdl g4 29 Kf1 Rf8 30 f3 gxf3 31 gxf3 Rf6 32 Rc2 Ka7 33 Rc7 Rh6 34 Rd2 a5 35 Kg2 Ka6 36 Re7 b6 37 Rc2 Kb5 38 Rc4 Rg6+ 39 Kh3 Rh6+ 40 Kg2 Rh5 41 Rd7 Rg5+ 42 Kh3 Rh5+ 43 Kg2 Bc5 44 Rg7 Rh6 45 Rg5 Rd6 46 Rxe5 Rd3 47 Rxf4 Rxb3 48 Rf7 a4 49 Rxh7 Rb2+ 50 Kg3 a3 51 Ra7 Kb4 52 f4 a2 53 Re4+ Kb3 54 h4 b5 55 Ra8 b4 56 Re5 Kc4 57 Kg4 Rg2+ 58 Kf3 Rf2+ 59 Kg4 b3 60 Re4+ Kd3 White resigns.

Sveshnikov Variation, 490 in the SICILIAN DEFENCE, a popular line in the 1980s. Although first played in a game Tal–Shamkovich, Riga 1955, it was analytical work in the 1970s, by SVESHNIKOV in particular, that led to its widespread adoption.

Swedish Variation, 123, the FOLKESTONE VARIATION.

swindle, a trap by means of which a player who has a lost position avoids defeat. If the trap fails to ensnare the opponent it is not called a swindle. The most renowned of swindlers, MARSHALL, was rightly proud of this specal skill: for any means of saving a lost position is as good as another. His habit of playing on long after others would have resigned was well known, and may on occasion have disarmed his opponent.

Marshall–Marco   Monte Carlo 1904   Scotch Gambit

1 e4 e5 2 Nf3 Nc6 3 d4 exd4 4 Bc4 Bc5 5 c3 d3 6 0–0 d6 7 Qxd3 Nf6 8 b4 Bb6 9 a4 a6 10 Re1 Ng4 11 Ra2 Nge5 12 Nxe5 Nxe5 13 Qg3 Nxc4 14 Qxg7 Rf8 15 e5 Nxe5 16 Kh1 Be6 17 Rae2 Qe7 18 f4 Nd3 19 f5 Ne5 20 fxe6 fxe6 21 Bh6 Qxg7 22 Bxg7 Rf5 23 Bxe5 Rxe5 24 Rxe5 dxe5 25 g3 Rd8 26 Kg2 Rd3 27 Rxe5 Kf7 28 Re2 Be3 29 Rc2 Bh6 30 Rf2+ Ke7 31 Rf3 Rd1 32 Rf1 Rd3 33 Rf3 Rd1 34 Na3? Rc1 35 c4 Ra1 36 c5 Bc1 37 Nc4 Rxa4 38 Ne5 Bb2 39 Nd3 Bc3 40 Rf4 a5 41 Rh4 axb4 42 Rxh7+ Kd8 43 Nf4 b3 44 Nxe6+ Kc8

45 c6 (a desperate move in a lost position) 45 ... Be5? (Black, who has been winning since his 34th move, suspects nothing, but falls into White's trap—an eleven-move combination or swindle: 45 ... bxc6 wins.) 46 cxb7+ Kb8 47 Nc5 Ra2+ 48 Kh3 b2 49 Re7 Ka7 50 Re8 c6 51 Ra8+ Kb6 52 Rxa2 b1=Q 53 b8=Q+ Bxb8 54 Rb2+ Qxb2 55 Na4+ Kb5 56 Nxb2 c5 57 Kg2 c4 58 Kf3 c3 59 Nd3 Kc4 60 Ne1 Kd4 61 h4 Bd6 62 g4 Be7 63 g5 Ke5 64 Kg4 Bf8 65 Nc2 Ke4? (65 ... Ke6 draws) 66 h5 Kd3 67 Na1 Ke4 68 h6 Ke5 69 Kh5 Kf5 70 Nc2 Bd6 71 Nd4+ Ke4 72 Ne2 c2 73 g6 Ba3 74 g7 Kd3 75 g8=Q Kxe2 76 Qa2 Black resigns.

Swiss Gambit, 1317, variation in the BIRD OPENING, so named by WAGNER. He introduced the gambit, which is sometimes called after him, in a Swiss correspondence tournament game Wagner–Kostin, 1910–11.

Swiss system, a method of playing a tournament that allows more players to take part than would be possible in an ALL-PLAY-ALL tournament with the same number of rounds, and that does not have the disadvantages of the KNOCK-OUT TOURNAMENT method. The basic principle is that players are paired for each round against opponents who have the same score at that time, and whom they have not played before. Players should have an equitable number of games with each colour by the end of the event. Swiss tournaments usually have an odd number of rounds, greatly easing one of the organizers' main burdens, that of colour balancing. The administrative details can become quite complicated.

The reliability of the system is approximately shown by this formula:

$$\frac{(5 \times \text{number of rounds}) - \text{number of players}}{7}$$

$$= \text{number of places}$$

A twelve-round tournament with 32 players would thus give four reasonably accurate places, or rather eight, because the bottom four are also reliable. The other 24 are only crudely sorted. Therefore the Swiss system should not be used for a competition within a competition, such as awarding a championship to the highest placed local person in an international tournament. Obviously if the number of players is more than five times the number of rounds, then in theory no places can be regarded as satisfactory; but in practice ratings are used to effect an approximate balance, and so to make a satisfactory tournament possible.

This popular system, which on account of the numbers that can play often makes tournaments self-financing, was suggested by Dr Julius Müller of Brugg, Switzerland, and first used for a chess tournament at Zurich in 1895.

Swiss Variation, 1197 in the FRENCH DEFENCE, played in the game Lasker–Bogoljubow, Zurich 1934, but known earlier. Also 188, the HENNE-BERGER VARIATION of the QUEEN'S GAMBIT Declined; 311, the MILNER-BARRY VARIATION.

switchback, a composition term for the return of a piece to the square from which it came. The piece may return after weakening the defence in some way, as in the SIERS RÖSSEL THEME. In the so-called Mousetrap Theme a white piece returns after its square of origin has been crossed by a black line-piece, which is thus cut off from play.

symbols, see CONVENTIONAL SYMBOLS.

Symmetrical Defence, 11 in the ENGLISH OPENING (see GAVRIKOV; MANŒUVRE; MATULOVIĆ; TIMMAN); 77, the AUSTRIAN DEFENCE in the QUEEN'S GAMBIT Declined.

Symmetrical Variation, 131 in the TARRASCH DEFENCE to the QUEEN'S GAMBIT; 839 in the FOUR KNIGHTS OPENING; 1306 in the ZUKERTORT OPENING.

synthetic. The solution of a problem is given, perhaps accompanied by SET PLAY and TRY-PLAY, and the solver is required to construct the position. The earliest known synthetic was set in the *Chess Palladium and Mathematical Sphinx*, 1846.

synthetic game problem, see SHORTEST GAME PROBLEM.

synthetic method, a technique for playing chess without analysis of the position, but by applying military theory. Its advocate, Franklin Knowles Young (1857–1931), published half a dozen books between 1894 and 1923 to advance his method, but readers without a thorough grasp of military jargon found the books unintelligible, and readers with such a grasp found them useless. Reviewing the last book of the series in its December 1923 issue, the *Chess Amateur* said: 'We have read the book assiduously, confident that nobody can get everything wrong . . .'

system, a series of moves that can be made by one side independently, to some extent, of the opponent's play. The moves are not necessarily made in a fixed order. The idea of building up a middlegame position in this way, customary in the old game (see TA'BI'A), was introduced to the modern game by STAUNTON in the 1840s. For examples, see COLLE SYSTEM; LENGFELLNER SYSTEM; LENINGRAD SYSTEM; PIRC–ROBATSCH VARIATION; STAUNTON SYSTEM. The term is less appropriate for the FISCHER, PANNO, and PETROSYAN SYSTEMS. On the other hand the word 'system' might be applied to the traditional lines of the KING'S INDIAN DEFENCE, also to the BARCZA OPENING, LONDON VARIATION, and RÉTI OPENING.

systematic movement, a study term for a series of manœuvres, each of a similar kind, and each involving movement in the same direction. (See also GURGENIDZE.)

+

A study by CHEKHOVER, *64*, 1937. The theme is stalemate-avoidance; the means, a systematic movement slowly advancing the pawn. 1 Kh1 (1 Kg1? Rg8=. Other moves also fail) 1 ... Rd8 2 Kh2 Re8 3 e3 Rd8 4 Kh3 Re8 5 e4 Rd8 6 Kh4 Re8 7 e5 Rd8 8 Kh5 Re8 9 e6 Rd8 10 Kh6 Re8 11 e7 Rc8 12 Kh7 Rg8 13 e8=Q+ Rxe8 14 f7.

Szabó, László (1917–), International Grandmaster (1950), International Arbiter (1954), leading Hungarian player for about 20 years and in his prime one of the world's best dozen. His first notable successes came at the unusually early age of 18: he won the Hungarian championship (for the first of eight times—he lost the play-off on two other occasions), won a tournament at Tatatóváros (+10=6−1), and played in the Warsaw Olympiad, impressing competitors with his attacking style.

His next important tournament achievements came after the Second World War: Groningen 1946, fourth (+9=5−5) equal with NAJDORF, after BOTVINNIK, EUWE, and SMYSLOV, ahead of BOLESLAVSKY and KOTOV; Saltsjöbaden interzonal 1948, second (+8=9−2), after BRONSTEIN, ahead of Boleslavsky, Kotov, and Najdorf; Budapest 1948, first (+9=6); Saltsjöbaden interzonal 1952, shared fifth; Göteborg interzonal 1955 (+6=12−2), fifth equal. In his third and last CANDIDATES tournament, Amsterdam 1956, Szabó made his nearest approach to being challenger for the world championship, taking third place (+3=13−2) equal with Bronstein, GELLER, PETROSYAN, and SPASSKY, after Smyslov and KERES.

Subsequently he had several excellent victories: Zagreb 1964 (+6=7); Budapest 1965 (+7=8), equal with POLUGAYEVSKY and TAIMANOV; Sarajevo 1972 (+8=6−1), ahead of Petrosyan, HORT, and Keres; Hilversum 1973 (+6=7−1), equal with Geller, ahead of LJUBOJEVIĆ and Polugayevsky; and Hastings 1973–4, equal with KUZMIN, TIMMAN, and TAL. Hilversum was Szabó's best win, a fine achievement for a player in his fifty-seventh year. Over a period of 33 years (1935–68) Szabó played for his country in eleven Olympiads, five times at first board. In 1979 he retired, shortly after sharing first place with Hort and Westerinen in a small tournament in Helsinki.

His autobiography, *50 év—100 000 lépés* (1981) ('50 years—100,000 moves'), contains 222 games as well as details of his career.

Eliskases–Szabó Stockholm–Saltsjöbaden 1952 Queen's Pawn Opening Blumenfeld Variation

1 d4 Nf6 2 c4 e6 3 Nf3 c5 4 Nc3 cxd4 5 Nxd4 Bb4 6 Bd2 Nc6 7 Nxc6 bxc6 8 e3 0–0 9 Be2 Rb8 10 0–0 Be7 11 Qc2 d5 12 Rfd1 e5 13 cxd5 cxd5 14 Be1 Be6 15 Rac1 Qd7 16 Bf3 Rfc8 17 Qd2 Rd8 18 Ra1 Bb4 19 a3 Ba5 20 b4 Bb6 21 a4 d4 22 exd4 Bxd4 23 b5

23 ... Bb3 24 Rdb1 Qe6 25 Bc6 e4 26 Qf4 e3 27 Qf3
Bc2 28 Rc1 Bg6 29 h3 Bh5 30 g4 Bg6 31 a5 h5 32 g5
Nd7 33 Bxd7 Rxd7 34 b6 axb6 35 a6 b5 36 Rd1 Ba7
White exceeded the time limit.

Szabó Variation, 155 in the ANTI-MERAN GAMBIT,
introduced in the game Szabó–Euwe, Hastings
1938–9; 384, also called the Boleslavsky Variation,
in the GRÜNFELD DEFENCE; 420 in the KING'S INDIAN
DEFENCE, played by SZABÓ in the Amsterdam Candidates tournament 1956, but known much earlier.
Also 29, the BREMEN VARIATION.

Szén (pron. sen), József (1805–57), Hungarian
player, one of the world's best half-dozen in the
1840s, famed for his ENDGAME skill in both analysis
and play. 'Of a mild nature, thoughtful, active-
minded, patient, shy, and timid in manner', Szén
lacked worldly ambition. After a long period in his
father's office he became a paid official in the
Department of Archives. He had wanted to study
mathematics but in deference to his father, a
notary, he studied law, without success. At Paris in
1836 he went daily to the CAFÉ DE LA RÉGENCE; the
players could see him coming from a distance on
account of his conspicuous hat, calling him affec-
tionately 'l'Hongrois au chapeau blanc'. He met
BOURDONNAIS who gave him odds (pawn and move,
or pawn and two), and they played many games.
The advantage lay with Szén, but whether he led by
a narrow or decisive majority of games is not
known. He acquitted himself well in other cities, his
worst result a narrow defeat by BLEDOW at Berlin in
1839.
    In 1837 WALKER notes that Szén was stronger
than any player in Vienna, that he could beat all the
London players, that he was about as strong as
SAINT-AMANT but 'plays the endgame better'. From
1842 to 1846 Szén led a Hungarian team in a
correspondence match against Paris; Hungary's
decisive victory marked her coming of age in the
chess world, with Szén her first great master.
    He eagerly accepted an invitation to the world's
first international tournament, an unseeded series
of knock-out matches, London 1851. After defeating Samuel Newham (1796–1875), England's leading provincial player, he lost to ANDERSSEN, the
eventual winner, in the second round. (After the
third game of this match Szén was leading, +2−1,
and the players agreed that if either won the first
prize he would give a third of his winnings to the
other.) Szén won the third round against HORWITZ
(+4), the fourth and last round against KENNEDY
(+4=1), and was placed fifth overall. In 1853 Szén
lost a match to HARRWITZ (+1=1−3), then in his
prime. Szén's health, never robust, was now failing.
He returned to Pest where, during his last days, 'the
chessboard and the men were his constant companions.' (See THREE PAWNS PROBLEM.)

Szén Variation, 550, sound line in the SICILIAN
DEFENCE, played successfully by SZÉN against
ANDERSSEN at the London 1851 tournament, and
regarded as so strong that the Sicilian Defence went
out of fashion for most of the 1850s.

Szily Variation, 542, name sometimes given to the
CHEKHOVER VARIATION of the SICILIAN DEFENCE.
József Szily (1913–76), of Hungary, was one of the
world's best in the late 1940s.

T

ta'bi'a (pl. ta'bi'āt), an opening system used in SHAṬRANJ. Each ta'bi'a consists essentially of a PAWN FORMATION which a player should try to set up; this might be prevented by the opponent, or might remain incomplete because a better course of action presents itself. Generally the pawns are supported by pieces from the rear. A player tries to gain space, perhaps establishing one or more pawns on the fifth rank (e.g. for White, b5 and f5, the strong squares, or c5 and g5, to keep out the black FIRZĀN), and also tries to make holes in the enemy pawn formation so that the firzān may be advanced to the fifth rank or beyond.

As in the modern game, the initiative confers advantage, for the player moving first has the greater influence on the shape of the pawn formation. The pawn or pawns that are to be advanced beyond the third rank are usually moved first, but a player is advised, when the opponent moves a pawn, to make a reply that will 'stand against it', to prevent the gain of space by the opponent in any part of the board. For example, White might begin 1 f3 answering 1 ... f6 by 2 f4 or 1 ... c6 by 2 c3. The pieces shown as queens and bishops are firzāns (F) and FĪLS (A) respectively.

In the Saif opening a player attempts an early advance of the d-pawn (the saif pawn or sword pawn), not a good idea: for example, 1 d3 c6 2 d4 b6 3 c3 c5 4 d5 Nf6 5 c4 b5 (compare the BENKO GAMBIT) 6 b3 bxc4 7 bxc4 Aa6 8 Na3 Axc4 9 Nxc4 Nxd5, with advantage to Black.

The mujannaḥ, meaning flank opening, a solid formation that the opponent cannot easily prevent. White concedes no space, holds the weak square f4 firmly, and can link rooks on the second rank, for action on any part of the board. Of the pawn advances that White might now prepare al-LAJLĀJ comments: on the king's-side (best), in the centre (the most popular), on the queen's-side (the least effective).

The sayyāl, meaning torrent. White's aim is to advance the f-pawn (the torrent pawn) to f5. This and the mujannaḥ were the two openings most favoured by aṣ-ṢŪLĪ.

The muwashshaḥ, invented by aṣ-ṢŪLĪ. The name means richly-girdled, and White has indeed a promising position: but a strong opponent would not permit the completion of this ta'bi'a.

al-Lajlāj gives many fictitious games showing how advantage might be sought in the middlegame: by making use of strong squares on the fifth rank, by making a path for the firzān, or by advancing a group of pawns. To this end he does not always give the best moves by the defender. Some of his examples follow.

1 f3 f6 2 f4 f5 3 c3 c6 4 c4 c5 5 Nf3 Nf6 6 Nc3 Nc6 7 e3 e6 8 g3 g6 9 b3 b6 10 d3 d6 11 Rg1 Rg8 12 Rb1 Rb8 (the double mujannaḥ) 13 h3 Rb7 14 Rb2 Rbg7 15 Rbg2 h6 16 g4 fxg4 17 hxg4 g5 (else White advances the g-pawn) 18 f5 d5 19 fxe6 dxc4 20 bxc4 Axe6 21 Nd5 Fe7 22 Nxf6+ Fxf6, and 'White's firzān has a clear road to the centre of the board' (via f3 to d5). A variation on black's 14th move: 14 ... Rf7 15 Rf2 h6 16 g4 fxg4 17

hxg4 g5 18 f5 exf5 19 gxf5 Nd7 20 Nd2 Ne7 21 Ah3 (not 21 e4, leaving holes for the black firzān) 21 . . . g4 22 Rfg2 h5 23 Nde4 Rh8 24 Ng5 Rg7 25 Nf3 Rgg8 26 Nh4 gxh3, and, having a firm grip on f5, White has the advantage.

1 f3 f6 2 f4 e6 3 c3 c6 4 c4 d6 5 Nf3 g6 6 Nc3 b6 7 e3 Nd7 8 g3 Ne7 9 b3 Fc7 10 d3 d5 11 Rg1 e5 (Black plays the mashāʾīkhī, meaning the Sheikh's opening, characterized by the advance of both centre pawns. al-Lajlāj shows how a CLASSICAL CENTRE may be broken by the flank attack of the mujannaḥ. 11 . . . a6, the chanaj, would be better.) 12 Rb1 Fd6 13 b4 h6 14 Aa3 Ae6 15 fxe5 fxe5 16 c5 (confining Black's firzān) 16 . . . Fc7 17 b5! cxb5 18 Nxb5 Kd8 19 Nc3 bxc5 20 Axc5 Nxc5 21 Nxe5, and Black's centre is broken, the d-pawn isolated on a weak square.

1 g3 (aiming for the sayyāl) 1 . . . h6 2 g4 f6 3 h3 h5 (the recommended defence, after which White must find a new plan) 4 g5 f5 5 h4 g6 6 f3 Rh7 7 f4 Rf7 8 e3 e6 9 d3 d6 10 c3 c6 11 b3 b6 12 Nd2 Nd7 13 Ah3 Ne7 14 Ne2 Fc7 15 Rf1 Rb8 16 Ng3 a6 17 e4 fxe4 (if 17 . . . b5 18 exf5 exf5 19 Rf3 followed by Nf1 and Ne3 renewing the attack of f5) 18 dxe4 e5 (or 18 . . . d5 19 f5) 19 f5 gxf5 20 exf5, and 'White has two united passed pawns and Black's h-pawn is fixed.' An opening that would have pleased PHILIDOR.

table, see CROSSTABLE; PAIRING TABLE.

at-Tabrīzī, 'Alāʾaddīn (14th cent.), commonly known as Kwāja 'Alī ash-Shaṭranjī, the best player of his day. A lawyer from Samarkand, he became attached to the court of TIMUR and travelled extensively, for the court was almost continually on the move. His play was rapid and he claimed that he could play four simultaneous blindfold games while conversing with friends. He ascribed his strength to assistance from Allāh, who in a dream had once given him a set of chessmen. With Timur he played only GREAT CHESS. His book on chess has not survived, but positions from his games or composed by him have been copied into other manuscripts.

tabular notation, a notation that is written in column form, as, for example, on a SCORE SHEET. In many books the moves played are in tabular notation with annotational analyses in RUNNING NOTATION, as in the game under POSITIONAL PLAY.

tactics, the art of conducting the game, the means by which the strategic plans are carried out. Tactics are most evident in a COMBINATION and when dealing with immediate threats, but most, perhaps all, moves have a tactical ingredient, usually the preparation or prevention of threats. Chess has been described as a strategic game that is 99 per cent tactical, another way of saying that no move should be made without consideration of its tactical consequences. Tactics cannot be learned by rote: they vary from game to game, even when the same strategic plan is used. Beginners should play as many different opponents as possible, and analyse for themselves the games played by masters, thus becoming familiar with a wide range of tactical ideas.

Taimanov, Mark Yevgenyevich (1926–), Soviet player, International Grandmaster (1952), and one of the world's best ten from about 1950 to 1956, concert pianist. At the age of eight Taimanov already showed talent for both chess and music. A few years later he joined a group of young chessplayers receiving instruction from BOTVINNIK. In 1948 he won the Leningrad championship, and then competed in the USSR championship, a chastening experience, for he shared the last place. (At about the same time he was taking his final examinations at the Leningrad Conservatoire.) Soon afterwards his chess successes began: USSR championship 1949, third (+7=1−1) equal with GELLER, after BRONSTEIN and SMYSLOV; Leningrad championship 1950, first, and 1952, first; interzonal tournament, Saltsjöbaden 1952, second (+7=13) equal with PETROSYAN, after KOTOV; USSR championship 1952, first (ⅰ 11=5−3) equal with Botvinnik, who won the play-off; CANDIDATES tournament, Neuhausen–Zurich 1953, eighth (+7=14−7) equal with Kotov.

Some time elapsed before Taimanov made another attempt to gain the world title. He followed his career as a pianist, and chess successes came intermittently: USSR championship 1954, second (+7=12) equal with KORCHNOI after AVERBAKH; Moscow 1956, third (+6=9), after Botvinnik and Smyslov, ahead of Bronstein and KERES; USSR championship 1956, first (+8=7−2) equal with Averbakh and SPASSKY, and champion after a play-off; Leningrad championship 1961, first equal with Spassky; Dortmund 1961, first (+6=4−1), ahead of Smyslov and LARSEN; USSR championship 1962, second (+10=7−2) equal with TAL, after Korchnoi; Budapest 1956, first (+7=8) equal with POLU-GAYEVSKY and SZABÓ; and Copenhagen 1965, first (+8=6−1) equal with GLIGORIĆ and SUETIN, ahead of Larsen.

In 1969 and 1970 Taimanov played with renewed vigour, winning three international tournaments in succession: Zalaegerszeg 1969 (+7=8); Wijk aan Zee 1970 (+7=8), ahead of HORT; and Skopje 1970 (+7=8), a tie with VASYUKOV. He then played in the interzonal, Palma de Majorca 1970, scored +8=12−3, shared fifth place, and became a Candidate. In the quarter-final, played at Vancouver in 1971, he met FISCHER, and lost every game. There were few comparable precedents for such a CLEAN SCORE, and this crushing defeat effectively ended Taimanov's chess career. He was a marked man. His luggage was searched when he returned, and one of Solzhenitsyn's books was found. He did not declare money given to him by EUWE for FLOHR, but the authorities knew (from listening on the telephone) that he was carrying it. He became *persona non grata.*

'At least', he said, 'I still have my music.' Further troubles followed, however. His concert repertoire included piano duets, but these ended and he lost the greater part of his income when he left his wife of twenty-six years, who had been his musical partner, and re-married. The deserted wife complained about Taimanov's behaviour; he was excluded from the USSR team, and his salary as a chess professional withheld.

Slowly he became rehabilitated. He was third at Sukhumi 1972 (+7=8), after Tal and SAVON, won the Leningrad championship in 1973, for the fifth time, and in 1976 played in his twenty-third USSR championship, a number matched only by Geller. After that his successes were in minor events, but in due course he was allowed travel privileges again, and he ended his career sharing third prize at New Delhi 1982.

Taimanov made several contributions to openings knowledge, with his books on the NIMZO-INDIAN DEFENCE in particular. He also wrote *Zarubezhnye vstrechi* (1958), a diary of his travels. (See WEAKNESS.)

Evans–Taimanov New York 1954 USA–USSR King's Indian Defence Aronin–Taimanov Variation

1 d4 Nf6 2 c4 g6 3 Nc3 Bg7 4 e4 d6 5 Nf3 0–0 6 Be2 e5 7 0–0 Nc6 8 d5 Ne7 9 Ne1 Nd7 10 Nd3 f5 11 exf5 gxf5 12 f4 e4 13 Nf2 Nf6 14 Be3 Kh8 15 Kh1 Rg8 16 Rg1 c5 17 h3 Ng6 18 g4 fxg4 19 hxg4

19 ... Nh5 20 gxh5 Qh4+ 21 Kg2 Nxf4+ 22 Kf1 Bh3+ 23 Nxh3 Qxh3+ 24 Kf2 Raf8 25 Bf3 Nd3+ 26 Ke2 Rxf3 27 Qd2 Rxe3+ 28 Qxe3 Qxh5+ 29 Kd2 Bh6 30 Rxg8+ Kxg8 31 Nxe4 Bxe3+ 32 Kxe3 Qh3+ 33 Kd2 Ne5 34 Rg1+ Kf8 35 Rg3 Qh4 White resigns.

Taimanov Variation, 15 and 17 in the ENGLISH OPENING, the same plan in slightly different positions, as Smyslov–Taimanov, Moscow 1968; 284 in the MODERN BENONI, examined by TAIMANOV, who published his analysis in 1956, and played by him against TRIFUNOVIĆ in the USSR–Yugoslavia match, 1957; 319, a variation of the NIMZO-INDIAN DEFENCE favoured by Taimanov in the 1950s, but known earlier; 404 in the KING'S INDIAN DEFENCE, as Taimanov–Ciocaltea, Moscow 1956.

Also three unrelated lines, in the SICILIAN DEFENCE; 546, as Krogius–Taimanov, USSR championship 1959; 551, with the idea of following by Ra8–a7–b7; 552, the BASTRIKOV VARIATION.

Tal, Mikhail (1936–92), Latvian player, International Grandmaster (1957), World Champion

1960–1. Born in Riga, the son of a physician, he became interested in chess when he saw a game played in his father's waiting-room. At eight years of age he joined the chess section of the Pioneers at Riga, and five years later he began to study the game with Alexander Koblencs (1916–), a leading Latvian player. They became close friends. At this time Tal was not unduly skilled at the game; he was no child prodigy. A bright pupil at school, he went to university at the age of 15 to study Russian language and literature. He first became widely known in the Soviet Union when he won the chess championship of Latvia in 1953, after which he made rapid progress: USSR championship 1957, first (+9=10−2); USSR championship 1958, first (+9=5−3 and one win by default); Portorož interzonal 1958, first (+8=11−1); Zurich 1959, first (+10=3−2); Bled-Zagreb-Belgrade CANDIDATES tournament 1959, first (+16=8−4). By winning this last event, one of his best tournament achievements, Tal became challenger. In 1960 he defeated BOTVINNIK (+6=13−2) to become the youngest world champion up to that time.

A year later Tal lost the return match. He wanted to play in Tallinn, where he had enthusiastic support, but to the privilege of a return match, Botvinnik added another, the choice of venue, and they played in Moscow. Before the match Tal had been unwell with kidney trouble, but he declined a postponement offered by his opponent. The chief cause of his loss was lack of study and preparation. Botvinnik expressed this differently: 'If Tal would

Tal, going on to share first place at the Interzonal Tournament, Amsterdam 1964

learn to program himself properly then it would become impossible to play him.'

Shortly after losing the title Tal made the second of his great tournament performances, taking first prize (+11=7−1), one point ahead of FISCHER and two points ahead of GLIGORIĆ, KERES, and PETRO-SYAN, at Bled 1961. Tal began to play in the next Candidates tournament, Curaçao 1962, but withdrew before completing his games, to undergo hospital treatment for his kidney trouble. In the USSR championship later that year he came second (+11=5−3) equal with TAIMANOV, after KORCH-NOI, and at Miskolc 1963 he was first (+10=5), two points ahead of BRONSTEIN. After scoring +11=12 to share first place in the Amsterdam interzonal of 1964, Tal again became a Candidate. He then defeated PORTISCH (+4=3−1) and LARSEN (+3=5−2), but lost the final match to SPASSKY. At Kharkov in 1967 the Soviet championship was organized on the Swiss system for the first time, and Tal tied with POLUGAYEVSKY for the title, which they shared. Tal won the first of his Candidates matches in 1968, defeating Gligorić (+3=5−1), and then lost to Korchnoi. In 1969 he had an operation to remove a kidney, and declared he felt better as a consequence. A heavy smoker and drinker, Tal did not pamper his remaining somewhat unhealthy kidney, and was never free from bouts of ill-health.

Tal's best subsequent victories are: Tallinn 1971 (+9=5−1), shared with Keres; USSR championship 1972 (+9=12); Wijk aan Zee 1973 (+6=9); Tallinn 1973 (+9=6); Halle 1974 (+8=7); USSR championship 1974 (+6=7−2), equal with BELYAVSKY; Leningrad 1977 (+7=9−1) with ROMANISHIN; USSR championship 1978 (+5=12), equal with TSESHKOVSKY; Montreal 1979 (+6=12), equal with KARPOV; Riga interzonal 1979 (+11=6); Riga 1981 (+7=8); Porz 1981–2 (+7=4); Moscow 1982 (+5=8), equal with VAGANYAN; Sochi 1982 (+5=10); Tallinn 1983 (+6=8−1), equal with Vaganyan; Jurmala 1985 (+5=8), equal with M. GUREVICH; Tbilisi 1986 (+6=8), equal with AZMAI-PARASHVILI; Jurmala 1987, equal with GIPSLIS, PSAK-HIS, and RAZUVAYEV; and Termes de Rio Hondo 1987 (+5=6). In the Candidates match following the Riga interzonal of 1979 he lost to Polugayevsky. At the Montpellier Candidates tournament 1985, from which four players went forward, Tal was equal fourth with TIMMAN, drew the play-off (+1=4−1), but lost on tie-break.

Apart from world championship events, Tal competed in about 55 strong all-play-all international tournaments from 1949 to 1990, winning or sharing 19 first and 7 second prizes. He took first place in six Soviet championships, a record equalled only by Botvinnik, and played in seven Olympiads from 1958 to 1980, making a total score of +59=31−2.

Full of nervous energy, chain-smoking, pacing restlessly between moves, Tal was obsessed with chess. These characteristics are those of ALEKHINE, who, however, studied the game more assiduously.

Tal preferred to play, and even between games of a tournament indulged in fast chess until the early hours. When having an operation he talked chess until the mask was placed on his face; on more than one occasion when recuperating he made his escape to a chess club, to be recaptured and taken back to hospital. A great improviser, he had a genius for bold and attacking middlegame play that has rarely been equalled, and he was widely liked for both his scintillating style and his infectious enthusiasm for the game.

Tal was editor of the Latvian chess magazine *Sahs* from 1960 to 1970, and was probably the most prolific Soviet chess journalist. A compilation of material written by him was published in English as *Life and Games of Mikhail Tal* (1976). He has had a part in a few other books but the only one for which he was solely responsible is an account of his successful championship match against Botvinnik in 1960. It appeared in Latvian and Russian editions, and an English translation, *Tal–Botvinnik 1960—Match for the World Championship*, was published in 1970.

P. H. Clarke, *Mikhail Tal's Best Games of Chess* (1961), contains 50 games from 1951 to 1960; B. Cafferty, *Tal's 100 Best Games* (1975), contains 100 games and 21 parts of games played from 1960 to 1973; H. Thomas, *The Complete Games of Mikhail Tal* (1979–80), is a three-volume work going up to 1973.

Tal–Ftáčnik   Naestved 1985   Sicilian Defence Najdorf Variation

1 e4 c5 2 Nf3 d6 3 d4 cxd4 4 Nxd4 Nf6 5 Nc3 a6 6 Be2 e6 7 0–0 Be7 8 f4 0–0 9 Kh1 Qc7 10 a4 b6 11 e5 Ne8 12 exd6 Bxd6 13 f5 e5 14 Nd5 Qd8

15 f6 exd4 16 Qxd4 Nc6 17 Qh4 Bg3 18 Qxg3 Qxd5 19 Bf3 Qc4 20 Bh6 g6 21 b3 Qc3 22 Qh4 Bb7 23 Bxf8 Kxf8 24 Qxh7 Nxf6 25 Qh8+ Ke7 26 Rae1+ Kd6 27 Qg7 Nd5 28 Qxf7 Nd8 29 Qxg6+ Kc5 30 Re4 b5 31 Rd1 Black resigns.

Tal–Hjartarson   Reykjavik 1987   Spanish Opening Close Defence

1 e4 e5 2 Nf3 Nc6 3 Bb5 a6 4 Ba4 Nf6 5 0–0 Be7 6 Re1 b5 7 Bb3 0–0 8 c3 d6 9 h3 Na5 10 Bc2 c5 11 d4 Qc7 12 Nbd2 Bd7 13 Nf1 cxd4 14 cxd4 Rac8 15 Ne3 Nc6 16 d5 Nb4 17 Bb1 a5 18 a3 Na6 19 b4 g6 20 Bd2 axb4 21 axb4 Qb7 22 Bd3 Nc7 23 Nc2 Nh5 24 Be3 Ra8 25 Qd2 Rxa1 26 Nxa1 f5 27 Bh6 Ng7 28 Nb3 f4

29 Na5 Qb6 30 Rc1 Ra8 31 Qc2 Nce8 32 Qb3 Bf6 33 Nc6 Nh5 34 Qb2 Bg7 35 Bxg7 Kxg7

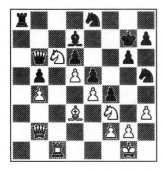

36 Rc5 Qa6 37 Rxb5 Nc7 38 Rb8 Qxd3 39 Ncxe5 Qd1+ 40 Kh2 Ra1 41 Ng4+ Kf7 42 Nh6+ Ke7 43 Ng8+ Black resigns because of 43 ... Kf7 44 Ng5 mate.

talia, an unorthodox piece used for some forms of GREAT CHESS. A talia is moved like a bishop but not to the nearest diagonal square, over which it leaps. For example, a talia at e5 controls all the squares that a bishop would control except d4, d6, f4 and f6, whether or not these squares are occupied. This piece, half FĪL, half bishop, may have represented a stage in the development of the modern move of the bishop; there is, however, no evidence that the talia was invented before the game of COURIER in which the bishop already has its modern powers. The idea of a piece that 'jumps and glides' led to the invention, by the English composer George Peter Jelliss (1940–   ), of a class of 'ski-pieces' for use in FAIRY PROBLEMS.

Tal Variation, 523 in the SICILIAN DEFENCE, played by TAL in his Candidates match with LARSEN in 1965. Tal knew of two earlier games, both by SUETIN, in what has since become a popular way of handling the SCHEVENINGEN DEFENCE. Also 282, the MODERN BENONI.

tandem chess, games for which two players move the pieces of one colour making alternate moves without consultation. Sometimes two masters will give a simultaneous display playing in tandem. In social chess one tandem pair might compete against another.

Tarjan, James Edward (1952–   ), American player, International Grandmaster (1976). A member of the US team that won the World Student Team Championship in 1970, he also played for the USA in the five Olympiads from 1974 to 1982, on the first occasion winning the prize for best score (+ 9 = 4) of those playing second reserve, and on the second occasion, 1976, the prize for best score (+ 8 = 3) of the first reserves. He was second in the US championship 1978, and first (+ 7 = 4 − 2) equal with NIKOLIĆ and AGZAMOV at Vršac 1983. After being placed equal third in the US championship of 1984,

Tarjan turned his attention to the creation of a satisfactory career outside chess.

Tarrasch, Siegbert (1862–1934), one of the best four players in the world for about twenty years. Originally from Breslau, he was, for most of his life, a general practitioner in Nuremberg, and there he won the German master title in 1883. After playing at Hamburg in 1885 and Frankfurt in 1887, sharing second and fifth places respectively, Tarrasch won five strong tournaments consecutively: Nuremberg 1888; Breslau 1889 (+ 9 = 8); Manchester 1890 (+ 12 = 7); Dresden 1892 (+ 9 = 6 − 1); and Leipzig 1894 (+ 13 = 1 − 3). He won matches against TAUBENHAUS in 1891 (+ 6 = 1 − 1) and WALBRODT in 1894 (+ 7 = 1), and drew with CHIGORIN in 1893 (+ 9 = 4 − 9), a match in which the clash of chess styles produced many fine games. Around 1893 Tarrasch was probably playing as well as or better than anyone else, and he might have challenged STEINITZ for the world championship, but he let the opportunity pass, partly because of his duties as a doctor. At Hastings 1895 he was fourth after PILLSBURY, Chigorin, and LASKER; and at Nuremberg 1896 he was third (+ 9 = 6 − 3) equal with Pillsbury, after Lasker and MARÓCZY. Two of his best achievements followed: Vienna 1898, first (+ 21 = 13 − 2) equal with Pillsbury, whom he defeated in the play-off (+ 2 = 1 − 1); and Monte Carlo 1903, first (+ 17 = 6 − 3), ahead of Pillsbury and SCHLECHTER.

At this time Tarrasch had won more strong tournaments than any other living player (7 out of the 13 in which he had competed) and he challenged Lasker for the world championship. Terms were agreed in October 1903, the match to begin about a year later. Tarrasch injured himself while skating and asked for a year's postponement; Lasker declined and there was no match. Tarrasch scored + 14 = 8 − 4 to share second place with JANOWSKI after Maróczy at Ostend in 1905, failed badly at Nuremberg in 1906, and then won (+ 8 = 9 − 3) the quadruple-round grandmaster tournament at Ostend in 1907, ahead of Schlechter; ostensibly this event was for the world tournament championship, although few recognized the title. In 1908 Tarrasch finally played a world championship match and was decisively beaten by Lasker.

After this defeat Tarrasch played in about 23 strong tournaments, achieving his best result, a fourth prize (+ 9 = 5 − 5), at San Sebastián in 1912. He drew a match with Schlechter in 1911 (+ 3 = 10 − 3), and defeated MIESES in 1916 (+ 7 = 4 − 2). Tarrasch played for Germany in the Olympiad of 1927. A patriot who bravely bore the loss of his only surviving son in the First World War, he was hounded by anti-Semites in his last days.

The fastidiousness and elegance of Tarrasch's dress and manner were part of his vanity. His books and the many chess columns he edited were written with style and wit, and also with arrogant self-assurance. Germany was then the leading chess nation, and although he enjoyed the title of

Praeceptor Germaniae his writings were influential well beyond the boundaries of his country. His chess thinking was straightforward: in the early part of a game a player should, above all, seek mobility for the pieces. An isolated pawn or a loose pawn formation was of little account if one had compensating mobility, a view accepted with some reservation by posterity; to concede one's opponent a PAWN CENTRE, or even a HALF-CENTRE, or to accept a DEFENSIVE CENTRE, must be bad because mobility might thereby be limited, a view which disregarded the advances made by Steinitz, and is no longer held. Presumably Tarrasch mellowed. In the 1920s he sometimes played the new openings of the HYPER-MODERN movement, itself largely a reaction to his dogmatic notions regarding the centre.

Tarrasch published *Dreihundert Schachpartien* (1895), an autobiographical games collection, and *Die moderne Schachpartie* (1912), a selection of more than 200 games. *Das Schachspiel* (1931), an instructional book, was translated as *The Game of Chess* (1935), and is still being reprinted in both languages. He also contributed to the last edition of Bilguer's HANDBUCH. F. Reinfeld, *Tarrasch's Best Games of Chess* (1947) contains 183 games. (See SPACE.)

Tarrasch–Walbrodt   Hastings 1895   Spanish Opening
Tarrasch Variation

1 e4 e5 2 Nf3 Nc6 3 Bb5 a6 4 Ba4 Nf6 5 Nc3 d6 6 d4 Bd7 7 Bxc6 Bxc6 8 Qe2 exd4 9 Nxd4 Bd7 10 0-0 Be7 11 b3 0-0 12 Bb2 b5 13 a4 b4 14 Nd1 c5 15 Nf3 Bc6 16 Nd2 d5 17 e5 Ne8 18 Ne3 Qd7 19 Rad1 d4 20 Nec4 Qe6 21 f4 f5 22 Na5 Bd5 23 Qd3 Kh8 24 Qg3 Ra7 25 Nac4 Rg8 26 Rde1 g5 27 Re2 Bd8 28 Qd3 Rag7 29 g3 gxf4? (29 ... Bc7 with advantage to Black, according to Pillsbury) 30 Rxf4 Rg5 31 Ref2 Ng7 32 Nd6 Qxe5 (Here, too, 32 ... Bc7 is best.) 33 Nxf5 Nh5?

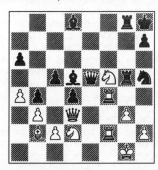

34 Rxd4 Nxg3 35 Nxg3 Rxg3+ 36 hxg3 Rxg3+ 37 Kf1 Rxd3 38 Rg4 Black resigns.

Tarrasch–Catalan Variation, 217, the TARRASCH DEFENCE response (Pc7–c5) to a CATALAN OPENING treatment of the QUEEN'S GAMBIT Declined.

Tarrasch Defence, 118 in the QUEEN'S GAMBIT Declined. Black is likely to get an ISOLATED PAWN after 4 cxd5 exd5, but then gains active play for the pieces. Believing this to be a good defence, TARRASCH fought a long battle with his contemporaries,

many of whom abhorred the isolated pawn; and in the 1930s it seemed that he had lost. Since the 1940s, however, masters have been less sensitive about isolated pawns. Using this defence five times in his world championship match with PETROSYAN in 1969, SPASSKY scored a win and four draws. (See CAPABLANCA; TIME (1).)

Also 707, the OPEN DEFENCE to the SPANISH OPENING. Here, too, Tarrasch believed that the mobility of Black's pieces outweighs the vulnerability of the queen's-side PAWN FORMATION.

Tarrasch Gambit, 120 in the QUEEN'S GAMBIT Declined, a line given by TARRASCH in his book *Die Verteidigung des Damengambits* (1924).

Tarrasch Trap, two different traps in the SPANISH OPENING. If, instead of 11 ... Nxe5 12 f3 Bd6, the BRESLAU VARIATION (722), Black plays 11 ... Qd7, then White wins a piece by 12 Nxe6, because whichever way Black recaptures the d-pawn is pinned. Two grandmasters fell into this trap when playing Tarrasch: ZUKERTORT at Frankfurt 1887 and GUNSBERG at Manchester 1890. In 780 Black's castling is an error that loses at least a pawn, e.g. 8 Bxc6 Bxc6 9 dxe5 dxe5 10 Qxd8, where a game Tarrasch–Marco, Dresden 1892, continued 10 ... Raxd8 (10 ... Rexd8 also loses) 11 Nxe5 Bxe4 12 Nxe4 Nxe4 13 Nd3 f5 14 f3 Bc5+ 15 Nxc5 Nxc5 16 Bg5 Rd5 17 Be7 and Black resigned, for if 17 ... Rf7 18 c4 wins the exchange. Every move of this game had been published by TARRASCH in an annotation in *Deutsche Schachzeitung*, Feb. 1891, 18 months earlier.

Tarrasch Variation, 692, sometimes called the Blackburne–Marco Gambit, or Four Knights Variation, in the SPANISH OPENING played twice against MORPHY in 1858, adopted by TARRASCH (see game there) in the 1890s, and regarded for some years afterwards as one of the strongest lines at White's disposal; 844 in the SPANISH FOUR KNIGHTS GAME, introduced in 1908 by LASKER, in the 16th game of the world championship match. Tarrasch lost, and became an advocate of the move.

Also 910 in the ITALIAN OPENING, played Tarrasch–Alekhine, Baden-Baden 1925, but already known from Leonhardt–Rotlewi, Carlsbad 1911; 996 in the SCOTCH GAME, recommended by Tarrasch and put to the test by Lasker in an exhibition game with ALEKHINE in 1914 (see REPETITION OF POSITION); 1089 in the FALKBEER COUNTER-GAMBIT, played Réti–Tarrasch, Göteborg 1920; 1218 (see GELLER; SEVENTH RANK ABSOLUTE), also called the Leonhardt Variation, in the FRENCH DEFENCE, played by Tarrasch at Nuremberg 1888, superseded by the RUBINSTEIN VARIATION, 1216 (see ZWISCHENZUG).

A popular line, 1230 in the French Defence, introduced by FRASER in 1874, STAUNTON remarking that it was 'a novelty not undeserving attention'. Tarrasch adopted this variation in the 1880s but abandoned it because he believed that White would be at a disadvantage on account of Black's gaining an ISOLATED QUEEN'S PAWN (the normal outcome). Masters now play the variation because they hope to prove that Black's IQP is disadvantageous, and not a source of strength, as Tarrasch supposed. In his matches against KORCHNOI in 1974 and 1978 KARPOV played it nine times, resulting in nine draws.

Tartakower, Saviely Grigoryevich (1887–1956), International Grandmaster (1950), a professional player ranking about eighth or ninth in the world at his best (1926–30). A Jew of Austrian and Polish parentage, he was born in Rostov-on-Don, and learned the moves at the age of ten. In 1899, after both his parents had been murdered, he left Russia and completed his education, first in Geneva and then in Vienna, where he lived for many years, and where he obtained his doctorate in law in 1909. He gained the German master title in the Nuremberg HAUPTTURNIER 1906, and from then until 1914 played in about 18 tournaments, with varying results. He won matches against SPIELMANN in 1913 (+5=5−2) and RÉTI in 1914 (+3=1−2).

After serving in the Austro-Hungarian army during the First World War, Tartakower recommenced his chess career, taking second prize (+3=8−1), after VIDMAR, ahead of SCHLECHTER, in the quadruple-round Vienna tournament 1917–18. In the following years he twice defeated Réti in match play (1919, +3=5−2, and 1920, +3=3) and achieved several good tournament results: The Hague 1921, second (+5=4), after ALEKHINE, ahead of RUBINSTEIN; Vienna 1922, second (+7=6−1), after Rubinstein, ahead of Alekhine; and Vienna 1923, first (+7=4), ahead of Réti.

In 1924 Tartakower settled in Paris. Playing in three or four tournaments a year, he then won or shared first prize in five strong events: Ghent 1926 (+5=4−1); Bad Niendorf 1927 (+4=3), a tie with NIMZOWITSCH; London 1927 (+6=4−1), a tie with Nimzowitsch, ahead of Vidmar and BOGOLJUBOW; Liège 1930 (+6=5), two points ahead of a field that included SULTAN KHAN, Nimzowitsch, and Rubinstein—Tartakower's best achievement; and Łódź 1935 (+5=3−1), ahead of FINE. In 1933 he defeated LILIENTHAL in match play (+3=9). In six consecutive Olympiads, from 1930 to 1939, Tartakower played for Poland, although he had neither lived there nor learned the language, and on the second occasion, 1931, he made the best second-board score (+10=7−1). During the Second World War he served with the Free French forces under the name Lt. Cartier, and he subsequently took French nationality, playing for France in the Olympiad of 1950.

Tartakower often chose opening variations that were neither well known nor highly regarded, remarking that 'as long as an opening is reputed to be weak it can be played'. To explore uncharted ground suited his ingenious style and stimulated his imagination: conventional openings would have served him no better. Many of his inventions were considered bizarre, the fate of most new ideas, but

some, e.g. the TARTAKOWER VARIATION of the Queen's Gambit Declined and the TARTAKOWER ATTACK (882), have become standard play. He pioneered a revival of the DUTCH DEFENCE. He was equally creative in naming new lines, sometimes to the extent of giving more than one name to a move, and he even called one sequence the 'Nameless Variation'. He was also one of the best endgame players of his generation. (See STAUNTON GAMBIT.)

Besides his many writings on chess and other subjects, Tartakower wrote poems in French, German, and Russian. He was an admirable man—all speak of his high principles, honest dealings, and generosity—except for a weakness for gambling. Perhaps his extensive literary output was prompted by the need to finance his betting. His best book may be *Die hypermoderne Schachpartie* (1924–5), and his best books in the English language are *Breviary of Chess* (1937), *My Best Games 1905–1930* (1953), and *My Best Games 1931–1954* (1956). Epigrams proliferated in both his conversation and his writing; best known, perhaps, is his classic definition (freely translated): 'Tactics is what you do when there's something to do, strategy is what you do when there's nothing to do.' He also gave a proof of his existence that will be understood by every chessplayer, *Erro ergo sum*.

Tartakower–Schlechter   St Petersburg 1909   King's Gambit Declined Classical Defence

1 e4 e5 2 f4 Bc5 3 Nf3 d6 4 fxe5 dxe5 5 c3 Nf6 6 Nxe5 0–0 7 d4 Bd6 8 Nf3 Nxe4 9 Bd3 Re8 10 0–0 h6 11 Nbd2 Nf6 12 Nc4 c5 13 Nfe5 cxd4

14 Nxf7 Kxf7 15 Qh5+ Kg8 16 Rxf6 Re1+ 17 Rf1 Rxf1+ 18 Bxf1 Bf8 19 Bxh6 Qf6 20 Bg5 Qf5 21 Nd6 Bxd6 22 Bc4+ Be6 23 Rf1 Qxf1+ 24 Bxf1 Nd7 25 Bd3 Nf8 26 cxd4 Bf7 27 Qf3 Ne6 28 Be3 Rb8 29 g4 g5 30 Qf6 Bf8 31 Bh7+ Kxh7 32 Qxf7+ Ng7 33 Bxg5 Black resigns.

Tartakower Attack, 260 in the STAUNTON GAMBIT, as Tartakower–Mieses, Baden-Baden 1925; 882, the best way for White to avoid the LASKER DEFENCE to the EVANS GAMBIT, first played in 1855 by MORPHY; 436, the TORRE ATTACK.

Tartakower Gambit, 1114, name sometimes given to the LESSER BISHOP'S GAMBIT.

Tartakower Variation, 117, the ALAPIN VARIATION in the QUEEN'S GAMBIT Declined; 206 in the same opening, the STEMGAME being Capablanca–Tartakower, London 1922. In this variation, which comes in and out of fashion, Black seeks a central pawn majority, and from e6, rather than b7, the bishop is better placed to support the HANGING PAWNS that are likely to come about. In the QUEEN'S PAWN OPENING, 230, played twice by TARTAKOWER at Nottingham 1936.

Four lines in the SICILIAN DEFENCE: 478, as Réti–Tartakower, New York 1924; 502, a delayed MORRA GAMBIT; 554, the PIN VARIATION, played by Tartakower, but more frequently by ANDERSSEN; 566, the STEINITZ VARIATION, 'dubious, therefore playable' said Tartakower.

'New and good' was his verdict on 591 in the CARO–KANN DEFENCE, Tartakower–Przepiórka, Budapest 1929, known since Harmonist–Bardeleben, Berlin 1890; 731 in the SPANISH OPENING, a line known since the 1860s; 816 in the PONZIANI OPENING, recommended in *Die hypermoderne Schachpartie* as an improvement on the *Lärobok*'s 8 d4 e4 9 Qg3; 883 in the EVANS GAMBIT, introduced by Tartakower during the gambit tournament held at Baden-bei-Wien in 1914; 938, an analytical suggestion in the HUNGARIAN DEFENCE as an alternative to CHIGORIN's line, 5 . . . Na5; 999 in the SCOTCH GAME, played Maróczy–Tartakower, Vienna 1920, and fervently advocated in *Die hypermoderne Schachpartie*. This last is sometimes called the Blackburne Attack.

Also 1090 in the FALKBEER COUNTER-GAMBIT, an old line endorsed by Tartakower; 1209 in the FRENCH DEFENCE, as L. Steiner–Tartakower, Hastings 1927–8, with the idea of countering 7 Qg4 by 7 . . . Bf8; 1226 in the same opening, played Steinitz–Paulsen, friendly game at Vienna 1873, reintroduced by the Manchester player Rhodes Marriott (1856–1932) in 1897, and taken up by Tartakower (see DOUBLE CHECK); 1261 in the ALEKHINE DEFENCE, the subject of five pages of analysis in *Die hypermoderne Schachpartie*.

task, 'a problem [or study] which has maximum or minimum characteristics in relation to space, medium, limitations, and thematic features' (DAWSON). To compose a study with, say, the aim of showing a number of pawns that are promoted to a rook, would be a task; the greatest number of such promotions yet shown would be a task record; but if other studies showed as many, then the one with the fewest men on the board would be the task record. If each of the eight pawns was promoted to a rook this would be a maximum task. In problems, tasks may be shown in the post-key play, the set play, or the try-play.

Some examples of tasks are ALBINO, ALLUMWANDLUNG, EXCELSIOR, KNIGHT WHEEL, PICKANINNY, PLUS-FLIGHTS, and STAR-FLIGHTS. (See also CONSTRUCTION TASK; LONG-RANGE PROBLEM.)

Taubenhaus, Jean (1850–1919), Polish-born player who went to live in Paris in 1883 as a professional player and teacher, and became a French citizen. In 1889 he operated MEPHISTO during its visit to Paris. After playing in New York 1893 he went to Buenos Aires for two years, and on his way back defeated the Cuban player Vásquez in match play. In 1901 he defeated ALBIN (+ 3 = 1) in Paris. Other than these, his tournament and match results were unremarkable. (See TARRASCH.)

Tchigorine, the French spelling of CHIGORIN.

team match, a match between two teams of players. There is a contractual or at least a moral requirement that members of teams should be arranged in order of strength. When a series of different team matches is combined into one event, such as an Olympiad, it is usually called a team tournament. The earliest known occasion when each member of one team met every member of the other team, an arrangement identical to SCHEVENINGEN PAIRING SYSTEM, was at Thousand Islands, USA, in 1897. New York State scored + 22 = 7 − 20 to defeat Pennsylvania, each team fielding seven players.

technique, generally, the skill applied to win a won position, or defend a difficult position that should, with correct play, be drawn; but there is no precise definition. Although the term is commonly used to describe play in the later stages of the game, it could be used in reference to the correct handling of any strategic plan. Technique is not necessarily a dull and mechanical process, as is sometimes supposed; always specific to a position, its application frequently offers scope for creative ideas, for breaking new ground. In *Anglo-Soviet Chess Match* (1947) KLEIN writes '. . . how tenaciously a lost position may be held and how difficult it is to find a master plan against the best defence. Commonly referred to as technique this is the intrinsic art of chess, while the achievement of advantage is more often than not the opponent's work.'

Teichmann, Richard (1868–1925), German player, among the first ten in the world for about 20 years. At Berlin as a student of modern languages (in several of which he became fluent) he greatly improved his chess, in particular playing many games against von SCHEVE. In the winter of 1890–1 he won the city championship ahead of WALBRODT. In 1892 Teichmann moved to London where he remained for about ten years as a language teacher. His international tournament career began at Leipzig 1894, when he took third prize (+ 10 = 4 − 3), after TARRASCH and LIPKE. At Monte Carlo 1902 (won by MARÓCZY) he took fourth place (+ 12 = 11 − 3) ahead of SCHLECHTER and Tarrasch. In the next five years he was fifth in 7 of the 15 tournaments in which he played, so he was nicknamed Richard the Fifth; and during this period his love of chess so grew that he decided to become a chess professional, for which purpose he settled in Berlin.

In the 36-player five-stage Ostend tournament of 1906 he was placed finally equal fourth, but in the strong fifth stage he came second ($+3=4-1$) after the overall winner, Schlechter. Teichmann won a small but strong quadrangular event ($+4=1-1$) at Munich in 1909, and then achieved his finest victory at the great Carlsbad tournament of 1911: first prize ($+13=10-2$), ahead of RUBINSTEIN, Schlechter, and VIDMAR. At Breslau 1912 Teichmann was third, half a point behind the winners, DURAS and Rubinstein, and ahead of Schlechter, Tarrasch, and MARSHALL. Among his matches were victories over MIESES in 1895 ($+4=1-1$) and 1910 ($+5=2$), BARDELEBEN in 1910 ($+3=2-1$ and $+5=4-1$), and SPIELMANN in 1914 ($+5-1$).

Suspected in Germany of British sympathies, he lived in Switzerland during the First World War, after which his only notable chess achievement was a drawn match with ALEKHINE in 1921 ($+2=2-2$). Teichmann was blind in his right eye, and the other sometimes gave him trouble. His appearance was impressive: a black eye patch, full brown beard, a large head, and a high forehead. Among chessplayers, writes Ed. LASKER, 'he seemed like Wotan holding forth in the company of minor gods'. Teichmann was always willing to examine openings and games over-the-board, but when it came to writing he was notoriously lazy, and his annotations suffer accordingly; but he made a useful openings contribution to the last edition of Bilguer's HANDBUCH.

J. Spence, *The Chess Career of Richard Teichmann* (1970) contains 146 games, as well as tournament and match results.

Teichmann–Schlechter Carlsbad 1911 Spanish Opening Pilnik Variation

1 e4 e5 2 Nf3 Nc6 3 Bb5 a6 4 Ba4 Nf6 5 0–0 Be7 6 Re1 b5 7 Bb3 d6 8 c3 0–0 9 d3 Na5 10 Bc2 c5 11 Nbd2 Qc7 12 Nf1 Nc6 13 Ne3 Bb7 14 Nf5 Rfe8 15 Bg5 Nd7 16 Bb3 Nf8 17 Bd5 Ng6 18 Bxe7 Ngxe7

19 Bxf7+ Kxf7 20 Ng5+ Kg8 21 Qh5 Nxf5 22 Qxh7+ Kf8 23 Qxf5+ Kg8 24 Qg6 Qd7 25 Re3 Black resigns.

Teichmann Variation, 208 in the QUEEN'S GAMBIT Declined, recommended by TEICHMANN; 1224 in the

CHATARD–ALEKHINE ATTACK, originated by Teichmann in his annotations to a game in *British Chess Magazine*, 1899; 309, the CLASSICAL VARIATION of the NIMZO-INDIAN DEFENCE; 743, the PILNIK VARIATION of the SPANISH OPENING, played many times by Teichmann at the Carlsbad 1911 tournament.

telechess, a generic name for chess played at a distance. The earliest and still the most important is CORRESPONDENCE CHESS, but the name is more often used in connection with later forms—TELEGRAPH CHESS (see also CABLE MATCH), TELEPHONE CHESS, RADIO CHESS, teletext and television chess. Since 1977 FIDE has run Telechess Olympiads, the games of which may be played by telephone, telex, telegram, fax, or radio. No doubt television will be permitted. In 1979 a closed circuit television tournament was won by MILES against one player each from Ireland, Scotland, and Wales. It was a quickplay event with each contestant in a different city. In 1974 TAL, in Moscow, scored $5\frac{1}{2}-2\frac{1}{2}$ in a simultaneous display against eight players in Melbourne, Australia, using telex and telephone. Orbiting astronauts on different satellites have played. Other, perhaps fanciful, modes of telechess have been recorded such as between opposing troops in the First World War using megaphones, and between neighbouring clergymen (or, in another version, squires) using church bells.

telegraph chess, games for which the moves are transmitted by telegraph. At the end of 1823 Le Cercle de Philidor, Paris, challenged the London Chess Club to a pair of correspondence games, whereupon a member of the London club argued that as national honour was at stake the government should re-establish telegraphic communications between the two countries, shortening the time needed for the games and costing the country not more than £10,000. The Paris club had to withdraw. Semaphore telegraph was intended in this case, as was used between two friends who lived five miles apart near Birmingham in 1868. The first games using signals at sea were between the ships *Barham* and *Wellesley* on a passage from India to London in 1853.

The first electric telegraph match was in 1844 between Washington and Baltimore, just linked by the first American telegraph line. In 1858 STAUNTON offered to play MORPHY by the new transatlantic cable. Fortunately the challenge arrived after Morphy had left for England, for the cable failed after a month and was not successfully replaced until 1866. Staunton, a keen advocate of telegraph chess, was one of the players in the first European game played in that way when he and an ally, in Gosport, played a team of opponents in London, April 1845.

The earliest game played by means of submarine cable was between Liverpool chess club and Dublin Library Club in 1861. The same Liverpool club took part in the first intercontinental match, playing Calcutta in 1880–1; this was not played at a sitting, the telegraph being used to replace the mail. The age of the CABLE MATCH had arrived and at first there were conflicting transmission codes until GRINGMUTH NOTATION became standard.

telephone chess, games for which the moves are spoken on a telephone, usually with the line between opponents open throughout the game(s). The first such game documented was played in January 1878 between F. Thompson and J. Cooper, separated by the three miles between Belper and Milford in Derbyshire. In 1880 a consultation game was played between the clubs of Brighton and Chichester, and in September 1884 an eight-a-side match was played between Bradford and Wakefield. The organizational problems are similar to those of TELEGRAPH CHESS which has been more popular, perhaps because the printed evidence of the moves limits error.

tempo, (1) (pl. tempi), the unit of TIME (1). To lose a tempo is to play in *n* moves that which could be played in *n − 1* moves. Occasionally the loss of a tempo is unimportant, but far more often it is disadvantageous. The loss of three tempi, which may happen in a badly played opening, is usually regarded as equivalent to the loss of a pawn.

To LOSE A TEMPO does not mean to LOSE THE MOVE, an endgame manœuvre in which a player intentionally and advantageously thrusts the move (i.e. the turn to move) upon the opponent.

tempo, (2) a name used sometimes for RAPID CHESS.

tempo-move, a move of a pawn that is made or held in reserve in order to LOSE THE MOVE; loosely, any other move that does not carry a direct threat. Tempo-moves with pawns are a common feature of pawn endings, but rarely significant in other kinds of endgame. There may be a limited number of such moves, for the pawns may eventually become blocked. A player should conserve tempo-moves and if possible reduce those available to the opponent.

In this position after White's 39th move in the game Nunn–Bischoff, Lugano 1986, Black resigned. he must lose his d-pawn on account of White's having an option of tempo-moves with the a-pawn. For

example, 39 ... Kc6 40 Kd4 a5 41 a4, or 39 ... Kc7 40 Kd4 Kc6 41 a3 a5 42 a4. (See OPPOSITION.)

tempo-play, waiting moves played with the object of LOSING THE MOVE, including play by pawns (TEMPO-MOVES) and by pieces, thus setting up a SQUEEZE or a ZUGZWANG. See the game under BONDAREVSKY. Such moves are often featured in studies (see GURVICH; KRALIN).

Tennison Gambit, 605 or 1299, also known as the Lemberg Gambit, the dubious invention of the Danish-born American Otto M. Tennison (1834–1909), who published his analysis in the *New Orleans Times Democrat*, 1891. Tennison graduated from Heidelberg as an engineer and went to America. When the civil war broke out he mustered a regiment of Union soldiers but was then placed in command of a Black regiment. He rebelled at the idea of having real (as opposed to wooden) black and white men opposed, and was dismissed. He went south to join the Confederates, and after being held prisoner as a possible spy he was duly enlisted. When the war ended he maintained a military command known as Tennison's Rifles.

theatre and chess. Chess is a powerful device for subterfuge in *The Spanish Curate* (1622), taken directly by Fletcher and Massinger from *Gerardo, the unfortunate Spaniard, or a Pattern for lascivious Lovers* (1622), an English version of a Spanish novel by Gonzalo de Céspedes y Meneses. A woman is wooed, sometimes in front of her husband, by her chess opponent who conveys his feelings by using remarks that appear to refer to the state of the game. Chess is used in *Le Bourru bienfaisant* (1771) by Goldoni, *Götz von Berlichingen* (1773), Goethe's first drama, *Nathan der Weise* (1779) by Lessing, and several times more fleetingly by Shakespeare. The best-known play to have the game in a central position is the musical *Chess* (1986) by Rice, Andersson, and Ulvaeus.

In the most famous of the ALLEGORIES, *A Game at Chess* (1624) by Middleton, the parallel is with politics, while *Dierdre* (1907) by Yeats is mystical. A number of plays revolve around a chess AUTOMATON, the most successful being *Die Schachmaschine* (1797) by Heinrich Beck, allegedly from an English original which has never been traced. A one-act play, *Mat* (1883), by Joliet portrays actual characters from the CAFÉ DE LA RÉGENCE in about 1870.

In the ballet *Checkmate* (1937), choreography by de Valois, music by Bliss, the actual moves of the pieces influence the form of the dancing. Another ballet, *Pawn to King 5* (1968), uses chess only to indicate conflict in a general sense, but *Ana* (1990), choreography by Chopinet, based on Carroll's *Through the Looking Glass*, has a specially created game of 73 moves as its text. In *Sinbad the Sailor on Ice* (1953) the skaters gave a LIVING CHESS performance of MORPHY'S most famous FRIENDLY GAME, to music by Reginald Charles Noel-Johnson

(1904–   ), Kent chess champion on more than one occasion.

The inner technique of drama has been compared to that of a chess game. The phases of a typical three-act play, exposition, development, and resolution, compare to opening, middle, and endgame. The characters (pieces) are introduced and developed, the game and the drama have their own unity in that every move is towards a final goal, and the great creative artists in each field combine logic and surprise. The analogy was taken to great lengths by the German poet and chessplayer Rudolf von Gottschall (1823–1909). Among the more successful chess-playing playwrights are MORTIMER and the German problemist Oskar Blumenthal (1852–1917), author of *White Horse Inn.*

thematic try, a TRY that forms part of a composer's idea. Such a try should relate in some way to the POST-KEY PLAY and should be defeated by only one black reply. Thematic tries, and the TRY-PLAY that follows, may show CHANGED PLAY or TASKS (see PETROVIĆ; STAR-FLIGHTS), are ingredients of logical problems and the DOMBROVSKIS THEME, and may be seen in many other kinds of problems and, on occasion, in studies.

thematic variation, one of the main variations that reveal the problem composer's idea, as distinct from BY-PLAY. For an example, among many, see STOCCHI THEME with its three thematic variations and two lines of try-play.

theme. 'The theme of a problem [or study] consists of the line or lines of play which were uppermost in the composer's mind when he made the problem [or study] and which presumably will chiefly interest the solver'—A. C. WHITE, *The Good Companion Two-Mover* (1922). Other and subordinate lines of play are likely to be present; the study composer

Title page of Middleton's play *A Game at Chess* (printed 1625)

calls these SIDE VARIATIONS, the problemist BY-PLAY. There are numerous well-known themes, and their use in original settings need not involve PLAGIAR-ISM.

Compositions sometimes lack themes in any meaningful sense of the word, as, for example, in the problem given under BLOCK: there are many variations of about equal merit, and a good key, all of which solvers may find no less enjoyable than a highly thematic problem.

theme tourney, a tourney for which composers are required to show a particular theme or idea.

theoretical novelty, or TN, a move in the opening which is thought not to have been played before. Strong players study the latest games in the hope of finding an innovation which might put them at an advantage in a future game, and at worst will not be sprung upon them.

In the San Francisco 1987 tournament the game Miles–Christiansen began 1 e4 e5 2 Nf3 Nf6 3 Nxe5 d6 4 Nf3 Nxe4 5 Nc3 Bf5 6 Nxe4 Bxe4 7 d3 and was drawn on move 20. The game was published, with 5 . . . Bf5 indicated as a TN. At Biel 1988 ANAND played it against Zapata, who replied with 6 Qe2 and Anand resigned. This is one of the quickest losses by a grandmaster, notable because he did not play a single move of his own. The players in the earlier game had not overlooked this decisive reply, but their game was an AGREED DRAW and the moves they played were merely to observe formalities.

theory, a word with several chess connotations. Players commonly speak of opening theory although opening variations have arisen empirically and are not evaluated constantly over a period of time; in this sense theory means consensus, broadly represented by current literature on the subject. So-called endgame theory consists of information about the basic endgame; true statements may be made regarding many specific positions, or positions of a similar type, but there are few generalizations of universal application.

There is a well-accepted theory, attributed to STEINITZ, as to how the game should be conducted. This 'general theory' begins with the premiss that a correctly played game should end in a draw. In a level position a player might make a move that maintains the EQUILIBRIUM or one that concedes an advantage to the opponent. To make a move that gains the advantage is, however, impossible. A sustained attack should not be launched unless the equilibrium is already disturbed in one's favour; if this is not the case a player should manœuvre, or jockey for position, setting problems for the opponent in the hope of inducing error. (See POSITIONAL PLAY.)

In the 1860s attacks on the king were the order of the day, but PAULSEN showed that these often succeeded only because of incorrect defence, and that the attacker might be forced to retreat in disorder, perhaps thereby losing the game. (For an example, see ANTOSHIN.) In the 1870s Steinitz, influenced by Paulsen, recognizing that an error by the opponent was a precondition for victory, changed his style. He sought positional objectives, attacking only when the time was ripe. Followed by a mere handful of masters in the 1880s he was eventually followed by them all. The inference that victory depended upon a mistake by the loser was not well received, because it seemed to deny the possibility of creative play. In fact, this subsists in the positional and tactical manœuvres that precede the mistake (it is a small triumph to induce a master to play incorrectly) and in the subsequent play. An error may be so slight that it can be detected only by a master; and its exploitation may be far from obvious, often requiring subtle and imaginative play. In many annotations and in part I of his *Modern Chess Instructor* (1889), Steinitz makes clear that he embraced this new approach to the game; but he never postulated the theory in precise terms, a task that fell to LASKER many years later.

Therkatz–Herzog Variation, 12 Bg5 Bxg5 13 Nxg5 0–0 14 Nxh7, an alternative to the BAYONET ATTACK (914) in the ITALIAN OPENING, analysed by Wilhelm Therkatz (c.1850–1925), who edited the chess column of the *Krefelder Zeitung* from 1908 until his death, and by R. Herzog. Analysis by KERES and UNZICKER suggests that White's sacrifice should lead to a game with about even chances.

Thomas, George Alan (1881–1972), English player, International Master (1950), International Arbiter (1952), British champion 1923 and 1934, London champion 1946. His mother, who taught him chess, was winner of one of the first women's tournaments, Hastings 1895. He played in more than 80 tournaments and achieved his best result at Hastings 1934–5, when he scored +6=1−2 to share first place with EUWE and FLOHR, ahead of BOTVINNIK and CAPABLANCA. Thomas played in seven Olympiads from 1927 to 1939, and in the first of these made the highest percentage score (+9=6), equalled by the Danish player Holger Norman-Hansen (1899–1984) (+11=2−2). A leading English player for more than 25 years, Thomas fought many battles at the famous City of London club, winning 16 of its annual championships from 1913–14 to 1938–9. In his sixty-ninth year he gave up competitive chess when, after a hard game, 'the board and men began to swim before my eyes'.

A man of few words, imperturbable, of fine manners, Sir George Thomas was respected throughout the chess world for his sportsmanship and impartiality, and his opinion was often sought when disputes arose between players. The inheritor of both a baronetcy and private means, he devoted his life to games and sports. He was a keen hockey player, and a competitor in international lawn tennis, playing in every Wimbledon from 1919 to 1926, and reaching the last sixteen in 1922. His greatest sport, which brought him more recognition among the general public than did his chess, was badminton. He won about 90 titles, notably the All-England men's singles championship four times consecutively, 1920 to 1923.

Thorold Variation, 1171, attack in the ALLGAIER GAMBIT suggested by R. B. Wormald and practised by the English player Edmund Thorold (1832–99) in the 1870s.

threat, the possibility, if not countered, of a move that leads to advantage. The word customarily refers only to moves that have an overt tactical purpose, but there is a sense in which most good moves either make or defend against threats. After 1 d4 d5 2 c4, for example, White threatens to gain space by capturing on d5; the continuation 2 ... e6 3 Nc3 leaves Black in no immediate danger; White's third move, however, increases pressure on the central squares, threatening in a general way to gain space, and Black cannot ignore this entirely. Most threats are active, i.e. they are concerned with capturing material, the gain of space or time, or the gain of some other positional advantage. Occasionally a threat is passive, as when a player would profit by withdrawing an attacked man.

Problemists use this word only for a threat that also meets the STIPULATIONS. For example, in a TWO-MOVER that is not a BLOCK problem White's key makes a threat to mate next move. Neither a 'threat' to gain material nor a 'threat' to mate in two moves instead of one would be threat in this special context.

threat problem, a problem in which the KEY makes a threat (in the problem sense) as distinct from a key that maintains or sets up a BLOCK.

three-dimensional chess, or space chess, an unorthodox game. Allegedly KIESERITZKY showed such a game to ANDERSSEN at London in 1851, but details are not known, and it may have been a game played on the six outer surfaces of a cube. The man who did most work on the subject was Ferdinand Maack (1861–1930) of Germany. He proposed using eight 8 × 8 boards, one above another (512 cells), and orthodox pieces whose moves, however, were extended to three dimensions. The array follows the pattern of orthodox chess, White's pieces on the lowest tier, from Aa1 to Ah1, Black's on the top tier Ha8 to Hh8, and the pawns placed above and below the white and black pieces respectively. Maack, who believed the original form of chess to have been three-dimensional, described his game for the first time in the *Frankfurter Zeitung*, 1907, in several books, and in two magazines founded for the purpose.

A more manageable form was described by DAWSON in a series of articles running from July to December 1926 in *Chess Amateur*. Five 5 × 5 boards are superimposed (125 cells). The moves are: rook through cell faces; bishop through cell edges; unicorn through cell corners; queen, combin-

ing powers of other three; knight, normally in all planes. The king's move is like the queen's, but only in single steps, so that a king on Bb2 has a field of 26 cells. The pawn's move is in single steps forward through cell faces, but capturing through cell edges. The array is as follows: White, R, N, K, N, R from Aa1 to Ae1, and B, U (unicorn), Q, B, U from Ba1 to Be1, ten pawns Aa2 to Ae2 and Ba2 to Be2 (promotion rank = Ea5 to Ee5); Black R, N, K, N, R from Ea5 to Ee5, and U, B, Q, U, B from Da5 to De5, ten pawns Ea4 to Ee4 and Da4 to De4. Dawson also described other versions, including a conceptual four-dimensional game using hypercells.

In 1945 the English player Charles Beatty introduced 'total chess', rather like Maack's version but using four 8 × 8 boards (256 cells). A similar set was used by Buñuel in his film *Tristaña* (1974). Other attempts have been made, but none has caught the imagination of the chessplaying public, although composers of FAIRY PROBLEMS have used many varieties. Dawson composed his first, using Maack's version, in 1915.

three-handed chess, an unorthodox game for three players. Of less importance historically than four-handed chess, the three-handed game has never been popular. The earliest special board, dating from 1722, consisted of the normal 64 squares with 24 squares (8 × 3) added to three sides. Mate could not be given by two players combined and both adversaries had to be mated. This shape of board does not give each player equal opportunities. To obviate this defect a symmetrical board was designed in 1837 consisting of three wedge-shaped pieces joined together. Each wedge had 4 × 8 ordinary squares and then, along one of the long sides, six tapering squares and beyond them two more tapering squares, the whole board comprising 120 squares. (In effect the 24 tapering squares filled a triangle formed by the three 'half-boards' touching at their far corners.) Pawn promotion could be achieved on either back rank, otherwise the rules were more or less orthodox. A version introduced by the Marseilles player Antoine Demonchy (c.1827–95) in 1882 avoided the need for special boards. Three boards and three sets are used. The boards are placed so that each of two corners of each board adjoins one corner of another board, the empty space between all three forming a triangle. Outside, the edges of the boards form a nine-sided shape with three re-entrant angles in which the players sit. Each player faces two boards having the white pieces on one and the Black pieces on the other. In effect each is playing two games simultaneously against the other two. There have also been three-handed versions of ROUND CHESS. (See also HEXAGONAL CHESS.)

Three Knights Opening, 826, line dating from the 18th century, played in a game between STAUNTON and COCHRANE, 1841. It may also arise as 612 in the VIENNA GAME. (See LEONHARDT.)

Three Knights Variation, 329, sometimes called the Bogoljubow Variation, in the NIMZO-INDIAN DEFENCE (see ANTOSHIN; BARCZA); 378, also known as the Russian Variation, in the GRÜNFELD DEFENCE; 686, a little-played line in the SPANISH OPENING.

three-mover, a problem requiring three moves for its solution, i.e. three SINGLE-MOVES for White and two, or three, for Black.

Three Pawns Gambit, 1123 in the KING'S GAMBIT Accepted. Sometimes the name is given to the BERTIN GAMBIT, 1122, but at that stage White is not committed to sacrificing the third pawn.

three pawns problem, a study in which a king is opposed to three united passed pawns, or in which both kings are so opposed. In various forms this study, examined by CARRERA in 1617 and probably known earlier, attracted the attention of analysts until solved by SZÉN in 1836.

Whoever plays wins, e.g. 1 Ke2 Kd7 2 Kf3 Kc6 3 a4 h5 4 c4 f5 5 Kg3 Kb6 6 b4 g5 7 a5+ Ka7 8 c5 h4+ 9 Kh2 Kb8 10 b5 f4 11 Kg2 g4 12 Kg1 g3 13 Kg2 Kb7 14 b6 (White sets up the last of four successive ZUGZWANGS after which Black can no longer hold up White's pawns.) 14 ... Kb8 15 a6 Kc8 16 c6 Kb8 17 a7+ Ka8 18 c7.

Visiting Paris in 1836 Szén offered to play this position as a game for a stake of 20 francs, and among those who accepted the challenge was SAINT-AMANT. He and Szén played 20 games making the first move alternately, and Szén won nearly every time. In the new year he found the game equally profitable in London where he defeated WALKER and other players. Soon afterwards Walker and the English problemist William Bone (1810–74) rediscovered the solution which they published in the *Philidorian*, 1838, and *Bell's Life*, 1840. An understanding of the analysis is not without practical value.

A position (below) from the game Euwe–Botvinnik, Nottingham 1936. Having played 56 e6?, EUWE drew. He could have won by 56 Kb3 Kb5 57 e6 a4+ 58 Ka2 Ng6 59 h7 Kc6 60 e7 Kd7 61 Bf6 c4 62 Kb1 Ke8 63 e5 Kf7 64 e6+ Ke8 65 Bg5 (White LOSES THE MOVE by TEMPO-PLAY.) 65 ... Nh8 66 Bh4 Ng6 67 Bf6 and Black is in a SQUEEZE:

having to move his pawns, he will lose them all, e.g. 67 ... a3 68 Ka2 c3 69 Kb3, or 67 ... b3 68 Kb2.

tie-breaking. In ALL-PLAY-ALL tournaments the NEUSTADTL SCORE is both widely accepted and frequently used, mostly under the wrong name. For SWISS SYSTEM tournaments many different methods, such as BUCHHOLZ, COONS, HARKNESS, MEDIAN, and SOLKOFF scores, have been used. (See AUXILIARY SCORING METHODS.) A more recent method, growing in popularity, is the SUM OF PROGRESSIVE SCORES.

The preferred method of deciding the winner of a tied match is a SUDDEN DEATH play-off. In the early 1980s FIDE suggested the use of dice, and shortly afterwards, in 1983, a tied CANDIDATES match between SMYSLOV and HÜBNER was decided by the spin of a roulette wheel. In 1990 the second place in the British Zonal tournament, a qualification for the interzonal, was decided by the use of an electronic bingo machine.

In England an old method for deciding matches between teams is known as the elimination method. Beginning with the bottom board, results are discounted until a decisive score is reached. In 1950 the British Chess Federation adopted the board count proposal of David Vincent Hooper (1915–   ). Each win is given a numerical value which corresponds to the winner's board number. The numbers are added and the team with the lower number wins the match. For example, a team with wins on boards 1, 4, 7, and 12 (=24) wins against a team with victories on boards 2, 3, 9, 11 (=25), but would lose by the elimination method.

Tietz system, an AUXILIARY SCORING METHOD intended as a basis for the distribution of tournament funds among the competitors. The fund is first divided, two-thirds for prizes, one-third for a consolation fund. All players who score more than 50 per cent get a prize, each receiving a sum directly proportional to the number of points by which his score exceeds 50 per cent. All players who win one or more games share in the consolation fund, each receiving a sum directly proportional to the number of games he has won.

Victor Tietz (1859–1937), patron of the great Carlsbad tournaments of 1907, 1911, 1923, and 1929, wrote an article on his system in *Wiener Schachzeitung*, 1900. In several tournaments in the next few years funds were allocated in this way. His intention was to encourage competitors to play at their full strength and to strive for wins, thus providing interest for the onlookers. The greater the amount by which a player's score exceeded 50 per cent the larger the prize; even so, tournament leaders were not inclined to take undue risks. Although regarded as practical and just his system was suitable only for tournaments for which a large fund was available.

time, (1) a positional factor that concerns the minimum number of moves needed (not necessarily those taken) to reach a given position. Players rightly seek to gain time, which is measured quantitatively for lack of a better yardstick. However, the significance of the time gained can be determined only by considering the effectiveness of the 'gained' moves and other factors. After 1 e3 e5 2 e4 White has lost a TEMPO and Black has gained the advantage of the initiative. Such simple cases are not typical. In the game given under YATES Black plays 7 ... Nc6 with the intention of provoking 8 d5 and thereby weakening White's grip on c4. After 8 ... Nb8 9 e4 Nbd7 White has gained two tempi at the cost of a slight positional weakening. In the game under CLOSE GAME Black makes a similar manœuvre in order to use the bishop on the long diagonal. In the opening a gain of time usually goes hand in hand with a lead in development, but there are exceptions. A gain of three tempi in the opening, said to be worth a pawn, normally brings a decisive advantage.

Time is of importance throughout the game. In the endgame one tempo may be decisive. In the basic endgame, however, ZUGZWANGS and SQUEEZES sometimes occur: these are 'anti-time' positions in which a player does not want to have the move.

Rotlewi–Rubinstein Łódź 1907–8 Queen's Gambit Declined Tarrasch Defence

1 d4 d5 2 Nf3 e6 3 e3 c5 4 c4 Nc6 5 Nc3 Nf6 6 dxc5 Bxc5 7 a3 a6 8 b4 Bd6 9 Bb2 0–0 10 Qd2? (the queen will move again, losing time) 10 ... Qe7 11 Bd3? (White loses another tempo) 11 ... dxc4 12 Bxc4 b5 13 Bd3 Rd8 14 Qe2 Bb7 15 0–0 Ne5 16 Nxe5 Bxe5 17 f4? Bc7 18 e4 Rac8 19 e5 Bb6+ 20 Kh1 Ng4

A count of the moves needed to reach this position shows 11 for White, 12 for Black. (Moves required by men no

longer on the board are ignored.) The question is, who has spent his time the more effectively? Black has developed pieces while White has moved pawns. As it happens, White's pawn advances are seen to be irrelevant, for the game is dominated by piece play. If the tempo count excludes pawn moves then Black has gained three tempi (9:6), a decisive advantage. The game ended brilliantly: 21 Be4 Qh4 22 g3 Rxc3 23 gxh4 Rd2 24 Qxd2 Bxe4+ 25 Qg2 Rh3 White resigns.

time, (2) the time allotted for the moves of each player. (See TIME-LIMIT.) Sometimes a player repeats a short sequence of moves to anticipate time-trouble, to 'save time on the clock'. The opponent either connives to the same end or complies for lack of anything better (see, for example, the game under TUKMAKOV). Occasionally a player who has the advantage repeats the position once too often.

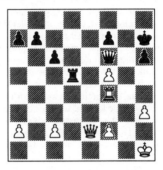

A position from the 3rd match game between FISCHER (White) and PETROSYAN in the final Candidates match, 1971. Black has the advantage. He attempts to gain time on the clock: 30 ... Qe5 31 Qh5 Qf6 32 Qe2 Re5 33 Qd3 Rd5. Fischer, indicating that he intended to play 34 Qe2, successfully claimed a draw by repetition of position. Unable to recover after this lost opportunity, Petrosyan drew two and lost four of the remaining six games of the match.

time control, see TIME-LIMIT.

time-limit, the time, as measured by a CLOCK, allotted for a number of moves to be made by each player; the point in time (sometimes called the time control) by which a player's moves must be made. A player who does not complete the required number of moves is said to have exceeded the time limit.

The TIMING OF MOVES was introduced in the middle of the 19th century to avoid undue slowness of play. Organizers, realizing that games are often marred by blunders made by players in time-trouble, sometimes inflicted no penalty other than a fine for exceeding the time-limit. This practice was virtually abandoned by 1914, although time-trouble blunders are no less frequent. Article 10.13 of the LAWS states that a game is lost by a player who has not completed the prescribed number of moves in the allotted time.

time-trouble, the situation in which a player has little time on the CLOCK to complete the stipulated number of moves. Competition play at all levels is dominated by the clock. Taking time to find the right move in a difficult position may be worth the risk of time-trouble, with its tendency to lead to errors, later on. Skill at fast play is desirable for all players. Nobody is immune from time-trouble.

timing of moves. In a competition a player failing to make a given number of moves within a specified period of time loses. The moves are timed by a CLOCK. If this is defective the player must inform the arbiter, who is empowered to deal with all complaints and disputes concerning the clock. A player complaining after exceeding the time limit would be unlikely to obtain redress. Both players' clocks may be stopped and play temporarily suspended if the clock is defective, if an illegal move is made, if a substitute piece is not available after promotion, or if there is outside interruption, as for example a lighting failure. Checkmate, resignation, or stalemate end the game, and neither player can subsequently lose on time.

When formal competitive play began to emerge, a demand for some kind of time control arose. The timing of moves was discussed by SAINT-AMANT in *Le Palamède*, 1836. In the same year, when DESCHA-PELLES offered to play a match with a leading English player, one of the suggested rules was that after a game had lasted two hours, each player should be limited to a maximum of two minutes for each move 'with five bisques'. (French players may well have remembered the slowness of McDONNELL'S play in his matches with BOURDONNAIS in 1834.)

In 1844 Deschapelles, commenting on the match between STAUNTON and Saint-Amant the previous year, said that the games 'averaged nine hours, that is, nine times longer than the games of the grand masters'. This was an extreme view, but he had correctly identified a change in the speed of play. In the abortive negotiations for a return match with Saint-Amant, Staunton offered a time limit of '10, or 15, or 20, or 25, or 30 minutes, at your pleasure', adding that a player who exceeded his time limit should be fined one guinea.

At that time players were concerned to prevent an opponent from sitting too long over a move, the overall time for a game being of less consequence. Playing in a match in which each move was timed separately, HARRWITZ ridiculed the idea by taking the full allowance for his first move. Another suggestion was made: if a player has not moved within a specified time the opponent may demand that a move be completed within a further period, also predetermined. Applying a time limit to each move became the standard method in draughts, but found favour only in LIGHTNING CHESS.

'A. Cantab' wrote in the *Chess Player's Chronicle*, 1852, 'Juries, ere now, have convicted men, and judges have hanged them, to save time. Railway companies at the present day break our legs, and sometimes our necks, to save time. Our chess-players are the only men in the country who disregard it.' He proposed that each player should have a three-hour SANDGLASS which would run only during that player's turn to move, and that the game would end either with mate or the sand running out. A similar system, a specified number of moves in a specified time, first suggested by von der LASA, and now generally used, was introduced in 1861 as a result of the influence of the London player George Webb Medley (c.1826–98). He played a match with KOLISCH in 1860 and then wrote: 'Herr Kolisch won the match, but in one or two of the games I was fortunate enough to run him rather hard. In one game some position of difficulty arose, and over three successive moves he took more than two hours, occupying 55 minutes over one of them. Now, Sir, although this was complimentary to my skills, it was, as you may imagine, a weariness of the flesh, and I set my wits to work . . .'

As a consequence of Medley's recommendation a time limit of 24 moves in two hours, measured by sandglasses, was used for the match between Kolisch and ANDERSSEN, August 1861, and the Bristol tournament of September 1861. The time control varied in subsequent events: Paris 1867, 10 moves every half-hour; Dundee 1867, 30 moves in two hours; Baden-Baden 1870 and Leipzig 1871, both controlled by Kolisch, 20 moves an hour. When the great tournament at London 1883 came along a time limit of 15 moves an hour was used, and Medley, sole surviving trustee of the LÖWEN-THAL·fund, the balance of which was given to the congress, pressed successfully for the use of clocks. Also, the practice of stopping the clocks while a sealed move was being considered, a privilege that had led to abuse, was abandoned. Since then rates of play have varied, but the timing method is unchanged.

In 1900 Samuel Walker, a Liverpool watch-maker, took out a PATENT for 'Improvement in Time Indicators for Chess or other Games'. The hands move clockwise for one player, anti-clock-wise for the opponent, the game being decided if the difference exceeds a specified limit. Although not without merit this radical idea made little impression. In the second half of the twentieth century weekend tournaments became increasingly popular. Crowded programmes left no time for adjournment, and SUDDEN DEATH time-limits were introduced. For example, after a four-hour playing period with a time-limit of 48 moves in two hours, the players' clocks are set back ten minutes and the game must be completed in the remaining time. With the advent of electronic clocks new possibilities arose and in 1990 the recluse FISCHER emerged to publicize a chess clock which he had patented. The basis of its novelty is the ability to add available time whenever a player makes a move. He suggested that each player should begin with one hour on the clock and that two minutes be added each time the clock is pressed, thus avoiding the worst features of a time scramble.

Although the technique has changed little, the attitude of players towards time control is different from the early days, when it was regarded as a spur, and a claim on time unsporting. Such scruples have long since disappeared. In 1882 a barrister and keen chessplayer, Wordsworth Donisthorpe (1847–1914), wrote: 'The object of the time limit is to insure a reasonable rate of progress, and not to afford a means of snatching a game out of the hands of the winner if he should by oversight or mistake miscount his moves or forget to watch his clock.' Donisthorpe's statement was provoked by an incident in the Vienna 1882 tournament. In the third round MASON, playing BIRD, overstepped the time-limit, but went on to win four hours later. Although Bird made no claim, STEINITZ successfully appealed to the tournament committee that the game be awarded to him. After thirty-four rounds the tournament ended with Steinitz and WINAWER scoring 24 points, while Mason, with 23 points, took third place.

Timman, Jan Hendrik (1951–), the strongest Dutch player to follow EUWE, national champion 1974, 1975, 1976, 1978 (shared), 1980, 1981, 1983, and 1987, regular member of his country's OLYMPIAD team from 1974, International Grandmaster (1974). His first win in a strong event was at Hastings 1973–4 when he shared the prize with KUZMIN, SZABÓ, and TAL. An outright victory at Natanya 1975 and a win at Reykjavik 1976 (+9=4−2), shared with F. ÓLAFSSON, were followed by three wins in strong tournaments: Nikšić 1978 (+7=5−1), a tie with GULKO; Amsterdam 1978 (+7=5−1); and Bled–Portorož 1979 (+7=8), ahead of LARSEN. Also in 1979 Timman played a practice match with POLUGAYEVSKY (+2=5−1) and entered the Rio de Janeiro interzonal; in this he came fourth (+6=10−1), half a point behind the joint winners HÜBNER, PETROSYAN, and PORTISCH, failing by this narrow margin to become a CANDIDATE.

Timman continued to make good results: Bugojno 1980, third (+3=7−1), after KARPOV and Larsen, ahead of Tal; Amsterdam 1980, second (+4=10), after Karpov; Tilburg 1980, third (+3=7−1), after Karpov and Portisch, ahead of SPASSKY and Tal; Buenos Aires 1980, second (+6=6−1), after Larsen, ahead of Karpov; Wijk aan Zee 1981, first (+6=4−2) equal with SOSONKO; Amsterdam 1981, first (+4=7), ahead of Karpov and Portisch; Las Palmas 1981, first (+7=3), ahead of Larsen and KORCHNOI; Mar del Plata 1982, first (+8=3−2), two points ahead of a field that included Karpov; Tilburg 1982, second (+3=8), half a point behind Karpov. In 1982 he was ranked number three in the world.

Successes continued regularly, the major wins in strong tournaments being: Bugojno 1984 (+4=9); Wijk aan Zee 1985 (+5=8), in front of NUNN and BELYAVSKY; Amsterdam 1987 (+2=4), shared with Karpov; Tilburg 1987 (+4=9−1), in front of HÜBNER and NIKOLIĆ; Linares 1988 (+7=3−1),

ahead of Belyavsky and YUSUPOV; Amsterdam 1989 (+3=3), in front of SHORT and SALOV; and Rotterdam 1989 (+7=7−1), ahead of Karpov and VAGANYAN. Timman was sponsored for some years to play an exhibition match against a leading opponent. In these he drew with Spassky +1=4−1 in 1983, beat Portisch +2=3−1 in 1984, lost to Kasparov +1=2−3 in 1985, drew with Yusupov =6 in 1986, defeated LJUBOJEVIĆ +3=3 in 1987, lost to Tal +1=3−2 in 1988, and drew with Short +2=2−2 in 1989.

In 1985, after sharing fourth place with Tal at Montpellier and drawing the play-off match (+1=4−1), Timman went through on tie-break to become a Candidate. After winning the first game of his semi-final match with Yusupov in 1986, Timman collapsed, losing +1=4−4. Again a Candidate in 1988, he defeated Salov +1=5, then in 1989, in the quarter-final, Portisch +2=3−1, and, in the semi-final, Speelman +2=5−1, but lost in 1990 to Karpov, who thereby became the challenger. Seeded to the next Candidates cycle Timman defeated Hübner +2=5, and Korchnoi +2=5 in 1991. In 1992 he won from Yusupov +4=4−2, to face Short in the final.

Timman–Adorján Wijk aan Zee 1974 English Opening
Symmetrical Defence

1 c4 c5 2 b3 Nf6 3 Bb2 d5 4 cxd5 Nxd5 5 Nf3 Nc6 6 a3 f6 7 e3 e5 8 Qc2 Be6 9 Bd3 g6 10 h4 Bg7 11 Nc3 Nxc3 12 Bxc3 Rc8 13 h5 Nd4 14 exd4 cxd4 15 hxg6 dxc3 16 dxc3 Qb6

17 Bc4 Bxc4 18 bxc4 Qe6 19 Rb1 b6 20 gxh7 f5 21 Ng5 Qg6 22 Qa4+ Kf8 23 Qd7 Re8 24 Nf3 f4 25 Rd1 e4 26 Nh4 Bxc3+ 27 Kf1 Qe6 28 Rd6 Qxd7 29 Rxd7 Re6 30 Rxa7 Rd6 31 Kg1 e3 32 fxe3 fxe3 33 Ra8+ Kf7 34 Rxh8 Bxh8 35 Nf3 Kg6 36 Rh4 Rd1+ 37 Kh2 Kf5 38 Kg3 Rf1 39 Rf4+ Kg6 40 Nh4+ Black resigns.

Timur, or Timur-Leng (Timur the lame) (1336–1405), known as Tamerlane, Mongol emperor who named one of his sons Shāh-Rukh, meaning CHECK-ROOK. In his court was the Persian lawyer and historian Alā'addīn at-TABRĪZĪ (the Aladdin of children's stories), known as Alī ash-Shaṭranjī because of his skill at chess. Timur said he had no rival as a ruler, Ali ash-Shaṭranjī none as a chessplayer. Timur also played GREAT CHESS and ROUND CHESS.

Timur's chess, see GREAT CHESS.

Tinsley, Samuel (1847–1903), chess editor of *The Times*. A self-educated man, he and his two brothers founded a publishing firm, Samuel Tinsley & Co. Contrary to the usual pattern, his playing strength increased in his middle age, and he became a chess professional. He shone at simultaneous displays but rarely took a high place in master events, where he was handicapped by the need to report for the press. Perhaps his best result was in a tournament in Simpson's Divan, 1893, when he was equal second with MASON and TEICHMANN, behind BLACKBURNE. He was well liked by the readers of his column, and had a good understanding of master chess.

titles, see FIDE TITLES. Commenting on ZUKERTORT's spurious claim to be a doctor of medicine, STEINITZ said that if one could become a doctor of chess then Zukertort would fully deserve it. Proposals for a chess professional body that would award grades of membership, perhaps based on examination, have not been realized.

TN, a THEORETICAL NOVELTY.

Tolstoy, Leo Nikolayevich (1828–1910), great Russian novelist and chess fanatic. Aylmer Maude writes '. . . when Tolstoy was a young officer in the Caucasus he was promised a St George Cross for bravery; but, absorbed in a game of chess, he failed to go on duty the night before the awards were to be distributed. It unluckily happened that the commander of the division visited the guns which should have been in Tolstoy's charge, and, not finding him at his post, placed him under arrest. The next day, when the crosses were distributed, Tolstoy was a prisoner and missed the coveted honour . . .' (*Times Weekly Edition*, 3 May 1907). He played countless games with URUSOV during the siege of Sevastopol (1854–5).

Tolush, Alexander Kazimirovich (1910–69), Soviet player, International Grandmaster (1953), International Correspondence Chess Master (1965), chess journalist. Though he was an outstanding master of attack, his play was never sound enough for the highest honours. A citizen of Leningrad, where he coached SPASSKY from 1951 to 1961, he won the city championship jointly in 1937, 1947, and 1954, outright in 1938 and 1946. The best of his ten attempts to win the USSR championship were: 1950, second (+8=6−3) equal with ARONIN and Lipnitsky, after KERES; 1952, fourth (+8=7−4) equal with BOLESLAVSKY, after BOTVINNIK, TAIMANOV, and GELLER, ahead of BRONSTEIN; and 1957, fourth (+10=6−5) equal with Spassky, after TAL, Bronstein, and Keres. Tolush achieved his best international tournament result at Bucharest 1953 when he was first (+10=8−1), ahead of PETROSYAN, SMYSLOV, Boleslavsky, and Spassky. At Keszthely 1958 he came second (+7=3−1) after PORTISCH.

Alexander Tolush (1983), compiled by his wife Valentina, is a biography and 92 games.

Kasparyan–Tolush Leningrad 1947 15th USSR Championship French Defence Hanham Variation

1 e4 e6 2 d3 d5 3 Nd2 Nf6 4 g3 dxe4 5 dxe4 Bc5 6 Bg2 Nc6 7 h3 e5 8 Ngf3 Be6 9 0–0 Qd7 10 Ng5 0–0–0 11 Nxe6 fxe6 12 c3 h5 13 Qe2 Qd3 14 Qxd3 Rxd3 15 Nb3 Bb6 16 Kh2 a5 17 a4 h4 18 g4

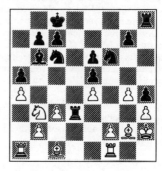

18 ... Nh7 19 Be3 Bxe3 20 fxe3 Rxe3 21 Rf7 Rg8 22 Raf1 b6 23 R1f2 Nd8 24 R7f3 Rxf3 25 Rxf3 Ng5 26 Rf2 Nc6 27 Bf1 Rd8 28 Ba6+ Kb8 29 Kg2 Ne7 30 Rd2 Rf8 31 Rd7 Ng6 32 Rxg7 Nf4+ 33 Kh1 Nfxh3 34 Nd2 Rf2 35 Rd7 Nf4 36 Rg7 Ngh3 37 Rd7 Rg2 White resigns.

Tolush–Geller Gambit, 97 and 98, the SLAV GAMBIT and its GELLER GAMBIT.

Tomlinson, Charles (1808–97), English player and writer, pioneer of research into surface tension. From 1841 to 1844 he ran a chess column in the *Saturday Magazine*. In 1891 he published, in the *British Chess Magazine*, his reminiscences of English chess life in the middle of the 19th century, a valuable insight.

Torre, Eugenio (1951–), Filipino player, International Grandmaster (1974). He has appeared regularly in his country's Olympiad team since 1970, and in 1974 scored +9=10 on first board. A high point in his career came in 1982 when he was equal first (+5=7−1) with PORTISCH, ahead of SPASSKY, at the Toluca interzonal, and became a CANDIDATE. In the quarter-final he lost to RIBLI. Other good results are: Manila 1976, first (+3=3), ahead of KARPOV, LJUBOJEVIĆ, and BROWNE; Manila 1979, first (+7=6), ahead of F. ÓLAFSSON; Hastings 1980–1, second (+6=8−1), after ANDERSSON; Bugojno 1984, third (+4=7−2), after TIMMAN and Ribli, ahead of Spassky, Andersson, Tal, and BELYAVSKY; Biel interzonal 1985, fourth (+7=7−3) equal with SHORT and van der WIEL, after VAGANYAN, SEIRAWAN, and A. SOKOLOV; Brussels 1986, third (+3=7−1) equal with Timman and MILES, after Karpov and KORCHNOI; and Biel 1988, third (+3=7−1) equal with TUKMAKOV, after I. SOKOLOV and GULKO.

Karpov–Torre   Manila 1976   Sicilian Defence Richter Attack

1 e4 c5 2 Nf3 Nc6 3 d4 cxd4 4 Nxd4 Nf6 5 Nc3 d6 6 Bg5 e6 7 Qd2 a6 8 0–0–0 Bd7 9 f4 b5 10 Qe1 Nxd4 11 Rxd4 Qb6 12 Rd2 Be7 13 Bd3 b4 14 Nd1 Bb5 15 Nf2 h6 16 Bh4 g5 17 fxg5 hxg5 18 Bg3 Nh5 19 Ng4 Nxg3 20 hxg3 Rxh1 21 Qxh1 Rc8 22 Kb1 Bxd3 23 cxd3 Qd4 24 Qd1 a5 25 Nh2

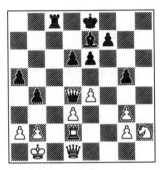

25 ... g4 26 Nxg4 Bg5 27 Rc2 Rxc2 28 Kxc2 a4 29 a3 b3+ 30 Kb1 d5 31 exd5 Qxd5 32 Nf2 Qxg2 33 Ne4 Be3 34 Nc3 Qc6 35 d4 Qc4 36 d5 e5 37 Qh1 Qd3+ 38 Ka1 Bd4 39 Qh8+ Kd7 40 Qa8 Qf1+ 41 Nb1 Qc4 (41 ... Bxb2+ 42 Kxb2 Qf2+ mates.) 42 Qb7+ Kd6 43 Qb8+ Kxd5 44 Qd8+ Ke6 45 Qe8+ Kf5 46 Qd7+ Kg6 47 Qg4+ Kf6 48 Nc3 Qf1+ White resigns.

Torre Attack, 432, QUEEN'S PAWN OPENING variation from the game C. Torre–Sämisch, Marienbad, or as 428 in the game C. Torre–Verlinsky, Moscow 1925, or as 436, sometimes called the Tartakower Attack, in Kmoch–Znosko-Borovsky, Budapest 1921. Although 432 was known from the 4th match game Kostić–Capablanca, 1919, it was made famous by the Mexican grandmaster.

Torre Repetto, Carlos (1905–78), Mexico's first International Grandmaster (1977), whose career had some parallels with that of MORPHY. Torre was born in Yucatán, and in 1915 moved with his family to New Orleans. In 1924, after proving himself the best player in Louisiana, he travelled north, where he won the New York State championship, and the Western championship. In 1925 he went to Europe and played in his only top-class events: Baden-Baden, Marienbad, and Moscow, coming tenth, equal third ($+6=8-1$), and equal fifth respectively. Asked why he gave no exhibitions in Europe he replied 'because I can learn nothing thereby'.

But the high promise of his European achievements was not fulfilled. In 1926 he won the Mexican championship by defeating each of his three opponents twice, and was told that he would be given a post teaching chess at the National University of Mexico. At Chicago later that year, just before the last round of the Western championship (in which he tied for second place), Torre received two letters by the same post, one informing him that he would not get the teaching post for lack of academic qualifications, and the other from his fiancée saying she had married someone else. He suffered a ner-

vous breakdown, returned to Mexico at the end of the year, took an ill-paid job in a drug-store, and played no more serious chess. Misfortune may have been only the immediate cause of his retirement. Of a mild and artistic temperament, he appreciated the beauty and logic of chess, but lacked the spirit of aggression needed for success in play. In 1934 he scored $=1-1$ in friendly play against FINE, who was then visiting Mexico. Torre never married. He retained an interest in chess throughout his life, and greatly admired FISCHER's play. (See KEVITZ-TRAJKOVIĆ DEFENCE.)

Torre–Duz-Khotimirsky   Moscow 1925   Polish Defence

1 d4 Nf6 2 Nf3 b5 3 Bf4 Bb7 4 Nbd2 e6 5 e3 a6 6 Bd3 c5 7 c3 Nc6 8 Qe2 Be7 9 h3 0–0 10 0–0 Qb6 11 Bg5 cxd4 12 exd4 Nd5 13 Be4 Bxg5 14 Nxg5 Nf6 15 Bd3 Ne7 16 Nde4 Ned5 17 Rfe1 h6 18 Nxf6+ Nxf6 19 Ne4 Nd5 20 Qd2 d6 21 Ng3 Nf6 22 Re2 Rac8 23 Rae1 Bd5 24 Bb1 Rfd8 25 Re3 a5 26 Ne2 b4 27 Rg3 Kf8 28 Nf4 bxc3 29 bxc3 Qc6 30 Qd1 Be4 31 Nh5 Bxb1 32 Nxf6 Bg6 33 d5 exd5 34 Nxd5 Rd7?

35 Rge3 Rcd8 36 Qf3 Qb7 37 Nf6 Qc8 (37 ... gxf6 38 Qxf6 Bh7 39 Qh8+ Bg8 40 Qxh6 mate) 38 Re8+ Rxe8 39 Rxe8+ Qxe8 40 Nxe8 Kxe8 41 Qa8+ Ke7 42 Qxa5 Be4 43 Qb4 f5 44 a4 Rb7 45 Qd4 Rb1+ 46 Kh2 Rb2 47 Qxg7+ Ke6 48 Qxh6+ Kd5 49 Qe3 Kc4 50 Qd4+ Kb3 51 Qxd6 Kxa4 52 h4 Kb3 53 h5 Kxc3 54 h6 Rb7 55 f3 Black resigns.

Torre Variation, 1290, sometimes called the Moscow Variation, a line in the RÉTI OPENING played in the game Réti–C. Torre, Moscow 1925. At an earlier date CAPABLANCA had played 3 ... Bg4, leading to the same line of play, and some give the variation his name.

touch and move law, the popular name for Article 7 of the LAWS. A player who first expresses the intention (e.g. by saying J'ADOUBE) may adjust pieces on their squares. Without the warning the player who deliberately touches (a) one or more pieces of the same colour, must move or capture the first piece touched that can be moved or captured, or (b) pieces of both colours, must capture the one with the other if legal, otherwise as in (a). If no legal move can be enforced there is no penalty. A player who makes a move loses the right to claim for previous infringements.

This law applies only to the player with the move. If the other player acted in this manner an arbiter might use Article 15 (see BEHAVIOUR), but there has not been a general problem.

tournament. The word 'tournament' owes its modern meaning to chess. Originally martial sports for knights, tournaments died out, after more than 600 years, during the Renaissance. In 1839 the Earl of Eglintoun re-created the tournament, with a lavish feast, as an entertainment. The event stirred the imagination of the public in general, and WALKER in particular. In *Bell's Life* he began to use jousting terms in his accounts of chess events, and described a gathering of Yorkshire players in Leeds in 1841 as a 'tournament'. The term caught on and was firmly established by the time of the first international event of this kind, London 1851, won by ANDERSSEN. The most important tournaments of the next 40 years were Vienna 1882, won by STEINITZ and WINAWER, and London 1883, won by ZUKERTORT.

From the 1890s there was a steady growth in the number of tournaments of all kinds, among them Hastings 1895, won by PILLSBURY; St Petersburg 1895–6 (the first great MATCH TOURNAMENT), Nuremberg 1896, and London 1899, all won by LASKER; and San Sebastián 1911, Spain's first international tournament, in which CAPABLANCA gained fame almost overnight. The most memorable tournament before the First World War was St Petersburg 1914. The world's strongest two players, Capablanca and Lasker, raced neck and neck for 18 rounds, Lasker winning by a short head, while the third-prize winner, ALEKHINE, was far behind. Four great international tournaments were played between the two world wars (winners' names in brackets): New York 1924 (Lasker), New York 1927 (Capablanca), Nottingham 1936 (BOTVINNIK and Capablanca), and AVRO 1938 (FINE and KERES).

Botvinnik won the match tournament for the world title in 1948. Five CANDIDATES tournaments followed. After these ceased in 1962 the strongest international tournaments were Santa Monica 1966 (SPASSKY), Montreal 1979 (TAL and KARPOV), Tilburg 1979, Bugojno 1980, Tilburg 1980, Moscow 1981, all won by Karpov, Tilburg 1981 (BELYAVSKY), Turin 1982 (Karpov and ANDERSSON), Tilburg 1983 (Karpov), Tilburg 1985 (MILES, HÜBNER, and KORCHNOI), Bugojno 1986 (Karpov), Tilburg 1986 (Belyavsky), Tilburg 1987 (TIMMAN), Linares 1988 (Timman), Belfort 1988 (KASPAROV), Brussels 1988 (Karpov), Tilburg 1988 (Karpov), Linares 1989 (IVANCHUK), Barcelona 1989 (Kasparov), Rotterdam 1989 (Timman), Skellefteå 1989 (Karpov and Kasparov), Tilburg 1989 (Kasparov), Belgrade 1989 (Kasparov), Linares 1990 (Kasparov), Tilburg 1990 (Ivanchuk and KAMSKY), Linares 1991 (Ivanchuk).

In 1890 there were two international master tournaments, in 1990 well over a hundred. Besides these there are many tournaments to which entry is restricted to national players, youths, students, blind players, or women. (See CANDIDATE (2); INTERZONAL TOURNAMENT; NATIONAL TOURNAMENT; ZONAL TOURNAMENT.)

J. Gaige, *Chess Tournament Crosstables, 1851–1900, 1901–1910, 1911–1920, 1921–1930* (4 vols., 1969–74); R. J. McCrary, *The Birth of the Chess Tournament* (1982).

tournament category, a classification based on the average ELO RATING of the competitors. Each category embraces a span of 25 points, category 1 being 2251–2275, category 16 2626–2650. These categories determine the percentage score needed by a player to achieve a NORM. For example a category 7 tournament, 2401–2425, the lowest for which a GM norm is possible, demands a 76 per cent score for a GM norm, 57 per cent for an IM norm, 43 per cent for an FM or WGM norm, and 30 per cent for an IWM norm.

An early attempt to classify tournaments was made by an Austrian architect, Franz Drobny (1863–1924), in *Deutsches Wochenschach*, 1899. Using statistical methods he classified 31 tournaments played between 1870 and 1899, listing them in order of strength. His list may be compared with the results obtained by applying Elo rating retrospectively. Sometimes Drobny's placings differ markedly, but 24 of them are accurate to within five places.

tournament controller, an officer responsible for enforcing the tournament rules, which are not necessarily the same for every event, and for ensuring compliance with the FIDE LAWS. For major events there are often other officers who have specific functions such as seeing that clocks are set correctly, watching the clocks of players in TIME-TROUBLE, ensuring that SEALED MOVES are made properly, or acting as referee in disputes between players or between a player and an official. Those with sufficient experience of controlling tournaments may qualify for the FIDE title of INTERNATIONAL ARBITER, and the control of the highest level events would be in such hands. A controller can impose penalties for infringements of the laws and rules if, for example, a player were to analyse in the tournament room, or consult books, and he may also penalize players for other kinds of misconduct such as fixing a game beforehand or losing or drawing a game for payment. Unfortunately the practice of 'selling' games to players seeking title norms is not uncommon. These and other malpractices such as 'accidentally' exceeding the time-limit or intentionally sealing an illegal move are often hard or impossible to prove. In grandmaster tournaments a committee that includes players and officials is elected before the event and may act as an ultimate court of appeal.

tourney, a competition for the composing of problems or studies; a SOLVING TOURNEY. (Sometimes used as synonymous with TOURNAMENT, but such confusion should be avoided.) In an informal (composing) tourney, compositions published during a set period, usually in one publication, are submitted to judges. For a formal tourney unpublished compositions are submitted by a given date, and the composers' names are not known to the judges. Besides prizes, competitors may be awarded 'honourable mentions' and, after this, 'commendations'. Sometimes 'special prizes' are awarded, an evaluation that may mean much or little.

The first informal tourney, for problems published in the *Illustrated London News* in 1854, was won by Walter Grimshaw (1832–90). The first formal problem-composing tourney in 1856, and the first study-composing tourney in 1862, both international events, were organized by LÖWENTHAL. The former was won by BAYER closely followed by F. Healey, the inventor of BRISTOL CLEARANCE, while the latter was won by HORWITZ. In 1956 FIDE initiated the title of International Judge of Chess Compositions.

trainer, a recent arrival on the chess scene. There have always been chess teachers or coaches, and it is now common for a player taking part in an important event to have a SECOND who will help the player to prepare. In the Soviet Union a player who was thought to be a potential world champion would have a permanent trainer whose duties went far wider than practice games and analysis. For example on one famous occasion BOTVINNIK'S trainer, RAGOZIN, had to smoke incessantly during practice games to accustom the champion to playing in a smoky atmosphere. A second is appointed on an event-by-event basis, and has to probe the weaknesses of the opposition. A trainer is permanent, and has to probe the weaknesses of the player. There must be mutual confidence.

Traité de Lausanne, see ASPERLING.

Trajković Variation, 737, an unusual line in the SPANISH OPENING.

transpose, to bring about a given position by an alternative and perhaps less conventional series of moves. A traditional variation of the QUEEN'S GAMBIT Declined, for example, is 1 d4 d5 2 c4 e6 3 Nc3 Nf6; the sequence 1 c4 Nf6 2 Nc3 e6 3 d4 d5 is a transposition. This is still a Queen's Gambit Declined although White begins with the ENGLISH OPENING (1 c4). A position arising from the FRENCH DEFENCE, 1 e4 e6 2 d4 d5 3 exd5 exd5 4 Nf3 Nf6, can also arise from the PETROFF DEFENCE, 1 e4 e5 2 Nf3 Nf6 3 Nxe5 d6 4 Nf3 Nxe4 5 d3 Nf6 6 d4 d5; in this case each line of play retains its name. In the opening phase transposition is an additional weapon. A player may transpose to a preferred variation or one known to be favourable. To this end some players begin 1 Nf3 or 1 c4, or in reply to either of these moves play the non-committal 1 ... Nf6.

Transpositions (for White) are unacceptable in the ORTHODOX PROBLEM, but a more lenient view is taken for STUDIES, depending on the nature of the transposition.

trap, generally an attractive line of play that is less advantageous than it appears and which may have been deliberately set as a temptation by the opponent. As much could be said of many possibilities in a game, and there is no precise definition of a trap, nor is the element of temptation essential.

A game Mayet–Harrwitz, Berlin, 1848, began 1 d4 d5 2 c4 e6 3 Nc3 Nf6 4 Bg5 Nbd7 5 cxd5 exd5 and Mayet played 6 Nxd5?, falling into a trap

This travelling set has two flaps that fold over the pieces to hold them in place, and then the whole board folds to lock everything together. The position on the board shows the Tarrasch Trap.

and losing a piece after 6 . . . Nxd5 7 Bxd8 Bb4+ . However, this trap is incidental to Black's purpose, and few masters would suggest that Black tempts White. After 1 e4 e5 2 Nf3 Nc6 3 Bb5 Nf6 4 d3 Ne7 (MORTIMER TRAP) 5 Nxe5? c6 wins a piece. If 5 Nc3 instead, White gets more advantage than he would otherwise expect in this opening. Traps like this, which leave a player worse off if the opponent avoids them, should not be set unless a player already has a lost position. A trap that succeeds in such a case is called a SWINDLE. There are many traps in the opening: four well-known ones are the LASKER, TARRASCH (two), and WÜRZBURGER TRAPS.

travelling set, a three-dimensional set designed for use on journeys (two-dimensional sets are usually called POCKET SETS). In the early 18th century French noblemen had chessmen with spikes at the base and cushions embroidered as chequered boards, but, by the end of the century, sets having boards with a hole in the middle of each square and every man with a peg at the bottom were in use. With a suitable lid the set can be closed and put away without disturbing the position. A more sophisticated design, *In Statu Quo*, has a folding board with a locking device to keep the men in place when the board is folded. Later sets use magnetism to keep pieces on their squares while the players are in motion.

Traxler Variation, 953 in the TWO KNIGHTS DEFENCE. Karel Traxler (1866–1936), a well-known Czech problemist, played this line at Prague in 1890 in a game Reinisch–Traxler; it is also known as the Wilkes–Barre Variation.

Trebitsch, Leopold (1842–1906). Austrian industrialist who learned chess half-way through his life and became a generous patron. A series of 20 Trebitsch Memorial tournaments took place in Vienna from 1907 to 1938; the strongest of them were the first (1907, won by MIESES), the seventh (1915, won by SCHLECHTER), the twelfth (1928, won by GRÜNFELD and Takács), and the eighteenth (1935, won by ELISKASES and L. STEINER).

trébuchet, a type of ZUGZWANG shown in the diagram.

Whoever has the move loses the game. A similar situation could arise on other ranks and files. *Le trébuchet* could be interpreted as meaning 'the trap': either player must avoid reaching this position unless he can ensure that it would be his opponent's turn to play. When DURAND and PRETI introduced the term in 1871 they used it for a different position: White Kf5, Pd4, Black Kb5, Pd5. White to play 1 Ke6 Kc6=, or 1 Kf4 Kb4, b6, or c6=, but not 1 Ke5? Kc4. Black to play 1 . . . Kc6 or b6=, but not 1 . . . Kb4? 2 Ke6 Kc4 3 Ke5. Play might proceed 1 Kf4 Kb4 2 Kf5 Kb5 and so on, the up and down movements of the kings suggesting the operation of a balance, another meaning of *trébuchet*.

triangulation, a manœuvre by the king that LOSES THE MOVE and sets up, or leads to, a SQUEEZE or a ZUGZWANG. In the following example White's king is moved on a triangular path (b3–a3–b2–b3). The term probably originated because this is the pattern of moves most frequently seen, but other patterns occur from time to time.

A position published in 1841 by WALKER, who supposed it to be drawn. Subsequently KLING showed the winning procedure: 1 Ka3 (the beginning of a triangulation) 1 . . . Kb6 2 Kb2 Ka5 3 Kb3 (The triangulation ends. Having to move, Black must withdraw the king.) 3 . . . Kb6 4 Kc3 Ka5 5 Kd2 Ka4 6 Ke3 Kb4 7 Kd3 Ka3 8 Ke4 Ka4 9 Kd5 Kb4 10 a3+ .

Triangulation was understood in the 10th century, and perhaps earlier. Kling was probably the first analyst of modern chess to perceive that this manœuvre had a wide application in pawn endings.

Trifunović, Petar (1910–80), International Grandmaster (1953), champion of Yugoslavia 1945, 1946, 1952, and 1961, joint champion 1947, lawyer and government official. In 1948 he came tenth in the Saltsjöbaden interzonal; eight of those above him became CANDIDATES. Trifunović was moderately successful in several master tournaments: Prague 1946, second equal with STOLTZ, after NAJDORF; Cheltenham–Birmingham–Leamington 1951, second equal with PIRC and STÅHLBERG, half a point after GLIGORIĆ; Belgrade 1954, third, after BRON-STEIN and MATANOVIĆ, ahead of PETROSYAN and Gligorić; Beverwijk 1962, first; and Sarajevo 1962, third, after PORTISCH. In a small tournament at Noordwijk in 1965 he came second after BOTVINNIK. He played in seven Olympiads from 1935 to 1962, making the best third-board score ($+8 = 4 - 1$) in 1950, and contested one important match, drawing with Najdorf ($+1 = 10 - 1$) at Opatija in 1949.

Trifunović was a hard man to beat, and enjoyed a fight (he had been a wrestler in his youth). However, his cautious positional style was not conducive to greater successes: he was more concerned to avoid a loss than to win. At the Leipzig tournament in 1965 he played 15 games and drew them all.

Pachman–Trifunović   Bled 1961   Queen's Gambit Declined Semi-Slav Defence

1 d4 d5 2 c4 c6 3 Nc3 Nf6 4 e3 e6 5 Nf3 Nbd7 6 Bd3 dxc4 7 Bxc4 b5 8 Bd3 a6 9 e4 c5 10 d5 exd5 11 e5 Ng4 12 Bg5 f6 13 exf6 Ndxf6 14 h3 Nh6 15 Qe2+ Qe7 16 Bxf6 Qxe2+ 17 Kxe2 gxf6 18 Nxd5 Kf7 19 Be4 f5 20 Ne5+ Ke6 21 f4 fxe4

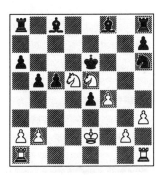

22 Nc7+ Kf5 23 Nxa8 Kxf4 24 Nf7 Nxf7 25 Rhf1+ Ke5 26 Rxf7 Be6 27 Raf1 Bc4+ 28 Ke1 Bxf1 29 Kxf1 c4 30 Nc7 Bd6 31 a3 Bxc7 32 Rxc7 h5 33 a4 Kd4 34 axb5 axb5 35 Ke2 Rg8 36 Rd7+ Kc5 37 Kf2 e3+ 38 Kf3 h4 White resigns.

Trifunović Variation, 83 in the SLAV DEFENCE, as the game Botvinnik–Trifunović, Moscow 1947; 802 in the SPANISH OPENING, an old line (Winawer–Schütz, Berlin 1881) revived in 1963 by TRIFUNOVIĆ with a new idea. After 7 Nxe5 Bd7 8 Nxd7 he played 8 . . . Nxd4 9 Ne5+ c6 (Nemet–Trifunović, Vrnjačka Banja 1963) and after 8 Bxc6 Bxc6 9 Re1 Bd7 (Shamkovich–Trifunović, Sarajevo 1963).

Two other old lines revived by Trifunović: 1061 in the PETROFF DEFENCE; 1265 in the ALEKHINE DEFENCE, first played in a game Marco–Kostić, The Hague 1921, and reappearing in Wade–Trifunović, Staunton Memorial Tournament, 1951. Again Trifunović had a new idea, to continue 6 Nf3 e6 7 Nc3 Na6.

Tringov, Georgi Petrov (1937–), International Grandmaster (1963), Bulgarian champion 1963, 1981, and 1985. He played for his country in eleven Olympiads between 1956 and 1982, and came first in five international tournaments: Kecskemét 1964 (a zonal event); Vršac 1973, equal with PARMA; Smederevo 1981, also shared; Prague 1984, shared with four others; and Asenovgrad 1986, shared with two others. His best result was at Vinkovci 1976 when he was third ($+5 = 10$) equal with POLUGAYEVSKY, after HORT and SAX.

triple, to place two rooks and a queen of the same colour on the same file or rank, with no other men intervening. For an example, see FIXED CENTRE.

tripled pawns, three pawns of the same colour on the same file.

Tröger Variation, 19 in the ENGLISH OPENING, an idea of the German player Paul Tröger (1913–92), and often played by LJUBOJEVIĆ. One German chess encyclopedia describes Tröger as a solid positional player, strong in defence, while another says he loved risky play.

Troitzky, Alexei Alexeyevich (1866–1942), widely regarded as the founder of the modern art of study composition. (Henri RINCK also played a part, but Troitzky was the more inventive.) As a student at Leningrad he met many of Russia's chess enthusiasts, among them CHIGORIN who edited a chess column in *Novoye Vremya* and invited Troitzky to contribute studies. Two years later, in 1897, Troitzky left for the country to take up a post as assistant forester in the district of Smolensk, his interest waned, and after a few years his first composing period was over. He had shown many new ideas but, as he said later, some were crudely expressed.

His return to chess in 1906 was marked by the publication in *Deutsche Schachzeitung* of his examination of the endgame two knights against pawn. It remains the most thorough and recondite noncomputer analysis of any one kind of endgame, and was the basis for a change in the FIFTY-MOVE LAW many years later. He resumed composing and was especially prolific between 1908 and 1913. In 1910 he wrote an article, published in the periodical *Niva*, laying down the principles for the composition of studies. (An English translation appeared in *EG*, Jan. 1968.) He also composed problems and became one of the world's leading exponents of RETROGRADE ANALYSIS. This period ended during the troubled times of 1917 when he lost all his papers.

In 1923 he began his third composing phase 'mellowed and still rich in ideas'. In 1928 the government of the Russian Soviet Federated Republic awarded Troitzky the title of Honoured Art Worker—the first time that chess composition was officially regarded as an art form. An unassuming man who spent much of his life in remote places, with chessmen for companions, he died of starvation during the siege of Leningrad. All his papers perished with him.

Troitzky published *500 Endspielstudien* in 1924, a selection of his own studies. In 1934 the first volume of a Russian edition of his studies appeared, the second volume, scheduled for 1940, being a victim of the war. The volume that was published contains 360 studies and the whole of the analysis of the endgame two knights against pawn. It was translated as *Chess Studies* (1937): the reprint of 1968 excludes the endgame analysis, his most important contribution to the game.

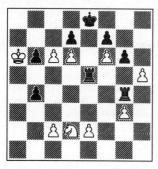

A study by Troitzky, *Neue Leipziger Zeitung*, 1935.
1 c7 Rc5 2 h6 Rxg3 3 Ne4 Ra3 + 4 Kb7 Rxc2 5 Nc3 (Plachutta interference—see CUTTING-POINT THEMES):

5 ... Raxc3   6 c8 = Q+ Rxc8   7 h7
5 ... Rcxc3   6 h7 Rh3   7 c8 = Q mate.

Trompowsky Opening, 437, the OPOČENSKÝ OPENING. The one-time Brazilian champion Octavio Siqueiro F. Trompowsky (1897–1984) tried it in the 1930s and 1940s, at about the same time as did OPOČENSKÝ.

try, a move (other than a COOK) which could be mistaken for the key of a composition. A try may be merely incidental, a trap for the solver, or a THEMATIC TRY. In England in the 1890s tries were called 'almosts'.

try-play, or virtual play, a THEMATIC TRY together with the play that could follow.

Tschigorin, the German spelling of CHIGORIN.

Tseitlin, Mikhail Semyonovich (1947–), Byelorussian player, International Grandmaster (1987), International Correspondence Chess Grandmaster (1990). He was co-champion of Moscow 1976, champion in 1977, and has won four international tournaments: Naleczów 1979, shared; Pernik 1981 (+8=3−2), again shared; Prague 1985 (+7=5−1); and Budapest 1990 (+6=7).

Tseshkovsky, Vitaly Valerianovich (1944–), Russian player, International Grandmaster (1975). After winning tournaments at Leipzig 1975 (+8=6) and Dubna 1976 (+5=10), he played in the interzonal at Manila 1976 and was fourth (+8=8−3) below MECKING, HORT, and POLU-

GAYEVSKY, the three who qualified as CANDIDATES. In 1978 Tseshkovsky was equal third (+4=8−2) at Lvov, first (+6=2−1) at Malgrat, equal with ANDERSSON, and, in the USSR championship, first (+6=10−1) equal with TAL. They shared the title. In 1986, on the ninth of his ten attempts, he became undisputed Soviet champion. After each of his two victories he was last in the succeeding year.

In the interzonal at Riga 1979 Tseshkovsky scored only moderately, but he had good results subsequently: Yerevan 1980, first (+8=5−2) equal with PETROSYAN, ahead of Tal; Banja Luka 1981, first (+9=2), three and a half points clear of the field; Riga 1981, second (+7=7−1), after Tal; Sochi 1981, first (+8=5−2), ahead of Polugayevsky; Minsk 1982, first (+8=5−2); Halle 1984, first equal with UHLMANN; Krasnodar 1986, first; Baden-Baden 1988, first; and Wijk aan Zee 'B' tournament 1988, first.

Tseshkovsky–Chandler   Minsk 1982   Sicilian Defence

1 e4 c5 2 Nf3 c6 3 d4 cxd4 4 Nxd4 Nf6 5 Nc3 Nc6 6 Ndb5 d6 7 Bf4 e5 8 Bg5 a6 9 Na3 Be6 10 Nc4 Rc8 11 Bxf6 gxf6 12 Bd3 Ne7 13 Ne3 Bh6 14 0–0 Bxe3 15 fxe3 Qb6 16 Qf3 h5 17 Nd5 Bxd5 18 exd5 Rh6 19 Rab1 Rc7 20 c4 f5

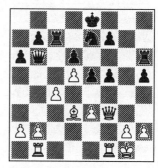

21 b3 f4 22 Rbe1 Ng8 23 Kh1 fxe3 24 Qg3 Kf8 25 Qg5 f6 26 Qh4 Rg7 27 Bf5 Rg5 28 Be6 Kg7 29 Rxf6 Nxf6 30 Qxg5+ Rg6 31 Qxe3 Qa5 32 a3 Ng4 33 Bxg4 Rxg4 34 b4 Qa4 35 h3 Rg6 36 Rf1 Qc2 37 Qf3 Black exceeded the time limit.

Tukmakov, Vladimir Borisovich (1946–), Ukrainian player, International Grandmaster (1972). He competed in fourteen USSR championships between 1967 and 1989, being second on three occasions: 1970 (+9=11−1), after KORCHNOI, ahead of STEIN; 1972, after TAL; and 1983 (+5=8−2), after KARPOV. Tukmakov's best results in international tournaments are: Buenos Aires 1970, second (+7=9−1), after FISCHER; Moscow 1971, fourth (+3=14) equal with PETROSYAN, after Karpov, Stein, and SMYSLOV; Madrid 1973, second (+7=7−1), half a point behind Karpov; Amsterdam 1974, first (+6=8−1) equal with IVKOV and JANSA; Děčin 1977, first (+8=7); Las Palmas 1978, first (+7=7−1) equal with SAX; Vilnius 1978, first (+6=9); Yerevan 1982, second (+7=6−2) equal with PSAKHIS, after YUSUPOV; Tilburg 1984, second (+2=9) equal with

BELYAVSKY, HÜBNER, and RIBLI, after MILES; Moscow 1985, third (+3=8), behind ROMANISHIN and VAGANYAN; Szirák 1985, first (+5=7−1) equal with PINTÉR; Kuibyshev 1986, first; Dortmund 1987, second (+4=6−1) equal with ANDERSSON, after BALASHOV; and Reggio Emilia 1987–8, first (+3=6), ahead of Belyavsky, CHRISTIANSEN, PORTISCH, Ribli and Korchnoi, his finest win. In a Swiss system event at Lugano 1985 he was first from 168 players. Tukmakov was in the Soviet Olympiad team of 1984, and in the same year played against the Rest of the World for the USSR, on fourth board for two rounds and third board in the last round.

Tukmakov–Kuzmin Sverdlovsk 1987 Queen's Gambit Declined

1 d4 Nf6 2 c4 e6 3 Nf3 d5 4 Nc3 dxc4 5 e4 Bb4 6 Bg5 c5 7 Bxc4 cxd4 8 Nxd4 Nbd7 9 0-0 Bxc3 10 bxc3 Qa5 11 Bh4 0-0 12 Re1 Qc5

13 Bxe6 fxe6 14 Nxe6 Qc6 15 Qb3 Kh8 16 Nxf8 Nxf8 17 Bxf6 Qxf6 18 Rad1 Qe7 19 Qb4 Qxb4 20 cxb4 Be6 21 a3 b5 22 f4 g6 23 h3 h5 24 f5 gxf5 25 exf5 Bxf5 26 Rd5 Bd7 27 Re7 a5 28 Rxh5+ Kg8 29 Rg5+ Kh8 30 Rh5+ Kg8 31 Rg5+ Kh8 32 Rd5 axb4 33 axb4 Be8 34 Rde5 Bd7 35 Rh5+ Kg8 36 Rg5+ Kh8 37 g4 Rb8 38 Rh5+ Kg8 39 Rg5+ Kh8 40 Kf2 Be6 41 Kc3 Bc4 42 Rh5+ Kg8 43 Rg5+ Kh8 44 h4 Rd8 45 Rh5+ Kg8 46 Rg5+ Kh8 47 h5 Ne6 48 Re5 Rd1 49 Kf2 Rf1+ 50 Kg3 Rg1+ 51 Kh3 Nd4 52 Re3 Nc2 53 Rf3 Kg8 54 Kh4 Nxb4 55 h6 Rf1 56 Rxf1 Bxf1 57 g5 Nd5 58 Rd7 Nf4 59 Rd8+ Kh7 60 Rd7+ Kh8 61 Rd8+ Kh7 62 Kg4 Ng6 63 Rd7+ Kh8 64 Rd8+ Kh7 65 Kf5 Ne7+ 66 Ke6 Ng8 67 Rd7+ Kh8 68 Kf7 Black resigns. A game showing generous use of repetition to gain time on the clock.

Turk, the nickname which became attached to the first chess AUTOMATON. Made by KEMPELEN, and first shown in the court of the Empress Maria Theresa in 1769, it immediately aroused great interest. The machine played chess well, could make the KNIGHT'S TOUR, and could answer questions by pointing to letters and numbers inscribed on a chess board. Four years later, wishing to give more time to serious work, Kempelen dismantled the apparatus, which he considered unimportant, although he was proud of the mechanism that moved the arm.

In 1781 Maria Theresa's successor, Joseph II, ordered the Turk's refurbishment for the entertainment of Grand Duke Paul, future Tsar of Russia,

and his wife. This was another triumph and as a consequence the Emperor gave Kempelen leave to tour Europe with the machine. He visited Paris in 1783, Germany in 1784, and went on to Amsterdam. Although defeated by PHILIDOR, his talented countryman Bernard, and VERDONI, the android maintained its high reputation. Exhibitions were relatively few until after Kempelen's death in 1804. In the following year Johann Nepomuk Maelzel (1772–1838) bought the machine which he operated successfully, first in Europe and from 1826 in the USA. Shortly after Maelzel's death the Turk was placed in a Chinese museum in Philadelphia, where it was destroyed by fire in 1854.

The apparatus consisted of a life-size figure sitting at a desk little more than a metre wide, about 80 cm high, and about 60 cm deep. On the front were three doors, and at the foot a drawer running the length of the desk. The procedure was to open a door on the left side, then go to the back and open a door behind it and shine a candle so that the spectators could see through the 'machinery'. The rear was closed, the drawer and the other two doors at the front were opened, and another door behind the right-side front door was opened and a light shown at the back. The inside of the figure was exposed while all the front doors and the drawer were open, and the spectators believed they were seeing the entire interior. Some educated observers thought that the Turk was a true automaton, others that it was operated by remote control. Most scientifically-minded observers believed that there must have been a man inside; but how was he concealed, how did he make the moves, and how did he know what was happening on the board?

By 1790 there were already more than a dozen books devoted solely to solving the mystery. One author, Baron Racknitz, made a scale model which he thought explained everything. He was right in supposing the Turk's arm was moved by a pantographic device, and near the mark on two other secrets. However, his solution wrongly supposed the operator to be a boy or a dwarf, an opinion shared by others, and still parroted more than a century and a half after the truth was known. Illustrations of Racknitz's model are frequently printed as being pictures of the real Turk. It was not until 1820 that Robert Willis, then a young man, published a book in which he analysed the Turk logically and deeply, showing how a full-grown man could be concealed without detection. The method of signalling moves had already been guessed, so that by 1820 the whole method had been deduced by a combination of three people, but no one could be certain they were right. In 1827 two youths looking from a rooftop saw the operator emerge when Maelzel opened the chest after a performance; their discovery, published in several papers, was regarded as an unworthy attempt by Maelzel to get publicity. In 1834 one of the former operators, MOURET, sold the secret to a magazine. This was the only betrayal by an operator, and the only authentic explanation published during the machine's existence. Curiously, the Turk's reputation was unaffected by these revelations, perhaps because most of them were in more or less inaccessible sources.

In 1836 Edgar Allan Poe's famous article appeared. Although the Turk's secret had been first deduced, then observed, and finally revealed by a former operator, Poe's essay has been credited with discovery of the secret by deductive logic. Ironically, although Poe added nothing new, and was wrong about much that was already known, the public's belief in the Turk was irreparably damaged.

Who operated the machine during Kempelen's life is not known. Among the operators after his death were ALLGAIER, ALEXANDRE, Mouret, and his equally gifted compatriot Boncourt, an Englishman Peter Ungar Williams, and Wilhelm Schlumberger (c.1800–38) who travelled to the USA for the purpose, and was perhaps the strongest player in the country at that time. Napoleon is said to have played the machine with Allgaier inside, and there are varying accounts of the engagement. This might be true, but the game often published as arising from the encounter is spurious, like the other two games supposedly played by Napoleon and published from time to time.

A romanticized fiction based on the Turk developed after its destruction. For a play, *La Czarine*, published in Paris in 1868, the famous magician Robert-Houdin made a chess machine with a dummy looking more like a medieval alchemist than a Turk. A novel, *The Turkish Automaton*, by Sheila Braine was published in London in 1899, and a silent film, *Le Joueur d'échecs*, appeared in 1926, to be followed by a talking version in 1938.

Robert-Houdin's imagination was responsible for the myth that whilst in Poland [which he never was] Kempelen had created the Turk as a device to conceal an heroic patriot who had lost both legs, and was being sought by the Russian army. The American academic, Donald Fiene, suggested (*British Chess Magazine*, 1979) that Robert-Houdin probably took his inspiration from Józef Maria

The full-size working replica of Kempelen's Turk made by John Gaughan

Wróski (1778–1853), a colourful Pole who lived in Paris from 1806 onwards.

In 1989 John Gaughan, an internationally renowned expert on stage magic, demonstrated a full-size reproduction of the Turk (see photograph) on which he had been working for several years. 'I discovered that the Chess Automaton was the first to use several principles of magic. Magicians had long assumed that they discovered these principles in the nineteenth century', said Gaughan.

C. M. Carroll, *The Great Chess Automaton* (1975); H. Leonhardt, *Der Taktmesser* (1990), is a biography of Maelzel.

Turton, Henry (1832–81), English problem composer active in the early 1850s, co-founder of a chess club in Burton-on-Trent in 1854. A year or two later he gave up composing and married.

Turton doubling, see DOUBLING THEMES.

twins, two or more compositions consisting of almost identical positions but with distinctly different solutions. The dissimilarities of the set positions, however, should be slight: the removal, addition, or repositioning of one man, replacement of one man by another, or a shift of the whole position, intact, to another part of the board. Composers have sometimes amused themselves and solvers with progressive twins: position A is changed to position B which is in turn changed to C, and so on. Each change is slight but the last position of the series may differ considerably from the first.

h#3   b) Pa3–c2

Helpmate twin by PÁROS, third prize, BCF 27th tourney, 1938. Black moves first (as in all helpmate problems). The twin, (b), is formed by moving the Pa3 to c2.

(a) 1 Ba4 Bd4   2 Rb5 Nb6+   3 Kb4 Nc6#
(b) 1 Re2 Bb4   2 Be4 Nf5   3 Kd3 Ne5# .

(See also HELPMATE; KOPNIN.)

Twiss, Richard (1747–1821), English writer who travelled 27,000 miles and made 16 sea voyages, recording his observations. In 1787 he published anonymously *Chess*, which he introduced thus: 'The following trifle is offered to Chess-players as a

Compilation of all the Anecdotes and Quotations that could be found relative to the game of Chess; with an account of all Chess-books that could be procured.' A second volume came out in 1789.

Many years later, under his own name, Twiss published a two-volume work, *Miscellanies* (1805), the second volume of which contained a substantial supplement to his earlier work as well as 100 pages of stories about draughts, and many topics such as Kolf-play (golf) 'not known in any other country [than the Netherlands], a very pleasant salutary exercise, and not attended with the fatigue of Tennis.'

Twiss missed little of importance in chess, although LUCENA was unknown to him. He copied his extracts carefully, in type style as well as spelling, and made literal translations of the foreign extracts. His own recollections were not always reliable. 'I ... was with [PHILIDOR] in Paris in 1783, where I saw his wife. He had at that time 19 [sic] children living, to none of whom he had taught chess.'

two bishops. To say that a player has the two bishops usually implies that the opponent has bishop and knight or two knights instead. Advantage might subsist in the possession of the two bishops, especially if they can operate on open diagonals and if the opposing knight or knights cannot find anchorage in the CENTRAL ZONE. A player who 'gains' the two bishops in the opening might consider this a potential advantage, hoping to open diagonals for the bishops later in the game. However, to have two bishops is not necessarily advantageous. Many other factors, not least the nature of the PAWN FORMATION, must be taken into account.

The power of the two bishops was first pointed out by PAULSEN, and STEINITZ pioneered the appropriate technique by means of which the mobility of the opposing knight or knights could be restricted. From the many games he won in this way masters also learned how to conduct play with the knight or knights. Today a master might voluntarily lose the MINOR EXCHANGE, that is, exchange a bishop for a knight in the opening phase, expecting to arrange matters in such a way that the opponent's two bishops will not gain extensive scope. For examples which demonstrate the bishops' power in the endgame or middlegame, see JANOWSKI and MAKOGONOV. In the game under SPEELMAN, White gets an open position but never gets his bishops actively placed. (See also COLLE; ENGLISCH; JANOWSKI; MASON.)

Petrosyan–Lilienthal USSR Championship 1945 Four Knights Opening Double Ruy López

1 e4 e5 2 Nf3 Nc6 3 Nc3 Nf6 4 Bb5 Bb4 5 0–0 0–0 6 d3 Bxc3 7 bxc3 d6 8 Bg5 Qe7 9 Re1 Nd8 10 d4 Ne6 11 Bc1 c5 12 Bf1 Qc7 (Either 12 ... cxd4 or 12 ... Nc7 is better.) 13 d5 Nd8 14 Nh4 Ne8 15 g3 Qe7 16 Nf5 Bxf5 17 exf5 Qf6 18 Qg4 Qe7 19 Bg5 Qd7 20 a4 f6 21 Bd2 g6 22 Bh3 Qxf5 23 Qxf5 gxf5 24 Bxf5 Ng7 25 Bd3 f5 (25 ... Nf7 is better. Now White opens up the centre, gaining

active play for the two bishops.) 26 f4 e4 27 Be2 Rc8 28 c4 Ne8 29 h3 Nf6

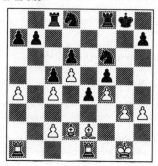

30 g4 fxg4 31 hxg4 Rc7 32 Kf2 h6 33 Rh1 e3+ 34 Bxe3 Ne4+ 35 Kg2 Nf7 36 Bd3 Re7 37 Rae1 Rfe8 38 Bc1 Nc3 39 Rxe7 Rxe7 40 a5 b6 41 axb6 axb6 42 Bd2 Ne2 43 c3 b5 44 Kf2 Black resigns.

Two Knights Defence, 940, a good alternative when Black wants to avoid defending the ITALIAN OPENING. After 4 Ng5 Black may need to sacrifice a pawn, for which the resulting attack provides compensation. This old opening, found in GIANUTIO (1597) and known to POLERIO, is sometimes called the Bilguer Defence, or Prussian Defence. (See ANASTASIA'S MATE; CHAROUSEK; LASA.)

Two Knights Variation, 568, line in the CARO–KANN DEFENCE popular in the 1950s.

two-mover, a problem requiring two moves for its solution, i.e. two SINGLE-MOVES by White, one or two by Black.

Two Pawns Attack, 1256, the LASKER VARIATION of the ALEKHINE DEFENCE.

U

Uedemann Code, the name incorrectly given by FIDE and others to GRINGMUTH NOTATION. The code devised by Louis Uedemann (1854–1912) was never used. He saw an account of the RUTHERFORD CODE and wrote a letter published in *Brentano's Chess Monthly*, Feb. 1882, saying 'it is totally unpractical for several reasons. I did not read the article entirely...' It was his code, given here, that was 'unpractical': Rutherford's remained in use.

AP	EP	IP	OP	PO	PI	PE	PA
AL	EL	IL	OL	LO	LI	LE	LA
AK	EK	IK	OK	KO	KI	KE	KA
AH	EH	IH	OH	HO	HI	HE	HA
AG	EG	IG	OG	GO	GI	GE	GA
AF	EF	IF	OF	FO	FI	FE	FA
AD	ED	ID	OD	DO	DI	DE	DA
AB	EB	IB	OB	BO	BI	BE	BA

Ufimtsev Variation, 237, the Soviet name for the PIRC DEFENCE. Anatoly Gavrilovich Ufimtsev (1914–   ) developed the system in 1934. He was born Ufintsev, but when the secret police took his father away for execution in 1937 they recorded the name as Ufimtsev and it was deemed prudent to let that version stand.

Uhlmann, Wolfgang (1935–   ), professional player, International Grandmaster (1959), champion of East Germany eleven times between 1954 and 1986, he played first board in ten Olympiads from 1956 to 1988, notably scoring +13=4−1 at Tel Aviv in 1964. At first his international results were uneven but from the mid-1960s he won or shared first prize in several strong events: Sarajevo 1964 (+6=9), equal with POLUGAYEVSKY; Havana 1964 (+11=10), equal with SMYSLOV; Zagreb 1965 (+9=9−1), equal with IVKOV, ahead of PETROSYAN; Szombathely 1966 (+8=7), equal with BRONSTEIN; Berlin 1968 (+8=5−2), equal with Bronstein; Raach 1968, a zonal tournament (+11=9−1), two points ahead of PORTISCH, who shared second place; Hastings 1975–6 (+5=10), equal with HORT and Bronstein; Vrbas 1977 (+5=6); Halle 1978 (+6=6−1), equal with FARAGÓ and KNAAK; Halle 1981 (+7=6); Halle 1984, equal with TSESHKOVSKY; Potsdam 1985; Stary Smokovec 1985.

At the Palma de Majorca interzonal 1970 Uhlmann scored +10=8−5, shared fifth place, and became a CANDIDATE; but he lost the quarter-final against LARSEN. Uhlmann is one of the few masters of his time to pin his faith in the FRENCH DEFENCE; he has strengthened many variations from Black's point of view, although none has been named after him.

Uhlmann–Osmanović   Děčin 1979   English Opening Sicilian Variation

1 c4 e5 2 Nc3 Nf6 3 Nf3 Nc6 4 g3 Bb4 5 Bg2 0–0 6 0–0 e4 7 Ne1 Bxc3 8 dxc3 h6 9 Nc2 d6 10 Ne3 Re8 11 Qc2 a5 12 Bd2 Qe7 13 f4 exf3 14 exf3 Bd7 15 Rae1 Qf8 16 f4 Rab8 17 Qd3 Ne7 18 h3 Bc6 19 Nd5 Nexd5 20 cxd5 Rxe1 21 Rxe1 Be8 22 b4 axb4 23 cxb4 b5 24 Bc3 Bd7 25 Bd4 Qd8 26 Qc3 Ra8 27 a3 Rc8 28 Kh2 Ra8 29 Re3 Rc8 30 Bf3 Ne8 31 Kg2 Ra8 32 Qe1 Nf6 33 g4 Nh7 34 Bb2 Rc8 35 Qc3 Qf6 36 Qxf6 Nxf6 37 g5 hxg5 38 fxg5 Nh7 39 Re7 Nf8

40 g6 Nxg6 41 Rxd7 Nh4+ 42 Kg3 Nxf3 43 Kxf3 Kf8 44 h4 Ke8 45 Bxg7 Kxd7 46 h5 Game adjourned. Black resigned without resumption.

Uhlmann Variation, 287 in the HROMÁDKA DEFENCE, played several times by UHLMANN, e.g. Uhlmann–Planinc, Skopje 1969, but also twice by BOTVINNIK in his 1960 world championship match with TAL.

Ujtelky Defence, 1276, the ROBATSCH DEFENCE.

Ulvestad Variation, 963 in the TWO KNIGHTS DEFENCE, analysed in *Chess Review*, 1941, by the American player Olav Ulvestad (1912–   ), who played for Andorra in the Siegen Olympiad, 1970, after retiring to Spain. Also 875, an EVANS GAMBIT variation popular in the second half of the 19th century and played, for example, by KOLISCH against ANDERSSEN in their match of 1861.

unblock, to make a FLIGHT in the KING'S FIELD by moving away a man of the same colour as the king;

the move made for this purpose. The term is used by composers; a player would call this making an ESCAPE SQUARE.

uncapture, to retract (take back) a move that involves a capture; the move so retracted. The term may be used by composers when describing RETRO-GRADE ANALYSIS.

underpromotion, promotion of a pawn to any piece other than a queen. For a practical example in which underpromotion is necessary, see DIDACTIC POSITION. Such events are rare in play but are sometimes featured in problems (see ALLUMWAND-LUNG; BABSON TASK) and in studies.

+

A study by the Czech composer Mario Matouš (1947–), first prize *Československý Šach*, 1982. 1 Nc5 b2 2 Nb3+ Kb1 3 Nd5 a1=N (3 . . . a1=Q 4 Nb4 and 5 Rd1 mate) 4 Nxd4 Kc1 5 Rc2+ Nxc2 6 Nb3+ Kd1 7 Kf1 b1=N 8 Kf2 and wins.

For compositions showing more than one under-promotion see BRON, CALVI, GANDEV, HARING, HELP-MATE, KRALIN, PETKOV.

undouble, to make a move so that a pawn no longer remains doubled. A player may wish to undouble pawns if they are likely to become a source of weakness, as in the game given under WYVILL FORMATION.

united pawns, pawns on adjoining files. Given free rein, either may guard the other. Suppose white pawns on d2 and e4 with a black pawn on d3, then White's pawns are said to be artificially isolated, but they have the potential to become 'properly' united should the black pawn be moved out of the way. In the ARRAY all the pawns on each side are united.

unorthodox chess, versions of the game that do not conform to the international LAWS OF CHESS. Forms such as CHATURANGA, CHATRANG, SHAṬ-RANJ, and MEDIEVAL CHESS were orthodox in their time, and some like CHINESE CHESS and SHOGI still are orthodox in their regions. Some of the features that have fallen out of use during the game's evolution, or were proposed but never adopted, are still used in the unorthodox field.

Suggestions to make the game more difficult are occasionally made by masters, but more frequently by comparatively weak players of the normal game. (See GREAT CHESS; HEXAGONAL CHESS; ROUND CHESS; THREE-DIMENSIONAL CHESS.) New pieces invented for these games are sometimes used in FAIRY PROBLEMS. (Conversely, pieces invented for fairy problems are seldom used in games.) To dispense with the need to study books on the openings the ARRAY may be altered by changing the places of the black king and queen. Another possibility is to switch bishops and knights. Opening such a game BLACKBURNE played 1 Ng3, remarking that it threatened mate in two moves. The array is changed more extensively in RANDOMIZED CHESS.

In Italy LOSING CHESS and PROGRESSIVE CHESS became popular in the 1970s. The Associazone Italiana Scacchi Eterodossi (AISE) was formed, a magazine, *Eteroscacco*, appeared, and *Manuale di scacchi eterodossi* (1980) by Leoncini and Magari was published, all centred on these two unorthodox versions, which have been featured in correspond-ence tournaments.

In 1930 B. Walker Watson invented Petty Chess for lunch-hour games, played on a board of five files and six ranks. White's back rank, left to right, reads Q, K, B, N, R, and the second rank is full of pawns. Black mirrors this arrangement. The laws are normal except that there is no double move for the pawn. Other back-rank arrays have been used. AISE has a version on a 5 × 5 board, the back ranks, left to right, K, Q, B, N, R, which is playable (e.g. 1 b3 cxb3 2 axb3 a3 3 Qa2 e3 4 Nb2 exd2 5 Bxd2 Nc3 6 Bxc3 bxc3 7 Nc4+ Qxc4 8 bxc4 Bb4 9 Qb3 Re3 10 Rb1 1:0).

Some uses of chessmen and board create a new game rather than a version of chess, although it is impossible to define the boundary. An example is chess draughts, introduced by H. Richter of London in 1883. Play is on dark squares only. Reading from left to right each player has pawn, FIRZĀN, bishop, pawn on the back rank, and four pawns on the next. Pawns are moved diagonally forward and capture in the same way. Captures are not compulsory. Pawns reaching the back rank are promoted to bishops. The object is to capture the opposing firzān.

(See also ALICE CHESS; BEROLINA PAWN; CHECK-LESS CHESS; CIRCE CHESS; COURIER; DOUBLE-MOVE CHESS; FOUR-HANDED CHESS; KRIEGSPIEL; PAWNS GAME; POCKET KNIGHT CHESS; RIFLE CHESS; THREE-HANDED CHESS.)

J. Boyer, *Les Jeux d'échecs non orthodoxes* (1951) and *Nouveaux Jeux d'échecs non orthodoxes* (1954). In 1990 G. Jelliss began a quarterly, *Variant Chess*.

unorthodox problem, see FAIRY PROBLEM.

unpin, to free a pinned man; a problem term for the freeing move. Unpins are occasionally featured in compositions. For an example, see KASPARYAN.

unseen mate, or blind mate, a mate not seen by the winner. In former times when it was obligatory to announce check and checkmate an unseen mate might earn the victor only half the stakes.

unsound, said of opening play that is incorrect, of a combination that should not succeed, or of a composition that has no solution or too many solutions. Sometimes the failure of the intended KEY and the discovery of another makes a composition sound, but probably of little merit.

Unzicker, Wolfgang (1925–), International Grandmaster (1954). Winner of the German championship six times from 1948 to 1963, co-winner with PFLEGER in 1965, Unzicker was the strongest West German player from 1945 to about 1970. From 1950 to 1978 he competed in twelve Olympiads, and on one of the ten occasions when he led his team, Dubrovnik 1950, he scored +9=4−1 to share with NAJDORF the prize for the best top-board score. As presiding judge of an administrative court Unzicker had little time for international tournament play. He competed in two interzonals, taking ninth place at Saltsjöbaden 1952 and sixteenth at Göteborg 1955. The best of his other achievements are: Sochi 1965, first (+6=9) equal with SPASSKY; Santa Monica 1966, fourth (+2=15−1) equal with PORTISCH, after Spassky, FISCHER, and LARSEN, ahead of PETROSYAN, then world champion; Maribor 1967, first, ahead of RESHEVSKY; Hastings 1969–70, second (+4=5), after Portisch, ahead of GLIGORIĆ and SMYSLOV; South Africa 1979, second (+3=7−2) to KORCHNOI; and Amsterdam 1980, first equal with REE. After his retirement he again entered the chess fray, winning tournaments at Almada 1988 and Daugavpils 1990 (shared).

Unzicker–Ligterink Amsterdam 1980 Sicilian Defence Richter Attack

1 e4 c5 2 Nf3 d6 3 d4 cxd4 4 Nxd4 Nf6 5 Nc3 Nc6 6 Bg5 e6 7 Qd2 Be7 8 0-0-0 0-0 9 f4 h6 10 Bh4 Bd7 11 Nf3 Qa5 12 Qe1 Rfc8 13 e5 dxe5 14 fxe5 Nb4 15 exf6 Rxc3 16 bxc3 Nxa2+ 17 Kd2 Bc5

18 Bd3 Nxc3 19 Ra1 Qb4 20 Qe5 Bc6 21 Be1 Bxf3 22 gxf3 Rd8 23 Kc1 Bd4 24 Qa5 Be3+ 25 Bd2 Black resigns.

In 1956 Unzicker, his style modelled on the teachings of TARRASCH, lost a match against KERES, another classical player (although not cast in the same mould). In every one of the eight games they played the SPANISH OPENING as if this, the most traditional of all openings, were the only 'correct' way to begin a game. Unzicker's good manners, his

sportsmanship and sense of fair play, made him popular at home and abroad.

Urusov, Sergei Semyenovich (1827–97), the elder and better-known of two brothers, both chess-playing Russian princes. In a letter dated 1899 TOLSTOY writes that during the battle of Sevastopol (1854–5) Urusov, 'a brave officer, a great eccentric, and one of the best European chess-players', proposed to play a game of chess with an Englishman to determine the possession of the first trench of the fifth bastion which had long been contested at the cost of many lives; and that Urusov approached his commanding officer, General Saken, who summarily dismissed the proposal. Tolstoy, although sympathetic, implies that he was only a bystander, but there may have been complicity, for he and Urusov played chess endlessly throughout the campaign. His name is attached to several opening lines. (See GAMBIT; KOLISCH; PETROFF.)

Urusov Attack, 1170, variation in the ALLGAIER GAMBIT named after URUSOV.

Urusov Gambit, 655, 1058, sometimes called the Keidanski–Urusov Attack, a gambit that may arise from the BISHOP'S OPENING, CENTRE GAME, PETROFF DEFENCE, or SCOTCH GAMBIT. If Black takes the pawn, 4 ... Nxe4, White gets a compensating attack by 5 Qxd4. Although his analysis was published in *Schachzeitung* in 1857, URUSOV had played the gambit as early as 1853 in a game against PETROFF. Also 1169, the WALKER ATTACK.

useless check, a check that achieves nothing and often loses time, a common fault among beginners although masters are sometimes guilty. A game van Steenis–Wechsler, Premier Reserves, Hastings 1946–7, went 1 e4 e6 2 d4 d5 3 Nc3 Bb4 4 exd5 Qxd5 5 Qg4 Ne7 6 Qxg7 Qe4+? (to guard h7 before playing Rg8) and after 7 Kd1 Black resigned.

A position from the game Filip–Darga, European Team Championship, Oberhausen 1961. White could win by 33 g4+ Ke5 34 Rc5+ Kd6 35 Qf8+. Instead he played 33 Qxh7+?? Kg4 and resigned, having overlooked ... Kh3.

Facetiously, beginners may be told 'Always check, it might be mate', but they would be better advised to sit on their hands.

V

Vaganyan, Rafael Artemovich (1951–), Soviet player from Armenia, International Grandmaster (1971). A cheerful, extroverted, and popular player, Vaganyan first attracted attention outside his own country when he tied for the European Junior Championship 1968–9. When he was 19 he won the Vrnjačka Banja tournament in 1971 (+7=8), ahead of LJUBOJEVIĆ and STEIN, and clinched his GM title. Subsequently Vaganyan won tournaments at Kragujevac 1974 (+8=7), São Paulo 1977 (+7=6), Kirovakan 1978 (+7=8), Las Palmas 1979 (+9=6), Manila 1981 (+9=2), Moscow 1982 (+6=6−1), shared with TAL, Hastings 1982–3 (+9=4), Tallinn 1983 (+6=8−1), equal with Tal, Lvov 1984 (+6=6−1), equal with DORFMAN, Biel interzonal 1985 (+8=0), and Naestved 1985 (+5=3−3), equal with BROWNE and LARSEN.

Yusupov–Vaganyan Montpellier 1985 Candidates Tournament Queen's Pawn Opening Old Indian Defence

1 d4 Nf6 2 c4 d6 3 Nf3 Nbd7 4 Nc3 c6 5 e4 e5 6 Be2 Be7 7 0–0 a6 8 Qc2 0–0 9 Rd1 Qc7 10 Bg5 h6 11 Bh4 Re8 12 h3 b6 13 Bg3 Bb7 14 c5 bxc5 15 dxc5 dxc5 16 Na4 Rad8 17 Bh2 Nh7 18 Qb3 Ng5 19 Nxg5 hxg5 20 Bc4 Rf8 21 Rd3 Bd6 22 Rg3 Nf6 23 Qe3 Nh7 24 Nxc5 a5 25 Nxb7 Qxb7 26 b3 Qe7 27 Qb6 Nf6 28 Qxc6 Rc8 29 Qb5 Nxe4 30 Re3 Rc5 31 Qa6 Nd2 32 Rd1 Nxc4 33 bxc4 Bc7 34 Red3 e4 35 Rd7 Bxh2+ 36 Kxh2 Qe5+ 37 Kg1 e3 38 fxe3 Qxe3+ 39 Kh1 g4 40 R7d3 Qe2 41 R3d2 Qe7 42 Rd7 Qg5 43 R7d5 Rxd5 44 cxd5 gxh3 45 gxh3 Qe5 46 Qd3 Rb8 47 Rd2

A KING HUNT now begins. 47 . . . Qe1+ 48 Kg2 Rb1 49 Re2 Qg1+ 50 Kf3 Rf1+ 51 Ke4 Qg6+ 52 Kd4 Qb6+ 53 Kc3 Qb4+ 54 Kc2 Qb1+ 55 Kc3 Qb4+ 56 Kc2 Qb1+ 57 Kc3 Rc1+ 58 Kd4 Qb4+ 59 Ke5 Rc4 60 Kf5 g6+ 61 Kg5 Rf4 62 a3 Qd6 63 Re6 (thus White gets two SPITE CHECKS) 63 . . . fxe6 64 Qxg6+ Kf8 65 Qh6+ Ke7 White resigns.

Vaganyan shared first place at the CANDIDATES tournament Montpellier 1985 (+5=8−2) with A. SOKOLOV and YUSUPOV, but was crushed by Sokolov

in the first Candidates match. Further tournament victories followed: Sochi 1986 (+7=3−4), equal with BELYAVSKY and GLIGORIĆ; Leningrad 1987 (+4=8); Marseille 1987 (+5=4); and Toronto 1990 (+8=3). Meanwhile, in 1988, he had another set-back in Candidates events, losing a match with Portisch, but in the following year, 1989, after eleven attempts beginning in 1967, he won the USSR championship (+5=8−2). At Reggio Emilia 1991 he was second (+1=11) equal with GULKO, after Ljubojević.

G. Akopyan, *Po puti bolshikh shakhmat* (1979), is a biography, in Russian, of Vaganyan, with 33 games, published before he had reached full strength.

Vajda–Rellstab Variation, see RELLSTAB VARIATION.

Valencia Opening, 47, the Spanish name for the MIESES OPENING.

value of pieces. A popular scale is P=1, N=3, B=3¼, R=5, Q=9. This answers most purposes, except that three minor pieces are usually regarded as superior to the pair of rooks, because they work better together. Also, a rook and a knight are not as superior to the two bishops as the scale suggests. See the game under SCHLECHTER for an example.

Every writer on this subject, without exception, rightly stresses that the values of this or any other scale are not to be relied upon for every kind of position, or for every phase of the game; all values depend on the nature of the position. For example, in the basic endgame king and two knights against king, the knights have no value whatsoever, and a rook would be worth a great deal. Indeed, there are positions in which a man can have a negative value.

Great players like TARRASCH and FISCHER have valued a bishop above a knight, yet there are positions in which the knight is plainly superior. (See MINOR EXCHANGE for a comparison.) A knight firmly anchored in the basic centre is not greatly inferior to a rook. If well placed, a piece may be of more value than its counterpart. If a player has many better-placed men a sacrifice may be the best way to break through, and the nominal value of the pieces is then of no account. Perhaps the best use of a scale of values is as part of an EVALUATION OF POSITION, balancing the loss of material against positional or tactical gain (or vice versa), often a matter of judgement rather than exact calculation.

Quasi-scientific attempts have been made to establish values. Early in the 19th century PRATT worked out six scales, based on general range of action, general facility of transit, power of transitive attack, dislodging faculty, extra points of support, and circumscribing powers. After complicated consolidation he arrived at the values P = 1, N = 3, B = $3\frac{1}{2}$, R = $5\frac{1}{2}$, and Q = 10. In Bilguer's HANDBUCH, 1843, a scale based on the activity of the pieces throughout the game gave the result P = 1.5, N or B = 5.3, R = 8.6, Q = 15.5, which seems to undervalue the pawn slightly. In his *Handbook* (1847) STAUNTON gave P = 1, N = 3.05, B = 3.50, R = 5, Q = 9.94. In *Revue d'échecs*, 1916, Vogler based a scale on the squares controlled by pieces on an empty board, summing the values for each of the 64 squares: N = 336, B = 560, R = 896, Q = 1,456: but he understated the value of the pawn, neglecting its queening capabilities. The Soviet chess encyclopedia/dictionary, 1990, gives N or B = 3 Ps, N or B and 2 Ps = R, 2 Rs or 3 minor pieces = Q, again emphasizing the unreliability of such figures if used without reference to the position. Most players regard two rooks as stronger than a queen, but this may not be so at the beginning of a game, or in a game played by beginners.

Computers need values for chess purposes. One set is P = 2, B = 7, N = 8, R = 14, Q = 27. The king has two values: for general purposes 8, but for exchanges 1,000 (so that the computer never tries to exchange it). The low value of the bishop here is because it can reach only half the board, and two bishops are usually worth more than twice this value.

valve, a problem composer's description of a move, made by Black, that opens a line for a black line-piece (LINE VACATION) and closes a line previously commanded by the same line-piece (INTERFERENCE). (For an example, see BIVALVE.) The term valve first appeared in *The Good Companion Two-Mover* (1922).

Van Geet Opening, 288, the Kevitz–Trajković Defence, favoured by Dirk Daniel van Geet (1932–) of Rotterdam.

vanished centre, a position without centre pawns. For example 1 e4 e5 2 Nf3 Nf6 3 d4 exd4 4 e5 Ne4 5 Qxd4 d5 6 exd6 Nxd6. In such wide open positions the game is likely to favour the player who first develops active play with his pieces, but control of the central squares may nevertheless remain of consequence.

Van 't Kruijs Opening (pron. vant-cries), 440, given by LUCENA. Maarten van 't Kruijs (1811–85) of Amsterdam, winner of the sixth Dutch championship in 1878, liked its transpositional possibilities. He played it against ANDERSSEN in 1851, but it was known earlier to Dutch players. (See BLACKBURNE.)

vao, a piece invented for use in FAIRY PROBLEMS. It is moved on diagonal lines, making non-capturing moves like a bishop, but capturing only when the man to be captured stands (at any distance) beyond an intervening man of either colour. For example, place a white vao at c3, a man of either colour at e5 and a black man at f6, g7, or h8. The vao can be moved as far as a5, a1, e1, or d4; it neither threatens nor guards the man at e5, but can capture the man that lies beyond.

This piece was invented by the Czech composer Julius Zdeněk Mach (1877–1954) in 1939, and is akin to the PAO. (See CHINESE FAMILY.)

variants of chess, see UNORTHODOX CHESS.

variation, any alternative line of play, especially one that could occur in the opening phase of the game. A treatise on the openings may contain hundreds or even thousands of variations beginning with either white or black moves at various stages of the opening. All of these variations have evolved empirically and are subject to reassessment as they are exposed to combat conditions. Nevertheless, some that have been widely accepted over a period of time are called main variations, or main lines.

One or two main lines form the essence of a study, and other lines that begin with a black move are called side variations: they merely serve to demonstrate that Black cannot achieve a better result by avoiding the main line or lines. In a DIRECT MATE PROBLEM variations are lines of play commencing with a black move, and some of them form an important part of the composition. For example, in a two-mover threat problem the KEY threatens instant mate, and the essence of the solution subsists in the variations that avoid this particular mate. In a HELPMATE a variation is any line of play so designated by the composer.

Vásquez Variation, 901 in the EVANS GAMBIT Declined, recommended by the Cuban player Andrès Clemente Vásquez (1844–1901).

Vasyukov, Yevgeny Andreyevich (1933–), Russian player, International Grandmaster (1961), journalist. From 1959 he averaged one strong international tournament a year, usually taking a high place, and gaining twelve first prizes: Moscow 1961 (+5 = 5 − 1), equal with SMYSLOV; Moscow 1962 (+7 = 6 − 2), equal with AVERBAKH; Berlin 1962 (+9 = 5 − 1); Varna 1964; Reykjavik 1968 (+7 = 7), equal with TAIMANOV; Skopje 1970 (+8 = 6 − 1), equal with Taimanov; Varna 1971 (+8 = 6 − 1); Manila 1974 (+8 = 5 − 1), ahead of PETROSYAN and LARSEN—Vasyukov's finest achievement; Zalaegerszeg 1977 (+6 = 6); Moscow 1986 (shared); Budapest 1989; and Græsted 1990.

In the USSR Vasyukov entered the national championship 11 times from 1959 to 1980–1, scored +7 = 10 − 3 to share fourth place in 1961, and came third in the first Swiss system event at Alma-Ata 1967. He has the rare distinction of having won the Moscow championship six times, 1955, 1958, 1960, 1962 (shared with Averbakh), 1972, and 1978.

Vasyukov–Parma USSR–Yugoslavia match 1963 Sicilian Defence Dragon Variation

1 e4 c5 2 Nf3 d6 3 d4 cxd4 4 Nxd4 Nf6 5 Nc3 g6 6 Be3 Bg7 7 f3 Nc6 8 Qd2 0–0 9 Bc4 Bd7 10 h4 Rc8 11 Bb3 Ne5 12 h5 Nxh5 13 0–0–0 Nc4 14 Bxc4 Rxc4 15 g4 Nf6 16 Rdg1 e6 17 Kb1 Qa5 18 Nb3 Qc7 19 Bf4 e5 20 g5 Nh5 21 Nd5 Qd8 22 Be3 Be6

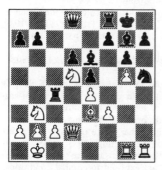

23 Nf6+ Nxf6 24 gxf6 Qxf6 25 Bg5 Qxf3 26 Qh2 Qh5 27 Qf2 Bh3 28 Qe3 h6 29 Nd2 Black resigns.

Velimirović, Dragoljub (1942–), Yugoslav champion 1970 (joint) and 1975 (ahead of GLIGORIĆ and LJUBOJEVIĆ), International Grandmaster (1973). His best results are: Vrnjačka Banja 1973, first (+8=6−1); Novi Sad 1976, second (+8=4−3); Zemun 1980, first equal with Vukić; Titograd 1984, first (+4=7) equal with KORCHNOI; Vršac 1985, first (+6=5); and Vršac 1987, first (+5=6) equal with EHLVEST. A short, energetic man, Velimirović is an aggressive combinative player, a characteristic that has made his games popular. His mother, Jovanka Velimirović (1910–72), was Yugoslavia's first woman champion.

Velimirović–Skembris Pula 1987 Tito Cup final Caro-Kann Defence Exchange Variation

1 e4 c6 2 d4 d5 3 exd5 cxd5 4 c4 Nf6 5 Nc3 e6 6 Nf3 Be7 7 cxd5 Nxd5 8 Bd3 Nc6 9 0–0–0 10 Re1 Bf6 11 Be4 Nxc3 12 bxc3 Bd7 13 Ne5 g6 14 Bh6 Bg7 15 Bxg7 Kxg7 16 Qf3 Rc8 17 Rad1 Rc7 18 Nxd7 Qxd7 19 h4 Ne7 20 h5 f5 21 Bc2 Nd5

22 Bb3 Rxc3 23 Qe2 Rf6 24 h6+ Kf7 25 Qd2 Rc7 26 Re5 Qd8 27 Rde1 Rd7 28 Qe2 Nf4 29 Qe3 Rxd4 30 Bxe6+ Nxe6 31 Rxe6 Re4 32 Rxe4 fxe4 33 Qb3+ Qd5 34 Rxe4 Qb6 35 Rf4+ Ke7 36 Qc3 Rf6 37 Qe5+ Re6 38 Qb8 Qb1+ 39 Kh2 Qe1 40 Qc7+ Ke8 41 Qf7+ Kd8 42 Rd4+ Kc8 43 Qd7+ Black resigns.

Velimirović Variation, 472, also called the Yugoslav Variation, in the SICILIAN DEFENCE, used by VELIMIROVIĆ from c.1962.

Venice Attack, 499, the MOSCOW VARIATION, 517 and 539 in the SICILIAN DEFENCE, each showing the same move.

Venice Variation, 172 in the QUEEN'S GAMBIT Declined, from the game Tartakower–Canal, Venice 1948, and sometimes called the Canal or Peruvian Variation.

Verdoni (d. 1804), Italian who, unusually, learned chess only in his middle age and yet became a strong player. With three French players, Bernard, Carlier, and Leger, he wrote *Traité théorique et pratique du jeu des échecs* (Paris, 1775). Popularly known as the *Traité des amateurs*, the book ran to four editions, the last in 1873. After PHILIDOR's death (1795) Verdoni was engaged to take his place at Parsloe's club in London and spent the rest of his days in England; SARRATT was his pupil. (See PAWN AND TWO MOVES.)

Veresov Variation, 58, sometimes called the Betbeder Variation, or Parisian Opening, in the QUEEN'S PAWN OPENING, a continuation of the RICHTER ATTACK, 56, which also sometimes bears Veresov's name; 535 in the SICILIAN DEFENCE.

Verlinsky, Boris Markovich (1888–1950), Soviet player, International Master (1950). He took first prize, ahead of BOGOLJUBOW, in the Odessa tournament 1910, and subsequently played in a number of national events, to reach his best form in the early 1920s. He won the Moscow championship in 1928, and competed in the USSR championship five times, winning the title in 1929. Verlinsky played in only one international event, the strong Moscow tournament of 1925 (won by Bogoljubow), when he shared twelfth place with RUBINSTEIN and SPIELMANN.

version, a term used by composers to indicate that a composition has been amended subsequent to its first publication. For examples of how this may be done, see INDIAN THEME and DOUBLING THEMES.

vertical line, a FILE.

Vicent, Francesch (15th cent.), author of the first practical chess book to be printed. In 1495 his Catalan book *Libre dels jochs partitis dels schachs en nombre de 100* was published in Valencia. A copy was known to exist in the Benedictine monastery of Montserrat, but unfortunately the library was scattered by occupying French troops in 1811, and no copy is now known.

Vida, Marcus Antonius Hieronymus (c.1490–1566), poet, writer, and, from 1532, Bishop of Alba. In

1513 or a little earlier he wrote a Latin poem, in the style of Virgil, 'De Ludo scaccorum', or 'Scacchia ludus', printed first, without Vida's approval, in 1525 (probably in Basle), and in a revised form in 1527. It became widely admired and copied— JONES'S 'Caïssa', for example, was inspired by it. Some 150 editions have appeared of which about half have been in translation. The poem is not a thinly disguised sermon, as might have been expected from such an exalted churchman, but a pagan account of an exciting game of chess between Apollo and Hermes.

It was played according to the then new rules, giving the poem importance to the chess historian. The best-known English version, formerly attributed to Oliver Goldsmith, has these lines:

Soon after this, the heavenly victor brought
The game on earth, and first th'Italians taught.
For (as they say) fair Scacchis he espied
Feeding her cygnets in the silver tide,
(Scacchis, the loveliest Seriad of the place)
And as she stray'd, took her to his embrace.
Then, to reward her for her virtue lost,
Gave her the men and chequer'd board emboss'd
With gold and silver curiously inlay'd;
And taught her how the game was to be play'd.
Ev'n now 'tis honour'd with her happy name;
And Rome and all the world admire the game.

Vidmar, Milan (1885–1962), Yugoslav player, International Grandmaster (1950), International Arbiter (1951), electrical engineer, Dean of Ljubljana University. For about 20 years he was ranked among the world's best half-dozen players. He was born at Laibach (Ljubljana) and while studying in Vienna (1902–7) took the opportunity to play in strong tournaments at Coburg 1904, Barmen 1905, Nuremberg 1906, Vienna 1907, and Carlsbad 1907. His first notable win ($+6=2-1$) was at Göteborg 1909. At San Sebastián 1911, one of the strongest four tournaments held up to that time, he scored $+5=8-1$ and shared second prize with RUBINSTEIN, half a point after CAPABLANCA, and ahead of SCHLECHTER and TARRASCH. When the First World War began in 1914, the Mannheim tournament was broken off, 11 of the 17 rounds having been played. Having the highest percentage, ALEKHINE was awarded the first prize, but Vidmar was undefeated and had met stronger opposition. (See AUXILIARY SCORING METHODS.)

During the war Vidmar won two strong tournaments: Vienna 1917–18 ($+5=6-1$), ahead of Schlechter; and Berlin (Apr.) 1918 ($+3=3$), ahead of Schlechter and Rubinstein. Subsequently he achieved five excellent tournament results: London 1922, third ($+9=4-2$), after Capablanca and Alekhine, ahead of Rubinstein and BOGOLJUBOW; Hastings 1925–6, first ($+8=1$) equal with Alekhine; Semmering 1926, third ($+9=6-2$), after SPIELMANN and Alekhine, ahead of NIMZOWITSCH and Rubinstein; New York 1927, fourth ($+3=14-3$), after Capablanca, Alekhine, and Nimzowitsch; and Bad Sliač 1932, first ($+6=7$) equal with FLOHR, ahead of Bogoljubow. In 1936–7 he won a strong correspondence tournament, and in 1939 won the strongest Yugoslav championship held up to that time. After an unsuccessful foray at Groningen 1946 he ended his playing career, but was chief arbiter at the first world championship controlled by FIDE, that of 1948. In match play Vidmar defeated TARTAKOWER twice, in 1906 ($+4=3-2$) and 1918 ($+2=4-0$), and while on a visit to USA in 1936 he defeated RESHEVSKY ($+3=1-2$).

'I am lucky that Vidmar is torn between engineering and chess; otherwise my title would be seriously threatened', said Capablanca. His achievements are all the more remarkable in that he played throughout his life as an amateur among professionals, creating his ideas in play, and not in preparation. He wrote 35 books on engineering, and two autobiographical accounts of his hobby: *Pol stoletja ob šahovnici* (1951) includes 100 annotated games and much biographical detail; *Goldene Schachzeiten* (1961), an outstanding book, also includes a number of annotated games, not all involving Vidmar, and, looking more widely at the chess scene, contains a fund of information about his contemporaries. Neither has been translated into English. His only tournament book, *Carlsbad 1911* (1912), written in German, reprinted 1969–70, was not, he said, as good as it should have been because he was paid too little.

Vidmar's son, also called Milan (1909–80), an electronics engineer, competed in a few tournaments and the Olympiad of 1950, obtained the title of International Master (1950), and retired from master play soon afterwards.

Vidmar–Tartakower   London 1922   Dutch Defence

1 d4 e6   2 c4 f5   3 e3 Nf6   4 Nc3 Bb4   5 Bd2 0–0   6 Nf3 Qe7   7 Bd3 d6   8 Qc2 g6   9 a3 Bxc3   10 Bxc3 Nbd7   11 0–0–0 e5   12 dxe5 Nxe5   13 Nxe5 dxe5   14 f4 e4   15 Be2 Be6   16 h3 a5   17 g4 Ra6   18 g5 Nd7

White's dark bishop dominates the long diagonal. 19 h4 Bf7   20 h5 gxh5   21 Bxh5 Bxh5   22 Rxh5 Rf7   23 Rd5 a4   24 Qd1 c5   25 Rh6 Rg6   26 Rxg6+ hxg6   27 Rd6 Nf8   28 Qd5 Qc7   29 Be5 Qa5   30 Kb1 Qe1+   31 Ka2 Qxe3   32 Rf6 Qb3+   33 Ka1 Ne6   34 Rxe6 Kh7   35 Re8 Rg7   36 Qd7 Black resigns.

Vidmar Variation, 13 Qc2 in the CLASSICAL VARIA-
TION (200) of the QUEEN'S GAMBIT Declined, played
in the game Vidmar–Stoltz, Bled 1931.

Vienna Defence, 1132, the HERZFELD DEFENCE to
the KING'S GAMBIT Accepted.

Vienna Gambit, 613, the KING'S GAMBIT move Pf2–
f4, played in the VIENNA GAME after 2 ... Nc6. The
play is akin to the King's Gambit, but reputedly less
favourable for White.

Vienna Game, 608, the name now used for the
Hamppe Opening, also known as the Queen's
Knight Opening, given by PONZIANI and first ana-
lysed by JAENISCH.

Vienna Variation, 213 in the QUEEN'S GAMBIT Declined, played in the game Bogoljubow–Wolf,
Carlsbad 1923, tested in a series of consultation
games between the Viennese players GRÜNFELD,
KAUFMANN, Baldur Hönlinger (1905–90), and WOLF
in 1933, and analysed by another Viennese player,
Hans Müller (1896–1971). (See GRÜNFELD.) Also
713, the ST PETERSBURG VARIATION.

Viennese Variation, 712, the ITALIAN VARIATION of
the SPANISH OPENING.

Villemson Gambit, 1113 in the KING'S GAMBIT
Accepted, sometimes called the Steinitz Gambit
(perhaps because of its resemblance to 614, but
STEINITZ did play it in a consultation game in 1880),
or the Krause, Polerio, or Rosentreter Gambit.
Martin Villemson (1897–1933) of Pärnu, Estonia,
editor of the chess magazine *Eesti Maleilm,* played
it in the first International Correspondence Tournament of the *Deutsche Schachzeitung.* He was a
strong correspondence player and may well have
inspired KERES to try that activity, in which they
overlapped.

Vinken Variation, 450, the GRAND PRIX ATTACK,
much played by the German-born Dutch player
Joseph Alexander Vinken (1919–83), for example in
his match with Kramer in 1942.

virtual play, see TRY-PLAY.

Visserman, Eeltje (1922–78), Dutch composer, International Judge of Chess Compositions (1958),
civil servant in Ministry of Housing and Building.
He was one of the first four to be awarded the title
of International Grandmaster for Chess Compositions when it was introduced in 1972. Although he
composed FAIRY PROBLEMS successfully, he is better
known for his orthodox TWO- and THREE-MOVERS;
in this field he was rivalled, in his generation, only
by LOSHINSKY. During the period 1957–70 Visserman edited the Dutch problem magazine *Probleemblad.* In 1964 he published *64 Nederlandse
componisten,* containing short biographies.

#2

A problem by Visserman, *Chess Correspondent,*
1947. The key is 1 b8 = Q, and the variations show
CYCLIC PLAY:

1 ... Rde6	2 Nc3 ‡
1 ... Rxd5 (Black CORRECTION)	2 Bb1 ‡
1 ... c4	2 Bb1 ‡
1 ... cxd4	2 Nxg3 ‡
1 ... Rf ~	2 Nxg3 ‡
1 ... Rxf5 (Black correction)	2 Qg2 ‡
1 ... g4	2 Qg2 ‡
1 ... gxf4	2 Nc3 ‡.

Considering the 4th and 8th of these variations
also to show Black correction, DAWSON gave this
problem as an example of cyclic correction.

Vistaneckis Variation, 1227 in the FRENCH
DEFENCE, a line dating back to Noa (1885). It was
played by NIMZOWITSCH and TARRASCH and more
recently in a game Mikenas–Vistaneckis, Lithuanian championship, 1947. The Lithuanian-
born correspondence player Isakas Vistaneckis
(1910–) became Itzchak Vistanietzki when he
emigrated to Israel.

visualization. Hazy visualization of positions yet to
come leads to poor evaluation of them: moves that
would be easily seen if such positions were set on
the board are overlooked, and games are frequently
lost in this way. The power to visualize is rarely
perfected, as masters admit, but it can be improved.
The student should practise by working out variations given by annotators or conceived by himself
and assessing the end positions without moving the
men.

Vitolins Variation, 519 in the SICILIAN DEFENCE,
developed by the Latvian player Alvis Vitolins
(1946–) in the mid-1970s.

Vitzthum Attack, 978, premature assault in the
SCOTCH GAMBIT played in the game Vitzthum–
Falkbeer, London, 1856. Count Conrad Woldemar
Vitzthum von Eckstädt (1802–75) came second in
the tournaments at Düsseldorf in 1864 and Cologne
in 1867.

Vladimirov, Yakov Georgievich (1935–), Russian
composer of orthodox problems. International

Judge of Chess Compositions (1965), International Grandmaster for Chess Compositions (1988), International Solving Master (1982). He won the more-mover section of the USSR composing championship four times: 1959–61, 1962–4, 1969–70, and 1975–6. Problem editor for the Soviet periodical *64* from 1973, he is an outstanding columnist.

#3

A problem by Vladimirov, second prize, Loshinsky Memorial Tourney 1981–2. showing a Roman DECOY THEME. Three tries fail: 1 Ke7? Qd3; 1 Nb5? Rf1; 1 Bc8? Rxh6. The key is 1 Ba6 threatening 2 Qf4+

```
1 ... Qxb2   2 Ke7
1 ... Rh5    2 Nb5
1 ... Rf1    2 Bc8.
```

Vogt, Lothar Helmut (1952–), German player, International Grandmaster (1976), East German champion 1977 and 1979. His best results in international play are: Kecskemét 1977, first (+5=6); Halle 1978, fourth (+5=7−1); and Tastrup 1990, first equal.

Volga Gambit, 279, the Russian name for the BENKO GAMBIT, played by B. Argunov of Kuibyshev, who published his analysis in *Shakhmaty v SSSR* in February 1946.

Von Hennig–Schara Gambit, 119, the SCHARA-HENNIG GAMBIT.

Vukcevich, Milan Radoje (1937–), composer and player, International Grandmaster for Chess Compositions (1988), a distinguished scientist, nominee for a Nobel prize. Vukcevich played for his native country, Yugoslavia, in the Olympiad of 1960 and developed his composing skills at about the same time. During the 1960s he emigrated to the USA and around 1970 began an intensive period of composition, winning tourney awards for problems of all kinds. A year or so later he renewed his interest in play, and in 1975 he took third prize after BROWNE and Rogoff in the US championship (which on this occasion was also a zonal tournament). *Chess by Milan* (1981) contains 216 game positions and problems. For problems by him see BRISTOL CLEARANCE; SQUARE VACATION.

Vuković, Vladimir (1898–1975), Yugoslav player and author, International Master (1951), International Arbiter (1952). He played in the Olympiad of 1927 and in five strong tournaments: Vienna 1922, Debrecen 1925, Kecskemét 1927, Rogaška-Slatina 1937, and the Yugoslav championship 1939. In his time he was his country's leading writer on the game. He wrote a two-volume work on world championship matches *Od Steinitza do Botvinika* (1949–50), and some books on the MIDDLEGAME including *Škola kombiniranja* (1951), *The Art of Attack* (1965), and *The Chess Sacrifice* (1968): he also wrote some chess primers and edited the magazine *Šahovski Glasnik* for many years.

Vyzhmanavin, Alexei Borisovich (1960–), Russian player, International Grandmaster (1989), winner of tournaments at Naleczów 1986, Tashkent 1987, Moscow 1988 (shared), Sochi 1989 (+6=8), and Gorky 1989 (USSR championship semi-final). He won the Rilton Cup (Swiss system, 205 players) at Stockholm 1990 by a clear point.

Wade Variation, 147, also known as the Modern Variation, in the QUEEN'S GAMBIT Declined, MERAN VARIATION, from Bogoljubow–Wade, Oldenburg 1949; 1239 in the FRENCH DEFENCE, introduced by Wade in a match against SCHMID in 1950. New Zealand-born Robert Graham Wade (1921–) won the championship of his homeland three times before moving to England as a young man. He won the British championship twice and trained many young English players.

Wagner, Aleksander (1868–1942), Polish/Ukrainian player, and openings analyst. (See LEMBERG GAMBIT; POLISH DEFENCE; SWISS GAMBIT.)

Wagner Gambit, 433, a QUEEN'S PAWN OPENING variation named after the Hamburg master Heinrich Wagner (1888–1959) who played it in a match against BECKER in 1924; 1317, the SWISS GAMBIT, named after Aleksander WAGNER.

Wagner Variation, 130, in the QUEEN'S GAMBIT Declined, introduced by Heinrich Wagner in 1921.

waiter, see BLOCK.

waiting move, generally, any move that carries no threat; specifically, such a move in an endgame or study that is played with the object of LOSING THE MOVE and thereby setting up a SQUEEZE or, on occasion, a ZUGZWANG. For some endgame examples, see SQUEEZE, TEMPO-MOVE (a waiting move by a pawn), TEMPO-PLAY, and THREE PAWNS PROBLEM.

Walbrodt, Carl August (1871–1902), German player born in Amsterdam, manufacturer. He learned the moves when he was ten, played at master level in 1890, and between then and 1898 entered about a dozen tournaments and played in matches. One of his best achievements was at Kiel 1893, when he came first (+6=2) equal with BARDELEBEN, but he had fair results in other strong tournaments: Dresden 1892, a share of fourth prize; Leipzig 1894, again equal fourth; Berlin 1897, second (+11=6−2), after CHAROUSEK, ahead of JANOWSKI, SCHLECHTER, and CHIGORIN. In match play Walbrodt defeated Bardeleben in 1892 (+4=4), drew with SCHEVE in 1891 (+4=2−4) and MIESES in 1894 (+5=3−5), but lost to Janowski, PILLSBURY, and TARRASCH. Although he had undoubted talent, he lacked application. From the early 1890s he suffered from tuberculosis, and he sought to enjoy life fully, while he had time, allegedly hastening his death by 'unruly living'.

Pillsbury–Walbrodt Nuremberg 1896 Spanish Opening Steinitz Defence Deferred

1 e4 e5 2 Nf3 Nc6 3 Bb5 a6 4 Ba4 d6 5 d4 exd4 6 Nxd4 Bd7 7 Nc3 Nxd4 8 Bxd7+ Qxd7 9 Qxd4 Ne7 10 Bf4 Nc6 11 Qe3 Be7 12 Nd5 0–0 13 0–0–0 Rae8 14 Qg3 Kh8 15 e5 dxe5 16 Bxe5 Nxe5 17 Qxe5 Bd6 18 Qd4 Re6 19 Rhe1 Rxe1 20 Rxe1 Rd8 21 Qe4 h6

22 h3 Bc5 23 Rd1 Bxf2 24 Rd3 f5 25 Qf4 Qe6 26 c4 c6 27 Qxf2 cxd5 28 Qd4 Rc8 29 c5 b6 30 b4 bxc5 31 bxc5 Qe1+ 32 Kb2 Qe2+ 33 Ka3 Rxc5 34 Qxc5 Qxd3+ 35 Kb4 Qc4+ 36 Qxc4 dxc4 37 Kxc4 g5 38 a4 h5 39 a5 h4 40 Kd5 Kg7 41 Ke6 Kg6 42 Ke5 g4 43 Kf4 gxh3 44 gxh3 Kf6 45 Kf3 Ke5 46 Ke3 f4+ 47 Kf3 Kf5 48 Kf2 Ke4 49 Ke2 f3+ 50 Kf1 Kd4 51 Kf2 Kc4 52 Kxf3 Kb5 53 Kg4 Kxa5 54 Kxh4 Kb5 55 Kg5 a5 56 h4 a4 57 h5 a3 58 Kg6 a2 59 h6 a1=Q 60 Kh7 Qf6 White resigns.

Walker, George (1803–79), English chess writer and propagandist. Born over his father's bookshop in London, he later became a music publisher in partnership with his father. At a time when he was receiving odds of a rook from LEWIS he had the temerity to edit a chess column in the *Lancet* (1823–4); the first such column to appear in a periodical, it was, perhaps fortunately, short-lived. He tried his hand at composing problems, with unmemorable results; but his play improved. In the early 1830s he was receiving odds of pawn and move from McDONNELL, after whose death (1835) Walker was probably, for a few years, London's strongest active player.

Walker's importance, however, lies in the many other contributions he made to the game. He founded chess clubs, notably the Westminster at Huttman's in 1831 and the St George's at Hanover Square in 1843. From 1835 to 1873 he edited a column in *Bell's Life*, a popular Sunday paper featuring sport and scandal. Many of his contributions were perfunctory, but on occasion he wrote at length of news, gossip, and personalities in a rollicking style suitable for such a paper. As with many of his writings he was more enthusiastic than accurate. He edited England's first chess magazine, *The Philidorian* (1837–8). Above all, Walker published many books at a low price: they sold widely and did much to popularize the game. The third edition of his *New Treatise* (1841) was as useful a manual as could be bought at the time and its section on the EVANS GAMBIT was praised by JAENISCH. Walker established the custom of recording games, and his *Chess Studies* (1844), containing 1,020 games played from 1780 to 1844, has become a classic. For the first time players could study the game as it was played and not as authors, each with his own bias, supposed it should be played. Throughout his life Walker helped chessplayers in need. He raised funds for BOURDONNAIS, W. D. EVANS, and other players, and often for their destitute widows.

After his father died (1847) Walker sold their business and became a stockbroker, reducing his chess activities but continuing his many kindnesses. With an outgoing personality he enjoyed the company of those, such as Bourdonnais, whom he called 'jolly good fellows', an epithet which might well be applied to himself. He was occasionally at odds with Lewis, who was jealous of his own reputation, and STAUNTON, imperious and touchy; but it seems unlikely that the easy-going Walker, who believed that chess should be enjoyed, intentionally initiated these disputes. He left a small but excellent library of more than 300 books and his own manuscript translations of the works of COZIO, LOLLI, and other masters.

He should not be confused with William Greenwood Walker who recorded the games of the Bourdonnais–McDonnell matches 1834, and died soon afterwards 'full of years'.

Walker Attack, 1169 in the ALLGAIER GAMBIT, recommended by WALKER in 1846. Also known as the Urusov Gambit.

Waller Attack, 880 in the EVANS GAMBIT. George Waller of Dublin sent his analysis to the *Chess Player's Chronicle* in August 1846. (See EVERGREEN GAME.)

Ware Gambit, 4 in the WARE OPENING, an inferior move in an inferior opening.

Ware Opening, 3, also known as the Meadow Hay Opening. Preston Ware (1821–90) of the USA had an independent attitude to openings. He also liked the STONE–WARE DEFENCE and the STONEWALL Attack.

wazir, an unorthodox piece that may be moved one square laterally. Placed on d4 it attacks c4, d5, e4, and d3. This piece was used in some forms of GREAT CHESS and, under the name *Schleich*, in COURIER: the general (king) of CHINESE CHESS is moved in the same way. The name wazir (vizier) has also been used to describe unorthodox pieces that are moved in other ways; for example, the combined piece B + N (now called a PRINCESS) was called a wazir in an 18th-century Persian manuscript. (See CYLINDER BOARD.)

weakness, a pawn or a square, or a group of pawns or squares, that is hard to defend. In practice, weaknesses are associated with PAWN FORMATION. An immobile group of pawns, a group of squares of one colour (see COLOUR-WEAKNESS), or a square (see HOLE) might be a weakness. Conventionally some of these characteristics have been regarded as inherently weak, a view no longer held.

'Anything is weak which can be attacked, and anything that cannot be attacked is not weak' KLEIN, *Anglo-Soviet Chess Match* (1947). This view became better understood in the 1940s, and in consequence some new openings ideas were developed. In one of these, pioneered by BOLESLAVSKY in the Sicilian Defence, a black pawn advances to e5, leaving a backward pawn at d6; Black gets a hold on the centre, and free play for his pieces. In another, an idea pioneered by Boleslavsky and BRONSTEIN in the traditional King's Indian Defence, Black plays . . . c6, obtaining a flexible pawn formation on the queen's-side; Black's pawn at d6 cannot be defended by other pawns. In neither case is the pawn at d6 intrinsically weak. The verdict depends on the skill of the players: White might prove the pawn to be weak, Black might prove it to be strong, or it might be merely a feature of no account.

Unzicker–Taimanov Saltsjöbaden 1952 Interzonal Tournament Sicilian Defence Boleslavsky Variation

1 e4 c5 2 Nf3 Nc6 3 d4 cxd4 4 Nxd4 Nf6 5 Nc3 d6 6 Be2 e5 7 Nf3 h6 8 0–0 Be7 9 Re1 0–0 10 h3 a6 11 Bf1 b5 12 a3 Bb7 13 b3 Rc8 14 Bb2 Rc7 15 Nb1 (Or 15 Nd5 Nxd5 16 exd5 Nb8, when the Pd6 is screened from frontal attack. Black might later gain space by Pf7–f5.) 15 . . . Qa8 16 Nbd2 Nd8 17 Bd3 Ne6 18 Rc1 Rfc8 19 Nh2 Nd7 20 Nhf1 Ndc5 21 Ng3 g6 22 Ne2? Bg5 23 Nc3 Nd4 24 Ncb1

24 . . . d5 (The triumph of the BACKWARD PAWN. Black gains advantage in the centre.) 25 exd5 Nxd3 26 cxd3 Rxc1 27 Bxc1 Bxd5 28 f3 Rc7 29 a4 b4 30 Kh1 Qc6 White resigns. There is no immediate danger, but White

has hardly any moves he can play, and prefers not to wait until he is crushed.

Smyslov–Denker   Moscow 1946, USSR–USA match
Sicilian Defence Close Variation

1 e4 c5 2 Nc3 Nc6 3 g3 g6 4 Bg2 Bg7 5 d3 e6 6 Be3 Nd4 7 Nce2 (the Smyslov Variation) 7 . . . d6 8 c3 Nc6 9 d4 cxd4 10 Nxd4 Nxd4 11 Bxd4 e5 12 Be3 Ne7 13 Ne2 0–0 14 0–0 Be6 15 Qd2 Qc7 16 Rfc1 f5 (if 16 . . . b5, 17 a4) 17 c4 fxe4 18 Nc3 Nf5 19 Nxe4 Nxe3 20 Qxe3 h6 21 Rd1 Rfd8 22 Rac1 Rac8 23 b3 b6 24 Nc3 Qe7 25 Bd5

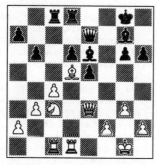

After the forced exchange of the light bishops, the pawn at d6 becomes a fatal weakness. 25 . . . Kh7 26 Bxe6 Qxe6 27 Rd3 Rc7 28 Rcd1 Rf7 29 Ne4 Bf8 30 Rd5 Qg4 31 R1d3 Be7 32 Nxd6 Bxd6 33 Rxd6 Rdf8 34 Qxe5 Rxf2 35 Rd7+ R2f7 36 Rxf7+ Rxf7 37 Rd8 Rg7 38 Qe8 g5 39 Qh8+ Kg6 40 Rd6+ Kf7 41 Qxh6 Qf5 42 Rd1 Qc5+ 43 Kg2 Qe7 44 Rf1+ Kg8 45 Qf6 Qe8 46 Qf5 g4 47 Rf2 Qe7 48 Qd3 Rg5 49 Re2 Qf8 50 Qe4 Rg7 51 Qd5+ Qf7 52 Re6 Qc7 Black resigns.

Boleslavsky–Euwe   Zurich 1953 Candidates Tournament
Sicilian Defence Boleslavsky Variation

1 e4 c5 2 Nf3 Nc6 3 d4 cxd4 4 Nxd4 Nf6 5 Nc3 d6 6 Be2 e5 7 Nb3 Be7 8 0–0 0–0 9 Be3 Be6 10 Bf3 Na5 11 Nxa5 Qxa5 12 Qd2 Rfc8 13 Rfd1 Qb4 14 Rab1 h6 15 a3 Qc4 16 Rbc1 a6 17 Be2 Qc7 18 f3 Nd7 19 Bf1 b5 20 a4 b4 21 Nd5 Bxd5 22 Qxd5 Nc5 23 b3

23 . . . Bg5 24 Bxg5 hxg5 (Black exchanges his BAD BISHOP, protecting the d-pawn indirectly.) 25 Kh1 a5 26 h3 Rab8 27 Bb5 Rd8 28 c3 bxc3 29 Rxc3 Qe7 30 Qc4 g6 31 b4 axb4 32 Qxb4 Kg7 33 Qc4 Qa7 34 Rc2 Ne6 35 Qc3 Nd4 36 Rb2 Rdc8 37 Qd2 Kf6 38 Rc1 Rxc1+ 39 Qxc1 Qc5 40 Qd2 Rc8 41 Kh2 Qa3 Drawn.

For some examples of the move Pc7–c6 in the traditional King's Indian Defence, see SMEJKAL, ZAITSEV.

weak square, a square that cannot be defended satisfactorily.

Weenink, Henri Gerard Marie (1892–1931), Dutch composer, player, and author. He played in several national tournaments, notably a two-stage event, Amsterdam 1927–8, when he and EUWE tied for first place well ahead of the field, and in a small tournament at Amsterdam 1930, when he came first (+4 = 1) ahead of Euwe, whom he defeated, and SPIELMANN. Weenink played for the Netherlands in four Olympiads from 1927 to 1931.

Besides composing problems he wrote a book on the subject, *Het Schaakprobleem* (1921). He is chiefly remembered for a greatly expanded version of this book, *The Chess Problem* (1926). Probably the best of all books on the subject, this comprehensive work from the hand of an artist contains a history, a detailed discussion of themes and problem construction, 374 compositions, and biographical information about some eight or nine hundred composers. He had nearly completed a book in English (published posthumously) about another all-rounder, PRZEPIÓRKA when he died of tuberculosis.

Euwe, Niemeijer, Rueb, and Van Trotsenburg, *H. G. M. Weenink* (1932), contains games, articles, 350 problems, and 33 studies by Weenink.

Weenink Attack, 1255, the STEINER VARIATION of the ALEKHINE DEFENCE.

Weiss, Miksa or Max (1857–1927), Hungarian-born player who studied mathematics in Vienna, where he made his career in Rothschild's bank. Throughout the 1880s his chess improved steadily, as shown by his results in strong tournaments: Vienna 1882, tenth; Nuremberg 1883, tenth; Frankfurt 1887, second equal with BLACKBURNE, after MACKENZIE and ahead of TARRASCH; and New York 1889, first equal with CHIGORIN, ahead of GUNSBERG and Blackburne (all four games of the play-off match were drawn). This last tournament was organized to find a challenger for the world championship, but neither Chigorin, who had already lost a title match, nor Weiss wanted to go further.

Having reached a position among the world's first five or six players, Weiss now gave up international chess, probably because it would conflict with his banking career. Later he played in a few Viennese events, notably a first (+7 = 8), ahead of BAUER and ENGLISCH, in 1890; a match against MARCO in 1895 (which he won +5 = 1 − 1); and a winter tournament, 1895–6, in which he shared first place with SCHLECHTER but was awarded first prize because he had won more games. From about 1896 Weiss devoted his energies to setting up and maintaining a Viennese 'school' of chessplayers.

He should not be confused with Max Ignaz Weiss (1870–1943) of Bamberg, who wrote more than a dozen books on both problems and the game.

Gunsberg–Weiss   New York 1889   Petroff Defence

1 e4 e5 2 Nf3 Nf6 3 Nxe5 d6 4 Nf3 Nxe4 5 d4 d5 6 Bd3 Nc6 7 0–0 Be7 8 Re1 Bg4 9 c3 f5 10 Nbd2 0–0 11 Qb3 Kh8 12 Qxb7 Rf6 13 Qb3 Rb8 14 Qc2 Rg6 15 b3 Bd6 16 Be2 Bh3 17 Bf1 Qf6 18 g3 Bxf1 19 Kxf1 Rf8 20 Nxe4 fxe4 21 Nh4

21 ... Rxg3 22 hxg3 Bxg3 23 Kg2 Bxh4 24 Be3 Qf3 + 25 Kh2 Be7 26 Kg1 Rf6 27 Kf1 Qg4 28 Qd1 Rf3 29 Rc1 Qh3 + White resigns

Wenigsteiner, a composition with four or fewer men on the board, including kings.

West Indian Defence, 1307, an Indian Defence in which Black fianchettoes on the queen's (west) wing, as opposed to the king's (east) wing.

Westphalia Defence, 173 or 182, the MANHATTAN DEFENCE, analysed aboard the passenger ship *Westphalia* by several masters on their way to play in the New York tournament of 1927.

WGM, see WOMAN GRANDMASTER.

White, the player who moves the lighter coloured pieces and pawns. These are called white regardless of their actual colour.

White, Alain Campbell (1880–1951), American problem composer, author, and patron. From his father he acquired a lifelong interest in chess problems. Each Christmas from 1905 to 1936 he published one or more problem books at his own expense, a total of 44 volumes known as the Christmas Series. Besides famous classics such as DAWSON and HUNDSDORFER'S *Retrograde Analysis* and WEENINK'S *The Chess Problem*, the series includes collections of problems by A. F. MACKENZIE, LOYD, HEATHCOTE, SHINKMAN, MANSFIELD, and other leading composers. For many years from 1908 White collected and classified TWO-MOVERS and from the 1920s this work was taken over by HUME, the result of their labours being known as the White–Hume collection. Hume also helped White with some of his books.

White's other interests included English, French, and Italian literature (he wrote on Dante and Carlyle), botany, on which he wrote two books, and the Litchfield (Connecticut) Foundation which administered his gift of about 3,500 acres (1,420 ha)

of land, including a wild-life sanctuary. He also wrote books on the history of Litchfield, where he lived for many years. (See ALTSCHUL.)

White, John Griswold (1845–1928), founder and donor of the world's largest chess library, at Cleveland, Ohio. As a boy White was left with a book dealer when his mother shopped, and he developed both a love of books and rapid-reading ability. He could grasp essentials quickly but was unable to remember numbers or to learn by heart. A lawyer, as his father had been, he achieved high honours in his profession. White could play a fair game of chess; in friendly combat with ZUKERTORT during the 1880s, although he lost most of the games, he is said to have acquitted himself well; but he is remembered for his chess library, which, founded upon his father's collection, eventually consisted of 12,000 books and 428 beautifully carved chessmen, some bone, some ivory. He assisted the chess historian MURRAY by sending him many photographic copies and transcripts of rare oriental manuscripts. White's other interests included collecting fungi and sailing (he was a founder member of the Cleveland Yacht Club). Able to read, to varying standards, 29 languages, a skill stemming from his need to know more about his chess books, he was inspired to collect 60,000 volumes of folklore and orientalia which he presented to the Cleveland Public Library. Every year White took a holiday in the mountains, on one occasion a guide saying, 'They ain't no cow man in these here parts c'n throw the diamond hitch on a cayuse better'n him'; and in the mountains he died, in a remote camp at Jackson Lake, Wyoming. He bequeathed his chess books and chessmen, valued at $300,000 for estate purposes, to the Cleveland Public Library and provided adequate endowment for the future. Further additions since his death have doubled the size of the collection.

white correction, see CORRECTION.

Wiel, John C. van der (1959–), Dutch player, International Grandmaster (1982), Netherlands champion 1984 and 1986, European Junior Champion 1978–9. He played in the Olympiads 1980–90, and in all-play-all international events had a number of successes: Wijk aan Zee master tournament 1981, first (+ 5 = 4); Wijk aan Zee 1982, third (+ 5 = 5 − 3) equal with HORT, after BALASHOV and NUNN; Novi Sad 1982, first (+ 4 = 9); Montpellier zonal 1985, first (+ 8 = 2 − 1); Amsterdam (OHRA) 1986, second (+ 4 = 4 − 2), after LJUBOJEVIĆ; Wijk aan Zee 1986, second (+ 4 = 8 − 1) equal with Ljubojević and NIKOLIĆ, after SHORT; Amsterdam (OHRA) 1987, first (+ 3 = 7) in front of CHANDLER, TIMMAN, and GULKO; Ter Apel 1987, first (+ 2 = 3) equal with LOBRON and REE; Haninge 1989, second (+ 2 = 9) equal with ANDERSSON, after FTÁČNIK.

Wiesbaden Variation, 93 in the SLAV DEFENCE, played by BOGOLJUBOW in the third game of his championship match with ALEKHINE in 1929, and thus sometimes called the Bogoljubow Variation. The first six games of the match took place at Wiesbaden. This line became the answer to 6 Ne5 when the CARLSBAD VARIATION, 92, went out of fashion around 1937. (See POLUGAYEVSKY.)

Wilder, Michael Joseph (1962–), US champion 1988, International Grandmaster (1988).

Wild Muzio Gambit, 1136, or Greco–Lolli Gambit, an unsound line in the KING'S GAMBIT Accepted first given by POLERIO and named on account of its violent nature.

Wilkes-Barre variation, 953, the TRAXLER VARIATION of the TWO KNIGHTS DEFENCE. Claiming to be the first to analyse and publish this line, MARSHALL named it after a town in Pennsylvania.

Williams, Elijah (1809–54), English player, apothecary. A native of Bristol, from where he edited one of the earliest chess columns (*Bath and Cheltenham Gazette*), and of whose chess club he was president, Williams gave up his job in 1844 and moved to London where he attempted to earn a living at chess. In a tournament at Simpson's Divan, 1849, he was knocked out in the second round by BUCKLE but the following year he led +3−1 in an unfinished match against the same player. In the London international tournament of 1851, a knock-out event, Williams defeated LÖWENTHAL in the first round but, after leading 3–0, lost to WYVILL in the third and penultimate round. He won the third prize after defeating STAUNTON (+4=1−3). He admired Staunton's play and, like several of his contemporaries, adopted the positional style of the English school; but after this match the master never forgave the pupil. Staunton challenged Williams to a match seven up in 1851, giving Williams three games start; of the games actually played, Williams won four, drew three, and lost six, but won the match.

In 1851 Williams also defeated Medley 4–0 and Mongrédien 4–0, and in 1852, he won against HORWITZ (+5=9−3). Williams has a reputation of being a slow player, but the facts suggest that this was so only in exceptional cases: Horwitz wrote that most of the games in his match were over in two hours, and none lasted longer than five. He played at least three matches with HARRWITZ, 1846, 1852, and 1853, without success. When cholera broke out in London he posted a notice on his door offering preventive medicine free. Supplies had run out when, feeling unwell, he left home for the last time; seized with violent pain in the Strand, he entered Charing Cross Hospital where he died of the disease two days later, leaving his wife and children destitute.

He wrote two books, *Souvenir of the Bristol Chess Club* (1846) and *Horae Divanianae* (1852), and edited a chess column in *The Field* from January 1853, when the magazine was founded, until his death.

Williams–Staunton   London 1851 5th game   Bird Opening

1 f4 d5   2 e3 c5   3 Nf3 e6   4 Bb5+ Bd7   5 Bxd7+ Nxd7
6 0–0 g6   7 c4 d4   8 Qe2 Bg7   9 e4 Nh6   10 d3 0–0   11 h3 f5
12 Nbd2 a6   13 Ng5 Re8   14 e5 b5   15 b3 Rb8   16 Ndf3
Bf8   17 Qf2 Rb7   18 Qh4 Nb8   19 Ba3

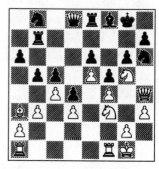

19 ... Qc7? (19 ... b4 is correct)   20 Nxd4 b4   21 Ndxe6
Rxe6   22 Nxe6 Qe7   23 Qxe7 Rxe7   24 Nxf8 bxa3   25
Nxg6 hxg6   26 b4 cxb4   27 d4 Rc7   28 Rac1 Kf7   29 d5
Rc5   30 Kf2 a5   31 Ke3 a4   32 Kd4 Na6   33 Rb1 Ra5   34
Rfc1 b3   35 c5 Nb4 (White's phalanx cannot be stopped
without loss of material.)   36 Kc4 Na6   37 c6 Ng8   38 d6
Ke6   39 c7 Nxc7   40 dxc7 Ne7   41 Kb4 Ra8   42 Kxa3
Kd7   43 axb3 axb3+   44 Kxb3 Nc6   45 Rxc6 Kxc6   46
Rc1+ Black resigns.

Williams Gambit, 1315, a curious experiment in the BIRD OPENING, an opening to which WILLIAMS showed great partiality in the 1840s and 1850s.

Winawer, Szymon (1838–1920), Polish player, merchant. Previously unknown to players of western Europe he 'dropped from the clouds' (LÖWENTHAL) to share second prize with KOLISCH in the Paris tournament 1867. For the next 15 years Winawer stood among the world's best half-dozen players. At Paris 1878 he came first (+14=5−3) equal with ZUKERTORT, ahead of BLACKBURNE and MACKENZIE, taking second prize after a play-off; at Berlin 1881 he shared third place with CHIGORIN, after Blackburne and Zukertort; and at Vienna 1882, the strongest tournament held up to that time, he achieved his greatest success, first (+22=4−8) equal with Steinitz, ahead of Blackburne, Mackenzie, and Zukertort (a play-off was drawn +1−1).

A businessman first and chessplayer second, Winawer was often out of practice, and after a poor start at London 1883 he decided to give up competitive chess, a course of action that was delayed for six weeks on account of a curious incident. In urgent need of a dentist while on his way to Vienna, he stopped off at Nuremberg where a tournament was about to begin. Waylaid by the organizers when he was about to resume his journey, he was persuaded to play and came first (+13=2−3), ahead of Blackburne. After a long absence he returned to the chess scene in the 1890s to find himself outclassed by a younger generation. At the age of 76 he declined an invitation to participate in the St Petersburg 1914 tournament.

In his games Winawer was often adventurous (a 'kill or cure style', wrote Steinitz) but he could also play positionally, as when he successfully exploited the WYVILL FORMATION against both NEUMANN and Steinitz at Paris 1867. Contrary to the opinions of most masters Winawer preferred knights over bishops. In particular he would exchange bishop for knight in order to double pawns, and then play for the endgame.

Marshall–Winawer Monte Carlo 1901 Queen's Gambit Declined Winawer Counter-gambit

1 d4 d5 2 c4 c6 3 Nc3 e5 4 cxd5 cxd5 5 e4 dxe4 6 d5 Nf6 7 Bg5 Qb6 8 Bxf6 gxf6 9 Bb5+ Bd7 10 Bxd7+ Nxd7 11 Nge2 f5 12 Qa4 0–0–0

13 d6 Kb8 14 Qc4 Nc5 15 0–0 Qxd6 16 Qxf7 Qg6 17 Qc4 Rg8 18 g3 Qe6 19 Qxe6 Nxe6 20 Rad1 Nd4 21 Kg2 Bc5 22 Na4 Be7 23 Nac3 h5 24 Nxd4 exd4 25 Ne2 Bf6 26 b3 Be5 27 Rfe1 d3 28 Ng1 h4 29 Nh3 Rc8 30 Rc1 hxg3 31 Rxc8+ Rxc8 32 hxg3 Rc2 33 Nf4 Bd4 34 Rf1 Bxf2 35 Kh3 Rxa2 36 Kh4 d2 37 Rd1 Bd4 White resigns.

Winawer Counter-gambit, 80 in the QUEEN'S GAMBIT Declined, introduced against MARSHALL, Monte Carlo 1901, in the game given under WINAWER.

Winawer Defence, 828 in the THREE KNIGHTS OPENING, introduced in the game Leffmann–Winawer, Leipzig 1877, but demolished by the game Breyer–Balla, Piešt'any 1912. Also 1247, the BARNES DEFENCE.

Winawer Variation, 808, SPANISH OPENING variation played twice by WINAWER against ZUKERTORT in the play-off match for first prize, Paris 1878; 1099, the STEINITZ VARIATION of the KING'S GAMBIT.

One of the most popular lines in the FRENCH DEFENCE, 1184. White, needing to do something about the threatened e-pawn, usually advances it to e5. This leads to a BLOCKADE in which White has chances on the king's-side, and will gain the TWO BISHOPS if Black plays Bxc3, while Black has counterplay on the queen's-side.

Black's third move, played twice by KOLISCH against PAULSEN in their match of 1861, was ana-

lysed in detail by Hirschbach in *Schachzeitung*, 1867, and later by ALAPIN. The name may have arisen from WINAWER's having played it against STEINITZ at Paris 1867, and three times at London 1883. For a long time the variation was considered inferior for Black. Revived in the 1930s, mainly on account of the influence of NIMZOWITSCH, whose name it sometimes bears, the Winawer Variation at last became popular. For example, BOTVINNIK played this defence throughout his long career. (See BRONSTEIN; CHANDLER; LJUBOJEVIĆ; NOGUEIRAS; J. POLGÁR; PSAKHIS; SKEWER; USELESS CHECK.)

windmill, see SEE-SAW.

wing, see FLANK.

Wing Attack, 701 in the SPANISH OPENING.

Wing Blumenfeld, 1294, variation in the RÉTI OPENING, liked by RUBINSTEIN and sometimes called the Reverse Benoni. (See BALASHOV.)

Wing Gambit, 445 in the SICILIAN DEFENCE, given by GRECO and favoured by BIRD and MARSHALL, but of dubious merit; 640 in the BISHOP'S OPENING, introduced by McDONNELL in his 24th match game against BOURDONNAIS, 1834.

Wing Gambit Deferred, 498 in the SICILIAN DEFENCE. Introduced in the 1930s by KERES, whose name it sometimes bears, played successfully by him against ELISKASES at Semmering–Baden 1937, this speculative pawn sacrifice is harder to meet than the older form of the gambit, 445.

Wing Variation, 677 in the SPANISH OPENING. Although most 'wing' names refer to pawns, this one is because of the remote placing of the knight. Known since the 1880s, the line was reinvented in 1901 by SCHLECHTER, when RANKEN wrote in the *British Chess Magazine*: 'We shall be much surprised if this mode of defence to the Ruy López does not obtain a large amount of favour, for it certainly seems to cope with the attack more speedily and effectively than the ordinary defences to this difficult opening.'

The line was revived in the 1950s and called the Furman–Taimanov Variation. Current opinion supports 6 0–0 in reply; the sacrifice 6 Bxf7+ is unsound.

Winter Variation, 254 in the DUTCH DEFENCE, from the game Winter–Mikenas, Łódź 1935.

win the exchange, to gain a rook for a MINOR PIECE.

Wisker, John (1846–84), English player, journalist. After moving from Yorkshire to London in 1866 Wisker improved rapidly, so that in the early 1870s he could be ranked among the world's best ten, and second only to BLACKBURNE among English-born players. In 1870 Wisker won the British championship ahead of Blackburne (the holder) after a play-off against BURN, and in 1872 he again won the title after a play-off against DE VERE (winner of the first British championship). By winning twice in succession Wisker retained the trophy and the contests ceased until 1904 (when NAPIER won). Against two of his contemporaries Wisker played six matches: BIRD in 1873 ($+6=1-6$ and $+4=3-7$) and again in 1874 ($+10=3-8$ and $+3=1-5$); and MACDONNELL in 1873 ($=1-3$) and 1875 ($+7=4-4$). Discovering that he had tuberculosis, Wisker emigrated to Australia in the autumn of 1876, hoping to improve his health. In England he edited excellent chess columns in the *Sporting Times* and *Land and Water*, and was co-editor of the *Chess Player's Chronicle* from 1872 to 1876; in Australia he edited a chess column in the *Australasian*.

Wittek, Alexander (1852–94), Austrian player, architect. Wittek's tournament career at master level lasted from 1880 to 1882. He came equal fifth at Berlin 1881 (won by BLACKBURNE) and ninth in the great Vienna tournament of 1882, a double-round event of 18 players including 8 of the best 9 in the world; he won one game against each of the winners, STEINITZ and WINAWER. Wittek played in one more tournament later that year and then withdrew from serious play because it interfered too much with his professional work.

Wolf, Heinrich (1875–1943), Austrian who played in 17 strong tournaments in two periods: 1900 to 1908, and April 1922 to July 1923. Although usually finishing somewhere between fifth and tenth place, he had three notable results: Vienna 1902, first equal with JANOWSKI, ahead of SCHLECHTER and MARÓCZY; Vienna 1905, second after Schlechter; and Vienna 1922, third ($+7=5-2$) after RUBINSTEIN and TARTAKOWER, ahead of ALEKHINE and BOGOLJUBOW, both of whom he defeated. After the Hanover tournament of 1902 he played a match with BERNSTEIN, $+1=6-1$. Wolf's victory in 168 moves over DURAS at Carlsbad 1907 was, for many years, the longest game in master chess.

Wolf Variation, 196 in the QUEEN'S GAMBIT Declined, from the game Grünfeld–H. Wolf, Ostrava 1923; 778 in the SPANISH OPENING, as in Maróczy–H. Wolf, Monte Carlo 1903.

Woman Grandmaster (WGM). Introduced in 1977, this is the highest-ranking FIDE title restricted to women except for that of Women's World Champion.

won position, a position that one side will win if played correctly by both contestants.

wood-pusher, or wood-shifter, a player who makes unco-ordinated moves to little purpose; or one who merely pushes the wood (chessmen) around in a routine fashion.

world championship. In 1886, two years after MORPHY'S death, STEINITZ and ZUKERTORT played a match agreeing between themselves, but to the general satisfaction of the chess public, that the winner should be the individual world champion. Steinitz won; and the title then passed successively to LASKER, CAPABLANCA, ALEKHINE, EUWE, and back to Alekhine. Holders chose their opponents, devised their own terms, and set the stakes to be raised by the challengers, who often found this 'gold barrier', as TARTAKOWER called it, insurmountable. All matches were won by the first player to score a predetermined number of wins, first ten, then eight, and lastly six. (See LONDON RULES.)

With the death of Alekhine in 1946 FIDE was able to take over the control of world championship events. In August 1947 the Federation decided that the vacant title should revert to Euwe pending a new competition. Shortly afterwards the delegation from the USSR arrived, delayed on the journey, the matter was re-opened, and a match-tournament was arranged for the following year, the title being left in abeyance meanwhile. Five players competed, BOTVINNIK winning convincingly from SMYSLOV, KERES, RESHEVSKY, and Euwe. An elimination cycle produces a challenger every three years. FIDE decided in favour of a match of 24 games, the title-holder retaining the championship in the event of a tie, and having the right to a return match a year later should he lose.

Under these conditions Botvinnik remained champion until 1963, except for two one-year periods when Smyslov and then TAL held the title. Several of these matches ended with an anticlimax, short draws without a fight. For example the last two games of the 1957 match lasted 13 and 11 moves, of the 1963 match, 10 and 10 moves. (Both matches were lost by Botvinnik, allegedly a great fighter.) In 1963, the return match condition waived, PETROSYAN became champion, followed by SPASSKY in 1969, and FISCHER in 1972.

In 1975 KARPOV became champion by default. Fischer declined to play when not all of his conditions were accepted, but one of them, that the winner should be the first to score six wins, was used in the matches of 1978, 1981, and 1984. Then FIDE took the retrograde step of bringing back the revenge match rule. Unfortunately the marathon match between Karpov and KASPAROV in 1984, abandoned when still undecided after 46 games, led to a return to the 24-game limit. In 1985 Kasparov won the re-arranged match and drew the return match, to which Karpov was entitled, in 1986. In 1990 Kasparov retained the title.

The Women's World Championship has been organized from its inception in 1927 by FIDE. The first winner was MENCHIK, who held the title until her death in 1944. For many years all the champions were Soviet players: RUDENKO 1950–3; BYKOVA 1953–6 and 1958–62; RUBTSOVA 1956–8; GAPRINDASHVILI 1962–78; CHIBURDANIDZE 1978–91.

Reflecting the break-up of the USSR, Chiburda-nidze appeared as a Georgian when defending her title in 1991. The winner and new champion was XIE JUN of China. However, in recent years the strongest women players have chosen not to take part.

FIDE also organizes world championships for teams, juniors, blind players, etc.

E. G. Winter, *World Chess Champions* (1981); Morán, Wade, Whiteley, Keene, *World Chess Championships* (2 vols., 1986), gives the games of all championships from 1886 to 1985.

World Chess Compositions Tournament, a competition introduced in 1975 comprising seven sections with ten themes, judged neutrally. It met with lukewarm support, and appears to have lapsed after three tourneys.

World Cup, a kind of tournament world championship, the brainchild of the GRANDMASTERS' ASSOCIATION. In the first cycle, 1988–9, the world's strongest grandmasters played each other in six tournaments. Each player took part in four events and received points based on a combination of score and placing, the best three sets being added to give the final score. The outcome was a close affair won by KASPAROV, who was first twice and equal first twice, from KARPOV, who was first once, equal first once, and second twice. The only other player with an outright tournament victory was TIMMAN, and the only one with a shared win was LJUBOJEVIĆ.

World Team Championship, an event launched by

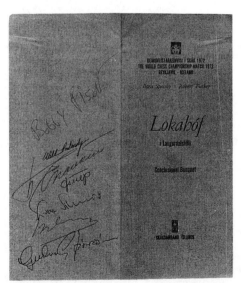

A menu from the Russell Collection. It was signed at the farewell banquet of the 1972 world championship match by Fischer, his second Lombardy, Spassky, his second Geller, Schmid the chief arbiter, Euwe, President of FIDE, and Gudmundur G. Thorarinsson, President of the Icelandic Chess Federation.

FIDE in 1985 as a supplement to OLYMPIADS. Representative teams from each of four continents, Europe, Asia, America, and Africa, the five leading teams from the previous year's Olympiad, and a team from the host nation play each other over four boards. In the first two events the African team was selected from several countries while the other continental teams were from leading countries which failed to qualify from the Olympiad.

Wormald Variation, 696 in the SPANISH OPENING, also called the Paulsen–Alapin Attack, and the Schlechter Variation. Robert Bownas Wormald (1834–76) wrote manuals on openings and completed STAUNTON's last book. His analysis of this opening appeared in *Chess World*, 1867.

Worrall Attack. 757 in the SPANISH OPENING, first played in the 1840s. Thomas Herbert Worrall (1807–78), subsequently appointed British Commissioner in Mexico, was afterwards transferred to New York.

wrong coloured bishop, SEE BISHOP OF THE WRONG COLOUR.

Würzburger Trap, 628 in the VIENNA GAMBIT, named around 1930 after the Berlin banker Max Würzburger, who spent much of the 1930s in Paris. Black's bishop on c2 is trapped (5 ... Qh4+ is probably an error).

Wurzburg–Plachutta theme, SEE CUTTING-POINT THEMES.

Wyvill, Marmaduke (1815–96), winner of second prize in the first international tournament, London 1851. He developed his chess skill in the 1840s, meeting DUBOIS in Rome, KIESERITZKY in Paris, and many players, including BUCKLE, in London, His style was that of the English school, and he understood well the positional ideas of the ENGLISH OPENING and the SICILIAN DEFENCE. In 1847 he was elected Member of Parliament for Richmond, Yorkshire, a seat he held until 1868 except for a break of two years. The London 1851 tournament consisted of a series of knock-out matches. After defeating WILLIAMS (+4−3) in the third round and losing to ANDERSSEN (+2=1−4) in the fourth and final round, Wyvill was placed second. His score against Anderssen was better than that made by other players (Kieseritzky =1−2, SZÉN +2−4, STAUNTON +1−4). Wyvill had proved himself one of the leading players of his time. Although he played in no more tournaments he retained an interest in the game throughout his life.

Wyvill formation, a name given by TARRASCH to a particular pawn formation with DOUBLED PAWNS. This formation was not unfamiliar to WYVILL, but could with more justification have been named after WINAWER, who so frequently doubled his opponent's c-pawns that this and similar formations became known as his trade-mark. The technique for attacking the Wyvill formation was also understood by NEUMANN, and before him by Carl Hamppe (1814–76), the leading Viennese player of the 1850s.

A Wyvill formation for White arises after the moves 1 d4 d5 2 c4 Nf6 3 Nc3 Bb4 4 a3 Bxc3+ 5 bxc3, and is characterized by the pawns on c3, c4, and d4. White strengthens his centre, with prospects of attack on the king's-side. On the other hand, the pawn at c4, which can be defended neither by a piece from the rear, nor by a pawn, may become a source of weakness. See the game under SÄMISCH.

Bogoljubow–Torre   Moscow 1925   Queen's Indian Defence

1 d4 Nf6 2 Nf3 b6 3 c4 Bb7 4 Nc3 g6 5 g3 Bg7 6 Bg2 Ne4 7 Qd3 Nxc3 8 bxc3 (White accepts the Wyvill formation.) 8 ... d6 9 h4 Nd7 10 h5 e5 11 Bg5 f6 12 Bd2 Qe7 13 h6 Bf8 14 Qc2 Rg8 15 Be3 a5 16 Rb1 Rd8 (Fearing the consequence of a colour-weakness on the light squares, Black declines to win the exchange by 16 ... exd4 and 17 ... Be4.) 17 Qb3 Be4 18 Rd1 g5

19 c5 (White undoubles his pawns, dissolving the Wyvill formation; if now 19 ... Rg6, 20 Nxe5.) 19 ... d5 20 cxb6 cxb6 21 dxe5 fxe5 22 Rh5 Rg6 23 Kf1 Nf6 24 Bxg5 Rxg5 25 Rxg5 Bxf3 26 Bxf3 Bxh6 27 Bh5+ Kf8 28 Rf5 Qe6 29 Bg4 Ke7 30 Bh3 Qd6 31 Qa4 Ne4 32 Rd3 Bg7 33 Bg2 Nf6 34 Qh4 Qe6 35 Rg5 Kf7 36 Rf3 h6 37 Rxd6 Rxd6 40 ... Nxd5 41 Bxd5+ Kh8 42 Be4 Qf6 43 Qg6 Kg8 44 Qh7+ Black resigns.

X

Xie Jun (pron. hsieh chūn) (1970–), the first Chinese player to qualify for a world championship at international chess. She won the Chinese Junior Championship in 1989, and while a student (of history) at the Beijing Sports Academy she qualified as a CANDIDATE at the interzonal in Malaysia in 1990. Later in the same year, while still 19, she was equal first at the women's Candidates tournament at Borzhomi and in January 1991 defeated her co-equal, Alisa Marić of Yugoslavia. This qualified her to challenge CHIBURDANIDZE for the title, and in September–October 1991 she won the match +4=9−2, becoming Women's World Champion the day before her 21st birthday. She is noted for her cheerful outlook on life.

Chiburdanidze–Xie Jun World Championship 1991, 8th game   Spanish Opening Pilnik Variation

1 e4 e5 2 Nf3 Nc6 3 Bb5 a6 4 Ba4 Nf6 5 0–0 Be7 6 Re1 b5 7 Bb3 0–0 8 d3 d6 9 c3 Na5 10 Bc2 c5 11 Nbd2 Re8 12 Nf1 Nc6 13 h3 Bb7 14 Ng3 Bf8 15 Nf5 Ne7 16 Nxe7+ Bxe7 17 a4 Bf8 18 Bg5 h6 19 Bh4 Be7 20 d4 Qc7 21 dxe5 dxe5 22 Qe2 c4 23 Red1 Qc5 24 Nh2 b4 25 cxb4 Qxb4 26 Nf3 Nh5 27 Bxe7 Qxe7 28 g3 Qe6 29 Kh2 Nf6 30 Ra3 a5 31 Re3 Bc8 32 Qf1 Rb8 33 Rb1 Ba6 34 Qe1 Rb4 25 b3 Reb8 36 bxc4

36 ... Nd7 37 Reb3 Qxc4 38 Rxb4 axb4 39 Bb3 Qd3 40 Qd1 Qxd1 41 Rxd1 Nc5 42 Rb1 Bd3 43 Rb2 Bxe4 44 Nxe5 Nxb3 45 Rxb3 Bd5 46 Rb2 b3 47 Nd3 f6 48 g4 Bc4 49 Nc5 Rc8 50 Ne4 Bd5 51 Ng3 Ra8 52 Ne2 Rxa4 53 Nc3 Ra2 54 Rb1 Rxf2+ 55 Kg1 Rg2+ 56 Kf1 Rh2 White resigns.

Y

Yankovich Variation, 961 in the TWO KNIGHTS DEFENCE, an idea of the Russian player Boris Alexeyevich Yankovich (1863–1918) who used it in a correspondence game against SCHIFFERS. However, it had been played by CHIGORIN in 1896 and LEONHARDT in 1907.

Yanofsky, Daniel Abraham (1925–), Canadian player, International Grandmaster (1964), International Arbiter (1977). At the OLYMPIAD in 1939 he made the highest percentage at second board (+12=3–1).

Yates, Frederick Dewhurst (1884–1932), English player, British champion 1913, 1914, 1921, 1926, 1928, and 1931. Around 1909 he gave up his job in accountancy to become a chess professional. Of the many international tournaments in which he competed, from Hamburg 1910 to Hastings 1931–2, he made his best results in the B Final, Kecskemét 1927, first (+4=2–1) equal with TARTAKOWER, and at San Remo 1930, the strongest tournament of the year, when he came fifth after ALEKHINE, NIMZOWITSCH, RUBINSTEIN, and BOGOLJUBOW, ahead of SPIELMANN, VIDMAR, and Tartakower. Yates represented Britain in the Olympiads of 1927, 1930, and 1931.

A tenacious player, Yates could be a dangerous opponent. In tournament play he defeated most of the greatest masters of his time on one occasion or another. Among those so conquered are Alekhine twice (Hastings 1922, Carlsbad 1923 — see below), Bogoljubow three times (London 1922, Baden-Baden 1925, Scarborough 1927), and Rubinstein three times (London 1925, Moscow 1925, Budapest 1926). A careful and conscientious writer, he conducted chess columns in the *Yorkshire Post* from 1910 until 1932 and the *Daily Telegraph* from 1925 to 1932, was chess correspondent for the *Manchester Guardian*, and wrote three books in collaboration with William Winter (1898–1955). A leak from a faulty gas fitting killed Yates while he was asleep. His book, *One-hundred-and-one of My Best Games* (actually 109), was completed by Winter and published in 1934. Yates himself selected for inclusion a loss to Capablanca at Barcelona 1929.

Alekhine–Yates Carlsbad 1923 King's Indian Defence
1 d4 Nf6 2 c4 g6 3 g3 Bg7 4 Bg2 0–0 5 Nc3 d6 6 Nf3 Nc6 7 d5 Nb8 8 e4 Nbd7 9 0–0 a5 10 Be3 Ng4 11 Bd4 Nge5 12 Nxe5 Nxe5 13 c5 dxc5 14 Bxc5 b6 15 Bd4 Ba6 16 Re1 Qd6 17 Bf1 Bxf1 18 Rxf1 c5 19 Bxe5 Qxe5 20 Qb3 Rab8 21 Qb5 f5 22 Rae1 f4 23 Qd7 Rbd8 24 gxf4 Qxf4 25 Qe6+ Kh8 26 f3 Qg5+ 27 Kh1 Rd6 28 Qh3 Be5 29 Re2 Rdf6 30 Nd1 Rf4 31 Ne3 Rh4 32 Qe6 Qh5 33 Ng4

33 ... Rxg4 34 fxg4 Rxf1+ 35 Kg2 Qxh2+ 36 Kxf1 Qh1+ 37 Kf2 Bd4+ 38 Kg3 Qg1+ 39 Kh3 Qf1+ 40 Rg2 Qh1+ 41 Kg3 Qe1+ 42 Kh3 g5 43 Rc2 Qf1+ 44 Kh2 Qg1+ 45 Kh3 Qh1+ 46 Kg3 Qd1 47 Rc3 Qg1+ 48 Kh3 Qf1+ 49 Kg3 Bf2+ 50 Kf3 Bg1+ Mate in two moves.

Yates Variation, 345 in the QUEEN'S INDIAN DEFENCE, a line that received little support until the 1960s.

Yepishin, Vladimir Viktorovich (1965–), Russian player, champion of Leningrad 1987, International Grandmaster (1990). He was equal second in an 11-round Swiss tournament, Berlin 1989, which had 320 players, equal second in New York 1990, 63 players, 9 rounds, and equal first at Linz 1990, 130 players, 9 rounds. He shared victory in an all-play-all tournament at Frankfurt 1990, and at Reggio Emilia 1991 he was fourth (+2=8–2) equal with BELYAVSKY and ROMANISHIN, after LJUBOJEVIĆ, GULKO, and VAGANYAN.

Young Variation, 1137, variation of the WILD MUZIO GAMBIT in which Black offers a third piece, apparently with decisive effect, named after an American engineer, William Wallace Young (1877–1940). A friendly game Young–Marshall, Bordentown, New Jersey, 1913, continued 10 ... Ne7 11 Bxf4 d6 12 Qh5+ Kg7 13 Bh6+ Black resigns. Instead of 7 ... Qf6? Black would gain the advantage by 7 ... d6, according to KERES.

Yudasin, Leonid Grigoryevich (1959–), Russian player, International Grandmaster (1990), engineer. He won the championship of Leningrad in 1984, and played in four USSR championships between 1981 and 1990, in the last of which he was first (+4=9) equal with BELYAVSKY (who was awarded the title on tie-break), BAREYEV, and VYZHMANAVIN. Yudasin was first at the Lvov zonal,

1990, equal with DREYEV, LPUTYAN, and SHIROV. At the interzonal tournament, Manila 1990, he was equal fifth and became a CANDIDATE, but was crushed by IVANCHUK in the ensuing match in 1991. Yudasin's best wins in other tournaments are Albena 1985, Leningrad June–July 1989, Leningrad September 1989, and Pamplona 1989–90 (+ 5 = 3 − 1), ahead of KORCHNOI.

Přibyl–Yudasin Leningrad 1989 Queen's Bishop Game

1 d4 Nf6 2 Nf3 d5 3 Bf4 c6 4 c3 g6 5 h3 Bg7 6 Nbd2 0–0 7 e3 Bf5 8 Be2 Nbd7 9 Qb3 Qc8 10 g4 Be4 11 Rg1 Bxf3 12 Bxf3 a5 13 a4

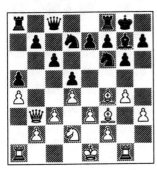

13 ... e5 14 dxe5 Nc5 15 exf6 Nxb3 16 fxg7 Nxa1 17 gxf8 = Q+ Qxf8 18 Ke2 Nc2 19 Kd3 Nb4+ 20 cxb4 Qxb4 21 b3 b5 22 Ra1 c5 23 Kc2 Rd8 24 axb5 c4 25 Rb1 Qxb5 26 bxc4 Qa4+ 27 Kc3 Qa3+ 28 Kd4 dxc4+ 29 Bd5 Qd3+ White resigns.

Yugoslav Variation, 180 in the CAMBRIDGE SPRINGS DEFENCE, first played in master chess by TARTA-KOWER at the Moscow 1925 tournament, but much analysed in the early 1920s by ASZTALOS and VUKO-VIĆ who, at that time, were both living in Yugosla-via; 387 in the GRÜNFELD DEFENCE, introduced around 1948; 417 in the KING'S INDIAN DEFENCE, closely studied in the 1950s by the Yugoslavs, particularly Mijo Udovčić (1920–84).

Also 237, the PIRC DEFENCE; 364 and 380, RUSSIAN VARIATION, two similar lines in the Grünfeld Defence; 472, the VELIMIROVIĆ VARIATION of the Sicilian Defence.

Yusupov, Artur Mayakovich (1960–), Russian player, International Grandmaster (1980), World Junior Champion 1977. In his first USSR cham-pionship, 1979, he was second (+ 6 = 9 − 2) to GELLER, a position he did not match in his next five attempts up to 1988. There followed other suc-cesses: Esbjerg 1980, first (+ 8 = 3 − 1); Vrbas 1980, second equal with ADORJÁN and PETROSYAN, after

MILES; Yerevan zonal 1982, first (+ 7 = 7 − 1); Sara-jevo 1983, third equal with van der WIEL, after KORCHNOI and TIMMAN; Linares 1983, fourth (+ 2 = 7 − 1) equal with Miles and SAX, after SPASSKY, KARPOV, and ANDERSSON; Denpasar 1983, third (+ 8 = 11 − 2), behind Timman and PORTISCH; Carthage 1985, first (+ 7 = 9), ahead of BELYAVSKY; Montpellier interzonal 1985, first (+ 4 = 10 − 1) equal with A. SOKOLOV and VAGANYAN.

This last event made Yusupov a CANDIDATE for the first time, but after beating Timman (+ 4 = 4 − 1) in 1986 he lost the next match to Sokolov. In the next Candidates cycle he defeated EHLVEST + 2 = 3 in 1988 and SPRAGGETT + 2 = 6 − 1 in 1989, but lost to KARPOV in the semi-final. He had some good results during this period, notably Linares 1988, third (+ 2 = 9) after Timman and Belyavsky, and a drawn match (= 6) with Timman in 1986. After coming close to death when he was shot near his home by a thief in mid-1990, the following year he defeated DOLMATOV in the Candi-dates match + 3 = 7 − 2, including the four-game rapid-play tie-break. Later in 1991 he defeated IVANCHUK + 3 = 3 − 2, including the two-game tie-break, but was defeated by Timman in the Candi-dates semi-final match in 1992.

At Linares 1991 he was fourth (+ 4 = 7 − 2) equal with SPEELMAN, after Ivanchuk, KASPAROV, and Belyavsky. He played for his country in the Olym-piads of 1984, 1986, and 1988, and against the Rest of the World in 1984.

Yusupov–Nogueiras Montpellier 1985 Candidates Tour-nament Queen's Gambit Declined Exchange Variation

1 d4 d5 2 c4 e6 3 Nc3 c6 4 Nf3 Nf6 5 Bg5 Nbd7 6 cxd5 exd5 7 e3 Bd6 8 Bd3 Nf8 9 Ne5 Qb6 10 0–0 Bxe5 11 dxe5 Ng4 12 Qa4

12 ... Qxb2? 13 Rac1 Bd7 14 Qd4 f6 15 exf6 gxf6 16 Bxf6 Rg8 17 Nb5 Qxb5 18 Bxb5 Ne6 19 Qb2 cxb5 20 Bh4 Black resigns.

Z

Zagorovsky, Vladimir Pavlovich (1925–94), Soviet player, International Correspondence Chess Grandmaster (1965), science historian. After winning the Moscow championship in 1952, and a few minor over-the-board events, he took up postal chess at which he became the most feared player of his time. He did not compete in the first three World Correspondence Championships, but in the next five he had an unrivalled series of results: first (+7=5) in the 4th championship, 1962–5; equal fourth in the 5th, 1965–8; second in the 6th, 1968–71; equal third in the 7th, 1972–5; and equal first (+9=4−1) in the 8th, 1975–9, a tie with SLOTH who was awarded the title on tie-break.

Zagoruiko theme, see CHANGED PLAY; PACHL.

Zagoryansky Variation, 360 in the CATALAN OPENING, used by the Soviet player Yevgeny Alexandrovich Zagoryansky (1910–61), for example Zagoryansky–Ravinsky, Moscow championship 1950.

Zagreb Variation, 507, line in the SICILIAN DEFENCE popular in the 1950s.

Zaitsev, Alexander Nikolayevich (1935–71), Soviet player, International Grandmaster (1967). He played four times in the USSR championship and on the third occasion, Alma-Ata 1968–9, was first (+6=13) equal with POLUGAYEVSKY, but lost the play-off. His best international tournament achievement was at Sochi 1967 when he scored +6=8−1 to share first prize with KROGIUS, SHAMKOVICH, SIMAGIN, and SPASSKY. Zaitsev came to a sad end. Wishing to marry, he decided first to remedy a limp by having one leg lengthened; although he was otherwise a robust and healthy man, he died of thrombosis as a consequence of the operation.

Alexander Zaitsev (1986) is a biography, 104 selected games, and other features such as all six games of the match with Polugayevsky, annotated.

Zaitsev–Lutikov   Moscow 1969 USSR Championships
King's Indian Defence

1 d4 Nf6 2 Nf3 g6 3 c4 Bg7 4 Nc3 0–0 5 Bg5 d6 6 e3 h6 7 Bh4 c6 8 Be2 Bg4 9 0–0 Nbd7 10 b4 e5 11 dxe5 dxe5 12 Nd2 Be6 13 Qc2 a5 14 a3 Qe7 15 c5 axb4 16 axb4 g5 17 Bg3 Nd5 18 Nxd5 cxd5 19 Rxa8 Rxa8 20 f3 f5 21 Rc1 f4 22 exf4 gxf4 23 Bf2 Nf6 24 Bh4 Qc7 25 b5 Ne8 26 Bd3 Bf8 27 Bf2 Nf6 28 b6 Qe7 29 Qb2 Bg7 30 c6 e4 31 cxb7 Rd8 32 fxe4 dxe4

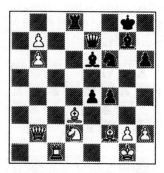

33 Qe5 Ng4 34 Qxe4 Nxf2 35 Kxf2 Qd6 36 Rc6 Qd4+ 37 Qxd4 Bxd4+ 38 Kf1 Bd7 39 Rc7 Be5 40 Nc4 Black resigns.

Zaitsev Variation, 543 in the SICILIAN DEFENCE; 772 in the SPANISH OPENING, recommended in 1973 and 1968 respectively by the Soviet player Igor Arkadyevich Zaitsev (1938–   ). Sometimes used for the LENZERHEIDE VARIATION, 747.

Zappas, Byron (1927–   ), the leading Greek problem composer of his time, International Master for Chess Compositions (1984), International Judge of Chess Compositions (1988). His best work is in the field of orthodox two- and three-move direct mates. *Skakistikes suntheseiz* (1990) is a Greek book containing 240 of his problems.

#2

A problem by Zappas, first prize *ex æquo*, *The Problemist*, 1980. The key is 1 Ne1, guarding c2 and threatening 2 Rd3#. The set play:

1 ... Nc5   2 Qc4#
1 ... Nde5 2 Qb3#
1 ... Nfe5 2 Qd4#.

The tries, other attempts to guard c2, are each refuted by one of the set-play moves:

1 Bb1? Nc5
1 Bb3? Nde5
1 Nd4? Nfe5.

zatrikion, see ROUND CHESS.

zebra, a LEAPER invented for use in FAIRY PROBLEMS. The co-ordinates of its leap are 3,2, and the length of its move $\sqrt{13}$. A zebra standing on d4 would attack a2, a6, b7, f7, g6, g2, f1, and b1.

zeitnot, German for TIME-TROUBLE. Russia adopted the word and it is sometimes used in other countries.

Zemch Variation, 11 ... Bb6, an alternative to the RUBINSTEIN VARIATION, 946, in the MAX LANGE ATTACK, an old line deeply analysed by S. Zemch of Kiev in the pages of *Deutsche Schachzeitung*, Nov. and Dec. 1900. Zemch attributes the line to Heinrich Abels of Hapsal, but GOSSIP ascribes it to Wormald.

Abels, Kossmann, Zemch (Saratov)–Chigorin (St Petersburg) Telegraph 1898–9

1 e4 e5 2 Nf3 Nc6 3 Bc4 Nf6 4 d4 exd4 5 0–0 Bc5 6 e5 d5 7 exf6 dxc4 8 Re1+ Be6 9 Ng5 Qd5 10 Nc3 Qf5 11 Nce4 Bb6 12 fxg7 Rg8 13 g4 Qg6 14 Nxe6 fxe6 15 Bg5 d3 16 cxd3 cxd3 17 Qxd3 Rxg7 18 Rad1 Rf7 19 h4 e5 20 Qd5 h5 21 Nc5 Bxc5 22 Rxe5+ Be7 23 Re6 Qc2 24 Rd2 Qb1+ 25 Kg2 Kf8 26 Bh6+ Kg8 27 Rd3 Kh8 28 Rg6 Rxf2+ 29 Kxf2 Qc2+ 30 Kf1. Game broken off, with White having a decisive advantage.

Zepler, Eric Ernest (1898–1980), German-born composer, International Judge of Chess Compositions (1957), International Master for Chess Compositions (1973), was one of the pioneer composers of the so-called New German school (see PROBLEM HISTORY; LOGICAL SCHOOL). He and Adolf Kraemer (1898–1972), both among the leading German composers between the two world wars, often composed together.

Of Jewish birth, Zepler became a refugee in 1935 and, abandoning all his possessions, fled in haste to England, where he settled. His considerable expertise in electronics was put to good use in the Second World War, and in 1949 he became professor of electronics at Southampton University, the first such chair in Britain and perhaps in the world. (The department is still housed in the Zepler Building.) Kraemer remained in Germany, but until his death he and Zepler maintained a close friendship. They published *Im Banne des Schachproblems* (1951), a collection of their compositions, and *Problemkunst im 20. Jahrhundert* (1957), which contained what they regarded as the best problems of the first half of the 20th century.

Zepler doubling, see DOUBLING THEMES.

zero-position, a position that is not a problem but to which slight changes or additions may be made, in different ways, to provide two or more problem twins.

This zero-position, from the CIVIS BONONIAE, may have been used for wagers; one gambler is to place the white king on the board and the other has to find a mate in two. With the king on a3 (or most other squares) the solution is 1 Rf7+ Nxf7 2 Ng6. If the king is placed on g5 (or d6, d8, h6) 1 Rf7+ Nxf7+ prevents mate in two, but the king on h6 permits a different solution by 1 Rxg7.

Zinnowitz Variation, 407 in the KING'S INDIAN DEFENCE, played in the tournament at Zinnowitz in 1966. (See PANNO.)

Znosko-Borovsky, Eugene Alexandrovich (1884–1954), Russian-born professional player, music and drama critic. He made his chess début by winning a local tournament at St Petersburg 1902–3. Between then and 1914 he began his writing career, editing some leading Russian chess columns, and he played in three international tournaments; he also played in four All-Russia (national championship) tournaments and in one of them, Łódź 1907–8, shared third prize with SALWE, after RUBINSTEIN and ALAPIN. After settling in Paris around 1920 Znosko-Borovsky played in two major events (London 1922 and Budapest 1926) and in many minor events, mainly in France and England, notably winning ahead of TARTAKOWER and LILIENTHAL at Paris 1930. Between the two World Wars he wrote several books; they are largely outmoded but their suitability for club players of that time and the fluent style of his writing made the books both popular and profitable, and they were published in several languages. A man of principle and a sporting opponent, he became widely known and liked.

Zollner Gambit, 532, an enterprising attack against the DRAGON VARIATION of the SICILIAN DEFENCE, analysed in the 1930s and early 1940s by Hans Zollner, who died towards the end of the Second World War while serving with the German army.

zonal tournament, the preliminary qualifying

event for the world championship. FIDE divides the world into geographical zones and many 'zonals' are held concurrently to determine who should play in the INTERZONAL TOURNAMENTS. The strength of zonal tournaments varies considerably. From a weak zone only the winner would qualify. One of the strongest such tournaments was a zonal in the USSR, 1964, won by SPASSKY ahead of BRONSTEIN, STEIN, KHOLMOV, KORCHNOI, SUETIN, and GELLER.

zugzwang, a German word, now anglicized, for a position in which whoever has the move would obtain a worse result than if it were the opponent's turn to play. All chess positions may be classified in one of three categories according to their time characteristics: (1) the great majority, in which both players could profit by having the move; (2) those in which only one player would be at a disadvantage on account of having the move; (3) those in which both players would be at a disadvantage if obliged to move. Some authorities refer to (2) and (3) as zugzwang and reciprocal zugzwang respectively. In this book, however, in order to emphasize the fundamental difference between the groups, the terms SQUEEZE and zugzwang are used respectively.

This position is a zugzwang. White to play must give stalemate (1 Kc6) or lose the pawn and draw; Black to play loses because the pawn can then be promoted. The example shows the characteristics of all zugzwangs: the result each player obtains if obliged to move is worse than if it were the opponent's turn to move; neither player can LOSE THE MOVE; and neither can make direct threats. Players who see zugzwangs coming may use them to their advantage. The position white king at d5, white pawn at c6, black king at c7 is drawn. Black to play puts White in zugzwang after 1 ... Kc8 2 Kd6 Kd8, and this may lead to the diagram above after 3 c7+ Kc8. The result is the same if White moves first: 1 Kc5 Kc8 2 Kd6 Kd8.

In practice zugzwangs occur only in the endgame, most frequently in pawn endings (see ISOLATED QUEEN'S PAWN; TEMPO-MOVE), occasionally with knights on the board, rarely with line-pieces. For some kind of endgames, computer analysis has identified all possible zugzwangs: Q v. B + B (see LOLLI), Q + R v. Q (see below), Q v. B + N, one

each; R + B v. R, 17; Q + B v. Q, 25; Q + N v. Q, 38; Q v. N + N, 229; B + N v. N, 922; R v. B, 5; R v. N, 18.

A player needs to know some zugzwangs, or their likely presence. For example, the position White Kf1, Qe6; Black Kd4, Rf4, Pf2 is a zugzwang that few would recognize unless they had advance knowledge. Black to play loses (1 ... Rf3 2 Qg4+ Ke3 3 Qc4 Rf4 4 Qd5 Rf3 5 Qe5+), but White to play only draws: 1 Qd6+ Ke4 2 Qe6+ Kf3 3 Qe2+ Kg3 4 Qh5 Rg4 5 Qe5+ Rf4 6 Qg5+ Kh3 and White is again in zugzwang. See OPPOSITION and CONJUGATE SQUARES for some examples in which one side may be held in zugzwang for several moves, or even in perpetuity.

A composer describing a problem position in which White makes no threats (using this word in its problem sense) may call it a zugzwang. To a player it is nothing of the sort, and to avoid confusion it should be called a BLOCK. On the other hand, zugzwangs are part of the stock-in-trade of study composers.

=

A study by T. Whitworth, *British Chess Magazine*, 1986. 1 Bg4 Rxg4 2 Nxd2 exd2 3 h8=Q d1=Q 4 Qb2+ Kf1 5 Qf6+ Kg1 6 Qc3 (zugzwang)=. If 6 ... Rd4, 7 Qe1+.

Zukertort, Johann Hermann (1842–88), Polish-born player, from about 1871 to 1886 second in the world after STEINITZ. In April 1861 Zukertort enrolled in the faculty of medicine at Breslau University but for the next five years he spent much of his time playing chess, including many friendly games with ANDERSSEN, and was struck from the register because of non-attendance. This brief brush with higher education enabled him to pass himself off as a doctor in later life, but it also allowed him to be useful as a medical orderly in the war between Prussia and Austria, which lasted from mid-June to mid-July 1866. That experience, too, provided material for later tales of glory (twice wounded, left for dead, seven medals, etc).

By 1867 he was second only to Anderssen in Breslau and had also become celebrated as a blind-fold player, at which he was able to play 16 games simultaneously (a record at that time). Then an opportunity arose for him to become co-editor (with Anderssen) of the *Neue Berliner Schachzeitung* when the previous editor NEUMANN had decided to move to Paris. Zukertort contributed excellent analysis and annotations but in 1869 he began to quarrel with MINCKWITZ, then editor of the [*Deutsche*] *Schachzeitung*, and the dispute was pursued through their magazines. Whether or not this was a factor, the *Neue Berliner Schachzeitung* folded at the end of 1871. At that time Zukertort was hardly known, but he built a reputation on a match victory against Anderssen (+5−2) in 1871. In fact Anderssen did not regard it as a proper match as there were no stakes, and the games were played casually. If they were to play a real match, he said, Zukertort must put down a stake and he would put down double. This duly happened and Anderssen won all three games.

At just that time a group of London players were trying to find somebody capable of beating STEINITZ, and thinking that Zukertort might be the man, gave him 20 guineas to move to London. This was an attractive offer because London was then the only place in the world where it was possible to scratch a living as a chess professional. Arriving there in 1872, Zukertort took third place, after Steinitz and BLACKBURNE, in the strongest tournament in which he had yet played, and later in the year was decisively beaten by Steinitz in match play (+1=4−7). Zukertort lived the rest of his life in London as a professional player. He won matches against POTTER in 1875 (+4=8−2), ROSENTHAL in 1880 (+7=11−1), and Blackburne in 1881 (+7=5−2). He also had a good record in tournament play: Leipzig 1877, second equal with Anderssen, after PAULSEN, ahead of WINAWER; Paris 1878, first (+14=5−3) equal with Winawer, ahead of Blackburne (Zukertort won the play-off, +2=2); Berlin 1881, second after Blackburne, ahead of Winawer; and Vienna 1882, fourth equal with MACKENZIE, after Steinitz, Winawer, and MASON. The world's best nine players were among the competitors in the double-round London tournament of 1883 when Zukertort achieved his greatest victory: first (+22−4) three points ahead of Steinitz, the second-prize winner. In seven weeks and a day he played 33 games (seven draws were replayed) and towards the end he relieved the strain by taking opiates, a factor in his losing the last three games.

This victory led to the first match for the world championship, a struggle between him and Steinitz played in New York, St Louis, and New Orleans, USA, in 1886. After nearly ten weeks of relentless pressure by his opponent Zukertort lost (+5=5−10), winning only one of the last 15 games. His spirit crushed, his health failing, he was advised to give up competitive chess, but there was nothing else he could do. 'I am prepared', he said, 'to be taken away at any moment.' Seized by a stroke while playing at London's famous coffeehouse, Simpson's Divan, he died the next day.

Like Anderssen, his teacher, Zukertort had a direct and straightforward style, and in combinative situations could calculate far ahead. Having a prodigious memory he could recollect at will countless games and opening variations, a talent which may have limited his vision. (For his match with Steinitz in 1872 his extensive opening preparation brought him only one win. Steinitz was the better player in unfamiliar situations.) As an annotator and analyst Zukertort was outstanding in his time, and much of his work in these fields appeared in the *Chess Monthly* which he and HOFFER edited from 1879 to 1888.

Zukertort read widely and what he read became, as he said, 'iron-printed in my head'. Hoffer recalls Zukertort holding a visitor from India spellbound with a detailed and convincing account of a tiger-hunt, although it must have been outside his own experience. This love of telling a yarn may have been behind the many absurd boasts he made about his non-chess skills.

Jimmy Adams, *Johannes Zukertort, Artist of the Chessboard* (1989), contains more than 300 annotated games, career results, and a compilation of biographical comments from many sources.

Zukertort–Blackburne London 1883 English Opening

1 c4 e6 2 e3 Nf6 3 Nf3 b6 4 Be2 Bb7 5 0–0 d5 6 d4 Bd6 7 Nc3 0–0 8 b3 Nbd7 9 Bb2 Qe7 10 Nb5 Ne4 11 Nxd6 cxd6 12 Nd2 Ndf6 13 f3 Nxd2 14 Qxd2 dxc4 15 Bxc4 d5 16 Bd3 Rfc8 17 Rae1 Rc7 18 e4 Rac8 19 e5 Ne8 20 f4 g6 21 Re3 f5 22 exf6 Nxf6 23 f5 Ne4 24 Bxe4 dxe4 25 fxg6 Rc2 26 gxh7+ Kh8 27 d5+ e5

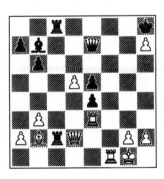

28 Qb4 R8c5 29 Rf8+ Kxh7 30 Qxe4+ Kg7 31 Bxe5+ Kxf8 32 Bg7+ Kg8 33 Qxe7 Black resigns.

Zukertort–Berger Variation, 993, the SCHMIDT VARIATION of the SCOTCH GAME.

Zukertort Defence, 617, VIENNA GAMBIT variation advocated by ZUKERTORT from 1871. After 6 exd5 Bg4+ 7 Nf3 Black castles, sacrificing a piece for a counterattack.

Zukertort Opening, 1283, abhorred by Ruy LÓPEZ, used by ZUKERTORT always as a preliminary to 2 Pd2–d4. Now the fourth most popular initial move (after 1 e4, 1 d4, or 1 c4) it was played in 17 of the 48 games in the first world championship match between KARPOV and KASPAROV. (See DORFMAN.)

Zukertort Variation, 226 in the QUEEN'S PAWN OPENING, but reached equally from 1 Nf3; 726 in the SPANISH OPENING, favoured by ZUKERTORT in the 1880s, but laid to rest soon after; 807, another abandoned line in the Spanish Opening; 1031, a sound line for White in the PHILIDOR DEFENCE.

Zurich Variation, 311, the MILNER-BARRY VARIATION; it became more widely known at the Zurich tournament of 1934.

zwischenzug, from German, literally an in-between move. Usually a move interspersed during an exchange or series of exchanges.

Geller–Ståhlberg   Stockholm Interzonal 1952   French Defence Tarrasch Variation

1 e4 e6 2 d4 d5 3 Nd2 Nf6 4 e5 Nfd7 5 Bd3 c5 6 c3 Nc6 7 Ne2 Qb6 8 Nf3 cxd4 9 cxd4 f6 10 exf6 Nxf6 11 0–0 Bd6 12 Nf4 0–0 13 Re1 Bxf4 14 Bxf4 Bd7 15 Bd6 Rfe8 16 Bc5 Qc7 17 Rc1 Qf4 18 Ne5 Rac8 19 Rc3 Nxe5 20 dxe5 Rxc5

If now 21 Rxc5, Ng4, or 21 exf6, Rxc3. Instead, two zwischenzugs displace the black queen. Later White's 25th and 26th moves might be regarded as in-between moves. 21 g3 Qb4 22 a3 Qb6 23 exf6 Kf7 24 fxg7 Rxc3 25 Qh5+ Kxg7 26 Qxh7+ Kf6 27 bxc3 Qd8 28 Bg6 Rf8 29 Bh5 d4 30 cxd4 Qa5 31 Qg6+ Black resigns.

Whether or not a move can be defined as a zwischenzug may depend on the view taken by the observer. The player might simply regard such moves as a natural part of the combination. See DORFMAN, in whose game 19 ... Rd5 might be called a zwischenzug, and DE VERE.

APPENDIX I

OPENINGS

OPENING lines given on the following pages are included because they have names. All major openings and most major variations have names; so have many unimportant lines of play. Entries for all the named lines listed here will be found in the main body of the text.

The openings are sequenced by the letter and then the number of the arrival squares but castling (0-0 or 0-0-0) comes last. If different men can be moved to the same square on the same move then pawn moves are given first and piece moves in alphabetical order (B, K, N, Q, R). Variations that can arise from more than one sequence of moves are usually given only once.

A few important named lines that arise later than the scope of these tables are indicated by an asterisk in the footnotes. For example, one of the Tarrasch Traps is an alternative to the Breslau Variation, 722. The asterisk in the footnote to the tables indicates the presence of another possibility. The text account of the Breslau Variation mentions the Tarrasch Trap as an alternative, and the text for Tarrasch Trap indicates that the Breslau Variation, 722, will give the preliminary moves.

Abbreviations: A Attack, C-A Counterattack, C-G Counter-gambit, D Defence, G Gambit, O Opening, S System, V Variation.

1 a3[1]
1 Na3[2]
1 a4[3] e5 **2** a5 d5 **3** e3 f5 **4** a6[4]
1 b3[5]
1 b4[6]
1 c3[7]
1 Nc3[8]
1 c4[9]   b5[10]
—   c5[11]   **2** Nc3   Nc6   **3** Nf3   Nf6   **4** d4   cxd4   **5** Nxd4 e6 **6** g3 Qb6[12]
—   —   —   —   **3** g3   g6   **4** Bg2   Bg7   **5** e4[13]
—   e5[14]   **2** Nc3   Nc6   **3** g3   g6   **4** Bg2   Bg7   **5** Rb1   Nh6[15]
—   —   —   —   —   —   —   —   **5** e3   d6   **6** Nge2 Be6[16]
—   —   —   —   —   —   —   —   —   —   —   Nh6[17]
—   —   —   d6   **3** Nf3   Bg4[18]
—   —   —   —   **3** g3   Be6   **4** Bg2   Nc6[19]
—   —   —   —   —   c6[20]
—   —   —   Nf6   **3** Nf3   Nc6[21]   **4** a3[22]
—   —   —   —   —   —   **4** d3[23]
—   —   —   —   —   —   **4** d4   exd4   **5** Nxd4 Bb4 **6** Bg5 h6 **7** Bh4 Bxc3+ **8** bxc3 Ne5[24]
—   —   —   —   —   —   —   —   e4[25]
—   —   —   —   —   —   **4** e3 Bb4 **5** Qc2 Bxc3[26]
—   —   —   —   —   —   **4** e4[27]
—   —   —   —   —   e4   **4** Ng5   b5[28]
—   —   —   —   **3** g3[29]   Bb4[30]
—   —   —   —   —   c6[31]
—   —   **2** Nf3[32]   e4[33]
—   f5[34]
—   Nf6[35]   **2** Nc3   d5   **3** cxd5   Nxd5   **4** Nf3   g6   **5** g3   Bg7 **6** Bg2 e5[36]
—   —   —   —   —   —   **4** g3   c5   **5** Bg2   Nc7[37]
—   —   —   —   —   —   —   g6   **5** Bg2   Nb6[38]
—   —   —   —   —   —   —   —   —   —   Nxc3[39]
—   —   —   e6   **3** e4[40]   c5[41]
—   —   —   —   —   Nc6[42]
—   —   —   —   —   d5[43]   **4** e5[44]
—   —   —   —   **3** Nf3   Bb4[45]
—   —   **2** Nf3   g6   **3** g3   Bg7   **4** Bg2   0–0[46]
1 d3[47]
1 d4[48]   b5[49]
—   c5[50]   **2** d5   d6   **3** Nc3   g6[51]
—   —   —   e5   **3** e4   d6[52]
—   Nc6[53]
—   d5   **2** Nc3[54] Nf6   **3** e4   dxe4   **4** f3[55]
—   —   —   —   **3** Bg5[56]   Bf5   **4** f3[57]
—   —   —   —   —   —   **4** Bxf6[58]
—   —   **2** c4[59]   dxc4[60]   **3** e4   f5[61]
—   —   —   —   **3** Nf3   a6   **4** e3 b5[62]
—   —   —   —   —   —   —   Bg4[63]   **5** Bxc4 e6 **6** d5[64]
—   —   —   —   —   —   **4** e4[65]
—   —   —   —   —   Nf6   **4** Qa4+[66]
—   —   —   —   —   —   **4** Nc3   a6   **5** e4[67]
—   —   —   —   —   —   **4** e3   e6   **5** Bxc4 c5[68]   **6** Qe2 a6 **7** dxc5 Bxc5 **8** 0–0 Nc6 **9** e4 b5 **10** e5[69]
—   —   —   —   —   —   —   —   —   —   **6** 0–0 a6 **7** a4[70]

1 d4 d5 2 c4 dxc4 3 Nf3 Nf6 4 e3 e6 5 Bxc4 c5 6 0-0 a6 7 Qe2 b5 8 Bb3 Bb7 9 Rd1 Nbd7 10 Nc3 Bd6[71]

—— —— —— —— —— —— —— —— — Nc6 **8** Rd1 b5 **9** Bb3 c4 **10** Bc2 Nb4 **11** Nc3[72]

—— —— —— —— —— —— —— — **7** e4[73]

—— —— —— —— —— —— —— — cxd4[74]

—— —— —— —— — Bg4[75]

—— —— —— —— — g6[76]

—— —— — c5[77]

—— —— — c6[78] **3** Nc3 dxc4 **4** e4[79]

—— —— — — e5[80]

—— —— — e6[81]

—— —— — **3** cxd5[82] cxd5 **4** Nc3 Nf6 **5** Nf3 Nc6 **6** Bf4 Bf5 **7** e3 e6 **8** Qb3 Bb4[83]

—— —— — **3** Nf3 Nf6 **4** Nc3 Qb6[84]

—— —— —— —— — dxc4 **5** a4[85] Na6 **6** e3 Bg4[86]

—— —— —— —— — — e6[87]

—— —— —— —— — — Bf5[88] **6** e3 Na6[89]

—— —— —— —— — — — e6[90] **7** Bxc4 Bb4 **8** 0-0 0-0 **9** Qe2 Ne4 **10** g4[91]

—— —— —— —— — — **6** Ne5 Nbd7 **7** Nxc4 Qc7 **8** g3 e5[92]

—— —— —— —— — — — e6[93] **7** f3 Bb4 **8** e4 Bxe4[94]

—— —— —— —— — — Bg4[95]

—— —— —— —— — **5** e3[96]

—— —— —— —— — **5** e4[97] b5 **6** e5[98]

—— —— —— —— — e6[99]

—— —— —— —— — g6[100]

—— —— —— — **4** Nbd2 Bf5 **5** e3 e6 **6** Be2 Bd6 **7** c5[101]

—— —— —— — **4** e3 e6 **5** Nc3[102]

—— —— —— — — — **5** Nbd2[103] Ne4 **6** Bd3 f5[104]

—— —— —— — — — **5** Bd3 Nbd7 **6** Nbd2[105]

—— —— —— — Bf5 **5** cxd5 cxd5 **6** Qb3 Qc8 **7** Bd2 e6 **8** Na3[106]

—— —— —— — — **6** Nc3 e6 **7** Ne5 Nfd7[107]

—— —— —— — g6[108]

—— —— Nc6[109]

—— —— e5[110] **3** dxe5 d4 **4** e3 Bb4+ **5** Bd2 dxe3[111]

—— —— —— — **4** Nf3 Nc6 **5** Nbd2[112] Qe7[113]

—— —— — — — f6[114]

—— —— — — — Bg4 **6** h3 Bxf3 **7** Nxf3 Bb4+ **8** Bd2 Qe7[115]

—— —— e6 **3** Nc3 a6[116]

—— —— — b6[117]

—— —— — c5[118] **4** cxd5 cxd4[119]

—— —— — — exd5 **5** dxc5 d4 **6** Na4 b5[120]

—— —— — — — **5** e4[121]

—— —— — — **5** Nf3 Nc6 **6** g3[122] c4[123] **7** e4[124]

—— —— — — — — Nf6[125] **7** Bg2 Be7 **8** 0-0 0-0[126] **9** dxc5 Bxc5 **10** Na4[127]

—— —— — — — — — **9** Bg5 Be6 **10** Rc1 b6[128]

—— —— — — — — — c4[129]

—— —— — — — — Bg4[130]

—— —— — — **4** e3 Nf6 **5** Nf3 Nc6 **6** Bd3 Bd6 **7** 0-0 0-0[131] **8** Qe2 Qe7 **9** dxc5 Bxc5 **10** e4[132]

—— —— — — **4** Nf3 Nf6 **5** Bg5[133]

—— —— — c6[134] **4** e4 dxe4 **5** Nxe4 Bb4+ **6** Bd2[135]

—— —— — — **4** Nf3 dxc4 **5** a4 Bb4 **6** e3 b5 **7** Bd2 a5[136]

—— —— —— —— — — Qb6[137]

—— —— —— —— — — Qe7[138]

—— —— — — Nf6 **5** e3 a6[139]

—— —— — — — Nbd7 **6** Qc2 Be7 **7** b3[140]

71 Smyslov V
72 **11** . . Nxc2 **12** Qxc2 Bb7 **13** d5 Qc7 Flohr V
73 Geller V
74 Steinitz V
75 Janowski–Larsen V
76 Smyslov V
77 Austrian D
78 Slav D
79 Alekhine V
80 Winawer C-G
81 see **2** . . . e6 (134)
82 Exchange V
83 Trifunović V
84 Süchting V
85 Alapin V
86 Smyslov V
87 Soultanbéieff V
88 Czech D
89 Lasker V
90 Dutch V
91 Sämisch V
92 Carlsbad V
93 Wiesbaden V

94 Krause V
95 Steiner V
96 Alekhine V
97 Slav G
98 Geller G
99 see **2** . . . e6
100 Schlechter V
101 Breyer V
102 see **2** . . e6 **3** Nc3 c6 **4** Nf3 Nf6 **5** e3 (139–52)
103 Semmering V
104 Stonewall V
105 Breyer V
106 Landau V
107 Amsterdam V
108 Schlechter V
109 Chigorin D
110 Albin C-G
111 Lasker Trap
112 Alapin V
113 Balogh V
114 Janowski V
115 Krénosz V
116 Janowski V

117 Alapin V
118 Tarrasch D
119 Schara–Hennig G
120 Tarrasch D
121 Marshall G
122 Schlechter V
123 Folkestone V
124 Rey Ardid V
125 Prague V
126 Normal position
127 Réti V
128 Stoltz V
129 Bogoljubow V
130 Wagner V
131 Symmetrical V
132 Levenfish V
133 Pillsbury V
134 Semi-Slav D
135 Marshall G
136 Abrahams V
137 Junge V
138 Koomen V
139 Alekhine V
140 Stoltz V

1 d4 d5 2 c4 e6 3 Nc3 c6 4 Nf3 Nf6 5 e3 Nbd7 6 Bd3 Bb4[141]
— — — — — — — — — — dxc4[142] 7 Bxc4 b5 8 Bd3 a6 9 e4 b4[143]
— — — — — — — — — — — — — — — — c5 10 d5[144]
— — — — — — — — — — — — — — — — — — 10 e5 cxd4 11 Nxb5[145]
— — — — — — — — — — — — — — b4[146]
— — — — — — — — — — — — — — Bb7[147]
— — — — — — — — Bd6[148]
— — — — — — — — Be7[149]
— — — — — — 6 cxd5[150]
— — — — — — 6 Ne5[151]
— — — — Ne4 6 Bd3 f5[152]
— — — — — 5 Bg5[153] dxc4 6 e4 b5 7 e5 h6 8 Bh4 g5 9 exf6 gxh4 10 Ne5[154]
— — — — — — — — — — — — — 9 Nxg5 hxg5 10 Bxg5 Nbd7 11 Qf3[155]
— — — — — — — — — — — — — — — — 11 g3[156]
— — — — — Be7[157]
— — — — — Nf6 4 cxd5[158] exd5 5 Bg5 Be7 6 e3 0–0 7 Bd3 Nbd7 8 Qc2 Re8 9 Nge2 Nf8 10 0–0–0[159]
— — — — — 4 Nf3 Bb4[160]
— — — — — c5[161] 5 cxd5 Nxd5 6 e4 Nxc3 7 bxc3 cxd4 8 cxd4 Bb4+ 9 Bd2 Qa5[162]
— — — — — — — — — — — — — — — Bxd2+ 10 Qxd2 0–0 11 Bb5[163]
— — — — — — 5 Bg5[164] cxd4 6 Nxd4 e5 7 Ndb5 a6 8 Qa4[165]
— — — — — — — — 6 Qxd4[166]
— — — — Nbd7 5 cxd5[167] exd5 6 Bf4[168]
— — — — — 5 Bg5[169]
— — — — 4 Bf4[170]
— — — — 4 Bg5 c5[171] 5 cxd5 Qb6[172]
— — — — — Nbd7 5 e3 Bb4[173]
— — — — — — c6 6 a3[174]
— — — — — — — 6 cxd5[175]
— — — — — — 6 Nf3 Qa5[176] 7 Nd2 Bb4 8 Qc2[177] 0–0 9 Bh4[178]
— — — — — — — — — dxc4[179]
— — — — — — 7 cxd5 Nxd5[180]
— — — — — — 7 Bxf6[181]
— — — — 5 Nf3 Bb4[182]
— — — — — c6 6 e4[183]
— — — — Be7 5 e3 Ne4[184]
— — — — — 0–0 6 Rc1[185]
— — — — — 6 Nf3 Nbd7[186] 7 Qb3[187]
— — — — — — — 7 Rc1 a6[188]
— — — — — — — — b6 8 cxd5 exd5 9 Qa4[189]
— — — — — — — — — 9 Bb5[190]
— — — — — — — — — 9 Bd3[191]
— — — — — — — c6[192] 8 Qc2[193] a6[194] 9 a3[195]
— — — — — — — — Ne4[196]
— — — — — — — 8 Bd3 dxc4 9 Bxc4 b5[197]
— — — — — — — — — Nd5[198] 10 Bxe7 Qxe7 11 Ne4[199]
— — — — — — — — — — 11 0–0[200]
— — — — — — — — 10 h4[201]
— — — — — 7 Qc2[202]
— — — — — 7 Bd3[203]
— — — — — 7 cxd5[204]
— — — — — h6[205] 7 Bh4 b6 8 cxd5 Nxd5 9 Bxe7 Qxe7 10 Nxd5 exd5 11 Rc1[206]
— — — — — — Ne4[207] 8 Bxe7 Qxe7 9 Qc2[208] Nf6 10 Bd3 dxc4 11 Bxc4[209]
— — — — — — — 9 cxd5 Nxc3 10 bxc3 exd5 11 Qb3[210]

1 d4 d5	2 c4	e6	3 Nc3	Nf6	4 Bg5	Be7	5 Nf3	c6	6 e4[211]				
— —	—	—	3 Nf3	Nf6	4 g3[212]								
— —	—	—	—	—	4 Bg5	Bb4+	5 Nc3	dxc4[213]					
— —	—	—	—	—	—	Nbd7	5 e3	c6	6 Nbd2[214]				
— —	—	—	—	—	—	h6[215]	5 Bxf6	Qxf6	6 Nc3	c6	7 Qb3[216]		
— —	—	—	3 g3	Nf6	4 Bg2	c5[217]							
— —	—	Bf5[218]											
— —	—	Nf6[219]											
— —	2 e3	Nf6	3 Bd3	c5	4 c3	Nc6	5 f4[220]						
— —	2 e4	dxe4	3 Nc3	Nf6	4 f3[221]								
— —	—	—	3 f3[222]										
— —	2 Nf3	c5[223]											
— —	—	Nc6[224]											
— —	—	Nf6	3 e3	c5	4 c3[225]								
— —	—	—	—	—	4 Nbd2	e6	5 b3[226]						
— —	—	—	—	—	4 Bd3	e6	5 b3[227]						
— —	—	—	—	Bf5	4 Bd3	e6[228]							
— —	—	—	3 Bf4[229]										
— —	—	—	3 Bg5[230]										
— —	2 Bf4[231]	c5[232]											
— —	2 Bg5[233]												
— d6[234]	2 e4	e6[235]											
— —	—	f5[236]											
— —	—	Nf6	3 Nc3	g6[237]	4 Be2	Bg7	5 g4[238]						
— —	—	—	—	—	—	—	5 h4[239]						
— —	—	—	—	—	4 f4[240]								
— e5[241]	2 dxe5	Nc6	3 Nf3	Qe7	4 Qd5	f6	5 exf6	Nxf6[242]					
— e6[243]	2 c4	Bb4+[244]											
— —	—	b6[245]											
— —	2 e4[246]												
— f5[247]	2 c4	e6	3 Nc3[248]										
— —	—	—	3 g3	Nf6	4 Bg2	Bb4+[249]	5 Bd2	Be7[250]					
— —	—	—	—	—	—	Be7	5 Nf3	0-0	6 0-0	d5[251]	7 b3[252]		
— —	—	—	—	—	—	—	—	—	—	d6	7 Nc3	Qe8[253]	8 Re1[254]
— —	—	—	—	—	—	—	—	—	—	Ne4[255]			
— —	—	—	Nf6	3 Nf3	g6	4 g3[256]							
— —	2 Qd3[257]												
— —	2 e4[258]	d6[259]											
— —	—	fxe4	3 Nc3	Nf6	4 g4[260]								
— —	—	—	—	—	4 Bg5	b6[261]							
— —	—	—	—	—	—	c6[262]	5 f3[263]						
— —	—	—	—	—	—	g6	5 f3[264]						
— —	—	—	—	—	—	—	5 h4[265]						
— —	2 g3[266]	Nf6	3 Bg2	d6	4 c4	c6	5 Nc3	Qc7[267]					
— —	—	—	—	e6	4 Nf3	Be7	5 0-0	0-0	6 c4[268]				
— —	—	—	—	—	4 Nh3[269]								
— —	—	—	—	g6[270]									
— —	—	g6[271]	3 Bg2	Bg7	4 Nf3	c6	5 0-0	Nh6[272]					
— —	—	—	—	—	4 Nh3[273]								
— —	2 g4[274]												
— Nf6[275]	2 Nc3	d5[276]											
— —	2 c4	b6[277]											
— —	—	c5[278]	3 d5	b5[279]									

1 d4 Nf6 2 c4 c5 3 d5 e5²⁸⁰ 4 Nc3 d6 5 e4 Be7²⁸¹
— — — — e6 4 Nc3 exd5 5 cxd5 d6²⁸² 6 e4 g6 7 f4²⁸³ Bg7 8 Bb5+²⁸⁴
— — — — — — — — — — 8 e5²⁸⁵
— — — — — — — 6 Nf3 g6 7 Nd2²⁸⁶
— — — — — — — — 7 Bg5²⁸⁷
— — — Nc6²⁸⁸
— — — d6²⁸⁹
— — — e5²⁹⁰ 3 dxe5 Ne4²⁹¹ 4 Qc2²⁹²
— — — — Ng4²⁹³ 4 e4²⁹⁴ d6²⁹⁵
— — — — — Nxe5 5 f4 Nec6²⁹⁶
— — — — 4 Bf4²⁹⁷
— — — e6 3 Nc3 Bb4²⁹⁸ 4 a3²⁹⁹ Bxc3+ 5 bxc3 c5 6 e3 Nc6 7 Bd3 0–0 8 Ne2 b6 9 e4 Ne8³⁰⁰
— — — — — — — 6 f3 d5 7 cxd5 Nxd5 8 dxc5³⁰¹ f5³⁰²
— — — — — — — — 7 e3 0–0 8 cxd5 Nxd5³⁰³
— — — — 4 Qb3³⁰⁴ c5 5 dxc5 Nc6 6 Nf3 Ne4 7 Bd2 Nxc5³⁰⁵ 8 Qc2 f5 9 g3³⁰⁶
— — — — — — — — Nxd2³⁰⁷ 8 Nxd2 0–0 9 0–0–0³⁰⁸
— — — — 4 Qc2³⁰⁹ c5 5 dxc5 0–0³¹⁰
— — — — — Nc6³¹¹ 5 Nf3 d6 6 a3³¹²
— — — — — d5³¹³ 5 a3 Bxc3+ 6 Qxc3 Nc6³¹⁴
— — — — — — — Ne4 7 Qc2 Nc6 8 e3 e5³¹⁵
— — — — 4 e3³¹⁶ b6 5 Nge2 Ba6³¹⁷
— — — — — c5 5 Bd3 Nc6 6 Nf3 Bxc3³¹⁸
— — — — — Nc6³¹⁹ 5 Nf3 0–0 6 Bd3 d5 7 0–0 dxc4³²⁰
— — — — — d5 5 a3 Bxc3+ 6 bxc3 c5 7 cxd5 exd5 8 Bd3 0–0 9 Ne2 b6³²¹
— — — — — 0–0 5 Bd3 d5 6 Nf3 c5 7 0–0 dxc4 8 Bxc4 b6 9 Qe2 Bb7 10 Rd1 Qc8³²²
— — — — — — — — — — Bd7³²³
— — — — — — — — — Nbd7 9 Ne2³²⁴
— — — — — — — — — Qe7³²⁵
— — — — — 5 Nge2³²⁶ d5 6 a3 Bd6³²⁷
— — — — 4 f3³²⁸
— — — — 4 Nf3³²⁹ c5 5 d5³³⁰ Ne4³³¹
— — — — 4 g3³³²
— — — — 4 Bg5³³³
— — — 3 Nf3 Bb4+³³⁴ 4 Bd2 Bxd2+ 5 Qxd2 b6 6 g3 Bb7 7 Bg2 0–0 8 Nc3 Ne4 9 Qc2 Nxc3 10 Ng5³³⁵
— — — — — — Qe7³³⁶
— — — — 4 Nbd2³³⁷
— — — — b6³³⁸ 4 a3³³⁹ Bb7 5 Nc3 d5 6 cxd5 Nxd5 7 Qc2 c5 8 e4 Nxc3 9 bxc3 Nc6 10 Bb2 cxd4 11 cxd4³⁴⁰
— — — — — 4 Nc3 Bb7 5 Bg5 h6 6 Bh4 g5 7 Bg3 Nh5³⁴¹
— — — — — 4 e3 Bb7 5 Bd3 c5 6 0–0 Be7 7 b3 0–0 8 Bb2 cxd4 9 Nxd4³⁴²
— — — — — 4 Bf4³⁴³
— — — — — 4 g3 Ba6³⁴⁴
— — — — — — Bb7 5 Bg2 Bb4+ 6 Bd2 a5³⁴⁵
— — — — — — — — Be7³⁴⁶
— — — — — — c5 6 d5 exd5 7 Ng5³⁴⁷
— — — — — — — 7 Nh4³⁴⁸
— — — — — — Qc8 6 0–0 c5 7 d5³⁴⁹
— — — — — — Be7 6 Nc3 Ne4 7 Bd2³⁵⁰
— — — — — — — 6 0–0 0–0 7 b3³⁵¹
— — — c5³⁵² 4 d5 b5³⁵³ 5 e4³⁵⁴
— — — — — 5 Bg5 exd5 6 cxd5 h6³⁵⁵
— — — Ne4³⁵⁶

1 d4 Nf6 2 c4 e6 3 g3[357] d5 4 Bg2 dxc4 5 Qa4+ Nbd7 6 Qxc4 a6 7 Qc2[358]
— — — — — —   — —   — Be7 5 Nf3 0–0   6 0–0 Nbd7 7 Qc2 c6 8 Nbd2 b6 9 b3 a5 10 Bb2 Ba6[359]
— — — — — —   — —   — —   — —   —   — —   — —   8 Rd1 b6 9 a4[360]
— — — — — —   — —   — —   — —   —   — —   7 Nc3 c6 8 Qd3[361]
— —   g6[362] 3 Nc3 d5[363] 4 Qb3[364]
— —   — —   — — 4 cxd5 Nxd5 5 e4 Nxc3 6 bxc3[365] Bg7 7 Bc4 0–0 8 Ne2 b6 9 h4 Ba6[366]
— —   — —   — —   — —   — —   — —   — — Nc6[367]
— —   — —   — —   — —   — —   — — c5 9 0–0 Nc6 10 Be3 cxd4 11 cxd4[368]
— —   — —   — —   — —   — — Qd7 9 0–0 b6[369]
— —   — —   — —   — —   5 g3[370]
— —   — —   — 4 e3 c6[371]
— —   — —   — Bg7 5 Nf3 0–0   6 Qb3 dxc4 7 Bxc4 Nbd7 8 Ng5[372]
— —   — —   — —   — — 6 b4[373]
— —   — —   — —   — — 6 Bd2[374]
— —   — —   — —   — — 6 Bd3 c6[375] 7 0–0 Bf5[376]
— —   — —   — —   — —   — — Bg4[377]
— —   — —   — 4 Nf3[378] Bg7 5 Qa4+[379]
— —   — —   — —   — — 5 Qb3[380] dxc4 6 Qxc4 0–0 7 e4 a6[381]
— —   — —   — —   — —   — — Na6[382]
— —   — —   — —   — —   — — b6[383]
— —   — —   — —   — —   — — c6[384]
— —   — —   — —   — —   — — Nc6[385]
— —   — —   — —   — —   — — Bg4[386] 8 Be3 Nfd7 9 Qb3 c5[387]
— —   — —   — —   — —   — — — — 9 Be2 Nb6 10 Qd3 Nc6 11 0–0–0[388]
— —   — — 4 Bf4 Bg7 5 e3 0–0[389] 6 Rc1[390] c5 7 dxc5 Be6[391]
— —   — — 4 g3[392]
— —   — — 4 Bg5[393] Ne4 5 Nxe4 dxe4 6 Qd2 c5[394]
— —   — Bg7 4 e4 d6 5 Be2 0–0 6 Bg5[395]
— —   — — — — 5 f3[396] e5 6 d5 Nh5 7 Be3 Na6 8 Qd2 Qh4+ 9 g3 Nxg3 10 Qf2 Nxf1 11 Qxh4[397]
— —   — — — — 0–0 6 Be3 Nc6 7 Nge2 Rb8[398]
— —   — — — 5 Nf3 0–0 6 Be2 e5 7 d5[399] Nbd7 8 Bg5 h6 9 Bh4 g5 10 Bg3 Nh5 11 h4[400]
— —   — —   — — — —   — — 7 0–0 c6[401]
— —   — —   — — — —   — — Nc6[402] 8 d5 Ne7[403] 9 b4[404]
— —   — —   — — — —   — — — — 9 Ne1 Nd7 10 f3 f5 11 g4[405]
— —   — —   — — 6 Be3[406]
— —   — —   — — 6 Bg5[407]
— —   — — — 5 f4[408] c5 6 d5 0–0 7 Be2 e6 8 dxe6 fxe6 9 g4 Nc6 10 h4[409]
— —   — — — 5 h3[410]
— —   — — 4 Bg5[411]
— — — 3 d5[412] b5[413]
— — — 3 f3[414]
— — — 3 g3 Bg7 4 Bg2 d5[415] 5 cxd5 Nxd5 6 Nf3 0–0 7 0–0 c5[416]
— —   — —   — d6 5 Nf3 0–0 6 Nc3 c5[417]
— —   — —   — —   — — 6 c6 7 0–0 Qa5[418]
— —   — —   — —   — — Nc6 7 0–0 a6 8 h3 Rb8[419]
— —   — —   — —   — — — e5[420]
— —   — —   — —   — — — Bf5[421]
— —   — —   — —   — — — Bg4[422]
— —   — —   — — 6 0–0 Nc6 7 d5 Na5[423]
— — 2 Nf3 b5[424]
— — — b6[425] 3 g3 Bb7 4 Bg2 c5[426] 5 c4 cxd4 6 Qxd4[427]
— — — — 3 Bg5[428]
— — Ne4[429]

1 d4 Nf6 2 Nf3 e6 3 c4 Bb4+[430]
— — — — — c5 **4 d5** b5[431]
— — — — **3 Bg5**[432] c5 **4 e4**[433]
— — **g6**[434] **3 Bf4** Bg7 **4 Nbd2**[435]
— — **3 Bg5**[436]
— — **2 Bg5**[437]
— g6 **2 c4** Bg7[438]
— — **2 e4**[439]
1 e3[440]
1 e4[441] a6[442]
— b6[443]
— c5[444] **2 b4**[445] cxb4 **3 a3 bxa3**[446]
— — — — — d5 **4 exd5 Qxd5 5 Bb2**[447]
— — **2 c3**[448]
— — **2 Nc3**[449] Nc6 **3 f4**[450] g6 **4 Bc4 Bg7 5 Nf3 e6 6 f5**[451]
— — — **3 g3** g6 **4 Bg2 Bg7 5 d3 d6 6 Nge2 e5**[452]
— — — — — — e6 **6 Be3 Nd4 7 Nce2**[453]
— — — e6 **3 g3 d5**[454]
— **2 Bc4**[455]
— **2 d4**[456] cxd4 **3 c3**[457]
— — — **3 Nf3 e5 4 c3**[458]
— **2 Ne2**[459]
— **2 Nf3** a6[460] **3 c4**[461]
— — Nc6 **3 Bb5**[462] g6 **4 0–0 Bg7 5 Re1 e5 6 b4**[463]
— — — **3 Nc3 e6 4 Bb5 Nd4**[464]
— — — **3 d4 cxd4 4 c3**[465]
— — — — **4 Nxd4 Qc7 5 Nb5 Qb8**[466]
— — — — d5[467]
— — — — e5[468]
— — — — Nf6 **5 Nc3 d6 6 Bc4**[469]e6[470] **7 Be3 Be7 8 Bb3 0–0 9 f4**[471]
— — — — — — — — — **8 Qe2**[472]
— — — — — — **6 Be2 e5**[473] **7 Nxc6**[474]
— — — — — — — e6[475]
— — — — — g6[476] **7 0–0 Bg7 8 Nb3 0–0 9 Be3 Be6 10 f4 Na5 11 f5**[477]
— — — — — — — — — — — Qc8[478]
— — — — — — — — — **9 Kh1**[479]
— — — — — **6 Bg5**[480] e6 **7 Nb3**[481]
— — — — — — **7 Bb5**[482]
— — — — — — **7 Nxc6 bxc6 8 e5**[483]
— — — — — — **7 Qd2**[484] Be7 **8 0–0–0 0–0 9 f4 e5**[485]
— — — — — — **7 Qd3**[486]
— — — — — g6[487]
— — — — e5[488] **6 Ndb5 d6 7 Bg5 a6 8 Na3 b5**[489] **9 Bxf6 gxf6 10 Nd5 f5**[490]
— — — — — — — — — — Be6[491]
— — — — e6[492]
— — — g6[493] **5 c4**[494] Nf6 **6 Nc3 Nxd4 7 Qxd4 d6**[495]
— — — — — Bg7 **6 Nc2 d6 7 Be2 Nh6**[496]
— — — — — **6 Be3 Nf6 7 Nc3 Ng4**[497]
— d6 **3 b4**[498]
— — — **3 Bb5+**[499]Bd7 **4 Bxd7+ Qxd7 5 c4**[500]
— — — — **5 0–0 Nc6 6 c3 Nf6 7 d4**[501]
— — — **3 d4 cxd4 4 c3**[502]

1 e4 c5 2 Nf3 d6 3 d4 cxd4 4 Nxd4 Nf6 5 Nc3 a6[503] 6 Bc4[504]
— — — — — — — — 6 Be2 e5[505]
— — — — — — — — 6 Be3[506]
— — — — — — — — 6 g3[507] e6[508]
— — — — — — — — 6 Bg5 Nbd7 7 Bc4 Qa5 8 Qd2 e6 9 0-0-0 b5 10 Bb3 Bb7 11 Rhe1[509]
— — — — — — — — — e6 7 f4 b5[510] 8 e5 dxe5 9 fxe5 Qc7 10 Qe2[511]
— — — — — — — — — — Qb6 8 Qd2[512]
— — — — — — — — — Be7 8 Qf3 h6 9 Bh4 g5[513] 10 fxg5 Nfd7 11 Nxe6[514]
— — — — — — — — 6 h3[515]
— — — — — — — Nc6[516]
— — — — — — — e5 6 Bb5+[517]
— — — — — — — e6[518] 6 Bb5+[519]
— — — — — — — 6 Bc4[520]
— — — — — — — 6 Be2 a6[521]
— — — — — — — — Nc6 7 0-0 Be7 8 Kh1[522]
— — — — — — — 6 f4 Nc6 7 Be3 Be7 8 Qf3[523]
— — — — — — — 6 g4[524]
— — — — — — g6[525] 6 Be2 Bg7 7 Be3 Nc6 8 Nb3[526]
— — — — — — — — 8 Qd2[527] 0-0 9 0-0-0[528]
— — — — — — — — 8 0-0 0-0 9 Nb3 a5[529]
— — — — — — — — — Be6 10 f4 Na5 11 f5[530]
— — — — — — — — 9 Qd2[531]
— — — — — — — — 9 f4 Qb6 10 e5[532]
— — — — — — 6 Be3 Bg7 7 f3[533] 0-0 8 Qd2 Nc6 9 Bc4 a5[534]
— — — — — — — — 9 g4 d5[535]
— — — — — — — — 9 0-0-0[536]
— — — — — — 6 f4[537]
— — — — — 5 f3[538] e5 6 Bb5+[539]
— — — — g6[540] 5 c4[541]
— — — — 4 Qxd4[542] Nc6 5 Bb5 Qd7[543]
— — — Nf6[544]
— — e6 3 d4 cxd4 4 Nxd4 a6[545] 5 Nc3 Qc7 6 Bd3 Nc6 7 Be3 Nf6 8 0-0 Ne5[546]
— — — — — — 5 c4[547] Nf6 6 Nc3 Bb4 7 Bd3 Nc6 8 Bc2[548]
— — — — 5 Bd3 Nf6 6 0-0 d6 7 c4 g6[549]
— — — Nc6 5 Nb5[550] d6 6 c4 Nf6 7 N1c3 a6 8 Na3 Be7 9 Be2 0-0 10 0-0 Bd7 11 Be3[551]
— — — — 5 Nc3 Qc7[552] 6 Be3 a6 7 a3 b5 8 Nxc6 Qxc6 9 Be2 Bb7 10 Qd4[553]
— — Nf6 5 Nc3 Bb4[554] 6 Bd3 e5[555]
— — — — 6 e5[556]
— — — Nc6 6 Ndb5 Bb4[557] 7 Nd6+[558]
— — — — 6 Be2 Bb4 7 0-0[559]
— — — d5[560]
— — Nf6[561] 3 e5 Nd5 4 Nc3 e6 5 Nxd5 exd5 6 d4 Nc6[562]
— — g6[563] 3 c4[564]
— 2 f4[565]
— 2 g3[566]
c6[567] 2 Nc3 d5 3 Nf3[568]
— — — 3 Qf3[569]
— 2 d0[570]
— — 2 d4 d5 3 Nc3 dxe4 4 Nxe4 Nd7[571]
— — — — — — Bf5[572] 5 Ng3 Bg6 6 f4[573]
— — — — — — — — 6 Nh3[574]
— — — — — — — — 6 h4 h6 7 Nf3 Nd7 8 h5[575]

1 e4 c6 2 d4 d5 3 Nc3 dxe4 4 Nxe4 Nf6[576] 5 Nxf6+ exf6 6 Bc4[577]
— — — — — — — — gxf6[578]
— — — — — — 5 Bd3[579]
— — — — — g6[580]
— — 3 exd5[581] cxd5 4 c3 Nc6 5 Bf4 Nf6 6 Bd3[582]
— — — — 4 c4[583] Nf6 5 Nc3 Nc6 6 Bg5[584] Qa5[585]
— — — — — — — — Qb6[586]
— — — — — — — dxc4 7 d5 Na5[587]
— — — — — — — e6[588]
— — — 3 e5[589] Bf5 4 g4[590]
— — — 3 f3[591]
— — — Nf6[592]
— Nc6[593] 2 d4 d5 3 Nc3[594]
— d5[595] 2 exd5 Qxd5 3 Nc3 Qa5 4 b4[596]
— — — — — 4 d4 e5[597] 5 Nf3 Bg4[598]
— — — — — Nf6 5 Nf3 Bf5 6 Ne5 c6 7 g4[599]
— — — — — — Bg4 6 h3[600]
— — — Nf6[601] 3 Bb5+ Bd7 4 Be2[602]
— — — — 3 c4 c6 4 dxc6 Nxc6[603]
— — — — 3 d4 Nxd5 4 c4 Nb4[604]
— 2 Nf3[605]
— d6[606]
— e5 2 c3[607]
— 2 Nc3[608] Bc5 3 Na4[609]
— — Nc6[610] 3 d4[611]
— — — 3 Nf3[612]
— — — 3 f4[613] exf4 4 d4[614] Qh4+ 5 Ke2 b6[615] 6 Nb5 Ba6 7 a4 g5 8 Nf3 Qh5 9 Ke1 Kd8 10 g4[616]
— — — — — d5[617] 6 exd5 Qe7+ 7 Kf2 Qh4+ 8 g3 fxg3+ 9 hxg3[618]
— — — — 4 Nf3 g5 5 Bc4 g4 6 0–0[619] gxf3 7 Qxf3 Ne5 8 Qxf4 Qf6[620]
— — — — — 5 d4[621]
— — — — — 5 h4 g4 6 Ng5[622] d6[623]
— — — 3 g3[624]
— — Nf6[625] 3 Bc4 Nxe4 4 Qh5 Nd6 5 Bb3 Nc6 6 d4[626]
— — — — — Be7 6 Nf3 Nc6 7 Nxe5[627]
— — — 3 f4 d5 4 fxe5 Nxe4 5 d3 Qh4+ 6 g3 Nxg3 7 Nf3 Qh5 8 Nxd5 Bg4 9 Nf4 Bxf3 10 Nxh5 Bxd1 11 hxg3[628]
— — — — — 5 Nf3 Bb4 6 Qe2[629]
— — — — — Be7[630]
— — — — — Bg4 6 Qe2[631]
— — — — — 5 Qf3[632] f5[633] 6 d4[634]
— — — — 4 d3[635] Bb4 5 fxe5 Nxe4[636]
— — — 3 g3[637]
— 2 Bc4[638] Bc5[639] 3 b4[640] Bxb4 4 f4[641] exf4 5 Nf3 Be7 6 d4 Bh4+ 7 g3 fxg3 8 0–0 gxh2+ 9 Kh1[642]
— — — 3 c3[643] d5[644]
— — — — Nf6 4 d4 exd4 5 e5 d5 6 exf6 dxc4 7 Qh5 0–0[645]
— — — — Qg5[646]
— — — 3 Qe2[647]
— — — 3 Nf3 d6 4 c3 Qe7 5 d4[648]
— — — c6[649] 3 d4 d5 4 exd5 cxd5 5 Bb5+ Bd7 6 Bxd7+ Nxd7 7 dxe5 Nxe5 8 Ne2[650]
— — — f5[651] 3 d3[652]
— — — Nf6[653] 3 d4[654] exd4 4 Nf3[655] d5 5 exd5 Bb4+ 6 c3 Qe7+[656]

1 e4 e5 2 Bc4 Nf6 3 Nf3 Nxe4 4 Nc3[657]
—— —— ——   3 f4[658]
—— —— 2 d3[659]
—— —— 2 d4 exd4 3 c3[660] dxc3 4 Bc4 cxb2 5 Bxb2 d5[661]
—— —— —— ——   —— Qe7[662]
—— —— —— ——   —— d5[663]
—— —— —— 3 Qxd4[664] Nc6 4 Qe3[665] Bb4+ 5 c3 Be7[666]
—— —— —— ——   f5[667]
—— —— —— ——   Nf6[668] 5 Nc3 Bb4 6 Bd2 0–0 7 0–0–0 Re8 8 Bc4 d6 9 Nh3[669]
—— —— —— 3 Nf3 c5 4 Bc4 b5[670]
—— —— 2 Ne2[671]
—— —— 2 Nf3[672] Nc6 3 Bb5[673] a6[674] 4 Ba4 Bb4[675]
—— —— —— —— —— —— b5[676] 5 Bb3 Na5[677]
—— —— —— —— —— —— —— —— Bc5[678]
—— —— —— —— —— —— Bc5[679]
—— —— —— —— —— —— d6[680] 5 c3   Bd7 6 d4 Nge7[681]
—— —— —— —— —— —— —— —— —— Nf6 7 0–0 Be7 8 Re1 0–0 9 Nbd2 Be8[682]
—— —— —— —— —— —— —— —— —— g6[683]
—— —— —— —— —— —— —— —— f5[684] 6 exf5 Bxf5 7 0–0[685]
—— —— —— —— —— —— 5 Nc3[686]
—— —— —— —— —— —— 5 c4[687]
—— —— —— —— —— —— 5 Bxc6+ bxc6 6 d4 f6[688]
—— —— —— —— —— —— 5 d4 b5 6 Bb3 exd4 7 Nxd4 Nxd4 8 Qxd4[689]
—— —— —— —— —— —— Nge7[690]
—— —— —— —— —— —— f5[691]
—— —— —— —— —— —— Nf6 5 Nc3[692] Bc5 6 Nxe5 Nxe5 7 d4 Bd6 8 0–0[693]
—— —— —— —— —— —— 5 d3[694] d6 6 c4[695]
—— —— —— —— —— —— 5 Qe2[696] b5 6 Bb3 Be7 7 c3 d6 8 d4 Bg4[697]
—— —— —— —— —— —— 5 0–0 b5[698] 6 Bb3 Bb7[699]
—— —— —— —— —— —— —— —— d6 7 Ng5 d5 8 exd5 Nd4 9 Re1 Bc5 10 Rxe5+ Kf8[700]
—— —— —— —— —— —— —— —— Be7 7 a4[701]
—— —— —— —— —— —— —— —— Bc5[702]
—— —— —— —— —— —— —— —— d6[703] 6 Bxc6+ bxc6 7 d4 Nxe4[704] 8 Re1 f5 9 dxe5 d5 10 Nc3[705]
—— —— —— —— —— —— —— —— —— —— Bg4[706]
—— —— —— —— —— —— —— —— Nxe4[707] 6 Nc3[708]
—— —— —— —— —— —— —— —— 6 d4 b5 7 Bb3 d5 8 a4 Nxd4[709] 9 Nxd4 exd4 10 Nc3[710]
—— —— —— —— —— —— —— —— —— —— 8 c4[711]
—— —— —— —— —— —— —— —— —— —— 8 dxe5 Be6 9 c3 Bc5[712] 10 Nbd2[713] 0–0 11 Bc2[714]
—— —— —— —— —— —— —— —— —— —— —— —— 10 Qd3[715] Ne7[716]
—— —— —— —— —— —— —— —— —— —— —— —— Nc5[717]
—— —— —— —— —— —— —— —— —— —— —— —— Be7[718] 10 a4 b4 11 Nd4[719]
—— —— —— —— —— —— —— —— —— —— —— —— 10 Nbd2[720] 0–0 11 Qe2[721]
—— —— —— —— —— —— —— —— —— —— —— —— 10 Re1 0–0 11 Nd4[722]
—— —— —— —— —— —— —— —— —— —— —— 9 Qe2[723] Be7 10 c4[724]
—— —— —— —— —— —— —— —— —— —— —— 10 Rd1 0–0 11 c4[725]
—— —— —— —— —— —— —— —— —— —— —— Ne7[726]
—— —— —— —— —— —— —— —— —— 7 d5[727]
—— —— —— —— —— —— —— —— —— 7 Nxe5[728]
—— —— —— —— —— —— —— —— —— exd4[729] 7 Re1 d5 8 Bg5[730]
—— —— —— —— —— —— —— —— 6 Qe2[731]

1 e4 e5 **2** Nf3 Nc6 **3** Bb5 a6 **4** Ba4 Nf6 **5** 0–0 Be7[732] **6** c3 d6 **7** d4 Bd7 **8** Re1 0–0 **9** Nbd2 Be8[733]

— — — — — — — — **6** Bxc6[734]
— — — — — — — — **6** d4[735] exd4 **7** e5 Ne4 **8** c3[736]
— — — — — — — — **6** Re1 b5 **7** Bb3 Bb7[737]
— — — — — — — d6 **8** c3 Na5 **9** Bc2 c5[738] **10** d4 Qc7 **11** a4[739]
— — — — — — — — — — — **11** h3[740]
— — — — — — — — 0–0 **9** a3[741]
— — — — — — — — — **9** Bc2[742]
— — — — — — — — — **9** d3[743]
— — — — — — — — — **9** d4 Bg4[744]
— — — — — — — — — **9** h3 a5[745]
— — — — — — — — — Na5 **10** Bc2 c5 **11** d4[746]
— — — — — — — — — Bb7[747]
— — — — — — — — — Nb8[748] **10** d4 Nbd7 **11** Nbd2[749]
— — — — — — — — — — — **11** Nh4[750]
— — — — — — — — — Be6[751]
— — — — — — — — — h6 **10** d4 Re8[752]
— — — — — — — 0–0 **8** a4[753]
— — — — — — — — **8** c3 d5[754]
— — — — — — d6[755] **7** c3 Bd7 **8** d4 0–0 **9** Nbd2 Be8[756]
— — — — — — **6** Qe2[757]
— — — — — g5[758]
— — — — — g6[759]
— — — — **4** Bxc6[760] bxc6 **5** Nc3[761]
— — — — dxc6 **5** d4 exd4 **6** Qxd4 Qxd4 **7** Nxd4 Bd7[762]
— — — — — — Bg4[763]
— — — — — **5** 0–0 Bg4 **6** h3 h5[764]
— — — Na5[765]
— — — Bb4[766]
— — — Bc5[767] **4** c3 Bb6[768]
— — — — Qe7 **5** 0–0 f6[769]
— — — — f5[770]
— — — — Nf6 **5** 0–0 0–0 **6** d4 Bb6[771]
— — — **4** 0–0 Nd4 **5** b4[772]
— — — Nd4[773] **4** Nxd4 exd4 **5** d3 c6 **6** Bc4 Nf6 **7** Bg5[774]
— — — — — **5** 0–0 Ne7[775]
— — d6[776] **4** d4 Bd7 **5** Nc3 Nf6 **6** Bxc6[777]
— — — — — — **6** 0–0 exd4[778]
— — — — — — Be7 **7** Bxc6[779]
— — — — — — — **7** Re1 0–0[780]
— — — — — — — **7** Bg5[781]
— — — — — **5** c4[782]
— — — Nge7[783]
— — — f5[784] **4** Nc3[785] Nf6 **5** exf5 e4 **6** Nh4[786]
— — — f6[787]
— — — Nf6[788] **4** Nc3 Bb4[789]
— — — — **4** d3 Bc5 **5** Be3[790]
— — — — d6 **5** c4[791]
— — — — — **5** Bxc6+[792]
— — — — Ne7[793] **5** Nxe5 c6[794]

1 e4 e5 2 Nf3 Nc6 3 Bb5 Nf6 4 d4 exd4 5 0–0[795]
— — — — — — — — — Nxe4 5 0–0[796]
— — — — — — 4 0–0 Bc5[797]
— — — — — — — d6 5 d4 Nd7[798]
— — — — — — — Nxe4 5 d4 a6[799]
— — — — — — — — — Nd6 6 Ba4[800]
— — — — — — — — — — 6 dxe5[801]
— — — — — — — — — Be7 6 Qe2 d5[802]
— — — — — — — — — — — Nd6 7 Bxc6 bxc6 8 dxe5 Nb7 9 b3[803]
— — — — — — — — — — — — — — 9 Nc3 0–0 10 Re1[804] Nc5 11 Nd4[805]
— — — — — — — — — — — — — — — — — Re8 11 Qc4[806]
— — — — — — — — — — — — — — 9 c4[807]
— — — — — — — — — — — — — — 9 Nd4 0–0 10 Rd1[808]
— — — — — — — — — — — — Nf5[809]
— — — — — — — — — — 6 dxe5[810]
— — — — — g5[811]
— — — — — g6[812]
— — — — 3 c3[813] Bc5 4 b4[814]
— — — — — d5 4 Qa4 Bd7[815] 5 exd5 Nd4 6 Qd1 Nxf3+ 7 Qxf3 f5 8 Bc4 Bd6 9 d3[816]
— — — — — — — f6[817]
— — — — — — — Nf6[818]
— — — — Be7[819]
— — — — Nge7[820]
— — — — Nf6[821] 4 d4 Nxe4 5 d5 Bc5[822]
— — — — f5[823] 4 d4 d6 5 d5[824] fxe4 6 Ng5 Nb8 7 Nxe4 Nf6 8 Bd3 Be7[825]
— — — 3 Nc3[826] Bb4 4 Nd5 Nf6[827]
— — — — f5[828]
— — — — Nf6[829] 4 a3[830] d6 5 h3[831]
— — — — — 4 Bb5[832] a6 5 Bxc6[833] dxc6 6 Nxe5 Nxe4 7 Nxe4 Qd4 8 0–0 Qxe5 9 Re1 Be6 10 d4 Qd5[834]
— — — — — — Bb4[835] 5 0–0 0–0 6 Bxc6[836]
— — — — — — — — 6 d3 Bxc3 7 bxc3 d5[837]
— — — — — — — — — — d6 8 Re1[838]
— — — — — — — — — d6[839] 7 Ne2[840]
— — — — — — — — 7 Bg5 Bxc3 8 bxc3 Qe7[841] 9 Re1 Nd8 10 d4 Bg4[842]
— — — — — — — — — — — — h6 9 Bh4 g5 10 Nxg5 Nxe4[843]
— — — — — — — — — — Be6[844]
— — — — — — — — — Ne7[845] 8 Nh4 c6 9 Bc4 d5 10 Bb3 Qd6[846]
— — — — — — — — — Bg4 8 Nd5 Nd4 9 Nxb4 Nxb5 10 Nd5[847]
— — — — — — — — — Qe7 7 Ne2 d5[848]
— — — — — — — — 6 Nd5 Nxd5 7 exd5 e4[849]
— — — — — — Bc5[850] 5 0–0 0–0 6 Nxe5 Nd4[851]
— — — — — — — — — Nxe5 7 d4 Bd6 8 f4 Nc6 9 e5 Bb4[852]
— — — — — — Nd4[853] 5 Nxd4 exd4[854]
— — — — — — 5 Be2 Nxf3+ 6 Bxf3 Bc5 7 0–0 0–0 8 d3 d6 9 Na4 Bb6[855]
— — — — — — 5 Nxe5 Qe7 6 f4[856]
— — — — — — 5 0–0[857]
— — — — 4 Bc4[858]
— — — — 4 d4[859] Bb4 5 Nxe5[860]
— — — — — exd4 5 Nd5[861]
— — — — — d6 5 Bb5 Bd7[862]
— — — — 4 Nxe5[863]
— — — — g6[864] 4 d4 exd4 5 Nd5[865]

1 e4 e5 **2** Nf3 Nc6 **3** Bc4 Bc5[866] **4** b4[867] Bxb4 **5** c3 Ba5 **6** d4 b5[868]

— — — — — — exd4 **7** 0–0 Bb6 **8** cxd4 d6[869] **9** Nc3[870] Na5 **10** Bg5[871] f6 **11** Be3[872]

— — — — — — — — — — — Bg4 **10** Qa4[873] Bd7 **11** Qb3[874]

— — — — — — — — — **9** d5 Na5 **10** Bb2[875] Ne7[876]

— — — — — — dxc3[877] **8** Qb3 Qf6 **9** e5 Qg6 **10** Nxc3 Nge7 **11** Ba3[878]

— — — — — — — — — — — **11** Rd1[879]

— — — — — — d6 **8** Qb3[880]

— — — — — — d6[881] **7** Qb3[882] Qd7 **8** a4[883]

— — — — — — — — **8** dxe5 dxe5 **9** 0–0 Bb6 **10** Ba3 Na5 **11** Nxe5[884]

— — — — — — **7** Bg5[885]

— — — — — — **7** 0–0 Bb6[886]

— — — — — — Bd7[887]

— — — — — — Bg4[888]

— — — — — **6** 0–0 Nf6 **7** d4 0–0 **8** Nxe5[889]

— — — — — — Qf6[890]

— — — — — Bc5[891] **6** d4 exd4 **7** cxd4 Bb4+ **8** Kf1[892]

— — — — — Bd6[893]

— — — — — Be7 **6** d4 Na5[894]

— — — — — Bf8[895]

— — — — Bb6[896] **5** a4 a6 **6** Nc3[897]

— — — — **5** Bb2[898]

— — — — **5** b5 Na5 **6** Nxe5 Qg5[899] **7** Qf3 Qxe5 **8** Qxf7+ Kd8 **9** Bb2[900]

— — — — — — **7** Bxf7+ Ke7 **8** Qh5[901]

— — — — — Nh6[902] **7** d4 d6 **8** Bxh6 dxe5 **9** Bxg7 Rg8 **10** Bxf7+ Kx?7 **11** Bxe5[903]

— — — d5[904]

— — — **4** c3 d6 **5** d4 exd4 **6** cxd4 Bb4+ **7** Kf1[905]

— — — — — Db0[906]

— — — Qe7[907] **5** d4 Bb6 **6** d5 Nb8 **7** d6[908]

— — — — — — **6** Bg5[909]

— — — — — — **6** 0–0 Nf6 **7** a4 a6 **8** Re1 d6 **9** h3[910]

— — — Nf6 **5** b4[911]

— — — **5** d4 exd4 **6** cxd4 Bb4+ **7** Nc3 Nxe4 **8** 0–0 Bxc3 **9** bxc3 d5 **10** Ba3[912]

— — — — — — — — **9** d5[913] Bf6 **10** Re1 Ne7 **11** Rxe4[914]

— — — — — — — Nxc3[915] **9** bxc3 Bxc3 **10** Ba3[916]

— — — — — — — — — **10** Qb3 d5[917]

— — — — — — **7** Bd2 Nxe4 **8** Bxb4 Nxb4 **9** Bxf7+ Kxf7 **10** Qb3+ d5 **11** Ne5+[918]

— — — — — — **7** Kf1[919]

— — — — — **6** e5 d5 **7** Bb5 Ne4 **8** cxd4 Bb4+[920]

— — — — — — Ne4 **7** Bd5 Nxf2 **8** Kxf2 dxc3+ **9** Kg3[921]

— — — **4** Nc3 Nf6[922] **5** d3[923]

— — — **4** d3[924] f5 **5** Ng5 f4[925]

— — — — Nf6 **5** Nc3 d6 **6** Bg5[926] h6 **7** Bxf6 Qxf6 **8** Nd5 Qd8 **9** c3 Ne7 **10** d4[927]

— — — **4** d4 exd4[928] **5** c3 d6[929]

— — — **4** Bxf7+ Kxf7 **5** Nxe5+[930]

— — — **4** 0–0 Nf6 **5** d3 d6 **6** Bg5 h6 **7** Bh4 g5[931]

— — — — — **5** d4 exd4[932]

— — — — Bxd4 **6** Nxd4 Nxd4 **7** f4 d6 **8** fxe5 dxe5 **9** Bg5 Qe7 **10** Nc3[933]

— — — — — — — — **7** Bg5 h6 **8** Bh4 g5 **9** f4[934]

— — Nd4 **4** Nxe5 Qg5 **5** Nxf7 Qxg2 **6** Rf1 Qxe4+ **7** Be2 Nf3[935] mate

— — — d6[936]

— — — Be7[937] **4** d4 exd4 **5** c3 Nf6 **6** e5 Ne4[938]

— — — f5[939]

866 Italian O
867 Evans G
868 Leonhardt V
869 Normal position
870 Morphy A
871 Göring A
872 Steinitz V
873 Fraser A
874 11 .. Na5 12 Bxf7+ Rf8 13 Qc2 Fraser–Mortimer A
875 Ulvestad V
876 Paulsen V
877 Compromised D
878 Paulsen V
879 Potter V
880 Waller A
881 Alapin V
882 Tartakower A
883 Tartakower A
884 Levenfish V
885 Sokolsky V
886 Lasker D
887 Sanders–Alapin D
888 Alapin–Steinitz V
889 Richardson A

890 Steinitz V
891 most lines as Ba5
892 Jaenisch V
893 Stone–Ware D
894 Cordel V
895 Mayet D
896 Evans G Declined
897 Showalter V
898 Cordel V
899 Hirschbach V
900 Hicken V
901 Vásquez V
902 Lange V
903 11 .. Qg5 12 Nd2 Pavlov V
904 Evans C–G
905 Miss in baulk V
906 Bourdonnais V
907 Close V
908 Eisinger V
909 Mestel V
910 Tarrasch V
911 Bird A
912 Steinitz V
913 Møller A
914 11 .. d6 12 g4 Bayonet A*
915 Greco V

916 Aitken V
917 Bernstein V
918 11 .. Kf6 12 f3 Krause V
919 Cracow V
920 Andersson V
921 Ghulam Kassim V
922 Four Knights V
923 Giuoco Pianissimo Deferred, see 4 d3
924 Giuoco Pianissimo
925 Dubois V
926 Canal V
927 Normal V
928 Scotch G
929 see 4 c3 d6 (905–6)
930 Jerome G
931 Steinitz D
932 see 945–50
933 Holzhausen A
934 Rosentreter V
935 Blackburne Shilling G
936 Semi-Italian O
937 Hungarian D
938 Tartakower V
939 Rousseau G

1 e4 e5 2 Nf3 Nc6 3 Bc4 Nf6[940] 4 Nc3[941] Nxe4 5 0–0[942]
— — — — — 4 d3[943]
— — — — 4 d4 exd4 5 e5 d5 6 Bb5 Ne4 7 Nxd4 Bc5 8 Nxc6 Bxf2+ 9 Kf1 Qh4[944]
— — — — — — 5 0–0 Bc5 6 e5[945] d5 7 exf6 dxc4 8 Re1+ Be6 9 Ng5 Qd5 10 Nc3 Qf5 11 Nce4[946]
— — — — — — — — — — — — — — — 11 g4[947]
— — — — — — — — — — — — — — g6[948]
— — — — — — — — — — — 9 fxg7[949]
— — — — — — Ng4 7 c3[950]
— — — — — — Nxe4 6 Re1 d5 7 Nc3[951]
— — — — — — 7 Bxd5 Qxd5 8 Nc3 Qa5 9 Nxe4 Be6 10 Bg5 h6 11 Bh4[952]
— — — — 4 Ng5 Bc5[953]
— — — — — d5 5 exd5 Na5 6 Bb5+ c6 7 dxc6 bxc6 8 Be2 h6 9 Nf3 e4 10 Ne5 Qc7[954]
— — — — — — — — — — — Bd6 11 d4[955]
— — — — — — — — — — 9 Nh3[956]
— — — — — — — — 8 Qf3 cxb5[957]
— — — — — — — — Rb8[958]
— — — — — — — — Qc7 9 Bd3[959]
— — — — — — 6 d3[960] h6 7 Nf3 e4 8 Qe2 Nxc4 9 dxc4 Bc5 10 Nfd2[961]
— — — — — — — — — — — Be7[962]
— — — — — b5[963]
— — — — — Nd4[964] 6 c3 b5 7 Bf1 Nxd5 8 Ne4[965]
— — — — — Nxd5 6 d4[966]
— — — — — 6 Nxf7[967] Kxf7 7 Qf3+ Ke6 8 Nc3 Ncb4 9 Qe4 c6 10 a3 Na6 11 d4[968]
— — — — — — — — — — Nce7[969]
— — — 3 d4[970] exd4 4 Bb5[971]
— — — — 4 c3[972] dxc3 5 Bc4 Nf6 6 Nxc3 Bb4[973]
— — — — 4 Bc4[974] Bb4+ 5 c3 dxc3 6 bxc3 Ba5 7 e5[975]
— — — — — — — 6 0–0 cxb2 7 Bxb2 Nf6 8 Ng5 0–0 9 e5 Nxe5[976]
— — — — — Bc5 5 Ng5 Nh6 6 Nxf7 Nxf7 7 Bxf7+ Kxf7 8 Qh5+ g6 9 Qxc5 d5[977]
— — — — — — 6 Qh5[978]
— — — — — 5 0–0 d6 6 c3 Bg4[979]
— — — — — Nf6[980]
— — — — Be7[981]
— — — — Nf6[982]
— — — — 4 Nxd4 Bc5 5 Nb3[983] Bb4+[984]
— — — — — 5 Be3 Bb6[985]
— — — — — Qf6 6 Nb5[986]
— — — — — 6 c3 Nge7 7 Bb5[987] Nd8[988]
— — — — — — — 7 Nc2[989]
— — — — — — — 7 Qd2[990] d5 8 Nb5 Bxe3 9 Qxe3 0–0 10 Nxc7 Rb8 11 Nxd5[991]
— — — — Nxd4[992]
— — — — Nf6[993] 5 Nc3[994] Bb4 6 Nxc6 bxc6 7 Bd3 d5 8 exd5 cxd5 9 0–0 0–0 10 Bg5 c6 11 Qf3[995]
— — — — — — — — — — — Be6[996]
— — — — — — — 7 Qd4[997] Qe7 8 f3 c5[998]
— — — — — 5 Nxc6 bxc6 6 Nd2[999]
— — — — — — 6 e5 Qe7 7 Qe2 Nd5 8 Nd2[1000]
— — — — Qh4[1001] 5 Nb5[1002] Qxe4+ 6 Be2 Bb4+ 7 Bd2 Kd8 8 0–0 Bxd2 9 Nxd2 Qg6[1003]
— — — — — — — 7 Nd2 Qxg2 8 Bf3 Qh3 9 Nxc7+ Kd8 10 Nxa8 Nf6 11 a3[1004]
— — — — — 5 Nc3[1005]
— — — — — 5 Nf3[1006]
— — — — Nxd4[1007] 4 Nxd4 exd4 5 Qxd4 d6 6 Bd3[1008]
— — — — 4 Nxe5 Ne6 5 Bc4 c6 6 Nxf7[1009]

1 e4 e5 **2** Nf3 Nc6　**3** Be2[1010] Nf6　**4** d3 d5　**5** Nbd2[1011]
— — — —　**3** Nxe5 Nxe5　**4** d4[1012]
— — — —　**3** g3[1013]
— — — d5[1014]
— — — d6[1015]　**3** Bc4 Be7　**4** c3[1016]
— — — —　　— f5[1017]　**4** d4 exd4　**5** Ng5 Nh6　**6** Nxh7[1018]
— — — —　**3** d4 exd4　**4** Nxd4 d5　**5** exd5[1019]
— — — —　　— —　　— g6[1020]
— — — —　　— —　**4** Qxd4 Bd7[1021]
— — — —　　— Nd7[1022]　**4** Bc4 c6　**5** a4[1023]
— — — —　　— —　　— —　**5** c3[1024]
— — — —　　— —　　— —　**5** Nc3[1025]
— — — —　　— —　　— —　**5** Ng5[1026] Nh6　**6** f4 Be7　**7** c3 0–0　**8** 0–0 d5[1027]
— — — —　　— —　　— —　**5** 0–0[1028] Be7　**6** dxe5[1029]
— — — —　　— f5[1030]　**4** Nc3[1031]
— — — —　　— —　**4** dxe5 fxe4　**5** Ng5 d5　**6** e6[1032] Bc5　**7** Nc3[1033]
— — — —　　— Nf6[1034]　**4** Nc3 exd4　**5** Nxd4 Be7　**6** Be2 0–0　**7** 0–0 c5　**8** Nf3 Nc6　**9** Bg5 Be6　**10** Re1[1035]
— — — —　　— —　　— Nbd7[1036]　**5** Bc4　Be7　**6** Ng5 0–0　**7** Bxf7+[1037]
— — — —　　— —　　— —　— —　**6** 0–0 0–0　**7** Qe2 c6　**8** a4 exd4[1038]
— — — —　　— —　**4** Bc4[1039]
— — — —　　— —　**4** dxe5 Nxe4　**5** Nbd2[1040]
— — — —　　— —　　— —　**5** Qd5[1041]
— — — —　　— —　**4** Ng5 h6　**5** Nxf7[1042]
— — — —　　— Bg4　**4** dxe5 Nd7[1043]
— — — f5[1044]　**3** Bc4 fxe4　**4** Nxe5 d5[1045]
— — — —　　— —　　— Qg5　**5** Nf7 Qxg2　**6** Rf1 d5　**7** Nxh8 Nf6[1046]
— — — —　**3** Nxe5 Nc6[1047]
— — — —　　— Nf6　**4** Bc4 fxe4　**5** Nf7 Qe7　**6** Nxh8 d5[1048]
— — — —　　— Qf6　**4** d4 d6　**5** Nc4 fxe4　**6** Nc3 Qg6[1049]
— — — —　　— —　　— —　　— —　**6** Ne3[1050]
— — — f6[1051]
— — — Nf6[1052]　**3** Nc3[1053]
— — — —　**3** Bc4[1054] Nxe4　**4** Nc3[1055] d5[1056]
— — — —　**3** d4[1057] exd4　**4** Bc4[1058]
— — — —　　— —　**4** e5 Ne4　**5** Qe2[1059] Nc5　**6** Nxd4 Nc6[1060]
— — — —　　— Nxe4　**4** Bd3 d5　**5** Nxe5 Bd6　**6** 0–0 0–0　**7** c4 Bxe5[1061]
— — — —　**3** Nxe5 d6　**4** Nf3 Nxe4　**5** c4[1062]
— — — —　　— —　　— —　**5** d4 d5　**6** Bd3 Nc6　**7** 0–0 Be7　**8** Re1 Bg4　**9** c3 f5　**10** c4[1063] Bh4[1064]
— — — —　　— —　　— —　　— Bd6[1065]　**7** 0–0 Bg4　**8** c4 0–0　**9** cxd5 f5　**10** Re1 Bxh2+[1066]
— — — —　　— —　　— —　**5** Qe2[1067]
— — — —　　— —　**4** Nxf7[1068]
— — — —　　— Nxe4[1069]
— — **2** f4[1070] Bc5[1071]　**3** Nf3
— — — —　　— d6　**4** b4[1072]
— — — —　　— —　**4** c3　f5　**5** fxe5 dxe5　**6** d4 exd4　**7** Bc4[1073]
— — — —　　— —　　— Bg4　**5** fxe5 dxe5　**6** Qa4+[1074]
— — — —　　— —　**4** Nc3 Nd7[1075]
— — — —　　— —　　— Nf6　**5** Bc4 Nc6　**6** d3 Bg4　**7** h3 Bxf3　**8** Qxf3 exf4[1076]
— — — —　　— —　**4** fxe5[1077]
— — — d5[1078]　**3** Nc3[1079]
— — — —　**3** exd5 c6[1080]
— — — —　　— e4　**4** Bb5+[1081]
— — — —　　— —　**4** Nc3 Nf6　**5** d3 Bb4　**6** Bd2 e3[1082]

```
1 e4 e5  2 f4 d5  3 exd5 e4   4 Nc3 Nf6   5 Qe2^1083
— —  — —  — —     4 d3 Nf6    5 Nd2^1084
— —  — —  — —     — —         5 Qe2^1085
— —  — —  — —     5 dxe4 Nxe4  6 Qe2^1086 Qxd5  7 Nd2 f5  8 g4^1087
— —  — —  — —     — —          6 Nf3 Bc5       7 Qe2 Bf2+  8 Kd1 Qxd5+  9 Nfd2^1088
— —  — —  — —     — —          — Bf5           8 g4 0-0^1089
— —  — —  3 Nf3^1090
— —  exf4^1091 3 Nc3^1092
— —  3 Bc4^1093 b5^1094
— —  — d5^1095   4 Bxd5 Nf6^1096
— —  — —  —      Qh4+  5 Kf1 Bd6^1097
— —  — —  —      —     g5  6 g3^1098
— —  — —  Ne7^1099
— —  — —  f5^1100   4 Qe2 Qh4+  5 Kd1 fxe4  6 Nc3 Kd8^1101
— —  — —  Nf6^1102  4 Nc3 Bb4   5 e5^1103
— —  — —  —         — c6^1104
— —  — Qh4+  4 Kf1 b5^1105
— —  — —  —  d6         5 Qf3^1106
— —  — —  —  g5^1107    5 Nc3 Bg7  6 d4 d6  7 e5^1108
— —  — —  —  —          — —       6 — Ne7   7 g3^1109
— —  — —  —  —          — —       6 g3^1110 fxg3  7 Qf3^1111
— —  — —  —  —          5 Qf3^1112
— —  — 3 d4^1113
— —  — 3 Be2^1114
— —  — 3 Qe2^1115
— —  — 3 Nf3^1116 d5^1117  4 exd5 Nf6^1118  5 Bb5+ c6  6 dxc6 bxc6  7 Bc4 Nd5^1119
— —  — —  d6^1120
— —  — —  Be7^1121  4 Bc4 Bh4+  5 g3^1122 fxg3  6 0-0 gxh2+  7 Kh1^1123
— —  — —  f5^1124   4 e5^1125
— —  — —  Nf6^1126
— —  — —  g5^1127   4 Nc3^1128
— —  — —  —         4 Bc4 g4  5 Nc3^1129
— —  — —  —         — —       5 d4^1130
— —  — —  —         — —       5 Ne5^1131 Qh4+  6 Kf1 Nc6^1132
— —  — —  —         — —       — —             — f3^1133
— —  — —  —         — —       — —             — Nh6  7 d4 d6^1134
— —  — —  —         — —       — —             — —    — f3^1135
— —  — —  —         — —       5 Bxf7+^1136 Kxf7  6 0-0 gxf3  7 Qxf3 Qf6  8 d4 Qxd4+  9 Be3 Qf6  10 Nc3^1137
— —  — —  —         — —       5 0-0^1138 d5^1139
— —  — —  —         — —       — Qe7^1140
— —  — —  —         — —       — gxf3  6 Qxf3 Nc6^1141
— —  — —  —         — —       — —    — Qe7^1142
— —  — —  —         — —       — —    — Qf6  7 e5 Qxe5  8 d3 Bh6  9 Nc3 Ne7  10 Bd2 Nbc6  11 Rae1^1143
— —  — —  —         — —       — —    — —    — —      8 Bxf7+^1144
— —  — —  —         Bg7  5 h4^1145 h6  6 d4 d6  7 Nc3 c6  8 hxg5 hxg5  9 Rxh8 Bxh8  10 Ne5^1146
— —  — —  —         —    — —             — —    7 Qd3^1147
— —  — —  —         —    5 0-0^1148
— —  — —  4 d4^1149 g4  5 Ne5^1150
— —  — —  4 h4 g4  5 Ne5^1151 Nc6^1152
— —  — —  —        —         a5^1153  6 d4 Nf6  7 exd5 Qxd5  8 Nc3 Bb4  9 Kf2^1154
— —  — —  —        —         — —      — —       7 Bxf4 Nxe4  8 Nd2^1155
— —  — —  —        —         d6^1156
```

1 e4 e6 2 d4 d5 3 Nc3 Nf6   4 Bg5 Be7   5 e5   Ne4[1226]
— — — — —   — —   —   Ng8[1227]
— — — — —   — —   5 Bxf6[1228] Bxf6 6 e5 Be7 7 Qg4[1229]
— — — — 3 Nd2[1230] c5 4 exd5 Qxd5 5 Ngf3 cxd4 6 Bc4 Qd8[1231]
— — — — —   Nc6 4 Ngf3 Nf6 5 e5 Nd7[1232]
— — — — —   f5[1233]
— — — — —   Nf6 4 e5 Nfd7 5 Bd3 c5 6 c3 b6[1234]
— — — — —   — — 5 f4 c5 6 c3 Nc6 7 Ndf3 cxd4 8 cxd4 Nb6[1235]
— — — — 3 exd5[1236]
— — — — 3 Be3[1237]
— — — — 3 e5[1238] c5 4 c3 Qb6 5 Nf3 Bd7[1239]
— — — — —   — Nc6 5 Nf3[1240] Qb6 6 Bd3 cxd5 7 cxd5 Bd7 8 Nc3 Nxd4 9 Nxd4 Qxd4 10 0–0[1241]
— — — — —   — 4 dxc5[1242]
— — — — —   — 4 Qg4[1243]
— — 2 Qe2[1244]
— — 2 e5[1245]
— — 2 f4[1246]
— f6[1247]
— Nf6[1248] 2 Nc3 d5[1249] 3 exd5[1250]
— —   3 e5 Nfd7   4 e6[1251]
— — 2 Bc4[1252]
— — 2 d3[1253]
— — 2 e5   Nd5 3 Nc3[1254]
— — —   3 c4 Nb6   4 b3[1255]
— — —   — —   4 c5[1256]   Nd5   5 Bc4 e6 6 Nc3 d6[1257]
— — —   — —   4 d4 d6 5 exd6 cxd6 6 h3 g6 7 Nf3[1258]
— — —   — —   — — 5 Nf3 Bg4 6 Be2 dxe5 7 Nxe5[1259]
— — —   — —   — — 5 f4[1260] dxe5 6 fxe5 Nc6 7 Be3 Bf5 8 Nc3 e6 9 Be2 Qd7 10 Nf3 0–0–0 11 0–0[1261]
— — —   — —   — — — — 7 Nf3 Bg4 8 e6 fxe6 9 c5[1262]
— — —   — —   — — — — — Bf5 7 Nf3 e6 8 Nc3 Bb4 9 Bd3[1263]
— — —   — —   — — — — — — — Be7 9 Be2 0–0 10 0–0 f6[1264]
— — —   — —   — — Bf5[1265]
— — —   3 Bc4 Nb6 4 Bb3 c5 5 d3[1266]
— — —   3 d4 d6   4 Bc4[1267]
— — —   — —   4 Nf3 Nb6[1268]
— — —   — —   — dxe5[1269]
— — —   — —   — Bg4   5 c4[1270]
— — —   — —   — —   5 Be2   c6[1271]
— — —   — —   — —   5 h3[1272]
— — —   — —   — g6 5 c4 Nb6 6 exd6 cxd6 7 h3 Bg7 8 Be2 0–0 9 Nc3 Nc6 10 0–0 Bf5 11 Bf4[1273]
— — —   — —   — — 5 Bc4 Nb6 6 Bb3 Bg7 7 a4[1274]
— g5[1275]
— g6[1276] 2 d4 Bg7   3 Nc3 c6 4 f4 d5 5 e5 h5[1277]
— —   — —   — d6 4 f4[1278]
— —   — —   3 Nf3 b6[1279]
— —   — —   — d6[1280] 4 Nc3 c6[1281]
1 f3[1282]
1 Nf3[1283]   2 b3[1284]
—   d5 2 b4[1285]
—   — 2 c4[1286]   dxc4[1287] 3 e3 Be6[1288]
—   —   c6   3 b3 Nf6   4 g3 Bf5 5 Bg2 e6 6 Bb2 Nbd7[1289]
—   —   —   — —   — Bg4[1290]
—   —   —   — —   — g6[1291]
—   —   —   — Bg4[1292]

1 Nf3　　d5　　2 c4　　c6　　3 d4[1293]
—　　—　　—　　d4[1294]
—　　—　　—　　e6　　3 b3 Nf6　4 Bb2 Be7　5 g3 0–0　6 Bg2 a5[1295]
—　　—　　—　　—　　3 g3[1296]
—　　—　　2 d3[1297]
—　　—　　2 d4[1298]
—　　—　　2 e4[1299]
—　　—　　2 g3[1300] Nf6　3 Bg2 c5　4 d4[1301]
—　　f5[1302]　2 e4[1303]
—　　Nf6　2 b3[1304]
—　　—　　2 c4[1305] c5[1306]
—　　—　　2 d4 b6[1307]
—　　—　　—　　d5[1308]
—　　—　　—　　e6　3 Nbd2 d5　4 e3 Nbd7　5 Bd3 c5　6 c3[1309]
—　　—　　2 g3[1310] g6　3 c4 Bg7　4 Bg2 0–0　5 0–0 Nc6　6 Nc3 d6　7 d4[1311]
1 f4[1312]　d5　　2 c4[1313]
—　　—　　2 e3 Nf6　3 Nf3 c5[1314]
—　　—　　2 e4[1315]
—　　e5[1316]
—　　f5　　2 e4 fxe4　3 Nc3 Nf6　4 g4[1317]
1 g3[1318]　e5　2 Nf3[1319]
—　　—　2 Bg2 d5　3 Nf3 Nc6　4 d3[1320]
— Nf6　2 Bg2 d5　3 Nf3 e6　4 0–0[1321]
1 g4[1322]
1 h3[1323]
1 Nh3[1324] d5　2 f3 e5　3 e4 f5[1325]
—　　— 2 g3 e5　3 f4[1326]
1 h4[1327]

GLOSSARY OF CHESS TERMINOLOGY

THIS glossary lists the commonest chess terms in French, German, Italian, Magyar, Russian, and Spanish, and is intended as an aid to English readers wishing to consult chess books published in those languages.

FRENCH

abandonner, resign
accepté, accepted
attaque, attack
blancs (les), White
case, square
cavalier (C), knight
cinq, five
clouage, pin
colonne, file
combinaison, combination
couleur, colour
coup, move
dame (D), queen
début, opening
défense, defence
deux, two
diagonale, diagonal
échanger, to exchange
échec, check
échec et mat, checkmate
échecs, chess
échecs féeriques, fairy chess

échiquier, board
erreur, mistake
étude, study
fin de partie, endgame
finale, endgame
fou (F), bishop
gagner, win
gain, win
gambit, gambit
huit, eight
milieu de partie, middlegame
noirs (les), Black
nulle, draw
ouverture, opening
pat, stalemate
perdre, lose
perte, loss
pièce, piece
piège, trap
pion (P), pawn
position, position

prendre, take
prise, take
problème, problem
promotion, promotion (of pawn)
qualité, the exchange
quatre, four
rangée, rank
refusé, declined
reine, queen
remise, draw
roi (R), king
roque, castling
sacrifice, sacrifice
sept, seven
six, six
suite, variation
tour (T), rook
traverse, rank
trois, three
un, one
variante, variation

GERMAN

abgelehnt, declined (of a gambit)
Abspiel, variation
abtauschen, to exchange
acht, eight
angenommen, accepted (of a gambit)
Angriff, attack
Aufgabe, problem
aufgaben, resign
aufgegeben, resigned
Bauer (b), pawn
Brett, board
Dame (D), queen
Diagonale, diagonal
drei, three
ein, one
Endspiel, endgame
Eröffnung, opening
Falle, trap
Farbe, colour
Feenschach, fairy chess
Fehler, mistake
Feld, square

Fesselung, pin
Figur, piece
fünf, five
Gambit, gambit
Gewinn, win
gewinnen, to win
Horizontale, rank
Kombination, combination
König (K), king
Läufer (L), bishop
Linie, file
Märchenschach, fairy chess
Matt, (check) mate
Mittelspiel, middlegame
nehmen, take
Opfer, sacrifice
patt, stalemate
Problem, problem
Qualität, the exchange
Reihe, rank
Remis, a draw
Rochade, castling
Schach, chess
Schach!, check

Schachmatt, checkmate
schlagen, to capture
Schräge, diagonal
Schwarz, Black
sechs, six
sieben, seven
Springer (S), knight
Stein, chessman
Stellung, position
Studie, study
tauschen, to exchange
Turm (T), rook
Umwandlung (Bauern-), promotion (pawn)
unentschieden, draw
Variante, variation
verlieren, lose
Verlust, loss
Verteidigung, defence
Vertikale, file
vier, four
Weiss, White
Zug, move
zwei, two

ITALIAN

abbandonare, resign
accettato, accepted
alfiere (*A*), bishop
apertura, opening
arrocco, castling
attacco, attack
bianco, white
bizzarie, fairy chess
cambiare, to exchange
casa, square
catturare, take
cavallo (*C*), knight
cinque, five
colonna, file
colore, colour
combinazione, combination
diagonale, diagonal
difesa, defence
donna (*D*), queen
due, two

errore, mistake
finale, endgame
gambetto, gambit
inchiodatura, pin
linea, file
mangiare, take
medio giuoco, middlegame
mossa, move
nero, black
otto, eight
patta, draw
pedone (*P*), pawn
perdere, lose
perdita, loss
pezzo, piece
posizione, position
problema, problem
promozione, promotion (pawn)
quattro, four
re (*R*), king

regina, queen
rifutato, declined
sacrificio, sacrifice
scacchi, chess
scacchiera, board
scacco, check
scacco matto, checkmate
sei, six
sette, seven
stallo, stalemate
studio, study
svista, mistake
torre (*T*), rook
trappola, trap
traversa, rank
tre, three
uno, one
variante, variation
vincere, to win
vittoria, win

MAGYAR

áldozat, sacrifice
állás, position
átló, diagonal
átváltozás (*gyalog*), promotion
  (pawn)
báb, chessman
bástya (*B*), rook
csapda, trap
csel, gambit
csere, to exchange
döntö, decisive
döntetlen, draw (undecided)
egy, one
elfogadott, accepted
elhárított, declined
elsáncol, castles
elvesz, üt, take
feladja, resign
feladvány, problem
futár (*F*), bishop
gyalog (*gy*), pawn

három, three
hat, six
hét, seven
hiba, mistake
huszár (*H*), knight
két, kettő, two
király, king
kombináció, combination
kötés, pin
középjáték, middlegame
lekötés, pin
lépés, move
matt, checkmate
megnyitás, opening
mezö, square
minöség, the exchange
négy, four
nyer, wins
nyolc, eight
oszlop, file
öt, five

patt, stalemate
sakk, chess, check
sáncolás, casting
sor, rank
sötét, Black
szin, colour
tábla, board
támadás, attack
tanulmány, study
terv, plan
tévedés, error
tiszt, piece
tündérsakk, fairy chess
ütés, take
változat, variation
védelem, defence
végjáték, endgame
vesztett, lost
vezér (*V*), queen
világos, White
vonal, line

RUSSIAN

атака, attack
белые, white
вариант, variation
вертикаль, file
взять, take
восемь, eight
выигрывать, to win
выигрыш, win
гамбит, gambit
горизонталь, rank
два, two
дебют, opening
диагональ, diagonal
доска, board
жертва, sacrifice
задача, problem
защита, defence
качество, the exchange
комбинация, combination

конь (К), knight
король (Кр), king
ладья (Л), rook
ловушка, trap
мат, checkmate
миттельшпиль, middlegame
ничья, draw
один, one
отказанный, declined
ошибка, mistake
пат, stalemate
пешка (П), pawn
позиция, position
поле, square
принятый, accepted
провести пешку, to promote
   (pawn)
проигрывать, lose
проигрыш, loss
пять, five

разменивать, to exchange
рокировка, castling
связка, pin
сдаваться, resign
семь, seven
сказочные ш., fairy chess
слон, bishop
три, three
ферзь (Ф), queen
фигура, piece
ход, move
цвет, colour
черные, black
четыре, four
шах, check
шахматы, chess
шесть, six
зндшпиль, endgame
зтюд, study

SPANISH

abandonar, resign
aceptado, accepted
ahogado, stalemate
ajedrez, chess
alfil (A), bishop
apertura, opening
ataque, attack
blancas, White
caballo (C), knight
calidad, the exchange
cambiar, to exchange
captura, take
casilla, square
celada, trap
cinco, five
clavada, pin
color, colour
columna, file
combinación, combination
cuatro, four
dama (D), queen

defensa, defence
diagonal, diagonal
dos, two
empatada, draw
enroque, castling
error, mistake
estudio, study
fila, rank
final, endgame
gambito, gambit
ganar, to win
horizontal, rank
jaque, check
jaque mate, checkmate
jugado, move
medio juego, middlegame
negras, Black
ocho, eight
peón (P), pawn
perder, lose
pérdida, loss
pieza, piece

posición, position
problema, problem
problemas fantasía, fairy chess
promoción, promotion
rehusado, declined
rendirse, resign
rey (R), king
rinden, resign
sacrificio, sacrifice
seis, six
siete, seven
tablas, draw
tablero, board
tomar, take
torre (T), rook
trampa, trap
tres, three
uno, one
variante, variation
vertical, file
victoria, win